FOR LIBRARY USE ONLY

The Complete Guide to Antarctic Wildlife

*Birds and Marine Mammals of the
Antarctic Continent and the Southern Ocean*

Second Edition

Hadoram Shirihai

Illustrated by Brett Jarrett
With additional plates by John Cox

Edited by Guy M. Kirwan

Princeton University Press
Princeton and Oxford

Second edition – To Hans Jornvall, a friend, scientist and Southern Ocean aficionado.

First edition – this book stems from my enormous love of Antarctic wildlife, its marine mammals, particularly whales (of which almost incalculable numbers have been slaughtered by Man), and seabirds (which have suffered similar losses through predation by mammalian predators introduced by humans to their breeding grounds or have been killed en masse as bycatch of modern fishing techniques), as well as the Southern Ocean itself, which despite global warming and human interference remains the richest marine area on Earth, and its krill, the foundation of this wonderful ecosystem that I have come to love in recent years. I also acknowledge all of my fellows who share these sentiments.

Photographers: Cherry Alexander, Andris Apse, Simon Berrow, Klaus Bjerre, Andrea M. Booth, Michael and Malcolm Boswell, British Antarctic Survey, Dennis Buurman, Francisco Viddi Carrasco, Mike Carter, Neil Cheshire, Alfred van Cleef, Graeme Cresswell, Jim Cotton, John Croxall, Mike Danzenbaker, Grant Dixon, Paul Drummond, Falklands Conservation, Dick Forsman, Johan Fromholtz, Michel Gauthier-Clerc, Daisy Gilardini, Global Book Publishing, Chris Gomersall, Gonzalo González, Marc Guyt, Alan Henry, Steve Howell, Nic Huin, Mitsuaki Iwago/Minden Pictures, Alvaro Jaramillo, Brett Jarrett, Frédéric Jiguet, Morten Jørgensen, Ron LeValley, Nigel McCall, George McGallum, Colin McLeod, Tony Marr, P.J. Milburn, Thierry Micol, Hiroya Minakuchi/Sphere Magazine, Colin Miskelly, Paula Olsen, Jørgen Mortensen, Flip Nicklin/Minden Pictures, Tony Palliser, Gordon Petersen, Steve Pinfield, René Pop, Todd Pusser, Tony Pym, Peter Reese, Hans Reinhard, Research Program Dwarf Minke Whales/Undersea Explorer, Michael F. Richlen, Keith Robinson, Gabriel Rojo, Maria San Román, David Rootes, Tui de Roy/Minden Pictures, Peter Ryan, Keiko Sekiguchi, Hadoram Shirihai, Brent Stephenson, TAAF Collection, Brian Thomas, Roger Tidman, David Tipling/Windrush Photos, Barbara Todd, Frank S. Todd, Yann Tremblay, Kenji Tuda, Dylan Walker, Ross Wanless, Kim Westerskov, Richard White, Alan Wiltshire, Eric Woehler and Stephen Wong.

All artworks by Brett Jarrett, except plates 4, 5 and 11 by John Cox.

Marine mammal distribution maps: Peter G. H. Evans, Alison Gill
Map production: Pekka J. Nikander

Commissioning Editor: Nigel Redman
Project Editor: Julie Bailey
Designer: Julie Dando, Fluke Art, Cornwall

Published in 2008 in the United States, Canada, and the Philippine Islands by Princeton University Press, 41 William Street, Princeton, New Jersey 08540

In the United Kingdom and European Union, published in 2007 by A&C Black Publishers Ltd, 38 Soho Square, London W1D 3HB

First edition published 2002

Library of Congress Control Number 2007934874
ISBN: 978-0-691-13666-0

nathist.press.princeton.edu

Printed and bound in Malaysia by Imago
10 9 8 7 6 5 4 3 2 1

CONTENTS

List of colour plates

Preface

Less than five years after its original publication, this book now appears in a thoroughly revised edition, and under a new imprint, A&C Black. There has been no shortage of new material and ideas for the update. As readers will quickly realise, the new edition has photographs of nearly every species and covers the main variation. However, given that in recent months I was preoccupied with my studies of petrels in the Pacific, I decided that the short period available should be used to revise only the most important parts of the book, especially the tubenoses, with special emphasis on the great albatrosses. Other bird accounts were highly selectively but comprehensively revised, such as the Tristan da Cunha buntings (thanks to P. Ryan and his co-workers), and we also managed to source many of the missing photographs for some seabirds, seals and cetaceans, for which latter we fortunately could re-use the illustrations by Brett Jarrett from my recently published marine mammals guide. We were also fortunate to get the highly acclaimed bird artist John Cox on board, and he kindly produced two new plates of the great albatrosses and prions. John has a particular interest in studying and illustrating albatrosses and petrels, and is also illustrating my forthcoming tubenose monograph.

The Southern Ocean and Antarctica constitute a huge part of the globe and a true wilderness but, unlike some areas of the world to which this term is applied, it is largely inhospitable with very little habitat diversity, and, in consequence, hosts a rather depauperate avifauna and virtually no terrestrial mammals. Those vertebrates that do survive there are among the most interesting and highly adapted animals on Earth, making it a dream destination for both researchers and amateur naturalists. This guide was born of several reasons. With increasing interest in the conservation of many of the region's species, as well as the growth in ecotourism, I realised the need for an up-to-date field guide to these amazing birds and mammals, treating their identification using the modern approach. Thus, this is the first, and still the only, complete field guide to the birds and marine mammals of Antarctica and the Southern Ocean north to c.40°S. Because of the relatively small number of species involved, it is the largest area of the globe covered by a single-volume field guide. The history of human exploration is comparatively short but has already wrought very strong impacts on wildlife, making it impossible to describe the region's birds and mammals without referring to these processes. My hope is that both casual visitors and scientists will find this a complete guide, which will serve as a base for further research. I have also endeavoured to ensure the book serves as a swift reference – using a combination of illustrations and carefully chosen photos depicting identification features and typical behaviour – whilst also challenging the reader to delve deeper into some of the major identification and taxonomic subjects discussed.

As mentioned in the first edition, the present guide was in a way born of my tubenose monograph that is still in preparation, now for almost ten years. Shortly after commencing field work in the Southern Ocean for the latter, I found (like many before me) that I had become hooked on the region; my images and memories of this fantastic wonderland almost forced me to write the present work to commemorate the love I feel for it. This guide is not the product of one person but the cumulative work of a great many inquiring minds. My greatest hope is that the book will stimulate even greater interest in this, among our last (but unfortunately, far from untouched) wildernesses, and that it will play a role in the process of safeguarding the Antarctic continent and Southern Ocean from the ravages of humankind.

Hadoram Shirihai, August 2007

Referees for this book

I wish to record my deep appreciation of the referees for this guide, for their valuable comments, given freely and frequently with enthusiasm. They improved the work immeasurably, and possess the closest and most intimate relationship with the places covered herein. These, and others, have devoted their lives to studying the biology and conservation of birds and marine mammals in the region; their contributions to this book are as follows.

Bird species accounts

Andrea Booth (selected New Zealand subantarctic island breeding seabirds), Bill Bourne (albatrosses, gadfly petrels, prions and storm-petrels), Vincent Bretagnolle (prions), John Cooper (penguins and shearwaters), David Crockett (Magenta Petrel), John Croxall (penguins), Sheryl Hamilton (Shy Albatross), Mike Imber (gadfly petrels, prions and selected New Zealand subantarctic island breeders), Frédéric Jiguet (penguins, skuas, gulls and terns), Pierre Jouventin (penguins, albatrosses, prions and storm-petrels), Colin Miskelly (penguins, albatrosses, gadfly petrels and New Zealand subantarctic island breeders), Peter Moore (selected New Zealand subantarctic island breeders), Peter Reese (selected New Zealand subantarctic island breeders), Peter Ryan (Rockhopper Penguin, albatrosses, gadfly petrels, prions, storm-petrels, shearwaters, gannets, skuas, gulls, terns and Tristan da Cunha landbirds), Lars Svensson (*Stercorarius* skuas), Lance Tickell (albatrosses), Frank S. Todd (penguins), Tony Tree (gulls and terns), Henri Weimerskirch (albatrosses), Tony Williams (penguins), Alan Wiltshire (Shy Albatross), Eric Woehler (penguins) and Robin Woods (penguins and Falklands breeders).

Marine mammal species accounts

Annalisa Berta (cetaceans and seals), Peter Evans (cetaceans), Nick Gales (seals), Erich Hoyt (Killer Whale), Morten Jørgensen (cetaceans), Gary Miller (cetaceans), William Perrin (cetaceans), Robert L. Pitman (cetaceans), Randall Reeves (cetaceans) and Brent Stewart (seals).

Other subjects

Peter Baldwin (several introductory chapters), Dennis Buurman (Seabird and sea mammal viewing around New Zealand), Arthur Ford (Synopsis of the Region), Robert Headland (History of Antarctic Exploration and regional historical sections), Morten Jørgensen (Ushuaia, the Beagle Channel and sea area south of Tierra del Fuego), Roger Kirkwood (Islands off southern Chile and southern Argentina), Colin Miskelly (Synopsis of the Region and Seabird and sea mammal viewing around New Zealand), Tony Palliser (Observing Southern Ocean seabirds off Australia), Julieta Rajlevsky (Islands off southern Chile and southern Argentina), Graham Robertson (Islands off southern Chile and southern

Argentina), Peter Ryan (Seabird and whale viewing off South Africa), Sav Saville (Seabird and sea mammal viewing around New Zealand), Monika Schillat (History of Antarctic Exploration), David G. Senn (Synopsis of the Region) and José Valencia (Islands off southern Chile and southern Argentina).

Islands off South America (mainly the Falklands and South Georgia)

Tim & Pauline Carr, Andrea Clausen, John Croxall, Nic Huin, Becky Ingham, Amanda Lynnes, Sally Poncet, Brad Rees, Keith Reid, Monika Schillat, Tim Soper, Debbie Summers, Lance Tickell, Frank S. Todd, Richard White and Robin Woods.

Antarctic Peninsula and related areas

Ron Naveen, Sally Poncet, Brad Rheese, Monika Schillat, Ron Lewis-Smith and Frank S. Todd.

South Atlantic islands

Albert Beintema, Bill Bourne, Bianca B. Harck, Onno Huyser, Kjell Isaksen, Dave G. Keith, Fridtjof Mehlum, Beau Rowlands, Peter Ryan and Michael Swales.

Indian Ocean islands

Marthan Bester, Bill Bourne, Vincent Bretagnolle, John Cooper, Yves Frenot, Michel Gauthier-Clerc, Fabrice Genevois, Christophe Guinet, Frédéric Jiguet, Pierre Jouventin, Thierry Micol, Deon Nel, Peter Ryan, Henri Weimerskirch and Eric Woehler.

New Zealand and Australian subantarctic islands

Andrea Booth, David Crockett, Paul Dingwall, Rosemary Gales, Simon Goldsworthy, Sheryl Hamilton, Mike Imber, Nigel Milius, Colin Miskelly, Peter Moore, Mike Ogle, Brian Rance, Paul Sagar, Rodney Russ (co-author with HS of an earlier contribution on these islands in *Alula*), Lou Sanson, Graeme Taylor, Alan Tennyson and Alan Wiltshire.

East Antarctica, Weddell Sea and Ross Sea

Alan D. Hemmings, Frédéric Jiguet, Rodney Russ (co-author with HS of an earlier contribution on some of these regions in *Alula*), Frank S. Todd, Peter Wilson and Eric Woehler.

Acknowledgements

Due to lack of space, I will not repeat the extensive acknowledgments of the first edition, but must stress again that in a book such as this, it is unsurprising that I should have benefited from the assistance of many people and organisations. Above all, I wish to highlight the splendid contribution of the referees. Thereafter, I thank the book's editor, Guy Kirwan, for working intensively and mostly voluntarily on this edition, and above all for his encouragement and support of our many shared projects. Nigel Redman brought the project to A&C Black, a genial place to produce many more editions, whilst Julie Bailey and Julie Dando have indefatigably endeavoured to deal with many almost impossible requests. Maria San Román, my girlfriend, spent many hours selecting penguin photos. Photographers are credited on each image, but I would like to emphasise the ten world-class cetacean photographers who contributed to both editions: Robin W. Baird, Dennis Buurman, Graeme Cresswell, Morten Jörgensen, Todd Pusser, Michael F. Richlen, Gabriel Rojo, Kim Westerskov, Stephen Wong and Francisco Viddi Carrasco. Also, I thank Steve Howell for his Magenta Petrel images, Michael Force for sharing his observations of Chatham Petrel

and helping to acquire photos of the species, whilst Thierry Micol provided images of Saint Paul Prion. Tony Pym kindly commented on several identification topics, helped search out many important photos, and offered much general encouragement. Johan Fromholtz provided an extensive review of the Blue Petrel and prions section as part of our joint work on the identification of these birds. Hans Jornvall has travelled with me to many subantarctic islands, including our unforgettable visit to the breeding grounds of the Amsterdam Albatross, and some of the new images included here belong to our joint project, the *Photographic Handbook of Birds of the World*. I twice enjoyed the company of Tony Marr in the South Atlantic, and thank him for much encouragement and for contributing images. Peter Ryan provided new information and comments on the buntings in Tristan, as well as some of the best images in both editions. Robert Flood, Chris Gaskin, Brent Stephenson and Bryan Thomas kindly commented on my draft text for the New Zealand Storm-petrel, and both Brent, Chris and Sav Saville improved the New Zealand section at the end of the book. Robert L. Pitman commented on the Killer Whales and Rick LeDuc on the Blue Whales.

Background to the research work

During my studies in the Southern Ocean, related to the ongoing *Albatrosses, Petrels and Shearwaters of the World*, co-authored by Vincent Bretagnolle and John Warham, I have visited all but two subantarctic island groups. As a result, I have observed (and often photographed) virtually all bird species and subspecies, and most of the marine mammals recorded. My principal focus has been to study the taxonomy and identification of albatrosses, particularly the Royal and Wandering groups, both on their breeding grounds and at sea. Many of my observations were made in and around New Zealand waters, which for the last ten years I have visited for up to three months per annum. Many of the bird species covered here I have also examined in various collections, principally at the Natural History Museum (Tring) and Muséum National d'Histoire Naturelle (Paris).

Brett Jarrett based the plates on his field experience with many of the seabirds and marine mammals, both in the region and surrounding waters, backed up by studies of many important collections, principally those housed in the Smithsonian Institute (Washington) and American Museum of Natural History (New York). Other museums which he visited to examine seabird, whale and dolphin specimens were: the San Diego Natural History Museum, Chicago Field Museum of Natural History, Los Angeles County Natural History Museum, Monterey Aquarium, Museum of Victoria, National Museum of Australia, the Finnish Natural History Museum and the Natural History Museum of Tasmania.

As mentioned in the Acknowledgements, I have been fortunate

to work in partnership, learn from, and above all share data and experiences with many of the most active researchers in the region. In addition, extensive research into the mass of literature covering the region was also required, and whilst *The Handbook of Australian, New Zealand and Antarctic Birds* (*HANZAB*),

Watson's *Birds of the Antarctic and Subantarctic* and BirdLife International's *Threatened Birds of the World* were obvious starting points, it was also necessary to check many other, more obscure books and papers; a full bibliography is provided at the end of the book.

Layout of the Book

This work, designed for the knowledgeable naturalist, birder and researcher, is the first detailed overview of the natural history of Antarctica and the subantarctic islands, particularly its birds and marine mammals, and is divided into three principal parts. The first provides an introduction to the region, its general characteristics, marine environment and climate, and provides naturalists with a synthesis of our current knowledge of such issues. Based extensively on previous works, I have endeavoured to employ a fresh and original approach to my presentation. Coupled with this are descriptions of geology and habitat, background information to the birds and marine mammals, résumés of our knowledge of these groups, the future of conservation, and an outline of the region's human history.

Secondly, the plates illustrate all breeding and otherwise important birds and marine mammals in the region, whilst the species accounts discuss identification, plumage, in some cases moult, as well as general biology, populations, conservation and taxonomy. Both the text and plates are arranged by family/genus, similar species or regional groupings, but also endeavour to retain (as far as possible) conventional systematic order (as in *The Handbook of Australian, New Zealand and Antarctic Birds*, although several species covered here are not treated in the latter). Recommended literature is discussed within a series of introductions that open each section of species accounts. Throughout the book conservation is a particularly strong theme. Some of the issues facing the Southern Ocean, especially longlining, are among the most acute and damaging faced by bird populations anywhere. I have made every effort to give readers a flavour of these and to highlight the work being undertaken to address these problems.

The third main section treats the different island groups and regions of Antarctica, including the Falklands, Tristan da Cunha, Gough and Amsterdam, which are not usually covered by works on the subantarctic because they lie well north of the Antarctic Convergence. However, my approach to defining the boundaries of the Southern Ocean has necessitated their inclusion here, especially given the number of subantarctic breeding species present on them. They are of great interest to natural historians, especially birders, and some are often included in cruises to other parts of the region. Each section includes information on climate, geology, vegetation, birds, marine mammals, nature conservation, human history and visiting arrangements. Information concerning cetaceans is often relatively incomplete and this section may appear comparatively thin. Because independent travel is largely impossible (unless you own a private yacht), and it is much more likely that the visitor will join an organized cruise, the access sections are designed to give only general information concerning arrangements, any restrictions and what to expect. This is not designed to be a precise site guide as to where to locate specific species. Your voyage staff should be able to provide such information, as well as to advise on safety arrangements and access restrictions involved in any landings. With the exception of the species accounts and references elsewhere in the book

to species unknown from our main region, scientific names for birds and mammals are not presented in the main text, but can be found in the Checklist of Birds and Marine Mammals of Antarctica and the Southern Ocean.

This book is designed as a popular introduction to the Southern Ocean and I make no apology for the almost complete non-inclusion of references in the text. Full details of those works consulted are included in the Bibliography. I have deliberately refrained from mentioning the many papers, especially on birds, published on the region, and have generally restricted myself to citing more modern contributions to the periodical literature, updating main works such as *HANZAB* and *Encyclopedia of Marine Mammals* (Perrin *et al.* 2002). Some earlier works have been included because of their particular interest; needless to say such decisions have been highly arbitrary and selective.

Finally, this book is also designed as a photographic record of the amazing wildlife and scenery of the Antarctic and subantarctic (though the photographs have principally been chosen for identification purposes). If it produces an interest in the conservation of this marvellous region, and sparks a longing to visit or return to this incomparably wild part of the planet, then the book will have served its purpose.

The Maps
(see inside cover for island keys used in the maps)

Given the size of the region, one might expect that mapping bird and marine mammal distributions would be problematic. Fortunately, breeding censuses have been undertaken at virtually all subantarctic islands and many parts of Antarctica. In contrast, data on the oceanic dispersal of birds and ranges of many cetaceans are often limited to certain areas/seasons and frequently based on comparatively few observations. Therefore, the maps should, in many instances, be recognised as only providing an approximate indication of a species' distribution. Several keynote previous works have been utilized here, along with many other, more regional and species-specific works, all of which are listed in the Bibliography that closes this book. For birds, I have especially relied on Marchant *et al.* (1990–2001; only the first five volumes had appeared at the time of the first edition), and for marine mammals Jefferson *et al.* (1993), Kasamatsu & Joyce (1995), Kasamatsu *et al.* (1996), Perrin *et al.* (2002), Ridgway & Harrison (1981–99) and Riedman (1990). The mapping system and symbols are usually self-explanatory: where breeding occurs on a island/landmass the locality is indicated by a filled circle keyed below the map; medium pink areas depict the approximate/presumed oceanic dispersal/distribution of each species, though different shades are sometimes used for different populations and or densities; these are always explained in the relevant key. Although the northern limit of our region is largely defined by the position of the Subtropical Convergence and/or 40°S, to a certain extent and where relevant the distribution further north is usually also mapped.

Chinstrap Penguins Pygoscelis antarctica *on a rare blue iceberg (and Antarctic Prion* Pachyptila desolata *in flight). The iceberg has been sculpted by seawater and as it thaws melt water brings nutrients to the surface, attracting wildlife. South Sandwich Islands, Dec 1994. © Cherry Alexander.*

Synopsis of the region

The Antarctic and Subantarctic Environments: The Southern Ocean

The region covered by this book is somewhat amorphous. Most people reading this will have a clear vision of Antarctica, a barely explored continental wilderness of ice and mountains, surrounded by a frozen sea, inhabited only by penguins and a few other hardy others, as well as more recently by humans. What, on the other hand, constitutes the subantarctic or the Southern Ocean? The latter is a conglomeration of large parts of the S Pacific, S Atlantic and S Indian Oceans, each of which possesses its own distinctive attributes, leading some geographers to consider the Southern Ocean as the southern oceans. Here, however, I prefer to regard the Southern Ocean as a single unit. And, to users of this guide, whose primary interests are the birds and sea mammals of this region, the Southern Ocean is highly unitary in her fauna. Even those seabird species limited, as breeders, to perhaps a single rock or island, frequently range far and wide across much of, or the entire, Southern Ocean, not only during the non-breeding season but on foraging trips from the nest. Nonetheless, some species, for instance several penguins and a handful of petrels, are very closely tied to coastal Antarctica and the pack-ice region or to some specific oceanic latitudes and areas.

Boundaries

How does one define the Southern Ocean? Put simply, it is the oceanic region south of the Subtropical Convergence, and hence encompassing subantarctic and Antarctic waters (see Fig. 1, inside front cover, and Fig. 2). These represent distinct water masses of a complex oceanic system and are divided by the Antarctic Convergence or Polar Front, which marks the meeting point of cold Antarctic and warmer temperate waters, and is a significant biological boundary. Water salinity, temperatures and circulation patterns differ to some extent either side of the Antarctic Convergence, as do many animals. Many are mainly found one side of the convergence and are significantly rarer either north or south of it, leading some previous works to define, in different ways, the 'southern ocean' as principally the region south of the Antarctic Convergence or, more commonly, to refer to the latter zone as the Antarctic Ocean. The Commission for the Conservation of Antarctic Marine Living Resources (CCAMLR) considers the Southern Ocean to lie south of a line approximating to the Antarctic Convergence. In contrast, others have used the term 'southern ocean' for a much wider zone but limited to the Antarctic Circumpolar Current.

It could be argued, however, that vertebrates, marine mammals and chiefly birds of both localised and wider ranging forms, generally exhibit a smooth gradient of increasing species composition north through the Antarctic and subantarctic zones, without any division at the Antarctic Convergence. Nonetheless, several species are adapted to, and concentrated within certain oceanic areas, and can be related to sub-zonation within the Southern Ocean. In addition, higher animal diversity, principally among those groups particular to the Southern Ocean, occur in the subantarctic zone. The Antarctic Convergence does not occur at the same latitude at all longitudes, being c.15° further north in the E Atlantic than in the E Pacific. The mean position of the Antarctic Convergence also varies, within 120–240 nautical miles either side of its mapped position, due to atmospheric conditions. When the circumpolar low-pressure zone is strongly developed and strong westerly winds push Antarctic surface water further northeast, as well as preventing the southward movement of subantarctic waters, the convergence moves north in response. Given a weakly developed circumpolar low-pressure zone the convergence moves south.

The distribution and ecology of many of the Southern Ocean's birds and marine mammals are also related to the oceanic and environmental subzones, both sides of the Antarctic Convergence. For instance, the northern limit of the pack ice is another significant zonal boundary, as is the 10°C mean annual surface water isotherm. The northern limits of permanent pack ice and the East-wind-Drift region, which form a narrow belt around the continent, subdivide the Antarctic into continental and maritime subzones. Equally, the subantarctic can be subdivided into cold, transitional and temperate subzones. The Subtropical Convergence marks the meeting point between subantarctic and tropical waters (the Subtropical Life Zone) and, like the Antarctic Convergence, functions as a key biological boundary. Many of the subantarctic islands lie slightly south of, on or just north of the Antarctic Convergence, whilst other groups are located between the latter and the Subtropical Convergence. To a large degree these zones and their boundaries correlate with the water masses and wind regime discussed below.

Water Zones (the Water Masses and Currents)

Within the Southern Ocean, from the Antarctic Continent north to the Subtropical Convergence, the circulation patterns of several different water masses and currents can be discerned (Figs. 2–3). The various water bodies possess differing densities, due to their different temperatures and relative salt contents, and are usually relatively distinct. Current flow generally matches that of above-surface winds, but especially the subsurface currents are driven by density differences between the water masses.

Deep water at some point returns to the surface to replace water that has shifted through current circulation, thus mixing deeper waters with surface layers. Such upwelling/downwelling may also be caused by a combination of wind and proximity to the coast, especially at the continental shelves; all types of downwelling transport oxygen-rich surface water to lower depths, whilst upwelling of deep water brings nutrients close to the surface. Convergence is the process by which different water masses meet and often results in the sinking of surface water (downwelling), whilst divergence is the process by which water flows from a central area, and often results in upwelling. Many oceanic upwellings occur near obstructions to bottom currents, namely islands and (submerged) seamounts. Hence mineral-rich waters occur around breeding sites for birds and seals. A combination of minerals, oxygen and sun cause plankton concentrations to be enormous in such areas.

Easterly winds or East-wind Drift generates a relatively weak and narrow westerly flow close to the Antarctic continent (the Antarctic Continental Current) but north of c.65°S westerly winds or West-wind Drift push water east, forming the so-called Antarctic

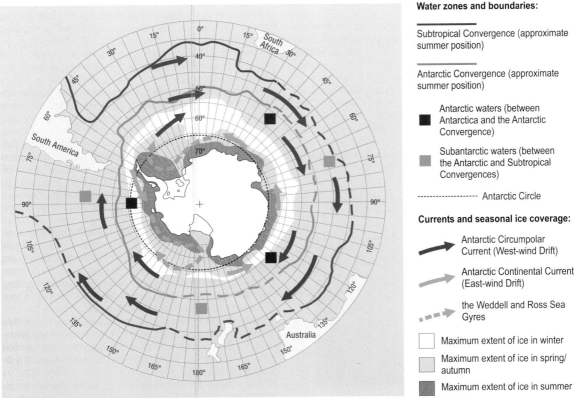

Water zones and boundaries:

Subtropical Convergence (approximate summer position)

Antarctic Convergence (approximate summer position)

Antarctic waters (between Antarctica and the Antarctic Convergence)

Subantarctic waters (between the Antarctic and Subtropical Convergences)

-------------------- Antarctic Circle

Currents and seasonal ice coverage:

Antarctic Circumpolar Current (West-wind Drift)

Antarctic Continental Current (East-wind Drift)

the Weddell and Ross Sea Gyres

Maximum extent of ice in winter

Maximum extent of ice in spring/autumn

Maximum extent of ice in summer

Figure 2. Water zones and currents in the Antarctic and subantarctic regions

Adélie Penguins Pygoscelis adeliae *leave Cape Royds in single file, heading past a frozen melt pool in the sea ice's buckled surface, on their way to the open sea to the north. Cape Royds, a protected site, has the southernmost Adélie Penguin colony on Earth. © Kim Westerskov.*

Circumpolar Current, which affects much of the Southern Ocean and is the most significant water current on Earth. In the Weddell Sea, the Peninsula blocks the East-wind Drift and deflects it north to meet the West-wind Drift, forming a circular current known as the *Weddell Gyre* (whose influence dissipates around the South Sandwich Is). Otherwise, sea-floor topography has a localised influence on the Southern Ocean system.

Of the five most prominent water masses in the Southern Ocean, the most distinct northward-flowing bodies are *Antarctic Bottom Water* (very cold, highly saline and extremely dense), which originates below winter pack ice, principally in the western Weddell Sea, and sinks over the continental shelf, and *Antarctic Surface Water*, which is relatively shallow (max. depth c.250 m) and exhibits characteristic seasonal variations in salinity. Close to the Antarctic Convergence these waters become warmer and partially lose their characteristic properties. Both carry cold water from the Antarctic to the tropics, and in the Southern Ocean sandwich the tongue of *Circumpolar Deep Water*—southward-flowing waters which penetrate from the Atlantic and, to much a lesser extent, from the Indian and Pacific Oceans, which is less dense

due to being relatively warmer. The *Antarctic Divergence* roughly marks the meeting point between the Antarctic Continental and Circumpolar Currents (or between the East- and West-wind Drifts), where surface water shifts and Circumpolar Deep Water rises to within 100 m of the surface and the three waters mix. Here also Circumpolar Deep Water rises and has a lower salinity as it begins to move north as Antarctic Surface Water. The rest is submerged and cooler Circumpolar Deep Water pushes toward the continent, where it sinks and augments Antarctic Bottom Water.

Around the Antarctic Convergence, warmer south-flowing *Subantarctic Surface Water* meets cold north-flowing Antarctic Surface Water, which generally sinks below the less dense Subantarctic Surface Waters, forming northbound *Antarctic Intermediate Water*. In consequence there is an approximate 2°C change in sea-surface temperatures over the short distance of 150 nautical miles. Below-surface expressions of the convergence are a rapid descent, below 200 m, of the minimum temperature layer and the position at which minimum salinity occurs. The *Subtropical Convergence*, where Subantarctic and Subtropical Waters mix and sink at a well-defined oceanic frontal system, also marks the northern limit of the east-flowing Antarctic Circumpolar Current.

Concluding remarks

Table 1 summarizes the various zones within the Southern Ocean and the present work's definition of the latter, based on several *combined* environmental and biological characteristics. The following assumptions should be explained.

1. Based on similarities in species distribution (or their gradient) and habitat types on the various islands in relation to the oceanic zones across the Antarctic and Subantarctic Zones, the latter two appear to represent a single large, complex faunal area. This circumpolar zone stretches from the Antarctic continent to the Subtropical Convergence and is defined as the Southern Ocean, forming a zoogeographical unit separate from adjacent oceans to the north.

2. This proposal demands research, as do several large-scale biogeographical and ecological relationships between the Southern Ocean fauna, e.g. the correlation between local and

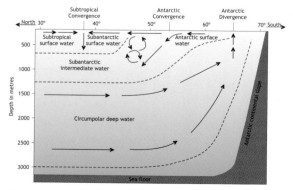

Figure 3. Schematic diagram of the Southern Ocean's principal water masses showing zonal flow of water.

Table 1. Oceanic zonation, habitat and wildlife diversity in the Southern Ocean (from the Antarctic coast to the Subtropical Convergence). For scientific names of birds and mammals see the Checklist of the Region (pages 31–34).

Climatic/oceanic limits	Main regions/islands within the Southern Ocean			Main habitat and significant breeding wildlife (inclusion of seabird and seal species largely corresponds to the presence of 10% or more of the world population in the combined islands/areas)		
	Islands/areas south of the Atlantic Ocean	Islands/areas south of the Indian Ocean	Islands/areas south of the Pacific Ocean	Habitat and Vegetation	Seabirds and others	Seals
Coastal Antarctic and immediate pack-ice zones Boundary: Antarctic continent coast to the northern limits of the permanent pack-ice zone. Mean summer surface temperature: -1.9°C to +1°C	Weddell Sea, Haakon VII Sea	East Antarctica	West Antarctica, Ross Sea	Mostly covered by ice. Moss, liverworts, lichens and algae (but very limited).	Emperor and Adélie Penguins, Southern Giant Petrel, Southern Fulmar, Antarctic, Cape and Snow Petrels, Wilson's Storm-petrel and South Polar Skua	Leopard, Weddell, Crabeater and Ross Seals.
The Pack-ice Zone Boundary: from the northern limits of previous zone north to the max. (winter) extent of the pack-ice zone (or roughly to the Antarctic Divergence). Mean summer surface temperature: -1°C to +2°C	South Shetlands, N Peninsula, South Orkney, South Sandwiches		Balleny Is, Scott, Peter I Øy	Snow-free ground is mostly bare and rocky. Moss, liverworts, lichens and algae reasonably abundant. Two spp. of flowering plants present.	Gentoo, Adélie and Chinstrap Penguins, Southern Giant Petrel, Southern Fulmar, Cape and Snow Petrels, Wilson's Storm-petrel, South Georgian and Antarctic Shags, Pale-faced Sheathbill, Subantarctic and South Polar Skuas, Kelp Gull and Antarctic Tern.	Leopard, Weddell, Crabeater and Ross Seals.
Antarctic Waters or the Periantarctic zones Boundary: between the Antarctic Divergence and Convergence. Mean summer surface temperature: +2°C to +6°C	South Georgia, Bouvetøya	Heard I		Patchy mature soil; snow-capped, bare rocky alpine terrain (in summer). Low and middle altitudes support abundant but patchy tree-less vegetation, including tussac and fellfield. Several spp. of flowering plants frequent close to sea level.	King, Gentoo and Macaroni Penguins, Wandering, Black-browed, Grey-headed and Light-mantled Sooty Albatrosses, Southern and Northern Giant Petrels, Southern Fulmar, Cape, Blue and White-chinned Petrels, Antarctic Prion, Wilson's and Black-bellied Storm-petrels, Common Diving-petrel, South Georgian and Heard Shags, Pale-faced and Black-faced Sheathbills, Subantarctic Skua, Kelp Gull and Antarctic Tern. Additionally, single species of pintail and pipit on South Georgia.	Antarctic Fur and Southern Elephant Seals.
The Cool Subantarctic Zone Boundary: from the Antarctic Convergence to approximately midway within Subantarctic Waters or to the 10°C isotherm in the warmest month. Mean summer surface temperature: +6°C to +10°C	Falklands	Crozet, Kerguelen, Prince Edward Is (the two latter groups are very close to the Antarctic Convergence)	Campbell, Macquarie	Soils mature and fertile (with extensive peat deposits). Abundant tree-less vegetation, including tussac and other grasses, herbs and meadows, admixed with small shrubs over most uplands.	King, Gentoo, Rockhopper, Macaroni, Royal, Yellow-eyed and Magellanic Penguins, Wandering, Black-browed, Campbell, Grey-headed, Indian Yellow-nosed, Sooty and Light-mantled Sooty Albatrosses, Southern and Northern Giant, Cape, White-headed, Soft-plumaged, Great-winged, Kerguelen, White-chinned, Grey and Blue Petrels, Antarctic, Salvin's and Slender-billed Prions, Wilson's, Grey-backed and Black-bellied Storm-petrels, South Georgian and Common Diving-petrels, Rock, Imperial, Crozet, Kerguelen, Macquarie and Campbell Shags, Black-faced Sheathbill, Falkland and Subantarctic Skuas, Dolphin, Kelp and Brown-hooded Gulls and Antarctic, South American and Kerguelen Terns. Relatively large numbers of landbirds on the Falklands and few on Campbell, Eaton's Pintail on Crozet and Kerguelen.	South American and Subantarctic Fur Seals, South American and New Zealand (Hooker's) Sea Lions and Southern Elephant Seal.
Temperate Subantarctic Zone Boundary: within Subantarctic Waters from the 10°C isotherm in the warmest month to the Subtropical Convergence (with exceptions). Mean summer surface temperature: above +10°C	Tristan da Cunha and Gough (situated in the transition zone between subantarctic and subtropical waters)	Amsterdam and St Paul (both situated north of the Subtropical Convergence)	Aucklands, Snares, Antipodes, Bounties, Chathams, Tasmania (the latter is marginally north of the Subtropical Convergence)	Soils mature and fertile (with extensive and deep peat deposits). Trees, shrubs, bushes, meadows and tussac in the lowlands; shrubs and fellfield, admixed with bushes, rather extensive in the upland.	Northern Rockhopper, Snares, Erect-crested, Yellow-eyed and Little Penguins, Tristan, Gibson's Antipodean, Amsterdam, Shy, White-capped, Salvin's, Chatham, Pacific, Buller's Atlantic and Indian Yellow-nosed, Sooty and Light-mantled Sooty Albatrosses, Northern Giant, Cape, White-headed, Great-winged, Atlantic, Kerguelen, Soft-plumaged, Mottled, Magenta, Chatham, Black-winged, White-chinned, Spectacled and Grey Petrels, Flesh-footed, Great, Sooty and Little Shearwaters, Broad-billed, Antarctic, Fairy and Fulmar Prions, White-faced, Grey-backed, and White- and Black-bellied Storm-petrels, South Georgian and Common Diving-petrels, Auckland, Campbell, Bounty, Chatham and Pitt Shags, Tristan and Subantarctic Skuas, Kelp and Red-billed Gulls, and White-fronted and Antarctic Terns. Relatively large numbers of landbirds on Chathams, and small/moderate numbers of indigenous landbirds on other groups.	New Zealand and Subantarctic Fur Seals, New Zealand (Hooker's) Sea Lion and Southern Elephant Seal.

Wandering Albatross D. [e.] exulans. In the enormous waves of the Southern Ocean, these massive birds appear small, but even in the fiercest of storms their supremely agile, effortless and relaxed flight is obvious. Experiencing these birds in such conditions is arguably the ultimate birding experience. Off Kerguelen, Mar 2004. © Hadoram Shirihai.

seasonal productivity of phytoplankton/zooplankton or certain squid and fish, and the seasonal abundance of seabirds and marine mammals, and how these can be related to various water masses and their circulation identified within the Southern Ocean. Such ongoing research should further recognize the zoogeographical uniqueness and unity of the Southern Ocean.

3. The present work presents a modified definition of the Southern Ocean, it being limited to the north by the Subtropical Convergence or latitude 40°S, and excluding continental waters off South America, Australia and mainland New Zealand, and southern Africa.

4. The following are the most productive wildlife regions within the various oceanic zones: most noticeable is the rich Antarctic Convergence Zone, and its islands, namely the Prince Edwards, Crozet, Kerguelen, Heard and Macquarie; and the New Zealand subantarctic groups are especially diverse due to their rich waters within a complex ocean-bottom topography and their proximity to the Ross Sea. All lands south of the Antarctic Convergence, which are affected by northward-flowing Antarctic waters, are remarkable for their birds and marine mammals, namely the South Sandwiches, South Georgia, South Orkneys, and the Peninsula and South Shetlands. The other rich Antarctic region is the Ross Sea. The richness of Tristan da Cunha and Gough is partially explained by the presence of the Subtropical Convergence, whilst high landbird diversity on the Falklands and among the New Zealand subantarctic islands is attributable to their proximity to landmasses.

The following chapters present a brief introduction to the evolutionary history, geology, geography, climate, habitats, sea environment, wildlife, human history and exploration, and conservation problems facing the region.

Geological History

The break-up of Gondwana

The pole to pole super-continent geologists call Pangea, containing all of the world's landmasses, came into being near the beginning of the Paleozoic era, c.500 million years ago. Near the beginning of the Mesozoic era, Pangea split along the line of a Paleo-Mediterranean Sea into two smaller super-continents, Laurasia to the north (North America and Asia) and Gondwana to the south (all of today's Southern Hemisphere continents). Rifting of Gondwana commenced c.190 million years ago and different lands separated from Antarctica at various times, firstly Africa and finally Australia and South America (c.50–20 million years ago). Gondwana broke up by a process of continental rifting, during which valleys foundered below sea level and eventually new oceans formed by the mechanism of sea-floor spreading, widening at rates of just c.5 cm per year. By 70 million years ago, in the early Cenozoic era, Antarctica was still basking in a temperate climate and was probably largely covered by dense forests. The Drake Passage apparently formed as recently as 20 million years ago, as the continents became widely separated, but it was 60–40 million years ago that Antarctica and Australia finally parted and the former assumed its present geographical position. Antarctica is considered to have been ice-bound for the last 25 million years, but was still able to support vegetation. In the 1980s plants and fossilized wood were discovered high in the Transantarctic Mountains, suggesting that even the interior of the continent was significantly warmer than it is today 2–5 million years ago.

The famous German naturalist Alexander von Humboldt was the first to notice, in the early 1800s, that the shapes of South America and Africa suggested that they might once have been joined. Ecological evidence began to appear as the 19th century wore on: Hooker noticed similarities among the plants of New Zealand, Tasmania, Kerguelen and the Falklands, and Snider-Pellegrini, discovered identical fossil deposits in North America and Europe. Edward Seuss was the first to formally propose the existence of Gondwana, taking the name from the Gond region of C India where fossil strata similar to those found in other disparate continents had been found. He soon found adherents, though Wegener – who was the first to propound the fully articulated theory of a super-continent, which he named Pangaea ('all lands') – was widely ridiculed among the scientific community. But, as the 20th century passed its midpoint, the evidence in support of Gondwana became irrefutable. Sea floors moving away from mid-ocean ridges provide the impetus for continental drift, while fossil evidence from Antarctica proves the existence there of a deciduous conifer, a fern and a terrestrial lizard, each of which has generic counterparts in India, Africa, South America and Australia. And, even to the casual travelling naturalist, the strikingly similar Southern Beech *Nothofagus* forest communities of S Chile and New Zealand provide an easily digestible pointer to Gondwana's existence. Fossils of *Nothofagus* show that similar forests once grew in Antarctica.

The icy landscapes of the Antarctic Peninsula are dominated by impressively rugged mountains. January 2001. © Hadoram Shirihai.

East and West Antarctica

The geological histories of East (Greater) and West (Lesser) Antarctica are different. The former is a stable platform of Precambrian rocks up to 3.84 billion years old overlain by marine and terrestrial sediments up to 590 million years old, which form the greater part of the Transantarctic Mountains separating East and West Antarctica. Being a geologically stable feature, they are arranged in horizontal layers and separate the ice sheets of the two parts of the continent. Though situated in West Antarctica, the Ellsworth Mountains consist almost entirely of sedimentary rocks of a similar age to those of the Transantarctic range, but their more deformed shape and position have led geologists to speculate that they may constitute a part of the Earth's crust that has been rotated. The rest of West Antarctica has enjoyed a considerably more turbulent geological history. It originally formed the Pacific rim of Gondwana and appears to have resulted from three major crustal fragments up to 700 million years old. Marie Byrd Land is separated from Thurston Island by the 2000 m-deep Byrd basin, whilst a very deep trough also divides the Peninsula and Thurston sections. The three blocks are united to each other and the rest of Antarctica by the overlying ice cap.

The Peninsula

The Antarctic Peninsula is a mixture of Mesozoic (65–225 million-year-old) and Tertiary (2–65-million-year-old) rocks as well as glacial deposits, and the mountains that form the spine of the Peninsula are a result of the same processes that wrought the Andes, providing further confirmation of the geological linkage between the continents. Indeed, they are still connected by the largely underwater Scotia Ridge, with several active volcanoes in the volcanic arc of the South Sandwiches, whilst other peaks in this range form the South Orkneys and South Georgia.

The subantarctic islands

Most of these islands are geologically young features (Amsterdam appeared just 200,000–400,000 years ago) and volcanic in origin, though some, e.g. South Georgia are the result of large-scale sedimentary activity. Many are mountainous with striking landscapes, though the Falklands are comparatively low-lying (especially that part of East Falkland known as Lafonia) and are also a product of the folding movements of sedimentary rocks, rather than volcanic activity. In the Falklands, which are older than many islands in the region, the folding activity gave rise to three montane ridges, some of which represent formidable terrain. In comparison to some subantarctic islands in the Indian Ocean sector, there is comparatively little evidence of glacial activity. Nonetheless, the heavily indented coastline is similar to several other 'true' subantarctic islands, e.g. the Kerguelen group.

Some of the subantarctic islands of the New Zealand region are of volcanic origin, rising from the Campbell Plateau, a submerged extension of the southern New Zealand continent. Its rocks principally date from the younger end of the scale, but Campbell itself contains some of the oldest rocks, dating from the Paleozoic era. The Snares and Bounties differ in being of the early Jurassic period (180–190 million years ago). Most islands became aerial 6–25 million years ago, but some are as young as 100,000 years old.

Unlike all other such islands, Macquarie is wholly oceanic in origin, being situated at the boundary of two tectonic plates, and within an area of considerable seismic activity. Few of the island's geological deposits formed sub-aerially and these are all very recent. Most of the island's rocks are 27–30 million years old, though Macquarie appeared above the surface 90,000–300,000 years ago. It forms the emergent portion of the Macquarie Ridge, part of a discontinuous complex of submarine ridges and trenches, some up to 5500 m deep. There is evidence of continuous tectonic activity along the ridge for 3–5 million years and it is possible that islands may have emerged and foundered at various points within the general vicinity of the present-day island on several occasions during this period.

Geography and Climate

Antarctica, the fifth-largest continent, is the only such landmass that exhibits regular changes in overall size. Even at its smallest, in summer, it covers an impressive 14.2 million km^2, with a diameter of c.4500 km and coastline of 32,000 km, it is marginally larger than Australia or Europe. But in September, in the depths of winter, its size effectively doubles due to the freezing of sea ice to almost 1000 km offshore, covering 20 million km^2 (or 57% of the Antarctic Ocean) and reaching north of the 60th parallel in

The spreading Commonwealth Glacier in the Dry Valleys, Ross Sea region. © Kim Westerskov.

some areas, though even at this season there are small pockets of open water. Sea ice is at its minimum in Feb–Mar when it covers 4 million km² (or 11% of the Southern Ocean). Surrounded by the Antarctic Ocean and separated from South America by 1000 km, Australia by 2500 km and Africa by 4000 km, Antarctica is the most isolated continent in the world. Despite the presence of several large under-ice lakes, it is also the most arid and, given a mean elevation of 2250 m, the highest.

Major geographical features

Viewed on a map, the principal geographical features dominating Antarctica are the Peninsula, which juts north like a tail towards South America, and the 2900 km-long Transantarctic Mountains, which separate East (Greater) and West (Lesser) Antarctica. Some geographers formerly regarded these as separate continents given their radically different ages, whilst others consider the Peninsula to be an offshore landmass connected to the main continent solely by the ice sheet. West Antarctica is significantly more mountainous than East Antarctica and has the continent's highest peak, the 4897 m Vinson Massif, at the base of the Peninsula. The Ellsworth Mountains and Marie Byrd Land separate the continent's two largest bays, the Weddell Sea and the Ross Sea, which are dominated by large ice shelves that act as continuations

of the Antarctic ice sheet. The Ross Ice Shelf, being the size of France, is the largest feature of its type in the world, being the product of seven major glaciers.

Ice features and formations

Given that Antarctica is *the* land of ice, with 99.77% ice-covered, it is unsurprising to find the world's largest glacier, the Lambert Glacier, which flows for over 400 km, in East Antarctica. Only c.5% of Antarctica's coastline is composed of rock. Ice flows downhill from the ridges and peaks, converging into major streams as it approaches the coast. The ice, whilst unevenly distributed, is up to 4776 m thick in places and has depressed the underlying bedrock by up to 2496 m. Ninety percent of the world's ice is in Antarctica, or nearly 30 million km³, i.e. 70–85% of Earth's fresh water. It is unevenly distributed, with 25.6 million km³ in East Antarctica. The ice sheet is subject to constant change as icebergs break off, particularly from the major ice shelves in the Ross and Weddell Seas.

Icebergs take 4–6 years to melt and may also be carried north by gyres into the Antarctic Circumpolar Current that moves them eastward. Bergs are usually tabular with steeply angled sides and are frequently 200–300 m thick. Several major bergs formed in 2000. One, which calved from the Ross Ice Shelf was c.295 km long by 37 km wide, with an area of c.10,600 km²; together with another huge berg it had, by Nov 2001, upset water currents and wind regimes in the Ross Sea, impeding the seasonal pack-ice break-up. Similar events occurred along the Ronne Ice Shelf, and the total area lost from the two ice shelves during the year 2000 was c.23,000 km², or around 1.5% of the area of all ice shelves in Antarctica.

Icebergs present fascinating forms, due to the action of waves, currents and upwellings, and colours, the blue and greens of solid ice being continually altered by the ever-changing light conditions of the Antarctic. Various estimates have been made concerning the frequency of icebergs and their production: one survey quantified 30,000 within 4400 km², whilst it is claimed that up to 1450 km³ of icebergs calve each year, most from ice shelves.

Currently, rates of build-up of new material, snow and ice on the surface of the continent, outstrip loss through iceberg formation, with an estimated 1700 km³ being added per annum. Complex studies using the most up-to-date technology are examining these processes in detail. Use of satellite data has demonstrated that, since 1992, 31 km³ of ice has been lost from Pine Island Glacier,

Huge plates breaking from the ice shelf are the principal source of immense icebergs. W Weddell Sea. © Hadoram Shirihai.

Ice

A. Formation of Sea Ice

- Frost smoke—wispy 'smoke' rising from the surface of the sea when new ice forms rapidly.
- Frazil ice—mushy first ice in sea, tiny spindles and discs of ice crystals form a thin and flexible layer (see grease ice).
- Grease ice—a soupy layer of new ice on the sea, with a greyish matte (greasy) appearance.
- Ice cakes—small plates of ice broken by sea swells and waves.
- Ice rafting—edges of thin cakes or floes slide over each other, thickening the sheet.
- Old ice—sea ice more than two years old, which may be up to 3 m thick (when severely weakened prior to melting it is known as rotten ice).
- Pancake ice—thicker cakes of new ice that collide with each other producing turned-up edges (new ice less than one year old).
- Pack ice—more or less continuous cover of ice on the sea, with annual thickness of c.3 m. Pancakes coalesce to form solid layer of floating ice. Often multi-year ice.
- Young ice—first stage in the formation of sea ice, when ice crystals start to appear in calm water and join together.

B. Some features of ice in the sea

- Anchor ice—submerged ice attached to the seabed.
- Bergy bit—1 m to 5 m-high fragments of broken floating ice, which often form during the break-up of an iceberg.
- Brash ice—floating ice consisting of broken pieces of pack ice and ice floes (floating slabs of ice usually smaller than 3 m thick and 2 m across)
- Fast ice—sea ice attached to the shore.
- Floe—a large sheet of ice detached from the pack and floating freely in the sea.
- Growler—piece of floating glacier, which is too small to be an iceberg. Growlers float low in the water, barely showing above the surface and are usually formed of old, hard ice. They can be dangerous because they are difficult to detect on ships' radar.
- Ice shelf—a sheet of very thick, generally floating ice attached to land, typically with an ice cliff or barrier at its front along the sea and fed by mountain glaciers and ice streams.
- Iceberg—large mass of floating ice that has broken away from a glacier or ice shelf (can be immense in size). A glacier berg is an opaque white iceberg formed from a glacier, commonly white but often with a soft green or blue colouring due to colour absorption and scattering, and often crevassed.
- Ice blink—silvery-white glare caused by the reflection of distant pack ice on the clouds.
- Lead—a large crack in the ice pack, used by ships for passage through the pack.
- Polynya—area of open water within pack ice, wider than a 'lead', which may be important to marine mammals.
- Shore lead—open water between pack and shore.
- Tabular berg—flat-topped iceberg derived from an ice shelf that can be immense in size (up to thousands of square kilometres).
- Water sky—dark-coloured underside of clouds due to reflection of open water within the pack ice.

C. Other ice features

- Bergschrund—a crevasse at the head of a valley glacier that separates the ice from the rock behind it.
- Calve—the formation of a berg by breaking off from a glacier or other large ice mass.
- Cirque—a hollowed basin on a mountainside formed by glacier erosion.
- Cirque glacier—an alpine glacier occupying a cirque.
- Crack—a fracture in floating sea ice, narrow enough to jump across.
- Crevasse—fissure formed in a glacier, often covered by a snow bridge.
- Glacier—a mass of snow and/or ice moving from higher to lower ground confined as in a valley (sometimes a glacier may float out onto the sea).
- Glacier tongue—extension of a valley glacier into the sea.
- Hanging valley—a small tributary valley that enters the main valley above a cliff, typically with waterfalls. The main valley was eroded deeper by a larger glacier than in the tributary valley.
- Moraine—ridge or deposit of rocky debris carried along by a glacier; a terminal moraine marks the farthest advance of a glacier, which is then left behind when the glacier melts and retreats.
- Nunatak—a rocky spur or mountain peak projecting from and surrounded by a glacier or ice sheet.
- Oasis—area of bare rock left without ice or snow as an ice sheet retreats or thins, e.g. the Dry Valleys (S Victoria Land) and Vestfold Hills.
- Pressure ridge—ridge formed on sea ice by pressure of ice floes upon each other or by tidal or current movements.

In late winter (just before the Emperor Penguins Aptenodytes forsteri *complete their breeding cycle and return seaward) the SW Weddell Sea is still mainly frozen.* © Hadoram Shirihai.

Ice cakes and tabular bergs off South Orkney. © Hadoram Shirihai.

Snow blowing off the Ross Sea Ice Shelf. © Gordon Petersen.

A small iceberg is calved at the tidewater edge of the Fortuna Glacier, South Georgia. © Keith Robinson.

Crevasses across glacier tongue. © British Antarctic Survey.

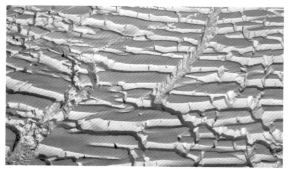

Pancake ice. © Hadoram Shirihai.

Formation of sea ice; here, calm seas have permitted the surface to freeze into glossy sheets, just a few cm thick. Disturbances from wind or sea have broken and moved these sheets so that they ride up over each other. © Kim Westerskov.

Pack ice in stormy weather. © Kim Westerskov.

Two icebergs in the W Weddell Sea sculpted by the sea. That in the foreground is of younger ice, more uniform in quality, whilst greater compression and thus density, with varying amounts of debris trapped therein, give that in the background its varied colours. © Hadoram Shirihai.

Tabular bergs, glowering skies and snow-covered fog-bound mountains are features of the South Orkneys. © Hadoram Shirihai.

the largest in West Antarctica, which has retreated over 5 km inland as a consequence. Data from another sensor indicates that the thinning is restricted to the area where the ice is flowing fastest, indicating a change in flow of the ice sheet, and not simply changed snowfall.

Eventually, it is predicted, the ice sheet will entirely melt, be it at more normal rates or due to climate change induced by human actions. At this point pressure on the continent will be relieved and the crust slowly rebound to a new altitude, which has been estimated by examination of the surrounding continental shelf to be 300–400 m.

There are several different types of sea ice. In the early stages of freezing, when the ice first floats to the surface, it is known as 'slush' or 'sludge' ice. When broken into fragments, it may form small circular floes with slightly raised sides known as 'pancake' ice. 'Young' ice is easily penetrated by ships, being unhummocked and unconsolidated; if a smooth sheet of water freezes under calm conditions, it may be known as 'black' ice. 'Fast' ice is also usually unhummocked, and also carries a heavy snow burden and is attached to the coast. An unbroken large area of ice is known as a 'field', whilst a free-floating area of known dimensions is called a 'floe'. Old ice, which has been thrown into ridges by internal expansion, water currents or winds, is known as 'hummocky' ice, while at sea 'drift' ice is an area of solid ice now broken so that the extent of open water exceeds that of the ice. 'Brash' ice, the final result of wave action on drift ice, is near detritus.

Snow is a rarer commodity in Antarctica than many people expect; much of the interior and Peninsula receive less than 10 cm annually and only coastal areas and parts of West Antarctica routinely exceed 30 cm per annum. Nonetheless, severe blizzards frequently redistribute existing snow and form deep drifts capable of burying buildings. In addition, glacial ice originates as snow, which accumulates and is compacted by ever-increasing younger layers, eventually fusing as ice under the great pressure. Whilst the ice sheet is c.25 million years old, probably none of the ice currently in existence is more than 700,000 years old.

Climate and weather systems

Given its location, almost uniformly high elevation, permanent ice cover (which reflects c.80% of the Sun's radiation back into Space) and lack of a protective water-vapour-filled atmosphere, it is unsurprising that Antarctica's climate is harsh and unforgiving. Mean temperatures in the interior range from -40°C to -70°C in

winter and -15°C to -35°C in summer, but on coasts overall temperatures are significantly 'warmer': -15°C to -32°C in winter and 5°C to -5°C in summer. The South Pole whilst cold is not the coldest place on Earth. Vostok station at 3500 m (almost 700 m higher than the Pole), a Russian-operated base in East Antarctica, recorded -89.2°C in Jul 1983. In contrast, the Peninsula records the highest temperatures in the continent on a year-round basis. The famed Antarctic blizzards are the most extreme winds on the planet and can reach up to 320 km/h, with the highest winds usually experienced in coastal regions. These are caused by denser, colder air being swept off the polar plateau coastwards by their own weight but in a layer that is only a few metres thick. Once clear of the coast these winds rapidly disappear. Little, if any, snow falls in such conditions, but snow whipped from the ground frequently reduces visibility to almost nothing. At Cape Denison, wind speeds reach hurricane force on average every three days and such conditions led Douglas Mawson to deem the area *The Home of the Blizzard*.

That Antarctica has by far the coldest climate on our planet is due to the drift of the continent into the southern polar region and the opening of the Drake Passage, which occurred roughly 20 million years ago. The appearance of the latter triggered the continuous flow of the most important oceanic current: the Westwind Drift, which could henceforth circum-flow Antarctica without obstacle, and has since acted as a barrier to warm Atlantic and Pacific currents. Thus Antarctica and most subantarctic islands (which are circum-flown by the West-wind Drift) are isolated from any 'heating' influence.

The climate of the subantarctic islands is different, though it shares some features in common with that of the Antarctic continent. With the exception of the Falklands, the islands covered here lie between the Antarctic Circle (66.5°S) and the Antarctic Convergence (or Polar Front), which roughly tracks the 50th parallel. South of the convergence, mean summer sea temperatures fall to 3.9°C (from 7.8°C), whilst in winter they are 1.1°C (north of the convergence they are 2.8°C). However, changes in sea temperature in this region are not gradual but occur as several fronts and are linked to the eastward flow of the Antarctic Circumpolar Current. The Circumpolar Current stretches over 20,000 km around the Antarctic continent and though its surface speed is comparatively modest, its carrying volume of 135 million m³ per second is almost incomprehensible. The current also permits the free interchange of water between all of the world's major oceanic basins.

The Cape Crozier Emperor Penguin Aptenodytes forsteri *colony at the easternmost tip of Ross I. © Kim Westerskov.*

All of the islands have windy climates, which are remarkably uniform due to the moderating oceanic influence. Sunshine is a comparatively rare but infrequently measured commodity (figures available for Campbell indicate that it receives 660 hours per annum, or c.16% of the possible total), although temperatures comparatively rarely dip below freezing on the Falklands, which experience mean winter temperatures of 7°C and in summer of 10°C, whilst those on Macquarie, though on average slightly lower, do not fall below freezing, even in midwinter. South of the convergence, at South Georgia recorded temperatures vary between -19°C and 24°C, but the annual range of mean monthly temperatures is just 7°C. South of this group, maximum temperatures typically decline and minimum temperatures significantly decrease. Rainfall and wind are predominant features, with periods of calm weather being rare. Mean wind speed in the Falklands is 16 knots. Precipitation, as mist, rain, sleet or hail occurs year-round and, on some islands, all can fall on the same day. Annual precipitation in the Falklands, at the wettest sites, is 630–650 mm. Whilst snow can fall at any season, it rarely lies more than one week and is usually brief. Even south of the Antarctic Convergence, snow rarely accumulates, except in winter, with rain more prevalent. Southern Hemisphere temperatures in general, but especially at higher latitudes, rose during the 20th century, and the South Georgia glaciers have known to be in retreat since the 1880s.

Political boundaries and human geography

Seven nations claim territory in Antarctica (though these are currently held in abeyance under the 1961 Antarctic Treaty) and others, e.g. Russia and the USA, have carefully preserved the right to do so. Australian Antarctic Territory is the largest national claim, covering much of East Antarctica, though a small strip of land bisecting the Australian-claimed land, the Terre Adélie, is part of the French Southern and Antarctic Territories (Territoire des Terres Australes et Antarctiques Françaises). The Ross Dependency, which neatly sandwiches the Ross Sea, is New Zealand's piece of the continental jigsaw. Four nations lay claim to parts of the Antarctic Peninsula, the Weddell Sea and related regions, Chile, Argentina, Norway and the UK. Thirty-four year-round stations have been established in Antarctica, including the South Shetlands, operated by Argentina, Australia, Brazil, Chile, China, France, Germany, India, Japan, New Zealand, Poland, Russia, South Africa, South Korea, the UK, Ukraine, Uruguay and the USA, with most bases being in the Peninsula and East Antarctica.

Biological research has been a significant feature of Man's most recent interest in the subantarctic islands. The Falklands, Tristan da Cunha (both to the UK) and the Chathams (New Zealand) are the only archipelagos to hold significant human populations. Scientists represent the vast majority of the inhabitants on all other islands. The UK also claims South Georgia, and has territorial interests in the South Shetlands, South Orkneys and South Sandwiches. Argentina has a base on the South Orkneys, and Gough, which is also claimed by the UK, has a South African base. Norway administers Bouvetøya, which has only been visited very occasionally, principally for scientific purposes, as well as Peter I Øy. South Africa maintains another scientific station on the Prince Edwards, whilst Australia exerts territorial rights over Heard and McDonald, with all of the other islands in this region belonging to France. New Zealand controls all of the subantarctic islands within the seas to its south, except Macquarie which is Australian and has been subject to some of the most intensive research, including ornithological, of any island in the entire region covered here.

A number of metrological and scientific bases are dotted through the South Shetlands and the Peninsula, such as this Chilean station, Gonzales Videla, Antarctic Peninsula, January 2001. © Morten Jørgensen.

Sea Environment

Within the sea ice surrounding the Antarctic continent and its nearby islands there is almost a complete absence of shallow-water flora and fauna. Anchor ice, which reaches the seabed in depths of up to 33 m, discourages such life forms, though the sea floor itself may hold some sponges, starfishes and algae, and some seaweeds, marine worms, starfishes and other animals inhabit the zone immediately below the low-water mark on colder coasts. Surprisingly, it is not temperature but available light that discourages life in such regions. However, the islands north of the pack-ice zone possess relatively rich intertidal and sub-littoral zones, especially in sunlit waters, marked by large banks of kelp off many coasts, and the seas of much of this region are the richest in the world; overall productivity is about four times greater than any other oceanic environment. Huge areas of discoloured water—green, brown or red—are actually plankton, which are among the essential links in the chain of Antarctic life (see the inset Food Chains in the Oceans, on p. 20). Algae can also survive well within the pack-ice zone.

Plankton

The Southern Ocean's low temperatures and high mineral content provide the necessary cocktail for extreme productivity. Cold water harbours more carbon dioxide and oxygen than warm water, providing plants with the required agents for photosynthesis, while the constant upwelling brings large quantities of phosphates, nitrates and other essential compounds close to the surface where, in summer, the long hours of daylight permit plants to almost continually photosynthesise. Conditions are most favourable for such growth within the East-wind-Drift region, where winds are weaker and the water more stable, and least favourable in the subantarctic oceans. Whilst the cold limits the number of species, those that are adapted to such extremes are able to occur in near-incalculable quantities.

Phytoplankton are the smallest of the small. Virtually all are diatoms, single-celled plants each contained within a box of glass-like silica, and coloured pale brown or green. Many have long, thin shapes and form strands or chains, with whiskers and bristles that permit them to remain near the surface, where they may stain the edge of ice floes red-brown. Dinoflagellates, another form of uni-cellular green plant, are much less common. These form the food of a myriad of small, floating animals, zooplankton (numerous tiny crustaceans). Chief are krill and other crustaceans and larval fishes, but pelagic molluscs, salps, jellyfish and arrow-worms sometimes feed on the herbivores and occasionally also number millions. Of the zooplankton, the Euphausiid crustaceans, especially krill, form the principal foodstuff for baleen whales, Crabeater Seals and many tubenoses. Krill are small luminescent shrimps and are extremely abundant in cold polar oceans. Of the 85 known species of krill, 11 are restricted to Antarctic waters, of which the best known is the 3–6-cm long Antarctic Krill *Euphausia superba*.

The standing crop of phytoplankton can be crudely estimated by observing the amount of chlorophyll discolouring the water, whilst the relative productivity of a sector of ocean can be established by a representative sampling of plants for radioactive carbon-14. Both standing crop and yield are not uniform, with areas of particularly low productivity in parts of the E Pacific and W Atlantic, the Drake Passage and Weddell and Bellinghausen Seas. Much higher productivity is located in the Scotia Arc, the SW Weddell Sea, west of the Peninsula and the Ross Sea. By inference, such areas are also much more productive feeding areas for birds and marine mammals. There is also seasonal, as well as distributional, variation in standing crop and yield values. These reach their lowest in Apr–Jul, when days are very short and sea ice is at its maximum extent. Productivity increases during Aug, but remains relatively low until Sep/Oct, when phytoplankton return to the surface in large numbers and commence 'blooming' in waters north of the pack ice. Standing crop and yield reach a maximum in Jan, but then rapidly diminish as day length and temperatures start to decrease.

Rich and colourful life encrusted on an underwater rock, 10 m below the surface of the entrance to Perseverance Harbour, Campbell I. 'Pink paint' coralline algae, sea anemones, sea squirts (solitary ascidians), mating white sea slugs (opisthobranch molluscs), bryozoans/polyzoans, compound ascidians, and predatory whelks are all visible. © Kim Westerskov.

Zooplankton, unsurprisingly, show similar patterns and levels of abundance. In May–Sep most of these winter at depths of 250–2000 m in the Warm Deep Current. This presents a lean period for birds and marine mammals, and many move considerably further north at this season. From Oct zooplankton also rise to the surface north of the pack-ice zone and spread south as the ice recedes closer to the continent. Areas where phytoplankton reach their highest density, e.g. within inshore and turbulent waters subject to a mixing of layers and commonly at the shelf edge, are also favoured by krill and copepods. Again the most important areas are within the Scotia Arc and the northern and western coasts of the Peninsula, the SW Weddell Sea and the less rich Ross Sea. The yield and standing crop of zooplankton are considerably more difficult to establish. Estimates are all likely to be conservative, though perhaps of the correct order of magnitude. It is thought that the total productivity of the Southern Ocean amounts to c.360 million tonnes of animal material per annum.

Antarctic Krill Euphausia superba is perhaps the most abundant species on Earth. Krill are food for whales, seals, birds and fish. This species can reach c.50 mm long. © Global Book Publishing.

Whales, seals and birds do not only take plankton, though these groups take particularly large and quantifiable quantities (e.g. seabirds are estimated to take 40 million tonnes of krill per annum). All of the seabirds breeding in our region are heavily dependent on plankton, whilst Crabeater Seal almost exclusively takes planktonic arthropods (probably 100 million tonnes of krill annually) and some baleen whales take up to 1 tonne of zooplankton per day during their short stay in Antarctic waters. Fishes and squid are also strongly reliant on plankton (perhaps taking 150–200 million tonnes of krill per annum) though their natural histories are much less well documented. Those of squid are almost wholly unknown, but they are known to be an important resource for birds, seals and whales, which may take as many as 34 million tonnes of squid annually.

Fish

Approximately 90 species of bottom-living and 60 surface-feeding fish species occur in Antarctic waters. Three-quarters of the former belong to the Notothenioidei, a suborder restricted to cold waters of the Southern Hemisphere and four of the group's five families are almost entirely limited to Antarctic waters: Antarctic cod, ice fishes, dragon fishes and robber fishes. The first of these is principally a group of heavy, bull-headed fish with very large mouths that browse organisms on the seabed. A small number do, however, form dense shoals in surface waters and follow the summer harvest of zooplankton, whilst young of some other species attach themselves to those parts of an iceberg that are submerged, where they feed on diatoms and crustaceans. Ice fishes remarkably lack any trace of red blood, and some of this family,

and dragon fishes, spend those seasons when plankton are close to the surface in attendance.

Most polar fishes would immediately die if they came into contact with ice, which may appear surprising, given that they spend much of their lives in waters with a temperature below freezing point. Others that live among ice floes have a special protein-carbohydrate compound in their blood, which effectively acts as an antifreeze device. Cold-water fish exhibit different degrees of tolerance to temperature changes. Those specifically adapted to very cold inshore continental waters are particularly sensitive. Others, used to the slightly warmer waters off the Peninsula and the Scotia Arc, do not appear to occur elsewhere around the continent. In fact, probably less than one-third of those fishes in Antarctic waters are truly circumpolar and approximately one-sixth occur solely off the Peninsula and in the Scotia Arc, emphasizing once again the richness of this region of Antarctica.

Food Chains in the Oceans

The principal food chain (continuous arrows) includes about six steps (stages I–VI). Stage I represents the *primary production of the phytoplankton* (mainly diatoms). Within the Antarctic there is typically one less step than in other oceans, and the efficiency of energy transfer at each stage may be as low as a few percent. The reproduction and development of phytoplankton and increasing biomass (organic compounds) is caused by photosynthesis. Biomass consists of purely inorganic components (water, carbon dioxide and minerals) and is the food for the *small zooplankton*, stage II. The *large zooplankton* (stage III) feed on small zooplankton. Fish and squid represent the *small nekton* (animals that are able to migrate over long distances by their own muscular power) or stage IV. They are food for the large nekton or stage V (tuna, dolphins, seals and penguins). Finally, there follows stage VI, the stage of the *end consumers* (large predators). In Antarctic waters Killer Whale and Leopard Seal belong to this group; in temperate waters the Great White Shark *Carcharias carcharodon* is a famous end consumer.

Stages of the food chain may be skipped (interrupted arrows). Sperm Whale (stage VI) feeds on squid (stage IV). Krill (crustaceans, principally *Euphausia superba*) of stage III feed on phytoplankton (stage I). On the other hand krill are eaten by the large baleen whales; many of the Antarctic seals and some penguins (stage VI).

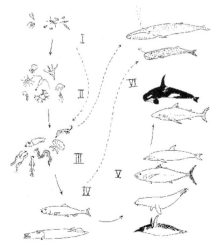

Figure 4. Diagrammatic representation of the Southern Ocean food chain.

Shortcuts in the system

Some important animals participate in the food chain by shortcuts. Famous are the large baleen whales (Blue, Fin, Humpback and right whales) which feed on astonishingly small food. For many of these end consumers (stage VI) krill is the major component of their diet (a Blue Whale consumes 3–4 tonnes of krill per day). Krill represents the third stage in the food chain; it feeds on diatoms, the first stage. The shortcut in the food chain omits stages II, IV and V (see p. 20): this appears to save energy in the flow of biomass and enables animals to grow larger.

Habitats and Vegetation

Given the climate and thin soils it is, of course, unsurprising that the Antarctic continent possesses a poorly developed flora. Plant distribution is controlled by temperature, the influence of mammals and birds, and the availability of water, wind, heat and suitable soils. The effect of Man around human bases is also of paramount importance, and some communities have been negatively influenced or even destroyed in such areas.

Antarctic vegetation

Algae (c.360 terrestrial and freshwater species) and lichens (c.350–400 species), which mainly grow on rocks and stones, are the most obvious components of the vegetation communities. Among these, endolithic algae are probably the hardiest plants other than bactos. There are also 75 species of moss and two

flowering plants, a grass, *Deschampsia antarctica* and a pearlwort, *Colobanthus quitensis*, both restricted to warmer maritime areas of the Peninsula; the latter reaches its southernmost extent at Neny I (68°12'S) and the grass at Refuge Islet (68°21'S).

Subantarctic Skua Catharacta [skua] antarctica *race* lonnbergi, *South Georgia, Nov 2001. Along with giant petrels,* Catharacta *skuas are the most aggressive avian scavengers and, to some extent, predators (here at a King Penguin* Aptenodytes patagonicus *rookery, searching for dead or weak chicks).* © Hadoram Shirihai.

Leopard Seal Hydrurga leptonyx *has a broad diet, but principally takes penguins and young seals (especially Crabeater). Penguins are killed and then skinned by banging the carcass against the water.* © Morten Jørgensen.

Killer Whale Orcinus orca *(probably Antarctic Type A) off the Crozets. In the Southern Ocean this species and Leopard Seal* Hydrurga leptonyx *are the top-end consumers in the food chain.* © TAAF collection.

Southern Giant Petrel Macronectes giganteus *feeding on dead bull Southern Elephant Seal* Mirounga leonina, *Livingston I.* © Frank S. Todd.

Colourful lichens, South Shetland Is, Feb 2002. © Morten Jørgensen.

Luxuriant vegetation on Enderby I, Aucklands, Feb 1997. © Daisy Gilardini.

Incubating Buller's Albatross Thalassarche [bulleri] bulleri in well-vegetated habitat on Solander I, New Zealand; this form is restricted as a breeder to the latter island and the Snares. © Kim Westerskov.

Growth is slow and neither species usually exceeds 3 cm in height; even in particularly suitable areas the ground will only be partially covered, with the grass usually growing in patches smaller than 25 m². Mosses reach 84°42'S and lichens 86°09'S and to altitudes of almost 2000 m. Most of the latter become inactive during the Antarctic winter, some of them freeze-drying, only rehydrating the following summer, and some are capable of surviving for 2000 years. Huge areas of Antarctica are devoid of vegetation, especially many of the inland peaks and many of the dry coastal areas appear similarly barren, as only the simplest microscopic organisms are able to exist in the sand or gravel. Within Antarctica it is only at the Peninsula, with its consistently more benign maritime climate that one finds better soils and shallow underground reservoirs of moisture that support thick mats of algae, lichens, liverworts and mosses. Precipitation is sufficiently high that harmful concentrations of minerals are washed out of the soil but, even here, the flora of the west is notably more diverse than the east, where the climate is noticeably more severe, and in some areas the soils are 'ornithogenic', deriving entirely from penguin and other seabirds' guano. Several fungi, some unique to the continent, occur in Antarctica, on the South Shetlands and the Peninsula.

The subantarctic islands

Given the relatively similar geology and and climate, the flora and vegetation of all of the subantarctic islands are unsurprisingly similar in many respects. Many islands have been subject to close botanical study and the different communities well described. All have very peaty soils of variable texture, composed almost entirely of plant debris, with minerals comparatively uncommon, except in areas of really thin soils. Landslips and tunnel gully erosion are natural and ongoing processes, and wind erosion is a feature on some islands, being exacerbated by trampling of the covering vegetation and to a lesser extent by the construction of nest burrows by tubenoses. Dense, tall tussac grassland, either *Spartina* or *Poa*, fernbush and shrub land form the principal plant communities on most islands. Tussac is of key importance to nesting tubenoses on virtually all of the islands on which it occurs, as it provides a particularly impenetrable cover against many natural predators. This habitat is also favoured by many of the small number of nesting landbirds resident in the subantarctic region. Areas of standing water, e.g. on the Falklands and Tristan da Cunha, attract several different species. Woody plants, e.g. Southern Rata *Metrosideros umbellata* and leatherwood *Olearia* spp, form a low dense forest on some islands, for instance within parts of the Auckland group and, especially, on the Snares and parts of the Chathams, whilst an introduced, 6 m-tall *Sicea* on Campbell is the most isolated tree in the world. Dwarf forests possess another-world type atmosphere, due to the low trees with their extremely gnarled and twisted formations, and are of extreme importance for breeding seabirds, e.g. the globally endangered Magenta Petrel on Chatham, and for a handful of landbirds. Until the mid-19th century, Amsterdam was also covered by dwarf forest. While the few remnants are now protected, Amsterdam has lost virtually all her seabirds, partially as a result. In marked contrast, the forested areas of New Zealand's subantarctic islands have survived relatively intact.

Floral diversity

Several islands boast native floras of 150–200 species of plants, including the Falklands and Antipodes, whilst the Aucklands support 233 taxa and the Chathams c.320 species, including at least 40 vascular plants endemic at varying rank. However, the indigenous vascular flora of many of the Indian Ocean islands and most other archipelagos in the New Zealand region are much less rich; Kerguelen supports most in the former region, at 29 species (just one endemic). Of those in the New Zealand region, even high-latitude Macquarie possesses 41 species. Long-distance dispersal is a feature on many islands and presumably accounts for the comparatively low rates of endemicity: the South Georgian and Falklands floras contain strong Fuegian elements, the Prince Edwards and Crozet a limited southern African affinity, and that of Macquarie a well-developed Australasian element.

Vegetation within much of the subantarctic is relatively uniform and comprises several distinct communities: fernbush of *Phylica*, *Empetrum* and *Blechnum*, with many lichens and other epiphytes; tussac grassland dominated by one or more species of *Poa* or *Spartina*, which may form a canopy; herbfield, the composition of which is subject to local conditions; heath for which typical constituents are *Juncus*, *Scirpus*, *Agrostis*, *Deschampsia* and, where there are peat bogs, *Sphagnum*; and feldmark, which dominates rocky highlands and is characterized by cushion plants of *Azorella*, with *Empetrum* and *Rhacomitrium* on some islands.

A tiny number of islands, including some at lower latitudes, e.g. the Bounties southeast of New Zealand, have naturally depauperate floras consisting entirely of lichens and algae. The vegetation of others, e.g. Amsterdam and parts of Tristan, have been negatively impacted by introduced herbivores and only fragments of their natural flora remain, mainly in less accessible regions. Recovery programmes are in operation on some islands, but alien vascular plants have become significant constituents within some communities due to accidental or, in some cases, deliberate introductions.

Avifauna

One of the major focuses of this guide is the avifauna, especially seabirds and endemics, of the subantarctic islands. Although no overview previously existed, the extremely detailed and immensely thorough *Handbook of Australian, New Zealand and Antarctic Birds* (HANZAB) serves as a comprehensive guide to much of the region. Unlike HANZAB, this guide, by combining the use of photographs, conventional field guide plates and species and regional texts, serves as an in-the-field identification reference to the birds (and marine mammals) of the Southern Ocean. The area included is broader than that treated by HANZAB. I include the Falklands (a regular port of call en route to the Antarctic Peninsula and destination for conventional bird tours), and the much less-visited Tristan da Cunha group, as well as sea areas north to the Subtropical Convergence (at 40°S).

Previous and ongoing work

Research into the Antarctic and subantarctic avifauna has only recently broken out of the first phase, documentation of existing and former diversity. Judging from fossil records, some of the area's former avifauna was truly remarkable. Even within the last 100–200 years several endemic forms have been lost and many local extirpations have occurred. Early seminal contributions came from Robert Cushman Murphy, whose *Oceanic Birds of South America*, published in the mid-1930s, remains a standard work even today, and George Watson. His work (published in 1975) on the birds of the Antarctic and subantarctic incorporated a mass of original research and, although *Birds of the Antarctic and Subantarctic* did not cover many of the New Zealand subantarctic islands or the Falklands, it has provided a foundation for many subsequent ornithological works.

During the last quarter century the dedicated work of a relative handful of field workers, most notably the British, Bill Bourne, John Croxall, Gary Nunn, the late Peter Prince, Ian Strange, Lance Tickell and Robin Woods; the South Africans John Cooper, Peter Ryan and their co-workers; the French, Pierre Jouventin and Henri Weimerskirch in particular, but also their many co-workers; the Australians Bill Fraser and Eric Woehler; and the New Zealanders Mike Imber, Chris Robertson, Rodney Russ and John Warham. In addition, Frank Todd and a number of other researchers from the USA have worked extensively on Antarctic birds, to name but a few of those involved in original and exciting research, which has provided our basic knowledge of the breeding populations of most species.

The avifauna of certain islands have been relatively well studied. Groundbreaking new approaches to the taxonomy of several groups, most notably albatrosses, have resulted within the last decade. Similar work on other groups, for instance shearwaters and petrels, skuas and penguins, may well follow and yield equally surprising results. Major monographs of albatrosses, penguins and petrels have been produced, providing detailed overviews of our knowledge of these important groups. The recently completed, multi-volume HANZAB also demands special mention. Since the publication of Peter Harrison's classic identification guide to the world's seabirds in 1983, numerous works have advanced our knowledge of the at-sea identification of seabirds. Details of many of these works can be found in the Bibliography. For a summation of our current knowledge of the identification, natural histories and conservation of most of the region's seabirds see the species accounts (pp. 42–272). As yet, there have been few popular but scientifically accurate and detailed guides available to the comparative layperson with an interest in this region, but is a tradition on which this guide seeks to build.

Ornithological research in the Southern Ocean is increasingly focusing on analysing breeding behaviours and diets of seabirds. Given that the dangers posed by longline fisheries are one of the more significant threats to the world's birds, basic biological

Moulting Adélie Penguin Pygoscelis adeliae, *Ross Sea, Jan 1999. Unlike Emperor Penguin* Aptenodytes forsteri, *this species, which is the only other Antarctic-breeding penuin, nests in the short summer season and moults immediately thereafter. © Hadoram Shirihai.*

Lesser Snow Petrel Pagodroma [nivea] nivea. *Snow Petrels are the 'angels' of Antarctica, as they search for cephalopods and crustaceans amidst the ice floes of Antarctica, by aerial- and contact-dipping, and surface-seizing (photo taken during the summer Antarctic night). Antarctic Peninsula. © Hadoram Shirihai.*

knowledge is essential to the formulation of conservation plans for those species at risk from such practices. Fortunately seabirds, given their faithfulness to ancestral nesting sites, provide comparatively model study subjects and such data is being rapidly accumulated. More complex questions of course remain: where, how and when do seabirds acquire food. New technology, such as tiny technological devices and satellite transmitters, is being harnessed to answer these puzzles and to provide key information to those who set catch limits and other controls for fisheries in the region.

Bird biology

Our knowledge of the life histories of many species has increased immeasurably in recent years. Elaborate displays used by penguins, albatrosses and gulls are well described, but those of nocturnal and more secretive tubenoses much less well known. More data are required, however, on seasonal variation in food resource utilisation, segregation between similar species and congenerics, and between different age classes. Breeding habits have been comparatively well studied in recent years, even among the burrow-nesting small petrels. Nonetheless, whilst many data have been gathered, there are still obvious gaps in our knowledge, such as the degree of intraspecific synchronicity in nesting at different colonies. Whilst most seabird species breed more or less synchronously at a given site, they may not do so across their entire range. Resource partitioning between species nesting at the same site or island has also been studied less thoroughly. Many other aspects of the natural histories of Antarctic and subantarctic birds have received attention in the literature and some are comparatively well known, for instance moult and, perhaps surprisingly, the incidence of ectoparasites.

The avifauna of the Southern Ocean, at least south of the Polar Front, is rather depauperate; c.45 species breed, including seven species of penguin, though just a handful nest on the Antarctic continent. These are adapted for extreme climatic conditions, with penguins and petrels possessing a dense layer of subdermal fat, a coat of heavy down and an outer surface of overlapping contour feathers. Even at rest such layers are virtually impermeable to cold, wind and precipitation, but the climate also enforces birds to moult at the warmest season and to seek sheltered conditions. The large fat reserves, most notably carried by penguins, also serve their

Spectacled Petrel Procellaria conspicillata *is one of the most bizarre-looking petrels, with its diagnostic, highly conspicuous and complex white headbands. It is an endemic breeder to Inaccessible (Tristan group). Off Tristan, Mar 2006. © Hadoram Shirihai.*

function during periods of enforced starvation, especially during moult and incubation. Young birds must also carry high fat reserves to ward off starvation during bad weather and nest sites are usually selected for their shelter from strong winds, closeness of moderating sea temperatures, or low risk of being inundated by snow. Breeding periods are usually established so that when chicks are ready for independence food availability is at its maximum.

Faunal zones in the Southern Ocean

Broad faunal zonation in the region covered by this work is discussed in The Antarctic and Subantarctic Environments: The Southern Ocean (see especially Table 1). In addition to coastal Antarctica, the pack-ice zone (including its maximum northerly winter extension) encompasses the Peninsula, the southern islands of the Scotia arc east to the South Sandwiches, whilst Peter I, the Balleny and Scott Is form part of the same zone. South Georgia, Bouvetøya and Heard and McDonald lie within the maritime Antarctic zone (i.e. south of the Antarctic Convergence). All other islands treated here are situated on or slightly north of the Antarctic Convergence, or between the latter and the Subtropical Convergence; a greater variety of habitats for breeding landbirds appears on these islands. Within the cold subantarctic zone (broadly commensurate with the Antarctic Convergence) lie Marion, Crozet, Kerguelen, Macquarie, Campbell and the Falklands, whilst the rest of New Zealand's subantarctic islands, Tristan da Cunha and Gough lie close to the Subtropical Convergence. Peaks of avian diversity are reached in these two zones, in the subantarctic and other islands off New Zealand, especially the Chathams, on Tristan da Cunha and Gough, as well as in the Falklands, where a combination of its close proximity to the South American continent and relatively high observer activity has led to the identification of over 200 species. Zonal speciation is evident within several genera and the avifaunal affinities of several taxa on the subantarctic islands provide clues as to colonization events and geological and evolutionary history: e.g. the pintail and pipit on South Georgia are clearly recent arrivals or radiations within South American groups, whilst of those landbirds on Tristan da Cunha and Gough,

the buntings are clearly derived from South American stock and the thrush appears to share a similar ancestral heritage, but the *Gallinula* spp. could have originated from either Africa or the Neotropics and the origin of the rail is wholly obscure.

Threatened species and the future

The enormous densities and vast overall numbers of several seabirds, a number of attractive and poorly studied endemics and the relatively large number of globally threatened species compensate for what the region lacks in numbers of species. Among globally threatened species that breed are six species of penguin, many albatrosses and petrels. Of landbirds (including wildfowl, raptors and shorebirds), two breeders in the Falklands, six in the Tristan da Cunha group (four of them passerines), one in the French Southern Territories (Eaton's Pintail) and a remarkable 16 in the subantarctic islands of New Zealand are considered threatened or nearly so. These figures illustrate, very graphically, that conservation is a burning issue in the Southern Ocean. Given growing interest in the taxonomy of the region's birds, the application of the Phylogenetic Species Concept and new approaches to the application of the Biological Species Concept, the number of conservation-dependent 'species' in the region is probably set to rise even further.

Marine Mammals

Seals

The most conspicuous marine mammals are seals. Five species are known from the Antarctic coast and pack-ice zones, all of them phocid ('true') seals, the most numerous being Leopard, Weddell and Crabeater, and the poorly known Ross Seal. On some islands, principally at the north end of the Peninsula and the southern islands of the Scotia arc east to the South Sandwiches, a few Southern Elephant Seals (also a phocid) and Antarctic Fur Seals also breed. These and several other fur seals and sea lions (the otariids or eared seals), mainly inhabit the subantarctic islands. Some islands host several taxa of the genus *Arctocephalus*, New Zealand (Hooker's) Sea Lion also

Pair of Southern Royal Albatross Diomedea [epomophora] epomophora, *Campbell I. The New Zealand subantarctic islands hold the largest number of albatross taxa in the Southern Ocean, among them this endemic.* © Andris Apse.

occurring on some of New Zealand's subantarctic territories. The current distributions and populations of most species are reasonably well known, with the exception of Ross Seal, which is strictly associated with the densest areas of pack ice and appears to be most common around Cape Adare and off King Haakon VII Land.

Phocids have no external testes or ears, but possess exceptional hearing both on land and in the water. They are a clumsy group on land, being unable to turn their hind flippers to assist their movements, and depend on their body muscles for locomotion, with the fore flippers principally being used for support. The group appears to have evolved from otter-like ancestors. In contrast, otariid seals can walk or lope using both sets of flippers in a rudimentary four-'footed' motion. They also possess external ears and testes.

Cetaceans

The other principal constituents of the marine mammal fauna are the cetaceans; whales, dolphins and porpoises. The distributions and life histories of many are very poorly known. Among baleen whales the most frequently recorded species in Antarctic and subantarctic waters are Blue, Fin, Sei, minkes, Humpback and Southern Right Whales, and among toothed whales, Sperm and Southern Bottlenose Whales. Baleen whales breed in tropical and subtropical waters, but generally migrate to Antarctic waters in summer to take advantage of the rich shoals of krill and establish sufficient food reserves to sustain them for the rest of the year. The species tend to arrive at different times and do not uniformly penetrate to the highest latitudes. The baleen whales use two feeding methods: shallow feeding involves the animal in simultaneously engulfing huge quantities of food and water, the latter being squeezed out by contraction of the throat grooves and raising the tongue to the roof of the mouth. In a variation of this, Southern

Weddell seal Leptonychotes weddellii *mother and pup on sea ice, Ross Sea. This species is endemic to Antarctic waters. Pups keep as close to the mother as possible for the first two months of life, sometimes even clambering onto the female. It's entertaining – and heartwarming – to spend some time watching pups with the females.* © Kim Westerskov.

Right and Sei Whales swim through a swarm of krill, their heads partially above the water surface and their mouths half-open, skimming the food. Humpbacks feed differently, swimming with a circular motion below the surface releasing a trail of air bubbles that entrap krill, which can then be engulfed by swimming through the area that has been encircled. Many species of toothed whale are extremely poorly known and have only rarely, if ever, been observed at sea. They possess only one nostril, although they

Antarctic Fur Seals Arctocephalus gazella *at a major rookery in South Georgia (right), where c.1% of the population is the honey-blond morph (left). Exploitation by sealers almost completely decimated the population, but since then it has recovered dramatically due to protection. However, some areas are now overpopulated and have been extensively damaged by seals to the detriment of burrow-breeding petrels and even albatrosses, as well as to plant communities.* © Hadoram Shirihai.

Southern Right Whale Eubalaena australis *mother and young calf near the Auckland Is. At least locally, this species appears to be slowly and steadily recovering, due to protection. Unfortunately, some nations are committed to renewing the hunting of large whales, apparently ignorant of the environmental and ecological well-being of our planet. © Kim Westerskov.*

do have two nasal passages. Some beaked whales are known only from beached animals and their entire life histories largely unknown; even their identification and colorations (as stranded individuals often change colour) are subject to much doubt. The growth of interest in voyages to the Antarctic and subantarctic regions, therefore, offers an exciting opportunity to garner new data for several of these species.

Marine mammals and Man

Almost concurrent with the first significant exploration of Antarctic and subantarctic seas, by Cook in the late 1700s and Bellinghausen in the early 1800s, came sealers lured by easy profits to be made from the huge numbers of fur seals then present on the subantarctic islands. British and American sealers led the way in a short-lived era of uncontrolled slaughter for fur, which could be used for slippers, book-binding, fashion items and cold-weather coats. Stocks of fur seals were rapidly exhausted; some populations were hunted to near extinction within just two decades. In the wake of this, sealers turned their attention to elephant seals and subsequently, on some islands, penguins, but even these stocks had been reduced to almost nothing by the end of the 19th century. In 1910, the British again permitted the killing, under license, of elephant seals on South Georgia, and this practice was only discontinued in 1964. By the 1930s fur seals were noticeably starting to recover, and dramatic increases were noted from the 1950s. Most populations are now thought to have almost reached pre-1800 levels. Most of the other 'true' seals have never been subject to commercial exploitation, and several seal reserves have been established, though it remains legal to take any number of any species for 'scientific' purposes.

The first whalers arrived in the Southern Ocean in 1839, as stocks in warmer subtropical areas were depleted, but the fast-moving baleen whales were difficult to catch and tended to sink upon being harpooned, although development of an explosive harpoon in the 1860s partially solved the problem. However, extensive and intensive commercial whaling, with long-lasting effects on the principal catch species, did not commence until the early 1900s. Thereafter an explosion in whaling occurred, with its epicentre at South Georgia (from 1904) and its famous factories, both on land and sea. Attention originally focused on Humpback

The former Grytviken whaling station, South Georgia. Whaling stations were originally all land-based, like this, but by the early 1920s floating factory ships, which undertook all processing at sea, became more practical. © Hadoram Shirihai.

Humpback Whale Megaptera novaeangliae *is often found near shore and is very active at the surface, making it a special attraction of an Antarctic cruise, especially around the Peninsula. Perhaps 200,000 were hunted in the Southern Ocean, but since the moratorium in 1966 some stocks have recovered. Antarctic Peninsula, Jan 2002. © Morten Jørgensen.*

and Blue Whales, but in the 1950s and 1960s switched to Fin, Sperm and, ultimately Sei Whales, until the final abandonment of such fishing practices in 1978. The foundation of the International Whaling Commission (IWC), in 1946, and more pertinently the growth in public support for conservation pressure groups advocating the cessation of whaling, brought total protection for most of the baleen whales and most countries to abandon commercial whaling during the third quarter of the 20th century. By 1969 only the former Soviet Union and Japan continued to operate whaling fleets in Antarctic waters and these countries still operate small-scale whaling missions under the loophole of 'scientific' whaling. Whilst a visit to Antarctica still offers the chance to see whales, the devastation wrought by over 100 years of whaling and new fishing techniques designed to exploit some of their food resources mean that it will prove near-impossible to witness a return to former numbers.

For an overview of general identification and taxonomy, as well as the life histories of the marine mammals, see the separate introductions to the seals and cetaceans which precede the species accounts, and where discussion of individual species information can be found.

Conservation in the Region

Undoubtedly, some of the 'hottest' conservation issues of the modern age are significant within the Antarctic environment: global warming and the effects thereof, as well as the ozone hole, longline fishing, whaling (even given the currently small numbers taken, theoretically for scientific purposes, this remains a contentious and extremely emotive issue) and over-fishing of the Southern Ocean.

The age of exploitation

Man's arrival in the subantarctic unleashed a holocaust for its marine mammals and, to a lesser extent, birds. The opening up of the Southern Ocean in the early-19th century provides a particularly graphic demonstration of the human capacity for destruction. Populations of fur and elephant seals were decimated within a few decades and, though less significant, the result of the not infrequent shipwrecks that occurred at some remote islands would be that the survivors were forced to 'live off the land': colonies of

albatrosses and penguins would often pay a brief price. Factory production of oil from penguins followed in the late-19th century on several archipelagos; these private enterprises swiftly proved unprofitable, but not before local populations of some species had been virtually annihilated. It was next the turn of the great whales. Exploitation in the name of 'research' by a tiny number of countries continues to the present, but the damage was again done in the initial years of the harvest, which reduced some species, e.g. Blue Whale, to between 1% and 20% of their pre-exploitation numbers. Whilst populations of seals and penguins have rebounded, due to subsequent, near-inviolate protection, baleen whales which may breed as infrequently as once every four years will probably never fully recoup their losses.

The first sealers were, however unwittingly, the indirect cause of another cataclysmic force in the Southern Ocean, which even today poses one of the greatest problems for conservationists: introduced alien mammals. Rats, cats, sheep, rabbits, goats, cattle, pigs and even Reindeer were deliberately or accidentally brought to many subantarctic islands. Some of these provided food for shipwrecked mariners, whilst cats were introduced to curb the rats that had arrived almost concurrently with humans. All had devastating effects on the populations of indigenous birds, particularly smaller tubenoses. On some islands, particularly the Falklands and Tristan da Cunha group, the human harvest of shearwaters, albatrosses and penguins contributed substantially to the decline in seabird numbers. At Tristan legal harvesting of some tubenoses continued until comparatively recently. But, on most islands in the subantarctic region, it was introduced mammalian predators that wreaked the most damage. The woeful tale of carnage is well illustrated by the example of Amsterdam, in the S Indian Ocean, where the introduction and arrival of a host of domestic mammals and others has reduced the numbers of breeding seabirds almost to none. The once-extensive forests on this island were largely destroyed by fires, which often raged for months, either deliberately or accidentally started by humans, whilst pigs and cattle have done much of the rest. Breeding seabirds are now largely confined to the most inaccessible areas of the island and populations of tubenoses are pitiful in comparison to other archipelagos in this ocean.

Redressing the balance

Today many of the subantarctic islands receive a significant degree of legal protection as reserves and, in some cases, World Heritage Sites. Four, the Tristan da Cunha group, Gough, the Aucklands and the Chathams, are Endemic Bird Areas (EBAs), as defined by BirdLife International, and thus essential to the conservation of global biodiversity. Several others are included in the Important Bird Area (IBA) programme of the same organization. An IBA inventory for Antarctica is in progress. Scientific bases have been established on several islands, notably in the Indian Ocean, and in Antarctica, principally on the Peninsula and South Shetlands. Seabird monitoring programmes and management plans have been developed for the future conservation of many islands, which despite Man's impact remain near-wilderness areas. Management strategies frequently take their key from a list of eight directives developed by a Scientific Committee on Antarctic Research (SCAR)/IUCN workshop held in 1980: 1) to assess the impact of introductions, introduce controls and monitor recovery processes in the ecosystem; 2) protect islands from further introductions; 3) establish maritime buffer zones for wildlife and to provide limited protection of their food resources; 4) formulate conservation plans; and 5) establish legal protection for islands and other sites of special scientific interest. Three additional recommendations were also set forth: control stations and programmes and their effects on wildlife; conserve and document sites of human historical importance; and educate the public in achieving these objectives.

Whilst many subantarctic and, to a slightly lesser extent, Antarctic stations were created to conduct climatic, floral and geological studies, other disciplines, including ornithology have also flourished, with the documentation of the life histories and breeding cycles of many of the bird species in the subantarctic. In harness with these have come novel taxonomic insights, a process liable to continue for some time as humans attempt to recognize real-world evolutionary relationships. New approaches to taxonomy have brought yet more headaches for conservationists, as priorities for protecting biodiversity have appeared to increase almost exponentially in recent years. A particularly notable example of the 'sea change' in avian systematics has been the application of new standards for 'species' recognition among albatrosses; of the 24 taxa recommended as species, practically all those occurring in the Southern Ocean are officially threatened. The 'new' taxonomy has not been without its critics, especially for its lack of consensus in the use of 'new' names and application of 'old' ones, though such contrary arguments are unlikely to stem ongoing work and similar re-analysis of other groups.

Such research has stimulated interest in the conservation of seabirds, especially in the Southern Ocean. Active eradication programmes against introduced mammalian predators are in progress in the New Zealand and Indian Ocean regions, and many notable successes have already been achieved. Where it has not proved feasible to eradicate or remove the main problem species, fencing programmes, e.g. on Amsterdam, have been used to good effect. Strict quarantine regulations govern landings on New Zealand's subantarctic islands to prevent the accidental arrival of rodents or alien plant species. Rodents have caused significant problems for some passerines on the Falklands and South Georgia, but their eradication is a long way off. Coupled with such work to reduce mammalian predators, at least on the Chathams, have been reintroduction and other projects designed to propagate, protect and research the populations and conservation requirements of several globally threatened species, most notably the Magenta Petrel and Black Robin.

Seabirds on the hook

Whilst land-based protection work is producing significant successes and redoubled survey work is providing new hope for several species previously considered at risk, a new and ghastly threat has arisen at sea: longlining, which involves vessels trailing lines up to 130 km long with up to 40,000 baited hooks seeking pelagic and deep-sea fish. Since the 1980s but especially after 1997, when a BirdLife International Seabird Conservation Programme was launched, longlining, which became increasingly fashionable following the banning of high-sea drift nets in 1993, has been recognised as a major threat to seabird populations throughout the globe. Up to 60 seabird species have been reported as bycatch in such operations: birds are caught as they attempt to scavenge the bait, become ensnared on the hook and subsequently drown as the line sinks. Longliners also discharge waste from processed fish, which supplements the diets of seabirds but also encourages them to remain in the vicinity of the boat, thereby further exposing them to line-setting operations when baited hooks are deployed.

The Southern Ocean with its internationally important numbers of many species has come under the spotlight, especially during the most recent BirdLife project: *Save the Albatross Campaign: Keeping the World's Seabirds off the Hook*. Increasing numbers of albatross and petrel species are considered globally threatened largely due to longlining activities; most are Southern Ocean breeders. Data on the numbers of seabirds killed by longlining are more difficult to catch than the birds, but the Patagonian Toothfish *Dissostichus eleginoides* industry, which only commenced in 1994, may have been responsible for 145,000 seabird deaths in a single year in the Southern Ocean. Such figures led the Commission for the Conservation of Antarctic Marine Living Resources (CCAMLR) to regard the threat to albatrosses, giant petrels and White-chinned Petrel as unsustainable. Mitigation techniques have been developed and, in some cases, voluntarily adopted by fishing vessels. Bird-scaring lines, line weighting, reducing discharge of fish waste and night setting can all help to reduce seabird bycatch, and all 23 signatory countries to CCAMLR have introduced some measures to minimise the effect of longlining on seabirds.

Unfortunately, the problem is acerbated by the fact that 'pirate' ships or non-signatories to CCAMLR operate many longline

Feeding concentration off Kaikoura, New Zealand, demonstrating how albatrosses are strongly attracted to fishing vessels. Many die when they become ensnared on longline hooks. © Hadoram Shirihai.

fisheries: indeed the scale is estimated to be up to ten times that of legal fisheries. Whilst the CCAMLR has the power to regulate fishing within its waters and at least some signatories police territorial waters outside the CCAMLR zones, some species are heavily over-fished in unregulated waters. The Southern Bluefin Tuna industry, which principally occurs in waters north of the Southern Ocean, is near collapse. Whilst the principal participatory nations, Australia, Japan and New Zealand, have formed the Commission for the Conservation of Southern Bluefin Tuna, among whose regulations is the mandatory introduction of measures to reduce seabird bycatch, other states continue to fish in an unregulated and potentially damaging manner.

Krill is the staple food of a wide range of species but is now being harvested by Man. Such fisheries have been acquiring importance in the Southern Ocean for two decades: in 1981–82, 500,000 tonnes were taken in Antarctic waters by Russian and Japanese trawlers, and eventually it may become food for humans. As we have seen, krill are of key importance within the marine food chain and over-fishing could have potentially disastrous effects on populations of many smaller seabirds that breed in Antarctic and subantarctic waters; clearly humans must find a way of sustainably harvesting krill without damaging the overall dynamics of the Southern Ocean ecosystem.

Saving the seabirds

Top priorities in the coming years are the adoption of National Plans of Action for Reducing Incidental Catch of Seabirds in Longline Fisheries, the development of a Southern Hemisphere Albatross and Petrel Agreement under the terms of the Bonn Convention on the Conservation of Migratory Species of Wild Animals, strict trade controls for Patagonian Toothfish in order to eliminate pirate fishing and, finally, to persuade regional fishery bodies to follow CCAMLR directives concerning mitigation techniques to reduce seabird losses from longlining. These directives were strengthened at CCAMLR meeting, in Hobart, in 2000. Additional support has come from the UN's Food and Agriculture Organisation (FAO), the Agreement on the Conservation of Albatrosses and Petrels (ACAP), which stems from the listing of 14 species of albatrosses with unfavourable conservation status in the appendices of the Convention for Migratory Species of Wild Animals, and the Global Environment Fund. Nonetheless, vigorous lobbying at international, inter-governmental and national levels will be required to make headway with such objectives, but official recovery plans for albatrosses and petrels may depend for their success on the ability of the BirdLife Seabird Conservation Programme and the BirdLife partnership to turn these into action.

The CCAMLR was founded, in 1980, under the terms of the Antarctic Treaty with the explicit aim of monitoring and controlling krill, squid and finfish fisheries. It arrived too late for many finfish species, which had already reached a state of commercial extinction, but nonetheless forms an essential plank of the Treaty, which was negotiated by the 12 participating nations in the International Geophysical Year of 1957–58. The Treaty came into force in 1961 and is frequently viewed as one of the most successful international agreements ever brokered, despite criticisms from some countries that are non-party to the agreement that it should be replaced by a UN governing body. There are currently 45 signatories to the Treaty, 27 of which are Consultative Parties that meet regularly to discuss scientific cooperation, environmental protection and regulation of tourism.

A key priority is protection of what is still a comparatively unspoilt ecosystem. Agreements approved under the Treaty include the Agreed Measures for the Conservation of Antarctic Fauna and Flora (1964), the Convention for the Conservation of Antarctic Seals (1978), the Protocol on Environmental Protection to the Antarctic Treaty (1991) and, under the auspices of the latter, the Antarctic Site Inventory Project (1994). These stipulate and provide for the establishment and management of protected areas, regular monitoring of wildlife colonies, particularly birds, conservation of the continent's flora and fauna, regulate waste disposal and commercial sealing, ensure that environmental impact assessments are properly conducted prior to new developments and prohibit mining in Antarctica until the year 2048, among many other guidelines.

Effects of tourism

The arrival in force of tourists in the 1960s brought both benefits and downsides for wildlife. Tourists were the first to comment on scientist-imposed damage on what was billed as a pristine ecosystem. The arrival of pressure groups, notably Greenpeace, added to the cries for change, and as a result many countries have introduced far-reaching clean-up campaigns and measures to mitigate environmental damage around their bases. The 1991 Protocol was a major result of the previous decade's developments but unsolved problems remain. Those associated with 'mass' tourism are still unclear and subject to debate, but it is unquestionable that some alien plants and animals have reached Antarctica aboard supply ships, although any deleterious effects are unknown. The impact of disturbance upon colonies of breeding birds, especially penguins, and other wildlife are also very poorly known, but repeated visits to a small number of colonies does impact negatively on birds, sometimes leading to a reduction in the number of individuals and, probably more frequently, increasing stress rates and possibly reducing breeding success. Stricter guidelines governing tourism and greater inter-company liaison and planning are clearly required by those operating tours to Antarctica, although the International Association of Antarctica Tour Operators has been largely successful in self-regulating responsible ecotourism to the region.

The ozone hole and global warming

The 1985 discovery of an ozone hole above Antarctica, which has been widening increasingly rapidly since 1976, is unquestionably *the* problem facing mankind. Global climate change has manifested itself in the rapid disintegration of certain ice shelves, a general warming in the region's climate and a possible decrease in the extent of sea ice, which has probably had a negative impact on some penguin species' breeding success. Climatic changes in the Antarctic environment are likely to have already had significant impacts on the availability of krill, which form the heart of the Antarctic food chain. Biologists from the British Antarctic Survey have discovered that seals, penguins and albatrosses are experiencing difficulties in rearing offspring successfully as demand for krill exceeds supply. Long-term monitoring of seabirds and seals at South Georgia has revealed an increase in the frequency of years when there is insufficient krill to feed seal pups and seabird chicks.

If the Antarctic ice sheet were to completely melt, the accumulated water would drown many of the major global cities and lead to massive human displacement. However, even given global warming, such a spectacle is not immediately likely (though there is now overwhelming agreement amongst scientist that some of the worst-case scenarios predicted at the time of the first edition of this book are seemingly well supported by evidence). Such problems are increasingly part of mainstream political agendas, although few countries are yet showing a willingness to take the necessary long-term and deep-rooted actions required to tackle them.

Checklist of Birds and Marine Mammals of Antarctica and the Southern Ocean

This is the first checklist of the birds and marine mammals known from Antarctica and the Southern Ocean north to c.40°S (for details, see The Antarctic and Subantarctic Environments: The Southern Ocean, pp. 8–12). The list also serves as a source for scientific names of birds and mammals mentioned in the regional descriptions. (Scientific names are included in the species accounts and for those species that have not occurred in the region.) Avian orders and nomenclature largely follow the Handbook of Australian, New Zealand and Antarctic Birds (HANZAB). Deviations from this, e.g. in the albatrosses, largely reflect new approaches to the taxonomy of a number of groups published since the relevant volume of HANZAB. Furthermore, the species accounts treat several taxa slightly differently (usually as allospecies) from the latter, but these are explained in the relevant taxonomy sections. For South American, African and other species not covered by HANZAB, the nomenclature of Sibley (1996) has largely been followed, with occasional deviations in the light of recent taxonomic proposals. Some unconfirmed records of vagrants have been denoted and others, not identified to species, are mentioned in the regional accounts. It should be emphasized that this list represents a first base, upon which future workers can build. For marine mammals I have followed the classification and names used in Rice (1998), Berta & Sumich (1999) and Perrin et al. (2002). The checklist covers all those species mentioned in the regional and species accounts, as well as a handful of vagrants (mostly to the Falklands) not mentioned elsewhere. The oceanic occurrence codes, in most cases, indicate which of the regional chapters the reader should refer for data concerning distribution, populations or records of vagrants. The region does not include coastal and nearby waters of South Africa, South America, Australia, and mainland New Zealand and its close offshore islands (with the exception, of course, of the Chathams).

Status is indicated by the following codes or symbols:
RB Breeds in the region*, either resident/dispersive** or as a partially/wholly circumpolar migrant within the region
MB Migrant breeder*, occurs in the region only to breed in summer
OB Occasional breeder in the region
e   Species/race endemic as a breeder to the region
X   Lost as a breeding species in the region: no recent records
N   Non-breeding regular visitor which migrates (or disperses) to and from the region
V   Irregular, of marginal occurrence or vagrant to the region
?   Status in doubt owing to lack of information
I   Introduced species

Regional distribution is indicated by the following codes: AO (=Southern Ocean/subantarctic islands sector south of Atlantic Ocean); IO (=Southern Ocean/subantarctic islands sector south of Indian Ocean); PO (=Southern Ocean/subantarctic islands sector south of Pacific Ocean, including the New Zealand region); AC (=Antarctic Coastal and/or immediate sea regions, including the South Shetlands, South Orkneys and South Sandwiches; **bold** indicates breeding (with the exception of extinct breeders) while other, unboldened, codes refer to non-breeding; those codes within [ ] refer to marginal occurrences within the checklist region).

For those species that breed in the region, Red Data List categories are presented in CAPITALS and follow IUCN/BirdLife International. It should be borne in mind that several forms treated as species/allospecies here have not been evaluated from the standpoint of their conservation status using such criteria.

With thanks to: **Birds** Andrew Clarke, John Cooper, John Croxall, Bruce Dyer, Mike Imber, Frédéric Jiguet, Tony Martin, Colin Miskelly, Peter Moore, Peter Ryan and Eric Woehler. **Marine Mammals** Annalisa Berta, Peter Evans and William Perrin.

Birds

ORDER Podicipediformes
Family **Podicipedidae**
Pied-billed Grebe *Podilymbus podiceps* V (AO)
Hoary-headed Grebe *Poliocephalus poliocephalus* V (PO)
White-tufted Grebe *Rollandia rolland rolland* RBe (**AO**)
Great Grebe *Podiceps major* RB (**AO**)
Silvery Grebe *Podiceps occipitalis* RB (**AO**)

ORDER Sphenisciformes
Family **Spheniscidae**
King Penguin *Aptenodytes patagonicus* RBe (**AO, IO, PO,** [AC])
Emperor Penguin *Aptenodytes forsteri* RBe (**AC**)
Gentoo Penguin *Pygoscelis papua* RBe (**AO, IO, PO, AC**) NEAR THREATENED
Adélie Penguin *Pygoscelis adeliae* RBe (**AC**)
Chinstrap Penguin *Pygoscelis antarctica* RBe (**AO, IO, [PO], AC**)
Rockhopper Penguin *Eudyptes [chrysocome] chrysocome* RB(e) (**AO, IO, PO,** [AC]) VULNERABLE
Northern Rockhopper Penguin *Eudyptes [chrysocome] moseleyi* RB(e) (**AO, IO**)

VULNERABLE (?)
Fiordland Penguin *Eudyptes pachyrhynchus* N ([PO]) VULNERABLE
Snares Penguin *Eudyptes robustus* RBe ([AO], **PO**) VULNERABLE
Erect-crested Penguin *Eudyptes sclateri* RBe ([AO], **PO**) ENDANGERED
Macaroni Penguin *Eudyptes chrysolophus* RBe (**AO, IO**) VULNERABLE
Royal Penguin *Eudyptes schlegeli* RBe (**PO**, [IO?]) VULNERABLE
Yellow-eyed Penguin Megadyptes antipodes RB (**PO**) ENDANGERED
Little Penguin *Eudyptula [minor] minor* RB (**PO**)
Magellanic Penguin *Spheniscus magellanicus* RB (**AO,** [AC]) NEAR THREATENED

ORDER Procellariiformes
Family **Diomedeidae**
Wandering Albatross *Diomedea [exulans] exulans* RBe (**AO, IO, [PO],** [AC]) VULNERABLE
Tristan Albatross *Diomedea [exulans] dabbenena* RBe ([IO?], [PO?]) ENDANGERED
Gibson's Albatross *Diomedea [exulans] gibsoni* RBe ([IO], **PO**) VULNERABLE

Antipodean Albatross *Diomedea [exulans] antipodensis* RBe ([IO], **PO**) VULNERABLE
Amsterdam Albatross *Diomedea [exulans] amsterdamensis* RBe (**IO**, [PO?]) CRITICAL
Southern Royal Albatross *Diomedea [epomophora] epomophora* RBe ([AO], [IO], **PO**) VULNERABLE
Northern Royal Albatross *Diomedea [epomophora] sanfordi* RB(e) ([AO], [IO], **PO**) ENDANGERED
Black-browed Albatross *Thalassarche [melanophrys] melanophrys* RBe (**AO, IO, [PO], [AC]**) NEAR THREATENED
Campbell Albatross *Thalassarche [melanophrys] impavida* RBe ([AO?], [IO?], **PO**) VULNERABLE
Shy (Tasmanian) Albatross *Thalassarche [cauta] cauta* N ([AO], IO, PO)
White-capped Albatross *Thalassarche [cauta] steadi* RBe ([AO], IO, **PO**) NEAR THREATENED
Chatham Albatross *Thalassarche [cauta] eremita* RBe (**PO**) CRITICAL
Salvin's Albatross *Thalassarche [cauta] salvini* RBe ([AO?], [IO], **PO**) VULNERABLE
Buller's Albatross *Thalassarche [bulleri] bulleri* RB(e) (**PO**) VULNERABLE
Pacific Albatross *Thalassarche [bulleri]* sp. RB(e) (**PO**)
Grey-headed Albatross *Thalassarche chrysostoma* RBe (**AO, IO, PO, AC**) VULNERABLE

---

* Only regular breeders are included; and marine mammals are considered 'breeders' only if they mate and/or give birth in the region.
** Some species in this category completely vacate their breeding areas and may perform short- or long-distance dispersions, but almost all remain within the region.

Atlantic Yellow-nosed Albatross *Thalassarche [chlorhynchos] chlorhynchos* RBe (**AO**, [IO], [PO]) NEAR THREATENED
Indian Yellow-nosed Albatross *Thalassarche [chlorhynchos] carteri* RBe ([AO], **IO**, [**PO**], [AC]) VULNERABLE
Laysan Albatross *Phoebetria immutabilis* V (IO)
Sooty Albatross *Phoebetria fusca* RBe (**AO**, **IO**, [PO]) VULNERABLE
Light-mantled Sooty Albatross *Phoebetria palpebrata* RBe (**AO**, **IO**, **PO**, [AC]) NEAR THREATENED
Family **Procellariidae**
Southern Giant Petrel *Macronectes giganteus* RBe (**AO**, **IO**, **PO**, **AC**) VULNERABLE
Northern Giant Petrel *Macronectes halli* RBe (**AO**, **IO**, **PO**, [AC]) NEAR THREATENED
Southern Fulmar *Fulmarus glacialoides* RBe ([AO], [IO], [PO], **AC**)
Antarctic Petrel *Thalassoica antarctica* RBe ([AO], [IO], [PO], **AC**)
Cape Petrel *Daption capense capense* RBe (**AO**, **IO**, **AC**)
New Zealand Cape Petrel *Daption capense australe* RBe (**PO**)
Lesser Snow Petrel *Pagodroma [nivea] nivea* RBe (**AO**, **AC**)
Greater Snow Petrel *Pagodroma [nivea] confusa* RBe (**AC**)
Great-winged Petrel *Pterodroma [macroptera] macroptera* RB (**AO**, **IO**, PO)
Grey-faced Petrel *Pterodroma [macroptera] gouldi* N (PO)
White-headed Petrel *Pterodroma lessonii* RBe (AO, **IO**, **PO**)
Atlantic Petrel *Pterodroma incerta* RBe (**AO**, [IO?], [AC]) VULNERABLE
Magenta Petrel *Pterodroma magentae* RBe (**PO**) CRITICAL
Tahiti Petrel *Pterodroma rostrata* V (IO)
Kerguelen Petrel *Pterodroma (Aphrodroma or Lugensa) brevirostris* RBe (**AO**, **IO**, PO, [AC])
Soft-plumaged Petrel *Pterodroma mollis mollis* RBe (**AO**, [AC])
Soft-plumaged Petrel *Pterodroma mollis dubia* RBe (**IO**, **PO**)
Mottled Petrel *Pterodroma inexpectata* RB (**PO**) NEAR THREATENED
Juan Fernández Petrel *Pterodroma externa* V (PO)
Barau's Petrel *Pterodroma baraui* V (IO)?
White-necked Petrel *Pterodroma cervicalis* V (IO)
Black-winged Petrel *Pterodroma nigripennis* RB ([**PO**])
Chatham Petrel *Pterodroma axillaris* RBe (**PO**) CRITICAL
Cook's Petrel *Pterodroma cookii* N ([PO]) ENDANGERED
Gould's Petrel *Pterodroma leucoptera* V (PO)
De Filippi's Petrel *Pterodroma defilippiana* V (PO)?
Blue Petrel *Halobaena caerulea* RBe (**AO**, **IO**, [**PO**], [AC])
Broad-billed Prion *Pachyptila vittata* RBe (**AO**, [IO], [AC])
Saint Paul Prion *Pachyptila [vittata/salvini] macgillivrayi* RBe (**IO**)
Salvin's Prion *Pachyptila salvini* RBe (**IO**, [PO])
Antarctic Prion *Pachyptila desolata* RBe (**AO**, **IO**, **PO**, [AC])
Slender-billed Prion *Pachyptila belcheri* RBe (**AO**, **IO**, [PO])
Fairy Prion *Pachyptila turtur* RB (**AO**, **IO**, **PO**)
Fulmar Prion *Pachyptila crassirostris* RBe ([**IO**], **PO**)
White-chinned Petrel *Procellaria aequinoctialis* RBe (**AO**, **IO**, **PO**, [AC]) VULNERABLE
Spectacled Petrel *Procellaria conspicillata* RBe (**AO**, [IO]) VULNERABLE
Westland Petrel *Procellaria westlandica* V (PO)
Black Petrel *Procellaria parkinsoni* V (PO)
Grey Petrel *Procellaria cinerea* RBe (**AO**, **IO**, **PO**) NEAR THREATENED
Cory's Shearwater *Calonectris diomedea diomedea* N/V (AO, IO, PO)
Cory's Shearwater *Calonectris diomedea borealis* N/V (AO)
Buller's Shearwater *Puffinus bulleri* V (PO)
Flesh-footed Shearwater *Puffinus carneipes* RB ([**IO**], [PO])

Great Shearwater *Puffinus gravis* RB (**AO**, [IO], [AC])
Sooty Shearwater *Puffinus griseus* RBe (**AO**, [IO], **PO**)
Short-tailed Shearwater *Puffinus tenuirostris* N/V ([IO], PO)
Manx Shearwater *Puffinus puffinus* V (AO, PO)
Fluttering Shearwater *Puffinus gavia* N/V (PO)
Hutton's Shearwater *Puffinus huttoni* N/V (PO)
Little Shearwater *Puffinus assimilis* RB (**AO**, **IO**, **PO**)
Family **Hydrobatidae**
European Storm-petrel *Hydrobates pelagicus* V (AO)
Wilson's Storm-petrel *Oceanites oceanicus* RBe (**AO**, **IO**, PO, **AC**)
Grey-backed Storm-petrel *Oceanites nereis* RBe (**AO**, **IO**, **PO**)
White-faced Storm-petrel *Pelagodroma marina* RB (**AO**, [IO], **PO**)
Black-bellied Storm-petrel *Fregetta tropica* RBe (**AO**, **IO**, **PO**, [AC])
White-bellied Storm-petrel *Fregetta grallaria* RB (**AO**, [IO])
New Zealand Storm-petrel *Pealornis maoriana* N/V? (PO)
Leach's Storm-petrel *Oceanodroma leucorhoa* V (AO, IO?, PO, AC)
Family **Pelecanoididae**
South Georgian Diving-petrel *Pelecanoides georgicus* RBe (**AO**, **IO**, [PO])
Common Diving-petrel *Pelecanoides urinatrix* RBe (**AO**, **IO**, **PO**, [AC])
Magellanic Diving-petrel *Pelecanoides magellani* N/V ([AO])?

ORDER Pelecaniformes
Family **Sulidae**
Cape Gannet *Sula capensis* OB ([IO]) VULNERABLE
Australasian Gannet *Sula serrator* N/OB ([IO], [PO])
Peruvian Booby *Sula variegata* V (AO)
Family **Phalacrocoracidae**
Great Cormorant *Phalacrocorax carbo* RB ([PO])
Pied Cormorant *Phalacrocorax varius* V (PO)
Red-legged Shag *Phalacrocorax gaimardi* V (AO)
Spotted Shag *Phalacrocorax punctatus* V (PO)
Pitt Shag *Phalacrocorax featherstoni* RBe (**PO**) VULNERABLE
Neotropic Cormorant *Phalacrocorax olivaceus* V (AO)
Imperial Shag *Phalacrocorax [atriceps] atriceps* RB (**AO**)
Antarctic Shag *Phalacrocorax [atriceps] bransfieldensis* RBe (**AC**)
South Georgian Shag *Phalacrocorax [atriceps] georgianus* RBe (**AO** [AC])
Heard Shag *Phalacrocorax [atriceps] nivalis* RBe (**IO**)
Crozet Shag *Phalacrocorax [atriceps] melanogenis* RBe (**IO**)
Kerguelen Shag *Phalacrocorax [atriceps] verrucosus* RBe (**IO**)
Macquarie Shag *Phalacrocorax [atriceps] purpurascens* RBe (**PO**)
Chatham Shag *Phalacrocorax [carunculatus] onslowi* RBe (**PO**) ENDANGERED
Auckland Island Shag *Phalacrocorax [campbelli] colensoi* RBe (**PO**) VULNERABLE
Campbell Shag *Phalacrocorax [campbelli] campbelli* RBe (**PO**) VULNERABLE
Bounty Shag *Phalacrocorax [campbelli] ranfurlyi* RBe (**PO**) VULNERABLE
Rock Shag *Phalacrocorax magellanicus* RB (**AO**)
Little Pied Cormorant *Phalacrocorax melanoleucos* OB ([PO])
Family **Fregatidae**
Lesser Frigatebird *Fregata ariel* V (PO)

ORDER Ciconiiformes
Family **Ardeidae**
New Zealand (Black-backed) Little Bittern *Ixobrychus novaezelandiae* X (PO)
Cocoi Heron *Ardea cocoi* V (AO)
Great Egret *Ardea alba* V (AO, PO)
Intermediate Egret *Ardea intermedia* V (AO)
White-faced Heron *Ardea novaehollandiae* RB ([**PO**])
Snowy Egret *Ardea thula* V (AO)
Eastern Reef Egret *Ardea sacra* V (PO)
Striated Heron *Ardea striatus* V (AO)
Cattle Egret *Bubulcus ibis* V (AO, IO, PO, AC)

Black-crowned Night-heron *Nycticorax nycticorax falklandicus* Rbe/V (**AO**, IO)
Family **Threskiornithidae**
Black-faced Ibis *Theristicus melanopsis* V (AO)
Glossy Ibis *Plegadis falcinellus* V (PO)
Roseate Spoonbill *Ajaia ajaja* V (AO)
Family **Ciconiidae**
White Stork *Ciconia ciconia* V (IO)
Maguari Stork *Ciconia maguari* V (AO)

ORDER Phoenicopteriformes
Family **Phoenicopteridae**
Chilean Flamingo *Phoenicopterus chilensis* V (AO)

ORDER Anseriformes
Family **Anatidae**
Coscoroba Swan *Coscoroba coscoroba* V (AO)
Black Swan *Cygnus atratus* I (**PO**)
Black-necked Swan *Cygnus melancoryphus* RB (**AO**, [AC])
Canada Goose *Branta canadensis* V/I (PO)
Paradise Shelduck *Tadorna variegata* V (PO)
Australian Shelduck *Tadorna tadornoides* V (PO)
Upland Goose *Chloephaga picta leucoptera* RBe (**AO**)
Kelp Goose *Chloephaga hybrida malvinarum* RBe (**AO**)
Ashy-headed Goose *Chloephaga poliocephala* RB (**AO**)
Ruddy-headed Goose *Chloephaga rubidiceps* RB (**AO**)
White-faced Whistling Duck *Dendrocygna viduata* V (AO)
Flying Steamer Duck *Tachyeres patachonicus* RB (**AO**)
Falkland Steamer Duck *Tachyeres brachydactyla* RBe (**AO**)
Crested Duck *Lophonetta specularioides* RB (**AO**)
Maned Duck *Chenonetta jubata* V (PO)
Spectacled Duck *Anas specularis* V (AO)
Chiloe Wigeon *Anas sibilatrix* V (AO, AC)
Speckled Teal *Anas flavirostris* RB (**AO**)
Brown Pintail *Anas georgica georgica* RBe (**AO**, [AC])
Yellow-billed Pintail *Anas georgica spinicauda* RB (**AO**)
Silver Teal *Anas versicolor* RB ([**AO**])
Grey Teal *Anas gracilis* V (PO)
Auckland Teal *Anas [aucklandica] aucklandica* RBe (**PO**) VULNERABLE
Campbell Teal *Anas [aucklandica] nesiotis* RBe (**PO**) CRITICAL
Brown Teal *Anas chlorotis* X (PO)
Eaton's Pintail *Anas eatoni* RBe ([IO]) VULNERABLE
Amsterdam Flightless Duck *Anas marecula* Xe (IO)
Mallard *Anas platyrhynchos* I ([**AO**], [IO?], **PO**)
Pacific Black Duck *Anas superciliosa* RB ([**PO**])
Blue-winged Teal *Anas discors* V (AO)
Cinnamon Teal *Anas cyanoptera* RB ([**AO**])
Red Shoveler *Anas platalea* V (AO)
Australasian Shoveler *Anas rhynchotis* V (PO)
Rosy-billed Pochard *Netta peposaca* V (AO)
New Zealand Scaup *Aythya novaeseelandiae* X (PO)
White-eyed Duck *Aythya australis* V (PO)
Auckland Merganser *Mergus australis* Xe (PO)
Lake Duck *Oxyura vittata* V (AO, AC)
Black-headed Duck *Heteronetta atricapilla* V (AO)

ORDER Falconiformes
Family **Cathartidae**
Turkey Vulture *Cathartes aura* RB (**AO**)
Family **Accipitridae**
Swamp Harrier *Circus approximans* RB (**PO**)
Long-winged Harrier *Circus buffoni* V (AO)
Cinereous Harrier *Circus cinereus* V? (AO)
Sharp-shinned Hawk *Accipiter striatus* V (AO)
Red-backed Hawk *Buteo polyosoma* RB (AO)
Family **Falconidae**
Southern (Crested) Caracara *Caracara plancus* RB (**AO**)
Striated Caracara *Phalcoboenus australis* RB (**AO**) NEAR THREATENED
Chimango Caracara *Milvago chimango* V (AO)
American Kestrel *Falco sparverius* V (AO)
Hobby *Falco subbuteo* V (IO)
New Zealand Falcon *Falco novaeseelandiae* RB (**PO**) NEAR THREATENED
Aplomado Falcon *Falco femoralis* V (AO)
Peregrine Falcon *Falco peregrinus* RB/V (**AO**, IO)

ORDER Galliformes
Family **Odontophoridae**
California Quail *Lophortyx californicus* X?/I ([PO])

ORDER Gruiformes
Family **Rallidae**
Austral Rail *Rallus antarcticus* V (AO)
Speckled Rail *Coturnicops notatus* V (AO)
Weka *Gallirallus australis* I (**PO**) VULNERABLE
Macquarie Island Rail *Gallirallus philippensis macquariensis* Xe (PO)
Dieffenbach's Rail *Gallirallus philippensis dieffenbachii* Xe (PO)
Chatham Island Rail *Rallus modestus* Xe (PO)
Giant Chatham Island Rail *Diaphorapteryx hawkinsi* Xe (PO)
Auckland Island Rail *Dryolimnas [pectoralis] muelleri* RBe (**PO**) VULNERABLE
Inaccessible Island Rail *Atlantisia rogersi* RBe (**AO**)
Baillon's Crake *Porzana pusilla* V (AO)
Spotless Crake *Porzana tabuensis* RB ([**PO**])
Paint-billed Crake *Neocrex erythrops* V (AO)
Plumbeous Rail *Pardirallus sanguinolentus* V (AO)
Corncrake *Crex crex* V (IO)
Purple Gallinule *Porphyrio martinica* V (AO)
Purple Swamphen *Porphyrio porphyrio* RB (**PO**)
Allen's Gallinule *Porphyrula alleni* V (AO)
Tristan Moorhen *Gallinula [nesiotis] nesiotis* Xe (AO)
Gough Moorhen *Gallinula [nesiotis] comeri* RBe (**AO**) VULNERABLE
Eurasian Coot *Fulica atra* V (PO)
White-winged Coot *Fulica leucoptera* V (AO)
Red-gartered Coot *Fulica armillata* V (AO)
Red-fronted Coot *Fulica rufifrons* V (AO)

ORDER Charadriiformes
Family **Chionidae**
Pale-faced Sheathbill *Chionis alba* RBe (**AO**)
Black-faced Sheathbill *Chionis minor minor* RBe (**IO**)
Black-faced Sheathbill *Chionis minor marionensis* RBe (**IO**)
Black-faced Sheathbill *Chionis minor crozettensis* RBe (**IO**)
Black-faced Sheathbill *Chionis minor nasicornis* RBe (**IO**)
Family **Haematopodidae**
Magellanic Oystercatcher *Haematopus leucopodus* RB (**AO**)
Blackish Oystercatcher *Haematopus ater* RB (**AO**)
South Island Pied Oystercatcher *Haematopus finschi* V (PO)
Chatham Island Oystercatcher *Haematopus chathamensis* RBe (**PO**) ENDANGERED
Family **Recurvirostridae**
Black-winged (Black-necked) Stilt *Himantopus himantopus mexicanus* V ([AO])
Black-winged (White-headed) Stilt *Himantopus himantopus leucocephalus* V ([**PO**])
Black-winged (White-backed) Stilt *Himantopus himantopus melanurus* V ([AO])
Family **Charadriidae**
American Golden Plover *Pluvialis dominica* V (AO)
Pacific Golden Plover *Pluvialis fulva* N/V (AO)
Grey Plover *Pluvialis squatarola* V (AO, IO, PO)
Ringed Plover *Charadrius hiaticula* V (IO)
Double-banded Plover *Charadrius bicinctus bicinctus* RB (**PO**)
Auckland Island Banded Plover *Charadrius bicinctus exilis* RBe (**PO**)
Large Sand Plover *Charadrius leschenaultii* V (IO)
Mongolian Plover *Charadrius mongolus* V (PO)
Oriental Plover *Charadrius veredus* V (PO)
Three-banded Plover *Charadrius tricollaris* V (IO)
Two-banded Plover *Charadrius falklandicus* RB (**AO**)
Rufous-chested Dotterel *Charadrius modestus* RB (**AO**)
Shore Plover *Thinornis novaeseelandiae* RBe (**PO**) ENDANGERED
Wrybill *Anarhynchus frontalis* V (PO)
Tawny-throated Dotterel *Eudromias (Oreopholus) ruficollis* V (AO)
Magellanic Plover *Pluvianellus socialis* V (AO)
Masked Lapwing *Vanellus miles* RB ([**PO**])
Blacksmith Lapwing *Vanellus armatus* V (IO)
Spur-winged Lapwing *Vanellus spinosus* V (PO)
Southern Lapwing *Vanellus chilensis* V (AO)
Family **Scolopacidae**
Latham's Snipe *Gallinago hardwickii* V (PO)
Magellanic Snipe *Gallinago magellanica* RB ([**AO**])
Fuegian Snipe *Gallinago stricklandii* OB/X? ([**AO**])

NEAR THREATENED
Chatham Island Snipe *Coenocorypha pusilla* RBe (**PO**) VULNERABLE
Snares Island Snipe *Coenocorypha [aucklandica] huegeli* RBe (**PO**)
Auckland Island Snipe *Coenocorypha [aucklandica] aucklandica* RBe (**PO**)
Antipodes Island Snipe *Coenocorypha [aucklandica] meinertzhagenae* RBe (**PO**)
Campbell Island Snipe *Coenocorypha [aucklandica] undescribed taxon* RBe (**PO**)
Black-tailed Godwit *Limosa limosa* V (PO)
Hudsonian Godwit *Limosa haemastica* V (AO, PO)
Bar-tailed Godwit *Limosa lapponica* N/V (AO, IO, PO)
Eastern Curlew *Numenius madagascariensis* V (PO)
Eskimo Curlew *Numenius borealis* V (AO)
Whimbrel *Numenius phaeopus* N/V (AO, IO, PO)
Common Greenshank *Tringa nebularia* N/V (AO, IO, PO)
Marsh Sandpiper *Tringa stagnatilis* V (PO)
Greater Yellowlegs *Tringa melanoleuca* V (AO)
Lesser Yellowlegs *Tringa flavipes* V (AO, PO)
Solitary Sandpiper *Tringa solitaria* V (AO)
Wood Sandpiper *Tringa glareola* V (IO)
Terek Sandpiper *Xenus cinereus* V (IO)
Common Sandpiper *Actitis hypoleucos* V (AO, IO)
Spotted Sandpiper *Actitis macularia* V (AO)
Grey-tailed Tattler *Heteroscelus brevipes* V (PO)
Wandering Tattler *Heteroscelus incanus* V (PO)
Ruddy Turnstone *Arenaria interpres* N/V (AO, IO, PO)
Red Knot *Calidris canutus* N/V (AO, PO)
Sanderling *Calidris alba* N/V (AO, IO, PO)
Little Stint *Calidris minuta* V (AO, IO)
Red-necked Stint *Calidris ruficollis* V (PO)
Semipalmated Sandpiper *Calidris pusilla* V (AO)
Least Sandpiper *Calidris minutilla* V (AC)
White-rumped Sandpiper *Calidris fuscicollis* V (AO, AC)
Baird's Sandpiper *Calidris bairdii* V (AO, AC)
Pectoral Sandpiper *Calidris melanotos* V (AO, PO, AC)
Sharp-tailed Sandpiper *Calidris acuminata* V (AO, PO)
Curlew Sandpiper *Calidris ferruginea* V (IO)
Stilt Sandpiper *Micropalama himantopus* V (AO)
Upland Sandpiper *Bartramia longicauda* V (AO, AC)
Surfbird *Aphriza virgata* V (AO)
Grey Phalarope *Phalaropus fulicarius* V (AO, IO, AC)
Wilson's Phalarope *Phalaropus tricolor* V (AO, AC)
Family **Thinocoridae**
White-bellied Seedsnipe *Attagis malouinus* X?V (AO)
Least Seedsnipe *Thinocorus rumicivorus* OB? (AO, AC)
Family **Stercorariidae**
Falkland Skua *Catharacta [skua] antarctica* race *antarctica* RBe (**AO**)
Tristan Skua *Catharacta [skua] antarctica* race *hamiltoni* RBe (**AO**)
Subantarctic Skua *Catharacta [skua] antarctica* race *lonnbergi* RBe (**AO, IO, PO**)
Chilean Skua *Catharacta [skua] chilensis* N (AO)
South Polar Skua *Catharacta [skua] maccormicki* MBe (**AC**)
Pomarine Jaeger *Stercorarius pomarinus* N/V (AO, IO, PO, AC)
Arctic Jaeger *Stercorarius parasiticus* N/V (AO, IO, PO, AC)
Long-tailed Jaeger *Stercorarius longicaudus* N/V (AO, IO, PO)
Family **Laridae**
Dolphin Gull *Larus scoresbii* RB (**AO**)
Kelp Gull *Larus dominicanus* RB (**AO, IO, PO**)
Yellow-legged Gull *Larus cachinnans* V (IO)
Lesser Black-backed Gull *Larus fuscus* V (IO)
Band-tailed Gull *Larus belcheri* V (AO)
Grey Gull *Larus modestus* V (AO)
Red-billed Gull *Larus scopulinus* RB (**PO**)
Black-billed Gull *Larus bulleri* V (PO)
Grey-headed Gull *Larus cirrocephalus* V (AO)
Brown-hooded Gull *Larus maculipennis* RB (**AO**)
Franklin's Gull *Larus pipixcan* V (AO, IO)
Sabine's Gull *Larus sabini* V (AO)
Family **Sternidae**
Elegant Tern *Sterna elegans* V (AO)
Sandwich Tern *Sterna sandvicensis* V (AO)
White-fronted Tern *Sterna striata* RB (**PO**)
Common Tern *Sterna hirundo* V (AO, IO, PO)
Arctic Tern *Sterna paradisaea* N (AO, IO, PO, AC)

Antarctic Tern *Sterna vittata* RBe (**AO, IO, PO, AC**)
Trudeau's Tern *Sterna trudeaui* V (AO)
Elegant Tern *Sterna elegans* V (AO)
Kerguelen Tern *Sterna virgata* RBe (**IO**) NEAR THREATENED
Black-fronted Tern *Sterna albostriata* V (PO)
South American Tern *Sterna hirundinacea* RB (**AO**)
Sooty Tern *Sterna fuscata* OB (AO)
Common Noddy *Anous stolidus* RB (**AO**)
Black Noddy *Anous minutus* V (AO)

ORDER Columbiformes
Family **Columbidae**
Chilean Pigeon *Columba araucana* V (AO)
Rock Pigeon *Columba livia* V/I (PO)
European Turtle-dove *Streptopelia turtur* V (IO)
Cape Turtle-dove *Streptopelia capicola* V (IO)
Laughing Turtle-dove *Streptopelia senegalensis* V (IO)
Eared Dove *Zenaida auriculata* V (AO)
Ruddy Ground-dove *Columbina talpacoti* V (AO)
Blue Ground-dove *Claravis pretiosa* V (AO)
Chatham Island Pigeon *Hemiphaga chathamensis* RBe (**PO**)

ORDER Psittaciformes
Family **Psittacidae**
Antipodes Parakeet *Cyanoramphus unicolor* RBe (**PO**) VULNERABLE
Red-crowned Parakeet *Cyanoramphus [novaezelandiae] novaezelandiae* RB (**PO**)
Antipodes Red-crowned Parakeet *Cyanoramphus [novaezelandiae] hochstetteri* RBe (**PO**)
Chatham Island Red-crowned Parakeet *Cyanoramphus [novaezelandiae] chathamensis* RBe (**PO**)
Macquarie Island Parakeet *Cyanoramphus [novaezelandiae/erythrotis] erythrotis* Xe (PO)
Yellow-crowned Parakeet *Cyanoramphus auriceps* RB (**PO**)
Forbes' Parakeet *Cyanoramphus [novaezelandiae/auriceps] forbesi* RBe (**PO**) ENDANGERED
Burrowing Parrot *Cyanoliseus patagonus* V (AO)
Austral Parakeet *Enicognathus ferrugineus* V (AO)

ORDER Cuculiformes
Family **Cuculidae**
Dark-billed Cuckoo *Coccyzus melacoryphus* V (AO)
Yellow-billed Cuckoo *Coccyzus americanus* V (AO)
Common Cuckoo *Cuculus canorus* V (IO)
African Cuckoo *Cuculus gularis* V (IO)
Oriental Cuckoo *Cuculus saturatus* V (PO)
Pallid Cuckoo *Cuculus pallidus* V (PO)
Lesser Cuckoo *Cuculus poliocephalus* V (IO)
Red-chested Cuckoo *Cuculus solitarius* V (IO)
Shining Bronze-cuckoo *Chrysococcyx lucidus* MB ([**PO**])
Long-tailed Cuckoo *Eudynamys taitensis* V (PO)

ORDER Strigiformes
Family **Tytonidae**
Barn Owl *Tyto alba* RB (**AO**)
Family **Strigidae**
Magellanic Horned Owl *Bubo magellanicus* V (AO)
Burrowing Owl *Athene cunicularia* V (AO)
Southern Boobook *Ninox novaeseelandiae* V (PO)
Short-eared Owl *Asio flammeus sanfordi* RBe (**AO**)

ORDER Caprimulgiformes
Family **Caprimulgidae**
Common Nighthawk *Chordeiles minor* V (AO)
Band-winged Nightjar *Caprimulgus longirostris* V (AO)

ORDER Apodiformes
Family **Apodidae**
White-collared Swift *Streptoprocne zonaris* V (AO)
Ashy-tailed Swift *Chaetura andrei* V (AO)
White-throated Needletail *Hirundapus caudacutus* V (PO)
Common Swift *Apus apus* V (IO)
Fork-tailed Swift *Apus pacificus* V (PO)
Family **Trochilidae**
Green-backed Firecrown *Sephanoides sephaniodes* V (AO)

ORDER Coraciiformes
Family **Alcedinidae**
Sacred Kingfisher *Todiramphus sanctus* V (PO)

33

Family Coraciidae
Broad-billed Roller *Eurystomus glaucurus* V (IO)

ORDER Passeriformes
Family Furnariidae
Blackish Cinclodes *Cinclodes antarcticus antarcticus* RBe (**AO**)
Bar-winged Cinclodes *Cinclodes fuscus* V (AO)
Thorn-tailed Rayadito *Aphrastura spinicauda* X? (**AO**)
Family Rhinocryptidae
Magellanic Tapaculo *Scytalopus magellanicus* X? (**AO**)
Family Phytotomidae
Rufous-tailed Plantcutter *Phytotoma rara* V (AO)
Family Tyrannidae
White-crested Elaenia *Elaenia albiceps* V (AO)
Tufted Tit-tyrant *Anairetes parulus* V (AO)
Fire-eyed Diucon *Pyrope pyrope* V (AO)
Black-crowned Monjita *Xolmis coronatus* V (AO)
Black-billed Shrike-tyrant *Agriornis montana* V (AO)
White-browed Ground-tyrant *Muscisaxicola albilora* V (AO)
Dark-faced Ground-tyrant *Muscisaxicola macloviana macloviana* RBe (**AO**)
Cattle Tyrant *Machetornis rixosus* V (AO)
Austral Negrito *Lessonia rufa* V (AO, AC)
Great Kiskadee *Pitangus sulphuratus* V (AO)
Eastern Kingbird *Tyrannus tyrannus* V (AO)
Fork-tailed Flycatcher *Tyrannus savana* V (AO)
Family Meliphagidae
New Zealand Bellbird *Anthornis melanura melanura* RB (**PO**)
Chatham Island Bellbird *Anthornis melanura melanocephala* Xe (**PO**)
Tui *Prosthemadera novaeseelandiae novaeseelandiae* RB (**PO**)
Chatham Island Tui *Prosthemadera novaeseelandiae chathamensis* RBe (**PO**)
Family Acanthizidae
Grey Warbler *Gerygone igata* V (PO)
Chatham Island Warbler *Gerygone albofrontata* RBe (**PO**)
Family Petroicidae
Chatham Island Tomtit *Petroica [macrocephala] chathamensis* RBe (**PO**)
Auckland Island Tomtit *Petroica [macrocephala] marrineri* RBe (**PO**)
Snares Tomtit *Petroica [macrocephala] dannefaerdi* RBe (**PO**)
Black Robin *Petroica traversi* RBe (**PO**) ENDANGERED
Family Rhipiduridae
New Zealand Fantail *Rhipidura fuliginosa fuliginosa* RB (**PO**)
Chatham Island Fantail *Rhipidura fuliginosa penitus* RBe (**PO**)
Family Laniidae
Red-backed Shrike *Lanius collurio* V (IO)
Family Alaudidae
Skylark *Alauda arvensis* I (**PO**)
Family Motacillidae
New Zealand Pipit *Anthus novaeseelandiae* RB (**PO**)
Correndera Pipit *Anthus correndera grayi* RBe (**AO**)
South Georgia Pipit *Anthus antarcticus* RBe (**AO**) NEAR THREATENED
Yellow Wagtail *Motacilla flava* V (IO)
Family Prunellidae
Dunnock *Prunella modularis* I (**PO**)
Family Passeridae
House Sparrow *Passer domesticus* I (**AO**, IO, **PO**)
Common Waxbill *Estrilda astrild* I (**IO**)
Family Fringillidae
Common Chaffinch *Fringilla coelebs* I (**PO**)
European Greenfinch *Carduelis chloris* I (**PO**)
European Goldfinch *Carduelis carduelis* I (**PO**)
Common Redpoll *Carduelis flammea* I (**PO**)
Black-chinned Siskin *Carduelis barbata* RBe (**AO**)
Family Emberizidae
Yellowhammer *Emberiza citrinella* I (**PO**)
Mourning Sierra-finch *Phrygilus fruticeti* V (AO)
Patagonian Sierra-finch *Phrygilus patagonicus* V (AO)
Black-throated (Canary-winged) Finch *Melanodera melanodera melanodera* RBe (**AO**)

Yellow-bridled Finch *Melanodera xanthogramma* X? (**AO**)
Gough Bunting *Rowettia goughensis* RBe (**AO**) VULNERABLE
Inaccessible/Tristan Bunting *Nesospiza acunhae* RBe (**AO**) VULNERABLE
Nightingale Bunting *Nesospiza questi* RBe (**AO**) VULNERABLE
Grosbeak Bunting *Nesospiza wilkinsi* RBe (**AO**) VULNERABLE (CRITICAL?)
Patagonian Yellow-finch *Sicalis lebruni* V (AO)
Rufous-collared Sparrow *Zonotrichia capensis* V (AO)
Family Troglodytidae
Grass Wren *Cistothorus platensis falklandicus* RBe (**AO**)
Cobb's Wren *Troglodytes cobbi* RBe (**AO**) VULNERABLE
Family Mimidae
Patagonian Mockingbird *Mimus patagonicus* V (AO)
Family Hirundinidae
Brown-chested Martin *Progne tapera* V (AO)
Grey-breasted Martin *Progne chalybea* V (AO)
Southern Martin *Progne modesta* V (AO)
Purple Martin *Progne subis* V (AO)
White-rumped Swallow *Tachycineta leucorrhoa* V (AO)
Chilean Swallow *Tachycineta meyeni* V/N (**[AO]**)
Blue-and-white Swallow *Notiochelidon cyanoleuca* V (AO)
Sand Martin *Riparia riparia* V (AO, IO)
Southern Rough-winged Swallow *Stelgidopteryx ruficollis* V (AO)
Tawny-headed Swallow *Alopochelidon fucata* V (AO)
Cliff Swallow *Petrochelidon pyrrhonota* V (AO)
Barn Swallow *Hirundo rustica* V (AO, IO, AC)
Welcome Swallow *Hirundo neoxena* RB (**[PO]**)
Tree Martin *Hirundo nigricans* V (PO)
Northern House Martin *Delichon urbica* V (IO)
Family Sylviidae
Common Whitethroat *Sylvia communis* V (IO)
Willow Warbler *Phylloscopus trochilus* V (IO)
Snares Islands Fernbird *Bowdleria [punctata] caudata* RBe (**PO**)
Chatham Island Fernbird *Bowdleria rufescens* Xe (PO)
Family Zosteropidae
Silvereye *Zosterops lateralis* RB (**PO**)
Family Muscicapidae
Mountain Chat *Oenanthe monticola* V (IO)
Familiar / Sicklewing Chat *Cercomela familiaris / C. sinuate* V (IO)
Family Turdidae
Common Blackbird *Turdus merula* I (**PO**)
Song Thrush *Turdus philomelos* I (**PO**)
Wood Thrush *Hylocichla mustelina* V (AO)
Austral Thrush *Turdus falcklandii falcklandii* RBe (**AO**)
Tristan Thrush *Nesocichla eremita* RBe (**AO**) NEAR THREATENED
Family Sturnidae
Common Starling *Sturnus vulgaris* I (**PO**)
Family Icteridae
Long-tailed Meadowlark *Sturnella loyca falklandica* RBe (**AO**)
Shiny Cowbird *Molothrus bonariensis* V (AO)
Family Corvidae
Rook *Corvus frugilegus* V/I (**PO**)

Marine Mammals

ORDER Carnivora Subgroup Pinnipedia
Family Otariidae
South American Fur Seal *Arctocephalus australis australis* RB (**AO**)
New Zealand Fur Seal *Arctocephalus forsteri* RB (**PO**)
Antarctic Fur Seal *Arctocephalus gazella* RBe (**AO**, **[IO]**, **[PO]**)
South African Fur Seal *Arctocephalus [pusillus] pusillus* V (IO)
Subantarctic Fur Seal *Arctocephalus tropicalis* RBe (**AO**, **IO**, **[PO]**)
South American (Southern) Sea Lion *Otaria flavescens* RB (**AO**)
New Zealand (Hooker's) Sea Lion *Phocarctos hookeri* RBe (**PO**) VULNERABLE

Family Phocidae
Leopard Seal *Hydrurga leptonyx* RBe (**[AO], [IO], [PO], AC**)
Weddell Seal *Leptonychotes weddellii* RBe (**[AO], [IO], [PO], AC**)
Crabeater Seal *Lobodon carcinophaga* RBe (**[AO], [IO], [PO], AC**)
Southern Elephant Seal *Mirounga leonina* RB (**AO, IO, PO, [AC]**)
Ross Seal *Ommatophoca rossii* RBe (**AC**)

ORDER Cetacea
Family Delphinidae
Commerson's Dolphin *Cephalorhynchus commersonii* RB (**AO, IO**)
(Short-beaked) Common Dolphin *Delphinus delphis* V/N (**[PO]**)?
Long-finned Pilot Whale *Globicephala melas* RB (**AO, IO, PO**)
Risso's Dolphin *Grampus griseus* V/N (PO)
Peale's Dolphin *Lagenorhynchus australis* RB (**AO**)
Hourglass Dolphin *Lagenorhynchus cruciger* RB (**AO, IO, PO, [AC]**)
Dusky Dolphin *Lagenorhynchus obscurus* RB (**AO, IO, PO**)
Southern Right Whale Dolphin *Lissodelphis peronii* RB (**AO, IO, PO**)
Killer Whale *Orcinus orca* (including 3 distinctive Antarctic ecotypes) RB (**AO, IO, PO, AC**)
False Killer Whale *Pseudorca crassidens* RB (**AO, IO, PO**)
Bottlenose Dolphin *Tursiops truncatus* V/N (**[AO], [IO], [PO]**)?
Family Physeteridae
Sperm Whale *Physeter macrocephalus* N (**AO, IO, PO**)
Family Ziphiidae
Arnoux's Beaked Whale *Berardius arnuxii* RB (**AO, [IO?], PO, [AC]**)
Southern Bottlenose Whale *Hyperoodon planifrons* RB (**AO, IO, PO, AC**)
Andrews' Beaked Whale *Mesoplodon bowdoini* RB (**[PO]**)
Ginkgo-toothed Beaked Whale *Mesoplodon ginkgodens* V/N (**[PO]**)?
Gray's Beaked Whale *Mesoplodon grayi* RB/N (**[AO], [IO?], PO**)
Pygmy (Peruvian) Beaked Whale *Mesoplodon peruvianus* V (IO)?
Hector's Beaked Whale *Mesoplodon hectori* RB/N (**[AO], [PO]**)?
Strap-toothed Whale *Mesoplodon layardii* RB (**AO, IO, PO**)
Shepherd's Beaked Whale *Tasmacetus shepardi* RB/N/V (**[AO], [PO]**)?
Cuvier's Beaked Whale *Ziphius cavirostris* RB/N/V (**[AO], [PO]**)?
Family Phocoenidae
Spectacled Porpoise *Phocoena (Australophocaena) dioptrica* RB/N (**[AO], [IO], [PO]**)
Family Balaenidae
Southern Right Whale *Eubalaena australis* RB/N (**[AO], [IO], [PO?]**)
Family Balaenopteridae
Dwarf Minke Whale *Balaenoptera [acutorostrata]* unnamed subspecies/allospecies N (**[IO], [PO]**)? ENDANGERED
Antarctic Minke Whale *Balaenoptera bonaerensis* N (AO, IO, PO, AC)
Sei Whale *Balaenoptera borealis* N (AO, IO, PO, [AC])
Southern Blue Whale *Balaenoptera [musculus] intermedia* N/V (AO, IO?, PO?, AC) ENDANGERED (CRITICAL?)
Pygmy Blue Whale *Balaenoptera [musculus] brevicauda* N/V (AO?, IO, PO, AC?) ENDANGERED?
Fin Whale *Balaenoptera physalus* N (AO, IO, PO) ENDANGERED
Humpback Whale *Megaptera novaeangliae* N (AO, IO, PO, AC) VULNERABLE
Family Neobalaenidae
Pygmy Right Whale *Caperea marginata* RB (AO, IO, [PO])

History of Antarctic Exploration

The European approach to the South Atlantic and subsequently Antarctica arose from the desire to explore a mythical continent, *Terra Australis Incognita*. Upon reaching the Southern Ocean the Europeans exploited it with a rapacity that equalled the conquest of the American West. The initial quest for Antarctica amazingly spanned the better part of four centuries and, despite the indelibly adverse impressions that some of the Antarctic islands left on the early explorers such as Bouvet and Cook, it rarely lost its attraction to those in search of fame, and perhaps fortune. Perhaps even more amazingly, the existence of a southern landmass had been predicted, if not actually assumed, for nearly 2000 years (and in c.700 BC a Phoenician fleet reportedly reached the Indian Ocean via S Africa). As early as 400 BC, Greek philosophers notioned that the world must be spherical and, based on their natural love of order and often-displayed fondness for symmetry, argued that there must be land to the south, balancing that in the north, known as Arktos because it lay below the constellation Arctos, the Bear. Through Arktos ran an imaginary line, the Arctic Pole, around which all the heavens appeared to revolve. It was easy to imagine another fixed point—the Antarctic Pole. As in many things intangible at the time, the ancient Greeks were subsequently proven to be correct.

First steps toward Antarctica

A concerted search for the southern continent commenced in the mid-15th century. If, as the ancient geographer Ptolemy had imagined, India and Africa were connected to *Terra Australis* (as was subsequently demonstrated to have been the case, millions of years prior to the arrival of Man in the Earth's scheme), then it would surely be possible to reach this elusive and potentially rich continent simply by sailing south via the W African coast. In 1418–60, Prince Henry the Navigator, of Portugal, sent ship after ship south, each expedition venturing a little further towards its goal, yet in real terms falling well short of achieving it. By mid-century, Portuguese vessels had crossed the equator and, in Feb 1488, Bartholomeu Diaz was driven by raging storms far beyond the previous farthest south attained (with the exception of the Greek expedition mentioned above), reaching what is now known as the Cape of Good Hope. To the south lay open sea. He turned east, rounding the southern tip of Africa and within nine years Vasco da Gama had finally reached India via this route, laying to rest Ptolemy's claim.

Columbus meanwhile had sailed west across the Atlantic, discovering the Caribbean islands, which he fancifully imagined were the East Indies, but were if anything to prove, along with the additional discoveries in the New World that quickly followed, even richer. Columbus also witnessed signs of a great landmass to the south. Portuguese expeditions, in 1501 and 1502, discovered Brazil and subsequently the Patagonian coast, confirming the presence of an American continent. Was this *Terra Australis*? A Portuguese captain, Fernão de Magalhães (Ferdinand Magellan) swiftly settled the question, in Nov 1520. His stated mission was to bypass the American continent, if possible, and sail west to China and Japan. He followed the eastern seaboard of South America, exploring every bay and river mouth, hoping to find a strait to reach the Pacific. If necessary, he would sail to the Pole, but such determination was to prove unnecessary. At 52°S, a channel appeared with salt water and a strong current. The small fleet passed through and discovered that it was a genuine strait

Icebergs and storms were perilous hazards of early expeditions to the Antarctic. Here the Erebus *and* Terror *collide during the James Clark Ross expedition, 12 Mar 1842. © Global Book Publishing.*

linking the oceans. To the south land was still visible. It seemed to Magellan to be continental land, perhaps the northernmost part of *Terra Australis*. He named it Tierra del Fuego, among the few names given by the early explorers to have persisted until the present. Magellan's fleet went on to become the first mariners to circumnavigate the globe (though their captain was killed in the Philippines in Apr 1521), discovering Amsterdam I during the return part of the voyage, in Mar 1522.

Cartographers were by now convinced of the existence of a huge land south of the Strait of Magellan. Not for many years, however, did any navigator venture to uncover the truth. When Francis Drake in the *Golden Hind* repeated Magellan's feat 60 years later (in Oct 1578) it was due to a chance storm and not through planned initiative. He found himself among a group of islands that he named the 'Elizabethides', but which were possibly those now known as the Wollaston Is. Francis Fletcher, the voyage's chronicler, remarked that to the south of their anchorage no land was visible, suggesting that Drake discovered the southernmost tip of South America. This area of sea, which marks the mixing of Pacific and Atlantic waters, now bears his name, the Drake Passage. However, a Dutch voyager, Willem Schouten, who landed on the Cape on 29 Jan 1616 and named it after his hometown Hoorn, has been accorded credit for the discovery of the southernmost islands of South America. The latter's claim to be the first European to reach Cape Horn was possible because Drake's discovery was declared an official state secret by Elizabeth I, who sought to protect knowledge of a second gateway to the Pacific particularly from the Spanish and Portuguese navies. The Strait of Magellan, under Spanish control, was thought to be the only passage and contemporary maps continued to depict a continent to the south, *Terra Australis*.

Further voyages now sought the mythical land. Some travelled further east in their efforts. In 1642, a Dutch captain, Abel Tasman reached Tasmania. Initially called New Holland, the main landmass (which Tasman virtually circumnavigated without ever seeing) swiftly became better known as Australia, 'The Southern Land'—a southern continent, but this was not *the* southern continent that explorers had been searching for the past 100 or more years. Tasman went on to discover New Zealand before returning to the Dutch East Indies. It was obvious that a polar continent, if it existed, did not reach very far north. Open water was now known to exist to the south of Africa, South America and Australia. Roaming buccaneers and merchantmen had gained high latitudes without witnessing the supposed last continent.

The late 16th and 17th centuries

The first recorded landfall in the Southern Ocean, in true Antarctic waters was in 1675. An English merchant, Antonio de la Roché, rounding Cape Horn en route home from Chile, was swept east in a gale to a snow-covered island, which appeared mountainous, stormy and uninhabited (South Georgia), at c.55°S. Continuing on his way north, de la Roché is also credited as being the first person to make landfall on remote Gough. Thereafter, buccaneers such as Sharpe and Davis reached beyond 60°S but reported seeing only floating ice. Storms and extreme cold, the lot of every Antarctic explorer, unsurprisingly discouraged further exploration until a young Frenchman, Bouvet de Lozier, persuaded the French East India Company to furnish two ships for another search for the fabled southern continent. On New Year's Day 1739, steep, snow-topped mountains loomed from the fog, but rough seas thwarted a landing. So dense was the fog, it was impossible to know whether an island or continent had been discovered, but it proved to be insular and is named Bouvetøya, the most isolated land on Earth and still among the most rarely visited, at 55°S 28°E. What lay beyond seemed deeply unattractive: Bouvet visualized a remote, unapproachable continent, ringed by icebergs, inhabited by only seals and penguins; ironically this has proved to be little short of the truth, but such harsh visions did not dampen some men's ardour for fame and potential glory.

Indeed, it was French mariners that subsequently returned to the quest, but it was only following the loss of the Seven Year's War (1756–63), which stripped France of most of her North American possessions, that it became urgent to repair her empire by claiming new land. Meanwhile, the British had stolen a march: Byron, in 1764, and Wallis and Carteret, in 1766, searched the S Atlantic and Pacific on behalf of the Admiralty for the undiscovered continent. They found nothing but scattered islands. In 1764 Antoine de Bougainville claimed what is now the Falklands, installing a settlement of French Canadians. The colony on East Falkland was known as Port Louis and the archipelago Îles Malouines, in reference to the French port of St.-Malo, from where the expedition had set sail. Only a year later and unaware of the French colony, John Byron took possession of West Falkland and established Port Egmont. British cartographers named the islands after the Viscount of Falkland, Commissioner of the Admiralty. Another Bougainville expedition, in 1767, to the Pacific found 'new' tropical islands, but still there was no sign of the southern continent. In 1772, the French made a last-ditch attempt to find the elusive land. Two small vessels under the command of Yves Joseph de Kerguélen-Trémarec discovered, on 12 Feb, fog-shrouded land at 49°40'S, in the S Indian Ocean. Kerguélen dubbed his discovery 'South France' and hastily and ill-advisedly returned to Paris ambitiously claiming to have found the central mass of the Antarctic continent. A year later, Kerguélen returned with instructions from the French crown to establish trade relations with the natives and to explore the coast between 40°S and 60°S. He found neither natives nor wood, nor the precious stones, which had also entered his tales of untold wealth and possibilities. The land was not even continental, but merely a small, barren island amidst an icy sea, which now bears the name of its discoverer, who must have deeply regretted his rash tongue: he spent six years (commuted from 20 years) in prison for being unable to fulfil his wild promises of glory for the French nation.

Captain Cook

The revelation of the true nature of the 'southern continent'—Antarctica—was to belong to the Englishman, Captain James Cook, perhaps the earliest and still one of the greatest of the true Antarctic explorers (though at the time of his first expedition he was a largely unknown, albeit capable, sea captain). Of most interest to the Royal Society, sponsor of his first voyage, was a transit of Venus, in Jun 1769, which would be visible as a black spot against the sun—a rare astronomical event capable of yielding important scientific information if observed from the best place, the S Pacific. But more was really involved: Cook's clandestine mission aboard *HMS Endeavour* was to search for the unknown southern continent and claim any island not ruled by a Christian prince. Cook was gone during Aug 1768 to Jul 1771. He first rounded Cape Horn, thereafter conducted astronomical observations at Tahiti, circumnavigated New Zealand, and followed the east coast of Australia in the process of which he discovered the Great Barrier Reef (claiming both lands for the crown), before returning to England via New Guinea and Java. The scientific results were important, as was the expedition's contribution to geography, Cook having mapped large areas of the Pacific Ocean.

But with the southern continent still intangible, a second expedition comprising *HMS Resolution* and *HMS Adventure* was planned. This time Cook's instructions specifically requested him to search for the southern continent, and this he did. In Jul 1772 he travelled the W African coast to the Cape of Good Hope and then further south. On 17 Jan 1773 the Antarctic Circle was crossed for the first time in history and Cook's small fleet entered the South Frigid Zone. On reaching 67°S the ice pack stretched ahead as far as the eye could see: there was no possibility of gaining further headway south (unknown to the expedition, they were within 130 km of the Antarctic landmass). Cook then sailed east for two months, landing on and then passing south of Kerguelen and thus bringing further proof its insular nature. Having found no southern continent south of Africa or in the E Pacific, Cook headed south again at 160°W, and then east at c.55°S, meeting heavy ice but no land until Tierra del Fuego, though in Jan 1774 he was able to reach as far as 71°S and during this period he effectively circumnavigated Antarctica. Early in 1775, after rounding Cape Horn and heading southeast, he came upon a fair-sized island, which

Portrait of James Cook. © Global Book Publishing.

Portrait of James Weddell. © Global Book Publishing.

was almost certainly that seen by de la Roché in 1675 and at least once during the intervening years. Cook explored its coast, landed three times, and took possession in the name of George III. The 'Isle of George' subsequently became known as South Georgia. For Cook, it was a dreadful place, 'wild rocks raised their lofty summits till they were lost in the clouds, and the valleys lay covered with everlasting snow. Not a tree was to be seen, nor a shrub even big enough to make a toothpick.' Nothing but penguins and thousands of seals, which proved to be among the most important discoveries of the voyage. Satisfied that South Georgia was not part of a continent, he pressed south again, naming its southeastern tip Cape Disappointment, and discovered more small islands, c.740 km to the southeast in a 350 km-long chain that he named for Lord Sandwich, First Lord of the Admiralty. On 7 Feb, he turned north to search again for Bouvetøya. He failed, like all others until 1898. By late Jul 1775 Cook was back in England with the map wiped clean of legendary continents.

The beginning of the commercial era

Despite the relative failure of the expedition to discover remarkable new lands, sealers and whalers swiftly followed in Cook's footsteps with the scent of money in their nostrils. Whales were by the late-18th century big business, as petroleum was not developed for fuel and oil lamps lighted homes. Whaling ships had already thoroughly fished the northern waters off Europe making the new whaling territory appear attractive. Seals too acquired importance: seal oil was also good for lighting and their pelts were valuable, particularly in the manufacture of warm slippers. This had been discovered on Cook's third voyage, which visited the Kerguelen Is but whose main purpose was to discover a North West Passage. Following his death in Hawaii in mid-Feb 1778, James King, who had assumed command of *HMS Discovery*, had continued to Canton, China. Aboard were seal pelts acquired during trade in the American northwest. Chinese merchants eagerly snapped these up at high prices and the Asian fur trade was born.

By 1815, 200 North American and British sealers were present in the waters south of Cape Horn, systematically stripping islands of their seals: one vessel reportedly killed 100,000 in five years. As known areas became depopulated sealers had to search for new territory. A British captain, William Smith, made the first recorded discovery (given that the sealers livelihood depended on discovery of bountiful new areas and that their interests lay with money not geography, it is possible that previous discoveries went unannounced). In Feb 1819, while rounding Cape Horn, Smith met

rough head winds and elected to veer south to avoid them. Some days later he thought he saw land through falling snow. With clear skies next day the discovery became certain. His position was 62°40'S 60°00'W. In Oct, on the same route, Smith refound the island and took formal possession for King George III. Originally named 'New South Britain', it is now South Shetland. It was a barren, disagreeable, icebound place, but along its shores were seals in abundance.

Antarctica at last

Confusion for many years surrounded the 'discovery' of Antarctica, because, as mentioned above, sealers were not overly interested in furthering geography and usually elected to keep good hunting grounds secret. Three candidates for the discovery emerged in 1820. Captain Bransfield, with Smith, was sent to survey the South Shetlands and raise the British flag. They sighted 'Trinity Land' on 30 Jan, which is actually part of Antarctica. Some North American maps named it 'Palmer Peninsula' as a sealer from Connecticut, Nathaniel Palmer, also discovered it that year (on 16 Nov). Like his predecessors, he was unable to land due to the ice. The third, Baron Bellingshausen, is rightly regarded as the first great Antarctic explorer in the wake of Cook and was indeed the first to sight the continent, on 27 Jan 1820.

The Russian expedition (whose discoveries went largely unacknowledged outside of the country until the 20th century) virtually circumnavigated the entire Antarctic continent but missed finding the Ross Sea due to unusually severe pack ice, and visited the newly discovered South Shetlands. Bellingshausen explored the group thoroughly, giving many islands Russian names. But Bransfield had already charted and named the islands, and consequently his names remain in use.

Bellingshausen returned to Russia in Jul 1821, following the most important voyage of exploration since Cook. He had discovered a total of 29 islands including small Peter I Øy and the larger, more mountainous Alexander I, as well as charting the small islands of South Georgia and another outlying group, the South Sandwiches. Further east, Bellingshausen had been the first to see continental Antarctica, though he had not realized it.

While surveying the South Shetlands Bellingshausen had, rather remarkably, met Palmer, who informed him of the profitable sealing there. But Bellingshausen did not consider it worthy to send Russian sealers to the islands without good cause; he correctly surmised that these mammals' populations would rapidly decrease. He was unquestionably correct: by 1830 these sealing grounds were exhausted. It was sealers, therefore, who also made the first discoveries elsewhere on the continent. Between 1831 and 1839, Biscoe, Kemp and Balleny all observed the Antarctic coast in the Indian Ocean sector, and in 1823 James Weddell aboard the *Jane* made a surprisingly easy passage to 74°S through what he termed the George IV Sea, which had been renamed by 1873 in his honour. Indeed, so remarkable was Weddell's achievement that several of his successors doubted its veracity, although it appears unquestionable, with the benefit of hindsight, that he was merely 'the right man in the right place at the right time'. Thereafter, for a brief period, national expeditions succeeded private sealing and whaling ventures in efforts to penetrate the ice pack.

In Jan 1840 a French expedition led by Dumont d'Urville, and the six-vessel and 400-man US Exploring Expedition, under Charles Wilkes, discovered—within hours of each other—separate sections of the same coast south of Australia. Miraculously, given their remote position, ships from the two expeditions passed each other by in dense fog with Wilkes in the *Vincennes* veering away from the French vessels to avoid contact. Dumont d'Urville's expedition occupied much of the four years between 1837 and 1840 and despite desertions, deaths and scurvy mapped significant areas of the Southern Ocean, including Graham Land and the South Shetlands, and the piece of Antarctica, Adélie Land, he eventually discovered bears the name of his wife. The equally long Wilkes' expedition was more notable for the trials and tribulations of its participants, subsequent recriminations (Wilkes was court-martialled on his return to North America) and failure to make notable geographical discoveries. Nonetheless, Wilkes followed the pack ice for over 2700 km and saw enough of the continent itself to be sure that it was a landmass rather than an island.

Spurred into immediate action by the successes of the North American and French voyages the Englishman, Sir James Clark Ross, already a popular hero and experienced Arctic explorer, led the third great expedition of the age. In Jan 1841, through information supplied by a British sealer, Balleny, he discovered Victoria Land and the sea named in his honour, but entered the latter only to eventually find his way blocked by a wall of ice up to 60 m high. This, the Ross Ice Shelf, and the island also named after him were, due to their proximity to the South Pole, to serve as starting points for some of the great journeys into the interior over 60 years later. Following a winter in southern Australia, Ross and his two ships returned south the next summer, reaching the Barrier again, despite more severe pack ice, and gaining 78°S before heading for the Falklands to winter. Thereafter his expedition spent a third summer in Antarctic waters, exploring the east side of the Peninsula in heavy pack ice, but failing to make any significant new discoveries prior to eventually returning to England after 4.5 years at sea. Ross had led a most successful expedition, which during the 1841 summer alone discovered Mount Erebus and Mount Terror, taken the first sea soundings in Antarctica, collected rocks and plants in the subantarctic islands of New Zealand and demonstrated that the South Magnetic Pole was much farther south than previously envisaged.

Interest wanes

In the wake of Ross, public interest in the Antarctic declined as the region beyond the ice was perceived as having no commercial value; which had, as we have seen with some of the French expeditions in particular, been the principal motivating force behind the pioneering journeys of the previous centuries. For many years, with the exception of the 1870s *Challenger* expedition, which obtained a wealth of oceanography data from the Southern Ocean, the only visitors were sealers who periodically exploited the remnants of the subantarctic seal colonies. But in the 1890s, with northern whale stocks reduced to commercial inviability, entrepreneurs again looked to the south. In 1892 whaling fleets from Norway and Scotland arrived in the Weddell Sea and made significant geographical discoveries in the Antarctic Peninsula. Though sketchy, the outline of Antarctica was taking shape. The great question was what lay in the interior? Henryk Johan Bull, a Norwegian who had emigrated to Australia in the mid-1880s, laid a foundation for the revolution in Antarctic exploration that was about to unfold. Bull was determined to lay a financial bedrock to continued Southern Ocean expeditions by combining these with whaling interests. Eventually he was able to raise Norwegian money for the venture and on 24 Jan 1895 Bull, Borchgrevink and Kristensen stood ashore at Cape Adare, being only the sixth-ever landing on the Antarctic mainland. The venture is perhaps best known for the subsequent disagreements that arose as to which of them or indeed a New Zealand seaman was *the* first to set foot on the continent and its singular failure to find an exploitable

population of great whales, but the expedition did also discover lichen on an island, subsequently named Bull, in the Possession group (the first vegetation to be found on continental Antarctica), as well as laying the ground for those who were to come.

Dawn of a new era

The sixth International Geographical Congress, which was held in London in 1895, proposed major new exploration of Antarctica and launched an era of government-sponsored scientific expeditions and the heroic age of Antarctic exploration, marked by much personal endurance and bravery. Much of this work is presented in greater detail in the chapter describing the Ross Sea region. Expeditions by Borchgrevink (the first to winter on the Antarctic mainland and which was beset by personal problems between its leader and men), Gerlache (whose 1898–1900 mission to the Peninsula produced a wealth of new scientific data, including the first meteorological information for the Antarctic winter and geological data to support a link between the Andes and Peninsula via the Scotia Arc, as well as some of the first photographs of Antarctica), Filchner, Nordenskjöld and Charcot charted the Antarctic Peninsula and elsewhere, while those of Shackleton, Scott, Mawson and Amundsen mapped the mountains and glaciers of the interior. Sketch maps of variable quality were published with expedition reports and a new map of Antarctica was published by Bartholomew in 1905 at a scale of 1:14 million. Both Scott and Drygalski in 1902 attempted to use balloons to extend observations of the distant terrain.

Portrait of Robert Falcon Scott © Global Book Publishing.

The Golden Age

This epoch of Antarctic exploration is chiefly remembered for 'the race to the Pole', which claimed the lives of Scott and his four compatriots, and still provokes much interest among Antarctic historians as to the relative merits of the different strategies employed, as well as those of the different expeditions leaders. Nonetheless, the glory attached to reaching the Pole was subsidiary to the work of most of these expeditions, which was scientific: geological, biological, geographical and meteorological data were all gathered, in abundance, by these pioneers. However, such work, to a certain extent, was only made possible through funding made available in the quest to be first at the South Pole. Opportunities for natural history and ornithological work were not ignored. Edward Wilson, naturalist and surgeon on Scott's expeditions to the southern continent, made many useful contributions to our knowledge of the region's seabirds. His remarkably life-like drawings of flying albatrosses, completed in an age when even the very best bird artists were unwilling to contemplate attempting to depict birds in flight, remain fine examples of such work even today.

Wilson's most heroic exploits were in his quest to understand the biology and relationships of the Emperor Penguin, which breeds during the long darkness of the Antarctic winter. Having become fascinated by this remarkable species during his first visit to the region, Wilson persuaded Scott to permit himself, Bowers and Cherry-Garrard the opportunity to visit the colony at Cape Evans during the early breeding season. The tale is marvellously told in all of its horrific detail by Cherry-Garrard in *The Worst Journey in the World*. Nevertheless, despite the superhuman efforts needed to collect the eggs and embryos, when Cherry-Garrard presented them to the British Natural History Museum, in 1913 (the other two men having died in the return from the Pole), they were received ungraciously and without thanks.

Shackleton's death, from a heart attack, on his third and uncharacteristically poorly planned expedition in 1922 marked the end of the 'heroic age'. Men and their animals hauling heavy sledges had penetrated the continent, but most of the land remained unknown. The future of Antarctic exploration lay now in the hands of mechanics and aviators. Motorized vehicles had, of course, been taken to Antarctica prior to the 1920s. Charcot in 1907, Shackleton in 1908 and Scott in 1911 had all experimented with their use, while Mawson had planned to use an airplane in 1911, but its wings were lost in an accident.

Toward the modern period

Mawson and Davis performed new exploratory work linking that undertaken by Scott, d'Urville, Ross and Wilkes with that of Drygalksi, tracing the coast between Gaussberg, in Kaiser Wilhelm Land, and King George V Land, near the Ross Sea. In 1928 aeroplanes started to provide a wealth of information, but also demonstrated the impossibility of making maps solely based on aerial photos and without complementary ground surveys. In that year, Sir Hubert Wilkins flew south from Deception I along 61°W to 71°S. Within hours he had seen more than earlier expeditions had observed in several seasons. Seven years later, the North American Lincoln Ellsworth made two flights over the east part of the peninsula. Neither mission was of great value for mapping purposes; navigation was by dead reckoning in unknown winds, over ground without surveyed points, but such flights were useful in gaining a general impression of the terrain below. In 1934–7 the British Graham Land Expedition led by John Rymill surveyed much of the Peninsula's west coast. The combination of ground surveys, based on sledge journeys, and aerial photographs produced accurate maps.

There were still three great unmapped stretches of coast: from the Weddell Sea to Enderby Land, Enderby Land and Kaiser Wilhelm Land, and between the Ross Sea and the Peninsula. Privately sponsored expeditions from the USA, Norway and Australia explored these blanks in the period 1928–38. Firstly, the Byrd expedition of 1928–9 visited the area between the Peninsula and the Ross Sea. It was the first from North America since that of Wilkes, 90 years before, and preceded an avalanche of US expeditions. Byrd's principal interest was the unknown sector between the Bellingshausen and Ross Seas. He mapped the western coast and its hinterland naming it Marie Byrd Land, in honour of his wife. Byrd was also first to use a fixed aerial survey camera. Ashley McKinley took photos of the Rockefeller Mountains and the coast east of the Bay of Whales. In 1929 Byrd made the first flight over the South Pole and disproved some former findings such as Amundsen's Carmen Land, south of the Queen Maud Mountains. Subsequently the British Graham Land Expedition of 1934–7 demonstrated that Marie Byrd Land was part of the continent, and that there was no channel linking the Weddell and Ross Seas.

By World War II most of the Antarctic coastline had been charted, if not entirely accurately. But while the broad shape of the continent was now well known, much of the interior was still unexplored. Generally, the war marked the end of private expeditions, with the work of Antarctic exploration being assumed by large well-equipped government organizations wintering in permanent bases. In 1946, the US Navy organized Operation Highjump, a massive effort to map Antarctica, again led by Byrd. Over 4700 men, 13 ships including two icebreakers, an aircraft carrier with two seaplane tenders, six aircraft equipped for trimetrogon photography, four helicopters, three light aircraft and a submarine were deployed. Prior to this only c.600 people had set foot in Antarctica. The chief task was to circumnavigate the 25,000 km Antarctic coast and map it thoroughly. Seaplanes explored the coast and its immediate hinterland, while ski-equipped planes made long photo reconnaissance journeys deep into the interior. The mission was three-pronged. In the east ships left the Balleny Is, south of New Zealand, and headed west. Another group commenced their work at 90°W and moved toward the Greenwich meridian in Queen Maud Land, east of the Weddell Sea. The two groups, now based at the Bay of Whales, subsequently explored the remaining coast. The war had brought a host of developments: new techniques for aerial photography and mapping; instruments to determine the depth of ice and structure beneath; fantastic new ice-breaking ships; and long-range planes that could cover thousands of miles without refuelling. Many of the problems faced by the earlier explorers no longer existed.

A true leader of men and hero of several Antarctic expedtions, Sir Ernest Shackleton (left). Much has been written on Shackleton, but the famous 17-day voyage of the James Caird *(right) from* Elephant I *to South Georgia, following the loss of the* Endurance*, is unquestionably one of the most famous journeys in Antarctic exploration and illustrates Shackleton's bravery and determination to save his men at all costs. Nonetheless, it was another five months before those marooned on Elephant I were to be rescued. © Global Book Publishing.*

The International Geophysical Year and the present day

The early 1950s also witnessed Norwegian, Swedish, French, British, Chilean and Argentine expeditions. The nations of the world were preparing for a monumental scientific enterprise, International Geophysical Year (IGY), a global effort to undertake simultaneous scientific observations in many fields throughout Earth. Research was conducted into cosmic rays, weather, the nature of the aurora and much else. Antarctica was selected as a key area for IGY studies, which were planned to run for 18 months. Late in 1954, 28 Antarctic observation sites were selected, ten on the mainland. The following 12 nations established stations in Antarctica and many of the periantarctic islands in this period: Argentina, Australia, Belgium, Britain, Chile, France, Japan, New Zealand, Norway, South Africa, Soviet Union and the USA, some of which were occupied from the 1955–6 season. The USA established three: at Little America, in Marie Byrd Land and at the South Pole. Among US achievements probably the most spectacular was the establishment of a permanent base at the South Pole. How incredible that would have been to Shackleton, Scott or Amundsen! Giant Air Force Globemasters dropped 760 tonnes of packaged building material, fuel and supplies at the Pole, during 84 round flights. Two dozen men, working in midsummer temperatures of 5°C to -25°C, erected seven tunnel-linked buildings. The outpost was suitably named Amundsen–Scott Station, after the leaders of the only two expeditions to have reached the South Pole overland prior to 1958.

Meanwhile thousands of men in 40 stations and from 11 countries subjected the southern continent to a detailed investigation that dwarfed all previous research. As part of the UK IGY programme, Vivian Fuchs, a British geologist who had previously worked in Africa and the Arctic, revived Shackleton's idea of a Trans-Antarctic land crossing. The plan owed much to Shackleton's original vision. A main party would travel from Vahsel Bay to McMurdo Sound on the Ross Sea, while a support team, starting from the Ross Sea side, would lay food and fuel depots en route. Rather than dog-drawn sledges, they would use trucks with tractor treads, while aircraft also dropped supplies. Fuchs led the main party, while Sir Edmund Hillary, who in 1953 had been part of the first expedition to climb Mount Everest, led the Ross Sea party. This expedition's geographical purpose was to explore the unknown area between the Weddell Sea and the Pole, and to map the west side of the mountains Shackleton and Scott had seen during their polar treks. This time, the Trans-Antarctic crossing was made, though the team was plagued by crevasses, severe sastrugi and health problems.

It was originally planned that when the IGY ended in mid-1958 most of the new bases would be closed. But it was obvious that too great an investment had been made to halt Antarctic research. Though some stations were closed, many others became permanent. Today, several parts of the continent are inhabited year-round, though the number of inhabitants necessarily decreases markedly in the winter season. As US Rear Admiral Tyree put it, 'we are in Antarctica to stay'. The Soviet Union, too, had an active Antarctic programme, with several permanent bases on the coast and deep in the interior. The UK, Chile, Argentina, France, New Zealand and others are also represented (for full details of the current human geography of Antarctica, see Geography and Climate). Formerly bitter political feuds over possession of Antarctic territory gave way to an international agreement, signed in 1959, which set Antarctica aside for peaceful and cooperative scientific research. No national claims have been renounced, but they are no longer put forward with great conviction. Gradually gaps in knowledge have been filled in even greater detail. Today,

modern techniques and equipment, especially satellites, have led to the production of very accurate maps. As will have been seen in the chapter dealing with Conservation in the Region, the Antarctic Treaty provides many inviolate accords for the preservation of the continent's natural resources, as well as the continuation of scientific and other work.

Some further reading

Those interested to explore Antarctic history in more detail will enjoy browsing Headland's 1989 book, *Chronological List of Antarctic Expeditions and Related Historical Events* (published by Cambridge University Press), as well as the recently published *The Complete Story: Antarctica* (edited by McGonigal & Woodworth, 2001). Both provide a wealth of detail on these and many other, lesser events and also present a panoply of background information concerning many of the major Antarctic explorers and adventurers, coupled in the McGonigal & Woodworth publication with many high-quality and extremely well-produced photographs.

Some key dates in the history of Antarctic and subantarctic exploration at a glance

1506 A Portuguese expedition discovers Tristan da Cunha.

1522 Elcano, Magalhães' (Magellan's) second-in-command, discovers Amsterdam I.

1618 A Dutch expedition is the first to officially sight St Paul I, in Apr, though Portuguese charts from the previous century mark its position.

1663 A Dutchman, Lam, sights the Prince Edward and Marion Is in early Mar.

1675 Antoine de la Roché sights South Georgia in Apr.

1739 Bouvet, working for the French East India Company, discovers Bouvetøya.

1764 Bougainville claims the Falklands for France and establishes a colony there. The British found a separate colony on West Falkland a year later.

1772 In Jan, Marion Dufresne discovers the Crozet Is, naming them for his second-in-command and claiming them for France. Independently, the following month, Kerguelen-Trémarec sights the islands that will bear his name, imagining them to be an outpost of the Antarctic Continent and to harbour untold riches. A subsequent expedition the following year proves his high-flown fancies to be false and causes his ignominious dismissal from the French navy.

1773 Captain James Cook and his crew become the first men to cross the Antarctic Circle.

1775 On the same monumental expedition, Cook sights South Georgia and goes on to discover the South Sandwich Is.

1788 William Bligh discovers the Bounty Is.

1791 Vancouver discovers the Snares Is, south of New Zealand, and Broughton becomes the first European to land at the Chatham Is.

1800 Waterhouse discovers the Antipodes Is.

1806 Bristow, a whaler, becomes the first human to sight the Auckland Is.

1810 In January, Hasselburg discovers the southernmost of the subantarctic islands of New Zealand, Campbell I, and goes on to find Macquarie I in Jul the same year.

1819 William Smith, a sealer, discovers the South Shetland Is.

1820 The Antarctic Peninsula is sighted for the first time, independently, by Bellingshausen, Bransfield and Palmer.

1821 Bellingshausen discovers Peter I, and charts the small islands of South Georgia as well as the South Shetlands and the South Sandwiches. He also sights the Antarctic

Continent for the first time, but fails to realise it. Captain John Davis, a North American sealer, becomes the first man to set foot in the Antarctic.

1823 James Weddell, a sealer, becomes the first man to enter the sea that will subsequently bear his name, reaching 74°S.

1831 John Biscoe sights Enderby Land.

1840 Charles Wilkes sights Wilkes Land. Dumont d'Urville discovers Terre Adélie.

1841 Sir James Clark Ross penetrates the pack ice of the sea that will later bear his name; in the process he discovers Victoria Land, Ross I, Mount Erebus and the Ross Ice Shelf.

1853 A North American, John Heard, discovers the island that bears his name, though at least three previous visitors may have sighted the island, including Cook in 1773, while two months after Heard, a British mariner discovers the nearby MacDonald Is.

1873 The first German expedition to enter Antarctic waters, led by Dallman, discovers the Bismarck Strait.

1874 *Challenger* becomes the first steamship to cross the Antarctic Circle during the course of a four-year expedition to study the oceanography of the Southern Ocean including several of the subantarctic islands.

1899 The *Southern Cross* expedition lands at Cape Adare and becomes the first to winter in Antarctica.

1901–4 Robert Falcon Scott in the *Discovery* leads the first extensive scientific expedition to Antarctica; the first flight over the continent is made in a balloon.

1902 Wilhelm II Land discovered by a German expedition. Scott, Wilson and Shackleton, in attempting to explore the interior mountains, almost reach the South Pole but are forced to turn back having reached 82°S.

1903 The Scottish National Antarctic Expedition, led by Bruce and Robertson, winters on Laurie I, in the South Orkneys, establishing a meteorological observatory, which has operated continuously ever since (under Argentine control since 1904).

1908 A four-man team under Shackleton attempt to reach the Pole, but are forced to turn back just 180 km short of their destination.

1909 The first visit to the South Magnetic Pole is made by Australian Edgeworth David.

1911 Amundsen's Norwegian expedition successfully reaches the South Pole on 14 Dec.

1912 Robert Falcon Scott's five-man team reaches the Pole on 17 Jan. All die during the return journey, with Scott, Wilson and Bowers being the last succumb just 20 km from a food depot. Filchner discovers the Luitpold Coast.

1914 Shackleton fails to make the first transcontinental crossing, but despite the loss of the *Endurance* saves the lives of all of his men.

1922 Shackleton's death at South Georgia, during the poorly defined *Quest* expedition marks the end of the Golden (or Heroic) Age of Antarctic exploration.

1928–9 Wilkins flies south from Deception I to 71°S. The Byrd expedition visits the area of the continent between the Peninsula and the Ross Sea, naming Marie Byrd Land and making the first flight over the South Pole.

1935 Lincoln Ellsworth makes two flights over the east coast of the Antarctic Peninsula. In Feb, the Norwegian Karoline Mikkelsen becomes the first woman to set foot in Antarctica.

1937 The three-year British Graham Land expedition draws to a close having surveyed much of the Peninsula's west coast.

1944 The British naval expedition, Operation Tabarin, establishes Base A at Port Lockroy, commencing the permanent human occupation of Antarctica.

1946 The US expedition, Operation Highjump employs huge numbers of personnel and 13 ships to circumnavigate and thoroughly map the entire Antarctic coast. The following year, a smaller project, Operation Windmill, uses helicopters to survey some of the major features identified by the earlier mission.

1954 The Australian National Antarctic Research Expeditions (ANARE) establish a permanent Antarctic base, Mawson Station in East Antarctica, with several other countries also establishing bases on the continent in the same year.

1955 Operation Deep Freeze establishes McMurdo Station in preparation for the International Geophysical Year (IGY).

1957–8 The IGY witnesses a wealth of scientific activity on the Antarctic continent, with many new bases being established and the completion of the first trans-continental journey, by Sir Vivien Fuchs. The first Antarctic tourists disembark briefly from a Pan American flight that lands at McMurdo Sound in 1957.

1966 Antarctic tourism commences in earnest when Lars-Eric Lindblad offers the first of what were to become annual trips to the frozen south.

1969 The first women to reach the South Pole arrive there by US transport plane.

1972–4 New Zealander David Lewis makes the first solo voyage to Antarctica.

1987–92 Greenpeace establishes World Park Base on Ross I to conduct year-round monitoring of human impacts on Antarctica. The base is removed upon the programme's completion.

1992–3 First all-woman trek to the South Pole (from Hercules Inlet) is led by a North American, Ann Bancroft, while the first person to man-haul a sledge solo to the South Pole is Norwegian Erling Kagge. In addition, Fiennes and Stroud become the first team to successfully man-haul across the breadth of the Antarctic continent without support.

The history of Antarctica is marked not only by stories of heroism but also Man's ability to unsustainably exploit the world around him; here two whales await processing. © Global Book Publishing.

Species Accounts

In preparing this work, I swiftly reached the conclusion that to include full details of all species ever recorded in the region, particularly extreme vagrants and introductions, would make for a needlessly large volume. Many of these birds are unlikely to be encountered by the visitor and are, in any case, well covered by many other guides. Indeed, in due course, the *Handbook of Australian, New Zealand and Antarctic Birds (HANZAB)* will provide an exemplary source for virtually all of them. Instead, I chose to concentrate my attention upon the select number of species or groups of most interest to researchers and visiting naturalists (especially issues of taxonomy and identification), and of key importance in determining conservation priorities for the region. This process had the happy outcome of enabling me to cover these species in far greater detail. Birds are presented first, followed by the marine mammals. The bird species accounts generally follow *HANZAB* nomenclature (except in the case of a few recent taxonomic revisions where other names in more common usage have been selected) and order, but with a few deviations in order to more closely follow plate layout. English and scientific names of those species not covered by *HANZAB*, principally taxa from the Falklands and Tristan da Cunha, follow Sibley (1996). As a result of following more traditional systematics, widespread oceanic species such as penguins and tubenoses are followed by other seabirds, the regional endemics and specialities. However, in some key groups, such as albatrosses, a slightly different order is employed for the sake of easier comparison between closely related and morphologically similar forms.

Penguins

Most of the world's 17 or so species occur in the northern cool temperate region of the Southern Ocean, many of them within our region, where penguin diversity reaches its highest in the sub-antarctic islands. In many parts of the Antarctic and subantarctic the group constitutes a substantial proportion of the entire avian community, up to 80% of biomass in most of Antarctica. Penguins are closely related to the petrels and albatrosses. Modern-day species are flightless but evolved from a small-sized ancestor that was capable of flight and was also a strong underwater swimmer, perhaps not unlike present-day auks or diving-petrels. Almost 40 species of penguins, within 17 genera, are known from the fossil record, with 14 of these being from mainland New Zealand. Many of these extinct taxa are known from sites which would then have been at high latitude, relative to present-day positions.

Penguin physiology is highly specialized in order to withstand the very low land and sea temperatures that most species endure for much of the year; various insulative, circulatory, metabolic and behavioural adaptations have evolved for this purpose. The feet and, in some species, parts of the facial region are unfeathered, the undersides of the flippers which are sparsely feathered, and all are served by an abundant blood supply near the surface in order to dissipate heat during high temperatures or periods of exercise such as when diving. Penguin feathers are unusual in being very stiff, relatively short and packed very densely over the entire body, which traps warm air next to the skin and waterproofs the body. Antarctic and subantarctic species are further insulated by dense subdermal fat, which is particularly important to down-covered King *Aptenodytes patagonicus* and Emperor Penguin *A. forsteri* chicks in winter when they largely fast, it being an important food store. While many species of penguins have prolonged fledging periods, none can match the King Penguin chick that takes almost a year to reach independence and to gain its first feathers.

Packed in blubber, the penguin body is superbly designed. The wings, which are reduced to flippers with the bones flattened and major joints fused, serve as high-propulsion paddles in the water.

Ad Adelie Penguins Pygoscelis adeliae *porpoising, Weddell Sea, Feb 2002. © Jørgen Mortensen.*

Plate 1 King and Antarctic penguins

Largest and most robust penguin; short decurved bill with smaller pale stripe; larger neck-side patches and longer 'trousers' than King

juv.

Red bill with distinctive white patch above eye

juv.

downy chick

Gentoo Penguin ad. (p. 53)

Chinstrap Penguin ad. (p. 59)

Black of head above eye level; narrow throat stripe; lacks feathering on bill

juv.

downy chick

Emperor Penguin ad. (p. 49)

downy chick

...ll/slim with longer and ...ler bill and more spoon-...aped neck patches than ...mperor

juv.

downy chick

juv.

Black of head reaches below eye level; white eye-ring in ad

juv.

King Penguin ad. (p. 44)

downy chick

Adélie Penguin ad. (p. 55)

Of all birds, penguins are *the* supreme swimmers and divers. All but three species porpoise, in which they leap out of the water in a graceful arc, thus enabling them to breathe without slowing their swimming speed. The short legs, set well back on the body, give them their characteristic, ungainly waddling gait ashore, and in the two most southerly species the feet serve to propel them over snow and ice when 'sledging' or 'tobogganing' on the belly.

The five species in this section occur on Antarctic coasts, those of the Peninsula and adjacent southern to mid-latitude subantarctic islands (where King, Gentoo *Pygoscelis papua* and Chinstrap Penguins *P. antarctica* are joined by some of the crested penguins). Despite the widespread misconception of penguins being exclusively Antarctic, the only species that breed on the continent are Emperor and Adélie Penguins *Pygoscelis adeliae*. Males of the former have adapted to fasting through much of the long winter breeding season, a system unique within the avian world, whereas the latter has a very short, conventional summer breeding season.

Among these five species, the two larger, rather closely related Emperor and King Penguins are well differentiated in most of their seasonal biology, reproduction and adaptation, which reflect their different distributions. For instance, male Emperor Penguins incubate their eggs through the coldest season in order that the chicks may fledge during the period of greatest food abundance in the following spring and summer, while King Penguin, which breeds farther north in the milder subantarctic, is also forced to resort to special tactics in order to rear its long-dependent young (breeding throughout the year in two breeding cycles spread across three years). The three smaller species, Adélie, Gentoo and Chinstrap Penguins, the so-called brush-tailed penguins, which mostly breed south of the Antarctic Convergence or Antarctic Polar Front (though many Gentoo nest north of it) all complete their breeding cycles within a polar summer. Adélie, the southernmost breeder of these, faces the greatest challenge, because it scarcely has sufficient time to breed and moult before the onset of the Antarctic winter.

The distributions of these five penguins often overlap, sometimes also with some of the more northern crested penguins. Emperor Penguin, however, only slightly overlaps in its range (and not during the breeding season) with Adélie, which in turn co-exists with Gentoo and Chinstrap (whose ranges in the north meet to some extent that of King). The southernmost subantarctic islands hold the most stunning assemblages of penguins: Macquarie, South Georgia and Kerguelen each support 4–5 breeding species. Thus, numbers and types of penguin species on the subantarctic islands are closely related to latitude and offshore water conditions (in relation to the Antarctic Convergence), which support each species' specific requirements.

King Penguin *Aptenodytes patagonicus*   Plate 1

Identification

Confusion risks: Emperor Penguin *A. forsteri* (especially imm at sea).

Main characters: Second-largest penguin, tall and has distinctly long slender bill (slightly decurved). **Ad** in fresh plumage has blackish head strikingly patterned with orange to orange-yellow patches on rear head-sides, narrowing on upper neck/breast-sides; upperparts appear dark to pale silvery-grey (depending on distance from observer and lighting), separated from white underparts by narrow black band on body-sides, with variable ill-defined orange wash on upper breast; underside of flipper white, broadly edged blackish-blue on leading edge and rather extensive black

Ad King Penguins Aptenodytes patagonicus *often raft in close formation near the breeding sites. With their long bills and bodies, and distinctively shaped rear head-side patches, this species is unmistakable even when distant. Andrews Bay, South Georgia, Jan 2001. © Hadoram Shirihai.*

tip (see also Emperor). Iris dark brown; black bill with rather broad pinkish stripe to base of lower mandible, and unfeathered grey tarsus. Sexes alike and seasonal variation limited to feather wear, and upperparts becoming duller/browner and auricular patches paler; breeders moult to fresh plumage c.1 month after nesting, chiefly Dec–Feb (mandible plates shed following moult, F. S. Todd pers. comm.), in non-breeders or failed pairs much earlier, from about Sep. **Imm** (juv plumage) similar to ad, but overall smaller and less bulky (in early stages), with head and dorsal areas duller and browner especially with wear (and fringed paler), and spoon-shaped auricular patches and upper breast duller (pale yellow to white); bill stripe slightly duller and much reduced in early juv stage. Attains ad plumage as third-year. **Chick** has dark brown down; when moulting to juv plumage and has partially lost its down, acquires a rather bizarre appearance.

Voice: Colonies very noisy (especially in early spring, rarely until autumn); usual ad display call a loud musical/polysyllabic trumpeting (higher pitched in female), with bill pointing skywards; contact

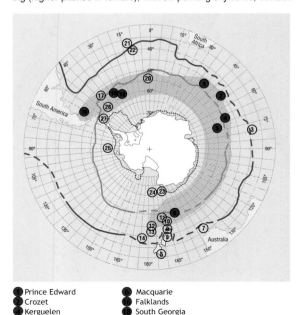

1 Prince Edward
2 Crozet
4 Kerguelen
5 Heard

Macquarie
Falklands
South Georgia
South Sandwich

King Penguins Aptenodytes patagonicus *usually form huge rookeries, often within breathtaking scenery. Ads and chicks (top left) often share the beaches with Southern Elephant Seals* Mirounga leonina *(top right), whilst paths to the colonies are busy with grimy-bellied birds (upper-middle right) en route to the sea to feed and clean-bellied ones returning from the ocean (lower-middle right). 'Kintergardens' are guarded by a few ads (bottom left), whilst chicks vary greatly in size and proportions (bottom right). Top two and two middle right images, Salisbury Plain/Gold Harbour, South Georgia; bottom left, Île de la Possession, Crozets, and bottom right, Ratmanof, Kerguelen, Oct–Mar 2001–06. © Hadoram Shirihai.*

King Penguins Aptenodytes patagonicus *in display and mutual preening and grooming behaviour, which may continue for hours, or even days, prior to copulation. Salisbury Plain and Gold Harbour, South Georgia, Oct–Mar 2001–06. © Hadoram Shirihai.*

Ad King Penguin Aptenodytes patagonicus in moult, with many fresh feathers already visible below the old feathers which appear to shed in blocks. Salisbury Plain, South Georgia, Mar 2006. © Hadoram Shirihai.

Well-grown King Penguin Aptenodytes patagonicus chick moulting its down, Ratmanoff, Kerguelen. © Hadoram Shirihai.

call a single monosyllabic, soft cooing *aark*; chicks/young imm give soft (but sometimes loud) triple whistle.

Size: 85–95 cm, weight 9.3–17.3 kg. Female averages smaller in flipper, bill and toe lengths in perhaps as many as 93% of pairs (sample of 75 pairs).

Similar species: Only possible confusion is with Emperor Penguin (mainly imm at sea), but latter is much more robust and has different head pattern, bill colour and proportions (see Emperor).

Distribution and biology

Distribution, movements and population: Principally restricted to high subantarctic and low-latitude Antarctic zones, and usually near colonies, which are mainly close to the Antarctic Convergence. Colonies on Macquarie, the Falklands (few), South Georgia, South Sandwich (only recently proven to breed), Prince

Two imm King Penguin Aptenodytes patagonicus (left) showing variation in coloration of rear head-side patches, and ad on right, Ratmanoff, Kerguelen, Nov 1999. © Hadoram Shirihai.

King Penguin Aptenodytes patagonicus on average breeds twice every three years, but due to its extended cycle colonies are always occupied with breeders at different stages; on the left an incubating bird and on the right breeders with chicks of varying sizes. Salisbury Plain, South Georgia, Mar 2006. © Hadoram Shirihai.

King Penguins Aptenodytes patagonicus *appear to resolve most disputes vocally, without recourse to using the wings or bill. Gold Harbour, South Georgia, Mar 2006. © Hadoram Shirihai.*

Many aspects of social behaviour and communication can be observed in King Penguin Aptenodytes patagonicus *rookeries. Gold Harbour, South Georgia, Mar 2006. © Hadoram Shirihai.*

Edward, Crozet, Kerguelen and Heard; none south of 60°S. Formerly bred in S Magellan region (in S Chile, on Horn I and S Argentina on Staten I), and numbers of moulting non-breeders currently increasing in this area. Wanders to S Australia, Tasmania, New Zealand, Brazil and South Africa, and very rarely south to Antarctic coast. Population generally increasing, most notably on Crozet, Kerguelen , South Georgia, Heard and Macquarie, with an estimated total population of 2.23 million pairs in recent decades.

Diet and feeding: Mainly small fish and some cephalopods taken by pursuit-diving. Specializes in lanternfish, and other species probably comprise only c.5% of diet. Capable of remaining underwater for c.10 minutes (and probably longer), mostly at around 25 m but recorded to 322 m.

Social behaviour: Monogamous and highly gregarious, but pair-bond fidelity lower than many other penguin species, perhaps due to long reproductive cycle and differing moult cycle between sexes.

Breeding biology: Nov–Dec onwards. Breeds on average twice every three years (unique among penguins and possibly among all birds) or in some areas biannually, in large colonies on flat ice-free areas, sometimes with tussac-grass thickets and on some islands, such as the Falklands and Macquarie, in association with other penguins, mainly Gentoo; many rookeries adjacent to seal colonies. Breeding cycle takes over one year, and as non-breeders (including unsuccessful breeders and imms) return to colonies to moult, a complex mix of birds is virtually always present in nesting areas. Those pairs that successfully raise a chick and lay later

A very crowded King Penguin Aptenodytes patagonicus *rookery, Salisbury Plain, South Georgia, Mar 2003. © Hadoram Shirihai.*

King Penguins Aptenodytes patagonicus form enormous rookeries that utilise every bit of land on flat and protected sites, with close access to the sea. Salisbury Plain, South Georgia, Mar 2006. © Hadoram Shirihai.

the following season generally fail as the chick will perish in winter. Except during moult, the species may breed at any time, but can only fledge two young within a three-year period. Most early breeders are birds that failed in their previous breeding attempt. Colonies very noisy, especially when birds display, using long-call trumpeting accompanied by neck-stretching, vertically tilting head and bill skywards. Single pale greenish-white egg, incubated on feet. Both sexes incubate (for total of 55–56 days), but during first two weeks usually male alone, while female takes responsibility for second fortnight; thereafter they alternate over shorter periods. Sometimes lays replacement egg. Both sexes care for young (for c.50 weeks). In larger colonies communal crèches of a few hundred chicks (c.5 weeks old and larger) may form, permitting both parents to forage simultaneously. By Apr chicks are almost full grown but lose weight during winter, regaining body size when food is ample from about Sep, and fledge in Nov–Dec. Thus, chicks undergo three distinct stages: initial growth from hatching to mid-Apr/early May; winter fast in Apr/May–Sep/Oct; and final growth and moult from Sep/Oct until fledging. Due to extended breeding cycle and long gap between nesting efforts, colonies are continuously occupied and breeders at different stages occur alongside each other. Breeds from c.4 years but most at 5–8 years old.

Conservation Not globally threatened. Several populations of penguins, especially this species, were almost extirpated during the late 19th century for their oil. Since then, there has been a long recovery process, with some colonies now apparently over-populated due to lack of competition for food with whales that have failed to recover from mass hunting. See also Conservation in the Region.

Taxonomy Two subspecies recognized: nominate patagonicus in S Atlantic and halli elsewhere in its range, but there is considerable variation in size between different insular populations, with those breeding on Kerguelen and Crozet genetically isolated from each other.

Emperor Penguin *Aptenodytes forsteri*   Plate 1

Identification

Confusion risks: King Penguin *A. patagonicus* (especially imm at sea). *Main characters*: Largest penguin and extremely robust, but slightly decurved bill is proportionately short. **Ad** in fresh plumage has blackish head grading to dark bluish-grey on upperparts, latter separated from glossy white underparts by black band, which extends upwards as distinctive mark on lower foreneck; note diagnostic large, oval-shaped pale lemon-yellow neck patches, variably tinged orange, and which meet on lower throat/upper breast, where almost enclosed by black above and below (shape and tone of neck patches and black marks on neck-sides alter with movement of head/neck and lighting). Underside of flipper white, narrowly fringed black on tip and leading edge. Iris dark brown; black bill with pinkish or lilac stripe on lower mandible. Sexes alike

One-year old Emperor Penguin Aptenodytes forsteri. The young achieve ad plumage at c.18 months, prior to which they appear like a drabber version of the ad. Note especially the poorly defined and whitish neck patches (lacking any orange-yellow), which grade into the white chin and throat. South-east Weddell Sea, Oct 2001. © Hadoram Shirihai.

Pair of Emperor Penguins Aptenodytes forsteri *with chick: both sexes provision the young. Dawson-Lambton Glacier, Antarctica, Nov 1998. © David Tipling/Windrush Photos.*

Emperor Penguin Aptenodytes forsteri *chicks in their so-called 'Biggles' suits. There is much variation in size due to different hatching dates and food supplied by the ads. South-east Weddell Sea, Oct 2001. © Maria San Román.*

and seasonal variation limited to feather wear, thus upperparts bleach browner and auricular patches become whiter; successful breeders moult after chick-rearing stage, chiefly Dec–Feb. **Imm** (juv) as ad, but overall smaller and slighter (in early stages, some fledge at less than 50% of ad size), paler/browner above and on head (also usually paler around eye), neck patches ill defined and whitish (lacking orange-yellow tinge) and grade into diagnostic white chin and throat, and bill stripe dull pinkish-orange; moult to ad plumage when c.18 months old. **Chick** mainly dusky silvery-grey to whitish, with distinctive white face bordered by black crown and neck-sides.

Voice: Colonies very noisy; both sexes deliver powerful, rhythmic duet in display, a cooing and cackling trumpeted *kra-a-a-a...* (syllables longer in male; very brief final note by female), uttered with neck/head crooked forward onto breast, then partially raised once 'song' complete and flippers often moved slowly while pair still facing each other; contact call a loud single *ah* note; chick/small juv gives modulated piping whistles.

Emperor Penguin Aptenodytes forsteri *colony with chicks at approximately the mid-stage of their development. South-east Weddell Sea, Oct 2001. © Maria San Román.*

Ad Emperor Penguins Aptenodytes forsteri 'tobogganing'; this means of locomotion requires far less energy than walking. © Frank S. Todd.

Ad Emperor Penguin Aptenodytes forsteri in breathing hole, Ross Sea region; relatively short-billed with elongated rear head-side patches reaching far onto neck and to water level (cf. King Penguin). © Kim Westerskov.

Size: 1.0–1.30 m, weight 20–41 kg. Female usually averages smaller in flipper and bill lengths, but tail usually slightly longer.

Similar species: King Penguin in all plumages is overall markedly smaller and has proportionally longer bill and different head pattern, with brighter, more spoon-shaped neck patches, which unlike Emperor are mainly on rear of head (not neck and sides), and continue as crescentic strap on upper neck/breast-sides. Also, Emperor has longer 'trousers' (lacking bare tarsus skin), whiter underside to flipper and narrower pale stripe on lower mandible; unlike King, when swimming neck patches clearly appear larger, tending to reach water surface.

Distribution and biology

Distribution, movements and population: Coastal Antarctica at 66–78°S, enduring the coldest conditions of any bird, being largely confined to pack ice, fast-ice and adjacent seas. Outside breeding season extends north, satellite-tracked fledglings and post-breeding pre-moulting birds are now known to move to the vicinity of the Antarctic Convergence, and the species rarely reaches New Zealand, N Argentina (to Buenos Aires province) and the Falklands, South Georgia, South Orkney, Kerguelen and Heard. Total population estimated at 220,000 breeding pairs and c.400,000–450,000 individuals in the late 1990s (most in East Antarctica and Ross Sea), with new colonies, albeit small in size, still being discovered.

Diet and feeding: Mainly takes fish, small cephalopods and crustaceans captured principally by pursuit-diving; can dive for 15–20 minutes, mostly at c.50 m, but also recorded to c.250 m (exceptionally c.500 m), well below the level of plankton abundance in summer.

Social behaviour: Highly gregarious. Monogamous, but low pair fidelity, with a comparatively high percentage of pairs not renewing their bond the following season.

Breeding biology: Unique cycle begins in early winter. Breeds on fast-ice in Mar–Dec, in areas where ice usually breaks up the following spring, when young acquire independence. On arrival in Mar/Apr ads, especially males, are very fat, weighing up to c.40 kg. Courtship chiefly involves trumpeting calls, displaying golden neck patches. Lays single large greenish-white egg in May/Jun, incubated on feet of male alone (large groups huddle together as conglomerate mass during coldest weather), for 62–67 days. While males fast during incubation, females are foraging at sea, timing their return for the chick's emergence; the male, which is usually first to feed the nearly naked chick a rich secretion of fat and protein, may lose c.45% of its body weight during the c.115-

Emperor Penguin Aptenodytes forsteri leaping out of the water, Ross Sea region; Emperors may look a little slow on land, but in the water they move with grace and speed, their streamlined shape being perfect for moving through the water with minimum drag. Their flippers beat at between 25–50 times per minute when swimming, each wing beat propelling them 2–5 m, and they can dive to depths of below 500 m and remain underwater for up to 20 minutes. © Kim Westerskov.

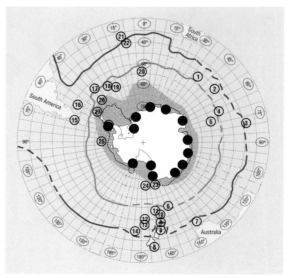

● Antarctica's coasts and offshore islands

'Maverick' ad Emperor Penguin Aptenodytes forsteri attempting to 'kidnap' a young chick. 'Mavericks' are non-breeders or ads that have lost their young but maintain the instinct to raise a brood (such disputes often end with the loss of the chick); Ross Sea region. © Kim Westerskov.

Ad Emperor Penguins Aptenodytes forsteri *displaying, McMurdo Sound, Ross Sea region, Jan 1999.* © Hadoram Shirihai.

Snow-covered Emperor Penguin Aptenodytes forsteri chicks (many die of starvation during extreme weather). © Frank S. Todd.

Moulting ad Emperor Penguins Aptenodytes forsteri with approximately half-grown chicks and a one-year-old imm. © Frank S. Todd.

day fast (exceptionally 134 days). Males then trudge seawards to feed, a journey that can occupy several days and cover 160 km. Subsequently, both sexes provision the chick. Many chicks die of starvation during extreme weather and if fast-ice persists. Chicks soon moult into their so-called 'Biggles' suit of down and fledge at c.150 days. They are abandoned prior to fully acquiring their first feathers (when they make a short walk to the sea, provided ice has disintegrated into floes). Juv plumage usually only partially acquired prior to complete break-up of ice and chicks fledge at only 9.9–14.8 kg, and may enter water still with some down. Return to colonies when aged c.4 years, breeding the following year.

Conservation Not globally threatened.

Taxonomy Monotypic.

Gentoo Penguin *Pygoscelis papua*   Plate 1

Identification

Confusion risks: None.

Main characters: Medium-sized (third-largest) penguin, proportionately very stocky with moderate length bill and obviously pointed tail. **Ad** in fresh plumage has dark bluish grey-brown head to upper breast and upperparts, sharply demarcated from white rear underparts. Orange-red bill with slightly darker tip and culmen. Most distinctive features are triangular white patch extending above and behind eye, and the white eyelids. Extent of patch varies, often being poorly defined, especially at rear, and usually narrowly meets on hindcrown. Variable white spotting on crown and head-sides especially when fresh. Underside of flipper white, with narrow black leading edge and rather small black tip; upperside also distinctive, being mostly as upperparts but has conspicuous white trailing edge. Iris dark brown; naked tarsus and feet dull red-orange. Sexes alike and seasonal variation confined to feather wear, bleaching much browner above; ad acquires fresh plumage following breeding, usually in Dec–Mar. **Imm** (juv) as ad, but overall smaller and less bulky (in early stages), paler/browner above and on head; eye-ring darker and white patch on rear head variably smaller, white head specks reduced and chin and throat variably paler; moult to ad plumage at c.1 year. **Chick** mainly greyish on head and rest of upperparts, white below including throat, with variable and diffuse whitish mark behind eye, and duller bill. *Voice*: Several calls, chiefly a loud crowing, repeated ah, aha, aha, aha, e, uttered with head up; contact call a short caw, usually

Gentoo Penguin Pygoscelis papua *colony, Antarctic Peninsula, Jan 2001. © Hadoram Shirihai.*

given when coming ashore; chicks give a modulated whistle and beg by cheeping.

Size: 75–90 cm, weight 4.5–8.5 kg. Female averages smaller in flipper and bill lengths, and overall weight; 96% of birds can be correctly sexed using bill size and depth.

Similar species: Unmistakable: no other red-billed penguin has distinctive white patch above eye.

Distribution and biology

Distribution, movements and population: Throughout Scotia Sea, on Antarctic Peninsula to c.65°S and north to South Shetland, South Sandwich and South Orkney; also subantarctic on Prince Edward/Marion, Crozet, Kerguelen, Heard, Macquarie, South Georgia and the Falklands; at least formerly on Staten I, S Argentina. Few range north to Tasmania, Campbell, New Zealand and Argentina north to 43°S. Population stable or increasing at southerly locations but decreasing in subantarctic, being estimated at 314,000 pairs in early 1990s, most south of the Convergence and mainly in N Peninsula, South Georgia and the Falklands.

Diet and feeding: Takes crustaceans and fish by pursuit-diving up to >100 m below surface, usually in waters within 10 km of land.

Social behaviour: Highly gregarious, most individuals remain near colonies year-round. Monogamous but pair-bonds rarely appear

The last few Gentoo Penguins Pygoscelis papua *prepare to depart the Antarctic Peninsula at the end of summer. Gentoos occupy a large breeding range, from the Antarctic Peninsula to those islands south of the Antarctic Convergence. Mar 2006. © Hadoram Shirihai.*

Gentoo Penguin Pygoscelis papua *feeding chick, Antarctic Peninsula, Jan 2001.* © Hadoram Shirihai.

Displaying Gentoo Penguins Pygoscelis papua *in territorial dispute, Ratmanoff, Kerguelen, Nov 1999.* © Hadoram Shirihai.

Almost full-grown Gentoo Penguin Pygoscelis papua *chicks 'testing the water'.* © Hadoram Shirihai.

Gentoo Penguin Pygoscelis papua *chick moulting to juv plumage.* © Hadoram Shirihai.

Despite often appearing clumsy and dumpy, ad Gentoo Penguins Pygoscelis papua can run fast (e.g. when 'escaping' their ever-hungry offspring) and are agile swimmers (right). Left South Georgia, 2003; right Antarctic Peninsula, Mar 2006. © Hadoram Shirihai.

to last more than 2–3 seasons.

Breeding biology: Breeds, usually in rather small colonies and occasionally with other species, in tussac-grass thickets, and on bare hillsides (to 200 m altitude and up to 8 km inland) and beaches. Mainly in south of range where principally takes crustaceans (c.85% of diet, unlike in north where more fish taken) some colonies now contain thousands of pairs, e.g. in the Peninsula. Inland colonies reached via circuitous routes and change slightly each year, possibly to provide relief from ticks and other parasites that survive within old nesting materials. Use all available materials for nesting, including pebbles, soil, moulted tail feathers and albatross bones. Two large white eggs, incubated by both sexes for c.35 days. Laying date varies latitudinally: Jun/Jul in north of range (e.g. Marion), on Macquarie from mid-Sep/early Oct (with replacement clutches until Dec), and in south not until Nov/Dec. Chicks gather in crèches at 4–5 weeks and become independent at three months, but unlike other penguins they fledge prior to independence, remaining in colony area until Mar. Fledging period also much shorter in south, 62–82 days, as compared to 85–117 days in north, and capable of breeding when two years old.

Conservation Near Threatened: while some Antarctic populations, which total 25% of overall numbers, have doubled within last two decades, most subantarctic colonies are in decline, possibly as a result of over-fishing of penguin prey species.

Taxonomy Two subspecies: nominate papua on subantarctic islands, which is generally larger, weighing as much as 6.2–8.0 kg, and *ellsworthii* breeding south of 60°S, on South Orkney, South Shetland, Antarctic Peninsula and adjacent islands, which is smaller, with shorter stubbier flippers, feet and bill, and is named after the American explorer, Lincoln Ellsworth, who first collected it. Marked intra-subspecific variability in body size.

Adélie Penguin *Pygoscelis adeliae*   Plate 1

Identification

Confusion risks: Chinstrap Penguin *P. antarctica* (only with juv. Adélie which has white throat).

Main characters: Medium-sized, with characteristic angular head and tiny bill. **Ad** in fresh plumage has upperparts entirely black

to bluish-black, including upperside of flipper (which has narrow white trailing edge) and head to lower throat, sharply demarcated from silky white underparts. Conspicuous white eye-ring. Underside of flipper white, with narrow black leading edge and rather small black tip. Bill largely feathered black as rest of head, leaving only extreme tip exposed, which is mainly black with indistinct dark red-brown tone. Iris black surrounded by white orbital ring and inner iris; mostly naked tarsus and feet pinkish. Sexes alike and seasonal variation limited to feather wear, bleaching browner above; moult of ad to fresh plumage takes place on sea ice, less often on land (though common in some areas), shortly after abandoning almost fledged chick (see below). **Imm** (juv) as ad, but overall smaller and

Ad Adélie Penguins Pygoscelis adeliae displaying, Paulet I, Antarctic Peninsula, Jan 2001. © Hadoram Shirihai.

Adélie Penguins Pygoscelis adeliae *after a snowstorm, Paulet I, Antarctic Peninsula, Jan 2001. © Hadoram Shirihai.*

less bulky (in early stages), with bluer-tinged upperparts, white chin and throat, and eye-ring dark or has much-reduced white until one year old. **Chick** entirely dark brownish-grey.

Voice: Colonies very noisy. Principally gives a rolling, loud throbbing display call, rendered *arr-rar-rat-rar-raah*, followed by a reverberating *kug-gu-gu-gu-gs-aaaa* (with head/neck fully extended and accompanied by head waving and flipper beating); common contact call a sharp guttural barking aark. Chicks beg by whistling (Watson 1975).

Size: 70–71 cm, weight 3.8–8.2 kg. Female significantly smaller in flipper and bill lengths and overall weight.

Similar species: Neither Gentoo or Chinstrap Penguins has entire head, including chin and throat, black. Imm Chinstrap also has white chin and throat (like ad), but is readily eliminated by less black on neck-sides and demarcation between white and black being above eye level (see this species for variation); bill longer/deeper based and lacks feathering.

Distribution and biology

Distribution, movements and population: Coastal Antarctica (including Peninsula and Enderby Land), South Sandwich, South Shetland, South Orkney, Bouvetøya, Balleny, Scott and Peter. One pair recently bred on South Georgia. Total population estimated at 2.4 million breeding pairs in 1990s. Overall numbers increased dramatically in 1950s to 1980s, and around Ross Sea more than one million pairs bred at c.40 localities, but numbers now decreas-

Adélie Penguin Pygoscelis adeliae *family (ads with well-fed young chicks), Paulet I, Antarctic Peninsula, Jan 2001. © Hadoram Shirihai.*

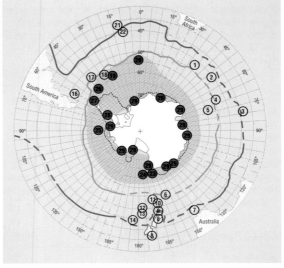

19 South Sandwich	26 South Orkney
20 Bouvetøya	27 South Shetland
23 Balleny	28 Antarctic Peninsula
24 Scott	29 Antarctica's coasts and
25 Peter I Øy	offshore islands

Adélie Penguins Pygoscelis adeliae *walking on fast ice (access to rookeries is not often not straightforward, and is patrolled by predatory Leopard Seals* Hydrurga leptonyx). *Paulet I, Antarctic Peninsula, Jan 2001. © Hadoram Shirihai.*

Ad Adélie Penguins Pygoscelis adeliae *can easily leap over 1 m vertically out of the water – and sometimes even higher – but do not always land gracefully on their feet. © Frank S. Todd.*

Adélie Penguin Pygoscelis adeliae *chick in snowstorm, Paulet I, Antarctic Peninsula, Jan 2001. © Hadoram Shirihai.*

Ad Adélie Penguins Pygoscelis adeliae *massing at favoured location before heading out to the sea; leaps of 3 m or more may be required to reach the water. © Frank S. Todd.*

ing in N Peninsula. Imms especially prone to northward dispersal, but scarcely above 60°S and rare or vagrant to S South America, Australia, New Zealand, the Falklands, South Georgia, Kerguelen, Heard and Macquarie.

Diet and feeding: Principally takes crustaceans, with some fish and cephalopods, caught by pursuit-diving. Most food taken 20–40 m below surface but recorded diving to 175 m. Krill favoured around Peninsula.

Different-sized Adélie Penguin Pygoscelis adeliae chicks, Paulet I, Antarctic Peninsula, Jan 2001. © Hadoram Shirihai.

In late summer, small gatherings of the last few penguins occur, here an Adélie Pygoscelis adeliae (middle), with three Gentoos P. papua (at the sides), and four Chinstrap Penguins P. antarctica (above and below). Antarctic Peninsula, Mar 2006. © Hadoram Shirihai.

Moulting ad Adélie Penguin Pygoscelis adeliae, Cape Royds, Ross Sea region, Jan 1999. © Hadoram Shirihai.

Social behaviour: Highly gregarious year-round. Monogamous but strength of pair-bond varies according to locality.

Breeding biology: Being a true Antarctic penguin and summer breeder, it uses an accelerated breeding cycle, from when coastal water temperatures rise above freezing, ensuring ample food. On arrival (males preceding females by c.4 days), fast-ice cover may still be extensive, and to reach some colonies birds must cross this most inhospitable barrier, which can range tens of km (individual colonies, on ice-free coasts, rocky outcrops and islands, sometimes far from sea, vary in size from a few hundreds to many thousands of pairs). Season generally Oct–Feb. Lays two greenish-white eggs in shallow scrape, in Oct–Nov, incubated 32–37 days. Chicks fledge at 41–64 days. Both ads incubate and provision young. No replacement clutch. At 2–3 weeks chicks join crèche, enabling both parents to feed simultaneously, and are abandoned shortly before fledging (when well fattened). Chicks

Snow-covered Adélie Penguin Pygoscelis adeliae after a snowstorm, Paulet I, Antarctic Peninsula, Jan 2001. © Hadoram Shirihai.

Displaying pair of Chinstrap Penguins Pygoscelis antarctica, Hannah Point, South Shetlands, Jan 2001. © Hadoram Shirihai.

especially vulnerable to adverse weather, particularly melting snow which wets their down. Typically moults away from colonies on ice floes and ice shelves.
Conservation Not globally threatened.
Taxonomy Monotypic.

Chinstrap Penguin *Pygoscelis antarctica*   Plate 1

Identification

Confusion risks: Adélie Penguin *P. adeliae* (especially imm with white throat).
Main characters: Medium-sized black-and-white penguin. **Ad** has diagnostic narrow black line across white chin and head-sides, and white around face reaches just above eye, thus black of head restricted to crown and neck, unlike Adélie Penguin (which see); rest of upperparts black to bluish-black, including upperside of flipper (which has thin white trailing edge), sharply demarcated from silky white underparts. Underside of flipper white, with narrow

black leading edge and rather small black tip. Bill black, contrasting with white feathering at base; iris dark orange-brown and mostly naked tarsus and feet pinkish. Sexes alike and seasonal variation confined to feather wear; moult of ad to fresh plumage undertaken close to completion of breeding, usually in Feb. **Imm** (juv) as ad, but overall smaller and less bulky in early stages, with face and throat speckled dark grey. Attains ad plumage at c.14 months. **Chick** uniform brownish-grey and paler below.
Voice: Colonies noisy. Display call a loud cackling (with bill open), soft humming, repeated *ah, kauk, kauk...*, with head raised, and accompanied by head swinging and flipper beating; contact call a low barking. Some similarities to Adélie (Watson 1975).
Size: 68–76 cm, weight 3.2–5.3 kg. Female averages smaller in flipper and bill lengths, and overall weight; 95% birds can be correctly sexed using bill size.
Similar species: Ad Adélie has black of head extending onto head-sides and throat, with smaller, blunter bill and no chinstrap line. Imm Adélie also has more black on head-sides, with demarcation between black and white below (not slightly above) eye level.

Surfacing Chinstrap Penguins Pygoscelis antarctica, showing their characteristic face markings and pointed tails. South Shetlands, Oct 2001. © Hadoram Shirihai

Chinstrap Penguin Pygoscelis antarctica *colony with ads and chicks, and an Antarctic Fur Seal* Artocephalus gazella, *Hannah Point, South Shetlands, Jan 2001. © Hadoram Shirihai.*

Distribution and biology

Distribution, movements and population: Chiefly spans zone between true Antarctic penguins and those of subantarctic islands, thus overlapping with northern populations of Adélie around Peninsula and with others in S subantarctic, generally close to c.60°S. Principally inhabits Scotia Sea, where vast majority gather to breed on South Sandwich, South Orkney, South Shetland and Antarctic Peninsula south to c.65°S, with few on South Georgia and Bouvetøya, Balleny and Peter I Øy. Total estimated breeding population 7.5 million pairs in 1980s. Very rarely disperses north to Tasmania, the Falklands, N Argentina (Buenos Aires province), Marion, Crozet, Kerguelen and Macquarie, and south to coastal Antarctica.

Diet and feeding: Takes crustaceans and some fish by pursuit-diving, for relatively short periods and close to surface.
Social behaviour: Highly gregarious. Monogamous and believed to form long-lasting pair-bonds.
Breeding biology: Returns relatively late to colonies, but season prolonged compared to that of Adélie and in areas where both occur Chinstrap breeds 3–4 weeks later than Adélie, and the former tends to favour and/or cope with steeper slopes and higher elevations. Nests Nov–Mar in large, dense colonies on rough, boulder-strewn slopes, at higher elevations than close relatives. Usually (perhaps always) lays two off-white to cream eggs, mid-Nov–Dec, incubated 31–39 days. Nest a simple gathering of small stones, sometimes a few feathers and bones. Chicks join crèche at c.3–4

Porpoising Chinstrap Penguins Pygoscelis antarctica *make short, flat, undulating leaps with much splashing. North-west Weddell Sea, Mar 2003. © Hadoram Shirihai.*

Ad Chinstrap Penguin Pygoscelis antarctica *during snowstorm, Deception I, South Shetland, Jan 2001. © Hadoram Shirihai.*

Ad Chinstrap Penguins Pygoscelis antarctica *intercepting a 'stranger' within the colony (the middle bird has chosen the 'wrong' way through the other territories and is being attacked by its conspecifics), South Sandwich, Nov 2001. © Hadoram Shirihai.*

Copulating Chinstrap Penguins Pygoscelis antarctica, *South Sandwich, Nov 2001. © Hadoram Shirihai.*

Chinstrap Penguins Pygoscelis antarctica *feeding juvs; having lost their down the juvs attain ad-like plumage, but some may show a variable dusky-tinged throat. © Hadoram Shirihai.*

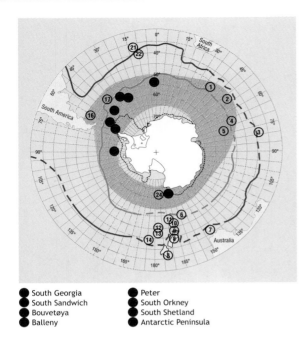

- ● South Georgia
- ● South Sandwich
- ● Bouvetøya
- ● Balleny
- ● Peter
- ● South Orkney
- ● South Shetland
- ● Antarctic Peninsula

weeks and fledge at 48–59 days. No replacement clutch. Both sexes incubate and provision young. Vacates colonies mainly in Mar and into Apr.

Conservation Not globally threatened.

Taxonomy Monotypic.

The crested penguins

The six crested penguins, or *Eudyptes*, combined populations equal c.45% of the total number of penguins (estimated at over 28 million breeding pairs). Though not a true 'crested penguin', recent research suggests that Yellow-eyed Penguin *Megadyptes antipodes*, whose overall population is perhaps the smallest of any penguin, is most closely allied to this group. However, in the following discussion, 'crested penguins' refers only to the genus *Eudyptes*, while *Megadyptes* appears on Plate 3. The group contains the world's commonest species, Macaroni Penguin *E. chrysolophus*, with at least nine million pairs, and the most threatened, Fiordland Penguin *E. pachyrhynchus*, of which there are possibly just 2500–3000 pairs. Populations are perhaps currently stable, with two obvious exceptions and several highly significant local declines. For example, on Campbell, Rockhopper *E. chrysocome* numbers have fallen by 94% since the 1940s and are decreasing at nearly all sites. Similar decreases in populations on the Aucklands and Antipodes have also occurred. Fiordland Penguin numbers have also declined, but due to the lack of earlier, accurate counts the scale of the decrease is unclear. However, for two species, the prognosis is more worrying: evidence suggests that Erect-crested *E. sclateri* numbers have fallen by up to 45% in recent years and those of Macaroni locally by as much as 50% in the S Atlantic.

In addition to the notable yellow or orange plume above the eyes, all crested penguins share several behaviours that mark them as different from other penguins. They do not reach sexual maturity until 5–6 years old, and Royal and Macaroni may not breed until 7–9 years. In common with virtually all penguins, they lay two eggs, but rather than being broadly the same size (as in other species), the first egg is 15–40% smaller. Of the two-egg

species, only crested penguins practice obligatory brood reduction. Thus, irrespective of food availability, usually either the smaller egg fails to hatch or the chick starves within ten days (though see Rockhopper). Uniquely, within this group the chicks are initially brooded and near-continuously guarded by the male (who fasts), and the female feeds them until they reach 3–4 weeks old, when they become mobile and join crèches. Thereafter they are fed by both parents, and leave the colony at c.8–10 weeks of age. First-years, some still with a pale throat/chin and insubstantial crest, and non-breeders, moult at the colonies or nearby, usually 1–2 months before breeders, who return to land following a short period spent foraging at sea immediately after breeding. Most complete their feather renewal by Mar–May and then depart the colonies, but timing varies according to species and locality. Winters are spent at sea in warmer waters further north, but dispersal distances vary between species. Commonly two species of crested penguin nest on the same island. In such instances, it is always Rockhopper and a larger species that are involved. Larger species invariably nest earlier. For example, on Macquarie, Royal Penguin arrives a month before Rockhopper and, in the Antipodes, Erect-crested Penguin lays 3–4 weeks before resident Rockhoppers.

Only two of the crested penguins (Rockhopper and Macaroni) are not endemic to New Zealand and its subantarctic islands (as treated here, i.e. including Macquarie). The others, which occur solely in the latter region (with the exception of occasional vagrants that have reached as far afield as the Falklands), are Fiordland, Snares *E. robustus*, Royal *E. schlegeli* (which is sometimes considered a race of Macaroni) and Erect-crested. Rockhopper is circumpolar.

Species identification, even on land, is not always straightforward, with Fiordland and Snares Penguins among the most difficult to separate, and at sea potentially extremely difficult. All should be identified using the shape, colour and distribution of the crest, particularly the point on the forehead at which it starts, the general shape and proportions of the bill, and extent of flesh at the gape, while the undersides of the flippers also possess, to some extent, diagnostic patterns (see Harrison 1983).

Rockhopper Penguin *Eudyptes chrysocome* Plate 2

Identification

Confusion risks: Erect-crested *E. sclateri,* Snares *E. robustus* and Fiordland Penguins *E. pachyrhynchus*, as well as Macaroni Penguin *E. chrysolophus*.

Main characters: The smallest of the crested penguins. **Ad** has (near-blackish) slate-grey upperparts, head and throat, sharply demarcated from white underparts; bright yellow eyebrow starts well behind bill base, ending as long yellow plumes projecting and falling sideways behind eye. Often-raised lateral and rear crown feathers form quite pronounced and shaggy occipital black crest. Underside of flipper largely white, amount of black varies both individually and geographically, but most have rather small black tip, narrow black leading edge and medium-sized black basal rear patch (neither reach tip). Bulbous but relatively small bill (accentuated by more extensive feathering at base and along lower mandible, reaching close to tip) is also not as deep based nor heavily grooved as other crested penguins; largely dark brown-red, usually with narrow pinkish-flesh margin at base in filholi, but black in nominate chrysocome. Iris bright red, rarely with gold inner ring; tarsus/feet pinkish-flesh, and soles dark. Sexes alike and seasonal variation confined to feather wear; before ads moult (Feb–Mar) dark areas duller and browner. **Imm** (juv) as ad, but overall smaller

Plate 2 Crested penguins

percilium narrower in front/above eye, and
est drooped/sparse

Erect-crested Penguin juv.

juv.

Erect crest on land

Extensive fleshy gape

ad.

ck

chick

Rockhopper
Penguin juv.

Rockhopper Penguin
(p. 62)

ordland
nguin juv.

Northern Rockhopper
Penguin ad. (p. 65)

Very long crest

chick

Erect-crested Penguin
(p.68)

Snares Penguin
(p. 66)

imm.

Crest from forehead
backwards

imm.

ad.

eshy gape;
ish cheek
es

ad.

chick

Fiordland
Penguin
(p. 68)

chick

Only
pale-faced
species

Royal Penguin
(p. 73)

chick

Macaroni Penguin (p. 71)

M.P. ad. br.

S.P. ad., pink gape

M.P. ad.

F.P. ad.

E.P. ad.

S.P. ad.

S.P. ad., white gape

M.P. juv.

F.P. juv.

E.P. juv.

R.P. ad.

E.P. ad.

S.P. juv.

RH.P. juv.

RH.P. ad.

Juvs or swimming birds, especially New Zealand's species, pose the greatest challenge (see main text)

Rockhopper Penguin Eudyptes [chrysocome] chrysocome (*race* filholi*), Heard. © Eric Woehler.*

Pair of Rockhopper Penguins Eudyptes [chrysocome] chrysocome *occupying an old albatross nest within a typical Falklands mixed colony of Rockhoppers, Imperial Shags* Phalacrocorax [atriceps] atriceps *and Blackbrowed Albatrosses* Thalassarche [melanophrys] melanophrys*; note rather sparse, short plumes, Falklands, Jan 2001. © Hadoram Shirihai.*

and slighter (in early stages), yellow superciliary almost absent or partially marked and no projecting crest plumes, at least in early stages (even subsequently, crest often still poorly developed), while chin and throat greyish with variable white mottling (becoming darker with age), and bill darker and iris dull brown. Attains ad plumage at c.2 years. **Chick** uniform brownish-grey above and whitish below.

Voice: Colonies very noisy. Trumpeting display call of mixed grating, loud barks and braying 'yells' with vibrating quality and repeated rhythmically, accompanied by head swinging and raising, and flipper beating. Contact call a short high-pitched monosyllabic bark.

Size: 45–55 cm, weight 2.0–3.8 kg. Female significantly smaller in flipper and bill measurements, but large overlap in weight.

Similar species: Smaller, with narrower and less obvious eye-

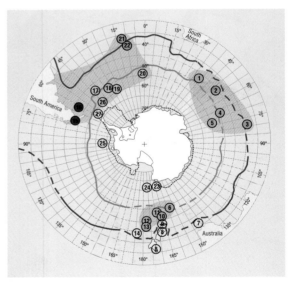

■ Rockhopper Penguin *Eudyptes [c.] chrysocome* (nominate)
▨ Rockhopper Penguin *Eudyptes [c.] chrysocome* (race *filholi*)
▨ Northern Rockhopper Penguin *Eudyptes [c.] moseleyi*

1 Prince Edward & Marion
2 Crozet
3 Amsterdam & St Paul
4 Kerguelen
5 Heard
6 Macquarie
10 Auckland
11 Campbell
12 Antipodes
13 Bounty
15 South American offshore islands
16 Falklands
21 Tristan da Cunha
22 Gough

Rockhopper Penguin Eudyptes [chrysocome] chrysocome (*of the race* filholi*, which is similar to the nominate but has a narrow pink, rather than black, stripe at the bill base, and usually a narrower and even shorter supercilium), Macquarie, Jan 1998. © Hadoram Shirihai.*

brow than Similar species, which diagnostically does not reach bill base nor join on forehead. At sea, unless all features seen well, identification almost impossible and given usual visibility in such conditions many can, at most, be determined only as crested penguins. It should be emphasized that separation from Similar species is best based on relative width and length of superciliary, and relative projection of crest plumes; the bill and underside of the flippers are always difficult to evaluate, but in comparison with Macaroni, the bill base lacks the latter's striking pinkish bare-skin gape and the underside of the flipper has less black, especially on the leading edge, which never reaches tip. Further complication is provided by the occasional presence of *E. [c.] moseleyi* on East Falkland, and several apparent hybrids between Rockhopper and Macaroni have also been recorded in the Falklands. Separation of young from most congeners is always challenging, especially lone birds at sea, but always tend to have narrower and shorter superciliary, be overall smaller, and bill lacks obvious pale bare skin at gape. For differences from Northern Rockhopper Penguin *E. [c.] moseleyi* see below.

Distribution and biology

Distribution, movements and population: Circumpolar, breeding on many subantarctic islands in Indian and Atlantic Oceans, colonies occur on islands of Cape Horn (S South America), the Falklands, Prince Edward, Marion, Crozet, Kerguelen, Heard, Macquarie, Auckland, Campbell, Bounty and the Antipodes. Currently c.1.1 million pairs (compilation of data from 1980s and 1990s), but numbers falling alarmingly at some sites (e.g. on the Falklands and Marion). Pelagic range c.44–55°S and mostly rare/vagrant to South Georgia (where formerly bred in tiny numbers) and north to South Africa, Australia and New Zealand, and south to Antarctica. *Diet and feeding*: Feeds on krill, squid, octopus and fish by pursuit-diving.

Social behaviour: Highly gregarious. Monogamous and apparently forms long-lasting pair-bonds.

Breeding biology: Breeds Oct–Mar in colonies on tumbling scree and lava slopes, often with tussac grass, sometimes inland. Commonly associates with Black-browed Albatross Thalassarche [melanophrys] melanophrys and shags. Two spheroid to ovoid greenish-blue eggs from mid-Nov, laid in shallow depression and incubated 32–38 days. In common with most crested penguins, first egg smaller and chick apparently never survives. Other chick fledges at 66–73 days. Both sexes incubate and care for young. Imm and non-breeders moult from mid-Feb, breeders slightly later, returning to land after short period foraging at sea, with most completing renewal by late Mar and departing colonies Apr/May.

Conservation Vulnerable. Overall has decreased by 24% in past 30 years, and is threatened by habitat loss and degradation, human disturbance and various types of pollution, as well as starvation due to commercial fishing of squid.

Taxonomy Two subspecies: nominate in South America and the Falklands and filholi throughout rest of range. Nominate chrysocome and filholi similar except former has narrow black (rather than pink) stripe at bill base, and usually a broader supercilium. Note that those on Marion, which have sometimes been assigned to filholi, do not have pink on gape. Herein I consider moseleyi from Tristan da Cunha, Gough, Amsterdam and St Paul separately (which see). Further study of the E. [chrysocome] superspecies is required, and may even confirm specific status for filholi (for which the English name Eastern Rockhopper Penguin has been suggested).

Northern Rockhopper Penguin
Eudyptes [chrysocome] moseleyi　　　Plate 2

Identification

Confusion risks: Other crested penguins, mainly at sea or with young birds.

Main characters: All features and plumage development as Rockhopper Penguin *E. [c.] chrysocome* (which see). For detailed separation see below.

Voice: Probably largely similar to Rockhopper. Local study at St Paul demonstrated clear differences from Crozet birds in

Ad Northern Rockhopper Penguins Eudyptes [chrysocome] moseleyi; note very dense, long plumes forming diagnostic, luxuriant crest, Saint Paul, Nov 1999. © Hadoram Shirihai.

Northern Rockhopper Penguin Eudyptes [chrysocome] moseleyi guarding a crèche, Saint Paul, Nov 1999. © Hadoram Shirihai.

Northern Rockhopper Penguins Eudyptes [chrysocome] moseleyi; *protecting chicks from a Subantarctic Skua* Catharacta [skua] antarctica *(race* lonnbergi*), Saint Paul, Nov 1999. © Hadoram Shirihai.*

frequency (Hz), length of phrases and number of syllables but no precise study of vocalizations related to geographical variation available across entire range.

Size: 48–58 cm, weight 1.5–4.3 kg. Female significantly smaller in flipper and bill measurements, but large overlap in weight.

Similar species: Compared to Rockhopper, ad has diagnostic very long plumes forming a luxuriant crest, larger size (see above) with longer flippers (175–190 mm versus 160–175 mm in Rockhopper), longer (but not deeper) bill and combination of black stripe at bill base and more extensive black on underside of flipper. Young possibly inseparable in the field but further study required. Being very similar to Rockhopper it is subject to similar potential confusion with other crested penguins (main problems are birds at sea or with young birds: see Rockhopper).

Distribution and biology

Distribution, movements and population: Tristan da Cunha, Gough, Amsterdam and St Paul. Currently c.300,000 pairs on Tristan da Cunha and Gough, and between 26,000 and 48,000 pairs on Amsterdam and St Paul. Pelagic range c.35–50°S; rare/vagrant to South Africa and Australia, very rare in New Zealand and has apparently wandered to the Falklands.

Diet and feeding: Few specific data, presumably much as chrysocome.

Social behaviour: Presumably much as chrysocome.

Breeding biology: Few specific data, largely as chrysocome, but some studies have revealed slightly earlier breeding period and different chick-rearing period (appears shorter in E. [c.] moseleyi); lays two eggs annually in early Sep–Oct, and young and ads depart colonies in Dec–early Jan when moult commences.

Conservation This form has not been subject to separate evaluation of conservation status, but, as Rockhopper, probably at least Vulnerable. Has decreased by 50% in past 30 years within Indian Ocean sector of its range but the much larger Atlantic population is overall stable, and even increasing on the main island of Tristan, following the cessation of exploitation.

Taxonomy Monotypic. The high phenotypic distinctness and different breeding cycle of this form, which is usually considered a subspecies of Rockhopper, appear sufficient to warrant specific status, although this requires confirmation. The length of the crest and voice appear to be behaviourally isolating mechanisms

(Jouventin 1982). *E.* [c.] *moseleyi* apparently differs from all other Rockhopper populations as much as the New Zealand crested penguins differ from each other. See also Rockhopper.

Snares Penguin *Eudyptes robustus*   Plate 2

Identification

Confusion risks: Fiordland *E. pachyrhynchus* and Erect-crested Penguins *E. sclateri*, especially at sea.

Main characters: Medium-sized, yellow-crested, black-and-white penguin. **Ad** has dark blue-black upperparts, head and throat, white underparts and bright yellow stripe above eye, almost from bill base, which forms only slight bushy crest behind eye (black feathers of crown uncrested). Viewed from front, supercilia almost form V, which especially when wet can appear much tighter. Large, heavily grooved, deep-based red bill has obvious bare pink skin at base, especially noticeable and becoming triangular at gape; very narrow black skin separates bill base from facial feathering. Iris bright red-brown; feet and tarsus pinkish-flesh. Underside of flipper white, with moderate black tip and entire leading edge, which almost always meet. Sexes alike and seasonal variation related to feather wear; before ads moult (around Mar) dark areas duller and browner, and yellow plumes paler. **Imm** (juv) as ad, but overall smaller and slighter (in early stages), with paler yellow (almost white with wear) and narrower superciliary, and at least in early stages lacks plumes; also duller and less robust bill with inconspicuous flesh-grey bare skin at base, and chin and throat variably whitish-grey, becoming darker with age. Even with age, crest is usually still poorly developed. Attains ad plumage at c.3 years. **Chick** uniform brownish sooty-grey (almost black) above and whitish below.

Voice: Display and contact calls largely similar to those of other crested penguins, especially Fiordland, and generally consist of lower pitched, longer phrases than Rockhopper (which see), but are more persistent and demonstrative.

Size: 51–61 cm, weight 2.4–4.3 kg. Female averages smaller in flipper and bill lengths, and overall mass.

Similar species: Snares and Fiordland Penguins are difficult to separate. Note exposed line of pale bare skin that extends from gape around bill base, which is very obvious in ad Snares but absent in ad Fiordland (which often has whitish cheek-stripes and shorter crest). Ad Erect-crested Penguin is taller with erectile, bushy crest. Separation of the three in non-ad plumages is possible with care

Porpoising Snares Penguins Eudyptes robustus, *Snares, Dec 1999. © Hadoram Shirihai.*

Ad Snares Penguins Eudyptes robustus *underwater, the Snares.* © Kim Westerskov.

Ad Snares Penguins Eudyptes robustus, *Snares, Dec 1999.* © Hadoram Shirihai.

and experience and if close views obtained on land. Snares has a narrower, yellower supercilium and generally darker cheeks than Fiordland; former also has relatively longer bill and typically some pink skin at gape. Erect-crested has supercilium starting nearer gape and rising obliquely over eye, a longer bill, larger chin and more domed head in profile.

Distribution and biology

Distribution, movements and population: Snares. Population 23,250 breeding pairs in 1985–6. Most are on Main and Broughton. In winter few range far, being scarce at Stewart I and S New Zealand mainland and very rarely recorded, mainly as vagrant, on Macquarie, Antipodes, Tasmania and S Australia.
Diet and feeding: Mainly takes krill, also squid and small fish by pursuit-diving, principally within inshore waters.
Social behaviour: Gregarious. Monogamous and pair-bonds sustained.
Breeding biology: Nests within forest in dense colonies, Aug–Jun.

Lays two pale bluish-grey eggs (mainly Sep/Oct) in shallow nest of twigs and mud, incubated 31–37 days. Chicks fledge at c.75 days. Both sexes incubate and provision young. In common with other crested penguins, the smaller chick usually starves. No replacement clutch. Probably first breeds at four years old.
Conservation Vulnerable. Not known to be declining and apparently not threatened by introduced predators, but a large squid fishery near the Snares may be competing with the species.
Taxonomy Monotypic.

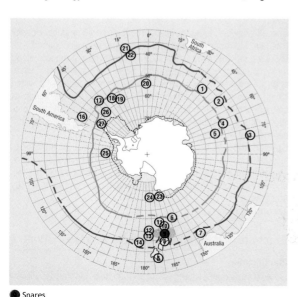

● Snares

Ad Snares Penguins Eudyptes robustus *with chick, the Snares, Nov 1987.* © Colin Miskelly.

Fiordland Penguin Eudyptes pachyrhynchus, *Open Bay Islands, S New Zealand, Aug 1985.* © Colin Miskelly.

Fiordland Penguin Eudyptes pachyrhynchus *(left) and Snares Penguin* E. robustus; *note the lack of pink skin around the bill base in the former. The Snares, Nov 1986.* © Colin Miskelly.

Fiordland Penguin *Eudyptes pachyrhynchus* Plate 2

Identification

Confusion risks: Snares *E. robustus* and Erect-crested Penguins *E. sclateri*, mainly at sea and in non-ad plumages.

Main characters: Medium-sized, yellow-crested, black-and-white penguin. The only crested penguin with white cheek-stripes (partially exposed bases to black feathers). **Ad** has dark bluish-grey upperparts with darker head to throat and broad yellow eyebrow from bill base, which droops behind eye and reaches neck (crest plumes never appear bushy, even less than in Snares), while black feathers of crown never form crest. Most have 3–6 whitish stripes on cheeks. Large orange-red bill lacks bare pink skin at base/gape, but still has rather noticeable bulbous culminicorn ridge; very narrow black skin separates bill base from feathers. Iris reddish-brown; feet and tarsus pinkish-flesh. Underside of flipper white, with moderate (but variable) black tip and narrow leading edge, which rarely meet. Sexes alike and seasonal variation related to feather wear; before ads moult (around Mar) dark areas duller and browner, and yellow plumes paler. **Imm** (juv) as ad, but overall smaller and slighter, with less deep-based, more

blackish-brown bill in early stages, and lacks bare skin at base; also has short, flattened head plumes (appear as short, narrow supercilia) and grey or even white throat and cheeks, becoming darker with age. Attains ad plumage at c.2 years. **Chick** uniform brownish black-grey above and whitish below.

Voice: Generally very similar to Snares Penguin (which see), but slightly less harsh.

Size: 55–60 cm, weight 2.1–5.1 kg. Female averages smaller, especially in bill depth and bill index (depth x width x culmen length), as well as flipper length and overall mass.

Similar species: For differences from Snares and Erect-crested Penguins see those species.

Distribution and biology

Distribution, movements and population: S New Zealand on South I, Stewart and neighbouring islets. Just 2500–3000 pairs in mid-1990s; the rarest of all penguins. Regular non-breeding visitor to the Snares where up to 30 imm moult annually. Vagrant to W and S Australia, Tasmania and perhaps the Falklands (provenance of latter specimen appears very doubtful; R. Woods pers. comm.).

Diet and feeding: Takes fish, squid, octopus and krill by pursuit-diving.

Social behaviour: Gregarious, but nests solitarily or in low-density colonies. Monogamous and pair-bonds apparently sustained.

Breeding biology: Breeds Jul–Nov in coastal rain forest and along rocky coasts or occasionally sandy beaches. Lays two dull white eggs in shallow scrape concealed by roots, boulders or within cave, in Jul–Aug, and incubated 30–36 days. Chicks fledge at c.75 days. No replacement clutch. Both parents incubate and provision young. First breeds at 5–6 years old. Other biological and behavioural aspects most similar to Snares Penguin.

Conservation Vulnerable. Principally threatened by introduced species (cats, stoats, rats and dogs) and Weka *Gallirallus australis*, but human disturbance and squid fishing may be taking a toll, and marine perturbations may bring substantial changes in prey abundance.

Taxonomy Monotypic.

Erect-crested Penguin *Eudyptes sclateri* Plate 2

Identification

Confusion risks: Fiordland *E. pachyrhynchus*, Snares *E. sclateri* and Rockhopper Penguins *E. chrysocome*.

Main characters: Medium-sized, yellow-crested, black-and-white

8 New Zealand and offshore islands

Ad Erect-crested Penguins Eudyptes sclateri *with Southern Elephant Seal* Mirounga leonine *in the background, Antipodes, Jan 2007.* © *Hadoram Shirihai.*

penguin. **Ad** has jet-black upperparts and head to throat, contrasting with white below. Broad, bright yellow eyebrow starts at bill base and forms striking, erect brush-like crest above and behind eye, presenting mohican-like crown when erect, but when matted down (often on land and more usually at sea) overall pattern does not clearly differ from several congeners, especially Snares Penguin. Distinctive profile with domed crown, longer bill and large chin cf. Snares and Fiordland. Long, reddish orange-brown bill has narrow bare pink skin at base and gape point, but less noticeable compared to Snares. Iris dark reddish-brown; tarsus and feet pinkish-flesh. Underside of flipper white, with largest amount of black among crested penguins, forming broad black tip and leading edge (which meet), and base. Sexes alike and seasonal variation related to feather

wear; before ads moult (in Mar–Apr) dark areas duller and browner, and yellow supercilium and crest paler. **Imm** (juv) as ad, but overall smaller and slighter (in early stages), with less deep-based, more blackish/brownish bill (in early stages) and inconspicuous bare skin at base; also head has short narrow supercilium, lacking (or with very short) erect plumes until first moult, and grey or even dirty white throat and cheeks, becoming darker with age. Note same distinctive profile as ad. Attains ad plumage as third-year. **Chick** uniform brownish black-grey above and whitish below.

Comparison of surfacing crested penguins in New Zealand's subantarctic waters, with (top to bottom) Snares Eudyptes robustus, *Erect-crested* E. sclateri, *Fiordland* E. pachyrhynchus *and Rockhopper Penguins* E. [chrysocome] chrysocome. *Snares and Erect-crested share a massive bill with a fleshy gape that extends as a pale line around bill base, which elements are better marked in Snares, and lacking in ad Fiordland. All species when wet fold their crest plumes, but in Snares the supercilium tends to appear more evenly broad and in Erect-crested it typically rises obliquely in front and over eye. Fiordland often has whitish cheek-stripes (albeit difficult to see), whilst Rockhopper is usually more easily separated from the others by its smaller size, less robust bill, and much shorter and narrower supercilium in front of the eye. Photographs taken in Snares, Bounty, Stewart and Antipodes, respectively, Dec–Jan 1999–2007.* © *Hadoram Shirihai.*

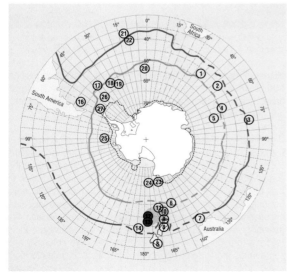

 Antipodes
Bounty

Erect-crested Penguin Eudyptes sclateri *colony in the Antipodes, where around two-thirds of the population breeds. Jan 2007. © Hadoram Shirihai.*

Erect-crested Penguins Eudyptes sclateri *usually choose sheltered access points to their island colonies, but often face difficult conditions and steep 'landings', forcing them to leap higher or to use their strong feet and claws to drag themselves ashore. Bounties, Jan 2007. © Hadoram Shirihai.*

Voice: Generally similar to Snares and Fiordland Penguins (which see), but distinctly lower pitched throbbing phrases, and more sonorous brief pulses.

Size: 60–67 cm, weight 3.3–7.0 kg. Female usually smaller and lighter, averaging smaller in flipper and bill lengths and overall mass, and some can be sexed according to bill index (depth x culmen length).

Similar species: Erect crest distinguishes it from other yellow-crested penguins (see above). Young, especially in early stages, very similar to Fiordland and Snares, differing by marginal characters that are prone to individual variation related to plumage development. Subtle differences such as in bare skin at bill base and underside of flipper patterns very difficult to judge at sea, especially as Erect-crested has characters intermediate between the others. At sea, when poor visibility can further hamper viewing, young are indistinguishable, as are many ads. Note that it shares breeding islands only with Rockhopper Penguin, separation from which is usually rather easy in ads, but less so in young. In latter plumage, Rockhopper is overall smaller, has smaller and less robust bill, much shorter and narrower supercilium (not reaching bill base), relatively much darker chin/throat (at least in early stages), and much less black on underside of flipper.

Distribution and biology

Distribution, movements and population: Two large populations on Bounty and Antipodes (which holds around two-thirds of the overall population) totalling c.77,000 pairs in three colonies in mid-1990s. A 1978 survey estimated 115,000 pairs on Bounties but only 28,000 pairs were found there in 1997; however differences between the survey techniques employed preclude the possibility of making direct comparisons. No recent breeding records from Campbell. In winter disperses from colonies, and some imms moult away from breeding islands. Ranges to most subantarctic islands in this region, but rare or vagrant to S Australia, Tasmania, Macquarie, mainland New Zealand, the Falklands and Kerguelen.

Ad Erect-crested Penguins Eudyptes sclateri*: note variation in crest plumes, which are often slightly folded when wet, as in the three birds on the left which just arrived from the sea, but held erect and brush-like when dry (right-hand bird). Bounties, Jan 2007. © Hadoram Shirihai.*

Diet and feeding: Krill and squid are principal foods, with some small fish.

Social behaviour: Nests colonially at high densities, some rookeries contain thousands of pairs, in association with vast colonies of Salvin's Albatross Thalassarche [cauta] salvini on Bounty, and on latter and Antipodes also with Rockhopper Penguin and fur seals. On Bounties a rather clear division is visible, with fur seals concentrated at the bottom, penguins in the centre and albatrosses at the top, depending upon physical structure of the island, but sometimes a complete mix occurs, forming an incredibly noisy spectacle.

Breeding biology: Breeds from Sep on bare exposed rocks, tussac-clad beaches and cliffs. Lays two pale bluish or greenish eggs in shallow depression between large boulders, in Oct, incubated c.35 days. Chicks fledge at c.70 days. Maximum of one young raised per nest. Probably no replacement clutch. Few data concerning

roles of sexes though, like other crested penguins, female feeds young more frequently than male during crèche stage.

Conservation Endangered: populations have decreased by at least 50% in last 45 years, with that on Campbell probably extirpated. Unknown marine changes and atmospheric pollution have been postulated as reasons for the decrease, as mammalian predators are unknown on Bounty and the Antipodes.

Taxonomy Monotypic.

Macaroni Penguin *Eudyptes chrysolophus* Plate 2

Identification

Confusion risks: Closely related to Royal Penguin *E. schlegeli* (see taxonomy), but less likely to be confused with it; younger birds, especially at sea, could be confused with other crested penguins (see below).

Main characters: Second-largest crested penguin, with orange crest and black-and-white plumage. **Ad** has black (slightly bluish-tinged) upperparts, contrasting with white below; head and cheeks dark grey to black. Golden-orange plumes (with black shaft-streaks) cover upper forehead and reach beyond eye, where they droop. Massive, deep-based bill (with noticeable series of grooves and bulbous culminicorn) is reddish orange-brown and has conspicuous bare pink skin at base, especially noticeable and becoming triangular at gape point. Iris dark reddish-brown; tarsus and feet pinkish-flesh. Underside of flipper white, with variable (often quite extensive) black forming broad tip and leading edge (often connected), and base. Sexes alike and seasonal variation related to feather wear; before ads moult (in Mar–May) dark areas duller and browner, and plumes paler. **Imm** (juv) as ad, but overall smaller in early stages, with head plumes either absent or very sparse, bill less robust and duller brown (with less conspicuous bare skin at base) and chin and throat dark grey. Attains ad plumage as second-year. **Chick** uniform brownish-grey above and whitish below.

Voice: Like other crested penguins, very noisy at colonies. Display call principally a repeated, loud harsh bray, deep throbbing or raucous trumpeting (lower pitched in male), accompanied by head swinging and raising, and flipper beating. Contact call a short bark.

Macaroni Penguin Eudyptes chrysolophus *colony at egg stage, Crozet Nov 1999. © Hadoram Shirihai.*

Pair of Macaroni Penguins Eudyptes chrysolophus *mutual preening on still empty nest, Hannah Point, South Shetlands, Jan 2001. © Hadoram Shirihai.*

Macaroni Penguin Eudyptes chrysolophus *has golden-orange plumes meeting on the upper forehead and drooping behind the eye; note, also, massive, deep-based bill with noticeable grooves and triangular bare pink skin at gape point. South Georgia Mar 2003. © Hadoram Shirihai.*

Size: 71 cm, weight 3.1–6.6 kg. Female averages smaller and lighter, and averages smaller in bill length and overall mass; c.90% can be sexed according to bill measurements.

Similar species: Distinguished from very similar Royal Penguin by colour of throat and cheeks, though pale-faced individuals reported within Macaroni colonies and vice versa. Ads of both species are only crested penguins whose crests meet on forehead, lack yellow supercilium/lateral crown-stripe of close congeners, and lack occipital crest of black central crown feathers (see Rockhopper). Both are noticeably larger, with more robust bills and very extensive exposed bare skin at base, than Rockhopper, but these features are less useful in respect to other crested penguins. Crest is more orange, rather than sulphur-yellow as in Rockhopper. Young Macaroni, however, is more likely to be confused, especially at sea, with young Rockhopper (which see) and with young of New Zealand's crested penguins, which do

not overlap in range. Its larger size, more robust bill with bright pink triangle of bare skin at gape, loose patch of chrome-yellow and white feathers on forehead and forecrown-sides are useful identification criteria.

Distribution and biology

Distribution, movements and population: S Chile, the Falklands (very few), South Georgia, South Sandwich, South Orkney, South Shetland, Bouvetøya, Prince Edward, Marion, Crozet, Kerguelen and Heard; periodically Antarctica (outer Peninsula). Population c.11.64 million pairs in 1992. Ranges north to islands off Australia, New Zealand, S Brazil, Tristan da Cunha and South Africa, and regularly reaches north of Antarctic Convergence in winter.

Diet and feeding: Principally takes small krill, along with small fish and tiny proportion of cephalopods by pursuit-diving. Mostly dives to c.20 m, but recorded as deep as 115 m.

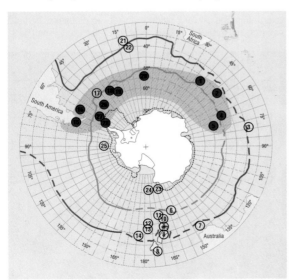

- ❶ Prince Edward & Marion
- ❷ Crozet
- ❸ Kerguelen
- ❹ Heard
- ❺ South American offshore islands
- ❻ Falklands
- ❼ South Georgia
- ❽ South Sandwich
- ❾ Bouvetøya
- ❿ South Orkney
- ⓫ South Shetland
- ⓬ Antarctic Peninsula

Ad Macaroni Penguin Eudyptes chrysolophus *is distinguished from the very similar Royal Penguin* E. schlegeli *by the dark throat and cheeks. South Georgia Mar 2003. © Hadoram Shirihai.*

Social behaviour: Gregarious, breeding in large, high-density colonies. Monogamous and pair-bonds long lasting.

Breeding biology: Breeds Sep–Mar on exposed, level or steep, rocky or tussac-covered ground, but usually on heavily denuded areas. Lays two white eggs in Nov (only larger, second egg usually hatches) in rudimentary shallow scrape, incubated 33–37 days. Chick fledges at 60–70 days. No replacement clutch. Both sexes incubate and provision young.

Conservation Vulnerable. Some populations have decreased by at least 50% in the last 36 years perhaps as a result of various types of pollution and, more probably, the impact of ocean warming, though some colonies stable since late 1980s.

Taxonomy Royal Penguin is often regarded as a subspecies or colour morph of this species; individuals with pale or white faces, but with plumage otherwise very similar to Royal are of unknown provenance. Many birds showing all criteria of Royal are present in breeding colonies at Kerguelen and Crozet, as well as intermediate individuals with a greyish throat.

Royal Penguin *Eudyptes schlegeli*   Plate 2

Identification

Confusion risks: Largely unmistakable, but see below for relationship to Macaroni Penguin *E. chrysolophus*.

Main characters: Large, orange-crested, black-and-white penguin. Plumage almost identical to Macaroni Penguin except variably pale face. **Ad** has black (slightly bluish-tinged) upperparts and crown, contrasting with white lower face (supercilium, ear-coverts and chin/throat), which is variably tinged greyish and yellow-buff. Long yellow, orange and black-coloured plumes project from forehead to behind eye, where they droop. Massive bill (slightly larger than Macaroni) is reddish orange-brown with conspicuous bare

Royal Penguin Eudyptes schlegeli, *Macquarie, Jan 1998. © Hadoram Shirihai.*

Royal Penguin Eudyptes schlegeli *and Macaroni-like* E. chrysolophus *Penguin; some on Macquarie with Macaroni-like appearance can be attributed to individual variation within Royal Penguin, Macquarie, Dec 1999. © Hadoram Shirihai.*

One-year-old imm Royal Penguin Eudyptes schlegeli, *Macquarie, Jan 1998. © Hadoram Shirihai.*

Hustle and bustle within the Sandy Bay Royal Penguin Eudyptes schlegeli *colony, Macquarie.* © Frank S. Todd.

pink skin at base, especially noticeable and becoming triangular at gape point. Iris blackish-brown; tarsus and feet pinkish-flesh. Underside of flipper white, with variable (but somewhat less extensive) black areas as in Macaroni, forming broad black tip and leading edge (which often meet), and base. Sexes alike (except female tends to have greyer lower face and is noticeably rather smaller and slighter) and seasonal variation related to wear; before ads moult (in Mar–May) dark areas duller and browner, and plumes paler. **Imm** (juv) as ad, but in early stages smaller and slimmer with duller, browner bill (and less conspicuous bare skin at base), greyish cheeks and throat, dense mat of yellow-white feathers on forehead and lacks long crest plumes. Yearlings prior to complete moult (Jan–Feb) at c.1 year have partial crest and

are bleached browner above. Attains ad plumage at c.2 years old.
Chick uniform dark brownish-grey above and whitish below.
Voice: Generally similar to Macaroni Penguin (which see).
Size: 65–75 cm, weight 3.0–8.1 kg. Female averages smaller in most measurements, including flipper and bill lengths and overall mass.
Similar species: This and Macaroni Penguin are the only species in which head plumes meet on forehead, but latter has jet-black/dark grey cheeks and throat, though pale-faced individuals reported at some localities. On Macquarie there are some Macaroni-like birds or intermediates between Macaroni and Royal. Some even appear indistinguishable from Macaroni according to most features (except perhaps bill and body sizes, Royal is 10–20% taller than Macaroni). Vagrancy and interbreeding between them has been suggested, but occurrence of such individuals perhaps implies that some Royals can look like Macaroni.

Distribution and biology

Distribution, movements and population: Confined to Macquarie, on all coasts and a few inland up to 200 m, and on adjacent islets. Over 50 colonies are known, ranging from c.60 pairs to more than 160,000 pairs. In 1984–85, 848,719 pairs. Winter movements and ecology unknown, though vagrants recorded in Australia, New Zealand and Antarctica. Claims from the Falklands lack substantiation, but several records from South Georgia (K. Reid *in litt*. 2002).
Diet and feeding: Fish, squid and euphausiids taken by pursuit-diving.
Social behaviour: Gregarious. Monogamous and sustained pair-bonds, though some extra-pair copulations take place.
Breeding biology: Breeds in huge high-density colonies on exposed, often rocky tussac-covered ground. Breeders return in mid-Sep and lay c.1 month later. Lays two white eggs in shallow depression, sometimes lined with grass, in Oct, incubated 35

Moulting ad Royal Penguin Eudyptes schlegeli, *Macquarie, Feb 1997.* © Daisy Gilardini.

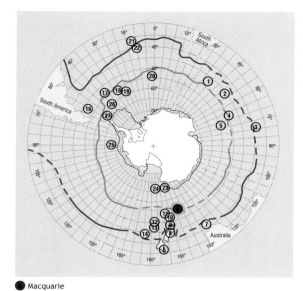

● Macquarie

days. The first egg is rarely incubated because birds fail to sit properly or (more typically) it is broken. Chicks fledge in c.65 days, mainly in late Jan. No replacement clutch. Both sexes incubate and provision young. Ads, after foraging at sea, go ashore in Mar to moult. Last individuals leave Macquarie in late Apr.

Conservation Vulnerable. The currently stable population is, however, threatened by introduced predators, human disturbance, marine and atmospheric pollution, habitat loss and degradation, though the effect of climate change on food supply may offer the most significant long-term threat.

Taxonomy Formerly regarded as a subspecies or morph of Macaroni Penguin, but now generally treated as a separate, sibling species.

Northern penguins

This group contains five species, of which four are Spheniscus penguins, a principally South American genus, which contains the only species found north of the equator, Galápagos Penguin *S. mendiculus*. The localized Humboldt Penguin *S. humboldti*, which breeds from C Peru to C Chile, is restricted to the nutrient-rich waters of the Humboldt Current. Their close relative, Magellanic Penguin *S. magellanicus* is reasonably widespread in S South America. Only one form recognized in this genus does not occur in the Western Hemisphere, African Penguin *S. demersus*, which has nearly reached the equator (in Gabon) as a vagrant. The other species belongs to the genus *Eudyptula*, which recent cladistics analysis demonstrates to be most closely related to *Spheniscus*. *Eudyptula* is usually considered monotypic, but its complex taxonomy (six taxa are recognized) demands further investigation and possibly revision. I tentatively recognise *albosignata* (White-flippered Penguin) as an allospecies here. Yellow-eyed Penguin *Megadyptes antipodes* is included on Plate 3, but is most closely allied to the crested penguins (see remarks above).

Both *Spheniscus* penguins recorded from our region are similar, largely black-and-white species, which principally differ in the number of breast-bands, while *Eudyptula* is very small and relatively nondescript, being blue-grey above and white below. Identification of a vagrant *Spheniscus* would pose considerable problems. Mem-

bers of this genus generally reach sexual maturity at 4–5 years, but *Eudyptula* is capable of breeding when 2–3 years old.

Unlike most other penguins, chicks of both genera do not form crèches (except very small ones in some African Penguin colonies), with both parents taking turns to feed and guard the young, sometimes leaving them unguarded during the day after c.30 days, and chicks leaving the colony at c.9–11 weeks.

Like the crested penguins, first-year and failed breeder *Eudyptula* penguins moult at the colonies or nearby, concurrently with successful breeders, who return to land following a period of up to 13 weeks spent foraging at sea after breeding. The *Spheniscus* behave differently; African and Galápagos Penguins have a pre-nuptial moulting system, with first-years and non-breeders renewing their feathers during the breeding season, while Magellanic moults following breeding, with first-years and non-breeders staggering their moults prior to those of breeders, which principally do so in the colonies. Galápagos Penguin is the only penguin to moult twice per annum. All species spend a brief period feeding at sea prior to feather renewal, and both African and Magellanic Penguins embark on relatively long migrations (particularly in the latter) into warmer waters in search of food during the non-breeding season; in contrast *Eudyptula* is largely sedentary.

Northern penguin numbers are generally decreasing, most markedly in African and Magellanic Penguins, both of which have suffered more as a result of oil spills than any other penguin species. Numbers of Galápagos and Humboldt Penguins are overall perhaps more stable, but experience dramatic declines in response to El Niño Southern Oscillation events, with both decreasing by up to 75% as a result of the 1982–3 event.

Yellow-eyed Penguin *Megadyptes antipodes*   Plate 3

Identification

Confusion risks: None: appearance unique.

Main characters: Medium-sized penguin. **Ad** has pale yellow eye (and narrow but distinct red orbital ring), which gives slightly fierce appearance; top of head neatly capped by yellow, black-centred feathers, bordered by broad bright lemon-yellow band extending through eye to around hindcrown. Upperparts and lower throat pale to dusky slate-blue, throat and neck-sides tinged brownish, and underparts contrastingly white. Upperside of flipper blue-black with yellow-white margins forming especially broad trailing edge; underside almost uniform white. Bill rather long, almost straight and not deep based, mainly flesh coloured with red-brown tip; tarsus and feet pinkish-flesh. Sexes virtually alike and seasonal variation limited to feather wear; prior to ad moult (in Feb–Apr) dark areas duller. **Imm** (juv) as ad but has olive-grey crown to

Ad Yellow-eyed Penguins Megadyptes antipodes, *Aucklands, Dec 1999.* © Hadoram Shirihai.

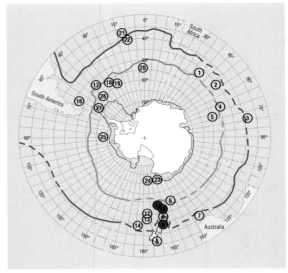

● Southern New Zealand
● Auckland
● Campbell

Juv Yellow-eyed Penguin Megadyptes antipodes, *Aucklands, Dec 1999. © Hadoram Shirihai.*

upper throat (lacking black streaks on crown), and slightly narrower yellow band on head, while eye more greyish-yellow and orbital ring grey-brown. Ad plumage of yellow-and-black crown may only develop at 14–18 months. **Chick** prior to acquiring juv feathers, possesses thick brown outer down and is further insulated by an underlying pale brown down; eye blue-grey, bill black and legs greyish-pink.

Voice: Relatively quiet, being the least colonial and most secretive penguin, and to some extent nocturnal. Several loud display calls, including musical trills, high-pitched throbbing and harsh 'yells' and grunts. Contact call two high-pitched, musical, disyllabic notes (*HANZAB*).

Size: 56–78 cm, weight 3.6–8.9 kg. Female averages smaller in most measurements, including flipper and bill lengths, and overall weight.

Similar species: None; voice is also markedly different from other penguins.

Distribution and biology

Distribution, movements and population: S New Zealand (South I north to Banks Peninsula), Stewart, Auckland and Campbell. Ranges north to Cook Strait but is largely sedentary. Population c.2000 pairs in 1995. Most juv to four-year-old birds vacate breeding areas, but very little is known of their whereabouts, though it has been suggested they move north.

Diet and feeding: Prey species vary according to availability. Primarily takes red cod, opal fish, sprat and squid by pursuit-diving. On breeding grounds, ads usually leave for sea at dawn, returning in evening to feed chicks.

Social behaviour: Secretive. Nests solitarily or at very low densities. Monogamous with high degree of pair-bond fidelity. Due to

their being more males than females, latter have wide choice of mates and pair-bond is not necessarily life-long. Only at few sites do older chicks form small crèches.

Breeding biology: Comes ashore to breed in traditional areas, largely in second half of Aug. Breeds Aug–Mar in tussac-grass thickets and coastal forest; each nest out of sight from those of neighbouring pairs. Lays two bluish-white eggs in shallow scrape of leaves, grass and twigs, in Sep–Oct, incubated 39–51 days (full incubation is delayed until up to ten days after eggs laid). Often one egg is left partially exposed. Two-year-olds lay only one egg that is often infertile. The chances of infertile eggs lessen with maturity, with older individuals usually laying two eggs. Studies indicate that hatching rate is rather high, with an estimated 85–90% of eggs producing young. However, at 14–18 weeks, when fledglings enter sea they face a critical period. Chicks fledge at 106–108 days. No replacement clutch. Both sexes incubate and provision young. An opportunity to breed may not arise until male is 3–10 years old, though females may generally achieve sexual maturity earlier.

Conservation Endangered (the world's rarest penguin), but given measures in place to halt habitat degradation and loss may warrant downgrading to Near Threatened in short term. However, fluctuating population remains at risk from introduced predators in some areas, as well as human disturbance, accidental fires and fishing-net mortality, especially in gillnets.

Taxonomy Monotypic.

Little Penguin *Eudyptula minor*   Plate 3

Identification

Confusion risks: White-flippered Penguin *E.* [*m.*] *albosignata* (Banks Peninsula, South I, New Zealand) is generally identical; otherwise none, though much larger Yellow-eyed Penguin *Megadyptes antipodes* presents similar profile in water.

Main characters: The smallest penguin, greyish and lacks crest. In water, almost only rear of rounded body and head are visible above surface. **Ad** appears almost uniform metallic grey-blue above and on head to just below eye (whitish bases and dark

Plate 3 Northern penguins

Only penguin with yellowish eye and mask

ad.

juv.

chick

juv.

Little Penguin (p. 76)

Smallest penguin; greyish above, pale-eyed and lacks crest

Yellow-eyed Penguin (p. 75)

chick

ad.

juv.

ad.

chick

White-flippered Penguin (p. 78)

As Little, but variable white flipper edges

Ad has single breast-band

juv.

ad.

ad.

Ad has double breast-band

juv.

African Penguin (p. 79)

chick

chick

Magellanic Penguin (p. 80)

Little Penguin Eudyptula [minor] minor, Chatham, Oct 1993. © *Peter Reese.*

shaft-streaks to blue-grey dorsal feathers visible only when very close). When wet can appear darker blackish slate-blue above, especially around eye and cheeks; underparts and throat white, but not sharply defined from upperparts. Upperside of flipper contrasting blue-black, with narrow white trailing edge; underside almost uniform white, with variable dusky tip. Rather stout, slightly hooked bill mainly greyish-black. Iris whitish-grey; tarsus and feet greyish-flesh. Sexes alike and seasonal variation related to feather wear; before ads moult (in Feb–Mar) dark areas duller or browner, with some white feather bases visible. **Imm** (juv) as ad, but in early stages smaller and slimmer, with smaller bill and upperparts often bluer. **Chick** pale greyish-chocolate above and whitish below.

Voice: Very noisy at colonies at night. Loud yaps, wails, trumpeting, deep growls and harsh grunts, but also long trills and brays, used in various communal on-land behaviours, including displays, e.g. *urrrrrrrrr...urrrrrrrraaaaawoooooo…rrr...aaaaowooo... raowooo* (HANZAB); contact call a short high-pitched monosyllablic *huk*.

Size: 40–45 cm, weight 0.5–2.1 kg. Female has on average shorter and less deep-based bill, marginally shorter flippers and weighs slightly less in all races.

Similar forms: White-flippered Penguin is slightly larger, with paler blue-grey upperparts and broad white margins to both edges of the flipper, which may join on centre in males. Yellow-eyed Penguin should be easily distinguished given its larger size and characteristic head markings.

Distribution and biology

Distribution, movements and population: Coasts and offshore islands in S Australia (from Perth to New South Wales), Tasmania, New Zealand, Stewart and Chatham. Vagrant to SE Queensland, Lord Howe I and Snares but most birds sedentary. Total population perhaps as many as one million individuals in 1980s.

Diet and feeding: Mainly takes small shoaling fish and cephalopods, less frequently crustaceans, by pursuit-diving.

Social behaviour: Gregarious. Monogamous and long-term pair-bond may be usual. Nests in loose colonies or often in solitary pairs.

Breeding biology: Lays Jul–Dec, peaking Aug–Nov, in 0.15–1.0 m-long burrow, lined with plant material, or hollow under bushes or rocks, in dunes and on vegetated slopes of coasts and islands (sometimes up to 500 m inland). Usually lays two white eggs incubated 33–39 days. Chicks fledge at 50–65 days. May lay replacement clutch and is unique among penguins in that true second clutches frequent at some locations (e.g. 23–40% of pairs at Phillips' I). Both ads incubate and provision young. Chicks brooded for first ten days, guarded continuously day and night for further two weeks, than guarded solely at night and when close to fledging only visited for feeding at night. First breeds at 2–3 years old.

Conservation Not globally threatened and overall population is stable or perhaps increasing, with main threats being predation by introduced predators, human disturbance and agricultural development.

Taxonomy Six subspecies usually recognized, with *albosignata* also frequently considered within this group: *minor* occurs around South I, New Zealand; *novaehollandiae* in W and S Australia and Tasmania; *iredalei* and *variabilis* around North I, New Zealand; and *chathamensis* in the Chatham group. The validity of several of these forms appears questionable.

White-flippered Penguin
Eudyptula [minor] albosignata   Plate 3

Identification

Confusion risks: As Little Penguin *E. minor.*

Main characters: Like Little Penguin, being small (perhaps slightly larger than latter) and similar in all features except following. Ad has pale blue-grey upperparts, white below, broad white leading and trailing edges to flippers, but amount of white varies individually (in extreme cases among males the white may meet in centre of flipper) and some may show virtually no white. Imm (juv) much as ad. Chick pale greyish-chocolate with pale underparts.

Voice: Like Little Penguin (which see), but no comparative study available.

Size: 41 cm, weight 1.0–1.5 kg. Few specific mensural data available for this form, though evidence suggests that the sexes overlap considerably in weight.

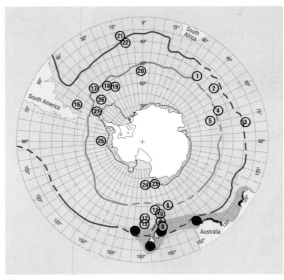

■ Little Penguin *Eudyptula [minor] minor*
▨ White-flippered Penguin *Eudyptula [minor] albosignata*
● Tasmania   ⑧ Southern New Zealand
● New Zealand and   ● Chatham
  offshore islands

White-flippered Penguin Eudyptula [minor] albosignata: note white margins to both edges of flipper. Kaikoura, South I, New Zealand, Feb 2001. © Hadoram Shirihai.

Breeding pair of White-flippered Penguin Eudyptula [minor] albosignata which, compared to slightly smaller Little Penguin E. minor, has paler blue-grey upperparts and broad white margins to the flippers. S New Zealand, Aug 1991. © Peter Reese.

Similar species: For differences from Little Penguin see that species.

Distribution and biology

Distribution, movements and population: Confined to Banks Peninsula and Motunau I, on east coast of South I, New Zealand.
Diet and feeding: Few specific data.
Social behaviour: No specific information.
Breeding biology: Differences, if any, from Little Penguin unknown.
Conservation Prospects inadequately known due to it being generally regarded as a subspecies of Little Penguin.
Taxonomy Often considered a subspecies of Little Penguin. Its status as an allospecies, species or subspecies requires further study of the biological and molecular differences, and relationships, between all forms within this group.

African Penguin *Spheniscus demersus* Plate 3

Identification

Confusion risks: None in range. See taxonomy.
Main characters: Medium-sized, distinctly patterned, black-and-white penguin, with black face and broad band on chest and belly-sides. **Ad** has black (tinged brownish) forehead to nape and rest of upperparts, including upperside of flipper, contrasting with white below, the latter with variable black spotting, especially on belly, bordered by black horseshoe-like band on belly-sides, broadening below flipper and separated from dark dorsal area by variable white band, widest on upper breast. Most striking, however, is isolated black face (head-sides to throat) encircled by broad and well-defined white band reaching white of breast. Black eye has distinctive pink orbital ring, which extends as patch to bill base. Variation includes some with hint of partial second darkish-mottled breast-band, but never as complete and broad as on Magellanic Penguin *S. magellanicus* (which see). Underside of flipper almost black with variable, though often quite extensive, ragged whitish stripes. Quite deep-based, stout bill mainly black with vertical sub-terminal band close to tip; tarsus and feet admixed pinkish-flesh and black. Sexes alike and seasonal variation related to feather wear; before ads moult (in Nov–Jan in South Africa and Apr–May in Namibia) dark areas become duller and browner. Male has deeper based bill. **Imm** (juv) well differentiated, having ill-defined pattern and is initially dark brownish slate-blue above and on head to breast, thus lacking striking head pattern and bands on body, but usually has diffuse pale head-sides and throat bar, darker

area around eye (bare pink skin obscured), and upper breast and flanks merge with dirty whitish belly. Becomes progressively browner with age, acquiring ad patterns in stages, but at c.2 years old much as ad. **Chick** initially all brown, thereafter medium brown on upperparts and head, and whitish below.
Voice: A donkey-like braying mainly heard at night.
Size: 60–70 cm, weight 2.1–3.7 kg. Female averages smaller in bill size and overall weight, but no significant differences in flipper length.
Similar species: Very rarely has double black breast-band, like Magellanic Penguin, but latter unknown in African waters.

Distribution and biology

Distribution, movements and population: Off coasts of S Africa, from C Namibia, at Hollandsbird I to Algoa Bay, South Africa. Ranges north to S Angola and as vagrant to Gabon, Congo and

Ad African Penguin Spheniscus demersus usually has just a single breast-band (cf. Magellanic Penguin S. magellanicus), whilst facial, bill and flipper patterns also help identify the species. South Africa. © Peter Ryan.

Ad African Penguins Spheniscus demersus, *South Africa. © Peter Ryan.*

C Mozambique. Population c.179,000 ads in 27 colonies in the late 1990s.

Diet and feeding: Sardine, anchovy and other pelagic school-fish captured by pursuit-diving form bulk of diet, also squid. Most dives reach 30 m, but recorded up to 130 m.

Social behaviour: Gregarious. Monogamous with sustained pair-bonds.

Breeding biology: Breeds mainly May–Aug on rocky ground with little or no vegetation. Nest burrows are usually dug colonially. Lays two (very rarely one) white eggs, mainly in either Mar–May (South Africa) or Nov–Dec (Namibia), incubated 36–41 days. Chicks fledge at 60–130 days. Replacement (or second) clutches may be initiated four months later. Both sexes incubate and provision young.

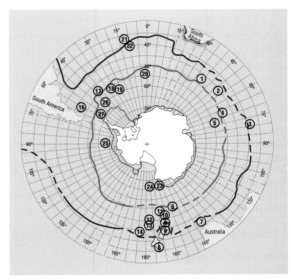

One-year old African Penguin Spheniscus demersus*: note diffuse head pattern with obscure bare pink skin on the lores and around eye, and upper breast-band and flanks merge with dirty whitish belly. South Africa. © Peter Ryan.*

Conservation Vulnerable. Currently undergoing a rapid decline, of c.2% per annum, due to food shortages and environmental fluctuations, while a large oil spill in 2000 would have affected 40% of the population but for resourceful, immediate and large-scale rescue effort. Some colonies are increasing. Human disturbance, principally by guano- and egg collectors, habitat degradation and loss, fishing-net mortality and shark and seal predation are additional threats.

Taxonomy Monotypic. Some past authorities questioned the validity of this species, suggesting that African, Humboldt and Magellanic Penguins constitute well-marked races of a single species; Humboldt and African Penguins interbreed in captivity and the former and Magellanic Penguin in the wild in Chile.

Magellanic Penguin
Spheniscus magellanicus   Plate 3

Identification

Confusion risks: Similar to Humboldt Penguin *S. humboldti* (not recorded from our region) and African Penguin *S. demersus* (no overlap, though African-like individuals have been reported in coastal Patagonia).

Main characters: Medium-sized, well-patterned, black-and-white penguin, with black face and bold black or white bands on head-

Pair of Magellanic Penguins Spheniscus magellanicus *by their nest hole: unlike African Penguins* S. demersus, *they have two black breast-bands. Falklands, Jan 2001. © Hadoram Shirihai.*

'Excited' Magellanic Penguin Spheniscus magellanicus; *the species is notoriously nervous, Falklands, Feb 2001. © Morten Jørgensen.*

sides, breast and belly, and overall very similar appearance to African Penguin except following. **Ad** has double black breast-bands (African usually has single band), the first very broad across foreneck (which connects with dark slate-brown upperparts on necksides) and a narrower horseshoe-like band on lower breast that demarcates white belly. Underside of flipper plainer and cleaner, mostly whitish/greyish at all ages (see Plate 3). Narrow bare pink skin at bill base, otherwise bare parts much as African. **Imm** lacks head pattern and breast-bands; also (and unlike similar-aged African) greyish-white head-sides and chin/throat (usually whiter on supercilium and ear-coverts) and diffuse greyish upper breastband and diagnostic pale and dark bands on flanks. Plumage progression slow and can produce intermediate, older imm resembling young African. Attains ad plumage at c.2 years old. **Chick** apparently as African Penguin.
Voice: At sea occasionally emits a single haaa contact call, while principal display call a loud braying, with head held skyward, while raising and flapping flippers.
Size: 70 cm, weight 2.3–7.8 kg. Female averages smaller in flipper and bill lengths, overall weight and especially bill depth (93% can be correctly sexed on this feature).
Similar species: African and Humboldt Penguins usually possess only single breast-bands, while latter has more pink at bill base (imm shares this feature, absent in imm Magellanic) and narrower white band on head-sides.

Distribution and biology

Distribution, movements and population: C Chile and S Argentina to Cape Horn; the Falklands and Juan Fernández. Population numbered over one million birds in late 1980s, but perhaps in decline. Ranges north to N Chile and NE Brazil (increasing numbers have been reaching SE Brazil in recent years), also vagrant to Australia, New Zealand, South Georgia and South Shetland.
Diet and feeding: Principally takes small crustaceans, small fish and small squid by pursuit-diving.

Social behaviour: Gregarious. Monogamous and pair-bonds long lasting.
Breeding biology: Breeds Sep–Apr in up to 2 m-deep burrows on open beaches, sand dunes and grassy slopes, and occasionally in forest. Two white eggs are laid mid-Oct to mid-Nov, incubated 39–42 days. Chicks fledge at 60–70 days. Rarely lays replacement clutch. Both sexes incubate and provision young.
Conservation Near Threatened. Declines of up to 10% noted at some Falkland colonies in recent years, apparently due to food shortages, while Argentine populations were apparently decreasing in 1990s due to losses caused by oil spills, direct competition with expanding commercial fisheries and human development for land.
Taxonomy Monotypic. Some authorities question the validity of this species, suggesting that African, Humboldt and Magellanic Penguins constitute well-marked races of a single species; Humboldt and African Penguins interbreed in captivity and the former and Magellanic Penguin in the wild in Chile.

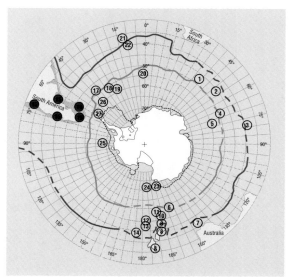

● South American offshore islands
● Falklands

Great albatrosses

Traditionally considered to consist of two species: Wandering Albatross *Diomedea exulans*, which is widespread in the Southern Ocean, and Royal Albatross *D. epomophora*, which is a breeding endemic to New Zealand and its subantarctic islands, but during dispersal ranges mainly east to S South America.

These are the largest albatrosses and the longest-winged flying birds on Earth. Both have wingspans that can exceed 3 m. (Mensural data can be useful for sexing the great albatrosses; females are usually smaller than males in several measurements; further information on these and the relative level of overlap, expressed in crude terms, are presented in the species accounts.) Their separation from any of the small/medium-sized albatrosses, the so-called mollymawks, *Thalassarche*, is easy, given that they are clearly larger and lack a dark 'bridge' across the mantle, linking the invariably all-dark upperwings. Also unlike the mollymawks, the underwing is largely white, whilst the pattern (a narrow dark trailing edge and primary tips) remains almost unchanged throughout their lifespans and scarcely varies among the different taxa. Other characters are detailed in the relevant species accounts.

Taxonomy and nomenclature of the seven taxa of great albatrosses are still highly controversial, subject to further study and I currently prefer to treat all recognized taxa as distinctive allospecies belonging to two superspecies. Thus, the *Diomedea* [*exulans*] superspecies, the so-called Wanderers, includes five specifically distinct forms and the *D.* [*epomophora*] superspecies, the Royals, two (see lists below, groups A and B). To simplify this, we can view these taxa as cases of speciation in progress, they being rather closely related according to genetic studies and exhibit rather modest morphological differences, although their very strong fidelity to natal colonies greatly restricts gene-flow between the different populations. For the results of such molecular analysis, which favours the recognition of all forms as species, see Robertson & Nunn (1998) and Nunn & Stanley (1998). Burg & Croxall (2004) and Brooks (2004) recently offered a slightly different arrangement, recognizing all Wanderers as separate species except *gibsoni* and *antipodensis* which they lumped as Antipodean Albatross. In complete contrast, however, Penhallurick & Wink (2004) recommended lumping all forms and recognizing just one Wandering and one Royal Albatross (though this arrangement was criticized by Rheindt & Austin 2005). I feel that application of a phylogenetic or the Biological Species Concept is insufficient for delimiting many seabird populations which clearly segregate geographically to breed though exhibiting often-limited morphological or molecular divergence. I thus prefer to maintain the superspecies approach for these groups and strongly recommend that all forms be regarded as more than 'just' subspecies. Each merits research and conservation measures because all populations, whether species or subspecies, are under immediate threat and in sharp decline.

The information presented here should be regarded as part of the ongoing attempt to understand the relationships between populations and their separation at sea. All seven taxa receive equal treatment here. I should remark that the complicated debate concerning the status of these forms should not deter the experienced observer from attempting to label these birds at sea, away from their breeding islands, in order to attempt a better understanding of their dispersal (and thus level of risk from oceanic longline fisheries) and to practise their identification (see below). The recognition and characterization of these forms is as follows.

Group A: Wandering Albatross
Diomedea [*exulans*] superspecies
These comments apply mostly to ads; juvs of all forms have all-brown bodies, with only the face and throat white. Acquisition

Younger imm Southern Royal Albatross Diomedea [epomophora] epomophora. *Note that some (especially young) Southern Royals may have a slight smudge on the leading edge of the carpal area. Kaikoura, South I, New Zealand, Feb 2001. © Hadoram Shirihai.*

Plate 4 Wandering Albatrosses

Wandering (Snowy) Albatross ad. ♂ (p. 90)

rger and heavier billed n all other forms

Wandering ad. ♂

Wandering ad. ♀

Plumage identical to similar-sized younger ad male Tristan and Gibson's

Wandering juv.

White face/throat and underwing contrast with uniform brown rest of plumage

Wandering younger/1st imm. So-called 'leopard' plumage

Cleaner white body

Similar in all forms of complex

Marbled uniformly above, but lacks solid black cap

d white upperwing- rts (only a few an become as e)

Wandering Mid/old imm. ♂ (and 1st ad. ♀)

First white appears on belly

Similar plumage occurs in all white-bodied Wanderers

Underwing pattern similar in all Wanderers/ages

Often has limited white on upperwing-coverts

Some darkening on crown

Some older imm. males develop extensive white fringes to upperwing (see Plate 5), as ad. male Tristan and Gibson's

Whiter body, but still has all-dark upperwing, variably blotched/vermiculated

Amsterdam ad. ♀ (and older imm.)

Tristan Albatross ad. ♂ (p. 93)

Overall slighter with smaller bill than similar Wandering

Near-identical to ad. female Gibson's, but note characteristic solid black cap

Antipodean ad. ♀

Black cap and cutting edge to bill

Brown juv-like plumage, but has clear white belly patch

Tristan imm.

Antipodean Albatross ad. ♂ (p. 99)

Solid black cap

ensive white ing and ral area on erwing- rts (like r imm or ger ad male dering)

Some darkening on crown

Similar to ad. Amsterdam and brown ad. female Antipodean, but lacks solid black cap

Near-identical to ad. Amsterdam, but no black cutting edge to upper mandible

Black cutting edge to upper mandible (near-diagnostic)

Amsterdam Albatross ad. ♂ (p. 101)

Upperwing almost uniform dark

Brownish plumage recalls younger imm. Wandering, but solid blackish cap/crown

Upperwing almost uniformly dark, plumage heavily blotched/ vermiculated

Tristan older ad ♀ (or younger ad ♂)

Gibson's ad. ♀ (and younger ad. ♂)

Body extensively blotched/vermiculated

Amsterdam older ad. ♂

Gibson's Albatross ad. ♂ (p. 96)

Some darkening on crown

Identical to same age/sex Tristan (and larger older imm. male or younger ad. female Wandering)

With age brownish plumage becomes more restricted

In few older ad. males more white on upperwing-coverts; body often less pure white

Identical to ad. male Tristan and larger younger ad. Wandering

Note slim/long-necked nd sloping head rofile of Royals

Black cutting edge to upper mandible near-diagnostic among Wanderers

Amsterdam Albatross ad. ♂

Paler bird with less solid brownish plumage and blackish cap

Southern Royal Albatross ad. (or older imm.)

cutting edge to bill! se view)

Darkening to bill tip varies in all Wanderers but often more distinct in Antipodean and especially Amsterdam

eaner white body and tensive (but ill-defined) ite on upperwing-coverts d white tail

ote squarer/ under head ofile of anderers

Antipodean Albatross ad. ♀ (and older imm.)

Wandering Albatross ad. ♂

Overall very large and heavier-billed

Note solid black cap but no black cutting edge to bill

Body and upperwing-coverts become whiter with age

Dark areas of upperwing may be concealed by white body feathers

In close view brown juv-like plumage has transversal barring (also in Amsterdam)

Mostly typical ads (also a juv and some young Wandering) and recognizable plumages are illustrated, with their main characteristics described, but see main text and photographs for further details. Identification possible only in comparative views and with typical birds!

of 'ad' plumage is protracted, with imms of paler forms having transitional plumage patterns identical to 'ad' plumages of forms that breed in darker plumages. However, even ad plumage varies according to sex, age and breeding locality, and, despite the general trends relating to these variables, it is also important to stress that, in well-studied populations, the range of individual variation among birds of the same age and sex is enormous.

1. Wandering Albatross D. [e.] exulans (including the synonym 'chionoptera', the so-called Snowy Albatross) breeds in South Georgia and the S Indian Ocean, with a few pairs at Macquarie. Ad has whitest upperwing-coverts.

2. Tristan Albatross D. [e.] dabbenena principally breeds at Gough. Relatively small compared to previous form (but mostly similar in size to others), with rather contrasting plumage; most ads have extensively dark upperwing-coverts, approaching ad gibsoni, but with age a few older males may become whiter as exulans. A characteristic of this form is its apparently delayed maturation which produces imm plumages identical to amsterdamensis (or ad female antipodensis). [Beware the sometimes different use of the names exulans, dabbenena and 'chionoptera' by different authors: see Taxonomy under the first two forms.]

3. Gibson's Albatross D. [e.] gibsoni breeds on the Auckland group. Approaches antipodensis in having extensive dark upperwing but never has as dark brown plumage as the latter (ad female).

4. Antipodean Albatross D. [e.] antipodensis breeds on the Antipodes, with a few on Campbell. In many respects very close to gibsoni. To some degree ads retains juv/imm-like brown plumages (especially females), similar to amsterdamensis. Often shows characteristic, but variable blackish cap.

5. Amsterdam Albatross D. [exulans] amsterdamensis breeds on Amsterdam. Brown in plumage generally very extensive, as in brownest female antipodensis. Dark cutting edge to upper mandi-

ble diagnostic whilst the dark greenish tip to bill is best developed in this form.

There is some evidence, based on identified birds, ringing data and satellite tracking to suggest that each of the Wanderers has separate 'home' ranges for foraging, but are capable of ranging very widely at sea; e.g. one exulans travelled 25,000 km in c.9 weeks, or almost the entire Atlantic and Indian Oceans from west to east, while a male from the Antipodes moved 8000 km to the S Pacific in 17 days. Recent GPS-tracking of Wandering Albatrosses has demonstrated that they achieve a mean 55 km/h in flight, travelling faster than 85 km/h almost 10% of the time. Distances and pattern of dispersal are very variable, and vary between breeders and non-breeders, sexes (with in some a tendency for females to forage to the north of males of the same form), and apparently also with age (dispersal of young birds is least known). Recent observations suggest the following tendencies, which should be considered when studying birds at sea (some additional details are presented in the species accounts). The taxa gibsoni and antipodensis, which breed in subantarctic New Zealand, are readily seen around their breeding islands most of the year and often occur together in the rich feeding areas between these archipelagos, or further north where they may mix with exulans off New Zealand and in Australian/Tasmania waters. Unknown numbers apparently regularly reach as far east as waters off western South America. Indeed, the various populations of exulans have been recorded widely in the Southern Ocean. Though a banded dabbenena has been caught off Australia, this form is restricted to the S Atlantic when breeding, and probably seldom ventures far into the Indian Ocean. Identifying its range is complicated because even ads are largely indistinguishable at sea from gibsoni or exulans. Both exulans and dabbenena reach coasts of South Africa, but there are almost no data on the dispersal of amsterdamensis. The separation of all these forms is discussed further within the relevant accounts.

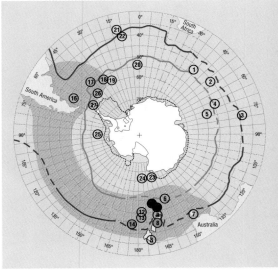

■ Wandering Albatross *Diomedea [e.] exulans*
  Tristan Albatross *Diomedea [e.] dabbenena*
  Gibson's Albatross *Diomedea [e.] gibsoni*
  Antipodean Albatross *Diomedea [e.] antipodensis*
  Amsterdam Albatross *Diomedea [e.] amsterdamensis*

● Prince Edward & Marion   ⑩ Auckland
● Crozet   ⑪ Campbell
③ Amsterdam   ⑫ Antipodes
● Kerguelen   ● South Georgia
● Heard & McDonald   ㉑ Tristan da Cunha
● Macquarie   ㉒ Gough

■ Southern Royal Albatross *Diomedea [e.] epomophora*
  Northern Royal Albatross *Diomedea [e.] sanfordi*

⑧ New Zealand   ● Campbell
● Auckland   ⑭ Chatham

Map showing main breeding areas and principal regions of dispersal of both forms of Royal Albatross Diomedea [epomophora] *but not limited occurrences in S Atlantic and S Indian Ocean.*

Plate 5 Royal and Wandering Albatrosses

Southern Royal Albatross ad. (p. 103)

Jizz distinctive, especially sloping head profile

Dark cutting edge to bill (in close view)

Cleaner white body and all-white tail

Extensive white on upperwing, concentrated on smaller coverts (often partly flecked) and 'elbow'

Diffusely pale-fringed larger coverts

Southern Royal ad.

No (or limited) black carpal mark on leading edge of underwing

Diffuse pale 'dusting' to fore upperwing-coverts

Southern Royal young ad. (or older imm.)

Compared to Wanderers with similar white on upperwing, has whiter body and almost all-white tail.

Wavy-vermiculated scapulars

Dark cutting edge to bill

In close view, diffusely/narrowly pale-fringed upperwing-coverts

Whiter body and more limited black in tail than any Wanderer with mostly dark upperwing

Southern Royal young juv. (and 1st imm.)

Classic 'dusting' effect (with diffuse greyish-toned whitish fringing) to upperwing-coverts

In this stage, narrow white leading edge is supporting character

Small white feathering on 'elbow'

Southern Royal young imm.

Often appreciably smaller/slighter than Southern Royal

Northern Royal Albatross ad. (p. 106)

Northern Royal ad.

Dark cutting edge to bill (in close view)

Black carpal mark on leading edge of underwing

Blotched scapulars (less barred)

Solidly dark upperwing contrasts with white body and tail

Northern Royal juv.

Variable black centres to tail feathers

As ad, but a few dark blotches on crown and lower back to rump (variable)

Body more extensively blotched/vermiculated, and tail usually darker

Wandering Albatross old imm. ♂ (and ad. ♀)

Superficially Southern Royal-like, but bolder white fringing on upperwing-coverts

Black-and-white 'checkerboard' pattern, with clear-cut 'elbow' patch

Gibson's younger ad. ♀ (or old imm. ♂)

Wandering juv.

Tristan ad. ♀

Amsterdam ad. ♀ (and old imm.)

Wandering mid/older imm.

Tristan ad. ♂

Wandering older ad. ♀ (or old imm. ♂)

Antipodean ad. ♂

Gibson's ad. ♂

Salvins ad.

Antipodean ad. ♀

Southern Royal ad.

Amsterdam ad. ♂

Northern Royal ad.

Southern Royal juv.

Wandering older ad. ♂

Southern Royal younger imm.

Great albatrosses, especially Wanderers, are often more safely identified if several forms of different ages/sexes can be directly compared (for both size and plumage): mainly identifiable plumages are illustrated, and their main features are described in the captions to the flying birds (see photographs and main text).

Possible Gibson's Albatross Diomedea [exulans] gibsoni *with Westland Petrel* Procellaria westlandica. *The Wanderers and Royal Albatrosses are the longest-winged flying birds on Earth, with wingspans that can exceed 3 m. Kaikoura, South I, New Zealand, Feb 2001. © Hadoram Shirihai.*

Group B: Royal Albatross
Diomedea [epomophora] superspecies

Characterized by largely white tail at all ages, black cutting edges to paler, yellower bill, and lacks pink neck mark of many ad *D. [e.] exulans* and some other pale Wanderer forms. Head shape and, to some extent, bill (and nostril) shape also differ from latter; superficially, wing of Southern Royal appears to whitens from leading edge back (in *exulans* from the centre of the wing outwards).
1. Southern Royal Albatross *D. [e.] epomophora* breeds only on Campbell with a few on Auckland (some individuals hybridizing with Northern Royals at Taiaroa Head). Develops ill-defined (but quite extensive in ad) white upperwing-coverts and always has white leading edge.
2. Northern Royal Albatross *D. [e.] sanfordi* breeds at Chatham (on the Sisters and Forty Fours), with a few at Taiaroa Head, New Zealand. Has solid dark upperwing. Smaller, less heavily built and narrower winged than *epomophora*, with characteristic broader black leading edge to carpal; lacks white leading edge of *epomophora*.

Approach to identification

Distinguishing ads of these forms on or around the breeding islands is usually straightforward, but when dealing with birds far from these areas several points must be considered. The following notes summarize the key identification issues, but for further details see the relevant accounts.

Wanderers versus Royals. The various Wanderers with imm-like plumages, which have some brown feathering, are easily separated from Royals of any age. When dealing with non-brown Wanderers, identification is complicated by variation within both groups, but usually should not pose a major problem, especially if the upperwing-covert and tail patterns can be correctly judged, in combination with any head markings, bill colour and sometimes extent and type of makings on chest and body-sides; in some cases markings on the scapulars or leading edge of the underwing (near the carpal) are also useful features. With experience the two Royals can be also distinguished from Wanderers by general shape and structure (jizz). Beware that Royals' diagnostic black cutting edges to the bill can be judged only in optimal views, i.e. on some birds or in certain circumstance is easily detected, in others not. The greatest confusion risk is between some, mainly distant, ad white Wanderers and same-age Southern Royal, or more often between older imm plumages of these two (especially if tail colour is not seen and the upperwing is only seen poorly or briefly). Such

pitfalls are illustrated with photos (see p. 87) and detailed under Southern Royal (see also Plate 5).

The main challenge, identification of Wanderers. Identification of the different forms of Wanderer is limited by many uncertainties! Keen observers should bear in mind that practice and experience in identifying these birds is a key starting point. As summarized in the species accounts, Wanderers at sea, away from or even sometimes near the breeding colonies, may only be reliably identified to a taxon in ad plumage (and perhaps some older imms possessing typical ad-like characters). (All other younger plumages, of most taxa, based on present knowledge, lack the distinctive marks of their respective ads, or possess no definitive characters independent of age and sex.) It should also be realized that many individuals cannot be certainly ascribed to a specific taxon, even in ad plumage. In many instances, the degree of overlap significantly complicates matters, e.g. a few older male *dabbenena* attain white plumage identical to *exulans*, whilst *gibsoni* females (especially well-marked younger ads) are very similar to paler ad male *antipodensis*, and well-marked brownish ad female *antipodensis* can appear very similar to any other brownish imm Wanderer, especially to both *amsterdamensis* and imm female *dabbenena*. Also, location or principal home range are only of limited use because of the extensive overlap in dispersal, but should be always taken into account, especially when faced with large numbers of birds. For example, *exulans* is the most abundant form in S Atlantic and Indian Oceans, but less frequent than other forms in the S Pacific; *gibsoni* principally occurs in Australasian waters and *antipodensis* mainly east of New Zealand to Chile, with some reaching E Australia, whilst *dabbenena* is principally confined to the S Atlantic. Thus, identification of Wanderers should always rely on a combination of features and, in most cases, an analysis of age and sex should be made in tandem with specific identification. It is important for the observer to be fully aware of plumage progression in those taxa for which data are available. However, this process is often very difficult, notably with birds at sea, and very often impractical at long distance. It is beyond the scope of this guide to comprehensively cover all aspects of plumage maturation, but some comments are worth making, whilst Plates 4 and the photographs should provide a stimulus to practise identifying members of the group. I also recommend that observers leave unidentified those lacking clear-cut characteristics of any taxon of assumed age/sex, or any showing atypical or intermediate characteristics. As repeated several times, the information presented here represents an ongoing study of the field identification of the *Diomedea [exulans]* group and should be regarded as work in progress.

Plumage maturation and variation in Wanderers. Learning the plumage differences of the various age classes, their variability and progression to adulthood, and the sexual differences of each of the five Wanderers is integral to the identification process. Initially this can be practised at colonies, especially if many birds have been tagged, when they can be photographed and compared, permitting a more reliable knowledge of plumage maturation within a given taxon. Such information may later be used with birds away from the breeding grounds. Bear in mind, however, that the plumages of birds aged 1–4/5 years (which are away from the colony) are rather poorly known. Though some return as early as three years old, it is unknown if these individuals are a random subset of three-year olds or perhaps fast-maturing birds that return to the colony early. Ageing, and sometimes sexing, should be carefully assessed by a combination of plumage pattern on the upperwing and tail, and on the body; see also comments below regarding use of size differences, which sometimes acquire importance. At sea, such efforts will be most reliable if dealing with a close group

Left two images Wanderers: Wandering Albatross D. [e.] exulans (top), probably younger ad male or older ad female. Off South Georgia, Mar 2006; and older ad male Gibson's Albatross D. [e.] gibsoni (bottom), Chatham Rise, New Zealand, Jan 2007. Right two images Southern Royal Albatrosses D. [e.] epomophora: younger imm (top) and ad (bottom), Kaikoura, South I, New Zealand, Jan 2005 and 2003. © Hadoram Shirihai.

These photographs illustrate some of the principal differences between non-brown Wanderers (namely exulans, dabbenena, gibsoni and whiter male antipodensis) and Southern Royal Albatross. When comparing younger or less white birds (upper images), note Southern Royal's greyish-white 'dusting' on the upperwing-coverts, creating a more uniform and diffuse pattern, which when older will appear to whiten from the leading edge back (in exulans, white markings bolder and concentrated on the central upperwing-coverts, and appears to whiten from this area outwards). Narrow white leading edge to upperwing of young Southern Royal is rarely solid but is of even width and consistently present (this feature is, however, not useful in ads, as both species have extensive white leading edges). Comparing older ad plumages, when both species possess almost similar amounts of white on the upperwing-coverts, note the pattern in Southern Royal is more diffuse due to same 'dusting' effect on fore coverts and around the smaller 'elbow' patch. Also note that: tail colour is age-dependent, Wandering's pink neck mark varies individually (absent in bottom left bird), and the black cutting edge to the bill is a diagnostic of Royal but is often difficult to see in flight. These all require consideration when arriving at an identification (see species accounts). Northern Royal (not shown here) is less likely to be confused with non-brown Wanderers due to its combination of solid dark wings and purer white plumage (Wanderers with uniform dark wings usually show less clean white plumage and more black in tail), whilst other characters that separate Southern Royal also apply to Northern (see account and photographs).

of birds (of mixed taxa/ages) on the water, when useful comparisons can be made. Occasionally, some taxa can be reliably but approximately aged, and sometimes even sexed, given a reasonably close view, especially with prior knowledge and experience. Due to limited space here moult patterns are not described, as they are of limited use for ageing birds at sea, but occasionally offer some clues, especially if birds are seen and photographed well in flight. Some authors have proposed use of a single plumage index to describe all Wanderers and their variation, but this is problematic because plumage maturation differs considerably between taxa and is also sex-related. Such an index for the entire group is also insufficient (and will probably never satisfy keen observers) to be useful in field separation of the five forms, since it lacks unique characteristics that can assist to separate the different taxa. Instead, I have found it preferable to separately describe each distinctive plumage, comparing it with those of other taxa. It is convenient to consider plumage maturation within four broad age classes. The first plumage (**juv**) is that acquired upon fledging, which is moulted at sea from c.1 year old (in second-winter), and is dusky-/chocolate-brown with a white face in all taxa. With each successive moult (**younger imm**, until c.3–4 years old), the brown body feathering is replaced with progressively whiter basal feathers in *exulans*, *dabbenena*, *gibsoni* and some pale male *antipodensis*; this process is more rapid on the underparts (especially belly, which whitens first) than the upperparts, with both becoming extensively blotched and, subsequently, vermiculated (generally more patchy on the neck- and body-sides, but more boldly mottled on the mantle to rump). With age (**older imm**, 4–5 to c.9 years old), as birds start to visit their natal islands, these marks reduce in

extent and below are limited to the sides, especially on the breast (which can appear as a pectoral band), with variable dark feathers on the head/neck, especially cap, and narrower wavy vermiculations usually being retained until this stage, if not for life. The uniform dark upperwing is last to whiten, mainly from the central/inner upperwing-coverts (except in *amsterdamensis* and *antipodensis* and, to a lesser extent, in *gibsoni* and *dabbenena* which remain largely dark). Finally ad plumage (**ad**) is acquired, which initially and often variably, continues to show vestiges of immaturity and to change with age (see below). Observers should be aware that the degree of whitening again varies between taxa and in relation to sex (process more rapid and extensive in males), being subject to greater acceleration in some taxa and further complicated because most female *amsterdamensis* and *antipodensis*, and to some degree *dabbenena*, variably retain some dark juv-/imm-like features. All forms, however, continue to whiten with increasing age, even at 10–20 years old or more. But, even within forms, the details differ. For instance, detailed studies of *exulans* at Crozet and South Georgia reveal that those at the latter whiten faster and become overall whiter. It appears that whitening is to some extent a clinal character linked to latitude (South Georgia being further south than Crozet).

Use of size differences. Especially without previous experience and if observing lone birds, size is of very limited use in ageing/sexing and identification of Wanderers at sea (much overlap between all taxa). However, where several forms and sexes mix, e.g. around a boat (mainly if closely grouped on the water), thus permitting accurate size comparisons, this may be used, with care, as a supporting character. Examples include the smaller

Imm Southern Royal Albatrosses Diomedea [epomophora] epomophora. *Witihin colonies of both Royals and Wanderes, birds of both sexes and all ages, including non-breeders and breeders prior to laying, congregate to display; however, most birds involved in such displays are unmated subads. Campbell I, Jan 1999. © Hadoram Shirihai*

dabbenena (Atlantic) and *gibsoni* (Pacific) against *exulans*, where in some cases differences are rather obvious. It is important to remember that females of all forms are usually noticeably smaller and slighter, especially around the head/neck, and the bill can be less deep-based and more delicate. When considering size differences between the forms, this is most reliably used as an identification aid by simultaneously endeavouring to age and sex the birds, and compare their plumage patterns.

Separation, ageing and sexing of Royals. Away from the breeding islands separation of Northern and Southern Royals is rather easy (ads and imms) and even, with practice, most juvs can be reliably identified (see above and the relevant accounts). Unlike Wanderers, both Royals have a first plumage almost as white as ads, and only Southern Royal exhibits age differences in upperwing pattern. Both young Royals also have some dark-tipped tail feathers, and whilst Northern Royal remains almost unchanged in upperwing pattern, it has a variable dark-mottled back and rump markings which disappear with age. Like Wanderers, the sexes differ rather considerably in size and structure (in direct comparison on the nesting grounds or on the water the differences are noticeable). For further details see relevant accounts.

New comments (2nd edition). Even after ten years of field work, on or around the breeding grounds of all taxa, and in attempting their identification elsewhere in the S Indian, Pacific and Atlantic Oceans (backed-up by studies of plumage variation in photographs of over 1000 individuals), I still feel very cautious about offering hard and fast 'rules'. Mostly ad Wanderers (and only under optimal and/or comparative circumstances) should be identified. My recent observations show that there is great variability and overlap, making seperation of the various forms away from the breeding islands very problematic. Since the first edition, I visited the breeding areas of all these forms again, being especially fortunate to photograph over 130 individuals of *dabbenena* during two visits to Gough and the Tristan group in 2003 and 2006, and to study the plumages of nearly 40 *amsterdamensis* during my visit to Amsterdam Island's central plateau, in 2004. My recent observations concur with Ryan's (2000) report of delayed maturation in *dabbenena*, and reveal that the latter has imm plumages virtually identical to *amsterdamensis* (or ad female *antipodensis*). This type of non-breeding imm (see photographs, p.94) perhaps went unrecorded because the birds apparently mostly gather around Gough, but very seldom visit the island itself. This plumage is probably sometimes confused with juv plumage, as in the recently published photograph (no. 3, p.65, *Field guide to Tristan de Cunha and Gough Island*, 2007). Furthermore, such an *amsterdamensis*-like *dabbenena* was subject to much controversy (see photograph on p.100, first edition). Only following these recent observations is it possible to certainly determine the latter to be imm *dabbenena*, and further suggests that probably all (or most) claims of *amsterdamensis* / *antipodensis* in the Atlantic involve such imm *dabbenena*.

Life cycles and conservation of the great albatrosses

Being oblivious to the threat posed by humans, on the breeding islands these remarkable seabirds permit stunningly close approach and thus detailed study. Much has been written about the displays of the great albatrosses, certainly far more than can be condensed here. The seven forms share many common or similar displays; nonetheless, even interspecific variation between populations of the same taxon on different islands has been noted. A few of the main displays that might be witnessed by visitors to the breeding islands are described below, but for those interested to delve further into this facet of the lives of the great albatrosses, Tickell's book

(2000) now provides a well-written and readily accessible source.

Within colonies, groups of birds of both sexes and all ages (prior to laying), including non-breeders, congregate to display (though ads arrive earlier). These displays involve similar repertoires in both Royal and Wandering Albatrosses, with the full wing-stretch being unique to this group of albatrosses (although breeding-ad Royals rarely perform full wing displays, except perhaps on first returning to the colony at the start of breeding season). However there are some clear differences in behaviour and vocalizations between Royal and Wandering Albatrosses. The most dynamic and elaborate displays ('dances'), which are accompanied by neighs, groans, wails, croaks, cackles and bill-snapping/-clapping, are often given around nest sites, but other areas may also be used and serve as a kind of 'lekking' site. Most birds involved in these displays are unmated subads, or inexperienced breeders, but, in Wanderers, breeding males may join in early in the season. The main components of these 'dances' and other singular displays are as follows: billing is usually performed by 2–3 individuals facing each other with their bills often touching and mandibles partially open; yapping involves the head being moved vertically up and down with the bill open, emitting loud trilling calls; head-shake and wing-stretching comprise the head being rapidly waved from side to side (gradual stop), tail fanned and wings fully outstretched in a curve towards other individuals, and usually involves distinct bill-clapping; and the gawky-look, where the head is pushed forward, giving the bird a peculiar appearance, which suggests interest in the action of other individuals.

The breeding biologies and life cycles of many of the penguins are remarkable, but in some respects are certainly matched by those of the great albatrosses, which because of their extended immaturity and long breeding seasons can apparently live to 60+ years, the oldest known being a Northern Royal Albatross, the late 'Grandma', which nested at Taiaroa Head, New Zealand. Pair-bonds are usually for life, but Wanderers may re-páir if a mate dies and a system of temporary partners is established prior to the first breeding attempt. Imms first return to the colony at 3–8 years old, but breeding does not occur until 6–22 years of age, though most Wanderers will have bred once by the time they are 13 years old. The presence of varying numbers of younger non-breeders in many colonies provides useful opportunities to study plumage development among imms and to compare these with ads. Between four and five weeks prior to nesting, the breeders return to their colonies. All albatrosses lay one egg, with the date varying according to location and year, e.g. Amsterdam Albatrosses have been noted to commence breeding between 12 Feb and 8 Mar (i.e. two months after other forms within *exulans*). The large white egg weighs c.390–560 g. All forms are loosely colonial, with tens (occasionally hundreds) of metres between nests, which are low mounds of vegetation and soil, often on flat ground near a ridge, where individuals can easily use the wind in take-off. If breeding is successful, ads miss a year before nesting again, usually in the same area (if breeding fails sufficiently early in the season, a replacement clutch may be attempted the following year or even the same year, although always unsuccessfully in the latter case). This system is due to the long breeding cycle: incubation, by both sexes in alternating shifts of usually 2–12 days but occasionally much longer, occupies c.74–85 days; the chicks are then brooded or guarded for 4–6 weeks, with the parents making short feeding visits. Fledging is at c.7–10 months, whereupon the chick is immediately independent. If one of the ads dies once the nestling is beyond the guard phase, a single parent can, at least occasionally, rear the chick successfully.

Historically, the major threats to great albatrosses were direct

Wandering Albatrosses Diomedea [exulans] exulans, *South Georgia, Jan 2001. Left, most probably ad male; such white birds are easily identified at rest or in flight (see p.95, top right photo). © Hadoram Shirihai. Right, probably a younger ad female, which often possess many vestiges of immaturity and, as in this case, may be superficially similar to (and largely unidentifiable from) most ad female* gibsoni *and* dabbenena *or male* antipodensis, *though some have more white in the upperwing-coverts. © Jørgen Mortensen.*

exploitation of ads, chicks and eggs for food, and possible disturbance and predation by introduced animals, namely pigs, sheep, cattle and goats, on some of the subantarctic islands of New Zealand, Tristan and elsewhere. Subsequently, climate events have wrought habitat deterioration on several islands: large storms destroyed significant nesting habitat of Northern Royal Albatross on the Forty Fours and Sisters (Chatham). Most recently, longline tuna and Patagonian toothfish fisheries have induced large-scale mortality in Wanderers. Because males and females, especially among Wanderers, often range over different areas at sea, they are exposed to different risks. (While Wanderers are principally deep-sea birds, Royal Albatrosses most often occur over the continental shelf.) In some populations there is evidence that female Wanderers are more likely to be taken as bycatch at longliners causing significant localized population imbalances. An acute lack of accurate historical counts of breeding colonies has frustrated attempts to obtain information on population trends, but declines in many taxa are now obvious. These require quantification in order that much-needed conservation management programmes can be undertaken, and so that fishing industry and conservation agencies can enforce mitigation measures. Some taxa within the Wandering Albatross superspecies have experienced population declines in excess of 20% over most of their range within recent generations.

Wandering (Snowy) Albatross
Diomedea [*exulans*] *exulans*   Plates 4

Identification

Confusion risks: All forms of Wanderers, principally in younger plumages; also Southern Royal *D.* [*e.*] *epomophora*.
Main characters: The largest Wanderer and when older the whitest. **Ad** in all stages appears very white on body and upperwings, becoming ever purer white with age. Dark vermiculations on body and upperwing-coverts strongly reduced, and oldest/whitest birds (especially males, which more rapidly attain white final plumage) often appear entirely white except black remiges and perhaps some coverts. Old female almost as pale or even whiter than younger ad male but rarely as pure white as whitest old male. Tail varies from wholly or partially black (younger ad and female) to mainly pure white in older males. Massive flesh-coloured bill and pale greyish-pink legs (both may appear reddish when breeding).

(See *antipodensis* for records of occasional Wanderers with black cutting edge to bill.) Many breeding ads have a variable crescentic pink-stained rear ear-covert patch (e.g. c.75% of those at South Georgia); this feature, unique to Wanderers, is more prominent in males than females. **Juv** huge, long-winged and long-bodied; overall blackish chocolate-brown (with wear at sea becomes duller), but contrasting white face from forehead to upper foreneck, and white underwing (small dark extension from body to base of leading edge, otherwise as ad). **Younger imm** typically heavily mottled/blotched and vermiculated, most strongly marked above and on neck/chest and body-sides, with largely uniform dark upperwing (at most only a hint of small white patches on centre of wing near body and elbow region). **Older imm** (many intermediates between this and previous stage) much whiter, though body still has extensive (but narrower) vermiculations; head and neck mostly whitish (crown usually still dark); brown upperpart feathering and that on neck/chest strongly reduced and, when most upperwing-coverts have moulted, has bold black-and-white

Wandering Albatross Diomedea [exulans] exulans *with limited white on upperwing-coverts probably suggesting a ad female (here feeding a chick); thus superficially similar to (or inseparable from) most ad male* gibsoni *and* dabbenena. *Kerguelen, Nov 1999. © Hadoram Shirihai.*

(checkerboard-like) pattern typical of form. Upperwing-coverts pattern usually unbroken and distinctive in fresh birds (note extensive white covert fringes in very close views), thus making coverts appear very pale, contrasting with darker remiges and offering an important character for the identification of this taxon (see below). With bleaching often has large white panel on coverts, disrupting checkerboard pattern, and pattern even of fresh birds, if seen distantly, is difficult to appreciate and may appear different side-on (best appreciated close to and from above). Tail still wholly or largely black. Such birds approach **younger ad**, which becomes progressively much purer white (including upperwing-coverts).

Voice: See introduction concerning vocal and nuptial displays on breeding grounds, but note that the same sounds, mainly the guttural and croaking noises, and bill-clapping, are also used at sea during disputes over food. No comparative analyses across geographical variation of Wanderers. Some single-island vocalization studies are summarized in Tickell (2000).

Size: 1.1–1.35 m, wingspan 2.5–3.5 m (these figures refer to the entire *exulans* complex), wing 62–79 cm, weight 6.35–11.3 kg. Female averages smaller than male in culmen, tarsus, tail and wing measurements, and overall weight, but reasonably extensive overlap in all.

Similar forms: Juv and younger imm usually unidentifiable from most other Wanderers in similar plumages. Older imm and especially older ads possess more extensive white plumage, most notably on upperwing-coverts, than any other form (except extremes of *dabbenena*, which see; compare also extreme white *gibsoni*). As mentioned, older imm attains upperwing-coverts with alternate white and black fringes, forming distinctive checkerboard pattern that may extend across entire coverts and which is characteristic in both form and extent (again, a few ad male *dabbenena* and *gibsoni* may show a very similar pattern, but white fringes tend to be less extensive and the overall pattern less bold). Also note comparatively larger overall size and robust bill. Separated from both Royal Albatrosses by lack of black cutting edge to upper mandible and, depending on age, both Royals exhibit different wing/tail patterns to any form of Wandering (see Royal Albatrosses for some problematic cases; this pitfall is also discussed and illustrated in the introduction to the great albatrosses).

Distribution and biology

Distribution, movements and population: Southern Ocean on South Georgia, Prince Edward, Marion, Crozet, Kerguelen, Heard, McDonald and Macquarie, ranging at sea mostly south of 22°S and a rare vagrant north of the equator. Annual breeding population estimated at 8500 pairs, with perhaps an overall total of 55,000 individuals (28,000 mature) based on 1980s and 1990s counts.

Diet and feeding: Cephalopods, largely scavenged, with some fish and rarely crustaceans, mostly taken by surface-seizing, some shallow-plunging and pursuit-plunging. Max. diving depth 1 m. Attracted to boats, where regularly consorts with other tubenoses and is dominant over most seabirds in such feeding 'frenzies', but avoids such dense feeding groups at trawlers off S Africa. Also associates with several cetacean species.

Social behaviour: Gregarious in breeding season, less so at sea, though small groups may congregate at food sources; exceptionally up to 500 scavenging offal at a longline vessel near the Prince Edwards. Monogamous, pair-bond life-long, though divorces not unknown. Well-defined aggressive and courtship displays (for details see introduction to the great albatrosses).

Breeding biology: Breeds (biennially if successful) in mid-Dec–Feb onwards, in areas of short vegetation with near-bare area for take-off, on coastal plains and valley floors, and sometimes with giant petrels *Macronectes* spp. Nest a truncated cone of grass, twigs, roots and soil with central depression. Lays one whitish egg with some diffuse red spots at broad end, incubated 75–83 days. Chicks fledge in 258–288 days. Single-brooded. Both sexes incubate and provision young.

Non-breeding Wandering Albatross Diomedea [exulans] exulans *on South Georgia, with younger ad males (two left-hand birds; note relatively large size and heavy build, and reduced amount of white on upperwing, but clean white crown and well-vermiculated white upperparts) and younger ad female (at right; slighter appearance and virtually all-dark upperwing). In the left-hand birds note the bold black and white fringes forming the checkerboard-like pattern on upperwing-coverts. In this plumage the taxon is largely indistinguishable from many ad male Tristan* D. [e.] dabbenena *and whitest older ad male Gibson's Albatrosses* D. [e.] gibsoni. *South Georgia, Mar 2006. © Hadoram Shirihai.*

Fresh juv Wandering Albatross Diomedea [exulans]. Juv plumage (uniform brown except white face and underwing) is similar in all forms of the complex, but the relatively small size (and location) suggest gibsoni *or* antipodensis *in this case. Subantarctic waters off New Zealand, Feb 2007. © Hadoram Shirihai.*

Young imm Wandering Albatross Diomedea [exulans] exulans showing characteristic mottled upperparts and uniform upperwing-coverts and dark cap emphasizing whitish face. Taxon identification by range alone (such plumage also exists in other forms of Wanderers). Between Kerguelen and Crozet, Nov 1999. © Hadoram Shirihai.

Wandering Albatross Diomedea [exulans] exulans. Combination of extensive brown neck and chest, but whiter upperparts and rear underparts, and already some white on elbow region, suggests young imm exulans*, which tends to whiten rather rapidly; also large strong bill supports* exulans*, whilst location is an important aid to identification. Off South Georgia, Jan 2001. © Hadoram Shirihai.*

Wandering Albatross Diomedea [exulans] exulans, probably imm male or younger ad female, with still quite extensive dark feathering on head, back and breast, mostly dark upperwing, but clean white belly. Taxon identification by range (such plumage also exists in near-ad, mostly female dabbenena *and* gibsoni*). Off Kerguelen, Mar 2004. © Hadoram Shirihai.*

Wandering Albatross Diomedea [exulans] exulans, apparently younger ad female given already extensively white body, but tail and upperwing largely black (small white patch at 'elbow'); taxon identification by location as, in such plumage, is indistinguishable from many ad Tristan D. [e.] dabbenena and Gibson's Albatrosses D. [e.] gibsoni. Off South Georgia, Mar 2006. © Hadoram Shirihai.

Wandering Albatross Diomedea [exulans] exulans, probably ad female or older imm male, showing relatively large amount of white in upperwing-coverts, forming typical checkerboard-like pattern. Taxon identification by range (such plumage, mostly in ad males, also exists in dabbenena *and* gibsoni*). Off Kerguelen, Nov 1999. © Hadoram Shirihai.*

Wandering Albatross Diomedea [exulans] exulans. *Many older imm, younger ad males or older ad females show such extensive white on central upperwing. Taxon identification by range (such plumage also exists in older male* dabbenena *and* gibsoni). *Off South Georgia, Mar 2006.* © *Hadoram Shirihai.*

Ad male Wandering Albatross Diomedea [exulans] exulans; *extensive white on upperwing-coverts conclusive for sexing; taxon identification by range (only separable from whitest* dabbenena *by overall larger size and heavier bill). Off Kerguelen, Mar 2004.* © *Hadoram Shirihai.*

Conservation Vulnerable and some populations declining. Numbers taken as bycatch in S Atlantic, Indian and Pacific Oceans by longliners is almost certainly the most significant threat. The tiny Macquarie population has again been brought to a critically low level, possibly because of this practice, having previously recovered from the devastation wrought by sealers in the 19th century. Rates of decline in different insular populations have been ascribed to fishing grounds used by each and extent of overlap with commercial fisheries, but some colonies (e.g. at Possession) have declined by up to 50% during last two decades and those breeding at South Georgia at rate of 1% per annum since 1979.

Taxonomy Recent advances in understanding of albatross taxonomy have affected this species, which was formerly considered polytypic, with nominate *exulans* throughout most of the species' range, being replaced by *dabbenena* on Gough and Inaccessible (and formerly Tristan da Cunha), *antipodensis* on the Antipodes and Campbell groups, and *gibsoni* in the Auckland group. All may be sufficiently distinct to warrant specific status, but see introduction to the great albatrosses. According to the rules of nomenclature, Tristan Albatross may take the name *exulans* with *dabbenena* a synonym, whilst '*chionoptera*' is perhaps applicable to those populations at southern latitudes (South Georgia and S Indian Ocean, with a few pairs at Macquarie, here treated as nominate *exulans*).

Tristan Albatross
Diomedea [*exulans*] *dabbenena*   Plate 4

Identification

Confusion risks: Other Wandering Albatrosses.

Main characters: Large, but comparatively slighter, more compact and smaller than *exulans*, and ad typically less extensively white. **Ad** has relatively delayed and reduced whitening process. Upperwing predominantly black-brown, white being limited to central ('elbow') and inner-covert patches; whiter/older male has rather extensive white 'elbow', but on rest of coverts only small white spots, barely approaching strong black-and-white pattern of most older imm or younger ad *exulans* (which see), whilst most females retain almost uniformly dark upperwing-coverts. Body rather purer

white with narrow, dark, pencil-thin vermiculations (especially older males), but young ad males and all females tend to be extensively vermiculated and irregularly blotched greyish or dusky, especially on body-sides, producing prominent breast-band. Thus, substantial sexual dimorphism apparent, overall not dissimilar to that in Gibson's Albatross *D.* [*e.*] *gibsoni* (which see). Tail variable, most largely or almost all black. Nevertheless, older ad males with almost all-white upperwing-coverts and no dark feathers visible in tail have been photographed on Gough (P. Ryan & M. de Villiers pers. comm.), and such extreme white males also recently noted by HS in the surrounding waters (see photographs). Such males are identical in plumage to ad males of nominate *exulans*. Bare parts mostly as *exulans* (which see); see also *antipodensis* for records of Wanderers with black cutting edge to bill. Only a relatively small number of breeding ads have the prominent crescentic pink patch on rear ear-coverts. **Juv** has characteristic paler, greyer tone to dark chocolate-brown plumage (Ryan 2000), otherwise as other Wanderers. **Younger imm** largely unknown, but presumably not dissimilar to *exulans* and especially *gibsoni*, being heavily mottled/blotched and vermiculated, most strongly marked above and on neck/breast and body-sides; birds assigned to this form apparently have uniformly dark upperwings. **Older imm** (many intermediate between this and previous stage) males generally approach ad females, having much paler body at this stage, though tends to have greyish wash to white feathers, which are still extensively and densely vermiculated, affording typical dusky appearance, whilst crown often still dark, and nape and neck/chest still rather extensively blotched brown, emphasizing whitish face and darker mottled breast-band; also, upperwing-coverts still largely uniform dark, with at most only hint of small white patch in centre of wing near body and elbow region; tail still wholly or extensively black. Female *dabbenena* of this age class (or probably even when younger, perhaps 3–4 years old) highly characteristic, being very similar in pattern to *amsterdamensis* (or brown ad female *antipodensis*), with mostly brown upperparts, solid dark upperwings and dusky brown body-sides, neck and head, contrasting with rather well-defined whitish face and belly (see photos). Some such birds have a rather obvious dusky bill tip on the unguis.

Voice: See Wandering Albatross *D.* [*e.*] *exulans*.

Size: Noticeably smaller/slighter build than *exulans*, but much overlap between male *dabbenena* and female *exulans*; culmen

Ad female Tristan Albatross Diomedea [exulans] dabbenena. Note duskier appearance with numerous marks on head/neck, mantle, breast and flanks. Gough, Sep 2001. © Peter Ryan.

Ad male Tristan Albatross Diomedea [exulans] dabbenena. Extensively white plumage, but on upperwing-coverts white is restricted to elbow region and white over rest is rather weak (not forming bold checkerboard-like pattern of exulans though much individual variation and overlap in this character between forms). Plumage identical to younger ad female D. [e.] exulans and ad male Gibson's Albatross D. [e.] gibsoni. Gough, Sep 2001. © Peter Ryan.

length can discriminate all birds, especially if sex known (max 151 mm in one sample, sexes combined, against minimum 155 mm for exulans); as in other Wanderers females clearly average smaller than males. Very similar in size to gibsoni and antipodensis.

Similar forms: Faced with birds away from the breeding islands, dabbenena, exulans and gibsoni may prove inseparable. Juv dabbenena leaves nest with paler, greyer wash to brown plumage than exulans, but it is unknown how this changes at sea. Ad dabbenena appears to have much-delayed process of plumage whitening, retaining dark barring and duskier wash on underparts for longer (relative to upperparts), and can appear to possess promi-

nent breast-band as a result, whilst upperwing usually appears almost solidly dark and very contrasting (with limited white patch near base and elbow region). It seems that only very few, oldest ad male dabbenena attain amount of white feathering on upperwing-coverts of exulans; most dabbenena also seem to have less strongly marked black-and-white upperwing-covert pattern of older imm and ad exulans, but much overlap now known. Perhaps, with

Tristan Albatross Diomedea [exulans] dabbenena, apparently younger imm female (probably of 3 or 4 years old, at age of first return to Gough). In the Atlantic, this plumage appears highly characteristic, but is virtually identical to amsterdamensis and brown ad female antipodensis, with mostly uniform brown upperparts, dusky body-sides, neck and head, contrasting with rather well-defined whitish face and belly. Note slight dusky/greenish bill tip on mandibular unguis. Off Gough, Mar 2003 and 2006. © Hadoram Shirihai.

Older/whitest ad male Tristan Albatross Diomedea [exulans] dabbenena. Extensive white on body and upperwing-coverts. Plumage identical to ad male D. [e.] exulans but note smaller size and slighter build, with smaller bill, as well as location. Off Gough, Mar 2003. © Hadoram Shirihai.

Ad male Tristan Albatross Diomedea [exulans] dabbenena, showing extensively white plumage, but on upperwing-coverts white restricted to 'elbow' and white tips on rest of coverts rather extensive but narrower and less bold than exulans (overall plumage slightly less advanced than that of incubating male; see p. 94). Note also slighter build. Off Gough, Mar 2003. © Hadoram Shirihai.

Tristan Albatross Diomedea [exulans] dabbenena, apparently older imm male (or ad female): dirty whitish body, blotched brownish on mantle and chest, dark cap and uniform dark upperwings, all of which are characteristic. Species identification is, however, still based on location (and perhaps by apparently slight build), as in such plumage is indistinguishable from imms of several other Wanderers. Off Gough, Mar 2006. © Hadoram Shirihai.

experience and in direct comparison, some *dabbenena*, including whiter examples, can be separated by their overall relatively smaller size, especially the slighter head and bill. Furthermore, imm *dabbenena* females (see above) with *amsterdamensis*-like (or brown ad female *antipodensis*-like) plumages are, at least in Atlantic, characteristic. In comparison, many younger imm *exulans* with such generally brown plumage tend to lack a well-defined pale belly and whitish face, these areas being already more ill-defined or broken due to more strongly mottled and blotched dark surrounding plumage. Such imm *dabbenena* females are virtually inseparable from brown ad female/imm *antipodensis* (and are also rather similar to some younger imm *gibsoni*), and are only separated from *amsterdamensis* by lack of latter's Royal-like black cutting edge to the upper mandible. In such plumage many (but not all) *amsterdamensis* and especially *antipodensis* have the characteristic dark cap and head-sides, whilst at least in most younger imm *dabbenena* these are definitely lacking, but this character is often difficult to appreciate at moderate or long distances. I have not found a single consistent character useful at sea to separate *dabbenena* from *gibsoni* (most ages). Fortunately, the degree of overlap in ranges between *dabbenena* and *gibsoni/antipodensis* is relatively minimal. For comparison with Royal Albatrosses see these forms.

Distribution and biology

Distribution, movements and population: Tristan da Cunha group (Gough, Inaccessible, and formerly Tristan da Cunha), ranging at sea through S Atlantic Ocean (between at least 23°S and 42°S) to W coast of South Africa and to within c.300 km of the coast of Brazil, although as yet there are only six records for the latter country, and SW Indian Ocean, with one record from SE Australia. Annual breeding population estimated at c.1000 pairs, with an overall total of perhaps 9000 individuals in 1999–2000.

Diet and feeding: As Wandering Albatross (which see).

Social behaviour: As Wandering Albatross (which see).

Breeding biology: Breeds (biennially if successful) presumably between Dec and Feb onwards (but few concrete data), in areas

Tristan Albatross Diomedea [exulans] dabbenena: ad male (foreground) showing extensive white plumage, large white elbow patch extending as broad white fringes to rest of upperwing-coverts, creating same checkerboard pattern to smaller coverts as in typical exulans (apparently only a few, very old dabbenena achieve such white in plumage); the bird behind is perhaps an ad female but its relatively strong build is also suggestive of a male, and is thus probably a younger ad or older imm male. Off Gough, Mar 2003. © Hadoram Shirihai.

Tristan Albatross Diomedea [exulans] dabbenena, *apparently older imm by combination of extensively brown lower neck and chest, heavily mottled brown upperparts but whiter body below, uniform dark upperwings, dark cap, and white of face extending to upper neck and nape. Taxon identification is still based solely on location (as in such plumage indistinguishable from imms of several other Wanderers). Off Gough, Mar 2003. © Hadoram Shirihai.*

devoid of shrubby vegetation above 300 m (principally at 400–700 m), with near-bare area for take-off. Loosely colonial. Nest a truncated cone of grass, twigs, roots and soil with central depression. Lays one whitish egg with some diffuse red spots at broad end, incubated for c.68 days, but no information concerning fledging period. Single-brooded. Both sexes incubate and provision young. **Conservation** Endangered and overall population has declined, though numbers currently stable on Gough and a recent proposal suggests it should be downlisted to Vulnerable. Feral pigs and humans considerably reduced numbers on Inaccessible (where not more than three pairs have been recorded since 1950s) and its extirpation from Tristan da Cunha (where birds have recently been observed prospecting) was also primarily through direct exploitation, though rat predation perhaps hastened decline. Numbers taken as bycatch in S Atlantic, Indian and Pacific Oceans by longliners is almost certainly the most significant current threat, but these have yet to be quantified except off Brazil; data from elsewhere are urgently required.
Taxonomy Formerly considered a subspecies of *exulans* but molecular work suggests it is sufficiently distinct to warrant specific status, a treatment underscored by further such data (it being genetically the basal taxon within the group). Obviously, more awaits discovery concerning relationships within the great albatrosses (see introduction for further information regarding the taxonomic debate). See note under *exulans* concerning nomenclature of the latter and Tristan Albatross.

Gibson's Albatross
Diomedea [exulans] gibsoni   Plate 4

Identification
Confusion risks: All forms of Royal (but only when viewed distantly and in the case of a few confusingly plumaged birds) and Wandering, but most similar to (and unidentifiable in some plumages from) *antipodensis* and *dabbenena*.
Main characters: Large, but smaller and slighter than *exulans*. **Ad**

generally appears less pure white on body than *exulans* and upperwing predominantly black-brown, with usually limited white central patch on inner coverts near body and around 'elbow'. All ads tend to be rather clearly sexually differentiated, with most females having more extensive dark caps (lost with age and wear in most males), heavier barring, dirtier white parts and darker upperwing, but individual and age-related variation obscure differences. When older, becomes overall purer white with finer dark vermiculations on body, especially in males. Furthermore, some older males (the whitest) develop quite extensive white on wing, similar to the extent in younger ad male *exulans* (see below). Tail varies from wholly to partially black, only in some older males does it appear pure white or almost so. Bare parts mostly as *exulans*. (See *antipodensis* for records of Wanderers with black cutting edge to bill.) A relatively small number of breeding ads have crescentic pink patch on rear ear-coverts, but is often quite reduced when present. **Juv** No known differences from *exulans*. **Younger imm**, presumably of this form and age (around New Zealand), has heavily mottled/blotched and vermiculated body, uniformly dark upperwing, with no unique character to separate it from same-age *exulans* (though latter may have some white on coverts) or, especially, from *dabbenena*, though usually paler than most, but not all, similar-age *antipodensis*. Thus, identification of youngest *gibsoni* currently appears impractical at sea, except on range. Older imm (many intermediates between this and previous stage) has much paler body, but tends to retain dirtier

Older ad male Gibson's Albatross Diomedea [exulans] gibsoni *with relatively extensive white 'elbow' and inner coverts, whilst fore-coverts extensively fringed white, creating very similar checkerboard pattern to advanced imm and ad* exulans. *Body overall white with limited vermiculations on mantle and scapulars, and few dark flecks on crown, though tail still mainly black. Note relatively slighter build, including head and bill, characterizing this form. Even in known range,* gibsoni *in such plumage can be extremely difficult to separate from* exulans, *especially without prior experience of the group, whilst outside such area separation from* exulans *and* dabbenena *is impractical. Chatham Rise, New Zealand, Jan 2007. © Hadoram Shirihai.*

the wing-coverts are probably still never completely white (unlike older ad male *exulans*) and usually exhibits a less bold checkerboard pattern than younger ad male or older female *exulans*. Even in New Zealand's subantarctic, and Tasmanian, waters separation of *gibsoni*, *antipodensis* and *exulans*, even of ads, will often prove impractical. Separation from the extremely similar *dabbenena* is virtually impossible at sea, except using range. Separated from both Royal Albatrosses by lack of black cutting edge to upper mandible and, depending on age, they usually have clearly different upperwing patterns, but for possible confusion plumages see the latter forms.

Distribution and biology

Distribution, movements and population: Auckland group, females range to Tasman Sea and males northeast to the mid-Pacific and slightly west at lower latitudes, at least during breeding season. Annual mean breeding population is 5800 pairs, with perhaps an overall total of 40,000 individuals in late 1990s.

Diet and feeding: As Wandering Albatross (which see).

Social behaviour: As Wandering Albatross (which see).

Breeding biology: Breeds (biennially if successful) from mid-Jan, in areas of short vegetation with near-bare area for take-off, on coastal plains and valley floors. Nest a truncated cone of grass, twigs, roots and soil with central depression. Lays one whitish egg with some diffuse red spots at broad end, but no specific data concerning incubation or fledging periods. Single-brooded. Both sexes incubate and provision young.

Conservation Vulnerable (treated as conspecific with *antipodensis* in most-recent examination of conservation status; BirdLife International 2004). Feral pigs and cats have reportedly considerably reduced numbers, though their effect has declined significantly. Its breeding grounds form part of a nature reserve and World Heritage Site, but significant numbers were taken as bycatch in New Zealand

Gibson's Albatross Diomedea [exulans] gibsoni, ad, probably older female, showing mostly black upperwing and tail, extensive dark vermiculations above and flecking on crown. Relative size and range are important aids to identification. Chatham Rise, New Zealand, Jan 2007. © Hadoram Shirihai.

and densely vermiculated white feathering, often admixed with brownish blotches; crown frequently extensively dark, upperwing-coverts largely uniformly dark or possess small white patch on central inner coverts, and tail still entirely or mainly black. Such birds approach younger ad, both of which most likely to be confused with *antipodensis*, especially male (but see below).

Size: Averages smaller than *exulans* in most measurements and overall weight of both sexes. Wing 60–70 cm, weight 5.5–11.0 kg. Culmen length can discriminate many birds (range 133–162 mm in one sample, sexes combined, against 155–180 mm of *exulans*). Female averages smaller than male in culmen, tarsus, tail and wing measurements, and overall weight, but considerable overlap in all of these.

Similar forms: Juv and younger imm probably unidentifiable from other Wanderers. Older imm and ad always paler than similar-aged female and most male *antipodensis*, and generally less pure/extensively white than *exulans* of same age/sex. Unlike *antipodensis*, usually has more extensive white patch on inner upperwing-coverts and around 'elbow', and black on crown usually smaller and blotchier. Also lacks characteristic brown ad female *antipodensis*-type plumage, with mostly but variable brown body and distinctive white belly and face pattern. Compared to ad *exulans*, typical ad *gibsoni* combines relatively smaller size and slighter build (including bill) with less clean white body and often some blotching on crown (but body relatively white compared to still mostly dark upperwing-coverts). Especially in comparative situations, when dealing with classic individuals and with previous experience such differences can be useful, but range remains an important factor. Furthermore, in the case of whitest older ad male *gibsoni*

Gibson's Albatross Diomedea [exulans] gibsoni, probably older imm male or younger ad female: note mostly black upperwing and tail, extensive dark blotches and vermiculations above and on chest, and dark-flecked crown. Such birds can be extremely difficult to separate from exulans; relative size and range are important aids to identification. Chatham Rise, New Zealand, Feb 2007. © Hadoram Shirihai.

Older imm or young ad Gibson's Albatross Diomedea [exulans] gibsoni. *Upperwing-coverts still almost uniformly dark. Auckland. © Alan Wiltshire.*

waters and Tasman Sea by longliners until recently, though none has been caught in the last two years for which data is available.

Taxonomy Two recent molecular studies produced differing results, the first suggesting that *gibsoni* is sufficiently distinct to warrant specific status, but the other that *gibsoni* and *antipodensis* should be considered conspecific. Traditionally, *gibsoni* was considered a subspecies of *exulans* and, as mentioned previously, more awaits discovery concerning relationships within *Diomedea* [*exulans*] (see introduction for further information concerning the taxonomic debate).

Classic imm Gibson's Albatross Diomedea [exulans] gibsoni: *the rather large size and strong build (compared with other* gibsoni*) suggest a male, indicating that it is probably an older imm male. Note rather pale body plumage and dark-flecked crown (lacking solid dark cap of* antipodensis*). Away from New Zealand subantarctic and Tasmanian waters, separation of such birds from* exulans *is impractical. Also note the very clear dark cutting edge to the upper mandible, as in Royal Albatrosses and* amsterdamensis *(very rare in all other Wanderers). Chatham Rise, New Zealand, Feb 2007. © Hadoram Shirihai.*

Ad Gibson's Albatrosses Diomedea [exulans] gibsoni *showing variation in white on 'elbow' and dark of cap. The bird in the foreground is the probably the oldest and an ad male, given its larger size and heavy build, including head and bill, and relatively large 'elbow' patch; rest of wing-coverts lack the bolder checkerboard patterns of advanced imm and ad* exulans *though this is variable in both forms. Its body is also overall whiter with only a few dark flecks on crown. Note the quite well-developed crescentic pink ear-coverts patch. Such a bird can be extremely difficult to separate from* exulans *without considering age- and sex-related differences in relative size and plumage characteristics, and range. Kaikoura, South I, New Zealand, Jan 2003. © Hadoram Shirihai.*

Antipodean Albatross
Diomedea [exulans] antipodensis   Plate 4

Identification

Confusion risks: All forms of Wandering Albatross, but most similar to and unidentifiable in certain plumages from *gibsoni*, *dabbenena* and *amsterdamensis*.

Main characters: Large, but smaller and slighter than *exulans*, comparatively dark and very variable. **Ad** often shows clear-cut sexual differences, as most females are (variably) almost all brown and superficially resemble juv. Typical brown ad (most females) appears almost uniform brown, though looks variably blotched (due to slight pale feather bases) on nest or water; in flight most upperparts, neck and very broad breast-band visibly brownish, becoming solid dark brown on fore flanks (below wings) and around legs, vent and undertail-coverts, with extensive white belly and face. Extremely pale ad male has whiter appearance to body, but in close view entire neck, chest and upperparts are blotched brownish-cream and heavily vermiculated, thus almost indistinguishable from many ad female or older imm *gibsoni*. In common with other Wanderers, much individual variation and overlap between sexes, with many intermediates between these examples. Some (especially younger) ad males can be almost as extensively brown as typical ad female, whilst some ad females are rather pale but always have very extensive brown-mottled areas, which can appear as large smudges on neck/breast and body-sides. Ad *antipodensis* almost invariably lacks extensive white feathering on upperwing-coverts, which at the most (and virtually only in ad males) is confined to a small white patch on elbow and inner coverts; they are often also characterized by a clear-cut jet black or blackish-brown crown patch, often (in browner birds) extending as bold dark ear-coverts patch, emphasizing whitish face. Be aware that solid black upperwing and crown cannot be used alone to distinguish *antipodensis* from other imm Wanderers, as nearly all advanced imms, especially females, of all forms can acquire some dark/black marks on crown, superficially like *antipodensis*, which in turn may have a smaller/more smudged black cap. Use of as many features as possible in combination is essential, and ageing/sexing should proceed in tandem with

Ad female Antipodean Albatross Diomedea [exulans] antipodensis. *Combination of extensive brown body with whitish belly and solid dark cap and ear-coverts eliminates juvs and some imm plumages of the complex. Note also, lack of dark cutting edge to bill of Amsterdam Albatross* D. [e.] amsterdamensis, *though probably indistinguishable from latter in plumage. Antipodes, Jan 2000. © Hadoram Shirihai.*

Extreme white ad male Antipodean Albatross Diomedea [exulans] antipodensis, *Antipodes, Jan 2000. © Hadoram Shirihai.*

Ad male (right) and female Antipodean Albatross Diomedea [exulans] antipodensis. *Note high sexual dimorphism, with ad male approaching female Gibson's Albatross* D. [e.] gibsoni *and the brown female similar to Amsterdam Albatross* D. [e.] amsterdamensis. *Antipodes. © Alan Wiltshire.*

Probably older (pale) ad female Antipodean Albatross Diomedea [exulans] antipodensis. Note solid dark upperwing but rather pale body, whilst solid black cap and ear-covert patch, and dark mottling above, are all characteristic, making such birds identifiable even away from the breeding grounds. Between Chatham and Bounties, Feb 2007. © Hadoram Shirihai.

identification. Tail wholly or extensively black. Bare parts mostly as *exulans* (which see) but perhaps more often than latter a few birds, especially young, show a hint of dusky or greenish smudges on unguis. In recent years, I recorded *antipodensis*, as well as *exulans* and *gibsoni* with a dark cutting edge to upper mandible (see photograph in Gibson's account), like Royal Albatrosses and *amsterdamensis*, and P. Ryan (pers. comm.) has noted a similar case in *dabbenena*. I have very occasionally noticed birds of the first three named forms with a hint of dark on the cutting edge (especially if in shadow), but this is never as black or as clear-cut as *amsterdamensis* and the Royal Albatrosses. Small numbers of pale breeding ads, most males, have a much-reduced pink crescent on rear ear-coverts (which apparently also occurs in dark birds, but is invisible). **Juv** not known to differ from *gibsoni* or *exulans* (which see). **Younger imm** never certainly recorded at sea (only dead birds examined); almost all dark/pale buff-brown, with contrasting darker feather centres; blackish crown and head-sides weak (often take form of black crown-sides and ear-coverts patch), though whitish face as contrasting as juv and whitish belly patch is variably developed. Others, presumably of this form, generally slightly paler with stronger mottling (possibly males), but still very dark, especially on neck/breast and body-sides. Possibly never acquires heavy mottling/blotching or dark vermiculations of similar-age *gibsoni* or, by implication, young *exulans*. This plumage requires further documentation. **Older imm** of both sexes darker/browner (especially females) with less white body feathering than corresponding ages/sexes of *gibsoni*; upperwing of this and previous age class still uniformly dark. Such birds may already approach **younger ad** (see ad) and perhaps prove more readily identifiable.
Voice: See Wandering Albatross *D. [e.] exulans*.
Size: Averages smaller than *exulans* but virtually identical to *gibsoni* in most measurements and weight in both sexes. Wing 62–66 cm, weight 5.84–7.46 kg. Female averages smaller than male in culmen, tarsus, tail and wing measurements, and overall weight (extent of overlap unclear).
Similar forms: Until further data available on variation in young birds become available, most will probably be impossible to identify at sea, especially as ageing and sexing is so problematic, though location and season should be kept in mind. It is recommended to only identify ads (and perhaps some older imms) possessing

the classic characters described above, e.g. extensively dark brown females are distinguished (including from juv/younger imm of other Wanderers) by combination of contrasting blackish cap (often extending as dark ear-coverts patch), rest of brown plumage usually mottled slightly paler and belly always whitish, contrasting with dark brown rear underparts and fore flanks. Other extreme is ad male with whitish, extensively vermiculated body, but characteristic solid black crown and upperwing-coverts may distinguish it from very similar, mainly female, *gibsoni*. However, such differences difficult to appreciate unless observed close to, and unless correctly aged/sexed. Extensively brown plumages, mostly female/imm, very similar to *amsterdamensis*, as well as to imm *dabbenena* females (see these forms). Easily distinguished from both Royal Albatrosses given overall dark plumage.

Distribution and biology
Distribution, movements and population: Most occur on the Antipodes, with very few on Campbell, ranging at sea in non-breeding season east to Chile and probably the Patagonian shelf, and west to the Tasman Sea. Annual breeding population estimated at 5150 pairs, with perhaps an overall total of 33,000 individuals in 1995.
Diet and feeding: As Wandering Albatross (which see).
Social behaviour: As Wandering Albatross (which see).
Breeding biology: Breeds (biennially if successful) from mid-Jan (mid-Feb on Campbell), among tussac grass in coastal plains and valley floors. No differences known between this form and *gibsoni* (which see).
Conservation Vulnerable (treated as conspecific with *gibsoni* in most-recent review of conservation status; BirdLife International 2004). Cattle and sheep have been removed from Campbell and its entire breeding grounds form part of a nature reserve and World Heritage Site, but significant numbers have been taken as bycatch in New Zealand waters by longliners, and given its long migrations it is probably also affected by mid-ocean longline fishing. Lack of comparable data prevent accurate estimation of the extent of the problem.
Taxonomy See note under *gibsoni* concerning the current taxonomic status of *antipodensis*.

Classic ad male Antipodean Albatross Diomedea [exulans] antipodensis. Note extensive dense vermiculations to whitish body and strikingly solid black crown and upperwing-coverts. Kaikoura, South I, New Zealand, Jan 2005. © Hadoram Shirihai.

Amsterdam Albatross
Diomedea [exulans] amsterdamensis   Plate 4

Identification

Confusion risks: All juv and younger imm forms of Wanderer; most similar to, and often indistinguishable from, many young and female *antipodensis* (see below).

Main characters: Large, but smaller and somewhat slighter than *exulans*, comparatively darker and rather variable. **Ad** does not show clear-cut differences between sexes, both having largely dark brown body, with slightly darker or blacker crown and head-sides, white face/throat and upper foreneck, variably producing near all-dark (juv-like) brown plumage, but has whitish belly and brown less uniform, with paler feather bases and some wavy vermiculations to white below. Like other Wanderers, especially males, with age becomes much paler/whiter, especially below, so that dark on underparts is virtually confined to rather narrow breast-band and vent-side patches, but much individual variation and overlap between sexes, and plumage development of both sexes obscures differences. Large pink-coloured bill, with black cutting edge to upper mandible as in Royal Albatrosses, and variable dusky tip; otherwise bare parts mostly as *exulans* (which see). Tail wholly or almost completely black. For further details and similarity to *antipodensis* see below. **Juv** not known to differ from other juv Wanderers, but bill has diagnostic black cutting edge to upper mandible and variable duskier tip (reports that some fledglings, and probably even a few ads, exhibit weak black cutting edges are unconfirmed, and require documentation; all c.40 individuals I observed recently on Amsterdam had very clear black cutting edges). **Younger imm** completely unknown as does not return to the breeding island during this period and has apparently never been recorded at sea with certainty. **Older imm** differs little from **younger ad**, as in both sexes they are predominately brown. I have examined only a few

Older ad Amsterdam Albatross Diomedea [exulans] amsterdamensis. *With age, especially males, whiten rather considerably (especially around neck and chest), and sexual variation in breeders can be rather obvious. Amsterdam I, Mar 2004. © Hadoram Shirihai.*

apparently advanced non-breeding imms at the colony. Main differences from ad are overall darker, more extensive and solid brown neck, chest and upperparts (few or virtually no pale feather bases visible), with pale belly also restricted and often flecked brown, as well as better-defined white face and upper foreneck. Very similar to darker ad breeding female, making separation of such birds from ad very difficult (see below).

Voice: See Wandering Albatross *D. [e.] exulans*.

Size: 1.1 m, averages smaller than *exulans* in culmen and tail measurements and overall weight in both sexes. Wing 62–67 cm,

Ad male (right) and female Amsterdam Albatross Diomedea [exulans] amsterdamensis. *Note slight sexual differences (male paler). With exception of dark cutting edge to bill and perhaps less intense black cap, on plumage apparently indistinguishable from brownish female Antipodea Albatross D. [e.] antipodensis. Amsterdam I, Mar 1994. © Yann Tremblay.*

Ad/near-ad Amsterdam Albatrosses Diomedea [exulans] amsterdamensis. *At the top centre is probably a non-breeding older imm or younger ad female, given more intense dark brown plumage. Black cutting edge to bill diagnostic in all plumages, but can be difficult to see in flight, whilst combination of brown plumage, uniform dark upperwings, darker cap and clear white face, and whitish belly patch with well-defined dusky sides are characteristic but not diagnostic (see text). Amsterdam I, Mar 2004. © Hadoram Shirihai.*

weight 5–8 kg. Female averages smaller than male in culmen, tarsus, tail and wing measurements, and overall weight (with comparatively little overlap in culmen and wing data).

Similar forms: On present knowledge the black cutting edge to the upper mandible of *amsterdamensis* is its only constant diagnostic character, but note that under certain conditions this can be difficult to detect or judge, and very rarely other Wanderers can appear to show vestiges of this character (see comment under *antipodensis*). Compared to latter, ad *amsterdamensis* also has less clear-cut sexual dimorphism; both sexes are brown and males, even the oldest/palest, are presumably never as whitish as male *antipodensis*. Brown (mainly female) *antipodensis* and typical ad *amsterdamensis* are almost identical, with no single constant or diagnostic plumage characters, though the latter apparently tends to have a browner (less black and clear-cut) crown patch. Other characters claimed to separate *amsterdamensis*, such as dark patches extending more conspicuously from body onto leading edge of underwing and on vent, are based on descriptions made before *antipodensis* was known to be so similar, and appear of no use in their separation. Thus, *amsterdamensis* and *antipodensis* appear very close, perhaps invalidating previous claims concerning the distinctness of *amsterdamensis*. Furthermore, the recent finding that certain plumages of imm (mainly female) *dabbenena* with *amsterdamensis*-like (or brown ad female *antipodensis*-like) plumages further complicates the issue, suggesting that in plumage these three forms away from the breeding grounds are practically inseparable (though *dabbenena* seems quite constantly to lack the solid back/dark cap). The fact that the black cutting edge has (rarely) been recorded in *antipodensis* and *dabbenena* means

Probably older ad male Amsterdam Albatross Diomedea [exulans] amsterdamensis. *Note overall relatively pale plumage. Amsterdam I, Mar 1994. © Yann Tremblay.*

Possible Amsterdam Albatross Diomedea [exulans] amsterdamensis. *On plumage probably indistinguishable from brown ad female Antipodean Albatross but note apparent Amsterdam-like dark cutting edge to bill. Off Sydney, Australia, Oct 1999. © Tony Palliser.*

that any vagrant *amsterdamensis* could only be proven through DNA testing or by reading any ring (most, but not all, *amsterdamensis* are ringed).

Distribution and biology
Distribution, movements and population: Confined as a breeder to Amsterdam I, ranging at sea within S Indian Ocean, possibly east as far as south of Tasmania. Annual breeding population estimated at 15 pairs (in 2000), with perhaps an overall total of c.120 individuals.
Diet and feeding: No specific data, though presumably similar to other Wanderers.

Social behaviour: Gregarious in breeding season, its sociality at sea is more or less unknown. Monogamous; pair-bond life-long. Well-defined aggressive and courtship displays.
Breeding biology: Breeds (biennially if successful) in mid-Feb–early Mar, in areas of tussac grass unaffected by cattle grazing on the island's central plateau, at 470–640 m. Nest a truncated cone of grass, twigs, roots and soil with central depression. Lays one whitish egg with some diffuse red spots at broad end, but no specific data concerning incubation or fledging periods. Single-brooded. Both sexes presumably incubate and provision young.
Conservation Critical, though population has been slowly increasing since advent of monitoring procedures in mid-1980s. Degradation of breeding sites by introduced cattle has led to its being restricted to the island's difficult-of-access central plateau, which has been subject to two fencing operations designed to ensure the area is not subject to incursions by livestock. The population is monitored annually and all birds are banded. Cats may still destroy some eggs and chicks. Some individuals perhaps taken as bycatch by longliners in the 1970s and early 1980s.
Taxonomy Frequently considered sufficiently distinct to warrant specific status from *exulans*, but see above.

Southern Royal Albatross
Diomedea [epomophora] epomophora   Plate 5

Identification
Confusion risks: Imm with Northern Royal Albatross *D.* [e.] *sanfordi* and also with superficially similar whitish plumages of Wanderers.
Main characters: Large, with extensively white plumage at all ages. **Ad** has pure white body and head, with wavy vermiculations almost restricted to scapulars; variable white on upperwing-

Ad Southern Royal Albatross Diomedea [epomophora] epomophora. *Combination of dark cutting edge to bill, and large amount of white in wings and white tail identify it from all congeners. Kaikoura, South I, New Zealand, Feb 2001. © Hadoram Shirihai.*

coverts quite extensive, but generally more so in males, and birds continue to whiten even when quite old. Typically, upperwing-coverts possess ill-defined pattern of whitish-grey/white inner coverts and purer white (small) 'elbow' and marginal/fore coverts, merging with darkish brown-grey (narrowly fringed white) larger and outer coverts, and dark brown remiges. Extremes, usually older males, have purer and more extensively white coverts but, like other ads, in flight overall pattern appears rather uniform, with the greyish fringes/centres creating a 'dusted' look. Superficially, the wing appears to whiten from the leading edge backwards, forming a diagonal border with the darker areas. Tail invariably pure white or almost so. Never has pink-stained rear ear-covert patch of ad Wanderer. Bill massive, flesh-coloured with black cutting edge to upper mandible. Legs and feet pale pinkish-grey. Bare parts pinker with vasodilation and during chick-rearing. **Juv** has body similar to ad, being very white overall, but with some black flecks on rump, back, carpal and crown, and mostly dark upperwing. All upperwing-coverts (see ad) have fewer and much narrower whitish fringes and hence appear almost uniform (depending on angle, some appear rather dark brownish, others more grey-brown). Most usually appear paler on fore- and innermost coverts, and usually has at least a few feathers with white tips/fringes around 'elbow'. With wear upperwing bleaches browner and becomes more uniform. Tail mainly white, with variable black centres especially near tip, forming a, usually indistinct, terminal band. Bare parts as ad but duller. **Younger imm** very similar to juv, but has perhaps slightly purer white body and more extensive whitish fringes to fore and inner-wing coverts, but mostly

Young imm Southern Royal Albatross Diomedea [epomophora] epomophora. *Some white on upperwing (and already quite extensive white leading edge) prevent confusion with Northern Royal D. [e.] sanfordi; note dark cutting edge to bill not always easily detected, but combination of almost all-white tail and diffuse pale flecks on fore/smaller upperwing-coverts separate this individual from any of superficially similar pale plumages in Wanderers D. [exulans]. Kaikoura, South I, New Zealand, Feb 2001. © Hadoram Shirihai.*

Young Southern Royal Diomedea [epomophora] epomophora *(bottom) and Northern Royal Albatrosses D. [e.] sanfordi. Note white leading edge already well developed in former (thus separating them), but this feature, especially in juv/young imm, is often very thin, like many Northern (necessitating care in its use). Kaikoura, South I, New Zealand, Oct 2001. © Hadoram Shirihai.*

Ad Southern Royal Albatross Diomedea [epomophora] epomophora. *Note typical white fore/smaller coverts and triangular elbow patch, and diffuse pale flecking on central and outer coverts. Campbell, Jan 2000. © Hadoram Shirihai.*

unmoulted larger coverts often bleached browner, whilst tail has less black than juv. **Older imm** (some intermediates between this and previous stage) overall much whiter and closer to younger ad in amount of white on wing and tail. However, in both this and previous stage, often has slightly more contrasting white patches on central/inner coverts and 'elbow', and at certain angles in flight may appear superficially similar to whitish Wanderers (older imm and ad), but see below for discussion of such problems.

Voice: See Wandering *D. [e.] exulans* and Northern Royal Albatrosses.

Size: 1.07–1.22 m, wingspan 2.9–3.51 m (figures refer to the entire *epomophora* complex), wing 61–70 cm, weight 6.52–10.3 kg. Female averages smaller than male in culmen, tarsus, tail and wing

Southern Royal Diomedea [epomophora] epomophora *(bottom right) and Gibson's Albatross* D. [exulans] gibsoni, *showing superficial similarity in upperwing pattern (when Royal's diagnostic black cutting edge to bill undetectable). However, Southern Royal appears 'dusted' on the fore-coverts, whereas the pattern is more clean-cut in Wanderers). Note the pure white tail of the Royal but tail colour is age-dependent (and can be similarly white in older Wanderers). Chatham Rise, New Zealand, Jan 2007. © Hadoram Shirihai.*

measurements (no overlap in first three), and overall weight.

Similar forms: In most instances readily differentiated from Northern Royal Albatross by amount of white on upperwing (any Royal with clear white on upperwing is Southern), jizz and leading edge pattern to underwing. The main pitfall is separation of juv Southern, which has the darkest upperwing (superficially like Northern), but even so still possesses at least some pale/whitish feathering on 'elbow' (also noticeable at rest), as well as to some degree the characteristic diffuse, paler inner and fore upperwing-coverts. Some young Southern already develop the broader white leading edge, best seen head-on (usually narrower or lacking in Northern, but much overlap in this feature). Also, differences between the two forms in the dark carpal mark on the underwing seem less consistent in young birds, but is still useful in classic individuals. At close range, easily distinguished from all Wanderers by different upperwing pattern, lack of brown mottling on body in non-ad, and black cutting edge to upper mandible. (See *antipodensis* for notes concerning incidence of this character in Wanderers). As mentioned under older imm, some may appear confusingly similar to white-bodied Wanderers, but usually only prior to examination of upperwing-coverts pattern. In Southern Royal, the whiter fore-coverts extend diffusely and diagonally backwards, with small white 'elbow' surrounded by greyish-fringed/centred coverts visible at some angles. In Wanderers, white is more blotchy, with bold marks concentrated across central wing outwards, usually contrasting with fore-coverts. Some advanced imm or ad *exulans* (and older ad *gibsoni* and *dabbenena*) have distinctive bold checkerboard-like pattern to upperwing-coverts, quite unlike the diffuse pattern of Southern Royal. Moreover, many Wanderers with confusing upperwings have much more extensive black on tail (predominately white in *epomophora*), but some older male Wanderers acquire clean white tails too. With experience, there are some trifling structural differences: Southern Royal tends to be more humpbacked, less narrow-winged with a broader wing base and often appears longer/thicker necked in flight. This pitfall is also discussed and illustrated in the introduction to the great albatrosses.

Distribution and biology

Distribution, movements and population: Campbell, with a much smaller population on Enderby in the Auckland group. Annual breeding population estimated at 8200–8600 pairs, with an overall total of perhaps 28,000 individuals in the late 1990s. Ranges at sea between 36°S and 63°S in S Atlantic and Indian Oceans, and Australian waters. Reaches north to 18°S off Chile.

Diet and feeding: Cephalopods with some fish, crustaceans and salps, mostly taken by surface-seizing and some shallow-plunging. Attracted to boats, where regularly consorts with other tubenoses.

Social behaviour: Gregarious in breeding season, less so at sea, though groups may congregate at food sources. Monogamous; pair-bond life-long. Well-defined aggressive and courtship displays.

Breeding biology: Breeds (biennially if successful) in late Nov–Dec onwards, usually on ridges, peat bogs or leeward slopes with tussac grass. Nest a mound of grass, moss, ferns and other vegetation with central depression. Lays one whitish egg with some red spots at broad end, incubated 78–80 days. Chicks fledge in 224–253 days. Single-brooded. Both sexes incubate and provision young.

Conservation Vulnerable. Numbers thought stable or slightly increasing, but interpretation of counts is difficult due to different census techniques. Humans and introduced mammals had wrought large declines and local extirpations by the late 1800s, and pigs and cats may still take eggs and chicks on Enderby. The spread of scrub on Campbell and Enderby, as a result of climatic changes, may have an effect, but numbers taken as bycatch mid-ocean and in New Zealand and Australian waters by longliners are miniscule, just 15 individuals in the last ten years. Collisions with netsonde monitor cables largely eliminated since abolition in the early 1990s.

Taxonomy Usually considered polytypic, with nominate epomophora on Campbell and Auckland, replaced by sanfordi on South I, New Zealand and Chatham, and overlapping on Enderby, in Auckland group (where they hybridize). Recent molecular evidence suggests that sanfordi is sufficiently distinct to warrant specific status, but the taxonomic debate is ongoing.

Northern Royal Albatross
Diomedea [epomophora] sanfordi   Plate 5

Identification
Confusion risks: Imm Southern Royal Albatross D. [e.] epomophora.

Main characters: Large, with white body and black upperwing. **Ad** has pure white body and head (though females have variable dark patch on crown in early breeding season), and almost lacks wavy vermiculations, except on very limited part of scapulars, where boldly blotched and barred dark brown, and perhaps extending fractionally onto lower back and rump (cf. juv); upperwing, including coverts, wholly jet-black (bleached slightly browner). When on nest or water no whitish area visible around elbow region. Near diagnostic is black smudge parallel to leading edge of underside of primary bases (near carpal). Tail often pure white, but variable numbers (57% in one analysis) have some black-tipped rectrices. Never has variable pink-stained rear ear-coverts of ad Wanderer. Bare parts as epomophora (which see). **Juv** very similar to ad, being overall largely white, with sometimes a few dark brown flecks on crown and variable, but often quite extensive, bold dark brown blotches on lower back and rump; upperwing-coverts very indistinctly fringed whitish when fresh, otherwise upperwing very similar to ad. Tail mainly white, with variable black centres, especially near tip, forming indistinct terminal band. Bare parts duller than ad. **Younger imm** very similar to juv, but perhaps has slightly purer white body, upperwing often bleached browner on

coverts and tail has less black. **Older imm** progressively ad-like and hardly separable in field.

Voice: See introduction concerning vocal and behavioural displays on breeding grounds. At sea quieter than D. [exulans], but may give some harsh screams and 'yells', and bill-clap, especially in disputes over food; like Wanderers, full range of vocal and behavioural displays is observed at sea, even tens of kms from breeding island (pers. obs.). Tickell (2000) summarized the main vocal and other display differences between Royals and Wanderers, the principal one being the more rapid and musical (less harsh) yapping of the former.

Size: Averages smaller than epomophora in culmen and wing measurements and overall weight (with apparently no overlap in former), wing 61–67 cm, weight 6.53–6.8 kg. Female averages smaller in all measurements and weight, with no overlap as far as is known.

Similar forms: At close range, easily separated from all Wanderers by combination of solid blackish upperwing, pure white body plumage and black cutting edge to upper mandible (as in Southern Royal, which also lacks brown body mottling of non-ad Wanderers). Confusion possible only with extremely dark-winged young Southern Royal Albatross (see below), but Northern still has clearly more uniform and solid, darker/blacker upperwing (lacking obvious white; at most slight flecking in worn plumage or very indistinct narrow white covert fringes in fresh juv). Some young Southern Royal superficially appear to have more uniform upperwings, especially at long range or in brief/side views, or due to increased wear. Thus, such 'trickier' young Southern should be checked more closely for pale elements on the upperwing (i.e. pale/whitish feathering on 'elbow' or for any indication of the characteristic paler inner and fore upper-wing coverts. Supportive characters are: black smudge parallel to leading edge of underside of primary bases and near carpal, though be aware that some Northern Royal may possess a narrower and less obvious black smudge, and that some Southern Royal have a slight smudge (this character is best used only in obvious cases); and some, but not all, Northern Royal (see above) have rather extensive bold dark brown blotches on lower back and rump, a feature not shared by most (except juv) Southern Royal. Northern Royal is distinctly smaller and, more importantly, less heavily built and narrower winged, with the body always appearing smaller in proportion to the wings, and the neck is narrower and shorter than Southern Royal. Use of these structural characters in New Zealand waters suggests most individuals can be correctly identified on shape alone.

Scavenging Northern Royal Albatrosses Diomedea [epomophora] sanfordi *(on left and in middle foreground: former probably male, by its larger size, and latter female),* Gibson's Albatross D. [exulans] gibsoni *(middle back, ad but sex undetermined), and* Southern Royal Albatross D. [e.] epomophora *(far right; ad, probably male). Note distinctive differences in shapes of the three forms, as well as in inner scapular patterns and amount of white on coverts and 'elbow' (between the Royals). The Wanderer has the least 'clean' body, it being heavily vermiculated. Chatham Rise, New Zealand, Jan 2007. © Hadoram Shirihai.*

Southern Royal Diomedea [epomophora] epomophora, younger imm (top two images), and Northern Royal Albatross D. [e.] sanfordi, with bottom left bird probably imm and bottom right probably ad. Their separation becomes an issue with dark-winged juv or imm Southern, though note Northern's more solidly dark wings and predominantly blotched upper/inner scapulars (chiefly wavy vermiculations in Southern). Northern also lacks Southern's white feathering on 'elbow' and diffuse whitish-fringed and greyish-toned forewing-coverts. All images taken close to Chatham group or over Chatham Rise, New Zealand, Jan 2000, 2007. © Hadoram Shirihai.

Ad Northern Royal Albatross Diomedea [epomophora] sanfordi. *Note solid black upperwing and rather lighter build than Southern Royal D. [e.]* epomophora. *Off Chatham, Jan 2000. © Hadoram Shirihai.*

Juv Northern Royal Albatross Diomedea [epomophora] sanfordi. *Note characteristic dark marks on lower back and rump and solid black upperwing. Kaikoura, South I, New Zealand, Oct 2001. © Hadoram Shirihai.*

Distribution and biology

Distribution, movements and population: Chatham (nearly 99% of total population) and South I, New Zealand (c.30 pairs at Taiaroa Head, Dunedin) and Enderby, in the Auckland group (a handful of mixed pairs with Southern Royal). Range at sea circumpolar, being commonest between 30°S and 52°S, with most wintering in Chilean, Argentine and Uruguayan waters, returning by way of South African (where rare) and Australian waters. Annual breeding population estimated at 5200 pairs, with perhaps a total of 28,000–34,000 individuals in the 1990s.

Social behaviour: As Southern Royal (which see) but less regularly attracted to boats and always remains at greater distance from vessels.

Breeding biology: Breeds (biennially if successful, but nest failure rates are high, leading many pairs to lay annually) in late Oct–early Dec onwards, usually on flat-topped, small rocky islets. Nest a mound of soil, rock chips and small woody herbs with central depression. Lays one whitish egg with some red spots at broad end, incubated 76–86 days. Chicks fledge in 216–252 days. Single-brooded. Both sexes incubate and provision young.

Conservation Endangered and population declining. Stoats and cats still take eggs and chicks on South I, but a species of blowfly is the main predator of chicks. A huge storm, in the mid-1980s, which destroyed much vegetation and soil cover, has significantly affected subsequent breeding success (currently 18%). Numbers taken as bycatch mid-ocean and in New Zealand and Australian waters by longliners is tiny. Small-scale, illegal harvesting of chicks is thought to still occur on Chatham.

Taxonomy Formerly considered a subspecies of *epomophora* but *sanfordi* is now thought sufficiently distinct to warrant specific status, but see introduction to the great albatrosses for more information concerning the current taxonomic debate.

Ad Northern Royal Albatross Diomedea [epomophora] sanfordi. *Note diagnostic black carpal mark on leading edge of underwing. Off Chatham, Jan 2000. © Hadoram Shirihai.*

Small and medium albatrosses

The small to medium-sized albatrosses of the Southern Ocean, the mollymawks, are generally large, long-winged seabirds, though all are clearly far smaller than the great albatrosses and easily separated from them by the dark mantle 'bridge', linking the uniformly all-dark upperwings, and unlike Wanderers and Royals their underwing patterns may change with age and can be used to separate some of the various forms. The dark tail, like the upperwing pattern, is uniform across age and taxa. All share a triangular loral patch and white crescent on the lower rear eye-ring, but bill patterns can be complex and usually offer an important character for identification.

Five to 11 species are recognized, but species limits are currently subject to intense debate (like the great albatrosses). For now, I regard the many recently suggested 'splits' as allospecies, which signals their distinctiveness and is a term especially appropriate to island taxa whose reproductive isolation cannot be examined. I follow the proposal, which has gained widespread support, that all small and medium-sized albatrosses should be placed within the genus *Thalassarche*, rather than *Diomedea*.

Of paramount importance in identification are the combined underwing and head patterns, which vary with age in some taxa. Thus, it is always advisable to attempt ageing first. Bill colour is very important, but be aware that the true pattern may be detected only at close range and in optimal light, and is also subject to age-related variation. Shape and jizz are useful with experience.

Mainly for identification purposes, the small and the medium albatrosses can be divided into two major groups as follows.

Group A: The Shy *Thalassarche* [*cauta*] superspecies
Four closely related medium-sized taxa, some clearly differentiated.

- Shy (or Tasmanian) Albatross *T.* [*c.*] *cauta* breeds mainly on Albatross and Mewstone, as well as Pedra Branca, Tasmania.
- White-capped Albatross *T.* [*c.*] *steadi* breeds mainly at Auckland (principally on Disappointment).
- Salvin's Albatross *T.* [*c.*] *salvini* breeds mainly on the Bounties and Snares.
- Chatham Albatross *T.* [*c.*] *eremita* breeds at The Pyramid (Chatham).

All are usually noticeably larger than the next group, the small albatrosses, and share (at all ages) a narrow dark outline to the underwing and small dark patch at the base of the leading edge. None of the small albatrosses is likely to be confused with these four taxa, given the striking combination of underwing and head/neck patterns, bill colour and generally larger/heavier build. Note that Salvin's and Chatham have all-grey hoods and broader black wingtips than the whitish-hooded Shy and White-capped, and differ from each other by amount of grey in head and yellow in bill, chiefly in ads (both noticeably more extensive in Chatham). Juvs and imms differ in similar respects, mainly combination of underwing-tip pattern and amount of grey in hood, but the bill is very similar between forms. However, differences are sometimes difficult to appreciate at sea or from land, mainly because hood colour differences are not as clear as in ads and the amount of grey can be affected by wear, while intermediates also exist. I find *steadi* to be almost indistinguishable in

Small and medium albatrosses of the genus Thalassarche *involve a handful of species in the Southern Ocean, here ad Pacific* T. [bulleri] *sp. (left) and Salvin's Albatrosses* T. [cauta] salvini *(representatives of two superspecies groups). Although superficially similar, both being grey-hooded, they differ considerably in their underwing and bill patterns, and in overall size. Off Chatham, Jan 2007 © Hadoram Shirihai.*

Shy Albatross Thalassarche [cauta] cauta. *Very similar to, or indistinguishable from, White-capped* T. [c.] steadi, *except usually by more yellowish bill of typical ad, but some are identical to* steadi *(like this bird). Albatross I, Tasmania, Oct 2001. © Alan Wiltshire.*

the field from *cauta*, unless size and, in ads, bill colour is correctly judged. For further details see relevant accounts.

Group B: Small albatrosses

Four distinctive groups, each of which may be regarded as a superspecies of 1–2 distinct populations (allospecies).

The Black-browed *Thalassarche* [*melanophrys*] superspecies
• Black-browed Albatross *T.* [*melanophrys*] *melanophrys* breeds widely in the S Atlantic, with the overwhelming majority in the S Atlantic.
• Campbell Albatross *T.* [*m.*] *impavida* breeds on Campbell.

The Grey-headed *Thalassarche* [*chrysostoma*] superspecies
• Grey-headed Albatross *T. chrysostoma* breeds widely in the Southern Ocean.

The Buller's *Thalassarche* [*bulleri*] superspecies
• Buller's Albatross *T.* [*bulleri*] *bulleri* breeds on the Snares and Solander.
• Pacific Albatross *T.* [*b.*] sp. breeds at Chatham and Three Kings.

The Yellow-nosed *Thalassarche* [*chlororhynchos*] superspecies
• Atlantic Yellow-nosed Albatross *T.* [*chlororhynchos*] *chlororhynchos* breeds on the Tristan da Cunha group and Gough.
• Indian Yellow-nosed Albatross *T.* [*c.*] *carteri* breeds on Prince Edward, Crozet, Kerguelen, Amsterdam and St Paul, and Chatham (irregularly one pair).

The four groups are usually well separated, producing only a few cases of overlap (given birds of known age), but separation of the different taxa within each superspecies can be difficult outside the breeding ranges and if not seen well; most young birds are almost identical. Some key points and the main identification issues are highlighted briefly below.

Black-browed and Grey-headed vary considerably in underwing pattern with age; the former also differs geographically (darker underwing in *impavida*). Separation of ad Black-browed and Grey-headed is straightforward. The most reliable character for young birds is bill colour; pale brownish (gradually becoming yellowish), with conspicuous black tip in Black-browed, and uniform shiny black in Grey-headed. If aged correctly, both are also separable by the amount of grey on the head in non-ad plumages (see relevant accounts).

Beware of possible confusion at sea between ad Grey-headed and Buller's, which is sometimes underestimated, but careful study of head, bill and underwing patterns should produce correct identifications. Moreover, underwing, head and bill patterns of correctly aged young birds is often crucial when dealing with separation of Grey-headed/Buller's and Buller's/ Black-browed.

Using overall shape and underwing pattern, which do not vary with age, identification of Buller's and Yellow-nosed Albatrosses is easy. Bill colour in both varies with age, but differs between taxa and at close range can clinch identification. Note that the South Atlantic form of Yellow-nosed Albatross has a grey head (approaching Buller's though usually paler).

Ageing and sexing

Sexing in all *Thalassarche* is possible only by measuring individuals: males are usually larger than females, but there is no sexual dimorphism in plumage. (As with the great albatrosses, mensural

Ad Shy Albatross Thalassarche [cauta] cauta *or White-capped* T. [c.] steadi *(front) and Salvin's Albatrosses* T. [c.] salvini. *Separation of the latter from the other two is usually rather straightforward given the darker grey head/neck and dusky brown-yellow bill. Kaikoura, South I, New Zealand, Oct 2001. © Hadoram Shirihai.*

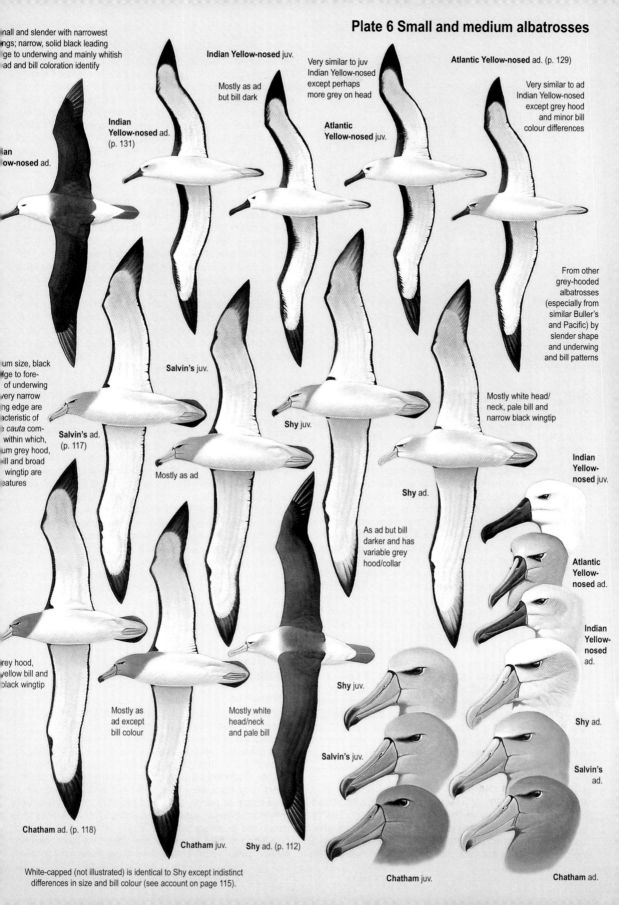

Plate 6 Small and medium albatrosses

...all and slender with narrowest ...ngs; narrow, solid black leading ...ge to underwing and mainly whitish ...ad and bill coloration identify

...ian ...ow-nosed ad.

Indian Yellow-nosed ad. (p. 131)

Indian Yellow-nosed juv.

Mostly as ad but bill dark

Very similar to juv Indian Yellow-nosed except perhaps more grey on head

Atlantic Yellow-nosed juv.

Atlantic Yellow-nosed ad. (p. 129)

Very similar to ad Indian Yellow-nosed except grey hood and minor bill colour differences

From other grey-hooded albatrosses (especially from similar Buller's and Pacific) by slender shape and underwing and bill patterns

...um size, black ...dge to fore- ...of underwing ...very narrow ...ng edge are ...acteristic of ...*cauta* com- ...within which, ...um grey hood, ...ill and broad ...wingtip are ...eatures

Salvin's ad. (p. 117)

Salvin's juv.

Mostly as ad

Shy juv.

Mostly white head/ neck, pale bill and narrow black wingtip

Indian Yellow- nosed juv.

Shy ad.

As ad but bill darker and has variable grey hood/collar

...rey hood, ...yellow bill and ...lack wingtip

Mostly as ad except bill colour

Mostly white head/neck and pale bill

Shy juv.

Salvin's juv.

Atlantic Yellow- nosed ad.

Indian Yellow- nosed ad.

Shy ad.

Salvin's ad.

Chatham ad. (p. 118)

Chatham juv.

Shy ad. (p. 112)

Chatham juv.

Chatham ad.

White-capped (not illustrated) is identical to Shy except indistinct differences in size and bill colour (see account on page 115).

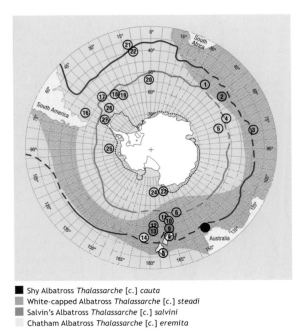

■ Shy Albatross *Thalassarche [c.] cauta*
▨ White-capped Albatross *Thalassarche [c.] steadi*
▨ Salvin's Albatross *Thalassarche [c.] salvini*
□ Chatham Albatross *Thalassarche [c.] eremita*

② Crozet   ⑫ Antipodes
● Tasmania   ⑬ Bounty
⑨ Snares   ⑭ Chatham
⑩ Auckland

Map showing the main breeding areas and principal regions of dispersal of Shy Albatross Thalassarche [cauta] *but not limited occurrences in SAtlantic Ocean.*

data are often extremely useful for sexing purposes: females are usually smaller than males in several respects, and further information on these and the relative level of overlap, expressed in crude terms, are presented in the species accounts.) Ageing young birds may be possible using a combination of plumage and moult patterns, but this is far from easy at sea. For the purposes of field identification, it is most convenient to describe the major plumage classes and general maturation of each taxon, and analyse the confusion risks. Only when crucial to ageing is moult pattern mentioned. Plumage maturation is considered using the following four broad age classes. The first plumage is that acquired on fledging (juv), which is moulted at sea from c.1 year old; in most taxa juv plumage distinctly differs from ad, mainly on the head and in bill colour, and in some taxa the underwing is wholly different. With wear, some changes to head/neck pattern often occur in first-year birds. With partial moult (**younger imm**, aged 2–3 years), plumage becomes intermediate, especially on head and, in some forms, partially on underwing, but bill-coloration changes are more protracted. With age (**older imm**, aged 3–5 years, when start to visit natal islands), plumage is overall much like ad, but younger birds show clearer vestiges of immaturity, mostly on bill and, perhaps, head. Finally, ad plumage (**ad**) is acquired, which also changes with age. Be aware that the degree of plumage change from juv to ad varies significantly between the different groups listed above.

Life cycles of the small albatrosses

Probably more than 50% of the estimated total of six million breeding pairs of mollymawks are Black-browed Albatrosses. Like the great albatrosses, these forms share many similar displays, which are generally much more restricted and less elaborate because of the denser colonies that they inhabit. A few of the main displays

are described below, but for those with the interest to delve further, Tickell's book (2000) serves as an excellent source. Croaking calls are the most common behaviour in all mollymawks, being even occasionally heard during feeding frenzies at sea, and accompanied on land by various head-nodding and bowing and tail-fanning movements. Other calls are wails, given as birds arrive at the colony. Bill-pointing, -touching, -rubbing and -nibbling are common duelling actions, while a variety of other social interactions have been described, including several preening motions that have ritual significance.

Breeding biologies, like those of the great albatrosses, are reasonably well described. Imms return to the colonies earlier than great albatrosses (some as early as when 2–3 years old), but first breeding is still delayed until 8–17 years old. Between two and four weeks prior to nesting, breeders return to the colonies. All lay one egg, with the date usually varying by up to three weeks. The whitish egg weighs 186–333 g, with the smallest eggs belonging to the yellow-nosed albatrosses. All mollymawks are colonial, nesting on tussac-covered ridges, flat or gently sloping rocky ground, or narrow ledges on steep crags, with up to tens of metres between nests (some colonies are much denser even when more than one species is present), and occasionally in association with penguins, cormorants and gannets. Nests are long-lasting mounds of peat and soil or guano (rocky sites). All except Grey-headed breed annually, usually at the same nest site. Breeding cycles are much shorter than in the great albatrosses: incubation, by both sexes in 5–20 alternating shifts, occupies 68–75 days; the chicks are brooded or guarded for 18–25 days and fledging occurs at 115–167 days, whereupon the chick is immediately independent. Most mollymawks abandon their colonies at the end of the southern summer, but *bulleri* is unusual in rearing its young during winter.

Threats to the mollymawks closely match those of the great albatrosses, with longline toothfish, swordfish and bottom longlining and trawler tuna fishing posing the most significant latter-day problem. The lack of accurate historical counts of breeding colonies has frustrated efforts to obtain information on population trends, but declines in many taxa are now obvious. While debate currently rages concerning the taxonomy of albatrosses, such discussions have had the undoubtedly beneficial effect of bringing the conservation status and threats to all forms into much sharper and prominent focus. The time is ripe for clear-sighted and far-reaching legislation governing human use of the marine environment and the effect upon pelagic birds and other wildlife, though see Conservation in the Region for some recent encouraging developments in this respect.

Shy (Tasmanian) Albatross
Thalassarche [cauta] cauta   Plate 6

Identification

Confusion risks: Virtually inseparable from White-capped *T. [c.] steadi* and could also be confused with young Salvin's *T. [c.] salvini* or even Chatham Albatrosses *T. [c.] eremita*.
Main characters: Medium-sized, with extensive white head, underparts and underwings, the latter with narrow black margins at all ages. Distinctive black 'thumb mark' where anterior underwing meets body; black wingtip relatively small, with large amounts of white visible on primary bases. **Ad** has white head with variable greyish smudging on ear-coverts emphasizing white forehead and crown, and prominent black eye and blackish triangle surround, broadening in front of eye as loral patch, but much narrower behind, giving typical 'unhappy' facial expression. Bill yellowish

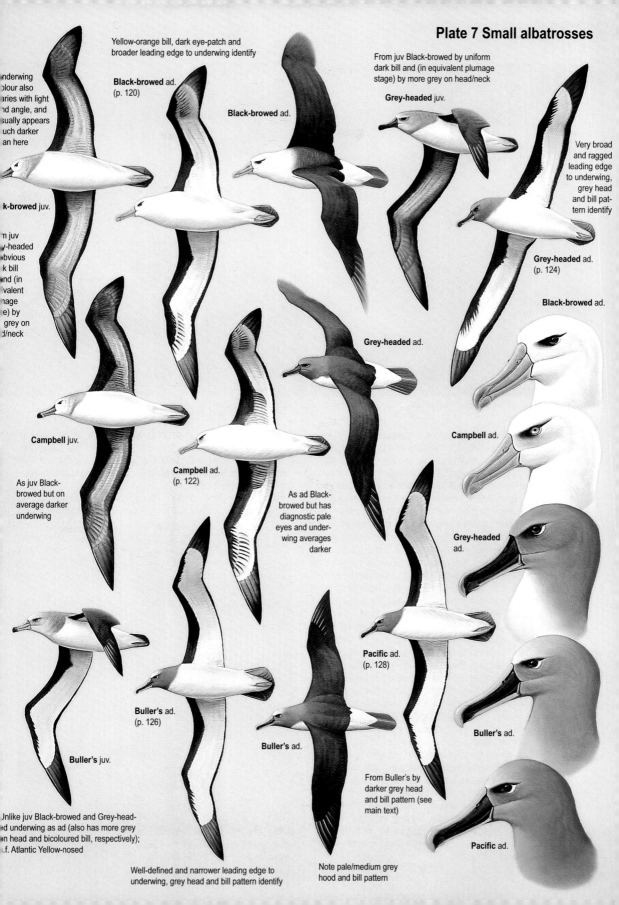

Plate 7 Small albatrosses

Yellow-orange bill, dark eye-patch and broader leading edge to underwing identify

...underwing ...olour also ...aries with light ...nd angle, and ...sually appears ...uch darker ...an here

Black-browed ad. (p. 120)

Black-browed ad.

From juv Black-browed by uniform dark bill and (in equivalent plumage stage) by more grey on head/neck

Grey-headed juv.

...k-browed juv.

...m juv ...y-headed ...obvious ...k bill ...nd (in ...valent ...mage ...e) by ...grey on ...d/neck

Very broad and ragged leading edge to underwing, grey head and bill pattern identify

Grey-headed ad. (p. 124)

Black-browed ad.

Grey-headed ad.

Campbell juv.

Campbell ad.

Campbell ad. (p. 122)

As juv Black-browed but on average darker underwing

As ad Black-browed but has diagnostic pale eyes and underwing averages darker

Grey-headed ad.

Pacific ad. (p. 128)

Buller's ad. (p. 126)

Buller's ad.

Buller's ad.

Pacific ad.

Buller's juv.

From Buller's by darker grey head and bill pattern (see main text)

Unlike juv Black-browed and Grey-head-ed underwing as ad (also has more grey ...n head and bicoloured bill, respectively); ...f. Atlantic Yellow-nosed

Well-defined and narrower leading edge to underwing, grey head and bill pattern identify

Note pale/medium grey hood and bill pattern

Ad Shy Albatrosses Thalassarche [cauta] cauta, *Albatross I, Tasmania, Aug 1996. © Alan Wiltshire.*

white-grey with bright yellow tip (unguis), and pale yellow culmen (culminicorn) ridge (especially bright near base) and cutting edge to upper mandible; dark mark at lower tip usually lacking or indistinct (but see older imm). Legs and feet bluish-grey tinged pinkish. **Juv** similar to ad, except some differences to head/neck and bill. Latter generally rather uniform, pale/medium brownish horn-grey, with conspicuous black tip. Grey wash on head/neck varies in extent and depth, sometimes rather pronounced forming slight hooded appearance, extending variably onto crown and almost entire neck, leaving forecrown/forehead, throat and upper (or in paler birds entire) foreneck whiter, and appearing as partial greyish collar. Usually has diffuse dusky hindneck patch, emphasizing otherwise whitish head. With wear at sea, grey areas become blotchy and whiter around head and foreneck. Black wingtip slightly more extensive than ad. **Younger imm**, following first moult, has neck/head-sides progressively whiter/paler grey, but some darker/greyer birds can appear slightly grey-hooded (like Salvin's Albatross, which see); others much whiter and some have grey on hindneck tapering at foreneck (but lack true collar). Only in third-/fourth-year does bill colour develop, though yellowish and greyish-horn still limited and tip largely dark, while head/neck become whiter and less grey, and in some latter coloration is restricted to cheeks. **Older imm** not always clearly separated from previous stage or **younger ad**, unless moult pattern carefully evaluated. Advanced birds much whiter on head/neck, but may be separated from ad by duller, greyish-brown bill with extensive blackish tip. Variably retains vestiges of immaturity around head, with some having very slight greyish hue to head-sides and hindneck, but most five- to six-year olds are inseparable from ads at sea.
Voice: See group introduction concerning vocal and nuptial displays on breeding grounds (chiefly braying croaks, cackling, wailing and 'gaping display'), but no comparative studies on differences from *steadi*, *salvini* and *eremita*; harsh croaking when squabbling over food.

Size: 90–100 cm, wingspan 210–260 cm (both figures refer to entire *cauta* complex), wing 53.5–59.0 cm, weight 3.2–5.1 kg. Female averages smaller than male in culmen, tarsus, tail and wing measurements, and overall weight, but varying degrees of overlap (some extensive) in all these.
Similar forms: Shy reliably separated from White-capped Albatross only in classic ad, by combination of smaller size and

Juv Shy Albatross Thalassarche [cauta] cauta *at the nest, Albatross I, Tasmania, Aug 1997. © Alan Wiltshire.*

Ad Shy Albatross Thalassarche [cauta] cauta *or White-capped Albatross* T. [c.] steadi. *Rather prominent yellowish tone to bill suggests* cauta. *Note black mark at forewing base and narrow black underwing edges (both diagnostic of the* T. [cauta] complex), *and relatively reduced black wingtip (broader in* salvini/eremita). *Off New Zealand, Jan 1998.* © Hadoram Shirihai.

depression. Lays one whitish egg with reddish-brown spots at broad end, incubated c.73 days, with most chicks hatching early to late Dec. Fledging period also imprecisely known, but most depart colony in Mar/early Apr. Single-brooded. Both sexes incubate and provision young.

Conservation Status not separately evaluated, but certainly demands Red Data listing. Problems of separation from *steadi* at sea and its uncertain taxonomic status have prevented accurate assessment of its conservation prospects, but see *steadi* for general analysis of the threats facing these forms. All three breeding islands are protected, Mewstone and Pedra Branca as World Heritage Sites and Albatross as a nature reserve. Large numbers of albatrosses were exploited for their feathers on latter in early 1900s, and numbers have probably still not fully recovered, but are currently increasing despite this form constituting 12% of bycatch of Japanese tuna longliners in Australian waters in 1989–95. Commercial squid and fish exploitation in Bass Strait may also constitute a significant threat, as may avian-pox virus.

Taxonomy Recent molecular work has led to a radical reinterpretation of relationships within the *Thalassarche* [*cauta*] group. Formerly considered polytypic, the nominate is now considered to comprise two species-level taxa, *cauta* and *steadi* (latter was formerly only doubtfully accorded taxonomic status), and both other taxa, *salvini* and *eremita*, also now considered sufficiently distinct to warrant specific status. However, further study is required to demonstrate the true biological relationships of all these.

more delicate overall structure, but most noticeably bill, which is typically extensively yellowish, especially on culmen (from base to level with tubes) and on cutting edge of upper mandible, and generally appears bright yellowish-grey (rather than dull bluish horn-grey). However, such differences readily appreciated only when observed at very close quarters on water. Younger ad Shy often has less yellow on bill, being generally very similar to bill of ad White-capped, thus identification is best attempted only of advanced breeding ads, which have complete yellow tip (with at most a slight darkening on lower mandible), and by checking area near base of culmen and cutting edges (yellow in Shy and dark in White-capped). Those with obvious dark on tip or an intermediate bill should be left undetermined. Field observations demonstrate that young are inseparable, though bill of newly fledged juv Shy is usually paler and less dusky than White-capped, but varies individually, with much overlap, and it is unknown how subsequent imm plumages develop. For separation from Salvin's and Chatham Albatrosses see those accounts.

Distribution and biology

Distribution, movements and population: Albatross, Mewstone and Pedra Blanca, off Tasmania. Disperses in Southern Ocean west to South Africa and Namibia (most ads remain comparatively close to natal area) at 15–60°S, with one record from N Pacific, off North America, but distribution at sea unclear due to difficulties of separation from *steadi* and may be much more widespread than supposed from these certain records. Not uncommon around Amsterdam and St Paul during austral winter (*cauta* or *steadi*). Population 12,250 pairs in 1993–4.

Diet and feeding: Fish and cephalopods, as well as barnacles and crustaceans, mostly taken by surface-seizing and pursuit- and surface-plunging. Feeds with other albatrosses and seabirds, including around boats, and in association with cetaceans. Also takes offal.

Social behaviour: Colonial, generally gregarious on land and, at least in some areas, attends breeding colonies for much of year. No data on length of pair-bond. Well-defined aggressive and courtship displays.

Breeding biology: Breeds annually in early Sep–mid-Oct, in sheltered crevices on bare rocky slopes, cliffs and ledges. Builds low mound of mud, guano, feathers and other material with central

White-capped Albatross
Thalassarche [cauta] steadi   Not illustrated

Identification

Confusion risks: Virtually inseparable from Shy *T.* [*c.*] *cauta* and could also be confused with young Salvin's *T.* [*c.*] *salvini* or even Chatham Albatrosses *T.* [*c.*] *eremita*.

Main characters: Plumage development and features as Shy (which see), and for details concerning both see similar forms in previous account. Only major differences between them are bill coloration and various measurements, especially wing, which do not overlap with sex. Due to overall duller and greyer bill of *steadi*, with limited yellowish pigment and tendency to have slightly darker tip, age-related differences in bill colour are generally less marked, which should be borne in mind when ageing individuals of these forms.

Voice: See Shy Albatross.

Size: Averages larger than *cauta* in culmen, tarsus, tail and wing measurements, overall weight in male and, in some instances, in female. Wing 57–62 cm, weight 2.6–5.3 kg. Female averages smaller than male in all measurements, with only marginal overlap in culmen data and almost none in wing.

Similar forms: For separation from Shy, Salvin's and Chatham Albatrosses see those accounts.

Distribution and biology

Distribution, movements and population: Three islands in Auckland group, and Bollons in the Antipodes group, with one pair on Forty-Fours (Chatham) in 1991 and 1996. Disperses in Southern Ocean east to W South America, scarcely into S Atlantic, commoner off South Africa but few in S Indian Ocean, at 10–65°S. Breeding population estimated at 70,000–80,000 pairs (the vast majority on Disappointment in the Aucklands), with perhaps an overall total of 350,000–375,000 individuals in 1992–4.

Diet and feeding: As *cauta*, which see.

Social behaviour: As *cauta*, which see.

Breeding biology: Breeds, probably annually, in Nov–Dec, in

White-capped Albatross Thalassarche [cauta] steadi, *Auckland Is, Dec 1999. © Hadoram Shirihai.*

White-capped Albatross Thalassarche [cauta] steadi, *off the Auckland Is, Dec 1999. © Hadoram Shirihai.*

sheltered crevices and on well-vegetated slopes. Builds mound of mud, guano, tussac, herbs, feathers and other material, with central depression. Lays one whitish egg with reddish-brown spots at broad end, incubated for an unknown period, but most hatch in Jan–Feb. Fledging period also imprecisely known but most depart colony in mid-Aug. Single-brooded. Both sexes incubate and provision young.

Conservation Near Threatened, but few population or trend data, and classification based on assumption that *steadi* and *cauta* are conspecific. Longline fishing perhaps constitutes greatest threat to this distinctive form. *Steadi* formed 15% of bycatch of longliners in New Zealand waters in 1988–97 and 85% of deaths at squid trawlers in same waters (with an estimated 2300 ads alone taken in 1990) until netsonde monitor cables were prohibited in 1992. However, more recent totals from New Zealand-registered vessels are more encouraging: during the period 1996 to 2001, a total of 346 was taken as bycatch of longline fisheries and trawlers. Effects of feral cats, on Auckland, unknown. Pigs have significantly restricted available breeding habitat on main Auckland island.

Taxonomy Often considered a subspecies of Shy Albatross, but see that form. Some have questioned the validity of *steadi*, but my examination of museum material and large numbers of photographs suggests that *steadi* deserves recognition, given the bill colour (see above) and clear size differences, with insignificant overlap, between same sexes of it and *cauta*.

White-capped Albatross Thalassarche [cauta] steadi, *off the Auckland Is, Dec 1999. © Hadoram Shirihai.*

Juv Shy Thalassrche [cauta] cauta *or White-capped Albatross* T. [c.] steadi. *Most birds of these forms are distinctinctly paler/whiter on head/neck than young* salvini *(and have less black at tip of underwing than latter). Possibly off Australia. © Brett Jarrett.*

Salvin's Albatross
Thalassarche [cauta] salvini   Plate 6

Identification

Confusion risks: Shy *T.* [*c.*] *cauta*, White-capped *T.* [*c.*] *steadi* and Chatham Albatrosses *T.* [*c.*] *eremita* (mainly young birds).

Main characters: Medium-sized, grey-headed albatross with extensive white underparts and underwings, the latter with narrow black margins at all ages. Distinctive black 'thumb mark' where anterior underwing meets body; black wingtip relatively large, covering much of visible primaries. **Ad** has pale to medium greyish head and neck, forming hood (which varies individually and with light; looks paler in bright sunlight) and merging into darker brown-grey mantle, with ill-defined variable white forehead/forecrown, and grey neck variably demarcated from white underparts. Typical 'unhappy' facial expression formed by black triangular eyestripe, broader on lores and much narrower behind eye. Dull/dusky olive-brown bill with slightly yellower (ivory-horn) culmen and lower mandible, and nearly always has ill-defined dark smudges on tip of both mandibles, sometimes only or mainly on lower. Legs and feet bluish-grey tinged pinkish. **Juv** similar to ad. Bill generally darker, dusky grey-brown (lower mandible darker), with conspicuous broad black tip; darkness of grey wash to plumage varies, but rather extensive on head and almost entire neck, leaving ill-defined whitish-grey forehead (or entire crown) and upper throat, sometimes reaching foreneck; and many have variable but pronounced darker half-collar on hindneck to neck-sides. With wear at sea all grey parts become paler and slightly patchy. **Younger imm** is little changed, with grey on head/neck more irregular and perhaps concentrated on head-sides and lower neck-sides as slightly darker collar; plumage only noticeably changes in third-/fourth-year, when bill becomes largely dull brownish, often with limited yellowish and greyer pigments, but tip usually still mostly blackish. **Older imm** can be almost ad-like, neat uniform grey on head and neck, with diffuse white forecrown. However, bill usually

Ad Salvin's Albatross Thalassarche [cauta] salvini, *Kaikoura, South I, New Zealand, Feb 2001. © Hadoram Shirihai.*

retains extensive blackish tip, and others may still be less uniform grey with some darker areas on neck.

Voice: See Shy Albatross.

Size: Averages larger than *cauta* in tail and wing measurements of male. Wing 55–60 cm, weight 3.3–4.9 kg. Female averages smaller than male in culmen, tarsus, tail and wing measurements, and overall weight, but extensive overlap in almost all of these.

Similar forms: Given full ad, elimination of other members of *T.* [*cauta*] complex rather easy: Shy has brighter yellowish-grey bill, with no, or limited, dark tip to lower mandible, narrower black wingtip, and white head/neck, and White-capped shares these features, but has overall bill colour intermediate between Shy and Salvin's. Chatham Albatross has much darker grey head/neck and bright yellow bill. Confusion possible in following instances. Younger imm Shy and White-capped have darkish bill with darker tip and may attain sufficiently greyish head/neck to appear superficially grey-hooded. Extremes close to palest grey Salvin's (such as very pale/bleached individuals, or in bright light). Fortunately, most Shy/White-capped possess greater contrast between dark mantle and paler grey neck, more contrasting pure white forecrown, diffuse whiter feathering on face near bill base, on throat, foreneck and lower border of hood, with often a faint collar created by even whiter lower hindneck, emphasized by variable dusky mid-hindneck patch characteristic of very young Shy/White-capped. Young/extremely pale grey-hooded Salvin's still more evenly grey on head/neck, only slightly admixed whitish on lower foreneck, and whiter crown not as contrasting. Also useful is narrower black wingtip in *cauta/steadi*, which usually separates them (but some almost overlap). For further comparison with Chatham Albatross see below. Among small albatrosses, Salvin's might only be confused with Buller's/Pacific Albatrosses *T.* [*bulleri*], but only if underwing and age-related bill coloration, or size/structure are incorrectly judged.

Distribution and biology

Distribution, movements and population: Breeds on Crozet (few pairs), Snares (c.1200 pairs) and Bounties (over 90% of total population). One has regularly built a nest within a Black-browed Albatross colony on Kerguelen in recent years. Disperses in Southern Ocean west to SW Indian Ocean, east to W South America at 14–50ºS, where very common off C Chile, and rarely into S

Ad Salvin's Albatross Thalassarche [cauta] salvini, *Kaikoura, South I, New Zealand, Feb 2001. © Hadoram Shirihai.*

Juv Salvin's Albatross Thalassarche [cauta] salvini. *Even in juv/imm plumage the hood is more extensive/darker grey than juv Shy/White-capped* T. [c.] cauta/steadi, *but less so than juv Chatham* T. [c.] eremita; *bill colour of juvs is very similar (dusky olive-brown with a conspicuous broad black tip) in all members of the complex. Off Chile, Nov 2006. © Alvaro Jaramillo.*

Atlantic. Breeding population estimated at 76,500 pairs on Bounties (in 1978), with perhaps an overall total of 350,000–380,000 individuals, but only 30,750 pairs were counted on the Bounties in the 1990s, suggesting a significant decline, although differences between the survey techniques employed limit the usefulness of a comparison between them.

Diet and feeding: Probably as *steadi* (which see).

Social behaviour: Probably as *steadi* (which see).

Breeding biology: Breeds, presumably annually, in early Oct–mid-Nov (hatching dates 5–21 Nov in 1997 on Bounties), in open colonies on level ground. Builds low mound of mud, guano, feathers and rock chips, with central depression. Lays one whitish egg

with reddish-brown spots at broad end, incubated 68–75 days. Fledging period unknown. Single-brooded. Both sexes incubate and provision young.

Conservation Vulnerable. Apparently particularly at risk from extreme weather events and gradual ocean warming, and resulting changes in food availability may also be having an effect. Longline fishing is undoubtedly a significant threat, though only 108 individuals were taken as bycatch by New Zealand-registered boats in 1996–2001. Given scale of apparent decline (only very recently recognized) this may be a significant additional risk to populations of the species.

Taxonomy Formerly considered a subspecies of *cauta*, but in common with all other forms of this complex is possibly best considered sufficiently distinct to warrant allospecies status.

Chatham Albatross
Thalassarche [cauta] eremita   Plate 6

Identification
Confusion risks: Shy *T.* [*c.*] *cauta*, White-capped *T.* [*c.*] *steadi* and Salvin's Albatrosses *T.* [*c.*] *salvini* (mainly young birds).

Main characters: Represents extreme (dark end) of *T.* [*cauta*] complex. Medium-sized, dark grey-headed albatross, and has extensive contrasting white underparts and underwing, with narrow black margins at all ages. Distinctive 'thumb mark' as in rest of complex and relatively broad black wingtip like Salvin's. **Ad** has uniform dark grey head and neck (forecrown may be slightly paler), forming contrasting hood clearly demarcated from white underparts (grey varies only slightly and with lighting) and concolorous with dark brown-grey mantle. Typical 'unhappy' facial expression created by triangular black loral patch, which rarely extends far behind eye. Bright deep-yellow bill with blackish subterminal tip to lower mandible. Legs and feet pinkish bluish-grey. **Juv** rather similar to ad, but bill darker, dusky olive-brown (lower mandible darker), with conspicuous broad black tip; grey head and entire neck, lacking any whitish parts or collar effect, but face and throat usually appear marginally darker. With wear at sea grey hood becomes paler and may be slightly patchy and darker on lower part. **Younger imm** possibly has slightly paler bill (by fourth-year), with more yellowish and horn elements, though

Ad Salvin's Albatross Thalassarche [cauta] salvini. *Note combination of narrow black margins to underwings with black 'thumb mark' at base, typical of* T. [cauta] *complex, and the medium grey head, relatively large black wingtip and dull yellowish bill, which separate* salvini *from rest of group. Kaikoura, South I, New Zealand, Feb 2001. © Hadoram Shirihai.*

Juv Chatham Albatross Thalassarche [cauta] eremita *is similar to ad but has blackish-tipped dusky bill; head and neck more evenly and darker grey than salvini (creating more contrast with white underparts), but also note how grey tone varies with the light, whilst the slightly paler crown is a frequent characteristic of bleached birds. Off Chile, Nov 2006. © Alvaro Jaramillo.*

still largely dull brownish-olive; rest of plumage much as juv. **Older imm** usually almost ad-like, with uniform dark grey head/neck, but bill typically younger in appearance, being extensively washed dusky, mainly on sides.

Voice: See Shy Albatross.

Size: Averages larger than *cauta* in tail and wing measurements of male. Wing 54–59 cm, weight 3.1–4.7 kg. Female averages smaller than male in culmen, tarsus, tail and wing measurements, and overall weight, but considerable overlap in all of these.

Similar forms: Shy and White-capped lack dark grey head contrasting sharply with white underparts. Salvin's has much paler grey hood, with clearly whitish/paler forecrown, and bill never as conspicuously yellow as ad Chatham. Separation, however, possibly difficult in case of a few atypical younger imm Salvin's and Chatham Albatrosses with superficially intermediate shade of grey to hood (especially if comparing birds of dissimilar ages or

moult, or in certain lights/angles, e.g. in harsh evening light Salvin's can seem much darker hooded and imm Chatham with slightly bleached grey hood and partially dark bill could be mistaken for Salvin's). Unfortunately, both have similarly broad black wingtips, making it advisable in any intermediate cases (especially if dealing with birds outside the normal ranges) to carefully review each feature in relation to age. However, the vast majority of both species, even imms, are quite easily identified, especially if seen well.

Distribution and biology

Distribution, movements and population: Chatham, on Pyramid Rock, with birds occasionally seen ashore and at least one unsuccessful breeding attempt on the Western Chain (Snares). Recent satellite-tracking initiatives have established extent of distribution at sea, west to Tasmania and east to Chile, where regular, and Peru, where greater part of population now thought to winter, returning to breeding areas by way of lower latitudes. Many ads remain at 38–48ºS in waters east of New Zealand, but there are two recent records off South Africa (with one videotaped on 27 May 2001) and several off Tasmania. Breeding population occupied 5333 sites in 1999–2000, with perhaps overall 18,000–20,000 individuals, though there is a chronic need for continued and up-to-date census work at the main colony.

Diet and feeding: Fish and cephalopods, as well as barnacles and crustaceans, mostly taken by surface-seizing and pursuit- and surface-plunging. Feeds with other albatrosses and seabirds. Also takes offal. Ranges up to several tens of kms when foraging during breeding season, but no records from further away at this season.

Social behaviour: Colonial, but generally not gregarious in non-breeding season. No data on length of pair-bond. Well-defined aggressive and courtship displays.

Breeding biology: Breeds, annually in Aug–Sep, on slopes, cliffs and ledges. Builds low pedestal of mud, guano, feathers and other material with central depression. Lays one whitish egg with reddish-brown spots at broad end. Incubation lasts 66–72 days and chicks probably fledge in Feb–Apr. Single-brooded. Both sexes incubate and provision young.

Ad Chatham Albatrosses Thalassarche [cauta] eremita, *ff Chatham, Dec 1999. © Hadoram Shirihai.*

Ad Chatham Albatross Thalassarche [cauta] eremita. Amongst the Shy T. [cauta] superspecies, this form is characterised by having the darkest and most uniformly grey head, and rather pure, deep yellow bill. Off Chatham, Jan 2007 © Hadoram Shirihai.

Conservation Critical. A number of extreme storms, in 1985 and since, have significantly reduced extent of available vegetation for nest-building and have also removed much soil, increasing likelihood of nest collapses. Conditions have improved somewhat since 1998, but first reports of individuals taken as bycatch by longliners occurred in late 1990s and recent introduction of small-scale longlining in Peruvian waters, where 60% of population winters, must be viewed with alarm (though most fishing is apparently in summer), as the estimated total number of albatrosses (this species and Waved Albatross *Phoebastria irrorata*) caught annually by this fishery is thought to be 2370–5610 individuals. Some illegal harvesting of chicks may still occur.

Taxonomy Formerly considered a subspecies of *cauta*, but in common with all other forms in this complex now considered sufficiently distinct to warrant specific status, on basis of molecular work.

Black-browed Albatross
Thalassarche [melanophrys] melanophrys   Plate 7

Identification
Confusion risks: Campbell Albatross *T. [m.] impavida* in all plumages, and young Grey-headed *T. chrysostoma* and, to lesser extent, Buller's/Pacific Albatrosses *T. [bulleri]*.
Main characters: Small, black-and-white, pale-headed albatross, with underwing pattern varying with age. **Ad** has prominent black eye and slight dark triangle around it which does not reach bill base, and rest of head and underparts white. Underwing-coverts largely white, bordered by noticeable black trailing (and up to three times broader) leading edge and wingtip; black/white areas mostly well demarcated, with some diffuse streaking, mainly on larger primary-coverts and, variably, at elbow region where leading edge broadest. Bill yellowish-orange with reddish tip. Legs and feet bluish-grey tinged pinkish. **Juv** mainly white-headed with small ill-defined dusky eye-patch and variable amounts of grey; extremes may have head-sides wholly grey as nape, hindneck and narrow collar (i.e. partial or complete upper breast-band extending from mantle), though crown, throat and much of foreneck like whiter headed juv. With wear at sea, all grey parts including collar are reduced, and may soon appear almost all white on head/neck. Underwing black, with diffusely paler (whitish-grey) coverts, formed by whitish feathers with broad black centres; thus underwing appears to have ill-defined greyish panel or even seems black at distance. Bill also variable: most pale brownish with prominent black tip, but some (mainly recent fledglings) have darker grey bill, with tip even darker, while others have more extensive yellow on upper ridge and cutting edges. **Younger imm**, following first moult, much as bleached juv, but neck/head whiter and underwing even more so. Only as third-year does bill change dramatically, though still variable, usually becoming much paler and yellower at base, while head whitens (emphasizing short black brows) with reduced grey wash on hindneck/neck-sides and perhaps cheeks, and

Ad Black-browed Albatrosses Thalassarche [melanophrys] melanophrys displaying, the Falklands, Jan 2001. © Hadoram Shirihai.

Younger imm Black-browed Albatross Thalassarche [melanophrys] melanophrys. Bill colour diagnostic. Off Tristan group, S Atlantic, Mar 2006. © Hadoram Shirihai.

Ad Black-browed Albatross Thalassarche [melanophrys] melanophrys. Note more extensive cleaner white underwing-coverts, black eye and somewhat narrower black eye-patch compared to Campbell Albatross T. [m.] impavida. Orange bill and underwing pattern diagnostic (both melanophrys and impavida). South Atlantic, Mar 2006. © Hadoram Shirihai.

underwing-coverts can be almost as white as ad (but more black streaks, formed by black tips/centres). **Older imm** not always very different, though advanced birds have much whiter body and underwing-coverts, being mainly separated from ad by dull yellow bill with some blackish and/or reddish on tip. Some have slight vestiges of immaturity on head and perhaps underwing, but most five/six-year olds are inseparable at sea from ad.

Voice: See group introduction concerning vocal and nuptial displays on breeding grounds (chiefly braying croaks, accompanied by bill-fencing and mutual bowing, nibbling and preening), but no comparative study of differences from *impavida*; croaks noisily in squabbles over food.

Size: 80–96 cm, wingspan 210–250 cm (both figures refer to entire *melanophrys* complex), wing 50–56 cm, weight 2.9–4.6 kg. Female averages smaller than male in culmen, tail and wing measurements, and overall weight, but considerable overlap in all of these.

Similar forms: Very similar to Campbell Albatross and only ads may be identifiable if seen well, principally using underwing pattern. Campbell has more prominent and extensive eyebrow, pale eye and more black on underwing (see this form for more details). Both Black-browed/Campbell Albatrosses may be confused with Grey-headed when young (though latter has diagnostic shiny black bill), and problems may also arise with young Buller's/Pacific Albatrosses. Best distinguished from these by underwing pattern and general silhouette, and bill pattern given good views. However, identification is more problematic if attempted prior to ageing (primary moult pattern and bill coloration are useful for this). For details see Grey-headed and Buller's/Pacific Albatrosses.

Juv Black-browed Thalassarche [melanophrys] melanophrys or Campbell Albatross T. [m.] impavida. Melanophrys and impavida are generally inseparable in juv/imm plumages, but relatively extensive pale underwing-coverts and narrower eye-patch in these birds suggest former (much individual variation and overlap). Note, in both forms collar varies greatly in extent and shape but is usually incomplete and often restricted to neck-sides. Olive or grey-brown bill with black tip and thin pale ring in front also typical of T. [melanophrys] (cf. Grey-headed Albatross). Off Lord Howe Island, Jul 2005 (left) and South I, New Zealand, Feb 2001. © Hadoram Shirihai.

Advanced/older imm (probably late third-year) Black-browed Albatross Thalassarche [melanophrys] melanophrys, *still with extensive black on underwing, grey wash to head and duller orange bill. Off Kerguelen, Nov 1999. © Hadoram Shirihai.*

Juv Black-browed Thalassarche [melanophrys] melanophrys *or Campbell Albatross T. [m.] impavida. A juv with extensive white on underwing. Underwing pattern superficially very similar to imm Grey-headed Albatross T. chrysostoma but note relatively whiter head, clear black eye-patch and blacker bill-tip. Off Auckland Island, Jan 2004. © Hadoram Shirihai.*

Distribution and biology

Distribution, movements and population: Southern Ocean on South Georgia, Crozet, Kerguelen, Heard and McDonald, Macquarie, Bishop and Clerk Is, Snares, Campbell and Antipodes; also islands off S Chile and the Falklands. Disperses at sea in Southern Ocean, in winter reaching north to 20°S, in summer principally at 40–70°S, and vagrant to N Atlantic north to Greenland, Iceland and Norway. Population perhaps three million individuals, with up to 80% in the Falklands, in mid- to late 1990s.

Diet and feeding: Fish and krill, with some cephalopods and jellyfish, mostly taken by surface-seizing, pursuit-plunging, surface-plunging and surface-diving. Follows boats, where regularly consorts with other tubenoses, and is a regular scavenger, stealing prey from other seabirds. Also follows cetaceans.

Social behaviour: Gregarious year-round. Monogamous; pair-bonds probably long-lasting. Well-defined aggressive and courtship displays.

Breeding biology: Breeds annually in late Sep–mid-Nov onwards, usually on terraces or steep slopes of tussac grass, occasionally bare rocky areas and islets, and sometimes in association with other albatrosses or penguins. Nest a column of soil, grass and roots with central depression. Lays one whitish egg with fine red-brown spots at broad end, incubated 65–72 days. Chicks fledge in 110–125 days. Single-brooded. Both sexes incubate and provision young.

Conservation Endangered and possibly faces most severe threats

Ad Black-browed Albatross Thalassarche [melanophrys] melanophrys *with chick, the Falklands, Jan 2001. © Hadoram Shirihai.*

of any albatross. A Nov–Dec 2000 survey in the Falklands noted a decline of over 86,000 pairs since previous survey, in 1995, with over 27,500 pairs lost on Beauchêne I alone. Longline fishing and over-fishing of food sources probably threaten virtually all populations, including small numbers breeding in Australasian waters and those on Kerguelen and Macquarie, which also fish in former area (over 1500 were estimated to be killed annually in 1989–95 in this region alone). Larger colonies in Falklands threatened by longline operations over Patagonian shelf and those from South Georgia, where a significant decrease has been noted since 1990, are affected by development of similar practices in South African waters. It is known to be one of the commonest species taken as bycatch in Australian waters, and a decline has been noted at Kerguelen since 1990 due to low juv recruitment.

Taxonomy Usually considered polytypic, with nominate *melanophrys* throughout range, except Campbell, where replaced by *impavida*. Recent molecular work suggests *impavida* is sufficiently distinct to warrant specific status, but more research into the relationships of these forms is clearly required as, in recent years, they have freely hybridized on Campbell. Those on the Falklands exhibit genetic differences from other *melanophrys* populations.

Campbell Albatross
Thalassarche [melanophrys] impavida   Plate 7

Identification

Confusion risks: Black-browed Albatross *T. [m.] melanophrys* in all plumages, and young Grey-headed *T. chrysostoma* and, to lesser extent, Buller's/Pacific Albatrosses *T. [bulleri]*.

Main characters: All features and plumage development as Black-browed (which see); for detailed separation see below.

Voice: See Black-browed.

Size: 88–90 cm, averages smaller than *melanophrys* in culmen, tail and wing measurements and overall weight of male. Wing 49–54 cm, weight 2.2–3.8 kg. Female averages smaller than male in culmen, tarsus, tail and wing measurements, and overall weight, but considerable overlap in all of these.

Similar forms: Compared to Black-browed, ad has diagnostic straw-coloured irides and, albeit with much individual variation and overlap, triangular black eyebrow of *impavida* is usually more prominent and extensive (especially in front of eye where reaches

Ad Campbell Albatross Thalassarche [melanophrys] impavida: *right bird has more black around 'elbow', inner coverts and trailing edge, whilst the bird on the left is extreme in showing reduced black streaking and larger white area (as many ad* melanophrys). *On the other hand, older imm or younger ad* melanophrys *have less clean white coverts with more extensive black markings. Note the great individual variation (and overlap with* melanophrys) *in the dark triangle around the eye, thus leaving the straw-coloured irides as the single, most reliable diagnostic for identifying* impavida, *but bear in mind that it is only detectable in very close views and at certain angles. Between Antipodes and Snares, Jan 2007. © Hadoram Shirihai.*

base of bill), while yellow bill has orange tip (less reddish). Underwing usually has slightly more black, which can appear less clearly separated from white centre of wing. More extensive black especially apparent on elbow region and (mostly inner) trailing edge, usually separating white coverts from secondary tips, thus black of secondaries more exposed and almost reaches elbow, whereas in *T. [m.] melanophrys* trailing edge narrower and white of coverts tends to reach tip of inner secondaries, with black elbow region and trailing edge well separated. However, these features are often very hard to appreciate in the field (except in extremes), with much overlap and individual variation in both forms; also it is important to realise that younger/near-ad *melanophrys* may appear to have similar amount of black to ad *impavida*, making it inadvisable to rely on underwing alone. Young tend to exhibit similar degrees of overlap, with *impavida* generally having less white on underwing (especially on secondaries), but this is of little use at sea. Otherwise inseparable in the field in such plumages. Being very similar to Black-browed, also likely to be confused with young Grey-headed, and some problems may arise with young Buller's/Pacific Albatrosses (which see).

Distribution and biology

Distribution, movements and population: Restricted to Campbell and tiny offshore islet of Jeanette Marie, where total population was 19,000–26,000 pairs in the 1990s. One recently observed in a Black-browed Albatross colony on Kerguelen. Disperses through S Pacific, the Tasman and Ross Seas, and once to Indian Ocean in non-breeding season, when principally occurs at 24–48°S.

Diet and feeding: Few specific data, presumably much as Black-browed Albatross.

Social behaviour: Presumably much as Black-browed Albatross.

Breeding biology: Few specific data, largely as Black-browed Albatross, but lays single egg annually during period 24 Sep–8 Oct. Chicks and ads depart colonies in Apr–May.

Conservation Vulnerable but numbers stable or increasing since 1984, though between 1960s and 1980s may have decreased by as much as 33% at some colonies, perhaps due to natural changes in marine environment. The only significant on-land threat is natural, namely predation of eggs and chicks by skuas *Catharacta* and, at sea, giant petrels *Macronectes* spp. Tuna

Juv Campbell Thalassarche [melanophrys] impavida *or Black-browed Albatrosses* T. [m.] melanophrys. *In close views this bird appeared to have dull orange-brown irides (suggesting the diagnostic eye colour of* impavida *may already develop at a young age, but still not as obviously honey-coloured as imm and ad); also very limited pale on underwing-coverts and perhaps broader eye-patch may suggest* impavida *rather than* melanophrys. *Off Lord Howe I, Jul 2004. © Hadoram Shirihai.*

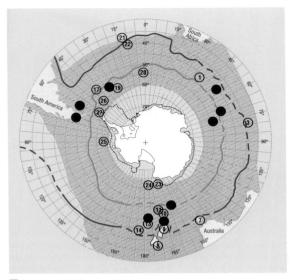

Ad Grey-headed Albatross Thalassarche chrysostoma. *Grey hood, bill colour (bright yellow edges and reddish tip) and very broad and ragged leading and trailing edges to underwing (see photo below) readily identify ads. Some have paler grey heads that can wear even lighter. Off Kerguelen, Nov 1999. © Hadoram Shirihai.*

■ Black-browed Albatross *Thallassarche [m.] melanophrys*
▓ Cambell Island Albatross *Thallassarche [m.] impavida*

● Crozet
● Kerguelen
● Heard & McDonald
● Macquarie
● Snares
⑪ Campbell

● Antipodes
● South American offshore
  islands
● Falklands
● South Georgia

longline fishing off New Zealand and S Australia took significant numbers of juvs and smaller quantities of ads as bycatch (although this problem had almost been eliminated off New Zealand by 2001); of banded albatrosses killed by longliners off Australia in 1987–94, 13% were this form.
Taxonomy Recent molecular analysis has suggested that this form, which was formerly considered a subspecies of *melanophrys*, is sufficiently distinct to warrant specific status, but this is not yet confirmed by other data. Both taxa breed sympatrically on Campbell, where *melanophrys* is extralimital.

Grey-headed Albatross
Thalassarche chrysostoma   Plate 7

Identification
Confusion risks: Young Black-browed/Campbell Albatrosses *T. [melanophrys]*, and to certain extent Buller's/Pacific Albatrosses *T. [bulleri]*.
Main characters: Small, compact black-and-white and grey-hooded albatross; underwing pattern (which changes with age) most closely resembles Black-browed. Jizz slightly different, with shorter and slimmer 'hand', more rounded head and shorter and stockier neck, but difficult to judge at sea without appropriate experience. **Ad** has medium to dark grey hood (forecrown perhaps slightly paler), merging with (but sometimes clearly demarcated from) white foreneck and lower whitish-grey hindneck; rest of underparts white and has restricted black triangular loral patch very near black eye. Bill glossy black, with bright yellow line on outer edges of both mandibles, narrower on culmen to tip, where becomes pink subterminally, while on lower mandible yellow outline reaches three-quarters of bill length from base, before tapering out. Underwing-coverts largely white, bordered by clear black trailing and (two to three times broader) leading edges and wingtip; black/white areas sharply demarcated, with more diffuse

streaking on larger primary-coverts and elbow region, where leading edge reaches widest point. Primary bases generally all dark. Legs and feet pinkish bluish-grey. **Juv** grey-hooded, the entire head/neck can appear medium to dark grey, but usually has variable amounts of whitish-grey on foreface/lower cheeks, and paler grey foreneck, imparting darker hindneck and indistinct broad neck-side collar merging with dark mantle and white underparts on lower foreneck (appears sharply demarcated in flight). Small ill-defined dusky eye-patch. Bill mostly dark greyish brown-black with prominent blacker tip, but at sea almost invariably appears uniform black. Underwing generally uniform black; at sea pale grey coverts hardly visible, unless catch light at close quarters. With wear at sea grey hood becomes paler, especially on face. **Younger imm**, following first moult, much as juv, but neck and head whiter, and underwing becomes whitish-grey, streaked black on coverts (varies individually and with light/distance). Crown, upper neck-sides and throat, and perhaps much of foreneck,

Ad Grey-headed Albatross Thalassarche chrysostoma. *Amount of white on underwing-coverts and intensity of hood varies individually (this is an extreme example). Note, even in close views, the bright yellow on the bill is not obvious. Off Kerguelen, Nov 1999. © Hadoram Shirihai.*

Juv Grey-headed Albatross Thalassarche chrysostoma. *When still fresh, grey hood appears more complete (often with characteristic pale fore-cheek area) and easily eliminates juv Black-browed/Campbell Albatross* T. [melanophrys]. *Unlike the latter, note uniform dark bill. S Atlantic, Mar 2006. © Hadoram Shirihai.*

Young imm Grey-headed Albatross Thalassarche chrysostoma. *Following first moult and/or feather abrasion, grey of head is reduced and pale underwing-coverts develop, thus becoming superficially very similar to juv Black-browed* T. [melanophrys] melanophrys, *and Campbell Albatrosses* T. [m.] impavida, *but bill still largely evenly dark, lacking obvious dark tip. Off Kerguelen, Nov 1999. © Hadoram Shirihai.*

ill-defined whitish-grey and ear-coverts pale grey, while darkest grey is hindneck, tapering on lower foreneck to form typical dusky collar, emphasizing pale face. Only as third-year does bill clearly change (though still variable) to partial and/or dull yellowish on culmen and base of lower mandible (visible only at close range), but still appears all black at distance. Head becomes whiter (with reduced or paler grey wash), emphasizing narrower collar, and underwing-covers variably whiten (some intermediate between juv and ad-like, others much as ad, but black streaks still numerous, especially on outer coverts and elbow region, where black of coverts reaches trailing edge). **Older imm** not always clearly separable, unless moult carefully assessed. However, advanced birds already approach ads, with much whiter underwing-coverts, but latter variably more streaked black and less boldly patterned, while bill usually has duller and less extensive yellow edges, and most still show some vestiges of immaturity on (paler) greyish head. Many five/six-year olds inseparable from ads at sea.

Voice: Vocabulary and call structure like other small albatrosses, particularly Black-browed (which see); see also group introduction.

Size: 70–85 cm, wingspan 220 cm, wing 48–55 cm, weight 2.6–4.35 kg. Female averages smaller than male in tarsus, tail and wing measurements, and overall weight, but quite considerable overlap in all of these.

Similar forms: For identification of all plumages (even very distant birds), overall shape, especially compared to Black-browed/Campbell, is distinctive, being smallish and rather compact, proportionately slimmer winged ('hand' shorter and more pointed) and shorter necked, with rounded head profile. Most likely to be confused with young Black-browed/Campbell, especially if incorrectly aged. Primary moult pattern and bill coloration, and knowledge of overall age-related plumage patterning, are useful to avoid this. The importance of correct ageing is demonstrable: second-/third-year Grey-headed, which lacks solid dark hood, but typically has whiter head and dusky neck-collar, as well as relatively more white in underwing, may thus strongly resemble juv Black-browed/Campbell. But, if aged correctly (note visibly renewed three outer blacker primaries) observers can exclude latter by blackish bill (not mainly dull olive-/yellowish-brown with black tip like juv and second-/third-year Black-browed/Camp-

bell). Greyish head and blackish bill are important characters for older imm, as underwings are very similar. For details of separation from Buller's/Pacific Albatrosses see latter.

Distribution and biology

Distribution, movements and population: Southern Ocean on Diego Ramírez and Ildefonso (off Tierra del Fuego), South Georgia, Prince Edward, Marion, Crozet, Kerguelen, Macquarie and Campbell. Ranges at sea, mainly in cold waters, south of 25°S (46°S in summer), occasionally reaching 15°S in Humboldt Current. Population estimated at 92,300 breeding pairs and perhaps 600,000 individuals (principally based on 1990s counts).

Diet and feeding: Fish and cephalopods with some krill and

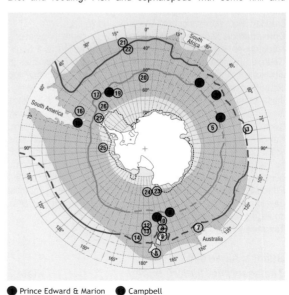

Prince Edward & Marion
Crozet
Kerguelen
Macquarie
Campbell
South American offshore islands
South Georgia

Older imm Grey-headed Albatross Thalassarche chrysostoma. Underwing-coverts already have much white but still less than ad, and pattern typically more ragged; bill already approaches ad but much duller and from most angles looks uniformly dark (cf. Black-browed/Campbell Albatross T. [melanophrys]); note also traces of imm greyish collar. Off Kerguelen, Nov 1999. © Hadoram Shirihai.

carrion, mostly taken by surface-seizing, as well as surface-diving and shallow-plunging. Congregates around boats in the Falklands, but more rarely elsewhere. Regularly consorts with other tubenoses and cetaceans (except around New Zealand).

Social behaviour: Solitary or in small groups year-round, but congregates in much larger flocks at food source. Monogamous; pairbonds probably life-long. Well-defined aggressive and courtship displays. Colonial nester.

Breeding biology: Breeds biennially in late Sep–Oct, usually on cliff ledges with tussac grass, often in association with other albatrosses. Nest a column of soil, grass and roots with central depression. Lays one whitish egg with fine red-brown spots at broad end, incubated 69–78 days. Chicks fledge in c.140 days. Singlebrooded. Both sexes incubate and provision young.

Conservation Vulnerable and declining, in some populations markedly so, e.g. a decrease of c.20% documented at a South Georgia breeding island in recent years and general declines in all colonies in group evident since the late 1980s. This archipelago supports over 50% of the global breeding population. Elsewhere, those breeding on Campbell have declined by up to 85% since the 1940s, apparently largely due to environmental factors. Only the relatively small Marion population is known to be increasing. Pelagic fishing poses greatest threat, with large numbers of imms (80% of 400 individuals annually in 1989–95) taken as bycatch by Japanese tuna longliners in Australian waters, with significant numbers also taken by Patagonian toothfish longliners off the Prince Edwards and unknown numbers at Kerguelen. Potential development of commercial squid fisheries in the Southern Ocean could, if implemented, offer a significant threat.

Taxonomy Monotypic.

Buller's Albatross
Thalassarche [bulleri] bulleri   Plate 7

Identification

Confusion risks: Pacific *T.* [*bulleri*] sp., Grey-headed *T. chrysostoma* and Salvin's Albatrosses *T.* [*c.*] *salvini*. Atlantic Yellow-nosed

Albatross *T.* [*chlororhynchos*] *chlororhynchos* (being grey-headed) and young Black-browed/Campbell Albatrosses *T.* [*melanophrys*] may also offer pitfalls.

Main characters: Small, slightly built, black-and-white, grey-hooded albatross, with underwing pattern (which does not change with age) midway between Grey-headed and Yellow-nosed Albatrosses. **Ad** has pale to medium grey hood, with quite extensive whitish forehead to about mid-crown, where becomes ill-defined, bordered by whitish-grey lower foreneck and white underparts; triangular black loral patch near black eye extends only indistinctly behind it. Bill glossy black with broad bright yellow line on outer edges of both mandibles, covering entire culmen to tip, while on lower mandible yellow reaches black tip. Underwing-coverts largely clean white, bordered by broad and clearly demarcated black leading edge, broader near body, becoming gradually narrower toward carpal and extending noticeably across 'hand' (sometimes appearing slightly ragged); trailing edge very narrow (and indistinct), and wingtip almost uniform black. Legs and feet pale pinkish bluish-grey. **Juv** approaches ad, being grey-hooded, entire head/neck sometimes appearing uniform medium grey, but duller usually more extensively whitish crown (sometimes entire crown), variable paler/whitish-grey throat/upper foreneck, imparting ill-defined, darker (more greyish-brown) and broader collar merging with dark mantle, and white upper breast; small ill-defined dusky eye-patch. Bill mostly pale greyish-horn with prominent black tip (or subterminal mark). Underwing generally as ad (see above), but sometimes mark diffuse, mainly near primary-coverts and elbow region. With wear at sea grey hood becomes progressively whiter especially on crown and face, until almost white-headed, recalling same-age Black-browed/Campbell Albatrosses (see below). **Younger imm** much as juv, but purer grey neck and head, and dusky-grey collar less pronounced, but with wear becomes progressively whiter and more patchy on crown, upper neck-sides, throat and foreneck, emphasizing collar. Only in third-year does bill visibly change (though still variable), usually becoming darker (blackish-brown) on sides, with pale yellowish-brown lines on culmen and lower mandible, and newly moulted hood overall purer grey, with further-reduced collar. **Older imm** not always separable, unless moult carefully assessed (often depends on state of wear); advanced birds strongly approach ads (perhaps inseparable at sea), but bill usually has duller and less sharply demarcated yellow ridges.

Voice: See group introduction concerning vocal and nuptial displays on breeding grounds, which generally resemble Black-browed (which see), but no comparative study of differences; croaks noisily in squabbles over food.

Size: 76–81 cm, wingspan 200–213 cm (both figures apply to entire

Juv Buller's Thalassarche [bulleri] bulleri or Pacific Albatross T. [b.] sp. Combination of grey hood and ad-like pattern to leading edge to underwing, as well as dark bill tip, eliminates juvs of all congeners. South of Sydney, Oct 2001. © Hadoram Shirihai.

Ad Buller's Albatrosses Thalassarche [bulleri] bulleri. *Combination of extensive whitish forecrown to grey hood and well-defined and even-width leading edge to underwing, as well as extensive yellow edges to bill identify it from superficially similar Grey-headed Albatross* T. chrysostoma *and Atlantic Yellow-nosed Albatrosses* T. [chlororhynchos] chlororhynchos; *from latter also by overall shape. Very similar to Pacific Albatross* T. [bulleri] sp. *Off the Snares, Dec 1998. © Hadoram Shirihai.*

bulleri complex), wing 49–54 cm, weight 2.05–3.35 kg. Female averages smaller than male in culmen, tarsus, tail and wing measurements, but considerable overlap in all of these.
Similar forms: Very similar to Pacific Albatross and perhaps only classic ad identifiable at sea, and only if seen well (for their separation see Pacific). Both ad Buller's/Pacific could be confused with superficially similar grey-hooded plumages of several congeners, especially Grey-headed and Salvin's. Former also has very similar bill pattern and latter (especially in later stages) can appear to have yellowish lines on bill (see these forms for bill differences). In my experience, the yellow lines in ad Buller's/Pacific are nearly always far more visible at long range, but very hard to see in Grey-headed, sometimes even when close. Moreover, both Grey-headed and Salvin's (all ages) are further eliminated, especially if seen well, using underwing pattern. In ad/imm Grey-headed the leading edge, especially, is broader than in Buller's/Pacific (all ages). If difficult to judge differences in width of black leading edge, concentrate on its shape: it is less sharply defined in Grey-headed, being more ragged, especially on the 'elbow' (where broadest), and thus more triangular between body and carpal, but narrows smoothly and solidly from body to carpal in Buller's/Pacific (see above). Salvin's has black underwing margins much narrower, especially on leading edge, and distinctive 'thumb' mark. Grey-headed is also more compact, with rounder head and less robust bill, whilst Salvin's is distinctly larger and broader winged compared to Buller's/Pacific. For separation of Buller's/Pacific and Yellow-nosed see latter. Problems may arise with young Grey-headed and Black-browed/ Campbell. Juv Grey-headed and Black-browed/Campbell have diagnostic dark underwings, but on the water very few features can be used to separate them from juv Buller's/Pacific. However, latter when not heavily worn has distinctive pale scaly fringes to scapulars and inner upperwing-coverts (lacking or indistinct in equivalent plumages of others). Note, most juv Black-browed/Campbell have narrow whitish subterminal line just before tip, but bill of juv Grey-headed is essentially uniform black, both unlike juv Buller's/Pacific. Several other differences in head pattern in fresh juvs can be used, but these parts wear very soon, obscuring differences. Furthermore, separation of Buller's/Pacific from Grey-headed on the water is complicated because bills of juv or younger imm Grey-headed and imm Buller's/Pacific can appear almost uniformly dark, whilst their upperparts wear uniform dark brown. This pitfall was well illustrated recently by a bird photographed off Chile (T. Pym pers. comm.). A few features may be used in combination to separate

them: in profile, the crown of Buller's/Pacific peaks further behind the eye whilst, importantly, the length of the jowl or chin is noticeably longer in Buller's/Pacific, giving them a longer faced appearance. Also the sloping forehead produces a less rounded crown than Grey-headed. Furthermore, the eye position may in Buller's/Pacific be closer to the bill and higher, whilst the white eye mark is more of a narrow crescent in Buller's/Pacific (larger, more triangular on Grey-headed). Several differences in bill structure separate the two on close inspection.

Distribution and biology
Distribution, movements and population: Restricted to Solander and the Snares. This form and Pacific Albatross (few specific at-sea records) range in Southern Ocean west to S Australia and east to S South America and SW Atlantic, with one record (of three individuals) at entrance to Falkland Sound. No records from Indian Ocean, but recorded recently (Aug 1995) off South Africa, and during breeding season principally at 38–50°S. Population

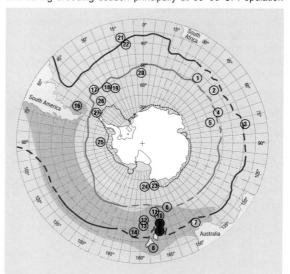

■ Buller's Albatross *Thalassarche* [bulleri] bulleri.
▨ Pacific Albatross *Thalassarche* [bulleri] sp.
● New Zealand offshore islands
⑧ New Zealand offshore islands
● Snares
⑭ Chatham

estimated at 11,400 breeding pairs, with perhaps 50,000–58,000 individuals, in the late 1990s.

Diet and feeding: Squid, with some fish and krill, mostly taken by surface-seizing and shallow-plunging. Follows boats.

Social behaviour: Usually solitary or in very small groups away from colonies, though large feeding flocks have occasionally been noted around boats. Monogamous; pair-bonds probably life-long. Well-defined aggressive and courtship displays.

Breeding biology: Most breed annually in late Dec/mid-Jan–late Feb, in dense vegetation (sometimes within forest) on slopes and ledges overlooking sea, occasionally among rocks in more open situations. Nest a column of soil and grass with central depression. Strong site fidelity. Lays one whitish egg with fine brownish-red spots at broad end, mean incubation period 69 days. Mean fledging period 167 days. Single-brooded. Both sexes incubate and provision young.

Conservation Vulnerable. Data on population trends from the Snares (where c.75% of population breed) suggest a very significant increase in last 30 years (from 4664 pairs in 1969 to 8877 pairs in 1997), but longline fishing is a significant threat, especially to ads, which winter in waters where such effort is concentrated at that season. Weka *Gallirallus australis* may take eggs on Solander.

Taxonomy Usually considered polytypic, with nominate *bulleri* in Solander and the Snares, replaced by Pacific Albatross on Chatham and Three Kings. Latter now considered sufficiently distinct to warrant specific status based on DNA analysis, but further research appears desirable.

Pacific Albatross
Thalassarche [bulleri] sp.   Plate 7

Identification

Similar species: Buller's *T. [bulleri] bulleri*, Grey-headed *T. chrysostoma*, and Salvin's Albatrosses *T. [c.] salvini*. Young Black-browed/Campbell Albatrosses *T. [melanophrys]* may also provide a pitfall.

Main characters: Plumage development and features as Buller's Albatross (which see); for detailed separation see below.

Voice: See Buller's Albatross.

Size: Averages smaller than *bulleri* in wing measurements and overall weight of male. Wing 47–53 cm, weight 2.15–3.3 kg. Female averages smaller than male in culmen, tarsus, tail and wing measurements, and overall weight, but considerable overlap in most of these.

Juv Buller's Thalassarche [bulleri] bulleri *or Pacific Albatross* T. [b.] *sp., in fresh plumage has characteristic pale scaly fringes above (see text). Off Chile, Oct 2006. © Gonzalo González.*

Similar forms: Compared to Buller's, ad Pacific has medium to dark (rather than pale to medium) bluish-grey hood and more restricted silvery cap, which reaches forecrown or almost mid-crown (rather than nearly always to mid-crown); thus cap appears more contrasting, and, in most, blackish lores reach nearer to bill base, usually covering two-thirds to three-quarters of area between eye and bill (half to two-thirds in Buller's). But large degree of overlap and individual variation, and effects of lighting, angle/distance of view and degree of feather wear can all render these features of little use. Pacific has deeper based bill and, in most, the yellow stripe on lower mandible is narrower relative to the width of the exposed lower mandible: the former being less than half width of latter (half or more in Buller's). But value of this very limited at sea, as often difficult to calculate such proportions, while border between mandibles is rarely visible, even at moderate/close ranges, and some overlap and individual variation exists, further negating usefulness of this feature. I recommend labelling only typical ad with all of above-mentioned features. Like ad, juv and imm of these two also tend to differ in darkness of grey, but only when fresh, and in extent of dark lores, but even greater overlap makes separation in such plumages unreliable. Being very similar to Buller's, also confusable with Grey-headed, and some problems may arise with young Black-browed/Campbell, but see Buller's for details.

Distribution and biology

Distribution, movements and population: Restricted to Chatham and Three Kings (only tiny numbers on latter). Range rarely reach-

Ad Pacific Albatrosses T. [bulleri] sp. *Almost identical to ad Buller's* T. [b.] bulleri, *except has darker grey hood with better defined and smaller white forecrown, broader black loral patch and relatively narrower yellow lower edge to bill, and perhaps somewhat broader leaing edge to underwing (see right photo). Off Chatham, Jan 2000 © Hadoram Shirihai.*

Left, imm (second/third-year) Grey-headed Albatross Thalassarche chrysostoma. Off Australia, Aug 2006 © P. J. Milburn; and right, imm, probably third-year T. [bulleri], probably Pacific Albatross. Off Chile, Nov 2004 © Tony Pym. Imm Grey-headed and Buller's/Pacific of this age can be very difficult to separate on the water. In profile, Buller's/Pacific appears longer faced with a less rounded head, the eye is closer to the bill and the white eye mark forms more of a narrow crescent rather than a triangle. Note the noticeably longer jowl than in Grey-headed. In flight they are easily separated by their underwing patterns.

es New Zealand coast but occurs at sea in Southern Ocean west to S Australia and east to S South America (though see remarks under *bulleri*). Breeding population estimated at 18,000 pairs, with overall perhaps 80,000–90,000 individuals in 1990s.

Diet and feeding: Probably largely as *bulleri* (which see).

Social behaviour: Probably largely as *bulleri* (which see).

Breeding biology: Breeds annually in late Oct–late Nov, on ledges and in holes in cliffs, usually near top, and on flat to rolling rocky-topped islets. Nest a column of soil and herb stems, with central depression. Lays one whitish egg with fine brownish-red spots at broad end, incubated 69 days. Nestling period unknown, but most chicks fledge May–Jun. Single-brooded. Both sexes incubate and provision young.

Conservation Not globally threatened but no data concerning population trends or potential threats available, though ads known to forage during breeding season in waters fished by longline vessels. Two deaths were reported in 1996–2001.

Taxonomy Formerly considered a subspecies of *bulleri*, but recent molecular studies suggest that this (unnamed) form is sufficiently distinct to warrant specific status (though see comments under *bulleri*). The form has been afforded the name *platei* but this has apparently been invalidated due to the designated type specimen being a misidentified immature *bulleri*.

Atlantic Yellow-nosed Albatross
Thalassarche [chlororhynchos] chlororhynchos
Plate 6

Identification

Confusion risks: Indian Yellow-nosed Albatross *T. [chlororhynchos] carteri*, and Buller's/Pacific *T. [bulleri]*, Grey-headed *T. chrysostoma* and Salvin's Albatrosses *T. [c.] salvini* could also offer pitfalls.

Main characters: Small albatross with slender profile, very narrow pointed wings, proportionately very slim neck and body, small head and long narrow bill; generally black and white with slight grey hood, and underwing pattern (which does not vary with age) has narrowest black margins of smaller albatrosses. **Ad** has uniform pale to medium grey hood, quite extensive whitish forehead to about mid-crown where becomes ill-defined, and no clear-cut border with whitish-grey lower foreneck (sometimes entire throat and foreneck). Dusky triangular loral patch between bill and black eye, indistinctly extending behind it. Bill glossy black with rather narrow bright yellow culmen to tip, where becomes orange-red, but at distance usually appears all black. Underwing-coverts largely clean white, bordered by clear-cut black leading edge

(relatively narrower than in *T. [bulleri]* but clearly broader than *T. [cauta]*), broadening slightly near body, mainly near elbow region; overall appearance is of almost even-width leading edge, but trailing edge very narrow (and indistinct), and wingtip almost uniform black. Legs and feet pale pinkish bluish-grey. **Juv** approaches ad, grey hood duller, may appear uniform medium grey, but darker on hindneck and usually has more extensive and/or ill-defined whiter crown, and variable paler/whitish-grey on face, throat and foreneck, imparting diffuse and incomplete darker (slightly brownish-tinged) collar. Smaller ill-defined dusky eye-patch. Bill mostly greyish-black. Underwing generally as ad (see above) but sometimes has slightly diffuse streaking, mainly near primary-coverts and elbow region. With wear at sea grey hood whitens sufficiently, especially on crown/face, to appear almost white-headed, not un-

Ad Atlantic Yellow-nosed Albatross Thalassarche [chlororhynchos] chlororhynchos. Overall slender appearance and typical underwing-pattern: amongst small albatrosses, both Yellow-nosed Albatrosses have the black leading edge narrowest, but only slightly so than Buller's/Pacific T. [bulleri]. Note grey hood can vary in intensity and is not always easily visible (cf. Indian Yellow-nosed). Off Inaccessible I, Tristan group, Mar 2006. © Hadoram Shirihai.

Atlantic Yellow-nosed Albatrosses Thalassarche [chlororhynchos] chlororhynchos. *Very similar to ad Indian Yellow-nosed* T. [c.] carteri, *except more extensive grey of head/neck, forming hood with restricted white forecrown, and slightly different bill pattern. Gough, Sep 1999 © Peter Ryan.*

like Indian Yellow-nosed Albatross of same age but fresher condition (see below). **Younger imm** still much as juv, but purer and somewhat more extensive grey on neck and head, and whiter than ad, becoming progressively patchier with wear; duskier grey hindneck less pronounced than juv. During second/third-year bill changes more obviously (though still variable), with brownish-cream culmen gradually becoming paler dull brownish-yellow, but upper tip often dark subterminally; newly moulted hood becomes overall purer greyer with further reduced collar. **Older imm** not always clearly separable, unless moult pattern carefully assessed (often also depends on wear), but bill generally develops to enable separation of advanced imm from ad. At sea some are difficult or impossible to separate from full ad.

Voice: See group introduction for vocal and nuptial displays on breeding grounds (chiefly high-pitched clattering cry, so-called braying and, like congeners, mutual bowing, tail fanning, bill touching and preening), but no comparative study of differences from *carteri*; croaks noisily in squabbles over food.

Size: 71–82 cm, wingspan 180–200 cm (both figures refer to entire *chlororhynchos* complex), wing 45–52 cm, weight 1.87–2.84 kg. Insufficient comparative material is available to comment on any sex-related differences in mensural data.

Similar forms: Very similar to Indian Yellow-nosed Albatross, principally differing in bill and hood colour (for identification features separating them see latter). Both, especially grey-headed Atlantic Yellow-nosed Albatross, are likely to be confused with several superficially similar congeners. But given distinctive slender wing and body shapes (see above), together with distinctly narrower, even-width leading edge to underwing, is readily separated from all other greyish-headed small albatrosses, namely Buller's/Pacific, Grey-headed and Salvin's. When close, slender bill and colour diagnostic. Both Atlantic and Indian Yellow-nosed when sat on water (and underwing pattern cannot be evaluated) may be confusable with young Buller's/Pacific, Grey-headed and Black-browed/Campbell *T.* [*melanophrys*], but overall structure, head profile, and colour and shape of bill (as described above) can still be used for identification. Juv Buller's/Pacific has pale bill with dark tip, but it becomes overall darker in imm plumage and hence closer to juv/imm to Atlantic Yellow-nosed, which also has greyish head, making separation more difficult if underwing pattern not seen. However, in most cases the grey hood is paler and less complete in juv/imm Atlantic Yellow-nosed and the bill-base meets the head in a straight line, giving the impression that the bill is 'stuck on' (Buller's/Pacific usually has a c.45° angle at the junction of the base of the lower mandible). On the water, both Yellow-nosed Albatrosses in juv/imm plumages can appear superficially similar to Grey-headed and Black-browed/Campbell, which otherwise are separated by the same bill-base structure described above, whilst Black-browed/Campbell also always have pale bill with dark tip. Nevertheless,

Ad Atlantic Yellow-nosed Albatross Thalassarche [chlororhynchos] chlororhynchos. *Note, grey hood can be rather washed out and limited (here scarcely reaching throat and foreneck, whilst crown is almost all white like many Indian Yellow-nosed). Compared to Indian Yellow-nosed dark eye/loral patch is, usually, more extensive, almost reaching bill-base. Off Inaccessible I, Tristan group, Mar 2006. © Hadoram Shirihai.*

Fresh juv Atlantic Yellow-nosed Albatross Thalassarche [chlororhynchos] chlororhynchos. *Very similar or indistinguishable from juv Indian Yellow-nosed, except for variable greyer tinge to head and neck (mostly sides), and perhaps better-developed dark eye/loral patch. Both Yellow-nosed Albatrosses can be confused with several other dark-billed small albatrosses in juv and imm stages, especially if underwing patterns are not seen (see main text). Nightingale I, Tristan group, Mar 2003. © Hadoram Shirihai.*

young Yellow-nosed Albatrosses in flight are readily separated from all these forms by underwing pattern, as well as structure.

Distribution and biology

Distribution, movements and population: S Atlantic on Tristan da Cunha group and Gough, and dispersing at sea in Southern Ocean, west to South America (where common at 23°S–45°S), north to 15°S off W Africa, rarely as far as N Atlantic, and east into Indian Ocean and as far as Chatham (where collected). Most remain in local waters or move to W South Africa. Breeding population estimated at 36,800 pairs, with perhaps an overall total of 165,000–185,000 individuals (principally based on 1970s and 1980s data); there is a chronic need for accurate and up-to-date census work.

Diet and feeding: Fish with some cephalopods, mostly taken by surface-seizing and variety of other techniques. Feeds with shearwaters, in association with cetaceans and follows boats.

Social behaviour: Gregarious year-round, but occasionally breeds solitarily. Monogamous; no data on length of pair-bond, but speculated to be shorter than in other albatrosses. Well-defined aggressive and courtship displays.

Breeding biology: Breeds, probably annually, mid-Sep–early Oct, in sheltered ravines and depressions within tussac grass. Lays one whitish egg with fine brown spots at broad end. Incubation period unknown. Chicks fledge in c.130 days. Single-brooded. Both sexes incubate and provision young.

Conservation Near Threatened, and only available data concerning population trends suggests that Gough colony has declined significantly since 1980s and 1990s. With the now-complete cessation of the once-dramatic human exploitation of this species, the greatest threat it now faces (like most albatrosses) is longline fishing. Given its only recently acquired (possible) specific status, its distribution at sea is still imperfectly known, but reports of large numbers of 'Yellow-nosed Albatross' taken as bycatch by tuna fisheries off SE Brazil (14% of all seabirds caught during such operations, equivalent to 900 individuals per annum) would appear to almost certainly involve this form. More concrete data may confirm that it

requires upgrading to Vulnerable in future Red Data listings.

Taxonomy Recent molecular studies have considered this form sufficiently distinct to warrant specific status; it was formerly considered polytypic, with nominate *chlororhynchos* on Tristan da Cunha, replaced by *carteri* in the Indian Ocean, but further work is clearly desirable.

Indian Yellow-nosed Albatross
Thalassarche [chlororhynchos] carteri   Plate 6

Identification

Confusion risks: Atlantic Yellow-nosed Albatross *T.* [*c.*] *chlororhynchos* and perhaps other congeners, if not seen well.

Main characters: Plumage development and features as Atlantic Yellow-nosed Albatross (which see); for detailed separation see below. However, much of head, neck and underparts are essentially white at all ages: in ad, grey is confined to face, from bill base and lower throat to entire head-sides, and in juv these parts are whiter, but has pale grey hindneck extending as indistinct narrow collar to sides of lower neck, and slightly onto cheeks, becoming whiter and fading with each successive moult. Ageing often relies on assessing moult pattern and bill-coloration development.

Voice: See Atlantic Yellow-nosed Albatross.

Size: Probably averages smaller than *chlororhynchos* but lack of mean data for former prohibits detailed analysis. Wing 45–50 cm, weight 1.75–2.93 kg. Insufficient comparative material is available to comment on any sex-related differences in mensural data.

Similar forms: Compared to Atlantic Yellow-nosed, ad Indian has medium grey face, often rather sharply defined and emphasizing white cap, which reaches hindcrown (mid-crown in Atlantic form), where it merges with greyish-white nape; thus white on head and

Ad Indian Yellow-nosed Albatrosses Thalassarche [chlororhynchos] carteri, *off Amsterdam I, Nov 1999 © Hadoram Shirihai.*

neck much more extensive than in Atlantic Yellow-nosed. In most, blackish loral patch restricted to diffuse patch immediately in front of eye, or at most reaches c.½ of distance between eye and bill (rather than as more contrasting patch extending further toward bill base, usually reaching it or almost so in Atlantic Yellow-nosed). But large degree of overlap and individual variation, and effects of lighting, angle/distance and degree of feather wear, may all render these features less useful. Some Atlantic Yellow-nosed have grey confined to head- and neck-sides and hindneck, leaving rest of face and foreneck whiter, but often the restricted white forecrown and more extensive loral patch are still useful features. Some ad Indian Yellow-nosed are extensively greyish washed, but never as much as classic of Atlantic form (though indicates need for caution with less well-marked individuals). Ad Indian Yellow-nosed has yellow stripe on upper mandible ending on bill base in sharp-pointed symmetric arrow shape, whereas it is more rounded in Atlantic Yellow-nosed, but this character is of very limited use at sea, and some (of both forms) appear to be almost intermediate, so this character is also best used only in clear-cut cases. Juv and imm of both forms, like ad, also tend to differ in amount of grey, es-pecially in fresh plumage, and in extent of loral patch, both being more extensive in Atlantic Yellow-nosed. But again some overlap makes separation in younger plumages sometimes unsafe, espe-cially as individual variation caused by wear can make it impos-sible to evaluate precise age and whether degree of white/grey is wear-induced. Nevertheless, many classic-plumaged young can be safely identified. As Atlantic Yellow-nosed, could be confused with Buller's/Pacific T. [bulleri] and perhaps others, but see Atlantic Yellow-nosed for details.

Distribution and biology

Distribution, movements and population: Prince Edward, Crozet, Amsterdam and St Paul, Kerguelen and Chatham (one pair), dis-persing in Southern Ocean, where abundant off S and E coasts of South Africa, and reaches east as far as Australia and New Zealand. Corpses recently found in Brazil. Breeding popula-tion estimated at 36,500 pairs, with perhaps an overall total of 160,000–180,000 individuals (based on 1980s and 1990s counts); there is a chronic need for up-to-date census work at its colonies, other than the crucially important Amsterdam population (which constitutes 70% of world population).

Diet and feeding: Fish with some cephalopods, mostly by surface-seizing and other techniques. Feeds with Australasian Gannet *Sula serrator*, and in association with cetaceans. Like other alba-trosses follows boats.

Social behaviour: Probably as *chlororhynchos* (which see).

Breeding biology: Breeds annually in mid-Sep–early Oct, on rocky cliffs, in dense grass or on bare soil. Lays one whitish egg with

Ad Indian Yellow-nosed Albatrosses Thalassarche [chlororhynchos] carteri. Very similar to ad Atlantic Yellow-nosed T. [c.] chlororhynchos, aside of whiter head and bill pattern. Both forms are typically slender in structure and have anrrow black edges to the underwing. Off Amsterdam I, Nov 1999 © Hadoram Shirihai.

fine brown spots at broad end, incubated 71–72 days. Chicks fledge in c.115 days. Single-brooded. Both sexes incubate and provision young.

Conservation Vulnerable. The only information available con-cerning population trends is from Amsterdam, where colony has declined by c.30% since 1981 and continues to decrease by 7% annually. Tuna longlining in Australian waters and Patagonian toothfish longline fisheries around the Prince Edwards are prob-ably the principal reasons for this marked decline. 'Yellow-nosed Albatrosses' constitute up to 13% of all seabirds taken as bycatch during such operations in recent years. The only other significant identified threat is a viral disease, which causes up to 95% chick mortality in some years.

Taxonomy Formerly considered a subspecies of *chlororhynchos*, recent molecular studies suggest that *carteri* is sufficiently distinct to warrant specific status, but see comments under *chlororhyn-chos*. Debate persists over whether the name *bassi* has prece-dence over *carteri*.

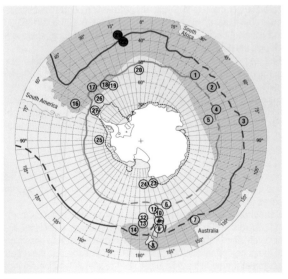

■ Atlantic Yellow-nosed Albatross
Thalassarche [chlororhynchos] chlororhynchos
■ Indian Yellow-nosed Albatross
Thalassarche [chlororhynchos] carteri
① Prince Edward & Marion ④ Kerguelen
② Crozet ㉗ Tristan da Cunha
③ Amsterdam & St Paul ㉒ Gough

Nearly one-year-old Indian Yellow-nosed Albatrosses Thalassarche [chlo-rorhynchos] carteri. Very similar to ad but bill mostly dark and unpatterened; underwing as ad. Off Amsterdam I, Nov 1999 © Hadoram Shirihai.

Sooty albatrosses, giant petrels and other distinct petrels

Ad Sooty Albatross Phoebetria fusca. *Note even, brownish-shaded, plumage; bill proportionally deeper based with yellowish-pink bill-stripe, and higher eye position and somewhat more extensive white to eye-ring (cf. Light-mantled Sooty* P. palpebrata). *Inaccessible I, Sep 1999. © Peter Ryan.*

This section and Plate 8 cover some of those species typical of the coldest waters and others of more northern latitudes, including two sibling-species groups, the sooty albatrosses and giant petrels. The distinctive petrels included here also range widely: among Cape, Antarctic and Snow Petrels, and Southern Fulmar, the former is widespread across the Southern Ocean, except in near-frozen waters surrounding Antarctica, which are the principal feeding areas of the others. Most or all can be observed during a voyage to the Peninsula or other Antarctic areas, e.g. the Ross Sea. Identification, as well as matters of annual cycle and general biology, differ considerably between them and are fully discussed within each account. (Like other albatrosses, female sooty albatrosses are usually smaller than males in several respects; further information and the relative level of overlap, expressed in crude terms, are presented in the species accounts.)

Sooty Albatross *Phoebetria fusca*   Plate 8

Identification

Confusion risks: Light-mantled Sooty Albatross *P. palpebrata*.
Main characters: Medium-sized, uniform sooty-brown albatross with characteristic long narrow wings and wedge-shaped tail. Plumage varies little with age/season, and sexes alike. **Ad** almost uniform, being dark to greyish chocolate-brown, with little contrast, including variably darker head to upper foreneck, belly, wings and tail; even in extremely pale birds, these tracts grade smoothly into paler areas. Plumage tone also varies with light, e.g. when observed close or in strong lighting, contrast between paler/darker

areas enhanced, whereas at distance in cloudy conditions appears overall uniformly darker, with paler parts less contrasting. With wear pale areas, especially nape to upper mantle, bleach paler and browner. White shafts to outer primaries (upperwings)

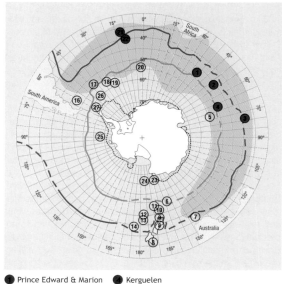

① Prince Edward & Marion ④ Kerguelen
② Crozet ⑪ Tristan da Cunha
③ Amsterdam & St Paul ⑫ Gough

Ad/imm Sooty Albatross Phoebetria fusca. *Note almost uniformly dark brownish plumage, exhibiting little contrast, even with the darker face to upper foreneck and body (which always grade smoothly into the paler plumage tracts). Off Inaccessible I, Mar 2003. © Hadoram Shirihai.*

Ad/imm Sooty Albatross Phoebetria fusca: *note almost two-thirds of white eye-ring is broad, but narrower and broken on lores, whilst bill has yellowish-pink stripe on sides of lower mandible. Off Tristan da Cunha, Mar 2006. © Hadoram Shirihai.*

conspicuous, even at distance. Almost two-thirds of white eye-ring is broad, but narrower and broken on lores. Bill proportionately narrow-based, and yellowish-pink stripe on sides of lower mandible. Legs and feet pale pinkish/bluish-grey. **Juv/imm** overall approaches ad, but neatly and narrowly fringed paler, especially on head and mantle; bill-stripe and eye-ring greyer and outer primary shafts browner, but all difficult to observe at sea. With wear, paler fringes and exposed basal feathering may coalesce to form patchy buffish-grey collar, from nape onto neck-sides and upper mantle. Subsequent imm similar to ad, but when worn appears more strongly bleached and patchier, with some newly moulted dorsal feathers being slightly mottled. Ageing after second-/third-year possible if able to assess moult pattern.

Voice: Largely silent at sea; at breeding sites gives double-syllable calls, the first shrill and second a descending, lower pitched trumpet-like note, also a more drawn-out scream (like a young goat), uttered on ground and in flight; lower pitched than Light-mantled Sooty.

Size: 84–89 cm, wing 49–54 cm, wingspan 203 cm, weight 1.8–3.03 kg. Female averages smaller in culmen, tarsus, tail and wing measurements, and weight (but much overlap in most of these).

Similar species: Easily distinguished from Light-mantled Sooty Albatross given reasonable view due to relative lack of contrast between wings and head/rest of body, but see above for variation caused by lighting and feather wear. However, even on extremely bleached Sooty pale area reaches at most mantle and neck/chest, leaving back to uppertail-coverts and abdomen dark brown (entire body near-uniform greyish in Light-mantled). I have experienced greater problems with darker Light-mantled, which superficially resembles Sooty, than vice versa. Note also differences in ad bill-stripe and eye-ring, the former bluish and latter more restricted in Light-mantled. Note also differences in eye position, higher in Sooty compared to more central point in head on Light-mantled. Sooty averages smaller than Light-mantled, but bill proportionately deeper based, and at sea appears to have broader wings and relatively heavier body, though experience required to appreciate these features. Both could be confused with superficially similar dark (mainly young) giant petrels, but given their distinctive overall shape with heavy thickset body, longer broader neck, shorter tail, rather massive pale-coloured bill and characteristic flap-and-glide flight on differently proportioned wings, should be readily eliminated.

Distribution and biology

Distribution, movements and population: S Atlantic and Indian Oceans with majority on Tristan da Cunha and Gough, Prince Edward and Marion, and much smaller numbers on Crozet, Kerguelen (only a few pairs), Amsterdam and St Paul. Ranges through Southern Ocean south of 30°S, preferring deep waters (mostly north of Antarctic Convergence and in subantarctic to subtropical waters) but reaching 64°S in SW Indian Ocean. Vagrant to New Zealand. Population estimated at 42,000 individuals in late 1970s and early 1980s.

Diet and feeding: Mostly cephalopods and also takes crustaceans, fish and carrion, principally by surface-seizing and presumably mostly nocturnally. Often alone or in small groups of fewer than

Chick Sooty Albatross Phoebetria fusca. *Both Sooty and Light-mantled Sooty have bizarre, mask-faced chicks. Inaccessible Island, Sep 1999. © Peter Ryan.*

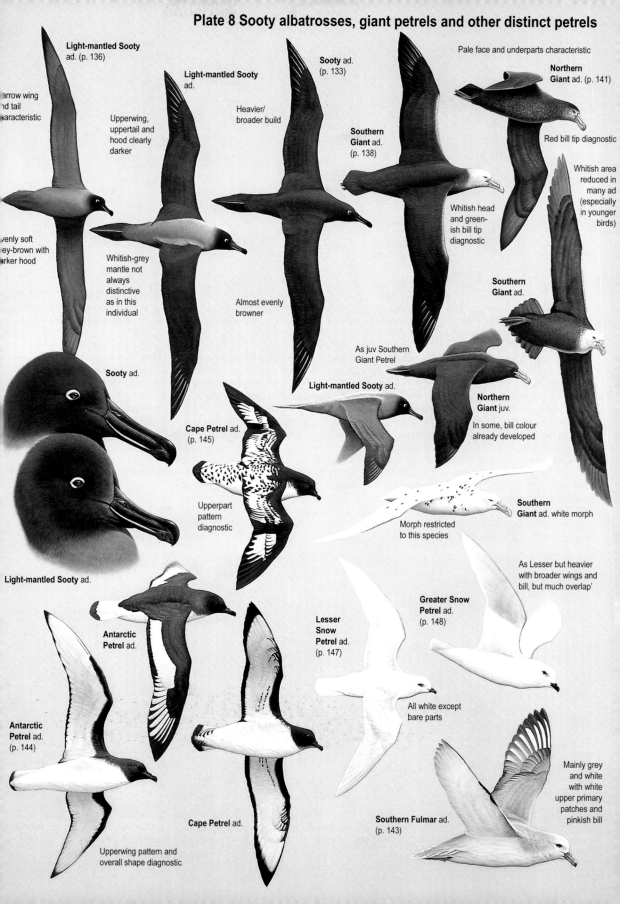

Plate 8 Sooty albatrosses, giant petrels and other distinct petrels

Light-mantled Sooty ad. (p. 136)

arrow wing nd tail aracteristic

Upperwing, uppertail and hood clearly darker

Light-mantled Sooty ad.

Heavier/ broader build

Sooty ad. (p. 133)

Pale face and underparts characteristic

Northern Giant ad. (p. 141)

Red bill tip diagnostic

Southern Giant ad. (p. 138)

venly soft ey-brown with arker hood

Whitish-grey mantle not always distinctive as in this individual

Almost evenly browner

Whitish head and greenish bill tip diagnostic

Whitish area reduced in many ad (especially in younger birds)

Southern Giant ad.

Sooty ad.

Cape Petrel ad. (p. 145)

Light-mantled Sooty ad.

As juv Southern Giant Petrel

Northern Giant juv.

In some, bill colour already developed

Upperpart pattern diagnostic

Morph restricted to this species

Southern Giant ad. white morph

Light-mantled Sooty ad.

As Lesser but heavier with broader wings and bill, but much overlap'

Greater Snow Petrel ad. (p. 148)

Antarctic Petrel ad.

Lesser Snow Petrel ad. (p. 147)

Antarctic Petrel ad. (p. 144)

All white except bare parts

Mainly grey and white with white upper primary patches and pinkish bill

Cape Petrel ad.

Southern Fulmar ad. (p. 143)

Upperwing pattern and overall shape diagnostic

Ad/imm Sooty Albatross Phoebetria fusca. With wear and bleaching develops (variable) buff fringing to mantle and patches on hindneck, contrasting more with darker face to upper foreneck, but still overall appearance is almost uniformly dark and brownish; note also chunkier body and broader wings compared to Light-mantled P. palpebrata. Off Amsterdam I, Mar 2003. © Hadoram Shirihai.

five, occasionally with other albatrosses, shearwaters and terns, and also associates with cetaceans. Less often and more briefly investigates boats than most albatrosses. May travel up to 1200 km on foraging trips from breeding colonies.

Social behaviour: Solitary or in small groups both when feeding and nesting (colonies usually larger than Light-mantled Sooty Albatross). Monogamous and forms life-long pair-bonds.

Breeding biology: Breeds, biennially (if successful) in Oct in small, loose colonies on vegetated, sheltered cliff ledges (including inland on Gough) or steep slopes. Constructs low nest mound of mud and plant material, lined with grass. Lays one white egg marked reddish-brown, incubated 65–75 days. Chicks fledge in 145–178 days. Single-brooded. Both sexes build nest, incubate eggs and provision young.

Conservation Vulnerable and declining. Humans substantially exploited populations on Tristan da Cunha, though these practices are now illegal, and introduced predators still exert significant threat to breeding success on Kerguelen and Amsterdam. Decline also noted, since 1980s, on other French subantarctic islands due to high ad mortality and low recruitment. Recent reports indicate that tuna longline fishing in Australian Fishing Zone, at least, may be taking a toll on populations.

Taxonomy Monotypic.

Light-mantled Sooty Albatross
Phoebetria palpebrata   Plate 8

Identification
Confusion risks: Sooty Albatross *P. fusca*.
Main characters: Medium-sized, slender, grey-bodied albatross

Ad Light-mantled Sooty Albatross Phoebetria palpebrata in typical flight around nesting cliffs. Compared to Sooty Albatross, note the more slender and pointed wings, and slimmer body, whilst from both above and below with the darker head clearly contrasts, especially with the silvery back. Crozet Is, Mar 2004. © Hadoram Shirihai.

Ad Light-mantled Sooty Albatross Phoebetria palpebrata; head/neck and wings are darkest parts and mantle the palest; bill proportionately rather small with bluish bill-stipe and mid-head eye position with somewhat reduced wite to eye-ring (cf. Sooty P. fusca). South Georgia. © Frank S. Todd.

with sooty-brown head and wings, darkest on flight feathers, long pointed wings and wedge-shaped tail, imparting pointed silhouette. Plumage varies little with age/season, and sexes alike. Flight typically graceful, even more so than Sooty. **Ad** has predominantly medium greyish to greyish-white body, tinged slightly pale brown, forming slight but obvious contrast with sooty-brown head and wings (especially noticeable is contrast between dark wings and pale mantle to rump area), while almost blackish-brown head to upper foreneck grades into paler/greyer rest of body, though usually appears clearly dark-hooded. Tone varies with light, e.g. when observed at close range, especially in strong light, contrast between paler/darker areas more obvious, whereas at distance and in cloudy conditions appears unpatterned and over-

all darker, with paler parts difficult to appreciate. Also varies individually, with some birds slightly darker, tinged more brownish and less contrasting. With wear, pale areas, especially nape/neck to mantle, bleach paler and buffier. White outer primary shafts rather obvious, mainly at close and mid-distances. Rear half of eye-ring broad and noticeable at close to mid-ranges. Bill proportionately rather slender, with bluish stripe on sides of lower mandible. Legs and feet pale greyish-pink. **Juv/imm** overall like ad, but feathers

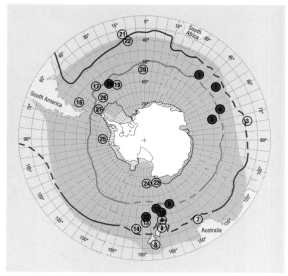

1. Prince Edward & Marion
2. Crozet
4. Kerguelen
5. Heard & McDonald
6. Macquarie
10. Auckland
11. Campbell
12. Antipodes
13. South Georgia

Ad Light-mantled Sooty Albatross Phoebetria palpebrata. Some extremely worn birds (apparently mostly imms) typically develop a variable, blotchy white, collar and patches on mantle/back, making black of head more clear-cut. Such wear is shared by Sooty Albatross (but the head never become so contrastingly black). Such variants need to be taken into account when identifying distant or atypical birds. South Georgia, Nov 2001. © Hadoram Shirihai.

narrowly fringed paler, especially on mantle; bill-stripe and eye-ring greyer and outer primary shafts browner, but all difficult to observe at sea. With wear, some fringes and exposed paler bases form patchy whitish-grey areas and variable collar, from nape onto neck-sides and mantle. Subsequent imm similar to ad, but when worn appears more strongly bleached, with variable patchy/blotchy appearance, sometimes with dark area limited to smaller mask. Ageing after second-/third-year possible if able to assess moult pattern.

Voice: Largely silent at sea, at breeding sites gives double-syllable *pee-ow*, the first note low and shrill (with open bill) and second a descending, horse-like noise, uttered on ground and in flight. Also other less distinct calls.

Size: 78–90 cm, wing 48–57 cm, wingspan 180–220 cm, weight 2.5–3.7 kg. Female averages smaller in culmen, tarsus, tail and wing measurements, and weight (but much overlap in most of these).

Similar species: Easily distinguished from Sooty, given reasonable view, by virtue of very pale body feathering. However, as mentioned under latter, there is a greater risk of confusion between darker Light-mantled Sooty and Sooty.

Distribution and biology

Distribution, movements and population: Circumpolar in Southern Ocean, mostly in Antarctic and subantarctic waters (close to Antarctic Convergence), breeding on South Georgia, Prince Edward, Marion, Crozet, Kerguelen, Heard and McDonald, Macquarie, Auckland, Campbell and Antipodes (largest numbers on South Georgia, Kerguelen and Auckland). Disperses at sea generally south of 30°S (to northern edge of Antarctic pack ice), but regularly reaches 20°S off Chile, recorded on several occasions

Ad Light-mantled Sooty Albatross Phoebetria palpebrata; note elongated shape and pale greyish-brown plumage and dark-hooded contrast. Crozet, Nov 1999. © Hadoram Shirihai.

to 12°S in Brazil and once to California. Distribution at sea generally more southerly than *P. fusca*. Overall population probably 19,000–24,000 pairs (and perhaps 140,000 individuals) in 1990s.

Diet and feeding: Mostly cephalopods and crustaceans, and also takes fish and carrion, principally by surface-seizing, but also surface-diving, surface-plunging and shallow-diving. Usually alone or in small groups of fewer than five, occasionally with other albatrosses and also associates with cetaceans. Less often and more briefly investigates boats than most albatrosses. May travel up to 1000 km on foraging trips from colonies.

Social behaviour: Solitary or in small groups both when feeding and at colonies. Monogamous and forms long-term pair-bonds.

Breeding biology: Breeds, biennially (if successful) in Oct–Nov, in small, loose colonies on vegetated and sheltered cliff ledges (including inland on Prince Edward), sometimes in association with other albatrosses/cormorants. Constructs low nest mound of mud, grass and plant material, lined with grass. Lays one white egg marked brown or reddish-brown, incubated 65–71 days. Chicks fledge in 141–170 days. Single-brooded. Both sexes build nest, incubate eggs and provision young.

Conservation Near Threatened but populations probably overall stable, at least in New Zealand portion of range and on Macquarie. Decline noted, since 1980s, on French subantarctic islands due to high ad mortality and low recruitment. Humans exploited populations on Kerguelen and perhaps Prince Edward in 19th century. Tuna and toothfish longline fishing in Southern Ocean possibly now taking a toll, and may, if quantified, require it to be upgraded to Vulnerable.

Taxonomy Monotypic.

Southern Giant Petrel
Macronectes giganteus   Plate 8

Identification

Confusion risks: Northern Giant Petrel *M. halli*.

Main characters: Large, thickset albatross-sized petrel, with protruding neck and humpbacked appearance, relatively short tail and narrow pointed wings. Typically flies on stiff wings. Two colour morphs, one all white with a few scattered blackish feathers, other greyish-brown, often with some white feathering on face to neck. Very large horn-coloured bill with greenish tip and prominent single nostril-tube. Sexes alike. ***Dark morph ad*** variable,

Light-mantled Sooty Albatross Phoebetria palpebrata chick, Macquarie. © Grant Dixon.

White-morph (possibly ad) Southern Giant Petrel Macronectes giganteus. *Of the two giant petrels, a white morph is only found in this species.
Kaikoura, South I, New Zealand, Oct 2001. © Hadoram Shirihai.*

but most have combination of whitish iris (perhaps subject to
individual, sex-/age-related and geographic variation) and whitish-cream (slightly flecked pale brown) head/neck almost to upper
or mid-breast. Legs dull pinkish-grey. **Juv** predominantly glossy
grey-black, soon bleaching browner; bill pale yellowish-horn, with
indistinct (and may appear to lack) pale green tip, iris dark and
legs greyer. **Imm** plumage develops slowly; generally heavily
mottled but with moult progressively paler, becoming especially
whiter on head, commencing on face/throat, and subsequently
closer to ad as white (usually still heavily flecked brown) extends
onto foreneck; and eye becomes paler brown. Much individual
variation, thus correct ageing impossible unless moult carefully
assessed (beware all-dark-brown ad). Full ad plumage and bill
colour probably develop only at 7–10 years (reported as late as 13
years, when already breeding for several seasons). **White morph**
Entirely white with exception of a few irregular dark brown feathers on body, wing-coverts and, sometimes, flight feathers (number
varies individually); juv and imm indistinguishable from ad except
by bare parts, which are as dark morph (see above). Very rare
all-white birds (so-called leucistic variant) with uniform yellowish
bill and pink legs and feet may result from mixed pairs with white-
morph birds (but unconfirmed).
Voice: Generally silent at sea, except croaking sounds when competing over food. Courtship calls include a drawn-out tremulous

cry, described as 'like the neighing of a colt' and cat-like mewing, uttered when two birds face each other, nibble faces or wave
heads and touch bills; voice perhaps softer but higher pitched than
Northern Giant; also other guttural rattles (Voisin 1968, Watson
1975, Bretagnolle 1988, *HANZAB*).
Size: 85–100 cm, wing 46.0–57.7 cm, wingspan 150–210 cm,
weight 3.8–5.0 kg. Female averages smaller in culmen (little overlap), tarsus and wing measurements, and weight.
Similar species: White morph unique, and ad with all-white head
and neck apparently only found in Southern. Confusion risk with
Northern greatest given uniformly dark or only partially pale-faced
younger imm Southern. Main distinction is bill colour: at most
ages, green tip of Southern is usually visible at close to mid-
ranges, and bill appears near uniform at distance, thus lacking
red-coloured tip of Northern (which is visible at longer range).
Bear in mind that fledglings and young juvs of both often have
only faint suggestion of tip colour, making separation using this
character unsafe; moreover, in certain lights and at distance, tip
coloration may be incorrectly assessed. But, even ad Southern
tends to have darker underparts (concolorous with upperparts)
from breast, rather than clearly paler underparts than upperparts
(typical of Northern), and more extensive and contrasting whitish
lower face and foreneck. However, some pale ad Northern often
appear paler on head/neck (extremes have limited whitish-grey
face/throat and breast patch), but usually distinctly sullied and/or
heavily mottled grey and almost same on much of underparts,
thus not exhibiting sharp contrast between white head/neck and
much darker upperparts and underparts of most Southern. Imm
and ad Southern tend to have clearly pale leading edge to inner
underwing, which is usually absent on Northern (though it may be
obvious on paler/older birds).

Distribution and biology

Distribution, movements and population: Southern Ocean on the

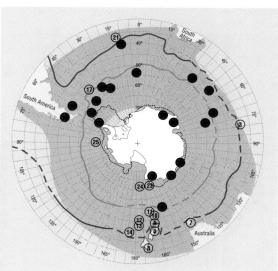

Ad dark-morph Southern Giant Petrel Macronectes giganteus; *note diagnostic clear whitish head/upper-neck contrast and greenish bill-tip.
Macquarie, Jan 1998. © Hadoram Shirihai.*

Prince Edward & Marion	South Sandwich
Crozet	Bouvetøya
Kerguelen	Gough
Heard	South Orkney
Macquarie	South Shetland
South American offshore	Antarctic Peninsula
islands	Antarctic coasts and
Falklands	offshore islands
South Georgia	

Young/mid-imm dark-morph Southern Giant Petrels Macronectes giganteus. The species is often gregarious and competes for food around boats. Species identification by greenish bill tip, but note that some (like the second bird in the foreground) develop a paler face and thus appear similar to imm/ad Northern Giant M. halli. Off Gough I, Mar 2006. © Hadoram Shirihai.

Falklands, South Georgia, South Sandwich, South Orkney, South Shetland, Bouvetøya (no recent breeding records), Prince Edward, Marion, Crozet, Kerguelen, Heard and Macquarie; also S Chile and coastal Antarctica, on Peninsula, Adélie Coast, Windmill Is and Enderby Land. Ranges widely south of equator, north to 20°S in winter, though most recoveries of Indian Ocean breeders have been in Australia and New Zealand. One verified record in N Atlantic. Population estimated at c.31,000 pairs.

Diet and feeding: Scavenger and predator, often attending penguin and seal carcasses on land, but also kills live birds, catching them by head; at sea principally by surface-seizing. Usually alone or in small groups of fewer than five, often gathering at food sources, e.g. around trawlers and at sewage outfalls. Principally locates food by smell.

Social behaviour: Gregarious on land, much less so at sea (and less so than Northern). Colonial breeder. Monogamous and forms long-term pair-bonds.

Breeding biology: Breeds Aug–Oct in small, loose colonies on ridges, exposed flats, sandy beaches and gravel areas, sometimes in dense tussac grass. Constructs low cup-shaped nest of grass, moss, gravel and bones. Lays one white egg, incubated 55–66 days. Chicks fledge in 104–132 days. Single-brooded. Both sexes build nest, incubate eggs and provision young. Those breeding sympatrically with Northern usually breed six weeks later, from Sep.

Conservation Vulnerable and declining. Evidence of substantial declines at several colonies between 1960s and 1990s, especially in Antarctica. Reduction in numbers of Southern Elephant Seals *Mirounga leonina* (an important carrion source), human disturbance and persecution have all been blamed for the decline, while recent reports indicate that Patagonian toothfish longline fishing in the Indian Ocean also may be taking a substantial toll on populations.

Taxonomy Monotypic.

Young imm Southern Giant Macronectes giganteus (left) and older imm Northern Giant Petrels M. halli (right). These birds have already developed the diagnostic bill-tip colorations. Kaikoura, South I, New Zealand, Oct 2001. © Hadoram Shirihai.

Ad Northern Macronectes halli *(left) and ad Southern Giant Petrels* M. giganteus *(right), illustrating the classic ad plumages of both (paler underparts with no sharp contrast between head and breast in the former, and whitish head and neck in latter). Such birds are safely identified at sea, even without seeing the diagnostic bill-tip colour. S Atlantic Ocean, Mar 2006. © Hadoram Shirihai.*

Juv/younger imm Northern Macronectes halli *(left) and Southern Giant Petrels* M. giganteus *(right). These birds have already developed traces of their diagnostic bill-tip colorations, but even in such close views the reddish and greenish tones, respectively, are ill-defined and can be difficult to detect. S Atlantic Ocean, Mar 2006. © Hadoram Shirihai.*

Northern Giant Petrel *Macronectes halli*   Plate 8

Identification

Confusion risks: Southern Giant Petrel *M. giganteus*.

Main characters: Large, stocky and thickset albatross-sized petrel. Structure and jizz identical to Southern (which see). Diagnostic brownish-red (rather than olive-green) bill tip is single most reliable character distinguishing it from Southern. Compared to latter lacks white morph, but identical juv plumage and other plumages very similar to dark-morph Southern, though some characters may be used as subsidiary identification features, especially if aged correctly. **Ad** typically has dark to medium grey-brown body (fringed paler), with silvery brownish-grey on head and ill-defined whitish face and throat (slight dark mask through eye); slightly duskier capped appearance, but indistinct compared to imm; whitish

throat often appears to be bordered by duskier collar, while rest of underparts blotched/mottled silvery grey-brown (paler than upperparts), with older birds being distinctly whiter. Dark red tip well developed, contrasting with pale yellowish pink-horn of rest of bill. Legs dark bluish-grey. **Juv** overall glossy sooty-black, with almost completely pinkish-horn bill that often lacks (or almost lacks) red tip, and thus inseparable from juv Southern until bill develops red colour (process is usually swift). Hardly moults as first-year, but plumage progressively wears/fades to dark greyish-brown, creating more mottled appearance, slightly paler face and pale-spotted head/neck. Iris black and legs flesh-grey. **Imm** exhibits much individual variation, making correct ageing difficult/impossible, but vast majority of younger imms typically mottled, with only slightly paler face/body. Older imm clearly paler, browner and greyer, and typically has darker crown and nape contrasting with whitish-grey

Ad Northern Giant Petrels Macronectes halli; with age imm and ad become paler and even whiter on face and underparts (varying individually). Off Auckland, New Zealand, Jan 1998. © Hadoram Shirihai.

Ad Northern Giant Petrel Macronectes halli; note reddish bill tip and paler face and underparts. Off Kerguelen. © Hadoram Shirihai.

lower face, throat and foreneck (producing more capped impression); underparts from breast whitish-grey, mottled darker; dark/reddish bill tip becomes darker (as ad), and iris usually whitish (unlike Southern in which development may appear slower). Thus strongly approaches ad and many are inseparable.

Voice: Generally similar to Southern (which see).

Size: 80–95 cm, wing 47–56 cm, wingspan 150–210 cm, weight 3.8–5.0 kg. Female averages smaller in bill (almost no overlap), tarsus and wing measurements.

Similar species: Despite much variation in coloration and age-related individual variation among both Southern and Northern Giant Petrels, some characteristic plumage patterns exist. Unlike Southern, Northern lacks white morph and ad and imm apparently never have all-whitish head and neck. See similar forms under Southern for further details of differences in plumage contrast and pattern of more confusing plumages.

Distribution and biology

Distribution, movements and population: Southern Ocean on South Georgia, Prince Edward, Marion, Crozet, Kerguelen, Macquarie, Auckland, Campbell, Antipodes, Stewart and Chatham. Disperses as far as Namibia, E Australia, C Chile and once to São Paulo, Brazil, but principally between 25°S and 45°S in winter and most of those recovered from Indian Ocean populations were

in Australia and New Zealand. Total population c.11,500 pairs in the 1990s.

Diet and feeding: Scavenger and predator, with males often attending penguin and seal carcasses on land and females taking live prey on water, principally by surface-seizing, but also surface-diving/pursuit-plunging. Usually feeds alone or in small groups. Often follows ships for offal.

Social behaviour: Solitary or in small groups both when feeding and at colonies. Monogamous and forms long-term pair-bonds.

Breeding biology: Breeds Aug–early Sep in small, loose colonies on well-vegetated areas near sea level and usually close to ocean. Constructs low cup-shaped nest mound of grass, twigs and other plant material. Lays one white egg, incubated 57–62 days. Chicks fledge in 106–120 days. Single-brooded. Both sexes build nest, incubate eggs (with shifts lasting up to 17 days) and provision young. In areas where breeds sympatrically with Southern Giant, usually nests six weeks earlier than latter.

Conservation Near Threatened. Recent population increase of

Older ad Northern Giant Macronectes halli, showing the palest stage in maturation. Note the overall pale head and underparts (contrasting with the darker upperprts). This plumage does not exist in Southern M. giganteus, and such birds are safely identified even without checking the bill-tip colour. S Atlantic Ocean, Mar 2006. © Hadoram Shirihai.

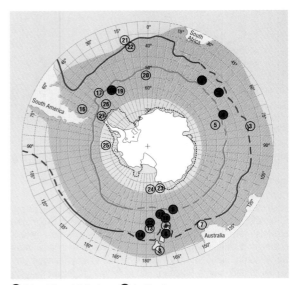

● Prince Edward & Marion   ● Auckland
● Crozet   ● Campbell
● Kerguelen   ● Antipodes
● Macquarie   ● Chatham
● New Zealand (off   ● South Georgia
   Stewart)

Southern Fulmar Fulmarus glacialoides. *Off Kaikoura, South I, New Zealand, Oct 2001. © Hadoram Shirihai.*

Southern Fulmar Fulmarus glacialoides. *Medium-sized, overall grey and white, bull-headed petrel with distinctly pinkish bill (prominent blackish tip and tubes). Off Kaikoura, South I, New Zealand, Sep 2003. © Hadoram Shirihai.*

34% in a decade may be a result, in part, of better monitoring, though some populations have certainly increased or at least remained stable during relevant period (1980s–1990s). The greater availability of carrion has undoubtedly contributed to this. Introduced predators on Auckland may limit colony distribution and breeding success. Of greater concern are recent reports which indicate that toothfish longline fishing in the Indian Ocean may be taking a substantial toll on populations.

Taxonomy Monotypic.

Southern Fulmar *Fulmarus glacialoides*   Plate 8

Identification

Confusion risks: None.

Main characters: Medium-sized, bull-headed petrel with overall grey-and-white, gull-like pattern. Flight typical of a petrel, characteristically consisting of shallow, stiff-winged fluttering and long glides. Identifiable on silhouette alone. Plumage features almost constant, varying only slightly with age/season, and sexes alike. In all plumages bill distinctly bicoloured, with pinkish base and prominent blackish tip and tubes (may have whitish subterminal band). **Ad** has whitish underparts and head, and pale bluish-grey upperparts, darker on upperwing; both wing surfaces have conspicuous whitish blaze at base of primaries, bordered by broad

Southern Fulmar Fulmarus glacialoides *is the only species in the Southern Ocean to possess such a wing pattern and bill colour. Balleny Is, Jan 1999. © Hadoram Shirihai.*

black trailing edge (paler on inner primaries), black outer primaries and some forewing feathers. Legs and feet pinkish-grey. **Juv/imm** overall as ad, but slightly and narrowly fringed paler, especially on mantle and inner upperwing-coverts. With wear may appear slightly patchy whitish-grey above. Subsequent imm similar to ad, but in worn plumage appears more strongly bleached. Ageing at sea unsafe unless moult pattern assessed.

Voice: Generally silent at sea, except if competing over food, when utters shrill rattling cackle. Display call involves a repeated, soft (but loud) droning, and guttural croaks, uttered when two birds face each other, nibble faces or wave heads and engage in mutual preening.

Size: 45–50 cm, wing 31.5–36.0 cm, wingspan 114–120 cm, weight 0.7–1.0 kg. Female averages smaller in culmen, tarsus and wing measurements, and overall weight.

Similar forms: Could perhaps be confused with a gull at long distance, but petrel-like flight should rapidly eliminate any identification problems.

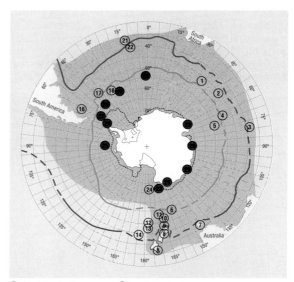

19 South Sandwich	**22** South Shetland
20 Bouvetøya	**23** Antarctic Peninsula
23 Balleny	**25** Antarctic coasts and
25 Peter I Øy	offshore islands
26 South Orkney	

Distribution and biology

Distribution, movements and population: Subantarctic on South Sandwich, South Orkney, South Shetland, Bouvetøya, and in coastal and insular Antarctica. In summer close to pack ice and rarely recorded north of 50°S. Ranges widely at sea south of 30°S in non-breeding season, also north to Ecuador and Brazil, and rarely to S Africa, Australia and New Zealand. Total population estimated at up to two million pairs in mid-1980s.

Diet and feeding: Mostly crustaceans, fish and squid, principally taken by surface-seizing and surface-diving. Gregarious when feeding, occasionally with other seabirds. Follows ships, including trawlers.

Social behaviour: Solitary or in small groups in non-breeding season. Nests in large colonies. Monogamous and forms long-term pair-bonds. Territorial only in immediate vicinity of nest.

Breeding biology: Breeds in colonies on steep slopes and cliffs in first half of Dec, sometimes with other petrels. Constructs simple scrape on flat rock or gravel, lined with stones or gravel. Lays one white egg, incubated 43–50 days. Chicks fledge in 48–56 days. Single-brooded. Both sexes build nest, incubate eggs and provision young.

Conservation Not globally threatened. Populations appear stable, though competition with commercial fisheries may pose long-term threat.

Taxonomy Monotypic.

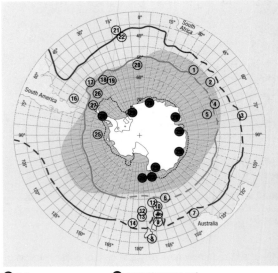

Balleny
Scott
Antarctic Peninsula

Antarctic coasts and offshore islands

Antarctic Petrel *Thalassoica antarctica*   Plate 8

Identification

Confusion risks: Cape Petrel *Daption capense*.

Main characters: Strikingly patterned medium-sized petrel, with dark brown and bold white pattern. Identifiable on silhouette alone. Performs characteristic stiff-winged glides on proportionately long narrow wings. Plumage varies little with age/season, and sexes alike. **Ad** has brownish head, upperparts, neck and wings, except broad white wingbar on secondaries to inner primaries. Underparts and tail white, latter has brown terminal band; underwing has broad dark brown leading edge and narrower trailing edge. Brown parts (when seen close) slightly paler fringed, and often has whitish flecks on chin, and blacker crown and face. In summer, bleaches paler and has slightly patchy brown dorsal feathering, often with greyish collar. Greyish-black bill. Legs and feet fleshy pinkish-grey. **Juv/imm** overall as ad, but slightly and narrowly fringed paler, especially on mantle and inner upperwing-coverts; bill blacker. Subsequent imm similar to ad but in worn plumage appears more strongly bleached. Ageing at sea unsafe unless moult pattern assessed.

Voice: Mostly silent at sea. During display at nest site gives churring, clucking and cackling calls (stronger and more resonant than those of Southern Fulmar *Fulmarus glacialoides*).

Size: 40–46 cm, wing 29.2–33.1 cm, wingspan 100–110 cm, weight 675 g. Female averages smaller in tarsus and wing measurements, but much variation in tail measurements and overall weight.

Similar species: Could be confused with slightly smaller Cape Petrel, but latter has well-differentiated checkerboard upperwing pattern, more rounded wing shape and different flight. Identification problems only likely with birds at very long distance.

Distribution and biology

Distribution, movements and population: Coastal Antarctica (to 350 km inland). A total of 35 colonies containing c.500,000 breeding pairs known in 1980s, but studies in Ross and Weddell Seas and elsewhere suggest existence of large, undiscovered

Antarctic Petrel Thalassoica antarctica *has essentially brown plumage and extensive white wings, tail and underparts, and flies on stiff wings, making it unmistakable. Off Possession I, Ross Sea, Jan 1999. © Hadoram Shirihai.*

Amongst the region's tubenoses, Antarctic Petrel Thalassoica antarctica *has a unique underparts pattern. NW Weddel Sea, Mar 2003. © Hadoram Shirihai.*

Antarctic Petrel Thalassoica antarctica *is often gregarious and is most abundant in the iceberg and pack-ice zones.* © Nigel McCall

colonies, particularly in W Antarctica and Victoria Land, and much higher total population of 4–7 million breeding pairs (or 10–20 million individuals). In summer most abundant in iceberg and pack-ice zones. Ranges widely in Southern Ocean north to S South America, South Africa, Tasmania and New Zealand, and regularly reaches 56°S in summer and 48°S in winter.

Diet and feeding: Mostly cephalopods, crustaceans and small fish, principally by surface-seizing, but uses wide variety of other techniques. Congregates in large flocks around whaling ships, and often associates with cetaceans, more occasionally other petrels (especially in winter) and terns.

Social behaviour: Gregarious at sea and when breeding. Monogamous and probably forms long-term pair-bonds.

Breeding biology: Breeds from late Nov in colonies on level snow-free surfaces, often on steep slopes and cliffs. Constructs shallow depression in rock, lined with gravel. Lays one white egg, incubated 40–46 days. Chicks fledge in 42–47 days. Single-brooded. Both sexes probably build nest, incubate eggs and provision young.

Conservation Not globally threatened and population considered stable. Inhospitable location of breeding colonies provides main protection, though potential development of krill fisheries may pose long-term threat.

Taxonomy Monotypic.

Cape Petrel *Daption capense*　　　　　　Plate 8

Identification

Confusion risks: Antarctic Petrel Thalassoica antarctica.

Main characters: Unmistakable medium-/pigeon-sized, round-headed petrel with highly distinctive black-and-white checkered upperparts and upperwing, and white underparts and underwing.

Flight silhouette consists of rounded, almost neckless head, small stocky body and rounded wings. Manoeuvrable flyer, with fast, shallow, stiff wingbeats and short glides. In all plumages has short black bill and legs. Plumage generally varies only with seasonal feather wear, and sexes alike. **Ad** has black head to upper neck and rest of upperparts, which from mantle/back are spotted/botched white, but usually has rump/uppertail-coverts almost

Cape Petrel Daption capense, *the dark hood and black-and-white upperparts make the species unmistakable even on the water. Off Kaikoura, South I, New Zealand, Sep 2003.* © Hadoram Shirihai

pure white (though some have far more white than black between mantle and uppertail-coverts). Upperwing also variable, but white primary patches always very conspicuous and in extremely white individuals can form broad, ragged white band on wing, in darker birds, white restricted to spots/streaks and small irregular patches, thus white panel at base of primaries more prominent. White underwing has (moderately broad) black leading and (narrow) trailing edges and wingtip. Tail contrastingly black. **Juv/imm** overall as ad, but slightly and narrowly fringed paler, especially on black upper mantle and inner upperwing-coverts. With wear at sea may appear patchier whitish-grey above than ad. Subsequent imm similar to ad but in worn plumage appears more strongly bleached. Ageing at sea unsafe unless moult pattern assessed.

Voice: At sea, competes over food with an aggressive sharp chattering or purring, *courrrrr*, and other cackling sounds, e.g. *cac-cac, cac-cac* with increasing tempo. Greeting displays involve same sounds, accompanied by mutual head swaying.

Size: 35–42 cm, wing 24–28 cm, wingspan 80–91 cm, weight 440 g. Female averages smaller in culmen, tarsus and wing measurements, and weight.

Similar species: Antarctic Petrel (which see) slightly larger, with some structural differences and quite different upperwing pattern, but identification problems only likely with birds at very long distance.

Distribution and biology

Distribution, movements and population: Southern Ocean on South Georgia, South Sandwich, South Shetland, South Orkney, Bouvetøya, Crozet, Kerguelen, Heard, Macquarie, Balleny, Peter, Chatham, Snares, Auckland, Campbell, Antipodes and Bounty, and coastal Antarctica. Ranges widely at sea, north to W Africa, NE Brazil, Vanuatu in W Pacific, and Galápagos and S Ecuador in E Pacific, though most populations are only partially migratory. Subantarctic islands of New Zealand population estimated at 5000–10,000 pairs prior to 1984, when overall population was 120,000–300,000 pairs.

Diet and feeding: Mostly cephalopods, crustaceans and fish, principally taken by surface-seizing, but also wide variety of other techniques including pattering and hydroplaning. Forms large flocks, especially around trawlers, occasionally with other seabirds and also in association with cetaceans. Scavenges at carcasses and appears to rely to some extent on smell to locate food.

Social behaviour: Solitary or, more frequently, in loose colonies when nesting. Gregarious at sea and habitually follows ships. Monogamous and forms long-term pair-bonds.

Two unmistakable petrels: Cape Petrel Daption c. capense *is widespread across the region, whereas Snow Petrel* Pagodroma [nivea] *(here Lesser,* nivea*) is confined to cold Antarctic waters, and is a specialty of the iceberg and pack-ice zones. Weddell Sea, Nov 2001. © Hadoram Shirihai.*

Breeding biology: Breeds Nov–Dec onward in loose colonies on level rocky ground or gravel, and moderately high cliffs with many ledges, often with other seabirds. Constructs scrape of stones and gravel. Lays one white egg, incubated 41–50 days. Chicks fledge in 45–57 days. Single-brooded. Both sexes build nest, incubate eggs and provision young.

Conservation Not globally threatened. Inhospitable location of breeding colonies provides main protection, although those on Kerguelen, Auckland and Cochons affected by cat and rat predation.

Taxonomy Two subspecies: *australe*, which breeds on New Zealand subantarctic islands, is overall darker and mantle/back

Cape Petrel Daption capense, *nominate race (on right) in S Atlantic and race* australe *off New Zealand. In extreme examples, the two forms differ markedly in the amount of white in the upperwings, but many birds are intermediate, and the amount of white and its pattern also varies very strongly, both individually and with wear. © Hadoram Shirihai.*

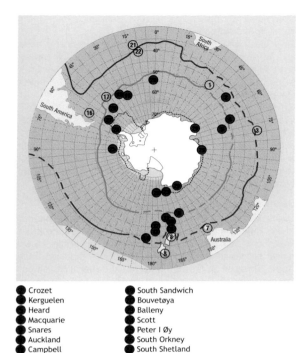

● Crozet	● South Sandwich
● Kerguelen	● Bouvetøya
● Heard	● Balleny
● Macquarie	● Scott
● Snares	● Peter I Øy
● Auckland	● South Orkney
● Campbell	● South Shetland
● Antipodes	● Antarctic Peninsula
● Bounty	● Antarctic coasts and
● Chatham	offshore islands
● South Georgia	

and upperwing have white patches on latter separated by more extensive black; circumpolar nominate has much whiter upperwing/upperparts, flecked black only on larger coverts and mantle/back. However, much individual variation, some intermediates, and effects of wear and bleaching make subspecific identification difficult in all but classic individuals of each taxon.

Lesser Snow Petrel
Pagodroma [nivea] nivea   Plate 8

Identification
Confusion risks: Greater Snow Petrel *P.* [*n.*] *confusa*.
Main characters: Generally unmistakable small- to medium-sized, nondescript, all-white petrel. Contrasting black eye and bill are most prominent features. However, when seen over wilderness pack-ice environment, characteristic shape and flight make its appearance very special, particularly as it is among the most sought-after specialities of the region, often being termed the 'angel of Antarctica'. Relatively long wings and almost square-ended tail (only slightly wedged when fanned). Flight highly characteristic: in windless conditions or slight wind has elastic slow wingbeats interspersed by short glides, low over water and between floating ice. Wingbeats looser and less stiff than other petrels, and may fly rather high, when appears like a white pigeon overhead. **Ad** as described above, but when fresh tinged slightly greyer, and upperwings and upperparts perhaps very slightly and finely vermiculated (only rarely visible even at close range). **Juv/imm** overall as ad, but somewhat more washed grey and finely vermiculated above, though at distance appears largely white. Subsequent imm similar to ad but with wear appears more strongly bleached. Ageing at sea unsafe unless moult pattern assessed.
Voice: Mostly silent at sea. Calls at breeding sites include harsh

guttural sounds, also churrs, clucks and screeches, e.g. a repeated *teck-teck-teck* or *k-k-k-kaa- kaa- kaa- kaa- kaa*. Larger individuals have lower pitched voices, while male vocalizations are typically lower than those of females, and intersyllabic duration is longer in males.
Size: 30–40 cm, wingspan 75–95 cm (both figures refer to *nivea* as a whole), wing 24.5–27.8 (though 28 cm has been suggested as cut-off point between *nivea* and *confusa*), weight 200–378 g. Female probably averages smaller in most mensural data.
Similar forms: Very similar to Greater Snow Petrel; principally differs in size/structure (for identification features separating them see latter). Both could be confused with other superficially similar-sized albino petrels, and perhaps, given distant views, small whitish gulls or terns, but all should easily be eliminated once shape, flight mode and other features are appreciated.

Distribution and biology
Distribution, movements and population: Coastal and inland (up to 300 km) regions of Antarctica, including the Peninsula, South Georgia and islands of Scotia Arc. Pure colonies known from Davis, South Georgia, Cape Denison and Svathamaren, but other sites within 'known' range apparently occupied by both *nivea* and *confusa*. Ranges north at sea during non-breeding season, principally south of 60°S, though little attention has been paid to differentiating the two forms at sea. Vagrant (form unknown) to Heard, Kerguelen and in Argentine waters at 50°30'S 56°57'W. Overall population unknown.
Diet and feeding: Mostly cephalopods, crustaceans and fish, principally taken by aerial- and contact-dipping, surface-diving and surface-seizing, but pattering and pursuit-diving also employed. Feeds among ice floes and occasionally in association with Antarctic Petrel *Thalassoica antarctica* and Antarctic Minke Whale *Balaenoptera bonaerensis*.
Social behaviour: Loosely gregarious and partially nocturnal at sea. Forms large concentrations at breeding grounds, but colonies rather loose. Monogamous and forms long-term pair-bonds, but natal philopatry unusually low for a petrel (though nest-site fidelity is high).
Breeding biology: Arrives at colonies from Oct, exceptionally Aug. Breeds Nov–Dec onward in loose colonies on cliffs and steep slopes, using crevices and clefts under boulders. No nest lining.

Lesser Snow Petrel Pagodroma [nivea] nivea *in a snowstorm, showing the typical flight action and shape. The white plumage and black bare parts make this petrel unmistakable, while the relatively small size and lighter build, especially the bill, are key features to separate it from* confusa. *Weddell Sea, November.* © Hadoram Shirihai.

147

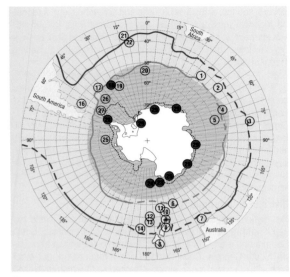

■ Snow Petrel *Pagodroma* [*nivea*] complex
● South Georgia
● Balleny
● Scott
● Antarctic Peninsula
● Antarctic coasts and offshore islands

Lays single smooth white egg, incubated 41–49 days. Chicks fledge in 42–54 days. Presumably single-brooded. No replacement clutch. Both sexes build nest, incubate eggs and provision young.

Conservation Not globally threatened. Inhospitable location of breeding colonies provides main protection, but also can mean that significant numbers (up to 44% in one study) of nests remain frozen during summer and cannot be used. Ad mortality appears to increase during winters with more extensive sea-ice cover, which may reduce prey abundance and availability, particularly in May–Jul, i.e. immediately following the breeding season.

Taxonomy Formerly considered polytypic, with nominate *nivea* in circumpolar Antarctic waters, being replaced by *confusa* in Balleny Is and probably elsewhere (cf. *HANZAB* for suggested far broader range), but controversy exists over their recognition as subspecies/allospecies/species (see Sibley & Monroe 1990, 1993, Sibley 1996 and *HANZAB*) due to reportedly extensive hybridization zone (28% of pairs at Pointe Géologie Archipelago, Terre Adélie, apparently mixed, almost certainly because competition for nest sites is high at this locality, perhaps forcing birds to choose mates according to this criterion). Further information on their relationships is clearly required, though it has been proposed that the two forms were isolated within separate refugia during the most recent Ice Age, on islands (*confusa*) and the mainland (*nivea*), with hybrid zones being established as they recolonized suitable breeding areas following the end of this event. At least in part of the range, the two forms differ in size, weight and some behavioural characteristics, and several inland colonies are occupied only by smaller birds.

Greater Snow Petrel
Pagodroma [*nivea*] *confusa*   Plate 8

Identification

Confusion risks: Lesser Snow Petrel *P.* [*n.*] *nivea*.
Main characters: Plumage development and features as Lesser

Snow Petrel (which see); for separation see below.
Voice: No information.
Size: 30–40 cm, wingspan 75–95 cm (both figures refer to *nivea* as a whole), wing 28.5–31.1 (data from Balleny Is; 28 cm has been suggested as cut-off point between *nivea* and *confusa*), weight 317–570 g. Female probably averages smaller in most mensural data.
Similar forms: Very similar to Lesser Snow Petrel, principally differentiated by size and structure. *Confusa* averages often noticeably larger and is heavier, with proportionately broader wings and, perhaps, deeper based bill. Differences impossible to appreciate at sea unless observed side by side and in case of extremes. Occurrence of intermediates is related to reported hybridization (see below). Further study urgently required.

Distribution and biology

Distribution, movements and population: Coastal and inland (up to 345 km) regions of Antarctica (to 2500 m), with pure colonies known only from the Balleny Is. Other colonies within 'known' range (suggested as being Pointe Géologie Archipelago, Terre Adélie, Peterson Is, Ardery I [a degree of segregation between the two forms has been noted at this site], Proclamation I, the South Sandwiches, Cape Hallet and Cape Hunter) apparently all mixed. Ranges north at sea during non-breeding season, principally south of 60°S, though little attention has been paid to differentiating the two forms at sea. Vagrant (form unknown) to Heard, Kerguelen and in Argentine waters at 50°30'S 56°57'W. Overall population unknown.
Diet and feeding: No known differences from *nivea* except that feeding trips away from the colony, when the ads have chicks, average c.50 hours (compared to over 70 hours in *nivea*).
Social behaviour: No known differences from *nivea*.
Breeding biology: Similar to *nivea*, though egg-laying dates apparently differ.
Conservation Not globally threatened. Inhospitable location of breeding colonies provides main protection.
Taxonomy Formerly considered a subspecies of *nivea*, but see comments under latter.

Greater Snow Petrel Pagodroma [nivea] confusa; *the relatively larger size and heavier build, especially the thicker bill and somewhat broader wings, are key features to separate from* nivea. *On Balleny there is apparently a pure population of* confusa, *which makes separation easier, otherwise the two forms mix freely, with many intermediates, and identification of the two is generally impractical at sea. Balleny Is, Jan 1999. © Hadoram Shirihai.*

Gadfly Petrels

Disregarding a handful of instances where taxonomy is uncertain, c.30 species are recognized in the genus *Pterodroma* (including Kerguelen Petrel for which a separate monotypic genus, *Aphodroma*, was recently proposed; though Bourne (2001 and *in litt.* 2001) argues that *Lugensa* is available and suitable for the taxon). These are the so-called gadfly petrels, most of which breed in tropical and subtropical oceans, mainly on undisturbed offshore islands and remote islets. They are among the most truly oceanic birds, coming to land only to breed. Approximately half of the total number of species have been recorded from our region, of which nine are known to breed within the Southern Ocean as defined here, the rest being vagrants or more or less regular visitors. Southern Ocean breeders involve two completely dark (Soft-plumaged Petrel *P. mollis* also has a very rare and variable dark morph), two white-bellied and an almost completely white-bodied form (the latter has dark wings), while the rest are mainly grey and white with slightly more complex wing and, in some, head patterns. The latter comprise the balance of the *Cookilaria*, a subgenus coined for nine smaller, predominantly grey-and-white species, of which several occur in our region. Here, I have attempted to present them in a logical order to facilitate comparisons between the most easily and frequently confused species.

Most species conform to a basic pattern: they have short, comparatively deep-based black bills, long rounded, narrow or relatively broad-based wings with the carpal held well forward, tapering, slightly wedge-shaped tails and plumage dominated by darker/blacker primaries and median/greater coverts, which form an open M mark that continues across the lower back/rump. The underparts and underwing are largely white, but the latter has a dark trailing edge and primary tips, and variable dark diagonal mark continuing across some (or all) of the underwing-coverts. In moderate to strong winds, most typically engage in remarkable, highly manoeuvrable flight consisting of rapid, towering arcs and strong glides, when they appear to almost bound through the air.

Given the complexities of identifying *Pterodroma* petrels, I have tried to limit my discussions to the principal characters visible *in the field*, and have especially attempted to emphasize each species' most pertinent and diagnostic characters, in the hope that observers can use these in order to build their own storehouse of impressions with the different forms. Identification should never be underestimated at sea: face and underwing marks are difficult to appreciate, mainly due to these species' fast and dynamic flight patterns; sea conditions/visibility, including any glare reflecting from the water surface and other light effects, often hamper viewing; and typical distances at which they are observed further complicate identification. Upperwing/upperparts markings vary substantially, according to light, distance and angle of view, and, most dramatically, with wear and bleaching. Structural or jizz differences are also difficult to appreciate, because flight patterns also significantly vary in response to wind direction/strength. I have attempted to emphasize the possibilities of, and problems raised by, these pitfalls in the appropriate places within the species accounts. Sex-/age-related variation is even more difficult to appreciate; even in-the-hand mensural data, which is decidedly incomplete for many species, cannot be reliably used to sex the majority of these taxa, there being very considerable overlap among most species for which comparative data are available (and these still do not exist for several forms). In summary, nothing compensates for time spent gaining experience with the group.

The group's behaviours are relatively uniform in most respects: their short stubby bills are adapted for seizing cephalopods, small fish and crustaceans (which form the main diet) from the surface of the water, with prey apparently being mainly taken at night. The general life and breeding cycles are very similar between species; the age at which birds first return to their natal colonies and that at which breeding is first attempted are unknown, but may be several years. Ads arrive at the colonies principally 6–8 weeks prior to breeding (when copulation takes place) and then disperse briefly to nearby marine feeding areas to gain weight prior to nesting (*pre-laying exodus*). Most nests are in self-excavated burrows, ads laying a single, usually smooth white egg, which is incubated 6–8 weeks, and chicks take anything from 8–16 weeks to fledge. Most species are nocturnal around the colonies, when they can be heard displaying; usually visiting their burrows just before dusk and returning to the sea sometime prior to dawn. Given their largely nocturnal lifestyles and that their colonies are usually located on remote islands, with birds feeding well offshore, it is unsurprising that *Pterodroma* petrels are among the least-known tubenoses.

Like other burrow-nesting seabirds, many *Pterodroma* petrels have been the unintentional victims of Man's arrival on their breeding islands: rats, feral cats, pigs and other introduced mammals have all caused significant losses among eggs, young and even ads. The most recent Red Data listing (BirdLife International) regards a staggering 21 *Pterodroma* as globally threatened (being categorized as Vulnerable, Endangered or Critical), with another three qualifying as Near Threatened. Fortunately many islands are currently subject to conservation work designed to tackle the problem of introduced predators and significant advances have already been made in a number of instances. Much, however, remains to be done.

Mottled Petrel *Pterodroma inexpectata*   Plate 9

Identification
Confusion risks: None.
Main characters: Medium-sized, characteristic gadfly petrel, with robust/solid build and dark frosty-grey head and upperparts,

Mottled Petrel Pterodroma inexpectata *is a medium-sized gadfly petrel with a characteristic dumpy and solid appearance. A very fast and powerful flier, its plumage makes it unmistakable: extensive dusky belly-patch (variable) and strong facial marks. Stewart I, New Zealand, Jan 2007. © Hadoram Shirihai.*

Mottled Petrel Pterodroma inexpectata, here banking steeply and arcing into headwind. When not heavily worn, frosty grey upperparts and upperwings are neatly fringed whitish, affording a mottled appearance when close, whilst broad blackish M pattern also distinctive. Stewart I, New Zealand, Jan 2007. © Hadoram Shirihai.

variably fringed paler/whitish, presenting mottled appearance when close, and obvious broad blackish M across upperparts/upperwing. White underparts, with large dark grey (or reddish-grey) belly patch (diagnostic) and crescent-shaped, broad black diagonal bend to white underwing. Given close views, head pattern distinctive, with pronounced whitish (variably streaked/mottled darker) forehead, supercilium and throat, forming whitish face pattern and emphasizing dusky rear eyestripe (or patch) and black bill; often appears to have darker grey neck-sides forming partial collar. Legs and feet pink with black toes. Bulky bodied and tail mid length, wings long but rather rounded and especially broad-based, giving bird large appearance, but when seen with White-headed Petrel *P. lessonii* (with which it shares New Zealand subantarctic waters) true size becomes apparent. Its powerful structure is

emphasized by its direct and vigorous flight; in strong wind performs deep arcs and long glides. **Age/seasonal variation** indistinct. Juv as ad, but flight feathers unmoulted and whitish fringes above perhaps more conspicuous when fresh. Subsequent imm and ad wear strongly, especially above and around head, when white mottling is reduced.

Voice: Not known to call at sea. Rather noisy around colonies at night. Generally like other gadfly petrels though quite diverse; loud, repeated staccato sounds, e.g. far-carrying hysterical *ti-ti-ti...*, others deeper pitched and more resonant, e.g. *quurrr, quurrr* or *goo-oo* from burrows, including in display (Warham in *HANZAB*).
Size: 34–35 cm, wing 24.2–27.1 cm, wingspan 85 cm, weight 315 g. Highly extensive overlap in wing length between sexes, though male may have slight tendency to average marginally longer.
Similar species: The boldly patterned upperwing and large dark belly patch should immediately separate it from all other grey-and-white gadfly petrels.

Distribution and biology

Distribution, movements and population: Islands of New Zealand including Snares, islets off Stewart I and, formerly, highlands of North and South Is of New Zealand. Trans-equatorial migrant, reaching N Pacific and Gulf of Alaska in winter, it disperses south to the Indo-Pacific Antarctic ice in late summer. Migrants occur offshore from W North America west to E Australia and south to Tierra del Fuego, with a recent record southeast of the Falklands. Total population exceeds 400,000 pairs (BirdLife International 2000).
Diet and feeding: Cephalopods, some fish and crustaceans, taken by surface-plunging, surface-seizing and pursuit-plunging. Sometimes associates with Soft-plumaged Petrel *P. mollis* and Sooty Shearwater *Puffinus griseus*. Does not usually follow boats.
Social behaviour: Solitary or in small groups at sea and breeds colonially, sometimes at high density. Monogamous and sustained pair-bonds.
Breeding biology: Breeds in self-excavated burrows, c.1 m long, on steep, well-vegetated slopes, cliffs and ledges, but generally avoids areas of tallest vegetation. Lays one white egg during 14–26 Dec (extreme dates 7 Dec and 10 Jan), incubated 48–53 days. Chicks fledge at 90–105 days. Single-brooded. Both parents incubate egg and provision young.
Conservation Near Threatened. Introduced rats and Weka *Gallirallus australis* may be major predators of eggs and chicks on some islands, and on others harvesting of Sooty Shearwater *Puffinus griseus* may also adversely affect this species.
Taxonomy Monotypic.

Kerguelen Petrel
Pterodroma (Aphrodroma or Lugensa) brevirostris
Plate 9

Identification
Confusion risks: Especially distant birds, could be confused with dark-morph Soft-plumaged Petrel *P. mollis* and any other dark *Pterodroma* (e.g. Great-winged Petrel *P. macroptera*), or some dark petrels and shearwaters.
Main characters: Medium-sized, bull-necked gadfly petrel, almost entirely dusky, blackish-slate or greyish-brown, but uniformly dark especially on head/neck, giving somewhat darker hooded impression, with or without ill-defined pale grey chin patch, darkening around eye (indistinct, even when close). Rest of body appears unpatterned, only in flight and mainly when strong light catches underwing is bright silver wash to base of primaries, greater primary-coverts and on lesser and marginal forewing-coverts

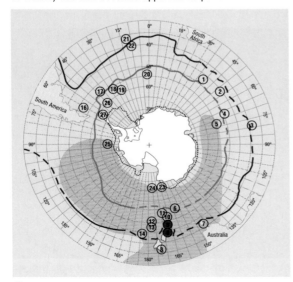

● New Zealand and offshore islands
● Snares

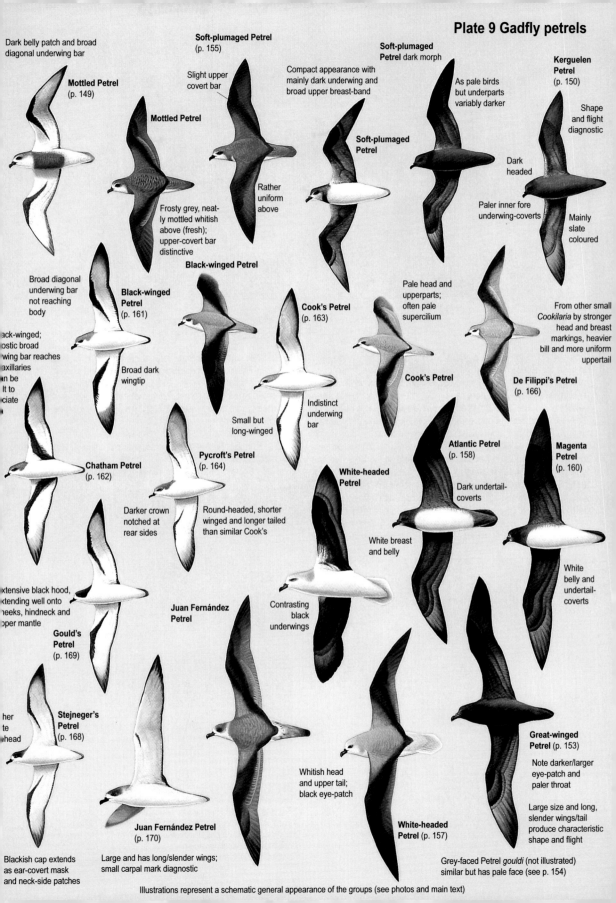

Plate 9 Gadfly petrels

Dark belly patch and broad diagonal underwing bar

Mottled Petrel (p. 149)

Mottled Petrel

Soft-plumaged Petrel (p. 155)

Slight upper covert bar

Compact appearance with mainly dark underwing and broad upper breast-band

Soft-plumaged Petrel dark morph

As pale birds but underparts variably darker

Kerguelen Petrel (p. 150)

Shape and flight diagnostic

Rather uniform above

Soft-plumaged Petrel

Dark headed

Frosty grey, neat-ly mottled whitish above (fresh); upper-covert bar distinctive

Paler inner fore underwing-coverts

Mainly slate coloured

Black-winged Petrel

Broad diagonal underwing bar not reaching body

Black-winged Petrel (p. 161)

Cook's Petrel (p. 163)

Pale head and upperparts; often pale supercilium

From other small *Cookilaria* by stronger head and breast markings, heavier bill and more uniform uppertail

ack-winged; ostic broad wing bar reaches axillaries n be lt to ciate

Broad dark wingtip

Small but long-winged

Cook's Petrel

De Filippi's Petrel (p. 166)

Indistinct underwing bar

Chatham Petrel (p. 162)

Pycroft's Petrel (p. 164)

White-headed Petrel

Atlantic Petrel (p. 158)

Dark undertail-coverts

Magenta Petrel (p. 160)

Darker crown notched at rear sides

Round-headed, shorter winged and longer tailed than similar Cook's

White breast and belly

White belly and undertail-coverts

extensive black hood, xtending well onto heeks, hindneck and pper mantle

Gould's Petrel (p. 169)

Juan Fernández Petrel

Contrasting black underwings

her te head

Stejneger's Petrel (p. 168)

Great-winged Petrel (p. 153)

Note darker/larger eye-patch and paler throat

Large size and long, slender wings/tail produce characteristic shape and flight

Whitish head and upper tail; black eye-patch

White-headed Petrel (p. 157)

Juan Fernández Petrel (p. 170)

Blackish cap extends as ear-covert mask and neck-side patches

Large and has long/slender wings; small carpal mark diagnostic

Grey-faced Petrel *gouldi* (not illustrated) similar but has pale face (see p. 154)

Illustrations represent a schematic general appearance of the groups (see photos and main text)

Kerguelen Petrel Pterodroma (Aphrodroma or Lugensa) brevirostris is squat-bodied and large-headed with characteristically proportionately long arched wings (often flies high above surface). Left-hand bird shows silver-grey flashes to primaries, greater primary-coverts and on lesser and marginal forewing-coverts, which are especially evident in strong light (right-hand bird). Off Gough I, Mar 2006. © Hadoram Shirihai.

(broadening near body) evident, and slightly paler rump and base of tail-sides may also be visible. In close views, fresh birds have pale fringes to upperwing (especially broad on greater and median) coverts, scapulars and uppertail-coverts. Underparts generally appear slightly paler. Stubby black bill, and black and pink legs and feet. Body relatively slim, with tapering, slightly wedge-shaped tail, and broad and moderately protruding neck/head, producing slightly fore-heavy appearance. Wings proportionately very long and narrow, with relatively stiff long 'arms' and long pointed 'hands'; in rough weather typically held half-bowed/arched towards body, imparting strong anchor-like shape. Spectacular rapid flight in stronger winds, often in high sweeping arcs and long glides. Characteristically hovers at great height (20–30 m), sometimes in kestrel *Falco*-like manner, unlike any other Southern Ocean petrel. **Age/seasonal variation** indistinct. Juv as

ad, but has unmoulted flight feathers in first-year. All ages bleach browner, with pale fringes above strongly reduced or worn off, and somewhat paler throat.

Voice: Appears rather quiet, nocturnal calls at colonies described as wheezy *chee-chee-chay* (*HANZAB*); other calls higher pitched and more drawn-out.

Size: 33–36 cm, wing 24.6–27.2 cm, wingspan 80–82 cm, weight 357 g. Female averages very marginally smaller in wing length, but extensive overlap.

Similar species: Shape (long wings, proportionately squat body

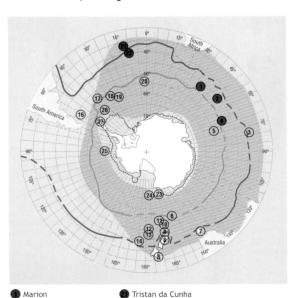

① Marion	㉑ Tristan da Cunha
② Crozet	㉗ Gough
④ Kerguelen	

Kerguelen Petrel Pterodroma (Aphrodroma or Lugensa) brevirostris in fresh plumage (here juv) and close views shows pale fringes to upperwing-coverts, scapulars and uppertail-coverts, forming scaly appearance. Also note the typical slate blue-grey tone to plumage (detectable in certain angles/lights). Off Gough I, Mar 2006. © Hadoram Shirihai.

and high-crowned, large head), characteristic fast flight and overall dark brown plumage, with rather short bill, and pale leading edge to underwing-coverts and basal remiges, separate this species from slightly smaller and overall more rotund Soft-plumaged and much larger and heavier Great-winged Petrels. Flies higher above water than latter. Kerguelen Petrel presents a common identification problem: the observer lacking experience of the species will find it difficult to appreciate the distinctiveness of the characteristic shape and flight; only patience in waiting for the 'Real McCoy' will prevent misidentification of the other two species.

Distribution and biology

Distribution, movements and population: S Atlantic and S Indian Oceans, on Gough and probably the Tristan da Cunha group, Marion, Crozet and Kerguelen. Disperses through Southern Ocean north to 40°S and to South Africa, Australia and New Zealand, more occasionally west to the Falklands and South Georgia. Total population in early 1980s probably 100,000–200,000 pairs.

Diet and feeding: Cephalopods, some fish and crustaceans, taken by surface-plunging and dipping. Occasionally associates with small cetaceans. Will occasionally fly above other tubenoses attending trawlers, but ignores ships.

Social behaviour: Solitary at sea, though small flocks congregate at food. Breeds in colonies. Probably monogamous. Only defends burrow.

Breeding biology: Breeds in burrows 0.8–2.8 m long, lined with plant material, on level or gently sloping ground and usually sheltered from prevailing winds. Lays one white egg in Oct, incubated 46–51 days. Chicks fledge in 59–62 days. Single-brooded. Both ads incubate egg and provision young.

Conservation Not globally threatened and most populations probably secure, though cats present around colonies on Kerguelen and rats on Île de la Possession (Crozet), whilst cats, rats and dogs may have exterminated population on Tristan da Cunha, and cats that on Île aux Cochons (Crozet).

Taxonomy Monotypic. Long placed in *Pterodroma*, it was subsequently transferred to the resurrected genus *Lugensa*, but dispute exists as to whether this name is technically available, leading Olson (2000) to propose a new genus, *Aphodroma*, for the taxon.

Great-winged Petrel
Pterodroma [macroptera] macroptera   Plate 9

Identification

Confusion risks: Especially distant birds, could be confused with any similar-sized dark *Pterodroma* or other dark tubenoses, e.g. Black *Procellaria parkinsoni* or White-chinned Petrels *P. aequinoctialis* and Flesh-footed Shearwater *Puffinus carneipes*. See also Grey-faced Petrel *Pterodroma [m.] macroptera*.

Main characters: Large, almost entirely blackish-brown gadfly petrel, sometimes with restricted and ill-defined pale wash around bill and on throat, whilst dark eye-patch often is pronounced and extensive (both in front and behind eye), if seen close. Rather deep-based black bill, and black legs and feet. In strong light, underwing has indistinct greyish wash to base of primaries, even less obvious on bases of greater primary-coverts. Body relatively heavy, though less so than Grey-faced, neck/head broad and protruding, and longish, slightly wedge-shaped tail. Long narrow wings with abrupt pointed 'hand', imparting somewhat swift-like appearance at distance. Spectacular rapid flight in stronger winds, with moderately high sweeping arcs and prolonged glides, 'towering' at intervals. **Age/seasonal variation** indistinct. Juv perhaps separable by freshness of plumage, and is blacker at fledging, with unmoulted flight feathers in first-year. Imm and ad bleach

Great-winged Petrel Pterodroma [m.] macroptera: *note rather extensive dark eye-patch and paler throat, but lack of pale forehead. Off Gough I. © Peter Ryan.*

browner, often with some patchy exposed white bases to upper-wing-coverts, neck and belly.

Voice: Not known to call at sea, except sometimes when disputing food. Nocturnal calls around colonies most like White-headed Petrel *P. lessonii*: typical calls are sharp, liquid whistles given by pairs in flight; burrow call is high–pitched *ki-ki-ki-ki*, or more squeaky

Great-winged Petrel Pterodroma [m.] macroptera: *note lack of pale face, but darker/larger eye-patch and paler throat often characteristic; bill is less heavy than gouldi. Both* macroptera *and* gouldi *have greyish wash to base of primaries, extending slightly onto greater primary-coverts. Off Crozets, Mar 2004. © Hadoram Shirihai.*

kik-kik-kik, or *kee-ik kukee-ik*; other calls include squeaks, and occasional gruff and slurred *quaw-er*.

Size: 38–40 cm, wing 29.3–32.0 cm, wingspan 97–100 cm, weight 440–680 g. Insufficient data to establish relative differences (if any) in wing lengths between sexes.

Similar species: Shape, especially long wings, stocky body and rounded head, powerful and dynamic flight, and overall dark brown plumage, with deep-based chunky black bill (lacking pale base), as well as indistinct flashes at bases of primaries, should eliminate the many, largely dark, confusion species. Differences from Grey-faced Petrel discussed under latter.

Distribution and biology

Distribution, movements and population: S Atlantic and Indian Oceans, with 10,000 estimated on Gough, 1000 on Tristan da Cunha, perhaps a few on Inaccessible, tens of thousands on Prince Edward and the Crozets, whilst Kerguelen population is perhaps 100,000–200,000 pairs, with only a few tens of pairs on Amsterdam. Further east, breeds on islands off W Australia, with perhaps 10,000–20,000 pairs in this region. Generally ranges at sea at 27–50°S.

Diet and feeding: Cephalopods, some fish and crustaceans, taken by surface-seizing and dipping. Associates with other tubenoses and cetaceans. Attends trawlers, forming monospecific tight groups, separate from other tubenoses.

Social behaviour: Solitary at sea, though small flocks congregate at food sources. Breeds in colonies. Monogamous and forms sustained or long-term pair-bonds. Only defends burrow.

Breeding biology: Breeds in self-excavated burrows, sometimes shared with summer-breeding species, and which are 0.6–2.9 m long, lined with leaves and twigs, in coastal forest. Sometimes nests on surface, under bush, between rocks or roots. Lays one white egg in late Jun–Jul, incubated 51–58 days. Chicks fledge in 108–128 days. Single-brooded. Both ads incubate egg and provision young.

Conservation Endangered, with reports of declines at some important colonies due to introduced predators, with especially feral cats and rats making severe inroads. Fortunately, human exploitation has decreased in recent years.

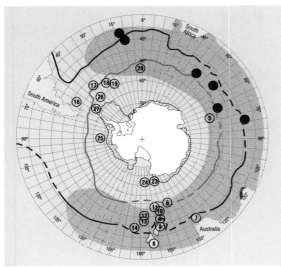

■ Great-winged Petrel *Pterodroma* [*macroptera*] *macroptera*
□ Grey-faced Petrel *Pterodroma* [*macroptera*] *gouldi*

● Marion
● Crozet
● Amsterdam
● Kerguelen
⑧ New Zealand and offshore islands
● Tristan da Cunha
● Gough

Grey-faced Petrel Pterodroma [macroptera] gouldi: *note overall brownish plumage, very long wings, which in close views typically appear less pointed, stocky body with fore-heavy appearance, broad neck and rounded head, slightly wedge-shaped tail, and deep-based black bill; the pale face is variable, but here is extensive and contrasting. Off Lord Howe I, Jul 2004. © Hadoram Shirihai.*

Taxonomy Often considered polytypic with two subspecies, but here *gouldi* (mostly New Zealand waters) is regarded as an allospecies. The two forms appear to differ sufficiently in size and plumage, and perhaps in calls, though further study is needed.

Grey-faced Petrel
Pterodroma [*macroptera*] *gouldi*   Not illustrated

Identification

Confusion risks: As Great-winged Petrel *Pterodroma* [*m.*] *macroptera*.

Main characters: Averages larger than Great-winged, with usually quite extensive, though still ill-defined, pale cream surround to bill, reaching forehead and onto throat. Extent of dark around eye also varies, but usually less pronounced than in *macroptera*, more restricted to area in front of eye. Bill quite noticeably deeper based.

Age/seasonal variation as Great-winged; young, especially juv, often overall darker and lack or have reduced pale area on face, but unknown whether such differences are entirely age-related or also reflect individual variation.

Voice: Some similarities with Great-winged, but *bor-r-r* and braying *eee-aw*, or *ohi* and *o-hee* or *aw-hee* (the first part almost pigeon-like, the second part shrill) described solely or mainly for *gouldi*. Further study required.

Size: 40–43 cm, wing 29.6–33.2 cm, wingspan 100–102 cm, weight 595–750 g.

Similar species: Differs from other dark petrels as Great-winged.

Differs from latter as described above, but note such features require optimal views, and age, individual variation, and wear, can all mask such differences. That some *gouldi* (chiefly juvs) lack the pale face makes identification even harder, or impossible in many instances. The above-mentioned differences await further testing at sea, on larger numbers of birds and of different ages.

Distribution and biology

Distribution, movements and population: Total population probably 200,000–300,000 breeding pairs on many islands, stacks and headlands around North I, New Zealand. Mostly ranges at sea around New Zealand, north into Tasmanian waters and beyond, as well as to subantarctic waters of this region, but western and eastern limits (and overlap with *macroptera*) poorly known (the map shows the range of the superspecies).

Diet and feeding/Social behaviour/Breeding biology: Mostly as Great-winged.

Conservation See Great-winged.

Taxonomy Often regarded as conspecific with Great-winged (but see latter for discussion of rationale for separate treatment).

Soft-plumaged Petrel *Pterodroma mollis*   Plate 9

Identification

Confusion risks: Two morphs and two races (though some commentators consider such variation unworthy of taxonomic recognition), both prone to confusion with other dark or pale petrels.

Main characters: Medium-sized gadfly petrel with rotund and almost neckless appearance. Brownish mid grey above, with dark M on upperparts/upperwing (not always obvious), but upperwing appears darkish and almost unpatterned, especially when fresh, whilst underwing also nearly always looks uniformly dark. Underparts white with variable grey breast-band. Chin/throat white, with variable whitish and dark scaling on forehead and dark oval eye-patch, perhaps with vague supercilium (markings can be difficult

Grey-faced Petrel Pterodroma [macroptera] gouldi: the very deep-based black bill and pale face are typical of gouldi, but in this bird the pale forehead is rather ill-defined and small. Note dark eye-patch restricted to lores. Off Lord Howe I, Jul 2004. © Hadoram Shirihai.

Soft-plumaged Petrel Pterodroma mollis. Whilst the bold grey breast-band and white throat are distinctive in close views, the species can appear to have an all-dark hood at longer range (left-hand bird), and although the underwing often looks uniformly dark (at distance or when overcast), in strong light, it imparts a more variegated in pattern. Off Gough I, Mar 2006. © Hadoram Shirihai.

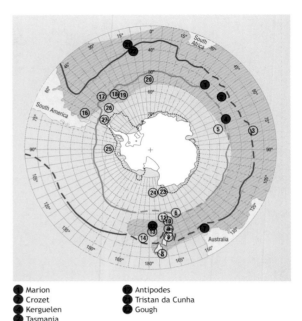

● Marion
● Crozet
● Kerguelen
● Tasmania

● Antipodes
● Tristan da Cunha
● Gough

Soft-plumaged Petrel Pterodroma mollis: pale forehead, short whitish su-percilium, dark oval eye-patch and rather obvious white throat abutted by bold grey breast-band are all characteristic in these unusually close views. Also overall uniform grey mantle to tail, whilst dark M mark varies with lighting and wear (here, the worn and bleached greater coverts make the pattern more distinctive). Off Gough I, Mar 2006. © Hadoram Shirihai.

to appreciate). In strong light, underwing may show indistinct greyish wash to base of primaries and across inner fore-coverts, and perhaps base of secondaries and their larger coverts, but usually underwing appears uniformly dusky or black. Black bill; pinkish legs and feet with dark tips to toes. **Dark morph** rather rare, mostly encountered in S Indian/Atlantic Oceans, and is partially (mottled) to wholly dusky-brown/sooty-grey on underparts,

with variable breast-band, but rest of plumage as pale morph. Unclear if such individuals represent gradual variation, and are thus phases rather than morphs, but extremes can look almost all dark at sea. Relatively chunky, squat jizz, with short round tail, proportionately broad-based wings and short round 'hands', especially apparent given partially bowed wings (carpals set forward), even when gliding or arcing. In moderate/strong winds performs lower arcs, with short glides and some zigzagging. **Age/seasonal variation** indistinct. Juv perhaps separated by freshness of plumage, with unmoulted flight feathers and indistinct paler mottling on upperwing-coverts and mantle in first-year. Imm and ad bleach browner, but (variable) dark M often more contrasting, and has some patchy exposed white bases above; also paler on face, enhancing dark eye-patch and whitish forehead.

Soft-plumaged Petrel Pterodroma mollis (right) and Cook's Petrel P. cookii: Soft-plumaged is usually clearly larger, longer- and broader-winged than the typical small Cookilaria Cook's, which lack the mostly dark underwing and breast-band of the former – here in excellent comparison – but these differences are not always easy detected at sea. South of Chatham Is, Dec 2006. © Hadoram Shirihai.

Dark-morph Soft-plumaged Petrel Pterodroma mollis: this variant is highly variable, but classic individuals (as here) have mostly sooty-grey underparts, whilst the dark breast-band grades into the throat and head to afford the typical dark-hooded appearance. Also note darkening on mid-section of underwing, though lacks Kerguelen Petrel's P. (Aphrodroma or Lugensa) brevirostris silver-grey flashes on lesser and marginal forewing-coverts; these forms are often more readily distinguished using structure and flight pattern. Off Gough I. © Peter Ryan.

Voice: Not known to call at sea. At colonies nocturnal calls distinctive, principally a repeated, low-pitched musical wail, suddenly increasing in frequency, interspersed by shrill squeaks. Also moaning cries in flight and aerial courtship display, *tree-pee* or shriller *uuuuuuu-hi*.

Size: 32–37 cm, wing 23.5–27.6 cm, wingspan 83–95 cm, weight 279–312 g. No significant differences between sexes.

Similar species: Smallish, noticeably rotund shape, near-uniform dark grey underwing, white vent, faint dark M above and grey breast-band are all key features from other gadfly petrels in the region. Several superficially similar *Pterodroma* are only likely to be misidentified in poor conditions or when distant, especially if observer lacks experience of size, shape and flight action, and because of variable appearance. Often appears misleadingly dark-hooded, with all-dark wings. Thus, especially from rear, can resemble white-bodied species, e.g. Magenta *P. magentae* and Atlantic Petrels *P. incerta*, but these are usually noticeably larger and can be distinguished using other features. Extremely rare dark morph easily confused with other dark petrels, but unlike Kerguelen *P. brevirostris* and Great-winged Petrels *P. macroptera* still has diagnostic upperwing marks, and different underwing pattern, size and shape.

Distribution and biology

Distribution, movements and population: S Atlantic and S Indian Oceans; on Tristan da Cunha, Gough, Marion, Crozet (East), Kerguelen, Antipodes (where increasing) and Maatsuyker I (Tasmania, where discovered 2001–2), dispersing through same sea

areas, though nominate apparently recorded sporadically between Réunion and Crozet. Population probably several hundred thousand pairs in 1980s.

Diet and feeding: Cephalopods, some fish and crustaceans, taken by surface-seizing. Sometimes associates with cetaceans and occasionally follows ships.

Social behaviour: Generally social at sea (but aggregations perhaps not indicative of truly gregarious behaviour) and breeds colonially, sometimes with other *Pterodroma* at periphery. Probably monogamous with sustained pair-bonds.

Breeding biology: Breeds in self-excavated burrows, c.0.6–2.8 m long, on steep, well-vegetated slopes and coastal lava fields. Lays one white egg in Nov–Dec, incubated 50 days (single dataset). Chicks fledge at 90–92 days. Single-brooded. Both ads probably incubate egg and provision young.

Conservation Not globally threatened. Feral cats, on Marion, and rats, on Possession, take a severe toll.

Taxonomy Two subspecies recognized: nominate in Atlantic (averages paler/greyer, with narrower breast-band) and darker *dubia* in Indian Ocean. Formerly considered conspecific with Cape Verde Petrel *P. feae* and Madeira Petrel *P. madeira* of N Atlantic. Further study is required to demonstrate true biological relationships of this group.

White-headed Petrel *Pterodroma lessonii*   Plate 9

Identification

Confusion risks: None in our region.

Main characters: Large, rather robust gadfly petrel with striking white, variably grey-tinged, head and tail (latter and whiter rump are most striking features from above), and conspicuous black smudge around eye. Grey (slightly mottled) mantle and upperwing, with ill-defined dark M pattern and grey cast may extend as pale grey neck-sides. Underwing greyish-black (usually appears uniform black, providing most striking feature from below); coverts slightly darker than remiges and contrasting with white rest

White-headed Petrel Pterodroma lessonii is among the most characteristic petrels of the region given its white head and tail, with contrasting blackish underwings. Off Pitcairn Is, Jul 2006. © Hadoram Shirihai.

Fresh juv White-headed Petrel Pterodroma lessonii, *showing striking white head and tail, grey-fringed back and upperwing (dark M pattern ill-defined), and conspicuous black smudge around eye, all of which render this gadfly petrel unmistakable. Off Pitcairn Is, Jul 2006. © Hadoram Shirihai.*

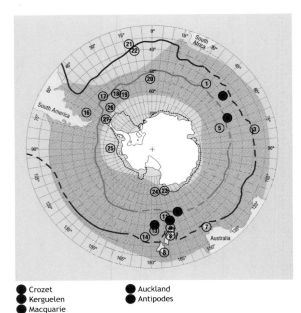

● Crozet
● Kerguelen
● Macquarie
● Auckland
● Antipodes

of underparts. Deep-based black bill, and pinkish legs and feet with dark tips to toes. Body relatively bulky and neck broad and protruding; head rounded and has mid length, slightly wedge-shaped, round-tipped tail. Wings proportionately long; flight not so fast and at moderate heights, in deep arcs and, often, short glides even in strong breezes, when from below may appear like distant, miniature juv Black-browed Albatross *Thalassarche* [*melanophrys*] *melanophrys*. **Age/seasonal variation** indistinct. Juv as ad, but perhaps separated by freshness of plumage, with unmoulted flight feathers. Subsequent imm and ad wear strongly, especially above and around head, with grey wash becoming limited.
Voice: Not known to call at sea. Nocturnal calls around colonies loud and throaty, *tewi, tew-i; wi-wi-wi-wi; wik-wik-wik* or long slurred *ooo-er, kukoowik, kukoowik, kukoowik* in flight and from burrow; in display a soft squeaky *si-si-si*. Vocalizations most like Great-winged Petrel *P. macroptera* (Watson 1975, HANZAB).
Size: 40–46 cm, wing 29.1–33.2 cm, wingspan 109 cm, weight 580–810 g. No specific sexual data apparently available.
Similar species: No similar species in our region, though some Soft-plumaged Petrel can appear very pale-headed in bright light.

Distribution and biology
Distribution, movements and population: Southern Ocean on Crozet, Kerguelen, Macquarie, Auckland and Antipodes, and perhaps Prince Edward and Campbell, dispersing throughout circumpolar regions south of 33°S, but commonest in S Pacific. Overall population not assessed but probably at least 200,000 pairs in New Zealand region alone.

Diet and feeding: Cephalopods and crustaceans taken by surface-seizing but not well known. Associations with other tubenoses recorded. Rarely follows ships for long, though is attracted to them.
Social behaviour: Solitary or in small groups at sea and breeds colonially, but sometimes dispersed. Monogamous with sustained pair-bonds.
Breeding biology: Breeds in large self-excavated burrows, c.1–2 m long with sparse lining, on flat ground with tussac grassland. Lays one white egg in Nov–Dec, incubated for c.60 days. Chicks fledge at c.102 days. Single-brooded. Both parents incubate egg and provision young. Some successful breeders may nest only in alternate years.
Conservation Not globally threatened.
Taxonomy Monotypic.

Atlantic Petrel *Pterodroma incerta*   Plate 9

Identification
Confusion risks: Trindade *P. arminjoniana* and Soft-plumaged Petrels *P. mollis* (see below).
Main characters: Large, robust gadfly petrel, with near-uniform dark brown upperparts, including entire head, upper breast and tail, darker smudge around eye and paler chin (both quite pronounced when observed close and in strong light), dark underwing and white underparts, but upper flanks and vent/undertail-coverts variably dark. In strong light, underwing has indistinct greyish wash to base of primaries, which may appear darker on both surfaces. Deep-based black bill, and pinkish legs and feet with dark tips to toes. Body relatively bulky, neck broad, head rounded, and has tapering mid-length, slightly wedge-shaped tail. Wings proportionately long and narrow, with short 'hands', especially apparent in frequent-flapping flight, even when gliding (at peak of arcs), but flight very rapid in moderate/strong winds, with moderately high sweeping arcs and short glides. **Age/seasonal variation** indistinct. Juv as ad, but perhaps separated by freshness of plumage and unmoulted flight feathers, and indistinct paler mottling on upperwing-coverts and mantle (rapidly abraded) in first-year. Subsequent imm and ad wear strongly to bleach

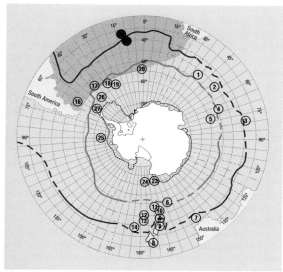

Atlantic Pterodroma incerta *(bottom) and Soft-plumaged Petrels P. mollis. Atlantic is usually rather noticeably larger and more robust, with near-uniform dark brown upperparts, head to upper breast and underwing; the white belly contrasts with the diagnostic dark vent/undertail-coverts and variably smudged flanks. However, in some instances, Soft-plumaged can also appear superficially dark-hooded and, as its underwings are also mostly dark, could be confused with Atlantic, making it often important to rely on the vent/undertail-coverts pattern. With experience, these species are easily separated using structure and flight pattern. Off Gough I, Mar 2006. © Bryan Thomas.*

● Tristan da Cunha
● Gough

browner, often with some patchy exposed white bases to brown areas, and typically has ill-defined pale greyish/buff-brown face, extending to throat and even neck, sometimes to whitish of belly, enhancing dark patch around and in front of eye.

Voice: Not known to call at sea. Nocturnal calls around colonies most like Great-winged Petrel *P. macroptera* (which see), but lower pitched and flutier (Watson 1975).

Size: 43 cm, wing 31.3–33.5 cm, wingspan 104 cm, no weight data. Large overlap in measurements between sexes and though mean female wing is marginally smaller, some have longer wing than longest male.

Similar species: Overlaps with Trindade Petrel in S Atlantic northeast of Tristan. Without previous experience, especially distant birds, could be confused with superficially similar, but smaller and much greyer Soft-plumaged Petrel, although Atlantic is a large, long-winged uniformly bronze form, with a distinct white, well-defined oval belly patch. Otherwise well separated geographically from other similarly patterned/sized white-bellied gadfly petrels of Southern Ocean, e.g. Magenta Petrel *Pterodroma magentae*, and those of the tropics not included here. Soft-plumaged Petrel (which see) can be eliminated by distinctly smaller size, bold dark breast-band and white throat (not always obvious and birds can superficially appear dark-hooded), and more contrastingly patterned upperparts/upperwing, with clear dark M (not always striking). Due to its smaller size, shorter tail and wings, its flight mode/silhouette are also different.

Distribution and biology

Distribution, movements and population: Tristan da Cunha group and Gough, principally dispersing west at sea to C and SW Atlantic Ocean as far as 65°S in the Weddell Sea, chiefly close to Subtropical Convergence, and reasonably frequent at 24°S–56°S off South America (being most abundant at 42°S–46°S); also in smaller numbers in SE Atlantic, at 12°S–48°S, including off South Africa. Few penetrate Indian Ocean east to 105°E. Population estimated (very approximately) at 40,200 individuals (BirdLife International 2000).

Diet and feeding: Fish and squid. Occasionally follows ships,

Atlantic Petrel Pterodroma incerta *is a rather striking, large and robust gadfly petrel. Note the brown head to upper breast and underwing (the coverts usually even darker still), and white belly contrasting with the diagnostic dark undertail-coverts, and variably smudged vent and flanks (brown flecking/mottling can extend to lower breast and belly). Off Gough I, Mar 2006. © Hadoram Shirihai.*

usually inspecting the vessel once before departing.

Social behaviour: Little known, but presumably much as congeners.

Breeding biology: Virtually unknown. Presumably much as close relatives. Burrows in lowlands. Lays in midwinter (Jun), with protracted nestling period, only fledging Nov–Dec.

Conservation Vulnerable, though populations apparently stable. It had become very scarce on Tristan by the 1940s due to human predation for winter food, but this has largely ceased today. Rats still take those breeding on Tristan da Cunha and skuas those on Gough (where its remains are abundant), but cats were successfully eradicated from the former in the 1970s.

Taxonomy Monotypic.

Magenta Petrel (Chatham Island Taiko)
Pterodroma magentae   Plate 9

Identification

Confusion risks: None in Southern Ocean.

Main characters: Medium to large, rather robust gadfly petrel with sooty greyish-brown upperparts, including tail, and even darker head and neck, and dark upper- and underwings. Underparts white, well demarcated from brown neck, but often reaching lower foreneck. Usually has inconspicuous pale facial area around bill and black smudge in front of eye; underwing has slightly darker coverts than remiges. Stout black bill, and pink legs and feet with black toes and webs. Body relatively bulky, neck broad and short, head generally large and rounded, with tapering mid-length, slightly wedge-shaped, round-tipped tail. Wings proportionately very long; flight relatively slow at moderate heights, with short arcs and glides even in strong breezes. **Age/seasonal variation** indistinct. Juv as ad, but perhaps separated by freshness of plumage, with unmoulted flight feathers. Subsequent imm and ad wear strongly, especially above and around head, where becomes abraded brownish, paler around face, with some exposed white basal feathering.

Voice: In flight a long moaning *wooo*, on the ground and in flight *oor-wick oor-wick*.

Size: 38–42 cm, wing 29.8–31.2 cm, wingspan 102 cm, weight

420–560 g. No data on sex-related differences in size (if any).

Similar species: White-bellied plumage pattern occurs only in slightly larger Atlantic Petrel *P. incerta* (which has oval shape to white belly, unlike Magenta), and also note former's proportionately longer tail, dark undertail-coverts/vent and bronze (not grey) upperparts; they are well separated geographically. All other petrels in our region lack solid sooty-grey head and underwing of *magentae*, which contrast markedly with white underparts. Several tropical-water petrels share similar plumage, but all are unlikely in our region. Beware possible confusion with smaller Soft-plumaged Petrel *P. mollis* (which see) that can appear superficially dark and white-bellied, but many structural and plumage differences distinguish them, if seen well.

Distribution and biology

Distribution, movements and population: Chatham and thought to range east of there in winter but no certain pelagic records have been made far from the group, though first collected in C Pacific and has possibly been seen off Chile. Population estimated at 120–180 individuals in Nov 2001 (of which 112 individuals have been banded) but real total probably closer to first-named figure.

Diet and feeding: The only available information is that it takes squid, fish and crustaceans.

Social behaviour: Solitary at sea and is a solitary or loosely colonial breeder. Ignores ships.

Breeding biology: Returns to colonies from mid-Sep and departs Apr–May. Non-breeders arrive at the breeding grounds from early Sep and depart in Dec–Jan. Breeds in self-excavated burrows on forested ridges or fern-covered slopes. Lays one white egg in late Nov–early Dec, incubated for c.52 days. Chicks fledge in c.90 days. No other information.

Conservation Critical but apparently increasing due to intensive management. Prior to 1900 the local Maori probably took large numbers for food, and the spread of agriculture in the archipelago probably caused widespread destruction of its breeding sites. Introduced predators would account for many ads, chicks and eggs but for intensive trapping and poisoning, and were known to take all chicks in some breeding seasons. Flooding of burrows may also negatively affect nesting success. Conservation efforts are proceeding on several fronts: poison baits and traps are being

Magenta Petrel Pterodroma magentae, one of the world's rarest gadfly petrels: the white underparts from lower breast to undertail-coverts is a key feature; note the proportionately long wings and slightly darker underwing-coverts than remiges, and the black smudge in front of eye. These photos are the only ones ever taken at sea, between the Chathams and Bounties (45°08'S 177°12'W), 24 Dec 2004. © Steve Howell.

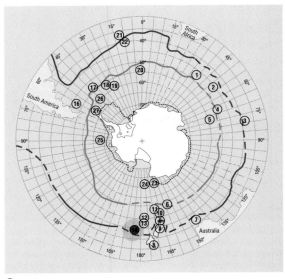

● Chatham

used against introduced mammalian predators, intensive nest monitoring and banding programmes are in place, and a detailed study of the similar Great-winged Petrel *P. macroptera* is ongoing in order to develop hand-rearing techniques and a secure-breeding programme for *magentae*. Additional funding for conservation programmes in Chatham was announced in Oct 2000, and in Feb 2001 a new breeding area for the species, holding at least five pairs (three non-breeding), was discovered. Sponsorship (NZ$150,000) is currently required to construct a predator-proof fence, which is essential to provide a secure breeding ground. At present, when young Taiko return to breed for the first time it is almost impossible to locate their burrows within the dense forest. This leaves them unprotected from predators, and breeding is liable to fail due to predation by rats and cats. If sponsorship can be raised, then a predator-proof fence will be constructed and Taiko lured to this safe site. Further details can be gained from the Department of Conservation or Taiko Expeditions (David Crockett).

Taxonomy Monotypic. Bred on Chatham into the 20th century, followed by a period when the species seemed to be extinct. Rediscovered on 1 Jan 1978 and since then Chatham Island Taiko Expeditions have used radio telemetry to locate breeding burrows.

Black-winged Petrel
Pterodroma nigripennis   Plate 9

Identification
Confusion risks: Mainly Chatham Petrel *P. axillaris*, but also smaller Cook's *P. cookii*, Pycroft's *P. pycrofti* and (vagrant) De Filippi's Petrels *P. defilippiana*; also compare vagrant Gould's (White-winged) *P. leucoptera* and Stejneger's Petrels *P. longirostris*.
Main characters: Comparatively small- to almost mid-sized gadfly petrel (larger and bulkier than Cook's and Pycroft's Petrels, but smaller than Soft-plumaged *P. mollis*), with overall compact structure, especially head and wings, but body quite narrow and has mid-length round-tipped tail. Dark grey to greyish-brown upperparts and head, with dusky crown, mottled paler especially on forehead, and conspicuous dark smudge below and around eye. May have vague pale supercilium; lores flecked dark in front of eye, whiter near bill. Upperwing has ill-defined dark M, but generally appears darkish and almost unpatterned (depend-

Black-winged Petrel's *Pterodroma nigripennis* compact and rotund appearance is very evident in this view. Also note the slightly duskier crown, neck- and (broad) breast-side patches, and eye-patch (with narrow whitish supercilium), whilst it also has an ill-defined dark M and tail-band. Off Kermadec Is, Jan 2006. © Hadoram Shirihai.

Black-winged Petrel *Pterodroma nigripennis is a medium-sized and compact gadfly petrel, with a rather rounded head and wings; the dark grey of the head extends to the neck- and breast-sides and it may show a conspicuous dark eye-patch, whilst the underwings possess a bold and very broad, diagonal black covert-band, almost reaching the body, where it narrows, as well as a broad black trailing edge and primaries. Underwing pattern is the most important identification aid. Off Kermadec Is, Jan 2006. © Hadoram Shirihai.*

ing on light), slightly darker than mantle/back, which are, in turn, darker than pale grey tail. Underwing and underparts mainly white, the former conspicuously marked by a diagonal, bold and very broad black covert-band from bend of wing, almost reaching body, where narrows slightly, and broad black trailing edge and primary tips. Variable dark grey nape extends to neck- and breast-sides to form bold breast-side patches, very prominent on most and noticeably usually extending to upper flanks. Deep-based black bill, and pinkish legs and feet with dark tips to toes. Relatively small size and proportionately broad-based wings with short round 'hands'. In moderate/strong winds, flight appears rather manoeuvrable with sudden sharp turns (making it difficult to evaluate underwing pattern and face marks), and rather short lower arcs and short glides. Like other gadfly petrels, also performs switchback movements or hangs motionless in wind, revealing underwing pattern (though still not easy to observe). **Age/seasonal variation** indistinct. Juv as ad, but perhaps separated by freshness of plumage, with unmoulted flight feathers (rapidly abraded) in first-year. Subsequent imm and ad wear strongly to bleach browner dorsally (variable), with some patchy exposed white bases above, and head greyer, enhancing dark eye-patch.
Voice: Not known to call at sea. Noisy around colonies at night; most notably gives a loud high-pitched *wi-wi-wi*, and hysterical *ha-ha-ha* from burrows. Generally like Mottled Petrel *P. inexpectata* (see *HANZAB*).

● New Zealand's offshore islands
● Chatham

Size: 28–30 cm, wing 21.5–23.6 cm, wingspan 63–71 cm; weight 170–200 g. Female perhaps averages smaller than male (in wing length), but considerable overlap.

Similar species: Cook's, Pycroft's and De Filippi's Petrels are smaller, narrower winged and lack extensive black markings on underwing, while similar-sized Chatham Petrel has more extensive black underwing-coverts and axillaries and a paler crown, but as mentioned elsewhere I find such differences difficult to appreciate in flight, even when close and in relatively calm conditions; experience and an observer's ability to quickly locate the critical features are of paramount importance. Could also be confused with vagrant and principally black-headed Gould's (White-winged) and Stejneger's Petrels (which see).

Distribution and biology

Distribution, movements and population: S Pacific Ocean off New Caledonia, Lord Howe, Norfolk, North I (New Zealand), Kermadec, Three Kings, Chatham, Tubuai, and probably off NE Queensland and New South Wales. Disperses through SC Pacific west to E Australia, north to 49°N and even Japan, and into E Pacific. Population probably 1.0–1.5 million pairs in 1980s.

Diet and feeding: Cephalopods and prawns taken by surface-seizing, dipping and pattering. Associates with a number of other tubenoses. Usually ignores ships, but occasionally follows them, sometimes in comparatively large numbers.

Social behaviour: Solitary or in small loose groups at sea. Breeds colonially, sometimes in huge numbers. No information concerning pair formation and longevity.

Breeding biology: Breeds in self-excavated burrows, c.50–100 cm long with lining of fresh leaves and litter, or in crevices in rocks. Lays one white egg in Dec–Jan, but no information on incubation or fledging periods, number of broods or roles of ads.

Conservation Not globally threatened. Feral cats account for some individuals on several islands and may prevent the species becoming established on other (in other respects suitable) islets. Elsewhere the species is doing well, having recently become established, or is expanding its range, on a number of predator-free islands.

Taxonomy Monotypic. Sometimes treated as a race of *P. hypoleuca*.

Chatham Petrel *Pterodroma axillaris*   Plate 9

Identification

Confusion risks: Principally Black-winged Petrel *P. nigripennis* but could also be confused with smaller Cook's *P. cookii*, Pycroft's *P. pycrofti* and (vagrant) De Filippi's Petrels *P. defilippiana*; also compare vagrant Gould's (White-winged) *P. leucoptera* and Stejneger's Petrels *P. longirostris*.

Main characters: Rather small- to almost mid-sized gadfly petrel; size and structure as Black-winged, with darkish to mid grey upperparts, including nape and neck-side patches (may appear like a breast-band) to tail, and conspicuous dusky (blackish) smudge at rear of and below eye (with ill-defined paler supercilium). Upperwing usually clearly darker than mantle, with rather broad but faint blackish M. Underparts white, with broad, deep grey breast-side patches at most only slightly extending onto fore flanks (see Black-winged). Underwing has strikingly broad diagonal dark mark, narrowest at wing bend, broadening inwards and diagnostically covering much of inner lesser and median coverts, humeral and axillaries, leaving only narrow whitish inner fore-coverts; broad blackish-grey trailing edge and primary tips. Forehead and forecrown mottled whitish, lores almost clean white. Deep-based black bill, and pinkish legs and feet with dark tips to toes. Flight much as Black-winged.

Voice: Not known to call at sea. Around colonies recorded to give a few sharp, rather quiet calls in flight, generally like Black-winged Petrel (Imber in *HANZAB*).

Size: 30 cm, wing 20–22 cm, wingspan 63–71 cm, weight c.200 g. Male averages smaller than female (in wing length), though largest males have longer wings than largest females.

Similar species: Differs from Black-winged Petrel in following combination of characters: broader (and widening) black band on underwing-coverts, which extends to axillaries (rather than almost equal-width, slightly tapering band that does not reach wing base in Black-winged), and grey of neck at most only slightly extends to upper flanks (often distinctive in Black-winged). Subsidiary features include slightly more contrasting pale grey areas above, emphasizing slightly dark-crowned appearance, though lacks contrast between mantle/back and tail, and has cleaner, broader white loral patch. Breast-side patches perhaps better developed and often appear to create a more complete and wider breast-band. However, these are all very difficult to appreciate at sea, even in close views; the main problem being to exclude Black-winged Petrel that appears to have more black. I have also noted the appearance of the underwing of Chatham Petrel change with the light and flight action. Much practice is needed to judge the underwing pattern correctly when following these fast-flying petrels at sea; I am unable to detect any differences in shape and flight pattern, even when observing them together. Cook's, Pycroft's and De Filippi's Petrels are smaller, narrower winged and lack extensive black underwing markings. Could also be confused with vagrant (and principally black-headed) Gould's (White-winged) and Stejneger's Petrels.

Distribution and biology

Distribution, movements and population: Chatham, only on South East; recently few pairs reintroduced on Pitt. Range at sea unknown. I recorded the species several times south of the Chatham group and even further south, nearer the Bounties (max 11 on 1 Jan 2000). The only confirmed record away from the breeding grounds is the observation by M. Force *et al.* (*in litt.*) during a NOAA cetacean research voyage, on 11 Oct 2006, c.820 nm west of the Paracas Peninsula, Peru, c.13°10'S 90°17'W (see photograph herein). Population estimated at 800–1000 individuals (BirdLife International 2000).

Chatham Petrel Pterodroma axillaris *is one of the world's rarest gadfly petrels and an endemic breeder in the Chathams. The right-hand photo is the first ever of the species taken at sea, and the only confirmed record away from the breeding grounds (see text), Oct 2006. Off Peru. © Jim Cotton. At left, ad outside its nest burrow in the Chathams. © Colin Miskelly. Overall close to Black-winged Petrel but has diagnostic diagonal black band across underwing-coverts, broadening on inner wing and reaching axillaries; breast-band well developed but flanks cleaner.*

Diet and feeding: Cephalopods recorded in a sample from breeding grounds, but no data available on techniques or possible associations with other seabirds and cetaceans. Not attracted to boats.

Social behaviour: Breeds colonially, in scattered situations amongst other tubenoses, but no concrete information from non-breeding season. No other details.

Breeding biology: Breeds in self-excavated burrows, c.0.4–2.0 m long with lining of dead leaves and twigs, on moderate, well-vegetated slopes and level ground. Lays one white egg in Dec–Feb, hatches Feb–Mar after 44–47 days, and fledges May–Jun at 77–98 days old. One brood per season, ads share incubation and chick-feeding duties.

Conservation Critical but apparently increasing due to intensive management. The principal threat is competition for nest burrows and attacks by Broad-billed Prion *Pachyptila vittata*, which may result in low breeding success and high pair-bond disruption. Exploitation by humans for food and introduced predators led to the species' disappearance from other islands in the group.

Taxonomy Monotypic. Sometimes treated as a race of *P. nigripennis* or *P. hypoleuca*.

Cook's Petrel *Pterodroma cookii*   Plate 9

Identification

Confusion risks: Principally other small *Cookilaria*, namely Pycroft's *P. pycrofti* and (vagrant) De Filippi's Petrels *P. defilippiana*; also vagrant Stejneger's *P. longirostris* or slightly larger gadfly petrels such as Black-winged *P. nigripennis*.

Main characters: Small gadfly petrel, with overall size, structure and plumage characteristics as Pycroft's (which see). Pale grey over much of upperparts and tail, which is tipped dark (and edged whitish when fresh); upperwing has dark M. Forehead indistinctly mottled/freckled paler, with rather conspicuous dark smudge below, around and behind eye, bordered above by faint whitish supercilium. White border to cheeks does not extend behind ear-coverts and grey nape and neck-sides hardly, or very faintly, extend to upper breast; hence dark border to head/neck appears straight and breast-/neck-side patches are rarely developed. In many, grey wash continues onto upper flanks. Underwing and underparts white, with indistinct (but variable) diagonal narrow black carpal/covert-bar extending towards body, narrow black tips and trailing edge. Black bar often difficult to see at sea, terminates level with elbow point, where narrows and fades. Thin black bill, and mauve legs and feet with black toes and webs. Wing proportionately long, narrow and pointed; tail short, slim and round-tipped. In moderate/strong winds, flight appears rather erratic and manoeuvrable, with sudden sharp turns and typically rather short lower arcs and short glides. **Age/ seasonal variation** indistinct. Juv as ad, but perhaps separated by unmoulted flight feathers in first-year, and upperparts usually more extensively fringed whitish than fresh ad. Subsequent imm and ad wear strongly to bleach duller and slightly browner/duskier above; M pattern reduced and may appear darker headed.

Voice: Not known to call at sea. Around colonies vocal at night, commonest call a nasal *kek-kek-kek* or *nga-nga-nga*, with almost duck-like quality, sometimes in long sequences; reportedly rather similar to Chatham *P. axillaris* and Mottled Petrels *P. inexpectata* (Imber in *HANZAB*).

Size: 25–30 cm, wing 22.3–24.5 cm, wingspan 65 cm, weight c.190 g. Female averages smaller than male in wing length, but some overlap.

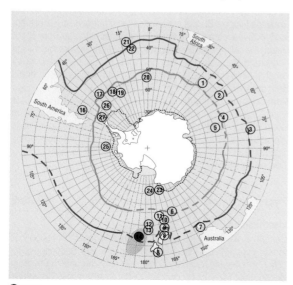

● Chatham

At this angle, Cook's Petrel Pterodroma cookii *is probably only plausibly separable from Pycroft's Petrel* P. pycrofti *by the apparently longer and more pointed wings (with relatively shorter tail), longer/stronger bill and, on average, more obvious whitish supercilium. Off New Zealand, Jan 2006. © Hadoram Shirihai.*

Cook's Petrel Pterodroma cookii, *compared to the near-identical Pycroft's Petrel* P. pycrofti, *has longer/more pointed wings but somewhat restricted black primary tips, purer white outer tail feathers, and a longer/stronger bill, with on average a better-marked whitish supercilium and dark eye-patch, as well as straighter lower border to cheeks. Off New Zealand, Jan 2006. © Hadoram Shirihai.*

Similar species: Pycroft's Petrel (which see) virtually indistinguishable at sea. Black-winged Petrel is larger and has broader, more extensive black lines and trailing edges to underwing, as well as obvious grey breast-sides. However, I find it very difficult to appreciate size, structure and plumage differences, even between small *Cookilaria* and mid-sized Black-winged and even given close views; the main problem being to exclude an example of

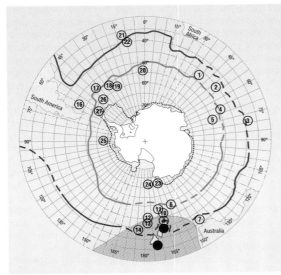

● New Zealand's offshore islands

latter that appears to have less black on underwing. All characters prone to change according to light/angle/flight mode; thus considerable experience is required to correctly judge those characters discussed under the following three species against Cook's.

Distribution and biology
Distribution, movements and population: New Zealand on Little and Great Barrier (off North I) and off Stewart I. Trans-equatorial migrant to N Pacific, off California, Oregon (rarely) and Baja California, and Peru. Total population estimated at 100,000 individuals in 1980s.
Diet and feeding: Cephalopods, some fish and crustaceans, taken by surface-seizing, dipping and pattering. Associates with other shearwaters and storm-petrels.
Social behaviour: Solitary at sea; breeds in loose colonies. Sustained or long-term pair-bond.
Breeding biology: Breeds in self-excavated burrows, c.1–5 m long, lined with leaves and twigs, and sometimes adopted from Black Petrel *Procellaria parkinsoni*, within subtropical forest on high ridges and steep slopes. Lays one white egg in late Oct–Dec, incubated 47–51 days. Chicks fledge in c.88 days. Single-brooded. Both ads incubate egg and provision young.
Conservation Endangered, though apparently increasing. Cats were a major predator of eggs and chicks on Little Barrier, and on Great Barrier numbers were reduced by both cats and rats, while Weka *Gallirallus australis* took a toll on Codfish, but latter eradicated by 1985 and cats on Little Barrier likewise by 1980.
Taxonomy Monotypic.

Pycroft's Petrel *Pterodroma pycrofti*　　　Plate 9

Identification
Confusion risks: Cook's Petrel *P. cookii* is main confusion risk (broad overlap); De Filippi's *P. defilippiana* and Stejneger's Petrels *P. longirostris* also very similar, but only vagrants to Southern Ocean; less likely to be confused with slightly larger *Cookilaria*, e.g. Black-winged *P. nigripennis*.

Only with experience and in optimal views are some better-marked Pycroft's Petrels Pterodroma pycrofti separable from the near-identical Cook's Petrel P. cookii. In this image note the more compact appearance, more rounded head and wings, and proportionally longer tail; the entire head-/neck-sides appear more extensive and progressively darker, and are variably notched on the crown-sides, emphasizing the collar. It also tends to have a reduced (or to lack a) supercilium or separate ear-coverts patch; outer tail feathers greyer (less pure white). Off New Zealand, Jan 1998. © Hadoram Shirihai.

Pycroft's Petrel Pterodroma pycrofti. Compared to Cook's Petrel P. cookii, note the apparently more extensive black on the primaries, the shorter/more rounded wings, more solid and duskier head, broader breast-side patches and smaller bill. Off New Zealand, Jan 1998. © Hadoram Shirihai.

Main characters: Small, dorsally grey and ventrally white gadfly petrel, with overall size, structure and plumage characteristics (and apparently age/seasonal variation) almost identical to those of Cook's Petrel.
Voice: Not known to call at sea. Around colonies noisy at night, commonest flight call a high-pitched ti-ti-ti, softer than Cook's Petrel; also calls from burrows (see HANZAB).
Size: 28 cm, wing 20.7–22.9 cm, wingspan 53 cm, weight 127–201 g. Male averages smaller than female in wing length, with some overlap.
Similar species: The following comparisons refer to the separation of Pycroft's from Cook's in fresh (or moderately worn) plumage, and are mainly based on my experience in New Zealand waters where they often occur side by side. However, when heavily worn

and bleached the two are far less easily separated on plumage. In general, I find their overall relative proportions often reliable to separate them, with Pycroft's having slightly shorter, more rounded wings, a proportionally longer tail and more rounded head, with a dusky more solid hood, affording it a more compact appearance than Cook's (bill also very slightly smaller, but extremely difficult to appreciate). Compared to Cook's, upperparts slightly darker/duller, grey-tinged brown and thus M mark is less pronounced. The entire crown, head-sides, nape and neck-sides are darker and more concolorous dusky-grey (slightly darker than mantle). Whitish supercilium usually indistinct (shorter and thinner) or lacking altogether, whilst dark ear-coverts patch appears to merge with crown, or often relatively darker and appears as a large oval or triangular patch (but can also be restricted to a dark smudge below/behind eye). In Cook's, however, dark ear-coverts patch often appears bolder, straighter and enhanced by better-developed white supercilium. The cheek-border often appears more variegated in Pycroft's; especially note the slight ill-defined

Pycroft's Pterodroma pycrofti (right) and Cook's Petrels P. cookii. In this rare comparative image, one can practice the separation of these near-identical petrels. Pycroft's is slightly smaller with a somewhat more rounded/smaller head and shorter/thinner bill compared to Cook's. The overall plumage, including the head, appears more dusky, grey, and Pycroft's tends to lack or to have a very short and thin whitish supercilium; the darker ear-coverts appear as a large oval or triangular patch which tends to merge into the crown (in Cook's the patch is usually smaller but bolder and enhanced by the longer, thicker whitish supercilium). Note the ill-defined pale notch behind the ear-coverts (which appears as a pale extension from the lower cheeks, but in some is almost lacking), whilst grey neck-sides (collar) better developed and darker. Interestingly, note that the Pycroft's appears to sit lower on the water with less white body plumage exposed than Cook's. Many of these characters vary individually and there is much overlap, so it is best to only attempt to identify classic individuals, meaning that many must be left unidentified. Off New Zealand, Jan 2006. © Hadoram Shirihai.

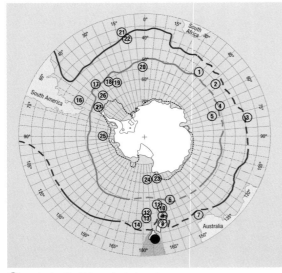

New Zealand's offshore islands (breeding season)

pale notch behind/below the ear-coverts (which may appear as a pale extension, but is variable and in some almost lacking). Thus, entire head-/neck-sides (collar) appear more extensive and progressively darker, with border variably notched on crown-sides, a pattern somewhat more reminiscent of De Filippi's than Cook's Petrel. Pycroft's slightly higher/rounded forecrown and greyer head make the white forehead and lores appear more extensive than most Cook's, again somewhat like De Filippi's. Furthermore, though perhaps only apparent in photographs, it has slightly less visible white in the outer tail feathers, and usually more extensive dark primary tips, edges and diagonal covert-bar, but much overlap and only extremes perhaps separable using these characters. Photos of several Pycroft's seem to suggest that it tends to have reduced (or to lack) grey on the upper flanks and below the wings (more extensive in most Cook's), but this feature needs checking. In sum, separation of these two species probably represents the most difficult challenge in *Pterodroma* identification, because no single character can be used alone to separate them (even in photographs). Thus, I recommend only attempting to identify those classic individuals by using a combination of shape, jizz and plumage characters. Also, beware the effects of light and angle which strongly influence the appearance of the above-mentioned characters.

For differences from vagrant De Filippi's and Stejneger's Petrels, see these texts. Both Chatham and Black-winged Petrels (which see) are larger, have broader and more extensive black lines and trailing-edges to underwing, and more extensive grey breast-sides.

Distribution and biology

Distribution, movements and population: Islands off NE New Zealand. Ranges at sea in equatorial Pacific east to 110°W. Total population estimated at 10,000–20,000 individuals (BirdLife International 2000).
Diet and feeding: Small cephalopods found as stomach contents but diet otherwise unknown.
Social behaviour: Breeds in low-density colonies. No information concerning longevity of pair-bond. Often breeds in association (sharing same burrows) with the endemic reptile *Sphenodon punctatus*.
Breeding biology: Breeds in self-excavated burrows, c.30–130 cm

long, lined with leaves and twigs, in well-drained forested areas on floor or sides of valleys. Lays one white egg in late Nov–early Dec, incubated c.45 days. Chicks fledge in 77–84 days. Single-brooded. Both ads incubate egg and provision young.
Conservation Vulnerable, though apparently increasing. Introduced rats are a major predator of eggs and chicks, and *Sphenodon punctatus* a natural predator, while Little Shearwater *Puffinus assimilis* may out-compete it for nesting burrows. A rat-eradication programme has been implemented on a number of islets. Chick transfers to establish a new colony on Cuvier I began in 2001.
Taxonomy Monotypic. Often regarded as race of *P. longirostris*, but differences in morphology and vocalizations, as well as their widely disjunct breeding ranges, suggest treatment as allospecies or full species more appropriate.

De Filippi's Petrel *Pterodroma defilippiana*   Plate 9

Identification

Confusion risks: Other small gadfly petrels, namely Cook's *P. cookii*, Pycroft's *P. pycrofti* and Stejneger's *P. longirostris*, but less likely to be confused with slightly larger *Cookilaria*, e.g. Black-winged *P. nigripennis*.
Main characters: Small gadfly petrel with grey upperparts including cap, white forehead, conspicuous dark smudge below eye, and dark M on upperwing. Rather pronounced grey half-collar on upper breast. Underwing and underparts white with narrow black marking extending towards body from wing bend, and narrow black tips and trailing edge. Relatively deep-based black bill, and pale legs and feet with black toes and webs. Otherwise, overall size, structure and plumage characteristics (and age/seasonal variation) almost identical to those of Cook's and Pycroft's Petrels (which see). Main differences from these, as well as from Stejneger's Petrel, discussed below.
Voice: Only nocturnal calls around colonies. Not known to call at sea.
Size: 26 cm, wing 22.9–24.1 cm, wingspan 66 cm, no weight data.

De Filippi's Petrel Pterodroma defilippiana *is best distinguished from other small* Cookilaria *treated here by its more distinctive face pattern (rather extensive, bold white forehead/lores and supercilium in front of eye, broad black eye/ear-coverts patch and well-developed dark grey half-collar). White of throat curves up behind ear-coverts to enhance half-collar, affording altogether bolder pattern than Pycroft's* P. pycrofti *or, especially, Cook's* P. cookii, *but not as extreme as Stejneger's* P. longirostris. *Also note the proportionately long, deep-based bill, but overall structure is otherwise closer to Pycroft's and Stejneger's. Off Chile, Nov.* © Tony Marr.

De Filippi's Petrel Pterodroma defilippiana (in advanced moult): note distinctive face and breast patterns, with extensive dark grey half-collar, bold white forehead/lores and supercilium in front of eye, and distinct black eye/ear-coverts patch; white of throat reaches behind ear-coverts. Proportionately long, deep-based bill, and relatively long full tail appear more uniform grey without or with very limited dark tip. Eastern Tropical Pacific, Sep 2003. © Hadoram Shirihai.

Moulting De Filippi's Petrel Pterodroma defilippiana: underwing very similar to other small Cookilaria but note the characteristic relatively extensive white on the wingtips; face and breast patterns also highly distinctive at this angle, especially the dark grey half-collar and white reaching behind ear-coverts, whilst the proportionately deep-based bill, and relatively long full tail are also evident. Eastern Tropical Pacific, Sep 2003. © Hadoram Shirihai.

No information concerning sex-related differences in size (if any). *Similar species*: From other small *Cookilaria*, De Filippi's is best distinguished at sea by following criteria. For its small size, it has an overall chunky/robust appearance, with proportionately long, deep-based bill, somewhat full, long wedge-shaped tail, and broad rounded wings (thus closer in shape to Pycroft's and Stejneger's Petrels, or even to Gould's *P. leucoptera*, than to relatively longer winged and shorter tailed Cook's). Usually has more distinctive facial marks, with rather extensive and bold white forehead/lores and supercilium in front of eye, often broader black eye/ear-coverts patch and well-developed dark grey half-collar to lower neck- and breast-sides, while in most (and again somewhat in common with Stejneger's, but little with Pycroft's) white of cheeks curves up behind ear-coverts to enhance half-collar affect, giving altogether bolder pattern than Pycroft's, especially compared to Cook's, but not as extreme as Stejneger's. Tail has on average

less broad white edges than Cook's, but more extensive than the others, and compared to any of these, tail appears, but not always is, uniform grey without or with very limited dark tip. Be aware that individual variation and wear and bleaching effects can render these differences of little use. Further, although De Filippi's and Stejneger's appear to share somewhat similar structural features, have quite slow, less erratic flight patterns, and extensive grey neck-sides, they differ from each other by latter's slightly larger/heavier and usually clearly overall darker upperparts, notably with contrasting darker/blacker crown/nape and higher white forehead (even sometimes extending to forecrown); also bill of De Filippi's relatively much deeper based. Separated from medium-sized gadfly petrels of Southern Ocean, e.g. Black-winged (which see), by smaller size and largely white underwing with reduced black markings, but as mentioned previously a good view is often required for reliable identification.

Distribution and biology

Distribution, movements and population: SE Pacific Ocean off SW South America (on San Félix, San Ambrosio, Más-á-Tierra and Santa Clara in Juan Fernández Is), ranging at sea perhaps to our region (no certain records, but clearly can be expected in southernmost waters of South America), from near its breeding grounds to south of the Galápagos and the C Pacific. Population placed at 10,400–10,600 individuals in 1990s.

Diet and feeding: No information from our region.

Social behaviour: No information from our region. Does not follow ships.

Breeding biology: Breeds on sheltered ledges, in crevices and among boulders in lava fields. Lays one egg in Jul–Sep.

Conservation Vulnerable. Feral cats and coatimundis *Nasua nasua* have brought the species to the verge of extinction on Robinson Crusoe and significantly reduced numbers on San Félix. The archipelago was designated a national park in 1935 and a biosphere reserve in 1977. Habitat restoration commenced in the late 1990s and several breeding islands are still predator free.

Taxonomy Monotypic. Sometimes treated as a race of *P. cookii*.

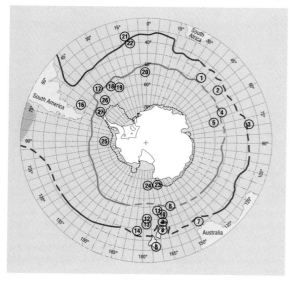

Fresh-plumaged Stejneger's Petrels Pterodroma longirostris *(probably juvs). In the degree of black on crown and nape, and strength of the upperparts pattern, Stejneger's is generally midway between Gould's* P. leucoptera *and all other small* Cookilaria *covered here. In most instances, readily separated from these latter by the contrasting blackish cap, and more extensive, higher, white forehead (sometimes very conspicuous and can extend to forecrown) and extension behind ear-coverts (creating two large round dark patches, an ear-covert mask and neck/breast-side patches in profile views), whilst the M mark is usually more contrasting too. Right: off Juan Fernández, Chile, Nov 2005. © Alavaro Jaramillo. Left: off Hawaii, Sep 2005. © Hadoram Shirihai.*

Stejneger's Petrel *Pterodroma longirostris* Plate 9

Identification

Confusion risks: Other small gadfly petrels, including Cook's *P. cookii*, Pycroft's *P. pycrofti* and (vagrant) De Filippi's *P. defilippiana*; also perhaps slightly larger Gould's *P. leucoptera*, Black-winged *P. nigripennis* and Chatham Petrels *P. axillaris*.

Main characters: Small, contrastingly marked, gadfly petrel with medium to dark grey upperparts, conspicuous darkish (or dark slaty) cap to nape, concolorous with dark smudge below and around eye, and bordered by extensive white forehead/lores (sometimes to forecrown) and lower cheeks, which reach behind ear-coverts, emphasizing tiny blackish area on nape. Lower neck medium grey, extending as broad half-collar on upper breast, concolorous with rest of upperparts to (darker tipped) tail and upperwing, which has broad, rather pronounced dark M. Upperwing slightly darker than mantle/back. Underwing and underparts white with diagonal narrow black carpal/coverts-band extending towards body, and narrow black tips and trailing edge. Black band, which is generally difficult to see, terminates well before wing base, reach-

ing level of elbow, where narrows and fades. Thin black bill, and pale legs and feet with black toes and webs. Comparatively small and slim, as, or marginally larger, than Cook's and Pycroft's, but generally appears to have narrower wings and proportionally longer (wedge-shaped) tail, like many other large *Pterodroma*. Head characteristically rounded and neck rather short. In moderate/strong winds, flight appears less erratic and manoeuvrable, with fewer sudden sharp turns than other small gadfly petrels; arcs shorter and lower, with short glides. **Age/seasonal variation** indistinct. Juv as ad, but perhaps separated by unmoulted plumage in first-year. Subsequent imm and ad wear strongly to bleach duller and slightly browner on dorsal parts, and M variably reduced, but head still blackish to dark slate-grey. With extreme wear has confusingly paler grey nape.

Voice: Only nocturnal calls around colonies. Not known to call at sea.

Size: 26–31 cm, wing 19.8–22.0 cm, wingspan 53–66 cm, weight (one) 88 g. No information on any sex-related differences in size (if any).

Similar species: From most medium-sized gadfly petrels (e.g.

Moderately worn Stejneger's Petrel Pterodroma longirostris. *Like all other small* Cookilaria *covered here, has extensively white underwing with relatively short narrow diagonal black covert-bar, but note contrasting blackish cap (diagnostic). Mid Pacific (55°48'S 83°11'W), Feb 2004. © Brent Stephenson.*

Moderately worn Stejneger's Petrel Pterodroma longirostris. *In worn plumage the neat grey scaling and M pattern is reduced considerably and the species looks browner. Note the diagnostically blackish cap, with higher white forehead (extending to forecrown). Stejneger's is also longer tailed than most small* Cookilaria, *especially Cook's* P. cookii. *Mid Pacific (55°48'S 83°11'W), Feb 2004. © Brent Stephenson.*

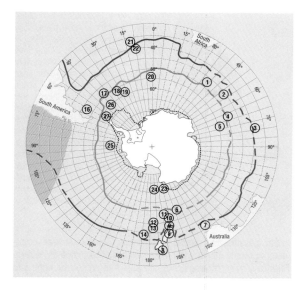

Gould's Petrel Pterodroma leucoptera caledonica. *When fresh, silvery grey upperparts with strong M resembles Stejneger's* P. longirostris, *but unlike latter and other small* Cookilaria *covered here, has diagnostic half-hood extending onto head, cheeks, breast-sides and hindneck to upper mantle. New Caledonia, Feb 2007. © Hadoram Shirihai.*

Black-winged and Chatham) by smaller size and largely white underwing. In latter, and other respects, very similar to other small *Cookilaria*, namely Cook's, Pycroft's and De Filippi's, from which best distinguished by contrasting blackish cap and nape (with stronger contrast than rest of grey dorsal areas), more extensive higher white forehead/lores (very conspicuous in some and can extend to forecrown), with better developed mark on neck-sides (see above), more extensive breast-sides, and virtual lack of paler outer tail feathers in these species. Stejneger's is also overall darker above and longer tailed than any of these, especially Cook's. See others for subsidiary structural, face, neck, upper-/underwing and tail-pattern differences. See also Gould's.

Distribution and biology

Distribution, movements and population: Breeds on Alejandro Selkirk in the Juan Fernández Is. Trans-equatorial migrant in apparent clockwise pattern around Pacific Ocean to Japan, N Pacific and off California. In Southern Ocean few records, mainly from SE Pacific, to c.49°S. Population estimated at 262,000 individuals in 1990s.

Diet and feeding: No information from our region.

Social behaviour: No information from our region.

Breeding biology: Unrecorded in our region.

Conservation Vulnerable and perhaps declining as a result of predation by introduced cats, dogs and, principally, rats, which in mixed colonies of this species and Juan Fernandez Petrel prefer to take the smaller *P. longirostris*. There is increasing human disturbance on its breeding island and a fire, in 1995, destroyed part of the suitable habitat for the species. However, sheep were removed from the island in the 1980s and the entire archipelago has been a designated national park since 1935 and a biosphere reserve since 1977.

Taxonomy Monotypic.

Gould's (White-winged) Petrel
Pterodroma leucoptera   Plate 9

Identification

Confusion risks: Other small-/medium-sized gadfly petrels, but in Southern Ocean might only be confused with another vagrant, Stejneger's Petrel *P. longirostris*, though Black-winged *P.*

nigripennis could offer a pitfall, especially given distant and/or worn birds. Otherwise very distinctive.

Main characters: Small to almost medium-sized, generally very strikingly plumaged gadfly petrel, with medium brownish-grey upperparts, white forehead, lores, lower cheeks and throat, and notable blackish-brown hood encompassing sides of head, neck and breast, and upper mantle, thus imparting unmistakable dark-faced or half-hooded pattern. Upperwing grey-brown, with broad, rather pronounced dark M. Much of upperwing, hood and rump to tail appears evenly and usually clearly much darker than greyish mantle/back and inner upperwing-coverts (subject to light and wear). Tail not long but rounded and darker tipped, indistinctly edged paler. Underwing and underparts white with moderately broad diagonal black carpal/coverts-band extending towards (but not reaching) body, with moderately broad black tips and trailing edge. Thin black bill, and pale legs and feet with black toes and webs. Comparatively smaller and slighter than Black-winged Petrel, and compared to small *Cookilaria*, e.g. Cook's, averages slightly larger and mainly bulkier, broad-necked and large-headed,

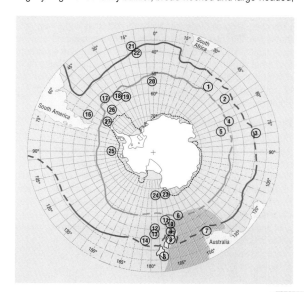

Gould's Petrel Pterodroma leucoptera: this bird appears to have purer white outer tail feathers and paler bases to the primaries, suggestive of the race caledonica, *rather than the much rarer nominate. Apparently, most birds seen around Tasmania and to the south, and thus within our region, refer to cal-edonica which also has on average paler upperparts, a perhaps narrower dark tail tip and somewhat weaker diagonal black carpal/coverts bar on underwings. However, the two subspecies are only doubtfully separable at sea. Also, note the extensive solid black hood (extending unbroken onto the neck-sides), which distinguishes it from all other* Cookilaria. *Off Tasmania.* © Mike Carter.

Gould's Petrel Pterodroma *leucoptera caledonica, showing the unmis-takable half-hooded pattern, extending well onto head/neck, cheeks and breast-sides, and especially on hindneck to upper mantle, thus making confusion with other small* Cookilaria *covered here unlikely. Note, also, diagonal black carpal/coverts bar is broader and extends further towards body than any of the others. New Caledonia, Feb 2007.* © Hadoram Shirihai.

with proportionately broader based, longer wings. In moderate/strong winds, flight appears less swift, but rather erratic and ag-ile, interspersed by manoeuvres, switchbacks, arcs (not high) and rather long glides. **Age/seasonal variation** indistinct. Juv as ad, but perhaps separated by unmoulted plumage in first-year. Subsequent imm and ad bleach strongly to have duller/markedly browner upperparts and reduced M, but head and upperwing re-tain diagnostic characters.

Voice: Only nocturnal calls around colonies. Not known to call at sea.

Size: 30 cm, wing 21.3–23.8 cm, wingspan 70–71 cm, weight 134–220 g. Female averages markedly smaller than male in cul-men and tarsus lengths, but not in wing/tail measurements.

Similar species: In our region, perhaps only confusable with vagrant Stejneger's Petrel, but unlike this and other smaller *Cookilaria*, namely Cook's, Pycroft's and De Filippi's, has more extensive black hood (in others black does not extend so exten-sively onto head/neck and cheeks to breast, and especially on hindneck to upper mantle) and diagonal black carpal/coverts-band, which is broader and extends further towards body than other species. Separated from most mid-sized gadfly petrels in region (e.g. Black-winged and Chatham) by smaller size and less extensive diagonal black carpal/coverts-band on underwing, and markedly different head pattern if seen well (experience is required to evaluate even such obvious differences at sea). See elsewhere for further structural, face, neck, upper-/underwing and tail-pattern differences. Has closer relationships and there is a greater risk of confusion with other tropical gadfly petrels not yet recorded in Southern Ocean.

Distribution and biology

Distribution, movements and population: SW Pacific Ocean off E Australia (Cabbage Tree I, New South Wales), Fiji, Cook and pos-sibly Solomons, New Caledonia and perhaps only historically on Vanuatu. Ranges at sea in S Pacific south to New Zealand, south of Tasmania (vagrant) and off S Australia, and east in tropical Pacific to 10°N and to 90°W, south of Galápagos. Population placed at 3000–21,000 individuals in 1990s.

Diet and feeding: No information from our region. Does not usually follow ships.

Social behaviour: No information from our region.

Breeding biology: Unrecorded in our region.

Conservation Vulnerable and apparently declining, but lower

threat classification perhaps warranted. Small Australian popu-lation currently increasing (since 1993) due to active protection. Prior to this, currawongs *Strepera* spp. had preyed on eggs and young, and rabbits damaged vegetation to the detriment of the petrel. In New Caledonia, rats and cats are potential threats and pigs certainly destroy nesting burrows.

Taxonomy Several forms recognized: nominate breeds only on Cabbage Tree and Boondelbah, *caledonica* on New Caledonia (the latter two barely separable at sea), and *brevipes*, which has been treated specifically (Collared Petrel), on Fiji, the Cooks and perhaps the Solomons, with populations elsewhere in the SW Pa-cific, e.g. Vanuatu, yet to be assigned to race (though previously considered as *brevipes*). All or some of these appear to form a distinctive superspecies.

Juan Fernández Petrel
Pterodroma externa   Plate 9

Identification

Confusion risks: Common in subtropical waters of E Pacific, and likely to be confused with related White-necked *P. cervicalis*, Vanuatu *P. occulta* and Barau's Petrels *P. baraui*, but not with any gadfly petrels of the Southern Ocean.

Main characters: Large, typically long, narrow-winged gadfly petrel, with grey upperparts, dusky cap, white forehead and con-spicuous blackish smudge below and around eye; white of face may extend beyond eye-patch, and upperwing has dark M. Grey half-collar on upper breast. Underwing and underparts white with short, crescent-shaped black carpal extending only slightly (and tapering) inwards, usually visible at close range, and narrow black primary tips and trailing edge. Whitish on rump is highly variable, both individually and due to degree of feather wear. Thin black bill, and pale legs and feet with black toes and webs. Relatively elon-gated, with proportionately long narrow wings especially 'hands', protruding narrow neck/head and longish rear body; flight even in moderate/strong winds never manoeuvrable and vigorous, con-sisting of effortless direct progress, no zigzagging, and graceful glides and arcs. **Age/seasonal variation** indistinct. Juv as ad, but unmoulted body and flight feathers, and slight (indistinct) paler fringes apparent to upperwing-coverts and mantle, which abrade rapidly in first-year. Subsequent imm and ad wear strongly to bleach browner on upperparts, dark M across upperparts/upper-wing often reduced, and some bleach whiter around face (enhanc-ing dark eye-patch) and hindneck.

Voice: Only nocturnal calls around colonies. Not known to call at sea.

Juan Fernández Petrel Pterodroma externa *(in advanced body moult, but wings mostly unmoulted and bleached). The new feathers on the mantle / back are neatly grey tipped whitish, whilst the dusky cap, blackish eye-patch and grey half-collar are well evident. However, the upperwings are heavily worn and bleached browner, with the dark M much reduced. Whitish on rump varies individually. Between Mexico and French Polynesia, Apr 2006. © Ron LeValley.*

The large Juan Fernández Petrel Pterodroma externa *typically has long narrow wings which are characteristically white below with a short, crescent-shaped black carpal mark extending only slightly inwards (very variable and detectable only close to), with small black primary tips and trailing edge. Also, note dusky cap, conspicuous blackish eye-patch and grey half-collar on upper breast-sides. Eastern Tropical Pacific, Sep 2003. © Hadoram Shirihai.*

Size: 43 cm, wing 30.2–33.3 cm, wingspan 97 cm, weight c.500 g. Apparently extensive overlap between sexes in most measurements.

Similar species: Several tropical-water petrels share, to some degree, a similar plumage pattern, but are unlikely in our waters. Buller's Shearwater *Puffinus bulleri* is only non-*Pterodroma* tubenose occurring widely in region that shares same size and extensive pale plumage, but many other characters should prevent confusion.

Distribution and biology

Distribution, movements and population: Juan Fernández Is. Ranges through Pacific, south and east of Hawaii, off W Mexico and,

exceptionally, to Tristan da Cunha in S Atlantic, and vagrant off E Australia and New Zealand. Population estimated at two million individuals in 1990s. In Southern Ocean recorded south to 50ºS.

Diet and feeding: No information from our region. Rarely follows ships.

Social behaviour: No information from our region.

Breeding biology: Unrecorded in our region.

Conservation Vulnerable. Predation by introduced cats, dogs and, principally, rats may be causing a decline. Increasing human disturbance of its breeding island and a fire in 1995 destroyed part of the suitable habitat for the species. Goats and the few cattle are also destroying breeding habitat. It is possible that fisheries may also be negatively affecting this species by depleting stocks of its food. Sheep were removed from the island in the 1980s and the entire archipelago has been a designated national park since 1935 and a biosphere reserve since 1977.

Taxonomy Monotypic, but has been considered conspecific with White-necked Petrel *P. cervicalis*.

Juan Fernández Petrel Pterodroma externa *(in advanced moult). Short, crescent-shaped black carpal mark on mostly white underwing can be very small or, as here, virtually lacking. Flight typically consists of effortless direct progress with long arcs and glides. Between Mexico and French Polynesia, Apr 2006. © Ron LeValley.*

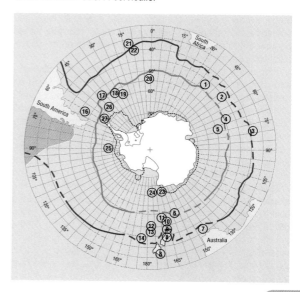

Procellaria petrels and shearwaters

The species featured in Plate 10 belong to two genera, *Procellaria* and *Puffinus*. The former consists of 4–5 species (according to taxonomy), all of which are largely confined to the Southern Ocean. On the other hand, the shearwaters are a rather large, widespread group, found throughout both hemispheres, and some species are among the world's greatest migrants; nonetheless the Southern Ocean is still an important area, as at least eight species have been recorded.

Both genera are clearly separable from the gadfly petrels by their proportionately longer and/or thinner bills, with less bulbous maxillary unguis and tubes, making the bill appear much less chunky and deep-based. Bills are usually pale (rather than all black), at least at the base. The head and neck are usually less rounded and somewhat narrower, while the wings are proportionately longer, pointed and appear more stiff, while the tail is almost never as proportionally long and wedge-shaped as most gadfly petrels. In plumage, most have very simple patterns, some are all black, sooty-brown or medium brown, while others are dark dorsally and largely whitish below, and only a few have more distinct markings on the head and upperwing. Sex and age-related variation is generally almost wholly lacking, and even mensural data show considerable overlap. The other genus close to this group is *Calonectris* (Cory's *C. diomedea* and Streaked Shearwaters *C. leucomelas*), which is midway in appearance between *Procellaria* and *Puffinus*, but neither has been regularly recorded in the Southern Ocean. All have powerful flight, which in most winds consists of shallow and rather few wingbeats, often with towering arcs and long glides.

I have attempted to present the species in a logical order to facilitate comparison between the most frequently confused species. Note that at-sea identification is often challenging, even for experienced observers, especially with some closely related species, such as the three dark *Procellaria* in New Zealand waters, or with Short-tailed *Puffinus tenuirostris* and Sooty Shearwaters *P. griseus*. Moreover, at sea it is often very difficult to appreciate any differences, mainly due to their fast flight, harsh sea conditions/visibility and often misleading lighting, as well as typical viewing distances. A combination of features must be taken into account, including size, structure/jizz (bill and head, wings and tail, and body), overall coloration/plumage pattern, especially tone, and perhaps some (not always distinct) differences in underwing/upperwing markings, as well as on the head/breast areas, underparts and perhaps rump.

The general behaviour, life and breeding cycles are rather uniform between species. Most *Procellaria* and *Puffinus* breed on undisturbed offshore islands, remote islets and continental coasts with dense grass or forest. Being truly pelagic, they come to land only to breed. Most prefer shelf-break and pelagic waters and are rarely sighted inshore, except near their breeding areas. Cephalopods, small fish and crustaceans constitute their principal diet, and are taken on or near the surface of the water. The age at which birds first return to their natal colonies and that at which breeding is first attempted are often unknown, but in at least some species the latter may be as late as nine years. Ads arrive at the colonies several weeks prior to breeding (when copulation takes place) and then disperse for up to two weeks to nearby marine feeding areas to gain weight prior to nesting (*pre-laying exodus*); most nests are in self-excavated burrows, ads laying a single, usually smooth white egg, incubated 7–9 weeks, and chicks take 10–20 weeks to fledge. Most are nocturnal around the colonies,

when they can be heard displaying; usually visiting their burrows just before dusk and returning to the sea sometime prior to dawn.

Like other burrow-nesting seabirds, many have been the unintentional victims of Man's arrival on their breeding islands: rats, feral cats, pigs and other introduced mammals have all caused significant losses among eggs, young and even ads. Several are globally threatened, with others qualifying as Near Threatened. Fortunately many islands are currently subject to conservation work designed to tackle the problems caused by introduced predators, and significant advances have already been made.

White-chinned Petrel
Procellaria aequinoctialis   Plate 10

Identification

Confusion risks: Westland *P. westlandica* and Black Petrels *P. parkinsoni*, and other large and dark petrels and shearwaters, such as Flesh-footed Shearwater *Puffinus carneipes*. The recently split Spectacled Petrel *P. [a.] conspicillata* is usually easily separated (see below).

Main characters: Large, heavily built, long-winged and almost uniform brownish-black petrel; in very close views often appears blacker on head and neck, whilst rest of upperparts and upperwings can be indistinctly paler-fringed. The small white chin/throat patch is highly variable individually and apparently to some degree also geographically, but in most birds and across much of the range it is restricted to a few white feathers at the base of the lower mandible and is practically invisible. However, I find that a few birds, mostly in the subantarctic Indian Ocean, can develop a quite sizeable white chin (and throat) patch, albeit irregular in shape. Strong, rather chunky (bulbous) bill, diagnostically appears largely pale yellow, even at long range (a principal identification feature), but note that a few may show some darkening on maxillary unguis (but less extensive than most individuals of the following three *Procellaria*). Feet mainly black and hardly project (at most only very slightly) beyond rather short, slightly wedge-shaped tail. According to the light, underwing varies but paler, silvery-tinged (mainly basal) primaries and often secondaries. At sea almost invariably appears bulky and long-winged, appearing midway in size between much larger giant petrels and all other dark, but smaller petrels and shearwaters. Given this, the distinctive yellowish bill and that it is the most regular boat-

White-chinned Petrel Procellaria aequinoctialis. *A few birds, apparently mostly in the subantarctic Indian Ocean, can develop an extensive, but rather patchy white chin/throat (as here); however, in most individuals and in much of the range, the white chin is very restricted and hardly visible at sea. Off Amsterdam, Nov 1999. © Hadoram Shirihai.*

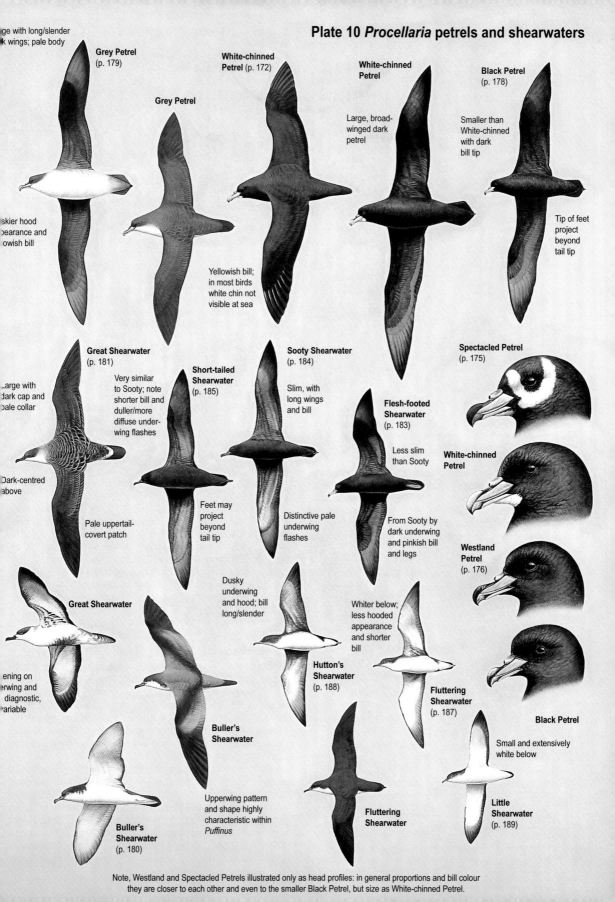

Plate 10 *Procellaria* petrels and shearwaters

ge with long/slender
k wings; pale body

Grey Petrel
(p. 179)

Grey Petrel

**White-chinned
Petrel** (p. 172)

**White-chinned
Petrel**

Large, broad-
winged dark
petrel

Black Petrel
(p. 178)

Smaller than
White-chinned
with dark
bill tip

skier hood
pearance and
owish bill

Yellowish bill;
in most birds
white chin not
visible at sea

Tip of feet
project
beyond
tail tip

Great Shearwater
(p. 181)

Very similar
to Sooty; note
shorter bill and
duller/more
diffuse under-
wing flashes

**Short-tailed
Shearwater**
(p. 185)

Sooty Shearwater
(p. 184)

Slim, with
long wings
and bill

**Flesh-footed
Shearwater**
(p. 183)

Less slim
than Sooty

Spectacled Petrel
(p. 175)

**White-chinned
Petrel**

Large with
dark cap and
pale collar

Dark-centred
above

Pale uppertail-
covert patch

Feet may
project
beyond
tail tip

Distinctive pale
underwing
flashes

From Sooty by
dark underwing
and pinkish bill
and legs

**Westland
Petrel**
(p. 176)

Great Shearwater

Dusky
underwing
and hood; bill
long/slender

Whiter below;
less hooded
appearance
and shorter
bill

**Hutton's
Shearwater**
(p. 188)

**Fluttering
Shearwater**
(p. 187)

Black Petrel

ening on
erwing and
diagnostic,
ariable

**Buller's
Shearwater**

Small and extensively
white below

**Buller's
Shearwater**
(p. 180)

Upperwing pattern
and shape highly
characteristic within
Puffinus

**Fluttering
Shearwater**

**Little
Shearwater**
(p. 189)

Note, Westland and Spectacled Petrels illustrated only as head profiles: in general proportions and bill colour
they are closer to each other and even to the smaller Black Petrel, but size as White-chinned Petrel.

White-chinned Petrel Procellaria aequinoctialis *in typical flight profile. A large, heavily built* Procellaria *with long wings, almost entirely sooty/ blackish-brown plumage, and feet hardly project (if at all) beyond rather short, slightly wedge-shaped tail; note pale bill without dark tip. Off Crozet Is, Mar 2004. © Hadoram Shirihai.*

follower of the group make identification usually straightforward. Flight typically appears relatively powerful and vigorous, but direct and effortless with long glides, and slow/few and shallow wing-beats. **Age/seasonal variation** indistinct. Juv as ad, but plumage and flight feathers unmoulted in first-year and become gradually abraded at sea. Both subsequent imm and ad wear strongly, be-

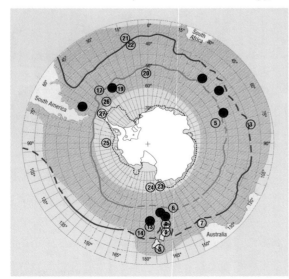

- ● Prince Edward & Marion
- ● Crozet
- ● Kerguelen
- ● Auckland
- ● Campbell
- ● Antipodes
- ● Falklands
- ● South Georgia

White-chinned Petrel Procellaria aequinoctialis *banking into a steep arc in strong winds. Though it occurs throughout Southern Ocean, often following ships for long periods and being attracted to food in large numbers, e.g. at trawlers, the species' population is in sharp decline. Off South Georgia, Mar 2006. © Hadoram Shirihai.*

coming slightly browner and, in extreme cases, patchy with pale upperwing panels. Leucistic individuals, up to c.10% of population, have some white, especially on belly.

Size: 51–58 cm, wing 35.5–41.5 cm, wingspan 134–147 cm, weight 1.28–1.39 kg. Highly extensive overlap in most measurements between sexes, though male has deeper based bill and slight tendency to average marginally longer in wing length.

Voice: Quite often heard at sea, around trawlers. At colonies ads very noisy at night, with ear-piercing, high-pitched squeals or screaming (chattering and rattling) trills, *chiky-chiky-chiky...* and other similar calls.

Similar species: Easily confused with Westland and, considerably smaller, Black Petrels (which see); identification of all three, under certain conditions, can be challenging. Generally, however, both lack white chin, but perhaps only safely separable when the (almost) diagnostic dark-tipped bill is visible (though White-chinned may also have a slightly darker tip whilst, more commonly, Westland may have a duller or partially paler maxillary unguis, requiring that such birds be checked more carefully). Flesh-footed Shearwater is clearly smaller and browner, with a pinkish bill and flesh-coloured feet. Spectacled Petrel (which see for problem cases) typically has diagnostic and usually very conspicuous white bands encircling the head.

Distribution and biology

Distribution, movements and population: Southern Ocean, breeding on the Falklands, South Georgia, Prince Edward, Marion, Crozet, Kerguelen, Auckland, Campbell and Antipodes. Disperses at sea north along coasts of South America to 6°S and Africa to 15°S. The total population was estimated at c.5 million individuals in the 1990s, but there is evidence from several areas of decreases in recent years, and this species is at great risk from current longlining practices.

Diet and feeding: Cephalopods, fish and crustaceans taken by surface-seizing, deep-plunging (to 13 m) and pursuit-plunging, and apparently located by scent. More reliant on fish and offal in non-breeding season. Feeds alone or in loose flocks, including mixed groups of seabirds, frequently associates with several species of cetaceans when feeding, and follows ships.

Social behaviour: Solitary or gregarious at sea and breeds in loose colonies, being territorial around burrow entrance. Probably monogamous. No further information.

Breeding biology: Breeds in self-excavated burrows, 1–2 m long with little nest lining, on well-vegetated slopes and level ground. Lays one white egg in Nov–Dec, incubated 57–62 days. Chicks fledge at 87–106 days. Single-brooded. Both sexes take full role in breeding cycle.

Conservation Vulnerable and in decline. Significant numbers are probably taken as bycatch in longline fishing off South Africa, Australia and Brazil. Estimates suggest that up to 80% of many thousands of seabirds killed by such fishery practices in the late 1980s were of this species. At a small number of breeding localities, rats pose a threat to nesting success and fur seals degrade its habitat. Population monitoring studies have been initiated in several breeding areas and others are sited within protected areas.

Taxonomy Monotypic. Formerly regarded as polytypic, the form *conspicillata* (Spectacled Petrel), which now breeds only on Inaccessible (Tristan da Cunha) is regarded as a separate species (based on cytochrome-*b* gene differences).

Spectacled Petrel
Procellaria conspicillata   Plate 10

Identification

Confusion risks: White-chinned Petrel *P.* [*a.*] *aequinoctialis* and other large/dark congeners.

Main characters: Generally similar in size, structure and plumage to White-chinned and Westland Petrels *P. westlandica* (which see), but has diagnostic, very conspicuous and complex head pattern consisting of broad white bands from white chin to behind and encircling ear-coverts (may connect on hindneck), and from base of latter across foreface, over lores and forecrown. Individual variation (extensive) mainly involves the width and distinctness of these bands, which may appear more ragged or partially/distinctly broken and taper at either end, but in many instances are very broad and well defined. Yellowish-horn bill is more similar to Westland Petrel, with distinctive black linings to plates, nostrils and on bill tip, and the feet rather clearly project beyond the tail as in the latter species. **Age/seasonal variation** is in general probably similar to White-chinned Petrel, but it is unclear if the variability in the white bands represents age/sex variation or merely a broad spectrum of individual variation (pending further study).

Voice: Largely similar to White-chinned Petrel, but much deeper pitched and repertoire also includes remarkably harmonious

Spectacled Petrel Procellaria conspicillata *has extensive and diagnostic white head markings. Its distribution in the Indian Ocean is poorly known, though the species may formerly have bred in Amsterdam I. This image represents the only (or one of the very few) Spectacled Petrels seen or photographed so far east in the Indian Ocean. Off Amsterdam, Nov 1999. © Hadoram Shirihai.*

groans never recorded in latter. Does not respond to calls of White-chinned Petrel.

Size: 55 cm, wing 36.9–39.7 cm, no wingspan data, weight 1.01–1.31 kg. Highly extensive overlap between sexes in most measurements.

Similar species: Given reasonable view of diagnostic head markings, generally unmistakable, e.g. when head-on white forehead is very obvious. Dusky bill tip and foot projection recall other dark *Procellaria*, but differ from White-chinned. Partially leucistic White-chinned Petrels are poorly documented and I have no experience of such birds, though P. Ryan (pers. comm.) reports that such variants never show white spectacles, but quite frequently possess white on the nape.

Distribution and biology

Distribution, movements and population: Southern Ocean, breeding only on Inaccessible (Tristan da Cunha). Some remain in the area year-round. Population 10,000 pairs in 2006 and has increased dramatically, despite longlining activities off S South America, where up to 700 taken as bycatch in non-breeding season. Some also winter in Benguela Current off southern Africa and it has penetrated Indian Ocean east to Amsterdam I (Nov 1999; HS pers. obs.), where it may formerly have bred, with 19th-century specimen records off Australia.

Diet and feeding/Social behaviour: Much as White-chinned Petrel.

Spectacled Petrels Procellaria conspicillata *showing the spectrum of individual variation in the species' white facial bands. In the foreground, note the third bird from the right with the rather partial and broken white bands. Off Inaccessible I, Mar 2003. © Hadoram Shirihai.*

Spectacled Petrel Procellaria conspicillata in fast steep arc and sideways banking, showing the head-on profile of bold white forehead and white band below and around ear-coverts; the feet are just visible beyond the tail-tip. Off Inaccessible I, Mar 2003. © Hadoram Shirihai.

Mainly visits colonies at dusk, but also regularly during day, especially from mid-afternoon.

Breeding biology: Breeds in self-excavated burrows in wet heath at 380–500 m in marshy areas and along sides of river valleys on western plateau of Inaccessible. Lays one white egg in second half of Oct and early Nov (up to five weeks earlier than White-chinned Petrel), but incubation and fledging periods unknown. Single-brooded. Both sexes take full role in breeding cycle.

Conservation Recently downlisted by BirdLife International to Vulnerable (from Critically Endangered). Greatest threat is from

longlining in S Atlantic, where large numbers taken annually off Brazil (see above) and perhaps elsewhere. Tristan Skua *Catharacta* [*skua*] *hamiltoni* is a natural predator of young, but feral pigs have now been removed from the island. Livestock may also have caused its extirpation on Amsterdam (where plausibly bred formerly).

Taxonomy Formerly regarded as a race of White-chinned Petrel *P. aequinoctialis*, but the fact that the dusky bill tip and foot projection recalls Westland (and Black), rather than White-chinned Petrel may suggest a closer relationship with the more northerly breeders. Further study is required.

Westland Petrel
Procellaria westlandica   Plate 10

Identification

Confusion risks: White-chinned *P.* [*a.*] *aequinoctialis* and Black Petrels *P. parkinsoni*. Also, at long distance, might be confused with other large, dark petrels and shearwaters, e.g. Flesh-footed Shearwater *Puffinus carneipes*.

Main characters: Large and particularly heavily built, with deep chest and belly; flies on broad, long wings. In plumage, almost identical to White-chinned Petrel (which see), being all brownish-black, with ivory-yellow black-tipped bill (diagnostic). Black feet may project slightly beyond tail in flight. Thus very similar in most respects (including age/seasonal variation) to White-chinned, but see below for differences.

Voice: Mostly silent at sea. At colonies ads noisy at night (though less vocal than White-chinned Petrel), with rather similar chattering and rattling squeals to latter, but has richest repertoire among *Procellaria*.

Size: 50–55 cm, wing 36.2–40.0 cm, wingspan 135–140 cm, weight 1.2 kg. Highly extensive overlap between sexes in most measurements.

Similar species: Almost diagnostically, Westland lacks (usually invisible) white chin of White-chinned, and has dark bill tip, though this varies individually; in extremes, it is rather solid and covers the entire maxillary unguis onto the culminicorn, but in others is limited or appears greyish (especially in young birds and in strong sunlight). Such individuals perhaps difficult to separate from some White-chinned with hint of dark bill tip, but my experience with both species in New Zealand waters demonstrates that most are safely distinguished using this character alone, though it is

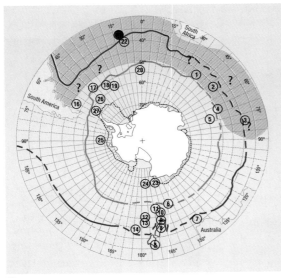

Westland Petrel Procellaria westlandica is relatively heavier built and the feet often project slightly less obviously beyond the tail than Black Petrel P. parkinsoni. Very similar to White-chinned Petrel P. aequinoctialis, but note dark bill tip. Kaikoura, South I, New Zealand, Oct 2001. © Hadoram Shirihai.

● Tristan da Cunha

detectable only at short (rarely moderate) distances and sometimes birds must be followed for some time to correctly evaluate it. Additional differences may be apparent with experience, e.g. Westland is proportionately heavier built, notably deep-chested and has a bulkier, more bulbous bill. Black Petrel (which see) also very similar in plumage and bill pattern, but rather smaller (intermediate between Sooty Shearwater *Puffinus griseus* and White-chinned Petrel), and has slightly different jizz, with feet perhaps projecting slightly further beyond tail; their ranges rarely meet. The species seems to moult rather earlier and/or closer to the breeding grounds, apparently chiefly in Aug–Jan (imms or non-breeders) and Oct–Feb (post-breeding ads), whereas Black Petrel moults mostly in tropical Pacific, in Mar–Nov, and most White-chinned Petrels moult in Jan–Mar. Furthermore, off South America where most Westland Petrels are in active primary moult or have pale upperwing panels in Aug–Dec at least, they are separable by moult and feather wear (with care and in reasonable views). Flesh-footed Shearwater is clearly smaller and browner, with a pinkish bill and flesh-coloured feet.

Distribution and biology

Distribution, movements and population: Coastal S New Zealand on South I. Disperses at sea west to Australia, at 33–45°S, and regularly east to South America, where there are now at least 46 records (one involving 340 individuals) over the Humboldt Current north to 16°S and south to Cape Horn and (recently) the Drake Passage. The total population has been estimated at fewer than 20,000 individuals in recent years.

Diet and feeding: Cephalopods and fish, with some crustaceans, taken by surface-seizing and pursuit-plunging. Feeds alone or in loose flocks, including mixed groups of seabirds, and scavenges offal behind ships.

Social behaviour: Gregarious at sea and breeds colonially, being territorial around burrow entrance and also aggressively defends food from conspecifics at sea. Long-term monogamous.

Breeding biology: Breeds in self-excavated burrows, 1–2 m long with sparse nest lining, cavities, hollow logs and among roots of trees in dense coastal hill forest, but also in areas without ground vegetation. Lays one white egg in May–Jun, incubated 51–68 days. Chicks fledge at 120–140 days. Single-brooded. Both

Westland Petrel Procellaria westlandica *is heavily built and long-winged, but only at certain angles are the darker underwing-coverts appreciable; otherwise, it appears as an all-dark* Procellaria. *This bird is probably young, with a paler bill tip (enhanced by the bright sunlight) and is undertaking its first (annual) complete moult (the species moults rather earlier and often closer to the breeding areas than Black* P. parkinsoni *and White-chinned Petrels* P. aequinoctialis). *Kaikoura, South I, New Zealand, Nov 2003. © Hadoram Shirihai.*

parents take full role in breeding cycle.

Conservation Vulnerable but considered stable. Some numbers are taken as bycatch of longline fishing off Australia and New Zealand. The breeding locality is situated within a national park, but introduced mammals pose a threat to nesting success and ads, as well degrading the species' habitat, and mining and agriculture have destroyed some nesting habitat. Birds are occasionally killed by flying into electricity pylons. Long-term monitoring studies were initiated in 1969 and public access to the colony was recently restricted.

Taxonomy Monotypic.

Westland Petrel Procellaria westlandica *is endemic as a breeder to New Zealand, and is a large, heavily built all-dark* Procellaria, *with a large head, thick neck, deep chest and robust yellowish-white bill with a darker tip. Kaikoura, South I, New Zealand, Jan 2006. © Hadoram Shirihai.*

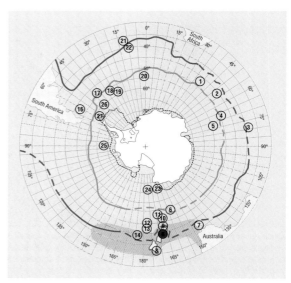

● Southern New Zealand

Black Petrel *Procellaria parkinsoni*   Plate 10

Identification

Confusion risks: White-chinned *P.* [*a.*] *aequinoctialis* and Westland Petrels *P. westlandica*. At long distance, might also be confused with other large, dark tubenoses, e.g. Great-winged Petrel *Pterodroma macroptera* and Flesh-footed Shearwater *Puffinus carneipes*.

Main characters: The smallest *Procellaria*, but still characteristically large and entirely brownish-black, and particularly close in plumage and bare-parts coloration to larger Westland Petrel, including dark-tipped pale yellow bill, which separates both from White-chinned Petrel. The dark feet usually project slightly more clearly beyond the tail than either of the latter species. See below for further details. **Age/seasonal variation** indistinct. Juv as ad, but plumage and flight feathers unmoulted in first-year and become gradually abraded at sea. Also bill of juv (at least in early stages) tends to have reduced yellowish tone, but some tinged greyish, bluish or pink; like Westland, at least some juv/imm have partially paler/greyer bill tip too. Both subsequent imm and ad wear strongly to become slightly browner, sometimes patchily paler, mainly on upperparts.

Voice: Probably mostly silent at sea. At colonies ads rather noisy at night, with loud, harsh, far-carrying calls, mainly a high-pitched squawk and repeated *clack-clack-clack-...*

Size: 46 cm, wing 32.6–35.9 cm, wingspan 115 cm, weight 587–855 g. Extensive overlap in most measurements, though male tends to average marginally larger in most.

Similar species: Compared to almost identically plumaged Westland Petrel, Black is noticeably smaller, less heavily built and slender necked, has a compact bill and is usually clearly narrower winged, which produces a lighter and less laboured flight, with quite relaxed and slower wingbeats; thus somewhat shearwaterlike, unlike Westland and White-chinned. Note also tendency for feet to project further beyond tail (difficult to see). Great-winged Petrel has deeper-based all-black bill and to some degree pale face (especially in race *gouldi* breeding on North I, New Zealand), whilst Flesh-footed Shearwater is overall slimmer with smaller head, longer, thinner bill and narrower, shorter wings, and is tinged browner, with a diagnostically mostly pinkish bill and legs, whilst the feet do not project beyond tail. These last two species also differ considerably in shape and flight action.

Black Petrel Procellaria parkinsoni *is very similar to Westland Petrel* P. westlandica, *and is best separated (with practice) by being quite noticeably smaller and less heavily built with a slender neck, more compact bill and, usually, clearly narrower wings. The more obvious foot projection beyond the tail tip is usually a good character, but there is some overlap between them. New Zealand, Jan 1998. © Hadoram Shirihai.*

Comparison between the three dark Procellaria. *P. parkinsoni (Black Petrel, top) has relatively smaller proportions, a smaller head, and narrower neck and bill, but shares the dark bill tip with the relatively larger and heavier* westlandica *(Westland Petrel, middle). Bill-tip pattern separates both from* aequinoctialis *(White-chinned Petrel, bottom). Some (apparently young)* westlandica, *e.g. that in the middle image, have a partially dark bill tip and are thus less easily separated from the similar-sized* aequinoctialis. *Note the very small, almost invisible white chin of* aequinoctialis. *Off New Zealand. © Hadoram Shirihai.*

Distribution and biology

Distribution, movements and population: New Zealand on Little Barrier and Great Barrier Is. Ranges widely at sea in Pacific east to Peru, north to SW Mexico, west to E coast of Australia and south into the Ross Sea. Total population estimated at 5000 individuals in recent years.

Diet and feeding: Cephalopods, some fish and crustaceans, taken by surface-seizing, surface-plunging and pursuit-plunging. Feeds alone or in loose flocks, including mixed groups of seabirds, associates with some small species of cetaceans when feeding, and scavenges behind ships.

Social behaviour: Solitary or occasionally gregarious at sea and breeds in loose colonies, being territorial around burrow entrance. Long-term monogamous. No other data.

Breeding biology: Breeds in self-excavated burrows, 1–3 m long with sparse nest lining, cavities, hollow logs and among roots of

Black Petrel Procellaria parkinsoni is endemic as a breeder to New Zealand but migrates across the eastern tropical Pacific, and is the smallest of the dark Procellaria. The photo shows the species in typical profile, but note that sometimes (as here), owing to its slimmer head and neck, the bill can look confusingly large. Off New Zealand. © Hadoram Shirihai.

trees on steep forested slopes and high ridges. Lays one white egg in Nov–Jan, incubated c.56 days. Chicks fledge at 96–122 days. Single-brooded. Both parents take full role in breeding cycle.

Conservation Vulnerable, though currently considered stable. Taken as bycatch of longline fishing off New Zealand and in the E Pacific, but no estimates of numbers caught by such practices appear to be available. Rats, dogs and feral pigs have all had a detrimental affect on breeding colonies, and decimated the Little Barrier population over several seasons until cats were eradicated there. Fledgling transfer from Great Barrier was attempted, with mixed success, in the wake of the eradication programme. Population monitoring studies have been initiated on both breeding islands.

Taxonomy Monotypic.

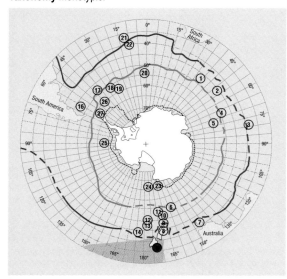

● New Zealand's offshore islands

Grey Petrel *Procellaria cinerea*   Plate 10

Identification

Confusion risks: Large shearwaters, e.g. Buller's *Puffinus bulleri*.
Main characters: Distinctive. Robust, heavy bodied, narrow/long-winged and ashy-grey petrel, with darkish crown/face and upperparts/upperwings, white below, grey wedge-shaped tail, dark grey underwings, slender greenish-yellow bill and pinkish-grey feet. Identification usually very straightforward, but see below. Often described as shearwater-like in jizz, but my experience suggests that it has a unique shape, consisting of long and very narrow/pointed wings, which are usually held stiff and straight. Flight, in most conditions, appears relatively direct, effortless (slow/few and shallow wingbeats) and almost albatross-like, with long glides, arcs and banks typical only in strong winds. **Age/seasonal variation** indistinct. Juv as ad, but plumage and flight feathers unmoulted in first-year.
Voice: Probably mostly silent at sea. At colonies ads vocal at night, with weaker repertoire than congeners, but during pre-laying season may contain some repeated quite melodious moans, *aaargh-hoo-errhooer...* on rising and falling pitch; also rattling calls.
Size: 50 cm, wing 29.0–36.4 cm, wingspan 115–130 cm, weight 0.76–1.52 kg. No data concerning any sex-related differences in measurements.
Similar species: Given combination of above-mentioned characters, unmistakable. Even in distant views, upperparts/upperwing pattern, shape and flight mode readily exclude confusion with large shearwaters. Inexperienced observers could misidentify White-headed Petrel *Pterodroma lessonii* (which see), mainly because of the superficially similar dark underwing and whitish belly, and in strong winds and distant views White-headed may appear very narrow/long and stiff-winged, but once this problem is appreciated, they are ready separated by different size, shape/jizz, head and upperparts patterns, and (in close view) different bill shape and colour.

Distribution and biology

Distribution, movements and population: Southern Ocean breeding on Tristan da Cunha, Gough, Marion, Crozet, Kerguelen, Campbell, Antipodes, and possibly St Paul. Formerly bred Macquarie, where population is currently attempting to re-establish itself. Disperses at sea, generally south of 25°S. The total population

Identification of Grey Petrel Procellaria cinerea *is usually straightforward, it being a large, drab grey petrel, with long/narrow stiff wings, a darkish hood, whitish body (with contrastingly dark underwings) and, in close views, a slender greenish-yellow bill. Note also the slight darkening on the flanks, vent and undertail-coverts, and the foot projection. Off Gough I, Mar 2003. © Hadoram Shirihai.*

179

Grey Petrel Procellaria cinerea in typical flight. A rather robust petrel, heavy with long narrow wings, an ash-grey tone to the plumage and darker face and underwings, which combined with its characteristically direct, effortless and sometimes almost albatross-like flight, with long glides or arcs, usually makes identification easy. Off Gough I, Mar 2006. © Hadoram Shirihai.

appears to be several hundred thousand pairs, with most apparently on Gough, but figures for the latter island are based on very few data and may represent a considerable overestimate.

Diet and feeding: Cephalopods, fish and crustaceans taken by surface-seizing and pursuit-plunging. Feeds alone or in loose flocks, including mixed groups of seabirds, associates with some small species of cetaceans when feeding, and scavenges behind ships.

Social behaviour: Solitary or gregarious at sea and breeds colonially. Probably monogamous. No further information.

Breeding biology: Breeds in self-excavated burrows, 1.5–3.0 m

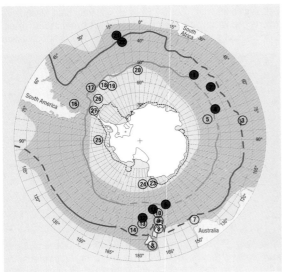

● Marion	● Campbell
● Crozet	● Antipodes
● Kerguelen	● Tristan da Cunha
● Macquarie	● Gough

long, on steep, well-vegetated slopes. Lays one white egg in Mar–Jul, incubated 52–61 days. Chicks fledge at 102–120 days. Single-brooded. Both parents probably take full role in breeding cycle.

Conservation Near Threatened. Historic decline, which has perhaps not stabilized, and appears to be significantly affected by longline fishing off New Zealand (c.45,000 killed in the last 20 years), Australia and in S Indian Ocean. Introduced predators, particularly rats and cats, may also take substantial toll on some breeding islands, and responsible for extinctions and near-extinctions on Macquarie and Amsterdam.

Taxonomy Monotypic.

Buller's Shearwater *Puffinus bulleri*   Plate 10

Identification

Confusion risks: None if seen well, but see below.

Main characters: Large, greyish-brown, slender bodied shearwater with notable *Cookilaria*-like dark carpal bars forming broad M on upperwing, joining on lower back and emphasized by pale greater coverts and innermost lesser coverts. Long wedge-shaped tail and largely white underparts/underwings. Rather long but quite rounded wings, with relatively small head, which may appear slightly capped, and typically shearwater-like bill proportionally less slender and mainly dark greyish, while legs/feet generally pinkish-grey. Uppertail-coverts/rump and outermost tail feathers paler than surrounding tracts. Outer primaries and tail blackish, like diagonal carpal bar, and contrasting, adding to distinctive overall dorsal pattern. Dark on underwings very inconspicuous, but dark breast-side patches poorly/moderately developed. Identification usually straightforward, but see below. Wings tend to be held in noticeable downward arc and/or with carpal bowed prominently forward. Flight usually appears graceful, effortless and unhurried (with slow/few and shallow wingbeats), typically with short glides and arcs. **Age/seasonal variation** indistinct. Juv as ad, but body plumage and flight feathers unmoulted in first-year; all ages wear browner.

Voice: Probably mostly silent at sea. At colonies ads very vocal at night, with high-pitched, far-carrying calls, described as howls, wails and screams, most similar to those of Sooty Shearwater *P. griseus*.

Size: 46–47 cm, wing 27.5–30.9 cm, wingspan 97–99 cm, weight 278–499 g. Extensive overlap between sexes in measurements.

Similar species: Among shearwaters, distinctive upperwing pattern

Buller's Shearwater Puffinus bulleri: dainty shape and highly characteristic upperparts pattern (with dark M, tail, remiges and crown) make this shearwater almost unmistakable. South I, New Zealand, Oct 2001 © Hadoram Shirihai.

Feeding frenzy of Buller's Shearwaters Puffinus bulleri *at a school of fish. The birds in flight show the typical 'flexible' wings and the distinctive marks above and below, whilst those on the water are also unmistakable due to their grey mantles, scapulars and breast-side patches contrasting with dusky crown, wings and tail, and snowy white underparts. Off North I, New Zealand, Jan 2006. © Hadoram Shirihai.*

unique. Sometimes, in poor weather and only at first glance, may appear superficially like large gadfly petrel, chiefly Juan Fernández Petrel *Pterodroma externa*.

Distribution and biology

Distribution, movements and population: New Zealand (on Poor Knights, possibly other islands off North I). Ranges at sea through Pacific Ocean north to Japan and Alaska, east to the Americas (occasionally as far south as Chile) and west to Australian waters. Vagrant to W Atlantic Ocean off New Jersey. Population c.2.5 million individuals in 1980s.

Diet and feeding: Chiefly fish and crustaceans, chiefly taken by variety of techniques at surface. Feeds in loose flocks, often with other tubenoses in mixed groups of seabirds, and sometimes scavenges offal behind ships. Perhaps more prone to feed nocturnally than other shearwaters.

Social behaviour: Gregarious at sea and breeds colonially, being territorial around burrow entrance. Long-term monogamous.

Breeding biology: Breeds in self-excavated burrows, 0.6–3.2 m long with sparse nest lining, in dense coastal hill forest, occasionally in more exposed areas and will also utilize crevices, caves and holes in walls. Lays one white egg in Nov–early Dec, incubated c.51 days. Chicks fledge at c.100 days. Single-brooded. Both parents take full role in breeding cycle.

Conservation Vulnerable. Some are probably taken as bycatch of longline fishing and it was formerly caught in N Pacific drift-nets. The eradication of pigs from one of its major breeding islands in 1936 was responsible for an increase from c.200 pairs at that time to c.200,000 pairs in 1981.

Taxonomy Monotypic.

Great Shearwater *Puffinus gravis*   Plate 10

Identification

Confusion risks: None.

Main characters: Distinctive. Large, dorsally dusky greyish-brown shearwater with noticeable dark cap (emphasized by ill-defined whitish collar) and noticeably pale (almost scaly) fringes to

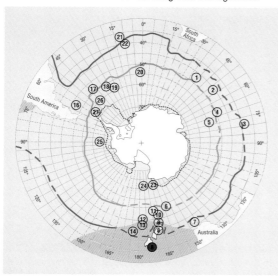

● New Zealand's offshore island

Great Shearwater Puffinus gravis; *the dark crown, whitish collar and rump patch, dark breast-sides and highly variable, but distinctive, dark marks on the underwing and belly identify this large shearwater. Off the Falklands, Jan 2001 © Hadoram Shirihai.*

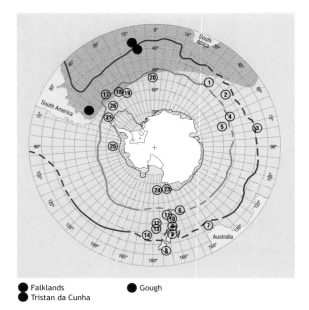

● Falklands   ● Gough
● Tristan da Cunha

that tend to be held straight and stiff, though often slightly bowed and lowered, with slightly forward-pointing carpals. Flight usually appears relatively powerful, with long glides and banks close to surface, interrupted by series of rapid wingbeats. **Age/seasonal variation** indistinct. Juv as ad, but body plumage and flight feathers unmoulted in first-year.

Voice: Probably mostly silent at sea. At colonies ads very vocal at night, with high-pitched, far-carrying howls and rhythmic calls, most similar to those of Sooty Shearwater *P. griseus*.

Size: 43–51 cm, wing 30.1–34.8 cm, wingspan 100–118 cm, weight 715–950 g. There is a tendency for females to average smaller, particularly in wing length.

Similar species: Unmistakable in our region.

Distribution and biology

Distribution, movements and population: S Atlantic Ocean on the Falklands and Tristan da Cunha (including Gough, Nightingale, Inaccessible and at least formerly on Tristan itself). Disperses in Atlantic north to Arctic Circle, and is vagrant in Pacific to Chile and C California, with a recent documented record in the Chathams (Dec 2006: HS pers. obs.). Total population estimated to be at least five million pairs in 1980s, with at least four million on Nightingale and Inaccessible alone in the 1990s.

Diet and feeding: Cephalopods, squid, fish and crustaceans taken by surface-seizing and pursuit-plunging. Feeds in flocks, including within mixed groups of seabirds, and scavenges offal behind ships.

Social behaviour: Gregarious at sea and breeds colonially, being territorial around burrow entrance. Long-term monogamous.

Breeding biology: Breeds in self-excavated burrows, c.1 m long with sparse nest lining, in dense tussac grassland and low woodland. Lays one white egg in Oct–Nov, incubated c.56 days. Chicks fledge at c.120 days. Single-brooded. Both parents take full role in breeding cycle. Arrives abruptly at breeding grounds in Sep, spending several weeks courting and cleaning burrows, before pre-laying exodus, returning en masse late Oct–early Nov (later at Gough) and lays shortly thereafter. Forms massive rafts around islands during day, coming ashore at dusk, but once chicks hatch visits more frequently in day.

Conservation Not globally threatened.

Taxonomy Monotypic.

upperwing-coverts and rest of upperparts (strongest on scapulars), while mostly white underparts/underwing often have (variable) suite of characteristic dark marks. Outer primaries and tail blackish, the latter bordered by ill-defined pale horseshoe on up-pertail-coverts/rump, and dark breast-side patches poorly/moderately developed. From some angles may appear to have hint of darker carpal bar on upperwing-coverts, but too indistinct to offer confusion with Buller's Shearwater *P. bulleri*. Underwing conspicuously dark over broad area, including tips. Dark feathering on rest of white underparts/underwing varies individually, but white underwing-coverts typically smudged dark on axillaries, median and lesser coverts (as double broken bars) and perhaps on marginal and primary-coverts, while markings on body include ragged brownish central belly patch (often very limited or wholly absent), dusky vent and undertail-coverts. Typical shearwater-like bill proportionately rather slender and mainly dark greyish, while legs/feet usually pinkish-grey. Rather long, quite broad wings

Great Shearwaters Puffinus gravis *in banking formation. In head-on views note the dark crown, whitish collar and dark breast-side patches; some birds also show the distinctive dark belly patch. This shearwater is endemic as a breeder to the S Atlantic Ocean, but disperses north as far as the Arctic Circle. Tristan da Cunha, Mar 2006. © Hadoram Shirihai.*

Flesh-footed Shearwater Puffinus carneipes: *pinkish bill base and feet, dark underwing-coverts and bulkier body, relatively less slender head, rather more robust bill, quite long and rounded broad-based wings, and round-tipped mid-length tail, identify this from several dark similar-sized tubenoses, especially Sooty Shearwater. Off New Zealand, Jan 2006. © Hadoram Shirihai.*

Flesh-footed Shearwater Puffinus carneipes: *pinkish base and dark tip to bill, rounded head, and overall brown plumage (here moderately worn but still showing some neat pale fringes to mantle, coverts and scapulars), readily identify this species. Off New Zealand, Jan 2006. © Hadoram Shirihai.*

Flesh-footed Shearwater
Puffinus carneipes   Plate 10

Identification

Confusion risks: *Procellaria* petrels and Sooty Shearwater *Puffinus griseus*.

Main characters: Large all-dark shearwater with dark-tipped pale pinkish bill and pinkish legs/feet. Plumage predominantly chocolate-brown, but has more uniform, sootier looking head and neck, while upperwing-coverts, rest of upperparts and belly are variably fringed slightly paler, though only visible in close views. Compared to Sooty Shearwater appears heavier and rounder bodied, with noticeably rather long, but typically quite rounded broad wings, rather round-tipped mid-length tail, head relatively less slender and bill more robust. Flight usually appears relatively graceful and unhurried, with slow/few wingbeats, typically short glides and arcs. **Age/seasonal variation** indistinct. Juv as ad,

but body plumage and flight feathers unmoulted in first-year; both ages wear to duller brown.

Voice: Probably mostly silent at sea. At colonies ads very vocal at night, with rather loud harsh calls, similar to those of Sooty and especially Great Shearwaters *P. gravis*.

Size: 40–45 cm, wing 30.9–34.0 cm, wingspan 99–107 cm, weight 533–750 g. There is a very slight tendency for females to average smaller in most measurements, but much overlap exists.

Similar species: Black Petrel *Procellaria parkinsoni* is blacker with ivory-coloured bill, and black feet that project beyond tail in flight. Other dark *Procellaria* are also larger. Sooty Shearwater has pale underwings and all-dark bill. All other dark tubenoses are also easily eliminated by combination of different plumage tones, overall structure, bare-parts coloration, and different flight patterns. Thus, only in poor conditions might it be confused.

Flesh-footed Shearwater Puffinus carneipes; *the almost evenly dark brown plumage, pinkish bill base and characteristic shape identify this species from several congeners; in closer views it may be possible to detect some neat pale fringes to the coverts and scapulars. Off Chatham, Dec 1997. © Hadoram Shirihai.*

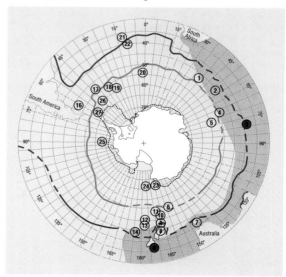

● St Paul
● New Zealand and offshore islands

Distribution and biology

Distribution, movements and population: S Indian Ocean (St Paul) and Australasian region off W Australia, Lord Howe I and islands off N New Zealand. Disperses at sea through Indian Ocean west to Mascarenes and Seychelles, north to Arabian Sea and through N Pacific to Japan, Gulf of Alaska and W USA. Overall probably several hundred thousand pairs in 1980s.

Diet and feeding: Cephalopods and fish taken by surface-seizing, surface-plunging and pursuit-plunging. Feeds alone or in loose flocks, often with Buller's Shearwater *P. bulleri* off New Zealand, and scavenges offal behind ships.

Social behaviour: Less gregarious at sea than other shearwaters, but nonetheless numbers congregate at food sources and when loafing, roosting or on migration, and breeds colonially, being territorial around burrow entrance. Long-term monogamous.

Breeding biology: Breeds in self-excavated burrows, 1–2 m long with sparse nest lining, on gentle to steep coastal slopes with forest or scrub, and occasionally in level ground. Often nests in association with other tubenoses. Lays one white egg in two-week period of Nov–Dec, incubated up to 60 days. Chicks fledge at c.92 days. Single-brooded. Both parents take full role in breeding cycle.

Conservation Not globally threatened. Breeding colonies are susceptible to introduced predators such as foxes and some ads are certainly drowned in longline fisheries. Few data concerning population trends, but most colonies are now protected and very little illegal human exploitation occurs.

Taxonomy Monotypic.

Sooty Shearwater Puffinus griseus *is almost evenly sooty-brown with dark bare parts and distinctive greyish underwing patches, and a characterisitic slender shape. Kaikoura, South I, New Zealand, Feb 2001. © Hadoram Shirihai.*

Sooty Shearwater *Puffinus griseus* Plate 10

Identification

Confusion risks: Flesh-footed Shearwater *P. carneipes* and perhaps *Procellaria* petrels, but main identification challenge is Short-tailed Shearwater *P. tenuirostris*.

Main characters: Rather large, all-dark shearwater, with silvery panel across centre of underwing, and dark bill and legs. Plumage predominantly sooty chocolate-brown (tinged slightly greyish when fresh) and rather uniform, except belly and throat, which are variably tinged slightly paler. For further details of underwing pattern see Short-tailed Shearwater. Sooty has very characteristic shape and flight, most noticeable is slim posture, especially head/neck (appears flat-crowned) and long/slender bill. Wings not long, but typically appear broad-based with pointed tips and held bowed, while tail rather short and slightly wedge-shaped (feet may project very slightly beyond tip). Flight usually relatively very fast and agile, often with strong wingbeats, and typically consists of long glides and short arcs, though quite manoeuvrable. **Age/seasonal variation** indistinct. Juv as ad, but body plumage and flight feathers unmoulted in first-year; both wear duller brown.

Voice: Probably mostly silent at sea. At colonies ads very vocal at night, with loud rhythmic, repeated eerie cat-like howls, *wheeoohar* or hoarse moans, *der-rer-ah* and a high-pitched *oo-oo-ah*, accelerating and becoming louder.

Size: 40–46 cm, wing 26.0–31.8 cm, wingspan 94–105 cm, weight 650–950 g. While females generally average smaller in wing length, they usually have longer tails, bills and tarsi, but extensive overlap exists.

Similar species: *Procellaria* petrels generally much larger/heavier and have more robust bicoloured bills, and dark underwing-coverts. Flesh-footed Shearwater has uniform dark underwing and

Sooty Shearwaters Puffinus griseus *showing the characteristic slender head (right image, apparently worn ad/imm), but this can appear to differ individually and with age/wear; especially fresh young birds (left image, possibly juv) can appear to have a more rounded head and less slender bill. © Hadoram Shirihai.*

Typical flight formation of Sooty Shearwaters Puffinus griseus *(part of a huge concentration off Ushuaia, S Argentina, Mar 2006): note characteristic slender body and silvery underwing flashes in the otherwise all-dark plumage.* © Hadoram Shirihai.

pinkish-flesh bare parts. Short-tailed Shearwater (which see) is most similar, only differing by vestigial underwing colour and shorter bill.

Distribution and biology

Distribution, movements and population: Islands in Australasian region, off SE Australia, New Zealand, Macquarie, Chatham, Antipodes, Campbell, Auckland and Snares; also S South America, including the Falklands, and in very small numbers on Tristan da Cunha. Disperses widely and follows well-known migration routes through E and C Pacific and Atlantic Oceans north to Arctic Circle, and Indian Ocean to SE Africa. One record from New Caledonia. Total population estimated to be in excess of 20 million individuals in 1980s.

Diet and feeding: Cephalopods, fish and crustaceans taken by wide variety of techniques including surface-seizing, surface-diving and pursuit-plunging. Usually feeds in large flocks, often with other seabirds and sometimes in association with cetaceans. Probably attracted to food by smell and by sighting congregations of seabirds.

Social behaviour: Highly gregarious at sea, occurring in enormous

Sooty Shearwater Puffinus griseus *diving underwater. Off New Zealand.* © Kim Westerskov.

flocks both on wintering grounds and on migration, and breeds in dense colonies, where defends burrow entrance. Long-term monogamous, but pair-bonds may also last only one season.

Breeding biology: Breeds in self-excavated burrows, 0.3–3.0 m long with sparse lining, or cavities on well-vegetated slopes, principally on offshore islands. Lays one white egg in Nov–Dec, incubated 50–56 days. Chicks fledge at 86–106 days. Single-brooded. Both parents take full role in breeding cycle.

Conservation Not globally threatened. Commercial exploitation still permitted around Stewart I by local Maori population, who take up to 250,000 young per annum. Breeding range elsewhere in New Zealand has contracted due to effects of introduced predators and habitat changes. On Snares, it has been out-competed for nesting sites by Snares Penguin *Eudyptes robustus*.

Taxonomy Monotypic.

Short-tailed Shearwater
Puffinus tenuirostris   Plate 10

Identification

Confusion risks: Sooty Shearwater *P. griseus*.

Main characters: Largish all-dark shearwater, almost identical to Sooty Shearwater, but some differences, especially with practice, should permit identification of at least most individuals. Averages slightly smaller and more compact, notably the shorter, somewhat stubbier bill, which never appears as slender as Sooty, more rounded head with higher forehead (less angular than Sooty) and shorter, broader neck. These features appreciable both on water and in flight, but note that the shorter tail and wings make birds at rest appear shorter bodied and, in flight, the wings appear shorter

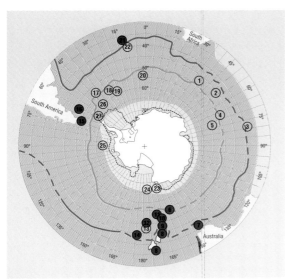

6 Macquarie
7 Tasmania
8 New Zealand's offshore
  islands
9 Snares
10 Auckland
11 Campbell
12 Antipodes
14 Chatham
15 South American
  offshore islands
16 Falklands
21 Tristan da Cunha

Short-tailed Shearwater Puffinus tenuirostris *compared to Sooty Shearwater* P. griseus *averages slightly smaller and is more compact, with a notably shorter, somewhat stubbier bill, more rounded head and higher forehead (giving it a more 'naïve' facial expression), and shorter, broader neck. Off New Zealand, Jan 2006. © Hadoram Shirihai.*

but narrower and more even in width (parallel edges), with less pointed tips, while, in most, the feet clearly project further beyond the tail than in Sooty. They are also separable using the pattern of the pale area on the underwing, but beware that some overlap and individual variation exist, and the effects of light and angle of view can be marked, making identification based on this character occasionally difficult or impossible. Short-tailed has the greyish panel on underwing generally duskier and duller (rarely as bright or as white as Sooty), but with fewer dark streaks, and is limited to the primary- and secondary-coverts, forming a continuous narrow central panel on the median coverts. In Sooty it is almost silvery-white and covers both greater and median coverts, but is mainly apparent, more solid and extensive on the primary-coverts, being interrupted on the secondary-coverts by exposed dark centres that limit the greyish to the tips, and appears as pale lines rather than a solid patch. These differences refer only to classic individuals. Short-tailed tends (albeit with much overlap) to have duller/darker brown plumage and a darker hooded appearance. Flight usually

relatively fast and more hurried, with faster wingbeats and relatively shorter glides and arcs, and often quite sharp manoeuvres. **Age/seasonal variation** indistinct. Juv as ad, but body plumage and flight feathers unmoulted in first-year; both wear duller and browner dorsally.

Voice: Probably mostly silent at sea. Ads vocal at night around burrows: loud harsh screeches, cackles and wails described, and a repeated harsh squealing *ee-ee-a-a-*, faster and more hysterical than Sooty Shearwater.

Size: 40–45 cm, wing 26.1–28.8 cm, wingspan 95–100 cm, weight 480–800 g. Extensive overlap between the sexes in mensural data.

Similar species: Sooty Shearwater is marginally larger, with a flatter head and longer bill, and has slightly different pale pattern to underwing (see above). For other possible confusion risks see Sooty Shearwater.

Distribution and biology

Distribution, movements and population: Islands off S and W Australia and Tasmania. Disperses widely at sea in Pacific west to Guam, the Marshall Is and Japan, north to Kamchatka and Alaska, and along Pacific coast of N America and W Mexico. Northern migration in W Pacific and southern migration in C Pacific. Total population c.23 million individuals in 1980s.

Diet and feeding: Cephalopods, fish and krill taken by wide variety of techniques including hydroplaning, deep-plunging, surface-seizing and pursuit-plunging. Feeds in loose flocks, often associated with cetaceans.

Social behaviour: Gregarious at sea, often joining other seabirds, and breeds in dense colonies, where defends area around burrow entrance. Long-term monogamous.

Breeding biology: Breeds in self-excavated burrows, 0.83–1.85 m long with sparse material, in level to steeply sloping, well-vegetated ground, but also in areas without vegetation, usually on offshore islands. Lays one white egg in Nov–Dec, incubated 52–55 days. Chicks fledge at 82–108 days. Single-brooded. Both parents take full role in breeding cycle.

In flight, Short-tailed Shearwater Puffinus tenuirostris *appears shorter-winged with more even-width parallel edges and less pointed tips; the feet clearly project further beyond the tail than in Sooty Shearwater. Here the overall more compact feel is evident, especially the shorter bill, and more rounded head. Off New Zealand, Jan 2006. © Hadoram Shirihai.*

Short-tailed Shearwater Puffinus tenuirostris *in classic flight profile, with shorter, more round-tipped wings, more compact body, more rounded head, and stubbier bill. Also, compared to Sooty Shearwater* P. griseus *the greyish area on the underwing is generally duller and appears as a narrower central panel on the median coverts, thus virtually lacking Sooty's dark and pale linings on the secondary-coverts. Off New Zealand, Jan 2006. © Hadoram Shirihai.*

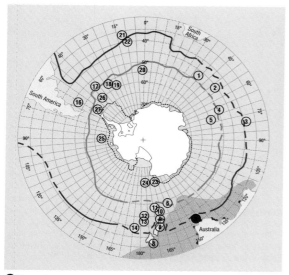

● Tasmania

Fluttering Shearwater Puffinus gavia *is less dark on the underwing and around the head/neck than the similar, but slightly larger, Hutton's Shearwater* P. huttoni. *This extremely pale individual is readily identified, but others are darker and closely approach Hutton's. Note the relatively short bill compared to the latter. Off New Zealand, Jan 1997 © Hadoram Shirihai.*

Conservation Not globally threatened and numbers apparently increasing despite long history of human exploitation, harvesting both eggs and chicks in huge numbers, with many others probably lost due to being trampled during such activities. In some areas it was still legal to collect ads as recently as the mid-1970s, but most exploitation banned in the early-20th century. Grazing and trampling by introduced herbivores may still damage colonies, but controls have been established in many areas. The effect of introduced pasture grasses and weeds, which may eventually cause substantial erosion and make existing colony sites untenable, is more problematic to address.
Taxonomy Monotypic.

Fluttering Shearwater *Puffinus gavia*   Plate 10

Identification

Confusion risks: Hutton's *P. huttoni* and Little Shearwaters *P. assimilis*.
Main characters: Medium-sized with dark brown upperparts, dark face and white below. Dorsal plumage predominantly dark to medium brown (according to wear and lighting, and may appear paler/greyer) and has only slightly (but variable) darker remiges, crown and foreface. Underparts largely contrastingly white, except dark breast-sides, which are poorly/moderately developed (small and diffuse in most); dark vent, but undertail-coverts invariably white. Underwing pattern varies, but most have predominantly white coverts, except some dark on fringes of lesser/inner coverts and axillaries (which appear as ill-defined dark lining), and dusky remiges. For further details of underwing pattern see Hutton's Shearwater. Bill mainly dark brownish-grey (perhaps with paler lower mandible) and legs/feet brownish to pink. Characteristic shape and flight, most noticeable (in comparison with Hutton's) is rounder and stubbier posture, especially head and relatively shorter bill. Wings rather narrow and not as long and stiff, tail short and feet project only very slightly beyond tail tip. Flight usually relatively very fast and direct, often on deep rapid wingbeats, and typically with short glides and arcs, but quite manoeuvrable. **Age/seasonal variation** indistinct. Juv as ad, but body plumage and flight feathers unmoulted in first-year; both wear duller brown above, losing pale fringes to upperwing-coverts of fresh plumage.

Voice: Probably mostly silent at sea. At colonies ads vocal at night, with typical repeated cackling *pa-ka-ha* (like Maori name), also a *ka-hek* or *ka-how*, accelerating and becoming louder; higher pitched than Sooty Shearwater.
Size: 32–37 cm, wing 18.0–22.1 cm, wingspan 76 cm, weight 230–415 g. Extensive overlap between the sexes in mensural data.
Similar species: Hutton's Shearwater is slightly larger with longer bill, duskier head/face, breast-sides and underwings, while Little Shearwater is smaller and usually significantly darker dorsally, and contrastingly whiter below, with different shape and flight pattern. See below for further details.

Distribution and biology

Distribution, movements and population: New Zealand (islets off North I and in Cook Strait). Ranges at sea west to S Australia and north to New Caledonia, reaching Vanuatu as a vagrant. Total population estimated at c.100,000 pairs in 1980s.
Diet and feeding: Largely fish, principally pilchards and sprats, with some coastal krill, taken by surface-seizing, pursuit-diving and pursuit-plunging. Feeds in flocks, often with other tubenoses and terns.
Social behaviour: Gregarious at sea and usually breeds colonially, being territorial around burrow entrance. Probably long-term monogamous.

Fluttering Shearwater Puffinus gavia *shows much individual variation in pigmentation on the head, breast-sides and underwing; this is a relatively dark individual, but still not as dark on these tracts as a typical Hutton's Shearwater* P. huttoni, *or as long-billed as the latter. Also, the flanks are cleaner white than most Hutton's. Off New Zealand, Nov 2005 © Hadoram Shirihai.*

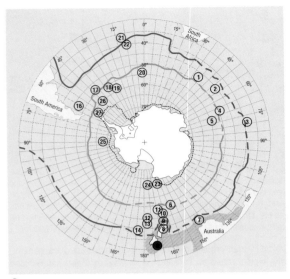

● New Zealand and offshore islands

Hutton's Shearwater Puffinus huttoni: *individual variation in underwing-coverts pattern is considerable, some being much whiter (as here) and less readily separated from darker Fluttering Shearwaters P. gavia. Note Hutton's deeper and sootier head and neck (appearing rather hooded), flanks and breast-sides, and noticeably longer/slenderer bill. Kaikoura, South I, New Zealand, Oct 2001. © Hadoram Shirihai.*

Breeding biology: Breeds in self-excavated burrows, 0.5–1.0 m long with sparse nest lining, on forested islands, in coastal scrub and sometimes more exposed slopes, often in association with other tubenoses. Lays one white egg in Sep–Oct, but no data concerning incubation or fledging periods. Single-brooded. Both parents take full role in breeding cycle.

Conservation Not globally threatened. Some colonies have been destroyed or substantially reduced by introduced predators, usually rats or cats.

Taxonomy Monotypic.

Hutton's Shearwater *Puffinus huttoni*   Plate 10

Identification

Confusion risks: Fluttering Shearwater *P. gavia*.

Main characters: Medium-sized with dark brownish-black upperparts, dark face, white underparts, well-patterned dark underwing-coverts and brownish mottling on neck- and chest-sides. Virtually identical to Fluttering Shearwater, but combination of slight differences, especially with practice, should permit identification, at

Hutton's Shearwater Puffinus huttoni *is progressively darker above, around the head/neck and on the underwing, and is relatively longer billed than the similar but slightly smaller and compact Fluttering Shearwater P. gavia. Kaikoura, South I, New Zealand, Oct 2001. © Hadoram Shirihai.*

least of typical individuals. Averages slightly larger and less compact, and the less-rounded head (often looks flatter crowned) and noticeably longer/slenderer bill, which never appears as stubby as Fluttering, adds to the angular head profile. These features are only appreciable when the two are observed together, and many intermediates cannot be identified using structure or without some previous experience of at least one species (see below). They may also be separated on some plumage characters. Aside of atypical and intermediate examples, classic Hutton's has deeper and sootier dorsal coloration, especially on crown and neck, extending more diffusely further onto cheeks, sometimes even reaching edges of throat and foreneck, and below, where forms well-developed dark breast-sides, as well as across flanks to vent-sides. Dark on head/neck gives rather hooded impression, especially in flight. Effect of individual variation on pattern of underwing-coverts considerable, but classic Hutton's clearly has a far larger area of dark markings, even covering the entire axillaries, lesser and most greater coverts, with only limited whitish centres to the median primary- and secondary-coverts. Others, with much whiter underwings (almost like darker Fluttering) and limited dark on neck/chest and flanks, are also identifiable on structure alone, mainly the longer bill (though also variable). Many are intermediate between such extremes. In flight, wings appear proportionately (in relation to body) short and narrow, while the feet of most project well beyond the tail. Flight, in most conditions, identical to Fluttering (which see), but generally less hurried. **Age/seasonal variation** indistinct. Juv as ad, but body plumage and flight feathers unmoulted in first-year; both wearing much duller brown on upperparts.

Voice: Probably mostly silent at sea. At colonies ads vocal at night, with quire variable high-pitched calls, which differ little from both Fluttering and Sooty Shearwaters.

Size: 36–38 cm, wing 20.3–23.3 cm, wingspan 72–78 cm, weight 242–378 g. Extensive overlap between the sexes in mensural data.

Similar species: Fluttering Shearwater slightly smaller and has shorter bill, with more limited dark markings on inner underwing-coverts and less mottling on neck-/breast- sides (see above).

Distribution and biology

Distribution, movements and population: S New Zealand (South I): only two colonies known, c.4 km inland in the Seaward Kaikoura

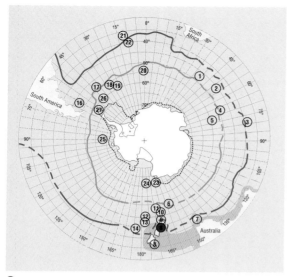

● Southern New Zealand

Mountains (at 1200–1800 m), where occurs in nearby coastal waters year-round. Also ranges west to waters around Australia and Tasmania, and reported from N Territory, with possible record from N Coral Sea. Total population estimated at c.94,000 pairs in recent years.

Diet and feeding: Principally small fish and krill taken by plunge- or surface-diving. Feeds alone or in loose flocks, congregating at small shoaling fish.

Social behaviour: Gregarious or solitary at sea and breeds colonially, being territorial around burrow entrance. Probably long-term monogamous.

Breeding biology: On Seaward Kaikoura gathers in huge numbers in Sep–Oct, awaiting snow-melt before moving to their burrows. Breeds in self-excavated burrows, 0.6–2.5 m long with sparse nest lining, in high alpine forest and tussac grassland. Lays one white egg in late Oct–early Dec, incubated 50–60 days. Chicks fledge at c.80 days. Single-brooded. Both parents take full role in breeding cycle.

Conservation Vulnerable. Some probably taken as bycatch of longline fishing off Australia and New Zealand. Population principally threatened due to heavy grazing by introduced herbivores, and predation by stoats, cats and pigs, though the two latter have been largely eradicated from its breeding areas and effects of former far less than initially feared, while grazing animals are now largely controlled. Heavy or late snowfall can delay or prevent breeding. Population monitoring studies have been initiated and many burrows are sited within protected areas.

Taxonomy Monotypic.

Little Shearwater *Puffinus assimilis*   Plate 10

Identification

Confusion risks: Fluttering *P. gavia* and Hutton's Shearwaters *P. huttoni* and Common Diving-petrel *Pelecanoides urinatrix*.

Main characters: Small compact shearwater (the smallest), with greyish-black upperparts and predominately white below and on underwing; some populations have diagnostic white face around eye. Two principal races in our region: *elegans* (widespread in the Southern Ocean) and *haurakiensis* (endemic to New Zealand), which are to some degree confusingly larger and dark-faced on

head-sides, lacking or with very limited white around and behind eye; they are also greyer and less black above, have somewhat less extensive white to underside of remiges, and thus might be confused with larger Fluttering and Hutton's Shearwaters (see below). Two other forms occur marginally, in Australia and New Zealand, nominate *assimilis* and *tunneyi*, both of which are distinctly smaller, blacker above and have rather conspicuous white around eye, imparting a white-faced appearance (variable, but in most there is an isolated dark rear ear-covert patch and only a hint of a white supercilium) and narrow blackish crown when viewed from behind. The four races appear to belong to two quite distinct groups (see below), only appreciable in optimal conditions. Both groups share the following characters: the typical shearwater-like bill is proportionately rather slender and short, mainly dark with a greyish-blue hue to pale parts, with same tone (and same fleshy elements) to pale areas of legs/feet, but both bill and legs/feet appear generally appear dark grey/blackish. When fresh, rather noticeable but ill-defined pale (almost scaly) fringes to upperwing-coverts and rest of upperparts (strongest on scapulars), best developed in *elegans*. Underwing always predominately white, with only limited dark trailing edge and primary tips, but often some grey flecking on axillaries, mainly in *elegans*. Dark neck-sides often poorly developed and relatively small, and never appear to reach breast-sides, while dusky vent-sides very small and undertail-coverts invariably white. Wings proportionately rather short, narrow and rounded near tip (longer in larger populations in Southern Ocean), and appear quite small compared to body size; typically of even width (with parallel edges) and tend to be held noticeably straight and stiff. Tail also relatively short and feet project only slightly. Flight usually relatively fast on series of rapid shallow wingbeats, short glides and banks close to surface, generally with limited shearing. **Age/seasonal variation** indistinct. Juv as ad, but body plumage and flight feathers unmoulted in first-year. Both wear duller and even slightly browner, losing whitish fringes above, and when strongly abraded white basal feathering on central upperwing exposed.

Voice: Probably mostly silent at sea; at colonies ads vocal at night, giving typical, variably loud, harsh shearwater calls, described as a repeated hoarse, asthmatic *wah-i-wah-i-wah-ooo*; no detailed

Little Shearwater Puffinus assimilis *of the subantarctic form* elegans: *note extensive white underside to the remiges and underwing-coverts (narrow dark edges and tip), and mostly white underparts, including undertail-coverts. Also characteristic is the overall slightly larger size and no white around eye, compared to other forms of Little Shearwater in the tropics. Off Gough I, Mar 2003.* © Hadoram Shirihai.

study of vocalizations linked to geographical variation.

Size: 25–30 cm, wing 17.3–18.9 cm (nominate *assimilis*) or 17.0–19.7 cm (*elegans*), wingspan 58–67 cm, weight 220–260 g. There are very few sex-specific data available for most forms of Little Shearwater, and these are especially deficient for *elegans, assimilis* and *haurakiensis*.

Similar species: Fluttering and Hutton's Shearwaters slightly larger with browner upperparts and dark faces, much darker undersides to remiges and usually far darker on axillaries and underwing-coverts; also differ in bare-parts coloration, shape and flight. Common Diving-petrel smaller and shorter winged, and offers only slight confusion risk due to superficially similar fast wingbeats, but is otherwise very different.

Distribution and biology

Distribution, movements and population: The subspecies *elegans* breeds on Chatham, the Antipodes, Tristan da Cunha and Gough; and *haurakiensis* on islets off east coast of North I, New Zealand. Largely sedentary around breeding colonies. No overall breeding population estimates, though at least 100,000 pairs are known from the Antipodes, but only c.150 pairs on Chatham.

Diet and feeding: Cephalopods, small fish and krill, principally taken by surface-diving, pursuit-diving and pursuit-plunging. Usually feeds alone but occasionally consorts with dolphins. Most, if not all, feeding is diurnal.

Social behaviour: Rarely flocks at sea, except offshore from breeding colonies. Territorial around burrow entrance. Probably long-term monogamous. Remains around colonies for much of year.

Breeding biology: Breeds in self-excavated burrows, 0.3–2.0 m long with sparse nest lining, in coastal forest, scrub and tussac grass; occasionally occupies rock crevices or cavities. Lays one white egg in late Jun–Sep, incubated 52–58 days. Chicks fledge at 70–75 days. Single-brooded. Both parents take full role in breeding cycle.

Conservation Not globally threatened. Status considered stable, but introduced predators and human disturbance have wrought declines and local extinctions. The species is capable of persisting, albeit in reduced numbers, in presence of rats.

Taxonomy Little Shearwater consists of seven subspecies breeding in the S Indian, Pacific and Atlantic Oceans, reaching north

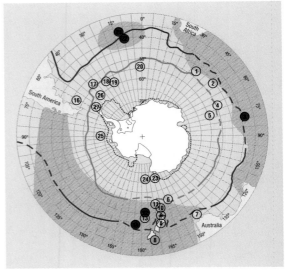

■ Little Shearwater *Puffinus assimilis elegans*
▨ Little Shearwater *Puffinus assimilis haurakiensis*
☐ Little Shearwater *Puffinus assimilis tunneyi*

● St Paul
⑧ New Zealand's offshore islands
● Antipodes
● Chatham
● Tristan da Cunha
● Gough

of the equator off NW Africa (*baroli*) and in C Pacific (*myrtae*). The mainly Southern Ocean and New Zealand forms, *elegans* and *haurakiensis*, are quite distinct in size and plumage from the principally Australian forms *assimilis* and *tunneyi*, and these two groups might be best considered as allospecies. The race *myrtae* and the Kermadec form *kermadecensis* show affinity with the former group, while *assimilis* and *tunneyi* are close to the disjunct C Atlantic *baroli* or intermediate between it and the larger, Southern Ocean group. The other form, *boydi* of the Cape Verdes, may not even belong within the *assimilis* superspecies. Some pitfalls exist in such proposals and relationships between the forms are still unclear.

Little Shearwater Puffinus assimilis *of the subantarctic form* elegans *in fresh plumage, showing characteristic slate-blue tinge to upperparts, rather noticeably pale-scaled upperparts (most obvious on scapulars) and white tips to upperwing-coverts. Also note white extending onto rear body-sides, hint of white supercilium (typical) and only limited greyish wash to breast-sides. Off Gough I, Mar 2003. © Hadoram Shirihai.*

Little Shearwater Puffinus assimilis *of the subantarctic form* elegans*: in fresh plumage note the characteristic white tips to upperwing-coverts (forming neat wingbars); also typical are the white extensions behind the ear-coverts and rear body-sides. The compact structure with the wings held noticeably straight and stiff is evident (flight fast on rapid shallow wingbeats close to surface). Off Gough I, Mar 2003. © Hadoram Shirihai.*

Blue Petrel and prions

Two genera, *Pachyptila* and *Halobaena*, are covered in the following accounts and Plate 11. The latter is a monotypic genus consisting of Blue Petrel *H. caerulea*, whilst the prions constitute 6–7 (perhaps more) species. All breed only in the Southern Ocean and are rarely found away from there. If there is a group of tubenoses that are harder to identify at sea than gadfly petrels it is the prions; even given current knowledge and experience, some forms are usually unidentifiable at sea. On the other hand, Blue Petrel is easily separated, and is included here only because of its superficial resemblance to prions.

Prions are well separated from all other petrels, having overall unique appearance and habits, mainly in their pale cryptic plumage (largely greyish and white), flight shape, very peculiar bill structure, and different flight mode and feeding techniques. In all species, the bill is characteristically broad and deep-based, becoming pointed at the tip (appears triangular from above), but the maxillary unguis and tubes are rather indistinct; all have a lamellae ridge (=bill-comb) on the cutting edges of the upper mandible, which filters plankton, and a gular skin patch that can distend if transporting food long distances. Bill size, comb and dimensions vary considerably between species, suggesting that each may have a slightly different diet and feeding technique. Most foraging is at night. Head shape and size also vary, being in some rather round and small, though others are larger and squarer. Wings are proportionately rather short, pointed and appear stiff and bowed downward, especially at the carpal, and tails are proportionately long and wedge-shaped. Legs and feet are blue with flesh-coloured webs.

In plumage, most have a very simple pattern, with an open M (on the carpals and outer primaries) connected on the lower back and emphasized by the paler remiges, black subterminal tail-band, bluish-grey dorsal parts and mainly whitish underparts. Varying facial patterns of whitish supercilium and loral patch emphasize a dusky eyestripe. Sex-/age-related variation is almost non-existent, even in measurements.

Approach to identification Separation of all species is complicated and requires a combined assessment of the following three major sets of clues (by order of general priority and/or visibility): 1) overall size and heaviness, and breadth of the dark tail-band – separating the genera only into main general groups – see below; 2) bill size/dimensions (and in some the colour) – often the most vital character – compare photographs and head/bill profiles in Plate 11; and 3) a set of subsidiary characters selectively supporting identification in one species or another – including head shape, the development of the grey breast-sides/collar, and face pattern (principally darkness of crown/head and relative development of white supercilium and lores, in contrast to the dark eyestripe), as well as the relative intensity of the upperparts ground colour, the breadth and/or intensity of the dark upperwing M, and perhaps the black pattern on the undertail. At sea it is often very difficult to appreciate these differences, because of their subtlety and due to these species' fast flight, poor sea conditions/visibility and/or various lighting effects. Correct identification also usually depends upon observer experience and highly favourable viewing conditions. The six (or seven) species can be divided into **two main groups**; separation of the first, comprising Broad-billed *P. vittata*, Salvin's *P. salvini* and Antarctic Prions *P. desolata*, is especially problematic in the case of *salvini* versus *desolata*. The distinctive Saint Paul Prion *P. [vittata/salvini] macgillivrayi* from the Indian Ocean is generally midway between Salvin's and Broad-billed. The other most significant problems lie within the species-pair Fairy *P. turtur* and Fulmar

Prions *P. crassirostris*, and between them and Slender-billed Prion *P. belcheri*, which although quite distinctive in colour and bill dimensions could easily be confused with both.

In general, **the first group**, Broad-billed, Salvin's (including Saint Paul) and Antarctic Prions comprises slightly/moderately larger species with a rather narrow tail-band (c.¼ of tail length), clear facial marks (especially in Salvin's/Saint Paul and Antarctic Prions) and distinct grey breast-side patches. Within the group, Broad-billed Prion is identifiable at sea by its characteristic squarer head and the most massive and duck-like bill (which is diagnostically blackish rather than bicoloured and greyer). Salvin's/Saint Paul Prions are similarly shaped but have a distinctly smaller bill, and in Antarctic Prion the bill is even smaller though stouter and lacks the odd duck-like shape. The latter three forms, especially Salvin's versus Saint Paul, are mostly inseparable at sea. Furthermore, the group is characterized by well-developed bill-combs which are exposed on the closed mandible in Salvin's/Saint Paul and Broad-billed Prions (in most populations of Antarctic the closed mandibles conceal the small palatal lamellae).

Of the **second group**, Fairy and Fulmar Prions are decidedly smaller and separated from all others by the broader tail-band (c.⅓ of tail length), with Fulmar (versus Fairy) having a rounder head with a more bland pattern, compressed bill, and is typically softer grey above and washed below. However, the latter characters are subject to complex geographical variation in both species.

Slender-billed Prion can be assigned to its own group, and has the most distinctive facial pattern, narrowest bill and can even be separated from all other species by the weaker M above.

All species have remarkable flight, being highly manoeuvrable and some being sufficiently distinct as to be of assistance in at-sea identification (see below). To try to simplify the problems, I intend emphasizing the main characters and diagnostic marks, both in the texts and accompanying summaries (Table 1).

Prions all have very similar calls, and only 'experts' are capable of separating them by ear (though *turtur* and *crassirostris* are probably inseparable except through analysis of sonograms): *belcheri* and *desolata* are relatively easy to distinguish, but require sufficient experience, whilst *vittata* and *salvini* are much more difficult to separate. In addition, male and female vocalizations strongly differ, further complicating the matter. Thus, the descriptions presented here, which are largely based on information presented in *HANZAB* and earlier works, are mostly inadequate for identification purposes, especially given observer inexperience. For further information the reader is advised to refer to Bretagnolle (1990).

The general behaviour, life and breeding cycles are rather uniform amongst the prions. Being truly oceanic, they come to land only to breed. Most nest on offshore and remote islands with dense grass or forest cover. Small fish and crustaceans constitute their principal diet, taken on or near the surface of the water. The age at which birds first return to their natal colonies and that at which breeding is first attempted are unknown. Ads arrive at the colonies prior to breeding and then disperse for up to two weeks to nearby marine feeding areas to gain weight prior to nesting (*pre-laying exodus*). Most nest in self-excavated burrows, with ads laying one, usually smooth white, egg, which is incubated 6–7 weeks. Chicks take 7–8 weeks to fledge. Most are nocturnal around the colonies, where they can be heard displaying. They usually visit their burrows just before dusk and return to the sea sometime prior to dawn.

Like other burrow-nesting seabirds, many prions have been the unintentional victims of Man's arrival on their breeding islands: rats, feral cats, pigs and other introduced mammals have all caused significant losses amongst eggs, young and even ads. Fortunately many islands are currently subject to conservation work designed to tackle the problems caused by introduced predators, and significant advances have already been made in several instances.

Broad-billed Prion *Pachyptila vittata*   Plate 11

Identification

Confusion risks: Other prions and Blue Petrel *Halobaena caerulea*.
Main characters: Proportionately large overall size, with large head (high steep forehead), and disproportionately large, very broad-based and all-grey-black bill (with high rounded upper mandible; in the hand bill-comb visible on closed mandibles, and cutting edges strongly curved). Blue-grey above and white below, with black M on upperwing and black tip to tail. Head usually appears darker (eyestripe too), and the white supercilium is individually variable, but usually narrow (and rather well-defined), confined mostly to above and behind the eye, whilst the conspicuous dusky-grey breast-sides, which almost form a complete collar in some, augment the dark-hooded appearance. Flight slower and less erratic than other prions, and more inclined to glide than congeners. For further characteristics, shared by all prions, see group introduction. For distinguishing features from similar species see below.
Voice: Probably silent at sea. At colonies ads vocal at night, with harsh cooing, varied *rerky-rickik-kikkik* or *ggrarr ka ka* and *pop poor popper pop* (by male), also rattling *per-per-per-per* and often a shrill *pihihihi...* in distress (for further details see *HANZAB*).
Size: 25–30 cm, wing 18.1–22.5 cm, wingspan 57–66 cm, bill length 3.15–3.68 cm, bill width 1.95–2.43 cm, tarsus 3.5–4.1 cm, weight 170–237 g. Very few sex-specific data available, but no evidence to suggest significant dimorphism.
Similar species: Blue Petrel has white-tipped tail. Distinguished from other prions by larger size, large squarer head with steeper forehead, and relatively massive all-dark bill (bicoloured, but mostly

Broad-billed Prion Pachyptila vittata: *the massive bill appears duck-like especially from above, whilst note also the large square head and steep forehead, giving a 'baseball cap' impression, and the pronounced breast-sides collar. Off Gough I, Mar 2006. © Hadoram Shirihai.*

bluish in Salvin's *P. salvini* and Antarctic Prions *P. desolata*); also has dark-headed appearance, highly pronounced collar and relatively narrow dark tail-band (broader in the smaller Fairy *P. turtur* and Fulmar Prions *P. crassirostris*). Be aware, however, that it is not always easy to appreciate the broad bill, which often requires prolonged views to accurately appreciate the true dimensions (which also vary individually). Furthermore, Broad-billed often closely approaches Salvin's in jizz (large-headed appearance), flight action and the heavy breast-side patches (see latter species). Fortunately, the breeding sites of the two do not overlap. Slender-billed Prion *P. belcheri*, in addition to being structurally smaller (bill conspicuously and unmistakably narrower), has an even narrower tail-band and less well-defined M marking on the upperwing.

Distribution and biology

Distribution, movements and population: Breeds on islands close

Broad-billed Prion Pachyptila vittata: *note the heavy and large appearance, especially the large squarer head with steep forehead and rather massive all-dark bill, and pronounced breast-sides collar; facial marks vary but here the white supercilium is rather narrow and well defined (mostly above and behind the eye). Off Nightingale I, Mar 2006. © Marc Guyt.*

Broad-billed Prion Pachyptila vittata: *note the relatively narrow tail-band (compared to Fairy and Fulmar Prions, but more similar to others), heavy bill, squarer and darker head with steep forehead but inconspicuous facial markings; the open dark M is typical of the genus. Off Gough I, Mar 2006. © Hadoram Shirihai.*

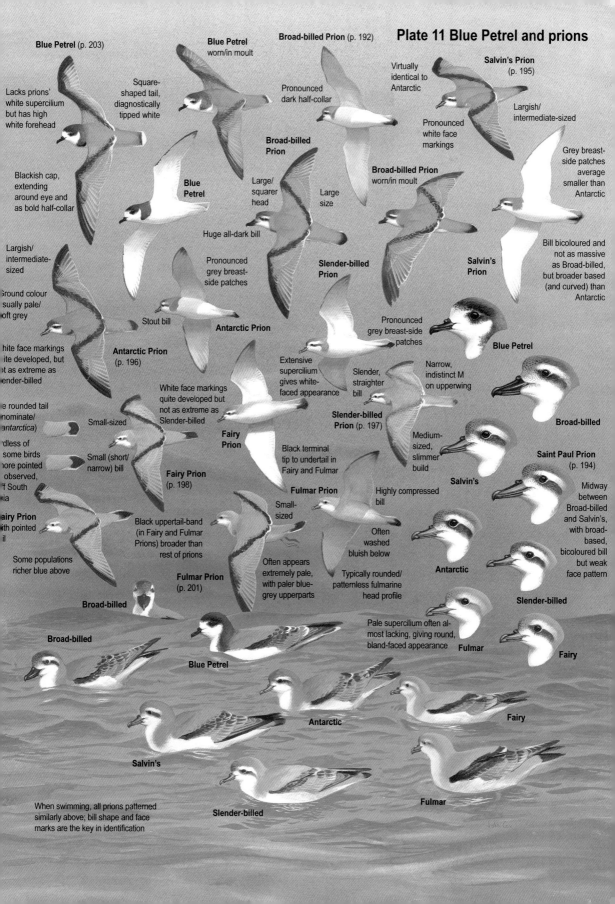

Plate 11 Blue Petrel and prions

Blue Petrel (p. 203)

Lacks prions' white supercilium but has high white forehead

Blue Petrel worn/in moult

Square-shaped tail, diagnostically tipped white

Blue Petrel

Blackish cap, extending around eye and as bold half-collar

Broad-billed Prion (p. 192)

Pronounced dark half-collar

Broad-billed Prion

Large/squarer head

Large size

Huge all-dark bill

Pronounced grey breast-side patches

Broad-billed Prion worn/in moult

Virtually identical to Antarctic

Pronounced white face markings

Salvin's Prion (p. 195)

Largish/intermediate-sized

Grey breast-side patches average smaller than Antarctic

Bill bicoloured and not as massive as Broad-billed, but broader based (and curved) than Antarctic

Largish/intermediate-sized

Ground colour usually pale/soft grey

White face markings quite developed, but not as extreme as Slender-billed

Stout bill

Antarctic Prion (p. 196)

Antarctic Prion

White face markings quite developed but not as extreme as Slender-billed

Slender-billed Prion

Pronounced grey breast-side patches

Extensive supercilium gives white-faced appearance

Slender, straighter bill

Slender-billed Prion (p. 197)

Blue Petrel

Narrow, indistinct M on upperwing

Broad-billed

Medium-sized, slimmer build

Salvin's

Small-sized

Small (short/narrow) bill

Fairy Prion

Fairy Prion (p. 198)

Black terminal tip to undertail in Fairy and Fulmar

Fulmar Prion

Small-sized

Black uppertail-band (in Fairy and Fulmar Prions) broader than rest of prions

Fulmar Prion (p. 201)

Often appears extremely pale, with paler blue-grey upperparts

Highly compressed bill

Often washed bluish below

Typically rounded/patternless fulmarine head profile

Saint Paul Prion (p. 194)

Midway between Broad-billed and Salvin's, with broad-based, bicoloured bill but weak face pattern

Slender-billed

Antarctic

Pale supercilium often almost lacking, giving round, bland-faced appearance

Fulmar

Fairy

Some populations richer blue above

Broad-billed

Broad-billed

Blue Petrel

Antarctic

Fairy

Salvin's

Slender-billed

Fulmar

When swimming, all prions patterned similarly above; bill shape and face marks are the key in identification

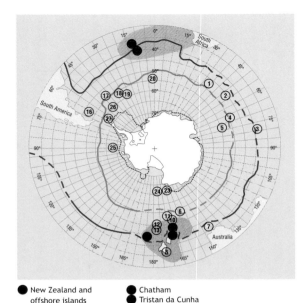

- New Zealand and offshore islands
- Snares
- Chatham
- Tristan da Cunha
- Gough

to Subtropical Convergence, principally in the New Zealand region (coasts of Foveaux Strait, islets off Stewart I, Snares and Chatham) and in Tristan da Cunha and on Gough. Ranges at sea in Southern Ocean south of 30°S, and to W and S Australia and South Africa. The population is estimated at more than 8 million pairs with the main breeding grounds on Gough and Nightingale in S Atlantic.

Diet and feeding: Gregarious at sea, taking crustaceans in summer and small squid in winter, which are caught by hydroplaning, surface-filtering, surface-seizing and surface-diving and dipping.

Social behaviour: Not known to follow ships. Gregarious year-round. Monogamous.

Breeding biology: Nests on slopes and steep banks, or depressions between rocks and caves, in self-excavated burrows 1.2 m deep, with nest lining of leaves, grass or twigs. Season Aug–Sep, with most laying one white egg. Incubation period probably c.50 days and fledging period similar. Both sexes take full share of all parental duties. Single-brooded.

Conservation Not globally threatened. Predation at some New Zealand colonies by Weka *Gallirallus australis*, cats and rats, and on Tristan da Cunha such predation has wrought serious declines. However, it remains abundant on predator-free Gough.

Taxonomy Monotypic.

Saint Paul Prion
Pachyptila [vittata/salvini] macgillivrayi   Plate 11

Identification
Confusion risks: Other prions, but chiefly Broad-billed *P. vittata* and Salvin's Prions *P. salvini*, with which it has complicated affinities.

Main characters: Overall large size, with large, broad-based, bicoloured bill. Latter recalls *salvini* but its shape and size approach *vittata*, or is intermediate between them, thus justifying its treatment as an allospecies. Affinities and relationships to Broad-billed and Salvin's Prions unresolved (see taxonomy). Otherwise, like latter, has (medium) blue-grey upperparts and is mainly white below, with moderately pronounced black M on upperwing and rather narrow black tip to tail; medium to dark head, with narrow and rather indistinct white supercilium, and quite conspicuous dusky-grey breast-sides add to dark-hooded appearance, thus somewhat approaching *vittata*. Flight does not apparently differ from either of the others. **Age/seasonal variation** indistinct; juv as ad, but plumage and flight feathers unmoulted in first-year. Upperparts usually wear duller grey and carpal M fades browner.

Voice: Probably silent at sea; sometimes calls during daylight like other prions, but no recordings known.

Size: Few data, wing 19–21 cm, bill length 2.95–3.25 cm, bill width 1.57–1.92 cm, tarsus 3.4–3.8 cm, no weight data.

Similar forms: Possibly indistinguishable at sea from both Broad-billed and Salvin's Prions; distinguished in the hand by bill, tarsus and wing measurements, and combination of plumage and bill colour.

Distribution and biology
Distribution, movements and population: Endemic to St Paul (and formerly Amsterdam), where population currently numbers 150–200 pairs on the offshore rock of Roche Quille. Range at sea within Southern Ocean unknown.

Diet and feeding: Unknown.

Social behaviour: Unknown.

Breeding biology: Unknown, but presumably very similar to closely related species.

Conservation Not evaluated according to IUCN criteria. Status precarious on Roche Quille, which is a tiny islet. It has apparently recently recolonized St Paul, where it was formerly extremely abundant.

Taxonomy Compared to *salvini*, *macgillivrayi* has a broader based, strongly compressed bill and slightly longer wings. Often considered a race of *salvini*, but strikingly heavier (approaching *vittata*) and bicoloured bill (as *salvini*) suggest that it is better treated within *vittata* or specifically (Bretagnolle *et al*. 1990, V.

One of the least known tubenoses, Saint Paul Prion Pachyptila [vittata/salvini] macgillivrayi *is somewhat midway between Broad-billed* P. vittata *and Salvin's Prions* P. salvini*: both ad (left) and fledgling have a broad-based, bicoloured bill with bluish elements (distinctly darker in the latter). Also, rather narrow black tail tip and weak face pattern perhaps closer to Broad-billed (but supercilium appears rather strong on fledgling). Saint Paul. © Thierry Micol.*

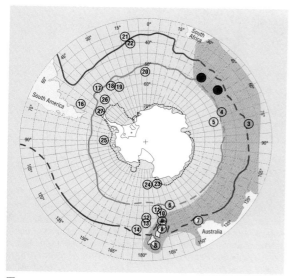

Salvin's Prion *Pachyptila salvini*
Saint Paul Prion *Pachyptila [salvini/vittata] macgillivrayi*
Prince Edward & Marion
Crozet
③ St Paul

Salvin's Prion Pachyptila salvini: *note the broad-based and bowed bill, somewhat approaching Broad-billed Prion* P. vittata *(but clearly smaller and less robust), which is the single most important character identifying this species from the otherwise virtually identical Antarctic Prion* P. desolata. *The strong white supercilium is evident. Off Crozet, Mar 2004. © Hadoram Shirihai.*

Bretagnolle pers. comm.). *Salvini, macgillivrayi* and *vittata*, may constitute allospecies, but relationships between them, as well as to *desolata* are unresolved and require further study.

Salvin's Prion *Pachyptila salvini*   Plate 11

Identification

Confusion risks: Other prions, especially Antarctic Prion *P. desolata*.

Main characters: Virtually identical to Antarctic Prion (which see) and not always separable from it at sea. Generally has pure pale blue-grey upperparts with pronounced broad black M pattern to upperwing, and white below with less extensive grey breast-sides. Head has quite pronounced broad white supercilium above and behind eye, and extensive pure white lores, enhancing dusky eyestripe and imparting white-faced appearance. Bill broad-based, intermediate in dimensions and distinctively bicoloured (bluish and greyish in tone); in the hand bill-comb visible and cutting edges appear clearly curved, thus somewhat approaching Broad-billed Prion *P. vittata* in shape, but size/dimensions clearly smaller and less robust, and in latter bill is all dark. Narrower black tail-band than Fairy *P. turtur* and Fulmar Prions *P. crassirostris*. For further characteristics, shared by all prions, see group introduction above. See below and Antarctic Prion for further details. **Age/seasonal variation** indistinct. Juv as ad, but body plumage and flight feathers unmoulted in first-year. Upperparts of both age classes wear paler and carpal M fades and becomes browner; prior to moult bleached upperwing is patchily white.

Voice: Probably silent at sea. At colonies ads vocal at night, but only limited information available concerning characters. Described as a four-syllable *ka-kakadu*, resembling rhythm of *what-have-to-do*, with emphasis on first and last syllables (*HANZAB*). Marked differences exist in male and female vocalizations.

Size: 27–28 cm, wing 17.6–21.0 cm, wingspan 57 cm, bill length 2.82–3.18 cm, bill width 1.35–1.59 cm, tarsus 3.1–3.5 cm, weight 130–210 g. No evidence to suggest significant sexual dimorphism.

Similar species: Almost identical to Antarctic Prion in size, shape,

flight action and plumage, and they are probably inseparable at sea, though bill slightly longer and broader in *salvini*.

Distribution and biology

Distribution, movements and population: Breeds on islands very close to the Antarctic Convergence, in SW Indian Ocean, on Prince Edward, Marion and Crozet, ranging at sea east to Australia and New Zealand, and west to South Africa. Population numbered in the millions.

Diet and feeding: Takes crustaceans and small fish, which are caught by hydroplaning, surface-filtering, surface-seizing and surface-diving, shallow-plunging and pursuit-plunging.

Social behaviour: No data.

Breeding biology: Nests in all suitable areas where not restricted by predators, in self-excavated burrows 0.93–1.35 m deep, with nest lining of leaves and twigs. Three-week laying season in

Salvin's Prion Pachyptila salvini *is virtually identical to Antarctic Prion* P. desolata *and the two are practically inseparable away from the breeding islands (although the slightly broader bill and perhaps stronger facial markings are sometimes detectable in optimal views). At sea, it is also not always readily distinguishable from Broad-billed Prion* P. vittata, *but note the smaller and more rounded head, less steep forehead, bicoloured and distinctly smaller bill (though still broad-based), stronger facial marks (including broader white supercilium) and, on average, smaller breast-side patches. Off Crozet, Mar 2004. © Hadoram Shirihai.*

Salvin's Prion Pachyptila salvini *is probably inseparable at sea from Antarctic Prion* P. desolata, *though it has fractionally larger bill dimensions, purer white face marks and less grey on the breast-sides. Off Crozet, Nov 1999. © Hadoram Shirihai.*

Antarctic Prion Pachyptila desolata *is almost identical to Salvin's Prion* P. salvini, *albeit with a slighter bill. It lacks the broad duck-like and all-black bill of Broad-billed Prion* P. vittata *and is usually overall paler. From the smaller Slender-billed Prion it differs in being less white-faced with a broader bill and more pronounced tail and upperwing markings, whilst compared to Fairy* P. turtur *and Fulmar Prions* P. crassirostris, *it has more obvious grey beast-side patches, a broader bill, but narrower black tail-band. Off South Georgia, Mar 2003. © Hadoram Shirihai.*

Nov–Dec, with most laying one white egg. Incubation 44–55 days. Fledging period 54–65 days. Both sexes take full share of all parental duties. Single-brooded.

Conservation Not globally threatened. Populations of *salvini* are secure, although rats (on Possession) and cats (on Marion) restrict breeding areas, take young and have reduced overall numbers on these islands.

Taxonomy Two subspecies generally recognized: *salvini* on Prince Edward and Crozet, and *macgillivrayi* (which is considered specifically here, see above), which has broader based, strongly compressed bill and slightly longer wings (though these features are probably impossible to accurately assess at sea) on St Paul. They may constitute allospecies, though *macgillivrayi* is sometimes considered within *P. vittata*, but striking differences in bill structure and colour suggest that it is better treated with *salvini* or at specific rank. V. Bretagnolle (pers. comm. 2001) considers it to be probably a species (and this is followed here) most closely related to *vittata*. Relationships between *salvini*, *macgillivrayi* and *vittata*, as well as *desolata*, are unresolved and demand further study. Moreover, nesting overlap and apparent hybridization with *P. belcheri* are known.

Antarctic Prion *Pachyptila desolata*   Plate 11

Identification

Confusion risks: Other prions.

Main characters: Very similar to Salvin's Prion *P. salvini* (which see) and the two are not always separable at sea. Characteristically, upperparts pure blue-grey with rather narrow but distinct black M on upperwing, while predominately white underparts have quite substantial dark grey breast-sides. Head has quite pronounced, broad white supercilium and lores, and distinct dusky eyestripe; generally appears less white-faced than Salvin's. Bill rather short and less broad-based than Salvin's and is pale greyish; in the hand it does not have visible combs and has straighter edges than Salvin's (which, like Broad-billed *P. vittata*, has a more duck-like bill outline). Narrower black tail-band than Fairy *P. turtur* and Fulmar Prions *P. crassirostris*. Flight fast, buoyant and erratic, with twisting glides broken by short bursts of shallow wingbeats, often high above surface of water. Also 'floppier' slower flight in calm weather. For further characteristics see group introduction. See below for further details.

Age/seasonal variation indistinct. Juv as ad, but body plumage and flight feathers unmoulted in first-year. Upperparts of both age classes wear paler and carpal M fades and becomes browner; prior to moult bleached upperwing is patchily white.

Voice: Probably silent at sea. At colonies ads vocalize at night; described as twittering, loud shrill squawks and squeals, with a throaty cooing *uc coo uc coo u-u-u-u-uc cuc coo o-o-o-o*, resembling turtle dove *Streptopelia* sp., most frequent (*HANZAB*).

Size: 25–27 cm, wing 17.1–20.9 cm, wingspan 58–66 cm, bill length 2.45–3.10 cm, bill width 1.10–1.55 cm, tarsus 2.9–3.5 cm, weight 95–224 g. Extensive overlap between sexes in measurements.

Similar species: Probably indistinguishable from Salvin's Prion at sea. Bill slightly narrower but this is obvious only in the hand. Given reasonable views distinguished from Broad-billed Prion by

Antarctic Prion Pachyptila desolata *in typical flight showing the soft pale grey plumage (also typical are the pronounced black tail and upperwing markings, face pattern and grey beast-side patches), which is virtually identical to Salvin's Prion* P. salvini, *from which it might be separated by the slightly shorter narrower bill. Off South Georgia, Nov 2001. © Hadoram Shirihai.*

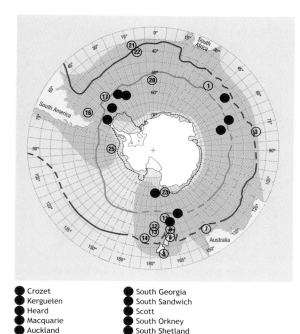

● Crozet
● Kerguelen
● Heard
● Macquarie
● Auckland

● South Georgia
● South Sandwich
● Scott
● South Orkney
● South Shetland

smaller size, especially bill, which is greyish (not blackish), and is overall paler above, mainly around head/neck. Also strongly resembles Slender-billed Prion *P. belcheri*, but differs in being less white-faced, with more pronounced tail-band and black M, and in being heavier/larger (flight is less dainty, manoeuvrable and aerobatic), with a less slender body, head, neck and bill, but much experience with the entire group is required to appreciate these differences. Broader bill, better-developed grey beast-side patches, but narrower black tail-band separates it from Fairy *P. turtur* and Fulmar Prions *P. crassirostris* (which see for further details).

Distribution and biology

Distribution, movements and population: Widespread in Antarctic waters, principally south of the Antarctic Convergence, breeding on South Georgia, South Sandwich, South Orkney, South Shetland, Crozet, Kerguelen, Heard, Macquarie, Auckland and Scott, and formerly in coastal Antarctica (at Cape Denison on King George V coast). Ranges at sea south of 35°S, and to Australia, New Zealand, S South America and South Africa. The world population is probably in excess of 20 million pairs.

Diet and feeding: Takes crustaceans, cephalopods, gastropods and small fish, which are caught by hydroplaning, surface-filtering, surface-seizing and surface-diving.

Social behaviour: Gregarious at sea and on land. Probably forms long-lasting pair-bonds.

Breeding biology: Nests in plateaux, gullies, screes and cliffs, in self-excavated burrows 23–100 cm deep, and rock crevices, with nest lining of twigs, mosses, pebbles and lichens. Four-week laying season in Dec. One white egg. Incubation 44–46 days. Fledging period 45–55 days. Both sexes take full share of all parental duties. Single-brooded.

Conservation Not globally threatened, though long-term survival may be affected by krill harvesting. Nesting areas restricted by presence of introduced predators, e.g. rats, rabbits, cats, pigs and cattle.

Taxonomy Polytypic with up to three subspecies recognized (*desolata* on Crozet, Kerguelen and Macquarie; *alter* on Auckland and Heard; and *banksi* in Antarctica, SW Atlantic, South Georgia,

South Sandwich and Scott), and recent biological studies suggest at least two are warranted. Tail, wing and bill lengths vary between populations, birds in South Atlantic having longest tails, wings and bills, these variables becoming smaller to the east, towards the subantarctic waters of Australia and New Zealand, especially in tail length which is shortest in Auckland Is birds. Some populations differ clearly between different localities, even in the same region, and there may be undescribed clades that warrant subspecies status. Sometimes considered a race of *P. vittata*, but same biological study regards this suggestion as invalid.

Slender-billed Prion *Pachyptila belcheri*   Plate 11

Identification

Confusion risks: Other prions.

Main characters: Upperparts dull blue-grey, with rather narrow tail-band and less pronounced M on upperwing, being usually ill-defined or faint and narrower, but slight individual variation, and in some more distinct; especially note fainter carpal bar (compared to darker outer primaries). Also smaller overall than previous species and is slimmest prion, especially on head/neck and rear body, with the narrowest (greyish) bill (edges straight when viewed from above and combs virtually absent and not exposed when mandible closed). Head has well-pronounced (broad and sharply demarcated) white supercilium and lores, and distinct dusky eyestripe, imparting extensive white-faced appearance, further emphasized by slightly darker crown. Predominantly white underparts offset by quite substantial, pale grey breast-sides. Flight fast and buoyant (manoeuvrable and aerobatic) in all weathers, low over water with brief bursts of shallow wingbeats, and wings regularly held straighter (more bowed at carpals in Antarctic Prion *P. desolata* and others). **Age/seasonal variation** indistinct. Juv as ad, but body plumage and flight feathers unmoulted in first-year. Upperparts of both age classes wear paler and carpal M fades; prior to moult bleached upperwing shows whitish patches.

Voice: Probably silent at sea. At colonies ads vocal at night, with guttural cooing, churring or trills the most frequent elements. Marked differences exist in male and female vocalizations.

Size: 25–26 cm, wing 16.6–19.1 cm, wingspan 56 cm, bill length 2.30–2.73 cm, bill width 1.02–1.25 cm, tarsus 3.1–3.6 cm, weight

Slender-billed Prions Pachyptila belcheri (worn plumage), showing the broad well-demarcated white supercilium and lores, which afford the species an extensively white-faced appearance (the most useful field mark), but also note the less pronounced M, fainter carpal bar (compared to the darker outer primaries), overall rather small and slim structure, especially the narrow bill, and the quite substantial pale grey breast-sides. Off the Falklands, Feb 2005. © Tony Marr.

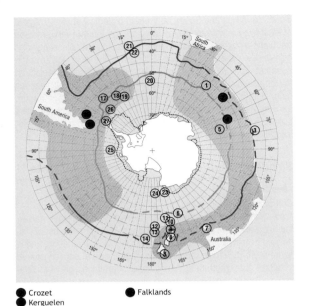

● Crozet　　　　　　● Falklands
● Kerguelen
● South American offshore
　islands

Fairy Prion Pachyptila turtur *is the smallest prion, with a broad black tail-band, short narrow bill and rather short collar, but intensity of bluish hue above, amount of greyish wash below and strength of facial marks all vary greatly, both individually and geographically. Kaikoura, South I, New Zealand, Oct 2001. © Hadoram Shirihai.*

115–180 g. Extensive overlap between sexes in measurements, but males average larger in culmen length, bill depth and width, head and tarsus lengths, with the greatest difference being in bill sizes.
Similar species: Combination of following marks useful for separation from all other prions: striking white-faced appearance (produced by broad and extensive white supercilium), overall pale plumage, narrow and indistinct M on upperwing, narrow tail-band and slender bill. Bear in mind that it is never easy to appreciate any of these characteristics, even if alongside other species at close range, and even for experienced observers. See above and other species for further comparisons.

Distribution and biology
Distribution, movements and population: Southern Ocean (principally close to Antarctic Convergence and to the north) on the Falklands, Crozet (East), Kerguelen, and possibly South Georgia, also in S Chile, dispersing north to Java, W Australia, New Zealand, W Peru, S Brazil and South Africa. The population is probably in excess of 2 million pairs.
Diet and feeding: Takes crustaceans, cephalopods and small fish, which are caught by dipping and pattering, surface-seizing and surface-diving.
Social behaviour: Gregarious at sea, often with Antarctic Prions *P. desolata*, and on land. Probably forms long-lasting pair-bonds. Rarely follows ships. Monogamous. Aggressive to conspecifics on land.
Breeding biology: Nests in self-excavated burrows 0.6–3.5 m deep, with nest lining of grass and feathers. There appears to be some interspecific competition for nest sites with Blue Petrel *Halobaena caerulea* on Kerguelen. Two-week season in Nov, laying one white egg. Incubation 46–47 days. Fledging period 49–50 days. Both sexes take full share of all parental duties. Single-brooded.
Conservation Not globally threatened. Eradication of predators has had beneficial affect on populations in the Falklands, which have long history of exploitation. Elsewhere cats and rats have detrimental affect on some populations.
Taxonomy Considered monotypic. Report of possible hybrids with *salvini* from Kerguelen considered erroneous.

Fairy Prion *Pachyptila turtur*　　　　　Plate 11

Identification
Confusion risks: Other prions, especially Fulmar Prion *P. crassirostris*.
Main characters: Smallest prion, with pale blue-grey upperparts and white to greyish-white below, characteristic broad black M and terminal tail-band (almost ¹/₃ of tail length). Bill stout with straight edges and is pale blue; in the hand has obvious maxillary unguis, sharply separated from the nasal tubes, but combs poorly

Probable Fairy Prion Pachyptila turtur, *race* subantarctica: *populations designated as this race, especially Antipodean birds, to some extent approach Fulmar Prion, including in bill dimensions. They are barely separable at sea, but note relatively well-defined white supercilium, emphasized by dark eyestripe. Off Antipodes, Jan 2007. © Hadoram Shirihai.*

198

Fairy Prion Pachyptila turtur *in feeding frenzy at krill. Most species of prions can form such dense concentrations at extremely rich food sources (plunging their head into the water to filter the prey). Note the broad tail-band, deep blue plumage, shorter grey collar and rather indistinct head pattern. Off North I, New Zealand, Sep 2003. © Hadoram Shirihai.*

Probable Fairy Prion Pachyptila turtur, *race* subantarctica. *Note greyish wash to body-sides, approaching Fulmar Prion P. crassirostris but, unlike latter, face pattern well developed and bill less compressed (with maxillary unguis well separated from nasal tubes). A cautious approach to identification of* subantarctica *is recommended. The relationship and variations of* turtur/crassirostris *are still poorly known. At sea between Snares and Stewart Is, New Zealand, intermediate birds with bill structure more like Fulmar and plumage more like Fairy have been observed by the author. Off Antipodes, Jan 2007. © Hadoram Shirihai.*

appearing as a central streak, but difficult to appreciate at sea. Wings proportionately short, broad and rounded, whilst tail rather long and quite wedge-shaped. Typically flies low over water with shallow wingbeats on fixed wings, though still capable of rapid manoeuvres. When feeding, wings held straighter or slightly above level of back (only bowed slightly at carpal), characteristically tilting and flitting from wave to wave, moving slowly into wind, often with some leg paddling (appearing to run across water), and banking in high winds. **Age/seasonal variation** indistinct. Juv as ad, but body plumage and flight feathers unmoulted in first-year. Upperparts of both age classes wear paler and carpal M becomes browner; prior to moult heavily bleached birds have patchy white upperwing. *Voice*: Probably silent at sea. At colonies ads vocal at night, giving staccato or rhythmic guttural cooing; commonest calls rather harsh and repeated *poor popper, popper, popper pop* or *kuk kuk coo-er* and *cup-a-curr*, often rising to crescendo in final syllables

developed and not exposed. Rounded head generally appears very pale and variably marked (both individually and geographically), with ill-defined to quite bold, but usually short to moderate and thin whitish supercilium, small whitish lores and rather indistinct/moderate greyish eyestripe (hardly darker than crown, which in turn is barely darker than rest of upperparts). Predominately white underparts (amount of grey varies individually and geographically), with rather obscure pale grey breast-sides half-collar. Black undertail mark more pronounced at tip, rather than

Fairy Prion Pachyptila turtur. *Birds breeding at lower latitudes or in cooler waters of Indian and Atlantic Oceans, like these birds from South Georgia, are generally paler and/or brighter blue, with smaller bill dimensions, and to some extent approach race* subantarctica, *but geographical variation in Fairy Prion is poorly understood and begs further study. Off South Georgia, Mar 2003 and 2006. © Hadoram Shirihai.*

Fairy Pachyptila turtur *(right-hand bird in both images) and Antarctic Prions* P. desolata. *Around South Georgia these two may be observed together and these remarkable photographs permit direct comparison. Note Fairy Prion's overall rather small, slim structure, relatively broader tail-band (despite being in moult), and clearly smaller bill dimensions than Antarctic; undertail has diagnostic black terminal tip, rather than central mark. Its face pattern is perhaps a feature of South Atlantic birds, here they superficially almost match those of Slender-billed Prion* P. belcheri. *Antarctic Prion also varies geographically, in this region the species has a relatively long bill. Off South Georgia, Nov 2005. © Johan Fromholtz.*

(see *HANZAB*). Marked differences exist in male and female vocalizations.

Size: 23–28 cm, wing 16.8–18.9 cm, wingspan 56–60 cm, bill length 2.03–2.43 cm, bill width 0.90–1.25 cm, tarsus 3.1–3.8 cm, weight 88–175 g. Extensive overlap between sexes, but significant differences appear to exist in bill length, with males having longer culmens.

Similar species: Small size, short bill, broad tail-band, often richer blue plumage, shorter collar and paler head with often indistinct to moderate pattern separate it from most other prions, except Fulmar Prion. Latter, though appreciably shorter necked with a rounder head and slightly larger/heavier bill, often a more obscure face pattern (affording a pigeon-like profile), paler blue-grey above (with perhaps on average a clearer M and somewhat broader tail-band) and

typically a bluish wash to the body-sides, largely on the vent, is virtually indistinguishable at sea. See below for further comparisons.

Distribution and biology

Distribution, movements and population: Widely but patchily distributed, principally north of the Antarctic Convergence in Australasia, in SE Australia, New Zealand (off North, South and Stewart Is), including the Chathams, Snares and Antipodes, and on Macquarie (see taxonomy); in rest of Southern Ocean on both sides of Antarctic Convergence, on the Falklands, South Georgia, Marion, St Paul, Kerguelen and Crozet (Hog). Disperses at sea south of 30°S, with some populations apparently moving north post-breeding. Probably 1 million pairs in 1980s.

Diet and feeding: Takes small crustaceans, small fish and

Fairy Prion Pachyptila turtur: *all prions share the same upperparts pattern when swimming, with grey upperparts and contrasting black on tertials, coverts and remiges. Also note here the wide individual variation in face pattern, though this is generally rather weak compared to some species. Off North I, New Zealand, Sep 2003. © Hadoram Shirihai.*

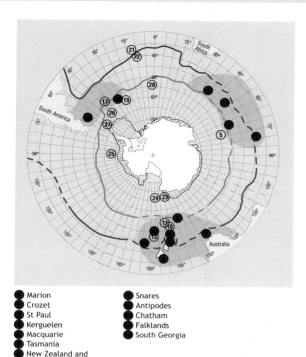

- ● Marion
- ● Crozet
- ● St Paul
- ● Kerguelen
- ● Macquarie
- ● Tasmania
- ● New Zealand and offshore islands
- ● Snares
- ● Antipodes
- ● Chatham
- ● Falklands
- ● South Georgia

Fulmar Prion Pachyptila crassirostris *has a rather bland face pattern, fulmarine head profile with a rather deep swollen bill and clearly curved maxillary unguis, which is hardly separated from nasal tubes, whilst the underparts are extensively sullied grey. Off Bounties, Jan 2007. © Hadoram Shirihai.*

pteropods, which are caught by dipping and pattering, surface-seizing and surface-plunging.

Social behaviour: Usually gregarious at sea and on land. Forms long-lasting pair-bonds and uses same burrow each season. Monogamous.

Breeding biology: Nests in rock crevices, self-excavated burrows 20–80 cm deep, even beneath trees, with nest lining of leaves and twigs. Laying season Oct–Dec, varying across range, laying one white egg. Incubation 44–55 days. Fledging period 43–56 days. Both sexes take full share of all parental duties. Single-brooded.

Conservation Not globally threatened, though nesting areas restricted by presence of introduced predators, e.g. rats, cats and Weka *Gallirallus australis*. Soil erosion may have caused deterioration in quality of some breeding areas, and fires during breeding season may also have detrimental affect.

Taxonomy The extensive variation within Fairy Prion populations requires further study and present taxonomy seems inadequate. Subspecific characters unstable and somewhat controversial owing to much variation (including bill size) between and within populations. Polytypic, with two subspecies recognized to date: nominate (most of range) and *subantarctica* (Antipodes, Snares and Macquarie). Separated by slight differences in bill size and plumage tones (*subantarctica* to some degree approaches Fulmar Prion, being paler overall, especially around face, and apparently lacks dark feathering on forehead and crown), but such differences cannot be appreciated at sea. Furthermore, the bill profile of Antipodean birds seems to approach Fulmar Prion whilst those on Heard and Motunau are rather intermediate in appearance. In some areas, e.g. New Zealand region, many birds have a variable greyish-blue wash to underparts, whilst larger billed populations tend to show variable dark on the crown, and smaller billed birds of cooler waters are paler. There is also apparently geographical variation in response to latitude and water temperature, as well as differences between oceans, e.g. S Atlantic vs. S Pacific. Relationship to Fulmar Prion is also to some extent unresolved.

Fulmar Prion *Pachyptila crassirostris*   Plate 11

Identification

Confusion risks: Other prions, especially Fairy Prion *P. turtur*.

Main characters: Rather small, distinctly pale prion. Upperparts pale (soft) blue-grey, with black M on upperwing and extensive black terminal tail-band (c.¹⁄₃ of tail length, i.e. as Fairy Prion or perhaps slightly broader). Bill stouter and slightly more robust than Fairy Prion (appears deeper and more swollen), due to larger and more clearly curved maxillary unguis which is hardly separated from nasal tubes; combs unexposed. Rounded head generally very pale, with featureless face, poorly defined whitish supercilium, often virtually lacks or has highly restricted loral patch (appearing as pale crescent above eye) and a rather indistinct greyish eyestripe, which is even paler than crown (latter usually slightly darker than rest of upperparts). Predominately white underparts with poorly developed pale grey breast-sides, but quite characteristically washed greyish on flanks, extensively so at rear, just in front of vent. Black

Fulmar Prion Pachyptila crassirostris: *combination of more rounded head and stubbier bill, as well as relatively paler blue-grey plumage (here M also relatively contrasting) identify it from very similar Fairy Prion* P. turtur. *However, this individual lacks the typical face pattern, having a stronger white supercilium (though still fades at rear). Off Bounties, Jan 2000. © Tony Palliser.*

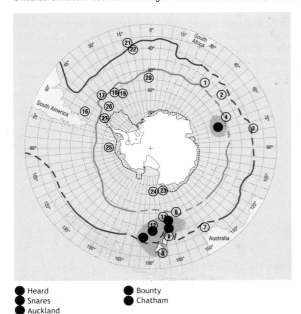

Both Fulmar Pachyptila crassirostris *(right-hand two images) and Fairy Prions* P. turtur *share a broad tail-band, but Fulmar tends to have a rather more fulmarine head proile (and virtually lacks the whitish supercilium and greyish eyestripe of Fairy which can vary individually, as shown here). Note also the rather more compressed (deeper and more swollen) bill, and pale bluish-grey tone to the plumage in Fulmar. Top right: Fulmar Prion, between Campbell and Antipodes, Dec 2005. © Michael & Malcolm Boswell. Bottom right: Fulmar Prion. Off Bounties, Jan 2007. Left: Fairy Prions. Off North I, New Zealand, Sep 2003. © Hadoram Shirihai.*

● Heard
● Snares
● Auckland

● Bounty
● Chatham

undertail mark more pronounced at tip, but difficult to appreciate at sea. Wings proportionately short, broad and rounded, whilst tail is rather long and noticeably wedge-shaped. Flight often very agile, with rapid manoeuvring and looping, but otherwise typically prion-like. **Age/seasonal variation** indistinct. Juv as ad, but body and flight feathers unmoulted in first-year. Upperparts of both age classes wear paler and carpal M becomes browner; prior to moult heavily bleached birds have white flecking on upperwing.

Voice: Probably mainly silent at sea. At colonies ads vocal at night and during day (at least on the Bounties), with varied cooing, gurgling, growling and squeaking; e.g. *coore-corr-corr* (*HANZAB*).

Size: 24–28 cm, wing 15.6–19.0 cm, wingspan 60 cm, bill length 2.12–2.50 cm, bill width 1.22–1.36 cm, tarsus 3.3–3.6 cm, weight 102–185 g. Extensive overlap between the sexes in measurements.

Similar species: Small size, short stout bill, very pale appearance and very broad tail-band separate it from most other prions, except Fairy. Compared to latter, Fulmar Prion is paler, typically softer blue-grey above, which often highlights the more pronounced M (but bear in mind individual variation and effects of light, viewing angle and feather wear), and generally has even weaker face pattern, often looking very bland, augmenting the more pigeon-like head. Furthermore, it is often washed bluish on body, with a slightly more fulmarine compressed bill structure, and tail-band perhaps averages slightly broader, but in practice the two species are extremely difficult to separate at sea. Variation within especially Fairy Prion (see Taxonomy under the latter) further obscures differences between them. It is therefore recommended to label only those birds exhibiting a complete suite of the above-mentioned characters as Fulmar Prion.

Distribution and biology

Distribution, movements and population: Southern Ocean on Heard, Snares, Auckland, Bounty and Chatham. Range at sea unknown, but appears largely sedentary, though has been recorded from SE Australia and South Africa. Overall population probably in region of 100,000 pairs in 1980s but only c.29,000 pairs estimated on Bounties in 1997 as opposed to an estimated 76,000 pairs in 1978. However, the different census methods employed mean that no firm conclusions can be drawn as to whether the population has declined.

Diet and feeding: Largely takes small crustaceans by surface-seizing or shallow-diving, principally close to shore.

Social behaviour: Usually gregarious at sea and on land. Forms long-lasting pair-bonds and is occasionally diurnal at colonies (often active in open during day on Bounties, where ads even feed chicks in daytime). Monogamous.

Breeding biology: Nests in rock crevices, caves, screes and beneath rock slabs with nest lining of debris and feathers, often in dense colonies in close proximity to albatrosses. Lays one white egg in Oct/Nov (with laying completed by the end of first week of Nov), and hatching occurs mid to late Dec on Bounties. No information concerning fledging. Both sexes take full share of all parental duties. Single-brooded.

Conservation Not globally threatened, though nesting areas and success presumably subject to similar constraints as other prions.

Taxonomy Two subspecies: nominate on Chatham, Snares and Bounty, and *eatoni*, which is smaller with smaller bill and different tail pattern, on Heard and Auckland. Those on Chatham have been separated as *pyramidalis*, but this form is no longer generally recognized. Sometimes considered a race of *P. turtur*, and further data are required to determine the validity of such treatment.

The white tail tip of Blue Petrel Halobaena caerulea *is a diagnostic field character that permits identiifcation even at long range. Off Wollongong, Australia, Jul 1999 . © Tony Palliser.*

Blue Petrel *Halobaena caerulea*   Plate 11

Identification

Confusion risks: Any of the prions.

Main characters: Small, prion-like-patterned petrel, greyish-blue above with white-tipped tail (latter also has narrow black subterminal bar), unique among petrels and prions, and often easy to see, even in poor sea conditions or at distance. Other conspicuous characters are the blackish cap, extending to and around eye, bordered by white forehead, lower cheeks and rear ear-coverts, and bold, broad dark patches on lower neck to breast-sides, enhancing white-throated appearance. Ill-defined, but dark and distinct M on upperwing. Rest of underparts/underwing predominately very clean white. Bill more petrel-like in shape, but rather small and mainly bluish-black; legs and feet blue with flesh-coloured webs. Flight resembles large prion, but less erratic, more buoyant and unlike prions sometimes flies higher above water, with action and pattern more like small *Pterodroma*. **Age/seasonal variation** indistinct. Juv as ad, but body plumage and

Blue Petrel Halobaena caerulea: *note conspicuous blackish cap, extending to and around eye, contrasting with white forehead, lower cheeks and rear ear-coverts, as well as broad dark lower neck to breast-sides, enhancing white-throated appearance. Off South Georgia, Mar 2006. © Hadoram Shirihai.*

Blue Petrel Halobaena caerulea *is a small compact petrel with greyish-blue upperparts and a dark M, affording it a somewhat prion-like pattern, but note diagnostic white-tipped tail-band, the conspicuous blackish crown and eye, and petrel-like bill. Off South Georgia, Mar 2006. © Hadoram Shirihai.*

Four Blue Petrels Halobaena caerulea (in front) and two Antarctic Prions Pachyptila desolata (at right). Blue Petrel has a conspicuous blackish cap, extending to and around eye, but lacks Antarctic Prion's white supercilium, and also shows a diagnostic white-tipped tail (rather than the black band of the prions); shape and flight behaviours also differ markedly. Off South Georgia, Mar 2006. © Marc Guyt.

flight feathers unmoulted in first-year.

Voice: Probably mainly silent at sea. At colonies ads vocal at night, giving pigeon-like cooing, somewhat similar to prions, *kuk-kuk-kuk coo-coo (HANZAB)*. Significant geographic variation in male (but not female) calls exists between different archipelagos and even between islands of same group (Bretagnolle & Genevois 1997).

Size: 26–32 cm, wing 19.8–23.3 cm, wingspan 62–71 cm, weight 152–251 g. Extensive overlap in measurements between the sexes, though males may tend to be heavier and slightly longer winged.

Similar species: Separated from all prions by darker cap with white forehead, largely black bill, lack of supercilium behind eye, white undertail and square, not wedge-shaped tail, which is tipped white. Latter is often the first feature to be noticed.

Distribution and biology

Distribution, movements and population: Circumpolar in Southern Ocean, principally close to and south of the Antarctic Convergence, breeding on South Georgia, Prince Edward, Marion, Crozet (East), Kerguelen and Macquarie, and in S Chile. Ranges north to S Australia, New Zealand, S South America and South Africa but some remain close to breeding colonies year-round. Young may wander throughout range prior to breeding. Population several tens of thousands.

Diet and feeding: Takes crustaceans, fish, cephalopods and

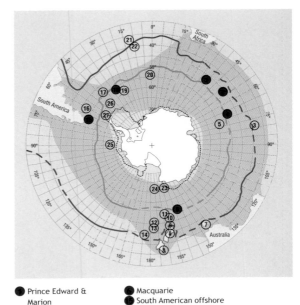

- Prince Edward & Marion
- Crozet
- Kerguelen
- Macquarie
- South American offshore islands
- South Georgia

occasionally insects by surface-dipping, surface-seizing, surface-diving and occasionally pursuit-diving.

Social behaviour: Often joins prion flocks and occasionally follows ships and associates with cetaceans. Gregarious throughout the year. Nocturnal at colonies.

Breeding biology: Nests on lower seaward-facing slopes, often with dense tussac grass, in self-excavated burrows 15–37 cm deep, sometimes with nest lining of leaves or twigs. There appears to be some interspecific competition for nest sites with Slender-billed Prion *P. belcheri* on Kerguelen. Season Sep–Feb, with most laying one white egg in Oct. Incubation 45–49 days. Fledging period 43–60 days. Both sexes take full share of parental duties.

Conservation Not globally threatened, but has been subject to predation by introduced mammals at breeding colonies. Rats have substantially reduced numbers on Macquarie and exterminated breeding population on Possession. Cats also take a toll of those breeding on Kerguelen and Prince Edward. Sometimes 'wrecked' in large numbers on beaches.

Taxonomy Monotypic.

Table 1. Quick reference to the main field marks between the prions Pachyptila.

Taxon	Overall size	Black tail-band	Bill size/ dimensions	Breast-side patches	Face pattern: mainly extent of white supercilium	Darkness of head	Darkness and depth of upperpart ground colour	Broadness and intensity of upperwing M pattern	Dark undertail mark
Broad-billed Prion *P. vittata*	Largest; also squarer head and steep forehead unique	Medium to narrow	Huge and very broad; duck-like	Very extensive	Indistinct	Dark	Dark to medium	Distinct	Central streak
Salvin's Prion *P. salvini*	Medium to large	Medium	Medium and broad	Rather extensive	Rather pronounced	Medium to pale	Medium	Distinct	Central streak
Saint Paul Prion *P. [vittata/salvini] macgillivrayi*	Medium to large	Medium	Large and broad	Rather extensive	Moderately developed	Medium to pale	Medium	Distinct	Central streak
Antarctic Prion *P. desolata*	Medium to large	Medium	Medium to small, but rather stout	Extensive	Rather pronounced	Dark to medium	Dark to medium	Distinct	Central streak
Fairy Prion *P. turtur*	Small	Very broad	Small	Obscured to moderate	Obscured to moderate	Pale or very pale (*subantarctica*)	Medium to pale	Distinct and broad (nom.) or narrow (*subantartica*)	Terminal tip
Fulmar Prion *P. crassirostris*	Small	Very broad	Small and rather stout	Obscured	Highly obscured	Pale	Pale	Distinct	Terminal tip
Slender-billed Prion *P. belcheri*	Medium	Narrow	Medium to small and narrow	Moderate	Pronounced	Rather pale	Pale	Obscured	Central streak

Storm-petrels and diving-petrels

These species, covered by Plate 12, constitute distinct groups of tubenoses, belonging to the families Hydrobatidae and Pelecanoidiidae. Both are amongst the smallest Procellariiformes. In the Southern Ocean, only five or six species of storm-petrels breed or occur regularly (of c.20 species in total), but three out of four diving-petrels do so. In this new edition we include an account for the recently rediscovered (long-lost) New Zealand Storm-petrel *Pealeornis maoriana*.

Identifying the storm-petrels of the Southern Ocean is rather straightforward as all are distinctively marked, except Black-bellied *Fregetta tropica* and White bellied Storm-petrels *F. grallaria*, but separating the diving-petrels is usually far more difficult, especially South Georgian *Pelecanoides georgicus* versus Common Diving-petrels *P. urinatrix*, which are often unidentifiable at sea. The latter still attracts controversy concerning how many forms merit recognition.

Storm-petrels have a unique overall appearance and habits: they are small with strongly hooked bills, which have prominently united nostrils and a single tube opening, and wings with a longer second functional primary, whilst their general plumage is mainly black to grey above with paler upperwing bars, often a variably shaped grey/white rump and vent, and some have more extensive whitish on the underparts and face. All five storm-petrels in our region belong to the largest subfamily, the Oceanitinae, which comprises four genera, characterized by relatively short/rounded wings with only ten secondaries, squarer (rather than forked) tails and longer tarsi than toes. When foraging they progress by hopping and fluttering (rather than 'walking'). Otherwise, they are characteristically restless, rather erratic and agile fliers. The Oceanitinae have, at least in some species, only a single coat of nestling down (rather than two). Diving-petrels comprise a single genus *Pelecanoides* and are characteristically stocky, compact birds with very dense plumage, generally dark above and white below. They appear to converge in form and behaviour with the small Northern Hemisphere Alcidae, apparently occupying a niche for small aquatic species that feed on plankton left unoccupied by penguins. They also have gular pouches for storing food. Their short wings and tail and well set back legs (no hind toe) are used for underwater propulsion. Some at least become flightless during moult. Fly close and very direct above water surface, on very fast whirring wingbeats, and dive straight into water without settling on surface first. On sea, float quite well above surface and if flushed from distance either make long escape flight or dive for prolonged period, but often when surprised nearby they first make short flight then dive (depending on stage of moult). Both storm- and diving-petrels exhibit no or almost no sex/age-related variation, even in mensural data.

The general behaviour, life and breeding cycles are rather uniform amongst the storm-petrels. Being truly pelagic, they come ashore only to breed, and then usually at night. Most nest on offshore and remote islands with dense grass or other vegetation. Food is mostly cephalopods, gastropods, carrion and pelagic crustaceans taken on or very close to the surface. Long-term monogamous pair-bonds and high fidelity to nesting sites are notable characteristics of their breeding behaviour. They vocalize with churring or purring calls around colonies at night, and nest colonially (except Grey-backed Storm-petrel), sometimes with other tubenoses or seabirds, in natural holes (storm-petrels, except Grey-backed), or self-excavated holes, burrows, and caves

(diving-petrels). The age at which birds first return to their natal colonies and that at which breeding is first attempted are often unknown, but some species do not reach maturity until 4–5 years old. Ads lay a single, usually smooth white, egg incubated 7–8 weeks, and chicks take 8–10 weeks to fledge. Usually nocturnal around the colonies, when they can be heard displaying; they visit borrows just before dusk and return to the sea sometime prior to dawn. The diving-petrels are also burrow nesters and breed colonially, with twittering voices around colonies, and with rather similar breeding biology to that described for the storm-petrels (see also species accounts).

Like most burrow-nesting seabirds, many of these petrels have been the unintentional victims of Man's arrival on their breeding islands: rats, feral cats, pigs and other introduced mammals have all caused significant losses to eggs, young and even ads. Fortunately, many islands are currently subject to conservation work designed to tackle the problems caused by introduced predators, and significant advances have already been made on a number.

Wilson's Storm-petrel
Oceanites oceanicus   Plate 12

Identification

Confusion risks: Black-bellied *Fregetta tropica*, White-bellied *F. grallaria* and New Zealand Storm-petrels *Pealeornis maoriana*; all potentially confusing white-rumped storm-petrels are only vagrants or have never been recorded in our region, thus, virtually unmistakable in the Southern Ocean.

Main characters: Small compact storm-petrel with blackish sooty-brown upperparts, including head and square tail, and bold white rump patch extending to vent-sides. Pale cream-brown greater coverts wingbar evident in flight; underwing predominately sooty-

Wilson's Storm-petrel Oceanites oceanicus *is readily identified by the pale carpal bar on upperwing-coverts, mostly dark underwing (indistinct pale wash on coverts) and the extensive white rump wrapping round onto vent-sides; the feet project the tail. South Georgia, Mar 2006. © Hadoram Shirihai.*

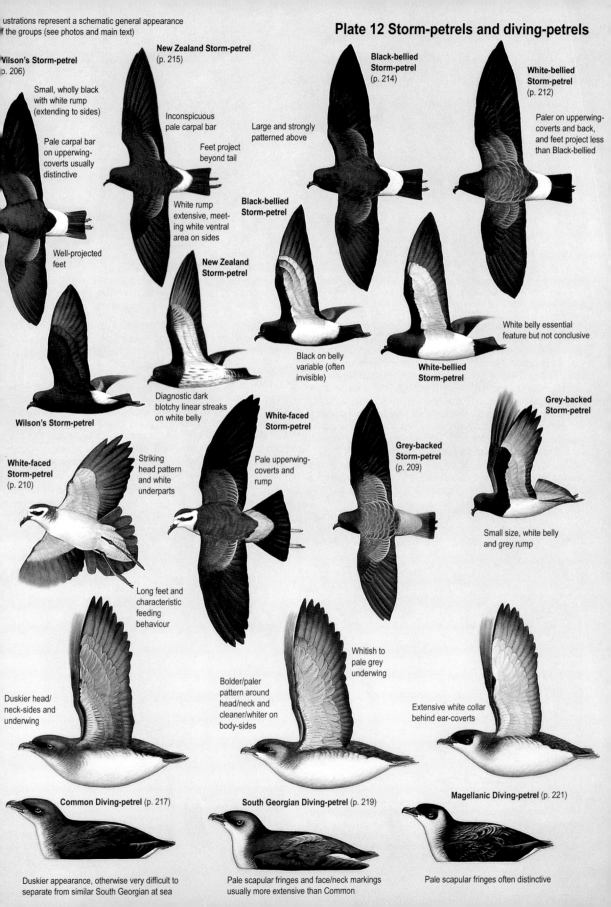

ustrations represent a schematic general appearance
f the groups (see photos and main text)

Plate 12 Storm-petrels and diving-petrels

Wilson's Storm-petrel
(p. 206)

Small, wholly black
with white rump
(extending to sides)

Pale carpal bar
on upperwing-
coverts usually
distinctive

Well-projected
feet

Wilson's Storm-petrel

New Zealand Storm-petrel
(p. 215)

Inconspicuous
pale carpal bar

Feet project
beyond tail

White rump
extensive, meet-
ing white ventral
area on sides

New Zealand
Storm-petrel

Diagnostic dark
blotchy linear streaks
on white belly

**Black-bellied
Storm-petrel**
(p. 214)

Large and strongly
patterned above

**Black-bellied
Storm-petrel**

Black on belly
variable (often
invisible)

**White-bellied
Storm-petrel**
(p. 212)

Paler on upperwing-
coverts and back,
and feet project less
than Black-bellied

White belly essential
feature but not conclusive

**White-bellied
Storm-petrel**

**White-faced
Storm-petrel**
(p. 210)

Striking
head pattern
and white
underparts

Long feet and
characteristic
feeding
behaviour

**White-faced
Storm-petrel**

Pale upperwing-
coverts and
rump

**Grey-backed
Storm-petrel**
(p. 209)

**Grey-backed
Storm-petrel**

Small size, white belly
and grey rump

Duskier head/
neck-sides and
underwing

Bolder/paler
pattern around
head/neck and
cleaner/whiter on
body-sides

Whitish to
pale grey
underwing

Extensive white collar
behind ear-coverts

Common Diving-petrel (p. 217)

Duskier appearance, otherwise very difficult to
separate from similar South Georgian at sea

South Georgian Diving-petrel (p. 219)

Pale scapular fringes and face/neck markings
usually more extensive than Common

Magellanic Diving-petrel (p. 221)

Pale scapular fringes often distinctive

Wilson's Storm-petrel Oceanites oceanicus is amongst the most widespread tubenoses in the Antarctic and Southern Ocean; here in typical short, low bouncing flight against the wind whilst feeding. Yellowish webs just visible, but pale carpal bar on upperwing-coverts and white vent-sides conspicuous. South Georgia, Mar 2006. © Hadoram Shirihai.

brown (paler than upperparts) with variable greyish-white wash to coverts (not always visible). Rest of underparts all dark. Bill, yellow-webbed feet and legs black, latter project beyond tail (though may be retracted into belly feathers, making this feature not always useful). Flies on typically rather short rounded wings, with hirundine-like jizz and action, almost without glides. Also generally less erratic or buoyant, almost without bounding, and usually flies very close and rather slow above surface, especially when foraging. However, can be more direct and fast, with rapid wingbeats interspersed by short glides, but mainly in active flight and windy conditions. **Age/seasonal variation** indistinct; juv as ad.

Voice: Probably mainly silent at sea, but low squeaks heard when feeding. At colonies ads more vocal at night, with 2–3 loud, wheezing notes or a nasal, grating disyllabic *aark-aark*, sometimes a monotonous *aark-uh-ah-ah-ah-uh-uh*.

Size: 15–19 cm, wing 13.6–16.2 cm, wingspan 38–42 cm, weight 28–50 g. Extensive overlap in mensural data between the sexes.

Similar species: Black-bellied, White-bellied and New Zealand

Storm-petrels all have white underparts from breast down, white underwing-coverts (emphasized by broad dark leading edge), and latter is also diagnostically streaked on the belly.

Distribution and biology

Distribution, movements and population: Southern Ocean on islets off Cape Horn, the Falklands, South Georgia, South Sandwich, South Orkney, South Shetland, Bouvetøya, Crozet (East), Kerguelen, Heard, Balleny, Scott and Peter; also coastal Antarctica. Disperses widely at sea through Atlantic and Indian Oceans north to Labrador, Persian Gulf, Greater Sunda Is, and in Pacific to Marshall Is and along coast of Americas and Japan. No overall population estimate available, but probably several million pairs.

Diet and feeding: Cephalopods, gastropods, carrion and pelagic

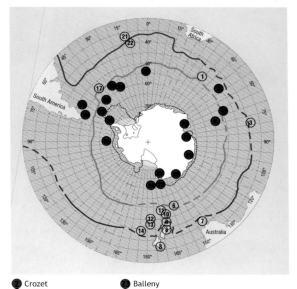

Crozet	Balleny
Kerguelen	Scott
Heard	Peter I Øy
South American offshore islands	South Orkney
	South Shetland
Falklands	Antarctic Peninsula
South Georgia	Antarctic coasts and
South Sandwich	offshore islands
Bouvetøya	

Wilson's Storm-petrels Oceanites oceanicus feed by dipping and pattering the surface, as well as by surface-seizing, shallow-plunging and sometimes even surface-diving. Note the distinctive pale carpal bar on upperwing-coverts, and extensive white rump and vent-sides; the yellow webs are well shown on the right-hand bird. South Georgia, Mar 2006. © Hadoram Shirihai.

crustaceans taken by dipping and pattering, as well as surface-seizing, shallow-plunging and, rarely, surface-diving. Feeds in large flocks, often associated with cetaceans and other seabirds, and routinely follows ships.

Social behaviour: Gregarious year-round. Monogamous and at least 50% of pair-bonds apparently long-lasting.

Breeding biology: Breeds colonially in crevices and 20–50 cm-long holes in cliffs and screes, usually with feathers lining nest chamber, partially associated with prions or other petrels. Lays one white egg spotted at broad end, in Nov–Feb, incubated 33–59 days. Chicks fledge at 46–97 days (considerable intra- and inter-colony variation). Mostly single-brooded, though some populations may lay replacement clutch. Both parents probably take full role in breeding cycle.

Conservation Not globally threatened, though cats and rats may predate ads, chicks and eggs on some islands, and pesticides and heavy metal residues may pose a potential threat to some populations.

Taxonomy Two poorly differentiated subspecies described, with nominate breeding on subantarctic islands and *exasperatus* on Antarctic mainland and in Scotia Sea, but probably best regarded as monotypic. New Zealand Storm-petrel was formerly believed to be an extinct race or pale morph of Wilson's, but was recently rediscovered and appears distinctive from both *Oceanites* and *Fregetta*.

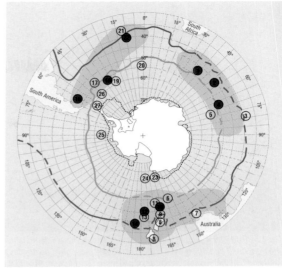

● Prince Edward & Marion
● Crozet
● Kerguelen
● Auckland
● Antipodes
● Chatham
● Falklands
● South Georgia
● Gough

Grey-backed Storm-petrel
Oceanites nereis   Plate 12

Identification

Confusion risks: *Fregetta* storm-petrels.

Main characters: Tiny, diminutive storm-petrel with dark head, throat, neck, upperparts and square tail, pale grey rump and white underparts. Tail rather short (with feet just projecting beyond tip in flight), but often appears elongated and slim at rear. Head and upperparts/upperwing predominantly slate grey-black (but may appear contrastingly blacker hooded), with ill-defined, dull silvery-grey coverts evident in flight and broad pale grey rump (which can seem darker/indistinct or sometimes quite white, according to light conditions), extending to base of tail, but sharply demarcated from blackish terminal tail-band. Slate grey-black head reaches upper breast, where sharply demarcated from white underparts; underwing mostly white, bordered by broad dark area on remiges and very broad, black lesser covert bar. Bill and legs black. Flight (on rather short rounded wings) quite direct, fast and fluttery with shallow bat-like wingbeats interspersed by very short glides, never conspicuously buoyant and almost without bounding; usually very close to surface, especially when feeding. **Age/seasonal variation** indistinct; juv as ad.

Voice: Probably mainly silent at sea. At night around colonies

Grey-backed Storm-petrel Oceanites nereis *showing the characteristic slate-black hood reaching the upper breast, where sharply demarcated from white underparts, whilst white underwing-coverts are bordered by very broad, black leading edge; sharply demarcated blackish terminal tail-band also visible from below. Some may show a few very fine dark streaks on rear flanks. Off Chathams, Jan 2007. © Hadoram Shirihai.*

Grey-backed Storm-petrel Oceanites nereis: *note slate-black hood that continues as broad black leading edge to underwing. The grey rump/uppertail-coverts appear paler in strong sunlight, accentuating this feature. Off Chathams, Jan 2007. © Hadoram Shirihai.*

Grey-backed Storm-petrel Oceanites nereis. These images demonstrate the effect of light and viewing angle on the grey rump/uppertail-coverts. On the right-hand bird this area is quite distinctively paler grey, contrasting with the blackish terminal tail-band and darker grey upperparts, while on the left-hand bird the upperparts appear much more concolorous. Note that the square-shaped tail can appear rather elongated and slim, with the feet just projecting beyond tip; ill-defined, dull silvery-grey tone to upperwing-coverts evident at some angles. Off Chathams, Jan 2007. © Hadoram Shirihai.

ads not as vocal as congeners, uttering harsh cricket-like calls (*HANZAB*). Similar to but slower than *Oceanites*. Also some soft calls.

Size: 16–19 cm, wing 12.4–14.0 cm, wingspan 39 cm, weight 21–44 g. Extensive overlap in mensural data between sexes, but females tend to be larger in most measurements, e.g. wing and tail lengths.

Similar species: White-bellied and Black-bellied Storm-petrels are larger and have white (not grey) rumps, and perhaps less extensive white on underparts (see below). Unlikely to be confused with White-faced Storm-petrel *Pelagodroma marina* (see below), which is much larger with strongly patterned face.

Distribution and biology

Distribution, movements and population: Southern Ocean on the Falklands (formerly?), South Georgia, Gough, Crozet (East), Kerguelen, Auckland, Antipodes, Chatham and possibly Macquarie. Ranges at sea, usually near breeding grounds. Overall population unknown, but perhaps fewer than 100,000 pairs.

Diet and feeding: Imm barnacles with some other crustaceans and, occasionally, small fish, taken by pattering and aerial-dipping, as well as shallow-plunging. At sea often associated with floating kelp. No additional information.

Social behaviour: Solitary or gregarious year-round. Generally avoids ships, being rarely observed aft of the bows looking forward. Assumed monogamous and pair-bonds presumed to be long-lasting.

Breeding biology: Breeds colonially or alone, usually on or near ground in dense tussac grassland or other vegetation on flat, sloping or occasionally steep ground (in Chatham and Kerguelen in tunnels 0–50 cm long), and nest virtually unlined. Lays one white egg spotted at broad end, in Sep–Dec, incubated c.45 days. Fledging period unknown. Single-brooded. Both parents take full role in breeding cycle.

Conservation Not globally threatened and overall population considered stable, although cats and rats may predate ads, chicks and eggs on some islands. There is also evidence of substantial predation of ads by Short-eared Owls *Asio flammeus* in the Falklands.

Taxonomy Monotypic. Also placed in the genus *Garrodia*.

White-faced Storm-petrel
Pelagodroma marina   Plate 12

Identification

Confusion risks: None.

Main characters: Medium to large, but rather slender and elegant storm-petrel with noticeably long legs (which project well beyond tail), notably rounded wings and square-ended, moderately long tail. Plumage characterized by white face, forehead and supercilium, and dark brown-grey eyestripe. Also distinctive are grey crown and neck, greyish-brown upperparts (flight and tail feathers darkest), variable paler rump (can appear much whiter) and cream-brown upperwing-coverts, with paler fringes producing ill-defined (narrow or broad) dull cream-grey wing panel. Otherwise, mainly white below, including throat, except quite distinct greyish breast-sides from lower neck; underwing mostly white, bordered by broad dark area on remiges and very narrow leading edge.

White-faced Storm-petrel Pelagodroma marina is readily identified by its large size, distinctive flight and feeding techniques, and diagnostic face and upperparts patterns. Note long legs and yellow webs to feet. Off New Zealand, Jan 2006. © Hadoram Shirihai.

White-faced Storm-petrels Pelagodroma marina *'walking' on surface. This photo illustrates this species' feeding technique: by facing into the wind with open wings, the birds partially lift-off, and by pushing forward using their long legs, progress slowly in short hops and sometimes appear to walk. Face and underwing pattern, with clear breast-side patches diagnostic. Off New Zealand, Jan 2006. © Hadoram Shirihai.*

Bill, yellow-webbed feet and legs black. Flight typically erratic, banking and weaving, with short glides, and when wings held stiffly, especially in windy conditions, interspersed by short jerky wingbeats. But, in windless conditions and when feeding, wing-beats looser and wings held bowed at carpals, raised above level of back. Legs typically dangle as proceeds by gentle hops with spring-like quality, legs pushing forward from water surface when facing into wind; usually flies very low, especially when feeding. **Age/seasonal variation** indistinct; juv as ad, but in freshest plumage tends to have broader pale fringes above; can appear grey or brown according to moult.
Voice: Probably mainly silent at sea, but when feeding in groups heard to make soft squeaking notes (audible at short range in calm conditions). At colonies ads more vocal (but not noisy) at night, giving a repeated mournful *coo* or *wooo*, sometimes *ooo-aaa-ooo*.
Size: 18–21 cm, wing 14.5–17.3 cm, wingspan 42–43 cm, weight 40–70 g. Extensive overlap in mensural data between sexes, but females tend to have longer wings and tail.
Similar species: Combination of white face and underparts, and dark eyestripe/mask distinguish it from all other storm-petrels. In our region almost unmistakable, but see *Fregetta* storm-petrels and Grey-backed Storm-petrel *Oceanites nereis*. Flight silhouette and pattern, especially when feeding, a good field mark among Southern Ocean species.

Distribution and biology

Distribution, movements and population: Atlantic Ocean on the Salvages, Canaries, Cape Verdes and Tristan da Cunha; off W and S Australia, New Zealand, Auckland, Chatham, Kermadec Is, and formerly on St Helena and Amsterdam. Disperses at sea in Indian and Pacific Oceans generally south of equator, but to 5°N in E Pacific and NE Atlantic in spring, and NW Atlantic in autumn. Overall population unknown, but several tens of thousands of pairs bred in Australia alone in 1970s.
Diet and feeding: Surface plankton, small fish and pelagic crustaceans taken by dipping and pattering and surface-seizing. Only occasionally follows ships, but is very quickly attracted to chum, sometimes in large numbers (e.g., in Jan 2007, off the Chathams

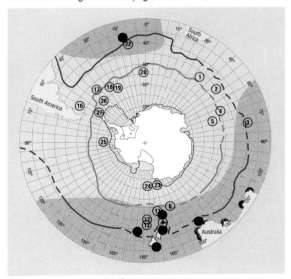

White-faced Storm-petrel Pelagodroma marina *gently hops on long legs. Note ill-defined cream grey panel on upperwing-coverts, and whitish-grey rump patch. Diagnostic face pattern also evident. Off New Zealand, Jan 2006. © Hadoram Shirihai.*

● Tasmania
● New Zealand's offshore islands
● Auckland
● Chatham
● Tristan da Cunha

*c.*2000 were observed at a fish oil slick; HS pers. obs.). Most feeding probably nocturnal.

Social behaviour: Gregarious in small parties at sea and in larger groups close to breeding colonies. Strongly colonial. Monogamous and pair-bonds sustained. Strictly nocturnal visits to land. Territorial around burrow entrance.

Breeding biology: Breeds in shallow self-excavated burrows, 0.3–1.2 m long, usually well lined with dry plant material, in areas with dense ground vegetation. Lays one white egg spotted at broad end, in Oct–Dec, incubated 50–59 days. Chicks fledge at 52–67 days. Single-brooded. Both parents take full role in breeding cycle.

Conservation Not globally threatened, although cats and rats may predate ads, chicks and eggs on some islands, and human disturbance is a factor on mainland Australia.

Taxonomy Six subspecies recognised, of which *marina*, *dulciae*, *maoriana* and *albiclunis* occur in the Southern Ocean. The form *albiclunis* may represent a different species, 'Kermadec White-faced Storm Petrel', differing mainly in its white rump and larger size.

White-bellied Storm-petrel
Fregetta grallaria   Plate 12

Identification

Confusion risks: Black-bellied Storm-petrel *F. tropica*.

Main characters: Robust but rather compact/small-looking storm-petrel, closely related to Black-bellied, with both exhibiting complex geographical variation in their underparts patterns. Size and structure as Black-bellied, but feet project at most only marginally beyond tail and usually difficult to see (even lacking in many). Plumage also very similar, with blackish-brown head, neck and upperparts, including tail, and white rump and belly; division between black and white areas runs across mid/upper breast and is well demarcated. Underwing-coverts mostly white, sharply delimited from broad leading edge and narrow black trailing edge and dark remiges; centres to primary-coverts partly dusky in some birds but in others purer white. Undertail-coverts and vent (mostly outer coverts) black with pale fringes. When fresh (and in close views) shows quite pronounced pale-fringed mantle,

White-bellied Storm-petrel *Fregetta g. grallaria*: *note characteristic white belly and sharply demarcated black and white underparts at mid/upper breast level. Note also indistinct flecks and streaks on flanks, a feature of birds at this locality. Off Kermadec Is, Jan 2006.* © Hadoram Shirihai.

back, scapulars and greater coverts, but marked geographical, individual and wear-induced variation. Generally, ground colour of upperwing-coverts paler than remiges, dull grey-brown, with less obvious carpal bar on greater-coverts (though enhanced by wear). Bill and legs black. Variation in white underparts includes those with pure white belly well demarcated from black throat/breast and vent/undertail-coverts (most); a tiny number are extensively black-bellied (dark morph; though central abdomen usually still paler) or partially so (intermediate), but birds fortunately also have dark rumps, preventing confusion with Black-bellied. Such dark

White-bellied Storm-petrel *Fregetta grallaria (race undetermined). These birds were photographed in the S Pacific roughly between where* segethi *(Juan Fernández) and* titan *(Rapa) breed. The extensive white fringes to the fresh mantle and scapulars (left-hand bird) are suggestive of* titan*, but the birds appeared rather small (more like* segethi*). On the left-hand bird, note the indistinct paler coverts panel with small pale tips to upper greater coverts, whilst on the right-hand bird note the species' characteristic white belly with the division between the black and white on the underparts sharply demarcated on the upper breast; legs do not appear to project beyond tail. E Tropical Pacific, Oct 2003.* © Hadoram Shirihai.

Possible White-bellied Storm-petrel Fregetta grallaria leucogaster. *This bird was identified as White-bellied, but given paucity of information concerning the white-bellied race, melanoleuca, of Black-bellied F. tropica (and their separation), which occurs in same region, it is impossible to be certain. Note the relatively extensive black on chest, reaching the mid/lower breast (approaching Black-bellied) and it appears to have isolated black feathers between the legs. Identification of this bird and others photographed off Tristan da Cunha, including Gough I, await verification. Off Gough, Mar 2006. © Hadoram Shirihai.*

birds found mainly off Lord Howe I where sizeable percentage are of intermediate appearance, with dark-smudged white rump and variable dusky blotches and streaks on body-sides. Most upper- and underwing-coverts in dark morph are wholly or almost entirely dark, but slightly paler than remiges. Flight generally recalls Black-bellied, but perhaps more varied and erratic, often more zigzagging, and may include more glides. In bouncing flight, sometimes appears marginally top-heavy. **Age/seasonal variation** indistinct; juv as ad.
Voice: Presumably mostly silent at sea. At colonies reported to have similar calls to Black-bellied (which see).
Size: 18–22 cm, wing 14.6–18.8 cm, wingspan 46–48 cm, weight 45–74 g. Sexual dimorphism apparently minimal except at Tristan da Cunha, where females notably larger than males.
Similar species: In much of our region Black-bellied Storm-petrel

is readily differentiated if its diagnostic black central belly stripe is reliably detected (lacking in White-bellied, as a rule). Other differences from Black-bellied are detailed under the latter. In the case of dark White-bellied (nominate *grallaria*), dark feathers are usually concentrated on body-sides rather than across middle as in Black-bellied, and they are also distinguished by their mainly dark upperparts, sometimes with highly restricted white rump. Nevertheless, the two species only occur locally in sympatry: White-bellied very rarely penetrates cooler subantarctic waters, whilst Black-bellied is principally found in Antarctic and subantarctic waters, but reaches subtropical waters in the non-breeding season. Separation from Black-bellied of the white-bellied *melanoleuca* (on Gough) has apparently never been attempted at sea and it seems doubtful if such birds could be reliably identified. Compare also Grey-backed and New Zealand Storm-petrels.

Distribution and biology
Distribution, movements and population: Indian Ocean on St Paul and formerly on Amsterdam; New Zealand on Admiralty, Lord Howe group and Kermadec; S Pacific Ocean on Rapa and Juan Fernández; and S Atlantic Ocean (Tristan da Cunha and Gough). Disperses at sea north to Samoa, Marquesas and Galápagos, Brazil and W and S Africa. Insufficient data to attempt overall population estimate.
Diet and feeding: Cephalopods and crustaceans taken by dipping and pattering. Follows ships and sometimes congregates with gadfly petrels, shearwaters and boobies to exploit food source.
Social behaviour: Very poorly known. Colonial, but not particularly gregarious and visits land principally at night (though frequent in day at colonies on Inaccessible). No other information.
Breeding biology: Breeds in shallow burrows with lining of plant material, in flat or sloping, grass-covered ground, or among loose rocks. Lays one white egg almost covered with spots, in Jan–Mar. No information on incubation or fledging periods, number of broods or detailed knowledge of parental roles, though presumably similar to close relatives.
Conservation Not globally threatened, although cats may predate ads, chicks and eggs on some islands (e.g. Lord Howe, where now extirpated), and skuas and Tristan Thrushes *Nesocichla eremita* exact a similar toll on Inaccessible I.

Possible White-bellied Storm-petrel Fregetta grallaria leucogaster, *showing many freshly moulted feathers with the species' characteristic broad white tips, and lack of clear feet projection. This bird showed an obvious white belly and was identified as White-bellied, but given lack of details concerning the potentially very similar white-bellied form of Black-bellied F. tropica* melanoleuca, *certain identification is impossible. Off Gough, Mar 2003. © Hadoram Shirihai.*

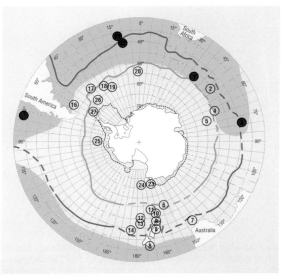

Prince Edward — St Paul — Tristan da Cunha — Gough

Taxonomy Marked geographical variation with four subspecies recognized: nominate *grallaria* on Admiralty, Lord Howe group and Kermadec; *leucogaster* on St Paul, Amsterdam and the Tristan da Cunha group, including Gough; *segethi* on the Juan Fernández; and *titan* on Rapa in the S Pacific. Taxonomic status of (some perhaps specifically distinct) and relationship with *F. tropica* unresolved. Larger *leucogaster* is closer in biometrics to Black-bellied, whilst *titan* is almost as large as Polynesian Storm-petrel *Nesofregetta fuliginosa* and is also much more heavily mottled white above (when fresh). Nominate on Lord Howe is polymorphic with pale, intermediate and dark birds, whilst in Kermadec group mostly pale and few intermediates are found. See also taxonomic note under *F. tropica*.

Black-bellied Storm-petrel
Fregetta tropica Plate 12

Identification

Confusion risks: White-bellied Storm-petrel *F. grallaria*.
Main characters: Medium to large and well-built, but rather compact/small-looking storm-petrel (size at sea never appears as large as measurements suggest), with rounded wings and square-ended, relatively short tail. Blackish-brown head, neck and upperparts, including tail, and distinct white rump and belly, with variable black vent and central belly stripe. Variation in white underparts includes those with well-pronounced, but always ragged black central mark, connecting black throat/breast to vent/undertail-coverts, but even in most-extensively black-bellied birds this is difficult to see or invisible at sea, and it is claimed that some are entirely white-bellied, like White-bellied Storm-petrel (but see below). Most upperwing-coverts browner than blackish remiges, but also some pale fringes to scapulars and tips of greater upperwing-coverts (mainly when fresh), which appear as indistinct panels. Underwing has rather limited white at centre, bordered by broad dark area on remiges and broad leading edge. Bill and legs black, latter projecting well beyond tail. Flight typically erratic and zigzagging, as repeatedly drags feet or 'bounds' off water, while rocking from side to side, on shallow wingbeats and very low. **Age/seasonal variation** indistinct; juv as ad.
Voice: Presumably mostly silent at sea. At colonies mainly high-

Black-bellied Storm-petrel Fregetta tropica. *These photos illustrate how the black belly patch can be very difficult to detect in the field, even in full profile view. Often, prolonged view are required to correctly evaluate this feature. Off South Georgia, Mar 2006. © Hadoram Shirihai.*

pitched whistle *huuuuu* or softer sequence of repeated *pip-pip-pip-pip* calls.
Size: 20 cm, wing 15.4–18.3 cm, wingspan 45–46 cm, weight 43–63 g. Extensive overlap in mensural data between sexes, but females tend to have longer wings and tail.
Similar species: Separation from White-bellied Storm-petrel is main issue. Black-bellied has diagnostic black central belly stripe, and in most cases this character is reliable, but on many this is difficult to detect or sufficiently narrow (and consequently hard to see) that they appear white-bellied. Additional characteristics may be used under certain conditions. Black-bellied usually appears longer legged, the feet distinctly projecting beyond tail, but this varies individually and is, in general, very difficult to observe at sea; remember that some Black-bellied lack any projection and are thus inseparable on this character from White-bellied. Except in the case of larger races of White-bellied, the characteristic bulky

Black-bellied Storm-petrel Fregetta tropica. *The right-hand bird is a classic individual, with diagnostic clear and broad black belly patch enabling ready identification. In contrast, the left-hand bird has much-reduced black (appearing as a very narrow, faint stripe), which can be very difficult to detect at sea. These images also demonstrate the clear (albeit individually variable) foot projection, extensive black chest (reaching lower on breast, below the level of the black leading edge to the underwing), and characteristic bulky and flat-headed appearance of* Fregetta *(which is especially pronounced in Black-bellied). Note dirty underwing-coverts with distal 'hook' formed by dark centres to greater and median primary-coverts. Off South Georgia, Mar 2006. © Hadoram Shirihai.*

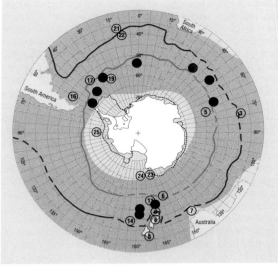

Black-bellied Storm-petrel Fregetta tropica *in fresh plumage has pale fringes to mantle, scapulars and back, but these are much narrower and less distinct compared to equivalent-plumaged White-bellied* F. grallaria. *Thus, in general, upperparts appear darker and wing-panels more contrasting and warmer brown than in White-bellied, but with wear these differences are reduced, and always difficult to detect at sea. Note lack of foot projection (on some the projection is much reduced or the legs may temporarily be concealed by the tail), making separation from White-bellied impossible using this character alone. Off South Georgia, Mar 2006. © Hadoram Shirihai.*

Prince Edward	Bounty
Crozet	South Georgia
Kerguelen	Bouvetøya
Auckland	South Orkney
Antipodes	South Shetland

and flat-headed appearance of *Fregetta* is often more pronounced in Black-bellied. Mantle, back and upperwing generally darker and warmer brown in Black-bellied, and paler and greyer in White-bellied; in general the pale upperwing bar is more contrasting in Black-bellied, but much overlap and effect of wear must be considered. In equivalent fresh plumage, Black-bellied has less extensive and distinctly narrower white tips to mantle, back, scapulars and upperwing-coverts, but these can be very pronounced in White-bellied (albeit with much individual, wear-induced and geographical variation). Also, border to black hood is slightly lower on breast than White-bellied and the demarcation is usually slightly more diffuse and smudgy. The white underwing-coverts tend to be smudged darker (almost always with dark distal 'hook' formed by dark centres to greater and median primary-coverts, which is apparently reduced or lacking in White-bellied). Chin/throat of Black-bellied often whitish (reduced or lacking in White-bellied), but much overlap. Observers should also note that on Gough there is reputedly a population of Black-bellied with white bellies and it is unknown how these can be separated from White-bellied, but fortunately such birds are apparently quite rare. On the other hand, White-bellied has dark and intermediate morphs, but these apparently mostly occur outside our region and can be distinguished by their mainly dark upperparts, sometimes with a highly restricted white rump. Especially in areas (and seasons) when both species can occur, some problematic birds or those seen poorly, are best left unidentified. Fortunately, in much of south of our region only Black-bellied occurs, and any White-bellied-like bird is almost certainly a Black-bellied. Separation from New Zealand Storm-petrel dealt with under latter.

Distribution and biology

Distribution, movements and population: Southern Ocean on South Georgia, South Orkney, South Shetland, Bouvetøya, Prince Edward (and perhaps formerly Marion), Crozet (East), Kerguelen,

Auckland, Bounty and Antipodes, at sea ranging north to Brazil, W Africa, Bay of Bengal, Australia, Coral Sea, Solomons and S Polynesia. Insufficient population data available to attempt overall estimate of numbers.

Diet and feeding: Surface plankton, small fish and pelagic crustaceans taken by dipping and pattering and surface-seizing. Rarely follows ships and most feeding probably nocturnal.

Social behaviour: Gregarious in small parties at sea and in larger groups close to breeding colonies. Monogamous and pair-bonds sustained. Strictly nocturnal visits to land. Territorial around burrow entrance.

Breeding biology: Breeds in slight and usually unlined depression in stable screes, among broken rocks and in burrows up to 50 cm long. Lays one white egg spotted at broad end, in Dec–Feb, incubated 35–44 days. Chicks fledge at 65–71 days. Both parents take full role in breeding cycle.

Conservation Not globally threatened, although cats and rats may predate ads, chicks and eggs on some islands, and late thaw in subantarctic breeding areas may delay or prevent nesting, while late snowfalls may block nesting cavities and lead to chick starvation.

Taxonomy Nominate *tropica* virtually throughout range, with white-bellied *melanoleuca* on Gough, though its status is presently unclear and this form has also been included within *F. grallaria*. Variation within *F. t. melanoleuca* and *F. g. leucogaster* and their relationship on Gough are wholly unknown, and until these issues are resolved the identification of the two species in the Atlantic, especially around Tristan and Gough, will remain troublesome.

New Zealand Storm-petrel
Pealeornis maoriana   Plate 12

Identification

Confusion risks: Black-bellied, White-bellied and Wilson's Storm-petrels.

Main characters: Smallish to mid-sized storm-petrel, mostly dark above with bold white rump, and whitish belly and underwing-coverts. Rather long-legged but tail rather short and square-ended, thus feet visibly project well beyond tail in optimal views. Superficially, shape more like Wilson's (also wings comparatively narrow and pointed) and plumage nearer Black-bellied. Head to chest and upperparts dark sooty-brown, with inconspicuous pale carpal bar. Body (below lower breast) mostly white and uniquely patterned with dark blotchy linear streaks, most intense on lower breast, flanks and thighs (the chief diagnostic at sea). On birds that are quite heavily streaked, the pattern can form two lateral lines either side of the central belly, but in others streaks less extensive and narrower, or mostly confined to lower breast and upper flanks. Underwing-coverts mostly white with broad dark leading edge, dark remiges and dark smudges on centres of coverts, especially primary-coverts; undertail-coverts dark with white tips. Bill, legs and feet black. Generally, flight and foraging much like Wilson's. In calm to moderate seas, flight hirundine-like, the wingbeats rapid and interspersed by quite long glides (wings normally held with trailing edge relatively straight), interspersed with a few short bounces. Usually low over surface, and less erratic or buoyant than Wilson's, but may temporarily make rapid changes of direction, especially when feeding. **Age/seasonal variation** Juv assumed to be like ad. Carpal bar appears to become more prominent with wear.

Voice: No data, but probably mainly silent at sea.

Size: (four birds in Hauraki Gulf) overall length c.18 cm, wing c.15 cm, wingspan c.38 cm, weight c.33 g (per the observers listed below; see Stephenson *et al.* in prep). No data concerning sexual differences, but overlap as in other storm-petrels possible.

Similar species: Black-bellied and White-bellied Storm-petrels have white underparts below breast level, and white rump. Both could resemble New Zealand Storm-petrel in poor views,

especially the darker-bellied form of White-bellied and paler-bellied examples of Black-bellied (geographical variation in both is complex). However, given optimal views both should be readily eliminated by New Zealand Storm-petrel's combination of smaller size, clearly streaked underparts and very different body proportions, including longer foot projection. Generally, the streaks on New Zealand Storm-petrel are concentrated on breast and flanks, rather than in dark area across central belly as in Black-bellied. Darker forms of the polymorphic White-bellied Storm-petrel (Lord Howe and, to some extent, Kermadec Is) are highly variable, and some possess fine streaking on body-sides (per. obs.). Black-bellied and, especially, White-bellied Storm-petrels usually possess some white fringes to dark tracts above, most noticeable when plumage fresh, unlike New Zealand Storm-petrel. With experience, jizz and foraging behaviour also differ. Given good views of underparts and white underwing-coverts, also readily separated from Wilson's, but note that variation in latter includes some with a whiter, smudged darker, lower belly and paler underwing-coverts, though never to extent to create confusion. Wilson's also has yellow webs to feet which New Zealand lacks. (In Hauraki Gulf, New Zealand, in Mar–Apr and Nov–Dec, Wilson's and New Zealand Storm-petrels observed together, sometimes side by side.) During chumming at this locality, also frequently observed feeding near White-faced Storm-petrel and, rarely, in same area as Grey-backed Storm-petrel, but both are readily eliminated by size and plumage differences.

Distribution and biology

Distribution, movements and population: Prior to its recent rediscovery known from only three 19th-century specimens collected (1827 and c.1895) off North I, New Zealand: the type specimen

New Zealand Pealeornis maoriana (*right*) and White-faced Storm-petrels Pelagodroma marina *in almost 'crane-like dance' posture while feeding on surface. In summer the recently rediscovered New Zealand Storm-petrel has been attracted to chum slicks, where it often joins large gatherings of the abundant White-faced Storm-petrel. White belly has unique dark blotchy linear streaks, most intense on sides, whilst the white underwing-coverts have a broad dark leading edge and the upper wing surface is almost uniform or shows an inconspicuous pale carpal bar. Hauraki Gulf, North I, New Zealand, Jan 2006. © Hadoram Shirihai.*

New Zealand Storm-petrel Pealeornis maoriana *skims the water surface, dragging its feet or 'bounding' forward. Note species' diagnostic dark streaking on underparts. Hauraki Gulf, North I, New Zealand, Jan 2005. © Hadoram Shirihai.*

The recently rediscovered New Zealand Storm-petrel Pealeornis maoriana *is small with well-streaked underparts and very 'different' structure, including long foot projection beyond tail tip; also note white underwing-coverts with broad dark leading edge, which makes species unmistakable if seen well. In this heavily streaked individual, the flank streaks appear as lateral lines either side of the cleaner central belly. Off Little Barrier I, North I, New Zealand, Nov 2003. © Bryan Thomas.*

held in Tring, and two in Paris. Subsequent authors considered these to represent a pale morph of Wilson's Storm-petrel and until 2003 *P. maoriana* was thought to be an extinct race of the latter. On 25 January 2003, off Coromandel Peninsula, North I, New Zealand, S. Saville & B. Stephenson rediscovered the species; they photographed a bird with odd characters which they originally identified as Black-bellied Storm-petrel. Subsequently, on the advice of Alan Tennyson of Te Papa/Museum of New Zealand, they concluded that the bird was closest to *P. maoriana* (Saville *et al.* 2003). The following summer, B. Flood & B. Thomas documented 10–20 similar storm-petrels on 17 Nov 2003 off Little Barrier I, New Zealand (Flood 2003), supporting the hypothesis that a relict population of New Zealand Storm-petrel survived. Over the following four summers K. Baird & C. Gaskin made over 70 excursions to study the birds in detail (Gaskin & Baird 2005), finding that the species is summer visitor, Oct–Apr, to the outer Hauraki Gulf, over the continental shelf edge, off North I, with counts of up to c.20. In collaboration with the Dept. of Conservation (DOC), New Zealand, Baird, Gaskin, M. Imber, Stephenson and others are conducting

a long-term study, to locate the breeding grounds and protect the potentially very small population. Outside the Hauraki Gulf there have been a few records off North Cape (once in late Mar, the rest in May). It is unknown to where the birds migrate from the Hauraki Gulf.

Diet and feeding: Birds attracted to boats using chum seen to feed near White-faced Strom-petrels, by dipping and pattering, as well as surface-seizing and shallow-plunging.

Social behaviour: Apparently mostly found alone, only gathering in small dispersed groups at food sources.

Breeding biology: Wholly unknown.

Conservation Critically Endangered. Seemingly very rare and probably highly threatened. Locating the breeding grounds and protecting these from human disturbance and alien predators are essential for the species' continued survival.

Taxonomy Morphologically those birds observed at sea match the three specimens and suggest that New Zealand Storm-petrel is a highly distinctive species, probably even meritorious of the monospecific genus, *Pealeornis,* it was originally awarded, a hypothesis also supported by its mallophaga (feather lice). Molecular analysis of captured birds is in progress.

Common Diving-petrel
Pelecanoides urinatrix Plate 12

Identification

Confusion risks: South Georgian Diving-petrel *P. georgicus*.

Main characters: Small, dumpy rather auklet-like petrel, dusky white below and blackish above, with mostly black bill and blue legs and feet. Usually inseparable from South Georgian Diving-petrel, as they differ in rather subtle characters that are inconsistent across range (especially present species which exhibits greater degree of geographical variation), and are very difficult or impossible to evaluate due to their fast flight and typical sea conditions. The following features broadly characterize the species in much of range, with emphasis on potential differences from South Georgian. When fresh, variable whitish scapular tips form ragged whitish stripe on either side of back, and fringes and trailing edge to secondaries usually (but not always) narrow and indistinct,

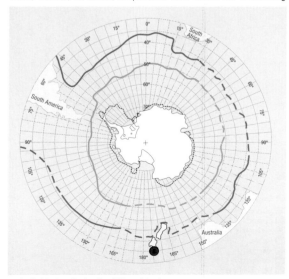

● Probably New Zealand's offshore islands
(Oct–Apr, but breeding grounds unknown)

Fresh-plumaged Common Diving-petrel Pelecanoides u. urinatrix (or chathamensis), showing species' characteristic quite large and bulky build, dusky underwing, extensively greyish-washed and mottled body-sides, and well-developed dusky half-collar. Head-sides rather uniform, with indistinct pale supercilium or extension onto neck-/rear head-sides, and lower border of dark ear-coverts diffuse and often appears to merge with dirty throat. Note rather noticeable foot projection beyond tail. Off North I, New Zealand, Sep 2003. © Hadoram Shirihai.

appearing obscured or invisible. Most appear quite dusky on underwing, with less white on underwing-coverts and bases/inner webs of remiges. However, some birds and populations tend to have paler or whiter underwings. Overall coloration of underwing also often affected by angle of view and light (see photos). Many (not all) tend to have extensive greyish-washed, mottled body-sides, extending as diffuse dusky half-collar on breast-sides (highly variable in extent). Head-sides less strongly patterned and appear overall dusky-tinged: pale grey crescents extend indistinctly onto neck- and rear head-sides, being usually concolorous with mid grey supercilium, offering indistinct contrast with darker crown and ear-coverts. Lower border of dark ear-coverts tends to be diffuse and often appears to merge with dirty throat. Larger

Identification pitfall in diving-petrels: fresh-plumaged Common Diving-petrel Pelecanoides urinatrix exsul; in bright sunlight, the pale face marks and white underparts are exaggerated, appearing superficially more like South Georgian Diving-petrel. Note Common's characteristically strong build, large thick bill, and lack of contrast between white crescent-shaped neck-sides and pale grey supercilium (as often shown by South Georgian). It lacks white scapular tips/ lines and has only thin whitish trailing edge to secondaries, as well as some mottling on flanks and apparently clear foot projection beyond tail tip, which together suggest Common. Off Crozet Is, Mar 2004. © Hadoram Shirihai.

and more heavily built than *georgicus*, but all above-mentioned characters difficult to reliably judge at sea, and subject to significant individual variation. Common tends to trail feet behind tail (especially noticeable on take-off). Flight typically direct on very whirring, short wings, bursting, quail-like, from surface and keeping low before plunging back to water. On water, somewhat like miniature penguin, the body quite high above the surface, but due to small size often hard to detect at rest. Capable of 'flying' underwater, using wings as flippers. **Age/seasonal variation** indistinct, but wears and bleaches browner above with reduced pale fringes, and becomes white below; juv as ad.

Voice: Not heard at sea. At colonies, mainly a rythmically repeated, double cooing or mewing note, *whooee-wihip*, quite different from South Georgian.

Size: 20–25 cm, wing 11.2–13.7 cm, wingspan 33–38 cm, weight 96–185 g. Significant overlap between sexes in mensural data, but in most populations (except *exsul*) males have longer wings.

Similar species: Partially separable by range from South Georgian, but where sympatric probably inseparable at sea except by using combination of plumage features, and if dealing with typical birds in optimal conditions at close range. In the hand usually separable by lack of black rear edge to tarsus, different bill shape/structure and measurements (for details and pitfalls, both at sea and in hand, see South Georgian). Compare also Magellanic Diving-petrel.

Distribution and biology

Distribution, movements and population: *P. u. urinatrix* occurs off SE Australia, off North I, in Cook Strait and Solander I (New Zealand), Snares and Chatham, and also S Atlantic on Tristan da Cunha group and probably islands along Pacific coast of S Chile. *P. u. berard* occurs in the Falklands and *P. u. exsul* in Southern Ocean on South Georgia, Marion, Crozet (Possession), Kerguelen,

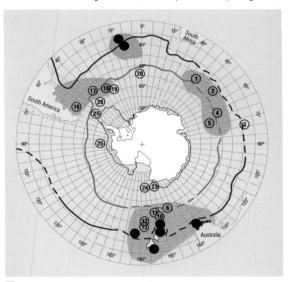

■ Common Diving-petrel *Pelacanoides [u.] urinatrix*
▨ Common Diving-petrel *Pelacanoides [u.] berard*
▨ Common Diving-petrel *Pelacanoides [u.] exsul*

① Marion	⑩ Auckland
② Crozet	⑪ Campbell
④ Kerguelen	⑫ Antipodes
⑤ Heard	⬤ Chatham
⑥ Macquarie	⑯ Falklands
⬤ Tasmania	⑱ South Georgia
⬤ New Zealand's	⬤ Tristan da Cunha
offshore islands	⬤ Gough
⬤ Snares	

Fresh-plumaged Common Diving-petrels Pelecanoides u. urinatrix, *showing individual variation in underwing coloration, and degree of greyish wash and mottling on body-sides (left bird noticeably paler, exaggerated by viewing angle and stronger light). Both have clearly less patterned head-sides, and the feet project beyond tail. Off South I, New Zealand, Jan 2007. © Hadoram Shirihai.*

Heard, Macquarie, Auckland, Campbell and Antipodes. All races range at sea in waters near breeding grounds. Overall population certainly several million pairs.

Diet and feeding: Mostly marine crustaceans taken by pursuit-diving and pursuit-plunging.

Social behaviour: Colonial and gregarious when breeding, but no information from feeding areas. Monogamous and pair-bonds sustained.

Breeding biology: Breeds in burrows, 0.25–1.5 m long, or crevices within screes, flat or sloping, sparsely vegetated ground, or among dense grass or roots. Lays one white egg in Jul–Dec (highly protracted season varies across range), incubated 53 days (only one dataset). Chicks fledge in 45–59 days. Single-brooded, although it appears possible that replacement clutches may be attempted. Both sexes incubate and provision young.

Conservation Not globally threatened, with most populations stable, some in decline. Cats and rats have taken a heavy toll on ads, chicks and eggs on some islands, causing extirpation of population on Marion, widespread decline in Chatham group, and

Identification pitfall in diving-petrels: Common Diving-petrel Pelecanoides urinatrix. *This bird, photographed off Stewart I, New Zealand, where Common is abundant and South Georgian* P. georgicus *apparently very rare, was originally suspected to be the latter due to the clear white scapular lines, quite extensive white fringes to upperwing-coverts and mostly white underwings and underparts, but it also has a quite well-developed dusky half-collar, duskier head with indistinct pale neck-sides and supercilium, heavier build and bill, and feet projecting beyond tail, all of which strongly suggest Common. The photo demonstrates the degree of overlap and that some Common can develop quite substantial white scapular lines and whiter underwings. In many instances, such birds with apparently mixed characters are best left unidentified. © Hadoram Shirihai.*

substantially reducing and restricting that on Macquarie. Natural predators include Short-eared Owl *Asio flammeus* and Peregrine Falcon *Falco peregrinus* on the Falklands. Cattle and sheep may also trample burrows and nesting habitat.

Taxonomy Six subspecies, of which three may perhaps warrant separation as allospecies, though some subtle forms are probably best regarded as synonyms: nominate, including poorly differentiated *coppingeri* (probably on islands off S Chile) and smaller *chathamensis* (on Snares, Chatham, Solander and islets off Stewart I, New Zealand); *exsul*, including poorly differentiated *dacunhae* (Tristan da Cunha and Gough), which may be best united with nominate; and *berard*. More information on their relationships and comparative museum studies of these forms are required.

South Georgian Diving-petrel
Pelecanoides georgicus   Plate 12

Identification

Confusion risks: Common Diving-petrel *P. urinatrix.*

Main characters: Small, dumpy rather auklet-like petrel, predominantly white below and dark above, with black bill and blue legs and feet (black line to rear edge of tarsus diagnostic). Typical individuals appear smaller and paler/whiter than Common Diving-petrel, but cannot usually be safely separated at sea. Several subtle, and somewhat inconsistent, plumage features are useful. When fresh, slate-black dorsal area has variable white scapular tips, typically coalescing to form broad lines either side of back, with quite pronounced broad white fringes and trailing edge to secondaries. Underwing usually appears overall whitish or greyish-white, less dusky, with whiter underwing-coverts and bases/inner webs to remiges than Common. South Georgian tends also to be cleaner/whiter on body-sides and breast, whilst head is overall, more open-faced (less dusky) and more strongly patterned. Neck-/rear head-sides paler, usually whiter than pale grey supercilium, and both appear sharply delimited from well-defined dark crown and ear-coverts patch; throat also usually purer white and tends to be sharply separated from lower border of ear-coverts. But, remember, these characteristics are all very difficult to evaluate at sea. **Age/seasonal variation** indistinct, but wears and bleaches browner and greyer above, with much-reduced pale fringes to scapulars and secondaries, and even whiter on body-sides; juv as ad.

Voice: Not heard at sea. At colonies mainly reported as a varying series of squeaked call-notes; limited information from across range, but some variation reported.

Size: 18–22 cm, wing 10.9–12.5 cm, wingspan 32 cm, weight

South Georgian Diving-petrel Pelecanoides georgicus *in fresh plumage, showing distinct white scapular lines, clear white fringes and trailing edge to secondaries, extensively white underwing and underparts with virtually no dusky half-collar on breast-sides, well-patterned face with distinctly paler neck-sides and supercilium sharply delimited from very dark crown and ear-coverts, the latter demarcated from whiter throat. Feet do not obviously project beyond tail. Off South Georgia, Mar 2006. © Hadoram Shirihai.*

90–150 g. Females probably slightly larger than males, but comparatively few data.
Similar species: At sea South Georgian is often not reliably separable from Common, unless views optimal and full suite of characters observed (and best confirmed from photos). The following lists features to focus on, followed by those features useful in the hand. Separation at sea: typical South Georgian shows combination of broad white scapular lines and relatively broad white trailing edge to secondaries; purer white underwings and almost pure white body-sides with very restricted and obscure dusky wash to upper-breast-sides. Should also exhibit clear-cut face pattern of whiter neck-sides, merging or contrasting with pale grey supercilium, both sharply delimited from dark crown and ear-coverts, and latter sharply distinct from purer white throat. A clear-cut example of Common has strongly reduced or lacks white scapular lines and trailing edge to secondaries, as well as duskier and ill-defined face pattern, and extensive dark wash to underwings and body-sides, forming pronounced breast-side patches. With experience, South Georgian appears relatively smaller and more compact with smaller/thinner bill. It also may appear to have shorter or lack foot projection beyond tail (often obvious in Common, but variation renders feature of little use). Birds with mixed features or lacking complete set of classic characteris probably best left unidentified

South Georgian Diving-petrel Pelecanoides georgicus. *Note rather strongly marked face pattern, with white throat and crescent-shaped neck-sides (contrasting with pale grey supercilium), sharply separated from dark crown and ear-coverts. Some South Georgian develop quite substantial (albeit variable) dark patches on uppermost flanks just below basal forewing base, but apparently never to extent of many Common. Rest of underparts rather pure white and pale underwing also typical, and note smallish, dainty and narrow-billed appearance, with small foot projection. White scapular lines and fringes to secondaries appear only moderately developed. Off South Georgia, Mar 2006. © Hadoram Shirihai.*

in most cases. A major pitfall is that some Common Diving-petrels have paler/whiter underwings and body-sides, and at certain angles and in some lights they appear substantially but superficially whiter below (especially in low-angle sunlight late in day). Bear in mind that some Common have quite substantial white tips to scapulars, whilst these can be much reduced through wear in South Georgian. Separation in the hand: quite frequently birds attracted at night to lights on vessels can be identified by many of the described above, but other features should be checked (see Murphy & Harper 1921, Payne & Prince 1978, and *HANZAB*). In much of range at least in ads, South Georgian has diagnostic black line to rear edge of tarsus (lacking in Common), but chicks of latter in South Georgia reportedly have black hind tarsus which may be retained post-fledging, whilst this feature may be indistinct in some South Georgian on Codfish I, New Zealand. South Georgian has different bill shape/structure and measurements. Note much smaller, less deep but relatively broader based bill (bill depth 5.0–5.7 mm, compared to 6.0–7.3 mm in Common, but southern populations of latter reportedly overlap with *georgicus*), and relatively shorter nostril with paraseptal processes in centre (rather than rear) of nostril, whilst viewed from underside, is more triangular with straighter lower border to gular patch. The bill edges also taper gradually towards the tip, converging into 'Gothic' arch at tip, and bill generally finer with broader base (in Common edges more parallel but converge sharply at tip). Averages smaller than Common Diving-petrel (see Size), but much overlap, at least in some populations.

Distribution and biology

Distribution, movements and population: Southern Ocean on South Georgia, Marion, Crozet, Kerguelen, Heard, Auckland, and possibly Macquarie. At sea remains in vicinity of breeding grounds, rarely north to SE Australia. Overall population totals several million pairs.
Diet and feeding: Cephalopods, marine crustaceans and some small fish taken by pursuit-diving, surface-diving, surface-seizing and pursuit-plunging. In one study at S Georgia, *georgicus* fed mainly on euphausids, *urinatrix* on copepods.
Social behaviour: Almost unknown. Colonial, but not particularly

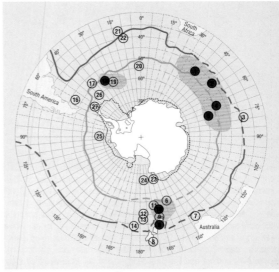

● Prince Edward & Marion
● Crozet
● Kerguelen
● Heard
● New Zealand offshore
  island (Codfish I)
● Auckland
● South Georgia

gregarious, especially at sea. Calls in flight, unlike *urinatrix*. No other information.

Breeding biology: Breeds in burrows, 0.3–1.7 m long without lining, or crevices within fine screes, flat or sloping, sparsely vegetated ground, or among grass hummocks. Lays one white egg in Oct–Dec, incubated 44–52 days. Chicks fledge in 43–60 days. Single-brooded. Both sexes incubate and provision young.

Conservation Not globally threatened, though skuas, cats, rats and Weka *Gallirallus australis* predate ads, chicks and eggs on some islands, and colony on Auckland was extirpated by sea lions. Cattle and sheep may also trample burrows.

Taxonomy Monotypic.

Magellanic Diving-petrel
Pelecanoides magellani   Plate 12

Identification

Confusion risks: Common Diving-petrel *P. urinatrix* (in the Falklands). *Main characters*: Small, dumpy rather auklet-like petrel, entirely white below with blackish upperparts and diagnostic broad white half-collar from neck to rear head-sides (just behind dark ear-coverts), in some even to edge of hindcrown. Scapulars and secondaries tipped white, forming clear diagonal shoulder stripe, and narrow white trailing edge visible in flight. Unless heavily worn, these plumage characters are exhibited by most individuals, but whitish markings on black upperparts often obscured in juv (or by feather wear). Black bill and blue legs and feet. Other characters include mainly white underwing-coverts and whitish-grey bases/inner webs to remiges, and relatively whiter body-sides and foreneck, with hardly any greyish wash or mottling to breast. Averages smaller and slighter than other *Pelecanoides*, but these and the above-mentioned characters are difficult to judge at sea, if not seen well, close to and in good light. Flight typically direct and whirring, but on proportionately slightly longer wings, and always very close to surface; swims low, like miniature penguin. **Age/seasonal variation** indistinct; juv as ad, but more uniform, with only limited whitish on black dorsal parts. With wear bleaches browner above with much-reduced whitish fringes to scapulars.

Voice: Not heard at sea, and apparently no published vocalization data from colonies.

Magellanic Diving-Petrel Pelecanoides magellani *in typical escape-flight. Even from behind the diagnostic white patch on neck-sides to edge of hindcrown is visible. Also note characteristic black-and-white appearance. On this individual the white scapular lines are virtually lacking. Off Ushuaia, S Argentina, Mar 2006. © Hadoram Shirihai.*

Size: 20–23 cm, wing 12.0–13.3 cm, wingspan 32 cm, no weight data. Extensive overlap in mensural data between sexes, but too few datasets to draw firm conclusions.

Similar species: Separable at close range from all other *Pelecanoides* (but principally Common Diving-petrel, which is the main, if not the only, species that is likely to cause confusion in our region) by extensive white half-collar behind dark ear-coverts.

Distribution and biology

Distribution, movements and population: Islands off S South America in Tierra del Fuego region, ranging at sea north along Chilean and Argentine coasts, and to the Falklands. Regarded as common, but no published population estimates.

Diet and feeding: Cephalopods, marine crustaceans and small fish taken by pursuit-diving and pursuit-plunging.

Social behaviour: Almost unknown. Colonial, but not particularly gregarious (especially at sea). No other information.

Breeding biology: Very few data. Breeds in burrows or crevices within fine screes, hill slopes and cliffs. Lays one white egg in Nov–Dec. Incubation and fledging periods unknown. Presumably single-brooded, and both sexes probably incubate and provision the young as in congenerics.

Conservation Not globally threatened.

Taxonomy Monotypic.

Magellanic Diving-petrel Pelecanoides magellani *differs quite distinctly from the other two diving-petrels in our region. Especially note diagnostic white patch on neck to rear head-sides that even extends slightly onto edge of hindcrown. Also characteristic are the clean white underparts and underwing, sharply contrasting with the blackish upperparts. Off Ushuaia, S Argentina, Mar 2006. © Hadoram Shirihai.*

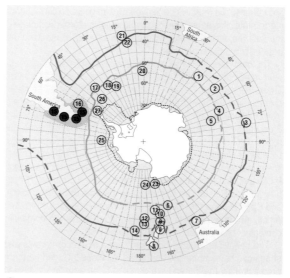

● South American offshore islands

Cormorants and shags

Cormorants and shags of the Southern Ocean

Plates 13–14 cover the distinctive, aquatic-adapted genus, *Phalacrocorax* (sometimes subdivided into other genera/subgenera), the cormorants and shags, of which only the purely marine and insular representatives in our region, from Antarctica north to c.45°S, are included. A few continental coastal species (see below), e.g. Rock Shag *P. magellanicus*, are also included if they occur regularly on a subantarctic island or the Falklands. Most forms depicted in Plate 13 belong to a distinctive group representing the superspecies *P. [atriceps]*, which occurs in the Atlantic and Indian Oceans (with the exception of Macquarie Shag *P. [a.] purpurascens*). All were variously considered forms of 1–2 species, under Imperial Shag and/or using the names King/Blue-eyed Shag (e.g. Harrison 1983), but have recently been treated more expansively (e.g. *HANZAB* 1990, Sibley & Monroe 1990). Here, I tend to follow a more 'flexible' arrangement, describing each distinctive taxon in detail and recognizing them as separate allospecies.

There is a case for recognizing three major subgroups, with the first, atriceps (consisting of two races/morphs, white-faced *atriceps* and black-faced *albiventer*) of South America and the Falklands, mostly frequenting areas from c.54°S north, the second, a white-faced subgroup comprising *georgianus* (South Georgia), *bransfieldensis* (Antarctic Peninsula) and *nivalis* (Heard) in southern cold waters mostly from 54°S south, and the third, in the subantarctic Indian Ocean, consisting of *melanogenis*, *verrucosus* and (Macquarie) *purpurascens* (roughly between 46°S and 54°S). Distinctions between these groups are very arbitrary, and further complicated by *verrucosus* being clearly different from *melanogenis* and *purpurascens*, which in turn exhibit certain affinities with *nivalis* and could, alternatively, be united within an expanded *atriceps/albiventer* group, leaving only *verrucosus*, *georgianus*, *bransfieldensis* as justifiably distinct.

The combination of amount of white on head-sides, upper back and forewing-coverts, and sometimes that on the outer scapulars may be used to separate members of the *P. [atriceps]* complex (young tend to have face patterns similar to ads, but there is more overlap between taxa). It must be stressed that these characters are rather subtle (mainly due to overlap, with variation corresponding to state of breeding plumage and other factors). Fortunately, the vast majority of forms never come into contact, reducing the possibility of much confusion.

The other two distinctive groups, illustrated in Plate 14, also appear rather close to *P. [atriceps]*, but are treated separately here. These are the New Zealand *P. [campbelli]* (comprising *campbelli*, *colensoi* and *ranfurlyi*) and Chatham Shags *P. [carunculatus]* onslowi, with the rest of the latter group, King *P. [c.] carunculatus* and Stewart/Bronze Shags *P. [c.] chalconotus*, breeding outside our region. Others also excluded, namely Spotted Shag *P. punctatus*, Little Black Cormorant *P. sulcirostris* and Black-faced Shag *P. fuscescens* of New Zealand/Australia, Neotropic Cormorant *P. brasilianus* (=Olivaceous Cormorant *P. olivaceus*), Guanay Cormorant *P. bougainvillii* and Red-legged Cormorant *P. gaimardi* of South America, and Cape *P. capensis* and Bank Cormorants *P. neglectus* of South Africa, also breed outside our region and are unlikely to come into contact, or be confused, with those treated here.

The behaviour, life and breeding cycles of the cormorants and shags can be summarized as follows. All those included here are predominately marine and are adapted to an aquatic life, having oil-gland feathers, plumage permeable underwater, swim and dive well, with well-developed webbed feet, strongly hooked bills, closed nostrils and a gular patch. Flight is powerful on broad wings. Most breed on offshore and remote islands, with those restricted to the latter in general apparently entirely sedentary. Diet is mostly small fish, crustaceans and cephalopods. They breed colonially, sometimes with other seabirds, herons etc., and use heaped nests of plant material, seaweed and debris. Well-developed advertising displays are described among males. Ads lay 1–7 oval pale-coloured eggs, incubated 4–5 weeks and chicks take 7–8 weeks to fledge but are usually dependent for another 8–12 weeks. Both ads take a full role in all aspects of the breeding cycle.

Recent reappraisals of the taxonomy of the groups included here has led to the recognition at specific level of several forms restricted to particular islands or island groups. Most of these have tiny populations and are considered globally threatened by BirdLife International (2000). Threats to such forms are those typical of insular taxa: predation by introduced mammals, competition with other bird species and marine mammals, and pressures associated with ecotourism etc. Fortunately, management plans and monitoring programmes are in place on a number of these islands, several of which also have protected status, which should enable these populations to remain stable or marginally increase, albeit at low levels.

Rock Shag *Phalacrocorax magellanicus*   Plate 13

Identification

Confusion risks: Unmistakable in range.
Main characters: Medium-sized distinctive marine shag. **Ad** easily identified by red facial skin (from bill base to around eye), otherwise mainly black, glossed green/violet, with lower breast and belly white, variably blotched black in some. In breeding season most have short black forehead crest, and head-sides and neck variably flecked white, usually as small white filoplumes on ear-coverts and some on upper foreneck (reduced with wear). Non-breeders duller and browner, with partially reduced white filoplumes and black forehead crest. Bill black and legs reddish. Eye-ring and iris largely red. Sexes similar except in size. Juv overall dark brown,

Ad Rock Shags Phalacrocorax magellanicus *at a nest in the Falklands, Jan 2001. Note variation in extent of white filoplumes on ear-coverts and upper foreneck. © Hadoram Shirihai.*

Plate 13 Shags of the Southern Ocean

Imperial Shag *atriceps*
ad. breeding
(p. 224)

Imperial Shag *albiventer*
ad. breeding

South Georgian Shag
ad. breeding
(p. 225)

Antarctic Shag
ad. breeding
(p. 226)

...ite-cheeked on
...inland South
...erica (as more
...thern forms)

Dark-cheeked
on Falklands
(and majority
lack white back
patch of most
atriceps)

Black-capped;
white on back
rather extensive

White cheeks not as high
and white back patch
limited in comparison with
similar Antarctic Shag

Macquarie Shag
ad. breeding
(p. 230)

Rock Shag
ad. breeding
(p. 222)

Small; red facial
skin and white
cheek patch

...nly lower part of
...eeks white; no
...hite on back

Heard Shag
ad. breeding
(p. 227)

Crozet Shag
ad. breeding
(p. 228)

Kerguelen Shag
ad. breeding
(p. 228)

Black-faced, with
limited white on
shoulders and none
on back

As South Georgian but
more extensive white on
back and shoulders

Most distinctive, being small and overall
darkest (black-faced; no or limited white on
shoulders and none on back)

In some ad Rock Shags Phalacrocorax magellanicus *the white underparts are variably blotched dark. Falklands, Jan 2005 © Klaus Bjerre.*

with slightly paler fringes, and has black facial skin, white throat and brownish legs; with age (imm) acquires white belly markings and faint indication of dull red facial skin patch and legs.
Voice: Chiefly a guttural *karrk*; in courtship utters a rapid rhythmic grunt *uk-uk-uk-uk* (Woods 1988).
Size: 66–71 cm, wing 23.3–25.8 cm, no weight data. Males average larger in most mensural data, particularly wing and tail lengths.
Similar species: None.

Distribution and biology

Distribution, movements and population: Coasts, cliffs and rocky shores of C Chile and SE Argentina south to Cape Horn, Staten I and the Falklands. Winters north to NE Argentina and Uruguay. Population estimated at 7,500 pairs in Patagonia, and 32,000–59,000 pairs in the Falklands in 1983–93.
Diet and feeding: Feeds alone or in pairs among kelp patches close inshore, taking small fish, crustaceans and cephalopods in relatively shallow water. Dives by jumping clear of water.
Social behaviour: Usually nests colonially and is also gregarious when roosting.

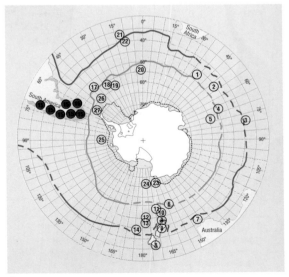

● South American offshore islands
◐ Falklands

Breeding biology: Nests, occasionally associated with Imperial Shag *P. [atriceps] atriceps*, are constructed of tussac grass, seaweed and other plant material. Lays 2–5 greenish-white eggs Nov–Dec, with fledglings leaving the nest in mid-Jan to late Feb.
Conservation Not globally threatened. Its widespread distribution should make it better able to withstand the impact of any environmental disasters.
Taxonomy Monotypic.

Imperial Shag
Phalacrocorax [atriceps] atriceps   Plate 13

Identification

Confusion risks: Unmistakable within range.
Main characters: Rather large black-and-white, blue-eyed marine shag. **Ad** breeding *'albiventer'* (Falklands) is pied, with black (glossed bluish and some green) upperparts including cheeks; demarcation between black and white on face arches across gape (not reaching eye level, leaving cheeks white, as in most *atriceps*); continuous white foreneck onto underparts; and variable white wing-covert bar, but almost invariably lacks white upper-back patch of most *atriceps*. Ragged white feathering on outer scapulars variable, in most as isolated white feathers or completely lacking. Rather long erectile crest, and variable number of white filoplumes (forming short supercilium) just above and behind eye present only during courtship or early stages of breeding (entire *P. [atriceps]* superspecies). Facial skin (gular and lores) mainly blackish-sooty, nasal caruncles ('knobs') yellow, eye-ring bright blue and irides dark reddish-brown; bill blackish-grey, and legs and feet dark pink. Sexes alike. Non-breeders lack crest and have faded/duller bare facial area, and white forewing patch reduced or lacking. **Juv** brown-and-white version of non-breeding

Ad Imperial Shag Phalacrocorax [atriceps] atriceps *(of the black-faced morph, sometimes recognized as albiventer), showing full display plumage of long erectile crest, white filoplumes behind eye and well-developed yellow 'knobs', Falklands. © Richard White/Falklands Conservation.*

Fresh juv Imperial Shag Phalacrocorax [atriceps] atriceps is a brown-and-white version of non-breeding ad; also note paler-fringed upper secondary-coverts. Off S Argentina, Mar 2006. © Hadoram Shirihai.

ad, lacks blue eye-ring and has dull facial skin, while bill is paler; tips of lesser and median coverts fringed paler, giving impression of vague wingbars when fresh. With age (**imm**) acquires patchy black feathering and (subsequently) faintly ad-like bare parts.
Voice: Chiefly a guttural *kork*, very noisy at colonies.
Size: 75 cm, wing 25.8–28.7 cm, no weight data. Males average larger in most mensural data, particularly wing and tail lengths.
Similar forms: All members of the complex, but does not overlap in range with any significant confusion species.

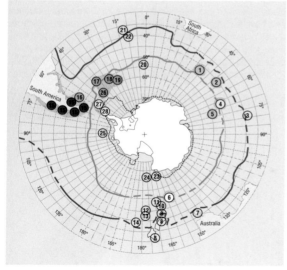

■ Imperial Shag *Phalocrocorax [a.] atriceps*
▨ Imperial Shag *Phalocrocorax [a.] atriceps* (form *albiventer*)
▨ South Georgian Shag *Phalocrocorax [a.] georgianus*
▨ Antarctic Shag *Phalocrocorax [a.] bransfieldensis*
▨ Heard Shag *Phalocrocorax [a.] nivalis*
▨ Crozet Shag *Phalocrocorax [a.] melanogenis*
▨ Kerguelen Shag *Phalocrocorax [a.] verrucosus*
▨ Macquarie Shag *Phalocrocorax [a.] purpurascens*

① Prince Edward & Marion ⑯ Falklands
② Crozet ⑰ Shag Rocks
④ Kerguelen ⑱ South Georgia
⑤ Heard ⑲ South Sandwich
⑥ Macquarie ㉖ South Orkney
● South American offshore ㉗ South Shetland
   islands ㉘ Antarctic Peninsula

Distribution and biology
Distribution, movements and population: Albiventer apparently restricted to the Falklands with 45,000–84,000 pairs estimated in 1983–93. Atriceps (and intermediates) breeds S Chile and S Argentina, inland in Neuquén and Río Negro, with population estimated at 40,000 pairs in Patagonia in the 1980s; during austral winter occurs north to Uruguay.
Diet and feeding: Mainly crustaceans and small fish caught by pursuit-diving. May travel some distance from shore to fish.
Social behaviour: Breeds in dense colonies and also gregarious at roosts and when feeding.
Breeding biology: Often breeds in close association with Rockhopper Penguin Eudyptes chrysocome and Black-browed Albatross Thalassarche [melanophrys] melanophrys on flat cliff tops. Nest a column of algae, mud and tussac grass, with lining of grass. Lays 2–4 pale green-blue eggs in Oct–Nov, incubated 28 days. Juvs usually fledge by mid-Feb.
Conservation Not globally threatened. Populations apparently stable and not significantly threatened by human activities. Commercially exploited prey species do not appear to be important within its diet.
Taxonomy The form *albiventer* is perhaps a morph of *P.* [*a.*] *atriceps*. *P.* [*a.*] *georgianus* and *P.* [*a.*] *bransfieldensis*, as well as *P.* [*a.*] *nivalis*, are often considered races of *atriceps*, though *bransfieldensis* may have been, or still is, sympatric with *atriceps* in extreme S South America (Siegel-Causey & Lefevre 1989, Condor 91: 408–415, in Sibley 1996). Other S Indian and Pacific Oceans forms and even groups (e.g. *P.* [*a.*] *verrucosus* and the *P.* [*carunculatus*]–*P.* [*campbelli*] complexes) are rather similar and may also belong to this assemblage. See group introduction and other species accounts.

South Georgian Shag
Phalacrocorax [atriceps] georgianus   Plate 13

Identification
Confusion risks: Unmistakable in range.
Main characters: Rather large, black-and-white, blue-eyed marine

Ad South Georgian Shag Phalacrocorax [atriceps] georgianus: demarcation between black and white on face is at eye level. The crest and white filoplumes behind the eye are usually lost rapidly. South Georgia, Jan 2001. © Hadoram Shirihai.

Younger imm South Georgian Shag Phalacrocorax [atriceps] georgianus. *Younger imms and juvs of the blue-eyed shag complex are generally alike, but usually possess the white/dark face pattern of the ads (though stilll best identified according to location). South Georgia, Jan 2001. © Hadoram Shirihai.*

shag. **Ad** breeding is pied, with black (glossed bluish/violet and oily green) upperparts (in some with restricted white upper back), including head and hindneck (appears dark-capped from behind), but not cheeks which are white, continuing onto foreneck and rest of underparts. Demarcation between black and white on face is at eye level or passes through upper ear-coverts. Rather long erectile crest. Also has variable (occasionally absent) white wing-covert patch, and usually a few isolated white feathers among outer scapulars. Eye-ring bright blue and iris dark reddish-brown; nasal caruncles ('knobs') yellow, bill pale greyish-black and bare facial skin (gular and lores) mainly blackish-sooty. Variable number of white filoplumes above and behind eye. Legs and feet dark pink. Sexes similar except in size. Non-breeders lack crest and have duller bare facial area, white forewing patch reduced or lacking, and are duller dorsally. **Juv** (and **imm**) mainly brown above and white below in early stages, and not reliably differentiated from same-age Imperial Shag *P. [a.] atriceps* (which see for further details).
Voice: Unstudied.
Size: 72–75 cm, wing 27.0–30.4 cm, weight 2.5–2.9 kg. Males average larger in most mensural data, particularly wing and tail lengths.
Similar forms: No other shag reported from South Georgia (see below).

Distribution and biology
Distribution, movements and population: Restricted to South Georgia, South Orkney and South Sandwich. Population subject to fluctuation, with perhaps up to 11,000 pairs.
Diet and feeding: Mainly fish caught by pursuit-diving, leaping clear of water.
Social behaviour: Monogamous, but most pair-bonds probably only last single season. Principally forages and roosts in small groups, and nests solitarily or colonially.
Breeding biology: Breeds on gentle tussac-grass slopes, building

truncated cone-shaped nests of dried kelp, grass and mud. Lays 2–3 greyish or bluish eggs in Nov–Dec, incubated by both sexes for 28–31 days. Chicks continuously brooded for 12–15 days, leave nest at two months and fledge at c.65 days.
Conservation Not globally threatened.
Taxonomy Monotypic. Forms superspecies with rest of Imperial Shag *P. [atriceps]* complex. Most closely related to *bransfieldensis* (Antarctic Peninsula) and especially similar to *nivalis* (Heard I). See also group introduction.

Antarctic Shag
Phalacrocorax [atriceps] bransfieldensis   Plate 13

Identification
Confusion risks: Unmistakable in range; no other blue-eyed shag overlaps with it.
Main characters: Rather large, black-and-white, blue-eyed shag of Antarctic Peninsula and nearby waters. **Ad** in breeding season pied, with black upperparts (glossed bluish and some green), but not including cheeks (entire ear-coverts), which are white reaching onto foreneck and rest of underparts. Demarcation between black and white on face arches across eye level, thus very similar to *georgianus*, but in some even reaches above eye at rear, thus imparting a somewhat black-capped appearance. Rather long wispy black erectile crest; white forewing-covert bar and white upper back rather prominent; and usually only a few isolated white feathers on outer scapulars. Sexes similar, except in size. Eye-ring bright blue and iris dark reddish-brown; nasal caruncles ('knobs') yellow, bill blackish-grey, and facial skin (gular and lores) mainly blackish-sooty. Legs and feet dark pink. Non-breeders lack crest and have faded/duller bare facial area; white forewing patch reduced or lacking. **Juv** (and **imm**) more brown and white, and early imm lacks blue eye-ring and has dull facial skin, while bill is paler; pale tips to lesser and median coverts suggest diffuse wingbars. Plumage progression noticeable, with patchy black feathering

Ad Antarctic Shag Phalacrocorax [atriceps] bransfieldensis; *the white face extends almost across the entire head-sides, leaving a black cap. Antarctic Peninsula, Jan 2001. © Hadoram Shirihai.*

Ad Heard Shags Phalacrocorax [atriceps] nivalis with remnants of the breeding-season wispy crest; in plumage closer to South Georgian Shag but white shoulder patches can be more extensive than any other form in the complex. Entirely restricted to Heard I. Left © Eric J Woehler; right © Neil Cheshire.

appearing above and, subsequently, ad bare-parts coloration.

Voice: Chiefly a guttural barking *aark*, very noisy at colonies.

Size: 77 cm, wing 32–33 cm, weight 2.5–3.0 kg. Males significantly larger and heavier, though overlap exists in mass, culmen depth, width and length, and tarsus and wing lengths.

Similar forms: Much larger than all other subantarctic blue-eyed shags, except highly range-restricted Heard Shag *P. nivalis*.

Distribution and biology

Distribution, movements and population: Breeds on Antarctic Peninsula, South Shetlands and Elephant I. Ranges at sea in this area, but not known to move further north even in winter. Total population c.11,000 pairs.

Diet and feeding: Fish and invertebrates (principally crustaceans) taken by pursuit-diving.

Social behaviour: Monogamous. Nests in small colonies. Congregates at good food sources, but usually roosts alone or in small groups.

Breeding biology: Breeds on cliff tops and rocky outcrops, building truncated cone-shaped nest or flattened mound of seaweed, moss, lichen, grass, guano and mud. Lays 2–3 greenish-white eggs in Oct–Nov, incubated by both sexes. Chicks continuously brooded when small, fledge at 40–45 days and provisioned and guarded by both parents.

Conservation Not globally threatened.

Taxonomy Monotypic. Forms superspecies with rest of Imperial Shag *P. [atriceps]* complex. Closely related to *georgianus* (South Georgia) and *nivalis* (Heard I), all having white cheeks. See also group introduction.

Heard Shag
Phalacrocorax [atriceps] nivalis　　　　Plate 13

Identification

Confusion risks: Unmistakable in range, no other shag breeds at Heard I.

Main characters: Rather large, black-and-white, blue-eyed marine shag. **Ad** in breeding season pied, with black upperparts (glossed metallic-blue or oily green, mainly on scapulars and upperwing-coverts); cheeks (much of ear-coverts) white, extending onto foreneck and rest of underparts. Demarcation between black and white on face is at lower eye level, thus very similar to *georgia-*

nus. Rather long, wispy black erectile crest and variable number of white filoplumes sometimes evident above and behind eye, and elsewhere on head, neck and back. White forewing-coverts, upper back and scapulars (isolated feathers) variable, occasionally very prominent but in some virtually absent. Sexes similar, except in size. Eye-ring bright blue and iris dark reddish-brown; nasal caruncles ('knobs') yellow, bill blackish-grey and facial skin (gular and lores) mainly blackish-sooty, sometimes with some orange/yellow. Legs and feet dark pink. Non-breeders lack crest and plumes and have faded/duller bare facial area, white forewing patch reduced/absent. **Juv** (and **imm**) more brown and white, lacks blue eye-ring and has dull facial skin; tips of lesser and median coverts paler. Plumage progression gradual, with black feathering being acquired above and, subsequently, ad bare-parts coloration.

Size: 77 cm, wing 30.5–33.5 cm, weight 2.8–3.3 kg. The very few female mensural data suggest that the sexes are broadly equal in size.

Voice: Described as a grunt, barking *aark*, very noisy at colonies.

Similar forms: None in range; see taxonomy of Kerguelen Shag *P. [a.] verrucosus*.

Distribution and biology

Distribution, movements and population: Entirely restricted to Heard I, where moves from northwest coast to southeast shorelines for non-breeding season. Population appears subject to broad fluctuations, but total estimated at 2500–3500 individuals in 2000.

Diet and feeding: Forages close inshore, taking squid, molluscs and fish by pursuit-diving.

Social behaviour: Probably monogamous. Breeds colonially, and roosts and feeds communally.

Breeding biology: Nests in tussac grass on cliffs and offshore stacks. Lays 2–4 eggs in Oct–Nov, but no data on incubation or fledging periods. Both ads incubate and tend young.

Conservation Not globally threatened, though very small overall population and lack of legal protection provide cause for concern. In November 2000 a previously unknown breeding colony, containing c.1000 nests, was discovered at Cape Pillar, which has led to a dramatic rethink in the total population size.

Taxonomy Monotypic. Forms superspecies with rest of Imperial Shag *P. [atriceps]* complex. Closely related to *georgianus* (South Georgia) and *bransfieldensis* (Antarctic Peninsula), all having white cheeks, but *nivalis* has plumage closer to former and larger size of latter. See also group introduction.

Crozet Shag
Phalacrocorax [atriceps] melanogenis Plate 13

Identification

Confusion risks: No other blue-eyed shag recorded within its breeding range.

Main characters: Rather large blue-eyed, black-and-white, black-faced marine shag. **Ad** in breeding season pied. Black upperparts (glossed bluish with some oily green mainly on upperwing-coverts); cheeks (much of ear-coverts) blackish, concolorous with crown and hindneck, and only lower edge of ear-coverts white, imparting almost all-black facial appearance, thus in this respect similar to purpurascens from Macquarie. Rather long, wispy black erectile crest and variable number of white filoplumes sometimes evident above and behind eye, and elsewhere on head, neck and back. White forewing-coverts generally limited in extent and (almost invariably) no white on upper back, with usually very few or no white feathers on outer scapulars. Rest of throat/foreneck and underparts white. Eye-ring bright blue and iris dark reddish-brown; nasal caruncles ('knobs') yellow, bill blackish-grey and facial skin (gular and lores) mainly blackish-sooty, sometimes with some orange/yellow. Legs and feet dark pink. Sexes similar except in size. Non-breeders lack crest and plumes, and have faded/duller bare facial area, with white forewing patch reduced/absent. **Juv** (and **imm**) generally brown and white, lacks blue eye-ring and has dull facial skin; tips of lesser and median coverts paler. Plumage progression gradual, with black feathering being acquired above and, subsequently, ad bare-parts coloration.

Voice: Described as a repeated barking *kok-kok-kok* or *heh-heh-hek*, noisy at colonies.

Size: 70 cm, wing 25.7–29.9 cm, weight 1.85–2.25 kg. Available data suggest that males are larger, particularly in wing and tail lengths.

Similar forms: None in range; see also taxonomy of this and next species.

Distribution and biology

Distribution, movements and population: Endemic to Prince Edward, Marion and Crozet, where largely sedentary. Population estimated at 1220 pairs in early 1980s, with just over half of these on Marion and Prince Edward.

Diet and feeding: Forages up to 6 km offshore, taking invertebrates, including octopuses and crustaceans, and fish by pursuit-diving.

Social behaviour: Monogamous but pair-bond apparently only lasts single season. Roosts and sometimes forages communally. Nests in small colonies.

Breeding biology: Nests on cliffs and beaches, building truncated cone of algae, grass, guano and mud. Lays 1–5 eggs in late Oct–early Feb. Both sexes incubate for 28–31 days. Fledging period 50–63 days. Both sexes tend the young.

Conservation Not globally threatened. Populations apparently stable. Prince Edward is a nature reserve and very little visited by humans.

Taxonomy Monotypic. Forms superspecies with rest of Imperial Shag *P. [atriceps]* complex. Closely related to *verrucosus* (Kerguelen) and *purpurascens* (Macquarie), all having mostly black cheeks. *Melanogenis* is larger and has more white on cheeks than *verrucosus* (both mostly lack white on upper back), and, compared to same-sized *purpurascens*, has relatively reduced white on forewing-coverts and mostly lacks white upper back. See also group introduction.

Kerguelen Shag
Phalacrocorax [atriceps] verrucosus Plate 13

Identification

Confusion risks: No other species of blue-eyed shag occurs on Kerguelen.

Main characters: Typical blue-eyed, black-and-white and black-faced marine shag, but is smallest of group. **Ad** in breeding

Ad Crozet Shag Phalacrocorax [atriceps] melanogenis is endemic to the Prince Edward and Crozet groups, and has extensive black on the head and limited white on the shoulders and back, Marion. © Peter Ryan.

Ad Kerguelen Shag Phalacrocorax [atriceps] verrucosus is the smallest and darkest of the complex. Note the lack of white on the back and outer scapulars, and limited extent on forewing-coverts. Morbihan Gulf, Kerguelen, Mar 2004. © Hadoram Shirihai.

Ad Kerguelen Shag Phalacrocorax [atriceps] verrucosus feeding in kelp, showing the characteristic all-black face of this and other Indian Ocean forms. Morbihan Gulf, Kerguelen, Mar 2004. © Hadoram Shirihai.

Imm Kerguelen Shag Phalacrocorax [atriceps] verrucosus: plumage progression is gradual, with black feathers being acquired above first, when still has variable brown streaking below. Morbihan Gulf, Kerguelen, Mar 2004. © Hadoram Shirihai.

Fresh juv Kerguelen Shag Phalacrocorax [atriceps] verrucosus is typically extensively brownish below. Morbihan Gulf, Kerguelen, Mar 2004. © Hadoram Shirihai.

season pied. Black upperparts (glossed metallic blue, with slight oily green and violet sheen, mainly on upperwing-coverts); cheeks (entire ear-coverts) and rather long, wispy erectile crest blackish, like rest of crown and hindneck, imparting almost all-black face, leaving throat and foreneck white, as rest of underparts (thus very similar to other Indian Ocean and the Macquarie forms). Unlike these (and other members of complex), apparently often lacks white upper back, forewing-coverts and filoplumes (sometimes a small number above and behind eye), with usually very few or no white feathers on outer scapulars (but see below). Sexes similar, except in size. Eye-ring bright blue and iris dark reddish-brown; nasal caruncles ('knobs') yellow, bill relatively short, slender and chiefly dark brownish horn-grey, and facial skin (gular and lores) mainly sooty-brown, occasionally with some orange. Legs and feet dark pink. Non-breeders lack crest and plumes and have faded/duller bare facial area, and no white plumes/patches. **Juv** (and **imm**) distinctive: generally dark brown above and white with variable brown streaking on throat, foreneck and belly, though some have predominately brown underparts; lacks blue eye-ring and has dull facial skin; tips of lesser and median coverts slightly paler. Plumage progression gradual, with black feathering being acquired above and, subsequently, ad bare-parts coloration.
Voice: Described as a hoarse croak (*HANZAB*), no other information.
Size: 65 cm, wing 24.8–28.1 cm, weight 1.5–2.2 kg. Males appear to average larger in wing and tail lengths.
Similar forms: None in range; see below under taxonomy.

Distribution and biology

Distribution, movements and population: Endemic to Kerguelen group, where sedentary, though individuals have been reported up to 70 km from the group. Estimated population 10,000–12,000 pairs in mid-1990s.
Diet and feeding: Presumably mostly fish and sea-urchins captured by pursuit-diving.
Social behaviour: Monogamous. Gregarious throughout year and colonies occupied virtually year-round.
Breeding biology: Uses sheltered sites on cliff ledges and rocky outcrops, building truncated cone of seaweed, twigs, mud and guano. Lays 2–4 pale blue/green eggs in Nov–Jan. No information on incubation and fledging periods.
Conservation Not globally threatened and populations apparently stable, and not reported to be affected by humans or introduced mammals.
Taxonomy Monotypic. Forms superspecies with rest of Imperial

Ad Kerguelen Shags Phalacrocorax [atriceps] verrucosus mutual preening, Morbihan Gulf, Kerguelen, Mar 2004. © Hadoram Shirihai.

Shag *P.* [*atriceps*] complex. Closely related to *melanogenis* (Crozet) and *purpurascens* (Macquarie), all having mostly black cheeks and backs, but is distinctly smaller with shorter/slenderer bill, more complete blackish appearance to head-sides and most lack (or virtually lack) white upper forewing-coverts. *HANZAB* summarizes individual variation and states that those with some (but usually limited/partial) white are restricted to Golfe du Morbihan and Presqu'île Jeanne D'Arc, with intermediates occurring there and on east coast of archipelago, and most apparent hybridization within a colony at Presqu'île Jeanne D'Arc. It has been suggested that such variation may have resulted from interbreeding between *verrucosus* and (recently arrived) *nivalis* from Heard, but possibility that invasion and interbreeding is with *melanogenis* from Crozet also demands consideration (including possibility of ship-assisted arrival). Recent colonization and subsequent hybridization theory is strengthened by lack of earlier records of partially white birds. Further morphological work and a molecular study would be interesting. See group introduction.

Macquarie Shag
Phalacrocorax [*atriceps*] *purpurascens*　　Plate 13

Identification
Confusion risks: No other shag occurs on the island.
Main characters: Typical blue-eyed, black-and-white and black-faced marine shag. Rather large. **Ad** in breeding season pied. Black upperparts (glossed bluish, with some oily green mainly on upperwing-coverts); upper/central ear-coverts blackish, like rest of crown and hindneck, leaving only lower cheeks white, thus imparting almost all-black face. White forewing-covert patch generally well developed, though variable, and therefore very similar to slightly smaller *melanogenis*. Usually only a few bold white feathers on outer scapulars and often lacks any white on upper back. Rather long, wispy black erectile crest and variable number of white filoplumes sometimes present above and behind eye, and elsewhere on head, neck and back. Rest of throat/foreneck and underparts white. Bright blue eye-ring and iris dark reddish-brown; nasal caruncles ('knobs') yellow, bill dusky-grey, and facial skin (gular and lores) mainly blackish-sooty, occasionally with some orange/yellow, especially near base of lower mandible (variable in extent). Legs and feet dark pink. Sexes similar except in size. Non-breeders lack crest and plumes and have faded/duller bare facial area, white forewing patch reduced/absent. **Juv** (and **imm**) generally brown and white, lacks blue eye-ring and has dull facial skin; tips of lesser and median coverts paler. Plumage progression gradual, with black feathering being acquired above and, subsequently, ad bare-parts coloration.
Voice: Described as a repeated loud raucous barking and honking, noisy at colonies (*HANZAB*). No further information.
Size: 75 cm, wing 27.8–32.2 cm, 2.2–3.5 kg. Males average significantly larger, particularly in wing and tail lengths.
Similar forms: Range does not overlap with any of the other blue-eyed shags.

Distribution and biology
Distribution, movements and population: Restricted to Macquarie and adjacent Bishop and Clerk Is. Largely sedentary. Population estimated at 760 pairs in 1970s, but may have declined slightly in recent years.
Diet and feeding: Pursuit-dives in search of fish, some crustaceans and other invertebrates.
Social behaviour. Principally monogamous. Forms groups for feeding, roosting and nesting.

Ad Macquarie Shag Phalacrocorax [atriceps] purpurascens *is taxonomically closest to Crozet* P. [a.] melanogenis *and Kerguelen Shags* P. [a.] verrucosus, *Macquarie, 1994. © Alan Wiltshire.*

Breeding biology: Uses same rocky site, just above high-water mark, on annual basis. Prolonged season, lays 1–3 eggs in late Sep–mid-Jan (peak Oct–Nov) in truncated cone-shaped nest of vegetation, mud and guano, constructed by both ads. Incubation, by both ads, takes 32–33 days. No information on fledging period.
Conservation Not globally threatened and population appears to be naturally small. Some are killed due to collisions with radio aerials, while skuas and cats predate chicks. Storm waves may also account for some nest failures.
Taxonomy Monotypic. Forms superspecies with rest of Imperial Shag *P.* [*atriceps*] complex. Closely related to *melanogenis* (Crozet) and *verrucosus* (Kerguelen), all having mostly black cheeks and backs. See also group introduction.

Cormorants and shags
of New Zealand's subantarctic islands

Plate 14 deals with a distinctive group from New Zealand and its subantarctic islands, the *P.* [*campbelli*] complex, namely *campbelli*, *colensoi* and *ranfurlyi*; also included in the following accounts is *onslowi* (Chatham Shag), which belongs to the *P.* [*carunculatus*] group (with King *P.* [*c.*] *carunculatus* and Stewart/Bronze Shags *P.* [*c.*] *chalconotus*). These groups appear closely related to each other and to *P.* [*atriceps*], which mainly occurs outside the Pacific. The relationships and affinities within *P.* [*campbelli*] and *P.* [*carunculatus*] are still not fully understood (see below).

Identification of all these taxa is often difficult, relying on subtle and variable differences (with much overlap), and some non-breeding plumages are unidentifiable, but fortunately most are well separated geographically and perhaps never or only occasionally come into contact, they being largely non-migratory.

Plate 14 and the following species accounts also treat three other *Phalacrocorax*, discussed here because they regularly occur on New Zealand's subantarctic islands. For further information on taxonomy see the introduction to Plate 13 and below. General information concerning behaviour, life history and breeding cycles are also presented in the introduction to Plate 13.

Auckland Shag
Phalacrocorax [campbelli] colensoi　　Plate 14

Identification
Confusion risks: None in the Auckland group.
Main characters: Typical black-and-white, black-faced marine shag of Southern Ocean. Rather small. **Ad** in breeding season pied, with black (glossed bluish-violet with partial oily green sheen) upperparts and head, including crown, ear-coverts and edges of throat, extending across hindneck and neck-sides, leaving only parts of throat and foreneck white. Extent of white varies from those with pure white foreneck to others with extensive black nearly meeting on foreneck, thus often enclosing white throat and appearing to have almost all-black neck, not unlike Campbell Shag *P. [c.] campbelli* (see taxonomy). Rest of underparts white. White forewing-covert patch generally well developed, though variable, being narrow and partial on some and bolder and more extensive in others; usually only a few scattered bold white feathers on outer scapulars; white on upper back variable, being rather prominent (in some males) or absent (most or perhaps all females). Rather short, sparse erectile crest; also several thin white nuptial filoplumes above and behind eye. Eye-ring bright blue-purple to orange-purple, iris dark reddish-brown, rest of bare facial skin reddish-yellow and dark purple (lacks nasal caruncles), gular pouch and gape orange-red, and bill blackish-grey with indistinct paler/yellowish mark at tip of lower mandible. Legs and feet pink. Sexes similar except in size. Non-breeders lack crest and have faded/duller bare facial area, white forewing and upper-back patches reduced/absent. **Juv** (and **imm**) a brown version of ad, lacking reddish facial skin and crest, and has white throat patch enclosed by (variable) brown neck; tips of lesser and median coverts and scapulars paler. Plumage progression gradual, with black feathering being acquired above and, subsequently, ad bare-parts coloration. See photo p. 495.
Voice: Chiefly repeated loud barking and ticking calls near nest (male), *ahr arr ohr... or ah ah ah...* etc; noisy at colonies.
Size: 63 cm, wing 23.7–29.1 cm, weight 2 kg. Males average marginally larger in wing length and distinctly longer in tail length.
Similar forms: No other shag of this complex, *P. [campbelli]*, occurs on Auckland, but note extensive variation within this species and its often great similarity to Campbell Shag. Most Auckland Shag readily separated by having at least some white on foreneck and the border between black/white areas usually ill-defined and mottled. In confusing all-black-necked individuals (quite common), study the demarcation between the lower foreneck/upper breast; in Auckland the white breast tends to curve upward, forming a white triangle, whereas in Campbell the black/white demarcation is almost invariably straight and sharply defined. However, I have noted some Auckland Shag with an almost identical neck pattern to Campbell Shag, though it is not known that the two species meet, either as vagrants or to interbreed, which might otherwise explain such intermediates. Note that Campbell Shag has a dark grey or blackish (not purple and orange) eye-ring and never has a white upper back, unlike some Auckland Shag (see above). For differences from Bounty Shag *P. [c.] ranfurlyi* see latter. Range does not overlap with any forms of the other bluish-eyed shag complexes, *P. [carunculatus]* and *P. [atriceps]*. Both Little Pied *P. melanoleucus* and Great Cormorants *P. carbo* are only vagrants to its range, and have longer wings and tails, black legs and feet, and no white on upperwing.

Distribution and biology
Distribution, movements and population: Restricted to Auckland and surrounding waters where entirely sedentary. Population c.1000 pairs in recent years.

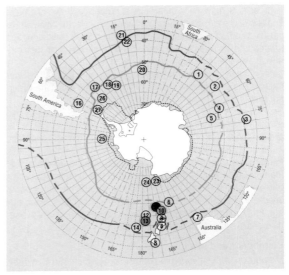

■ Campbell Shag *Phalacrocorax [c.] campbelli*
▨ Auckland Shag *Phalacrocorax [c.] colensoi*
▨ Bounty Shag *Phalacrocorax [c.] ranfurlyi*
🔟 Auckland
⬤ Campbell
⑬ Bounty

Diet and feeding: Takes crustaceans and fish.
Social behaviour: Solitary or gregarious, but is a colonial nester. Few other data.
Breeding biology: Nests colonially on ground, both ads constructing bulky bowl-shaped nest of grass, twigs, seaweed and debris. Lays three pale blue-green eggs Nov–Feb. Incubation 26–32 days, performed by both ads, which share provisioning duties. No information on fledging period.
Conservation Vulnerable due to predation by feral pigs, which have destroyed all accessible colonies, feral cattle and rabbits and potentially cats. Steps are being taken to eradicate livestock and other predators from the group, which is a nature reserve and World Heritage Site. Thus far, goats have been successfully removed and cattle and rabbits have been eliminated from at least two breeding islands.
Taxonomy Monotypic. Very similar to same-sized Campbell Shag, with which possibly best united specifically, but regarded as allospecies here pending further study of relationships within *P. [campbelli]*. Relationship and comparison to Bounty Shag discussed under latter.

Campbell Shag
Phalacrocorax [campbelli] campbelli　　Plate 14

Identification
Confusion risks: No other shags occur in the Campbell group.
Main characters: Typical, rather small pied, black-faced marine shag of Southern Ocean. **Ad** in breeding season very similar to closest congener, Auckland Shag *P. [c.] colensoi* (which see), except neck pattern and other minor differences. Invariably has complete black neck, sharply and squarely demarcated from white throat and upper breast, and thus lacks any white extensions onto foreneck as in Auckland Shag (see latter). Back and scapulars lack white markings (like some Auckland Shag). Eye-ring generally appears dark in field, being blackish-purple or dark grey, hardly differing

from facial skin, which is dusky-purple (in Auckland eye-ring paler and tinged orange, contrasting with surrounding face). **Juv** a brown version of ad, differentiated from juv Auckland Shag by sharper and lower border between brown foreneck and white breast, though otherwise extremely similar to latter. See photo p. 498.

Voice: Chiefly repeated loud barking, noisy at colonies. No other data and no comparative studies of vocalizations within the superspecies.

Size: 63 cm, wing 25.5–28.5 cm, weight 1.6–2.0 kg. Males tend to average marginally larger in wing and tail lengths.

Similar forms: No other shag of this complex, namely Auckland and Bounty Shags *P. [c.] ranfurlyi*, occur in the group (see these forms). Range does not meet any of the other bluish-eyed shags, *P. [carunculatus]* and *P. [atriceps]*. Little Pied *P. melanoleucus* (which has bred on the island) and Great Cormorants *P. carbo* (vagrant), should not be confused, having longer wings and tails, black legs and feet, and no white on upperwing. Distribution of white elsewhere in plumage and bare-parts colorations also differ.

Distribution and biology

Distribution, movements and population: Restricted to Campbell, where apparently sedentary, though possibly a vagrant to Antipodes. Population estimated at 8000 individuals in 1975.

Diet and feeding: Shells, marine invertebrates and small shoaling fish. Often feeds in large, occasionally dense, flocks of up to 200 individuals diving in unison.

Social behaviour: Little known, but nests and roosts communally.

Breeding biology: Few data, lays Aug–Dec on ground, in tussac grass or on ledges and steep cliffs. Often breeds in small, inaccessible colonies. Bowl-shaped nest of grass and other plant material and debris. Both ads incubate and provision the young, but very few additional data.

Conservation Vulnerable. Few threats, as feral cats and rats are thought to have had little effect on the species. Skuas predate eggs and, historically, livestock may have restricted breeding-colony expansion. The islands are a nature reserve and World Heritage Site, and a rat-eradication programme is planned.

Taxonomy Monotypic. Forms superspecies with rest of *P. [campbelli]* complex: see comments under Auckland and Bounty Shags.

Bounty Shag
Phalacrocorax [campbelli] ranfurlyi　　　　Plate 14

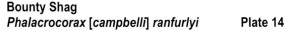

Identification

Confusion risks: No other shags occur in the Bounty group.

Main characters: The largest of the *P. [campbelli]* group. Typical pied, black-faced marine shag of Southern Ocean. Ad in breeding season almost identical to Auckland Shag *P. [c.] colensoi* (which see), but distinctly larger and heavier, with some differences in neck pattern and other minor plumage differences. Invariably has black hindneck and rear neck-sides, with extensive and sharply demarcated white foreneck, lacking any black extension onto latter as in most Auckland Shag (which can have similar amount of white on foreneck). Most have more extensive white forewing patch, but lack white feathering on scapulars (occasionally present in Auckland). Apparently lacks thin white nuptial filoplumes above and behind eye (not noted on specimens or in photographs), which are present on some/most displaying Auckland and Campbell Shags *P. [c.] campbelli*. **Juv** a brown version of ad, but lacks white forewing patch; aside of larger size does not clearly differ from juvs of other forms, but tends to have more extensive white on foreneck.

Voice: At colonies males deliver soft purring and ticking sounds. No other data.

Ad Bounty Shag Phalacrocorax [campbelli] ranfurlyi *is the largest of the* P. [campbelli] *complex, and typically has an extensively white foreneck and forewing patch, but lacks white on the scapulars. Bounty, Jan 2007.* © Hadoram Shirihai.

Size: 71 cm, wing 27.2–30.0 cm, weight 2.3–2.9 kg. Males average larger in all measurements.

Similar forms: Both Campbell and Auckland Shags (which see) are similar to some extent, but neither comes into contact with Bounty Shag. Larger size and some plumage differences (see above) separate latter from others (which see for further details).

Distribution and biology

Distribution, movements and population: Restricted to the Bounties, where apparently sedentary. No confirmed records away from the group though claimed once in Antipodes. Population c.1140 individuals in 1978.

Diet and feeding: Fish and marine invertebrates caught by large groups of up to 300 individuals in pursuit-dives, first jumping high above the surface. In breeding season males fish in afternoon and females in morning.

Social behaviour: Few data but nests and feeds communally.

Breeding biology: Principally on cliff ledges, where both ads construct a flattened bowl-shaped nest of seaweed, feathers, pebbles and mud. Lays 2–3 eggs in Oct–Nov, but no additional data.

Conservation Vulnerable but stable. Nesting areas may be

Ad Bounty Shag Phalacrocorax [campbelli] ranfurlyi *closely relates to* Campbell P. [c.] campbelli *and Auckland Shags* P. [c.] colensoi, *the three forming a distinctive superspecies (for photos of the latter two see Regional Accounts). Bounty.* © Andrea M. Booth.

Plate 14 Cormorants and shags of New Zealand's subantarctic islands

Auckland Shag
ad. breeding
(p. 231)

As Campbell and Bounty Shags but black on neck partially meets

Bounty Shag
ad. breeding
(p. 232)

As Campbell and Auckland Shags but extensive white foreneck

Campbell Shag
ad. breeding
(p. 231)

As Bounty and Auckland Shags but neck wholly black

Chatham Shag
ad. breeding
(p. 234)

Orange-red knobs (similar to King Shag of mainland New Zealand)

Pitt Shag
ad. breeding
(p. 235)

Double crests, dark spotty plumage and green facial skin

Great Cormorant
ad. breeding
(p. 238)

Largest and mainly dark

Pied Cormorant
ad. breeding
(p. 236)

Large and extensive white foreneck and underparts, except black thigh patch

Little Pied Cormorant
ad. breeding
(p. 237)

Very small, and white-faced

restricted due to competition with other birds and fur seals. Extreme weather conditions may affect numbers, but the introduction of mammalian predators, though a constant threat, appears only a remote possibility. The islands are a nature reserve and were recently declared a World Heritage Site.

Taxonomy Monotypic. Forms superspecies with rest of *P.* [*campbelli*] complex (see comments under Auckland Shag). White on foreneck, orange-tinged eye-ring and more extensive white on wings parallels Auckland Shag, but latter distinctly smaller, and sometimes has almost identical amount of black on foreneck to Campbell Shag. Such complex phenotypic characters should be analysed, along with acoustic and molecular data, to resolve the group's relationships.

Chatham Shag
Phalacrocorax [carunculatus] onslowi   Plate 14

Identification

Confusion risks: None: the only bluish-eyed, colourful-faced, black-and-white shag in the Chatham group.
Main characters: Typical pied, black-faced marine shag. Rather small. **Ad** in breeding season has black (glossed bluish-violet, with some oily green sheen) upperparts and head, including crown, ear-coverts and onto edges of throat, extending across hindneck and neck-sides, leaving throat and foreneck white. Rest of underparts white. White forewing-covert patch generally well developed though variable, on some narrow and partial; usually no or only very few bold white feathers on outer scapulars; white patch on upper back variable, rather prominent (in some males) or absent (in most or apparently all females). Rather short, sparse erectile crest, and perhaps some thin white nuptial filoplumes above and behind eye and on neck-sides. Eye-ring bright blue-purple, iris dark reddish-brown, bare facial skin dark purple with quite well-developed orange-red nasal caruncles ('knobs'), orange-red gular pouch, bare skin at base of lower mandible and gape, and relatively long, grey-brown bill, with slightly paler/yellowish tip. Legs and feet pink. Sexes similar except in size. Non-breeders lack crest and have faded/duller bare facial area; white forewing and upper-back patch reduced or absent. **Juv** (and **imm**)

Imm Chatham Shag Phalacrocorax [carunculatus] onslowi *is duller brown above and lacks the bright facial skin of ads. Chatham, Oct 2001. © Hadoram Shirihai.*

a dull brown version of ad, lacking reddish facial skin, caruncles and crest, and has rather pure, broad white throat and foreneck; tips of lesser and median coverts and scapulars paler, often quite extensive and bold, forming forewing-covert patch. Plumage progression gradual, with black feathering being acquired above and, subsequently, ad bare-parts coloration.
Voice: Chiefly repeated loud barking and ticking calls near nest (male), noisy at colonies. No other data.
Size: 63 cm, wing 26.1–29.2 cm, weight 2.0–2.5 kg. Males tend to average larger, but datasets are small.
Similar forms: No other shag of the *P.* [*carunculatus*] complex occurs in the group. Range does not overlap with any of the other bluish-eyed shags, i.e. the *P.* [*campbelli*] and *P.* [*atriceps*] groups. Both Little Pied *P. melanoleucus* (vagrant in range) and Great Cormorants *P. carbo* (scarce breeder) are easily differentiated, having longer wings and tails, black legs and feet, and no white on upperwing; pattern of white elsewhere in plumage and bare-parts colorations also differ.

Distribution and biology

Distribution, movements and population: Restricted to Chatham where sedentary. Population 842 pairs in 1997 in ten discrete colonies.
Diet and feeding: Apparently small fish, up to 10 cm long, as well as squid, cuttlefish and octopus taken principally in deeper offshore waters. No data concerning techniques.
Social behaviour: Monogamous. Nests colonially and may congregate to feed and roost.
Breeding biology: Nest, on level rocky ground slightly above high-tide mark, is of grass and plants. Lays 1–4 pale blue eggs Sep–Dec, but no information concerning incubation or fledging periods.
Conservation Endangered, with breeding restricted to four islands and the largest colonies being on predator-free islets. Introduced predators, gulls and human disturbance take a toll and fur seals have occupied several former breeding colonies. Ecotourism requires close monitoring and supervision. Illegal shooting and occasional capture in fishing pots and nets are also problems.
Taxonomy Monotypic. Most closely related and similar to Stewart/Bronze Shag *P.* [*c.*] *chalconotus*, and both are often placed within the King Shag *P.* [*carunculatus*] superspecies (e.g., by Sibley & Monroe 1990), but both Chatham and Stewart/Bronze Shags are very different from King Shag *P.* [*c.*] *carunculatus* and appear worthy of specific status (being much smaller, with more colourful bare facial areas).

Ad Chatham Shag Phalacrocorax [carunculatus] onslowi *is the only representative in our region of the King Shag* P. [carunculatus] *superspecies. Chatham, Oct 2001. © Hadoram Shirihai.*

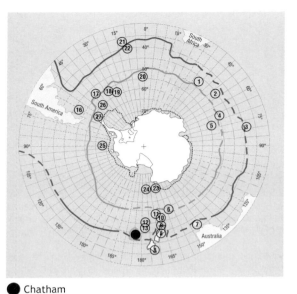

● Chatham

Pitt Shag *Phalacrocorax featherstoni*   Plate 14

Identification

Confusion risks: Distinctive and localized on Chatham, and thus unlikely to be misidentified by presence of Chatham Shag P. *onslowi* and others of group (see below).

Main characters: Small/medium-sized, but typically slender, grey-and-black marine shag. **Ad** in breeding season has almost uniform blackish olive-brown upperparts (glossed bluish and greenish), including entire head and upper neck, with lower foreneck and rest of underparts dull whitish-grey. At close range, delicate black terminal-spot pattern evident on mantle, scapulars and upperwing-coverts, with spotty/streaky white filoplumes behind eye and elsewhere on head and hindneck, and strange double crest (that on forehead being short and bushy, the other on hindcrown wispy). Restricted apple-green facial skin and eye-ring, and dark red-brown iris. Bill distinctly long, slender and mainly dusky-grey, with small yellow gular and gape, especially on lower mandible. Legs and feet dull orange-yellow. Sexes similar except in size. Non-breeders lack crests and plumes and have greyer/duller bare facial area. **Juv** (and **imm**) principally brown, with paler dorsal area, lacks crests and has dull greyish-yellow facial skin, and tips of upperwing-coverts paler. Plumage progression gradual, with black feathering being acquired above and, subsequently, ad bare-parts coloration.

Voice: At colonies, described as a repeated deep grunting, gargling and ticking, e.g. *argh-argh-argh*, or *ooo-argh, eh-argh-argh*; noisy (HANZAB).

Size: 63 cm, wing 20.9–25.5 cm, weight 0.6–1.3 kg. Males tend to average larger, but datasets rather small.

Similar species: Unlikely to be confused due to small size, slender build and greyish plumage. Spotted Shag P. *punctatus*, a plausible vagrant to Chatham, has diagnostic white stripes on head-sides and neck. Juv distinguished from same-age, non-marine Little Black Cormorant P. *sulcirostris* (which could also occur as vagrant) by different overall structure, especially shorter tail and longer/slenderer bill, and yellow-brown legs and feet.

Distribution and biology

Distribution, movements and population: Restricted to eight

Ad Pitt Shag Phalacrocorax featherstoni *is endemic to the Chatham group and unmistakable in its range. Main Chatham, Oct 2001. © Hadoram Shirihai.*

islands in Chatham group, where sedentary, with a total population of 729 pairs breeding at 63 locations in 1997–8.

Diet and feeding: Feeds solely on small fish and marine invertebrates caught in either offshore or inshore waters, sometimes in kelp beds.

Social behaviour: Virtually unknown, though frequently recorded in mixed-age small groups.

Breeding biology: Small colonies, usually separate from Chatham Shag, on cliff ledges or rocky islets. Platform nest of seaweed, grass and plants. Lays 1–4 pale blue eggs Aug–Sep, but no other data available.

Conservation Vulnerable but stable. Livestock and other intro-

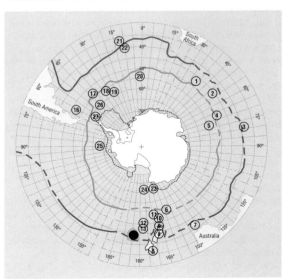

● Chatham

Ad Pied Cormorant Phalacrocorax varius *is a rare and irregular non-breeding visitor to several of New Zealand's subantarctic islands, where it is unlikely to be confused. South I, New Zealand, Jan 2003. © Hadoram Shirihai.*

Imm Pitt Shag Phalacrocorax featherstoni *is more uniform and browner, lacks the crests and bright facial skin of ads, whilst the wing-covert tips are paler (here bleached to create a 'shoulder' effect). Pitt, Chatham Is, Oct 2001. © Hadoram Shirihai.*

duced mammalian predators may adversely affect breeding success, though former have been removed from several breeding islands. Some are illegally shot by fishermen and others drown in lobster pots.

Taxonomy Monotypic. Has been placed in *Stictocarbo*.

Pied Cormorant *Phalacrocorax varius*   Plate 14

Identification

Confusion risks: Unlikely to be confused with any other species in our region, but cf. Little Pied *P. melanoleucus* and Great Cormorants *P. carbo*.

Main characters: Rather large black-and-white coastal cormorant, with long stout bill, long neck, short broad wings, and short tail and legs. Vagrant to our region. Following refers to nominate varius. **Ad** in breeding season has uniform metallic black upperparts (glossed bluish and bronze), including crown and hindneck, contrasting sharply with white lower face (reaching above eye level), foreneck and rest of underparts. Crown and hindneck may have, for limited period, short white nuptial plumes. Yellowish facial skin in front of eye, bluish-tinged eye-ring and narrow surround, and green iris. Bill (with pronounced terminal hook) mainly dusky-grey, with yellowish and reddish-pink elements especially on lower mandible, including gular and gape. Legs and feet mainly black. Sexes similar except in size (female smaller with shorter bill). Non-breeders lack plumes and have yellower/duller bare facial area, and browner upperparts. **Juv** (and **imm**) principally dark brown above, with variably paler underparts, being mostly mottled brown or has variably white-streaked brownish-grey underparts (especially marked on head-sides, neck and breast); dull greyish-yellow/greenish facial skin and dark brown iris; and tips of upperwing-coverts slightly paler. Plumage progression gradual, with black feathering being acquired above and, subsequently, ad bare-parts coloration.

Size: 65–85 cm, wing 27.4–35.6 cm, weight 1.0–2.2 kg. Males tend to average larger in all measurements.

Voice: Very noisy (males) at colonies, chiefly a repeated loud squeaking, grunting, gargling, gobbling or barking, consisting of two principal but variable notes, *ark* and *kerlike* (sometimes higher pitched, e.g. *ahrk, arrh-eh or aahr, whee-err*).

Similar species: Within our region, ad Great Cormorant (which see) of race steadi (New Zealand) is very dark/black below, and unlikely to be confused with ad Pied. Note that juv Pied can be superficially similarly dark below, but is still identifiable by smaller size, paler face, head-sides and foreneck, and whiter underparts, contrasting with darker (blackish-brown) crown, hindneck and upperparts, whereas juv steadi has mainly dark head and neck, with yellowish bare skin at bill base being only pale area on face, and neck and body-sides more extensively dark. Pied also has relatively longer bill, shorter wings and tail. Pied-morph Little Pied Cormorant is much smaller, with short, stubby yellowish bill, longer tail and no black thigh patch; white-faced morph also has diagnostic black body.

Distribution and biology

Distribution, movements and population: Local in Australia, except arid western interior, and New Zealand, including Stewart I. Vagrant to Lord Howe I and several of New Zealand's subantarctic islands. Population 5000–10,000 pairs in New Zealand during 1980s.

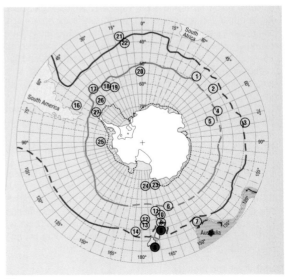

● New Zealand and offshore islands

Ad Pied Cormorant Phalacrocorax varius, *South I, New Zealand, Jan 2003.* © Hadoram Shirihai.

Diet and feeding: Takes fish and, to a much lesser extent, crustaceans caught by pursuit-diving. Sometimes jumps clear of surface prior to dive and will occasionally steal fish from nets.

Social behaviour: Breeds colonially, sometimes with other Phalacrocorax, pelicans or spoonbills. Colonies often shift location. Forms solitary or communal roosts, often with other cormorants.

Breeding biology: Colonies active year-round, but most laying activity in New Zealand is in Jul–Oct and Jan–Mar. Usually ground-based nests constructed of twigs, seaweed and refuse by female (male brings material). Lays 2–5 bluish-green eggs, incubated by both ads for 25–33 days. Chicks leave nest after c.28 days and fledge at 47–60 days, but fed for further 11 weeks.

Conservation Not globally threatened. Sometimes illegally shot by fishermen and occasionally caught in nets, but numbers are overall increasing.

Taxonomy Two subspecies: nominate in New Zealand and *hypoleucos* in Australia principally vary in slight head-pattern differences, plumage sheen and coloration at bill base.

Little Pied Cormorant
Phalacrocorax melanoleucos   Plate 14

Identification
Confusion risks: Unlikely to be confused with any other species in our region, but cf. Pied Cormorant *P. varius*.

Main characters: Small, squat, distinctly long-tailed, black-and-white cormorant, principally of Australian and New Zealand coastal and inland waters; vagrant to New Zealand's subantarctic islands. Highly distinctive. The endemic New Zealand form *brevirostris* is polymorphic. **Ad** *white-throated morph* in breeding season has uniform greyish-black upperparts (glossed green-bronze), including crown centre (cap) and hindneck, neck-sides and lower foreneck, with sharply defined white face (reaching well above eye level), throat and upper foreneck; rest of underparts from lower foreneck black. Nominate (Australia) has entire underparts and foreneck white, but *pied-throated morph* of *brevirostris* can also be white below. Intermediates of *brevirostris* like pied morph but have variable (blotchy) black on white underparts. Crown has short, spiky black crest on forehead and for a limited period short and erect frilly white plumes on rear head-sides. Yellowish-/greenish-/brownish-orange bill (short and stubby), restricted facial skin, gular pouch, eye-ring and surround, and dark brown iris. Legs and feet mainly black. Sexes similar except in size. Non-breeders lack crest and plumes and have yellower/duller bare facial area, and

browner upperparts. **Juv** (and **imm**) *brevirostris* principally dark brown; nominate and pied-morph *brevirostris* like non-breeding ad, but duller above with dark crown reaching below eye level; in intermediate juv *brevirostris* underparts variable. All have dull/darker and greyish-yellow/greenish facial skin and bill; tips of upperwing-coverts slightly paler. Plumage progression gradual, with black feathering being acquired above and, subsequently, ad bare-parts coloration.

Voice: Noisy at colonies or evening roosts, chiefly a repeated cooing *keh-keh-keh* or harsher *aark-aark-aark*.

Size: 55–65 cm, wing 22.0–24.6 cm, weight 410–880 g. Males tend to average larger in all measurements.

Similar species: Short stubby yellowish bill, overall size and wedge-shaped long tail unmistakable. Pied Cormorant shares basic plumage pattern but is much larger with shorter tail and longer bill. Little Black Cormorant *P. sulcirostris*, which could reach the subantarctic islands as a vagrant, is also small, but has slenderer, darker bill, and lacks yellowish facial skin.

Distribution and biology
Distribution, movements and population: Indonesia, New Guinea and New Caledonia south to Australia and New Zealand, including Stewart and small colony, either nominate or pied-morph *brevirostris*, briefly established on Campbell in 1967. Dispersive, being a vagrant to Lord Howe and Norfolk Is, and also reaches Snares and Auckland. Population 5000–10,000 pairs in New Zealand in 1980s.

Diet and feeding: Crayfish and other crustaceans, with smaller quantities of fish also taken, usually close inshore. Feeds alone or in small groups, diving frequently but for short periods.

Social behaviour: Roosts and breeds communally, sometimes with other cormorants and large tree-nesting species. Monogamous.

Breeding biology: Nests in large colonies, in trees or on sea-cliff ledges. Constructs a platform of twigs and leaves. Long season, from late Jul to Feb, with most activity in Oct–Nov. Lays 2–5 pale blue-green eggs, but no information concerning incubation or fledging periods.

Conservation Not globally threatened. Sometimes illegally shot by fishermen and occasionally caught in nets, but numbers are overall increasing.

Taxonomy Three subspecies: nominate in Australia, New Guinea

Ad Little Pied Cormorant Phalacrocorax melanoleucos *is a rare or irregular non-breeding visitor, and apparently occasional breeder on several of New Zealand's subantarctic islands. Small size and plumage render it unmistakable. South I, New Zealand, Jan 2003.* © Hadoram Shirihai.

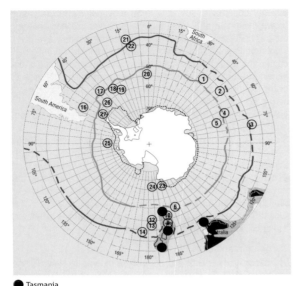

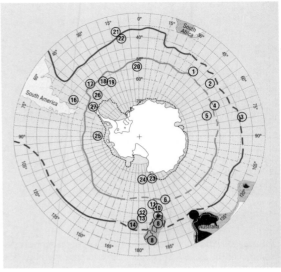

● Tasmania
● New Zealand and offshore islands
● Campbell

■ Great Cormorant *Phalacrocorax carbo carboides*
■ Great Cormorant *Phalacrocorax carbo steadi*
□ Great Cormorant *Phalacrocorax carbo lucidus*

● Tasmania
⑧ New Zealand and offshore islands
⑭ Chatham

and Indonesia, *brevicauda* on Rennell I, in the Solomons, and *brevirostris* in New Zealand, including Stewart I. Latter is polymorphic and may be sufficiently distinct, morphologically and behaviourally, to warrant specific status.

Great Cormorant *Phalacrocorax carbo*   Plate 14

Identification

Confusion risks: Unlikely to be confused with any other species in our region, but cf. Pied Cormorant *P. varius*.

Main characters: Rather large, principally black, coastal and inland-water cormorant, with stout bill, long neck, large, broad wings, mid-length tail and short legs. Largely vagrant to our region. Following refers to endemic New Zealand race *steadi*. **Ad** in breeding season almost entirely black, upperparts with bluish-green/bronze sheen (only fringed slightly paler/browner on upperwing-coverts), including head, neck and rest of underparts. Whitish throat patch (extends narrowly around eye), short black erectile crest on nape, and white thighs. Crown and upper neck may have, for limited period, short white nuptial plumes. Face in front of eye and eye-ring mainly blackish; bill (with pronounced terminal hook) largely dusky-grey, with some yellowish and reddish-pink, especially on skin around lower mandible, including gular and gape, and green iris; legs and feet mainly black. Sexes similar except in size. Non-breeders lack plumes, crest and white thighs, and have duller bare facial area, with browner upperparts. **Juv** (and **imm**) as non-breeding ad, but principally dark brown and also lacks bold white throat; facial skin duller, mainly greyish-yellow/greenish, and iris dark brown; tips of upperwing-coverts slightly paler. Overall shape neater compared to ad. Plumage progression gradual, with black feathering being acquired above and, subsequently, ad bare-parts coloration. Imm dull brown, with brown-and-white mottled underparts.

Voice: Very noisy at colonies and roosts, with complex variety of calls (louder in male), chiefly a repeated raucous, barking and grunting, e.g. *tock-gock-gock...cock* or *kro-kro-kro... roh-roh-roh...* etc. Also gargling and gobbling.

Size: 80–85 cm, wing 28.5–38.5 cm, weight 1.2–3.1 kg. Males tend to average larger in all measurements.

Similar species: For differences from young Pied Cormorant see that species. Little Black Cormorant *P. sulcirostris*, which could reach the subantarctic islands, is unmistakeably smaller, with a slenderer bill, longer tail and lacks yellowish facial skin, while all-brown juv of white-throated morph, race *brevirostris*, of Little Pied Cormorant is much smaller, has longer tail and short, stubby yellowish bill, and bronze morph of Stewart Shag *P. chalconotus* is wholly marine, smaller winged, shorter tailed, thicker necked and has pink legs.

Distribution and biology

Distribution, movements and population: Near cosmopolitan. Across much of the N Holarctic, from NE North America and Europe and south to E and SE Asia and Australia, Tasmania, New Zealand and Chatham Is (233 pairs in 1997–8). Also much of Africa. Northern populations move south for winter and it also wanders irregularly to New Guinea and Lord Howe, Norfolk, Macquarie, Snares and Campbell. Population 5000–10,000 pairs in New Zealand in 1980s.

Diet and feeding: Mostly fish with some insects and crustaceans, usually taken underwater in pursuit-diving.

Social behaviour: Colonial or solitary nester and also roosts and feeds communally. Monogamous.

Breeding biology: Very few data from our region, probably at any time of year depending on suitable conditions, but mostly Jun–Oct in New Zealand. Female constructs large stick platform (with help from male) in tree, bush or on ground. Lays 3–6 pale bluish or whitish eggs, incubated by both ads for 27–31 days. Chicks leave nest at 28 days and fledge at c.49 days.

Conservation Not globally threatened and few, if any, threats evident in our region.

Taxonomy Six subspecies recognized (though *steadi* of New Zealand and Chatham and *carboides* are not always afforded recognition), of which *lucidus*, in Africa, and *novaehollandiae*, in our region have occasionally been suggested to be specifically distinct. The six taxa form a superspecies.

Gannets

Plate 15 and the following text treat the very similar Australasian *Morus serrator* and Cape Gannets *M. capensis*, which are sometimes considered races of the same species. Together with Northern Gannet *M. bassanus* of the Northern Hemisphere, they appear to form a superspecies, with Australasian having somewhat intermediate characteristics, namely black secondaries as in Cape but the amount of white in the tail and length of the central black gular stripe approaches Northern.

Gannets are rather large seabirds, in size almost like small albatrosses, with characteristic long pointed wings and tails, and heavy pointed bills. Plumage maturation is prolonged, thus non-ad plumages are variably patterned: the juv is mainly dusky grey-brown, liberally streaked and spotted white, and ad is mostly white, with wing and tail quills black, and yellowish-buff head, while imms have several intermediate stages. Sexes alike.

Their presence in the Southern Ocean is rather limited and principally restricted to non-breeding dispersal when a few reach the north of our region, and Australasian Gannet occurs in the S Tasman Sea and even around New Zealand's subantarctic islands and S Indian Ocean. Both species have recently bred, with unknown success, on St Paul.

Both typically dive from the air to capture fish underwater. They usually form large and very crowded breeding colonies on coastal cliffs or on flat ground on small guano islands. Other interesting biological aspects of this group include their displays which recall some aspects of those of herons and pelicans. The general life histories and breeding cycles are very similar between gannets (some boobies are quite different): the age at which birds reach maturity is 4–6 years, nests are usually low mounds on the ground with a well-defined shallow cup, and the male is responsible for collecting any lining. They lay 1–4 pale green, blue or white eggs, incubated 40–55 days by both partners, and chicks take anything from 85 to 175 weeks to fledge. In two-egg clutches, usually only one chick survives.

Australasian Gannet *Morus serrator*, Kaikoura, South I, New Zealand, Feb 2001. © Hadoram Shirihai.

white areas, especially upper greater coverts, rump and tail, which are blotched, and bare-parts coloration perhaps less advanced, while golden-buff head less intense.

Voice: At sea largely silent, but very noisy at colonies, where utters a variety of calls, principally *urrah-urrah* (similar to Cape Gannet but much higher pitched; in South Africa this distinction is of sufficient use to permit field workers to locate the species among large colonies of Cape Gannet).

Size: 84–91 cm, wing 44.0–48.5 cm, wingspan 170–200 cm,

Australasian Gannet *Morus serrator*　　　Plate 15

Identification

Confusion risks: Cape Gannet *M. capensis*.

Main characters: Large, long/narrow-winged marine bird, very similar to Cape and Northern Gannets *M. bassanus*, and shares some features of both. Flight relaxed, steady and graceful, often with long glides. **Ad** has yellowish-buff tinge to head and neck, but extent and intensity varies individually and with season; rest of body plumage, including wing-coverts, essentially white, but upper primaries, their coverts and secondaries (except innermost) and central tail feathers contrastingly black, while underwing is similar except white primary-coverts. Mainly bluish-grey bill, bordered by blackish facial skin, with short central gular stripe; grey eye, blue eye-ring and mainly blackish-grey legs. **Juv** predominantly greyish-brown, heavily spotted/streaked white on head/neck, and on dark back and upperwing-coverts, but mainly whitish below with variable dark feathering on breast; flight feathers and tail black; bare parts duller, with bill and eye blacker. **Imm** in second–fourth-year becomes progressively white, at first rather patchily and irregularly patterned, with whiter head/neck and underparts than upperparts and upperwing-coverts. By third-year body largely white, but wing-coverts especially have some bold dark marks. Fourth- to fifth-year birds much as ad but vestiges of immaturity on

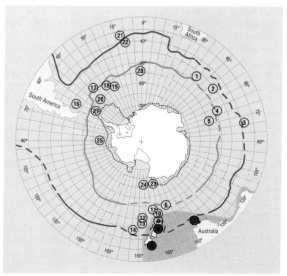

Tasmania
New Zealand and offshore islands

weight 2.0–2.8 kg. Much overlap between the sexes in mensural data and no clear trends discernable.
Similar species: For differences from Cape Gannet see that species.

Distribution and biology

Distribution, movements and population: Breeds off SE Australia in S Victoria, NE and S Tasmania; New Zealand off North I and islets south of South I; and with recent records from St Paul. Ranges at sea along coasts of S Australia north to C Western Australia and SE Queensland, west into Indian Ocean and southeast into New Zealand waters south to subantarctic islands. For comments concerning occurrence in South Africa see Cape Gannet taxonomy.
Diet and feeding: Largely small fish and occasionally cephalopods, taken by deep-plunging (from up to 20 m), but also surface-plunging. Prey caught underwater. Flocks of up to 500 may form at good fishing sources; also follows boats.
Social behaviour: Gregarious, both at colonies and at sea. Generally monogamous and pair-bonds may be life-long, though males may occasionally be promiscuous.
Breeding biology: Jul–Feb on rocky, usually inaccessible islands and stacks. Constructs low compact mound with shallow cup, on bare ground, rocks or within low vegetation. Lays 1–2 matt white eggs, incubated by both sexes for 35–50 days. Young fledge in 95–119 days and are usually immediately independent.
Conservation Not globally threatened and population increased between mid-1940s and early 1980s at rate of 2.3% per annum to almost 53,000 pairs, most of which were in New Zealand. Since then overall population considered probably stable. Disturbance by humans permits Kelp Gulls *Larus dominicanus* to rob eggs, and fisherman sometimes take chicks as bait, while Maori formerly exploited young.
Taxonomy Monotypic.

Cape Gannet *Morus capensis* Plate 15

Identification

Confusion risks: Australasian Gannet *M. serrator*.
Main characters: Large, long/narrow-winged marine bird, much like previous species, including plumage pattern and development. Flight and behaviour also similar, and both are like Northern Hemisphere counterpart, Northern Gannet *M. bassanus* (not recorded in Southern Ocean), differing from latter in ad plumage by black secondaries and tail. **Ad** tinged deep yellowish-buff on head and neck, but varies individually and with season; rest of body, including wing-coverts, essentially white; outer primaries, their coverts, secondaries (except innermost) and usually entire tail contrasting black, while underwing is similar except primary-coverts, which are also white. Bill mainly bluish-grey, bordered by blackish facial skin with rather long black gular stripe; eye pale grey, eye-ring blue and legs blackish. **Juv** predominantly dusky-brown, sparsely spotted white on head/neck, breast, back and upperwing-coverts, and variably paler below, but usually has darker breast. Remiges and rectrices black; bare parts duller, and bill and iris darker. **Imm** in second–fourth-year becomes progressively whiter, in second-year mainly upperwing-coverts and belly whiten, but still rather patchily and irregularly patterned, followed by head/neck and underparts, then rest of upperparts. By third-year body largely white. Fourth- to fifth-year birds essentially as ad but with variable dark feathering on white parts, especially above, and bare-parts coloration perhaps less advanced and golden-buff head less intense.
Voice: At sea largely silent, but very noisy at colonies (see Australasian Gannet).

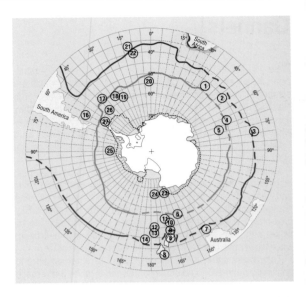

Size: 85–94 cm, wing 45–51 cm, wingspan 171–185 cm, weight 2.29–3.29 kg. Male slightly larger than female.
Similar species: Separated with certainty from ad Australasian Gannet only if seen close, when diagnostic, substantially longer black gular stripe can be observed; also usually has all-black tail (most often only central 2–4 feathers in Australasian), but some Cape can possess white outer feathers and some Australasian may have almost all-black tail, especially younger ads. Cape also tends to have paler iris. Juv and imm darker and less spotted white than Australasian, but due to great individual variation in both species, the most reliable feature is the length of the black gular stripe (about three times longer in Cape), which is difficult to see in the field. Other characters appear unreliable or not useful for field identification, but require further study.

Distribution and biology

Distribution, movements and population: Breeds at six colonies off S Africa at Mercury, Ichaboe and Possession Is (Namibia) to Lambert's Bay, Malgas I and Bird I, Algoa Bay (South Africa), with recent records from St Paul. Ranges north at sea to Gulf of Guinea and Kenya, east into Indian Ocean and west across Atlantic as far as Brazil (at least three records) and S Argentina (four records). One frequented an Australian Gannet colony near the entrance to Port Phillip Bay, south of Melbourne, throughout much of 1980s and another was caught off W Australia. Also, one at Cape Kidnappers, New Zealand, in 1997–2001. Population believed to total over 153,000 pairs in late 1990s (the overwhelming majority in South Africa), with evidence of decrease of 31% between 1956 and 1996.
Diet and feeding: Much as Australasian Gannet; often associates with dolphins.
Social behaviour: Like Australasian Gannet.
Breeding biology: Few data from our region, but for a general résumé see Brown *et al.* (1982).
Conservation Vulnerable; fully protected at colonies, as value in guano production well known. Occasionally killed by fishermen at sea.
Taxonomy Monotypic. Sometimes considered conspecific with Australasian Gannet, and vagrants of latter have occurred on several islands off South Africa and interbred with Cape Gannets on Malgas I, in Saldanha Bay.

Plate 15 Gannets

Australasian Gannet ad.

Usually only central (2–4)
tail feathers are black

Cape Gannet ad.

Most (but not all) have wholly or
largely black tail feathers

Australasian Gannet ad.

**Australasian
Gannet** juv.

Cape Gannet juv.

Darker overall

Paler and more
extensively
spotted

Australasian Gannet juv.

Cape Gannet ad.

Much longer black
gular stripe to throat;
all-black tail

Cape Gannet ad.
(p. 240)

Australasian
Gannet ad.

Much shorter black gular stripe
to throat; more white in tail

Australasian Gannet ad.
(p. 239)

Large skuas

Plate 16 and the following text deal with another taxonomically problematic group, the genus *Catharacta* or large skuas, which together with *Stercorarius* form the subfamily Stercorariinae. These are medium to large predatory and scavenging marine birds, clearly differentiated from gulls, but (with terns) belonging to the same family, Laridae. Separated from gulls by many phenotypic characters e.g., females larger than males (the opposite in gulls), stronger flight muscles and feathers, strongly hooked claws, hard scutes to the tarsi, and powerful, hooked and slightly more complex-structured bills. The large skuas differ from the smaller *Stercorarius* in their lack of tail streamers and different plumage patterns, while nearly all breed in the Southern Hemisphere, rather than the north.

Catharacta contains six diagnosable taxa, of which five nest in our region. Generally, from south to north they are, *maccormicki* on Antarctic coasts, lonnbergi mainly on islands either side of the Antarctic Convergence, with further north in the S Atlantic, *antarctica* and *hamiltoni*, and *chilensis* local in S South America. The sixth form, skua, Great Skua, is the only Northern Hemisphere representative, being confined to the NE Atlantic.

For many years the six forms were regarded as races of 1–2 species, but more recent works generally regard four as species: South Polar Skua *C. maccormicki* (monotypic), Subantarctic/Brown/Antarctic Skua *C. antarctica* (including lonnbergi and hamiltoni), Chilean Skua *C. chilensis* (monotypic) and Great Skua *C. skua* (monotypic). This arrangement was supported by Harrison (1983), Olsen & Larsson (1997) and del Hoyo *et al.* (1996), but Higgins & Davies (1996) favoured three, uniting *antarctica*, lonnbergi and hamiltoni within skua. Alternatively, Sibley & Monroe (1990) and Sibley (1996) treated *antarctica* and hamiltoni conspecifically (as Southern Skua) and separate from lonnbergi (Brown Skua), thus regarding the complex as consisting of five allospecies of *C. [skua]*, which has, unfortunately, been subject to erroneous interpretation by some subsequent authors.

The group's taxonomy begs further study and I currently prefer to tentatively treat all recognized taxa as distinctive allospecies of the superspecies *C. [skua]*. I view this group as containing several, well-diverged taxa with clear morphological differences, which have not yet reached a level of sufficient distinctness to avoid interbreeding when they come into contact. Moreover, I use the term 'brown skua', *C. [skua] antarctica*, to characterize the main Southern Ocean group, treating *antarctica*, lonnbergi and hamiltoni as distinct races, apportioning them equal weight to emphasize their distinctness and unresolved taxonomic status. The arrangement is as follows (English names follow Olsen & Larsson 1997):

1. Great Skua *C. [skua] skua* – NE Atlantic, not treated here (as outside our region)

2. The 'brown skua' group *C. [skua] antarctica* – Southern Ocean, three distinct populations:

   Falkland Skua the race *antarctica* – Falkland and Patagonia

   Subantarctic Skua the race *lonnbergi* – mainly on subantarctic islands

   Tristan Skua the race *hamiltoni* – Tristan da Cunha and Gough, and possibly this form on Amsterdam and St Paul

3. Chilean Skua *Catharacta [skua] chilensis* – S Chile and S Argentina to Cape Horn

4. South Polar Skua *C. [skua] maccormicki* – on Antarctic coasts.

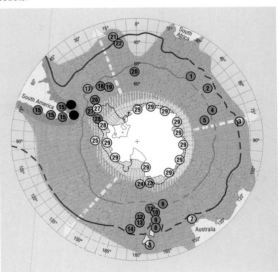

Falkland Skua *Catharacta [skua] antarctica* ssp. *antarctica*
Tristan Skua *Catharacta [skua] antarctica* ssp. *hamiltoni*
Subantarctic Skua *Catharacta [skua] antarctica* ssp. *lonnbergi*
Chilean Skua *Catharacta [skua] chilensis*
South Polar Skua *Catharacta [skua] maccormicki*
Overall summer range of the 'brown skua' group
Overall summer range of South Polar Skua
Northwards migration of South Polar Skua

1 Prince Edward & Marion
2 Crozet
3 Amsterdam & St Paul
4 Kerguelen
5 Heard
6 Macquarie
8 New Zealand and offshore islands
9 Snares
10 Auckland
11 Campbell
12 Antipodes
13 Bounty
14 Chatham
● South American offshore islands
15 South American offshore islands
● Falklands
18 South Georgia
19 South Sandwich
20 Bouvetøya
21 Tristan da Cunha
22 Gough
25 Peter I Øy
26 South Orkney
27 South Shetland
27 South Shetland
28 Antarctic Peninsula
28 Antarctic Peninsula
29 Antarctic coasts and offshore islands

Ad Subantarctic Skua Catharacta [skua] antarctica, *subsp.* lonnbergi. *Many of the southern skuas live close to penguin rookeries where they predate eggs or small chicks; here eating a King Penguin* Aptenodytes patagonicus *chick. Kerguelen, Mar 2004. © Hadoram Shirihai.*

Plate 16 Large skuas

Large, heavily built and evenly dark; underwing-coverts hardly contrast with paler body as in most pale/intermediate South Polar

Subantarctic Skua
lonnbergi ad.
(p. 246)

Slighter, rather pale body contrasts with darker wings; usually paler nape and lores

South Polar Skua
intermediate ad.

Chilean Skua ad.

and broad
ary flashes;
se view,
age
ularly
hed

Diagnostic pale
body contrast

Chilean Skua ad.
(p. 248)

Rusty-tinged body and underwing-coverts, dark cap and paler bill base identify most individuals

South Polar Skua pale ad.

Falkland Skua ad.
(p. 244)

South Polar Skua
intermediate ad.

rker cap and
re uniform
mage, otherwise
eparable from
ilar Subantarctic
ua

Usually paler (streaky) nape patch and lores; pale body contrasts with darker wings

South Polar Skua pale ad.
(p. 249)

alkland Skua
.

Young still
uniform

Falkland Skua ad.

South Polar Skua juv.

Difficult to separate from brown skuas, but slighter build, colder plumage with pale nape patch and loral mark (absent in juv)

South Polar Skua
dark ad.

Tristan Skua ad.
(p. 245)

ntermediate between Subantarctic
nd Falkland Skuas and largely
separable from both, except by
nge (see text)

Subantarctic Skua
lonnbergi ad./imm.

More uniform and narrowly streaked birds (and
even plainer juv – see photo p. 248) subject to
much confusion with dark/juv South Polar

Subantarctic Skua
lonnbergi ad.

Heavily built with large
head and bill; characteristic
blotchy upperparts

Using this conservative but flexible approach, I recognize the need for further evidence in the quest to arrive at a thorough understanding of the group's taxonomy, while emphasizing their distinctness by treating each in detail.

General size and overall proportion/shape, including head/bill, and to some degree differences in head and body coloration/pattern, including extent/shape and nature of pale body streaks/blotches, especially on neck, the specific pattern of dark on crown/head and the relative strength of the pale nuchal collar are important, but should be used in combination to correctly identify each of the *C. [skua]* complex. Other less distinct plumage features, such as the amount of white on the primary bases (flashes) and, in some, bill colour, may also prove useful. Moult timing and strategy can be an important identification aid (if the bird in question is correctly aged). For example, South Polar Skua moults on migration/in winter and very rapidly (juv much later than ad), whereas the entire 'brown skua' group commence their rather prolonged moult (which sometimes extends throughout the non-breeding season) at the end of, or immediately after the breeding season. It is vital to stress the difficulty of correctly appreciating all these characters, as they are often obscured, mainly due to overlap and individual variation, and further complicated by the presence of hybrids, which are quite common in some areas. I would also like to stress the importance of the following works, which have contributed to the ongoing process of understanding the identification and taxonomy of large skuas: Devillers (1977, 1978), Harrison (1983), Gantlett & Harrap (1992), Jiguet (1997), *HANZAB* (1996), Olsen & Larsson (1997) and Jiguet *et al.* (1999).

All six forms treated here are marine birds, which principally scavenge for food, as well as predating seabird eggs and young. Kleptoparasitism is an important means of acquiring food. They principally nest on offshore and remote islands. Diet is mostly small fish, crustaceans and cephalopods. They nest in loose colonies, sometimes close to other seabirds, using small, often unlined scrapes. Ads lay 1–4 (most usually two) eggs, incubated 4–5 weeks, and chicks take 7–8 weeks to fledge. Both ads take a full role in all aspects of the breeding cycle. Of the species considered here, all wander to some extent in the non-breeding season but only *maccormicki* performs regular long-distance migrations, perhaps mainly by imms, following a clockwise route from Antarctica to the N Pacific, thence south to 'summer' at sea just north of the equator, with a similar pattern having recently been established in the Atlantic, but the frequency of its occurrence in the N Indian Ocean is still unknown.

Falkland Skua *Catharacta* [*skua*] *antarctica*, subspecies *antarctica*   Plate 16

Identification

Confusion risks: Other southern *Catharacta*, but principally Subantarctic *lonnbergi*, Chilean *chilensis* and South Polar Skuas *maccormicki*.
Main characters: Generally brownish, large gull-like skua, with bold white primary flashes visible in flight; occurs principally in coastal and marine waters between the Falklands and S Argentina. Compared to similar Subantarctic and Tristan Skuas, distinctly smaller and slighter, with proportionally longer legs and stronger, powerful bill in relation to more rounded head shape (which approaches Tristan), thus not as heavy/large as Subantarctic; overall size close to South Polar but stockier. Somewhat intermediate between European *skua* and Subantarctic, but closer to former in shape and general plumage, though typically colder brown. **Ad** quite variable, but compared to Subantarctic has darker, often quite contrasting cap (in some reduced to dark mask near eye)

Ad Falkland Skua Catharacta [skua] antarctica, *subsp.* antarctica. *Characteristic in being relatively smaller, paler streaked above and usually obviously dark-capped. Falklands, Jan 1991. © René Pop.*

and numerous narrow straw-yellow streaks on neck and breast, though mantle, scapulars and upperwing-coverts usually lack obvious pale streaks/blotches, with larger pale blotchy streaking/mottling on body-sides and breast, especially in paler individuals. Thus, look for typical combination of paler-streaked/spotted neck/breast, emphasizing darker upper head and more uniform/unmarked dorsal areas, unlike most Subantarctic. Beware, however, often quite extensively mottled upperparts to palest birds, and some with rustier blackish-brown ground colour, which strongly resemble Subantarctic. Smaller underwing-coverts blackish-brown, contrast with greyer greater coverts and underside of flight feathers (but not solidly and contrastingly marked as in South Polar). Bill, irides, eye-ring and legs mainly black. Reported to have more prominent supra-orbital ridges than other *Catharacta* (Devillers 1978, Olsen & Larsson 1997). Sexes similar except in size. **Juv** principally dark brown, with darker hood and extensively tinged buffish-cinnamon below and on narrow/indistinct (U-shaped) fringes and bars to upperwing-coverts and scapulars. Underwing as ad, but may have reduced white primary flashes. Bill dusky with even darker tip, and rest of bare parts greyer, less intense or only partially black. Probably inseparable from juv *lonnbergi* and *hamiltoni*, but apparently more rufous-toned. **Imm** much as ad, but darker and more uniform with much-reduced or irregular pale streaks and blotches. Attains ad plumage at 3–4 years old, but ageing very difficult by second-year, and should only be attempted if possible to assess moult.
Voice: Apparently very similar to Subantarctic Skua (which see); regrettably there are no data concerning possible differences in

Ad Falkland Skua Catharacta [skua] antarctica, *subsp.* antarctica *in territorial long-call display, which characterizes the large skuas, Falklands, Dec 1990. © René Pop.*

long-calls and displays of the 'brown skuas'.

Size: 52–64 cm, wing 35.5–40.2 cm, wingspan 126–160 cm, no weight data. Females average larger in most measurements, most noticeably in wing length, though considerable overlap.

Similar forms: Differs from Subantarctic Skua in smaller size, paler-streaked neck/breast, darker upper head, and more uniform mantle, scapulars and upperwing-coverts, but the two are only doubtfully separable in the field. Also very similar to Tristan Skua from which mainly separated by range, but latter to some degree closer to Subantarctic in size and plumage, with less obvious dark cap, fewer yellow neck streaks and larger pale streaking/mottling on upperwing-coverts and scapulars than Falkland (see Tristan for further information). Could also be confused with Chilean Skua, with which it hybridizes (see latter). South Polar Skua distinguished from *antarctica* by same principal characters as from other 'brown skuas' (see *maccormicki* for details).

Hybridization: Apparently to a limited extent only with Chilean Skua in S Argentina.

Distribution and biology

Distribution, movements and population: Falklands and S Argentina from Chubut to Tierra del Fuego. Argentine birds may be *chilensis* rather than *antarctica* (Sibley 1996). Ranges at sea, during mid-Oct to mid-May, but rarely moves far, e.g. only a straggler as far north as Buenos Aires province, Argentina. Numbered c.5000–9000 pairs in the Falklands during 1983 to 1993.

Diet and feeding: Scavenges at refuse tips, but principally takes burrow-nesting seabirds at night, and predates penguin eggs, chicks and ads, as well as afterbirth and carcasses of seals.

Social behaviour: Sometimes establishes feeding territories.

Breeding biology: Oct–Nov onwards in loose colonies, though highly territorial, on flat grassy areas or short-grass heaths. Nest scrape unlined or only scantily so. Lays 1–3 eggs (two most common), incubated 28–32 days. Young leave nest within 1–2 days and fledge in 40–50 days. Reaches sexual maturity at six years.

Conservation Not globally threatened. Numbers possibly reduced in the Falklands through human persecution and perhaps as result of decline in Rockhopper Penguin *Eudyptes chrysocome*.

Taxonomy Genus frequently merged within *Stercorarius*. Occasionally regarded as conspecific with all congeners and the group almost certainly constitutes a superspecies. Often included with Subantarctic Skua or Great Skua *C.* [*s.*] *skua*, but this form appears as distinct as all other southern skuas. Tristan Skua, with which it is often united, also appears sufficiently distinct to warrant separate treatment. See also group introduction.

Tristan Skua *Catharacta* [*skua*] *antarctica*, subspecies *hamiltoni*   Plate 16

Identification

Confusion risks: Other southern *Catharacta*, but principally Subantarctic *lonnbergi* and South Polar Skuas *maccormicki*.

Main characters: Generally brownish, large gull-like skua, with bold white primary flashes visible in flight; occurs principally in waters around Tristan da Cunha and Gough. Generally intermediate between Subantarctic and Falkland Skuas *antarctica*. Compared to former, slightly smaller, with proportionally longer legs and bill, and squarer or rounder head shape (in latter approaches Falkland). **Ad** typically has uniform dark brown head and neck, but often appears quite obviously dusky-capped, intermediate between Subantarctic and Falkland. Narrow straw-yellow streaks on hindneck and neck-sides normally fewer than latter, but can be similar, even having warmer (more golden-buff) necklace than Subantarctic. Mantle, scapulars and upperwing-coverts usually have more obvious pale creamy-rufous streaks/blotches, strongly approaching Subantarctic. Blackish-brown smaller underwing-coverts clearly contrast with greyer greater coverts and underside to remiges (but pattern less marked than South Polar). Bill, irides, eye-ring and legs mainly black. Sexes similar except in size. **Juv** overall dark brown, with slightly darker hood; underparts rather extensively tinged warmer reddish-/cinnamon-brown, and upperwing-coverts and scapulars narrowly/indistinctly fringed buffy-rufous. Underwing as ad, but some have reduced white primary flashes. Bill has darker tip, and rest of bare parts greyer and less intense black. Generally intermediate between Subantarctic and Falkland, and probably inseparable from either, but apparently still rufous below, thus closer to latter. **Imm** (ageing difficult) darker and more uniform than ad, with much-reduced or irregular pale streaks and blotches. Attains ad plumage at c.3–4 years old.

Tristan Skua Catharacta [skua] antarctica, *subsp.* hamiltoni *is only separable by range from other 'brown skuas'. It approaches smaller Falkland* C. [s.] antarctica, *subsp.* antarctica *in slightly capped appearance (reduced or lacking in Subantarctic Skua* C. [s.] antarctica, *subsp.* lonnbergi*). Off Gough, Mar 2003. © Hadoram Shirihai.*

Tristan Skua Catharacta [skua] antarctica, *subsp.* hamiltoni *is generally intermediate between Falkland* C. [s.] antarctica, *subsp.* antarctica *and Subantarctic Skuas* C. [s.] antarctica, *subsp.* lonnbergi, *from which it is mainly separated by range. Gough. © Peter Ryan.*

Voice: Apparently very similar to Subantarctic Skua (which see); regrettably there are no data concerning possible differences in long-calls and displays of the 'brown skuas'.
Size: 52–64 cm, wing 37.2–42.3 cm, wingspan 126–160 cm, weight 1.17–1.8 kg. Females average larger in all measurements, most obviously in bill size and depth, and tarsus length.
Similar forms: Generally intermediate between Subantarctic and Falkland Skuas, with separation in the field from the latter probably impossible, except on range. It is also uncertainly distinguished in the field from Subantarctic, except perhaps by combination of somewhat smaller size, proportionately longer bill, slight cap and more straw-yellow (finely streaked) neck. See also South Polar Skua.
Hybridization: May hybridize to limited extent with Subantarctic Skua (see below for complications with latter in Indian Ocean).

Distribution and biology

Distribution, movements and population: Gough, Inaccessible and Tristan. Population c.2500 pairs in recent years. Range at sea poorly known, but most apparently remain close to breeding area, between 35°S and 55°S, though two ringed birds recovered in NE Brazil. For discussion concerning possibility of it breeding on Amsterdam and St Paul see taxonomy.
Diet and feeding: Principally catches burrow-nesting seabirds, and also predates penguin eggs, chicks and ads, as well as afterbirth and carcasses of seals.
Social behaviour: May establish feeding territories.
Breeding biology: Oct–Nov onwards in loose colonies, but highly territorial. Nest scrape unlined or only scantily so. Lays 1–3 eggs (two most common), incubated 28–32 days. Young leave nest within 1–2 days and fledge in 40–50 days. Reaches sexual maturity at six years.
Conservation Not globally threatened. Numbers have declined in Tristan da Cunha through human persecution.
Taxonomy Occasionally considered conspecific with all congeners and the group almost certainly constitutes a superspecies. Often united with Falkland Skua (e.g., by Sibley & Monroe 1990), but they appear sufficiently distinct to be treated separately. Birds on Amsterdam and St Paul have similar biometrics (especially shorter bill and wing) to *hamiltoni*, rather than *lonnbergi* of elsewhere in the Indian Ocean (*HANZAB*), but moult apparently as latter. Those on Amsterdam and St Paul have noticeably dark caps, like *hamiltoni*, and rest of plumage also approaches latter, except limits of fine yellowish streaks on neck. It is noteworthy that Tristan da Cunha and Gough, and Amsterdam and St Paul share several marine avifauna similarities, including Northern Rockhopper

Penguin *Eudyptes* [*chrysocome*] *moseleyi*, which may explain the similarity of the skuas on Amsterdam and St Paul to *hamiltoni*. The two latter populations and the previous form represent the northernmost representatives of their respective complexes in the Atlantic and Indian sectors of the Southern Ocean, principally breeding north of the Antarctic Convergence and in northerly subantarctic waters. The genus is frequently merged within *Stercorarius*. See also group introduction.

Subantarctic Skua *Catharacta* [*skua*] *antarctica* subspecies *lonnbergi* Plate 16

Identification

Confusion risks: Other southern *Catharacta*.
Main characters: Generally brownish, large gull-like skua, with bold white primary flashes in flight; occurs largely in subantarctic waters, but also on South Shetlands, northern Peninsula, South Orkney and South Sandwiches. Larger and heavier than preceding forms, with proportionately shorter legs and bill (latter still very powerful and stubby), somewhat flatter crown and very thick neck; most are medium warm brown (tinged dull rufous) with more pale blotches above and below. **Ad** has variably dark head, some having dusky crown and cheeks, or sometimes dusky mask (when bleached); also a few, rather indistinct, narrow straw-yellow streaks on hindneck and neck-sides (barely forming a patch). Rest of plumage also variable, some have blackish-brown ground colour (intensity of rufous hue varies individually/with wear, but generally stronger in pale/intermediate individuals, and can be strongly reduced); mantle, scapulars and upperwing-coverts usually rather broadly streaked/blotched pale, with pale, quite well-developed longitudinal blotchy streaks/mottling (and some ill-defined cross-bars) on body-sides and breast, especially on pale birds. With wear, also bleaches duller and spots/streaks obscured. Lesser and median underwing-coverts blackish-brown, contrasting with greyer greater underwing-coverts and underside to flight feathers, but less marked than South Polar Skua. Bill, irides, eye-ring and legs mainly black. Sexes similar except in size. **Juv** rather uniform dark chocolate-brown (or tinged rufous/cinnamon), lacking dark-hooded impression, and underparts only slightly tinged buffish-cinnamon; no or very narrow/indistinct streaks and blotches on back, scapulars and upperwing-coverts (later tipped paler when fresh). Underwing as ad, but white primary flashes slightly smaller. Bill dusky with even darker tip and rest of bare parts greyer, less intense or only partially black. **Imm** much as ad, but darker and more uniform, with strongly reduced/irregular pale streaks and

Ad Subantarctic Skua Catharacta [skua] antarctica, *subsp.* lonnbergi, *Snares. © Colin Miskelly.*

Ad Subantarctic Skua Catharacta [skua] antarctica, subsp. lonnbergi *is heavier than other 'brown skuas', with a very thick neck, chunky body, broader wings and stubbier bill; note heavily blotched, rufous-brown plumage, and blackish-brown underwing-coverts usually contrast less strongly than South Polar. South Georgia, Oct 2001. © Hadoram Shirihai.*

blotches. Attains ad-like plumage following first post-juv moult, but many imms very uniform brown without extensive pale blotching on mantle and only pale golden streaks on hindneck, making ageing (which requires accurate assessment of moult) thereafter difficult; fully ad at c.3–4 years old.

Voice: Generally silent, except typically raucous long-call of 5–9 loud guttural notes, given while stretching neck upwards, raising head and opening bill to widest possible extent, and sometimes extending and raising the wings backward, exposing white primary patches (especially in defence of territory); also in some food disputes; other calls, including alarm, quiet and low pitched. See *HANZAB* for details.

Size: 52–64 cm, wing 37.8–34.5 cm, wingspan 126–160 cm, weight 1.25–2.54 kg. Females average larger in all measurements, principally wing, bill and tail length, but considerable overlap.

Similar forms: Very similar to Falkland *antarctica* and Tristan

Ad/imm Subantarctic Skua Catharacta [skua] antarctica, subsp. lonnbergi *is variable, some have a blackish-brown ground colour with much-reduced pale streaks/blotches. Auckland, Dec 1999. © Hadoram Shirihai.*

Ad/imm Subantarctic Skua Catharacta [skua] antarctica, *subsp.* lonnbergi: *note very heavy build, especially thick neck, ad with short strong legs and short wingtip. Note rather reduced pale blotches and streaks due to wear. Kerguelen, Mar 2004. © Hadoram Shirihai.*

Fresh juv Subantarctic Skua Catharacta [skua] antarctica, *subsp.* lonnbergi: *more uniformly dark compared to ad, with diffuse and narrower pale tips, streaks and blotches to wing-coverts and scapulars. South Georgia, Mar 2003. © Hadoram Shirihai.*

Skuas *hamiltoni*, with differences discussed under these forms. See also Chilean *chilensis* and South Polar Skuas *maccormicki* for separation of these forms.

Hybridization: May hybridize to some extent with all southern *Catharacta*, but principally with *maccormickii* (which see for details).

Distribution and biology

Distribution, movements and population: Southern Ocean (principally close to the Antarctic Convergence) on South Georgia, South Sandwich, South Orkney, South Shetland, Bouvetøya, Prince Edward, Marion, Crozet, Kerguelen, Heard, Macquarie, Auckland, Campbell, Snares, Bounty, Antipodes, Chatham; also Antarctic Peninsula to 65°S, and S New Zealand, in Fiordland and on Stewart I. Ranges at sea to tropical oceans and in the Atlantic to the Lesser Antilles.

Diet and feeding: Scavenges at refuse tips, but principally catches burrow-nesting seabirds at night, and also preys on penguin eggs, chicks and ads, as well as the afterbirth and carcasses of seals.

Social behaviour: Sometimes establishes feeding territories.

Breeding biology: Oct–Nov onwards in loose colonies, but highly territorial. Sometimes several males to one female, especially in areas occupied year-round, and such communal breeding observed in up to 30% of territories in Chathams and Snares. Nest scrape unlined or only scantily so. Lays 1–2 eggs (latter more common), incubated 28–32 days. Young leave nest within 1–2 days and fledge in 40–50 days. Reaches sexual maturity at six years.

Conservation Not globally threatened. Numbers greatly reduced, particularly on Chatham, through human persecution. Breeding success usually high and numbers apparently increasing on Antarctic Peninsula, probably as a result of arrival of humans and consequent disturbance of seabird colonies.

Taxonomy Genus frequently merged within *Stercorarius*. Sometimes regarded as conspecific with all congeners and group almost certainly constitutes a superspecies, *C. [skua]*. Often treated as conspecific with Great Skua *C. [s.] skua*, and frequently merged with *antarctica* and *hamiltoni*, which together form the 'brown skua' group. See group introduction.

Chilean Skua *Catharacta [skua] chilensis*   Plate 16

Identification

Confusion risks: Other southern *Catharacta*, but principally Subantarctic *lonnbergi*, Falkland *antarctica* and South Polar Skuas *maccormicki*.

Main characters: Generally brownish, large gull-like skua, with bold white primary flashes visible in flight; occurs largely in waters around S South America. Compared to 'brown skuas', particularly Subantarctic, rather smaller and slighter/slenderer, with proportionately less powerful/stubby bill and has narrower wings, slimmer tail, body and neck, with jizz approaching South Polar. Angular head, emphasized by dusky cap, which with bicoloured bill and warmish rusty-cinnamon tinge to underparts are best field marks. **Ad** usually has clear-cut blackish-brown cap (only slightly obscured in a few), extending to lower eye level and covering entire crown. Dark cap appears uniform with upperwing/back and clearly contrasts with paler neck and rest of body (head to back usually paler than upperwing in 'brown skuas'). Neck and body to mantle extensively mottled/streaked cinnamon and rufous-buff to reddish-brown, with some extremes heavily marked on mantle. Vague darkish breast-band sometimes apparent. With wear, rusty/cinnamon hue and pale mottles/streaks reduced, and some bleach paler and greyer (with whiter patches). Apparently, blackish-brown examples, as variably exist in 'brown skuas' (especially Subantarctic) and well described in South Polar (dark morph), unknown, but further evidence required. Underwing dark brown, usually with rusty-tinged underwing-coverts, much like body, and not contrasting with underside of flight feathers; underwing white primary flashes typically narrower than 'brown skuas'. Bill mainly grey with black tip, and irides, eye-ring and legs mainly black. Sexes similar except in size. **Juv** generally much more uniform and richer cinnamon/rusty below, with broad scaly fringes (of same colour) to darker upperparts, and rump usually buffier. Underwing as ad. Bare parts greyer and less intense black. **Imm** generally as ad, but darker with reduced/irregular pale streaks and blotches. Attains full-ad plumage at c.3–4 years old.

Chilean Skua Catharacta [skua] chilensis: note dark cap, and cinnamon and rufous-buff mottling and streaks, including on underwing-coverts, which identify it from all other Catharacta. Off Ushuaia, S Argentina, Mar 2006. © Hadoram Shirihai.

Voice: Apparently very similar to Subantarctic Skua (which see); regrettably there are no data concerning possible differences in long-calls and displays from those of the 'brown skuas'.

Size: 53–59 cm, wing 36.8–41.8 cm, wingspan 130–138 cm, weight 1.1–1.7 kg. Females typically average larger in all measurements, especially wing length, but usually considerable overlap.

Similar forms: Falkland Skua, but latter and other southern *Catharacta* have all-dark (rather than bicoloured) bills, while ad *chilensis* also tends to have more capped appearance and, on average, much brighter cinnamon-coloured underparts and underwing; the latter is especially pronounced in juvs, which are unique among skuas in their strongly barred mantle feathering.

Hybridization: Apparently to limited extent with Falkland Skua in S Argentina.

Distribution and biology

Distribution, movements and population: Coasts and islands of SC Chile and S Argentina to Cape Horn. Ranges at sea north along both coasts of South America to Peru, at 14°S, and Brazil, to 22°S, and W Falklands. Population unknown but perhaps several thousand pairs.

Diet and feeding: Poorly known, but perhaps more gull-like than other skuas, though it apparently visits seabird colonies to predate eggs and young, and parasitizes other birds, it also feeds on

shores alongside Kelp Gull *Larus dominicanus*, follows trawlers and visits rubbish tips.

Social behaviour: Much less territorial and more colonial than other large skuas; perhaps less prone to attack humans entering nesting areas, though reports vary.

Breeding biology: Nov onwards in colonies, sometimes at high density. Nest scrape lined with dead grass. Lays 1–2 eggs (latter more common), incubated 28–32 days. Few other data.

Conservation Not globally threatened. Threats unknown, though eggs and chicks presumably harvested for food. No information on population trends or breeding success.

Taxonomy Occasionally regarded as conspecific with all congeners of *C. [skua]*. Genus frequently merged within *Stercorarius*. See also group introduction.

South Polar Skua
Catharacta [skua] maccormicki   Plate 16

Identification

Confusion risks: Other southern *Catharacta*, but principally Subantarctic Skua *lonnbergi*, and perhaps Pomarine Jaeger *Stercorarius pomarinus*.

Main characters: Highly variable. Polymorphic, with coldest cream, brownish to blackish-brown plumages. Large gull-like skua, with bold white primary flashes. Principally Antarctic waters, but performs longest migrations of *Catharacta*. Usually distinctly smaller than *Subantarctic*, but approximately same size as Falkland *antarctica*, Tristan *hamiltoni* and Chilean Skuas *chilensis*. Compared to all, especially former, slighter and less powerful, proportionately smaller headed, with flatter crown, shorter legs and slimmer bill (less pronounced gonys), and also not as thick-necked, wings somewhat narrower and longer. In flight, appears less heavy and more agile, and is less prone to kleptoparasitize than congeners.

Ad plumage has two, perhaps three morphs, pale, intermediate and dark, but, especially between first two, extensive variation.

Pale and intermediate morphs have head to underparts pale, greyish cream-brown or buffy-cream (pale morph), to medium or dark cold brown (intermediate morph), contrasting with very dark wing surfaces and rest of upperparts; typically, pale feathering below appears diffusely barred. Usually has quite conspicuous pale-streaked buffish nape/hindneck (sometimes to neck-sides), often appearing as broad patch (especially distinct in flight), further enhanced in summer by golden hackles (visible in close views). Pale

Chilean Skua Catharacta [skua] chilensis: strong reddish-cinnamon and buff pigments on underparts, dark cap and bicoloured bill render this form identifiable in most instances. Off Ushuaia, S Argentina, Mar 2006. © Hadoram Shirihai.

Ad South Polar Skua Catharacta [skua] maccormicki is smaller and slighter than Subantarctic Skua C. [s.] antarctica, subsp. lonnbergi, with pale morph (here) diagnostic amongst southern Catharacta. Cape Bird, Ross Sea, Jan 1999. © Hadoram Shirihai.

Ad South Polar Skua Catharacta [skua] maccormicki, *intermediate (left) and dark morphs: note slighter overall structure, smaller head, less thick neck, proportionately longer wings, well-marked buff hindneck, small whitish lores, and rather ill-defined barring below; smaller underwing-coverts appear solidly blackish. Antarctic Peninsula, Mar 2003. © Hadoram Shirihai.*

parts, especially head/neck, evenly and very narrowly lanceolated buff and white (shaft-streaks), often including darker mantle/scapular feathers. Most have small whitish-tinged forehead/loral patch (near bill base). To varying degree, all have slight dark-faced/cheeked appearance, and the dark around and in front of eye limited but often distinct. With the wear, bleach paler, almost becoming white-headed in extremes. Lesser and median underwing-coverts solidly blackish-brown to black, sharply contrasting with greyer greater coverts and underside to flight feathers. **Dark morph** (1–20% of ads) entirely cold, sooty blackish-brown, but usually has even darker face and upperparts and, at close range, appears highly symmetrically and narrowly streaked buffy on nape/neck and whitish on mantle/scapulars, while some may have tiny paler frontal spots. Buffy nuchal patch usually faint and rather sparse, being limited to a few streaks, and is rarely more conspicuous (most usually in flight) when tips to neck feathers coalesce. In breeding season develops golden hackles to nape/hind-neck like paler morphs. Underwing-coverts contrastingly blackish as in paler morphs. Intermediates between dark and paler morphs are dark morph-like, with paler barred underparts or fore body. All morphs have same, mainly black bill, irides, eye-ring and legs. Sexes similar except in size and, slightly, in tone (female larger and paler). **Juv** variable in darkness of overall body plumage, apparently unrelated to morphs and vast majority principally like ad intermediate morph, but distinctive in being overall plainer and greyer; upperparts almost uniform dusky-brown, narrowly/indistinctly fringed pale, with clear-cut, black-tipped grey bill and mainly greyish legs. Nape/neck patch of ad missing. Underwing as ad. **Imm** attains full-ad plumage at c.3 years old, but in second-year (following post-juv moult) ageing becomes difficult (and requires accurate moult assessment; juvs moult c.4 months later than ads); on breeding grounds, young imm lacks golden hackles on nape/hindneck. At least in earlier stages (2–3 years old), plumage generally more uniform, with strongly reduced/partial pale nape/hindneck and golden hackles, and reduced pale streaking. Paler bill base and legs sometimes still apparent in second-years. *Voice*: Some differences from Subantarctic Skua (which see), with somewhat lower pitched and faster and more raucous long-calls, but some variation and much overlap. Long-call displays like Subantarctic, but neck of latter tends to be held slightly more forward. *Size*: 50–55 cm, wing 37.0–42.1 cm, wingspan 126–160 cm,

weight 0.6–1.69 kg. Females average larger in all measurements, but considerable overlap.

Similar forms: Principally Subantarctic Skua, but most characters (except size) also apply to 'brown skuas'. Differs from much chunkier Subantarctic in being smaller, more compact, flatter crowned, slimmer billed, smaller headed, less thick-necked and slightly shorter legged. Wings project further beyond tail and tertials and, in flight, wings appear proportionately narrower and longer. **Pale and intermediate morphs** Pale buffy-cream individuals diagnostic, as this plumage does not exist in Subantarctic. Others differ from Subantarctic by structure and size, and usually conspicuous, pale buff hindneck and small, whitish forehead/lores (both absent or much reduced in Subantarctic). Also has greyer and colder-toned body, lacking reddish/rufous-brown pigments present to some degree in 'brown skuas'. Blackish-brown upperwing/upperparts contrast more sharply with paler rest, whilst below has more ill-defined barring (rather than blotching); when close, evenly lanceolate buff-and-white (shaft-streaks) on pale head/neck and darker mantle/scapulars (Subantarctic more broadly and unevenly streaked/spotted, and also diffusely blotched). Smaller underwing-coverts usually blacker and/or more solidly patterned, contrasting more noticeably with grey greater coverts and underside

Fresh juv South Polar Skua Catharacta [skua] maccormicki: *identification can be very difficult (pale nape and loral patches of ad missing) and often requires correct judgment of structure; note plainer dusky-brown plumage with very indistinct streaking (cf. juv Subantarctic Skua C. [s.] antarctica, subsp. lonnbergi p.246). Antarctic Peninsula, Mar 2003. © Hadoram Shirihai.*

Ad/imm South Polar Skua Catharacta [skua] maccormicki, *intermediate (left) and intermediate-dark morphs. Compared to Subantarctic Skua C. [s.]* antarctica, *subsp.* lonnbergi *is more compact, with smaller head, colder greyer body, with evenly pale shaft-streaks above; pale buff hindneck and small whitish lores conspicuous only on left bird. The other has slightly dark-faced appearance. Antarctic Peninsula, Oct 2001. © Hadoram Shirihai.*

to remiges than Subantarctic (but note that in some lights, latter could appear confusingly contrasting too). **Dark morph** Separation from darkest Subantarctic less straightforward, but note evenly symmetric, narrow pale upperpart/neck streaking, which may form buff nape patch, and darker face. Subantarctic usually has less regular spots/streaks, with very limited tiny streaks on neck, broader streaks and some blotches on mantle/scapulars, and seldom has dark face or buff nape. See introduction for moult differences. **Juv** Identification of juv South Polar and Subantarctic (and other 'brown skuas') is even more problematic due to their rather plain plumages, with the species-specific marks either lacking or strongly reduced. Thus, separation is often dependent upon correct judgment of structural and size differences. I find that most juv South Polar appear more uniform than Subantarctic, which tends to show better-marked pale fringes or broader shaft-streaks on upperwing-coverts and, especially, scapulars, but such differences evident only when close (and these pale marks wear rapidly). Differences in contrast of smaller underwing-coverts, described above, also useful.

Juv Pomarine Skua can be confusingly similar, especially when distant. Seen well, *maccormicki* is easily identified in flight by being noticeably heavier/chunkier and 'hunched' (lacking elongated appearance and more pointed wings of Pomarine), with contrastingly black underwing-coverts (paler and barred in Pomarine), usually bolder and broader white primary flashes (narrower, especially on inner feathers in Pomarine, which also has pale primary-covert bases, forming pale double 'comma'), and white flashes on upperwing far more conspicuous than in Pomarine. Furthermore, *maccormicki* never has the pale uppertail-coverts/rump of Pomarine, but often has broader and bolder pale hindneck.

Hybridization: Quite extensive wherever meets Subantarctic Skua, and especially well documented around Peninsula; Olsen & Larsson (1997), HANZAB (1996) and Jiguet *et al.* (1999) summarize extent of this. Up to 5% of combined populations may consist of mixed pairs, hybrids and backcrosses, but on South Shetlands c.10% of pairs are mixed or hybrids. Great variation in appearance of hybrids, most are roughly intermediate between the two forms in both structure and plumage, but in some areas may more closely approach one parent.

Distribution and biology

Distribution, movements and population: Coasts and nearby mountains of Antarctica north to South Shetlands. In Mar/Oct–Nov, ranges at sea to Alaska, Greenland, NW Africa, Indian and N Pacific Oceans. Population 5000–8000 pairs in recent years.

Diet and feeding: Principally fish, especially *Pleurogramma antarcticum*, taken at sea some distance from colony. Predation of penguin eggs and chicks of variable, but probably always secondary, importance.

Social behaviour: Few data.

Breeding biology: Nov onwards in loose colonies, but highly territorial. Nest scrape unlined or only scantily so. Lays 1–2 eggs (latter more common), incubated 28–31 days. Young leave nest within 1–2 days and fledge in 36–45 days. Infanticide common, with older chick typically killing younger bird. Reaches sexual maturity at six years.

Conservation Not globally threatened. Numbers possibly reduced through human persecution, but population trends unclear, though breeding success known to be low and compounded by harsh weather, which also affects chick survival and adult foraging success.

Taxonomy Occasionally regarded as conspecific with all congeners and group almost certainly constitutes a superspecies, but *maccormicki* also often considered a monotypic species. Apparently locally stable hybrid populations with Subantarctic Skuas recorded with some frequency in certain areas of Antarctica (see above). See also group introduction. Genus frequently merged within *Stercorarius*.

Ad intermediate South Polar Skua Catharacta [skua] maccormicki: *note well-marked buff hindneck and back/scapulars rather thinly streaked; bold white primary flashes long and conspicuous. Antarctic Peninsula, Mar 2003. © Hadoram Shirihai.*

Stercorarius skuas

The following accounts and Plate 17 treat another characteristic group of maritime predators and scavengers—the highly migratory Northern Hemisphere-breeding skuas or jaegers. *Stercorarius* comprises three species, Pomarine *S. pomarinus*, Arctic *S. parasiticus* and Long-tailed Jaegers *S. longicaudus*, which breed across the N Holarctic, on tundra, coastal moors and remote islands, but are included here because they regularly winter in the Southern Ocean.

Stercorarius are generally small or medium-sized skuas, phenotypically clearly different from the much larger, mostly brown *Catharacta* (large skuas), but molecular data somewhat contradict this, as mtDNA sequences of Pomarine and Great Skua *C. [skua] skua* are closer to each other than the former is to Arctic/Long-tailed (cf. also Pomarine, under voice). The introduction to the large skuas explains their separation from gulls *Larus*, which belong to the same family, Laridae.

Generally they are usually lightly built skuas; most are typically fast flyers on long/narrow wings with a pointed 'hand', and relaxed and elegant, rather shallow but powerful wingbeats. Most appear dark in the field, being extensively grey-brown and off-white, with pale primary bases, which is generally also true of light-morph and young birds. Projecting tail-streamers (spring/summer) and dark, light and intermediate morphs occur in ad *parasiticus* and *pomarinus*, but in Long-tailed dark and intermediate phases are apparently restricted to a few young individuals, whereas young Pomarine and Arctic are less obviously polymorphic. Sexes alike.

These three species present an identification challenge on which much has been written, most notably by Jonsson (1992), Olsen & Larsson (1997) and Svensson et al. (1999), which the following accounts largely follow. However, I have attempted to treat the group from a Southern Ocean perspective, dealing mainly with non-breeding ads and young, and hence the most confusing plumages. Nonetheless, as these are northern breeders, it is necessary to relate plumage to age and moult development based on the northern seasons, i.e. winter plumage/moult refers to Oct/Nov–Feb/Mar.

As highlighted by Svensson *et al.* (1999), correct identification of such difficult plumages requires much field practice. Size, overall proportion/shape and build, including width of the 'arm', and mode of flight are important starting points. Beware, however, illusions relating to size and jizz in respect of dark/light morphs and other plumages, or effects of lighting and distance in correctly judging these. All generally undergo prolonged complete moult in the winter range involving remiges/rectrices and body feathers (strategy, sequence and duration varies between species/ages), but only by Feb/Mar do the projecting central tail streamers usually reach full length, especially in breeding ads, when most have already migrated well north of the Southern Ocean. With those observed close, it is useful to note underwing pattern (mainly overall colour/pattern of coverts and contrast with body), as well as prominence of pattern on primaries and/or primary-coverts, while combined appearance of colour of head, breast-band and body, paleness and strength of bars on flanks, vent, tail-coverts and rump patch, and size and coloration of bill are also important. However, some characters apply only to certain species/plumages, so correct ageing is often crucial and characters should be used in combination. Do not expect to be able to identify all tricky plumages—it takes vast experience before more difficult individuals can be correctly assigned to species, and some may still have to be left

unidentified. The remote risk of confusion with the large skuas exists, especially between Pomarine and South Polar Skuas *C. [skua] maccormicki*.

All are circumpolar breeders on arctic tundra and seacoasts, wintering mainly in pelagic tropical and subtropical waters, some even in the cold waters of the Southern Ocean. Though maritime, some perform impressive non-stop overland migrations, including across Asia. When breeding they largely rely on inland foods, predominantly lemmings, eggs and young of other birds, fish, insects and berries (relative importance of these vary annually), while during rest of year takes mainly fish, as well as small mammals, carrion and offal. Fish are generally pirated. Such kleptoparasitism involves chasing other birds in rapid aerobatic flight; the victim, usually a smaller gull or tern, is pursued incessantly and very closely, until it disgorges the contents of its crop, which are caught in mid-air by the pursuant. Gulls and terns generally take off when a skua approaches, as if it were a bird of prey.

Other ecological and biological aspects of this group, which to some extent explain their occurrence and abundance in the Southern Ocean, are summarized in Cramp & Simmons (1983), Furness (1987) and *HANZAB*.

Pomarine Jaeger (Pomarine Skua)
Stercorarius pomarinus Plate 17

Identification
Confusion risks: Arctic Jaeger *S. parasiticus*, but problems may also arise with *Catharacta* skuas, chiefly South Polar Skua *C. [skua] maccormicki*.

Main characters: Largest *Stercorarius*; decidedly larger than Arctic Jaeger, especially in flight, and noticeably heavier chest/body, longer winged with characteristically rather broad 'arm'. Flight relaxed but purposeful on measured wingbeats, and path more direct (generally lighter and jerkier with energetic wingbeats in Arctic). **Ad** has (mainly) pale and (rarer) dark morphs. Pale primary patch above and below similar or somewhat broader than on Arctic, and considerably narrower than in *Catharacta*. In Nov–Feb/Mar characteristic long/broad, oval-ended tail streamers wholly or almost entirely absent, although those in advanced moult, from mid-/late winter, and sub-ads, may have partial broad/round tail elongation. All morphs have yellowish-/greyish-brown bill, tipped black, and mainly blackish irides, eye-ring and legs. Sexes similar except size (female larger) though pale-morph male may tend to lack or have only incomplete breast-band. **Light morph** in winter/Southern Ocean almost uniformly dark dorsally, but due to wear and newly moulted pale-fringed feathers, cap and head-sides less solid, and has well-developed dusky breast-band and barred flanks, rear abdomen and vent, on otherwise dirtier whitish underparts (than crisply patterned summer ad); rump/uppertail-coverts barred (unlike in spring/summer). Not dissimilar from younger birds, except black unbarred underwing-coverts. **Dark morph** (up to c.8% of breeding ads) all dark except whitish wing patches (which are usually slightly narrower than in pale birds), but in winter/Southern Ocean less uniformly black (than ad summer), being tinged browner and may have slightly paler neck-sides, and variable pale mottling below and fringes above. **Intermediate morph** (less than 1%) like dark morph, but often has neck and belly mottled/blotched paler. **Juv** varies little in overall pattern and coloration, most are uniformly cold dark brown, with indistinctly paler nape/neck (never

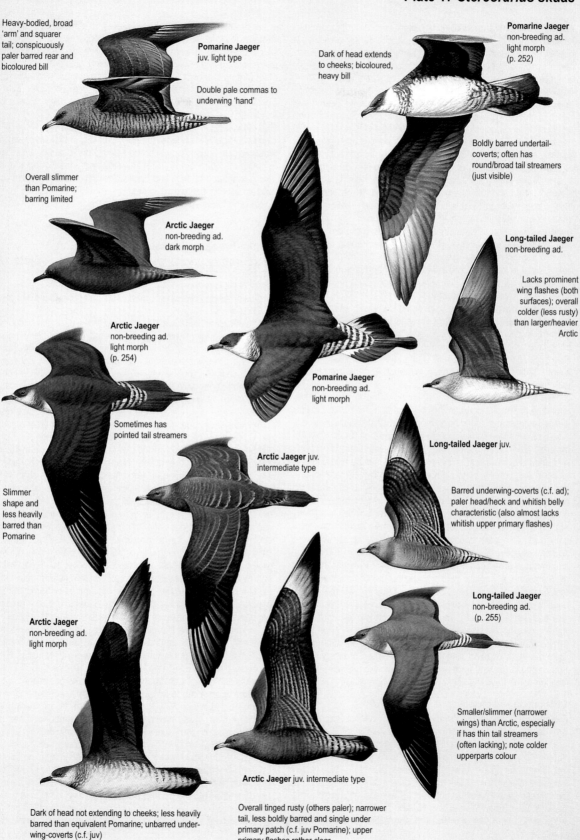

Plate 17 *Stercorarius* skuas

Heavy-bodied, broad 'arm' and squarer tail; conspicuously paler barred rear and bicoloured bill

Pomarine Jaeger juv. light type

Double pale commas to underwing 'hand'

Dark of head extends to cheeks; bicoloured, heavy bill

Pomarine Jaeger non-breeding ad. light morph (p. 252)

Boldly barred undertail-coverts; often has round/broad tail streamers (just visible)

Overall slimmer than Pomarine; barring limited

Arctic Jaeger non-breeding ad. dark morph

Arctic Jaeger non-breeding ad. light morph (p. 254)

Pomarine Jaeger non-breeding ad. light morph

Long-tailed Jaeger non-breeding ad.

Lacks prominent wing flashes (both surfaces); overall colder (less rusty) than larger/heavier Arctic

Sometimes has pointed tail streamers

Arctic Jaeger juv. intermediate type

Long-tailed Jaeger juv.

Barred underwing-coverts (c.f. ad); paler head/neck and whitish belly characteristic (also almost lacks whitish upper primary flashes)

Slimmer shape and less heavily barred than Pomarine

Long-tailed Jaeger non-breeding ad. (p. 255)

Arctic Jaeger non-breeding ad. light morph

Smaller/slimmer (narrower wings) than Arctic, especially if has thin tail streamers (often lacking); note colder upperparts colour

Dark of head not extending to cheeks; less heavily barred than equivalent Pomarine; unbarred under-wing-coverts (c.f. juv)

Arctic Jaeger juv. intermediate type

Overall tinged rusty (others paler); narrower tail, less boldly barred and single under primary patch (c.f. juv Pomarine); upper primary flashes rather clear has clear buffy collar of most Arctic), paler-barred rump/uppertail-coverts, vent and underwing (contrasting with darker body), and overall colder, never warm or rusty tinged as most Arctic. Pale panel on primary bases and primary-coverts (latter only visible when close), forming comma-shaped patches on underwing. Tar-black (still with pale primary patches and some pale spotting/barring on inner underwing-coverts) and palest extremes (with buffy head, neck-sides and abdomen) also occur, albeit very rarely, but all become progressively paler through bleaching in first-year. Bill has pale blue-grey base and dark tip more conspicuous than Arctic (see below). Central tail feathers only rarely and just visibly elongated, and rounded at tips. **Imm** light morph when younger has neck and belly paler than juv, central tail feathers (first-spring/summer) short and untwisted, but like ad usually absent/only partially grown while in Southern Ocean. Older imm (second/third-winter/summer) light morph has neck/belly paler with reduced dark bars and more obvious dark cap, but underwing-coverts still partially barred, not solidly dark like ad; longer central tail feathers develop only in early spring. Attains full-ad plumage at c.3–4 years, but due to age-related individual plumage progression and variation, by second-year (following post-juv moult) precise ageing not easy, even from winter ad.

Voice: At sea largely silent, except some low, harsh screams during food disputes. On breeding grounds performs long-call with wing-raising/aerial displays like *Catharacta* skuas, unlike Arctic/Long-tailed.

Size: 65–78 cm, wing 33.5–37.4 cm, wingspan 110–127 cm, weight 530–917 g. Much overlap, although juv and imm female may average larger than male.

Similar species: Non-breeders (winter ad/young) resemble corresponding plumages of Arctic, but larger and bulkier, with broader wings, rounder and 'fuller' belly, more 'even' flight and heavier bill. Also typically more conspicuously paler barred on rump/uppertail-coverts, rather boldly barred black-brown on vent/undertail-coverts and often across breast and flanks, and bill clearly bicoloured at all ages. Additionally, young almost invariably rather more uniform and duskier, with distinctly paler-barred underwing-coverts (than dark belly); often lacks contrasting paler head or belly (cf. Arctic/Long-tailed). Extreme dark individuals have uniform head/body and paler-barred rump/uppertail-coverts (unlike Arctic); diagnostically also have pale 'double patch' on underwing, i.e. primaries and primary-coverts basally pale (hard to see beyond 300 m), and blunt-ended, broad central tail-feathers project insignificantly, if at all. Pomarine, especially young birds, can be confused with distant *Catharacta*, especially South Polar Skua (which see). Latter usually distinctly heavier bodied, thicker necked and has shorter rear body/tail and broader, more triangular wings; also lacks contrasting pale-barred rump, vent or underwing-coverts of Pomarine, but head often slightly darker than rest of body (Pomarine usually uniformly dark or head slightly paler than chest), and generally has clearly larger and purer-white wing patches reaching to 'arm' (though some have restricted patches on upperwing).

Distribution and biology

Distribution, movements and population: Almost circumpolar breeder on arctic tundra, shores and coastal mountains; on migration in all oceans (though some use overland routes), mostly in Mar–May and Aug–Nov, to and from main winter areas off NW South America, the W Atlantic and Caribbean, off W Africa (where almost exclusively coastal, though some straggle to shelf break and rarely visits trawlers), the Arabian Sea and off Australia (especially New South Wales) and N New Zealand, reaching north edge of Southern Ocean in small numbers (but generally north of

winter ranges of Arctic and Long-tailed), with some to S Chile and vagrants to Uruguay and Antarctica (four records).

Diet and feeding: Breeds on tundra, where feeds largely on lemmings; during rest of year mainly fish, mostly obtained by pirating other birds (cf. above), being more aggressive than Arctic Jaeger and attacks birds up to size of gannets, even killing smaller gulls.

Social behaviour: The only jaeger that does not show mate and site fidelity between years.

Breeding biology: Breeds only in Northern Hemisphere.

Conservation No evidence available for any major changes in status or distribution, though breeding success is closely linked to lemming abundance and foxes are a major predator of eggs and young. Human predation and Snowy Owls *Nyctea scandiaca* may also account for some nest losses.

Taxonomy Monotypic.

Arctic (Parasitic) Jaeger (Arctic Skua)
Stercorarius parasiticus   Plate 17

Identification

Confusion risks: Pomarine *S. pomarinus* and Long-tailed Jaegers *S. longicaudus*.

Main characters: Mid-sized *Stercorarius*; like a dark gull with long all-dark narrow wings (typically long pointed 'hand' and less broad 'arm') and tapering rear body, slender head and flatter belly than Pomarine. Thus, more elegant, with rather fast dynamic flight and almost falcon-like wingbeats. Differences from heavier Pomarine and slimmer Long-tailed not always obvious (see below and group introduction). At close range, pale primary patches narrower and bill slightly less deep-based than Pomarine, making it appear uniformly darker at equal distance. Otherwise much as latter (which see), but see below for features relevant to winter/Southern Ocean. **Ad** has pale (up to 99% of those in Siberia, Greenland and Spitsbergen) and dark morphs. In Nov/Feb–Mar characteristic long, narrow tapering tail-streamers wholly or almost entirely absent, although those in advanced moult from mid-/late winter may have partially grown/exposed central feathers. All have almost uniform blackish grey-brown bill, indistinctly tipped darker, and mainly blackish irides, eye-ring and legs. Sexes similar except size (female larger). **Light morph** in winter/Southern Ocean recalls younger birds, though unlike latter has unbarred dark underwing-coverts and is almost uniformly dark above, but due to wear and newly moulted feathers becomes variably paler fringed and blotched, and like imm has less solid cap and paler-barred rump/uppertail-coverts. Also rather extensive ill-defined dusky breast-band, and barred flanks, rear abdomen and vent, on otherwise dirtier whitish underparts (unlike spring/summer). Some, however, have spring/summer-like dark cap of ad, which is less black than ad Pomarine, does not reach gape and is always separated from bill base by small pale area. As Pomarine, yellowish-buff lower cheeks and neck of spring/summer ad obscured or absent in winter. **Dark morph** (up to 95% of breeding ads in some parts of N Atlantic, but less than 50% and even as little as 1% in other populations) entirely sooty-brown except whitish primary patches on underwing, which are usually smaller (especially in darkest birds). In winter not as uniform on body as in summer, being variably lightly barred/mottled, with pale buff neck-sides enhancing darker cap. **Intermediate morph** (most frequent in N Atlantic and Baltic, where up to 50% of juvs may be this type) closer to dark morph, but dark areas more greyish-brown and has extensive paler areas on cheek/neck and/or belly (sometimes strongly mottled/barred paler), and often has rather pronounced blackish cap. **Juv** varies

quite considerably, even in overall pattern, the palest (usually lighter than Pomarine) having contrastingly cream-coloured head and neck to belly, with ill-defined dark barring on breast/body-sides (latter areas also finely streaked/spotted, discernible at close range). Dark juv completely tar-black and extremely similar to darkest Pomarine; most reliably identified by slimmer size/shape and overall proportions (see above). Like all other juvs has central tail feathers projecting 1–3 cm, forming tiny 'double point' at tail tip, and underwing has pale bases to primaries, but greater primary-coverts never pale like Pomarine, while bill generally looks dark, not strikingly pale-based (pale base hardly visible beyond 150 m). Also tends to have rusty-orange or cinnamon-brown tinge to nape and upperpart fringes (cf. Pomarine/Long-tailed). Important subsidiary characters, especially given close, perched birds, are streaked head and neck (see above; cf. Pomarine) and, in fresh plumage, pale primary tips, especially prominent in dark juv (lacking or indistinct in juv Pomarine). On upperparts, rump/uppertail-coverts generally darker and less regularly patterned; a rule of thumb is that, at distance, rump never appears paler than nape, and dark-headed/necked juv generally lacks pale rump (reverse usual in Pomarine). Palest individuals often have pale patch at base of primaries above and characteristic pale base to spread tail. Axillaries and underwing-coverts usually barred dark, but ground colour equal to or slightly darker than body, thus coverts often appear darker/less patterned than Pomarine; opposite is case on undertail-coverts/vent, which are usually less barred and paler than juv Pomarine. Some have dark, virtually unmarked underwing-coverts. Additionally, unlike Pomarine, tends to have paler leading edge to lesser upperwing-coverts. Younger **imm** light morph, through wear and/or subsequent post-juv moult, has neck and underparts paler and less warm, or less coarsely barred than juv, and central tail feathers (first-spring/summer) shorter, but like ad usually absent/only partially grown while in Southern Ocean. Older imm (second/third-winter/summer) light morph has neck and belly paler and less barred, and dark cap more pronounced, but underwing-coverts still barred, not solidly dark as ad; longer central tail feathers develop mainly in early spring. Attains full-ad plumage at c.3–4 years, but due to age-related individual plumage progression and variation, by second-year (following post-juv moult) precise ageing not easy, even from winter ad.
Voice: In winter/Southern Ocean and at sea largely silent, except some harsh calls during food disputes.
Size: 46–67 cm, wing 29.8–34.5 cm, wingspan 97–115 cm, weight 301–697 g. Females may tend to have longer wings and bill in some populations.
Similar species: Non-breeders (winter ad/young) resemble corresponding plumages of Pomarine (which see), but with practice can be identified by combined differences in size, proportions and jizz, as well as plumage, but it is important to age the bird and identify the type of morph before proceeding to species identification, e.g. in identifying juvs underwing-coverts pattern and contrast are important characters. The relative intensity of barring on the body, breast and rump/uppertail-coverts, and bill depth and colour are to some degree important in most plumages. In winter/Southern Ocean it is usually impossible to identify birds on the shape of the tail-streamers. Young are easily confused with Long-tailed Jaeger (which see).

Distribution and biology

Distribution, movements and population: Circumpolar breeder on arctic tundra, seacoasts and islands, locally in loose colonies; moves on broad front through all oceans, some overland, mostly in Mar–May and Aug–Nov, to and from winter areas between 30°S

and 50°S in Atlantic (largely inshore, associated with tern flocks, but common to the shelf break) and off SE Australia, New Zealand and in Humboldt Current of W South America, reaching Antarctic waters in small numbers, with some records to 65°S.
Diet and feeding: On tundra breeding grounds takes lemmings or scavenges eggs and chicks at seabird colonies; during rest of year mainly fish parasitized from other seabirds (terns are commonest victims).
Social behaviour: Monogamous with long-lasting (often life-long) pair-bonds. Large territories. Usually solitary outside breeding season though may migrate in groups.
Breeding biology: Breeds only in Northern Hemisphere.
Conservation No evidence available for any major changes in status or distribution, though breeding success is closely linked to lemming abundance and foxes are a major predator of eggs and young. Human predation and Snowy Owls *Nyctea scandiaca* may also account for some nest losses.
Taxonomy Monotypic.

Long-tailed Jaeger
Stercorarius longicaudus   Plate 17

Identification
Confusion risks: Arctic Jaeger *S. parasiticus*.
Main characters: Smallest *Stercorarius*; especially in flight is noticeably slighter, slender bodied, smaller headed and markedly narrower winged than Arctic, and particularly ad in spring/summer characteristically long-tailed. Bill short but proportionately heavy. Flight light, almost tern-like, less jerky and surprisingly relaxed, with elastic wingbeats, as might be expected given its small size. **Ad** apparently variable but no confirmation of existence of dark/intermediate morphs in ads (as in other *Stercorarius*), though there are very rare reports of such birds (see imm). Unlike other *Stercorarius*, lacks pale primary patches on underwing, these being restricted to whitish primary shafts (on both surfaces) of 2–3 outermost primaries. In Nov/Feb–Mar long tail streamers are wholly or almost entirely lacking. Only some, in advanced moult from mid-/late winter, may have partially grown central tail feathers. Furthermore, such ads in winter/Southern Ocean have less solid blackish cap and, unlike spring/summer, a dusky breast-band and faintly barred rear flanks, abdomen and vent on otherwise dirty whitish underparts (lacking pale breast that gradually darkens on belly of ad summer). Due to wear and newly moulted pale-fringed feathers above, mantle and scapulars less uniform than in summer and rump/uppertail-coverts usually also barred and paler (unlike spring/summer). Thus, not dissimilar from younger birds, though unlike them has dark, unbarred underwing-coverts and paler brown-grey upperwing-coverts, contrasting with brown-black flight feathers. Almost uniform dark grey-brown bill, blackish eye, dark grey to black legs and blacker feet. Sexes similar except size (female larger). **Juv** varies considerably in pattern and coloration, with pale and dark extremes, and range of intermediates. Palest juv has wholly creamy-white head and all-white belly (never shown by Arctic); darkest appear uniform dark brown-grey, always with some pale fringes above. Most have ground colour colder and/or greyer brown (never as warm/rusty as Arctic); variable buff nape patch, but except in extremely dark individuals rather obvious; conspicuous black-and-white bars on rump/uppertail-coverts (though virtually lacking in dark juv); pale primary bases on underwing (unlike ad, but still narrower than Arctic), and whitish shafts to outermost 2–3 primaries, making rest of upperwing primaries appear dark (and contrastingly darker than typically dull-coloured

upperwing-coverts). Unlike ads underwing-coverts/axillaries (except extreme dark individuals) and vent/undertail-coverts evenly and boldly barred black and white, thus contrastingly paler than underparts (except extreme whitish-bellied juv); and the paler upperwing-coverts and mantle/scapulars usually have narrow but noticeable fringes. Finger-like projecting central tail feathers (blunt at tip) protrude from tail tip, and are usually clearer narrower than on juv Arctic. Many have uniform, unbarred breast-band, faintly vermiculated flanks and paler abdomen. Primary tips quite rounded, normally dark but sometimes with narrow pale fringes. Blue-grey bill with black tip; legs mainly pale grey with contrasting blackish feet. **Imm** light/intermediate birds when younger have neck and belly paler than juv, often enhancing dusky-hooded and/or breast-band appearance, while central tail feathers (first-spring/summer) shorter and distinctly pointed, but (like ad) usually only partially grown or entirely absent in Southern Ocean. Older imm (second/third-winter/summer) light bird has neck and belly even paler, with weaker dark bars and more pronounced dark cap, thus strongly approaches ad, but most underwing-coverts at least partially barred, not solidly dark as ad; longer central tail feathers develop only in early spring. Attains full-ad plumage at c.3–4 years, but by second-year (following post-juv and subsequent moults), and because of individual variation, precise ageing is not easy, even from winter ad. Well-advanced dark morph-like second/third-winter/summer have been documented. They usually lack almost any pale barring on underwing-coverts or pale bases to primaries, and may be the source of claims of dark-morph ads, but plumage maturation in such dark imms is unknown.

Voice: At sea apparently largely silent.

Size: 35–58 cm, wing 23.8–35.0 cm, wingspan 92–105 cm, weight 218–444 g. Female (when breeding) has longer wings and is heavier than male.

Similar species: In winter/Southern Ocean most ads and young lack tail streamers, and are also similar in having barred winter plumage, ads lacking soft dusky wash to rear body of summer plumage. However, many other characters can be used, in combination, to distinguish it from Arctic: the slimmer silhouette (especially narrow body/wings, with flatter, longer looking rear, but compressed fore body), characteristic flight (see above), colder greyer toned plumage including upperwing-coverts (both ad and young) and usually only 2–3 whitish primary shafts (normally 4–7 in Arctic). A greyish juv with white head or juv with greyish head and breast-band and white belly is usually a Long-tailed. Other specific characters are more strictly age-related and are detailed above.

Distribution and biology

Distribution, movements and population: Almost circumpolar breeder on arctic tundra, coastal mountains (high above timberline in south). Markedly pelagic, migrates through all oceans, but some overland, mostly in Mar–May and Aug–Nov, to and from winter areas mostly around 35°S off Africa (where primarily offshore, typically in oceanic waters beyond the shelf break, though sometimes driven closer inshore by strong winds; also common off southeast coast of Africa north to at least S Mozambique with a strong movement around the Cape) and at 39–45°S off Patagonia and in Falkland Current, and perhaps at 40–50°S in S Pacific, apparently further south than other *Stercorarius*, regularly in subantarctic waters, with some to 65–70°S.

Diet and feeding: On tundra dependent on supply of rodents, mostly lemmings, for breeding, and numbers accordingly fluctuate annually; during rest of year mainly fish (often pirated from other birds, though kleptoparasitizm apparently rare off Africa).

Social behaviour: Monogamous with long-lasting pair-bonds. Large territories. Usually solitary outside breeding season though may migrate in groups.

Breeding biology: Breeds only in Northern Hemisphere.

Conservation No evidence available for any changes in status or distribution, though breeding success is closely linked to lemming abundance and foxes are a major predator of eggs and young.

Taxonomy Two poorly differentiated races: nominate *longicaudus*, from Scandinavia and NE Russia to about Taimyr, and a pale-bellied form, *pallescens*, from Taimyr to NE Siberia, the Nearctic and Greenland.

Gulls and terns

This section and Plate 18 cover the remainder of the family Laridae, those gulls and terns regularly recorded in the Southern Ocean. Most are comparatively widespread within our region, but some are endemic to a particular area, such as Dolphin Gull *Larus scoresbii* (mainly off S America and Falklands) and Kerguelen Tern *Sterna virgata* in the Indian Ocean.

Identification and taxonomy, as well as annual cycles and general biologies, are discussed at length within each account. Fortunately, there is no problematic gull complex as in the Northern Hemisphere (great albatrosses, prions, shags and skuas are probably enough!), but some identification challenges can be found among the terns.

Dolphin Gull *Larus scoresbii* Plate 18

Identification
Confusion risks: None in range.
Main characters: Attractive coastal S South American gull. Medium-sized, with short, rather strong bill, longish sloping forehead and high rounded crown. In flight, broad round-tipped wings typically appear strongly bowed at carpal with 'loose hands'. **Ad** unmistakable. Breeder (Jul–Mar) has soft grey wash to white head and underparts, with purer white lower back/rump and tail, very dark slate-grey/-black mantle, scapulars and upperwing, and all-black primaries with white tips and inner trailing edge which extends very broadly on secondaries. Underwing has dark 'hand' and whitish-grey 'arm'. Red legs and bill, and yellowish-white eye with red orbital. Non-breeder has darker, grey-mottled hood (variable). **Juv** unique in uniform dusky-brown head and upper breast, with whitish belly, slate-brown back and upperwing, and ill-defined broad dark subterminal tail-band. Broad white trailing edge as ad; bare parts mainly greyish-brown to blackish. **Imm**, in first-winter/summer like juv, but dark areas more slate, hood variably darker (often emphasized by ill-defined paler band on upper neck) and is whiter below. Becomes progressively paler and blotchier with wear in first-summer; bill base and legs paler. Second-winter/summer variably closer to non-breeding ad, with dusky hood, but neck and chest still greyish, part of neck and throat white, and vestigial dark subterminal tail-band; bill changes first to reddish-pink with dark tip or subterminal mark, and legs to reddish-brown; iris whitish by second-summer. Ad plumage acquired as third-year, but third-summer has variable, duskier, grey-mottled hood (as non-

Third-summer Dolphin Gull Larus scoresbii, *with dusky hood as non-breeding ad, and still has duller bare parts than ad; smaller white primary tips already completely worn off. Falklands, Dec 1990. © René Pop.*

breeding ad), and usually some vestiges of immaturity, e.g. duller bare parts and, when fresh, smaller white primary tips than ad.
Voice: Distinctive, short high-pitched *kyik*; also repeated rapid screams, *keear-keear-keear*, on breeding grounds (Woods 1988).
Size: 40–46 cm, wing 30.6–33.9 cm, wingspan 104–110 cm, weight 524 g. Male generally larger in all measurements, but much overlap.
Similar species: Given a reasonable view, unlikely to be confused with any gull in our region, including larger Kelp Gull *L. dominicanus*, which also has black back.

Distribution and biology
Distribution, movements and population: Seacoasts of S Chile and S Argentina south to Tierra del Fuego and islands of Cape Horn; also the Falklands. South American populations disperse north in winter. Overall population estimated at a few tens of thousands of pairs.

Ad breeding Dolphin Gull Larus scoresbii, *Falklands, Jan 2001. © Hadoram Shirihai.*

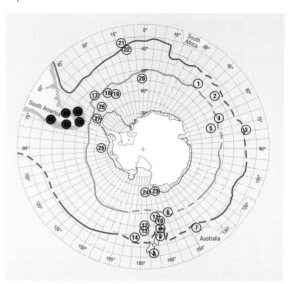

● South American offshore islands
◑ Falklands

Juv Dolphin Gull Larus scoresbii is mostly dusky- to slate-brown, with diffuse whitish belly, broad dark subterminal tail-band and white trailing edge, and dull bare parts. Ushuaia, S Argentina, Mar 2003. © Hadoram Shirihai.

Diet and feeding: Omnivorous, but principally scavenges carrion and offal, bird eggs and their chicks; also takes marine invertebrates, mussels, beach flies and other natural foods by probing seaweed and feeding at sewage outfalls. Pirates food from other gulls and cormorants.

Social behaviour: Usually in small dense colonies, whose sites change near annually. Regularly associates with Kelp Gull.

Breeding biology: Breeds from early Nov, most usually in Dec. Nest, usually sheltered by boulders or grass, of kelp and vegetation, lined with grass. Lays 2–3 olive-buff or grey-green eggs, incubated 24–27 days. Chicks leave nest at 2–5 days and may form crèche when older.

Conservation Not globally threatened, but no information on reproductive rate or population trends.

Taxonomy Monotypic. Taxonomic position uncertain: placed in *Larus* by many recent authors, but sometimes included with Pacific Gull *L. pacificus* in *Gabianus* on basis of bill shape, but other behavioural and morphological features suggest placement in monospecific genus, *Leucophaeus*, is most appropriate. Closest relatives unclear.

Kelp Gull *Larus dominicanus*   Plate 18

Identification

Confusion risks: None in range, though Baltic Lesser Black-backed Gull *L. fuscus fuscus* is a regular visitor in very small numbers to South Africa (and may present problems), while Heuglin's Gull *L. f. heuglini* is possibly a rare annual visitor to South Africa and may also require separation.

Main characters: Generally recalls large white-headed gulls of Northern Hemisphere, but is sole form of such appearance in Southern Ocean and ad is blacker on upperwing and young relatively pale. Powerful bill, short sloping forehead, flat crown and long broad wings. **Ad** breeding has uniform white head, underparts and tail, slate-black mantle, scapulars and upperwing, the latter with moderate-sized white 'mirrors' and tips to other primaries, and conspicuous trailing edge to inner primaries, broadening on secondaries. Underwing has blackish-grey outer primaries, greyer on rest of remiges and whitish coverts. Yellow bill with red gonys, yellow eye with red orbital ring, and greyish-green legs. Non-breeding ad has brown-streaked head and neck. **Juv** has

buff-brown and whitish speckling on head, neck-sides and chest, where heavily vermiculated, while back, scapulars and upperwing scaled and streaked grey-brown, with whitish-buff fringes (typical mottled pattern of young white-headed gulls), and tail has extensive black subterminal-band (white generally restricted to base of outer tail feathers). Bill and eye black, and legs flesh-grey with dark smudges on front of tarsus. **Imm** when younger (first-winter/ summer) similar to juv, but bleached duller and browner above, and becomes progressively whiter on head and below; bill base paler. Older imm (second/third-winter/summer) acquires still-whiter head and underparts (some slightly mottled/streaked brownish), and increasing number of slate-black feathers on mantle, scapulars and upperwing; with narrower black subterminal tail-band (very variable). Bill changes first to yellowish-grey flesh with dark tip or subterminal mark, and legs to pale yellowish-brown; iris already whitish in some second-summer. Ad plumage acquired as fourth-year, but usually still has some vestiges of immaturity, mainly in bare parts, and younger ad, when fresh, often has dark spots on head and neck, smaller white primary tips and smaller and fewer 'mirrors' than full ad.

Voice: Generally recalls range of vocalizations of several Northern Hemisphere congeners, with e.g. long-calls of African populations

Kelp Gull Larus dominicanus is unmistakable within much of its range, being the only 'large white-headed gull'. South Georgia, Jan 2001. © Hadoram Shirihai.

Plate 18 Gulls and terns

Smaller and shorter billed than Antarctic; greyer, including rump and tail, and overall darker

Kerguelen Tern breeding ad. (p. 271)

Kerguelen Tern non-breeding ad.

Largish and purer white, with long, slightly curved black bill

White-fronted Tern non-breeding ad.

ess dark outer primaries nd outertail

Greyer plumage than Arctic

Antarctic Tern non-breeding ad.

Antarctic Tern breeding ad. (p. 269)

Tail/legs rather short

Primary wedge

White-fronted Tern breeding ad. (p. 265)

Translucent primaries with distinct black edges

Strong bill

Limited greyish below

Arctic Tern non-breeding ad.

e grey

Primary wedge

Common Tern non-breeding ad.

Longer legs

Common Tern breeding ad. (p. 266)

Longer legs; long curved bill

Whitish plumage

South American Tern non-breeding ad.

South American Tern breeding ad. (p. 267)

Arctic Tern breeding ad. (p. 267)

Very short legs; long tail

White on p8

Only two primary mirrors

Extensive white to wingtips

region's only e gull and has d juv/imm ages

Large with black upper-wing and white body

Kelp Gull breeding ad.

Silver Gull ad.

Red-billed Gull ad.

Black-billed Gull ad.

Slender/longer blackish bill

Kelp Gull juv.

Dolphin Gull breeding ad. (p. 257)

Paler grey

Black-billed Gull breeding ad. (p. 263)

Medium-sized, white with dark upperparts and red bill and legs (some plumages darker headed)

Silver Gull breeding ad. (p. 261)

The only large white-headed gull in the region

Kelp Gull breeding ad. (p. 258)

Brown-hooded Gull breeding ad. (p. 264)

Red-billed Gull breeding ad. (p. 262)

The only dark-hooded small gull in the region

Shorter/deeper bill, darker grey above

Ad Kelp Gull Larus dominicanus. *Kaikoura, South I, New Zealand, Oct 2001. © Hadoram Shirihai.*

Juv/first-year Kelp Gull Larus dominicanus. *Kaikoura, South I, New Zealand, Oct 2001.© Hadoram Shirihai.*

of Kelp Gulls apparently harsher and coarser than Yellow-legged *Larus michahellis* or Lesser Black-backed Gulls, while long-calls of S Indian Ocean birds are close to those of Caspian Gull *L. cachinnans* (Jiguet *in litt.* 2002). However, little work has been conducted on geographical variation within Kelp Gull vocalizations, although it is certainly an important subject for future studies, following recent findings in plumage and bare-parts coloration variation, and revealing genetic studies. Vocalizations will be particularly important, given the recent proposal that five subspecies of Kelp deserve recognition (Jiguet 2002, *Bull. Brit. Orn. Club* 122: 50–73), and that S Indian Ocean birds belong to a new subspecies, not to the nominate form.

Size: 54–65 cm, wing 37.2–42.2 cm, wingspan 128–142 cm, weight 0.9–1.34 kg. Male generally larger, and very little overlap in wing and tail lengths in South American and Falklands populations.

Similar species: The only large white-headed and white-tailed gull in the Southern Ocean. Ad could be confused at distance with ad Dolphin Gull *L. scoresbii* (which see), but a range of features separate them.

Distribution and biology

Distribution, movements and population: W Ecuador and SE Brazil to Tierra del Fuego, principally on coasts; coastal Africa from Mozambique to Namibia, with a population on Madagascar and isolated breeding in Senegambia and (recently) Mauritania; W and S Australia, Tasmania, New Zealand; and Southern Ocean on the Falklands, South Georgia, South Sandwich, South Orkney, South Shetland, Bouvetøya, Prince Edward, Marion, Crozet, Kerguelen, Heard, Macquarie, Campbell, Auckland, Snares, Antipodes, Bounty and Chatham; also Antarctic Peninsula to 68°S. Vagrants have reached Tristan/Gough (where comparatively regular), the Caribbean, USA (where breeds and interbreeds with American Herring Gull *L.* [*argentatus*] *smithsonianus*), Mexico and France (one record of uncertain provenance). Some disperse in non-breeding season and nominate *dominicanus* has been recorded on several occasions in South Africa and may be overlooked to some extent there. World population estimated at 1.085 million pairs.

Diet and feeding: Varied, scavenges around human settlements, but also takes broad range of natural foods, by dabbling and plunge-diving in water, picking from ground and drops shellfish from height. Molluscs (principal diet on Kerguelen), fish, small mammals, birds (to size of goose), sickly lambs, termites, many invertebrates and amphibians all taken. Follows boats at sea and steals food from terns. In Antarctica main food is limpets.

Social behaviour: Few data.

Kelp Gull Larus dominicanus *in post nuptial moult. Like other large 'white-headed gulls' plumage maturation is slow. Note juv moulting to first-winter (left foreground bird) and second-winter (middle bird, second row); most others are ad or near-ad, some showing the brown-streaked head and neck of non-breeding plumage. Ushuaia, S Argentina, Mar 2003. © Hadoram Shirihai.*

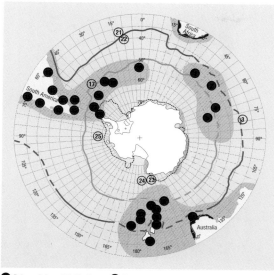

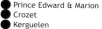
- Prince Edward & Marion
- Crozet
- Kerguelen
- Heard
- Macquarie
- Tasmania
- New Zealand and offshore islands
- Snares
- Auckland
- Campbell
- Antipodes
- Bounty
- Chatham
- South American offshore islands
- Falklands
- South Georgia
- South Sandwich
- Bouvetøya
- South Orkney
- South Shetland
- Antarctic Peninsula

Breeding biology: Principally Sep–Jan (over broad range). Forms dense and sometimes large colonies (though isolated pairs not uncommon). Nest is of dried plants or seaweed, often at base of bush or rock. Lays 2–3 variably coloured eggs, incubated 24–30 days. Chicks fledge at seven weeks.

Conservation Not globally threatened, being common and widespread over much of its expanding world range.

Taxonomy Often considered monotypic, though African population (apparently darker eyed) occasionally (almost certainly correctly) recognized as *vetula* (Cape Gull, which differs from other forms in its relative massive size, different head shape, eye and leg colour, and size of eye) and those on South Shetland separated as *austrinus*, though latter distinction appears unwarranted (subspecific differentiation only supported by measurements). A recent (1998) phylogenetic study suggests that the South American (*dominicanus*) and South African (*vetula*) forms are only distantly related and are therefore best regarded as species, though a subsequent study questions some of the earlier work, and work in preparation suggests that the Malagasy population may be among the strongly differentiated within this complex (certainly being worthy of taxonomic recognition at some level). The same work also proposes another new subspecies endemic to the Indian Ocean subantarctic islands and that henceforward five taxa within the Kelp Gull complex be recognized (Jiguet 2002).

Silver Gull *Larus novaehollandiae*   Plate 18

Identification

Confusion risks: Red-billed Gull *L. scopulinus*.
Main characters: Australian endemic. Medium-sized white-and-grey gull, almost identical to Red-billed Gull of New Zealand, but

perhaps separable by longer, less deep-based bill and more white in primaries; overall slightly larger than latter. Head typically has very long sloping forehead, thus appears flatter and less rounded than Red-billed Gull, while bill is proportionately slightly longer and stronger, with less-angled upper mandible. Wings broad with slightly more pointed tips. **Ad** breeding has white head, tail and underparts, and pale grey mantle/wing-coverts. Black on primaries extends broadly across outer feathers and as large subterminal tips to rest, leaving very extensive white on central primaries, forming diagonal panel which extends as white leading edge along entire carpal, and very extensive white 'mirrors' to outer two primaries (and small one on next innermost) that can meet white tips. Underwing has blackish primaries and whitish-grey rest of remiges and coverts. Bill and feet scarlet, and eye yellowish-white with narrow red orbital ring. Non-breeder has duller bare parts, with orbital ring often blacker (less pure red), and variable black mark on bill tip. **Juv** has characteristic buff-brown scaly subterminal marks to pale grey mantle/upperwing-coverts and centres of scapulars, and narrow black subterminal bar to secondaries and tail. Primaries similar to ad, but with reduced white. Bill and eye generally blackish/dark brown and legs yellowish-brown. **Imm** when younger (first-winter/summer) as ad, becoming progressively cleaner grey on mantle/scapulars than juv, but similar wing pattern to latter, chiefly in faint dark carpal bar across upperwing-coverts, while first-spring/summer bleached duller with browner wings. Bare parts even duller. Older imm (second-winter/summer) acquires almost ad-like plumage, without black subterminal tail-band. While bill, legs and eye often exhibit some vestiges of immaturity, colorations generally approach non-breeding ad, with smaller white primary tips and 'mirrors' than full ad.
Voice: Range of vocalizations given in variety of social contexts, mainly rasping or screaming calls.
Size: 36–44 cm, wing 26.8–31.9 cm, wingspan 91–96 cm, weight 265–315 g. Male larger than female, but broad overlap in most measurements; greatest difference is depth of bill at gonys.
Similar species: Not known to overlap New Zealand's endemic Red-billed Gull, but they could meet at sea in Tasmanian waters, when identification would be difficult unless typical wing pattern and bill shape observed. For differences see Red-billed Gull.

Distribution and biology

Distribution, movements and population: Coasts, islands and large lakes of Australia, Tasmania and New Caledonia. Most move only

Ad Silver Gull Larus novaehollandiae *is distinguished from almost identical ad Red-billed* L. scopulinus *by slightly paler upperparts, with more extensive white on primaries (including small white mirror on p8), and has a relatively longer bill. Australia, Oct 2001. © Hadoram Shirihai.*

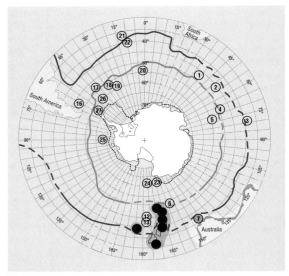

Ad Red-billed Gull Larus scopulinus *compared to ad Silver Gull* L. novaehollandiae *has darker upperparts, restricted white on outermost two primaries (and almost invariably lacks the small white mirror on p8) and a relatively deeper based, shorter bill. Kaikoura, South I, New Zealand, Oct 2001.* © Hadoram Shirihai.

Legend (map):

■ Red-billed Gull Larus scopulinus
▦ Silver Gull Larus novaehollandiae

⑦ Tasmania
● New Zealand and offshore islands
● Snares

● Auckland
● Campbell
● Chatham

short distances, but those in E Australia generally move north and those in W Australia move south, with some westerly movement along south coast. Considered to be increasing, with over 500,000 pairs in c.200 colonies in Australia in early 1990s.

Diet and feeding: Varied diet of refuse, fish, marine and terrestrial invertebrates, berries, seeds, insects and offal. Scavenges at picnic sites and refuse tips, as well as taking eggs of conspecifics and (in recent years) feeding in ploughed fields.

Social behaviour: Colonial and only rarely solitary. Often selects same mate and territory in consecutive years.

Breeding biology: Colonies number a small handful to several thousands of pairs, often close to terneries. Usually nests on ground, often in shade, occasionally to 2.5 m up in bush. Shallow cup nest constructed in any month, but principally Mar–Nov in W Australia. Lays 1–5 (usually three) eggs, incubated 21–27 days and chicks remain in colony for four weeks before leaving with parents, who cease to tend young after a further two weeks. Does not breed until 3–4 years old.

Conservation Abundant and increasing in Australia, especially in south, and reaching pest status in some areas, doubtless as a result of its ability to take advantage of new feeding opportunities.

Taxonomy Two races, with slightly larger *forsteri* in N Australia, New Caledonia and Loyalty Is, and nominate in rest of range. Forms superspecies with Hartlaub's *L. hartlaubii* and Red-billed Gulls *L. scopulinus* and all three have been treated as single species, but recent phylogenetic research suggests that *scopulinus* and *novaehollandiae* are not especially closely related.

Red-billed Gull *Larus scopulinus*   Plate 18

Identification

Confusion risks: Silver *L. novaehollandiae* and Black-billed Gulls *L. bulleri*.

Main characters: New Zealand endemic. Medium-sized white-and-grey gull, with diagnostic black pattern to wingtip. Bill rather short, stout and lacks prominent gonys, while head is rather rounded

with sloping forehead. Wings broad with rounded tips. **Ad** breeding has white head, tail and underparts, and pale grey mantle and wing-coverts; primaries mostly black with white tips, two distinct 'mirrors' and rather restricted diagonal white wing panel from outer to central primaries. Underwing has blackish primaries, greyish rest of remiges and whitish coverts. Often has ill-defined whiter leading edge on both surfaces. Bill and feet scarlet, and eye yellowish-white with narrow red orbital ring. Non-breeder has duller bare parts. **Juv** as ad, but has distinct buff-brown scaly subterminal marks to pale grey mantle/upperwing-coverts and centres of scapulars, while tail lacks black subterminal band (or has very narrow indistinct band). Wing pattern similar to ad, but white markings reduced and dark secondary subterminal bar faint. Bill and eye black and legs yellowish-brown. **Imm** when younger (first-winter/summer) as ad, becoming progressively cleaner grey on mantle/scapulars than juv, but similar wing pattern to latter (with reduced white in primaries) and has faint dark carpal bar on upperwing-coverts, while first-spring/summer bleached duller with browner remiges and narrow black subterminal tail-band. Bare parts even duller. Older imm (second-winter/summer) overall ad-like, without black subterminal tail-band.

Juv Red-billed Gull Larus scopulinus *tends to lack or have more reduced black subterminal tail-band than Silver Gull* L. novahollandiae. *Auckland, Dec 1999.* © Hadoram Shirihai.

Sub-ad Black-billed Gull Larus bulleri *is a New Zeland endemic that marginally reaches nearby subantarctic waters. Its distinctive bill shape and wing pattern readily separate it from similar Red-billed Gull* L. scopulinus. *Kaikoura, South I, New Zealand, Oct 2001. © Hadoram Shirihai.*

However, bill (brownish-yellow with black tip), legs and eye exhibit some vestiges of immaturity, being less advanced in coloration, and has smaller white primary tips and 'mirrors' than full ad.
Voice: Range of vocalizations given in variety of social contexts, mainly rasping or screaming calls.
Size: 37 cm, wing 26.3–28.9 cm, wingspan 91–96 cm, weight 245–360 g. Female slightly smaller and smaller billed, but much overlap in most measurements.
Similar species: Not known to meet Australian Silver Gull *L. novaehollandiae*, but they could meet in Tasman Sea, where Red-billed could be easily overlooked. Differs from ad Silver in somewhat darker grey upperparts, with more restricted white on primaries, including slightly squarer and smaller white mirrors on outermost two, and almost invariably lacks small white mirror on p8 (present on most, but not all, Silver). Also has relatively deeper based, shorter bill with slightly more angled upper mandible, and is overall slightly smaller (see taxonomy). Juv tends to lack or have reduced black subterminal tail-band than Silver, but apparently some variation. Further work on identification of Silver and Red-billed Gulls is urgently required, including imm plumages. Confusion also possible with Black-billed Gull (which see).

Distribution and biology
Distribution, movements and population: Coasts, islands and lakes of New Zealand, Chatham, Snares, Auckland and Campbell. Reported from Lord Howe I. Population estimated at 500,000 pairs.
Diet and feeding: Principally takes krill in breeding season, as well as other crustaceans, earthworms, insects and small fish, but at other times takes greater variety of fish and visits refuse tips. Frequently steals food from other seabirds and waders, and sometimes takes berries.
Social behaviour: Strong pair-bond and highly territorial. Usually returns to natal colony.
Breeding biology: Breeds from early Jul, eggs usually Sep–Dec (peak Oct–Nov). Sometimes in very dense colonies, but also nests alone. Lays 1–5 (usually two) eggs, incubated 22–26 days. Chicks fledge at 28–35 days.
Conservation Not globally threatened and has increased through 20th century having, like many other gulls, benefited from increased winter-food availability at human refuse tips and fish-processing plants.
Taxonomy Monotypic but often included within Silver Gull *L. novaehollandiae* (which see) and forms superspecies with it and Hartlaub's Gull *L. hartlaubii*.

Black-billed Gull *Larus bulleri*   Plate 18

Identification
Confusion risks: Red-billed *L. scopulinus* and Silver Gulls *L. novaehollandiae*.
Main characters: Endemic to inland New Zealand (though a rare visitor to Stewart I and Snares). Medium-sized gull with white-and-grey plumage and diagnostic black pattern to wingtip. Bill rather long and slender, while head has rather shallow/long sloping forehead. Wings proportionately narrow, with even narrower tip. **Ad** breeding has white head, tail and underparts, and very pale/whitish-grey mantle and wing-coverts. Most of primaries white except black subterminal tips and some fringes, thus has narrow restricted black area and no isolated white 'mirrors', as nearly all outer primaries are white. Underwing has very restricted black on primaries and much whiter rest of remiges and coverts. Often appears to have ill-defined whiter leading edge to both wing surfaces. Bill varies from all black to those with some dull reddish at base, and legs/feet and orbital ring mainly black or pale yellowish-/reddish-brown; eye yellowish-white. Non-breeder has paler and browner bare parts. **Juv** as ad, but has buff-brown scaly subterminal marks to upperwing-

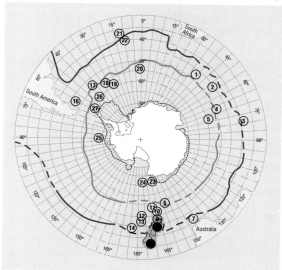

● New Zealand and offshore islands

coverts/mantle and centres of scapulars, occasionally some faint brownish mottling on crown/neck (wears swiftly), and tail is largely white. Wing pattern also like ad, but with reduced white. Bill (except black tip) and legs yellowish-brown and eye dark. **Imm** when younger (first-winter/summer) progressively cleaner grey dorsally than juv (hence approaching ad), but similar to juv in wing pattern, and first-spring/ summer bleached duller with browner remiges and perhaps faint dark carpal bar. Bare parts even duller and less intense black. Older imm (second-winter/summer) acquires almost ad-like plumage, without black subterminal tail-band, though bare parts perhaps less advanced in coloration and smaller white area on primaries than full ad.

Voice: Range of vocalizations given in variety of social contexts, mainly rasping or mewing calls.

Size: 35–38 cm, wing 27.4–31.0 cm, wingspan 81–96 cm, weight 109–277 g. Male consistently larger in most measurements and heavier than female.

Similar species: At all ages best identified from similar Red-billed by slender/longer bill and far more extensive white on primaries. Other differences described above.

Distribution and biology

Distribution, movements and population: Rivers and lakes of New Zealand, mostly on South I, and locally at several sites on North I; moves to coastal areas in winter and occasionally reaches Stewart I and Snares. Total population recently estimated at 100,000 pairs.

Diet and feeding: Occasionally visits refuse tips, but principally takes insects (sometimes aerially), fish, aquatic invertebrates and earthworms. Usually feeds gregariously and within 5 km of colony, following plough and using freshly tilled fields.

Social behaviour: Breeds colonially and pairs often use same nest site in consecutive years.

Breeding biology: Colonies occupied from mid-Sep and nesting commences synchronously in early Oct. Nest is deep depression of small sticks lined with grass. Lays 1–3 (usually two) eggs, incubated 20–24 days by both sexes and chicks fledge at c.26 days. Able to breed at two years, but more usually when 3–4 years old.

Conservation Has apparently increased since European colonization due to favourable agricultural practices providing additional feeding opportunities, but some colonies are vulnerable to habitat change as exotic lupins (*Lupinus*) invade suitable areas.

Taxonomy Monotypic.

Brown-hooded Gull *Larus maculipennis*   Plate 18

Identification

Confusion risks: None in range.

Main characters: Medium-sized gull with dark hood in breeding ad. Restricted to South America and the Falklands and generally recalls Black-headed Gull L. ridibundus of Europe. Plumage mainly white and grey, and best distinguished by diagnostic primary pattern. Bill not long, rather stout and has slightly drooped tip; head rather round-crowned. **Ad** breeding has well-defined dusky-brown hood, which reaches lower throat and upper nape, contrasting with white to pale greyish-white neck, underparts and tail. Mantle and upperwing pale to medium grey, slightly darker than underparts. Outer primaries and coverts diagnostically pure white, forming contrasting broad primary panel, well demarcated from paler (medium grey) remainder of both wing surfaces, while black of rest of primaries very extensive and contrasts on underwing (but only visible as black tips to upperwing). Bill and legs/feet vary from dark red-

Ad breeding Brown-hooded Gull Larus maculipennis. *Within our region only occurs in the Falklands, where it is unlikely to be confused with any other gulls. Falklands, Dec 1990. © René Pop.*

brown (most) to those with some dull reddish, and eye black-brown with narrow white eye-ring. Non-breeder lacks brown hood, with variable (but diffuse in most) dusky rear ear-coverts patch, and has duller bare parts. **Juv** as non-breeding ad, but has characteristic faint brownish wash to crown/nape, and streaky or scaly subterminal dark buff-brown marks to upperwing-coverts/mantle; tail has narrow black subterminal band. Remiges like ad, but white often considerably reduced: outer primaries only partially white with more black usually visible, forming broad mirror-like pattern close to tip; also more black and dark grey on inner primaries and secondaries, forming dark subterminal trailing edge. Bill (except black tip) and legs yellowish-brown and eye mainly dark. **Imm** when younger (first-winter/summer) progressively cleaner grey dorsally with whiter head than juv; hence approaching non-breeding ad, but similar to juv in wing and tail patterns (see above). First-spring/summer bleached duller with browner remiges and clear dark carpal bar; most develop only partial dark hood. Bare parts even duller and bill still has black tip. Older imm (second-winter/summer) acquires almost ad-like plumage, without black subterminal tail-band, though bare parts may be less advanced in coloration and has smaller white area on primaries than full ad.

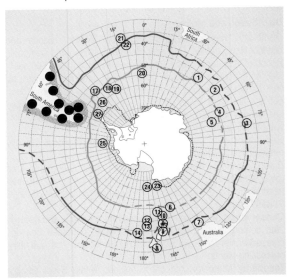

● South American offshore islands
❚ Falklands

First-winter Brown-hooded Gull Larus maculipennis *recalls non-breeding ad, but retains juv wing and tail feathers, with more black visible in primaries and dark subterminal tail-band, with duller bare parts. Ushuaia, S Argentina, Mar 2003. © Hadoram Shirihai.*

Voice: Flight call a short low-pitched *kip*; also a harsh guttural *kwarr* used at nest and when mobbing intruders (Woods 1988).
Size: 35–37 cm, wing 27.1–31.0 cm, weight 290–361 g. Male generally larger than female, but considerable overlap in measurements.
Similar species: Within our region unlikely to overlap with any confusing congeners.

Distribution and biology

Distribution, movements and population: Coasts, marshy lakes and rivers from C Chile, NE Argentina and Uruguay south to Tierra del Fuego; also the Falklands. Winters north to N Chile, N Argentina and E Brazil, though Falklands population apparently largely resident. Population estimated at 50,000–100,000 pairs in 1983–1993.
Diet and feeding: Largely insectivorous, following plough and hawking insects over marshy areas and grasslands, though also takes small fish, offal and carrion when available. Principally a scavenger in Tierra del Fuego.
Social behaviour: Few data.
Breeding biology: Breeds Oct–Jan in colonies of up to 500 pairs, sometimes with other species (usually Dolphin Gull *Larus scoresbii* or South American Tern *Sterna hirundinacea*). Often builds bulky grass nest, but may construct floating platform or usurp grebe nest. Lays 1–4 (usually 2–3) olive or buff eggs; few other data.
Conservation Not globally threatened; almost no data on population trends or recruitment rates, though solitary nesters are apparently often more successful than colonial breeders.
Taxonomy Monotypic and apparently most closely related to Brown-headed Gull *L. brunnicephalus* of Asia, or Red-billed Gull *L. novaehollandiae*, though it has in the past been occasionally treated as a race of Black-headed Gull.

White-fronted Tern *Sterna striata*   Plate 18

Identification

Confusion risks: None in range.
Main characters: Medium-sized distinctive tern, only marginal in our region (around New Zealand), where unlikely to be confused, and bears closest resemblance to Sandwich Tern *Sterna sandvicensis* of Northern Hemisphere. Plumage mainly white and pale grey and best distinguished by overall very whitish appearance. Tail deeply forked and moderately long, with quite substantial

pointed streamers (extending beyond folded wing); legs relatively short. Long, proportionately rather narrow wings with pointed tips.
Ad breeding has black cap extending broadly onto hindneck, with narrow white forehead, lores and cheeks, and very pale pearl-grey upperparts including upper tail; outer primaries distinctly duskier; underparts white sometimes with faint pinkish tinge to breast. Bill black and legs dark brownish. Non-breeding ad has more extensive white forehead, extending to mid/rear crown where spotted black; black on rear crown reaches forward to eye, but concentrated on nape and hindneck; and streamers shorter or lacking.
Juv as non-breeding ad, but has scaly subterminal brown marks on upperparts and upperwing-coverts (forming large dark carpal patch on inner forewing), and dark on head more extensive, reaching below eye where becomes more solid (more spotty black with brownish tinge), and diffuse whitish forehead; blackish outer primaries; and bare parts as ad, but legs browner. **Imm** when younger (first-winter/summer) cleaner grey dorsally, hence like non-breeding ad (also in head pattern), but similar to juv in darker outer primaries, faint dark carpal patch and shorter streamers.
Voice: Flight call a *crek*, or *ke-ke-ke*; also rasping and angry screams in defence of nest.

Ad White-fronted Tern Sterna striata. *Within our region this species only occurs marginally in New Zealand subantarctic waters (breeding on Chatham and Auckland), where readily identified by rather large size, long, slightly curved, all-black bill and very whitish plumage. Kaikoura, South I, New Zealand, Oct 2001. © Hadoram Shirihai.*

Ad White-fronted Tern Sterna striata: in flight, overall very whitish but outer primaries duskier. Breeders have long, deeply forked tails, black cap to hindneck, and narrow white forehead. Kaikoura, South I, New Zealand, Oct 2001. © Hadoram Shirihai.

Size: 35–43 cm, wing 26.0–28.8 cm, wingspan 79–82 cm, weight 103–160 g. Mensural data indicate large overlap between sexes, though tendency for female to average slightly smaller in wing, bill and tarsus measurements.
Similar species: In our region unlikely to be confused with any similar tern (on range).

Distribution and biology

Distribution, movements and population: Tasmania and Furneaux Is, New Zealand on North, South and Stewart Is; also Chatham and Auckland. Winters near breeding grounds and west to E Australia. Has reached Campbell. Approximately 50,000 pairs have bred in New Zealand in recent years. Usually associated with rocky coasts.

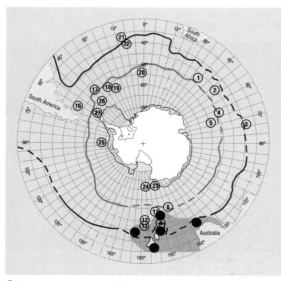

● Tasmania
● New Zealand and offshore islands
● Auckland
● Chatham

Diet and feeding: Flocks hunt fish and, to a lesser extent, shrimp in surf zone or up to several km out to sea by plunge-diving at 7–10 m, sometimes hovering, also by contact-dipping.
Social behaviour: Few data.
Breeding biology: Breeds Oct–Dec in colonies principally of 100–500 pairs, some annually changing location. Scrape in sand sometimes lined with grass. Lays 1–2 eggs, chicks brooded 4–6 days and then sometimes form crèche until fledging at 29–35 days, though remain dependent until 3–6 months.
Conservation Not globally threatened. Few data on breeding success, though winter storms considered to possibly cause high mortality among ads.
Taxonomy Three subspecies often recognized, though their validity is questionable and the species may be best regarded as monotypic: *incerta* (islands off NE Tasmania), *striata* (New Zealand) and *aucklandorna* (Chatham and Auckland), which is considered to be longer billed and heavier than mainland populations.

Common Tern *Sterna hirundo* Plate 18

Identification

Confusion risks: All other black-capped terns described below.
Main characters: Medium-sized (principally) Northern Hemisphere tern, pale grey above and white below. Winters marginally in north of our region. Most like Arctic Tern *S. paradisaea*, and both mainly occur in Southern Ocean in imm/non-breeding plumages, when best distinguished by primary pattern and slight differences in shape and feeding behaviour. Tail deeply forked with quite substantial, pointed streamers (absent in imm/non-breeding ad); legs relatively long. **Ad** breeding has black cap extending onto hindneck, pale grey upperparts and whitish-grey underparts, usually with whiter cheeks, while non-breeders have white lores, forehead and forecrown, and whiter underparts. Upperwing has large dusky area on outer primaries, forming dark wedge; only four inner primaries are paler (translucent against light); on underwing dusky feathers only visible at tips, forming clear dark trailing edge across much of primaries, with dark centre to outermost primary sometimes visible. Rump to tail mainly greyish-white, with darker outer webs to streamers. Black-tipped bill and legs red, becoming blacker/duller in non-breeding plumage. **Juv** as non-breeding ad but has scaly subterminal brown marks on grey-tinged, pale ginger-brown upperparts, and broad dark carpal bar. Dark on head has brownish tinge and extends slightly below eye level. Border of cap is not straight/solid and buff-white forehead is spotted black; dark on outer primaries more extensive and secondaries darker than upperwing-coverts. Bare parts as ad but legs generally dull brownish orange-red and bill has limited reddish at base. **Imm** when younger (first-winter/summer) cleaner grey dorsally (hence approaches non-breeding ad; also in head pattern), but similar to juv in darker outer primaries, faint dark carpal bar and short streamers.
Voice: Flight call harsher, more rasping and lower pitched than Arctic Tern.
Size: 32–37 cm, wing 23.9–28.7 cm, wingspan 72–82 cm, weight 92–140 g. Male slightly larger than female, most significantly in length and depth of bill.
Similar species: For separation from other black-capped terns see below.

Distribution and biology

Distribution, movements and population: North America to Caribbean; N Europe across Russia to W and N China, Kamchatka and Sakhalin, south to Azores and Madeira, as well as Tunisia (also breeding records in W Africa) and through Middle East to NW India, wintering generally south of Tropic of Cancer, locally south to S Africa, Australia and S South America. World population recently estimated at 250,000–500,000 pairs.

Diet and feeding: Principally small fish, with varying amounts of crustaceans, insects and fish offal, mainly taken by plunge-diving, contact-dipping and aerial-dipping, occasionally hawking. Some feed in dense flocks over ocean, but rarely over 15 km from shore.

Social behaviour: Colonial breeder, which usually returns to natal areas.

Breeding biology: Does not breed within our region. For a general summary see del Hoyo *et al.* (1996).

Conservation Populations greatly reduced in 19th century, but subsequently increased with active protection, and European population now stable. Human predation is a significant factor in W Africa and other threats include predation by mammals and birds, spring floods and pollution.

Taxonomy Two races apparently winter in Southern Ocean, nominate (described above) over most of breeding range and variable E Siberian *longipennis*, which has blacker bill and legs, and greyer underparts in breeding plumage, albeit with some overlap and intermediates.

Arctic Tern *Sterna paradisaea*　　　Plate 18

Identification

Confusion risks: Other black-capped terns.

Main characters: Northern Hemisphere tern, which in our region winters mainly in the north. Medium-sized, pale grey above and white below. Most like Common Tern; both mainly occur in Southern Ocean in imm/non-breeding plumages, when best distinguished by primary pattern and slight differences in shape and feeding behaviour. Tail deeply forked with rather long pointed streamers (absent in imm/non-breeding ad); legs relatively very short. **Ad** breeding has black cap extending onto hindneck, pale grey upperparts and whitish-grey underparts, usually with clearly whiter streak on cheek; non-breeders have white lores, forehead and forecrown, forming broad mask, and whiter underparts. Upperwing has limited dusky on primaries, which are pale whitish-grey and diagnostically translucent against the light (like secondaries); on both wing surfaces dark of primaries is confined to tips,

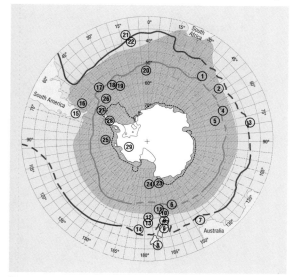

Distribution (wintering) during the austral summer

forming clear dark trailing edge across most. Rump to tail mainly greyish-white, with darker outer webs to streamers. Bill (sometimes tipped black) and legs red, darker in non-breeders. **Juv** as non-breeding ad but has scaly subterminal brown marks on grey upperparts (unlike Common these are rather limited, narrow and often faint, and grey ground colour is purer), broad dark carpal bar to upperwing and secondaries darker than upperwing-coverts. Dark on head has brownish tinge and extends slightly below eye level. Border of cap is not straight/solid and buff-white forehead is spotted black. Bare parts as ad, but legs dull brownish and bill mainly black with very limited reddish at base. **Imm** when younger (first-winter/summer) cleaner grey above (approaching non-breeding ad); also in head pattern), but similar to juv in (faint) dark carpal bar and short streamers.

Voice: Flight call a shrill piping tcheek and an occasional sibilant whistle is given by flocks in Antarctica (*HANZAB*).

Size: 33–36 cm, wing 23.9–29.0 cm, wingspan 76–85 cm, weight 86–127 g. Wing, tail fork and bill all longer in breeding male.

Similar species: Common Tern is paler below with conspicuous dark outer webs to 5–6 outermost primaries (forming a dark wedge), whereas Arctic usually has uniform upperwing (with translucent primaries and secondaries against light) and exhibits a number of structural differences, though most are best appreciated in summer plumage. Compared to Common tends to have more 'elastic' and deeper wingbeats, with body appearing to move up and down in flight (i.e. not as gull-like as Common), and tends to forage with more vertical plunges; with experience wings appear proportionally longer and narrower, set further forward on body (due also to more neckless appearance, smaller head and bill, and somewhat longer tail than Common). Antarctic Tern is longer legged and shorter tailed with paler webs to outermost feathers (for further comparisons see latter).

Distribution and biology

Distribution, movements and population: Strong migrant. Breeds throughout N Holarctic, from N North America, Greenland, Iceland and N Europe to N Russia, and N Siberia to Commander Is. Winters off South Africa and S South America, and in subantarctic and Antarctic waters, some even reaching E Pacific and Australia. Arrives in Southern Ocean in Oct and stragglers remain until May. Global perhaps 500,000 pairs.

Diet and feeding: Principally takes small fish and, to a lesser extent, crustaceans, molluscs and insects by plunge-diving following a short hover, also hover-dipping and surface-dipping.

Social behaviour: Few data from Southern Ocean.

Breeding biology: Breeds only in Northern Hemisphere.

Conservation Not globally threatened, but large declines reported in several parts of species' broad range.

Taxonomy Monotypic.

South American Tern *Sterna hirundinacea*　　Plate 18

Identification

Confusion risks: Antarctic *S. vittata*, Arctic *S. paradisaea* and Common Terns *S. hirundo* (only straggler to our region).

Main characters: Medium-sized, very whitish tern, pale grey above and even paler below. In our region restricted to the Falklands and S South America. Best distinguished by overall grey tone and plumage pattern, especially primaries, slight differences in shape, notably stronger more curved bill, and some feeding-behaviour differences. Tail deeply forked with rather long pointed streamers (absent in imm/non-breeding ad); legs relatively long. **Ad** breeding has black cap extending slightly onto nape/upper hindneck, very pale/whitish-grey upperparts (underparts only slightly paler, with ill-defined white cheeks and white undertail-coverts); rump to tail mainly whitish (hardly contrasting with pearl-grey rest of upperparts) and streamers usually lack visible darker edge to outer webs. Upperwing duskier on 5–6 outermost primaries, forming slight dark wedge. On underwing dark tips to same feathers rather diffuse and form only weak dark trailing edge, while inner primaries and secondaries have pure white trailing edge and often very narrow black streak on outer web of outermost primary, adding to uniformly very pale wing. Bill and legs red. Non-breeder has white lores, forehead and forecrown (forming broad mask), whiter underparts and duller red bare parts. **Juv** as non-breeding ad but has creamy-white crown, spotted and streaked darker, and more solid dark eye-patch, extending broadly well behind it. Greyish upperparts heavily mottled/barred blackish subterminally, most obviously on wing-coverts. Also, dark grey outer primaries (almost blackish on outermost), whitish-grey tail with dark outer webs, black bill and dirty yellow feet; broad dark carpal bar on upperwing and secondaries hardly contrast with upperwing-coverts; and face to chest often faintly buffish-brown. **Imm** when younger (first-winter/summer) cleaner grey above (thus approaches non-breeding ad; also in head pattern), but similar to juv in having (faint) dark carpal bar, darker outer primaries and secondaries, and, usually, greyer uppertail and short streamers.

Voice: In flight a short clear kyik, also harsh descending scream, keeeer or short ik-ik-ik (Woods 1988).

Size: 41–43 cm, wing 28.4–31.5 cm, wingspan 84–86 cm, weight 172–196 g. Much overlap in mensural data between the sexes, though males may tend to have longer tails.

Similar species: Around the Falklands and S South America most likely to be confused with Antarctic Tern, but is overall larger with stronger/longer bill which appears slightly drooped, paler, most noticeably on underparts, and also has clearly darker outer webs to 5–6 outermost primaries, forming dark wedge on upperwing (more uniform with rest of upperwing and has translucent primaries in Antarctic). From Arctic and Common Terns, which are usually in winter/imm plumage in our region (though least-advanced first-summer South American are winter plumage-like and most problematic), by larger overall size, with longer tail and bill; also greyer underparts than Common, and unlike Arctic has darker outer wedge to primaries above.

Distribution and biology

Distribution, movements and population: Coasts of Peru and E

Subad South American Tern Sterna hirundinacea *is distinguished from Antarctic Tern* S. vittata *by its overall larger size with strongly/longer and slightly drooped bill, paler grey underparts, and clearly darker outer webs to 5–6 outermost primaries on upperwing. Falklands, Jan 2001. © Hadoram Shirihai.*

Brazil south to Tierra del Fuego; also the Falklands. Most move north in non-breeding season, reaching Ecuador on Pacific coast. No total population data available.

Diet and feeding: Feeds principally on small fish and crustaceans, also probably insects, by vertical plunge-diving from c.7 m, also sometimes hovers before diving; often follows porpoises or predatory fish.

Social behaviour: Few data. Generally gregarious at all seasons.

Breeding biology: Breeds Oct–Jan in our region (Apr–Jun in Brazil) in dense colonies of up to 10,000 pairs at some localities, often close to gull nests in the Falklands. Nest a scrape or depression, sometimes with shells or pebbles, or lined with grasses and occasionally in dense vegetation. Lays 2–3 variably coloured eggs, incubated 21–23 days and chicks fledge at 27 days.

Conservation Not globally threatened. Few trend data, though some indicate moderate declines. Nonetheless still abundant at many Argentine colonies, despite effects of ecotourism. Breeding success is reasonable in populations for which data are available.

Taxonomy Monotypic.

Ad South American Tern Sterna hirundinacea. *Within our region only occurs in the Falklands where it could be confused with Antarctic Tern* S. vittata. *Falklands, Dec 1990. © René Pop.*

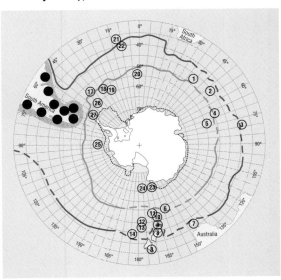

● South American offshore islands
● Falklands

Antarctic Tern *Sterna vittata*   Plate 18

Identification

Confusion risks: South American *S. hirundinacea*, Kerguelen *S. virgata* and Arctic Terns *S. paradisaea*; perhaps Common Tern *S. hirundo* (only straggler to our region, but very common off southern coast of South Africa and off SE Australia).

Main characters: Medium-sized, greyish and white, black-capped tern. Most widespread breeding tern in our region, found across Antarctic and subantarctic waters and on dispersal can overlap with all above species. Most similar to Arctic Tern, but both it and Common Terns occur in Southern Ocean in imm/non-breeding plumages (and occasionally breeding plumage farther north), though least-advanced first-summer Antarctic Tern is winter plumage-like and hence problematic. Separation from South American/Kerguelen Terns often difficult (see below). Best distinguished by combination of overall size, wing pattern and slight differences in shape and feeding behaviour. Tail deeply forked (at least in tristanensis) with rather long pointed streamers (absent in many imm/non-breeding birds at this season); legs relatively short (vary according to race) and afford stout impression. Strong bill is fairly stout and pointed. **Ad** breeding has black cap extending onto hindneck and very pale grey (as in *tristanensis*) to dark grey upperparts (as in nominate), white rump and tail (without darker outer web to streamers); underparts grey-white to dark grey (according to subspecies), usually with clear white cheek streak, and white undertail-coverts. Upperwing has limited dusky on primaries, which are mainly pale grey or only slightly darker than secondaries (both slightly translucent against light, but not as obviously so as in Arctic), with rather indistinct dark outer web to outermost primary. On both wing surfaces dark primary tips form faint dark trailing edge across two-thirds of outer primaries. Bill and legs range from dark coral-red to blood red according to race. Non-breeders have white lores, forehead

Ad breeding Antarctic Tern Sterna vittata, *South Shetlands, Nov 2001. © Hadoram Shirihai.*

and (dark-streaked) forecrown, forming broad mask, and usually most have more grey-mottled underparts. Bare parts, especially legs, duller and browner (though some retain red legs). **Juv** heavily barred dark brown on upperparts, cap black streaked buff and extends below eye level, border not straight and forehead white spotted/streaked black. Dark carpal bar and dark tips to secondary-coverts, throat and breast washed buff-brown, and belly white. Outermost tail feathers have darker outer webs. Legs and bill black. **Imm** plumage acquired during first winter/early summer; clean grey above with white underparts, darkish carpal bar (much paler than in Common Tern) and short streamers with some greyish edging; also black bill and legs acquire some reddish as season progresses.

Voice: Colonies are generally noisy, with a shrill high-pitched *trr-trr-kriah* being the commonest call (*HANZAB*, Watson 1975) while

Ad breeding Antarctic Tern Sterna vittata; *note deeply forked tail with rather long pointed streamers, and strong, fairly stout and pointed, red bill; dusky underparts emphasize white cheek stripe; also dark underwing, medium grey upperparts/upperwings with contrasting white rump and tail. South Shetlands, Nov 2001. © Hadoram Shirihai.*

Juv Antarctic Tern Sterna vittata *has heavily barred upperparts, dark mask behind eye, pale forehead and cap (latter streaked dark), throat and breast washed buff-brown, and black bare parts. Tristan group, Mar 2006. © Hadoram Shirihai.*

at communal roost sites a continuous, noisy chattering is maintained (A.J. Tree pers. obs.). Screams and squawks given in alarm and foraging birds utter a churring call when chasing other terns (*HANZAB*). A loud *chit…chit…chit…chirr, chirr, chirr…* in display.

Size: 32–40 cm, wing 23.8–28.7 cm, wingspan 74–79 cm, weight 114–205 g. Male tends to have longer bill in all subspecies, but differences marginal and much overlap.

Similar species: Arctic Tern (usually ad winter/first-winter in our region) separable from superficially similar first-year/non-breeding Antarctic by shorter legs and bill and longer tail with distinctly darker (not paler) webs to outer feathers, more obvious dark outer web to outermost primary and more translucent remiges. Restricted-range Kerguelen Tern (which see) slightly smaller, with shorter bill and wings, and darker overall plumage, having grey (not white) uppertail- and undertail-coverts. Confusion also possible with South American Tern (which see). From Common Tern by size, different jizz and lack of obvious dark wedge to outer primaries (like Arctic, problems only arise in certain plumages).

Distribution and biology

Distribution, movements and population: Southern Ocean on Tristan da Cunha, Gough, Bouvetøya, Crozet, Kerguelen, Amsterdam, St Paul, Heard, Macquarie, Campbell, Auckland, Snares, Antipodes and Bounty; and Antarctic Peninsula to 68°S, South Shetland,

First-summer Antarctic Tern Sterna vittata *recalls non-breeding ad, but has darkish carpal bar, and greyish-edged short streamers. Compared to Arctic Tern* S. paradisaea *is progressively more worn and bleached (note juv-retained, very worn scapulars). Antarctic Peninsula, Nov 2001. © Hadoram Shirihai.*

South Orkney, South Georgia and South Sandwich. Ranges at sea north to S South America, SE Atlantic Ocean and South Africa. Total population estimated to be at least 50,000 pairs.

Diet and feeding: Takes small fish and, to a lesser extent, limpets, euphausiids and crustaceans, occasionally insects or offal, mainly in inter-tidal or inshore waters around breeding sites but oceanic feeder in winter quarters, by plunge-diving and contact-dipping, typically hovers up to 10 m before dipping. Hunts singly or in flocks, occasionally follows boats and ads sometimes forage on ground, including in open pastures on Tristan.

Social behaviour: Few data.

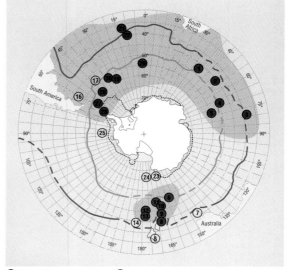

1 Prince Edward & Marion	12 Antipodes
2 Crozet	13 Bounty
3 Amsterdam & St Paul	18 South Georgia
4 Kerguelen	19 South Sandwich
5 Heard	20 Bouvetøya
6 Macquarie	21 Tristan da Cunha
7 New Zealand and	22 Gough
offshore islands	26 South Orkney
9 Snares	27 South Shetland
10 Auckland	28 Antarctic Peninsula
11 Campbell	

Ad Antarctic Tern Sterna vittata *of the distinctive race* georgiae, *South Georgia.* © Hadoram Shirihai.

Breeding biology: Breeds late Oct–Mar (according to locality) in loose colonies principally of 5–40 pairs, up to 1000 pairs at some localities, but in other areas also singly on cliff ledges to avoid predation. In Antarctic Peninsula and nearby localities arrives at colonies mid-Sep–early Oct though full breeding plumage may not be acquired until Nov. Nest a scrape or depression sometimes with shells or pebbles, constructed mid-Oct–mid-Nov. Lays 1–2 eggs in mid–late Nov, incubated 23–25 days and chicks fledge at 27–32 days, with some post-fledging feeding. Human disturbance and more especially skua predation are most important causes of breeding failure.

Conservation Not globally threatened. Few data on breeding success, though productivity known to be low on Heard, and tiny population (c.40 pairs) on Macquarie must be considered endangered owing to frequent nesting failure due to predation by cats and rats, as well as human disturbance. Skuas and gulls prey on ads, chicks and eggs. Studies in South African waters reveal low productivity of visiting populations in most years with only occasional good years—factors have not been determined but may be related to weather and food supplies (A. J. Tree pers. comm.).

Taxonomy Requires revision as cited differences in most subspecies insufficient to warrant such status. Probably only nominate form occurs in Indian Ocean, with cline of paler grey plumage and bill changing from blood-red to coral-red south to north, and many intermediates, while southern *vittata* is very dark. *S. v. sanctipauli* (on Tristan da Cunha and Gough) is a large, pale

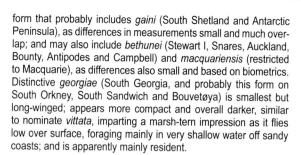

form that probably includes *gaini* (South Shetland and Antarctic Peninsula), as differences in measurements small and much overlap; and may also include *bethunei* (Stewart I, Snares, Auckland, Bounty, Antipodes and Campbell) and *macquariensis* (restricted to Macquarie), as differences also small and based on biometrics. Distinctive *georgiae* (South Georgia, and probably this form on South Orkney, South Sandwich and Bouvetøya) is smallest but long-winged; appears more compact and overall darker, similar to nominate *vittata*, imparting a marsh-tern impression as it flies low over surface, foraging mainly in very shallow water off sandy coasts; and is apparently mainly resident.

Kerguelen Tern *Sterna virgata*　　　Plate 18

Identification

Confusion risks: Antarctic *S. vittata* and Arctic Terns *S. paradisaea*. *Main characters*: Endemic to subantarctic islands of Indian Ocean, where overlaps with similar Antarctic Tern, but is not exclusively maritime, being also associated with inland fresh waters. Medium-sized, grey-plumaged, black-capped tern. Tail not as deeply forked and has shorter, less pointed streamers than most congeners (absent in imm/non-breeding ad), which do not project beyond wingtip. Legs very short. Bill fairly short and narrow. Habitat preference, feeding behaviour and general jizz impart a somewhat marsh tern-like impression. **Ad** breeding has black cap, hardly extending onto hindneck, and smoky-grey upperparts, including tail (without darker outer webs to streamers), with whiter rump/undertail-coverts. Underparts also smoky-grey, with prominent white cheek streak. Upperwing usually has duskier primaries, slightly darker than rest of wing and distinct dark outer web to outermost primary; on both wing surfaces dark primary tips rather obscure, barely forming dark trailing edge across two-thirds of outer primaries. Underwing diagnostically grey. Bill deep red and legs bright orange/dull red. Non-breeding ad has dull reddish to black bill and acquires white lores and forehead by Feb. **Juv** as non-breeding ad but vermiculated grey, brown and buff, with broad dark barring on pale buffish-grey upperparts, and broad dark carpal bar on upperwing. Primaries and secondaries variably darker than upperwing-coverts. Dark on head has brownish tinge and extends slightly below eye level. Border of cap is not straight/solid and buff-white forehead is spotted/streaked black. Underparts mainly whitish. Outermost tail feathers have slightly darker outer webs. Legs dull brown and bill mainly black. **Imm** when younger (first-winter/

Ad breeding Kerguelen Tern Sterna virgata *is separated from Antarctic Tern S.* vittata *by slightly smaller size, shorter bill and wings, and darker plumage, having grey (not white) uppertail- and undertail-coverts. Kerguelen. Left: Nov 1999* © Hadoram Shirihai. *Right: Jul 1996* © Frédéric Jiguet.

Ad winter Kerguelen Tern Sterna virgata: *note rather compact appearance with round wings, overall dark plumage and grey uppertail-coverts. Kerguelen, Mar 2004. © Hadoram Shirihai.*

summer) cleaner grey above and below, with dull reddish-black bill (thus approaching non-breeding ad; also in head pattern), but similar to juv in dark carpal bar and short streamers.

Voice: Described as high-pitched scream (Watson 1975), but also utters churrs and squeaks while foraging, and part of its repertoire appears very similar to Common Tern (*HANZAB*)

Size: 33 cm, wing 24.7–27.0 cm, wingspan 68–72 cm, weight 85–170 g. Insufficient data to draw conclusions concerning sex-related differences in measurements (if any).

Similar species: Kerguelen Tern, compared to more widespread Antarctic Tern, is slightly smaller, with shorter bill and wings and overall darker plumage, and has grey (not white) uppertail- and undertail-coverts.

Distribution and biology

Distribution, movements and population: Ponds, marshes and beaches of Prince Edward, Marion, Crozet and Kerguelen, in S Indian Ocean. Largely sedentary, dispersing only to inshore waters around breeding islands. Population c.2500 pairs, with most (2000) on Kerguelen.

Diet and feeding: Fish, crustaceans, molluscs, earthworms, insects and spiders taken according to quite strict seasonal preferences and availability, feeding in flocks of up to 20 inshore by plunge-diving and contact-dipping. Sometimes walks on kelp to capture invertebrates and flocks of up to 50 feed on insects in vegetation, both on ground and in flight. Contrary to some reports, the species is less strongly tied to inland waters than reported in

the literature, at least in parts of its range, e.g. 90% or more of foraging at the Prince Edwards is at sea.

Social behaviour: Few data.

Breeding biology: Breeds Sep–Jan (peak Nov to mid-Dec) in small, very loose colonies of up to 30 pairs, some solitarily, but all usually more than 200 m from shore. Nest a scrape often lined with plant material. Lays 1–2 eggs, incubated 24 days and chicks, which are brooded for five days, fledge at 31–39 days, but remain dependent for a further 20 days.

Conservation Near Threatened (formerly Vulnerable) and among the world's rarest terns. No data on population trends. Hatching success 73–88%, but high mortality among later-hatching chicks due to food shortages, and large population of feral cats on Kerguelen threaten most important subpopulation, which breeds on currently predator-free satellites of main island. Adverse weather conditions may pose most significant threat.

Taxonomy Monotypic, although those on Crozet have occasionally been separated as *mercuri*, on basis of more restricted grey forehead in non-breeders and subtle bare-parts coloration differences.

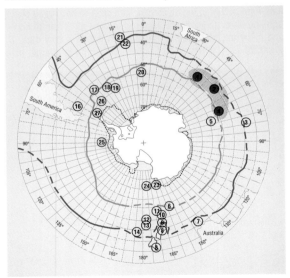

Ad winter Kerguelen Tern Sterna virgata: *rather small, short-billed and very dark grey, including undertail-coverts. Kerguelen, Mar 2004. © Hadoram Shirihai.*

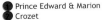

● Prince Edward & Marion
● Crozet
● Kerguelen

Endemic and indigenous species of subantarctic islands in the S Indian and S Atlantic Oceans and the Falklands

Plates 19–21 and the text below cover the indigenous endemic and speciality species breeding on subantarctic islands in the S Indian and Atlantic Oceans, and on the Falklands. A wide variety of species is treated, from herons to owls, with passerines from these regions being illustrated in Plate 22. The accounts and plates do not treat introduced or non-native colonists, only those taxa unique to the islands or which breed (usually regularly). Among non-passerines the latter includes several species that are principally South American (e.g. *Chloephaga* geese, steamer ducks and other waterfowl, and several raptors and waders). Among passerines several wide-ranging Patagonian or S Andean species occur on the Falklands. Here, I would like to emphasize the important contribution of Woods (1988). Though the illustrations in the latter work are relatively basic, the texts are excellent and provide a wealth of original information, which in terms of their approach are somewhat ahead of their time. Thus, I highly recommend it, and the *Atlas of Breeding Birds of the Falkland Islands* (Woods & Woods 1997), for use in the Falklands, especially to those visitors with a deeper interest in the archipelago's landbirds. Further details on those bird species recorded in these islands are presented in the relevant regional account, the associated table, and the checklist kindly prepared by Robin Woods.

White-tufted Grebe *Rollandia rolland*   Plate 19

Identification

Confusion risks: Rock Shag Phalacrocorax magellanicus.
Main characters: Relatively small, largely dark grebe with white tufts on ear-coverts the most striking plumage feature, especially when breeding. Sexes similar (except in bill size) but some age and seasonal plumage variation. Reasonably tame. **Ad** has head, neck and upperparts largely black with green sheen, striking triangular-shaped, white-tufted ear-coverts, and brown-fringed mantle and back feathers. Underparts uniform dull rufous, but sometimes mottled grey or brown, and secondaries white or pale grey with buffy tips (visible as pale trailing edge in flight). Pointed bill brown to black, legs and feet grey to olivaceous, and eye red. Non-breeding plumage duller, with white ear-coverts reduced or absent, browner upperparts with buffier fringes, chin, head- and throat-sides white, and underparts dull brownish-buff becoming white on undertail-coverts. **Imm** much like non-breeding ad, but neck- and throat-sides prominently streaked dusky-brown, and has much larger white wing patches (rarely seen).
Size: 24–36 cm, wing 12.9–14.5 cm, weight 262–269 g (two from Tierra del Fuego). Much overlap between sexes in most mensural data, but male has significantly larger bill in nominate.
Voice: Creaking or growling notes given in breeding season e.g. *hrrr* in aggressive situation and *jarrh* in alarm (Fjeldså & Krabbe 1990), while young have similar but higher pitched calls. Generally silent in winter.
Similar species: Rock Shag should not be easily confused, except at great distance, when horizontal carriage and shorter head and bill of grebe should still be obvious.

Distribution and biology

Distribution, movements and population: South America from NW Peru, Bolivia, Paraguay and S Brazil south to Tierra del Fuego;

Ad White-tufted Grebe Rollandia rolland. Falklands, Dec 1998. © Nic Huin/Falklands Conservation.

also the Falklands where population estimated at 750–1400 pairs in 1983–93.
Diet and feeding: Takes fish, arthropods, crustaceans and aquatic plants in short dives lasting 15–20 seconds.
Social behaviour: Territorial or loosely social year-round.
Breeding biology: Nests in mid-Oct–Jan, laying 1–3 white eggs (which soon become stained) in typical floating grebe nest of aquatic vegetation, placed close to bank or in fringe cover. Breeds year-round in Peru and multi-brooded at least in mainland South America.
Conservation Not threatened and no significant threats known.
Taxonomy Three races recognized, with *morresoni* confined to Lake Junín in C Peru, chilensis throughout rest of range except the Falklands, where replaced by nominate which is larger with no overlap in wing and bill measurements (R. Woods pers. comm.) and brighter rufous underparts than mainland populations, and was treated specifically by Wetmore (1926).

Silvery Grebe *Podiceps occipitalis*   Plate 19

Identification

Confusion risks: No significant identification problems.
Main characters: Relatively small, largely greyish-looking grebe. Sexes similar but some age and seasonal plumage variation. **Ad** bluish-slate above and silvery-white below, with straw-yellow and pale grey hair-like ear-covert plumes, grey breast-sides and flanks, prominent black patch on nape extending onto hindneck as narrow line, brownish-grey primaries (tipped white on innermost) and white secondaries (with some grey on outer webs of innermost). Bill, legs and feet dark grey to black, and eye crimson-red. Non-breeder similar but lacks ear-covert plumes. White neck and white wingbar obvious in flight. **Imm** much as non-breeding ad but has white nape faintly tinged brown, while small young are heavily striped on upperparts.
Size: 25.0–28.5 cm, wing 12.1–13.5 cm, weight 340–397 g. Male marginally larger, but much overlap in mensural data.
Voice: Short clucking and squeaky notes, e.g. *chook* or *djec* (Fjeldså & Krabbe 1990).
Similar species: Only other regularly occurring grebe in the Falklands is White-tufted *Rollandia rolland*, but latter is overall much

Ad Silvery Grebes Podiceps occipitalis, *Falklands, Feb 1991. © René Pop.*

Ad Black-crowned Night-heron Nycticorax nycticorax falklandicus, *Falklands, Jan 1991. © René Pop.*

darker with white ear-coverts in breeding plumage. They regularly breed on the same lakes.

Distribution and biology

Distribution, movements and population: W South America from SW Colombia south to Tierra del Fuego; also the Falklands where population estimated at 500–900 pairs in 1983–93. Southernmost populations winter north to C Argentina.

Diet and feeding: Takes fish and their eggs, insects and larvae, small crustaceans and vegetation in up to 20-second-long dives.

Social behaviour: Colonial and gregarious, with nests often in close proximity to form rafts. Pairs 'dance' and groups engage in parallel races in breeding season.

Breeding biology: In the Falklands probably lays two blue-white eggs in floating nest in Dec (at least occasionally earlier), with small young most frequently seen in Jan. In Patagonia eggs usually laid Nov–Jan, rarely to Feb–Mar in more northerly populations.

Conservation Generally relatively common and not threatened.

Taxonomy Two populations which may represent separate species, with *P. o. juninensis* (darker grey with grey-brown ear-covert plumes) in the Andes of Colombia, Ecuador, Peru and Bolivia to N Chile and NW Argentina, and the nominate in lowlands from NC Chile and W and S Argentina south to Tierra del Fuego, and the Falklands.

Black-crowned Night-heron
Nycticorax nycticorax falklandicus   Plate 19

Identification

Confusion risks: None in range.

Main characters: Stocky heron; in flight broad, rounded wings flapped slowly and feet project just beyond short tail. **Ad** has black cap, hindneck and upperparts, with two long white plumes extending onto nape; wings and flanks greyish-brown, forehead, face and neck whitish, becoming grey on rest of underparts. Red eye, black bill with yellow base and yellow legs; latter can be bright red during courtship. **Juv** (and younger **imm**) greyish-brown, heavily spotted yellowish-white on upperparts, slightly dark capped and heavily streaked dark on whitish neck and underparts; bill yellowish-brown, eye yellowish-orange and legs olive-green. Second-year more like ad but has browner cap and back, and some retained streaky feathers on wing-coverts and, perhaps, on less pure pale greyish neck and underparts.

Voice: Flight call a harsh *kwark*; other calls at colonies.

Size: 57 cm, wing 30.1–32.6 cm, no weight data available for *falk-*

landicus. Insufficient data relating to *falklandicus* to draw conclusions concerning any differences between the sexes.

Similar species: Unmistakable in the Falklands, where no herons have similar plumage or shape.

Distribution and biology

Distribution, movements and population: Near cosmopolitan, being absent only from Australasia. Falklands population placed at 1900–3600 pairs in the 1980s.

Diet and feeding: Feeds singly or in pairs, on beaches with rock pools.

Social behaviour: Gregarious at colonies and roost sites. Active at twilight and nocturnally, less often during day.

Breeding biology: On the Falklands nests in small colonies of up to 100 pairs, breeding in rushes, tussac grass and trees. Nest a substantial platform of grass and sticks. Lays 2–4 blue-green eggs from late Oct. Two broods may be attempted as eggs have been discovered as late as Jan.

Conservation Not globally threatened and no apparent threats to its survival in our region.

Imm Black-crowned Night-heron Nycticorax nycticorax falklandicus, *with still-heavily streaked neck and underparts, and yellowish-brown bill. Falklands, Jan 2005. © Klaus Bjerre.*

Plate 19 Endemic and indigenous non-passerines of the Falklands

Kelp Goose ad. ♀
(p. 277)

Kelp Goose ad. ♂

All white; yellow legs and small dark bill (pinkish culmen base)

Ruddy-headed Goose ad.
(p. 278)

Greyish lower neck sharply demarcated from pale chestnut upper neck

Upland Goose ad. ♀
(p. 277)

Warmer fulvous head, neck and chest

Upland Goose ad. ♂

Blackish-brown with white-barred underparts, whitish eye-ring and pink bill

Mostly white; barred on flanks and mantle

Black-necked Swan ad. ♂
(p. 276)

Black head and neck

Ash-grey head and upper neck; chestnut lower neck

(young male less pure white and more extensively barred)

Coscoroba Swan ad.
(p. 276)

All white except reddish bill

Ashy-headed Goose ad. ♂
(p. 279)

Flying Steamer Duck ad. ♂
(p. 280)

Duller (less white) head with small dull bill (often greyish near tip)

Flying Steamer Duck ad. ♀

Small bill with paler distal area; flight feather extensions

Black-crowned Night-heron
ad. ssp. *falklandica*
(p. 274)

Black cap and back, otherwise mainly grey (juv/imm brownish and streaky)

Thick bill

Falkland Steamer Duck ad. ♀

Very short wings

Falkland Steamer Duck ad. ♂
(p. 279)

Bright orange bill

White-tufted Grebe breeding ad.
(p. 273)

Largely black with green sheen, striking triangular, white-tufted ear-coverts; dull rufous below

Silvery Grebe breeding ad.
(p. 273)

Head becomes whiter with wear; second-year male has (variable) browner/darker head and duller bill

Relatively small; bluish-slate above and silvery-white below; yellowish ear-covert plumes

Black-necked Swans Cygnus melancoryphus, Chile. © Frank S. Todd.

Coscoroba Swans Coscoroba coscoroba, Chile. © Frank S. Todd.

Taxonomy The race *falklandicus* is endemic to the Falklands, being generally smaller and darker than other races, though there is considerable plumage variation between continental and insular populations, making recognition of such subspecific differentiation at best tentative.

Black-necked Swan
Cygnus melancoryphus   Plate 19

Identification
Confusion risks: None.
Main characters: Huge (the largest freshwater species in the Falklands), largely white, black-necked swan; by far the least approachable of the Falkland waterfowl. Sexes alike (except in size) and no seasonal plumage variation. **Ad** entirely clean white except black head and neck, with white chin and 'spectacles' (line around eye and across crown-sides to nape). Bill mainly blue-grey with scarlet base and large double-lobed frontal caruncle, legs and feet pale pinkish and eye dark brown. **Imm** lacks frontal caruncle and has head and neck brownish-black flecked grey, rusty-grey tips to dorsal feathers and fringes, and dark grey tips to primaries.
Size: 0.99–1.25 m, wing 40.0–46.3 cm, weight 4.0–5.4 kg. Male is heavier and has considerably longer wing and tarsus, but female has, on average, longer tail.
Voice: Typically a weak, wheezy whistle, *whee-her-her-her* and male gives *hooee-hoo-hoo* (Woods 1988), but usually silent.
Similar species: Unmistakeable.

Distribution and biology
Distribution, movements and population: Breeds from Uruguay and SE Brazil south through Argentina and S Chile to Tierra del Fuego and Cape Horn; also the Falklands where population estimated at 750–1400 pairs in 1983–93. Winters north in SE South America to Tropic of Capricorn and vagrants have reached South Shetlands and Antarctic Peninsula (though Falklands population present year-round).
Diet and feeding: Feeds by dabbling and submerging head and neck in shallow water.
Social behaviour: Gregarious in non-breeding season when forms moulting flocks of up to 6000 (exceptionally 20,000) individuals. Territorial in breeding season, being aggressive around nest, though pairs may occasionally build in close proximity.
Breeding biology: Breeds early Aug–mid-Sep onwards in the Falklands, constructing large nest of twigs and grasses within dense cover beside lake, occasionally on small islands or on floating vegetation in concealed position, and lays 4–7 cream-coloured eggs incubated five weeks. Both sexes care for young, carrying

them on back when smaller. Fledge at three months and first breed when several years old.
Conservation Few threats known though drainage of lowland wetlands has undoubtedly had an affect. Not threatened and reportedly increasing in Chile since cessation of hunting.
Taxonomy Monotypic.

Coscoroba Swan *Coscoroba coscoroba*   Plate 19

Identification
Confusion risks: None.
Main characters: Smallish white swan with comparatively short neck, black-tipped wings and bright pink bare parts. Swims with rear body somewhat raised. Sexes virtually identical and no seasonal plumage variation. **Ad** all white except black-tipped outermost primaries. Bill carmine becoming paler on nail, legs and feet pink and eye whitish (male) to dark brown (female), with pink eyelids. **Imm** much as female (including eye colour), with dark cap and brownish-grey mottling to upperparts.
Size: 0.9–1.15 m, wing 40.0–48.4 cm, weight 3.8–4.6 kg. Male considerably heavier and larger in most mensural data.
Voice: Trumpeted *cos-cor-oo* with emphasis on first note and overall higher pitched in female.
Similar species: None, it being the only all-white swan in our region though may sometimes require careful separation from domestic geese, especially in the Falklands, where several populations of feral geese (some capable of flight) are present.

Distribution and biology
Distribution, movements and population: Breeds in lowlands of N Paraguay, Uruguay and extreme SE Brazil south through Argentina and S Chile to Tierra del Fuego; several present on Pebble I from at least 1998, where a pair bred and raised four fledglings in 2000/1, the first recorded breeding in the Falklands since 1860. Winters north to C Chile and NE Argentina following moult.
Diet and feeding: Dabbles or wades in shallows, and occasionally grazes waterside vegetation.
Social behaviour: Forms small groups of up to 200 individuals in non-breeding season (exceptionally 1000 to 2000 in Chile). Pairs occasionally nest in small loose colonies.
Breeding biology: Builds bulky nest in tall lakeside cover or on small islands in shallow water. Very few breeding data from our region (small cygnets seen in May).
Conservation Status unclear, though apparently not globally threatened. The important Chilean population declined significantly in the 1970s.
Taxonomy Monotypic.

Family party of Upland Geese Chloephaga picta leucoptera, with male on left and female on right, Falklands. © Frank S. Todd.

Upland Goose
Chloephaga picta leucoptera   Plate 19

Identification

Confusion risks: Male could be confused only with male Kelp Goose *C. hybrida*, and female with Ashy-headed *C. poliocephala* and (more likely) Ruddy-headed Geese *C. rubidiceps*.

Main characters: Medium-sized, distinctly patterned goose. Within our region restricted to the Falklands, where represented by the endemic race, leucoptera, which is among the most widespread birds in the archipelago. Strong sexual dimorphism. **Ad** male has white head, neck and underparts, including tibia feathering, with greyish upperparts, black bill and legs; tail mainly black, though some have white outer tail feathers. Blackish barring on flanks and mantle, extends to neck and much of rest of underparts only in barred morph of nominate picta (on mainland). Female overall greyish-brown with warmer fulvous head, neck and chest, whitish belly, and closely barred lower neck to rear underparts, white wing-coverts (visible in flight), and black tail and vent; bill blackish and legs yellow-orange. **Juv** (and **imm**) as respective ad, but young male less pure white (washed grey) and more extensively barred (but variable), including young male leucoptera and unbarred morph of nominate, while young female duller with browner legs.

Voice: Main calls of male are whistles, with more rattling calls given by female.

Size: 60–65 cm, wing 40.0–46.2 cm (female 40.0–42.5 cm), weight c.3.3 kg (mean of both sexes). Male typically slightly larger.

Similar species: Male Kelp Goose (which see) considerably bulkier and overall purer white, with yellow legs and all-white tail. Both Ashy-headed and Ruddy-headed Geese smaller and exhibit very little sexual dimorphism. Former has grey head, rufous-brown neck, breast and mantle, and whitish, boldly barred black belly. Ruddy-headed Goose (which see) has smaller and daintier head than superficially similar female Upland, and unlike latter is more finely barred on greyish-white (not fulvous) neck and buffier underparts, becoming richer fulvous on abdomen and vent; also has narrow whitish eye-ring.

Distribution and biology

Distribution, movements and population: Breeds from S Tierra del Fuego north to c.38°S in Argentina and Chile; also the Falklands. Latter population estimated at 46,000–85,000 pairs in 1983–93, but may be significantly higher than even upper limit of this.

Diet and feeding: Feeds by grazing in open country, and rarely swims except when with young or moulting. Takes grasses and seeds, also very partial to seasonal berries on the Falklands.

Social behaviour: Highly gregarious and has been considered a pest for at least the past century; however, it is less persecuted now. Long-term pair-bond. Moulting concentrations form immediately after breeding season, but birds do not become truly flightless.

Breeding biology: Nests Aug–Jan, especially on coastal greens near settlements and ponds. Most lay in Sep–Oct on the Falklands. Grass nest within ferns or other cover, sometimes on tussac grass up to 1.5 m above ground. Lays 5–8 large cream-coloured eggs. Female alone incubates (one month). Fledging takes 9–10 weeks and both parents defend young from predators.

Conservation Not globally threatened. In the Falklands it has been labelled a pest for over a century due to claims that it consumes the best grass needed for sheep. It was viewed as a good alternative to mutton, particularly full-grown juvs and ads that had been feeding on berries in autumn. Fresh eggs are also taken. However, although the government and then farmers paid bounties for many thousands of bills collected from killed birds, the low human population has not significantly affected overall numbers. Thousands are thought to have died of starvation during winter 1995, when freak weather left large areas under a snow blanket for up to three months.

Taxonomy Two races: nominate in S South America, in which males have a barred and a white phase, and larger *leucoptera* in the Falklands, of which the male has no barred phase, though some first-years may have most of the underparts closely barred.

Kelp Goose
Chloephaga hybrida malvinarum   Plate 19

Identification

Confusion risks: Upland Goose *C. picta*.

Main characters: Rather heavy, medium-sized, variably plumaged goose. Within our region restricted to the Falklands, where represented by the endemic race malvinarum. **Ad** male all white with yellow legs and small, dark bill (black with pinkish culmen base). Female has pink bill, overall dark blackish-brown plumage, with cream-brown cap, conspicuous whitish eye-ring, white-barred underparts, dark primaries, white secondaries and lesser and median wing-coverts (visible in flight), and metallic green greater coverts, white tail, rump and vent. Legs yellow. **Juv** (and **imm**) much as female but has white forehead, lores and eyestripe, all-dark flight feathers and variable, reduced barring below. Young male gradually attains white plumage. In early stages both sexes have dull greenish-yellow legs.

Voice: Male's main call is a weak whistle; female gives loud resonant honking or hooting calls (Woods 1988).

Family party of Kelp Geese Chloephaga hybrida malvinarum, male on left and female on right, Falklands, Dec 1990. © René Pop.

277

Size: 55–65 cm, wing 39.0–39.6 cm (female 36.0–38.0), mean weight 2.6 kg (female 2.04 kg). Male typically larger, with apparently no overlap in wing length in either race.

Similar species: Male unmistakable, subad or advanced imm male could be confused with male Upland Goose, on account of having white plumage with partially barred underparts (and sometimes variably dark brown mantle), but latter less bulky and has longer, blackish legs.

Distribution and biology

Distribution, movements and population: Coastal Argentina north to 50°S and Chile to 42°S. Widespread throughout coastal regions of the Falklands. Some move to more sheltered coasts in winter, and mainland birds move north to c.39°S in Argentina and 33°S in Chile. Falklands population estimated at 10,000–18,000 pairs in 1983–93.

Diet and feeding: Feeds principally on algae on rocky coasts, but also visits freshwater ponds to bathe and drink, and grazes grass and takes berries in autumn.

Social behaviour: Small flocks form in spring and groups of up to several hundred non-breeders are common in summer. Post-breeding moulting groups form late Nov–late Feb. Rarely swims.

Breeding biology: Nests in mid-Oct to Nov, usually near shore in grass or rushes, occasionally on cliff ledge and rarely up to 1 km from coast. Rough grass nest lined with down holds 4–7 pale buff eggs. Female alone incubates.

Conservation Not globally threatened, though the Falklands population would be at risk from accidental spillages should potential oil exploration go ahead.

Taxonomy Two races: nominate in South America and *malvinarum* in the Falklands. Males very similar, but female *malvinarum* has broader and more conspicuous white breast and flank barring.

Ruddy-headed Goose
Chloephaga rubidiceps   Plate 19

Identification

Confusion risks: Ashy-headed *C. poliocephala* and female Upland Geese *C. picta*.

Main characters: Principally a Falklands species (see below). Medium-sized, ruddy-brown and extensively barred goose. Sexes very similar. **Ad** has closely barred body with sharply demarcated and unmarked warm buff/chestnut-brown upper neck and head (inconspicuous cream area around bill and narrow whitish eye-ring). Upperparts largely brown, becoming blackish on rump and tail. Breast, mantle and flanks finely barred black and buff, becoming whiter on rear flanks, buff on breast and warm cinnamon on vent. In flight has mainly white upperwing-coverts and secondaries, contrasting with black primaries and green-glossed greater coverts. Bill black and legs mainly orange, spotted black. **Juv** (and imm) much as ad, but duller with dull greyish-brown greater covert speculum.

Voice: Male's main call is a short, musical toonk, either given singly or on rising pitch if repeated; also a double-whistle call. Female gives very low, rasping guttural *quack* (Woods 1988).

Size: 45–50 cm, wing 33–35 cm (female 31–32 cm), weight c.2 kg. Male typically larger.

Similar species: Female Upland Goose has strong rufous tone to breast and fore flanks, and whitish-barred flanks. Fine barring extends further onto upper neck in Ruddy-headed. If seen together, Ruddy-headed appears obviously smaller, with smaller bill, different head shape (much flatter crown and forehead) and is overall slightly paler. These distinctions most obvious in the Falklands, where the larger race of Upland occurs. Ashy-headed has an obviously grey head and neck, very rufous unbarred breast and mantle, boldly barred flanks and a white belly.

Distribution and biology

Distribution, movements and population: Extreme S South America, in Tierra del Fuego, and principally the Falklands. Those on mainland chiefly winter (Apr–Sep) to north, mostly in Buenos Aires province (Argentina). Population 14,000–27,000 pairs in the Falklands during the 1983–93 Breeding Birds Survey, but probably fewer than 1000 birds in South America in late 1990s

Diet and feeding: Grazes open grassy plains and meadows, stubble fields and recently sown areas, taking plants by their roots.

Social behaviour: Sociable, occurring in large flocks in non-breeding season and regularly flocks with Ashy-headed and, to a lesser extent, Upland Geese. Strongly territorial in breeding season. During moult does not become flightless.

Breeding biology: Nest (late Sep–early Nov) well hidden in long grass or rushes, sometimes atop tussac grass or in old penguin burrow. Lays 5–8 creamy-buff eggs. Female alone incubates, but both sexes subsequently tend young. Few other data.

Conservation Not globally threatened, despite drastic decline over last 30 years in South American population due to introduction of foxes to control rabbits in Patagonia. Wetlands International was mandated in 2001 to implement concerted action for the management and conservation of the species in Chile and Argentina. It remains widespread and common in the Falklands.

Taxonomy Monotypic.

Ruddy-headed Geese Chloephaga rubidiceps, *Falklands.* © *Frank S. Todd.*

Ashy-headed Geese Chloephaga poliocephala, *Falklands.* © *Frank S. Todd.*

Ashy-headed Goose
Chloephaga poliocephala   Plate 19

Identification
Confusion risks: Ruddy-headed *C. rubidiceps* and female Upland Geese *C. picta*.

Main characters: Superficially resembles some plumages of other Falklands Chloephaga geese. Medium-sized, ruddy-brown, grey-and-white extensively barred goose. Sexes very similar. **Ad** has ash-grey head and upper neck, merging with chestnut lower neck, mantle and breast, while belly is clean white, with conspicuous bold black barring, mainly on sides, and buffish vent; inconspicuous paler area around bill and narrow whitish eye-ring. Upperparts largely greyish-brown, apart from ruddy mantle, becoming blackish on rump and tail, and in flight has mainly white upperwing-coverts and secondaries, contrasting with black primaries and green-glossed greater coverts. Bill and iris black. Legs mainly orange behind and black at front. **Juv** (and **imm**) much as ad, but duller, more heavily barred below, with dull greyish-brown greater covert speculum.

Voice: No specific information from the Falklands, but apparently recalls Ruddy-headed Goose.

Size: 50–55 cm, wing 35.5–38.0 cm (female 33.5–34.0 cm), mean weight 2.26 kg (female mean 2.2 kg). Male typically larger, with apparently no overlap in wing length.

Similar species: Diagnostic greyish head, unbarred breast and ruddy mantle should eliminate any confusion with Ruddy-headed and female Upland Geese; other characteristics are listed above.

Distribution and biology
Distribution, movements and population: S Chile north to Llanquihue and Bío-Bío and S Argentina north to Neuquén and Río Negro, south to Cape Horn and Tierra del Fuego; also the Falklands (breeds irregularly, but principally a scarce visitor). Winters (Apr–Sep) north to E Chile and NE Argentina in Buenos Aires.

Diet and feeding: Much as congeners.

Social behaviour: Usually in pairs or small parties of up to 100, sometimes with Ruddy-headed Geese. Forms long-term monogamous pair-bonds.

Breeding biology: Much as congeners, with nesting usually commencing in Nov, and nests may occasionally be placed in the low branches of a tree.

Conservation Not globally threatened, but undoubtedly rather uncommon. Farmers persecute this and other wintering geese in mainland South America, blaming them for crop damage, but total numbers killed unknown and no information on effects.

Taxonomy Monotypic.

Falkland Steamer Duck
Tachyeres brachypterus   Plate 19

Identification
Confusion risks: Flying Steamer Duck *T. patachonicus* (coastal areas of the Falklands) often very difficult to distinguish from this species.

Main characters: Flightless, large goose-like duck, with bulky and overall darkish appearance, particularly rounded head and massive bill. **Ad** male has cream-grey head with duskier cheeks (much paler when breeding) and whitish eye-ring, otherwise mottled scaly grey and brown on upperparts, chest and flanks, contrasting with whitish belly; legs and bill mainly pink-orange, latter has black nail. Female has generally darker and duskier head with characteristic whitish eye-ring, extending as line and curving around ear-coverts, and throat tinged reddish-brown; often has

Male (left) and female Falkland Steamer Ducks Tachyeres brachypterus, Falklands, Dec 1990. © René Pop.

ill-defined yellowish-buff ring to base of foreneck; bill greenish-yellow. Sexes have same wing pattern, with white secondary bar; also broad broken white bar across back. **Juv** (and **imm**) generally recalls female, with more uniform dusky-brown head and narrow eye-ring, but no line behind it; most can apparently be sexed on appearance of respective ads (head paler in male). Attains ad plumage as first-year, though second-year male may still have brownish head-sides.

Voice: Rather noisy, especially male's explosive and repeated (descending and sometimes 'vibrating') *cheeroo* calls, also repeated *kek-kek-kek* and short low honks, while female utters low, creaking or grating calls, as well as high-pitched *crek-crek-crek* (Woods 1988).

Size: 61–74 cm, wing 27.2–28.2 cm (female 25.1–27.2 cm), mean weight 4.33 kg (female 3.38 kg). Male considerably larger, with apparently almost no overlap in wing length.

Similar species: The only flightless steamer duck in the Falklands. Larger and more massive-billed than Flying Steamer Duck, with shorter wings (tips of latter reach upper rump level) and shorter, less curved tail. Plumage very similar, but *brachypterus* tends to have yellowish foreneck collar and uniform bright orange bill, without greyish distal area. Head of male may become as pale as that of Flying Steamer Duck.

Distribution and biology
Distribution, movements and population: Endemic to the Falklands where it is widespread and often abundant, ranging up to 5 km from shore. Population estimated at 9000–16,000 pairs in 1983–93.

Diet and feeding: Feeds by upending and diving, chiefly in shallow inshore waters, but also on nearby freshwater pools.

Social behaviour: In pairs and small parties; concentrations of non-breeders can reach several hundred, and may form mixed groups with Flying Steamer Duck in winter. Strongly territorial and very aggressive when breeding, defends territory year-round.

Breeding biology: Eggs found most months, but peak activity mid-Sep to late Dec. Nest usually a scantily lined depression in tussac grass or old penguin burrow and rarely up to 1 km from shore. Lays 5–8, occasionally up to 12, large cream-coloured eggs. Female alone incubates.

Conservation Not globally threatened. Eggs very occasionally taken for human consumption, but potential future oil exploitation constitutes a much greater threat, as accidental spillages would undoubtedly affect at least part of the population.

Taxonomy Monotypic.

Male (left) and female Flying Steamer Ducks Tachyeres patachonicus, Chile. © Frank S. Todd.

Male (right) and female Eaton's Pintails Anas eatoni, Kerguelen, Oct 1996. © Frédéric Jiguet

Flying Steamer Duck
Tachyeres patachonicus   Plate 19

Identification

Confusion risks: Falkland Steamer Duck *T. brachypterus*.
Main characters: Similar to Falkland Steamer Duck. Large goose-like duck, but smaller and slimmer than latter, with less massive bill. **Ad** male has whitish-grey head with reddish-brown patch on lower cheeks and throat (even paler when breeding), and whitish eye-ring, which extends as curved whitish line from eye around ear-coverts; otherwise predominantly mottled scaly grey and brown on upperparts, chest and flanks, contrasting with whitish belly; legs and bill mainly yellow-orange, the latter has greyish distal area, bluish around nostril and black nail. Female gener-ally darker with duskier head and whitish eye-ring extending as curved whitish line to above ear-coverts, and throat tinged red-dish-brown; bill yellowish with pale bluish cutting edges and in-distinct black nail. Sexes share wing pattern, dark with striking white secondary bar. **Juv** (and **imm**) generally recalls female, but more uniform, browner head, especially forehead, while cheeks and throat reddish-brown, and has narrow eye-ring but only very faint line behind it; juv male has paler head. Attains ad plumage as first-year, though second-year male may still have brownish head-sides.
Voice: No specific information from the Falklands.
Size: 66–71 cm, wing 28.7–31.7 cm (female 27.6–30.1 cm), mean weight 3.03 kg (female 2.42 kg). Male considerably larger.
Similar species: Bill smaller but wings longer (tips of latter reach to base of tail) than Falkland Steamer Duck. While plumages are very similar, *patachonicus* tends to have a less uniform, paler or-ange bill, with greyish distal area, and head of male is usually paler.

Distribution and biology

Distribution, movements and population: S Chile north to Concep-ción and Ñuble, and S Argentina north to Neuquén and Río Negro, south to Cape Horn and Tierra del Fuego including Staten I; also the Falklands.
Diet and feeding: Much as previous species (though occurs up to 50 km inland).
Social behaviour: As previous species (which see).
Breeding biology: Nov–Jan in Chile, but from Oct in the Falklands. Other aspects much as previous species.
Conservation Not globally threatened and no known threats.
Taxonomy Monotypic.

Eaton's Pintail *Anas eatoni*   Plate 20

Identification

Confusion risks: None in range.
Main characters: Small, short-necked pintail of subantarctic is-lands in S Indian Ocean, recalling Northern Pintail *A. acuta*. Sexes clearly differ in breeding plumage, with some seasonal/age-related plumage variation. **Ad** male darker, tinged more reddish-brown; in breeding plumage has elongated central tail and scapular feath-ers, and (at all times) green speculum bordered white, whilst at least some acquire whitish stripe on neck and trace of chocolate-brown on head (like *A. acuta*). Female generally duller and well scalloped, spotted and fringed pale buff, with brown speculum bordered white. Legs olive-brown and bill mainly bluish-grey. **Juv** generally like female, but paler and less richly coloured, and un-derparts streaked/fringed more longitudinally (less scalloped and spotted).
Voice: Male's main calls are whistles, with mostly quack notes been uttered by female.
Size: 35–45 cm, wing 20.0–23.5 cm, wingspan 65–70 cm, weight 430–502 g (female 400–500 g). Male apparently larger, especially in tail length, but much overlap in several measurements.
Similar species: None.

Distribution and biology

Distribution, movements and population: Restricted to Crozet and Kerguelen, where overall population in recent years considered fewer than 10,000 individuals.

Juv/imm Eaton's Pintail Anas eatoni, which recall female (see photo in Regional Accounts), but more evenly fringed, less scalloped and lacks spots. Kerguelen, Mar 2004. © Hadoram Shirihai.

Plate 20 Endemic and indigenous non-passerines of subantarctic islands in the S Indian and S Atlantic Oceans and Falklands

Southern Caracara ad.
(p. 287)

Black crown, reddish cere, body densely barred; extensive whitish primary bases visible in flight

Turkey Vulture ad.
(p. 285)

Entirely blackish with bright, bare red head; blacker underwing-coverts and long-fingered primaries in flight

Striated Caracara ad.
(p. 286)

Juv/imm confusingly streaked instead of barred

Red-backed Hawk ad.
(p. 286)

Crested Duck ad. ♂
(p. 285)

Mottled brown plumage, slight crest and dark patch round eye

Blackish-brown with white striations; reddish-orange lower belly; cere and feet orange-yellow (juv overall browner and lacks striations)

Peregrine Falcon ad.
(p. 288)

Black crown and moustachial

Barred underparts

Grey and white with chestnut mantle

Cinnamon Teal ad.
♂ (p. 284)

Small, rich reddish-chestnut (female/eclipse male brown and buff with mottled underparts); dark longish bill

Mottled brown with paler, scaly fringes; yellowish bill

Yellow-billed Pintail ad. ♂
A. g. georgigica
(p. 282)

Speckled Teal ad. ♂
(p. 283)

Small and short billed

Silver Teal ad. ♂
(p. 284)

Dark cap and brightly coloured bill; heavily barred flanks

Eaton's Pintail probably eclipse or young male
(p. 288)

Spotted breast and unmarked flanks separate from Yellow-billed/Brown Pintail

Chiloe Wigeon ad. ♂
(p. 283)

...ged reddish-brown (male) and ...f-brown (female), especially on ...d, with paler brown and mottled ... of plumage; greyish bill

Inaccessible Island Rail ad.
(p. 290)

Tiny and flightless dark rail; slate-grey underparts barred posteriorly

Gough Moorhen ad.
(p. 289)

Dark head with white frontal patch and green sheen; flanks orange (female duller)

Red forehead shield and yellow-tipped red bill (young duller throughout)

Eaton's Pintail Anas eatoni (apparently ad female): brown speculum and numerous scallops, spots and streaks. Kerguelen, Mar 2004. © Hadoram Shirihai.

Yellow-billed Pintail Anas georgica georgica. This race, 'South Georgian Pintail', is sometimes considered a separate species from South American spinicauda, but genetically they seem very close. South Georgia, Oct 2001. © Hadoram Shirihai.

Diet and feeding: Feeds on vegetation, worms, insects and marine crustaceans.

Social behaviour: Forms parties of up to 200 in non-breeding season, when it principally moves to coastal areas for winter, especially coastal lagoons, sheltered bays and offshore, but also remains inland on ice-free lakes.

Breeding biology: Breeds in Nov–Feb on small freshwater lakes, pools, marshes, peat bogs and streams. Minimum clutch five eggs.

Conservation Vulnerable. Though some of the smaller Kerguelen islands and four of the Crozet group are included within a National Park and part of a Specially Protected Area, introduced predators, especially feral cats, may take a toll. It is feared that a rapid decline is already well advanced. A population introduced to Amsterdam I in the 1950s disappeared by 1970. The species was formerly much hunted by sealers and scientific expeditions.

Taxonomy Nominate has shorter tarsus and longer wing. Slightly paler *A. e. drygalskii* of Crozet is also more buff on breast and some have finely vermiculated lower hindneck and flanks; it may represent a separate species. Both sometimes included within Northern Pintail.

Yellow-billed Pintail *Anas georgica*   Plate 20

Identification

Confusion risks: Speckled Teal *Anas flavirostris*.

Main characters: Small short-necked pintail of subantarctic islands in the S Atlantic. Sexes differ slightly and some seasonal or age-related plumage variation. **Ad** male has overall buff-grey and brown mottled plumage, crown slightly darker than cheeks and, unlike female, head is slightly rustier, glossed dark green (not dull blackish without gloss), with white-bordered speculum and pointed tail. Both sexes have fairly long, mainly yellow bill (duller in female) with grey nail and black culmen; legs pale brownish-grey. **Juv** generally recalls female, but even paler.

Voice: Main calls of male are weak short whistles, but more quacking notes given by female.

Size: 43–66 cm, wing 21–22 cm (female 19–20 cm), wingspan 71 cm, weight 610–660 g (female 460–610 g). Males tend to be larger than females.

Similar species: Speckled Teal is smaller and stockier (neck even shorter and less slender) with shorter bill and tail, almost unmarked flanks and uniform, contrastingly dark head. Form *spinicauda* (Yellow-billed Pintail), which is perhaps specifically distinct, has virtually identical slightly paler plumage, but is obviously larger.

Distribution and biology

Distribution, movements and population: Nominate georgica is restricted to South Georgia, though recorded as a vagrant on South Shetlands, and currently numbers c.1000 pairs. *A. g. spinicauda* considered to be one of the least common of the regularly breeding birds on the Falklands in the early 1990s.

Diet and feeding: Feeds by dabbling and upending, grazing on waterside grasses and also forages along shores. Also dives for shrimp. On South Georgia is also carnivorous, scavenging on seal carcasses along shore.

Social behaviour: Usually in small flocks in non-breeding season. Pair-bonds appear long-term.

Yellow-billed Pintail Anas georgica, *race* spinicauda *is widespread in South America, but in our region is confined to the Falklands.* © Frank S. Todd.

Male (right) and female Speckled Teals Anas flavirostris, Falklands, Jan 1991. © René Pop.

Breeding biology: Nests from Dec on ground, laying up to five eggs in dense vegetation close to water. Male assists in provisioning chicks but not incubation duties.

Conservation Not globally threatened.

Taxonomy Species status for the South Georgia form (Brown Pintail or 'South Georgian Pintail', *A. g. georgica*) has been proposed. The race *spinicauda* occurs throughout much of South America and the Falklands, with the now-extinct *niceforoi* in the E Andes of Colombia.

Speckled Teal *Anas flavirostris*   Plate 20

Identification

Confusion risks: Yellow-billed Pintail *Anas georgica*.

Main characters: Small short-necked teal, which in our region is restricted to the Falklands, where it is the smallest breeding duck. Sexes somewhat different in size, with minor age-related plumage variation. **Ad** overall mottled brown and buff, with contrastingly paler cream-buff, lightly black-speckled underparts; head darker with quite conspicuous blackish eyestripe; fairly short bill is mainly yellow (brighter in male) with black culmen, and legs grey. In flight, black-and-green speculum bordered buff on fore-coverts and white at rear. **Juv** generally recalls female.

Voice: Main call of male is a weak musical trill, with higher pitched quacking notes given by female.

Size: 35–45 cm, wing 19.0–20.2 cm (female 18.5–19.7 cm), wingspan 76 cm, mean weight 429 g (female 394 g). Male slightly larger than female.

Similar species: Yellow-billed Pintail (which see) readily separated by more pintail-like shape and larger size, lacks present species' blackish eyestripe and is more evenly mottled buff and brown above and below.

Distribution and biology

Distribution, movements and population: Andes of Colombia and NW Venezuela south to Bolivia, N Chile and N Argentina, and also lowlands of Chile, Uruguay and Argentina south to Tierra del Fuego, the Falklands and South Georgia. Winters north to Paraguay and S Brazil. Common over much of range and considered one of the commonest waterfowl during the Falklands Breeding Birds Survey of 1983–93, with population estimated at 6000–11,000 pairs.

Diet and feeding: Feeds primarily by dabbling, either while walking in shallow water or swimming, occasionally by diving.

Social behaviour: Pair-bonds appear semi-permanent, but also forms large groups in non-breeding season.

Breeding biology: Breeds from late Aug/early Sep. Uses holes in banks or more open situations on ground. Male often tends small young and two broods may be attempted.

Conservation No threats known.

Taxonomy Two subspecies groups recognized: the poorly differentiated *A. f. andium* and *A. f. altipetens* of the Andes in Colombia, NW Venezuela and Ecuador, and over the rest of the range *A. f. flavirostris* and *A. f. oxyptera*. The two groups appear quite different in several respects and may warrant specific status as suggested by Madge & Burn (1988).

Chiloe Wigeon *Anas sibilatrix*   Plate 20

Identification

Confusion risks: None.

Main characters: Small, black-and-white duck, with almost no sex-related plumage differences and little age-related variation. **Ad** male has black head and neck, except white forehead and fore face and white ear-covert patch, with variable green sheen behind eye, finely barred black and white breast, becoming white on rest of underparts, except variable orange breast-sides and flanks (in some quite extensive), and black mantle and scapulars streaked white. Wings and tail also black, with green sheen to speculum, white median and greater coverts, and entire tail-coverts white. Female duller, with less pure white on face, and less extensive and more mottled white wing-coverts. Bill blue-grey with black nail, legs and feet grey and eye dark brown. **Imm** like female, but overall distinctly drabber, has orange flank patches considerably reduced or lacking, duller speculum, and considerably less white on face and cheek patches almost lacking.

Size: 43–54 cm, wing 23.5–27.4 cm, weight 828–939 g. Male slightly heavier and larger in most measurements, but usually considerable overlap.

Voice: Male has distinctive whinnying *hoo-wee-ee-oo* used in courtship and rapid chattering whistle, while female gives high-pitched *quek-quek-quek* in flight (Woods 1988).

Similar species: Given good view should be unmistakeable due to largely black-and-white plumage and head pattern (which is not shared by any other species in our region). Even in flight dark flight feathers, white frontal head, white rump and wing-coverts and black tail provide easy identification features.

Distribution and biology

Distribution, movements and population: S South America from C Chile north to Atacama, C and NE Argentina north to Córdoba, Entre Ríos and Buenos Aires and south to Tierra del Fuego; also the Falklands where population estimated at 500–900 pairs in 1983–93. Winters rarely north to Uruguay and SE Brazil in Rio Grande do Sul and vagrant to South Georgia, South Orkney and South Shetland.

Ad male Chiloe Wigeon Anas sibilatrix, *Chile. © Frank S. Todd.*

Ad Silver Teal Anas versicolor, *Falklands. © Frank S. Todd.*

Diet and feeding: Grazes on short grass and mainly takes freshwater plants in ponds. Occasionally observed feeding on seaweed-covered rocky shores

Social behaviour: Usually in pairs or small groups, but in the Falklands sometimes recorded in gatherings of up to 40 birds and sometimes a few hundred (exceptionally 5000) birds in mainland South America. Pairs often noted throughout year, though bonds perhaps not permanent.

Breeding biology: Nests Sep–Dec, constructing well-hidden grass nest sometimes far from water and laying 5–8 white eggs. Male tends brood after hatching, though female alone incubates. Perhaps occasionally double-brooded.

Conservation Not globally threatened and no known threats, despite being extensively hunted in Chile.

Taxonomy Monotypic.

Ad male (left) and female Cinnamon Teals Anas cyanoptera, *Chile.* © Frank S. Todd.

Silver Teal *Anas versicolor*   Plate 20

Identification

Confusion risks: None.

Main characters: Small, black-capped duck with creamy-buff head markings. Sex-/age-related plumage variation rather limited. **Ad** has crown, hindneck and head-sides to below eye dark brown to blackish, lores, cheeks and ear-coverts pale buff speckled black, upperparts black with buff fringes to feathers and becoming barred on lower back, rump and tail, and wings grey, becoming brown on flight feathers, with bronze-green speculum; black-and-white bands on trailing edge of wing. Underparts reddish-buff, brightest on neck with larger black spots, becoming white posteriorly, heavily barred on flanks and less so on undertail-coverts. Axillaries and greater underwing-coverts white. Female overall duller with browner, less distinctly barred plumage. Bill mainly pale blue with orange basal patch and darker culmen and nail; legs and feet grey and eye dark brown. **Imm** duller than ad, with browner crown, duller speculum, less elongated tertials, and underparts spotting and barring less well marked.

Size: 38–45 cm, wing 18.8–21.1 cm, weight 373–442 g. Much overlap in mensural data between sexes, with male averaging larger in wing length, but female in tail length.

Voice: Male gives weak whistled *weeoo* and low rattle, and female gives descending series of up to ten low quacks.

Similar species: Unmistakeable within our region due to distinctive head pattern, especially dark crown and brightly coloured bill base.

Distribution and biology

Distribution, movements and population: S South America from C Chile, C Bolivia, Paraguay, extreme SE Brazil and Uruguay south through Argentina to Tierra del Fuego; also the Falklands where population estimated at 800–1500 pairs in 1983–93.

Diet and feeding: Takes clams, shrimps and insect larvae, largely by upending or dabbling below surface.

Social behaviour: Small groups, especially in winter, and often associates with congeners. In pairs much of the year and bonds perhaps long-term.

Breeding biology: Few data from our region, usually constructs well-hidden nest within dense vegetation from Oct (season perhaps chiefly Sep–Nov in our region) and lays at least five (perhaps up to ten) eggs; ads with small ducklings observed in Jan. Male helps tend brood.

Conservation Reasonably numerous, but rarely common anywhere in range, with no known threats.

Taxonomy Two races, with *fretensis* of S Chile and S Argentina (and the Falklands) being larger, overall slightly darker, having

paler and narrower fringes to mantle feathers, broader dark flank barring, more heavily spotted breast and decidedly heavier barred undertail-coverts than nominate, which replaces it to the north. Puna Teal *A.* [*v.*] *puna* has in the past sometimes been included within *versicolor*.

Cinnamon Teal *Anas cyanoptera*   Plate 20

Identification

Confusion risks: Blue-winged Teal *A. discors* (female).

Main characters: Small duck with distinct sexual dimorphism; male is largely reddish-chestnut and female brown and buff with mottled underparts. **Ad** male has rich chestnut-rufous head, neck and underparts, blackish crown and black-spotted breast-sides and flanks, black undertail-coverts and black upperparts, including tail, with mantle and scapulars narrowly fringed rufous. Wing-coverts cobalt-blue with white rear border and green/bronze speculum, and black flight feathers. Axillaries and wing lining white. Female (and eclipse male, Dec–Feb) mainly dark brown above, with buff head streaked brown, ill-defined loral spot and pale brown underparts mottled darker. Fairly long bill is black, legs and feet yellowish (dull greyish in imm) and eye yellow to orange. **Imm** much as female, but lacks any warm brown tones, and has more prominent loral spot and more streaked (rather than spotted) breast markings; attains more rufous-toned ad plumage in first autumn and male acquires ad iris coloration as first-winter.

Size: 38–42 cm, wing 17.6–20.8 cm, weight 362–408 g. Nominate male distinctly larger in most measurements (this does not apply to all forms).

Voice: Thin whistles given by male and high-pitched quacks by female, apparently indistinguishable from those of Blue-winged Teal.

Similar species: Over most of range female, eclipse male and imm require careful scrutiny to separate from Blue-winged Teal. However, latter is virtually unknown in our region (one vagrant record from South Georgia) and, in the Falklands, Cinnamon Teal only requires separation from Yellow-billed Pintail *Anas georgica* (black bill, yellow legs and black undertail-coverts are all useful features) and Speckled Teal *A. flavirostris* (larger size and black bill offer ready field marks).

Distribution and biology

Distribution, movements and population: Widespread breeder in New World, from W Canada, W USA and W Mexico (in N Baja California and central highlands of Chihuahua to Jalisco), thereafter South America in Colombia and N Ecuador (formerly) and C Peru, C and SW Bolivia, N Paraguay (rare) and extreme SE Brazil (accidental) south through Chile and Argentina to Strait of Magellan; also the Falklands where population estimated at 12–22 pairs in 1983–93. Winters from SW USA south to N South America, including W Venezuela, and rarely to Hawaii. North American population estimated at 300,000 in 1970s; no population information for South America, though resident Colombian birds are in strong decline.

Diet and feeding: Feeds in water by upending and dabbling, but no specific information from our region.

Social behaviour: Sociable and apparently forms pairs only for breeding, but very few specific data. Considered similar in most respects to Blue-winged Teal.

Breeding biology: Very few data from our region or even South America.

Conservation Not globally threatened and apparently at little risk, except diminishing N South American populations, which have declined for unknown reasons.

Taxonomy Closely related to Blue-winged Teal despite well-marked differences in males. Five races recognized: *septentrion-alium* in North America (wintering south to N South America, but no recent records from Ecuador where formerly occurred), *tropicus* in N Colombia, *borreroi* in E Andes of Colombia south (formerly) to N Ecuador, *orinomus* in S Peru and Bolivia south to N Chile and NW Argentina, and nominate in rest of range (including the Falklands). Latter relatively small compared to some other forms, with darker chestnut coloration in male, and female has paler crown and streaking on head- and neck-sides (compared to *orinomus*).

Crested Duck *Lophonetta specularioides*   Plate 20

Identification

Confusion risks: None.

Main characters: Medium-sized duck, which appears long-bodied, long-tailed and long-crested. Extremely limited age-/sex-related plumage variation. **Ad** has forecrown, head-sides and neck pale buffish, becoming deep brown on crown and crest (and darkest behind eye), whitish neck and cheeks, mottled brown upperparts, palest on mantle and becoming sooty-blackish on uppertail-coverts, with largely sooty-brown wings (black on primaries), conspicuously white-tipped secondaries (obvious in flight) and metallic purplish or coppery speculum. Underparts pale buffy-brown, mottled and spotted darker and becoming black on undertail-coverts, and dark underwing except white axillaries and tips to coverts. Bill, legs and feet dark grey and eye pale red to orange. Female slightly duller and smaller. **Imm** overall duller, with brownish neck and shorter tail than ad.

Size: 51–61 cm, wing 21.5–27.3 cm, weight 0.9–1.1 kg. Male heavier and larger in most measurements, but usually considerable overlap.

Voice: Fairly noisy, especially in spring. Male has buzzing *shweeoo* territorial call, also a repeated dry rattling in display, while female gives a low *grruf*, nasal *quek-quek-quek* when feeding, and short rapid quacks in display (Woods 1988).

Similar species: Head pattern of pale whitish neck, slight crest and dark patch round eye, along with rest of mottled brown plumage, provide ready distinction from other ducks in our region.

Distribution and biology

Distribution, movements and population: Breeds in Andes of Peru, Bolivia, Chile and NW and S Argentina south to Tierra del Fuego and Cape Horn; also the Falklands where population estimated at 7000–12,000 pairs in 1983–93. Winters north to NE Argentina.

Diet and feeding: Mainly sieves liquid mud for marine invertebrates including lice, shrimps and small bivalves; also upends in shallow water (often with neck and head wholly submerged) and occasionally observed diving.

Social behaviour: Aggressive and territorial (both towards specifics and other wildfowl), though occurs in groups of up to 80 in non-breeding season.

Breeding biology: Extended breeding season with eggs or young recorded in all months except May and Jul. Most nest in the Falklands in Sep–Nov, constructing grass/fern/tussac nest, lined with down, often far inland, and laying 5–7 (occasionally up to 11) cream-coloured eggs, incubated by female alone. Frequently double-brooded in the Falklands and three broods occasionally reported.

Conservation Generally appears common and widespread and no threats known.

Taxonomy Taxonomic relationships uncertain, some authorities (including Sibley & Monroe 1990) placing it between *Aix* and *Nettapus* and others considering it closer to Tadorna. Two races, with *alticola* in Andes of C Peru south to C Chile and NW Argentina being larger, overall browner and more uniform, and having darker (more purplish) speculum and more yellowish irides than nominate, which replaces it further south, but they appear to intergrade in Talca, Chile.

Turkey Vulture *Cathartes aura*   Plate 20

Identification

Confusion risks: None in our region.

Main characters: Almost all-black New World vulture with long-

Crested Duck Lophonetta specularioides. *Ushuaia, S Argentina, Mar 2003. © Hadoram Shirihai.*

Turkey Vulture Cathartes aura, *Falklands, Dec 1990. © René Pop.*

fingered primaries, long broad wings, long round-ended tail and small naked red head. No sexual dimorphism and limited age-related plumage variation. **Ad** has bright, bare red head, entirely black-brown body with buff fringes to secondaries and pale grey underside to flight feathers providing marked contrast with blacker underwing-coverts. Pale creamy, strongly hooked bill, dull grey-ish-crimson legs and feet, and brown eye. **Imm** similar but has dull grey head and brown legs; red head skin is gained as first-year.

Size: 63.5–76.0 cm, wing 46–55 cm, wingspan 180–200 cm, weight 0.85–2.0 kg. Female fractionally larger in most measurements.

Voice: Low hissing noises produced by young in nest and occasionally by ads (Woods 1988).

Similar species: Unmistakeable in our region, where Black Vulture *Coragyps atratus* is absent.

Distribution and biology

Distribution, movements and population: Widespread, from S Canada south through USA, Mexico and Central America, throughout South America south to Tierra del Fuego; also the Falklands (where it is the most common bird of prey and the population was estimated at 1900–3600 pairs in 1983–93), N Bahamas, Cuba and Isle of Pines and Jamaica. Range expanding north. Regularly recorded at South Georgia since early 1990s.

Diet and feeding: Scavenges carrion, attending carcasses of sheep, cattle, goats and seals, but probably only attacks very weak live animals. Hunts singly or in large parties of up to 100 individuals.

Social behaviour: Gregarious but nests alone.

Breeding biology: In the Falklands nests early Sep–late Nov (principally mid-Sep–late Oct), laying 2–3 white eggs with red-brown spots and lines, in scrape on ground, sheltered by scrub or rock, and sometimes in cave or old building. Incubation lasts 38–41 days and young fledge in 10–12 weeks. Fledglings seen from mid-Jan.

Conservation Widespread, common and increasing in parts of its range.

Taxonomy Six races recognized over its entire range, with *C. a. falklandica* in our region known from Ecuador and Peru south to Chile and the Falklands; it is possible that *C. a. jota* of the E Andes south to S Argentina has also wandered to the Falklands.

Red-backed Hawk *Buteo polyosoma*   Plate 20

Identification

Confusion risks: Southern *Caracara plancus* and Striated Caracaras *Phalcoboenus australis*.

Main characters: Large, largely white-tailed hawk with rufous

Ad Red-backed Hawk Buteo polyosoma, *Falklands.* © Nic Huin/Falklands Conservation.

mantle and usually all-white underparts. Quite extensive individual variation, but few sex-/age-related plumage differences. Glides on flat wings and often hovers, sometimes very high above ground. **Ad** has pale, dark and barred morphs, but all have white tail, broad black subterminal band and white tip, and female always has rich chestnut-brown mantle and back. *Pale morph* has white underparts with pale brown flank barring extending onto underwing, dark brown crown, nape and wing-coverts, and slate-brown flight feathers. Male usually entirely slate-grey above and white below. *Dark morph* has red-brown underparts and slate-brown upperparts, or is slate-grey above and below. *Barred-morph* ad female (male unknown) has blackish-grey head, with undertail-coverts and thighs heavily barred slate-grey or rufous, and blackish-grey admixed in rufous of upperparts. Bill blue-grey with black tip and yellow-green cere, legs and feet bright yellow with black claws, and brownish or yellowish eye. **Imm** mainly dark brown above, with variable red-brown on mantle, grey tail barred blackish and whitish patches on nape. Gradually acquires ad plumage.

Size: 46–56 cm, wing 35–45 cm, wingspan 110–120 cm, weight 950 g. Female averages 6% larger but much overlap.

Voice: Rarely calls outside breeding season when gives series of loud screams, most usually near nest and usually higher pitched in male (Woods 1988).

Similar species: Within our region only likely to be confused with one of the caracaras, but readily distinguished from either by short, square-ended, largely whitish tail, rounded head, usually red-brown mantle, less heavy bill, and from Southern (Crested) Caracara by lack of white primary bases, black cap and pale cheeks.

Distribution and biology

Distribution, movements and population: W and S South America from Colombia south through Ecuador and Peru to C and S Bolivia, Chile (to Cape Horn) and Argentina (to Tierra del Fuego); also the Falklands (where population estimated at 500–1000 pairs in 1983–93), and ranges to Uruguay and S Brazil.

Diet and feeding: Takes small mammals (hares, rats, mice, rabbits) and birds (e.g. young geese and waders) and occasionally carcasses and domestic fowl.

Social behaviour: Usually alone or in pairs.

Breeding biology: Repairs same stick nest each year, usually on high crag and lined with green leaves, moss, lichen and rubbish. Nests late Sep–Oct in the Falklands, where lays 2–3 almost elliptical whitish eggs marked red-brown. Incubates for 26–27 days and young fledge in 40–50 days.

Conservation Not globally threatened and generally common throughout wide range.

Taxonomy Two races, nominate throughout mainland range and *B. p. exsul* in Juan Fernández Is (Chile) on Más Afuera, which have occasionally been considered separate species.

Striated Caracara *Phalcobaenus australis*   Plate 20

Identification

Confusion risks: Southern (Crested) Caracara *Caracara plancus*.

Main characters: Heavily built with large round head. Sexes slightly different in size and pronounced age-related plumage variation. Typically inquisitive and quite tame; typically flies low above ground. **Ad** overall blackish-brown with white striations on nape, back and chest, forming slight collar. Flanks, lower belly and legs reddish-orange, and tail has white tip. Cere and feet orange-yellow, bill pale, and iris dark brown with clear yellow orbital ring. In flight, uniform upperwing with only indistinct pale bases to primaries, while underwing has more pronounced pale primary patch and variable buffish streaks on coverts. **Juv** overall browner, lacks

Striated Caracara Phalcobaenus australis is closely associated with seabird colonies, feeding on carcasses, eggs and young. Note orange cere, yellowish bill and white striations on nape of ad (left), whilst juv (right) is overall browner with rufous on chest and upperparts, greyish-yellow cere and darker bill. Falklands: left © Klaus Bjerre; right © Todd Pusser.

striations and has streaky buff collar, some rufous on upperparts, black bill, and greyish cere and legs; in flight primary patch quite conspicuous against overall dark plumage. **Imm** gradually develops blacker plumage and (patchy) finer whitish streaks, while reddish-orange abdomen and yellow bare parts often still little advanced even in older imm.

Voice: Rather varied, including wailing cat-like *waa-aow*, a strident *keee-ar*, a loud hoarse *kar* or *kaw* and very high-pitched strangulated shrieks; in courtship, the male utters a low guttural trill (Woods 1988).

Size: 55–62 cm, wing 39.4–41.0 cm (female 40.4–42.3 cm), wingspan 116–125 cm, weight (one) 1.19 kg. Female apparently larger, but comparatively few data.

Similar species: Similar-sized Southern Caracara is only other caracara breeding in the Falklands, and is scarcely mistakable, having a black crown contrasting strongly with much paler face and underparts, reddish cere, bluish bill and extensive whitish primary bases visible in flight; also, diagnostically, body is densely barred in ad and boldly streaked in juv.

Distribution and biology

Distribution, movements and population: Extreme S Chile and Argentina in Tierra del Fuego, Cape Horn archipelago, islands in the Beagle Channel and Staten I. Also the Falklands, where population estimated to be 500 pairs in the late 1990s.

Diet and feeding: Coastal predator and scavenger, dependent on albatross, prion, cormorant and penguin colonies, feeding on carcasses and waste, seabird eggs and young. Also attacks weak and stranded sheep and, in groups, wild geese.

Social behaviour: Alone, in pairs or in small groups. Juvs and imms congregate in flocks of up to 100 at some settlements in winter, where it is very inquisitive and even steals small manmade objects.

Breeding biology: Nest of twigs or grass is constructed on cliff or in shelter of tussac grass or rock, often close to a seabird colony. Eggs, 1–4 cream-coloured, laid in Oct–Nov. Sometimes forms small loose colonies with nests placed as close as 6–7 m apart.

Conservation Near Threatened. Formerly heavily persecuted in the Falklands but current population, while small, appears to face few threats and is obviously self-recruiting. A recent (1999) law provides additional protection for the species, with the threat of large fines for those found hunting it.

Taxonomy Monotypic.

Southern (Crested) Caracara
Caracara plancus   Plate 20

Identification

Confusion risks: Red-backed Hawk *Buteo polyosoma* and Striated Caracara *Phalcoboenus australis*.

Main characters: Large, heavy-billed caracara, with striking shaggy black crown and largely brown-and-grey plumage. Sexes alike and age-related plumage variation limited. Leisurely flight and walks and runs on ground easily. **Ad** has heavy black crown and crest, pale cheeks, dark brown upperparts, finely barred buff on back and pale fringes to flight feathers, large white, slightly curved, patches at base of primaries visible in flight, long whitish and square-ended tail with broad dark terminal bar, dark brown, closely barred neck and breast becoming uniform brown on belly and pale sandy-buff on sides of undertail-coverts. Bill cream or yellowish with dull pink to bright orange cere and surrounding facial skin, long yellow legs and feet, and orange to pink eye. **Imm** darker and more heavily streaked above and below, with bluegrey to yellowish bill, duller and darker cere and facial skin, and duller yellow legs.

Size: 49–63 cm, wing 35.8–45.5 cm, wingspan 120–132 cm, weight 0.83–1.6 kg. While females exhibit some tendency to be slightly larger than males in wing and bill lengths and bill depth, these differences are not statistically significant (unlike in *C. cheriway*, see taxonomy)

Voice: Loud harsh *kruk*, sometimes repeated, especially when perched; also a screaming *keeer* in courtship display.

Southern (Crested) Caracara Caracara plancus: *ads (right) and juv. In our region this raptor is confined to the Falklands, but confusion with the sympatric and similar-sized Striated Caracara* Phalcobaenus australis *is unlikely. Right: Falklands. © Frank S. Todd. Left: Brazil. © Hadoram Shirihai.*

Similar species: For separation from Red-backed Hawk see latter. Easily separated from Striated Caracara by heavy black cap, bold white primary bases and tail, heavier bill, pale cheeks and range of other plumage features.

Distribution and biology

Distribution, movements and population: Breeds in E and S South America from Brazil south of the Amazon south to S Chile and S Argentina; also the Falklands where population estimated at 400–800 pairs in 1983–93.

Diet and feeding: Takes carrion of all types and may attack wounded sheep or lambs, usually in pairs.

Social behaviour: Usually alone or in pairs, but small groups of imms occur.

Breeding biology: In the Falklands builds large, cliff nest of twigs, bones and grass lined with wool, which is repaired and added to annually. Lays 2–3 brownish-red eggs (or cream with brown-red blotches) in late Aug–Oct. Incubates 28–32 days but fledging period unknown.

Conservation Generally common and widespread throughout range, and no known threats.

Taxonomy Until recently *Caracara plancus* was considered a polytypic species consisting of three forms: *C. p. cheriway* (including *auduboni*, *ammophilus* and *pallidus*) in South and Middle America north of the Amazon to S USA and Cuba, nominate *plancus* south of the Amazon to Tierra del Fuego and the Falklands, and the extinct *C. p. lutosus* of Guadalupe (off Mexico), but a recent reassessment of their plumage characters and mensural data suggests that all warrant species status (Dove & Banks 1999), as they had been treated in the early-20th century. *Cheriway* and *plancus* exhibit limited evidence of intergradation/hybridization at localities close to the Amazon. Previously placed in the genus *Polyborus*, but this name was applied to a form of uncertain identity.

Peregrine Falcon *Falco peregrinus*　　Plate 20

Identification

Confusion risks: None.

Main characters: Large falcon with broad-based, pointed wings, long tail and overall very dark plumage. Sexes largely alike, though female noticeably darker (and larger), and comparatively little age-related plumage variation. Fast powerful flight. **Ad** is dark slate-grey above with sooty-black head reaching cheeks, and buffish throat, rest of underparts and underwing, all heavily barred dark brown. Bill slate blue, with cere, eye-ring, legs and feet bright yellow, and eye dark. **Imm** often darker than ad and even more heavily streaked on breast and belly; also has cere and eye-ring bluish or greenish, and blue-grey legs and feet.

Size: 34–50 cm, wing 28.4–35.8 cm (*F. p. cassini*), wingspan 80–120 cm (all races), no weight data available for *F. p. cassini*. Female larger.

Voice: Rarely calls outside breeding season, a sharp, sometimes repeated *kek*; harsh chattering notes in courtship, those of male being higher pitched.

Similar species: Much smaller American Kestrel *Falco sparverius* is only a vagrant to the Falklands and should offer no significant confusion risks.

Distribution and biology

Distribution, movements and population: Cosmopolitan, with populations in most parts of the world including through much of South America. Falklands population estimated at 500–900 pairs in 1983–93.

Ad Peregrine Falcon Falco peregrinus, *Falklands. © Richard White/Falklands Conservation.*

288

Diet and feeding: Catches birds to size of Upland Goose *Chloephaga picta* in dashing or stooping flight.

Social behaviour: Usually encountered singly, but strongly territorial and often in pairs around nest site.

Breeding biology: In the Falklands breeds late Sep–late Oct, laying 2–4 heavily marked red-brown eggs in large twig nest on cliff. Few other data available from our region.

Conservation Not globally threatened and local population in our region apparently stable and possibly no longer persecuted (previously birds were killed as it was alleged that they took domestic fowl).

Taxonomy Up to 19 subspecies recognized, with *cassini* of our region occurring from c.28°S in Chile and 42°S in Argentina to Tierra del Fuego and in the Falklands. Mainland populations winter as far north as Colombia and Uruguay.

Gough Moorhen
Gallinula [nesiotis] comeri Plate 20

Identification

Confusion risks: Common Moorhen *G. chloropus* (but no overlap).

Main characters: Medium-sized, dumpy, almost flightless rail, which is usually very secretive. Sexes alike with limited seasonal plumage change, but juv distinctive. **Ad** has sooty-black head, neck and underparts, and dark brown mantle; undertail-coverts and some rear flank feathers white. Red forehead shield and red bill with yellow tip; legs orange-red with greenish-yellow blotches and red garter. **Juv** mainly dark brown above, becoming paler on sides and whiter on belly, with mainly greenish-olive bare parts.

Voice: Main calls are repeated harsh tcherk *aaa kak*; alarm a metallic whistling shrill or staccato *chack-chack* (Watson 1975).

Size: 25–27 cm, wing 13.4–15.2 cm, weight 400–530 g. Male perhaps larger but much overlap in most measurements.

Similar species: None in range. Unlike Common Moorhen it has no, or very little, white on the flanks, and white restricted to the lateral undertail-coverts. Confusion also possible with Purple Gallinule *Porphyrio martinica* (up to 40 per annum arrive on Tristan, and probably other islands too).

Distribution and biology

Distribution, movements and population: Formerly endemic to Gough (restricted to 10–12 km² below 450 m), but reportedly introduced to Tristan in 1956, where Tristan Moorhen *G. [n.] nesiotis* apparently extinct by late 19th century, and has spread to most of Tristan (at 300–900 m; lower locally). Population recently 3500

Gough Moorhen Gallinula [nesiotis] comeri: *ad and full-grown chick. Gough, Mar 2003. © Hadoram Shirihai.*

pairs on Gough and 2000 pairs on Tristan, and still growing.

Diet and feeding: Vegetable matter, seeds, invertebrates and carrion, including petrel carcasses. Also seeks invertebrates around albatross nests and petrel burrows, and will investigate garbage for food.

Social behaviour: Shy and apparently constructs tunnels in dense vegetation to hide. Monogamous and territorial. Pair-bonds appear permanent and pairs remain in regular vocal contact and defend territory. Well-developed courtship ritual.

Breeding biology: Breeds Sep–Mar (peak Oct–Dec on Gough), in coastal bogs and near streams, being commonest in tussock grass and fernbush. Lays 2–6 pale buff to pinkish-cream eggs in well-concealed cup-shaped nest. Incubation 21 days and two broods per season recorded. Both sexes build nest, incubate and tend young. Young from first clutch may help provision second brood.

Conservation Vulnerable. Successful colonization of Tristan and current population levels on Gough suggest it could withstand some predation by invasive species, although it is probable that rats, hunting, feral pigs, cats, and habitat destruction through fire, accounted for probable extinction of *G. [n.] nesiotis*. Cats were successfully eradicated from Tristan in the 1970s and Gough is presently uninhabited except for a meteorological station.

Taxonomy Skeletal differences between *G. [n.] comeri* and the possibly extinct *G. [n.] nesiotis* exist. They are often considered a single species (formerly placed in the genus *Porphyriornis*), but Olson (1973) made a cogent argument for separate treatment. Recent work confirms that the original moorhens on Tristan are genetically distinct from the Gough birds. Both are very closely related to *G. chloropus*, but are most closely related to the S Af-

Ad Gough Moorhen Gallinula [nesiotis] comeri *on Gough (left) and on Tristan de Cunha (right). Are the moorhens on Tristan derived solely from introduced Gough Moorhens; why has Gough Moorhen persisted on Tristan when the Tristan Moorhen* G. [n.] nesiotis *could not; and could some Tristan Moorhens survive? Answers to some of these questions were partially addressed by a recent genetic analysis (see Taxonomy). Sep–Oct 2006. © Peter Ryan.*

rican subspecies, not that in S America. The same study indicted that present-day moorhens on Tristan are introduced Gough Moorhens, suggesting that Tristan Moorhen is indeed extinct. (A. Beintema pers. comm.).

Inaccessible Island Rail *Atlantisia rogersi* Plate 20

Identification
Confusion risks: None.
Main characters: The smallest flightless bird in the world. Tiny and very dark rail. Sexes poorly differentiated and no seasonal plumage change, but juv separable. **Ad** has sooty-brown, tinged rusty, head and neck; face to breast washed slate-grey, cheeks almost blackish and underparts usually paler/greyer. White or buffy transverse barring on flanks and belly, and even on upperwing-coverts, variable in extent, but usually indistinct and sometimes lacking. Short black bill (some reddish elements on sides and base), legs mainly greyish and eye red. Female paler (less sooty) with greyer ear-coverts and brown-washed underparts. **Juv** and similar imm plumages (retained 1–2 years) are overall browner, lacking pale bars and have dark eye. See photo p. 459.
Voice: Typical song is a *Rallus*-like descending trill; contact calls are various *chick* notes, and also utters a very distinct *weet-errr* call during the breeding season, possibly when accompanying chicks (P. Ryan pers. comm.).
Size: 13.0–15.5 cm, wing 5.1–5.9 cm, weight 34–49 g. Male may average slightly larger than female but much overlap in most data.
Similar species: None.

Distribution and biology
Distribution, movements and population: Restricted to Inaccessible I within the Tristan da Cunha group. Population most accurately estimated at 8400 individuals.
Diet and feeding: Takes broad range of invertebrates, including earthworms and moths, and berries and seeds. Forages, mouse-like, throughout available habitat, from favoured tussac grassland and fernbush to open beaches, marshy areas and short vegetation. Also active nocturnally.
Social behaviour: Occupies very small, flexible territories, some less than 20 m in diameter. Monogamous and pair-bond permanent. Elaborate courtship displays described.
Breeding biology: Poorly known. Nest is carefully woven domed structure with access track or tunnel. Two cream or buffy-white eggs laid Oct–Mar. Incubation and fledging periods unknown, but chicks precocial and attempt self-feeding at one week. Both sexes assume nest-building, incubation and feeding responsibilities, and vigorously defend nest against Tristan Thrushes *Nesocichla eremita*.
Conservation Vulnerable. Though deemed abundant and population may have reached carrying capacity, the species is restricted to a single island and at grave risk should introduced predators reach it. Tristan Thrush and the inclement climate are believed to be the chief sources of chick mortality, but neither appears to pose a significant threat. The island is currently listed as a nature reserve, subject to strict visitor controls and with a management plan in development.
Taxonomy Monotypic.

Pale-faced Sheathbill *Chionis alba* Plate 21

Identification
Confusion risks: Black-faced Sheathbill *C. minor* (no overlap).
Main characters: Medium-sized, plump hen-like, all-white bird; typically walks (often rather fast and restlessly) across open ground with pigeon-like bobbing of head; very tame. Sexes essentially alike (but see size) with limited seasonal plumage variation,

Ad Pale-faced Sheathbill Chionis alba, Antarctic Peninsula, Jan 2001. © Hadoram Shirihai.

but juv somewhat more distinctive. In flight, wings short and broad and wingbeats fast. **Ad** all dull white except pinkish facial caruncles, pinkish eye-ring, stout yellowish-horn bill with ill-defined black ridge and tip, and horny sheath; mainly dark grey legs and feet are strong with well-developed hind toe. **Juv** has smaller facial wattles and bill sheath. **Chick** has dense brown down, followed by mottled grey down. Fledgling may have trace of grey down.
Voice: Rather silent, sometimes utters short throaty, crow-like harsh calls.
Size: 34–41 cm, wing 23.4–26.0 cm, wingspan 74–84 cm, 460–780 g. Male larger, but high overlap in mensural data does not permit sexual identification based on any lone variable.
Similar species: No overlap with Black-faced Sheathbill, which has distinctive black facial caruncles, bill and sheath. At long range could be confused with a gull *Larus* or Kelp Goose *Chloephaga hybrida*, but separable due to smaller size, pigeon-like gait and swift movements.

Distribution and biology
Distribution, movements and population: Rocky seacoasts of South Georgia, South Orkney, South Shetland and Antarctic Peninsula to 65°S; also non-breeder north to the Falklands and SE South America in Patagonia, Uruguay and, exceptionally, NE Brazil. Ship-assisted vagrants have reached South Africa and even Europe. Overall population c.10,000 pairs in recent years.
Diet and feeding: Omnivorous, stealing krill, fish and other marine prey from penguins, as well as eggs and small chicks. Also carrion, faeces, algae, invertebrates and human refuse.
Social behaviour: Shows high fidelity to mate, territory and nest site, but unlike Black-faced Sheathbill is migratory, being absent from breeding sites in Apr–Oct, wintering in Patagonia, Tierra del Fuego and the Falklands, where occurs in close proximity to humans. Migrants will pause on icebergs.
Breeding biology: Usually breeds near penguin or cormorant colonies, Oct–Mar (eggs Dec–Jan, chicks Jan–Feb, fledging Mar). Nest a pile of debris in cavity. Usually 2–3 (range 1–4) eggs, incubated 28–32 days. Fledging occupies 50–60 days.
Conservation Not globally threatened and population considered stable, though poisoning from human-chemical waste products may have occurred in some areas in past.
Taxonomy Monotypic.

Black-faced Sheathbill *Chionis minor* Plate 21

Identification
Confusion risks: Pale-faced Sheathbill *C. alba* (but no overlap).

Plate 21 Endemic and indigenous non- and near-passerines of subantarctic islands in the S Indian and S Atlantic Oceans and Falklands

Short-eared Owl ad. ssp. *sanfordi* (p. 298)

Barn Owl ad. (p. 297)

Heart-shaped facial disk and black eyes

Pale-faced Sheathbill ad. (p. 290)

Black-faced Sheathbill ad. (p. 290)

The sheathbills are well separated geographically and in bare-parts colours

...und head (tufts ...t always visible); ...low eyes

Sooty Tern ad. (p. 296)

Square white forehead patch

Magellanic Oystercatcher ad. (p. 292)

White belly

Sooty Tern ad.

Black and white; elegant shape

Common Noddy ad. (p. 297)

Mostly dark; pale crown and shallow tail fork

Blackish Oystercatcher ad. (p. 293)

All-black plumage

Rufous-chested Dotterel breeding ad. (p. 294)

Markings obscured in winter

Two-banded Plover breeding ad. ♂ (p. 293)

Magellanic Snipe ad. (p. 294)

...east Seedsnipe ...d. ♂ ...295)

Coloration obscured in winter

...ale browner and duller ...ut obvious grey-and- ...k neck marks

Transversal underparts barring reaches undertail-coverts; *Scolopax* shape and no white trailing edge in flight

Fuegian Snipe ad. (p. 295)

Small and less heavily built; limited barring below but prominent sub-terminal tail-band; white trailing edge in flight

Ad Black-faced Sheathbill Chionis minor, *Crozet, Nov 1999.* © Hadoram Shirihai.

Ad Magellanic Oystercatchers Haematopus leucopodus, *Falklands, Dec 1990.* © René Pop.

Main characters: Generally similar to preceding species (which see) in size, shape, plumage and behaviour. Sexes essentially alike with limited seasonal plumage variation. **Ad** predominantly dull white with small black bill, bill sheath and facial caruncles; eye-ring pinkish. Leg colour variable (see taxonomy). **Juv** and **Chick** as *C. alba*.
Voice: Rather silent, generally utters short rattling harsh croaks (see also taxonomy).
Size: 38–41 cm, wingspan 74–79 cm, weight 450–760 g.
Similar species: No overlap with Pale-faced Sheathbill, which as its name suggests has a pale bill and loral region.

Distribution and biology

Distribution, movements and population: Occurs on rocky sea-coasts and moist inland meadows of Prince Edward, Marion, Crozet, Kerguelen and Heard. Total population estimated at 6500–10,000 pairs in recent years.
Diet and feeding: Omnivorous, scavenging fish, krill etc around seabird colonies, feeding on carcasses, human refuse and eggs and chicks, especially of penguins, as well as variety of terrestrial invertebrates, particularly in winter.
Social behaviour: Sedentary and ads rarely move farther than 1 km from breeding sites, though imms and non-breeders may wander a few tens of km, especially in response to food availability.
Breeding biology: Almost always nests in close association with penguin or other seabird colonies. Breeds Oct–Apr (eggs Dec–Jan, chicks Jan–Feb). Lays 1–4 (usually 2–3) eggs. Incubation 27–33 (mean 28) days. Chicks incubated constantly for first 14 days and fledge at 55–60 days. No replacement clutch. Success rate appears strongly dependent on ad experience and quality of breeding site.
Conservation Not globally threatened, though sharp declines due to feral-cat predation reported on Île aux Cochons and parts of Kerguelen. Mice may negatively affect numbers of invertebrates on Marion. Some populations increasing in response to growing penguin numbers.
Taxonomy Four subspecies recognized and no genetic mixing between these populations is known: *marionensis* on Prince Edward and Marion, *crozettensis* on Crozet, *minor* on Kerguelen, and *nasicornis* on Heard and McDonald. Differ in leg colour, which ranges from pinkish to purplish-black, as well as slightly in overall size and bill-sheath size. The four populations appear to consist of two groups, an eastern (Kerguelen and Heard) group, which is larger and heavier than the western group (Prince Edward and Crozet), with those from Kerguelen having lower pitched vocalizations than Crozet birds, and those on Heard having a shorter culmen, longer

tarsus and deeper bill sheath. Variation also exists at a micro-geographical scale in both the western group and on Kerguelen.

Magellanic Oystercatcher
Haematopus leucopodus   Plate 21

Identification
Confusion risks: Blackish Oystercatcher *H. ater*.
Main characters: Black-and-white shorebird with long red bill, which is often a conspicuous inhabitant of beaches. Strong flier and noisy. Sexual dimorphism is slight and age-related plumage variation also very minor. **Ad** has shiny black head, breast and most upperparts, with clean white belly to undertail-coverts, base and outer feathers to tail, uppertail-coverts and secondaries and most greater coverts (form striking wing and tail pattern in flight). Long orange-red bill, pale pink legs and feet, and eye-ring and iris bright lemon-yellow. Female has slightly longer and less deep-based bill, which is slightly duller in tone. **Imm** very similar and quickly assumes shiny black ad plumage, but has duller bare parts (brownish bill with a reddish base and greyish legs), brownish wing-coverts and otherwise buff-flecked black plumage.
Size: 42–46 cm, wing 23.7–26.7 cm, weight 585–700 g. Female may average slightly heavier and have a longer bill, but few comparative mensural data available.
Voice: Typical of oystercatchers, a piping *pee-pee*, a *peep* given in alarm or disyllabic *pee-you* in contact (Hayman *et al.* 1986).
Similar species: In our region overlaps only with Blackish Oystercatcher, but easily distinguished (even at some distance) by pied plumage pattern, with broad white secondary bar, uppertail-coverts and rump visible in flight, and blackish (not brownish) upperparts and white posterior underparts at rest.

Distribution and biology

Distribution, movements and population: Coastal beaches and inland meadows from C Chile north to Llanquihue and S Argentina north to Chubut, and south to Tierra del Fuego and islands of Cape Horn region; also the Falklands where population estimated at 7000–13,000 pairs in 1983–93.
Diet and feeding: Takes sand-worms, as well as mussels and limpets, using variety of techniques, chiefly hammering, prising, probing and stabbing at prey.
Social behaviour: May form large flocks (up to 100) in winter (Jan–Aug), but no information on length of pair-bond or extent of territoriality.
Breeding biology: Not well known. In the Falklands principally breeds late Sep–late Oct (c.1 month earlier than Blackish

Ad Blackish Oystercatchers Haematopus ater, *Falklands, Dec 1990.* © René Pop.

Ad Two-banded Plover Charadrius falklandicus, *Falklands, Jan 1991.* © René Pop.

Oystercatcher), with early clutches from mid-Sep and occasionally nests until mid-Dec. Lays two dark olive-brown or greenish eggs in scrape on sand or in dead kelp, often with some partial cover. No information on incubation or fledging periods.
Conservation Not globally threatened and population appears secure as its range is little populated by humans. Reasonably common to abundant throughout most of range.
Taxonomy Monotypic.

Blackish Oystercatcher *Haematopus ater*　Plate 21

Identification
Confusion risks: Magellanic Oystercatcher *H. leucopodus*.
Main characters: The only all-black oystercatcher in the Falklands, its dark plumage makes it more easily overlooked among kelp beds than the previous species, with which it frequently shares the same beaches. Limited age-/sex-related plumage variation. **Ad** has sooty-black head, neck and entire underparts, becoming dark brown on upperparts, wing and tail. Non-breeding female may develop whitish fringes to belly feathers. Heavy and long orange-red bill, becoming slightly yellowish at tip and broadening at nostril, legs and feet pale pink, eye-ring orange-red and iris bright lemon-yellow. **Imm** has duller upperparts, with paler, brownish-tipped coverts and duller bare parts (eye-ring and iris initially brownish).
Size: 43.0–45.5 cm, wing 26.2–28.2 cm, weight 585–708 g. Female averages larger, particularly in bill length.
Voice: Flight note is a loud *keep* or *keeup* with an abrupt end. Very loud vibrating whistles given in courtship (Woods 1988).
Similar species: For straightforward separation from Magellanic Oystercatcher see that species.

Distribution and biology
Distribution, movements and population: Rocky seacoasts and beaches from NW Peru, Chile and S Argentina to Tierra del Fuego, Juan Fernández (status unknown) and the Falklands where population estimated at 4000–8000 pairs in 1983–93. Largely sedentary but winters north to NE Argentina and (recently confirmed) Uruguay.
Diet and feeding: Principally takes limpets and mussels using similar techniques to Magellanic Oystercatcher.
Social behaviour: Much less social than previous species, but few data on many aspects of its life history.
Breeding biology: Not well known. In the Falklands breeds later than Magellanic Oystercatcher, with nest, late Oct–late Jan (latter probably a replacement), a simple scrape on sand or rock and often near high-tide mark. Lays 1–2 grey-buff eggs spotted yellow-brown/

purple-brown, but no information on incubation or fledging periods. Breeding success apparently often low due to predation by skuas.
Conservation Not globally threatened, though often at low density, occurs over extensive range that is little populated by humans.
Taxonomy Monotypic.

Two-banded Plover
Charadrius falklandicus　Plate 21

Identification
Confusion risks: None.
Main characters: Small, largely brown-and-white plover of sandy beaches in the Falklands. Limited age-/sex-related plumage variation; seasonal change is more marked. **Ad** breeding is pale grey-brown above, with a white forehead, lores and underparts, broad black crescentic breast mark and usually incomplete bar (complete on mainland birds) on lower neck. Latter connects with black line running from forehead through eye. Hindneck is chestnut, but crown more brownish. Female has less extensive breast-bands (especially upper), browner line through eye, and paler and more restricted chestnut on nape. Non-breeders have duller brown breast-bands and very little, if any, chestnut on head. In flight has dark tail with white outer feathers and faint white wingbar across primaries. Short stubby black bill, black or blackish-grey legs and feet, and dark brown eye. **Imm** much as non-breeding ad, with duller head pattern, bluff-flecked upperparts and even duller breast markings.
Size: 17–19 cm, wing 12.4–13.2 cm, weight 62–72 g. No information on sex-related differences (if any).
Voice: A thin *tseet* in contact, a plaintive *whiit* in flight and less plaintive, rapidly repeated calls in courtship (Hayman *et al.* 1986).
Similar species: The only small *Charadrius* plover to occur in the Falklands.

Distribution and biology
Distribution, movements and population: Breeds on sandy beaches from C Chile and Argentina south to Tierra del Fuego; also the Falklands (where sedentary and population estimated at 7000–13,000 pairs in 1983–93). Mainland populations winter north to Uruguay and SE Brazil (where recently proven to breed). Overall population estimated at 10,000–100,000 individuals in late 1980s (lower figure certainly appears too low given recently published results of the Falklands Breeding Bird Survey).
Diet and feeding: Small marine invertebrates picked from shoreline during characteristic small plover 'stop-and-run' action.
Social behaviour: Quite gregarious in non-breeding season, but nests solitarily.

Ad Rufous-chested Dotterel Charadrius modestus, *Falklands, Dec 1990.* © René Pop.

Magellanic Snipe Gallinago paraguaiae magellanica. *Falkland Islands, Jan 1991. © René Pop.*

Breeding biology: Breeds in the Falklands in Sep–mid-Jan (clutches from late Nov are probably replacements) on dry slopes up to 1.6 km from shore. Constructs scrape lined with a few wisps of grass, sometimes in kelp, and lays 2–4 (usually three) greenish/buff eggs spotted brown at larger end. Few other data.
Conservation Not globally threatened and no known threats.
Taxonomy Monotypic.

Rufous-chested Dotterel
Charadrius modestus   Plate 21

Identification
Confusion risks: None in range.
Main characters: Upright and attractive *Charadrius* plover of inland grasslands (and coastal areas in winter when unknown number of Falklands breeders move to mainland), with broad red-brown breast-band in breeding plumage and distinctive head pattern. Very limited sex-/age-related plumage variation but seasonal change is more marked. **Ad** breeding (mid-Aug–Dec when moult commences) has blue-grey face and throat, with white supercilium broadest and connecting on forehead, broad chestnut breast-band (bordered below by slightly narrower black crescentic band) and white rest of underparts, except small orange patch behind thighs. Crown, nape and rest of upperparts dark brown, with faint and narrow brighter fringes in fresh plumage. Female noticeably duller at this season. Non-breeders (Mar onwards) have buff supercilium and grey-brown neck and breast (though some may retain trace of lower black line). In flight has broad white outer feathers to otherwise blackish tail and white shaft-streaks to outer primaries. Slender, relatively short black bill, grey-brown legs and feet, and dark brown eye. **Imm** much like non-breeding ad but lacks all trace of supercilium, has brown breast, duller, sometimes yellowish-tinged bare parts, and is dark brown above with scaled pattern.
Size: 19–23 cm, wing 14.3–15.5 cm (Falklands only), weight 71–94 g. No known differences in size between sexes, but Falklands birds average larger in wing (mean 14.9 cm compared to 14.4 cm on mainland) and tarsus (mean 3.54 cm compared to 3.09 cm on mainland) measurements.
Voice: A tremulous *peeeoo*, becoming peu-peu-peu when extremely agitated, a wheezy *whee-ar* in territory defence and *pic-pic-pic* in high aerial display flight (Hayman *et al.* 1986).
Similar species: No significant confusion risks in the Falklands; vagrant Tawny-throated Dotterel *Oreopholus ruficollis* is larger, with longer, slimmer bill, long legs and dark belly patch in all plumages.

Distribution and biology
Distribution, movements and population: S South America in S Chile north to Llanquihue and S Argentina in Tierra del Fuego; also the Falklands where partially sedentary though parties are found on coastal grasslands. Winters north to N Chile, N Argentina, Uruguay and extreme SE Brazil. Falklands population estimated at 11,000–21,000 pairs in 1983–93 Falklands Breeding Birds Survey.
Diet and feeding: Apparently principally takes insects, including burrowing larvae, on breeding grounds, and small invertebrates, including molluscs and crustaceans, in winter.
Social behaviour: Gregarious (in flocks of up to 100) in winter, often with Two-banded Plover *C. falklandicus*, but territorial in breeding season and may also establish winter feeding territory of 10–100 m.
Breeding biology: Not well known, in the Falklands breeds on drier inland slopes in late Sep–mid-Jan, with peak in Oct and most laying 2–3 olive-brown eggs, heavily marked black or reddish, in typical plover scrape overhung by vegetation, and incubated by both sexes.
Conservation Not globally threatened and no threats identified.
Taxonomy Monotypic, though see size.

Magellanic Snipe
Gallinago paraguaiae magellanica   Plate 21

Identification
Confusion risks: Fuegian Snipe *G. stricklandii*.
Main characters: A typical snipe. Long-billed, cryptically plumaged rather small wader; in the Falklands, it is remarkably tame and unwilling to fly when disturbed. Extremely limited and, in some cases, perhaps no age-related, sexual or seasonal plumage variation. Zigzagging and (initially) towering escape flight when flushed by observer. **Ad** has blackish upperparts, heavily spangled and streaked chestnut and buff, with usually broad buff tramlines on mantle-sides, narrow central buff crown-stripe and broader (sometimes dull whitish) supercilium, dark eyestripe, buff and brown bands across face, and grey-white underparts, heavily spotted and streaked brownish-grey on breast and flanks and becoming clean white on belly, with perhaps no transversal bars on vent. Tail extends well beyond primaries at rest, barred whitish and dark brown, with narrow (but easily observed) chestnut subterminal band and white outer feathers most easily seen in flight. Long pale brown to yellowish bill with darker distal third, fairly long yellow-green (or greyish-green) legs, and large, staring

dark brown to black eye, often very prominent in face. **Imm** like ad but has darker bill, blue-grey legs and has neater pale buff fringes to median and greater coverts for several months after fledging. *Size*: 22–28 cm (*paraguaiae* as a whole), wing 12.8–14.4 cm (*magellanica*), weight 65–136 g (for *paraguaiae* superspecies). Female averages very fractionally larger in wing and bill lengths, but perhaps shorter in tail and tarsus data (Blake 1977).
Voice: Few specific data available for *magellanica*; *paraguaiae* stated to have a loud rasping alarm and (principally) nocturnal display flight (Hayman *et al.* 1986); also a staccato *yip-yip-yip…* (presumably same as *chippa-chippa-chippa* noted by Woods 1988) in long series from ground (perhaps in alarm), usually a grassy hummock (G. M. Kirwan pers. obs.). Display flights may commence up to three hours prior to sunset in Tierra del Fuego (G. M. Kirwan pers. obs.) and have been observed around midday and mid-afternoon in the Falklands (Woods 1988 and pers. obs.), who also notes *tik-tok-tik-tok* (and variations) from ad with young. Most calls are ventriloquial.
Similar species: Separation from Fuegian Snipe often difficult and covered under latter.

Distribution and biology

Distribution, movements and population: S South America in Chile west of the Andes from Atacama south to Cape Horn, and S Argentina from Neuquén and Río Negro south to Tierra del Fuego; also the Falklands where population estimated at 5000–9000 pairs in 1983–93. Winters north to N Argentina and Uruguay. *G. paraguaiae* (sometimes including *andina*, Puna Snipe) occurs over much of the rest of South America.
Diet and feeding: Mainly takes invertebrates, including earthworms and insect larvae in the Falklands.
Social behaviour: Poorly known and very few data, but several pairs may nest in relatively small area, and reasonably social like other *Gallinago* in non-breeding season.
Breeding biology: Few data, those in the Falklands breed in all months except Jul and Feb, though probably mainly Aug–Oct, laying 2–3 olive-green, pear-shaped eggs, heavily spotted and blotched black, in well-sheltered grass-lined nest in wet camp, often among rushes. No data on incubation or fledging periods.
Conservation Not globally threatened and *magellanica* is generally considered common through much of its range; no known threats.
Taxonomy Confused and subject to several different interpretations (e.g. Sibley 1996 considered *andina* specifically distinct from *paraguaiae* and *magellanica*, while other authors have considered *paraguaiae* only subspecifically distinct from *G. gallinago*). Increasingly the *paraguaiae* complex is being considered to represent three species-level taxa: *magellanica* in S South America, *andina* (form *innotata* is very doubtful) in high Andes of S Peru to N Chile and NW Argentina, and *paraguaiae* in much of rest of South America. Other members of the same complex, Common *G. gallinago*, Wilson's *G.* [*g.*] *delicata*, African *G.* [*g.*] *nigripennis* and Madagascar Snipes *G.* [*g.*] *macrodactyla* are frequently considered to represent species based on qualitative differences in morphology, vocalizations and drumming display.

Fuegian Snipe *Gallinago stricklandii*   Plate 21

Identification

Confusion risks: Magellanic Snipe *G. paraguaiae magellanica*.
Main characters: Plumage is that of a typical snipe, with long bill and comparatively long, strong-looking legs. More bulky than Magellanic with strongly rounded wings. Extremely limited and, in some cases, perhaps no age-related, sexual or seasonal plumage variation. Perhaps flushes with greater reluctance than *G. magellanica*. **Ad** has upperparts boldly variegated black, buff, brown and cinnamon, with coronal stripe even weaker than in Magellanic, mantle-sides lack obvious pale tramlines, wing-coverts heavily spotted and barred cinnamon-rufous, flight feathers largely barred cinnamon, buff and whitish, and whitish to pale buff underparts, finely speckled darker on throat, more heavily streaked on neck and breast, and narrowly barred brown on flanks and belly, extending to undertail-coverts. Face warm buffish-brown crossed by dark bars on lores and lower ear-coverts, supercilium rather indistinct, broadest, palest and most obvious in front of eye. Tail blackish-brown barred buffish-brown. Long, brownish-horn or olive bill (becoming darker, almost black, distally), legs and feet pale blue-grey or greyish-yellow, and eye dark brown to black. **Imm** poorly known and inadequately described in the literature.
Size: 29–30 cm, wing 14.4–16.5 cm, no weight data. Female averages larger in most mensural data, though sample sizes are small.
Voice: In display a *chip-chip-chip* is uttered in flight and a penetrating *char-woo* alternates with drumming during twilight and nocturnal displays (Hayman *et al.* 1986). Considered to be noisier and louder in display than *magellanica* (Couve & Vidal 2000).
Similar species: Magellanic Snipe differs from the present species by its shorter wings and less deep-based and shorter bill, and in flight, when Fuegian has an almost *Scolopax* wing shape (with no white trailing edge, unlike Magellanic), structural differences are heightened, but it is only in recent years that identification features to separate them have been clarified, and inexperienced observers should still exercise considerable caution in their separation, especially of lone birds. Fuegian, if seen well, has an almost kiwi-like rotund body shape, lacks a chestnut subterminal tail-band and transversal underparts barring reaches to undertail-coverts (rarely, if ever, in *magellanica*). Fuegian's willingness to occasionally perch in low branches of trees or bushes is considered a diagnostic difference from Magellanic. Subtle differences in head and upperparts patterns may be useful subsidiary features.

Distribution and biology

Distribution, movements and population: Breeds in grassy bogs and wet meadows of S Chile north to Cautín and Concepción and S Argentina in Santa Cruz, Tierra del Fuego and islands of Cape Horn region; also perhaps the Falklands where status rather unclear. No estimates or precise population estimates available.
Diet and feeding: Includes beetles but no other data.
Social behaviour: Very few data, but usually occurs alone or in pairs.
Breeding biology: Very few data. Two nests with eggs were found in Dec (with another pair perhaps having young nearby), on elevated ground with sparse rushes and grasses, and clutch size probably normally two eggs, which are deep olive, spotted cinnamon-brown.
Conservation Near Threatened and perhaps naturally rare over much of range; it is apparently only reasonably common on islands in Cape Horn region and a recent population estimate of 10,000 birds is largely surmise. No known threats.
Taxonomy Monotypic: form *jamesoni* now generally regarded as a separate species, Andean Snipe.

Least Seedsnipe *Thinocorus rumicivorus*   Plate 21

Identification

Confusion risks: None in the Falklands.
Main characters: Recalls a gamebird or sandgrouse on ground, and cryptic plumage often renders it invisible against favoured

Ad male Least Seedsnipe Thinocorus rumicivorus, *Chile.* © *Frank S. Todd.*

puna or steppe-like habitats, while in flight perhaps most closely resembles a plover. Little seasonal or age-related plumage variation, but strong sexual dimorphism. **Ad** male is streaked dark brown and buff on crown, nape and hindneck, with ash-grey neck-sides and forecrown, and white throat enclosed by black border, which continues as central line and joins broad black breast-band. Upper breast-sides grey and rest of underparts white. Rest of upperparts dark brown, densely mottled and fringed sandy-brown and white, with crescent-shaped subterminal tawny markings to most feathers, but plainer on mantle and rump. Flight feathers mostly brown. Female has buffish neck, with neck and breast pattern very indistinct and browner compared to male, and paler upperparts marked by broader fringes. In flight has narrow, pointed, dark brown wings and wedge-shaped tail with narrow white wingbar, tail-sides and terminal band (except to central feathers). Short, slightly curved and relatively deep-based yellow bill, tipped darker, very short legs and feet yellow, and eye dark brown. **Imm** much as ad female but throat and upper-breast pattern even weaker and more poorly defined, with broader upperparts barring and whiter fringes to wing-coverts.
Size: 15–19 cm, wing 11.0–13.2 cm, weight 50–60 g. Female averages marginally larger in wing and bill measurements but fractionally smaller in tail length.
Voice: Gives a snipe *Gallinago*-like call if flushed, also a disyllabic *kirik* in flight, a sharp *kikik* with young and mournful *piii*. Song is a repeated *wikiti-wikiti-wikiti*, followed by a dove-like hooting, either in flight or from ground (Hayman *et al.* 1986).
Similar species: Wholly distinctive within our region where no other seedsnipe has been recorded.

Distribution and biology
Distribution, movements and population: Breeds from SW Ecuador through Peru to NW Chile; also Andes of W Bolivia, and Chile from Atacama south to Magallanes and NW Argentina, in Jujuy and Tucuman, and from Río Negro south to Tierra del Fuego and Staten I; status on the Falklands unclear (perhaps formerly bred) but singles are reported less than annually, so probably vagrant. Winters north to NE Argentina and Uruguay, and a vagrant to South Shetland.
Diet and feeding: Principally takes buds and leaves of herbs, but also seeds.
Social behaviour: Generally in pairs or small family groups, and breeds solitarily.

Breeding biology: No data from our region, but eggs recorded Aug–Feb in Patagonia and perhaps multi-brooded. Nest a scrape in sandy soil, occasionally lined with animal dung and the four eggs are incubated c.26 days. Chicks fledge at seven weeks and are tended by both ads, and are capable of breeding at end of first summer.
Conservation Not globally threatened and generally common even in areas that have been heavily degraded by sheep grazing. No known threats to overall sparsely populated range.
Taxonomy Polytypic with the four subspecies differing according to size and overall coloration, and smaller and paler birds generally in north of range: *pallidus* occurs in SW Ecuador and NW Peru, *cuneicauda* in Peruvian Desert, *bolivianus* (the largest and warmest-coloured race) in extreme S Peru to N Chile and NW Argentina, and nominate *rumicivorus* in rest of range.

Sooty Tern *Sterna fuscata*   Plate 21

Identification
Confusion risks: Bridled Tern *S. anaethetus*.
Main characters: Elegant and medium-sized black-and-white tern, with long wings and tail, which has nested only once in our region. Limited seasonal and moderate age-related plumage variation.
Ad has deep black upperparts (sometimes with brownish cast, especially to remiges) including cap and broad loral stripe, and very clean white underparts (faintly tinged pale grey on undertail-coverts) and forehead patch, extending to above (but not behind) eye. White anterior margin to lesser wing-coverts visible at bend of closed wing. Deeply forked tail is largely black with clean white outer feathers, and underwing blackish-grey with immaculate white coverts. Bill and legs black or dusky, and eye dark brown. Non-breeder has variable white fringes to upperpart feathers, especially lores and crown. **Imm** has blackish-brown upperparts, finely vermiculated and flecked white, with grey-brown underparts, becoming paler posteriorly; first-summer acquires largely ad-like plumage except dark throat and upper breast.
Size: 35–44 cm, wing 27.2–31.0 cm (nominate), wingspan 76–90 cm, weight 95–150 g. Female smaller and lighter, at least in some Atlantic populations.
Voice: Well-known vocalization at colonies is *wide-awake* call.
Similar species: Bridled Tern has not been recorded in our region (but has occurred just outside it), and ad is distinguished by shorter-winged appearance, overall smaller size, paler upperparts contrasting with blacker crown and narrow white supercilium extending further beyond eye than in *fuscata*. Imm Sooty may require separation from similar-age noddy *Anous* sp., but whitish vent and undertail-coverts, paler underwing and forked tail are useful distinguishing features

Distribution and biology
Distribution, movements and population: Breeds on sandy or coral beaches on islands in Pacific from Ryukyu and Bonin, Hawaii; W Mexico and south to Philippines, off E Australia, Lord Howe, Norfolk, Kermadec, Tuamotu, Galápagos and off Chile; in Atlantic off S USA south to Belize, throughout West Indies to N South America, also off Brazil, and on Salvages, Ascension, St Helena and Príncipe; and in Indian Ocean in Red Sea and Persian Gulf, Madagascar, Mascarenes, Seychelles, off Djibouti, Somalia, Kenya, and on Laccadives, Maldives and Andamans, south to W Australia. Ranges at sea in tropical oceans and vagrant to S California, UK and also north to Japan and E Canada. In our region has bred once on St Paul. Population estimated at one million pairs in late 1980s.

Diet and feeding: Principally small fish and squid, with some crustaceans and occasionally insects and even offal, taken by aerial-dipping, contact-dipping and some plunge-diving. May feed nocturnally and sometimes up to 500 km from colony.

Social behaviour: Nests in dense colonies and typically gregarious in non-breeding season.

Breeding biology: Poorly known in our region. For general summary of nesting data see del Hoyo *et al.* (1996).

Conservation Not globally threatened and among the most abundant tropical-water seabirds, though some populations are locally at risk, usually due to predation by introduced mammals, especially rats and cats, but also through hurricane damage, egg harvesting by local people, tick infestation and viruses, and oil pollution, among other factors.

Taxonomy Eight races recognized of which (presumably) *nubilosa* has bred in our region on St Paul, and elsewhere in Red Sea and Indian Ocean east to the Philippines. The other races are nominate *fuscata* (S USA and West Indies south to C Atlantic), *infuscata* (C Indonesia), *serrata* (New Guinea, Australia and New Caledonia), *kermadeci* (Kermadec Is), *oahuensis* (Bonin, Hawaii and south through Pacific), *crissalis* (W Mexico to Galápagos) and *luctuosa* (Juan Fernández, off Chile).

Common Noddy *Anous stolidus*   Plate 21

Identification

Confusion risks: Black Noddy *A. minutus*.

Main characters: Large, rakish chocolate or sooty-brown tern with long narrow wings, which in our region breeds only on two islands in the Tristan da Cunha group and Gough. Tail has shallow fork (only visible when spread). No sexual dimorphism (except size) and very limited age-related plumage variation. **Ad** overall dark brown, with pale grey crown and superciliary region (sometimes almost white on forehead, and can be accentuated in heavily abraded individuals seen in strong light), slightly paler band across greater coverts, black primaries and long blackish, wedge-shaped tail. Underparts and hindneck also paler and more greyish, and underwing-coverts deep brownish-grey contrasting clearly with blackish-brown remiges. Narrow and incomplete white eye-ring, eye dark brown and bill, legs and feet black to blackish-brown (sometimes reddish-brown). **Imm** differs only slightly, having browner crown and pale fringes to upperpart feathers, gradually acquiring ad plumage over three years, becoming progressively more abraded above.

Size: 38–45 cm, wing 26.1–29.7 cm, wingspan 75–86 cm, weight 150–272 g. Female significantly smaller and lighter.

Voice: Gives low growling notes at colony, while feeding birds utter *eyeak* notes.

Similar species: Most closely recalls Black Noddy (not known from our region but occurs to north in Australia and breeds on St Helena in Atlantic), but latter is smaller and slimmer, with subtly blacker body plumage, greyer tail, more extensive white on head and proportionately longer, more slender bill. Voice also differs from *stolidus*.

Distribution and biology

Distribution, movements and population: Islands, in Pacific from Ryukyu and Bonin to Hawaii south to off Australia, Norfolk, Fiji, Tonga, S Polynesia, and off Mexico to Galápagos; in Atlantic from Dry Tortugas and Bahamas south through West Indies to Venezuela, Tobago, Trinidad and French Guiana, also Atlantic on Trindade, Ascension, St Helena, Tristan da Cunha and Gough (where a summer visitor) and islands off W Africa; and in Indian Ocean from Red Sea, Gulf of Aden and Laccadives south to Seychelles, Madagascar, and islands off Sumatra. Ranges at sea in tropical oceans, but many stay in general vicinity of breeding sites. Population estimated at 300,000–500,000 pairs in late 1980s.

Diet and feeding: Principally takes small fish and squid, with wide range of prey species documented in some populations. Mainly feeds by hover-dipping and contact-dipping, regularly foot patters the surface and may associate with other birds at rich food source.

Social behaviour: Rarely forms large colonies and nests sometimes almost solitarily.

Breeding biology: Poorly documented in our region except that it lays one egg and breeds both on sea cliffs and in trees (including introduced apple and pine trees), and some nest up to 1 km inland in *Phylica* trees at Tristan. For general summary of nesting data see del Hoyo *et al.* (1996).

Conservation Not globally threatened though some populations are locally at risk, usually due to predation by introduced mammals, especially rats and cats.

Taxonomy Five races recognized of which the nominate breeds in our region on Tristan da Cunha (Inaccessible and Nightingale) and Gough, and elsewhere on Caribbean and C and S Atlantic islands. The other races are *plumbeigularis* (Red Sea and Gulf of Aden), *pileatus* (Indian Ocean, Australia and much of Pacific range), *galapagoensis* (Galápagos) and *ridgwayi* (off W Mexico and W Central America).

Barn Owl *Tyto alba*   Plate 21

Identification

Confusion risks: Short-eared Owl *Asio flammeus*.

Main characters: Well known, its ghostly appearance has given it the local name in many regions of the world (including the Falklands) of the 'white owl'. Minimal sexual dimorphism or age-related plumage variation. **Ad** has both dark and pale morphs. Former has entire upperparts including crown, wings and tail mottled pale grey and buff, finely speckled white and with strong greyish cast in the Falklands (and South American) subspecies. Flight feathers and tail narrowly barred brown, with some white spots to tips of feathers. Pure white heart-shaped facial disk bordered by orange-brown, and underparts entirely very clean white, often marked by fine dark spots. Dark morph has underparts variably clay-brown, often lacking spots, but otherwise much as pale morph. Bill dark, long legs covered by white feathers, with black claws, and eye also black.

Size: 35–41 cm, wing 29.0–33.4 cm (*T. a. tuidara*), weight 250–480 g (all races). No evident differences in mensural data between sexes, though female may average heavier.

Voice: Variety of hissing, snoring and scream-like calls.

Similar species: Separation from Short-eared Owl is discussed under latter.

Distribution and biology

Distribution, movements and population: Cosmopolitan but in our region breeds only in the Falklands where population estimated at 7–10 pairs in 1983–93, after having been proved breeding there for the first time in 1987/8. Now known to be breeding at many settlements on East and West Falkland, where it usually nests in European Gorse *Ulex europaeus* (R. Woods pers. obs.). Has reached South Georgia.

Diet and feeding: Mainly takes small mammals (introduced House Mouse *Mus musculus* in the Falklands, R. Woods pers. obs.) by dropping onto them from above, in silent slow, wavering flight close to dusk or nocturnally.

Social behaviour: Usually alone or in pairs and bond often life-long.

Breeding biology: Very few data from our region, but several general summaries of such knowledge are available (e.g. del Hoyo *et al.* 1999).

Conservation Not globally threatened and no local threats known.

Taxonomy Approximately 30–36 races of *T. alba* have been described; that in the Falklands (and also in much of South America) is *T. a. tuidara*. A wide-ranging and exhaustive revision of this complex is apparently in progress.

Short-eared Owl *Asio flammeus sanfordi*   Plate 21

Identification

Confusion risks: Barn Owl *Tyto alba* is only other owl in the Falklands.

Main characters: Medium-sized, distinctly patterned owl, with large round head and small ear-tufts. Within our region only found in the Falklands, where represented by endemic race *sanfordi*. Sexes virtually alike, with indistinct seasonal or age-related plumage variation. **Ad** has pale buff-grey facial disc, white eyebrows and lores, and bright lemon-yellow eyes surrounded by blackish; predominantly mottled brown and buff on upperparts, and underparts whitish to warm buff, densely streaked brown on breast and body-sides; in flight, long, broad wings with darkish carpal and barred primary-tip marking on underwing. Female larger, browner above, and more buff below with heavier streaking. **Juv** barely separable in field; in hand by uniformly unmoulted remiges in first-year.

Voice: Described from the Falklands (mainly flight/territorial calls) as sharp *yip-yip-yip* or sneezing *wheechiz*; displaying male claps wings and utters a repeated low *boo-boo-boo* (Woods 1988).

Size: 33–41 cm, wing 28.1–33.5 cm, weight 206–505 g. Female averages heavier.

Similar species: The more strictly nocturnal Barn Owl appears all ghostly white when seen in flight at night, and has yellowish-buff (not brown) upperparts and white underparts when seen in daylight; always lacks distinctive dark underwing pattern of present species.

Distribution and biology

Distribution, movements and population: Throughout much of Eurasia, North and South America. The Falklands population was placed at 100–200 pairs in 1983–93.

Diet and feeding: Hunts Grey-backed Storm-petrels *Oceanites nereis* and Common Diving-petrels *Pelecanoides urinatrix* as they return to nest sites in dense tussac grass on offshore islands; also takes small mammals (House Mouse *Mus musculus* and rats), occasionally hovering low over ground to locate them or large insects. Diurnal, crepuscular and nocturnal.

Social behaviour: Territorial during breeding season, but may gather in small groups to hunt outside of this period; roosts communally and often active in day.

Breeding biology: In the Falklands nests in shelter of tussac grass, laying two round, white eggs. Nestlings heard calling in mid-Nov, suggesting that eggs are laid in early Oct.

Conservation Not globally threatened. Introduced rats and mice may form a significant proportion of its diet in the Falklands in winter, when its main food sources are unavailable. It may therefore be one of the few species to have benefited from such alien introductions.

Taxonomy At least ten races recognized, of which *sanfordi* is endemic to the Falklands and is paler and smaller than *suinda* in mainland South America.

Ad Blackish Cinclodes Cinclodes antarcticus, *Falklands. © Nic Huin/Falklands Conservation.*

Blackish Cinclodes *Cinclodes antarcticus*   Plate 22

Identification

Confusion risks: None.

Main characters: Within our region restricted to the Falklands, where represented by the endemic (nominate) race. Rather large passerine with stout-based, slightly decurved bill. The only landbird in the Falklands with all-dark brownish plumage, restless, but inquisitive and tame; flies low with rapid wingbeats. Sexes alike, with very slight seasonal/age variation. **Ad** entirely warm blackish-brown with slightly paler (buffy-brown) but indistinct supercilium, wingbar (not always present) and dull yellowish throat patch. Bill and legs black. Some, especially juvs, have yellow mark at base of bill.

Voice: Calls typically high pitched and often explosive, mostly sharp *chip* notes; song consists of musical trills interspersing more staccato notes, both from ground (when typically raises wings like all *Cinclodes*) or in flight display (Ridgely & Tudor 1994, Woods 1988).

Size: 19–23 cm, wing 10.5–12.5 cm, no weight data. No information on sex-related differences (if any) in mensural data.

Similar species: The only cinclodes in the Falklands.

Distribution and biology

Distribution, movements and population: Endemic to S Patagonia (in Chile and Argentina), where it occurs in S Tierra del Fuego, Beagle Channel islands, the Cape Horn archipelago, Staten I and the Diego Ramírez Is, and the Falklands, where the breeding population was estimated to be 15,000–28,000 pairs in 1983–93.

Diet and feeding: Animal matter taken on ground, especially small crustaceans and fly larvae captured on shorelines, but also closely associated with seabird and sea mammal colonies where it searches for food among excreta and takes regurgitated fish remnants. Can be remarkably confiding and take human foods.

Social behaviour: Alone, in pairs or small, loose groups.

Breeding biology: One to three glossy white eggs laid Sep–Dec, especially Oct, and incubated c.12 days. Young fledge at 12–15 days. Two broods often attempted. Nest is a shallow cup of grasses with a few feathers as lining, and sheltered by tussac grass or rocks, in a disused seabird burrow or other tunnel, and even placed below a house or in a bucket.

Conservation Not globally threatened, but considered rare in most parts of its South American range and has declined in the Falklands in those areas where rats and cats are present. Littoral pollution and the commercial removal of kelp, in which the species finds much of its prey, also pose potential threats.

Plate 22 Endemic and indigenous passerines of the S Atlantic Ocean and the Falklands

Black-chinned Siskin ad. ♂ (p. 304)

Black cap and bib; bold wingbars and extensive yellow pigments; female lacks black markings and overall duller

Tristan/Inaccessible/Nightingale Bunting ad. ♂ (p. 306, 307)

Diffusely streaked above, paler/yellower below; indistinct facial marks and small conical bill; female duller and streaked

Gough Bunting ad. ♂ (p.305)

Uniform olive-green, small black bib/lores, long conical bill; female duller with obscured facial marks

Chilean Swallow ad. (p. 300)

Falklands' only regular hirundine

Black-throated Finch ad. ♂ (p. 304)

n-grey , black and bib

Female/young duller, mainly buff-brown above, streaked blackish, whitish below

Grosbeak Bunting ad. ♂ (p. 307)

Large and chunky with massive bill; streaked underparts

Austral Thrush ad. ♂ (p. 302)

Female duller with no black on head

Grass Wren ad. (p. 303)

Tiny; narrowly streaked above and pronounced supercilium/eyestripe

Tristan Thrush ad. (p. 302)

Long legs, heavily streaked below; hops or runs

Long-tailed Meadowlark ad. ♂ (p. 308)

Female/young streaky and pale rosy-red on mainly greyish underparts

Cobb's Wren ad. (p. 303)

Uniform, mostly unstreaked, rather large

Blackish Cinclodes ad. (p. 298)

The only cinclodes and all-dark brownish bird in Falklands

Correndera Pipit ad. (p. 300)

The only pipit in the Falklands

ced Ground-tyrant ad.

Upright stance and flicks/fans tail; brownish-grey above with dark foreface, dull chestnut-brown crown and longish legs

The only passerine breeding in South Georgia

South Georgia Pipit ad. (p. 301)

Taxonomy Nominate race (described above) is endemic to the Falklands and is characterized in being slightly paler with a weaker (and finer/longer) bill (which is yellowish at the base) and more consistent wingbar than *maculirostris* in S South America.

Dark-faced Ground-tyrant
Muscisaxicola macloviana   Plate 22

Identification
Confusion risks: None in range.
Main characters: Within our region occurs only in the Falklands, where represented by endemic (nominate) race. Sexes alike and plumage variation very limited. A short-billed ground-tyrant, typically slim with upright stance; often runs rapidly, flicks and fans tail; is inquisitive and tame, but flies swiftly. **Ad** predominantly brownish-grey above, with characteristic black foreface, dull chestnut-brown crown to nape, dusky wings (fringed whitish), pale grey to whitish underparts, and black tail with some of outermost feathers white. Eye and thin pointed bill black, and longish legs dark grey. **Juv** generally as ad but has yellowish base to bill, streaked throat and buffy fringes to wing-coverts.
Voice: Rather unique calls, principally short squeaky *tseet*; also low harsh notes (often repeated), *tu* or *seet*; song an indistinct twittering (Woods 1988).
Size: 15.5–16.5 cm, no other data.
Similar species: The only ground-tyrant in the Falklands.

Distribution and biology
Distribution, movements and population: To 2500 m in S Chile and Argentina to Tierra del Fuego and Cape Horn; also the Falklands. Austral migrants reach W Peru, NW Argentina and Uruguay, and apparently S Ecuador, the Falklands and South Georgia. Falklands population estimated to be 4000–8000 pairs in 1983–93.
Diet and feeding: Insects, principally taken on ground, often after hovering to locate prey.
Social behaviour: Alone or in pairs, occasionally small groups.
Breeding biology: Nest, late Oct–late Dec, is of grass or roots and well lined. Usually placed in a crevice in a stone wall or cliff. Lays 2–3 closely marked, glossy white eggs. Possibly double-brooded.
Conservation Not globally threatened. In the Falklands it is apparently sufficiently adaptable to take advantage of higher insect numbers around settlements, though domestic cats appear to take a heavy toll.
Taxonomy Nominate *macloviana* (described above) endemic to the Falklands and is distinctly larger than *mentalis* of S South America.

Ad Dark-faced Ground-tyrant Muscisaxicola macloviana *feeding almost full-grown chick, Falklands, Dec 1990. © René Pop.*

Chilean Swallow *Tachycineta meyeni*   Plate 22

Identification
Confusion risks: Vagrant White-rumped *T. leucorrhoa* and Blue-and-white Swallows *Notiochelidon cyanoleuca*.
Main characters: Small, largely blue-and-white swallow with a distinctive white rump and slightly forked tail. Flies fast and low above ground, on relatively short triangular-shaped wings. Often found in urban areas. Only age-related plumage variation is well described. **Ad** has glossy blue-black or ultramarine upperparts and head to below eye (darkest on ear-coverts and brightest on wing-coverts and mantle), with occasionally a very slight white mark above lores, immaculate white underparts and rump, and brownish-black flight feathers and tail. Bare parts largely dark/black. **Imm** duller and browner, with only a very slight blue gloss to the mantle and lesser wing-coverts, but a much more noticeable white streak above lores.
Size: 12.0–13.5 cm, wing 10.5–11.7 cm, weight 15–20 g.
Voice: Most data is from Woods (1988), a buzzy *chrimp* or *chreez* varying in pitch while feeding, and a rapid chattering *chi-chi-chi…* when perched.
Similar species: Vagrant White-rumped Swallow is slightly larger and requires most careful separation, but latter has narrow white forehead patch extending slightly to lores (good views are required to determine this feature), greener sheen to upperparts, paler underwing-coverts and less forked tail. Blue-and-white Swallow (also a vagrant to the Falklands) possesses a similar overall plumage pattern but lacks a white rump. Differs much more substantially in flight action, size and silhouette from other hirundines recorded in the Falklands.

Distribution and biology
Distribution, movements and population: Breeds in C Chile north to Atacama and in S Argentina north to Neuquén and west Río Negro, south (in both countries) to Tierra del Fuego. Has bred only once in the Falklands (1983) but is an annual visitor in Oct–June, more numerous in autumn. Largely resident in north of range, during austral winter those in south migrate north and east across rest of Argentina to Uruguay, Paraguay, extreme SE Brazil (uncommon mid-May–mid-Sep), Bolivia (rarely) and S Peru.
Diet and feeding: Takes variety of flying insects such as beetles, flies, ants and others.
Social behaviour: Usually a solitary feeder and often nests singly, but also forms small groups to both breed and forage. Often associates with White-rumped Swallow in winter.
Breeding biology: Few data from our region, but elsewhere breeds Sep–Feb (often raises 2–3 broods in Chile), constructing a pad of grasses in eaves of a house or hole in a tree. Lays 4–6 white eggs, but no details on incubation or fledging periods and role of ads.
Conservation Not globally threatened.
Taxonomy Has been considered to be perhaps conspecific with *T. leucorrhoa*, although they are not known to intergrade, despite the existence of some apparently hybrid specimens.

Correndera Pipit *Anthus correndera*   Plate 22

Identification
Confusion risks: None in range.
Main characters: Within our region occurs only in the Falklands, where represented by the endemic race, *grayi*, often locally known as 'Falklands Pipit'. Small, chiefly brownish, medium-sized pipit. Sexes alike and plumage variation very limited. **Ad** has bold blackish and ochraceous-streaked upperparts, and two white longitudi-

Correndera (Falklands) Pipit Anthus correndera grayi. This race is confined to the Falklands. It differs markedly from South Georgia Pipit A. antarcticus, especially in the finer face and malar pattern and sparser streaking below. Falklands, November, 1994 © Mike Danzenbaker/avesphoto.com.

nal stripes on mantle, dusky tail with whitish outer feathers, and pale/warm buffy-white underparts with bold black breast streaking extending to flanks. Streaked face usually has quite distinct malar stripe and pale supercilium, and rather indistinct median-covert wingbar. Bill broad-based and mainly greyish-brown, and legs pale flesh-brown with relatively long hindclaw. **Juv** generally as fresh ad but buffier, especially below.
Voice: Flight call short and squeaky, e.g. *tipitip*; song (mainly Aug–Jan) a thin and rather squeaky short phrase of 3–4 notes followed by a harsh churr (Woods 1988).
Size: 14.3–16.0 cm, weight 15.0–26.5 g, no other data. Male perhaps larger and heavier (e.g. a sample of 16 males weighed 18–23 g and six females 15–22 g) but very few data and much overlap in these.
Similar species: None, the only pipit in the Falklands.

Distribution and biology
Distribution, movements and population: Sea level to 4000 m in South America from S Peru, Bolivia and S Brazil to Tierra del Fuego. Some southern populations migrate north in winter. Falklands population (*grayi*) estimated to be 8000–15,000 pairs in 1983–93.
Diet and feeding: Takes insects and their larvae on the ground, with young being fed small worms and moths, but few specific data.
Social behaviour: Alone or in loose pairs.
Breeding biology: In the Falklands prefers large areas of coarse white grass and wetter habitats than on mainland. Breeds late Sep–late Dec (perhaps all year in mainland South America). Nest of fine grasses well hidden. Two to four variably coloured eggs (often with some spotting). Two broods per season.
Conservation Not globally threatened. Grass burning and feral cats and rats pose greatest threats in the Falklands. New legislation is required to prohibit the burning of camp after mid-September, which may protect the species to some extent.
Taxonomy Five subspecies described (but intergradation reported between some populations): *grayi* in the Falklands (distinguished by larger size and apparently different voice to mainland South American birds); *chilensis* in S Argentina, Chile and Tierra del Fuego, *calcaratus* and *catamarcae* in the Andes, and the nominate in rest of range.

South Georgia Pipit *Anthus antarcticus*   Plate 22

Identification
Confusion risks: The only pipit on South Georgia.
Main characters: Closely related to Correndera Pipit *A. correndera*, but distinctly larger, with some plumage and vocalization differences. Sexes alike and plumage variation very limited. **Ad** has rather evenly-streaked bold blackish and ochraceous upperparts, without obvious white longitudinal stripes on mantle; buffy-white underparts almost wholly streaked dark from upper breast, most heavily on flanks, and malar stripe prominent. Tail dusky with whitish outer feathers; generally lacks pale supercilium but whitish median-covert wingbar rather distinct. Bill broad-based, mainly greyish-brown and legs pale flesh-brown with relatively long hindclaw. **Juv** generally as fresh ad but averages buffier, especially below.
Voice: In breeding season, display flight very conspicuous and monotonous, with repeated soft twittering and high-pitched sequences (lasting up to several minutes); when flushed gives indistinct short, soft notes.
Size: 16.5 cm, no other data.
Similar species: None.

Distribution and biology
Distribution, movements and population: Restricted to South Georgia, where confined to c.20 offshore islets and a handful of mainland areas enclosed by sea-level glaciers. Winters mainly on ice-free shorelines. Population estimated at 3000–4000 pairs in recent years.
Diet and feeding: Takes insects and their larvae in tussac areas, and insects and crustaceans on shorelines and along streams; springtails trapped in surface tension of small freshwater pools are favoured food in spring.
Social behaviour: No information.
Breeding biology: Breeds in low-altitude tussac grassland, laying up to 3–4 green or greyish, speckled red-brown eggs in mid Nov–Dec. Large, bulky nest of dry grass, with lining of feathers and tail-like appendage, covered by canopy of brown and green tussac grass. Possibly multi-brooded in order to combat high winter mortality.
Conservation Near Threatened; glacier retreat brings its mainland breeding areas under threat from invasive rats, and offshore islets must be considered under continual threat from infestation. Winter mortality of juvs high.
Taxonomy Monotypic.

Fresh South Georgia Pipit Anthus antarcticus. South Georgia's only endemic passerine recalls some European pipits. Note dense, diffuse streaking below, but quite plain head with pronounced white eye-ring; see also Regional accounts. Mar 2003. © Hadoram Shirihai.

Ad male Austral Thrush Turdus falcklandii, *Falklands, Jan 1991. © René Pop.*

Austral Thrush *Turdus falcklandii*　　　Plate 22

Identification

Confusion risks: None in range.
Main characters: Large, bulky-bodied, long-legged thrush, sometimes known as 'Falklands Thrush' as the nominate falcklandii race is endemic to the group. Distinctive, rather noisy and often seen hopping or running on semi-open ground. Sexual and age/seasonal plumage variation. **Ad** male has blackish head, grading into greyish cheeks, and olive-brown upperparts contrasting with yellowish rump, duskier flight and tail feathers; throat whitish heavily streaked blackish, breast pale brown and belly buff; eye-ring, bill and legs golden-yellow (duller in autumn). Female similar but less saturated, with less or no black on head, and buffish, narrowly streaked throat. **Juv** overall richer buff and conspicuously patterned, with pale fringes above and black spots below; bare parts duller.
Voice: Varied calls, mostly loud and harsh, e.g. *choyz-choyz-choyz*; song mainly whistles and harsh chuckles (Woods 1988).
Size: 23.0–26.5 cm, wing 12.8–14.2 cm, weight 100–111 g. Male typically has longer wings.
Similar species: The only thrush in the Falklands.

Distribution and biology

Distribution, movements and population: Resident to 2150 m, from 27°S in Chile and the Juan Fernández Is, and 37°S in Argentina

to Tierra del Fuego and Beagle Channel islands; also in the Falklands, where 4000–8000 pairs estimated in 1983–93.
Diet and feeding: Forages for grubs, worms and snails in typical thrush manner and will also take fruit and even human scraps in winter.
Social behaviour: Alone or in pairs, but appears to roost communally, at least in the Falklands. Small parties occur in winter at favoured feeding areas.
Breeding biology: Nest, Aug–Dec (occasionally mid-Jul, and until Feb in South America), a large deep cup of grass and roots in broad variety of sheltered areas. Lays 2–3 closely marked, blue-green eggs, incubated 14–16 days. Fledging takes 16–18 days and up to three broods per season may be attempted, with as few as 12–14 days between nesting periods.
Conservation Not globally threatened. Highly adaptable and able to withstand effects of introduced predators due to being multi-brooded.
Taxonomy Three races: nominate in the Falklands (described above), the slightly smaller *magellanicus* in mainland South America and *mochae* on Mocha I, off Chile.

Tristan Thrush *Nesocichla eremita*　　　Plate 22

Identification

Confusion risks: The only thrush in the islands.
Main characters: Largish, long-legged/tailed and heavily dark-streaked thrush, normally seen hopping or running across semi-open ground. Limited age/seasonal plumage variation; sexes alike. **Ad** has brown upperparts with pale orange-buff tips to wing-coverts, heavy dark bill, pale whitish throat and rest of buffy underparts heavily blotched and streaked dark brown; legs dark brown. Ad of race *procax* more rufous-brown above, with much less streaking below and brighter orange underwing (though *gordoni* approaches this), while *eremita* is smaller and duller than other forms. **Juv** strongly streaked pale orange-buff above, heavily mottled below and has broad pale orange-buff tips to tertials and wing-coverts.
Voice: Main calls a soft chirp or wheezing, given while flicking wings; song is a very quiet and rather varied warble (Fraser *et al.* 1994).
Size: 22–23 cm, wing 9.9–12.1 cm, weight 78–124 g (range 81–108 g on Inaccessible). Female perhaps averages shorter winged (at least in race *gordoni*), but no comparative data for other forms.
Similar species: None.

Tristan Thrush Nesocichla eremita *is a quite large (and long-legged/tailed) dusky-coloured thrush that inhabits ground levels of several islands in the Tristan Group: Nightingale and adjacent islets are occupied by race* procax *(left), while race* gordoni *(right) on Inaccessible approaches the former in size but is duller and less boldly marked. Left: Nightingale, Mar 2003; right: Inaccessible, Mar 2006. © Hadoram Shirihai.*

Ad Grass Wren Cistothorus platensis, *Falklands, Dec 1990. © René Pop.*

Ad Cobb's Wren Troglodytes cobbi, *Falklands. © Richard White/Falklands Conservation.*

Distribution and biology

Distribution, movements and population: Sheltered valleys and gullies, plantations, thickets and scattered trees on Tristan da Cunha (mostly above 100 m and relatively common only above 1400 m) and throughout Nightingale and Inaccessible. Total population 6000 individuals in 1980s.

Diet and feeding: Forages on ground beneath trees or in grassy clearings, taking broad variety of invertebrates, but also scavenges carrion, steals seabird eggs and takes eggs and nestlings of other endemic landbirds, and even ad storm-petrels on occasion.

Social behaviour: Usually alone or in pairs.

Breeding biology: Breeds Sep–Feb. Nest a large, neat cup-shaped construction, placed on ground or just above it, in vegetation or on rock, and usually well concealed. Two to four pale green eggs speckled reddish-brown. Chicks fledge in c.20 days and are fed by both ads.

Conservation Near Threatened. Numbers appear stable, though rat predation is potential problem on Tristan da Cunha. Introductions of forms from other islands and resulting hybridization remain a concern.

Taxonomy Three poorly marked races: nominate *eremita* on Tristan da Cunha, *gordoni* on Inaccessible, and *procax* on Nightingale, Middle and Stoltenhoff. Latter also illegally introduced to Tristan da Cunha.

Grass Wren *Cistothorus platensis* Plate 22

Identification

Confusion risks: Cobb's Wren *Troglodytes cobbi*.

Main characters: Typical wren, being tiny, short-winged, with pronounced tail cocking, and restless behaviour; occurring in our region only in the Falklands, where represented by endemic race, *falklandicus*. Usually in well-vegetated areas. Sexual or age-related plumage variation very limited. **Ad** has buff head narrowly streaked black, with indistinct whitish supercilium and dusky eyestripe; rest of upperparts (to rump) broadly streaked black and buffy-white, while wings and tail are rufous-brown, barred black; whitish underparts, washed buff on flanks and vent. Brownish bill rather short and straight, and legs mainly brownish-flesh. **Juv** as ad, but overall warmer with obscured facial markings.

Voice: Mainly a hard *tak-tak* or *ti-ti-ti*; song long and repeated, *sioo-sioo-sioo*, *chiwi-chiwi-chiwi* and *clee-clee-clee*, separated by low trill (Woods 1988).

Size: 10–11 cm, 9 g.

Similar species: Cobb's Wren has much more uniform, unstreaked plumage, and is more robust and slightly larger.

Distribution and biology

Distribution, movements and population: Widespread: occurs from NE USA and Canada south through the Andes to Tierra del Fuego, and SE Brazil. The Falklands population, which occurs from sea level to 200 m, was estimated at 1300–2300 pairs in 1983–93.

Diet and feeding: Few data but appears to feed, mouse-like, above ground level in tussac grass and preys mainly on insects, resorting to seeds in winter.

Social behaviour: Alone or in pairs, sometimes in loose colonies, but usually territorial. Flushes reluctantly and song is often best indication of presence.

Breeding biology: Nest an elaborate ball of grass, 0.3–1.1 m above ground, lined with wool or feathers and sometimes approached by a small grass tunnel. Breeds early Oct to mid-Nov (breeding recorded most months in South America). Four to seven white eggs and single-brooded, but few other data.

Conservation Not globally threatened. The endemic Falkland race inhabits dense tussac grass, wetter inland areas with rushes or long grasses and the shrub *Chiliotrichum diffusum*, also mixed upland vegetation of grasses and *Blechnum magellanicum*.

Taxonomy Many races described (and probably more than one species involved): *falklandicus* is distinguished by being the largest, with a heavier bill and less black-streaked plumage.

Cobb's Wren *Troglodytes cobbi* Plate 22

Identification

Confusion risks: Grass Wren *Cistothorus platensis*.

Main characters: Strongly built, long-billed and plain-plumaged wren; typically restless and vocal (raising tail). Frequents boulder beaches, especially those adjoining dense tussac grass and also occurs inland in shorter vegetation on islands without rats or mice, but tamer and less skulking than previous species. Sex-/age-related plumage variation very limited. **Ad** has dull featureless grey-brown head, and uniform red-brown back and wing-coverts. Flight and tail feathers chestnut, finely barred dark brown. Underparts whitish, suffused buff. Blackish bill rather long and slightly decurved, and legs mainly brownish-flesh. **Juv** more richly coloured, with buff underparts. Frequent aberration, with some white/grey on head (partial albino) described by Woods (1988).

Voice: Rather noisy; calls typically harsh and buzzing, *chiz*, *chiz-iz*, often becoming higher pitched, louder and explosive; song (Aug–Feb and occasionally mid-Apr) is rich, rather short and fast, with mixed trills, harsh notes and whistles, but often repeated in close sequences (Woods 1988).

Size: 12–13 cm, no other data.

Similar species: Grass Wren has much less uniform plumage, with heavily streaked upperparts and is less robust and slightly smaller.

Distribution and biology

Distribution, movements and population: Endemic to the Falklands, where a population of 4500–8000 pairs was estimated to be breeding on 29 islands in the late 1990s.

Diet and feeding: Prefers tussac grass in coastal areas and accumulated dead kelp on shores with large boulders, where it forages for invertebrates.

Social behaviour. Few data. Strongly territorial during breeding season and faithful to territories from year to year (R. Woods pers. comm.).

Breeding biology: Nest a dome of grasses, thickly lined and well hidden among tussac grass or a rock crevice. Three to four closely spotted pinkish eggs, Oct–Dec. Probably double-brooded.

Conservation Vulnerable. Almost completely restricted to predator-free islands and islets, it is highly susceptible to predation by rats, though can survive on larger islands with a few domestic cats. Cobb's Wren has not been found on any tussac island with rats, probably because it favours the same shoreline habitat that is used by the latter.

Taxonomy Although first described as a species in 1909, most authors followed Hellmayr (1921), who considered it a race of the widespread House Wren *Troglodytes aedon*. It is larger, with a longer bill and wings, and exhibits marked ecological differences that have led to it again being described as an endemic Falkland species (Woods 1993).

Black-chinned Siskin *Carduelis barbata*   Plate 22

Identification

Confusion risks: None in our region.

Main characters: Boldly marked finch with principally yellow, green and black plumage. Marked sexual dimorphism. **Ad** male has black cap extending across forehead to merge with chin and throat, yellowish-green face, including supercilium, olive-green mantle and back, yellow rump, wingbar (formed by broad tips to greater coverts) and bases to primaries. Underparts largely yellowish-green, becoming white on undertail-coverts. Mantle olive-green, streaked darker and wing-coverts and flight feathers largely brownish-black. Tail brownish-black with yellowish basal-sides and is slightly forked. Female is similar to male but lacks black chin to crown, is overall duller green, with paler underparts, which whiten from upper belly, and has duller, narrower wingbars and basal tail-sides. Bill short and slightly conical, dark brown to black-

ish with paler lower mandible, legs and feet dark brown, and eye dark. **Imm** most closely resembles female but is even paler, with streakier upperparts and broader pale buffish-yellow wingbars.

Size: 12–15 cm, wing 7.3 cm, weight 15.9 g. Insufficient mensural data are available to draw any conclusions concerning possible differences between the sexes.

Voice: Calls include a rising *tsooeet* and sparrow-like *chit*, also a very quiet *tsi-tsi-tsi* when feeding. In flight a short *chup*. Song loud, obvious and somewhat canary-like, consisting of repeated trills and sometimes sustained for up to ten minutes, principally given in May–Jul and Sep–Dec in the Falklands (Woods 1988).

Similar species: Unmistakable given a good view as no other siskin has occurred in the Falklands.

Distribution and biology

Distribution, movements and population: S South America in Chile from Atacama south and S Argentina from Neuquén and Río Negro south to Tierra del Fuego; also the Falklands, where population estimated at 1500–2800 pairs in 1983–93. Mainland birds move to lower elevations in non-breeding season.

Diet and feeding: Mostly takes seeds (including those of tussac grass), insects and their larvae on ground, though also known to feed in trees.

Social behaviour. Usually in pairs or small family groups, but occasionally forms flocks up to 100 strong in non-breeding season.

Breeding biology: Season principally early Sep–Dec in the Falklands, where up to three broods may be attempted. Nest is a neat cup of fine grass, lined with hair, wool or root fibres, in fork of large bush up to 1.8 m above ground or in mature tussac grass. Lays 3–5 pinkish-white eggs marked with red-brown spots. No information on incubation or fledging periods and role of sexes.

Conservation Not globally threatened, generally common throughout range and no known threats.

Taxonomy Monotypic though Woods (1988) suggested that those in the Falklands may deserve subspecific status.

Black-throated Finch
Melanodera melanodera   Plate 22

Identification

Confusion risks: Females may be confused with Correndera Pipit *Anthus correndera*.

Main characters: Medium-sized, distinctive finch, with pronounced sex-/age-related plumage variation; all plumages show considerable individual variation in amount of yellow and greenish

Ad male Black-chinned Siskin Carduelis barbata, *Falklands, Jan 1991.*
© René Pop.

Ad female Black-chinned Siskin Carduelis barbata, *Falklands, Jan 2005.*
© Klaus Bjerre.

Ad male Black-throated Finch Melanodera melanodera, *Falklands, Jan 1991.* © René Pop.

Ad Black-throated Finch Melanodera melanodera *(possibly female), Falklands.* © Frank S. Todd.

saturation. **Ad** male has conspicuous black lores and large throat patch, forming mask and bib pattern, the latter emphasized by white surround to forehead, supercilium and malar areas. Pale, rather bluish-grey crown and hindneck to upper mantle, merging into greyish-olive back, rump and breast-sides. Rest of underparts bright greyish-yellow, becoming white at rear/centre; blackish-centred wing-coverts, flight and outertail feathers broadly fringed canary-yellow (obvious in flight); bill dark grey, eye blackish and tarsus dark brown. Female duller, being buff-brown above, streaked blackish, whitish below with brownish streaks and buff-brown wash to breast, and duller wing and tail markings. Inconspicuous whitish supercilium, but some (older) females have vague darkening to lores and throat. **Juv** much as female, but more heavily streaked, with reduced greenish and yellow; bare parts duller. **Imm** has various stages between juv and ad, e.g. first-year male has duller facial marks and streaked body-sides; possibly does not reach ad plumage until second-/third-year (further study required).
Voice: Frequent call a simple high-pitched *si* (often repeated); song described as plaintive repetition of 2–3 phrases *peeoo-pay-oo-payoo* (Woods 1988).
Size: 14.5–15.0 cm, weight 24.8–35.0 g.
Similar species: Inexperienced observers may confuse females of this species with Correndera Pipit, though in flight the yellow outertail feathers provide a ready distinction and on the ground note their different bill structures. Outside our region observers should be aware of possibility of confusion with Yellow-bridled Finch *Melanodera xanthogramma*.

Distribution and biology

Distribution, movements and population: Extreme S South America, from c.47°S in Chile and Argentina to northern Tierra del Fuego, moving to coasts in winter, and the Falklands, where it occurs to at least 150 m and the population was estimated at 7000–14,000 pairs in 1983–93.
Diet and feeding: Inconspicuously picks seeds from ground or from seeding heads of grass.
Social behaviour: Pairs territorial around nest and form from mid-Jul. Flocks of up to 1000 (more commonly 6–25) from Dec, when some pairs are still breeding.
Breeding biology: Breeds mid-Sep to late Dec. Nest of fine grasses placed on ground, usually in grass or crevice, occasionally atop tussac grass, and lined with down or feathers. Female responsible for most construction. Clutch of 3–4 pale blue-grey or green eggs. Probably double-brooded.

Conservation Until recently listed as Near Threatened due to ongoing decline in mainland population (which is even locally extirpated) caused by overgrazing, but remains reasonably common and widespread in the Falklands.
Taxonomy Two races: nominate in the Falklands and *princetoniana*, which is slightly smaller and has considerably more yellow in wing, in South America. Plumage closely recalls Gough Bunting.

Gough Bunting *Rowettia goughensis*   Plate 22

Identification
Confusion risks: None.
Main characters: Chunky, bright green finch with deep-based bill. Plumage variation pronounced. All have dark bare parts. **Ad** male olive-green with ill-defined yellowish forehead and supercilium, and prominent black bib and lores. Greenish breast grades into yellowish abdomen; flight feathers blackish, coverts and tertials fringed whitish-yellow. Female duller, more olive-green and buffy-olive, with fainter dark face marks, but differences not always obvious. **Juv** rusty-brown and orange-buff, heavily streaked dark brown, usually except throat. **Imm**: various stages between juv and ads; possibly not reaching adulthood until second-/third-year.
Voice: Song, far-carrying high-pitched *tseeeeeuuu*. Female often responds with high *chissik* (P. Ryan). Watson (1975) described a penetrating *tissik*; a soft *pseep* while feeding.
Size: 16–18 cm.
Similar species: None.

Distribution and biology
Distribution, movements and population: Endemic to Gough, where fairly common to 800 m, especially above 600 m, in wet heath and feldmark; also along sea cliffs, but rare in fernbush. An estimated 1500 pairs (1991).
Diet and feeding: Primarily invertebrates, but also fruit, grass seeds and even scavenges broken eggs and dead birds.
Social behaviour: Few data.
Breeding biology: Breeds Sep–Dec. Cup-shaped nest placed on ground, within or under vegetation, usually on steep slopes or cliffs. Female alone incubates (mostly 2 pale blue, speckled brown, eggs): both sexes provision chicks (fledge at 20–26 days old).
Conservation Vulnerable. Population still decreasing due to egg and chick predation by introduced mice, whilst arrival of rats is a constant threat to be averted at all costs.
Taxonomy Monotypic.

Gough Bunting Rowettia goughensis *is rather large and chunky and exhibits gradual and variable plumage maturation (but rather weak sexual dimorphism in ads): left bird possibly dull ad male, being brighter greenish-yellow than females (though differences not always clear-cut); imm (middle) rather plain, lacking ad facial pattern or heavy streaking of juv (right). Some may attain full ad plumage only in second-/third-year, and some may breed in imm or intermediate plumages. Gough: middle photo, Sep, 2001 © Peter Ryan; others Mar 2006. © Hadoram Shirihai.*

Inaccessible/Tristan Bunting
Nesospiza acunhae   Plate 22

Identification

Confusion risks: Unlikely to overlap with similar Nightingale *N. questi* and Grosbeak Buntings *N. wilkinsi*.
Main characters: Almost uniform olive-green above but yellower below. Sex differences not always clear, but age-related variation can be. **Ad** male has ill-defined yellowish forehead and supercilium, even paler eye surround, and dark streaks mainly on mantle, with pale-fringed wings (especially tertials). Cleaner yellowish throat and duskier breast and flanks. Bare parts mainly dark grey. Female greyer and duller, and upperparts more heavily streaked. **Juv** buff-brown above and yellowish below, and characteristically heavily streaked dark brown. **Imm**: various stages between juv and ad; reportedly attains ad plumage only as second-/third-year.
Voice: Song simple and melodious; 3–4 repeated twittering notes or *chickory-chikky*, followed by wheezy *tweeyer*; recent study on Inaccessible suggests deeper and slower song in larger billed form.
Size: 17–21 cm.
Similar species: None in range.

Distribution and biology

Distribution, movements and population: Restricted to Inaccessible, where currently c.10,000 pairs. Three races occupy different altitudes and habitats, but young from higher elevations may descend to coastal areas in winter.
Diet and feeding: Seeds, fruits and invertebrates, but clear preferences amongst different races, e.g. large-billed form takes mainly fruit in *Phylica arborea* woodland.
Social behaviour: Mainly alone or in pairs.
Breeding biology: Open, oval or circular nest built by female, 0–120 cm above ground, in tussock; Nov–Jan. Lays 1–2 pale blue eggs with brownish-purple spotting. Incubation by female, 17–18 days. Both sexes tend young, which fledge at c.19 days.
Conservation Vulnerable. Population considered stable on Inaccessible. A small-billed form was 'common' on Tristan da Cunha, but now extirpated. Alien plants may be adversely affecting quality of favoured woodlands, and species is at permanent risk from accidental introduction of mammalian predators. Nonetheless, access to Inaccessible is strictly controlled.
Taxonomy Three subspecies in different habitats: *N. a. acunhae* in lowlands of Inaccessible, 'Lowland Bunting' (and, apparently, formerly on Tristan, the so-called 'Tristan Bunting'), with *N. a. fraseri* on upland plateau of Inaccessible ('Upland Bunting'), both of them smaller, weaker billed forms, though *fraseri* averages proportionately larger and thinner billed, and is more vivid yellow. Race *dunnei* ('Dunn's Bunting') of *Phylica* woodland on Inaccessible is distinctly larger billed (and males quite vividly coloured). Latter formerly considered within Grosbeak Bunting, but very recently P. Ryan *et al.* have removed it to *N. acunhae*. Relationships between races on Inaccessible (which apparently hybridize extensively), and

Fresh-plumaged male Inaccessible Bunting Nesospiza acunhae, *probably of the drab nominate race, 'Lowland Bunting', which occurs in lowlands and on coasts of Inaccessible. Inaccessible I, Mar 2006. © Hadoram Shirihai.*

Fresh-plumaged female Inaccessible Bunting Nesospiza acunhae, *probably nominate, is duller and streakier than male. Inaccessible I, Mar 2006. © Hadoram Shirihai.*

Male Inaccessible Buntings Nesospiza acunhae: on left race fraseri *('Upland Bunting') of the upland plateau (Ringeye Valley) showing characteristic thinner bill and vivid yellow underparts; centre: hybrid, note intermediate bill size (Denstone Hill); right: thick-billed race* dunnei *('Dunn's Bunting'), of* Phylica *woodland (Dragons Teeth, near West Road), Inaccessible I, Nov 2004. © Peter Ryan.*

taxonomic status of Nightingale and Grosbeak Buntings, are subject to ongoing behavioural and molecular research. Taxonomic status of recently extinct 'Tristan Bunting' also requires verification.

Nightingale Bunting *Nesospiza questi*   Plate 22

Identification

Confusion risks: Grosbeak Bunting *N. wilkinsi*.

Main characters: Virtually identical to small-billed forms of Inaccessible Bunting *N. acunhae*. Especially ad male, similar to brighter yellow male race *fraseri* on Inaccessible ('Upland Bunting'), but averages smaller.

Voice: Song a sharp and high-pitched, repeated *whit-wheu whit-wheu*; wheezy *tweeyer* and querulous whistles.

Size: 16–18 cm.

Similar species: Grosbeak Bunting larger and chunkier, with massive bill, but main confusion risk is potential interspecific hybrids. Note that Inaccessible Bunting appears to occasionally wander to Nightingale.

Distribution and biology

Distribution, movements and population: Occurs throughout Nightingale, Middle and Stoltenhoff, with a total of c.4,000 pairs.

Diet and feeding: Mostly forages on ground and in foliage, for seeds, fruits and invertebrates.

Social behaviour: Few data; occurs singly or in pairs.

Breeding biology: Season, Oct–Jan, otherwise presumably mostly as Inaccessible Bunting, but fewer data.

Conservation Presumably mostly as Inaccessible Bunting.

Taxonomy Previously considered a race of Tristan Bunting, with nominate *acunhae* on Inaccessible (and formerly mainland Tristan), and *questi* on Nightingale, Middle and Stoltenhoff, but other workers regard extinct population on Tristan da Cunha to be *questi*. Birds with apparently intermediate bill dimensions observed on Nightingale proven to be Inaccessible Buntings (P. Ryan pers. comm.). *Nesospiza* is most closely related to South American finches (Thraupini).

Grosbeak Bunting *Nesospiza wilkinsi*   Plate 22

Identification

Confusion risks: Nightingale Bunting *N. questi*.

Main characters: Massive, markedly conical bill; generally greenish above, and paler, mainly yellow, below. Sexes mostly alike, but young differ obviously. **Ad** male has yellow face and throat, vague yellow supercilium and forehead. Underparts yellowish-green with faint darker streaking on belly and flanks. Bare parts mainly blackish-grey, but base of lower mandible paler grey. Female

Nightingale Bunting Nesospiza questi, male that has almost completed moult. Nightingale I, Mar 2003. © Hadoram Shirihai.

Fresh-plumaged female Nightingale Bunting Nesospiza questi: duller and streakier than male. Nightingale I, Mar 2003. © Hadoram Shirihai.

Male Grosbeak Bunting Nesospiza wilkinsi: large, with markedly stout and conical bill (base of lower mandible paler grey). A threatened species: only 50 pairs survive. Nightingale I. © Peter Ryan.

generally duller and often slightly streakier. **Juv** olive-grey above and dull yellowish below, heavily streaked dark brown. **Imm** varies; ad plumage apparently attained in second-/third-year.
Voice: Resembles *N. acunhae*, but a more repeated flute-like whistling, *tweet-tweeyer* (Watson 1975) and perhaps deeper, slower and harsher than latter, e.g. *whut-prreu whut-prreu* (P. Ryan).
Size: 20–22 cm.
Similar species: Nightingale Bunting smaller, with smaller bill, brighter unstreaked yellow underparts, and more vivid greenish and finer streaked upperparts.

Distribution and biology
Distribution, movements and population: Restricted to *Phylica* woodland on Nightingale, where perhaps just 50 pairs (Ryan 2007).
Diet and feeding: Searches canopy of *Phylica* for seeds and fruit; also forages in tussock grass and ferns for invertebrates.
Social behaviour: Few data; usually alone or in pairs.
Breeding biology: Breeds Nov–Jan, with nests placed close to ground. Mean clutch 1.86.
Conservation Vulnerable. Long-feared arrival of alien mammals, and plants, potentially disastrous, whilst storm damage to *Phylica* woodland may negatively affect food supplies.
Taxonomy Monotypic: Ryan *et al.* (2007) removed race *dunnei* ('Dunn's Bunting') to within Inaccessible Bunting *N. acunhae*.

Long-tailed Meadowlark *Sturnella loyca*   Plate 22

Identification
Confusion risks: None in range.

Main characters: Unmistakable medium-sized terrestrial bird; within our region confined to the Falklands, where represented by the endemic race *falklandica*. The largest and longest tailed of its genus; bill conspicuously long, slightly decurved and sharp-pointed. **Ad** male scaled brown and streaked blackish on upperparts, blackish head-sides with prominent rose-red supercilium becoming white behind eye. Wing-bend and throat to chest brilliant red, grading into blackish lower belly (when fresh, underparts variably fringed whitish). Bill whitish, and eye and legs dark. Flight and tail feathers brown, barred black; in flight has white underwing-coverts. Female has all-whitish supercilium and throat, with rest of underparts pale rosy-red to mainly greyish, streaked dusky; bill greyer. **Juv** resembles female but browner with largely buffy-brown, dark-streaked underparts and narrow central pink streak on breast; bill shorter.
Voice: Flight call a typically high-pitched and often explosive *cheeoo*; song given by both sexes is delivered from ground, a perch or in flight, and is harsh and powerful, alternately rising and falling (Woods 1988).
Size: 24.0–25.5 cm, wing 11.4–13.1 cm, weight 67–131 g. Female markedly smaller (and often lighter), with apparently no overlap in wing length and little in tail length in *falklandica* (sample size small).
Similar species: None.

Distribution and biology
Distribution, movements and population: Lowlands to 2500 m, in Chile from Atacama south and Argentina from Jujuy and Buenos Aires south to Tierra del Fuego, and the Falklands, where the population was estimated to be 6000–10,000 pairs in 1983–93. Some evidence of austral migration in Argentina.
Diet and feeding: Principally invertebrates, including beetles, earthworms and larvae, dug from turf, prodding and opening the bill wide; digs up potatoes and makes substantial holes in them. Also takes grain from horse droppings.
Social behaviour: In pairs or family groups, and forms clustered territories. Flocks of up to 60 gather from Dec and disperse in Jul. Song given year-round.
Breeding biology: Breeds in late Aug–late Nov (until at least Jan on mainland, once in May in Chile), female builds nest of dry grass, well hidden on ground or in tussac grass, and incubates the 2–4 (3–5) blue-white eggs, blotched purple and black. Both parents feed young and probably raise two broods per season.
Conservation Not globally threatened, being very adaptable and persisting in close proximity to settlements.
Taxonomy Four races described in South America; *falklandica* in the Falklands is the largest, with the longest bill.

Ad male Long-tailed Meadowlark Sturnella loyca, Falklands, Dec 1990. © René Pop.

Ad female Long-tailed Meadowlark Sturnella loyca, Falklands, Jan 1991. © René Pop.

Endemic and indigenous non-passerines of New Zealand's subantarctic islands

The following accounts (and Plates 23–24) cover the indigenous land- and shorebird endemics and specialities breeding on New Zealand's subantarctic islands. A wide variety of species appears here, encompassing several different orders and families, from herons to waders. Other near-passerines, and passerines, are described thereafter and illustrated by Plates 25–26. Other non-passerines endemic to the region, including tubenoses, shags, skuas, gulls and terns are described and illustrated elsewhere in the book. The following accounts and plates do not treat introduced or species not native to New Zealand that have colonized the area, such as Black Swan *Cygnus atratus* and Mallard *Anas platyrhynchos*. Further information on all breeding birds in the region is presented in the island accounts and the relevant tables.

White-faced Heron *Ardea novaehollandiae*   Plate 23

Identification
Confusion risks: Could only be confused with vagrant Eastern Reef Egret *A. sacra*.
Main characters: Medium-sized, slim-bodied grey heron, with distinctive white face in ad. Bill fairly long, slender and slightly decurved. Occurs both on coasts and inland. Flight typically slow and rather high. **Ad** breeding predominantly pale blue-grey, with conspicuous white face reaching forehead, head- and throat-sides, pale foreneck and long, pale grey and whitish plumes above and cinnamon ones on lower neck and chest; most individuals possess slight ginger tone to chest year-round. Contrastingly darker remiges in flight (on both wing surfaces), when yellowish legs project beyond tail. Bill blackish-brown. Non-breeding ad generally duller and lacks plumes. **Juv** as non-breeding ad, but even duller, with browner bill and legs, usually lacks contrasting white face and has only ill-defined white throat and foreneck, and diffuse buff-cream hue to lower neck and belly.
Voice: Harsh *graaw* in flight and other loud, guttural and high-pitched calls.
Size: 66–68 cm, wing 28.2–34.1 cm, wingspan 106 cm, weight 450–880 g. Male generally larger, especially in wing length.
Similar species: Easily distinguished from similar-sized dark-morph Eastern Reef Egret, being slimmer, with paler, more bluish (not blackish slate-brown) plumage, darker bill and whitish feathering on face and foreneck. Both are vagrants to some New Zealand subantarctic islands, but within our region White-faced breeds only on the Chathams (see below), where no similar herons, including Eastern Reef Egret, are regular.

Distribution and biology
Distribution, movements and population: Coasts, marshes and lakes of Lesser Sundas, New Caledonia, Loyalty Is, Australia and Tasmania including outliers, S New Guinea, Norfolk and Lord Howe, New Zealand (breeding since 1941) and Chatham. Ranges widely including to Macquarie and other subantarctic islands of this region, Fiji and Vanuatu.
Diet and feeding: Broad range of aquatic vertebrates and invertebrates taken in typical heron manner.
Social behaviour: Few data, but often forms small loose flocks while feeding or roosting, but no information on pair-bond or mating system.

Breeding biology: Jun–Dec in New Zealand. Nests among boulders and on cliff ledges on Chatham. Builds rather flimsy stick nest, with male apparently responsible for collecting materials. Lays 3–5 pale bluish-green eggs, incubated 24–26 days by both sexes. Young probably fledge at c.43–46 days.
Conservation Not globally threatened. First recorded in New Zealand in mid-19th century, but bred only from early 1940s. Thereafter became widespread on both islands and a resident population established on Chatham in 1966.
Taxonomy Monotypic.

Auckland Teal
Anas [aucklandica] aucklandica   Plate 23

Identification
Confusion risks: None in range.
Main characters: Flightless, small round-bodied duck. **Ad** predominantly warm brown. Male has narrow white eye-ring and glossy greenish wash to head and indistinctly on (small and obscured) speculum. Bill blue-black and legs dark yellowish-brown. Eclipse male/female similar but plumage entirely warm brown, green hue reduced or lacking, while former often has distinctive darker mottled breast, and latter generally paler underparts with reduced white eye-ring. **Juv** (and **imm**) as non-breeding ad, but even duller. See photo p. 495.
Voice: Described (for entire complex) as soft, high-pitched wheezy whistles and popping calls by males, and low quacks and growls by females.
Size: 48 cm, wing 12.0–13.9 cm, weight 375–620 g. Male averages larger in all measurements, especially wing length.
Similar species: Very similar to Campbell Teal *A. [a.] nesiotis* (which see), also superficially resembles non-male plumages of Chestnut *A. castanea* and Brown Teals *A. chlorotis*, but no overlap with either.

Distribution and biology
Distribution, movements and population: Restricted to Auckland Is (see conservation).
Diet and feeding: Feeds at dusk and by night in peaty creeks, coastal platforms and in kelp beds, searching seaweed for invertebrates and algae.

Female Auckland Teal Anas [aucklandica] aucklandica *with chick. Auckland, Dec 1999. © Hadoram Shirihai.*

Social behaviour: Roosts communally by day, sometimes up to 200 m inland along small streams.

Breeding biology: Dec–Feb. Nest well-hidden bowl of grass. Lays 3–5 cream eggs, incubated for c.30 days by female alone. Young fledge in 50–55 days. Breeding success low.

Conservation Considered Vulnerable, with a stable population of 600–2000 individuals restricted to seven islands in Auckland group. Absent from main Auckland island due to presence of introduced cats and pigs.

Taxonomy Until recently *aucklandica*, including *nesiotis*, was treated within Brown Teal (*chlorotis*, a rare New Zealand endemic, principally restricted to Great Barrier I), but the two flightless forms have subsequently gained general acceptance as a single species, though a recent genetic study has demonstrated that *nesiotis* and *aucklandica* each demand specific recognition, at least under the Phylogenetic Species Concept, a view that has gained some acceptance within conservation planning. They are treated as allospecies here.

Campbell Teal *Anas [aucklandica] nesiotis* Plate 23

Identification

Confusion risks: None in range.

Main characters: Flightless, small round-bodied duck. Generally very similar to Auckland Teal *A. [a.] aucklandica*, also in plumage variation in relation to age, sex and season. See below for main differences between them.

Voice: No specific information for this form.

Size: wing 12.8–13.3 cm, weight 315–500 g. Extreme paucity of mensural data prevents analysis of any sex-related differences.

Similar species: Very similar to Auckland Teal but has more prominent, broader white eye-ring and apparently differs in behaviour (see below). Also superficially resembles non-male plumages of Chestnut *A. castanea* and Brown Teals *A. chlorotis*, but no overlap with either.

Distribution and biology

Distribution, movements and population: Restricted to Campbell (see conservation).

Diet and feeding: In contrast to Auckland Teal (which see), *nesiotis* inhabits dense tussac grass and is known to take insects and other invertebrates in captivity.

Social behaviour: Few data.

Breeding biology: Very few data available for *nesiotis*, though in captivity sometimes lays two clutches of 1–4 eggs.

Conservation Critical. Confined to Dent, off Campbell, with a population of 60–100 birds in 1990. Rats have had a highly detrimental effect. Rat eradication and captive-breeding programmes are now in place, and the first *nesiotis* were recently introduced to Codfish I, where they have now bred.

Taxonomy Monotypic (see comments under Auckland Teal).

Pacific Black Duck *Anas superciliosa* Plate 23

Identification

Confusion risks: Female-like plumages of Mallard *A. platyrhynchos*.

Main characters: Rather large and mainly grey-brown (sexes alike and seasonal variation limited). **Ad** has diagnostic and striking facial stripes, formed by dusky crown, eyestripe, white supercilium and broad whitish upper-cheek stripe bordered by streaky lower cheek band. Otherwise mottled greyish-brown with whitish-cream foreneck, extensive glossy greenish speculum, brownish eye, blue-grey bill and greenish-brown legs. **Juv** (and imm) hardly separable in the field.

Voice: Male gives soft, high-pitched *quek*, with louder quack by female; both strongly reminiscent of Mallard.

Size: 47–60 cm, wing 23–29 cm, wingspan 89 cm, weight 0.6–1.4 kg. Male generally larger in most measurements.

Similar species: Only superficially resembles non-male plumages of Mallard, and given good view when bold facial stripes and green (rather than blue) speculum should be noted, they are easily separated. Pacific Black Duck also averages smaller and slimmer than Mallard. Be aware, however, that Pacific Black Duck freely hybridizes with Mallard; the resultant offspring are paler with a less well-defined facial pattern, greyish bill, browner legs and bluer or intermediate-coloured speculum.

Ad Campbell Teal Anas [aucklandica] nesiotis *is very similar to Auckland Teal* A. [a.] aucklandica, *except in having a broader white eye-ring and being smaller, but much overlap and individual variation. Codfish I, New Zealand. © Peter Reese.*

Plate 23 Endemic and indigenous non-passerines of New Zealand's subantarctic islands

New Zealand Falcon ad. ♀
(p. 313)

Large and long-tailed; blackish-brown hood with broad moustachial; streaked and barred below; young overall more uniform and darker brown

White-faced Heron breeding ad.
(p. 309)

Pale grey plumage, white face and foreneck

Pacific Black Duck ad. ♂
(p. 310)

Bold facial stripes on buffy head/foreneck; green speculum

Swamp Harrier ad. ♂
(p. 312)

Campbell Teal ad. ♂ eclipse
(p. 310)

As Auckland Teal, but confined to Campbell. Full-plumaged male is similarly green on head; note broader white eye-ring

Long tail and broad wings (held in deep V in flight); paler facial marks, ginger below and bold whitish uppertail-covert patch; female as male but lacks prominent pale flight feathers of older males

Campbell Teal ad. ♀

Auckland Teal ad. ♂
(p. 309)

Flightless, small round-bodied duck; narrow white eye-ring

Auckland Merganser ad.
(p. 312)

Recently extinct on Auckland Island

Distribution and biology

Distribution, movements and population: Marshes, lakes, ponds and streams from W Indonesia to New Guinea, Admiralty Is, Louisiade and Bismarck archipelagos, Solomons, Vanuatu, New Caledonia, Loyalty Is, Fiji, Tonga, Samoa and Cook, the Society and Tubuai Is, and south to New Zealand, Australia and Tasmania, Kermadec, Chatham, Snares, Auckland, Campbell and Macquarie (principally resident on subantarctic islands). Overall population probably at least c.10,000 pairs but perhaps only a few hundred pairs in our region.

Diet and feeding: Principally aquatic vegetation, including seeds ingested with animal matter (e.g. insects and crustaceans), taken by upending.

Social behaviour: Solitary nester, but generally gregarious. Monogamous and forms sustained, sometimes life-long, pair-bonds. Largely active at twilight on Macquarie.

Breeding biology: Few data from our region, but elsewhere Aug–Jan in New Zealand. Usually nests in hole in tree, but also on ground, hidden by dense vegetation. Lays 7–14 pale cream or creamy-white eggs, incubated 26–32 days by female alone. Young fledge at 52–66 days and are entirely dependent on female for parental care.

Conservation Not globally threatened, but heavily hunted (particularly in Australia) and, in some areas, extent of hybridization with Mallard constitutes a significant threat to the integrity of this species' gene pool.

Taxonomy Considered monotypic by *HANZAB*, but other authors have recognised three weakly defined races: the nominate in the New Zealand region, *rogersi* in Australia, New Guinea and Indonesia, and *pelewensis* in the SW Pacific.

Auckland Merganser *Mergus australis*   Plate 23

Identification

Confusion risks: Extinct, probably since 1902 (see below); no similar species within former range.

Main characters: Medium-sized, shag-like bird that formerly inhabited coasts and was only capable of flying short distances. Sexes were possibly alike and seasonal plumage variation limited. **Ad** (both sexes) had red-brown neck and head, latter with quite long wispy crest at rear, otherwise chiefly dark grey-brown above and greyish, mottled whitish below. Bill was characteristically long and slender, prominently serrated along cutting edges and mainly dark brown, with reddish-orange lower mandible; legs described as orange. In flight white upperwing patch was visible. **Juv** (and **imm**) possibly hardly separable.

Voice: Undescribed.

Size: No information.

Similar species: None in former range.

Distribution and biology

Distribution, movements and population: Known with certainty only from the Auckland group, with a doubtful record from Campbell, and sub-fossil deposits indicate that a similar (or the same) form existed until comparatively recently on the Chathams, South and Stewart Is, New Zealand. No information on former population.

Diet and feeding: Apparently fish and molluscs.

Social behaviour: Sedentary, but otherwise unknown.

Breeding biology: No information.

Conservation Extinct. Only discovered in 1840, the last specimen was taken 1902, though uncertainty surrounds potential subsequent reports in 1905 and 1909. Appears to have died out as the result of introduction of alien mammals, as well as hunting by pre-Europeans and Europeans.

Auckland Merganser Mergus australis *is one of the recent extinctions from New Zealand's subantarctic islands.* © Peter Reese.

Taxonomy Presumably monotypic, though see Distribution, movements and population.

Swamp Harrier *Circus approximans*   Plate 23

Identification

Confusion risks: None.

Main characters: Typical long-winged and long-tailed harrier, with proportionally broad wings, in flight often held in deep V, and long-fingered primaries (almost buzzard-like). Most older ads can be sexed and young may be aged in the field. **Ad** male generally greyish-brown above and cream-cinnamon finely streaked dark below, with paler face, especially around ear-coverts, and bold whitish uppertail-covert patch. Usually becomes paler with age, when primaries and secondaries almost silvery-white, conspicuously paler than wing-coverts. Both flight and tail feathers barred darker, but reduce with age. Ad female as male but lacks prominent pale flight feathers of older males, though some older females can appear almost as pale; in general, body plumage browner than male. Eye and legs brighter yellow in most males than females. **Juv** (and younger **imm**) usually has more uniform, darker and warmer reddish-brown plumage, noticeably on underparts and face; also whitish nape patch, buffish uppertail-covert patch and prominent white primary patch, especially contrasting (with darker secondaries) from below; eye initially dark.

Voice: Main calls a whistle and during display flights male gives repeated high-pitched *kee-a*, and female a *kee-o* in response.

Size: 50–61 cm, wing 39.1–45.5 cm, wingspan 121–142 cm, weight 0.39–1.08 kg. Female significantly larger and heavier.

Similar species: None in range.

Distribution and biology

Distribution, movements and population: Wooded savannas, open marshes and wet grasslands of Australia, Tasmania, New Zealand, New Caledonia, Loyalty Is, Fiji, Tonga, Vanuatu, and Chatham (where common and widespread) and Kermadec. Vagrant to Macquarie, several of New Zealand's subantarctic islands, Norfolk and Lord Howe Is, and introduced to the Society Is.

Diet and feeding: Seizes mammals, birds and their eggs, reptiles, amphibians, fish and carrion in typical harrier fashion, dropping to ground or surface of water during slow quartering flights.

Social behaviour: Generally solitary but sometimes polygynous, and migrants may move in small parties.

Breeding biology: Breeds Sep–Dec, constructing a platform of sticks, grass and similar material on ground or above water in dense cover. Lays 2–7 (most usually 3–4) eggs, incubated 31–34 days and young fledge at 43–46 days, becoming fully independent 4–6 weeks later.

Conservation Local declines reported due to wetland drainage and vulnerable to human disturbance. Still common in suitable habitat.

Taxonomy Previously considered polytypic, with *gouldi* in New Guinea, Australia and New Zealand, but latter form recently demonstrated to be a synonym of *approximans*. Has been considered conspecific with Eurasian Marsh Harrier *C. aeruginosus*.

New Zealand Falcon
Falco novaeseelandiae Plate 23

Identification

Confusion risks: None.

Main characters: Distinctive, rather large endemic falcon of New Zealand, breeding in our region only on Auckland. Broad pointed wings and proportionately long tail. Fast flight, with rapid wingbeats and when soaring never holds wings in obvious V. Sexes alike, except in size (see below). **Ad** has blackish-brown crown, ear-coverts and broad moustachial, with narrow rufous supercilium. Generally greyish-brown, faintly barred cream-cinnamon above, and whitish, extensively and finely dark-streaked from throat downward, and boldly barred on flanks. Neck- and body-sides, abdomen, thighs and undertail-coverts tinged warm rufous. Flight feathers barred darker and tail almost uniformly dark. Bill and eye blackish, and cere and legs yellow. **Juv** (and younger **imm**) overall more uniform and darker brown, noticeably on underparts, with only throat paler; head pattern indistinct and bare parts mainly greyish

Voice: Main call a loud and far-carrying, rapid *kek-kek-kek*.

Size: 41–48 cm, wing 22.6–32.8 cm, wingspan 66–91 cm, weight 252–594 g. Female larger and heavier.

Similar species: None in range.

Distribution and biology

Distribution, movements and population: Endemic to New Zealand, on North and South Is, Stewart I (and outliers) and Auckland. Frequents forested areas and has occasionally wandered elsewhere within our region to Chatham. Total population recently estimated at 4000 pairs, of which the form breeding on Auckland and Stewart numbers just 200 pairs, of which ten were on Auckland in 1990.

Diet and feeding: Principally takes birds (including many introduced species, though prions and other small petrels are chief prey on Aucklands), as well as small mammals, insects, lizards and, occasionally, carrion. Hunts in typical dashing falcon flight, but also on ground and even robs bird nests situated in bushes.

Social behaviour: Monogamous and may form long-term pair-bonds, but evidence limited. Sedentary and usually observed in pairs or family groups.

Breeding biology: Sep–Dec. Nest a simple depression on cliff, steep hillside or occasionally in tree. Lays 2–4 eggs, incubated 29–35 days and chicks fledge at 32–35 days, becoming fully independent 70–90 days later.

Conservation Near Threatened. Perhaps still declining as result of forest clearance, illegal shooting by farmers and others, and possums which take eggs.

Taxonomy Monotypic: three morphologically and ecologically different populations (on North and in NW South Is; in Fiordland; on Stewart, the Auckland group and in the east of South I) are not recognized taxonomically.

Purple Swamphen (Pukeko)
Porphyrio porphyrio Plate 24

Identification

Confusion risks: None.

Main characters: Large-bodied, long-legged swamphen, which in our region breeds only on Chatham. Sexes alike, with little seasonal/plumage variation, though juv distinctive. **Ad** has red legs, eye, bill and 'shield', otherwise predominantly deep glossy blue, with blackish head, upperparts and upperwings, and contrastingly white undertail-coverts, obvious while walking or in flight. **Juv** (and younger **imm**) distinctly duller, being mainly dark brown on head and upperparts, and buffish-brown with limited blue suffusion below; also duller, pale orange-red bare parts.

Voice: Main call a loud, far-carrying screech.

Size: 38–50 cm, wing 25.1–29.4 cm, weight 0.68–1.31 kg. Female generally smaller, but differences in most measurements slight and much overlap.

Similar species: None in range.

Distribution and biology

Distribution, movements and population: Purple Swamphen is patchily distributed across much of the southern Old World (and has recently been recorded in Florida). The form occurring in our region is *P. p. melanotus*, which occurs from New Guinea, over much of Australia (except interior), Tasmania, New Zealand and Chatham. An occasional visitor to Campbell and islands in the S Pacific Ocean.

Diet and feeding: Principally vegetarian, takes roots, shoots, leaves and flowers of aquatic and semi-aquatic plants, but also variety of small animal and insect prey, e.g. molluscs, crabs, amphibians, small birds and their eggs and young, and small rodents. Forages at edge of cover, on shorelines and in shallow water, but rarely swims.

Social behaviour: Unlike other forms of the species, typically lives in communal groups.

Breeding biology: In New Zealand nests Aug–Feb, mainly Sep–Dec. Constructs large nest of dead stems and leaves concealed within dense vegetation. Lays 2–6 eggs, with several females of group laying in same nest. Incubation 23–27 days by both sexes and helpers, and young fledge at 60 days, becoming independent at 6–8 weeks. May lay up to three replacement clutches.

Conservation The form in our region, *melanotus*, is widespread and locally common in Australia and New Zealand, and appears to be increasing as a result of forest clearance in New Zealand.

Taxonomy Traditionally considered polytypic, with 14 subspecies having been described. However, recent work by Trewick (1997) and Sangster (1998) suggests that at least six subspecies-groups within the complex demand species status, with Australian Swamphen *P.* [*p.*] *melanotus* consisting of the nominate, *melanopterus*, *samoensis*, *bellus*, *chathamensis* and *pelewensis*.

Weka *Gallirallus australis* Plate 24

Identification

Confusion risks: None.

Main characters: Huge (male) to large (female) dry-land flightless rail, in our region breeding only on Chatham (see below). Historically introduced from mainland New Zealand, but now among the most abundant species on the main island and has important impact on other bird species (see below). Sexes alike and little age-related/seasonal plumage variation. Habitually runs very quickly. **Ad** predominantly dull olive-brown, with dark-

streaked upperparts and upperwings, and has some dark bars on latter and body-sides. Head rather featureless, much as upperparts, but slight pale supercilium. Pale brown from foreneck to mid-belly, merging with brownish breast-sides, abdomen and vent (where slightly barred); tail quite long. Strong pale orange-pink bill. Legs and eye orange-brown. **Juv** (and younger imm) generally as ad, but duller, tinged more olive-grey above and paler below; bare parts also duller. Fledgling appears slimmer with weaker bill. See photo p. 487.
Voice: Main call a loud, far-carrying repeated *coo-eet*, rising in pitch.
Size: 50–60 cm (male), 46–50 cm (female), wing 15.5–20.2 cm, weight 0.53–1.60 kg. Male distinctly larger and, especially, heavier, but considerable overlap in many measurements.
Similar species: None in range.

Distribution and biology
Distribution, movements and population: North and South I (New Zealand), and Chatham (introduced), where frequents forest, tussac grassland, scrub and beaches. Unsuccessfully introduced to the Auckland group and introduced (but now extirpated) on Macquarie. Mass migrations reported on several occasions in mainland New Zealand. Population currently in strong decline and estimated at 100,000–150,000 birds, of which 38,000–58,000 on Chatham.
Diet and feeding: An omnivorous scavenger, taking variety of molluscs, crustaceans, spiders, insects and their larvae, some birds, mammals to the size of rabbits, and leaves, seeds, shoots of grasses and aquatic plants. Both crepuscular and diurnal, and feeds mainly on ground. Its catholic diet and ability to kill quite large birds has caused problems for many native species, especially on islands where it was introduced as a food source.
Social behaviour: Monogamous and often territorial year-round. Pair-bonds often permanent, though polygamy recorded twice.
Breeding biology: Few specific data from subantarctic islands. Elsewhere season Aug–Mar. Nest of sedges, twigs and moss, constructed largely by male, within tussac grass, in burrows, under logs or shelter of tree, as well as in outhouses. Lays 3–6 glossy pinkish to white eggs, incubated 20–28 days by both sexes. Young fledge at c.56 days, but may not be fully independent until 108 days.
Conservation Vulnerable. Generally uncommon and populations subject to marked fluctuations. Readily colonizes new areas. Protected throughout its range, except Chatham, where hunters take large numbers (up to 5000 per annum). Introduced predators, poison bait and climate extremes (droughts and floods) considered main sources of local extinctions or declines. Surveys and translocations are planned.
Taxonomy Four subspecies recognised: *greyi* on North I, *australis* in the north and west of South I, *hectori* which is now confined to Chatham (where introduced; formerly also in east and interior of South I) and *scotti* on Stewart I.

Spotless Crake *Porzana tabuensis*   Plate 24

Identification
Confusion risks: None.
Main characters: Small, dark and rather elusive rail, which in our region breeds only on Chatham (see below). Sexes alike, with little age-related/seasonal variation. **Ad** largely bluish lead-grey on underparts, with whitish, dark-barred undertail-coverts, while upperparts and upperwings are dark brown and unstreaked. Rather thin, short blackish bill, and reddish legs and eye. **Juv** much as ad,

but duller, lacking blue gloss below (tinged greyer) and has whitish throat; eye and legs duller and browner.
Voice: Various calls, principally a loud sharp *pit-pit* and distinctive rolling *purrrrrrr*, decreasing in pitch.
Size: 15–18 cm, wing 7.8–9.2 cm, weight 21–58 g. Male larger and heavier, but considerable overlap in many measurements.
Similar species: None in range.

Distribution and biology
Distribution, movements and population: Philippines and New Guinea to much of Australia (except interior), Tasmania, New Zealand, Chatham, Kermadec and from the Carolines east to Marquesas, Tuamotu, and Society and Tubuai Is. No population estimates.
Diet and feeding: Omnivorous, taking variety of molluscs, crustaceans, spiders, insects and their larvae, eggs of some seabirds, and leaves, seeds, shoots of grasses and aquatic plants. Both crepuscular and diurnal.
Social behaviour: Monogamous and may pair for life. Territorial, perhaps year-round.
Breeding biology: In New Zealand breeds Aug–Jan, constructing shallow cup nest of grass and rushes in dense cover, often over water. Female may be principally responsible for nest building. Lays 3–4 eggs, incubated by both sexes for 19–22 days. Young fledge at c.40 days, but leave nest at 1–2 days (though perhaps dependent until 4–5 months old).
Conservation Considered widespread in New Zealand.
Taxonomy Three subspecies recognized: nominate on Philippines, New Caledonia and in SW Pacific, as well as in Australia, New Zealand and Chatham, with *edwardi* on New Guinea and *richardsoni* in Irian Jaya.

Auckland Island Rail
Dryolimnas [pectoralis] muelleri   Plate 24

Identification
Confusion risks: None in range.
Main characters: Relatively small, pale-coloured elusive rail. Within our region breeds only on Auckland group (see below). **Ad** has upperparts and upperwings to uppertail olive-brown, tinged cinnamon and streaked black, and crown, neck and head-sides pale rufous, with throat to breast grey and rest of underparts finely barred black and white. Legs yellow-brown, eye and long thin bill red. Sexes similar, but female duller with less red on head and neck. **Juv** overall duller, being tinged less rufous on head and browner below, with more pale streaking on crown and upperparts, darker bare parts and duller underparts barring.
Voice: Loud descending *crek* and whistle-like call, both uttered repeatedly; also variety of grunts and clicks.
Size: 17–21 cm, wing 7.6–8.5 cm, weight 63–100 g. No information concerning any sex-related mensural differences.
Similar species: None in range.

Distribution and biology
Distribution, movements and population: Restricted to Adams and Disappointment in the Auckland group, where it prefers coastal herb field, forest and tussac grass, and a stable population of c.2000 birds persists.
Diet and feeding: Apparently insects and other invertebrates.
Social behaviour: Few data. Active at night, but also, in summer, from just before sunrise to just after sunset. Flies very infrequently.
Breeding biology: Very few data, two well-hidden, cup-shaped

Plate 24 Endemic and indigenous non-passerines of New Zealand's subantarctic islands

New Zealand Snipe ad. (p. 318)

...und on some New ...aland subantarctic ...ands; considerable ...ial variation

Chatham Island Snipe ad. (p. 318)

Very compact, short bill; indistinct scaling above and slight barring below

Double-banded Plover breeding ad. ♂ (p. 316)

Broad chestnut and narrow black breast-bands; female duller with fainter pattern; breast markings mostly lost non-breeding and lacking in young

Spotless Crake ad. (p. 314)

Auckland Island Rail ad. (p. 314)

Head tinged rufous; barred black and white below; long thin red bill

Small, unstreaked dark and rather elusive rail (barred undertail-coverts)

Shore Plover ad. ♂ (p. 317)

Black forehead, face and throat (browner/fainter in female); red-orange bare parts

Weka ad. (p. 313)

Huge dry-land flightless rail; dark-streaked upperparts and some dark barring below; strong orange-pink bill

Black-and-white oystercatcher endemic to Chatham

Chatham Island Oystercatcher ad. (p. 316)

Purple Swamphen ad. (p. 313)

Masked Lapwing ad. ssp. *novaehollandiae* (p. 317)

Black-winged (White-headed) Stilt ad. (p. 316)

Black-and-white, long-legged stilt

...istinctive black ...ap/shoulder patch and ...n flight) remiges; vivid ...ellow facial marks ...reduced in young)

Large and long-legged; red legs, eye, bill and 'shield'; glossy blue plumage

nests found in Nov, suggest that eggs are usually laid Oct–Nov. Two cream eggs marked with brown to grey blotches.
Conservation Vulnerable. Both rail-inhabited islands are predator-free, but presence of feral cats, mice and pigs on Auckland must be considered a permanent risk. Both islands are nature reserves and part of a World Heritage Site.
Taxonomy Formerly considered a subspecies of widespread and geographically diverse Lewin's Rail *D. pectoralis* of Australia and New Guinea, but plumage differences and this form's extreme geographical isolation suggest species status is more appropriate (see Taylor & van Perlo 1998).

Chatham Island Oystercatcher
Haematopus chathamensis   Plate 24

Identification
Confusion risks: Both Pied *H. ostralegus* and pied phase of Variable Oystercatcher *H. unicolor* are similar, but infrequent overlap.
Main characters: Black-and-white oystercatcher endemic to Chatham. Sexes alike, with little age-related/seasonal plumage variation. **Ad** has jet black upperparts, head, breast and tail, with white underparts, red eye and long straight red bill. **Juv** (and **imm**) has black parts duller and browner, and bill pinker. Gradually acquires blacker plumage as second-/third-year. In flight all ages have white wingbar across upperwing-coverts. See photo p. 487.
Voice: Typical oystercatcher call, but appears higher pitched with shorter notes than congeners.
Size: 47–49 cm, wing 25.1–26.6 cm, 560–640 g. Female apparently larger and heavier, but comparatively few data.
Similar species: No overlap with other oystercatchers but has shorter bill and legs, and less smudged border to lower breast than Variable Oystercatcher. South Island Pied Oystercatcher *H. finschii*, which has occurred twice in Chatham group, has clean white uppertail-coverts and rump, sharp and slightly higher demarcation between white and black on underparts, slightly broader white wingbar, more white on underwing and is slightly smaller and less stocky, with a longer bill and less sturdy legs and feet.

Distribution and biology
Distribution, movements and population: Restricted to Chatham, where local feeding movements and short-distance juv dispersal noted. Population estimated at fewer than 200 individuals in 2000/1.
Diet and feeding: Takes molluscs, marine worms and other invertebrates, as well as small fish, on rocky shores and wave platforms, hammering through shells and probing and surface-picking for other prey.
Social behaviour: Ads appear to occupy breeding territory all year, but juvs and non-breeders may form small flocks on vacant shorelines.
Breeding biology: Breeds Oct–Mar, mostly Nov–Dec. Nest a shallow scrape protected by driftwood, rock or small bush. Lays 1–3 olive-grey eggs, incubated by both sexes for c.28 days. Chicks remain in nest for 1–2 days and then leave. Able to fly at seven weeks and to breed at two years.
Conservation Endangered. Population has increased markedly since 1970 due to predator control, nest manipulation, active protection and habitat management. Nonetheless, natural disasters, such as freak tides and storms, introduced mammalian predators, as well as trampling of nests by cattle and sheep, remain threats on some islands, and clearly, while protective measures are proving effective, these need to be continued.
Taxonomy Monotypic.

Black-winged (White-headed) Stilt
Himantopus himantopus   Plate 24

Identification
Confusion risks: No overlap with any congeners.
Main characters: Black-and-white, slim-bodied and disproportionately long-legged stilt. Within our region breeds only on Chatham. Sexes usually separable, but otherwise limited age-related/seasonal plumage variation. **Ad** male has jet black upperparts and wings, contrasting with white head, neck, underparts and tail, but most also have variable black on crown, hindneck and/or partial collar on lower neck, which is lacking or only very faint in female (which also has diagnostically browner wings and back). Long straight black bill; eye and long thin legs red. **Juv** closer to female, but has characteristic browner, buff-fringed upperparts and upperwings, and yellowish-green legs; also narrow white trailing edge to wing.
Voice: High-pitched piping notes and 'yelps' in alarm. Noisy in many situations.
Size: 33–40 cm, wing 19.7–24.6 cm, wingspan 61–73 cm, weight 138–205 g. Male larger than female in most measurements; also usually heavier.
Similar species: No similar species on Chatham.

Distribution and biology
Distribution, movements and population: Pan-continental (for broad ranges occupied by constituent taxa see below). In our region has occurred only on Chatham, with isolated records from New Zealand's subantarctic islands, Macquarie and the Falklands (records on latter involve *melanurus* with a recent record of *mexicanus*).
Diet and feeding: Aquatic and terrestrial invertebrates; also molluscs, crustaceans, insects and seeds taken while foraging (up to belly deep) in water or, more rarely, on land.
Social behaviour: Gregarious year-round. Monogamous, but pair-bonds last only one season.
Breeding biology: No specific data available from our region.
Conservation Not globally threatened and generally common.
Taxonomy Polytypic: nominate *himantopus* (including *ceylonensis*) in Eurasia and Africa, *leucocephalus* in Philippines, Indonesia, Australia and New Zealand, *mexicanus* in North America to N South America, *knudseni* in Hawaii and *melanurus* in C and S Andes and S South America. Sibley (1996) considered these to represent four species: *H. himantopus* (Black-winged Stilt), *H. leucocephalus* (White-headed Stilt), *H. mexicanus* (including *knudseni*) (Black-necked Stilt) and *H. melanurus* (White-backed Stilt).

Double-banded Plover
Charadrius bicinctus   Plate 24

Identification
Confusion risks: None in range.
Main characters: Medium-sized *Charadrius*, quite variable in plumage, geographically but mainly individually and strongly in relation to age/sex. Two distinct subspecies (see below). **Ad** male breeding mainly pale amber-brown above with white underparts marked by broad chestnut breast-band and thin black lower neck-band; dark or black line through lores, from eye along lower border of ear-coverts and on forecrown, bordering white forehead. Female not always clearly separable from less-advanced male, but most lack or have reduced black facial markings, and throat and breast-bands duller and narrower or faint. Short dark bill and yellowish grey-green legs. Non-breeding ad highly variable, black

and chestnut markings mostly lost but some remain at sides. **Juv** (and **imm**) as non-breeding ad, but retains (juv) paler fringed upperwing-coverts, and usually has some buff mottling on breast. All ages have narrow, rather indistinct pale wingbar across edge of upperwing-coverts and primary bases. See photo p. 495.
Voice: Mainly high-pitched, short loud *pit* notes and a fast rolling *che-ree-a-ree*.
Size: 18–21 cm, wing 12.9–13.3, wingspan 37–42 cm, weight 47–89 g. Much overlap in mensural data between the sexes.
Similar species: None on Auckland or Chatham.

Distribution and biology

Distribution, movements and population: Subspecies *exilis* confined to Auckland, where it breeds on Enderby and Adams (and formerly on main island), while nominate race occurs on Chatham and throughout much of New Zealand and its offshore satellites, with most from South I migrating to SE Australia in winter, and others moving north within New Zealand, but some as far as the SW Pacific.
Diet and feeding: Variety of terrestrial and aquatic invertebrates, taken in typical plover fashion, also some berries.
Social behaviour: Gregarious at roosts and often forms small flocks when feeding, but is also often territorial, especially when breeding.
Breeding biology: Few specific data for Auckland and Chathams populations. Elsewhere breeds Jul–Dec, laying 2–4 variable-coloured eggs in shallow scrape. Both sexes incubate for 25–27 days. Chicks quickly leave nest and become self-feeding, and fledge at 5–6 weeks.
Conservation Not globally threatened. Overall population c.50,000 individuals. Auckland population numbered 730 in 1989 (just 100–200 in early 1970s and increase perhaps largely attributable to greater availability of suitable breeding habitat following removal of grazing animals). Breeds at several localities on Chatham but no population estimates.
Taxonomy Two subspecies: nominate *bicinctus* throughout New Zealand and Chatham, and *exilis* on Auckland. Latter is plumper, heavier, longer legged than nominate, with the female having warmer brown upperparts and duller breast-bands.

Shore Plover *Thinornis novaeseelandiae*   Plate 24

Identification
Confusion risks: None.
Main characters: Small, stocky and distinctly patterned plover, now endemic to Chatham and among the rarest waders in the world. **Ad** male breeding has broad white diadem, black forehead, face and throat (brown and faintly patterned in female); otherwise crown and upperparts greyish-brown, and underparts white. Short black-tipped red bill, red eye-ring, black eye and short orange legs. **Juv** has dark bill and entirely dull brown upperparts, except short whitish supercilium. All ages have rather broad whitish wingbar across edge of secondary upperwing-coverts and primary bases.
Voice: Mainly high-pitched short *kleet* notes, and other calls during territorial disputes. See photo p. 488.
Size: 20 cm, wing 11.5–12.7 cm, weight 52–69 g. There appear to be no, or virtually no, differences in mensural data between the sexes.
Similar species: Wholly distinctive within limited range.

Distribution and biology

Distribution, movements and population: Inhabits wave platforms, marsh-turf and estuaries on South East and Mangere (Chatham).

Rarely wanders to other islands, though another group has recently been discovered on the Western Reef. Population fluctuates between 110 and 150 individuals. Recently introduced to Motuora I, in Hauraki Gulf (mid-1990s) and Portland I, Mahia Peninsula (1999).
Diet and feeding: Takes crustaceans, spiders, molluscs, insects and their larvae by gleaning and pecking tide-wrack, and foot-trembling on algae-covered rocks to disturb prey.
Social behaviour: Strongly territorial in breeding season, but forms small, loose flocks of up to 35 in winter.
Breeding biology: Two to three variably marked, pale buff eggs in mid-Oct to Jan and hidden beneath rock or dense vegetation. Incubation, by both sexes, lasts 28 days. Chicks fledge in 36–55 days and can breed at 2–3 years old.
Conservation Endangered. Cats and rats caused its extinction on South I, and removal of sheep from South East I, in 1961, has led to some loss of breeding habitat. Fire, storms, predation by skuas and other issues are threats, and limited success of translocation programme, due to dispersal and mortality caused by predators, is of concern.
Taxonomy Monotypic.

Masked Lapwing *Vanellus miles*   Plate 24

Identification
Confusion risks: None.
Main characters: Large, noisy and distinctly patterned plover, which within our region breeds only on Chatham. Rather limited seasonal, age- and sex-related plumage variation. **Ad** has pale greyish-brown upperparts and upperwing-coverts, the latter contrasting with blackish remiges in flight, underwing similar but coverts white (like underparts). Distinctive black cap and shoulder patch on lower hindneck, vivid yellow bill, facial patch and wattles. Longish pale pinkish-orange legs. **Juv** dull and has only restricted yellow on face, greyer legs and entirely pale brown upperparts, distinctly fringed buffish, and subterminally and narrowly barred dark.
Voice: Mainly high-pitched shrill *kleep* notes, and others when disturbed or in social contexts.
Size: 30–37 cm, wing 21.6–26.0 cm, wingspan 75–85 cm, weight 191–440 g. Broad overlap in mensural data between the sexes.
Similar species: None in range.

Distribution and biology

Distribution, movements and population: New Guinea to N, E and S Australia, Tasmania and New Zealand, including Chatham. Resident and dispersive; perhaps a regular non-breeding visitor to some parts of E Indonesia and numbers in coastal areas of Australia increase in autumn. Total population recently estimated at 287,000 birds, of which vast majority in Australia.
Diet and feeding: Principally insects, worms and spiders, with smaller proportion of molluscs, crustaceans, seeds and leaves, taken in typical plover fashion, but also by foot-trembling.
Social behaviour: Long-term monogamous and also highly faithful to breeding sites. Solitary breeder, but forms small parties immediately prior to breeding, which may play role in pair formation.
Breeding biology: Jun–late Nov in New Zealand. Depression in ground, lined with pebbles, usually in short grass and often near water. Lays 3–4 eggs, incubated 28–30 days. Young fledge at 6–7 weeks, but dependent for up to six months.
Conservation Not globally threatened. First bred in New Zealand in 1932 and range appears to be still expanding in this region.
Taxonomy Two subspecies recognized: nominate *miles* in New

317

Guinea and N Australia and *novaehollandiae* in E and SE Australia, Tasmania and New Zealand. Latter has smaller wattles and more extensive black cap reaching down hindneck to breast patches, but many intermediates known.

Chatham Island Snipe
Coenocorypha pusilla   Plate 24

Identification
Similar species: None.
Main characters: Endemic to Chatham group and among the rarest waders in the world. Short-legged and even smaller than similar New Zealand Snipe *C. aucklandica*. Very compact, with short thick bill. Limited seasonal, age- and sex-related plumage variation. **Ad** has typical snipe-like, dark brown and cream-buff stripes on crown and head-sides, while most of upperparts and upperwings are brown, tinged rufous, with scaly subterminal dark centres and buffy fringes, but pattern rather poorly defined. Lower breast and belly creamy-white, and rest of underparts have comparatively little barring, streaking and spotting. Female paler and less bright above. **Juv** has even less well-defined upperparts pattern, grey legs and bill base. See photo p. 486.
Voice: Male gives a *trerk trerk trerk…* loud call, in series of 5–15; also acoustic aerial displays at night, consisting of disyllabic whistles followed by non-vocal drumming. Various other notes, including a soft *chur* call, also given by female.
Size: 19–20 cm, wing 9.6–10.8 cm, wingspan 28–30 cm, weight 61–110 g. Very little difference between sexes.
Confusion risks: None.

Distribution and biology
Distribution, movements and population: Forest floor and scrub on South East, Mangere, Little Mangere and Star Keys in Chatham. Largely sedentary, though some inter-island movements reported. Total population previously estimated at 900–1050 pairs, with majority on South East, but 2001 estimate of only 1300 ads based on a more accurate technique.
Diet and feeding: Invertebrates in soil, including larvae and pupae, probing damp soil up to entire length of bill and swallowing prey whole.
Social behaviour: Little studied. Solitary, or in pairs with chick, and territorial, though may breed at comparatively high density, especially in forested areas. Apparently monogamous but can form small loose flocks in non-breeding season.
Breeding biology: Lays 2–3 pinkish-brown, variably marked eggs, in sheltered, leaf-filled but unlined nest, Sep–Mar. Sexes share incubation and other duties, but ads usually each take responsibility for one chick. Chicks fed for 2–3 weeks, able to fly at 21 days and become wholly independent at 41 days.
Conservation Vulnerable. Its historical range was reduced as a result of predation by introduced mammals, and this threat remains significant. Rats, cats, pigs and Weka *Gallirallus australis* are all known predators. Successfully reintroduced to one island following their eradication and removal of livestock has also resulted in regrowth of its habitat and a consequent increase in numbers.
Taxonomy Monotypic.

New Zealand Snipe
Coenocorypha aucklandica   Plate 24

Identification
Confusion risks: None.
Main characters: Small, compact, beautifully patterned snipe with

very short legs and long, slightly drooped bill. Considerable racial variation (see taxonomy) and female slightly larger; otherwise rather limited seasonal, age- and sex-related plumage variation. **Ad** has typical snipe pattern of boldly contrasting dark brown and cream-buff crown and head-side stripes. Rest of upperparts and upperwings predominately rufous-brown, with subterminal dark centres and buffy fringes, while below highly variable, but usually creamy-white and heavily streaked on throat and breast, and barred rufous-brown over rest of underparts. **Juv** like ad but black markings and streaking on underparts less distinct. See photos pp. 491, 496 and 501.
Voice: Main call a soft *trerk*, perhaps repeated several times; whistling aerial display call (caused by tail vibrating) given at night, and also described to give a *queeyoo queeyoo* (Heather & Robertson 1997).
Size: 21–24 cm, wing 10.0–11.3 cm, wingspan 30–35 cm, weight 82–131 g. Scarcely any differences between the sexes in measurements.
Similar species: None in range: larger than Chatham Island Snipe *C. pusilla* with longer bill, and stockier and smaller than *Gallinago* snipes, with shorter bill, neck, wings, legs and tail.

Distribution and biology
Distribution, movements and population: New Zealand region in Auckland, Antipodes and Snares, and formerly satellites of Stewart I. Total population estimated at 34,000 individuals with Auckland holding two-thirds of these.
Diet and feeding: Principally takes soil-dwelling invertebrates, including larvae and pupae, reached by probing ground to full length of bill. Rarely takes food from surface. Feeds in more open areas at night, and also active by day, especially on Snares. Often roosts in dense cover during sunny weather.
Social behaviour: Few detailed studies. Presumably largely sedentary, only evidence for dispersal may actually indicate presence of undiscovered populations. Usually solitary though may breed at comparatively high density.
Breeding biology: Mid-Aug to Apr (Nov–May on Snares). Elaborate courtship displays. Nests within cover, laying two pale brown, variably marked eggs. Incubation on Snares takes 22 days. Chicks fed by both parents for 2–3 weeks and able to fly at 30 days. Independent at 65 days. Single-brooded but can renest if first fails. Principally monogamous but some evidence of polygyny.
Conservation Not globally threatened. Populations stable but at permanent risk from accidental introduction of alien mammalian predators, which have already caused extinction of subspecies *iredalei* and *barrierensis*.
Taxonomy Three extant races: *huegeli* (Snares) has completely barred underparts, *aucklandica* (Auckland) has whitish belly and lower underparts, and *meinertzhagenae* (Antipodes) is darkest with most yellow on underparts. Two subspecies are extinct: *barrierensis*, of Little Barrier I, known only from a specimen taken in 1870, and *iredalei*, of islands off Stewart Island, last reported in 1964. Forms superspecies with Chatham Island Snipe *C. pusilla* and they were formerly regarded as conspecific. A *Coenocorypha* snipe was discovered in the Campbell group in 1997, but its taxonomic status is presently unclear.

Endemic and indigenous near-passerines of New Zealand's subantarctic islands

The following accounts (and Plate 25) cover all of the indigenous endemic and near-passerines breeding on New Zealand's subantarctic islands, including two cuckoos (scarce visitors from mainland New Zealand), the endemic Chatham Island Pigeon *Hemiphaga chathamensis* (treated specifically here), and the *Cyanoramphus* parakeet complex. Information on all other breeding near-passerines on these islands is presented in the regional accounts and associated tables.

Shining Bronze-cuckoo
Chrysococcyx lucidus   Plate 25

Identification
Confusion risks: None.
Main characters: Small, short-tailed and distinctly patterned green-and-white barred cuckoo, occurring within our region only as a scarce breeder on Chatham or very rare vagrant to the Snares (see below). Some seasonal and age-/sex-related plumage variation. **Ad** has crown to upperparts and upperwing-coverts glossed bronze-green, contrasting with white face and underparts, which are boldly barred green; eye usually reddish-brown, bill black and legs grey to blackish. **Juv** (and **imm**) similar, but vary in amount of green sheen to feathers, some much duller and completely lack any such tones just after fledging, with sides of underparts less heavily barred.
Voice: Song a distinctive series of high-pitched upslurred whistles, *tsooo-ee, tsoo-ee…* followed by 1–2 downslurred notes, *tsee-ew*, often given in flight at night (Heather & Robertson 1997).
Size: 13–18 cm, wing 9.7–11.2 cm, wingspan 25–32 cm, weight 16–32 g. Much overlap, but females may tend to be very marginally larger.
Similar species: None in range.

Distribution and biology
Distribution, movements and population: NW to SE and SW Australia, Vanuatu, Loyalty Is, New Caledonia, Solomons (resident in last four areas), New Zealand and Chatham, with most moving north to Lesser Sundas and New Guinea in winter. Vagrants have reached several subantarctic islands south of New Zealand.
Diet and feeding: Takes mainly caterpillars and other insects from within trees and shrubs, and occasionally on ground. Joins mixed-species flocks.
Social behaviour: May migrate in small groups, but generally solitary outside breeding season. Polyandry reported.
Breeding biology: In New Zealand mid-Oct to early Feb. On Chatham principally parasitizes Chatham Island Warbler *Gerygone albofrontata*. Lays one egg per host. Few other data from Chatham, but eggs usually take 13–16 days to hatch and young fledge after 18–20 days.
Conservation Considered locally common and widespread in much of Australian and New Zealand range, though has apparently declined in Vanuatu.
Taxonomy Sometimes placed in genus *Chalcites*. Between three and five subspecies recognized, with *plagosus* (from Australia) and *aeneus* (Vanuatu) often regarded as synonyms of nominate *lucidus* (Australia, Tasmania and New Zealand) and *layardi* respectively (New Caledonia, Loyalty Is and Vanuatu), with *harterti* in the S Solomons.

Long-tailed Cuckoo *Eudynamys taitensis*   Plate 25

Identification
Confusion risks: None.
Main characters: Large, long-tailed, brown-and-rufous cuckoo. Very rare visitor to some of New Zealand's subantarctic islands (see below). Some age-/sex-related plumage variation. **Ad** boldly barred dark brown and rufous on upperparts, upperwing and tail, dark-streaked buff-brown crown, contrasting with buffy-white and heavily streaked (with bold, long black and brown stripes) face and underparts; eye and bill yellowish-brown and legs olive-grey. **Juv** distinctive, being overall paler and more buff, with extensive whitish spots on crown and much of rest of upperparts, including upperwing-coverts, and fewer and shorter dark streaks below, usually with almost unmarked buff breast and whitish belly, pale buffy cheeks and contrasting dark eyestripe.
Voice: Main call a loud harsh *zzwheesht* given in flight or from lookout (Heather & Robertson 1997).
Size: 40–42 cm, wing 15.7–19.7 cm, wingspan 47–52 cm, weight 60–153 g. Much overlap between sexes.
Similar species: None in range.

Distribution and biology
Distribution, movements and population: Breeds in forest and scrub in New Zealand, migrating in non-breeding season to C Polynesia and elsewhere in C and S tropical Pacific. Has reached Chatham and several of New Zealand's subantarctic islands.
Diet and feeding: Takes insects, as well as crabs, lizards, eggs and nestlings of other birds.
Social behaviour: No pair-bond and ephemeral lek system appears to operate. May flock at favourable food source and prior to migration. Otherwise singly or in small groups of up to five.
Breeding biology: Breeds Nov–Dec, laying one whitish egg per host, incubated c.16 days and chick becomes independent at 21–29 days.
Conservation Population considered to require monitoring as certainly declining due to loss of forested habitat, which affects it both directly and through declines in host species.
Taxonomy Monotypic.

Chatham Island Pigeon (Parea)
Hemiphaga chathamensis   Plate 25

Identification
Confusion risks: None.
Main characters: Large, heavily built pigeon, noticeably larger even than mainland counterpart, New Zealand Pigeon *H. novaeseelandiae*, with which often considered conspecific (see below). **Ad** has dark glossy green head and breast, purple and bronze reflections on nape, mantle and scapulars, ash-grey back and rump, upperwing mainly green and purple (latter chiefly on coverts), with frosty cast to flight feathers, white underparts and dark tail. Bill, eye and cere red, and bill tip diagnostically yellow. **Juv** similar, but for short time after fledging and before moult is overall duller, with reduced sheen to plumage and paler bare parts. See photo p. 487.
Voice: Gives a soft *oooo* or *ku*, but generally silent; a scarcely audible *coo* in alarm.

Size: 48–49 cm (female 46–49 cm), wing 26.8–28.1 cm, wingspan 75 cm, weight 680–720 g. Male generally larger and heavier, but much overlap.
Similar species: The only pigeon on Chatham.

Distribution and biology

Distribution, movements and population: Restricted to Chatham, on main island (in forest at south end), Pitt and South East, with population 100–200 individuals in late 1990s.
Diet and feeding: Broad range of fruits, leaves and buds, responding strongly to seasonal abundance, and probably only dependent on a handful of species.
Social behaviour: Most frequently encountered in singles or pairs, with occasional loose groups of 5–13 forming at fruiting trees.
Breeding biology: Nov–Jul, peaking in Dec–Jan. Nest an insubstantial structure placed 3–9 m up in tree, but also near ground level. Single white egg incubated 30 days. Young fledge at 6–7 weeks. Low reproductive rate and high nest failure.
Conservation *Chathamensis* should qualify as threatened. Formerly abundant, a decline due to hunting, habitat degradation and predation by introduced mammals, and evident since the 1930s, had reduced the population to 30 birds in 1990, though it subsequently recovered to present level following cat control.
Taxonomy Well differentiated from New Zealand Pigeon (nominate throughout most of New Zealand and extinct *spadicea* on Norfolk I), in being distinctly larger and heavier, with broader, more hook-tipped bicoloured bill, duller head and breast, poorly marked reflections on neck, frostier duller green flight feathers and uppertail, no detectable pale tip to tail and paler grey underside to flight feathers, among other features. Given such morphological differences *chathamensis* is considered a distinct species by Millener & Powlesland (2001) and here.

Red-crowned Parakeet
Cyanoramphus [novaezelandiae] novaezelandiae
Plate 25

Identification

Confusion risks: Yellow-crowned Parakeet *C. auriceps*.
Main characters: Long-tailed, bright yellowish-green parakeet, with limited seasonal, age-/sex-related plumage variation. **Ad** virtually all green including long, graduated tail, with extensive deep blue patch on flight feathers and wing-coverts, deep red forehead extending as narrow stripe through eye, and red vent-sides. Underparts, especially breast, slightly yellowish and facial area emerald-green. May show pale yellow wingbar across inner primaries and secondaries on underwing. Bill grey with darker tip, legs pale grey and eye reddish-brown. **Juv** similar, but for short time after fledging and before moult is duller green, often with less red on head and rump, longer underwing bar, pink (or partially pink) bill, paler legs and feet, and eye initially black-brown.
Voice: Typically a rapid, loud and high-pitched chatter in flight and a variety of softer calls used to retain contact and when perched. Calls of those on Auckland group do not differ significantly from those on mainland New Zealand (*HANZAB*).
Size: 23–28 cm (female 21–26 cm), wing 10.4–14.0 cm, wingspan 32–38 cm, weight 43–113 g. Male generally larger and heavier than female, but considerable overlap in most measurements.
Similar forms: Within our region restricted to the Auckland group, where could only be confused with Yellow-crowned Parakeet (which see).

Ad Red-crowned Parakeet *Cyanoramphus* [*novaezelandiae*] *novaezelandiae*, Auckland Is, Dec 1999. © Hadoram Shirihai.

Distribution and biology

Distribution, movements and population: *C.* [*n.*] *novaezelandiae* is widespread throughout offshore islands of New Zealand and the Auckland group (currently known from five islands). Other red-crowed forms occur on some of New Zealand's subantarctic islands and are described below. No population estimate available from Auckland.

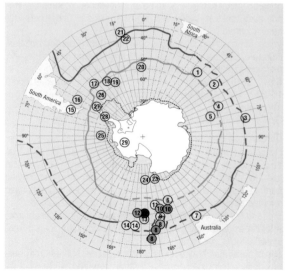

■ Antipodes Parakeet *Cyanoramphus unicolor*
▨ Red-crowned Parakeet
  Cyanoramphus [*novaezelandiae*] *novaezelandiae*
■ Antipodes Red-crowned Parakeet
  Cyanoramphus [*novaezelandiae*] *hochstetteri*
▢ Chatham Island Red-crowned Parakeet
  Cyanoramphus [*novaezelandiae*] *chathamensis*
■ Yellow-crowned Parakeet *Cyanoramphus auriceps*
▢ Forbes' Parakeet
  Cyanoramphus [*novaezelandiae*/*auriceps*] *forbesi*
⑧ New Zealand and offshore islands
⑧ New Zealand and offshore islands
⑩ Auckland
⑩ Auckland
● Antipodes
⑫ Antipodes
⑭ Chatham
⑭ Chatham

Plate 25 Endemic and indigenous near-passerines of New Zealand's subantarctic islands

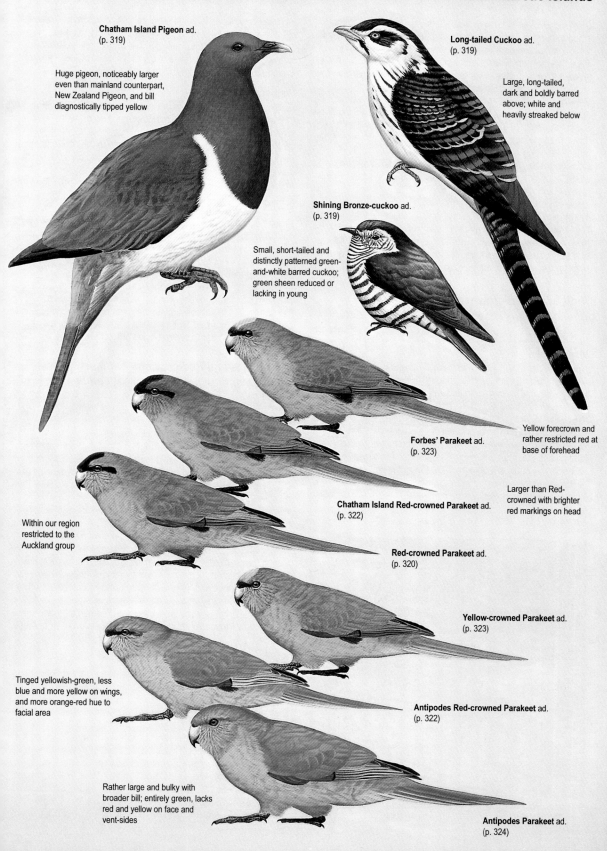

Chatham Island Pigeon ad.
(p. 319)

Huge pigeon, noticeably larger even than mainland counterpart, New Zealand Pigeon, and bill diagnostically tipped yellow

Long-tailed Cuckoo ad.
(p. 319)

Large, long-tailed, dark and boldly barred above; white and heavily streaked below

Shining Bronze-cuckoo ad.
(p. 319)

Small, short-tailed and distinctly patterned green-and-white barred cuckoo; green sheen reduced or lacking in young

Forbes' Parakeet ad.
(p. 323)

Yellow forecrown and rather restricted red at base of forehead

Chatham Island Red-crowned Parakeet ad.
(p. 322)

Larger than Red-crowned with brighter red markings on head

Within our region restricted to the Auckland group

Red-crowned Parakeet ad.
(p. 320)

Yellow-crowned Parakeet ad.
(p. 323)

Tinged yellowish-green, less blue and more yellow on wings, and more orange-red hue to facial area

Antipodes Red-crowned Parakeet ad.
(p. 322)

Rather large and bulky with broader bill; entirely green, lacks red and yellow on face and vent-sides

Antipodes Parakeet ad.
(p. 324)

Diet and feeding: Most active early and late in the day, gathering at food sources. Forages in trees and on ground on fruits, seeds, leaves, buds, invertebrates and nectar when available.

Social behaviour: Roosts communally and flocks also form at favoured feeding sites. Very territorial around nest and may use same site over several seasons.

Breeding biology: Oct–Mar, with peak in Oct–Dec. Nests in tree hollow, tussac grass or within shelter of rock crevice, laying 2–10 (most frequently 5–9) eggs, incubated by female alone for 18–20 days. Young fledge at 5–6 weeks and are fed by both parents, but female takes greater share.

Conservation Almost extinct on mainland New Zealand due to introduction of predators, but abundant on many predator-free islands. Range and population on Auckland have also decreased since introduction of cats and pigs.

Taxonomy Six extant and two extinct races recognized within Red-crowned Parakeet complex. Each of the remote forms on New Zealand's subantarctic islands is treated as an allospecies of a single superspecies here. For morphological differences from *hochstetteri* and *chathamensis*, see these forms.

Antipodes Red-crowned Parakeet
Cyanoramphus [*novaezelandiae*] *hochstetteri*

Plate 25

Identification
Confusion risks: Antipodes Parakeet *C. unicolor*.

Main characters: Long-tailed, bright yellowish-green parakeet. Description and (rather limited) seasonal age-/sex-related plumage variation essentially as *C.* [*n.*] *novaezelandiae* (which see). **Ad**, unlike latter, generally more yellowish-green, with less extensive blue on wings (mainly on wing-coverts), more orange-red hue to forecrown, lores, eyestripe and rump, and more obvious yellow leading edge to outer primaries. Eye orange. **Juv** similar, with correspondingly restricted amount of blue in wings and more orange-yellow tone to variable and reduced reddish areas.

Voice: Calls differ markedly from nominate *novaezelandiae*, being much lower pitched

Size: 21–27 cm, wing 13.1–15.0 cm, wingspan 32–38 cm, weight

Antipodes Red-crowned Parakeet Cyanoramphus [novaezelandiae] hochstetteri, *Antipodes, Jan 2007. © Hadoram Shirihai.*

91 g. Male averages larger in wing, bill and tarsus measurements, but much overlap.

Similar forms: Antipodes Parakeet, the only other parakeet species occurring on the island, is larger and slightly bulkier, lacks red in plumage and has more restricted blue in wing.

Distribution and biology
Distribution, movements and population: *Hochstetteri* is restricted to the Antipodes, with an estimated population of 4000–5000 individuals.

Diet and feeding: Most active early and late in the day, gathering at food sources. Forages in shrubs and on ground on fruits, seeds, leaves, buds, invertebrates, and nectar when available.

Social behaviour: Roosts communally and flocks also form at favoured feeding sites. Very territorial around nest and may use same site over several seasons.

Breeding biology: Nov–Mar; young in nests in Feb. Very few other data available for this taxon, though presumed to be similar to nominate *novaezelandiae*.

Conservation Not globally threatened and Antipodes population considered stable, though overall population of *C.* [*novaezelandiae*] has declined markedly and insular populations are clearly at risk from accidental introductions of mammalian predators.

Taxonomy While acknowledging the need for further study, each of the remote forms of Red-crowned Parakeet is treated as an allospecies of the same superspecies group here.

Chatham Island Red-crowned Parakeet
Cyanoramphus [*novaezelandiae*] *chathamensis*

Plate 25

Identification
Confusion risks: Forbes' Parakeet *C. forbesi*.

Main characters: Long-tailed, bright yellowish-green parakeet, most similar to *C.* [*n.*] *novaezelandiae* (which see), but larger than latter. **Ad** has brighter red markings on head and rump-sides and slightly bluer green facial area. **Juv** presumably very similar, but no specific data.

Voice: Differs from *novaezelandiae* in frequency and length of notes, but in other respects similar (*HANZAB*).

Size: 23–28 cm, wing 12.5–14.5 cm, wingspan 12.5–14.0 cm, weight 82–83 g. Male larger in most measurements.

Similar forms: *Chathamensis* overlaps only with Forbes' Parakeet, from which it is easily distinguished by its lack of yellow on head and much deeper and more extensive red on forecrown. Forbes' is restricted to Mangere and Little Mangere, where the two forms have hybridized, resulting in a range of intermediates and making it possible to identify only classic individuals on each of these islands.

Distribution and biology
Distribution, movements and population: Restricted to five islands in Chatham group. Population estimated at fewer than 1000 individuals.

Diet and feeding: Very similar to *novaezelandiae*, but varies seasonally, taking largely grass seeds in winter (and some leaves), mainly leaves, with seeds, flowers and invertebrates, in spring and principally seeds, especially *Geranium traversii* in late summer.

Social behaviour: Largely as *novaezelandiae*.

Breeding biology: Oct–Dec. Builds nest in tree hollow, tussac grass or in shelter of rock crevice, laying 5–7 eggs. No other data specific to *chathamensis*.

Conservation Insular Chatham populations certainly threatened,

Chatham Island Red-crowned Parakeet Cyanoramphus [novaezelan-diae] chathamensis, *Chatham.* © Peter Reese.

Forbes' Parakeet Cyanoramphus [novaezelandiae/auriceps] forbesi, *Mangere, Chatham, Oct 2001.* © Hadoram Shirihai.

being clearly at risk from accidental introduction of mammalian predators. Intermittently subject to human control on Mangere in order to reduce hybridization with Forbes' Parakeet.

Taxonomy While acknowledging the need for further study, each of the remote forms of Red-crowned Parakeet is treated as allospecies of the same superspecies group here.

Forbes' Parakeet
Cyanoramphus [novaezelandiae/auriceps] forbesi
Plate 25

Identification

Confusion risks: Chatham Island Red-crowned Parakeet *C. [n.] chathamensis*.

Main characters: Long-tailed, bright green parakeet; generally similar in size, structure and plumage to Red-crowned *Cyanoramphus [novaezelandiae]* and Yellow-crowned Parakeets *C. auriceps*, with indistinct age-/sex-related plumage differences. **Ad** largely green, with an extensive area of deep blue on flight feathers and wing-coverts, narrow orange-red lower forehead bordered above by large yellow forecrown patch, and red vent-sides. Underparts, especially breast, slightly yellowish. Some have pale yellow wingbar across inner primaries and secondaries on underwing. Bill grey with darker tip, legs pale grey and eye reddish-brown. **Juv** very similar, but prior to post-juv moult is overall duller with less orange-red on head.

Voice: No specific information available.

Size: 20–27 cm, wing 12.1–13.9 cm, wingspan 31–36 cm, no weight data. Male generally larger in most measurements.

Similar forms: Overlaps only with Chatham Island Red-crowned Parakeet, from which it is readily distinguished by yellow forecrown and much paler and less extensive red at base of forehead. Forbes' is restricted to Mangere and Little Mangere, where it sometimes interbreeds with Chatham Island Red-crowned Parakeet, resulting in range of intermediates.

Distribution and biology

Distribution, movements and population: Restricted to Mangere and Little Mangere in the Chatham group. Population placed at 500 birds in late 1990s.

Diet and feeding: Prefers dense, continuous woodland and scrub where it feeds on a variety of invertebrates, seeds, leaves, fruit, bark and flowers, with similar seasonal variation as in *C. [n.] chathamensis*.

Social behaviour: Gregarious like other parakeets.

Breeding biology: Few specific data. Nests in natural crevices, or holes in dead or living trees. Most data appertain to *auriceps*, which nests Oct–Mar and lays 5–9 white eggs, incubated for c.20 days by female alone, and young take c.40 days to fledge.

Conservation Endangered. Comprehensive conservation programme in place, which controls numbers of Chatham Island Red-crowned Parakeet on Mangere, has re-vegetated much of latter and is studying the species' population dynamics and mate-selection behaviour. Given the eradication of introduced predators from Mangere and managed habitat regeneration, the principal threat to its survival is continued hybridization.

Taxonomy Until recently regarded as a subspecies of Yellow-crowned Parakeet *C. auriceps*, but DNA research has demonstrated this taxon to be the most distinct of the entire *Cyanoramphus* group, making specific status warranted. Its biological and molecular relationships with *auriceps* and *novaezelandiae* require further study.

Yellow-crowned Parakeet
Cyanoramphus auriceps
Plate 25

Identification

Confusion risks: Red-crowned Parakeet *C. [n.] novaezelandiae*.

Main characters: Long-tailed, bright green parakeet. Sexes essentially alike and only limited seasonal, age-/sex-related plumage variation. **Ad** virtually all green, including long graduated tail; violet-blue on outer flight feathers and some wing-coverts, and red forehead bar extending narrowly from bill to eye, bordered above by large golden-yellow forecrown, and red vent-sides. Underparts, especially chest, slightly yellowish. Some have pale yellow wingbar across inner primaries and secondaries. Bill grey with darker tip, legs pale grey and eye reddish-brown. **Juv** similar, but prior to post-juv moult is duller, with reduced blue in wings, less red on head and rump, and more restricted yellow on forecrown, darker iris and pale pink bill.

Voice: Typically a rapid, but rather higher pitched, weaker chatter than Red-crowned Parakeet and its close allies.

Size: 20–27 cm, wing 9.5–11.4 cm, wingspan 31–36 cm, weight 37–55 g. Male has significantly longer and broader bill than female.

Similar species: Within our region only occurs on Auckland, where overlaps only with Red-crowned Parakeet, from which it is easily distinguished by smaller size, yellow on head and restricted red at base of forehead.

Distribution and biology

Distribution, movements and population: New Zealand, patchily on both North and South Is, and Stewart and some near-shore islands, also on two islands within Auckland group. No population data available from latter.

Diet and feeding: On mainland mostly gathers in pairs and small groups at food sources, sometimes with mixed-species flocks. Forages in trees and on ground on fruits, seeds, leaves, buds, invertebrates and bark. No specific data from Auckland.

Social behaviour: Very poorly known. No information on mating system. Usually seen in pairs or small groups of up to c.10.

Breeding biology: All data from mainland. May nest year-round, but most frequently in summer. Nests in hole in branch or trunk of dead or live tree. Lays 5–9 white eggs, incubated for c.18–20 days by female alone, and young take 39–46 days to fledge.

Conservation Mainland population currently regarded as stable, although range has contracted and subpopulations have declined due to forest clearance and impacts of introduced predators. Formerly considered a pest in the 19th century. Little specific information available for the Auckland population, though rates of hybridization with *C.* [*novaezelandiae*] are known to be high.

Taxonomy Monotypic given recent proposal to recognise Forbes' *C.* [*n./a.*] *forbesi* and Orange-fronted Parakeets *C.* [*a.*] *malherbi* at specific level (the latter was previously regarded as a colour morph and is confined to a small area of South I, New Zealand). Further study of the insular Auckland population required, particularly its relationships to *forbesi* and the *C.* [*novaezelandiae*] group.

Antipodes Parakeet
Cyanoramphus unicolor　　　　　　　　　Plate 25

Identification

Confusion risks: Antipodes Red-crowned Parakeet *C.* [*novaezelandiae*] *hochstetteri*.

Main characters: Long-tailed, bright green parakeet. Noticeably larger and bulkier than all above-mentioned parakeets. Sexes essentially alike, with limited plumage variation. **Ad** entirely green on head, body and graduated tail, with blue wing-coverts and some flight feathers, and yellow-tinged underparts. Red eye and dark grey legs and bill (latter tipped blackish). Lacks any red and/or yellow on forehead/forecrown, or on vent-sides. **Juv** prior to post-juv moult is duller, with darker eye and pinkish base to bill.

Voice: Compared to congeners, calls generally lower but at higher amplitude, with several unique vocalizations and lone individuals tend not to utter chattering calls. For details see *HANZAB*.

Size: 27–35 cm, wing 13.6–15.8 cm, wingspan 38–43 cm, weight 99–210 g. Male larger and heavier, with noticeably larger bill.

Similar species: Overlaps only with Antipodes Red-crowned Parakeet, but is overall larger and plumper, with larger head, broader bill, broader wings in flight and lacks red forecrown and vent-sides. Blue restricted to wing-coverts and some flight feathers.

Distribution and biology

Distribution, movements and population: Restricted to tussac grassland, scrub, bogs and swamps on Antipodes I, Bollons I and also on Leeward, Archway and Inner Windward Is, but only certainly breeds on two first-named. Population apparently stable and estimated at 2000–3000 individuals in 1985–95.

Diet and feeding: Prefers to walk or climb through vegetation when feeding. Principally feeds on leaves, but also takes seeds, berries, remains of dead seabirds and their eggs.

Social behaviour: Solitary or in family groups.

Breeding biology: Nests in well-drained and well-concealed burrows, or in tall tussac grass. Lays Oct–Jan. In wild perhaps only 1–3 white eggs, though up to seven in captivity. Female alone incubates, 24–28 days. Both sexes feed young, which fledge at 39–42 days and are wholly independent within another two weeks; probably mature at one year.

Conservation Vulnerable and given restricted range is clearly liable to predation by rats, should they reach the breeding islands. Mice may compete for food.

Taxonomy Monotypic.

Antipodes Parakeet Cyanoramphus unicolor, Antipodes, Mar 1985. © Kim Westerskov.

Endemic and indigenous passerines of New Zealand's subantarctic islands

The following texts and Plate 26 treat the indigenous passerines breeding on New Zealand's subantarctic islands (all references to the subantarctic islands below refer only to New Zealand territories and Macquarie). A wide variety of species from different families appears here. The following does not cover the introduced or naturally colonizing, but non-native New Zealand species, e.g. Skylark *Alauda arvensis*, Dunnock *Prunella modularis*, House Sparrow *Passer domesticus*, Common Chaffinch *Fringilla coelebs*, European Greenfinch *Carduelis chloris*, European Goldfinch *C. carduelis*, Common Redpoll *C. flammea*, Yellowhammer *Emberiza citrinella*, Common Blackbird *Turdus merula*, Song Thrush *T. philomelos* and Common Starling *Sturnus vulgaris*. Further information on these is presented in the relevant island accounts and table.

Welcome Swallow *Hirundo neoxena*   Plate 26

Identification
Confusion risks: None.
Main characters: Medium-sized, relatively short-tailed swallow, which in our region breeds only on Chatham. Sexes essentially alike with limited seasonal plumage variation, but juv distinctive. **Ad** virtually all blue-black above, contrasting with reddish face and breast, the latter poorly demarcated from dirty white rest of underparts. Dark tail rather deeply forked with moderately long streamers, which average longer in male. Bare parts mainly blackish. **Juv** (and younger **imm**) differ from ad in having duller, brownish-tinged upperparts, paler reddish on head and breast (heavily reduced on face), even less clean white underparts and only slightly forked tail.
Voice: Main call a twittering *twsit*.
Size: 15 cm, weight 14 g.
Similar species: No other swallows occur regularly in our region.

Distribution and biology
Distribution, movements and population: W Australia through N Territory to Queensland south throughout rest of Australia and Tasmania; reached New Zealand in 1958, Norfolk I in 1969 and Lord Howe I in 1972; vagrant to Macquarie and several of New Zealand's subantarctic islands.
Diet and feeding: Takes wide variety of insects, from dragonflies and beetles to moths and wasps in fast, agile flight, exceptionally at night.
Social behaviour: Gregarious, especially outside breeding season when may form roosts of up to 2000 individuals. Pairs will use same breeding site in several consecutive years, but no other information.
Breeding biology: Nests Aug–Mar in New Zealand, but no specific data available from Chatham.
Conservation Not globally threatened.
Taxonomy Most variation appears clinal and poorly defined, though up to three races have been described. The nominate occurs in E Australia, New Zealand, its outliers and Kermadec, with *carteri* in W Australia and the extremely doubtful *parsonsi* in Queensland.

New Zealand Pipit
Anthus novaeseelandiae   Plate 26

Identification
Confusion risks: None.
Main characters: Medium-sized, brownish, faintly dark-streaked pipit which exhibits some geographical variation across the subantarctic islands. Sexes alike, with limited seasonal plumage variation. **Ad** in most populations predominantly grey-brown, tinged buff (especially when fresh), and streaked rather heavily but coarsely on head and rest of upperparts; face slightly paler, highlighted by rather distinctive pale supercilium and dark eyestripe. Upperwing has indistinct whitish wingbars formed by fringes to greater and median coverts; underparts mainly dirty white, tinged pale greyish-buff on breast/flanks where profusely streaked darker, and has narrow dark malar stripe. Dark tail has distinctly whitish outer feathers in flight. Bill mainly dark grey-brown, with slightly paler base to lower mandible, eye blackish and rather long flesh-brown legs. **Juv** (and some less-advanced **imm**) differs from ad in having duller brownish upperparts with even more diffuse streaking, weaker facial marks but bolder dark centres to retained juv upperwing-coverts.
Voice: Main call a drawn-out shrill *thcrree* or *shweee*.
Size: 19 cm, weight 40 g.
Similar species: No other pipits occur in our region. Inexperienced observers could confuse it with Skylark *Alauda arvensis*, but note less deep-based bill, longer tail (sometimes wagged), and different plumage, as well as jerkier manner on ground.

Distribution and biology
Distribution, movements and population: New Zealand and Chatham, Auckland, Campbell and the Antipodes; vagrant to Lord Howe I.
Diet and feeding: Principally invertebrates, especially beetles, wasps, flies, crickets, moths and their larvae and pupae, and small percentage of seeds, taken on ground, but occasionally on wing; also sandhoppers on beaches.
Social behaviour: Very few data, but pairs are strongly territorial when breeding and may remain on territory year-round, though juvs may form flocks in non-breeding season.
Breeding biology: Breeds Aug–Feb throughout range (few specific data from our region), constructing deep cup nest of dry grasses well hidden in cover. Lays 2–5 (usually 3–4) cream eggs heavily blotched brown at broader end. Incubates 14–15 days and both ads tend young, which fledge in 14–16 days. Capable of attempting 2–3 broods per season.
Conservation Not globally threatened and no known threats.
Taxonomy Complex, but recent authors (e.g. Sibley 1996) have generally tended to regard formerly very wide-ranging 'Richard's Pipit' *A. novaeseelandiae* as a group of six species, *cinnamomeus* (over much of Africa south of the Sahara), *camaroonensis* (in montane W Cameroon), *hoeschi* (in Drakensberg Mountains of South Africa), *richardi* (across much of temperate Asia), *rufulus* (in the Himalayas and SE Asia to Indonesia and the Philippines) and *novaeseelandiae* (in Australasia). Sibley (1996) considers the latter to consist of *australis* in montane C New Guinea, Australia and Tasmania and the nominate in New Zealand and its outliers, but these latter forms are treated specifically here.

Silvereye *Zosterops lateralis* Plate 26

Identification

Confusion risks: None.

Main characters: Small, bright greenish warbler-like forest and bushland bird, extensively distributed through the subantarctic islands. Sexes alike, with limited seasonal or age-related plumage variation. **Ad** has diagnostic, conspicuous white eye-ring, with otherwise mainly bright olive-green upperparts, even brighter rump and soft grey lower hindneck, mantle and breast-sides (variable), while below is whitish with yellowish tinge to throat and cinnamon flanks. Bare parts mainly dark grey. **Juv** differs from ad in lack of white eye-ring and is duller above and entirely pale below. See photo p. 496.

Voice: Main call a drawn-out, high-pitched *chily-chily-chily*.

Size: 12 cm, wing 5.8–6.6 cm, weight 10.1–16.5 g (data from the Snares). No information from our region concerning any differences between sexes in mensural data.

Similar species: No congeners occur in our region.

Distribution and biology

Distribution, movements and population: Australia and New Zealand (latter colonized 1855), Chatham, Snares, Antipodes, Auckland and Campbell, and reached Norfolk I in 1904), Vanuatu, New Caledonia, Loyalty and Banks, Fiji and Tuamotu (on Makatea, since 1986). Tasmanian birds winter to SE Australia. No population data.

Diet and feeding: Varied, taking invertebrates (including caterpillars, spiders, bugs, flies and beetles), fruit and nectar.

Social behaviour: Forms small flocks in winter but pairs strongly territorial when nesting. Flocks appear to possess hierarchical structure.

Breeding biology: Nests Sep–Mar in New Zealand, but few data from our region.

Conservation Not globally threatened.

Taxonomy Polytypic: three races described, with nominate *lateralis* in New Zealand and its subantarctic islands, Oceania and E and SE Australia, *halmaturinus* in CS Australia and *gouldi* in SW Australia.

Chatham Island Warbler
Gerygone albofrontata Plate 26

Identification

Confusion risks: None.

Main characters: Small, short-tailed pale forest warbler on Chatham. Sexes only slightly differentiated and limited seasonal variation, but juv distinct. **Ad** male has olive-brown head and upperparts, darker wings and tail, prominent white forehead and supercilium, dark eyestripe and white underparts. Red eye. Flanks and undertail-coverts cream-yellow. Female lacks white forehead and has greyer underparts with pale yellowish supercilium, face and throat. **Juv** like female but yellower underparts and supercilium less noticeable. See photo p. 488.

Voice: Song consists of high-pitched, often prolonged, ringing notes. Female only utters subsong.

Size: 12 cm, wing 5.7–6.7 cm, weight 8.5–10.0 g. Male larger in all measurements, with comparatively little overlap in wing length.

Similar species: Unmistakable within tiny range. Similar to Grey Warbler *G. igata* of mainland New Zealand, but no known overlap.

Distribution and biology

Distribution, movements and population: Locally common in protected southern forests on main island of Chatham group, and also Pitt and several smaller islands, e.g. South East and Mangere, but no population estimates.

Diet and feeding: Entirely invertebrates, especially spiders, caterpillars, flies, beetles and bugs. Prey gleaned from leaves and crevices in branches, rarely hovering but occasionally venturing to ground to forage in leaf litter.

Social behaviour: Male strongly territorial, female less so. Small flocks of juvs may form in autumn, when population density high.

Breeding biology: Distinctive domed nest with side entrance, hung in open at end of branch (on offshore islands within dense foliage, at most 2–3 m above ground). Breeds Sep–Jan, mostly Sep–Dec. Lays 2–4 white eggs with reddish speckling, incubated by female alone for 17–21 days. Young fed by both parents and fledge sometime after 24 days, when parents each take care of 1–2 juvs. Sexually mature at two years.

Conservation Not globally threatened, but subfossil remains indicate that it was once widespread throughout the islands; it is now confined to better-forested areas of six islands. Nonetheless, despite the species' inability to adapt to human-modified habitats, predation by introduced mammals and perhaps parasitization by cuckoos, it remains the commonest native passerine in forested and scrub areas on the islands.

Taxonomy Monotypic.

Chatham Island Fantail
Rhipidura fuliginosa penitus Plate 26

Identification

Confusion risks: None

Main characters: Distinctive, small very long-tailed warbler-like bird. Quite well-marked geographical variation, but within our region occurs only on Chatham and Snares. Proportionately rather small round head with tiny bill. Very long tail often conspicuously fanned and typically moves restlessly with twists and jerks. Sexes largely alike with limited seasonal plumage variation, but juv distinct. Ad has grey head, white supercilium, brown upperparts with paler fringes to wing feathers, yellowish-cinnamon underparts and white and black bands on upper breast. Tail strongly patterned black (central feathers) and white (rest), but number of black tail feathers varies geographically (see below). Black morph of *fuliginosa* (12–25% of individuals), mainly restricted to South I (New Zealand) and is wholly sooty-black except small whitish spot behind eye and pale flight-feather fringes. Juv similar, but has browner body, rusty-brown wing-coverts and indistinct breast markings.

Chatham Island Fantail Rhipidura fuliginosa penitus, *Main Chatham, Jan 2007. © Hadoram Shirihai.*

Plate 26 Endemic and indigenous passerines of New Zealand's subantarctic islands

Auckland Island Tomtit ad. ♂ (p. 329)

Chatham Island Tomtit ad. ♀ (p. 328)

Rather clearly differentiated from male, being browner above and on breast, and dirtier/buffer below and on wingbar

Snares Tomtit ad. ♂ (p. 329)

All black, though male glossier (restricted to the Snares)

...ed, small robin-like ...psaltriidae (as male ...atham Island Tomtit); ...male has duller black ...perparts and upper ...east, merging with ...s clean white under-...rts and wingbars

Silvereye ad. (p. 326)

Small, bright greenish warbler-like bird; conspicuous white eye-ring

Snares Island Fernbird ad. (p. 328)

Very long-tailed, brownish, heavily streaked

Black Robin ad. ♂ (p. 331)

Entirely black, long legs and upright stance (restricted to Mangere and South East, Chatham)

Chatham Island Warbler ad. ♂ (p. 326)

Small and short tail; prominent white supercilium and dark eyestripe; juv duller with yellower underparts

Welcome Swallow ad. (p. 325)

Short-tailed swallow, which in our region breeds only on Chatham; young browner above and paler reddish on head/breast

Chatham Island Fantail ad. (p. 326)

Very long tail fanned and twisted restlessly; juv browner with indistinct breast markings

New Zealand Pipit ad. (p. 325)

Medium-sized, grey-brown and faintly dark streaked; pale supercilium and dark eyestripe

Tui ad. ♂ (p. 331)

New Zealand Bellbird ad. ♂ (p. 331)

Loud penetrating song (ringing bell-like whistles); female overall duller

Large, mainly blackish with green, blue and purple iridescences; white throat tufts and filaments on neck

Ad male (left) and female Chatham Island Tomtit Petroica [macrocephala] chathamensis *shows quite pronounced age-/sex-related and individual plumage variation, with some least advanced males duller, and some older females darker and may approach male coloration. Pitt, Chatham Is, Jan 2007. © Hadoram Shirihai.*

Voice: Song and calls varied. Main call, sometimes repeated, a penetrating but not very high-pitched *tchtee*, and song a harsh rhythmical 'saw-like' *tweet-a-tweet-a-tweet-a-tweet…*(Heather & Robertson 1997; pers. obs).
Size: 16 cm, weight 8 g.
Similar species: None: no other passerine exhibits similar combination of features.

Distribution and biology
Distribution, movements and population: Widespread in Australia and New Zealand; subspecies penitus restricted to Chatham. No population estimates.
Diet and feeding: Principally insectivorous, but may also take fruit. Fly-catches aerially as well as gleaning leaves and ferns; highly active and quite acrobatic.
Social behaviour: Strongly territorial in breeding season, but this breaks down in autumn when groups of 10–20 may form.
Breeding biology: Breeds Aug–Feb on New Zealand mainland, but shorter season (in which two broods are raised) on Chatham. Nest often near ground, but also 2–3 m above it, and usually protected by overhanging vegetation. Lays 2–5 white, lightly speckled eggs, incubated for 13–16 days by both parents. Nestlings fed for 11–16 days, until female commences second nest and male alone cares for juvs until fledging. Some juvs may breed after two months.
Conservation Not globally threatened, but strong annual population fluctuations, especially after severe winters or spring storms, which can lead to local extinctions.
Taxonomy Approximately ten subspecies recognized across broad range. Endemic race on Chatham, *penitus*, is characterized by having more white in the tail than the pied form of nominate *fuliginosa* on the Snares and South I (New Zealand).

Snares Islands Fernbird
Bowdleria [punctata] caudata   Plate 26

Identification
Confusion risks: None.
Main characters: Small-bodied but very long-tailed, brownish, heavily streaked passerine, which in our region is restricted to the Snares. **Ad** warm brown above with long, narrow, ragged-looking tail. Underparts whitish with heavy dark brown streaks and spots. Crown tinged chestnut, contrasting with white supercilium. No sexual or age-related variation. See photo p. 491.

Voice: Main calls (on mainland New Zealand) varied and rich, described as a short sharp *tchip*, and a mechanical, rather low sharp, metallic double-note, *uu-tick*, often produced by pair in duet; other calls include a *zrup* and a series of rapid clicking notes or a melodic warble (Heather & Robertson 1997); no information from the Snares.
Size: 18 cm, wing 6.5–7.2 cm, weight 30.5–40.4 g (data from Snares). No information from our region concerning any sex-related differences in mensural data.
Similar species: Unmistakable within tiny range.

Distribution and biology
Distribution, movements and population: *Bowdleria* [*punctata*] distributed throughout much of New Zealand and some offshore islands; the allospecies *caudata* is restricted to the Snares, where up to 1500 pairs are present.
Diet and feeding: Principally invertebrates taken on or near ground while moving, mouse-like, through vegetation; also takes maggots and flies around dead penguins or from seals and sea lions.
Social behaviour: Sedentary. Pairs or small groups remain together year-round and many pairs stay within their breeding territories all year. Inquisitive but shy and often difficult to flush.
Breeding biology: Season on Snares Oct (perhaps late Sep) to Mar. Both sexes build neatly woven nest of dry grasses within rushes or tussac grass, occasionally *Olearia* up to 2 m above ground. Lays 2–3 pink eggs heavily speckled purplish-brown. Both parents incubate, for 15–19 days, and tend young until they fledge at 20–21 days. Sexually mature at nine months.
Conservation Not globally threatened, but has declined due to habitat loss and predation by introduced alien mammals on mainland New Zealand. The commonest landbird on the Snares.
Taxonomy Five forms described within *Bowdleria* [*punctata*]: *vealeae* (North I), *punctata* (South I), *stewartiana* (Stewart I), *wilsoni* (Codfish I) and *caudata*. Latter is most distinctive and has been suggested to warrant specific status, but treated as an allospecies here.

Chatham Island Tomtit
Petroica [macrocephala] chathamensis   Plate 26

Identification
Confusion risks: None.
Main characters: Distinctively patterned, small, large-headed,

chat-like Australian robin (Eopsaltriidae; a variable group, see taxonomy). **Ad** male has black head with small white spot above bill, glossy black upperparts and breast, clean white wingbar and tail-sides, and yellowish-white underparts becoming brighter, more orange on breast. Female has dark brown upperparts with grey-brown chin and breast, becoming white on rear underparts, buff wingbar and tail-sides. **Juv** reminiscent of respective ad, but pattern and coloration obscure, e.g. juv male has duller greyish-brown tone, with whitish shaft-streaks to black above and is purer white below, while wingbar is narrower and buffish. Apparently both sexes in juv plumage have reduced or lack small white spot above bill; immediately after fledging has yellowish-orange gape. All plumages have mainly blackish bill and eye, and yellowish-brown legs.

Voice: Song and calls vary regionally. Former generally described as a loud jingling, and main calls *swee* or *seet* (Heather & Robertson 1997), but there no specific information for *chathamensis*.

Size: 13 cm, weight 11 g.

Similar forms: Wholly distinctive within tiny range: Black Robin *P. traversi* is all black (only overlap on Mangere and South East).

Distribution and biology

Distribution, movements and population: Chathamensis restricted to Chatham group, on Pitt, South East and Mangere. Population 770–900 birds.

Diet and feeding: Principally insectivorous, including spiders, beetles, caterpillars, moths etc, but also takes fruit in autumn. Typically prey is captured using watch-and-wait method, perching for longish periods before flying down to capture any located prey.

Social behaviour: Year-round territories are defended Jul–Feb; usually mates for life.

Breeding biology: Lays 3–4 eggs from mid-Oct to mid-Dec. Double-brooded. Female alone constructs nest and incubates eggs, for 17–18 days, and chicks fledge at 16–19 days.

Conservation Not globally threatened, though *chathamensis* declined during 19th century due to arrival of introduced mammalian predators. It disappeared from the main island in 1970s and was purposely removed from Mangere in the same decade to prevent competition with Black Robin. It has subsequently been reintroduced to Mangere.

Taxonomy Five forms described within *P.* [*macrocephala*]: *toitoi* (North I), *macrocephala* (South I), *dannefaerdi* (Snares), *marrineri* (Auckland) and *chathamensis*. These are often regarded as races of same species, though some have been considered specifically, but given lack of work on their relationships are treated as allospecies here.

Auckland Island Tomtit
Petroica [*macrocephala*] *marrineri*   Plate 26

Identification

Confusion risks: None.

Main characters: Small, large-headed Australian robin (Eopsaltriidae), with mainly black-and-white pattern, very much like male *P.* [*m.*] *chathamensis* but sexual dimorphism indistinct. **Ad** male has black head with small white spot above bill, glossy black upperparts and breast, clean white wingbar and tail-sides, and yellowish-white underparts becoming brighter, more orange on breast. Female has dull black upperparts and upper breast, becoming white on rear underparts, and buff wingbar and tail-sides. **Juv** like ad female, but even duller (greyer tinged) and pattern obscured, while wingbar is reduced and apparently both sexes have reduced

Ad male Auckland Island Tomtit Petroica [macrocephala] marrineri, *Auckland Is, Dec 1999. © Hadoram Shirihai.*

or lack small white spot above bill; immediately after fledging has yellowish-orange gape. All plumages have mainly blackish bill and eye, and yellowish-brown legs.

Voice: As in *chathamensis*, but pending further study.

Size: 13 cm, weight 11 g.

Similar forms: Wholly distinctive within narrow range.

Distribution and biology

Distribution, movements and population: *Marrineri* restricted to Auckland group, on Auckland, Adams, Ocean, Rose, Ewing and Enderby. No population data.

Diet and feeding: Principally insectivorous, including spiders, beetles, caterpillars, moths etc, but also takes fruit in autumn. Feeds in tussac grass, also on shorelines and even floating kelp.

Social behaviour: Year-round territories are defended Jul–Feb; usually mates for life.

Breeding biology: No specific data, but probably similar to Chatham or Snares birds.

Conservation Not globally threatened, but presumably at risk from ever-present threat of accidental arrival of introduced alien mammalian predators.

Taxonomy See Chatham Island Tomtit.

Snares Tomtit
Petroica [*macrocephala*] *dannefaerdi*   Plate 26

Identification

Confusion risks: None.

Main characters: Most distinctive form of *P.* [*macrocephala*] (see taxonomy), both sexes being all black and hardly differentiated;

Ad male Snares Tomtit Petroica [macrocephala] dannefaerdi; this, the only all-black form of the complex, is confined to the Snares. © Peter Reese.

size and structure otherwise as previous forms. **Ad** all black (with slightly greyish fringes to flight feathers), though male appears slightly glossier. **Juv** like ad female, but even duller with greyer tinge to black feathers; immediately after fledging has yellowish-orange gape. All plumages have mainly blackish bill and eye, and yellowish-brown legs.

Voice: As *chathamensis*, but pending further study.

Size: 13 cm, wing length 7.9–8.4 cm, weight 18.3–23.0 g. Female apparently heavier; much overlap in available mensural data, though female may also be longer winged.

Similar forms: Wholly distinctive within narrow range.

Distribution and biology

Distribution, movements and population: Restricted to the Snares. Approximately 500 pairs in 1987.

Diet and feeding: Principally insectivorous, including spiders, beetles, caterpillars, moths etc, but also takes fruit in autumn. Feeds in tussac grass, on shorelines and even floating kelp, and on flies around penguin colonies.

Social behaviour: Year-round territories are defended Jul–Feb; usually mates for life.

Breeding biology: Breeds Oct–Jan. Single-brooded and in exceptionally wet years may not attempt to breed. Nests within 1 m of ground in tree hollow or *Poa* roots. Lays 2–3 eggs incubated by female alone for 18–20 days, and chicks fledge at 17–22 days.

Conservation Not globally threatened, but presumably at risk from ever-present threat of accidental arrival of introduced alien mammalian predators.

Taxonomy See Chatham Island Tomtit.

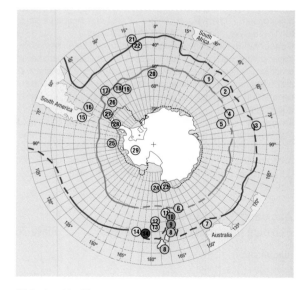

■ Chatham Island Tomtit
Petroica [macrocephala] macrocephala
▨ Aucland Island Tomtit
Petroica [macrocephala] marrineri
■ Snares Tomtit
Petroica [macrocephala] dannefaerdi
▨ Other New Zealand forms
■ Black Robin *Petroica traversi*

8 New Zealand and offshore islands   10 Auckland
9 Snares   14 Chatham   14 Chatham

Black Robin *Petroica traversi*　　　　Plate 26

Identification

Confusion risks: None.

Main characters: Medium-sized, large-headed Australian robin (Eopsaltriidae), with entirely soft black plumage, short fine bill, comparatively long legs and upright stance. Sexes and juv largely undifferentiated. **Ad** almost jet black in all plumages (bare parts same), but at certain angles may appear to have slight grey tinge. **Juv** immediately after fledging has yellowish-orange gape and indistinct greyish shafts to black body feathers. See photo p. 486.

Size: 15 cm, weight 22–25 g.

Similar species: None in limited range: male Chatham Island Tomtit *Petroica* [*macrocephala*] *chathamensis* has white underparts from breast down, with white wingbar and tail-sides.

Distribution and biology

Distribution, movements and population: Once widespread in Chatham group, but now restricted to Mangere and South East. Population 259 individuals in 1999.

Diet and feeding: Feeds on forest floor or low branches entirely on invertebrates, including caterpillars, spiders and larvae. Only rarely hawks for insects.

Social behaviour: Year-round territories especially marked in breeding season. Pair-bond may be life-long.

Breeding biology: Oct–Jan, mostly Oct–Dec. Female alone builds nest and broods eggs and young. Lays 1–3 cream eggs marked purplish-brown, incubated 17–19 days. Both parents feed young which fledge at 20–23 days and are sexually mature at one year, though rarely breed until second year. Single-brooded but can lay 1–2 replacement clutches if first fails.

Conservation Endangered. Subject of an intensive wildlife management programme, Black Robin has literally staged a comeback from the brink of extinction. In 1980 there were just five birds, including only one productive female, due to habitat degradation in their final refuge on Little Mangere. Following a detailed programme of foster parentage, reintroduction and relocation attempts, habitat management and nest protection, the species has been increasing consistently since 1981 and numbers continue to rise, albeit slowly.

Taxonomy Monotypic.

New Zealand Bellbird
Anthornis melanura　　　　Plate 26

Identification

Confusion risks: None.

Main characters: One of the most widespread New Zealand passerines (within our region confined to Auckland), generally in forest, but adapts to human settlement, and especially known for its vocalizations (more often heard than seen). Medium-sized, mainly greenish-olive, with short curved bill and slightly forked longish tail. Sexes largely alike and limited seasonal/age-related plumage variation. **Ad** male almost uniform olive-green, but paler (and yellower) below, with ill-defined dusky hood (visibly glossed purple if seen close) and variably darker, metallic blue-black wings and tail; characteristic yellowish patch at bend of folded wing. Female generally similar but overall duller, with less-hooded appearance (also only indistinctly glossed bluish), profusely streaked below and has diagnostic narrow yellowish-white stripe at lower border of cheeks. Bill and legs mainly dark slate-grey and eye bright red.

Juv differs from similar ad female in brown eye and is duller, less glossy on head and upperparts, but richer yellow (especially juv male) below including cheek stripe.

Voice: Song unmistakable except with Tui *Prosthemadera novaeseelandiae*, loud penetrating, liquid, ringing bell-like whistles, *whae-wee-whee-a…*

Size: 20 cm, weight 26–34 g. Male heavier.

Similar species: Within our region wholly distinctive.

Distribution and biology

Distribution, movements and population: New Zealand, including adjacent islands and Auckland. Extirpated from Chatham by c.1906.

Diet and feeding: Both this species and the next are nectarivorous (including on Southern Rata *Metrosideros umbellata*) and also take insects.

Social behaviour: Maintain long-term territories, but may be at least partially nomadic outside the nesting season, when usually solitary and may defend feeding territory, though other individuals share resources.

Breeding biology: Breeds Sep–Feb, but no specific data from our region.

Conservation Not globally threatened.

Taxonomy Four subspecies: *obscura* is confined to Three Kings I, with *oneho* breeding only on Poor Knights I (and visiting nearby E North I), nominate *melanura* on North I to Stewart and Auckland, and the now extinct *melanocephala* restricted to Chatham.

Tui *Prosthemadera novaeseelandiae*　　　　Plate 26

Identification

Confusion risks: None.

Main characters: Large, mainly blackish forest passerine, with some unique characters. Rather widespread in New Zealand, but within our region confined to Auckland and Chatham. Sexes alike and very limited seasonal/age-related plumage variation. **Ad** predominately sooty-black, with bronze-green and bluish-purple iridescences visible if seen close, cinnamon-brown tone to mantle, scapulars and flanks, and whitish upper wingbar. Also at close range has characteristic white throat tufts and filaments on neck. Legs, eye and slightly decurved bill mainly black. **Juv** differs from similar ad in duller, browner and less iridescent plumage, and lacks white throat tufts. See photo p. 488.

Voice: In mainland New Zealand, song varies regionally, but is usually high pitched, rather rich and melodic, intermixed with croaks, coughs, clicks, wheezes etc; no specific information from Auckland or Chatham.

Size: 30 cm, weight 110–150 g (Chatham). Male larger and heavier.

Similar species: Within our region unmistakeable.

Distribution and biology

Distribution, movements and population: New Zealand and adjacent outliers, Auckland, Kermadec and Chatham.

Diet and feeding: Nectarivorous (including on Southern Rata Metrosideros umbellata) and also take insects.

Social behaviour: Usually solitary, but may form small loose flocks in winter (when also roosts communally) while maintaining strict, closely guarded feeding territories.

Breeding biology: Breeds Sep–Feb, but few specific data from our region.

Conservation Not globally threatened.

Taxonomy Polytypic: the nominate form breeds throughout the range, apart from Chatham where replaced by *chathamensis*, which is now confined to Pitt and South East, and occasionally Mangere. Recently extinct on main Chatham island but may still occur as vagrant.

Seals

The following accounts describe all five phocid or 'true' seals (see Plate 29), namely Southern Elephant *Mirounga leonina*, Weddell *Leptonychotes weddellii*, Crabeater *Lobodon carcinophaga*, Leopard *Hydrurga leptonyx* and Ross Seals *Ommatophoca rossii*, and the otariids (eared seals), including all of the fur seals *Arctocephalus* spp. (see Plate 27) and South American *Otaria flavescens*, Australian *Neophoca cinerea* and New Zealand (Hooker's) Sea Lions *Phocarctos hookeri* (Plate 28). For a general introduction to the seals see the marine mammals section within the book's introduction.

Until recently, our knowledge of seals was largely confined to that part of their lives that brings them to land or sea ice, but electronic tagging during the last decade has brought increasing insights into their marine biology. They are wholly dependent on the ocean for food. As mentioned above seals of the Antarctic and subantarctic comprise two types, the eared (otariid) and 'true' or earless (phocid) seals. The former group includes fur seals and sea lions, which share the following general characteristics. The hind flippers can be pointed forwards or rotated beneath the body, the fore flippers are long and bent when walking; both sets have black leather soles, rather than fur, and can be splayed sideways to support the raised body. Some of the digits have nails, usually set well back from the trailing edges, and all species within this group can walk or run with their limbs tucked below the body. When moving on land their bodies appear sleek and tapered but heavy shouldered around the neck. Fur seals and sea lions also possess small, pointed ears and short free tails, while males have external testes. Mature males always appear larger than the cows

and have a matted lion-like mane. All species have less blubber than the true seals and because of their colonial behaviour may appear more lively and alert, having flexible necks (as do many phocids) and dog-like heads. The snout is squared and bristled and, in the water, the fore flippers are extended and used to propel the animal forward. Sea lions are more heavily built than fur seals and generally larger, but possess only a single, coarse layer of hair. They have more rounded, dog-like faces and muzzles (rather than being more pointed and otter-like), sandier coats in females and much denser manes and shoulders in bulls. Both sexes, especially males, appear to have smaller eyes than fur seals. Unlike fur seals, their snout appears shorter, the nose generally broader and blunter, and the earflaps relatively shorter and are held close to the head. In addition in areas where fur seals and sea lions coexist, the latter often select open beaches that are sheltered from heavy surf, feeding closer inshore than fur seals.

The phocid seals include all of the other species found in Antarctica, including Southern Elephant Seal. They spend much of their life in the water and are excellent swimmers and divers, and some species are capable of remaining submerged for up to two hours, reaching significant depths. Unlike eared seals they generally rely on their rear flippers for locomotion but on land the hind flippers cannot be rotated forward. All but the Southern Elephant Seal mate in the water, but the pups are always born on the ice or land. True seals can be identified by the following features: short paddle-like flippers with the hind limbs trailing, bristly fur with a thick layer of fat, and their ungraceful movements on land, as they are unable to use their hind flippers as aids. But, if they appear

Ad Weddell Seals Leptonychotes weddellii; *the bull is keeping watch on others in the water, ensuring they don't take over the hole in the sea ice that it has claimed. In early summer, while females rear their pups, fierce disputes are fought below the ice. Mature males spend most time underwater, defending territories around their holes. All females at a breathing hole mate with the male defending it. McMurdo Sound, near Ross I, Nov 1991.*
© *Kim Westerskov.*

Plate 27 Fur seals

New Zealand Fur Seal ad. ♂
(p. 336)

Subantarctic Fur
Seal ad. ♀

Subantarctic Fur Seal
ad. ♂ (p. 340)

Contrasting yellowish
and ginger pigments to
face/chest (both sexes);
bull on land may also have
diagnostic small crest on
forecrown

Long, straight sharp-
pointed snout and dark
fur, mainly greyish
olive-brown; often just
the fore snout is dis-
tinctly cream-coloured;
abundant whiskers

New Zealand
Fur Seal ad. ♀

South African Fur
Seal ad. ♀

South African
Fur Seal
ad. ♂
(p. 339)

Antarctic Fur Seal ad. ♂
(p. 337)

As Australian Fur Seal (not illustrated): generally somewhat
sea lion-like appearance (mane very large); long, pointed,
slightly upward-curved snout; darker/browner more even
coloured fur; long whiskers

ng neck and small head,
th distinctly convex
rehead and short, broad
out; well-developed,
ver-streaked mane; c.1%
population is honey-blond
orph (not illustrated)

Antarctic Fur Seal ad. ♀

Pups of all forms very similar

South American Fur
Seal ad. ♂ (p. 334)

Stocky body with moderately
pointed snout; mainly dark
brownish-grey, prominent
mane but rest of body much
slimmer

South American
Fur Seal pup

South American
Fur Seal ad. ♀

Note: all forms very similar and difficult to identify outside normal range, females/imms
even less separable; illustrations only depict animals with dry fur (wet animals darker
and usually indistinguishable); honey-blond morph occurs only in Antarctic Fur Seal.

very ungainly on land, in the water they are supremely agile creatures capable of surprising manoeuvres. Phocids also lack earflaps (pinnae), having only a small ear canal and, unlike male eared seals, the sexual organs are never visible but located inside the body cavity and protected below a thick layer of skin.

Elephant seals differ in some respects from other phocid seals. Sexual differences are much more pronounced. Mature males, in addition to being considerably larger, possess an inflatable proboscis or sac on the upper surface of the snout (hence their name). When fully inflated, for instance during territorial disputes, it overhangs the upper jaw adding considerably to the head's massive bulk. The proboscis may also serve to amplify the wide range of snorts and roars that accompany battles with rivals, but is not acquired until the third or fourth year.

Here I would like to pay short tribute to previous generalist contributions to our knowledge of the pinnipeds, including the excellent *Handbook of Marine Mammals* edited Ridgway & Harrison (1981), *The Sierra Club Handbook of Seals and Sirenians* by Reeves *et al.* (1992) and *Marine Mammals: Evolutionary Biology* by Berta & Sumich (1999), while many of the life history details in the following accounts, especially for Antarctic species, are based on *Antarctic Seals* edited by Laws (1993). The publication of Perrin *et al.* (2002) *Encyclopedia of Marine Mammals*, which I was fortunate to see in page proof, is likely to provide a new standard for both amateur and professional marine mammal enthusiasts seeking information on pinnipeds and cetaceans, while another very recent publication—the *National Audubon Guide to Marine Mammals of the World* (Reeves *et al.* 2002)—is also of interest.

Comments on field Identification

In attempting identification of seals, it is important to be aware that all species display great individual variation in size, shape and colour and pattern of their coat, reflecting complex age development, often the degree of sexual dimorphism and marked seasonal changes in overall bulk. Fur condition can substantially vary with wear (usually bleaching paler/browner or the mottled, streaked and spotted pattern fades), discoloration caused by local soil conditions, while texture and colour markedly change with degree of wetness (becoming much silkier, darker and less patterned when wet). Moreover, shape, coloration and jizz are completely different on land, in surface water and in deeper water. Identification at sea of several confusion species has been largely ignored by the literature. Fortunately, on the subantarctic island breeding grounds usually only one species of fur seal and Southern Elephant Seal are involved (though on some islands up to three species of fur seal may occur, giving rise to considerable potential confusion), and further south in the Antarctic, only Weddell, Leopard, Crabeater and Southern Elephant Seals are usually encountered, thus few identification problems should arise, especially given good views.

As mentioned above, categorization as either a 'true' or 'eared' seal should be easy. When dealing with similar species, however, it is best to use several features in combination, particularly overall size and proportions, head profile, flipper size and, in some, fur coloration and pattern. General behaviour and movements can also be very useful—identification of a sleeping seal on the ice is often not straightforward.

In summary, major confusion is possible only in areas where more than one species of fur seal or, to a lesser extent, where both a sea lion and fur seal coexist. Especially without previous field experience and if dealing with animals away from breeding areas, identification could be impractical under many circumstances. In Antarctica, it is surprising how much the appearance of an animal can alter when it moves and according to the angle of view, e.g.

Weddell and Crabeater Seals can sometimes pose problems and a distantly seen Leopard Seal could be mistaken for a young Crabeater; prolonged views will sometimes be required. Identification of Ross Seal is also often not easy.

Approaching seals on land and ice

A number of guidelines have been established by international treaties and agreements and within domestic statutes and regulations concerning this issue, and most Antarctic tour operators follow these conventions. True seals are far less aggressively territorial towards humans. In the case of Weddell, Ross and Southern Elephant Seals many animals will remain motionless even if an observer approaches closely, but Crabeater and usually Leopard will attempt to escape into water. Keep at least 10 m from the first three, and 50 m or more from Crabeater and Leopard. You should treat fur seals and sea lions with great respect, as they possess a somewhat aggressive reputation, and remember that you are an uninvited visitor to their breeding and feeding areas. Guides should advise you to maintain at least 10–20 m distance from these animals, depending on the number of individuals, the nature of the landing site and stage of the breeding season. Bulls, in particular, appear to regard the upright posture of humans as a threat, and move menacingly toward the observer. In such cases you should move immediately away, and always attempt to keep a wide berth because they are capable of fast movements despite their ponderous appearance. Experienced guides often find a good place that offers excellent opportunities for photography but does not disturb the animals. Eared seals have very sharp teeth and can run much faster than humans over most terrain so always keep a respectful distance.

Classification

The plates follow an order adopted by several field guides and related works, and are designed specifically for in the field use and to facilitate comparisons between easily confused species within a Southern Ocean context. The traditional classification of genera and families within the seals (which is followed by the text) are presented below. Only those families with representatives in the Southern Ocean are included and bear in mind that not all of the genera listed for each family occur in our region.

Order Carnivora Subgroup Pinnipedia: **Seals**

- Family Otariidae: **Eared Seals** (genera *Arctocephalus*, *Callorhinus*, *Eumetopias*, *Neophoca*, *Otaria*, *Phocarctos* and *Zalophus*)
- Family Phocidae: **True Seals** (genera *Cystophora*, *Erignathus*, *Halichoerus*, *Histriophoca*, *Hydrurga*, *Leptonychotes*, *Lobodon*, *Mirounga*, *Monachus*, *Ommatophoca*, *Pagophilus*, *Phoca* and *Pusa*)

South American Fur Seal
Arctocephalus australis   Plate 27

Identification

Confusion risks: Other fur seals and to some extent sea lions.
Main characters: Rather large and generally like Antarctic Fur Seal *A. gazella*. Size, structure and fur appearance varies strongly according to sex and age. **Ad** male dark brownish-grey with prominent mane of longer, paler/greyer fur; rest of body much slimmer and lower body tinged variably yellowish, and flippers dark reddish-brown. Female more uniform grey-brown, paler tan ventrally and sometimes inclining to greyish-black dorsally; most also have variable dusky eye mask and clearly paler areas around muzzle and ears, thus very similar to female *A. gazella*. **Pup** born with velvet-black short curled coat, moulting to blackish-grey after 3–4 months; the latter replaced several months later by an olive-grey

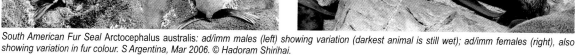

South American Fur Seal Arctocephalus australis: ad/imm males (left) showing variation (darkest animal is still wet); ad/imm females (right), also showing variation in fur colour. S Argentina, Mar 2006. © Hadoram Shirihai.

coat. **Imm** male still distinctly smaller and lacks heavy mane.

Physical notes: Male 1.8–2.0 m and 75–160 kg, female 1.4–1.5 m and 35–58 kg; pup at birth 3.5–5.5 kg (female), and 60–65 cm long (male) and 57–60 cm (female).

Chief identification at sea: See note under Antarctic Fur Seal *A. gazella* that refers to all fur seals; could also be confused at sea with South American Sea Lion *Otaria flavescens*, especially in poor visibility, and due to darker fur when wet and significant age/sex variation.

Voice: Includes 11 call types, which have been grouped into four functional classes: investigative, threat, submissive, and affiliative (Phillips & Stirling 2001).

Similar species: Very similar (especially nominate *australis*) to Antarctic Fur Seal, and they are probably indistinguishable outside normal ranges. Separation from other fur seals equally difficult, but see comparison with rather distinctive Subantarctic Fur Seal *A. tropicalis*. Could also be confused with South American Sea Lion (which see), but if seen well should be readily identified by many characters.

Distribution and biology

Distribution, movements and population: S South America, ranging north to Peru (at 6°S) and S Brazil south to 45°S in Argentina and 54°S in Chile, also Galápagos and the Falklands, and vagrant to

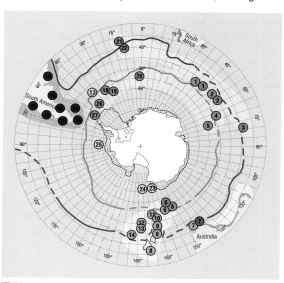

■ South American Fur Seal *Arctocephalus australis australis*
New Zealand Fur Seal *Arctocephalus forsteri*
Antarctic Fur Seal *Arctocephalus gazella*
Subantarctic Fur Seal *Arctocephalus tropicalis*
Australian Fur Seal *Arctocephalus [pusillus] doriferus*
South African Fur Seal *Arctocephalus [pusillus] pusillus*

1 Prince Edward & Marion
1 Prince Edward & Marion
2 Crozet
2 Crozet
3 Amsterdam & St Paul
4 Kerguelen
5 Heard & McDonald
6 Macquarie
6 Macquarie
6 Macquarie
7 Tasmania
7 Tasmania
8 New Zealand and offshore islands
9 Snares
10 Auckland
11 Campbell
12 Antipodes
13 Bounty
14 Chatham
15 South American offshore islands
16 Falklands
18 South Georgia
19 South Sandwich
20 Bouvetøya
21 Tristan da Cunha
22 Gough
26 South Orkney
27 South Shetland

Ad male South American Fur Seal Arctocephalus australis, S Argentina, Mar 2006. © Hadoram Shirihai.

Colombia and the Juan Fernández. Population 275,000–325,000 individuals in recent years but numbers may fluctuate negatively in response to El Niño events.

Diet and feeding techniques: Little information, but takes a variety of fish as well as sea snails, cephalopods and crustaceans.

Main social behaviour: Often occurs sympatrically with South American Sea Lion, but they separate in their choice of beaches; sea lions preferring more sandy shores and fur seals occupying rocky areas.

Breathing and diving: Usually reaches up to 40 m below surface and dives for up to three minutes, but may achieve depths of 170 m and remain underwater for up to seven minutes.

Breeding biology: Bulls reach breeding areas in Nov. Harems of 2–3 females to each bull. Most pups born in Nov–Dec in our region (possibly unlimited breeding season in Galápagos and mid-Oct–Dec in Peru), and ads mate again 6–8 days after birth, with breeding groups disbanding from late Jan. Postpartum females alternate between periods of 1.3 days ashore nursing pups and 4.6 days at sea feeding. Pups are weaned for 7–36 months, but there is no data on when they reach sexual maturity.

Conservation Lower Risk—least concern and CITES Appendix II. Commercially exploited off Uruguay in Jul–Aug, where up to 12,000 animals, largely young males, were taken annually into 1990s, while poaching may be a problem in a number of other localities, especially in Peru. Population is only 1000–2000 in Galápagos. In recent years populations in S Chile have been threatened by developing salmon industry, with seals becoming entangled in nets.

Taxonomy Previously considered polytypic, with nominate *australis* on the Falklands, *gracilis* in S Brazil, Uruguay, Argentina and Chile, occasionally Peru, and *galapagoensis* in Galápagos. Latter is smallest and is now accorded species status, while that in the Falklands is largest, though *gracilis* and nominate may not warrant separate taxonomic recognition.

New Zealand Fur Seal
Arctocephalus forsteri   Plate 27

Identification

Confusion risks: Other fur seals and to some extent sea lions.

Main characters: Rather large and generally approaches Antarctic Fur Seal *A. gazella*, especially in its more otter-like head with sharply pointed snout. Size, structure and fur appearance strongly varies according to sex and age. **Ad** male dark greyish olive-brown dorsally, including flippers, becoming to some extent paler grey-brown ventrally, but in comparison with congeners tends to appear more evenly dusky-olive (like others, appears blackish when wet); often just the fore snout is distinctly cream-coloured. Bull has moderately developed mane and rather heavy chest. Female distinctly smaller and paler greyish olive-brown above, becoming variably paler ventrally, but in some crème colour covers entire underparts. Both sexes have abundant whiskers, especially luxuriant and long in ad male. **Pup** born with velvet-black or blackish-brown short-curled coat, moulting to olive-grey at 2–3 months. **Imm** male still distinctly smaller and lacks heavy mane.

Physical notes: Ad male reaches 180–200 kg and 2 m, whereas female seldom exceeds 39 kg and 1.5 m; pup at birth up to 3.9 kg (male) and 3.3 kg (female), and reach 14 kg and 12.6 kg when ten months old.

Chief identification at sea: See note under Antarctic Fur Seal *A. gazella* that refers to all fur seals; the species may also be confused at sea with both sea lions in near range, mainly due to age/sex variation and poor visibility.

Voice: Probably much as other fur seals (see *A. gazella*).

Similar species: For comparison with Subantarctic Fur Seal *A. tropicalis* see latter; very similar to Antarctic Fur Seal, and outside main ranges might only be separated with certainty if typical bull of latter involved, which unlike present species has well-developed,

New Zealand Fur Seal Arctocephalus forsteri: *bull and female (right) with an intruder male. Both sexes have abundant whiskers, especially luxuriant and long in ad male, imparting more otter-like head with sharply pointed snout. Bounties, Jan 2007. © Hadoram Shirihai.*

New Zealand Fur Seal Arctocephalus forsteri: all otariids raft on surface with raised flippers, enabling them to lose heat via the bare parts, though such habits may also possess signaling functions. Chathams, Feb 2007. © Hadoram Shirihai.

silvery-streaked mane, and female tends to have better marked face (see latter for specific characters). Might also be confused with Australian Fur Seal A. [p.] doriferus, but latter in all corresponding age/sex classes is larger/stronger with darker/browner and less olive-tinged fur, and bull is heavier chested (mane very large) with somewhat more sea lion-like appearance. Australian Neophoca cinerea and New Zealand Sea Lions Phocarctos hookeri, especially if seen well on land, should be readily identified by many characters described in the introduction to the seal accounts, e.g. more pointed otter-like (rather than round dog-like) head/snout, and preference for rocky, less sandy coastal habitats; see also sea lions for further details.

Distribution and biology

Distribution, movements and population: Breeds on islands and coasts of New Zealand and S Australia. Total population perhaps 85,000–135,000 animals in 1990s and increasing, with 20,000–22,000 at Westland and Fiordland alone in 1989 and 35,000 in Australia. Seasonal movements in New Zealand take at least some bulls further north within islands and subad and juv animals appear on Macquarie in large numbers in Feb–Apr. Some propensity to wander, with three yearlings being discovered in New Caledonia in 1972–3.

Diet and feeding techniques: Principally takes squid and octopus, with some fish (largely non-commercial species). Lampreys, rock lobster, crabs and penguins also occasionally taken.

Main social behaviour: Much as other fur seals.

Breathing and diving: Reaches a max. depth of 274 m (more usually 30–74 m) and spends up to 11 minutes underwater. Diving behaviour varies seasonally and according to time of day.

Breeding biology: In rookeries usually on exposed, rugged coastlines. Bulls arrive in mid-Oct–Nov, followed by cows approximately 2–4 weeks later. Males fast for up to two months while defending territory. Pups born late Nov to mid-Jan with a peak in mid-Dec and ten days later cows mate again. Pups stay with mother for nearly a year, the female first visiting the sea nine days after birth then spending alternate periods of 2–7 days ashore nursing and 1–5 days feeding at sea. Males defend territories when ten years old but presumably reach sexual maturity earlier, while females are capable of breeding at five years.

Conservation CITES Appendix II. It was hunted almost to extinction in the late-18th and early-19th centuries, but has largely been protected since the 1890s and numbers are still increasing. Some limited sealing, under licence, is permitted. Some individuals have been killed in discarded fishing nets and by a hoki fishery established in 1989–90.

Taxonomy Monotypic but significant genetic differences have been noted between New Zealand and Australian populations, and also between different subpopulations within the former country.

Antarctic Fur Seal Arctocephalus gazella   Plate 27

Identification

Confusion risks: Any other fur seals.

Main characters: Rather slim fur seal, with relatively long neck, small head and pointed snout. Strong sex-/age-related and individual variation, mainly in size and tone and development of fur. **Ad** male generally dark brown, but fur appears much paler and greyer when ashore, due to grizzled silver-white hair on crown and heavy mane on neck, shoulders and breast (face darkish), with broad dusky yoke, flippers and back, but belly and rear sides paler, often tinged ginger. Especially when territorial, bull has moderately heavy mane. Female notably smaller (see below) and more delicately built, and variable fur is generally paler and greyer; darkest are flippers, and there is often a variable dark facial mask, which is bolder and darker around and behind eye, while muzzle/throat and belly are palest. Approximately 1% of population is honey-blond morph (both sexes and all ages). **Pup** born with velvet-black short-curled coat, moulting to olive-grey shortly after. **Imm** male still obviously smaller than ad male, has more uniform dark olive-brown fur and lacks heavy neck mane.

Physical notes: Averages 1.9 m in males and 1.2 m in females. Mean estimated weights 188 kg (males) and 45 kg (females, but reaches 50 kg); pup at birth up to 5.2 kg (male) and 5.9 kg (female), reaching 17 kg and 14 kg when weaned.

Chief identification at sea: Like other fur seals typically porpoises; often leaping clear of water to reveal head and other parts, and when close to shore often fans hind flippers with rest of body below surface. In wet conditions and especially in water largely appears very dark or black and almost unpatterned; identification from other fur seals thus often difficult and perhaps impossible at sea, given current knowledge.

Voice: All fur seals utter a complex series of vocalizations (see A. australis for a recent study), of which the most characteristic is a non-directional trumpet-like roar, which functions as a threat call among males.

Similar species: Especially away from breeding grounds could be confused with, or overlooked as, any other fur seal described here, but present species only known to meet Subantarctic Fur Seal A. tropicalis (which see) on several subantarctic islands, especially in

Young male Antarctic Fur Seal Arctocephalus gazella. All fur seals habitually use their hind-flippers for grooming, when they often appear to be pondering 'what to do next'. South Shetlands, Mar 2003. © Hadoram Shirihai.

Full-grown (right) and younger male Antarctic Fur Seal Arctocephalus gazella *in confrontation. Note grizzled silver-white crown to mane, with quite short and sparse whiskers. South Shetlands, Mar 2003. © Hadoram Shirihai.*

Indian Ocean, and to lesser extent with New Zealand Fur Seal *A. forsteri*. See also South American Fur Seal *A. australis*.

Distribution and biology

Distribution, movements and population: This species may have been the original fur seal on Macquarie Island that was decimated by sealers. Breeds from 61°S to Antarctic Convergence, with most on South Georgia and other colonies on South Orkney, South Shetland, South Sandwich, Bouvetøya, Marion, Kerguelen, Heard, McDonald and Macquarie. Wanders in non-breeding season to Weddell Sea, Argentina and recorded recently on Juan Fernández Is; females may perhaps migrate north of Antarctic Convergence. Current population numbers at least c.1.6 million (some suggest that it is perhaps as large as four million), with rapid expansion to many islands from South Georgia and increase in numbers until the present.

Diet and feeding techniques: Feeds largely on krill at night but takes fish in non-breeding season and away from South Georgia.

Main social behaviour: Males establish breeding territories for 20–40 days and very sociable at all seasons.

Breathing and diving: Mainly recorded at depths of 30–75 m with dives averaging two minutes (longest ten minutes), but may reach up to 181 m below surface. Males tend to forage significantly deeper than females.

Breeding biology: Breeds on land in late Nov–late Dec in large

Pup Antarctic Fur Seal Arctocephalus gazella: *c.1% of population on South Georgia is honey-blond morph (both sexes and all ages). South Georgia, Mar 2006. © Hadoram Shirihai.*

aggregations on rocky coasts. Females give birth c.2 days after arrival. Males have harems of 5–15 females, with additional attendant males and subordinates. Pups are nursed 5–8 days and females mate again at end of perinatal period, feeding at sea for 3–6 days and visiting the pup for 1–2-day periods for first four months of life. Males become sexually mature at 3–4 years old but do not usually breed until aged seven years, while females may reach sexual maturity at three years old and frequently the following year.

Conservation Lower Risk—least concern and CITES Appendix II. Following a long period of exploitation, which commenced in the 1790s, the population has recovered dramatically within the last 50 years colonizing (or recolonizing) many islands (though 95% still occur on South Georgia) and is growing at annual rate of 9.8%. The principal cause of mortality appears to be entanglement in fishing net and other debris, over 70% of recorded deaths involve males.

Taxonomy Monotypic. Hybridizes with both Subantarctic and New Zealand Fur Seals.

Cow Antarctic Fur Seal Arctocephalus gazella *(left) is smaller and more delicate than male of any age, here with her pup. When pups are a few months old they superficially resemble females, but have larger dark eye-patches and 'cleaner' chins. South Georgia, Mar 2006. © Hadoram Shirihai.*

South African Fur Seal *Arctocephalus* [*pusillus*] *pusillus colony with newborn pups; among the largest fur seals, they may bear a closer resemblance to sea lions than others. South Africa.* © Peter Ryan.

South African Fur Seal
Arctocephalus [*pusillus*] *pusillus*   Plate 27

Identification
Confusion risks: Any other fur seals.
Main characters: Largest fur seal and, in some respects, more like a sea lion than its congeners. Size, structure and appearance of fur strongly vary according to sex and age. **Ad** male dark greyish-black above, flippers darker still, slightly paler below; normally very heavy chested and has thick dark mane. Female distinctly smaller, paler and mainly brownish silver-grey above, becoming paler brown ventrally, some tinged slightly yellowish on chest and throat. **Pup** born with velvet-black coat of short-curled hair, moulting to olive-grey or even pale yellow at 3–5 months, which is in turn replaced after one year by silvery-grey coat. **Imm** male still distinctly smaller and lacks heavy mane of ad bull.
Physical notes: Male reaches 2.2 m and 247–350 kg, female 1.5–1.8 m and 57–120 kg; pup at birth up to 70 cm long and 6.4 kg (male) and 4.5 kg (female).
Chief identification at sea: See note under *A. gazella* that refers to all fur seals.
Voice: Reported to have less high-pitched voice than congeners.
Similar species: None in range; see note under *A. tropicalis* referring to potential confusion between seals outside normal range.

Distribution and biology
Distribution, movements and population: Abundant in coastal South Africa, from Algoa Bay, north and west to northern Namibia, where 20–25 breeding colonies are known. Prefers inshore waters, being rarely recorded up to 160 km from land, but is capable of making long-range (up to 1500 km) movements between colonies and has reached north to Angola and southeast to Marion. The total population was estimated at 1.7 million animals in the late 1990s and has been increasing for several decades.
Diet and feeding techniques: Ad principally takes small shoaling fish such as maasbankers and pilchards, though probably any available species taken, as well as broad range of cephalopods. Smaller fish may be swallowed whole underwater, but larger fish may be brought to the surface to be devoured. Usually hunts singly, though groups may congregate at large fish shoals. Principally feeds by day.
Main social behaviour: Most animals return to the rookery at night, but some sleep at sea.
Breathing and diving: Principally surface animals, the species rarely occurs below 50 m, exceptionally to 150 m, and females have been recorded to 204 m, remaining underwater for 7.5 minutes.

Breeding biology: Pups born on land in late Nov–early Dec (exceptionally late Oct to early Jan), with ads forming large aggregations on rocky coasts from mid-Oct. Bulls arrive at colonies first and may defend territories for up to six weeks. Mating occurs within a few days of the pups being born. During first three months female spends mean periods of 2.5 days ashore followed by 3–4 days feeding at sea. Age of sexual maturity appears to be unrecorded, but probably 4–5 years in males (though may not breed until 8–13 years old).
Conservation Lower Risk—least concern. Protected since 1973. Not threatened and not regarded as a threat to commercial fisheries, the population is increasing and in some areas ousting breeding seabirds from shared sites. The species' numbers may also be detrimental to some cetacean species with which it competes for food. Numbers controlled by regulated sealing in Oct–Nov (when c.2000 ads taken) and Jul–Aug (when c.60,000–80,000 pups are exploited).
Taxonomy Monotypic. Debate persists as to whether Australian Fur Seal *A.* [*p.*] *doriferus* is specifically distinct, mainly based on slight cranial differences, or should be considered a disjunct subspecies (the latter course is traditionally followed, e.g. by Rice 1998). In recognition of their widely separated ranges, I have elected to describe them separately.

Australian Fur Seal
Arctocephalus [*pusillus*] *doriferus*   Not illustrated

Identification
Confusion risks: Within range might be confused with New Zealand Fur Seal *A. forsteri*; perhaps also with Australian Sea Lion *Neophoca cinerea*.
Main characters: Characters as South African Fur Seal *A.* [*p.*] *pusillus* (which see). In the field possibly indistinguishable from latter, though slight cranial structural differences have been noted. Older females may develop a paler appearance than younger individuals.
Physical notes: Male reaches 2.2 m and 279–360 kg, female 1.7 m and 76–110 kg; pup at birth up to 80 cm long and 8.1 kg (male) and 7.1 kg (female), and reach 12 kg and 10 kg at one month.
Chief identification at sea: See note under *A. gazella* that refers to all fur seals; those at sea could also be confused with Australian Sea Lion, due to its relatively large size and sea lion-like character.
Voice: Undescribed for identification purposes from South African Fur Seal.
Similar species: Ashore most likely to be confused with New Zealand Fur Seal and, to much lesser extent, with Australian Sea Lion, depending on age/sex. See these species for details, though general distinctions between fur seals and sea lions are discussed in the introduction to the seals.

Ad female Australian Fur Seal Arctocephalus [pusillus] doriferus. *Lady Julia Percy I, Australia, Feb 1999.* © Brett Jarrett.

Ad male Australian Fur Seal Arctocephalus [pusilus] doriferus *is very similar to South African Fur Seal* A. [p.] pusilla; *both have a typical, slightly upward-pointed snout. Lady Julia Percy I, Australia, Feb 1999. © Brett Jarrett.*

Medium-sized Subantarctic Fur Seal Arctocephalus tropicalis *pup, with darker (wet) fur, during 'play' with same-aged pups whilst their mothers are feeding at sea. Gough, Mar 2006. © Hadoram Shirihai.*

Distribution and biology

Distribution, movements and population: Confined to SE Australia, primarily in waters off Victoria and Tasmania where known from nine islands in Bass Strait. Primarily restricted to same areas in non-breeding season, though small numbers wander as far as New South Wales. Population 35,000–60,000 in recent years and stable.

Diet and feeding techniques: Primarily takes fish (principally snook), cephalopods (including squid, cuttlefish and octopus) and crustaceans.

Main social behaviour: Much as other fur seals.

Breathing and diving: Males known to reach 102 m below surface and spend almost seven minutes underwater but females mainly recorded at 65–85 m and spend 2.5 minutes below surface.

Breeding biology: Pups born on land from late Nov, with ads forming large aggregations on rocky coasts from late Oct. Bulls usually arrive at colonies first. Mating occurs within a few days of the pups being born. During first three months female spends mean periods of 2–3 days ashore followed a similar number of days feeding at sea. Pups are occasionally suckled for 1–2 years. Age of sexual maturity is 4–5 years in males (though may not breed until 8–13 years old) and 3–4 years in females.

Conservation Lower Risk—least concern and CITES Appendix II. Original population estimated at 175,000–225,000 animals. Protected throughout its range since the 1970s and commercial exploitation was banned in 1923. A total of 11 colonies and 21 haul-out sites are known and c.10,000 pups are born annually. Overall population appears to have been stable since 1945 with some local increases of up to 6.2% per annum reported.

Taxonomy Monotypic. Considered conspecific with South African Fur Seal by Rice (1998) and others.

Subantarctic Fur Seal
Arctocephalus tropicalis   Plate 27

Identification

Confusion risks: All other fur seals.

Main characters: Similar to previous species, but several physical and structural differences (see below) and, at least on land when dry, coat rather conspicuously patterned. Strong sex/-age-related variation, mainly in size and fur appearance. **Ad** male generally dark olive-brown above and on flippers, merging with paler brown, tinged yellowish-cream, fore face to chest and darker ginger belly; bull normally has rather less heavy mane with fewer white hairs, and unlike congeners may have pale-tipped hair on top of head, often raised almost crest-like, especially when excited. Female smaller and slighter, and variable fur is generally paler/greyer, but approaches male in having essentially paler fore face and underparts; lacks hair on crown. Cheek teeth more prominent and less stained than previous species. **Pup** born with velvet-black or blackish-brown short-curled coat, moulting to olive-grey after 3–4 months. **Imm** male still distinctly smaller than ad male with more uniform dark olive-brown fur, but most tend to have characteristic paler underparts.

Physical notes: Males reach 2 m and weigh 88–165 kg, females 1.4 m and weigh 34–36 kg; pup at birth up to 4.4 kg (male) and 4 kg (female), and reach 12.9 kg and 9.5 kg at one year.

Chief identification at sea: See note under Antarctic Fur Seal A. gazella which also applies to this species, but given close views of well-marked animals with pale underparts may possibly be safely identified from congeners.

Voice: Probably much as other fur seals (but see previous species).

Similar species: Capable of wide dispersal and may reach areas occupied or visited by congeners, in south with *A. gazella*, and with any others further north. Ad has characteristic yellowish and ginger pigments to face/chest, unlike Antarctic Fur Seal, male on land may also have diagnostic crest, and average smaller and slighter than latter. Compared with South African and Australian

Bull Subantarctic Fur Seal Arctocephalus tropicalis: *note contrasting yellowish-orange face (to just above eyes), and often appears to have crest due to pale-tipped hair on forecrown. Abundant whiskers, especially in ad male. Gough, Mar 2006. © Hadoram Shirihai.*

Subantarctic Fur Seals Arctocephalus tropicalis *habitually form large harems on rocky coasts: note yellowish-orange face to chest in bulls and the noticeably smaller cows, with buff-tinged muzzle sides and cheeks, emphasizing dark eye patches and half-collar. Gough, Mar 2003. © Hadoram Shirihai.*

Fur Seals *A.* [*pusillus*] the present species lacks latter's sea lion-like appearance and darker more evenly coloured fur, and also has proportionally longer fore flippers, less prominent eyes and possibly less musky odour. New Zealand and South American Fur Seals *A. australis* larger and heavier, males heavy chested with extended mane and lack yellowish-cream underparts of present species, while females though pale tend to have less sharp contrast below. But all characters are of less use due to extensive individual variation, and without comparative views or field experience, it is doubtful if imms (especially) can be specifically identified. See also other species.

Distribution and biology

Distribution, movements and population: Isolated islands north of Antarctic Convergence, on Tristan da Cunha and Gough, Prince Edward, Marion, Crozet, Amsterdam, St Paul and recently established on Macquarie. There are many records of vagrancy in this species, with over 20 records from South Africa, several from South Georgia, singles from two states in Brazil, Madagascar, the Comoros, Australia and occasional stragglers have been reported on the west coast of New Zealand, the Snares and Antipodes. Increasing population numbered >310,000 individuals in late 1980s, with the vast majority (200,000) on Gough in the 1970s.

Diet and feeding techniques: A generalist taking squid, fish and krill, while those on Amsterdam also take some Northern Rockhopper Penguin.

Main social behaviour: Moult in summer in large groups. At sea, in small groups, often leaps clear of water like penguins and like other fur seals is playful, assuming various attitudes in water.

Breathing and diving: Varies seasonally and according to time of day but deepest recorded dive is 208 m and longest occupied 6.5 minutes.

Breeding biology: Breeds on land in late Nov–early Jan with most pups born in mid-Dec; forms large aggregations on rocky coasts. Males have harems of 5–15 females, with additional attendant males and subordinates. Females mate c.1 week after postpartum and then alternate between nursing pups for 2.5 days and feeding at sea over five-day periods. Males are sexually mature at 4–8 years but rarely breed before latter age, while females reach maturity at 4–6 years and most have usually bred by age five years.

Conservation Lower Risk—least concern. Not threatened and numbers increasing in most colonies except those on Crozet. Those colonies on Gough and Amsterdam appear to be increasing most rapidly.

Taxonomy Monotypic. Interbreeds with New Zealand and Antarctic Fur Seals. Known to interbreed with Antarctic Fur Seal on Macquarie, Marion and Prince Edward (where 0.1% of animals present in 1982 were hybrids) and lone bulls have also established themselves within colonies of the latter species on South Georgia. Hybridization with New Zealand Fur Seal also reported.

Australian Sea Lion *Neophoca cinerea*   Plate 28

Identification

Confusion risks: The only sea lion restricted to Australian waters; at least ashore unlikely to be confused with fur seals.

Main characters: Bulky and typically silver-grey, cream and fawn. Size, structure and fur appearance varies individually according to sex and age, most noticeably in bulls. **Ad** male coal choco-late-brown with longer, rougher neck hair forming moderate mane, and variably patterned yellowish-cream hairs on head and neck, though muzzle usually darker even in extremely pale individuals; rest of dorsal area usually greyer with duskier abdomen and paler throat/chest; flippers dark above. Female silver-grey, becoming

Bull (left) and female Australian Sea Lion Neophoca cinerea. All sea lions are larger and more dog-like, rather than otter-like, in head shape, and are paler than fur seals. Note relatively moderate mane development, blackish face, narrow snout and contrasting pale hindneck of the bull. Australia. © Mitsuaki Iwago/Minden Pictures.

fawn (greyish-brown) dorsally and paler, creamy-yellow below including head-sides and usually pale around eye, but muzzle and mouth-line clearly darker (contrast and demarcation variable). **Pup** born with short-curled natal, chocolate-brown coat, becoming greyer before moulting to mainly dusky creamy-brown at two months; latter replaced after several months by more female-like coat. **Imm** male resembles female in coloration for first two years

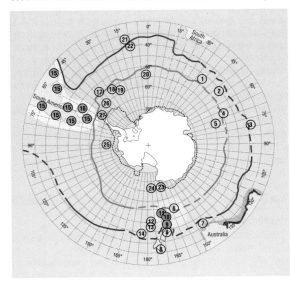

■ Australian Sea Lion *Neophoca cinerea*
■ South American (Southern) Sea Lion *Otaria flavescens*
■ New Zealand (Hooker's) Sea Lion *Phocarctos hookeri*

⑨ Snares
⑩ Auckland
⑪ Campbell

⑮ South American offshore islands
⑯ Falklands

of life, but thereafter larger and bulkier with poorly developed mane, slightly spotted chest and dark muzzle. Gradually, male acquires dark head with some white hairs, white nape and white ring around eye. Female exhibits indistinct age-related variation.

Physical notes: Males reach 2.0–2.5 m and 300 kg, females 1.7–1.8 m and 110 kg; newborn young weigh 6–8 kg and are 62–68 cm long.

Chief identification at sea: Especially paler coloured animals (see above) rather easily separated from any fur seal in region. Beware that all are much darker and appear unpatterned when wet, and separation not always easy, even of distinctive individuals.

Voice: Males produce barking directional calls, which serve to establish dominance within a group, while females utter distinctive vocalizations to their pups when returning from a foraging trip. Though several pups may respond to a female's calls, it appears that these are individually distinctive. When charging each other (or an observer) across beach, calls much like those of fur seals.

Similar species: None in range. Ashore, separation from fur seals generally not difficult, especially if seen well. See discussion under New Zealand Fur Seal *A. forsteri* and introduction to seal accounts.

Distribution and biology

Distribution, movements and population: Offshore islands from the mid-west coast of Western Australia to near Adelaide, South Australia. Known from more than 50 colonies of which just three are mainland sites. May formerly have occurred in N Tasmania and occasionally straggles to New South Wales and further north in Western Australia. Stable population estimated at just 9300–11,700 individuals in recent years, three-quarters in South Australia.

Diet and feeding techniques: Very few data, presumably largely fish and squid, including fiddler rays and cuttlefish, but also known to take Little Penguin *Eudyptula* [*minor*] *minor*. Prey usually caught in mouth and shaken violently above water surface.

Main social behaviour: Very aggressive; pups wandering in colony liable to attacks, occasionally lethal, from bulls, subad males and

Plate 28 Sea lions

South American Sea Lion
ad. ♀

South American Sea Lion ad. ♂
(p. 344)

Old bulls especially
develop huge, lion-like
shaggy mane, with
massive head; typically
short muzzle somewhat
curiously upturned at tip;
bull overall dark brown

Australian Sea Lion ad. ♀

Australian Sea Lion
ad. ♂
(p. 341)

Moderate mane with variable yellowish-
cream head/neck patch; long/narrow
muzzle usually darker; pale ring around
eye in female/young

pup

New Zealand Sea Lion ad. ♀

New Zealand Sea Lion ad. ♂
(p. 345)

Large head with short round muzzle; dense
coarser hair forms heavy mane, mainly around
neck and shoulders; older bulls have even
denser and richer coloured fur

even females, which may be dangerous to humans if possessing a pup. Bulls possess fluid territories, which change in response to availability of females or environmental conditions.

Breathing and diving: Dives recorded to 150 m and may last up to eight minutes, though most reach no deeper than 100 m.

Breeding biology: Poorly known. Inter-colony breeding seasons are apparently asynchronous. Harems usually contain 1–2 females and males practice sequential polygyny. Females come ashore just a few days prior to giving birth in early Oct–early Jan, with gestation occupying 17.5 months and pups being born almost year-round (varies according to site). Females may still be nursing pups from the previous breeding season when about to give birth, and may in consequence reject the newborn pup. Copulation occurs 7–10 days after birth of the pup, but female remains with the pup almost constantly for the first three months (with occasional feeding forays) and suckling continues for 15–18 months.

Conservation Near Threatened. Though protected, the population shows no evidence of having expanded as a result and fishermen continue to kill some. In some areas sea lions may become trapped in monofilament nets and at a site in Western Australia the species has apparently learned to rob salmon and rock lobsters from fisherman's pots, causing some conflict with the local community. The colony of Kangaroo I, South Australia is managed as a tourist attraction, with up to 100,000 visitors per annum.

Taxonomy Monotypic.

South American (Southern) Sea Lion
Otaria flavescens   Plate 28

Identification

Confusion risks: Within our region is the only sea lion in this part of its range and, at least ashore, is unlikely to be confused with fur seals.

Main characters: Large and heavily built. Strong sex-/age-related individual variation in size, structure and appearance, noticeably in fur development of bulls. Fore flipper proportionally very large. **Ad** male overall dark brown, becoming dull tan in summer and tinged yellow-brown on underside. Especially old bulls develop huge, lion-like shaggy yellowish-brown mane extending evenly to flipper level, creating smaller body appearance enhanced by massive head; typically short muzzle somewhat curiously upturned at tip. Ad female rather more strongly built than other sea lions treated here, with denser coat; head and neck paler than rest of body, smaller and more slender; generally dull yellowish-buff ventrally, becoming greyish-brown dorsally. **Pup** black or dark brown

The polygynous South American Sea Lion Otaria flavescens *forms large rookeries, here a bull (right), cow and her pup. Note compressed, blunt-tipped muzzle (all ages/sexes), though bull noticeably larger and darker, even when shaggy mane is held flat. S Argentina, Mar 2006. © Hadoram Shirihai.*

above, greyish-buff below, moulting to overall pale grey-brown at a few months, yearlings become reddish-brown, paler as first-year. **Imm**, at 9–18 months, young male resembles subad female in colour; subsequently acquires a darker, deeper and denser coat and partial mane, sometimes with paler face. Female has less clear age-related variation, but more than previous two species in general pigmentation and structure of fur.

Physical notes: Male reaches over 2.8 m and up to 350 kg, female 2.2 m and 144 kg; newborn males weigh 12–15 kg and are 75–86 cm long, with females being 10–14 kg and 73–82 cm.

Chief identification at sea: See note under Australian Sea Lion *Neophoca cinerea* that refers to all sea lions.

Voice: Probably much as other sea lions (see previous species).

Similar species: None in range. Ashore, separation South American Fur Seal *A. australis* generally rather easy (see note under previous species).

Distribution and biology

Distribution, movements and population: S South America, from SE Brazil (has occurred north to Bahia) and Peru (vagrant north to Galápagos, Colombia and Panama) south to Tierra del Fuego and islands south of Cape Horn, also the Falklands. Only breeds north

South American Sea Lion Otaria flavescens: *all these animals are apparently young non-breeding males, of different ages, which usually form separate gatherings. S Argentina, Mar 2006. © Hadoram Shirihai.*

Bull South American Sea Lion Otaria flavescens *killing pup Southern Elephant Seal* Mirounga leonina. *In all eared eals fur colour and shape varies, not only individually and with age/sex, but also if wet, when the fur becomes darker and silkier looking. Falklands, Mar 2001. © Morten Jørgensen.*

Bull South American Sea Lions Otaria flavescens fight constantly to defend their harems, when their huge, lion-like, shaggy rusty-brown mane is extended. Peru, Oct 2003. © Hadoram Shirihai.

to Uruguay and Peru but has wandered to several S Pacific atolls as far afield as Tahiti. Population c.275,000 individuals in early 1980s and decreasing, being sensitive to El Niño events.

Diet and feeding techniques: Principally takes squid and crustaceans, but small fish are also utilized and, on the Falklands, at least three species of penguins as well as young and female fur seals are taken. Penguins may sometimes be hunted by groups of sea lions.

Main social behaviour: Spends most time in water, but gregarious ashore where remains within a few hundred metres of the water. Males defend strict territories and their harems.

Breathing and diving: Mainly occurs in waters less than 300 m deep and max. recorded dive was to 175 m and for nearly eight minutes but most dives reach 19–62 m for periods of 2–3 minutes.

Breeding biology: Most data is from the Falklands. Ads arrive at colonies in first two weeks of Dec. Bulls form closely spaced territories and possess harems of 8–10 females. Pups are born mid-Dec–early Feb, only 2–3 days after females arrive at colony. Mating occurs c.6 days after birth and females visit sea for first time since giving birth 1–3 days later; thereafter they alternate between periods of three days fishing at sea and two days on land with the pup, which is dependent for 8–12 months. Pups may gather in groups but are recognized by mother using sound and smell. The age of sexual maturity is imprecisely known but may be 4–5 years in females and a year later in males.

Conservation Lower Risk—least concern. Numbers in many areas have declined strongly, principally due to hunting, which has forced colonies to relocate to less accessible areas, but also for unknown reasons. The Falklands population has declined from 300,000, in 1930s, to 30,000 at present, perhaps partially as a result of trawling. Many colonies are now protected but clandestine hunting continues in Uruguay, Chile and probably elsewhere.

Taxonomy Monotypic. Debate has centred over whether the name *flavescens* or *byronia* should be applied to this taxon but *A. Berta* (*in litt.* Mar 2002) reports that the latter may have priority as the holotype of (*Phoca*) *flavescens* is unidentifiable.

New Zealand (Hooker's) Sea Lion
Phocarctos hookeri   Plate 28

Identification
Confusion risks: The only sea lion restricted to S New Zealand waters; at least ashore unlikely to be confused with fur seals.

Main characters: Very large, heavy sea lion with marked sex-/age-related variation in size, structure and fur development, noticeably in bulls. **Ad** male predominantly dark brown to blackish-brown, with denser coarser hair forming heavy mane, mainly around neck and shoulders; older bulls have even denser and richer coloured fur (extremes are never matched by previous species); head large and round with short muzzle. Ad female superficially resembles previous species (see below), with generally dull yellowish-buff coat, indistinctly darker grey dorsally and variable ill-defined brownish hue to muzzle, crown/nape to eye level and flippers. **Pup** sexually dimorphic at birth. Newborn male pale chocolate-brown, paler on nose, top of head and neck. Female predominantly pale-coloured, darker on head and nape. **Imm** male at 9–18 months resembles subad female in colour. Gradually acquires darker thicker fur; tone and size of mane varies. Female exhibits indistinct age-related variation in overall pigmentation and structure of fur.

Physical notes: Male to 2.4–3.5 m and 320–450 kg, female 1.6–2.0 m and 90–230 kg; newborn young weigh 7.2–7.9 kg and are 70–100 cm long with males being larger from birth, achieving 13 kg (versus 11 kg) at 20 days.

Chief identification at sea: See note under Australian Sea Lion *Neophoca cinerea* that refers to all sea lions.

Voice: Probably much as other sea lions (see previous species).

Similar species: None in range. Ashore, separation from New Zealand Fur Seal *A. forsteri* generally rather easy. Note especially rounded dog-like face and muzzle (rather than more pointed and otter-like), sandy coat of female and much denser mane and shoulders of bull; general distinctions between fur seals and sea lions are discussed in the introduction to the seals.

Bull New Zealand Sea Lion Phocarctos hookeri. With age, the mane of bulls becomes broader and shaggier, but in this species the head fur is less dense. Auckland, Dec 1999. © Hadoram Shirihai.

Bulls (dark animals) and (mainly) female New Zealand Sea Lions Phocarctos hookeri. Auckland, Dec 1999. © Hadoram Shirihai.

Distribution and biology

Distribution, movements and population: Breeds on Auckland and Campbell, with very small numbers of pups apparently born on Snares. Regularly observed on New Zealand coast (where breeds on Otago Peninsula), Macquarie and Stewart (where formerly bred), especially young ads. Some non-breeders spend long periods up to 1 km inland within forest or on grass-covered cliffs on Enderby I. Total population stable at 11,100–14,000 individuals in recent years of which over three-quarters occur on Auckland and 95% of pups are born there.

Diet and feeding techniques: Broad variety of prey, mainly small fish, squid (especially octopus), crustaceans (including crabs, crayfish and prawns) and, occasionally, penguins. Some take fur seal and elephant seal pups, and frequently feeds at night.

Main social behaviour: Less aggressive than other sea lions. Highly polygynous, bulls defend territories against rivals, but most combats appear ritualistic, rather than real, and males show no aggression to pups. Some bulls fast for up to six weeks while on land. Moult commences in Feb soon after breeding season.

Breathing and diving: Capable of reaching depths of over 500 m (mean 123 m), at sea this species spends up to 45% of time submerged and up to 11 minutes (mean 4–6 minutes) underwater during each dive.

Breeding biology: Unlike fur seals prefers sandy beaches for breeding. Males arrive in Nov and females in late Nov–early Dec. Harems may number up to 25 females. Pups born over period of 35 days from early Dec and, like fur seals, females mate 7–10 days after giving birth. Territorial bulls generally depart colony mid-Jan. Pups taught to swim by, and leave colony with females at c.3–4 months. Females spend mean 1.7 days at sea foraging and 1.2 days ashore with pup, which gathers into groups with other young. Lactation continues for 8–10 months and pup may remain with female and be suckled for up to one year. Males become sexually mature at five years old, but not socially mature until age 8–10, while females reach breeding condition at three years old and have usually bred by the following year.

Conservation Vulnerable. The species receives total protection and its breeding grounds are all nature reserves. A large trawl fishery for squid, which commenced recently off the Aucklands, has caused 17–141 mortalities per year and exotic fauna introduced by humans, especially rabbits, formerly also had some impact on sea lions. As with all related species, tourism also requires monitoring to ensure that the species is not affected detrimentally. Epizootic diseases may produce large mortalities and 53% of pups died in Jan 1998 apparently as a result of an unknown bacterial infection.

Taxonomy Monotypic.

Leopard Seal Hydrurga leptonyx *smashing through thin ice in pursuit of an Adélie Penguin* Pygoscelis adeliae. *The seals can apparently see the birds crossing the translucent ice above them. The penguin is clearly aware of the danger and is running as fast as possible; it eventually escaped. Cape Crozier, Ross Sea. © Frank S. Todd.*

Leopard Seal *Hydrurga leptonyx*　　　Plate 29

Identification

Confusion risks: Crabeater *Lobodon carcinophaga*, Weddell *Leptonychotes weddellii* and Ross Seals *Ommatophoca rossii*.

Main characters: Long slim body with almost serpentine appearance and comparatively large reptilian head (long fore face/snout, powerful jaws, broad gape and relatively small dark eye), all of which make it easily recognizable if seen well. Fore flippers rather large and situated near centre of body. Rather marked sexual but mainly age-related variation, chiefly in size; tone/contrast of colour and spotted pattern varies mainly individually. On ice responds to human presence with deliberate movements. **Ad** very dark, almost black or blue-grey on flanks, with distinct boundary between dark dorsal and paler ventral colorations; dark area variably spotted darker grey, black and with few paler marks. Fore flipper, lower flanks and belly almost silver with more contrasting dark spots. In most, demarcation between dark/pale areas on head is just below eye, leaving rather contrasting paler, broad silver-grey band across gape and lower cheek. Very long canines and massive incisors with precise occlusion (less so in post-canines, which have fewer cusps). **Pup** similarly patterned but has denser softer fur. **Imm** in first-/second-year still distinctly smaller, sometimes slightly browner than ad, otherwise coloration at all ages similar. Coat colour generally fades only slightly prior to moult period.

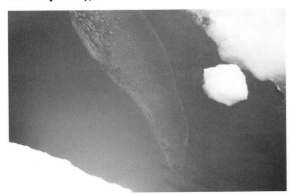

Leopard Seal Hydrurga leptonyx *patrolling the fast ice near a penguin colony for potential prey. Cape Crozie, Ross Sea. © Frank S. Todd.*

Leopard Seal Hydrurga leptonyx *taking an Adélie Penguin* Pygoscelis adeliae *chick. © David Rootes.*

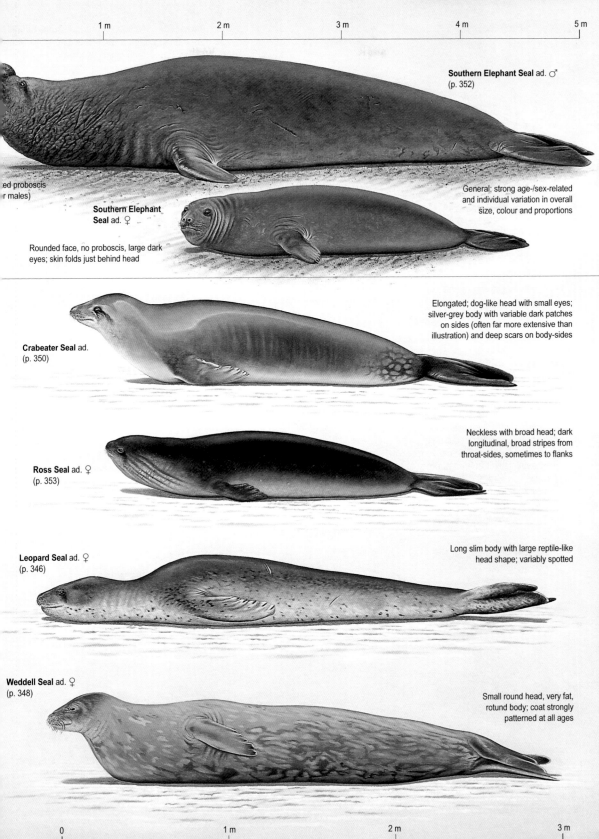

Plate 29 Phocid or true seals

1 m 2 m 3 m 4 m 5 m

Southern Elephant Seal ad. ♂
(p. 352)

...ed proboscis
...r males)

Southern Elephant Seal ad. ♀

Rounded face, no proboscis, large dark eyes; skin folds just behind head

General: strong age-/sex-related and individual variation in overall size, colour and proportions

Crabeater Seal ad.
(p. 350)

Elongated; dog-like head with small eyes; silver-grey body with variable dark patches on sides (often far more extensive than illustration) and deep scars on body-sides

Ross Seal ad. ♀
(p. 353)

Neckless with broad head; dark longitudinal, broad stripes from throat-sides, sometimes to flanks

Leopard Seal ad. ♀
(p. 346)

Long slim body with large reptile-like head shape; variably spotted

Weddell Seal ad. ♀
(p. 348)

Small round head, very fat, rotund body; coat strongly patterned at all ages

0 1 m 2 m 3 m

On the ice, identification of Leopard Seal Hydrurga leptonyx is usually straightforward due to the relatively huge reptilian head shape and greyish-brown dorsal skin, variably spotted, especially on the paler ventral and flank areas. Cape Crozier, Ross Sea. © Frank S. Todd.

Physical notes: Female larger, reaches 3.8 m and 500 kg, but records above that (up 4.5 m and 600 kg) are possibly rare cases and require verification; male 2.8–3.3 m (300 kg). Pup at birth recorded as c.1.0–1.2 m and 30 kg (1.5 m and 35 kg also reported).

Chief identification at sea: In water often holds head up and characteristically reveals back when submerging (head first, only sometimes tail first); characteristic head shape above surface permits immediate identification.

Voice: Underwater trills and moans at low, long frequencies, also gargles, grunts or higher pitched whistles, and vibrated guttural alarms described. Similar sounds also recorded on ice.

Similar species: Mainly due to superficially similar slim body appearance and elongated head profile, on ice Crabeater, especially young or distant animals, is the most likely confusion species. However, especially if able to appreciate Leopard Seal's characteristic massive head and reptilian facial appearance, identification is easy. Also, sometimes young and slimmer individual Weddell Seal could pose some confusion, but again, only temporarily when seen poorly or distantly, and only if observer inexperienced,

as latter has much thicker body and smaller rounded head, as well as different coat coloration to Leopard Seal. See also Ross Seal for comparison, the latter has very different structure but to some extent confusingly similar colours, mainly in young animals.

Distribution and biology

Distribution, movements and population: Widespread but uncommon in Antarctic and subantarctic zones south to 78°S (vagrants occur far north), breeding confined to Antarctic pack ice. An uncommon winter visitor to subantarctic islands (though numbers peak at several hundred in this region every 4–5 years and most frequent at Atlas Cove on Heard in Jul–Sep), and fairly frequently reaches S New Zealand, Australia, South America and South Africa, exceptionally to Tristan da Cunha, Lord Howe, Cook and Juan Fernández Is. Population at least 100,000 and perhaps 220,000–450,000 in 1980s.

Diet and feeding techniques: Broad diet, principally krill, fish, seabirds especially penguins (predation of latter varies according to locality) and young seals (particularly Crabeater and especially at seasons when other food is scarce), but probably mostly takes cephalopods: 1–2 animals often establish themselves close to penguin colony, catching birds as they return from fishing or taking young, killing and skinning them by banging carcass against water.

Main social behaviour: Usually solitary. Can behave aggressively near boats and their occupants, but its fierce reputation toward Man is not particularly warranted as it is unknown to directly attack humans.

Breathing and diving: No published information but presumably remains close to surface where most prey is located.

Breeding biology: Moult Jan–Feb (occasionally until Jun) and pup in Oct–Dec. Males highly vocal prior to and during breeding season in early Nov–Jan. Pups born on pack ice, following c.9-month gestation period, and lactation lasts c.1 month. During this period males are rarely seen. Mating is believed to take place in water in mid-Nov to Dec (though other sources place it as late as early Jan–Mar). Males become sexually mature at 3–6 years old and females at 2–7 years.

Conservation Lower Risk—least concern. Protected. This species has been subject to very little commercial fishing or hunting for research.

Taxonomy Monotypic.

Weddell Seal *Leptonychotes weddellii*　　Plate 29

Identification

Confusion risks: Crabeater *Lobodon carcinophaga*, Leopard *Hydrurga leptonyx* and Ross Seals *Ommatophoca rossii*.

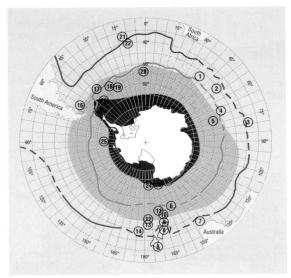

Weddell Seal Leptonychotes weddellii *covered by dusting of snow from a blizzard. McMurdo Sound, near Ross I, Nov 1991.* © Kim Westerskov.

■ Approximate main summer/breeding range
▨ Approximate main dispersal range

Mother and pup Weddell Seal Leptonychotes weddellii *remain close for the first two months of the pup's life. Six to seven weeks after birth, the mother ceases feeding the pup, which now weighs c.100 kg and is able to self-feed (for every kg gained by the newborn pup, the mother loses 2 kg; immediately after having given birth the female is 450 kg, but after feeding the pup for 6–7 weeks is only 300 kg). Ross Sea, Nov 1991. © Kim Westerskov.*

Weddell Seal Leptonychotes weddellii. *Although sleepy and awkward on land, Weddell Seal is alert and agile underwater. McMurdo Sound, near Ross I, Nov 1991. © Kim Westerskov.*

Main characters: Among the largest seals, with proportionately small flippers and head, and very fat, rotund body shape. Coat characteristically patterned at all ages; no obvious sexual differences and ages vary mainly in size. Round face with only slightly protruding fore face/snout and large dark eyes. Very placid and almost docile, ignores human presence (often remains asleep or may roll on its side with head and flipper raised in 'salute'). On ice and land moves very slowly with short 'humping' gait. **Ad** of both sexes similar in size and appearance, but female generally slightly larger and male has thicker neck and broader head and muzzle. Latter tends to be darker on upper surface, and hind flippers usually broader and shredded from fighting. Short dense coat is dark bluish-grey and variably/irregularly streaked and blotched greyish-white, these patches gradually increase in number and size chiefly between sides and abdomen. Can become browner and buffier prior to moult, and blotching on coats of both sexes may also be yellowish and silver. **Pup** has silver-grey, grey-brown or golden woolly coat, with dark stripe on back; initial coat is shed after 44 days. **Imm** in first-/second-year still noticeably smaller than ad; age of non-breeders best estimated by tooth condition.

Physical notes: 2.5–3.0 m and 400–600 kg (female 2.6–3.3 m); pup at birth c.1.2–1.5 m and 22–29 kg (gains 2 kg each day, and may reach 125 kg at weaning).

Chief identification at sea: Very rarely seen in open sea. Floats vertically with head pointing up or level and occasionally floats at angle, submerges tail first without revealing back; characteristic head shape and blotched body only slightly exposed.

Voice: Ashore may produce trills, pleasant musical whistles, guttural and gulping sounds. Also snaps teeth in defence and underwater produces broad range of buzzes, trills and chirps, which are apparently subject to some regional variation.

Similar species: Crabeater, which can have some blotchy marks on coat and more rounded head, is most significant confusion risk. With some experience, however, Crabeater (which see) usually clearly slimmer with more elongated and square-shaped head, and different behaviour, being more active and fast-moving. If present, blotches tend to be rather limited and very often is deeply scarred on body-sides. Some Weddell may also be confusingly pale and more uniform, but never like most Crabeater and coat never wears as pale as extreme, bleached-whitish Crabeater. For comparison with Leopard and Ross Seals see those species.

Weddell Seal Leptonychotes weddellii *with a large Antarctic Toothfish* Dissostichus mawsoni *caught in 300 m deep water under a large hole in the fast ice near Ross I, Ross Sea, Nov 1991. © Kim Westerskov.*

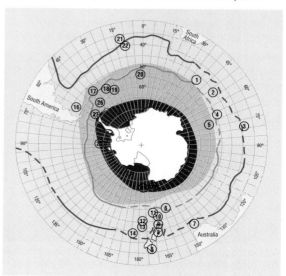

■ Approximate main summer / breeding range
▨ Approximate dispersal range

Distribution and biology

Distribution, movements and population: The most southerly breeding seal, circumpolar in distribution, being most abundant near Antarctic coast, inhabiting both pack and fast ice south to 78°S, and also reaches South Orkney, South Shetland, South Georgia and South Sandwich. Occasional sightings on Auckland, Campbell, Macquarie and other subantarctic islands, and vagrant to New Zealand, S Australia and South America (north to Uruguay and to Juan Fernández Is). Moves north with expansion of pack ice in winter and other more complex, seasonal movements reported. Population placed at 250,000–400,000 in 1980s, but it has recently been suggested that perhaps 500,000 to one million would be a more accurate estimate.

Diet and feeding techniques: Varied diet, mainly fish (but also cephalopods and crustaceans), usually hunted below ice using keen eyesight and high-speed swimming. Males defend three-dimensional territories in water adjacent to breeding colonies. Occasionally feeds in association with Crabeater Seal and also recorded taking Chinstrap Penguin *Pygoscelis antarctica*.

Main social behaviour: Barely social in non-breeding season but sometimes congregates around breathing holes in ice, which are kept open during winter by scraping away newly formed ice with its powerful canines and extended incisors. Mature males actively compete and fight for dominance at fishing holes.

Breathing and diving: Dives up to 750 m for up to 73 minutes, but most foraging dives occupy little more than 15–20 minutes at depths of 50–500 m; reaches deeper in spring than in summer. Diving and navigation abilities enable it to travel several km under thick ice and return to the same hole. Dives longer, deeper and more frequent in daylight than nocturnally.

Breeding biology: May form large colonies (some loose assemblages may number several hundreds) in late Sep–early Nov, giving birth on ice. Cows haul out on ice (or land in some parts of N Antarctica) from late Aug and pup in Sep/Oct (site fidelity varies and timing is earlier at lower latitudes). May occasionally produce two pups. Territorial males below ice attract females by unique vocalizations (see voice) and may mate with any female that enters territory. Generally courtship and mating occur in water, Nov–Dec; pups are weaned for 50–55 days and enter water at 10–14 days in order to extend diet. Females largely spend days 1–12 on ice with pup but thereafter 30–40% of each day is spent in water. Following this cows are ready to mate again. Males rarely seen around colony prior to this, and subad animals also rarely recorded at

Crabeater Seal Lobodon carcinophaga. *The long dark scars are usually attributed to Leopard Seal* Hydrurga leptonyx *attacks when young. The uniform pelage of Crabeater is diagnostic, but many are confusingly richly patterned like Weddell Seal* Leptonychotes weddellii. *Ross Sea, Jan 1999. © Hadoram Shirihai.*

colonies. Moult is Dec–Mar, with young taking c.17 days to replace their first coat. The mean age of first breeding is 6–8 years though may be significantly earlier in cows.

Conservation Lower Risk—least concern. Protected since 1961. There are no accurate and detailed overall estimates of abundance though some regional populations have been surveyed over time. The species has been little hunted for research purposes, though large individuals were taken to feed sled dogs in McMurdo Sound in the 1950s.

Taxonomy Monotypic.

Crabeater Seal *Lobodon carcinophaga* Plate 29

Identification

Confusion risks: Weddell *Leptonychotes weddellii*, Leopard *Hydrurga leptonyx* and Ross Seals *Ommatophoca rossii*.

Main characters: Comparatively slim and lithe, typically with elongated, square-shaped head, protruding dog-like foreface/snout and longer mouth opening, and flippers proportionally larger than Weddell. Eyes dark and small (set far apart). Marked seasonal and individual variation in coat colour and, to lesser extent, pattern; no obvious sexual differences and ages vary mainly in size. On ice, when approached, raises head as if 'pointing' and often moves quickly to water. **Ad** predominantly dark brown dorsally, becoming blond ventrally; variable chocolate-brown patches on silver-grey

Crabeater Seals Lobodon carcinophaga *hauled-out on an ice floe; note their pelage pattern/colour variation, which varies with age, state of bleaching or wetness and, above all, individually, but generally becomes paler and more uniform with age and bleaching. Antarctic Peninsula, Feb 2001. © Morten Jørgensen.*

Very old bull Crabeater Seal Lobodon carcinophaga *with head injuries attributable to fights with Leopard Seal* Hydrurga leptonyx. *With age pelage progressively bleaches whitish. Weddell Sea, Jan 2001. © Hadoram Shirihai.*

Crabeater Seal Lobodon carcinophaga *at breathing hole. © Paul Drummond.*

body-sides are largest near head/neck-sides, and smaller behind fore flippers and on rear body. With age, fur gradually becomes uniform blond after moult, hence name 'the white Antarctic Seal'. Thus many during summer, just before moult, are easily identified by typically uniform appearance, most also lack any blotches on sides. Many are diagnostically deeply scarred on back and body-sides due to attacks by Leopard Seal and sometimes Killer Whale; face and fore flippers also often heavily bleached and scarred (wounds reportedly inflicted in breeding season). Cheek teeth extremely complex, with two upper and one lower pair of incisors. The main cusps of the upper and lower teeth fit perfectly between each other, presumably to sieve invertebrates, especially krill, from water. **Pup** usually milk coffee-brown with darker hind flippers. **Imm** in first-/second-year still noticeably smaller than ad; non-breeders best aged by tooth condition, but 5–8 year-old apparently still distinctly smaller than older animals.

Physical notes: Ads reach 2.0–2.6 m and 180–410 kg (female averages slightly larger); pup at birth c.1.1 m and 36 kg (gains c.4 kg each day and may reach 110 kg at weaning, with a length of 1.6 m) and growth is nearly complete when two years old.

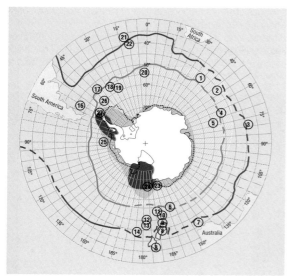

■ Approximate main summer / breeding range
▨ Approximate lower-density summer / breeding range
▨ Approximate dispersal range

Chief identification at sea: Very seldom seen at sea. In water head visible, submerges revealing back.
Voice: Apparently mainly silent underwater (unlike Weddell and Ross Seals), and only when disturbed on ice does it emit blowing/ hissing or snorting noises through nose/mouth (latter partially opened).
Similar species: Given slimmer body and elongated head, an inexperienced observer faced with a distant, especially young animal, the present species is more likely to be confused with Leopard and to some degree Weddell, and less so with Ross Seals, which see for comparison.

Distribution and biology

Distribution, movements and population: Almost exclusively on Antarctic pack ice south to 79°S, occasionally a very few reach the subantarctic islands and New Zealand, Australia, South Africa, the Falklands and South America north to SE Brazilian coast. Presumably migrates but pattern of movements unknown. Recorded up to 113 km from open water and to 1100 m altitude. Probably the world's most abundant pinniped: the best population estimate is 50–75 million in the early 1980s (though others place numbers substantially lower, perhaps 10–15 million).
Diet and feeding techniques: Feeds mainly on krill at night, when their prey is nearer surface, and often attacked by Leopard Seals or Killer Whales while so doing. Swims through shoals of krill, mouth open, sieving them from the water with its multi-cusped lower teeth (see above). Small fish taken in captivity.
Main social behaviour: Occurs singly or in small groups, but occasionally large concentrations of up to 1000 on ice or in water are reported. On ice is fastest moving and most active of true Antarctic seals.
Breathing and diving: Dives recorded to 530 m for up to ten minutes, but most foraging is at 20–30 m, spending 4–5 minutes underwater. Deepest dives are often during crepuscular periods.
Breeding biology: Moult Jan–Feb, occasionally Mar, but continue to feed and swim during this period. Apparently mainly in family pairs rather than harems, though other males may be in close proximity. Gestation occupies nine months. Pup in Sep–Oct, with lactation lasting 2–5 weeks and mating probably occurs two weeks after the pup has been weaned and continues until Dec. Sexual maturity is reached in 2.5–6.0 years with females (of which 80% breed annually) apparently reaching adulthood earlier than males.
Conservation Lower Risk—least concern. Protected since 1978. Although their meat is prized and their pelts are no less desirable than other Southern Ocean seals, commercial fishing is at present

Bull Southern Elephant Seals Mirounga leonine. *As a result of the species' polygynous breeding system, males must fight, which can result in serious injuries to the neck/chest and even face and flippers. St Andrews Bay, South Georgia. © Grant Dixon.*

Southern Elephant Seals Mirounga leonina *copulating; only dominant bulls will mate with the harem. South Georgia. © Hadoram Shirihai.*

Female Southern Elephant Seals Mirounga leonina; *the colour of the pelage varies individually according to state of bleaching or wetness, less so with age/sex, but also due to discoloration from the local soil, as they cover themselves as protection from the sun. Sea Lion I, Falklands, Jan 1991. © René Pop.*

unprofitable because of the species' broad but sparse distribution. Declines have been noted in recent years, but it appears unlikely that these are related to commercial fisheries or hunting to provide meat for sled dogs.
Taxonomy Monotypic.

Southern Elephant Seal *Mirounga leonina*   Plate 29

Identification

Confusion risks: Northern Elephant Seal *M. angustirostris* (no overlap).
Main characters: Heavily built, long-bodied seal with proportionately small flippers and some skin folds just behind head. Dark eyes large and round. Large age-/sex-related and individual variation in overall size, proportions, facial structure and appearance. Very clumsy on land, mainly using body for propulsion in caterpillar-

like fashion (so-called 'humping' gait). **Ad** has short stiff hair, usually dark grey dorsally (when newly moulted, though normally browner being discoloured by sand, mud and excrement) and paler ventrally. Male has square-shaped and larger head, with conspicuous proboscis, while much smaller female has more rounded face and no proboscis. Breeding male may weigh up to six times that of a breeding female. Elongated proboscis (normally limp) becomes inflated and acts as a resonating chamber when bulls roar at each other; neck of ad male often deeply scarred as a result of combats. Female tends to have paler 'yoke' on neck, due to bites during mating. Has two upper and one lower incisor. **Pup** has black coat, replaced after three weeks by a short dark brown (gradually becoming silver-grey) coat, darker above and paler below, when already has heavy body shape, typically rounded face and disproportionately large eyes. **Imm** in first-/second-year like female, but coat variably buff and brown; first-year male already conspicuously larger than ad female, with square-shaped head but proboscis only partially developed, being still short and flat. Moult mainly Dec–Apr, females and young preceding bulls (see below), when coat typically has irregular patchy appearance and becomes browner due to bleaching of old hair, dark brown-grey when in fresh moult.
Physical notes: Male 4.5–6.5 m and 3700 kg; female 2.5–4.0 m and 359–800 kg; pup at birth c.1.3 m and 36–50 kg (in first 23–25 days gains 3.6 kg daily and may then weigh 110–160 kg with a length of 1.6 m).

Female Southern Elephant Seal Mirounga leonina *with newborn pup, and giant petrels and skuas awaiting to scavenge the placenta. © Maria san Román.*

Cooling Southern Elephant Seal Mirounga leonina *with 'sun protection' of soil and sea plants. © Andris Apse.*

Bull and female Southern Elephant Seals Mirounga leonina. Bulls use their weight, fore flippers and elongated proboscis to hold the female while mating. South Georgia. © David Rootes.

Chief identification at sea: Apparently mainly underwater or elusive as rarely recorded at sea; close to breeding islands floats with head and hind flippers clear of water, submerges tail first, head pointing up and withdrawn vertically.

Voice: Ashore both sexes produce belching sounds; male has deep resonant roar while female barks, moans and howls. If disturbed displays fully-open reddish mouth and utters loud alarm.

Similar species: Very similar Northern Elephant Seal of W USA probably never comes into contact with this species. Inexperienced observers may sometimes confuse pups with other seals.

Distribution and biology

Distribution, movements and population: Widely distributed in Southern Hemisphere, breeding either side of Antarctic Convergence (sometimes even on Antarctic mainland and south to 78°S), in S Argentina and most cold temperate and subantarctic islands, where normally uses sandy and shingle coasts. Some individuals recorded far from breeding grounds (north as vagrant to Oman), but seasonal movements poorly known and dispersal may be random. Imms range south to Antarctica (reaching 77°S in the Weddell Sea) and north to Uruguay, South Africa (where occasionally breeds), Australia and New Zealand. Population 640,000 individuals in 1990s, when apparently declining in S Pacific and S Indian Oceans.

Diet and feeding techniques: Varied, but ads take mainly fish and cephalopods, caught in deep water.

Main social behaviour: Males sexually mature at c.4 (females 2–6) years old, but most bulls do not breed before age ten and inter-colony variation exists in age of first breeding of either sex, perhaps related to food supplies at different breeding sites. Due to high mortality (nearly 90% of males die before reaching social maturity) and intense competition for mates, most males never breed and only a few strong bulls breed in more than one season.

Breathing and diving: A remarkable diver, recorded at depths of up to 1444 m and for up to almost two hours underwater (shorter in males), though most dives last 20–27 minutes and reach 400–600 m.

Breeding biology: Highly polygynous, males arrive at breeding sites from late Aug and display aggressively (occasionally with bloodshed) for right to mate with groups of females (harems). A dominant bull may control up to 100 females (mean c.30), who come ashore late Sep–Oct to pup. Pups weaned at 3.0–3.5 weeks. Gestation occupies 49–50 weeks. Females mate following 18–19 days postpartum and then depart, though still occasionally feed pup; the latter remain ashore, fasting, for another 32–50 days. In post-breeding period, mostly from Oct/Nov, harems decline as most ad males and cows depart, but mean fasting period among females at colonies is one month and for breeding males three months. One- and two-year olds return in early Nov. In late Nov/early Dec imms return for 10–20 days, followed by cows in Dec/Jan and bulls 1–4 months later, all to moult, which lasts 21–23 days. By mid-Mar/Apr, most are gone and very few are seen in winter.

Conservation Lower Risk—least concern and CITES Appendix II. Hunted almost to extinction in the 19th and early-20th centuries, but now protected at almost all breeding sites. Commercial exploitation continued longest at South Georgia and eventually ended in 1964. A very significant decline has been noted on Campbell, where fewer than five pups are now born each season and a similar decline is thought to have occurred on the Antipodes. A substantial decline has also occurred on Macquarie.

Taxonomy Monotypic though low interchange between stocks in S Atlantic, S Indian Ocean, S Pacific and Argentina. Three subspecies proposed in late 19th century—*falclandicus* (the Falklands and dependencies), *macquariensis* (Macquarie and possibly Chatham) and *crosetensis* (Crozet and perhaps Kerguelen and Heard)—and as many as five recognized by some early-20th century authors but all have long been regarded as synonyms (see Rice 1998).

Ross Seal *Ommatophoca rossii*　　　　Plate 29

Identification

Confusion risks: Crabeater *Lobodon carcinophaga*, Weddell *Leptonychotes weddellii* and Leopard Seals *Hydrurga leptonyx*.

Main characters: The smallest Southern Ocean seal. Graceful, appears neckless and head broad and round, with indistinctly protruding fore face/snout and has short gape opening; dark eyes relatively large; body very thick around head/chest and appears

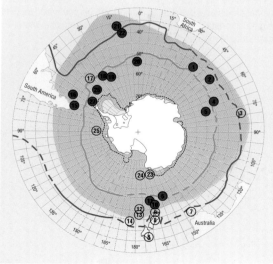

1	Prince Edward & Marion	16	Falklands
2	Crozet	18	South Georgia
4	Kerguelen	19	South Sandwich
5	Heard & McDonald	20	Bouvetøya
6	Macquarie	21	Tristan da Cunha
10	Auckland	22	Gough
11	Campbell	26	South Orkney
15	South America	27	South Shetland

to taper abruptly at rear. Fore flippers rather small, situated quite far forward on body. Some sexual, but strong age-related, variation mainly in size; tone and contrast of colour and streaked/spotted pattern varies mainly individually. On ice, including behaviour towards close observer, rather slow, typically raises head and foreparts almost vertically, with the back arched and chest enlarged (see voice). **Ad** has short, velvety fur, with back and flippers mainly dark grey (few streak-shaped spots) sharply demarcated from silvery or buff ventral surface. Most characteristic are dark (tinged chestnut or chocolate) longitudinally broad stripes or patches on throat-sides, head/neck and sometimes flanks; narrower variable spots and streaks on flanks, especially rear; dusky eye-mask sometimes apparent. Most ads also have pale scars on neck/shoulder. Small teeth recurved in canines and incisors, and cheek teeth barely pierce gum. **Pup** mainly dark brown, paler ventrally, with similar throat striping to ad. **Imm** still recognizably smaller, especially in first/second-year, but apparently does not distinctly differ in coloration from ad.

Physical notes: Averages 2 m in males and 2.1 m in females (max. 2.6 m). Mean estimated weights 173 kg (males) and 186 kg (females), but reaches 225 kg; pup at birth up to 1.2 m and 27 kg.

Chief identification at sea: No comparative information available on this species.

Voice: On ice, when approached by observer, lifts head high and opens mouth; out of water rather vocal and utters trilling, cooing and chugging sounds; siren calls uttered with closed mouth. Also reported to give similar underwater vocalizations, but characteristic moaning or buzzing at varying frequency also described.

Similar species: All above-mentioned congeners, especially younger animals, when asleep on ice or if observed distantly, can in different ways appears superficially similar to the scarcer Ross. For instance, younger Weddell with more striped body-sides, because of its often rounded head and heavy jizz, could be mistaken for Ross, while Leopard and some extremely blotchy, darker Crabeater are also pale ventrally and can appear to have similarly striped body-sides. It is recommended to rely on close views to confirm identifications. As always, once an animal's characteristics are known it is more readily recognized.

Distribution and biology

Distribution, movements and population: First discovered in 1840 (named by J. E. Gray, 1844, after James Clark Ross, British Antarctic Expedition) and probably still among the least-known pinnipeds. Circumpolar in pack ice of Antarctic Ocean south to 78°S but recorded north to S Australia, Kerguelen and Heard I. Though once considered rare, estimates suggest a total population of around 220,000 in early 1980s. Evidence suggests that it prefers

Ross Seal Ommatophoca rossii showing typical head-up posture, with mouth open when disturbed by observer. Formerly believed extremely rare, Ross Seals favour very dense pack ice, and thus are seldom encountered except aboard an icebreaker. East Antarctica. © Frank S. Todd.

heavy pack ice and it is for this reason that so little is known about the species.

Diet and feeding techniques: Few data but known to take krill, migrating squid and mid-water fishes, mainly nocturnally.

Main social behaviour: Appears solitary, especially in summer, but may be more sociable than known, as lone seals on ice are often associated with several others underwater.

Breathing and diving: Very poorly known and data relate to one individual, which was recorded diving to 212 m and for up to ten minutes; most periods underwater lasted up to six minutes and reached depths below 110 m.

Breeding biology: Pup in Nov–Dec and mate in late Dec–early Jan on pack ice, although impregnation is delayed until early Mar. Moult Jan–Feb. Females probably reach sexual maturity at three years old.

Conservation Lower Risk—least concern. Protected and considered to be the least-abundant phocid seal, but only miniscule numbers have ever been taken for research purposes and there is no data on population trends, even at a local or regional scale.

Taxonomy Monotypic.

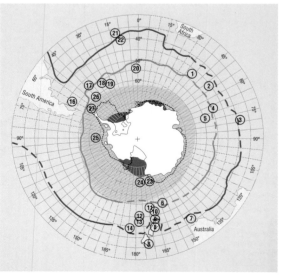

Ross Seal Ommatophoca rossii is relatively small, short-necked and has a short gape and diagnostic dark stripes on head-sides, neck and flanks. East Antarctica. © Frank S. Todd.

■ Approximate main summer/breeding range
▨ Approximate main dispersal range

Cetaceans

Plates 30–35 and the following species accounts are intended to assist field users, being arranged to facilitate rapid comparisons between similar and confusing species (for conventional taxonomy of these species see below). As a result, the species are grouped as follows: *Coastal dolphins and porpoises* in Plate 30, *Oceanic and coastal dolphins* in Plate 31, *Dark animals with similar, prominent dorsal fins* in Plate 32, *Small beaked whales* in Plate 33, followed by *Large beaked whales and small baleen whales* in Plate 34 and *Large rorquals and robust-bodied whales* in Plate 35. I have also attempted to follow a conventional and up-to-date taxonomic approach (see below) to the description of the 37 whales, porpoises and dolphins recorded in our region (between one-third and one-half of the world's c.85 recognized species) by organizing the species texts according to traditional systematics. For a general introduction to the cetaceans see the marine mammals section within the book's prefatory material.

Whales and dolphins, collectively known as cetaceans, offer one of the most exciting challenges to naturalists. The Antarctic and Southern Ocean ecosystem is richly populated by these mammals, with many species of baleen and toothed whales and dolphins (in all this region has been calculated to hold >50% of the world's marine mammals biomass). Knowledge of the life histories of many of these is limited, but more is known about the former group because of their commercial importance to whalers. In our region, the smaller toothed whales are virtually unknown, except through limited sightings and occasional strandings. Despite a vast increase in knowledge of several species since the 1980s, the distributions and movements of a number of cetaceans are still comparatively poorly known. Given that interesting and exciting discoveries are still being made in Northern Hemisphere waters concerning some species' distributions, the possibilities in the Southern Ocean for dramatic whale and dolphin watching appear almost infinite. It is as well to remember that many of our hypotheses concerning the behaviour of whales and dolphins are still subject to further testing. Our knowledge of many taxa is relatively limited simply because of the relative infrequency of sightings of some species: cetacean watching is not easy and, even at sea, demands patience and strong concentration: you must always be ready for the unexpected.

Identification is frequently based, in part, on an elimination process; with experience and by focusing on key features it should be possible to identify many individuals to species. Nonetheless, it should never be regarded as a defeat to admit that a briefly seen fin or blow could not be identified, and you should always take into account the sea state, weather conditions and the sun's glare in attempting to discern the colour, shape and size of the animal you are trying to observe. Some of the unique features of a species have been discovered only through examination of beach-stranded animals, and may never be visible at sea. Therefore it is wise to concentrate on studying as many of the following features as is possible during the observation period. Remember that the best conditions to observe cetaceans, especially whales, is a calm sea, when both the animals and their blows are far more obvious, therefore do not be surprised if you fail to observe any in a very rough sea, even in areas rich in cetaceans.

For the uninitiated observer identification of cetaceans can be daunting, given that views are often brief. The following list of features on which to concentrate are given in approximate order of importance and ease with which they may be appreciated by the less-experienced observer. Size is helpful to identification, but is often very difficult to judge (especially for the inexperienced observer), so where possible try and use surrounding objects as a gauge. The size, shape and angle of the blow (in large species), if visible, are all important to note, as is the relative position on the back and size and shape of the dorsal fin. Body and head shapes (e.g. if the animal lacks a beak or, if present, its relative size and structure, and the relative shape and bulk of the splashguard) are helpful features, as are the relative shapes of the tail flukes and flippers (if visible). Coloration patterns and scarring, particularly if striking, may be useful in species identification, but are often difficult to evaluate and, in any case, those of certain species are unknown at sea (the only descriptions being from strandings). Finally, it is important to note any behavioural characteristics such as fluking (raising the tail flukes above the surface of the water prior to a dive), breaching (raising the body above the surface before crashing down again), logging (lying motionless at or just below the sea surface), spyhopping (lifting and holding the head clear of the water) and porpoising (raising all or part of the body above the surface while in motion). Also, if there is more than one animal, the behaviour relative to other members of the group (travelling closely packed, loosely, or apparently individually, etc) may prove valuable in the identification process. It is also worth attempting to keep notes on the dive sequence, which may be of use in the identification of some species. Additionally, it is worth noting the general topography of the site, in particular water depth and possible vicinity of seamounts, underwater canyons or changes in the ocean floor such as banks, continental shelf limits, etc.

Dusky Dolphin Lagenorhynchus obscurus *performing impressive aerial jump. Kaikoura, South I, New Zealand.* © Barbara Todd.

General whale biology

Many Southern Hemisphere species of whales undertake long migrations, feeding during the austral summer in the rich Antarctic waters and breeding in winter at low latitudes where they undergo an enforced fast, relying on stored fat. Peak numbers of baleen whales are present in the Antarctic in Jan–Apr with Antarctic Minke Whale *Balaenoptera bonaerensis* being the most abundant. The different species arrive at various times: Blue Whales *Balaenoptera musculus* are earliest, Fin *B. physalus* and Humpback Whales *Megaptera novaeangliae* next, and then Sei Whale *Balaenoptera borealis*. Southern Right Whale *Eubalaena australis* may feed year-round between 30°S and 50°S; indeed there is circumstantial evidence from some areas to suggest that the species has become less migratory due to recent conservation efforts, the whales spending more time in areas where there is no hunting, though well-defined seasonal movements are known from W Australia.

Baleen whales are top predators in a very short food chain and therefore impact on plankton production. All filter-feed on plankton or small shoaling fish and their mouth structures are adapted to the size of food consumed. Smaller food organisms necessitate a finer baleen filter, while coarser filters catch larger organisms. Annual consumption of krill by Antarctic whales has been estimated at c.150 million tonnes. Some have suggested that reduced whale stocks must have produced an increase in krill, and that this surplus can be exploited by Man without affecting the dynamics of whale life cycles, i.e. it is acceptable to harvest both. But this is denied by those who maintain that other groups, such as seals, birds and fish, have taken advantage of the surplus, which is demonstrated by increases in their populations, thus establishing a new equilibrium in these waters.

Conservation of whales

Whaling has left some species seriously threatened. Commercial whaling began several centuries ago, but two relatively recent events precipitated an enormous increase in the Southern Ocean harvest: the development, in the 1860s, of a canon-fired harpoon and the introduction, in the mid-1920s, of floating factory ships that undertook all processing at sea. The former development was accompanied by other significant advances, namely the introduction of faster and more manoeuvrable ships, stronger and better machinery, improved navigational aids, better techniques for processing whale products and large new factory ships. As a result, a number of large-whale species were hunted to near extinction, until the advent of species-specific protective measures (the first taking affect in the early 1930s), which eventually culminated in a worldwide moratorium, enacted in the 1986 coastal and 1985/6 pelagic seasons. The International Whaling Commission (IWC) is an inter-governmental organization founded in 1946 (and currently numbering 40 member nations) which regulates whaling and conserves declining stocks of whales. It prohibits commercial take of large whales but some commercial whaling continues, despite the ban, mostly as a result of a loophole that permits their exploitation for 'scientific research'. The principal offenders are Japan and Norway, who annually exploit Antarctic Minke Whales (even within the 1994-established Ocean Whale Sanctuary which covers 50 million km2 around the continent), the N Pacific and N Atlantic Oceans, with the former also now taking several other species in the N Pacific through the scientific loophole. Indeed, over 20,000 individual whales have been taken by Japan, Norway, Iceland, Russia, Korea and others since 1985, and several of these countries are known to have falsified its whaling data over a period of up to several decades. Since the late 1990s, several nation members of the IWC have expressed their total opposition to whaling (in line with a vast body of public opinion), but it appears unlikely that some whale species will recover their former abundance in the foreseeable future. Whales are generally slow breeders, making any potential recovery period long, though there have been dramatic increases in some populations, e.g. of Southern Right Whales in South African and Australian waters.

Other works

Here I wish to mention some of the most important contributions to our knowledge of life history, identification, taxonomy and conservation of cetaceans, namely the *Handbook of Marine Mammals*, 3–6 (edited by Ridgway & Harrison, 1985–99), the *Sea Guide to Whales of the World* (Watson 1981, which despite its primary title also covers dolphins) and the outstanding *The Sierra Club Handbook of Whales and Dolphins* (Leatherwood & Reeves 1983), which was in many ways the first true field guide to offer modern techniques for the identification of whales at sea. Due to its original ideas and accuracy, I have extensively referred to it. These were followed by the well-illustrated *Marine Mammals of the World: FAO Species Identification Guide* (Jefferson et al. 1993), *Whales, Dolphins and Porpoises* (Carwardine & Camm 1995) and the *Collins Whales and Dolphins: The Ultimate Guide to Marine Mammals* (Carwardine et al. 1998), which have also been used extensively here, and are highly recommended. Most recently, Perrin et al. (2002) published the *Encyclopedia of Marine Mammals*. For those with more than a passing interest in pinnipeds and cetaceans, this is set to become an essential work. In addition the *National Audubon Society Guide to Marine Mammals of the World*, published by Knopf, and authored by Reeves et al. has also recently appeared.

Other recently published works which must be considered essential for those with a serious interest in the systematics, life history and conservation of marine mammals include *The Natural History of Whales and Dolphins* (Evans 1987), *Marine Mammals of the World: Systematics and Distribution* (Rice 1998), *Marine Mammals: Evolutionary Biology* (edited by Berta & Sumich 1999), and *Marine Mammals: Biology and Conservation* (edited by Evans & Raga 2001). The work of Rice, in particular, while comparatively technical, offers a detailed review of the taxonomy and distribution of all marine mammals, and can also be strongly recommended (to ornithologists as well as those interested in cetaceans) for its introductory sections, which discuss, in a knowledgeable but accessible style, the principles of zoological nomenclature, the merits of the various species concepts under current debate, use of English names and geographical variation. It should be remarked, however, that with respect to English names, equally cogent but alternative rationale governing the use of hyphens in compound group names have been presented (e.g. Inskipp et al. 1998, Borrow & Demey 2001)

Given such a wealth of published material, it might be questioned how the present work can contribute to our knowledge of marine mammals, especially cetaceans. Nevertheless, I have endeavoured to construct the following accounts from a Southern Ocean and Antarctic perspective, in terms of species inclusion, distribution and behaviour as well as identification difficulties. Above all, I would like to stress that in depicting these animals, the artist Brett Jarrett has followed a similar course. The plates are based on his personal field experience with most of the species included here.

Systematic classification

The plates follow an order adopted by several field guides and related works, and are designed specifically for field use and to facilitate comparisons between easily confused species within a Southern Ocean context. The most up-to-date classification and order of genera and families within the Cetacea are presented below. Only those families with representatives in the Southern

Ocean are included (bear in mind that not all of the genera listed for each family may occur in our region).

Order Cetacea: **Whales, Dolphins and Porpoises**
* Family Delphinidae: **The Dolphins** (genera *Cephalorhynchus, Delphinus, Feresa, Globicephala, Grampus, Lagenodelphis, Lagenorhynchus, Lissodelphis, Orcaella, Peponocephala, Pseudorca, Sotalia, Sousa, Stenella, Steno* and *Tursiops*)
* Family Physeteridae: **Sperm Whales** (genus *Physeter*)
* Family Kogiidae: **Pygmy Sperm Whales** (genus *Kogia*)
* Family Ziphiidae: **Beaked Whales** (genera *Berardius, Indopacetus, Hyperoodon, Mesoplodon, Tasmacetus* and *Ziphius*)
* Family Phocoenidae: **Porpoises** (genera *Neophocaena, Phocoena* and *Phocoenoides*)
* Family Balaenidae: **The Right Whales** (genera *Balaena* and *Eubalaena*)
* *Family* Balaenopteridae: **The Rorquals** (genera *Balaenoptera* and *Megaptera*)
* Family Neobalaenidae: **Pygmy Right Whales** (genus *Caperea*)

Commerson's Dolphin
Cephalorhynchus commersonii   Plate 30

Identification
Confusion risks: Spectacled Porpoise *Phocoena dioptrica*.
Main characters: Unmistakable but variably marked delphinid. Small, stocky and black and white, with large, variable, rounded dorsal fin, conical head, gently sloping forehead, small rounded all-black flippers, largely white body except rear third, face and around dorsal fin, and slightly notched round-tipped tail flukes. Black of face (extends beyond blowhole), flippers and breast surround large white throat patch, and most have black central belly. Distinct individual, age-/sex-related and geographical variation in purity of white and black patterning (see below). Oval blowhole on central crown. Each row of both jaws has 26–35 teeth. **Age/sex variation** in shape of ragged black central belly patch, which is more oval in male and U-like in female; younger imm smaller and has intermediate appearance between ad and calf. Age of sexual maturity apparently 5–8 (females) or 5–6 years old (males). Calf distinctive being initially wholly brown. With age the black areas become as ad but less sharply defined, merging with brownish-grey and black marks over much of body.
Physical notes: 1.2–1.7 m and 35–86 kg, female 5–10% larger. Calf at birth 0.55–0.75 m and 4.5–7.0 kg and one calf achieved

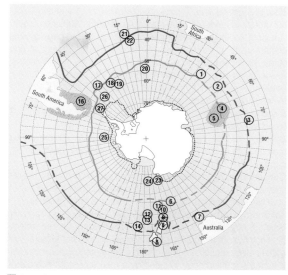

Approximate overall range

80% of its mother's size within one year.
Chief identification at sea: Resembles a porpoise but is a true dolphin in action and behaviour, making coloration far more striking. Frequently approaches boats, when it will swim upside-down, breach, bow-ride and perform erratic movements.
Similar species: Coloration wholly distinctive given a reasonable view but in poor light it may be possible to confuse this species with Spectacled Porpoise.

Distribution and biology
Distribution, movements and population: Extreme S South America (north to 34°S in Argentina and 50°S in Chile) south to 61°S in Drake Passage, the Falklands, perhaps South Georgia, near-shore waters of Kerguelen at 48°30'S to 49°45'S (where most frequent in the Golfe du Morbihan), and Heard I. Largely sedentary but appears less common inshore in austral winter and spring (Jun–Dec in Kerguelen). No overall population estimate but appears common around Tierra del Fuego (where c.3200 in 1984) and the Falklands.
Diet and feeding techniques: Fish, crab, krill and other crustaceans possibly largely taken inshore and near seabed. Sometimes feeds cooperatively, herding fish close inshore.

Adult Commerson's Dolphin Cephalorhynchus commersonii *is one of the most readily identified coastal dolphins, and most easily encountered in the Falklands. Feb 2001. © Morten Jørgensen.*

Ad Commerson's Dolphins Cephalorhynchus commersonii, *just below the surface, showing black face and narrow cape, which extends from dorsal fin to flukes, but black belly patch is more oval in male, U-shaped in female, and is usually difficult to see. © Gabriel Rojo.*

357

Main social behaviour: Typical group size is up to 15 (mostly 2–12) but groups of more than 100 may occur together (these represent seasonal, feeding or breeding aggregations). Some large groups contain up to one-third calves. Breaches very frequently: in one study, six individuals did so on 65–70 occasions in 17 minutes. Associations with Burmeister's Porpoise *Phocoena spinipinnis*, Peale's *Lagenorhynchus australis* and Black Dolphins *Cephalorhynchus eutropia* have been noted.

Breathing and diving: Dives for 15–20 seconds, breathing 2–3 times between dives.

Breeding biology: Largely unknown but the peak calving period may be early in the austral summer (Oct–Mar) with gestation occupying 10–12 months.

Conservation No information concerning population trends, but the species is hunted in S South America, principally for use as bait in crab fisheries, and it is also taken as bycatch in other fisheries.

Taxonomy The population around Kerguelen is geographically isolated, larger, has some grey in body (to some degree resembles calf in both populations; see above), possesses skeletal and genetic differences, and may deserve separate taxonomic status. It appears to have been founded by a relatively small number of animals perhaps as recently as 10,000 years ago. There is no information, as yet, concerning the recently discovered population around Heard.

Black (Chilean) Dolphin
Cephalorhynchus eutropia   Plate 30

Identification

Confusion risks: Burmeister's *Phocoena spinipinnis* and Spectacled Porpoises *P. dioptrica*.

Main characters: Small, stocky and appears largely dark at sea, with large rounded dorsal fin, indistinct beak, pale grey forehead, small rounded flippers, white lips, throat, mark behind flipper and belly, and distinctly notched point-tipped tail flukes. Pale grey forehead enhances black or dark grey face-sides, which continue ill-definedly along edge of slate-black sides, heightening contrast with white underside. Dorsal fin, flippers and flukes dark grey. Oval blowhole above forehead. Each row of both jaws has 28–34 teeth.

Age/sex variation restricted to differences in genital patches between sexes, while age of sexual maturity and development of young are unknown.

Mother and calf Black (Chilean) Dolphin Cephalorhynchus: note conical head with poorly defined beak, grey body, with broad black mask and dark lower jaw continuing as black band to flippers, and white throat. Ill-defined lateral band contrasts with large white belly patch. Chile. © Francisco Viddi Carrasco.

Physical notes: 1.2–1.74 m and 30–63 kg. No information on calf and its development.

Chief identification at sea: Appears black at sea, with at most only white of lips, throat/breast visible, while greyer fore face (enhancing broad black mask) and large round fin are distinctive, but usually inconspicuous even in calm conditions. Swims like sea lion, rarely breaching. Usually unobtrusive and difficult to approach but occasionally investigates boats, riding the bow or waist of the vessel.

Similar species: Dorsal fin shape distinguishes this species from two overlapping porpoises (Burmeister's and Spectacled, which see).

Distribution and biology

Distribution, movements and population: Coastal Chile north to 33°S and south to Tierra del Fuego and Cape Horn (Isla Navarino), and occasionally also into adjacent Argentine waters (e.g., a record of three in the Beagle Channel, close to Ushuaia, in Jan 2001; M. Jørgensen pers. comm.). Largely sedentary but appears

Black (Chilean) Dolphin Cephalorhynchus eutropia is a stocky, beakless and largely dark coastal dolphin, with a rather low, rounded dorsal fin and characteristic slow undulating swimming motion. Chile. © Todd Pusser.

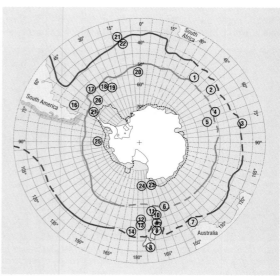

Approximate overall range

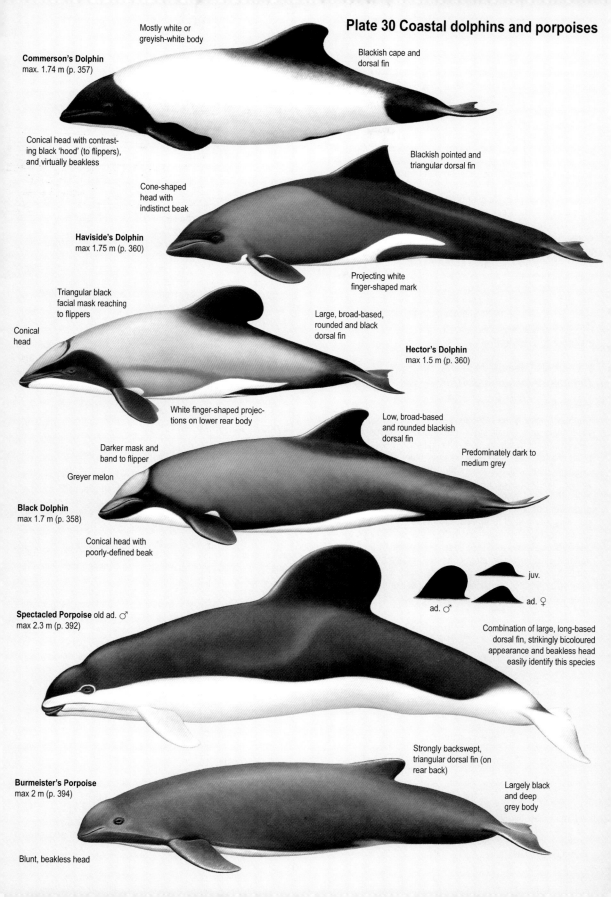

Plate 30 Coastal dolphins and porpoises

Commerson's Dolphin
max. 1.74 m (p. 357)

Mostly white or greyish-white body

Blackish cape and dorsal fin

Conical head with contrasting black 'hood' (to flippers), and virtually beakless

Cone-shaped head with indistinct beak

Blackish pointed and triangular dorsal fin

Haviside's Dolphin
max 1.75 m (p. 360)

Projecting white finger-shaped mark

Triangular black facial mask reaching to flippers

Conical head

Large, broad-based, rounded and black dorsal fin

Hector's Dolphin
max 1.5 m (p. 360)

White finger-shaped projections on lower rear body

Darker mask and band to flipper

Greyer melon

Low, broad-based and rounded blackish dorsal fin

Predominately dark to medium grey

Black Dolphin
max 1.7 m (p. 358)

Conical head with poorly-defined beak

juv.

ad. ♂

ad. ♀

Spectacled Porpoise old ad. ♂
max 2.3 m (p. 392)

Combination of large, long-based dorsal fin, strikingly bicoloured appearance and beakless head easily identify this species

Strongly backswept, triangular dorsal fin (on rear back)

Burmeister's Porpoise
max 2 m (p. 394)

Largely black and deep grey body

Blunt, beakless head

less common inshore in austral winter. Prefers areas of rapid tidal flow and shallow waters at entrance to fjords. No population estimates but appears to be probably in low thousands and perhaps declining.

Diet and feeding techniques: Fish, krill and other crustaceans. Herds fish using circular or zigzag movements. Often associates with feeding seabirds.

Main social behaviour: Typical group size is 2–10 but larger groups of 20–50 may occur (especially in north of range) and a concentration of possibly 4000 individuals has been reported. Sometimes recorded in association with Peale's Dolphin Lagenorhynchus australis.

Breathing and diving: No information.

Breeding biology: Poorly known but probably similar to better-known Cephalorhynchus species. Calves observed in Oct–Apr.

Conservation No precise information concerning population trends, but overall considered to be possibly (very) low and threatened by illegal hunting for use as bait in crab fisheries (1300–1500 may have been taken annually in western Strait of Magellan in late 1970s and early 1980s). Despite such hunting having been made illegal, the laws are practically impossible to enforce particularly when fishers are so poor. The species may also be caught incidentally in gill nets.

Taxonomy Monotypic.

Haviside's (Heaviside's) Dolphin
Cephalorhynchus heavisidii Plate 30

Identification

Confusion risks: None in range.

Main characters: Small, stocky and appears generally two-toned, with prominent triangular dorsal fin, indistinct beak, cone-shaped head, darker oval area around eye, blunt-tipped, small backswept flippers, white or pale grey diamond breast mark, side of flipper, trident-shaped belly-patch (with finger-shaped posterior extension), and distinctly notched point-tipped tail flukes. Face and throat often blackish as are flippers, merging with uniform purplish-grey rest of fore parts. Oval blowhole on rear of central crown, from where blacker line widens diagonally as an extensive blackish-blue cape and rear body to tailstock (where there is a variable paler horizontal streak). Each row of both jaws has 22–30 teeth. **Age/sex variation** expressed by slight differences in shape of white belly patch, especially where it meets anus. Age of sexual maturity unknown but apparently achieved when 1.56–1.59 m, and calf generally as ad.

Haviside's (Heaviside's) Dolphin Cephalorhynchus heavisidii is unmistakable in its coastal SW African range. South Africa. © Todd Pusser/ Danita Delimont Agent.

Physical notes: 1.2–1.74 m and 40–75 kg and sexes apparently same size. Calf at birth 0.85–0.87 m but no other information.

Chief identification at sea: Apparently shy; rarely breaches but performs rapid, forward somersaults up to 2 m high, bow- and wake-rides and may follow small vessels for several hours. Sometimes porpoises at high speed.

Similar species: Unmistakable in range.

Distribution and biology

Distribution, movements and population: Occurs outside of our region in SW Africa, from Cape of Good Hope north to Cape Cross, NC Namibia. Perhaps largely resident in near-shore areas, usually in waters shallower than 100 m. No population estimates. Included here as likely to be seen by observers using South Africa as a gateway to the Southern Ocean.

Diet and feeding techniques: Bottom-dwelling fish, octopus and crustaceans.

Main social behaviour: Typical group size is up to ten but as many as 30 may occur together. Sex and age composition of such groups is unknown but they have been speculated to be fluid.

Breathing and diving: No information.

Breeding biology: Poorly known but considered to be probably similar to congeners. Calves observed Oct–Jan.

Conservation No information concerning population trends, but some are hunted for food (perhaps up to 100 per annum) and similar numbers may become entangled in fishing nets.

Taxonomy Monotypic.

Hector's Dolphin
Cephalorhynchus hectori Plate 30

Identification

Confusion risks: None within its range.

Main characters: A New Zealand coastal endemic and the smallest (but stocky) delphinid, generally medium grey with contrasting black rounded dorsal fin (convex trailing edge), throat, small patch behind flipper and belly (finger-shaped creamy-white extension), almost beakless appearance, black round-tipped large flippers, and slightly notched and point-tipped tail flukes. Black beak and broad facial mask that narrows, passing through dark flipper and continuing as blackish stripe between dark blue-grey sides and white underparts. Oval blowhole above forehead. Each row of both jaws has 24–32 teeth. **Age/sex variation** in ads perhaps identifiable by male's smaller size (see below), though this is difficult to discern at sea, and by dark grey oval-shaped patch surrounding genital slit (reduced in female); younger imm clearly smaller and tends to have less developed convex dorsal fin, colour/pattern overall subdued and 4–6 pale bands on each side of body between flipper and tailstock (which disappear when c.6 months). Young become progressively paler. Sexual maturity apparently 6–9 (females) and 5–9 years old (males).

Physical notes: 1.2–1.5 m and 35–65 kg, females 5–10% larger. Calf at birth estimated to be 0.60–0.75 m and c.9 kg but no information on growth rates.

Chief identification at sea: In range, small size, contrastingly large, black, rounded dorsal fin, flippers and broad facial mask eliminate any possible confusion (no similar species come near). Strongly coastal. Rarely bow-rides but will follow boats. May breach, spyhop, lobtail and surf, but barely disturbs surface and prefers to investigate slow-moving or stationary boats, of which it is particularly inquisitive (though females with young can be shy).

Similar species: Unmistakable given limited range and striking combination of characters.

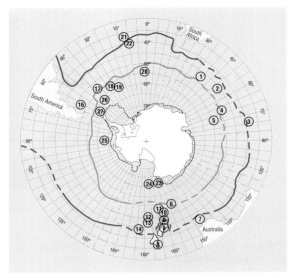

Hector's Dolphin Cephalorhynchus hectori. *Like other* Cephalorhynchus, *small with conical head lacking beak and has round, black dorsal fin. Characteristic grey, black and grey marks easily observed. Kaikoura, South I, New Zealand. © Hiroya Minakuchi/Sphere Magazine.*

▨ Approximate overall range

Distribution and biology

Distribution, movements and population: Occurs outside our region in coastal waters (less than 75 m deep and typically absent from areas deeper than 300 m) of New Zealand, where most common on east and west coasts of South I and only a very small population (perhaps fewer than 200 animals) on west coast of North I. Only local movements (of up to 30 km) reported but tends to favour areas further from shore in austral winter, though at all seasons has some preference for river mouths. South I population estimated at 7300 in recent years, of which c.5400 are on west coast. Included here as may be observed by those using New Zealand as a portal to the Southern Ocean.

Diet and feeding techniques: Small surface-schooling fish, squid, krill and other crustaceans. Those on east coast of South I have more varied diet than those on the west. May follow trawlers in summer.

Main social behaviour: Typical group size is up to 30 (most frequently 2–8) but as many as 100 may occur together. Associations within different subpopulations are relatively fluid.

Breathing and diving: Surfaces frequently, usually at intervals of less than 30 seconds, with c.6 short dives followed by a longer dive of c.90 seconds.

Breeding biology: Mating and calving occur in spring to late summer (early Nov–mid-Feb) and gestation occupies 10–11 months.

Lactation lasts at least six months. Mature females calve every 2–4 years and young remain with female for 1–2 years.

Conservation No precise information concerning population trends, but considered to be declining and recorded as incidental catch in gill nets; over 200 animals died as a result in 1984–88 off Banks Peninsula. In response, an 1170 km2 Marine Mammal Sanctuary was declared in 1989, within which gill netting was made illegal. Nonetheless smaller numbers (fewer than 20 per annum) continue to be caught north and south of the protected area. Pollution levels of several contaminants are cause for concern.

Taxonomy Monotypic though east- and west-coast South I populations appear to be genetically distinct, as is that on the west coast of North I, and there is an apparently isolated population in Te Wae Wae Bay, on South I.

Long-beaked Common Dolphin
Delphinus capensis Plate 31

Identification

Confusion risks: Short-beaked Common Dolphin *D. delphis*.

Main characters: Distinctively marked and even more slender with duller pigmentation than otherwise almost identical Short-beaked Common Dolphin (which see). Key distinguishing features are described below. As latter, much individual and geographical variation in overall pigmentation, especially patterns around face and sides. **Age/sex variation** much as *D. delphis*.

Physical notes: 1.93–2.6 m and to 235 kg, males average slightly larger. No information on calf and its growth.

Chief identification at sea: Easily distinguished from all congeners in our region with exception of Short-beaked Common Dolphin (which see). These two behave similarly at sea and require careful separation (see below).

Similar species: Longer, more slender beak is principal distinguishing mark from Short-beaked Common Dolphin, but is also overall more slender, with flatter head, less complicated beak pattern, poorly defined black spectacles, broader streak between lower jaw and flipper, and is less brightly coloured. Unlike latter also has narrow black eyestripe that extends back, bordering dull buff-yellow flanks. Plate 31 depicts typical examples of these very

Hector's Dolphin Cephalorhynchus hectori *is the smallest dolphin and endemic to New Zealand. Note compact body, striking black snout, broad triangular mask and black, rounded dorsal fin. Kaikoura, South I, New Zealand. © Dennis Buurman.*

Long-beaked Common Dolphin Delphinus capensis: note paler and more muted pattern of the younger animal in foreground. Eastern tropical Pacific, Aug 2000. © Brett Jarrett.

similar forms but observers should be aware that strong individual and geographical variation may cloud their separation.

Distribution and biology

Distribution, movements and population: Mainly inhabits inshore areas in warm-temperate and tropical oceans, reaching south to South Africa. Included here as may be observed by those using South Africa as a gateway to the Southern Ocean.

Diet and feeding techniques: Small fish, squid and krill. May take fish discarded from nets. Diet may vary seasonally as well as geographically.

Main social behaviour: Group size is generally large and frequently up to 500, although as many as 2000 may occur together, principally in the tropical Pacific. These may be the coalition of a large number of much smaller groups, which typically number 20–30 individuals. Some evidence of segregation within schools according to age and sex.

Breathing and diving: Dives for up to eight minutes, more usually ten seconds to two minutes, and capable of reaching depths of 280 m.

Breeding biology: Calving may peak in some regions in spring and autumn, and gestation occupies 10–11 months with 1–3 years between births. Near-term pregnant and lactating females may be separated from rest of population.

Conservation Presumably subject to similar threats as Short-beaked Common Dolphin though incidental catch in gill nets known to be more significant for this form.

Taxonomy Until recently regarded as conspecific with Short-beaked Common Dolphin. I follow Rice (1998) and previous authors in recognizing them as separate species, the present form mainly inhabits inshore areas while Short-beaked occurs offshore; other differences in typical ads are discussed above. All other described forms most probably represent only local variation, but the subject demands larger scale study.

Short-beaked Common Dolphin
Delphinus delphis Plate 31

Identification

Confusion risks: Long-beaked Common Dolphin *D. capensis*.

Main characters: Distinctively marked and slender, with grey, black or purplish-black upperside and V-shaped mark below tall, slightly rounded, dorsal fin, dark spectacles, complex face pattern and dark beak, yellowish patch on fore flanks, broad all-dark flippers, white underside with 1–2 broken yellow or grey lines, grey tailstock, and slightly notched, pointed tips to tail flukes. Much individual and geographical variation in overall pigmentation especially patterns around face, beak and area between flipper and beak, and darkness of tailstock and dorsal fin. Oval blowhole above forehead. Each row of both jaws has 40–60 teeth. **Age/sex variation** to some extent in coloration; male has slightly broader black blaze running just above genital region (narrower/paler in female), and younger animals identifiable by size and tendency to average paler. Sexually mature at c.2–7 (females) or 3–12 years old (males); appears to vary regionally. Calf as ad but less contrastingly patterned and paler.

Physical notes: 1.5–2.2 m and to 200 kg, male averages slightly larger. Calf at birth 0.7–0.9 m but no other information.

Chief identification at sea: Rather slim with well-defined black cape forming inverted V-like shape across centre of flanks, and the mainly dark fin, flippers, flukes and beak easily separate it from all but Long-beaked Common Dolphin (see below). Forms large, active schools, which are very acrobatic, porpoising, flipper-slapping, lobtailing, bow-riding, breaching and sometimes somersaulting. Very vocal, sometimes audibly so.

Similar species: Shorter beak is principal distinguishing mark from Long-beaked Common Dolphin (though very difficult to observe at

Long-beaked Common Dolphin Delphinus capensis *is similar to Short-beaked* D. delphis, *but has a longer, more slender beak, flatter melon and duskier face, whilst dark belt bordering duller thoracic area is diagnostic but variable. Mexico, Aug 2006. © Hadoram Shirihai.*

Short-beaked Common Dolphin Delphinus delphis *is separated from D. capensis by its more rounded head profile with shorter beak, and more contrasting pigmentation, lacking flank-stripe behind dark eye; thus white abdominal area appears to extend over flipper to merge with pale yellowish sides. Eastern tropical Pacific, Sep 1999. © Brett Jarrett.*

sea and beware juv has shorter beak than ad), but also, in older animals, has stronger gape to vent stripe, which may almost reach black eye-spot, as well as being overall less slender with more rounded head, more complicated beak pattern, more conspicuous black spectacles, more open-faced appearance (due to overall paler coloration), yellower (less buff) thoracic patch, narrower streak between lower jaw and flipper which passes below corner of gape (reaches it in Long-beaked), flipper to anus stripe tends to narrow and become fainter anteriorly, and is overall more brightly coloured.

Distribution and biology

Distribution, movements and population: Widespread outside polar regions and perhaps absent from our region (but included here to facilitate comparison with the previous species), mainly in warm-temperate to subtropical waters, but perhaps absent from the S Atlantic and Indian Oceans. Many populations appear to undertake seasonal movements and may follow warm-water currents. Principally found offshore. No population estimates.
Diet and feeding techniques: As Long-beaked Common Dolphin.
Main social behaviour: As Long-beaked Common Dolphin.
Breathing and diving: Most dives reach c.90 m and occupy c.3 minutes but known to reach 260 m and last up to eight minutes.
Breeding biology: As Long-beaked Common Dolphin.
Conservation Insufficiently known. No information concerning

population trends, but is often common. Threats include entanglement in nets (especially for tuna in tropical Pacific), pollution, hunting and human disturbance.
Taxonomy Previously regarded as conspecific with Long-beaked Common Dolphin. Variations within both these forms appear unworthy of taxonomic recognition, although at least three geographically separate populations in NE Pacific are distinguishable according to body length and cranial features.

Long-finned Pilot Whale
Globicephala melas   Plate 32

Identification

Confusion risks: Short-finned Pilot Whale *G. macrorhynchus* (but almost no geographic overlap) and, at distance, Killer Whale *Orcinus orca* and False Killer Whale *Pseudorca crassidens*.
Main characters: Long cylindrical black dolphin with variable, narrow diagonal, grey patch behind each eye and larger white (or grey) saddle behind dorsal fin, which is strongly curved or flag-shaped and situated well forward, almost level with long slender flippers. Bulbous forehead. Anchor-shaped grey-white patch on throat, which sometimes extends to abdomen (but poorly defined). Crescentic blowhole is slightly left of central crown. Concave-edged (median notch) tail flukes all black. Mouthline straight but slopes downwards, and 9–12 large conical teeth on each side of both jaws. **Age/sex variation** in overall size, which can be difficult to appreciate in the field, and dorsal fin (in male almost flag-like with deeply concave trailing edge, thick rounded tip and forms less upright triangle than female; sickle-shaped in young), and melon tends to be better developed in males, especially older animals when may overhang snout. Young tend to average paler and have pointed, more dolphin-like, dorsal fins positioned forward of centre. Sexually mature at 6–8 (females) to 12–14 years old (males) when 3.65–4.9 m. Calf as ad but uniformly paler.
Physical notes: Male 4.0–7.6 m and up to three tonnes, female 3.8–5.7 m and 2.0–2.5 tonnes. Calf at birth 1.75–2.0 m and c.75–80 kg and growth rates slow considerably at 2.5 years (in males) and six years (females).
Chief identification at sea: Quite visible on surfacing. Dorsal fin (though very variable) can be useful in separating species, and different ages and sexes, and Short-finned Pilot Whale may never have the saddle white in appearance, but diagnostic long flippers

Short-beaked Common Dolphin Delphinus delphis *is a fast swimmer, usually in large schools that whip the surface while porpoising. It may just enter our region seasonally, e.g. close to New Zealand waters. Eastern tropical Pacific, Oct 2003. © Michael F. Richlen.*

Long-finned Pilot Whale Globicephala melas. Note characteristic blackish coloration with very broad-based, falcate (highly concave rear edge to) dorsal fin located forward on body, as well as bulbous melon and lack of noticeable beak. The light streak behind the eye and saddle behind the dorsal fin are most pronounced in Southern Hemisphere populations, but also varies individually and are apparently reduced in young animals (left photograph apparently taken off New Zealand where these pale marks are often highly developed, while right photograph probably taken in Northern Atlantic where these marks reduced or lacking). Left. © Barbara Todd; right © Simon Berrow.

of *G. melas* usually invisible at sea. Typically has elongated wedge shape when viewed from above. Often lobtails and spyhops, and resting groups may closely approach slow-moving vessels. Bushy blow reaches up to 1 m and can be visible at some distance but is often indistinct. Infrequently breaches (usually younger animals) and is gregarious, being rarely seen alone.

Similar species: Range only slightly overlaps with very similar Short-finned Pilot Whale of warmer waters (occurring close to our region in temperate waters of Atlantic, off South Africa and Pacific) and *G. melas* has, at close range, a noticeably more conspicuous eye patch and saddle. *G. macrorhynchus* generally has a larger bulbous melon (and possibly more extreme overhang) in older males, less extensive white on belly, shorter (14–19% rather than 18–27% of body length), curved (rather than angled) flippers, and has possibly broader and less sharply defined saddle. Short-finned also has fewer (7–9) teeth on either side of both jaws but they are probably often indistinguishable at sea (except on range). Other similar species are Killer Whale and False Killer Whale. The former should, given reasonable views, be readily identified by its white markings and dorsal fin shape of at least one or more of the pod. Long-finned Pilot Whale, particularly young and/or females, could be mistaken for False Killer Whale, which may marginally reach our area. The latter, however, is generally more active, energetic and fast-moving, and lacks a paler-coloured cape.

Distribution and biology

Distribution, movements and population: The population in the

Long-finned Pilot Whale Globicephala melas. Highly gregarious and characteristic; within the region proper it does not overlap with the very similar Short-finned Pilot Whale G. macrorhynchus. Kaikoura, South I, New Zealand. © Dennis Buurman.

Southern Hemisphere is principally associated with the Humboldt and Benguela Currents and the Falklands. Reaches as far north as 14°S but generally replaced by *G. macrorhynchus* in tropical and subtropical seas. Disjunct population in N Atlantic. Prefers deep waters. Largely nomadic and penetrates south almost to edge of sea ice (having reached 68°S in C Pacific, though generally does not occur south of 60°S). The subspecies *G. m. edwardii* is thought to number 200,000 in Antarctic waters.

Diet and feeding techniques: Fish and squid, including some bottom-living species. Probably frequently feeds in very deep water and mostly at night but also occurs inshore.

Main social behaviour: Highly sociable, often in groups of up to several hundred or even 1000 but most commonly fewer than 50. No distinguishable pattern of age/sex segregation but as fewer males survive to adulthood, pods are likely to contain more females. Pod structure is generally stable. Groups are tighter when on move, or being chased, than when feeding. Regularly associates with several species of dolphin and occasionally large whales.

Breathing and diving: Most feeding dives last c.10 minutes (max. almost 16 minutes) and is capable of reaching at least 600 m, though it more commonly dives to 30–60 m.

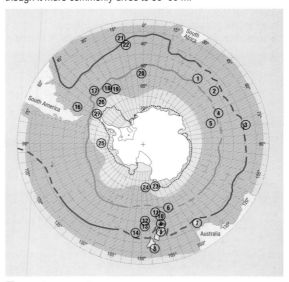

■ Approximate overall range; distribution refers mainly to the summer months

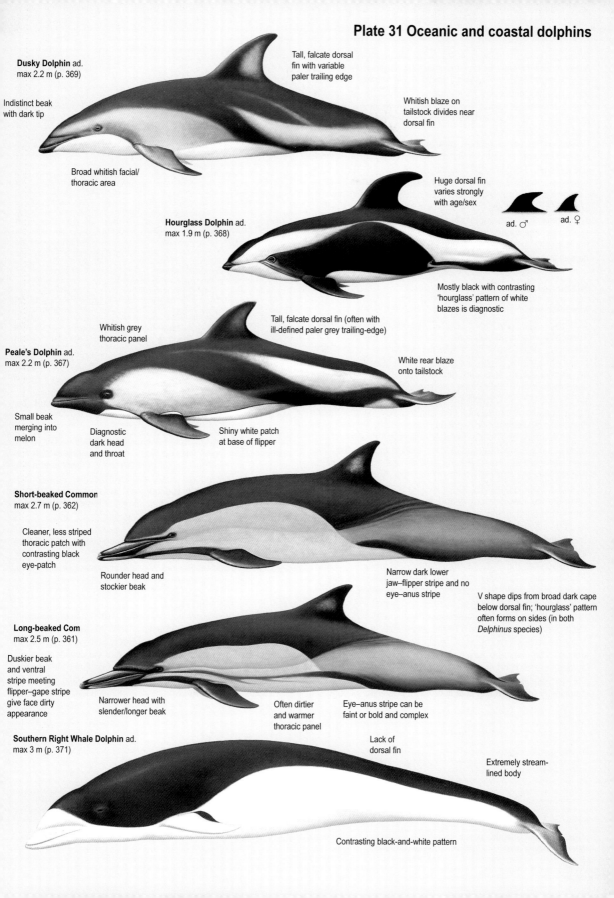

Plate 31 Oceanic and coastal dolphins

Dusky Dolphin ad.
max 2.2 m (p. 369)

Indistinct beak
with dark tip

Broad whitish facial/
thoracic area

Tall, falcate dorsal
fin with variable
paler trailing edge

Whitish blaze on
tailstock divides near
dorsal fin

Huge dorsal fin
varies strongly
with age/sex

ad. ♂   ad. ♀

Hourglass Dolphin ad.
max 1.9 m (p. 368)

Mostly black with contrasting
'hourglass' pattern of white
blazes is diagnostic

Whitish grey
thoracic panel

Tall, falcate dorsal fin (often with
ill-defined paler grey trailing-edge)

Peale's Dolphin ad.
max 2.2 m (p. 367)

White rear blaze
onto tailstock

Small beak
merging into
melon

Diagnostic
dark head
and throat

Shiny white patch
at base of flipper

Short-beaked Common
max 2.7 m (p. 362)

Cleaner, less striped
thoracic patch with
contrasting black
eye-patch

Rounder head and
stockier beak

Narrow dark lower
jaw–flipper stripe and no
eye–anus stripe

V shape dips from broad dark cape
below dorsal fin; 'hourglass' pattern
often forms on sides (in both
Delphinus species)

Long-beaked Com
max 2.5 m (p. 361)

Duskier beak
and ventral
stripe meeting
flipper–gape stripe
give face dirty
appearance

Narrower head with
slender/longer beak

Often dirtier
and warmer
thoracic panel

Eye–anus stripe can be
faint or bold and complex

Southern Right Whale Dolphin ad.
max 3 m (p. 371)

Lack of
dorsal fin

Extremely stream-
lined body

Contrasting black-and-white pattern

Breeding biology: Probably polygynous. Males move between family groups to mate during temporary large aggregations. Cows calve every 3–6 years, frequently in spring and autumn. Gestation takes 12–16 months and calves are weaned for 18–36 months (lactation may occasionally overlap with pregnancy). Older females act as 'wet nurses' for younger females' calves, after their own fertility has ended.

Conservation Large schools close inshore are easy prey for hunters (at least in northern waters) being readily driven ashore and stranded. Hunted since at least 16th century. In recent years significant numbers may have been taken as bycatch by other fisheries outside our region. Oceanic heavy metal and organo-chlorine contaminations are of long-term concern.

Taxonomy Two geographically and genetically well-separated forms are occasionally treated as species: nominate *G. melas* in the N Atlantic and *G. edwardii* in the Southern Ocean, with an unnamed form from the N Pacific known from the fossil record.

Risso's Dolphin *Grampus griseus*   Plate 32

Identification

Confusion risks: Killer Whale *Orcinus orca* and Bottlenose Dolphin *Tursiops truncatus* (at distance).

Main characters: Small but stocky and extensively scarred with linear white marks, largely dull grey body with tall, variable dorsal fin, slightly bulging forehead, almost beakless appearance, upward-sloping mouthline, long sickle-shaped flippers, variable pale underside and distinctly notched and point-tipped tail flukes. Unique crease on central forehead from blowhole to upper mouth; crescentic blowhole above forehead. Throat patch variable, solidly or partially dark, and body-sides and fin/flippers are usually clearly darkest parts, contrasting with anchor-shaped white breast/abdomen (see Plate 32). Has 2–7 large teeth on each side of lower jaw and occasionally very small teeth in upper jaw. **Age/sex variation** limited but young generally darker with no scarring (being initially silver-grey to chocolate-brown dorsally with creamy-white ventral area and around mouth, and anchor-shaped white patch between flippers, but then darken except on ventral area). With age (especially oldest) become considerably paler with whiter head (only tip of beak and area around eye remaining dark, and often have extensive scarring). Age of sexual maturity apparently unknown.

Physical notes: 2.6–3.8 m and 300–500 kg, female may average slightly smaller and body size may vary regionally. Calf at birth 1.1–1.5 m and males believed to attain sexual maturity when 3 m in length but no other information on growth rates.

Chief identification at sea: Overall small size but very robust body (especially area between fin/flippers), relatively tall falcate dorsal fin on mid-back, bulging face with square melon (bisected by deep crease) and heavily scarred pale skin, combine to make the species easy to identify. Many individuals may appear almost completely white and can clearly be seen swimming underwater.

Risso's Dolphin Grampus griseus *spyhopping. Small but stocky dolphin with broad head and cleft melon, relatively long flippers and dorsal fin, and generally pale coloration with extensive scarring. Costa Rica. © Flip Nicklin/Minden Pictures.*

Beware, however, that some are confusingly darker. Behaviour also important, sometimes spyhops, breaches, lobtails and flipper-slaps, and may bow-ride or swim alongside vessel or in wake, but more usually ignores boats and travels rather slowly; often porpoises, and especially younger individuals breach (half-breach when older). Forms lines when hunting. Blow very indistinct between typically short dives and surfaces at 45° angle, flukes sometimes visible when diving.

Similar species: Tall dorsal fin may recall female/young Killer Whale or Bottlenose Dolphin and the extensive scarring and whitish skin are shared by Cuvier's Beaked Whale *Ziphius cavirostris*, but combination of characters should eliminate any possible confusion.

Distribution and biology

Distribution, movements and population: Worldwide outside polar regions, reaching south to Argentina, Chile (to Cape Horn), South Africa, Australia and New Zealand. Records from approximately 60°N to 60°S usually in waters seaward of the continental shelf. Some populations appear to undertake seasonal movements, moving to cooler waters in summer. Prefers deep and continental shelf waters (0–1000 m). No overall population estimates.

Risso's Dolphin Grampus griseus *in typical surfacing formation, showing erect and falcate fin. Note very broad, pale body and, on some, the bulbous head and heavy scarring. Maldives. © Hadoram Shirihai.*

Risso's Dolphin Grampus griseus *showing surface profile: note cleft melon (lack of beak), relatively tall, erect dorsal fin, and generally pale coloration. California. © Todd Pusser/Danita Delimont Agent.*

Diet and feeding techniques: Fish and principally octopus, cuttlefish, squid and krill. Typically feeds in continental shelf areas and at night. May take fish from longlines.

Main social behaviour: Typical group size is 10–50 (mean 10–30 according to region) but as many as 4000 may occur together and solitary individuals or pairs occasionally observed. School composition appears to be fluid though subgroups may exhibit a higher degree of fidelity. Frequently observed in mixed-species aggregations with other cetaceans.

Breathing and diving: Dives for 1–2 minutes then takes up to 12 breaths at 15–20-second intervals, but capable of remaining underwater for up to 30 minutes.

Breeding biology: May calve year-round (though winter peak registered) with gestation perhaps occupying 13–14 months.

Conservation Insufficiently known. No information concerning threats or population trends, but considered to be probably abundant. Small numbers taken in gill nets in Southern Ocean and some deliberately killed because the species is known to take fish from longlines. Pollution may also pose some threat.

Taxonomy Monotypic. Hybrids with Bottlenose Dolphin have been reported in captivity.

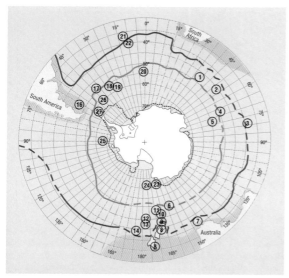

Approximate overall range

Peale's Dolphin
Lagenorhynchus australis　　　　　Plate 31

Identification

Confusion risks: Hourglass *L. cruciger* and Dusky Dolphins *L. obscurus.*

Main characters: Medium-sized dolphin, tinged dark grey/black, with dark face and back, paler (or even white) sides and flanks, white chest/abdomen, and distinctive pale longitudinal streak on upper flanks from tall recurved dorsal fin to tail. Dorsal fin sometimes two-toned, with paler greyish trailing edge (see Dusky Dolphin). Diagnostic shiny white patch at upper base of flippers. Extent of dark chin varies and some may have paler patch around eye, most a dark patch. Pointed snout with virtually no rostrum. Curved, long and pointed flippers contrastingly dark with convex leading edge, and dark tail flukes possess clear fork, pointed tips and distinct central notch. Oval blowhole above forehead. Tip of snout and lower jaw dark; 27–37 teeth in each row of both jaws.

Age/sex variation indistinct but younger animals separable by size and are overall paler grey with less distinct boundary between thoracic and flank patches. Flippers of older animals may have series of knobs on leading edge. Age of sexual maturity unknown.

Physical notes: 1.3–2.2 m and 100–115 kg. No other information except females may become sexually mature when 2.1 m long (though physically mature when smaller).

Chief identification at sea: Behaviour and appearance strongly recall those of Hourglass and Dusky Dolphins, and, like both, when moving fast it is not always easy to appreciate their distinctive patterns. Bow-rides large vessels and swims alongside smaller boats; spyhops and spins. Swims both slowly and in long, low leaps, interspersed by acrobatic high leaps. Seldom flukes and usually exposes blowhole and small part of back when surfacing.

Similar species: Peale's Dolphin is dark grey or black over back and upper flanks, with a pale curved flank patch behind the dorsal fin narrowing to a single line below it, and a larger pale thoracic patch rising towards the dorsal surface forward of the dorsal fin (delineated along its lower edge by a narrow black line). Closer to Dusky in size and close views may be required to observe all-dark fore face, small shiny oval-shaped white patch at upper base of flippers and dark lower border to pale grey area of fore body.

Distribution and biology

Distribution, movements and population: Restricted to nearshore, usually shallow, waters of S South America, often found at entrance to fjords, mostly south of 40°S and regularly around the Falklands, reaching as far south as at least 59°S in Drake Passage. Exceptionally north to 33°S in Pacific and 38°S in Atlantic.

Peale's Dolphin Lagenorhynchus australis, *Falklands . © Richard White/ Falklands Conservation.*

Peale's Dolphin Lagenorhynchus australis *recalls Hourglass* L. cruciger *and Dusky Dolphins* L. obscurus, *but is differentiated by body-side marks (dark diagonal stripe separates whitish fore and rear patches) and dark face, though when surfacing or porpoising it is difficult to appreciate such patterns.* © Simon Berrow.

Probably largely resident though some may move inshore in austral summer and sightings of animals similar to (or this) species have been made around Cook Is in the Pacific. No population estimates.
Diet and feeding techniques: Small octopus, squid and fish. Often feeds in kelp and may herd small fish.
Main social behaviour: Typical group size is 2–10 but may form larger temporary schools of 30–100. Often associates with Commerson's Dolphin Cephalorhynchus commersonii and less regularly with other dolphins.
Breathing and diving: Dives range up to 2.5 minutes (but typically slightly less than 30 seconds) with three short dives usually being followed by a longer period underwater.
Breeding biology: Unknown.
Conservation No information concerning population trends but was hunted for bait used in crab fisheries in late 1970s–1980s, especially in Chile (this practice was declared illegal in 1977) and is sometimes entangled in fishing nets. Pollution may also be a threat.
Taxonomy Monotypic but evidence of recent mtDNA studies indicates that it should be placed in the genus *Sagmatias*.

Hourglass Dolphin
Lagenorhynchus cruciger   Plate 31

Identification

Confusion risks: Dusky *L. obscurus* and Peale's Dolphins *L. australis*.
Main characters: Small oceanic dolphin, strongly patterned longitudinally with black, grey and white. Dark back with white hourglass pattern separating dark flank patch, extending as band from above eye to flipper, and along flanks towards dorsal fin as broad patch. Posterior white flank patch starts narrowly just below dorsal fin, then broadens as dips towards tailstock. Beak small and black with 26–35 teeth in each row of both jaws. Curved flippers are long and pointed with part of underside white, and dark tail flukes have concave trailing edge and distinct central notch. Oval blowhole above forehead. **Age/sex variation** indistinct, partially in coloration and overall size, although this can be difficult to appreciate in the field. Ad male has much larger, more lobed dorsal fin than female, which has a smaller and more pointed fin. Age of sexual maturity unknown and juv is undescribed.
Physical notes: 1.42–2.0 m and 73.5–94.0 kg. Calf at birth <1.1 m but no information on growth rates.
Chief identification at sea: Body pattern and surfacing behaviour make it usually unmistakable. Swims with long low leaps, both bow- (common in rough weather) and stern-riding. Undulating motion recalls a penguin. Often travels very close to surface with only the dorsal breaking the surface, raising a splash in front of it.
Similar species: Might be confused with Dusky or Peale's Dolphins but, as name suggests, coloration pattern differs and, in good view, should be virtually unmistakable. Especially note diagnostic horizontal broad black band from eye to flipper and on flanks (the others are extensively pale grey over much of the fore body-sides and Dusky has a whiter face, and both are larger). Hourglass also has a strongly hooked all-dark dorsal fin and is variably whiter grey posteriorly than Dusky.

Distribution and biology

Distribution, movements and population: Coldwater, circumpolar oceanic species that spends most time in subantarctic and Antarctic seas at 45°S–67°S (making it the southernmost dolphin

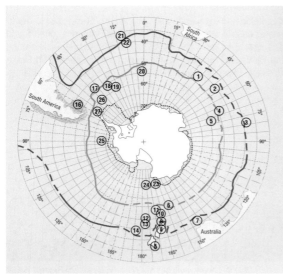

Approximate overall range

Hourglass Dolphin Lagenorhynchus cruciger: *such a view is the best an observer can hope for. Despite being an enthusiastic bow-rider, usually only the fin breaks the surface. White 'hourglass' divides black of upper body and flanks.* © Paula A. Olsen.

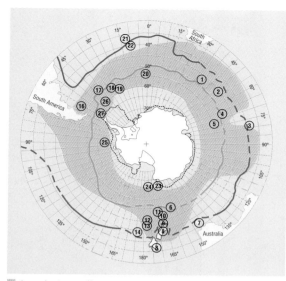

Approximate overall range; distribution refers mainly to the summer months

Dusky Dolphin
Lagenorhynchus obscurus   Plate 31

Identification

Confusion risks: Peale's *L. australis* and Hourglass Dolphins *L. cruciger*.

Main characters: One of the most acrobatic dolphins, easy to follow and identify. Virtually beakless, medium-sized dolphin, the head slopes evenly from blowhole to tip of snout. Bluish-black on back and tail, with dark band running diagonally across flanks from below dorsal fin onto tailstock. Underside white and whitish-grey on flanks. From sides of tailstock, two whitish streaks fork towards base of dorsal fin. Prominent two-toned dorsal fin with variably dark leading edge and usually greyer trailing edge. Curved, long and pointed flippers contrastingly dark, and dark tail flukes with clear fork, pointed tips and distinct central notch. Oval blowhole above forehead. Tip of snout and lower jaw dark, 22–36 teeth in each row of both jaws. **Age/sex variation** indistinct but younger animals separable on size. Age of sexual maturity appears to be 4–6 years old.

Physical notes: 1.5–2.2 m and 69–90 kg, male averages slightly larger. Calf at birth 0.55–0.91 m and 3–10 kg but no information concerning growth rate.

Chief identification at sea: Pale but distinctly marked and highly acrobatic. Frequently bow-rides. Sometimes leaps several dozen times, with entire group following the first to breach. Breaches in three ways: arc-shaped leaps returning headfirst, slams body against surface and lobtails, and in high somersaults.

Similar species: Peale's Dolphin has dark face and throat, and only a single whitish flank stripe. Less likely to be confused with Hourglass Dolphin (which see).

Distribution and biology

Distribution, movements and population: Three geographically separate populations: around New Zealand, Chatham, Auckland and Campbell; southern Africa, the Prince Edwards and Amsterdam (doubtfully also Kerguelen and Crozet); and South America north to Peru and N Argentina, including the Falklands. Records from Gough have not been identified to subspecies and reports from S Australia and Tasmania are unverified. Some populations appear to undertake seasonal movements of up to 780 km (principally following prey species) but other groups largely resident (e.g. off Argentina). No overall population estimates though 2665 animals counted during surveys over small part of range in

species) though recorded north to 33°S off Chile. Probably subject to seasonal movements, north in austral winter and south in summer. Most frequently observed in Drake Passage. A total of 144,300 was counted in waters south of Antarctic Convergence in early 1990s.

Diet and feeding techniques: Small fish, small squid and crustaceans. Often feeds among large flocks of seabirds and in plankton slicks.

Main social behaviour: Group size usually 4–8 but occasionally 60–100 may occur together. May accompany larger cetaceans including several species of large whales and Long-finned Pilot Whale *Globicephala melas*.

Breathing and diving: No information.

Breeding biology: Unknown but calves have been seen in Jan–Feb.

Conservation No information concerning threats or population trends but recent survey work has demonstrated it to be commoner than previously thought.

Taxonomy Monotypic but evidence from recent mtDNA studies indicates that it should be placed in the separate genus *Sagmatias*.

Dusky Dolphins Lagenorhynchus obscurus fitzroyi, *in typical surfacing formation. Separated from other* Lagenorhynchus *by prominent dark eye-patch, narrow pale stripe below fin, paler upper side to flippers and dark and light pattern to flanks. Off Peru, Oct 2003. © Michael F. Richlen.*

Dusky Dolphins Lagenorhynchus obscurus. *In New Zealand waters the species is represented by a still unnamed taxon. Kaikoura, South I, New Zealand.* © Dennis Buurman.

late 1970s and mid-1980s.

Diet and feeding techniques: Small fish (principally anchovies), squid, krill and other crustaceans.

Main social behaviour: Typical group size is 6–20 in winter, but in some rich coastal waters a few hundreds or thousands may sometimes occur together in summer, though off New Zealand this phenomenon appears to be reversed with larger schools in winter. May consort with other dolphin species.

Breathing and diving: Known to reach depths of up to 150 m (New Zealand) but activity patterns vary according to season and time of day, e.g., off Argentina, rarely below surface for more than 21 seconds at a time during night, but dive deeper and remain underwater longer during day, at least in spring and summer (pattern is apparently reversed in winter).

Breeding biology: Calves born in midwinter at some distance from shore (mainly Aug–Oct off Peru). Gestation estimated at 13

months and young may be weaned for up to 18 months.

Conservation Insufficiently known. Few data concerning threats or population trends but appears to be locally common despite being relatively frequently taken in gill nets off New Zealand. Some are hunted for human consumption off South Africa and incidental bycatch and intentional drift-net fisheries off Chile and Peru have been known for some years.

Taxonomy Evidence of recent mtDNA studies indicates that should be placed in genus Sagmatias. Two subspecies recently named: *L. o. fitzroyi* in South American waters and *L. o. obscurus* off South Africa, with an unnamed form in New Zealand. Perhaps conspecific with Pacific White-sided Dolphin *L. obliquidens*.

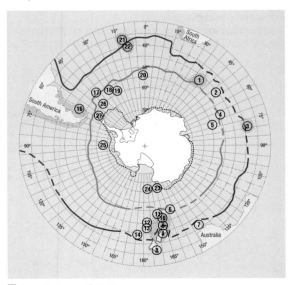

Dusky Dolphins Lagenorhynchus obscurus *are highly gregarious and acrobatic. Kaikoura, South I, New Zealand.* © Hadoram Shirihai.

▨ Approximate overall range

Southern Right Whale Dolphin
Lissodelphis peronii   Plate 31

Identification

Confusion risks: Northern Right Whale Dolphin *L. borealis* (no overlap).

Main characters: Streamlined dolphin that shares its name with right whales because both lack a dorsal fin. Very slender, particularly near tail, and lack of dorsal fin eliminates all other dolphins in our region. Coloration striking: dorsal surface jet-black, curving from forehead, passing between eye and corner of mouth, and sweeps up past flipper towards back, before dipping and levelling off at tail. Rest of body white, except rear edge of flipper, which is black. Head relatively small with elongated whitish snout and forehead (white reaches to just below blowhole level), and long mouthline. Flippers proportionally rather small, strongly curved and pointed, and vary in colour, some being all white, others have a narrow dark leading edge and some a broader dark leading edge. Tail flukes describe broad curve at rear with pointed tips and distinct middle notch, also largely dark but variably pale grey below and partially above. Oval blowhole above forehead. Each row of both jaws has 39–50 teeth, usually with more in the lower jaw. **Age/sex variation** indistinct but younger animals separable by size and newborn calves are dark grey/brown and only attain ad coloration at one year. Age of sexual maturity unknown.

Physical notes: 1.8–2.9 m and 60–116 kg, males tend to average larger. Calf at birth probably 0.9–1.1 m but no information on growth rates.

Chief identification at sea: Porpoises in a manner similar to penguins, with bouncing motion, and frequently leaps clear of water when moving fast in groups. Often lobtails and makes low-angle leaps clear of water, and small groups may bow-ride, but sometimes avoids vessels.

Similar species: Unmistakable in our region, although Spectacled Porpoise *Phocoena dioptrica* may be confused with this species by the inexperienced observer.

Distribution and biology

Distribution, movements and population: Circumpolar in subantarctic to temperate waters usually north of the Antarctic Convergence, at 25–65°S, and reaching 12°30'S off W South America and 23°S off Namibia. Northward movements reported in austral winter and spring off Chile and South Africa but appears to be largely sedentary. Prefers deep water and common in such waters off New Zealand, South Africa, in the Falkland Current and up to 450 km off Chile. No population estimates.

Diet and feeding techniques: Small fish, krill and squid.

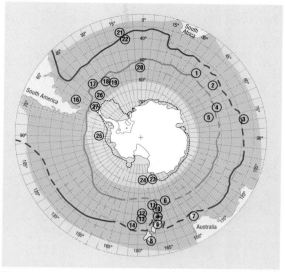

Approximate overall range; distribution refers mainly to the summer months

Main social behaviour: Often travels in large herds of up to 1000+ individuals though groups of 100–200 are more typical. Most frequently associates with Long-finned Pilot Whale *Globicephala melas* and *Lagenorhynchus* dolphins.

Breathing and diving: Dives last up to 6.5 minutes.

Breeding biology: Unknown.

Conservation Insufficiently known. Considered common but no information concerning trends. As with other dolphins, probably threatened by entanglement in nets and increasing numbers have been taken as bycatch in swordfish gill-net fisheries off Chile, while unknown numbers are taken in Peru and Chile for their meat and blubber and for use as crab bait.

Taxonomy Monotypic.

Killer Whale *Orcinus orca*   Plate 32

Identification

Confusion risks: Imm perhaps with False Killer Whale *Pseudorca crassidens*, Risso's Dolphin *Grampus griseus* and pilot whales.

Main characters: Largest member of the dolphin family. Strikingly

Mature male Killer Whale Orcinus orca *breaching off S New Zealand, where large animals are similar to Antarctic Type A (note lack of darker dorsal cape).* © *Dennis Buurman*.

Southern Right Whale Dolphin Lissodelphis peronii *is unlikely to be confused given its conspicuous shape and pattern; note also the lack of a dorsal fin. Kaikoura, South I, New Zealand.* © *Dennis Buurman.*

Killer Whales Orcinus orca, *mature male (right), taking South American Sea Lion* Otaria byronia *pup in Argentina, where populations are similar to Antarctic Type A.* © Gabriel Rojo.

black and white, or grey, black and white in the two Antarctic forms: throat to abdomen, part of flanks and oval blaze behind eye white (latter often stained yellow-orange by diatoms in two Antarctic types); rest mainly black, or grey with a black cape. Huge conical head with very slightly rounded beak (sometimes more pronounced in young). Flippers are large rounded paddles, and in ad males dorsal fin very tall (up to 1.8 m) and sharply triangular (may vary subtly). Female/young male have smaller, slightly curved dorsal fin (up to 0.9 m). Grey-white saddle behind fin not always detectable. Flukes broad, almost straight-edged in juvs and females, convex in adult males, with median notch and pale below. Blowhole V often slightly left of central forecrown, but varies. Mouthline straight, with 10–14 large conical teeth either side of both jaws. Three **Antarctic ecotypes** in our region, with pro-

nounced morphological and biological differences, and may be biological species. '**Type A**' has medium-sized, horizontal white eye-patch roughly parallel to body axis; lacks dorsal cape; inhabits offshore, ice-free waters; is circumpolar and preys predominantly on Antarctic Minke Whales. '**Type B**' similar, but eye-patch at least twice as large; clear-cut cape; inhabits inshore waters, closely associated with continental pack-ice (frequent around Peninsula); mainly preys on seals, but also Antarctic Minkes and Humpbacks. '**Type C**' most distinctive, having narrow, diagonal white eye-patch that slopes at front; distinct dorsal cape; inhabits inshore pack in E Antarctica, where feeds mainly on fish. Presumably only B and C possess white patches stained yellow-orange by diatoms, and chocolate-brown appearance to dark areas of body. Forms with dark cape have distinctive two-toned look in good light, with eye-

Killer Whale Orcinus orca, *probable ad female, in New Zealand waters (similar to Antarctic Type A). In Antarctic waters, Type A is circumpolar in off-shore and ice-free waters, and preys predominantly on Antarctic Minke Whales* Balaenoptera bonariensis. © Kim Westerskov.

Killer Whale Orcinus orca *in tight formation (females and young males), off S New Zealand, where similar to Antarctic Type A. Note medium-sized, horizontal white eye-patch and no darker dorsal cape.* © Kim Westerskov.

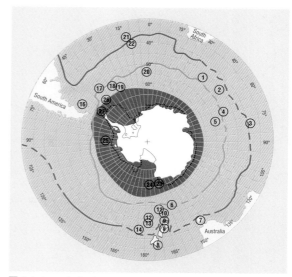

■ Main Antarctic distribution during the austral summer
▨ Overall distribution

patch in paler grey area. Length of male Type A up to c.10 m; Type C just over 6 m; no reliable size data size of Type B. **Age/sex variation**, in size and shape and height of dorsal fin, and tail flukes are strongly inward curved at tips in mature bulls. Calf as ad but saddle reduced, dorsal fin even lower and more falcate than imm/female, and white areas often tan to orange-yellow. Sexually mature at 8–16 years (or when male c.6.5 m 'Type A' and female 4.6 m).

Physical notes: (Type A) Male 7–9.8 m and 3.8–5.5 tones, female noticeably smaller in overall size (4.5–8.5 m), flipper length and dorsal fin. Calf at birth 2.1–2.6 m and c.160–200 kg. Type C adult males average 5.6 m, max 6.1 m; females 5.2 m, max 5.8 m. No reliable size data for Type B.

Chief identification at sea: Distinctive shape, black-and-white coloration, tall sword-shaped and strikingly visible dorsal fin, and spectacular behaviour almost unmistakable. Amongst the most exciting cetaceans, especially given its fast, unpredictable movements and behaviour. Inquisitive and approachable, in cold windless conditions the tall but fine bushy blow is conspicuous, but not so in the open sea. Flipper-slapping, lobtailing, breaching (graceful, with half-twist of body before landing sideways with great splash, all at high speed), spyhopping (slowly before gradually sinking) and logging (entire pod facing same direction in tight formation) all recorded (some commonly); capable of swimming at speeds up to 50 km/h.

Similar species: Females and young may be confused with similar-sized whales, due to less distinctive dorsal fin (than male), but head shape and coloration are unique distinguishing features. See

Mother and calf Killer Whale Orcinus orca, *of the small-sized Antarctic Type B. Note very large oval eye-patch and clear-cut dorsal cape.* © Todd Pusser.

Antarctic Killer Whale Orcinus orca, *of the small-sized Type B (mature male at left), which is closely associated with pack-ice. Body typically stained by diatoms, giving chocolate-brown appearance to dark areas and rusty-yellow tone to white areas, including the eye-patch. Antarctic Peninsula, Mar 2006.* © Hadoram Shirihai.

Spyhopping Killer Whales Orcinus orca of Antarctic Type C (the smallest, with narrow eye-patch, inhabits inshore pack in E Antarctica). Like other killer whales, it is a huge, black-and-white patterned dolphin. McMurdo Sound, Ross Sea, Jan 1992. © Kim Westerskov.

False Killer Whale, Long-finned Pilot Whale *Globicephala melas* and Risso's Dolphin for possible confusion with young animals.

Distribution and biology

Distribution, movements and population: Cosmopolitan, including throughout Antarctic waters, where it is a fairly common summer resident. Three distinctive ecotypes. Antarctic population estimated at 80,000 in 1980s though some researchers consider this optimistic.

Diet and feeding techniques: Feeds at ice edge and in open waters, taking fish, squid, penguins and other seabirds, seals and dolphins, and even makes group attacks on larger whales, but usually specializes on certain prey regionally. Frequently attacks seals on ice or shore in some areas; may spyhop to confuse potential prey and drive it into the water, where it is more easily caught, or deliberately beach themselves to seize inexperienced young animals. Even takes fish from longline hooks.

Killer Whales Orcinus orca, Antarctic Type C; the narrow, diagonal eye-patch is just visible in the animal in the foreground. Like Type B it has a dark dorsal cape and yellow-orange diatoms often make white areas appear rusty-yellow. Ross Sea. © Frank S. Todd.

Main social behaviour: Usually travels in tight herds of 2–50 (50% of pods in Antarctica have 5–10 animals), though sometimes be scattered over several km. Individuals or small groups often seen around subantarctic islands, patrolling the seas near penguin or seal colonies. Pods usually contain ads of both sexes, as well as calves and juvs, with the oldest female usually being dominant (and ad males frequently her offspring). Groups of over 100 presumably result from temporary amalgamation of several pods, whilst smaller pods usually contain at least one mature male. Often associates with other cetaceans without aggression but this may involve mainly fish-eating ecotypes.

Breathing and diving: Breathes every 10–35 seconds during series of a dozen short dives, followed by one lasting c.1–4 minutes, though capable of remaining underwater up to 17 minutes and reaching depths of 260 m.

Breeding biology: Probably breeds once every five years and gestation lasts 12–18 months. Calves apparently largely born in autumn and winter and remain dependent for up to one year.

Conservation Low Risk—conservation dependent. Rarely hunted, though occasionally taken with other dolphins (and Long-finned Pilot Whale), e.g. Soviet ships took 916 animals in Southern Hemisphere in 1979–80 (though just 26 p.a. in 1935–79), which could have caused local extinctions. Oil spills and other toxic pollutants, and the impact of human fisheries on prey species, are concerns elsewhere, as is habitat encroachment, as Killer Whale is apparently negatively impacted by human noise and maritime activities, at least in some parts of our region.

Taxonomy Traditionally considered monotypic, but with marked geographical variation, and in Antarctic waters genetic differences established among sympatric populations which differ ecologically and morphologically. Around Antarctica two names independently proposed (but not generally recognized): 'O. (o.) glacialis' (probably Type C) and 'O. (o.) nanus' (possibly Type B); Type A is probably the (nominate) worldwide form. Other forms may exist.

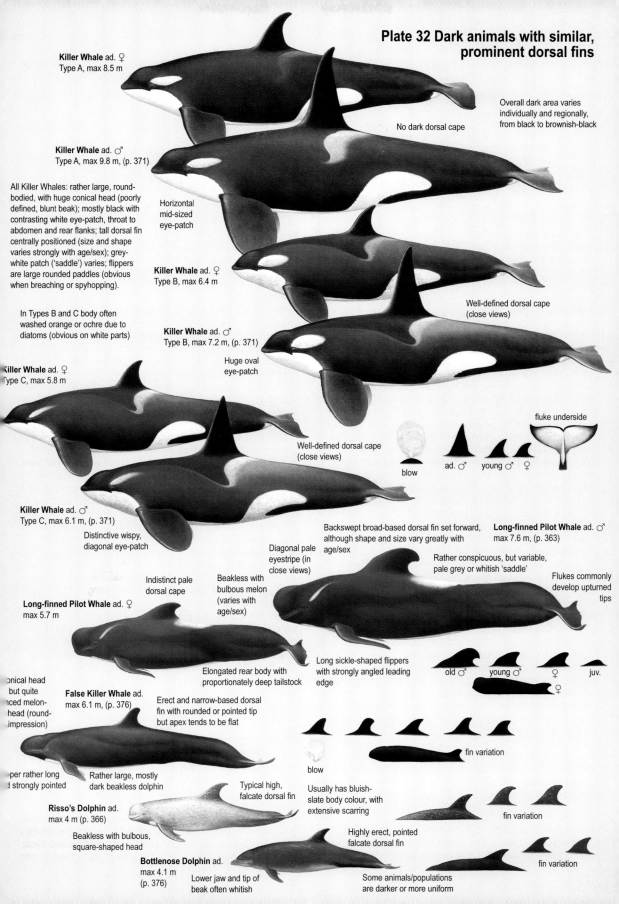

Plate 32 Dark animals with similar, prominent dorsal fins

Killer Whale ad. ♀
Type A, max 8.5 m

No dark dorsal cape

Overall dark area varies individually and regionally, from black to brownish-black

Killer Whale ad. ♂
Type A, max 9.8 m, (p. 371)

All Killer Whales: rather large, round-bodied, with huge conical head (poorly defined, blunt beak); mostly black with contrasting white eye-patch, throat to abdomen and rear flanks; tall dorsal fin centrally positioned (size and shape varies strongly with age/sex); grey-white patch ('saddle') varies; flippers are large rounded paddles (obvious when breaching or spyhopping).

Horizontal mid-sized eye-patch

In Types B and C body often washed orange or ochre due to diatoms (obvious on white parts)

Killer Whale ad. ♀
Type B, max 6.4 m

Well-defined dorsal cape (close views)

Killer Whale ad. ♂
Type B, max 7.2 m, (p. 371)

Huge oval eye-patch

Killer Whale ad. ♀
Type C, max 5.8 m

Well-defined dorsal cape (close views)

fluke underside

blow   ad. ♂   young ♂   ♀

Killer Whale ad. ♂
Type C, max 6.1 m, (p. 371)

Distinctive wispy, diagonal eye-patch

Backswept broad-based dorsal fin set forward, although shape and size vary greatly with age/sex

Long-finned Pilot Whale ad. ♂
max 7.6 m, (p. 363)

Diagonal pale eyestripe (in close views)

Rather conspicuous, but variable, pale grey or whitish 'saddle'

Flukes commonly develop upturned tips

Indistinct pale dorsal cape

Beakless with bulbous melon (varies with age/sex)

Long-finned Pilot Whale ad. ♀
max 5.7 m

Long sickle-shaped flippers with strongly angled leading edge

old ♂   young ♂   ♀   juv.

Elongated rear body with proportionately deep tailstock

onical head but quite nced melon-head (round-impression)

False Killer Whale ad.
max 6.1 m, (p. 376)

Erect and narrow-based dorsal fin with rounded or pointed tip but apex tends to be flat

fin variation

blow

per rather long d strongly pointed

Rather large, mostly dark beakless dolphin

Typical high, falcate dorsal fin

Usually has bluish-slate body colour, with extensive scarring

fin variation

Risso's Dolphin ad.
max 4 m (p. 366)

Beakless with bulbous, square-shaped head

Highly erect, pointed falcate dorsal fin

Bottlenose Dolphin ad.
max 4.1 m (p. 376)

Lower jaw and tip of beak often whitish

Some animals/populations are darker or more uniform

fin variation

False Killer Whale Pseudorca crassidens *is long-bodied, blackish/slate-grey and beakless, with a rather erect, falcate dorsal fin, like a flat-topped parallelogram, blunt head and rather long, elbow-shaped flippers. Fast-moving, it can be acrobatic and may raise much of body above surface. Marginal in the region. Left © Frank S. Todd. Right © Todd Pusser.*

False Killer Whale *Pseudorca crassidens*   Plate 32

Identification

Confusion risks: Pygmy Killer *Feresa attenuata*, Melon-headed *Peponocephala electra* and pilot whales *Globicephala* spp.
Main characters: Small, proportionally long-bodied black whale with little or no grey/white, and small blunt long head with broad curved mouth, distinctly point-tipped and notched tail flukes, which are small in comparison to overall body size, and tall recurved dorsal fin with variably pointed tip in mid-back. Fore flippers set forward on body and (uniquely) bent sharply in centre where they taper. Some have more obvious paler grey/whitish W on chest area (e.g. ad in Plate 32), others slightly paler behind and on sides of head. Oval blowhole above forehead, and 7–12 large conical teeth on each side of both jaws. **Age/sex variation** in overall size, although this can be difficult to appreciate in the field, and male has more forward-projecting forehead melon, while young tend to average uniformly paler. Considered to reach sexual maturity at 8–14 years old with males perhaps reaching adulthood later.
Physical notes: Male 3.7–6.1 m and 1.01–2.03 tonnes; female 3.5–5.0 m. Calf at birth 1.5–1.9 m and c.80 kg and achieves most growth in first two years, being 3.4–4.5 m at sexual maturity.
Chief identification at sea: Combination of overall long body, shape of dorsal fin (variable but frequently appears flat-topped) and flippers, and behaviour, are important features. Typically fast-moving and acrobatic: lobtails, breaches, bow-rides and frequently raises head and much of body above surface; frequently leaps gracefully clear of water (rising at varying angles). Blow inconspicuous and bushy. Schools may be scattered over several km.
Similar species: Larger than Pygmy Killer and Melon-headed Whales (both unrecorded in our region), and usually clearly darker (lacking white patches on flanks) than same-sized female/young Killer Whale, which may otherwise appear similar at distance. Distinguished from distant pilot whales by slender head and body, dolphin-like erect dorsal fin on mid-back and perhaps also by acrobatic behaviour. Given closer view, all are well differentiated by several other characters, e.g. the blunt but tapered head separates it from *Globicephala*, and the species' small puffy blows separate it from *Peponocephala* and *Feresa*.

Distribution and biology

Distribution, movements and population: Widespread between 50°N and 52°S in all but polar seas but only known to reach as far south as New Zealand, Peru, N Argentina, the seas south of South Africa and much of the N Indian Ocean, and no evidence for occurrence in our region (but included here to facilitate comparison with several potential confusion species known from the Southern Ocean). Usually in deeper waters (200 m to at least 2000 m) except where range approaches land. No seasonal migrations described though suspected in N Pacific and incidence of winter strandings suggest that some (perhaps food-related) movements may occur.
Diet and feeding techniques: Principally fish (sometimes taken from lines and nets) and cephalopods, but also mammals including dolphins. Occasionally attacks larger whales to size of Sperm Whale *Physeter macrocephalus* and may share food.
Main social behaviour: Small groups of 10–50 and, sometimes, larger herds of 300 (and a mass-stranding of 800). Herds usually contains animals of both sexes and all ages, are strongly cohesive and may associate with other cetaceans, especially Bottlenose Dolphin *Tursiops truncatus*.
Breathing and diving: Almost no information but estimated to reach up to 500 m below surface.
Breeding biology: Year-round, though perhaps peaking in late winter (Jan–Mar) and calves nursed 18 months to two years, with apparently long intervals of up to seven years between calvings. Gestation estimated at between 11 and 16 months.
Conservation Considered probably Secure. Mass strandings occasionally reported (and sometime deliberately induced in Japan) but few are hunted (off China and in the Caribbean). Tuna longline fishing responsible for some mortalities and also known to ingest plastic and toxins. No information concerning population trends.
Taxonomy Monotypic though some evidence for geographic differences in skull morphology exists.

Bottlenose Dolphin *Tursiops truncatus*   Plate 32

Identification

Confusion risks: Risso's Dolphin *Grampus griseus* and perhaps young Long-finned Pilot Whale *Globicephala melas*.
Main characters: Bottlenose or 'Cowfish' are among the largest dolphins and well known for their playfulness, being often observed 'riding' the bow waves of a vessel. Coloration varies, mainly individually but to some extent geographically, though usually rather uniform and unpatterned, dark or pale bluish- or brownish-grey on back, becoming gradually paler/whiter on lower jaw and throat, and even pinkish on belly. Beak relatively short, but varies, and

Bottlenose Dolphin Tursiops truncatus *is rather large with a robust body, short thick beak and very prominent, falcate dorsal fin; the body is generally grey with a slight dark dorsal cape and paler ventral area and lower flanks. Almost cosmopolitan but only of marginal occurrence in the Southern Ocean. Kaikoura, South I, New Zealand. © Dennis Buurman.*

stout with 18–29 pairs of teeth in each row of both jaws. Mouthline forms permanent 'grin'. High, broad-based and curved dorsal fin points towards broad tailstock. Flippers longish and pointed, and tail flukes distinctly notched and point-tipped. Crescentic blowhole above distinct bulging forehead. Sides and back sometimes scarred. **Age/sex variation** in overall size, which can be difficult to appreciate in the field, and young tend to average darker. Ads may have more extensive body scarring. Sexually mature at 5–13 (females) and 8–15 years old (males) but varies geographically.

Physical notes: 1.9–3.9 m and 150–650 kg, male typically averages slightly larger. Populations in warmer waters tend to be smaller and slimmer with proportionately larger flippers than those in cooler seas. Calf at birth 0.84–1.4 m and 15–30 kg, and achieves most of ad size by age 1.5–2.0 years, though may not reach physical maturity until 12–15 years old.

Chief identification at sea: Large powerful dolphin which is typically rather featureless. However, while some populations appear all grey at a distance, others have a conspicuous white belly; when bow-riding a cape pattern is usually clearly evident and the species often exhibits a shoulder blaze. Frequently lobtails, bow-rides, wake-rides and breaches up to several metres above surface. A strong swimmer, it often associates with boats and other cetaceans.

Similar species: Within our region only likely to be confused with Risso's Dolphin, but beak and body shapes distinctive. Young Long-finned Pilot Whale can appear superficially like Bottlenose Dolphin, but will normally be accompanied by older animals, substantially reducing the risk of any confusion.

Distribution and biology

Distribution, movements and population: Worldwide outside polar regions to 42°S, reaching south to Chile, Patagonia, the Indian Ocean between South Africa and Australia, and New Zealand, and thus only of marginal occurrence in our region. Some offshore populations appear to undertake seasonal movements of up to 4200 km but inshore groups are largely resident, although those in Argentina may move in response to El Niño Southern Oscillation events. No overall population estimates and none from our region.

Diet and feeding techniques: Wide variety of fish, krill and other crustaceans. Offshore populations exhibit strong preference for squid. Groups may cooperatively herd fish, disorienting their prey using leaps and occasionally pushing them shorewards where they may partially beach themselves. May also take advantage of small-scale human fisheries to seize prey.

Main social behaviour: Typical group size is up to 15 but as many as 1000 may occur together. Daily activity involves feeding over rocky areas where fish and other prey are common, resting and socializing. Group membership changes frequently but core members persist, with basic social units including nursery groups and mixed-sex groups of juvs.

Breathing and diving: Dives usually last 3–4 minutes but occupy

Bottlenose Dolphin Tursiops truncatus *is a strong swimmer and can be very playful; it often bow- or wake-rides large whales or boats. © Chris Gomersall.*

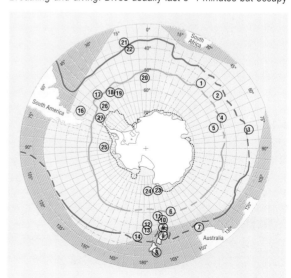

▨ Approximate overall range

up to 12 minutes (reaching depths as low as 535 m) in offshore populations.

Breeding biology: Calves every 2–6 years with births peaking in warmer months. Gestation occupies c.12 months and calves may be dependent for 6–12 months, becoming gradually independent during this period (though lactation may continue for as long as 3–7 years) and sometimes being cared for by other females. Strong bond between female and calf persists until next birth.

Conservation Insufficiently known. No information concerning population trends but threats include habitat destruction and degradation, entanglement in nets, overfishing of prey species and pollution—especially for the inshore form.

Taxonomy More than one species may be involved, with smaller, slimmer-bodied inshore and larger offshore forms known, with other differences and variation described between inter-ocean populations (e.g. inshore populations in the Atlantic are smaller, but in the E Pacific inshore populations are larger). Significant genetic differentiation has been discovered between neighbouring inshore populations off South Africa and the form *T. aduncus* is now generally recognized as a distinct species. Up to 20 forms have been described, though Rice (1998) considers geographical variation in *T. truncatus* to be so poorly known that subspecific designations are of very limited value.

Sperm Whale *Physeter macrocephalus* Plate 35

Identification

Confusion risks: Humpback Whale *Megaptera novaeangliae* and Arnoux's Beaked Whale *Berardius arnuxii*.

Main characters: The largest toothed whale. Distinctive due to huge box-like head (one-third of total body length in males) and low-slung narrow jaw which is rarely visible when mouth is closed. Series of hump-like ridges and a dorsal hump along midline of back towards tail. Almost uniform dusky purplish-brown but tone varies individually, usually appears dark grey-brown and in certain lights almost black or pale brown; in close view, skin characteristically rippled, with limited off-white around mouth. Belly-sides never visible during surfacing. Flippers proportionally small, triangular flukes often distinctly ragged (varies according to location and age/sex, and is caused by predators) and deeply notched on

Sperm Whale Physeter macrocephalus *is a bizarre shape, especially the huge square head, and a spectacular diver, reaching up to 3 km below the surface, hunting large squid using its spermaceti organ for echolocation in the darkness. Portugal, Jan 1998.* © Hiroya Minakuchi/Sphere Magazine.

trailing edge, while tailstock appears especially broad in profile and massive during fluking. Blunt snout has slight raised end and slit-like single blowhole on left side at front of rostrum. Eye disproportionately small. Long under-slung lower jaw has 40–52 large teeth. **Age/sex variation** perhaps estimable by overall size (see below); male often has greater number of narrow pale scars on head and back, a relatively large dorsal hump and snout projects further (due to more extensive spermaceti organ projecting from skull), while mature females are more liable to have a white or yellowish rough callus atop the dorsal fin. Sexually mature at 7–20 years old (female usually earlier than male which may be in puberty for as long as ten years) when 8.3–12.0 m, but reaches max. size only when up to 50 years old. Calf averages paler and greyer.

Physical notes: Male 15.0–18.3 m and 43.5–55.8 tonnes, female 8–17 m and 13.5–20.0 tonnes. Calf at birth 3.5–4.5 m and c.1 tonne (growth rate apparently unrecorded).

Chief identification at sea: Single nostril on left side of head spouts forward and leftward (up to 5 m high but usually 1–2 m, for up to 5–8 minutes continuously every 10–30 seconds). At surface

On surfacing, Sperm Whale Physeter macrocephalus *has a very long, log-like and usually finless body, with a triangular or rounded hump two-thirds of way along back (which may appear fin-like in some), wrinkled skin, blunt, slightly raised snout and slit-like blowhole on left side.* © Michael F. Richlen.

Breaching Sperm Whale Physeter macrocephalus *only rarely completely emerges (usually only partially in subantarctic waters), then mainly by young animals, and most frequently in poor weather.* © Stephen Wong.

Sperm Whale Physeter macrocephalus *typically raises its tailstock and flukes high prior to a feeding dive, leaving a few ripples on the surface as it sinks. Kaikoura, New Zealand, Jul 1993.* © Kim Westerskov.

usually has longitudinal log-like appearance, rather motionless or swims leisurely with very little of body visible. Lies low at surface, and can present impression of there being two animals, as the snout area and hump both protrude above the back. Often surfaces near same place. Blows repeatedly then dives vertically with raised flukes: on final blow typically slightly raises snout and dorsal hump, then partially submerges and accelerates with smooth well-exposed arching movement, tailstock and flukes raised vertically, leaving few ripples on surface.

Similar species: Virtually unmistakable (all rorquals have dorsal fin, rather than triangular-shaped dorsal hump, as well as vertical blow and rounded head) but at surface slightly similar (at distance) Humpback has entirely different blow sequence; both similarly arch back when commencing a dive, raising the fin or hump, and both show flukes, but these have different shape and colour. Seen close, when details of coloration and structure can be appreciated, they are rather different animals. In our region could also be confused with Arnoux's Beaked Whale—dense groups of the latter often surface simultaneously and respire rapidly, but possess very conspicuous scarring, vertical blows and do not usually fluke upon sounding.

Distribution and biology

Distribution, movements and population: Virtually cosmopolitan between 60°N and 70°S with non-breeding males periodically migrating to polar regions, though avoid areas of pack-ice. Females rarely found close to land, in waters shallower than 1000 m or south of 40°S. Often observed in areas where the continental shelf drops off dramatically and water depths reach 1000–3000 m. Within our region and nearby areas, records are concentrated

Sperm Whale Physeter macrocephalus *has a highly complex social organisation based on age and sex. In the Southern Ocean, males generally move south in the austral summer, returning north in winter. Kaikoura, New Zealand.* © Dennis Buurman.

Sperm Whale Physeter macrocephalus: *note triangular dorsal hump with series of smaller hump-like ridges and distinctly wrinkled skin. Kaikoura, New Zealand, Jul 1993.* © *Kim Westerskov.*

off E Australia and New Zealand, S South America and the Falklands, Tristan da Cunha and seas southwest of South Africa, and W Australia in Indian Ocean. Southern Ocean males generally move south in austral summer, returning north in winter. Population estimated at up to 1.9 million in late 1970s of which 780,000 in Southern Ocean and 30,000 reach Antarctic waters in summer.

Diet and feeding techniques: Principally squid, octopus and fish, including shark, salmon, rockfish, cod and skate in areas of upwellings and at continental shelf. Females are almost wholly reliant on squid, while males, in addition to preying on larger squid, take other items mentioned above and usually feed independently, unlike females.

Main social behaviour: Among the most intriguing cetaceans, being gregarious and polygamous, with a strong schooling instinct. Females, together with their offspring, form harems dominated by a single bull in mating season (older males usually associate with other animals only in breeding season, and bulls may migrate between groups of females). Younger males form separate herds during this period (but age at which they leave natal unit varies between four to 21 years old). Cows, calves and juvs form groups of 10–50 individuals in non-breeding season scattered over several km. Such units may occasionally travel together for several days, and females may switch groups. Breaching usually partial and rarely observed in subantarctic waters, mainly by young.

Breathing and diving: Deep divers, reaching depths of 3195 m for prolonged periods, up to 138 minutes, but normally depths of c.400 m for c.30–60 minutes or less; between dives remains on surface for usually no more than 8–15 minutes, exceptionally close to one hour when continues breathing and blowing (up to 50 times).

Breeding biology: Breeds every 3–5 years, with cows moving to warmer seas to give birth (Nov–Mar in Southern Hemisphere), but calves on independence increasingly move to cooler waters where feeding is better. Mating occurs in Jul–Mar in Southern Ocean (peak Sep–Dec). Gestation occupies 14–16 months and suckling (sometimes by females other than the mother) may continue for as long as 3.5 years. Reproductive rates may differ between populations according to rates of human exploitation.

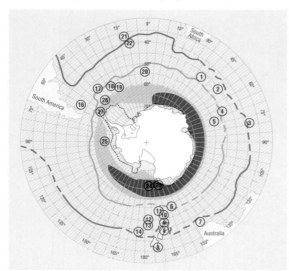

■ Higher Antarctic density recorded during the austral summer
▨ Lower Antarctic density recorded during the austral summer
▨ Approximate overall range (mainly during dispersal and austral summer)

Conservation Insufficiently known. Commercially hunted for several centuries, with up to 30,000 taken annually in 20th century until the 1988 moratorium, with males more susceptible to hunting due to their longer migrations to polar waters and the greater value of spermaceti. Stocks severely depleted due to this species' value for its oil which was used as fuel, a basis for cosmetics and leather dressing. Numbers taken in recent years have been smaller, in part due to overall reduced numbers but also the unfavourable public attitude towards whaling, and the Antarctic population, at least, appears to be increasing.

Taxonomy Monotypic. The name *macrocephalus* has precedence over *catodon*.

Arnoux's Beaked Whale
Berardius arnuxii   Plate 34

Identification

Confusion risks: Any other beaked whale, but size closest to Cuvier's Beaked *Ziphius cavirostris* and Southern Bottlenose Whales *Hyperoodon planifrons*.

Main characters: Rather large and elongated beaked whale, greenish-brown, dark grey or blue-black (may appear pale brown or even orange due to presence of microscopic algae on body) with paler flanks and abdomen, prominent dolphin-like beak and melon-shaped forehead. Heavily scarred whitish above and on sides. Very small, triangular or falcated dorsal fin, short broad flippers with parallel edges, and broad almost straight-edged tail flukes. Two flat triangular teeth either side of lower jaw. Crescent-shaped blowhole with rounded front on top/centre of head; single deep throat groove either side of head. **Age/sex variation** may exist in size (though few data on differences). Both sexes possess two teeth extruding from lower jaw (a smaller pair behind extrudes in later life; in most other beaked whales only extrude in ad male); ad generally becomes paler and more heavily scarred with age and, in older animals, the teeth may be so worn as to be invisible. No information on age of sexual maturity (estimated at 8–10 years in Baird's Beaked Whale) but only acquire teeth post-puberty, and calf unknown. Young animals apparently less heavily scarred whitish above.

Physical notes: 7.8–9.75 m and 7.1–10.1 tonnes (in better known Baird's Beaked Whale, males are up to 1 m smaller than females). No information concerning calf.

Chief identification at sea: Cruises at surface in compact groups, blowing 15 or more times prior to diving. Blow is low (to 2 m), bushy, angled forward (and perhaps slightly left) and diffuse, but may be quite distinct, even at a distance, and recalls that of Northern Bottlenose Whale *Hyperoodon ampullatus*. Groups may surface and breathe in unison, and always remain in very close contact. Rotund body appears proportionally very long and is generally very little exposed above surface, the long beak sometimes appears first when surfacing, when small round dorsal fin may also be visible, but high sloping forehead is not always obvious. Teeth could be visible in close view, and darker animals have contrasting heavy whitish scars on upperparts. Flukes sometimes slightly raised upon diving.

Similar species: All beaked whales, including this species, are distinguishable using dentition features, but these are rarely useful at sea. Southern Bottlenose Whale has a massive melon, stubby beak, very prominent dorsal fin and is usually a tan colour, whereas Arnoux's Beaked Whale has a low melon, long beak, and very small dorsal fin, and should be easily separable on the basis of fin size/shape alone. In addition, *B. arnuxii* is much more heavily scarred which, due to its darker ground colour, is more conspicuous. As both sexes have erupted teeth all ads are heavily scarred—in *Hyperoodon* only males have emergent teeth and ad females have little or no scarring. Plates 34 shows extreme and classic-coloured males, with dark Arnoux's and pale male Southern Bottlenose (with huge buffy-white bulbous forehead) but be aware that both can appear conversely dark or pale, and differences can be difficult to reliably appreciate at sea, especially as age-/sex-related variation is poorly known. Furthermore, bear in mind possible confusion with several (but usually clearly smaller and slimmer headed) *Mesoplodon*, especially with younger and paler Arnoux's. See also Cuvier's Beaked Whale.

Distribution and biology

Distribution, movements and population: Rare in the Southern Ocean. Occurs between 24°S and 78°S and apparently most abundant in Cook Strait and perhaps Ross Sea, with stranded individuals reported from New Zealand and Chatham (Dec–Mar), Australia, South Africa, S South America, the Falklands, South Georgia and Antarctic Peninsula (off Graham Land in Apr and Andvord Bay in Feb). Probably also occurs in S Indian Ocean. No population estimates or information concerning movements.

Diet and feeding techniques: Probably feeds on squid, octopus and fish in deep waters.

Main social behaviour: Occurs singly or in small tight groups of 6–10 but groups of up to 80 may congregate at favoured feeding areas (the latter consisted of several subgroups of 8–15 animals).

Breathing and diving: Usually dives for 12–25 minutes but capable of remaining below surface for over one hour and probably routinely dives 1000 m below surface (though recently recorded in comparatively shallow water on west side of Antarctic Peninsula); no other information.

Breeding biology: No information, though a female stranded in Dec was pregnant. Other aspects of cycle considered probably similar to Baird's Beaked Whale, e.g. gestation probably c.17 months.

Conservation Lower Risk—conservation dependent and placed on CITES Appendix I, but no information concerning threats or population trends.

Taxonomy Sometimes considered conspecific with Baird's Beaked Whale and recognition of the two taxa as species appears to be largely based on their apparent geographic separation, possible osteological differences and that *B. arnuxii* is apparently smaller than *B. bairdii*.

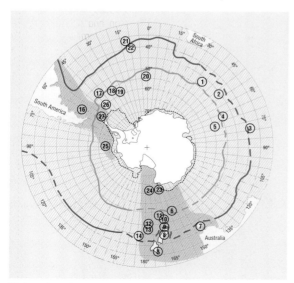

░ Approximate known range
▒ Possible range

Southern Bottlenose Whale Hyperoodon planifrons *is a large, robust beaked whale, with tall sickle-shaped dorsal fin and distinct bulbous melon (partially visible here); numerous scars (increase with age) are typical of male.* © Dylan Walker.

Southern Bottlenose Whale Hyperoodon planifrons: *note distinct pale and bulbous melon, but lack of scarring suggests an ad female or young.* © Paula A. Olsen.

Southern Bottlenose Whale
Hyperoodon planifrons   Plates 34

Identification

Confusion risks: Cuvier's Beaked *Ziphius cavirostris*, Arnoux's Beaked *Beradius arnuxii*, Dwarf Minke *Balaenoptera acutorostrata*, Antarctic Minke *B. bonaerensis*, and Long-finned Pilot Whales *Globicephala melas*.

Main characters: Medium-sized, stubby-beaked whale, which varies from yellowish olive-brown or dark brown (perhaps even black), most commonly tan, on upperside and is paler, creamy-brown to greyish-white below and on bulbous forehead (latter most pronounced when older, especially in males). Short but well-defined dolphin-like beak, small tapering flippers, unnotched, and broad deeply concave tail flukes. Large recurved, triangular or falcate dorsal fin set well back, and 0–4 (usually two) small cylindrical or oval teeth at tip of lower jaw visible in male. Heavily scarred whitish above and on sides (males, especially older animals). Rather broad crescentic blowhole on top/centre of head; single indistinct throat groove either side of head. May have some whitish spots on abdomen and sides. **Age/sex** can perhaps be judged using overall size, though difficult to appreciate, whilst females and young have teeth concealed by gums, or lacking, and tend to be much darker overall, with less bulbous foreheads than most males, which are typically paler olive-brown to blue-grey, with extensive pale scarring and well-developed, protruding, buffy-white bulbous forehead, beak and lower fore face to belly (see Plate 34). Both sexes, especially male, whiten with age and, consequently, melon contrast may reduce. No data on age of sexual maturity.

Southern Bottle-nosed Whale Hyperoodon planifrons: *body coloration varies from grey to yellowish-brown, but presence of scarring indicates a male. One of the most widespread beaked whales in the Southern Ocean. Drake Passage, Jan 2001.* © Morten Jørgensen.

Calf/juv dark grey-brown with more rounded dolphin-like head and conspicuous pale melon.

Physical notes: 6.0–7.5 m (but probably based on animals that had not reached max. size) and 6.9–8.1 tonnes; male probably much larger than female. Calf at birth 2.7–3.6 m but no information on growth rates.

Chief identification at sea: Tan coloration and tall, sickle-shaped dorsal fin usually identify the species, whilst a good view of the head, with its distinct melon and beak renders the species unmistakable. Bushy blow projects slightly forward and may be visible in favourable conditions; reaches 1–2 m high. When swimming fast, head may project above surface, and may raise it clear of water on surfacing.

Similar species: See Arnoux's and Cuvier's Beaked Whales. *Mesoplodon* spp in range usually smaller with less bulbous melon. Within our region proper, no known overlap with very similar Longman's Beaked/Tropical Bottlenose Whale *Indopacetus pacificus* (see Shirihai & Jarrett 2006).

Distribution and biology

Distribution, movements and population: Poorly known but circumpolar in deep waters of Southern Ocean, north to at least

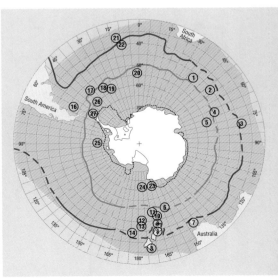

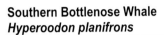 Approximate overall range

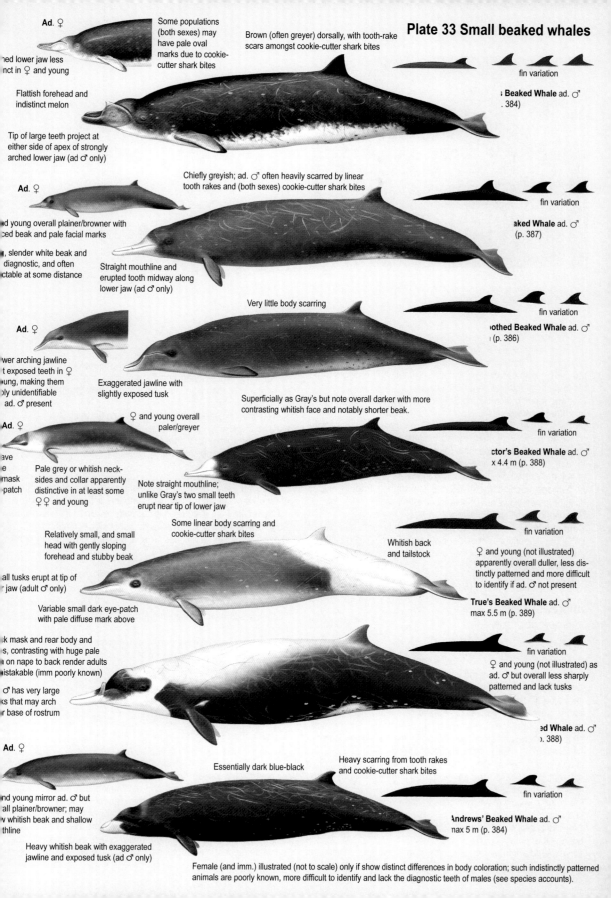

Plate 33 Small beaked whales

Ad. ♀

...ned lower jaw less ...nct in ♀ and young

Some populations (both sexes) may have pale oval marks due to cookie-cutter shark bites

Brown (often greyer) dorsally, with tooth-rake scars amongst cookie-cutter shark bites

fin variation

Flattish forehead and indistinct melon

... Beaked Whale ad. ♂
. 384)

Tip of large teeth project at either side of apex of strongly arched lower jaw (ad ♂ only)

Ad. ♀

Chiefly greyish; ad. ♂ often heavily scarred by linear tooth rakes and (both sexes) cookie-cutter shark bites

fin variation

...d young overall plainer/browner with ...ced beak and pale facial marks

...aked Whale ad. ♂
(p. 387)

..., slender white beak and ...diagnostic, and often ...ctable at some distance

Straight mouthline and erupted tooth midway along lower jaw (ad ♂ only)

Very little body scarring

fin variation

Ad. ♀

...oothed Beaked Whale ad. ♂
(p. 386)

...wer arching jawline ...t exposed teeth in ♀ ...oung, making them ...ly unidentifiable ...ad. ♂ present

Exaggerated jawline with slightly exposed tusk

Superficially as Gray's but note overall darker with more contrasting whitish face and notably shorter beak.

Ad. ♀

♀ and young overall paler/greyer

fin variation

...ave ...e ...mask ...patch

Pale grey or whitish neck-sides and collar apparently distinctive in at least some ♀♀ and young

Note straight mouthline; unlike Gray's two small teeth erupt near tip of lower jaw

...ctor's Beaked Whale ad. ♂
...x 4.4 m (p. 388)

Some linear body scarring and cookie-cutter shark bites

fin variation

Relatively small, and small head with gently sloping forehead and stubby beak

Whitish back and tailstock

♀ and young (not illustrated) apparently overall duller, less distinctly patterned and more difficult to identify if ad. ♂ not present

...all tusks erupt at tip of ...r jaw (adult ♂ only)

Variable small dark eye-patch with pale diffuse mark above

True's Beaked Whale ad. ♂
max 5.5 m (p. 389)

...k mask and rear body and ...s, contrasting with huge pale ...a on nape to back render adults ...istakable (imm poorly known)

fin variation

♀ and young (not illustrated) as ad. ♂ but overall less sharply patterned and lack tusks

...♂ has very large ...ks that may arch ...r base of rostrum

...ed Whale ad. ♂
.). 388)

Ad. ♀

Essentially dark blue-black

Heavy scarring from tooth rakes and cookie-cutter shark bites

fin variation

...nd young mirror ad. ♂ but ...all plainer/browner; may ...w whitish beak and shallow ...thline

Heavy whitish beak with exaggerated jawline and exposed tusk (ad ♂ only)

...Andrews' Beaked Whale ad. ♂
...nax 5 m (p. 384)

Female (and imm.) illustrated (not to scale) only if show distinct differences in body coloration; such indistinctly patterned animals are poorly known, more difficult to identify and lack the diagnostic teeth of males (see species accounts).

Southern Bottle-nosed Whale Hyperoodon planifrons: *small size, lack of body scarring, and sharply defined pale head indicate a young animal.* © Gary Friedrichsen.

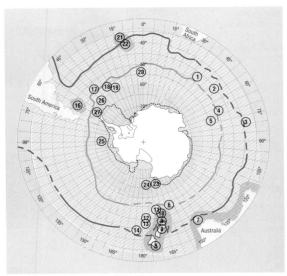

■ Approximate known range
▨ Possible range

20°S, with sightings off New Zealand, Australia, South Africa and South America (Argentina, Brazil and Chile), subantarctic islands off South America and to Antarctic continent in austral summer. No population estimates or information on movements (though may regularly migrate to warmer waters in winter) and appears to be reasonably abundant in Antarctic waters.

Diet and feeding techniques: Squid, with lesser quantities of fish and other invertebrates.

Main social behaviour: Occurs in small groups of 1–3, occasionally up to 25 but very rarely more than ten in Antarctica.

Breeding and diving: Capable of remaining below surface for up to two hours but typical dives are shorter. Perhaps among the deepest-diving whales (rarely found in waters shallower than 183 m) perhaps reaching up to 1000 m below surface. Prior to lengthy dive, breathes/blows at 20–30-second intervals.

Breeding biology: No information.

Conservation Lower Risk—conservation dependent and placed on CITES Appendix I. Insufficiently known. Rarely taken by whalers as stocks appear too small and widely scattered to be commercially hunted.

Taxonomy Monotypic.

Andrews' Beaked Whale
Mesoplodon bowdoini   Plate 33

Identification

Confusion risks: Other *Mesoplodon* species.

Main characters: One of the least-known beaked whales, the following is based on a few strandings, all in Australasia. Small and dark blue-black (some have brownish tone, white scratches and scars) with very slight melon-shaped forehead, predominantly white beak, small, pointed or round-tipped dorsal fin, short paddle-shaped flippers, and broad, all-dark tail flukes. Two broad flat teeth (in lower jaw) protrude from centre of strongly arched mouthline in ad male. Blowhole is on crown, with an indistinct throat groove on each side of head. **Age/sex variation** largely unknown though juvs and females lack visible teeth, being concealed by the gum in the latter, and only males are liable to show extensive and visible body scarring. Calf undescribed.

Physical notes: 4.0–4.7 m and 1.1–1.5 tonnes. Calf at birth 1.6 m but no other data.

Chief identification at sea: Requires study (see below), although

ad male should prove recognizable as a mesoplodont due to its conspicuous white-tipped beak (distal half) and heavy scarring; females will probably be indistinguishable from other female mesoplodonts.

Similar species: Apparently unknown at sea but even in close view may be impossible or difficult to identify from other mainly dark similar-sized congeners. Presumed range may offer a clue to distinguish it from some superficially similar species.

Distribution and biology

Distribution, movements and population: Cool temperate waters around New Zealand, including Campbell, and off S Australia. A 1970s record from Kerguelen is currently regarded as referring to Strap-toothed Whale *M. layardii*. No population estimates.

Diet and feeding techniques: Probably feeds on squid in deep waters.

Main social behaviour: Unknown.

Breeding and diving: No data.

Breeding biology: No information.

Conservation Placed on CITES Appendix I but no information concerning threats or population trends, although considered to be rare.

Taxonomy Probably conspecific with Hubbs' Beaked Whale *M. carlhubbsi*, which has a very similar skull and skeleton, and is currently treated as its northern counterpart.

Blainville's Beaked Whale
Mesoplodon densirostris   Plate 33

Identification

Confusion risks: Other *Mesoplodon* species.

Main characters: Medium-sized, mostly dark bluish slate-grey or generally brownish (to blackish or even orange-brown), with whitish-grey ventral areas and often-extensive greyish-white mottling and/or linear scarring (latter varies with range, age and sex). Dorsal fin rather large, triangular or falcate. Both sexes have gently sloping forehead and prominent, broad beak with clearly curved jawline. In mature male, lower jaw arches strongly upwards, appearing as forehead bump in profile, with two huge,

Ad male Blainville's Beaked Whale Mesoplodon densirostris *head-on: the tusk projects from the right-hand side at the apex of the strongly arched lower jaw; the left side is encrusted with barnacles; body heavily scarred white.* © Robin W. Baird.

slightly exposed, horn-like teeth. Small pale flippers and almost unnotched tail flukes (latter dark on upperside and pale below). Like most beaked whales, blowhole is on crown, with an indistinct throat groove either side of head. **Age/sex**: aside from dental differences (teeth only visible in full-grown male and, even then, often obscured by barnacles), female/young tend to have paler flanks, a much slighter head, and are more uniform above with indistinct or no scars. Plate 33 depicts a full-grown male with moderate markings above (some can have numerous linear whitish and buff scars on head and back, and are easier to identify). A nine-year-old female had only recently become sexually mature.

Calf much as female, but even paler and more uniform.
Physical notes: 4.5–6.0 m and 0.7–1.03 tonnes. Calf at birth 1.9–2.6 m but no other data.
Chief identification at sea: Mature male's heavy body scars, flattened head with strongly arched lower jaw projecting above head profile, with teeth sometimes just visible, are conclusive features. Female/young overall more uniformly patterned, but still have arched jawline. Mature animals of both sexes often have characteristic round mottling, produced by cookie-cutter shark bites (in animals that live or migrate thorough the tropics). On surfacing, usually emerges with beak pointing skywards, followed briefly by

Ad male Blainville's Beaked Whale Mesoplodon densirostris; *note slightly flacate dorsal fin, and long, rounded body, mainly medium grey, heavily blotched white. Bahamas, May 1999.* © Colin McLeod.

Ad male Blainville's Beaked Whale Mesoplodon densirostris: *note extensive linear body scars and moderately long beak, with large teeth just erupting from strongly arched lower jaw. East of Abaco, Bahamas, May 1999.* © Colin McLeod.

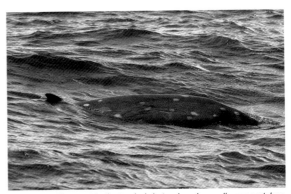

Blainville's Beaked Whale Mesoplodon densirostris*: presence of cookie-cutter shark bites (frequent in the tropics), but reduced or no linear scratches, and shallow-arched jawline, suggest an adult female; orange coloration probably due to diatoms. Hawaii. © Hadoram Shirihai.*

part of head on breathing (blow projects low and forward, but is inconspicuous), and back and prominent falcate dorsal fin usually visible only after head disappears from view. Usually in small groups. Observed to slap beak against surface.

Similar species: If recorded in our region, at least mature males should show combination of features to eliminate confusion, though be aware that those features portrayed in the plate and photos may be difficult or impossible to detect at sea. Moreover, *M. densirostris* is much more widespread and exhibits strong age/sex variation, including less well-marked animals; especially if there is no mature male in a pod, young and females are easily misidentified, which must be taken into account when claiming one of the poorer known Southern Ocean *Mesoplodon*.

Distribution and biology

Distribution, movements and population: Widely distributed in warm temperate and tropical seas with several reports close to northern limits of our area, e.g. off C South America south to Rio Grande do Sul (Brazil) and C Chile, South Africa and S Australasia. Included here primarily to facilitate comparison with several potential confusion species known from our region. No population estimates.

Diet and feeding techniques: Squid and fish in deep waters.

Main social behaviour: Occurs singly or in small groups of 1–6 but groups of up to 12 may congregate at favoured feeding areas.

Breeding and diving: Usually dives for 20–45 minutes but also shallow dives in series, at 15–20-second intervals.

Blainville's Beaked Whale Mesoplodon densirostris *is often predominantly greyish; the virtually unscarred body and shallow-arched jawline suggest a young animal, and the rusty-brown tinge is apparently due to diatoms. Canaries. © Graeme Cresswell.*

Breeding biology: No information.

Conservation Placed on CITES Appendix I but no information concerning threats or population trends.

Taxonomy Monotypic.

Ginkgo-toothed Beaked Whale
Mesoplodon ginkgodens   Plate 33

Identification

Confusion risks: Other *Mesoplodon* species.

Main characters: Small to medium-sized, smooth-headed beaked whale, with long sloping forehead, very dark grey to marine-blue body (paler, mid grey in female), white blotching around navel, and mid-length but relatively prominent, dolphin-like beak (variably tinged whitish). Uniquely among mesoplodonts, body usually unscarred (even males). Mature male has two triangular teeth near centre of lower jaw, which is strongly arched, whilst narrow upper jaw is sharply pointed and skin largely covers teeth. (The species' strange name is derived from the shape of the exceptionally broad [10-cm] teeth which recall the leaves of the Ginkgo tree, a common species in Japan, from where it was first described.) Small pointed dorsal fin with falcate trailing edge, short narrow flippers and almost straight-edged tail flukes. Crescentic blowhole behind sloping forehead, and single pale throat groove either side of head.

Age/sex: aside from differences in teeth and presence of white navel spotting (both only in full-grown males), females and young tend to be paler and less contrastingly patterned, paler and diffuse greyish-white below, possibly sometimes on face. Plate 33 depicts a classic full-grown male. Calf close to female in coloration.

Physical notes: 4.7–5.2 m and c.1.5–2.03 tonnes. Calf at birth 2.1 m but no other data.

Chief identification at sea: Even at close quarters, difficult to separate from other dark beaked whales, although if any heavily scarred males are evident within a group of beaked whales, this alone may eliminate *M. ginkgodens*.

Similar species: Among beaked whales in our region, male Blainville's *Mesoplodon densirostris* has diagnostic heavy whitish scarring to the dorsal areas and sides, which tend to be browner/greyer, with more extensive whitish on the belly, and a flatter head (both have pronounced arch to mouthline), which in profile has two high humps either side. Andrews' *M. bowdoini* is all dark with a white beak, and Cuvier's *Ziphius cavirostris* is larger with whitish-cream face and fore back, shorter beak and teeth near the jaw tip. Identification of females and young probably very difficult, even of specimens, and most are so poorly known in life as to make identification often uncertain.

Distribution and biology

Distribution, movements and population: Principally N Pacific and N Indian Oceans, but records in most sea areas, including off New Zealand and Chatham, and elsewhere in Indian Ocean. No population estimates but possibly uncommon.
Diet and feeding techniques: Squid and fish in deep waters.
Main social behaviour: Unknown.
Breathing and diving: No data.
Breeding biology: No information.
Conservation Placed on CITES Appendix I but no information concerning threats or population trends.
Taxonomy Monotypic.

Gray's Beaked Whale
Mesoplodon grayi   Plate 33

Identification

Confusion risks: Other *Mesoplodon* species, mainly Strap-toothed Whale *M. layardii*.
Main characters: Medium-sized, small-headed, dark bluish-grey, brownish-grey or black on upperside, with pale grey or white underside, very prominent, slender dolphin-like white beak (straight mouthline) and flat forehead. Pointed dorsal fin with concave trailing edge, short broad flippers and broad, almost straight-edged tail flukes (pointed slightly backwards at tips). Male has a single small triangular tooth on either side of lower jaw and both sexes have rows of 17–19 tiny vestigial maxillary teeth on upper jaw (unlike congeners) visibly embedded in gum, instead of bone. At close range shows scarring on body. Blowhole broad and slightly to left of top of crown, and single pale throat groove on each side of head. **Age/sex variation** aside from dental differences (teeth erupt only in full-grown males), females and young tend to be paler/browner, more uniform on sides and below, with less or no scarring, less white and muted facial coloration, and fewer yellowish spots around navel. Calf much as female, but perhaps even paler, with more uniform head and body, and some show a dark beak tip.
Physical notes: 4.5–5.6 m and c.1.01–1.5 tonnes. Calf at birth 2.0–2.4 m but no other data.
Chief identification at sea: Little information but known to breach at shallow angle (occasionally becoming entirely airborne several times in succession), porpoise in low arc-shaped leaps, and poke head above surface at 50° angle to breathe.
Similar species: Long snow-white beak and face distinctive amongst beaked whales, but less is known concerning appearance

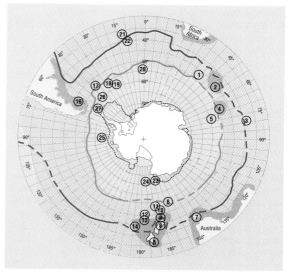

▨ Approximate known range
▨ Possible range

of females and young, which can be very similar to same-age Strap-toothed Whale (which also has long beak). However, latter still usually has some pale (though ill-defined) countershading on back and darker mask, and only distal half of beak is white. Compare also Blainville's *Mesoplodon densirostris*, Andrews' *M. bowdoini*, True's *M. mirus*, Hector's *M. hectori* and Ginkgo-toothed *M. ginkgodens* Beaked Whales, which can sometimes be eliminated by length and shape of beak, dentition and overall coloration.

Distribution and biology

Distribution, movements and population: Circumpolar south of 30°S, principally known from strandings in New Zealand and increasing number of records from Chatham, Australia, South Africa, the Falklands and Tierra del Fuego. Perhaps common in deep water south and east of Madagascar. Has wandered as far as N Atlantic (one record). No population estimates.
Diet and feeding techniques: Squid and fish in deep waters.
Main social behaviour: Occurs singly or in small groups of 2–6, but a group of 28 was stranded (Chatham, 19th century) and may be relatively social at sea.
Breathing and diving: No detailed information.
Breeding biology: No information.

Gray's Beaked Whale Mesoplodon grayi, *mother and calf: the latter still has a stubby dark-tipped beak, clearer dark eye patch and forehead; note lack of linear scarring on which has the species' quite large, pointed dorsal fin with concave trailing edge.* © *Paula A. Olsen.*

Gray's Beaked Whale Mesoplodon grayi, *mother and calf (foreground) in typical breathing roll of most Mesoplodonts, with beak often emerging first at steep angle. This species often swims slowly and rolls smoothly (revealing the diagnostic, conspicuously long, slender white beak).* © *Paula A. Olsen.*

Conservation Placed on CITES Appendix I. Appears to be widespread and reasonably common in Southern Ocean. Poorly known and no information concerning threats or population trends, though may be considered to be at risk long term from commercial squid fisheries and entanglement in nets.

Taxonomy Proposed monotypic genus, *Oulodon*, for this species has acquired little support.

Hector's Beaked Whale
Mesoplodon hectori   Plate 33

Identification

Confusion risks: Other *Mesoplodon* species.

Main characters: Small and small-headed, overall greyish-black (mature male) to brownish-grey on upperside, with pale grey or white below (female/young), and has short snow-white to pale grey, dolphin-like beak. Forehead rather flat with slight melon (and crescent-shaped blowhole). Male has some pale linear body scarring and both sexes have cookie-cutter shark bites, whilst female/young also appear to have characteristic large white patch on neck-sides and dark eye patch. All animals have small, variably triangular or rounded dorsal fin, short flippers with parallel edges, and broad, almost straight-edged tail flukes; single pale throat groove either side of head. Mature male has two small triangular teeth near tip of lower jaw. **Age/sex variation** apparent in coloration (see above), and teeth only erupt in full-grown males. Calf presumably much as female but perhaps even paler.

Physical notes: 3.9–4.4 m and c.1.01–2.03 tonnes. Calf at birth 2.1 m but no other data.

Chief identification at sea: Requires study; the above-mentioned characteristics are based on very few animals in the wild, and mature male coloration only recently documented, but following may prove useful: small size, short beak, pale or whitish beak and fore face, straight gape, and look for teeth at tip of jaw in animals with scarring.

Similar species: Few data but even when seen close it may be impossible or difficult to identify female/young from pale, similar-sized, congeners. Probably, if visible, male's small head, short white beak and diagnostic teeth are useful field marks; white patch on neck-sides and dark eye patch appear to be useful and consistent features of female/young. Some confusion species

include True's Beaked Whale *M. mirus* and juv Arnoux's Beaked Whale *Berardius arnuxii*; compare also Blainville's *M. densirostris*, Gray's *M. grayi* and Andrews' Beaked Whales *M. bowdoini*, the two latter of which have superficially similar white beaks in mature males, but differ strongly in head and beak structure, and dentition.

Distribution and biology

Distribution, movements and population: Occurs south of Tropic of Capricorn and apparently circumpolar. Most records are off New Zealand but also off Tasmania, South Africa and S South America (north to Brazil) and the Falklands. No population estimates.

Diet and feeding techniques: Squid in deep waters.

Main social behaviour: Few data but perhaps in pairs. May be inquisitive around boats.

Breathing and diving: No data.

Breeding biology: No information.

Conservation Placed on CITES Appendix I but no information concerning threats or population trends, although generally considered to be rare.

Taxonomy Monotypic.

Strap-toothed Whale
Mesoplodon layardii   Plate 33

Identification

Confusion risks: Other *Mesoplodon* species.

Main characters: The largest Mesoplodon, with prominent dolphin-like beak and slight melon-shaped forehead. Predominantly purplish-brown or bluish-black, with distinctive black mask and shoulder (from flipper), contrasting with white back and neck (in front of flipper), and sometimes fore part of rostrum, with considerable body scarring and grey or white patches around genital slit. Low, falcate dorsal fin, short narrow flippers, and broad unnotched, almost triangular, tail flukes. Male has two very long teeth (up to 30 cm) that curl around upper jaw. Both sexes possess short denticles at apices. Like most beaked whales, blowhole on crown with indistinct throat groove either side of head. **Age/sex** perhaps judged by size (though difficult to appreciate at sea), and full-grown male should have at least partially exposed whitish teeth; juv/female lack erupted teeth, though young male may have smaller, triangular-shaped teeth. Plate 33 depicts full-grown male with well-developed 'melon' and well-exposed teeth, but not to extent of some older males, in which teeth may curl over base of upper jaw and overlap. Female and young generally have reduced or no body scarring. Calf well differentiated, generally paler but pigmentation reversed, having pale facial mask, flippers, sides and rear body, with dark fore back, collar, abdomen patch and beak.

Breaching Strap-toothed Whale Mesoplodon layardii: note long white beak (dark at base) and dark melon contrasting with white shawl. The teeth can be difficult to see because they project where the black meets the white on the beak. South Atlantic. © John Hewitt.

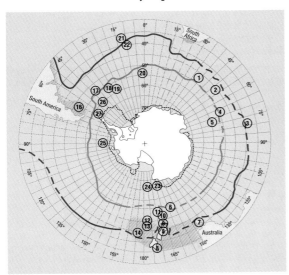

Strap-toothed Whale Mesoplodon layardii, apparently ad or imm male. On surfacing, beak appears first (at 45° angle), then part of head is briefly revealed to exhale (blow inconspicuous); part of back and low dorsal fin usually visible. Note long, white-tipped beak, black mask contrasting with white rear melon, and extensive pale shawl reaching to dorsal fin where it tapers. Habitually swims slowly. © Paula A. Olsen.

Physical notes: 5.0–6.15 m and c.1.1–3.4 tonnes. Calf at birth 2.5–3.0 m but no other data.

Chief identification at sea: Useful features are the long white-tipped beak and black head contrasting with white shawl from back of neck to dorsal fin. Teeth often difficult to see because they protrude at border between black and white areas of beak. Surfaces beak first (at 45° angle), then briefly reveals part of head to breathe (blow inconspicuous), with usually a little of back and low falcate dorsal fin visible; swims and dives very slowly, with flukes apparently never appearing above surface.

Similar species: Given unmistakable coloration and bizarre teeth of ad male, among the easiest beaked whales to identify at sea, though inconspicuous surfacing behaviour (see above) may reduce usefulness of these features, and be aware that pale head and fore back is not always obvious. Females and young may prove more difficult, appearing mainly greyish with a very long beak, and very similar to Gray's Beaked Whale *M. grayi*.

Distribution and biology

Distribution, movements and population: Widespread in Southern Ocean and nearby waters south of 30°S and north of Antarctic Convergence, with most records from New Zealand and Australia (and no strong evidence for seasonality in this region); also S South America (north to Uruguay), South Africa, Indian Ocean (Kerguelen) and the Falklands. No population estimates.

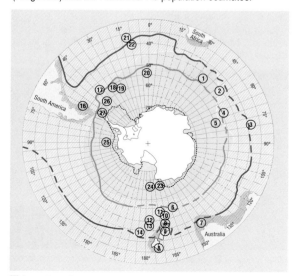

░ Approximate known range
▨ Possible range

Diet and feeding techniques: Squid, which are probably captured using intense suction, in deep waters. As with other beaked whales, the teeth may act as a 'guide' directing prey more swiftly into throat.

Main social behaviour: Occurs singly or in small groups of up to three. Shy of boats.

Breathing and diving: Usually dives for 10–15 minutes.

Breeding biology: Little information though calving reported in austral spring–summer.

Conservation Placed on CITES Appendix I. Appears to be widespread and reasonably common in Southern Ocean. Poorly known and no information concerning threats or population trends, though entanglement in nets and commercial squid fisheries may pose long-term threats.

Taxonomy Monotypic.

True's Beaked Whale *Mesoplodon mirus*　　Plate 33

Identification

Confusion risks: Other *Mesoplodon* species within region.

Main characters: Small, dark grey/bluish grey-black on upperside, with whitish (variably mottled grey) underside, much paler rear third, dark area around eye and on ridge of back, with mid-length, stubby dolphin-like beak (cheeks and lower jaw whitish) and distinctly bulging forehead. Small, falcate or triangular, dorsal fin with concave trailing edge, short dark flippers, and white tailstock and flukes with concave trailing edge. Scarred whitish. Male has two small triangular teeth near extreme tip of lower jaw. Blowhole on forecrown, with single brownish throat groove either side of head.

Age/sex variation limited, aside of differences in teeth (concealed or lacking in female/young, which tend to be paler and less patterned). Plate 33 (and description above) of Southern Hemisphere form. Calf more like female in coloration.

Physical notes: 4.8–5.3 m and c.0.89–1.5 tonnes. Calf at birth c.2.2 m and c.136 kg but no other data.

Chief identification at sea: Few positive identifications at sea though white tailstock is distinctive and permits even underwater identifications; may exhibit repeated breaching though generally moves unobtrusively at surface.

Similar species: Except in optimal and comparative views, probably not reliably identifiable from several congeners, especially if dealing with younger animals.

Distribution and biology

Distribution, movements and population: Principally N Atlantic but recently recorded several times in Southern Hemisphere, off South Africa, Australia and, possibly, New Zealand (where a specimen of Bahamonde's Beaked Whale *M. bahamondi* has also recently been discovered). Included here to facilitate comparison with several potential confusion species known from the Southern Ocean, and because of the possibility that it occurs in our region. No population estimates.

Diet and feeding techniques: Squid in deep waters.

Main social behaviour: Largely unknown but group size considered to be 1–6.

Breathing and diving: No data.

Breeding biology: No information.

Conservation Placed on CITES Appendix I but no information concerning threats or population trends.

Taxonomy Two populations, one in the North Atlantic which has a paler underside and lacks contrasting pale rear third of body, and that in Southern Hemisphere (described above).

Shepherd's Beaked Whale
Tasmacetus shepherdi　　　　　　　　　Plate 34

Identification
Confusion risks: Several *Mesoplodon* species.

Main characters: One of the least known cetaceans. Mid-sized to largish, robust and distinctly patterned beaked whale, with several dolphin-like characters. Diagnostic pattern includes pale flipper extending as round patch onto fore flanks, and bordered in front by diagonal dark shoulder band and cape, with contrasting creamy-white underside and tailstock; otherwise ground colour of dark areas is brownish-black. Steep, rounded forehead, often with well-defined, bulbous pale melon (both melon and cap-like mark on head probably more noticeable in mature male), and straight mouthline to prominent dolphin-like beak. Small, slightly falcate dorsal fin, short narrow and all-dark flippers, and broad, straight-edged or concave, all-dark tail flukes. The only beaked whale with a complete set of functional teeth in both jaws (17–21 in upper and 18–28 in lower jaw), but apparently only male has flat triangular first tooth protruding from gum on either side of lower jaw. Crescentic blowhole in centre of crown points slightly left, with a single indistinct throat groove either side of head. **Age/sex** perhaps can be judged by overall size (but always difficult at sea), and reportedly has duller, less-defined pattern in young/female, but chronic lack of data makes all such comments at best tentative. Illustration is of a full-grown male with moderately developed melon, set-off rather sharply from beak. Ad male also probably more heavily scarred with age.

Physical notes: 6.0–7.1 m and c.2.32–3.48 tonnes. Calf at birth 3.4 m (one) but no data on growth rates.

Chief identification at sea: Behaviour at sea largely unknown, but perhaps similar to some *Mesoplodon*, and possibly never gregarious.

Similar species: Possibly any similar-sized beaked whale with pale flanks, though coloration of Shepherd's possibly distinctive. Larger than most *Mesoplodon* with a steeper melon and distinctive flank pattern. Also *cf.* Southern Bottlenose Whale *Hyperoodon planifrons*, Arnoux's *Berardius arnuxii* and Cuvier's Beaked Whales *Ziphius cavirostris*. Any claimed at-sea record requires thorough documentation.

Distribution and biology
Distribution, movements and population: Perhaps circumpolar in temperate waters of Southern Ocean, with most records (12 strandings) from New Zealand, but also recorded from Argentina (three strandings), the Juan Fernández Is (twice), the South Sandwiches (once) and Australia (once). There are sight records from New Zealand and the Seychelles. No population estimates.

Diet and feeding techniques: Presumably squid and fish in deep waters.

Main social behaviour: Unknown.

Breathing and diving: Probably dives to great depths, like other beaked whales, but no available data.

Breeding biology: Unknown.

Conservation Placed on CITES Appendix I but no information concerning threats or population trends.

Taxonomy Monotypic.

Cuvier's Beaked Whale
Ziphius cavirostris　　　　　　　　　Plate 34

Identification
Confusion risks: *Mesoplodon* spp. and bottlenose whales *Hyperoodon* spp.; less likely to be confused with Arnoux's Beaked Whale *Berardius arnuxii*.

Main characters: Medium-sized, robust and highly variable in colour, from almost white (very old animals) to purplish-black, with cream-coloured blotches principally on underside and scars on back and sides, indistinct 'goose-like' beak and creamy-white forehead. Enormous individual variation and according to age/sex (see below), with that in Plate 34 being a distinctive ad male. Typically smallish round head is whitest part, with gently sloping forehead ending in poorly defined beak with clearly upturned mouthline. Relatively distinctive small, falcate (or more triangular) dorsal fin situated at rear of mid-back, tiny flippers, and broad almost straight-edged triangular tail flukes, which have prominent concave trailing edge. Male has two flat triangular, sometimes barnacle-encrusted, teeth either side of lower jaw. Thin crescentic blowhole just left of centre of head; single pale throat groove either side of head. **Age/sex variation** most marked in dentition; in both females and young animals they are concealed by the gums or lacking (though in males they may be obscured by stalked barnacles). Males have both long linear and white oval scars; females only the latter. All become paler with age, especially males (in which the white extends posteriorly with age, increasing on dorsal surface and slanting laterally forwards), some being even whiter than that in Plate 34, though females are usually dark grey to reddish-brown with a paler head and dark eye crescents. Melon in male becomes progressively more bulbous with age. No information on age of sexual maturity (although probably reached when 5.0–5.5 m) or growth rates. Calf/juv darker (including beak) and has more rounded dolphin-like head.

Physical notes: 4.7–7.0 m and 2.03–3.4 tonnes (no significant sexual size dimorphism). Calf at birth 2.0–2.7 m and c.270 kg but no other information concerning development.

Cuvier's Beaked Whale Ziphius cavirostris: *the lack of scarring indicates a subadult. Note well-defined pale head, almost beakless appearance and inconspicuous bushy blow, usually less than 1 m high and projecting slightly forward and left. © Todd Pusser.*

Cuvier's Beaked Whale Ziphius cavirostris: *extremely pale head and dorsal areas, extensive linear scarring, and two cone-like teeth readily distinguish this as a mature male. Note characteristic 'smile' and goose-beak profile.* © Todd Pusser.

Cuvier's Beaked Whale Ziphius cavirostris: *identified by robust body, pale head and stubby beak; orange patches are probably diatoms (often much more extensive than here). Breaching is considered rare in this species.* © Todd Pusser.

Chief identification at sea: Bushy blow (rarely visible, except after deep dive) projects slightly forward and left but is generally inconspicuous and usually less than 1 m high. When swimming fast, head may project above surface, revealing concave whitish face and very short beak, with dorsal fin and upper back rather exposed, usually showing large pale area and numerous pale scars. Arches back and may lift flukes in vertical descent of deep dive. Can appear confusingly overall reddish in bright sunlight. Occasionally breaches (vertically in dolphin-like jump).

Similar species: Three potentially confusing medium to large-sized beaked whales occur in the Southern Ocean (see Plate 34 for well-differentiated, classic-coloured male): blackish-blue or dark grey Arnoux's, paler brown male Southern Bottlenose *Hyperoodon planifrons* (with well-developed buffy-white bulbous forehead), and older Cuvier's with extensive pale marks. Young and females may be confusingly paler (Arnoux's) or darker (the others) and have less clear diagnostic head structure. Observers should bear in mind that even males can be difficult to identify at sea; close views and only those animals possessing clear combination of characters may be identifiable. Cuvier's best separated by more smooth-sloping forehead with indistinct beak, and paler parts usually extending from face to back rather than belly. Additional fin/flippers and behavioural distinctions are described under each. Potential confusion with smaller *Mesoplodon* is described under those species.

Distribution and biology

Distribution, movements and population: Worldwide in tropical, subtropical and temperate waters, being largely absent only from polar waters in both hemispheres. Sightings in our region and nearby waters reported from Tierra del Fuego, the Drake Passage, north of Shag Rocks, the Cape of Good Hope, Australia, New Zealand (including Chatham) and ad males occasionally recorded in Antarctic waters. No population estimates or information on movements (though apparently largely sedentary in some areas of Northern Hemisphere).

Diet and feeding techniques: Squid and fish in deep waters.

Main social behaviour: Occurs singly or in small groups of 3–12 but groups of up to 25 may congregate at favoured feeding areas. Single individuals are apparently usually old males but pods of 5–10 darker animals usually contain one (white) old male, which may migrate between groups. Avoids boats by diving but is sometimes inquisitive, logging or moving slowly within close proximity of a vessel.

Breathing and diving: Usually dives for 20–40 minutes; prior to lengthy dive breathes/blows at 10–20-second intervals.

Breeding biology: No significant information though appears to

Cuvier's Beaked Whale Ziphius cavirostris: *the mostly dark body and few scars suggest a young male.* © Graeme Cresswell.

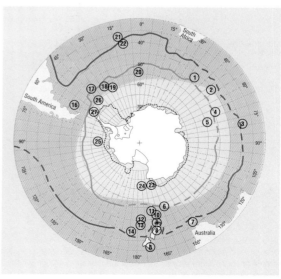

Approximate overall range

Cuvier's Beaked Whale Ziphius cavirostris *is robust-bodied with a fal-cate/ triangular dorsal fin, and distinctive coloration (dark grey-brown, though it may appear partially reddish-brown in bright sunlight), with many pale linear scars mainly in males.* © Todd Pusser.

Cuvier's Beaked Whale Ziphius cavirostris: *uniquely smooth-sloping forehead, with no obvious melon and appears almost beakless. The un-scarred body and limited white on face suggest a young male.* © Todd Pusser.

give birth year-round.
Conservation Data Deficient and placed on CITES Appendix II. No information concerning threats or population trends though Japanese *Berardius* fisheries have opportunistically taken the species.
Taxonomy Monotypic.

Spectacled Porpoise
Phocoena (Australophocaena) dioptrica　　Plate 30

Identification
Confusion risks: Black Dolphin *Cephalorhynchus eutropia*.
Main characters: Distinctively marked and stocky, with glossy blue-black upperside sharply demarcated from white underside, large, broad-based and rounded dorsal fin, white spectacles, small, vir-tually all-white flippers (with grey edges), and white/pale grey, dis-tinctly notched and point-tipped flukes. Along top of tailstock there is a narrow but clear white band. Oval blowhole above forehead. Mouthline short and straight with black lips. Each upper jaw has 16–26 teeth and lower jaws have 16–22 per side. **Age/sex varia-tion** marked in ads by shape of dorsal fin, being large and round in male but shorter and describing a shallow triangle in female, and same shape but smaller in respective young; also to some extent

in coloration, with young tending to be less pure white below, and dark stripe from lips to flippers often fades with age. Age of sexual maturity unknown but may be two years in females and four years in males. Young tend to be dark grey dorsally and pale grey ven-trally with darker streaks, including well-defined mouth to flipper stripe, which becomes paler and may disappear with growth.
Physical notes: 1.24–2.24 m and 60–115 kg (males may average larger). Calf at birth c.0.5 m but no other information.
Chief identification at sea: Dorsal fin (especially of male) unmis-takable at sea. Porpoising behavior—a slow roll or two at surface, then swims rapidly away just below surface—also distinctive.

Spectacled Porpoise Phocoena (Australophocaena) dioptrica, *female or young; even below the surface, the white, point-tipped flukes and top of the tailstock are visible.* © Paula A. Olsen.

Spectacled Porpoise Phocoena (Australophocaena) dioptrica, *probably female or young (note shorter, shallowly triangular fin, and grey body). Usually inconspicuous at the surface, it is often fast-moving in active travel.* © Paula A. Olsen.

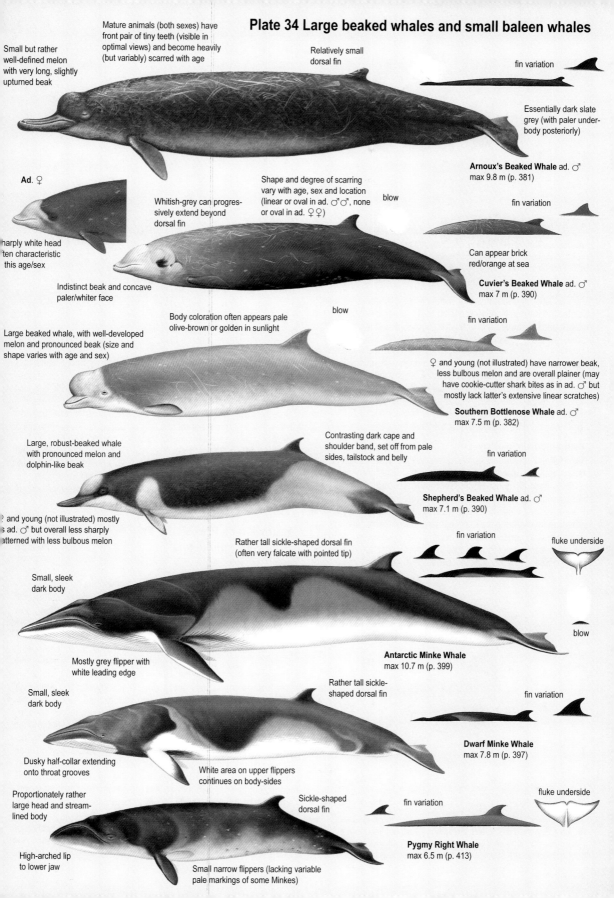

Plate 34 Large beaked whales and small baleen whales

Small but rather well-defined melon with very long, slightly upturned beak

Mature animals (both sexes) have front pair of tiny teeth (visible in optimal views) and become heavily (but variably) scarred with age

Relatively small dorsal fin

fin variation

Essentially dark slate grey (with paler under-body posteriorly)

Arnoux's Beaked Whale ad. ♂
max 9.8 m (p. 381)

Ad. ♀

Whitish-grey can progressively extend beyond dorsal fin

Shape and degree of scarring vary with age, sex and location (linear or oval in ad. ♂♂, none or oval in ad. ♀♀)

blow

fin variation

harply white head ten characteristic this age/sex

Indistinct beak and concave paler/whiter face

Can appear brick red/orange at sea

Cuvier's Beaked Whale ad. ♂
max 7 m (p. 390)

Body coloration often appears pale olive-brown or golden in sunlight

blow

fin variation

Large beaked whale, with well-developed melon and pronounced beak (size and shape varies with age and sex)

♀ and young (not illustrated) have narrower beak, less bulbous melon and are overall plainer (may have cookie-cutter shark bites as in ad. ♂ but mostly lack latter's extensive linear scratches)

Southern Bottlenose Whale ad. ♂
max 7.5 m (p. 382)

Large, robust-beaked whale with pronounced melon and dolphin-like beak

Contrasting dark cape and shoulder band, set off from pale sides, tailstock and belly

fin variation

Shepherd's Beaked Whale ad. ♂
max 7.1 m (p. 390)

? and young (not illustrated) mostly
s ad. ♂ but overall less sharply
atterned with less bulbous melon

Rather tall sickle-shaped dorsal fin (often very falcate with pointed tip)

fin variation

fluke underside

Small, sleek dark body

blow

Antarctic Minke Whale
max 10.7 m (p. 399)

Mostly grey flipper with white leading edge

Rather tall sickle-shaped dorsal fin

fin variation

Small, sleek dark body

Dwarf Minke Whale
max 7.8 m (p. 397)

Dusky half-collar extending onto throat grooves

White area on upper flippers continues on body-sides

Proportionately rather large head and stream-lined body

Sickle-shaped dorsal fin

fin variation

fluke underside

Pygmy Right Whale
max 6.5 m (p. 413)

High-arched lip to lower jaw

Small narrow flippers (lacking variable pale markings of some Minkes)

Spectacled Porpoise Phocoena (Australophocaena) dioptrica, probably young (note very shallow but still broad-based fin and grey body). Note typical porpoise shape; small-headed and virtually beakless. © Paula A. Olsen.

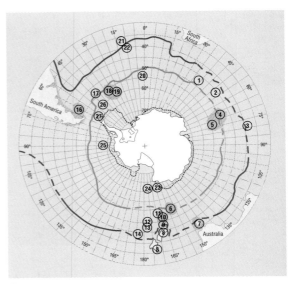

☐ Approximate overall range

Often elusive and fast in water, when white underside frequently visible, but swimming also reported to be 'slow and steady', and arches back strongly on diving when dorsal fin is also prominent. *Similar species*: Unmistakable among porpoises. No other similar-sized animal has such sharply demarcated black-and-white pigmentation midway across flanks, but beware confusion with Southern Right Whale Dolphin *Lissodelphis peronii* and Black Dolphin *Cephalorhynchus eutropia*, though both have many striking features that should readily eliminate any confusion (e.g. former lacks dorsal fin and latter has black on sides reaching belly and flippers, and both possess a different jizz).

Distribution and biology

Distribution, movements and population: Presumably circumpolar, though only recorded from Atlantic coast of South America north to 32°S, the Falklands, South Georgia (and south in Drake Passage to at least 59°S) and around some S Indian Ocean islands (Kerguelen and Heard), as well as in Australian and New Zealand subantarctic regions (once in Tasmania). Principally oceanic but also known to enter estuarine waters. No population estimates but apparently uncommon away from Patagonia (based on strandings and low incidence of sightings during surveys for other cetaceans).

Diet and feeding techniques: Fish, krill and probably squid (but data tiny).
Main social behaviour: Typical group size is apparently 1–3, but based on few sightings.
Breathing and diving: No information, although a calf was reported breathing 4–7 times per minute.
Breeding biology: Unknown but calves probably born Nov–Feb.
Conservation No information concerning population trends but probably, like most dolphins, at risk from some hunting and entanglement in nets. Apparently locally common off Patagonia.
Taxonomy Monotypic. Formerly classified as *Australaphocaena dioptrica*.

Burmeister's Porpoise
Phocoena spinipinnis   Plate 30

Identification

Confusion risks: Black Dolphin *Cephalorhynchus eutropia*.
Main characters: Stocky and appears all dark (slate) at sea, with low backward-pointing triangular dorsal fin (which has long, low leading edge, short, convex trailing edge and is placed well back on body), upturned mouth, flat forehead, blunt-tipped large flippers, variable paler area on underside and distinctly notched point-tipped tail flukes. Dark patch often observed around eye and dark grey stripe (broader on left side of body) from chin to base of flipper. Ventral region paler grey than rest of body with two abdominal stripes. Crescentic blowhole on top of forehead. Upper jaw has 10–22 teeth per side with 16–25 teeth in lower jaw (some variation between left and right sides). **Age/sex variation** indistinct (though abdominal stripes vary sexually) and age of sexual maturity unknown but females slightly smaller than males post-puberty. Tubercules on dorsal fin become sharper with age. Calf generally as ad.
Physical notes: 1.4–2.0 m and 40–105 kg (males usually significantly larger and more robust, and Atlantic animals may be slightly larger than those in Pacific). Calf at birth 0.86 m (mean) but no other information.
Chief identification at sea: Movement on surface inconspicuous and apparently rarely breaches; disinterested in vessels and does not porpoise or bow-ride when approached by boat. All-dark

Ad male Spectacled Porpoise Phocoena (Australophocaena) dioptrica, often arches strongly on diving, when huge rounded fin is prominent, and may show diagnostic black-and-white pattern. © Keiko Sekiguchi.

Breaching Burmeister's Porpoise Phocoena spinipinnis, *showing typical blunt, beakless head, and large, blunt-tipped flippers. Drake Passage. © Morten Jørgensen.*

appearance, shallow backward-sloping dorsal fin and low-profile swimming behaviour are characteristic in range.

Similar species: Separated from Black Dolphin by its different-shaped dorsal fin and behaviour on surfacing. Dorsal fin of latter is round, higher and situated on mid-back (rather than being straighter and a shallower triangle situated well back), and also has grey forehead and pure white throat and belly, unlike Burmeister's Porpoise.

Distribution and biology

Distribution, movements and population: To 50 km off South America (although most common inshore, occasionally frequenting estuaries and within the kelp-line), discontinuously from Tierra del Fuego north to N Peru (at 5°S) and S Brazil. No population estimates (but probably more common on Pacific coast where usually considered numerous) but may move north–south or inshore–offshore seasonally, at least in some parts of range (in others, e.g. Beagle Channel, appears resident).

Diet and feeding techniques: Fish, krill and other crustaceans.

Main social behaviour: Typical group size is up to eight but as many as 70 may occur together. Not recorded actively associating with other cetaceans.

Breathing and diving: Little information though unrecorded in waters deeper than 60 m and dives of 1–3 minutes are common.

Breeding biology: Largely unknown though calving may occur in early autumn, and females may give birth annually. Gestation probably occupies 11–12 months and conception and parturition may peak in Feb–Mar.

Conservation No information concerning threats or population trends but appears to be locally common. Heavily exploited, both directly and indirectly in Peru and Chile, being taken incidentally in gill nets and intentionally for bait. As many as 2000 per annum have been reportedly taken in Peru, and fisheries in Argentina and Uruguay are also known to incidentally take small numbers.

Taxonomy Monotypic.

Southern Right Whale
Eubalaena australis   Plate 35

Identification

Confusion risks: None.

Main characters: Large and very rotund, with no dorsal fin. Enormous head covered in callosities, strongly arched mouthline, uniformly black or dark brown body sometimes mottled grey, brown or blue, large all-dark spatulate flippers, narrow tailstock, broad, point-tipped, all-dark tail flukes, and irregular white patches on belly (incidence of piebald individuals is highest in S Atlantic). Long, dense baleen plates mainly black to brown, but greyish when younger. Well-spaced double-blowholes and splashguard rather indistinct; no narrow central rostrum ridge as in rorquals.

Age/sex variation perhaps estimable by overall size; male smaller and usually has more numerous callosities. Calf averages slimmer, paler and greyer (some even born white), and lacks or has only indistinct callosities (see below for size); age development apparently unknown for males, but females usually reach sexual maturity at 9–10 years old when 15.5 m.

Physical notes: 11.0–16.4 m and 20–30 tonnes; female usually slightly larger. Calf at birth 4.5–6.0 m and c.10 tonnes (at 10–12 months may reach 9–11 m).

Chief identification at sea: Extremely broad black body without dorsal fin. Highly acrobatic: regularly breaches, lobtails and flipper-slaps; also head-stands and waves flukes high above surface for up to two minutes, especially prior to deep dives. Emits broad

Burmeister's Porpoise Phocoena spinipinnis, *showing all-dark body, with triangular, strongly backswept dorsal fin set far back; note small ridge of tubercles on leading edge of fin. Usually inconspicuous at the surface, where its low-profile swimming behaviour is characteristic in range. Chile. © Francisco Viddi Carrasco.*

Southern Right Whale Eubalaena australis. *Although a very slow swimmer, the species is often surprisingly acrobatic, frequently breaching on the breeding grounds, sometimes up to ten times in close succession. Nuevo, Argentina, Oct 1993. © Hiroya Minakuchi/Sphere Magazine.*

V-shaped blows up to 5 m high, which sometimes appear as a single jet if seen from side or in wind.

Similar species: Virtually unmistakable. No overlap between this and other species of right whales, though may be mistaken for a Humpback *Megaptera novaeangliae* if logging at the surface.

Distribution and biology

Distribution, movements and population: Circumpolar in Southern Ocean at 35°S–60°S, with movement to colder Antarctic waters in austral summer when generally recorded south of 40°S (even on migration may pause in an area for several weeks), though some populations (e.g. in Golfo San Jose, Argentina), now protected, are exhibiting greater degrees of residency at lower latitudes than previously. Those that winter off South Africa and C Argentina principally spend the austral summer over the continental shelf near South Georgia. Clusters known from several subantarctic islands as well as coast of W Australia, New Zealand, South Africa

and S South America. Appears to be becoming more frequent in some waters around Antarctic Peninsula in recent years. Population c.7000 in recent years.

Diet and feeding techniques: Feeds on krill and other tiny crustaceans (including larvae), preferring to take copepods, with euphausiids a second choice. May feed year-round but most do so between Subtropical and Antarctic Convergences.

Main social behaviour: Groups of up to 12 (usually 2–3), but occasionally loose associations of up to 100 at favoured feeding grounds. Populations may have herding instinct. Inquisitive and often approachable. Curious of other objects in water and interacts peaceably with smaller cetaceans and pinnipeds. Members of group may surface in turn rather than simultaneously. Significance of its rather demonstrative actions, e.g. flipper-slapping and head-standing, not fully known but possess high social significance, for instance such movements in young are thought to indicate hunger, while may wave fluke in direction of intruders

In preparing to dive deep, Southern Right Whales Eubalaena australis *sink head first, the body shortly afterwards and finally the tail flukes, which are often raised quite high and submerge at an angle (varies); the flukes are broad with a smooth, concave trailing edge, central notch and pointed tips. Left © Stephen Wong; right © Gabriel Rojo.*

On surfacing Southern Right Whale Eubalaena australis *holds the body, and especially the head, high above the water; the callosities and strongly arched mouthline are visible. © Graeme Cresswell.*

Southern Right Whale Eubalaena australis *emits broad V-shaped blows up to 5 m tall (jets often asymmetric), which sometimes appear as a single jet, especially if seen side-on. © Stephen Wong.*

Southern Right Whale Eubalaena australis *showing typical rotund, dark appearance, with whitish callosities around head (especially on tip of rostrum), no dorsal fin, but broad triangular flukes. A slow deliberate swimmer (though capable of short bursts of acceleration), it is very inquisitive and approachable. Kaikoura, South I, New Zelaland. © Dennis Buurman.*

and explosive blowing may indicate alarm at close approach by another whale or boat.

Breathing and diving: Principally a shallow-water species and most dives occupy 10–20 minutes, but recorded underwater for up to 50 minutes and to 184 m.

Breeding biology: Females calve once every 2–4 years, usually close inshore, with traditional areas in our region including the Falklands, Tristan da Cunha, Kerguelen, Auckland and New Zealand. Several males may mate cooperatively with same female in or close to same areas. Calves born in winter (May–Aug), weaned at 12 months and return in subsequent years to their natal area. On winter grounds, calves remain with females, isolated from males in 'nursery', and there is a well-developed female/calf bond.

Conservation Lower Risk—conservation dependent and placed on CITES Appendix I with population currently increasing, due to protection, at c.7–8% per year. Protected since 1937, it was formerly taken in large numbers by whalers, being easy to catch, predominantly inshore and also of high commercial value. Current threats include human disturbance, entanglement in nets, habitat degradation and over-fishing of prey species.

Taxonomy Two species of right whales, Northern *E. glacialis* and Southern *E. australis*, are usually recognized (based on minor cranial differences and perhaps in positioning of callosities), though recent genetic data suggest that those in the N Pacific, *E. japonica*, represent a third species. Gene flow between different subpopulations of Southern Right Whale may be very low and preliminary data suggests incomplete separation of eastern and western South Atlantic stocks. Alternatively, Rice (1998) treated all right whales as a single species.

Dwarf Minke Whale
Balaenoptera [acutorostrata] unnamed sub-species/allospecies   Plate 34

Identification

Confusion risks: Principally Antarctic Minke Whale *B. bonaerensis* and to some extent with Sei *B. borealis*, Bryde's *B. edeni*, Pygmy Right *Caperea marginata* and perhaps several species of beaked whale.

Main characters: Generally as Antarctic Minke (which see) but differs in following. Considerably smaller with diagnostic solid white area across two-thirds of upper surface of flipper (only tip and trailing edge are black) continuing solidly as band behind the flipper, fading to greyish further up body. Top of rostrum/head and flanks paler grey and bordered by dusky collar, running from eye and flipper across and behind head (some animals may have ill-defined

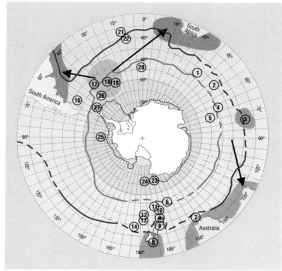

■ Approximate breeding range
▨ Approximate overall non-breeding range (mainly during the austral summer)
▧ Approximate higher Antarctic occurrences recorded during the austral summer
↗ Presumed migration/origin of feeding Antarctic summer populations

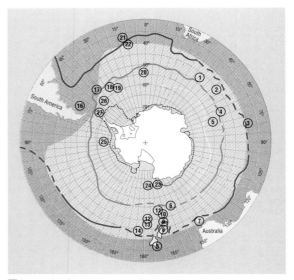

Presumed main range (year-round)
Presumed extended range south (mainly during the austral summer)

Dwarf Minke Whale Balaenoptera [acutorostrata]. *Unnnamed sub-species/allospecies in underwater head-on view, with solid white area on upper surface of flipper and dusky collar conclusive features.* © *Research Program Dwarf Minke Whales, Undersea Explorer.*

pale wavy pattern to sides of this collar, as depicted in Plate 34); belly often less pure white, affording greater contrast to white throat grooves (underside and flanks sometimes partially blotched or evenly coloured yellow, orange or even pink by diatoms and algae). No specific information concerning the baleen (which differs in northern and Antarctic forms of Minke). **Age/sex variation** probably mainly as Antarctic Minke.
Physical notes: Largest noted as 7.4 m (female) and 6.8 (male), and calf apparently up to 2.8 m at birth but no other information specific to this form.
Chief identification at sea: Blow diffuse and reaches 2–3 m high (dorsal fin visible almost simultaneously), and given 5–8 times in less than a minute, but rarely conspicuous except in cold weather; rolls high, humped and swift. Often appears completely black dorsally, and greyish tones and diagnostic white flanks are seldom apparent in brief view. When surfacing (which if performed at speed

creates a large splash), snout usually appears first at low angle (blow commences before back emerges), and following blows, arches almost vertically to dive, the tailstock exposed high above surface with dorsal fin still in view; flukes seldom visible. Rather fast swimmer and easily 'lost' while under observation but particularly approachable when feeding. May sometimes breach and spyhop.
Similar species: Both Dwarf Minke and Antarctic Minke are distinguished from all other rorquals by sharply pointed head, smaller/slighter build, different surfacing behaviour and blowing sequences, and colorations. Unlike Sei/Bryde's, Minke has extensive whitish flanks reaching far up dark back in undulating transition, usually the dark area of rostrum and upper lip extend equally to lip of lower jaw (which is whitish/pale grey in most Sei/Bryde's), and has diagnostic whitish undersides to the flukes (see other species for more details). Perhaps less likely to be confused with similar-sized Pygmy Right Whale and some beaked whales, as has straighter jawline, pointed and flat rostrum/head, and almost unscarred body, among many other obvious differences provided good views are obtained.

Distribution and biology

Distribution, movements and population: Perhaps circumpolar in Southern Ocean (occasionally to 60°S) but most records from waters off South Africa, Australia and the Indian Ocean, though occurs

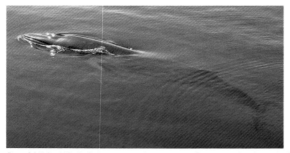

Dwarf Minke Whale Balaenoptera [acutorostrata] *unnamed subspecies/allospecies, differs from similar Antarctic Minke Whale B.* bonaerensis *by diagnostic combination of extensive solid white area on upper surface of flipper, extending broadly onto shoulder behind and bordered by broad dusky collar from eye and flipper across neck (downwards onto side of throat grooves). The pale flanks are usually lower and more clear-cut, and the white shoulder patch extends up as a tapering greyish mark with forward-pointing ends.* © *Research Program Dwarf Minke Whales, Undersea Explorer.*

Dwarf Minke Whale Balaenoptera acutorostrata *skyhopping, revealing the narrow pointed head and single rostrum ridge; the bow is rather indistinctive, Australia.* © Flip Nicklin/Minden Pictures.

year-round to 7°S in Atlantic and to 11°S in the Pacific. Sympatric with Antarctic Minke during austral summer and occurs off South Africa only in austral autumn/winter. No population estimates.

Diet and feeding techniques: Principally takes myctophid fishes and some euphausiids.

Main social behaviour: Few data for this form (see Antarctic Minke) but usually solitary or in pairs, occasionally up to eight. Often approaches slow-moving or stationary boats.

Breathing and diving: No specific information for this form (see Antarctic Minke).

Breeding biology: No specific information for this form other than that at least some breed annually, but probably most similar to northern forms of Minke Whale rather than Antarctic Minke.

Conservation Included with other minke whales on CITES Appendix I and classified as Insufficiently known but no specific information on this form (see Antarctic Minke). Presumably susceptible to same threats as facing Antarctic Minke but numbers taken are unknown.

Taxonomy See Antarctic Minke for brief overview of problems in categorizing this group. Dwarf Minke Whale is, in many respects (including genetically), apparently close to that form of Minke found in the N Atlantic but is restricted to the Southern Ocean (where it overlaps to an unknown extent with Antarctic Minke). N Atlantic form is the nominate, with *B. a. scammoni* in the N Pacific. The dwarf form, which may be better named White-shouldered Minke Whale, lacks a scientific name but I have considered it useful to highlight its potential uniqueness here.

Antarctic Minke Whale
Balaenoptera bonaerensis   Plate 34

Identification

Confusion risks: Dwarf Minke Whale *B. [acutorostrata]* unnamed subspecies/allospecies, Sei *B. borealis*, Bryde's *B. edeni*, Pygmy Right *Caperea marginata* and several species of beaked whale.

Main characters: Small, slim rorqual; head proportionately small, with sharply pointed snout, narrow central rostrum ridge from splashguard (and double blowholes) to snout tip, large sickle-shaped dorsal fin close to mid-back, and notched tail flukes. Head and back almost uniform dark bluish-grey, sharply contrasting, in undulating transition, with high pale grey/white flanks and belly (underside and flanks sometimes partially blotched or evenly coloured, yellow, orange or even pink, by diatoms and algae); up-

per surface of flipper (slim and pointed) usually appears greyish, with white only near leading edge or as diffuse central area which normally does not, or indistinctly extends to body; under flipper mostly white. Throat grooves (up to c.70) mainly white with slight dusky tone, reach just behind flipper. Underside of tail flukes white, bordered dark. Mouthline long and usually straight. Baleen short and dark/yellow-grey, becoming white on anterior plates, whilst posterior plates have white inner edges. **Age/sex variation** perhaps judged by overall size, although best done with experience and reference to surrounding objects or other cetaceans. Sexually mature at 5–8 years old (when 7.1–8.1 m), but only reaches maximum size up to seven years later. Calf averages darker with more rounded snout.

Physical notes: 7.2–10.7 m and 5.8–9.1 tonnes, female up to 1 m longer than male. Calf at birth 2.4–2.8 m and reaches 5.7 m when weaned and 7–8 m at one year old.

Chief identification at sea: See above for main features in relation to Dwarf Minke. Surfacing/blowing techniques probably mostly as latter (which see). It should be emphasized that the above-mentioned differences between these forms (and the depiction in Plate 34) relate only to typical individuals, and the extent of individual variation is unclear. Readily approaches boats and divers, and may breach and spyhop.

Similar species: Separation from Dwarf Minke is discussed under that form. Both are distinguishable from all other rorquals by virtue of those characters discussed under Antarctic Minke.

Distribution and biology

Distribution, movements and population: Circumpolar in Southern Hemisphere, between 65°S and 20°S in Atlantic, often found in shallow temperate coastal seas, large males and pregnant females migrating to Antarctic seas in austral summer, even reaching beyond ice edge (to at least 78°S in Ross Sea), but other animals rarely penetrating below 42°S at this season. Breeds in austral winter principally at 10–30°S but recorded once to Suriname in Northern Hemisphere and also occasionally in Antarctica at this season. Population 510,000–1.4 million.

Diet and feeding techniques: Krill is main diet in Antarctica.

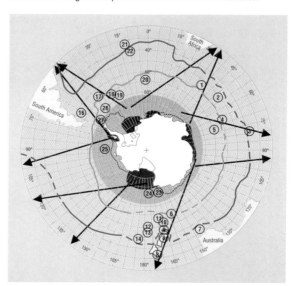

■ Approximate main Antarctic concentrations during the austral summer
▨ Approximate low-density Antarctic range during the austral summer
▫ Approximate non-breeding/migratory ranges
✦ Presumed migration/origin of feeding Antarctic summer populations

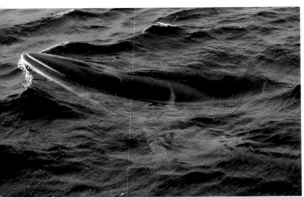

Surfacing Antarctic Minke Whale Balaenoptera bonaerensis: *note mostly grey flipper (diagnostic) and (cf. Dwarf Minke) no white shoulder patch or dusky collar in front of flipper, but very high pale flanks. On surfacing, head usually appears at low angle, following blow and smooth body roll. Fin may emerge whilst splashguard is disappearing and small blow is still settling.* © Paula A. Olsen.

Main social behaviour: Small groups of 5–10, occasionally aggregations up to 400 in productive feeding areas. Groups appear to segregate according to different age/sex classes. Visually inquisitive, it often spyhops around boats.

Breathing and diving: Usual dive lasts 3–8 minutes but capable of remaining underwater for up to 20 minutes.

Breeding biology: Breeds annually. Long mating season, from late austral winter to early summer (Jun–Dec, peaking Aug–Sep). Gestation occupies 10–11 months and calves are born in warmer waters mostly in late May–Aug.

Conservation Lower Risk—conservation dependent and placed on CITES Appendix I. It has been one of the most important commercial whales, having been exploited for over 50 years, primarily because small-whale coastal fisheries can take it (e.g. off South Africa and Brazil). With decline of great whales, commercial pelagic whaling fleets increasingly turned their attention to the species and in 1970s took up to 8100 per year, with hundreds more taken from land stations in Brazil and South Africa. The 1985–6 moratorium banned further commercial fishing. Currently the Japanese take over 400 Minkes from Antarctic waters annually for 'scientific' purposes.

Antarctic Minke Whale Balaenoptera bonaerensis. *Like all Minkes, rolls quite high, humped and swift, and animal easily 'lost'; swimming speed varies, but typically rather leisurely, just breaking surface once or twice to breathe before diving (does not raise flukes when diving). Ross Sea.* © Frank S. Todd.

Antarctic Minke Whale Balaenoptera bonaerensis *in typical Antarctic Peninsula landscape. Body often blotched yellow, orange or pink by diatoms and algae, mainly on underside and flanks.* © Morten Jørgenson.

Taxonomy Apparently best regarded as part of a superspecies, comprising several distinct forms, namely: Antarctic Minke (*bonaerensis*; Southern Hemisphere, the largest), Northern Minke (*acutorostrata*; Northern Hemisphere, the second-largest and generally resembles Dwarf Minke, but the upper surface of the flipper has a broad white band across its centre that does not continue onto body), and Dwarf Minke (unnamed; the smallest form and traditionally considered a dwarf form of Northern Minke, but overlaps widely with Antarctic Minke in Southern Ocean). Northern Minke also has distinctive N Pacific race, *B. a. scammoni*, and the least-known population, sometimes recognized as *B. a. thalmaha*, in waters around Sri Lanka. Genetic studies suggest that at least the northern and southern forms should be recognized at species level.

Sei Whale *Balaenoptera borealis* Plate 35

Identification

Confusion risks: Mainly with Dwarf Minke *B. [acutorostrata]* unnamed subspecies/allospecies., Bryde's *B. edeni* and Fin Whales *B. physalus* (but less likely with Blue *B. musculus* or other rorquals).
Main characters: Large slender whale with relatively pointed head. Chiefly dark bluish-grey on back, paler below. Relatively tall, hook-tipped fin, placed somewhat more forward, and, from above, head appears proportionately less pointed than in Fin. Blowholes and single central rostrum ridge large but lower above rostrum plate; given a close view, the single longitudinal rostrum ridge is a useful feature separating it from Bryde's. Snout in profile appears slightly arched downward near tip. Throat grooves (up to c.62 in the Southern Ocean) end just behind flippers and are white, usually forming a variable central white throat patch, whereas hind portion grades into bluish-grey. Lower jaw variably tinged darker. Dark undersides to short narrow flippers and relatively broad tailstock, which is relatively small compared to overall body size. Small uniformly dark tail flukes almost triangular with straight trailing edge, narrowing to pointed tips, with clear notch in base. Underside and sides sometimes mottled and scarred dull grey/white. Baleen plates mainly brownish-black, with variable number of pale grey tips. **Age/sex variation** can perhaps be judged by overall size and relative head size; sexually mature at 8–11 years old in Antarctica (slight regional variation) when 13–14 m, reaches max. size only several years later.
Physical notes: 12–21 m and 15.2–30.4 tonnes, female usually larger. Calf at birth 4.5–5.0 m and 0.65 tonnes (following 6–9

Dorsal fin of Sei Whale Balaenoptera borealis schlegellii *(Southern Ocean); here more Bryde's Whale-like, but still characteristically tall/erect. © Hadoram Shirihai.*

months weaning reaches 8–9 m).
Chief identification at sea: Rolls low at surface, dives often shallow and short; may appear to sink below surface (without raising tailstock). Compared to other baleen whales, has larger, more erect and variably hooked dorsal fin (less than two-thirds of distance from nose to tail), which becomes visible almost simultaneously with diffuse blow (to 3 m high, appearing like narrow cloud and given every 40–60 seconds, sometimes 20–30 seconds, for 1–4 minutes before diving). Dorsal fin visible longer than other baleen whales, which tend to feed below surface. Can skim-feed at surface, and sometimes turns on side when feeding, like Fin (blow is much less dense and lower than Fin's).
Similar species: Chief confusion risk, especially at distance, is Bryde's Whale, though range may help (in our region Sei ranges more widely and further south; Bryde's is marginal). Differences in dive sequences and head ridges are also useful pointers. At distance, the erect and taller dorsal fin is diagnostic (fin less sickle-shaped than Bryde's, but often has tiny backward bend at apex). Check for white right lip of usually (but not always) clearly larger Fin Whale, which usually has a more back-set fin, and different dive sequence and behaviour. From other much smaller or larger rorquals, look for tall fin, uniformly dark head on both sides, and relatively low blow, with fin visible almost concurrently. Also rarely arches tailstock prominently above surface and flukes only very infrequently and only fractionally visible.

Distribution and biology

Distribution, movements and population: Less well known than

Sei Whale Balaenoptera borealis schlegellii *(Southern Ocean). Compared to Fin and Bryde's, dorsal fin taller, more erect and less sickle-shaped (left), but often has tiny bend at apex (right), whilst in shallow roll fin is visible almost simultaneously with diffuse low blow (right), or with less than 1 second between their appearances. Rolls low at surface (and when diving, does not arch back/tailstock as much as Fin), and dives usually shallow and short; may appear to sink below surface or slip into shallow dive, dorsal fin disappearing last. Left: © Marc Guyt; right: © Paula A. Olsen.*

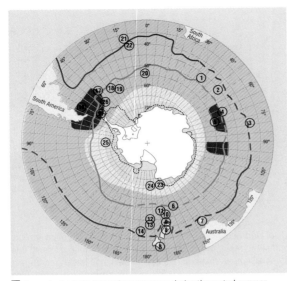

■ Approximate main Antarctic occurrences during the austral summer
▨ Approximate range during the austral summer
▨ Approximate southwards extension (rare/scarce)
   during the austral summer

other rorquals because its appearances in certain oceanic regions are much less regular than those of its congeners, favouring deep waters and is rare near coasts. Cosmopolitan, the Southern Ocean population spends a short part of the summer in Antarctic waters (below 40°S and mainly between the Subtropical and Antarctic Convergences), occasionally reaching the ice edge, and the rest of the year in the subtropics (below 30°S and mainly off South Africa, W and SE Australia, and Brazil). Southern Hemisphere population c.24,000 in 1980 but may have increased to as many as 70,000 since cessation of whaling (with c.10,000 in Antarctic waters).

Diet and feeding techniques: Zooplankton, small schooling fish (in Northern Hemisphere) and squid are main diet. Surface feeders, skimming the surface with baleen, sieving krill, tiny copepods and small fish. Usually feeds at dawn. Probably the fastest-swimming great whale, reported to reach 38 kph, which may assist them in capturing small schooling fish.

Main social behaviour: Usually alone or in pairs but also small groups of up to five, rarely 30–50. 'Shy' of boats. As other baleen whales, breaching (usually singly) is rare in Antarctic waters and generally at low angle, belly-flopping into water.

Breathing and diving: Dives for 5–20 minutes but often remains comparatively close to surface.

Breeding biology: Probably gives birth every 2–3 years with most calvings in Jun. Gestation occupies 11–13 months and calves are weaned at 6–7 months.

Conservation Endangered and placed on CITES Appendix I. During the 1940s–1960s this species formed the major part of the Antarctic whale catch in place of the protected Blue Whale and depleted Fin Whale, despite its relatively low oil yields. Its meat is prized in Japan. Whaling was prohibited for Southern Hemisphere populations in 1977 and numbers may have increased as a result.

Taxonomy Two subspecies are involved, as Northern (*B. b. borealis*) and Southern Hemisphere populations (*B. b. schlegellii*) are genetically distinct and subtly differ in number of throat grooves and baleen plates, with southern animals also typically larger.

Bryde's Whale *Balaenoptera edeni*   Plate 35

Identification

Confusion risks: Dwarf Minke *B.* [*acutorostrata*] unnamed subspecies/allospecies, Fin *B. physalus* and (principally) Sei Whales *B. borealis*.

Main characters: Size, shape and dorsal coloration largely as Sei Whale (which see). Smoky-grey upperside may appear chocolate-brown in some lights. Offshore populations (see taxonomy) may have extensive oval body scarring (caused by cookie-cutter shark bites). Prominent dorsal fin with deeply concave trailing edge which may be frayed or slightly notched; sited further behind mid back than Sei. Underside pale purple-grey, blue-grey or creamy-grey with some mottling or circular scars. Throat grooves (up to 56) may be partially yellowish-white or white but principally grey. Short slender flippers, broad tailstock and flukes, which may have dirty white undersides. Relatively large flukes with central fork, slight concave trailing edge and pointed tips, and clear notch in base. The two blowholes, at the flashguard and central rostrum ridge, are rather large but low above head; diagnostically there are two additional narrower rostrum lines, either side of the central ridge (only visible in close views). Short baleen plates vary (being broader in offshore population). **Age/sex variation** can perhaps be judged by overall size; sexually mature at 8–13 years old when 11–12 m (varies between sexes and different populations, with smaller inshore animals apparently achieving sexual maturity when 9–12 m), reaches max. size only several years later.

Physical notes: 10.0–15.6 m and 12.1–20.3 tonnes; female usually up to 1 m larger than male. Calf at birth 3.4–4.0 m and c.9 tonnes (following six months weaning reaches c.7–9 m) and may continue to achieve rapid growth until five years old.

Chief identification at sea: Typically makes rapid changes in direction. Blow tall and narrow, reaching 3–4 m and reasonably conspicuous at long distance; sequence irregular, typically 4–7 blows prior to dive. May sometimes blow below surface (thus invisibly). Breaches regularly (usually 2–3 times) in some areas outside our region, leaving water at steep (70–90°) angle, but infrequently in most of range.

Similar species: Bryde's has three parallel longitudinal ridges on head, unlike all other rorquals, which possess just one. Dorsal fin less erect than Sei and has less swept back (leading edge) than Fin Whale. Unlike Sei, tailstock often strongly arched prior to diving, and habitually surfaces more erratically than Sei (blowhole disappears from view before fin is visible). Note more conspicuous surfacing technique (often exposing most of head, followed by

Bryde's Whale Balaenoptera edeni; note diagnostic three parallel rostrum ridges. Eastern tropical Pacific, Oct 1999. © Brett Jarrett.

Bryde's Whale Balaenoptera edeni. *Sometimes the fin may emerge when splashguard still visible (more Sei-like), whilst fin shape and height do not always noticeably differ between the two, though here still is more sickle-shaped (i.e. less erect and has deeply concave, slightly notched trailing edge). This animal was identified as an inshore Bryde's Whale by the lateral rostrum ridges and more conspicuous surfacing technique. Hauraki Gulf, N Island, New Zealand, Jan 2006. © Hadoram Shirihai.*

sharp body roll), blows and swimming pattern, due to its smaller size and it being a deeper diver than latter. Also differs from Sei by mostly grey throat and chest, and ventral grooves extend further towards navel, whilst baleen are coarse and short, white in front of jaw and grey or black behind it (the two plates narrowly separated by a gap at front). See larger Fin and smaller Minke Whales for further comparisons.

Distribution and biology

Distribution, movements and population: Tropical and warm-temperate waters (above 20°C) in Atlantic, Indian and W Pacific Oceans, including off New Zealand. Migrations rarely take it to subpolar and cold temperate seas (to 40°S and equivalent in Northern Hemisphere) but perhaps, at most, a marginal visitor to our region and principally included here to facilitate comparison with other baleen whales. Some tropical-water populations may be largely sedentary (e.g. off Japan and Mexico). Population c.90,000 in recent years.

Diet and feeding techniques: Gulp feeder that probably takes larger plankton and pelagic schooling fish (including pilchards, mackerel, herring and anchovies), as well as crabs and perhaps even penguins among fish shoals. May use bubble-net feeding technique (see Humpback Whale *Megaptera novaeangliae*). Feeds year-round.

Main social behaviour: Typically 1–7 but loose groups of up to

10–30 may form over several km in good fishing areas. Sometimes inquisitive around boats.

Breathing and diving: Typically dives for less than two minutes, but occasionally up to 20 minutes. Known to be a deeper diver than most other rorquals.

Breeding biology: Probably breeds every second year. Breeds in austral autumn off South Africa (no other data for Southern Ocean), but apparently year-round in some more northerly and inshore populations. Gestation occupies c.11–12 months and calves are weaned at c.6 months.

Conservation Data Deficient and placed on CITES Appendix I. Poorly known, the species was largely ignored by whalers until the mid-20th century, once stocks of Blue and Fin Whales had been severely depleted. Commercial harvesting in the Southern Ocean was subject to a moratorium imposed in 1974, which was extended worldwide in 1987, with stocks in some areas already showing signs of recovery.

Taxonomy Uncertain, almost certainly involving at least two distinct forms, which overlap in some areas but are genetically distinct, the first (larger with broader baleen plates) occurring farther offshore and is at least partially migratory, and the other inshore and perhaps resident. Ecological attributes also appear to differ, at least off South Africa, where breeding and fishing behaviours differ. For a thorough discussion of the nomenclatural controversy surrounding the use of *B. brydei* versus *B. edeni*, and their possible application in relation to these forms see Rice (1998). Outside our region, in the WC Pacific to E Indian Ocean, there are 'dwarf' -type animals which were recently and controversially named as a separate species. Intermediate-looking individuals between this species and Sei Whale have been reported.

Southern Blue / Pygmy Blue Whales
Balaenoptera (musculus) intermedia / brevicauda
Plate 35

Identification

Confusion risks: Fin *B. physalus* and Sei Whales *B. borealis*.

Main characters: Among the largest animals ever known on Earth (max 33.6 m!). Blue whales share following characters: gigantic but long and graceful, with huge head and shoulder, and massive elongated rear. From above, rostrum broad and flat with well-rounded U-shaped tip, and prominent splashguard extends from base of double blowholes. Body varies from pale grey-blue or purplish-grey to dark slate with diagnostic pale/whitish-grey or silvery mottling. Also diagnostic is tiny triangular or nub-like, stubby dorsal fin placed well back. Triangular flukes relatively small but broad, with smoothly arched rear edges and slight basal notch. Up to 88 darkish throat grooves extend beyond navel. Dark slate

Approximate overall range

Surfacing Pygmy Blue Whale Balaenoptera (musculus) brevicauda: *rostrum breaks surface first, with splashguard still just below surface and closed (left), then blowholes open when head and shoulders exposed (right). Pygmy types are especially smaller than the largest blue whales in the Antarctic, but the ranges of both in the region are poorly known. Peruvian Current, Oct 2003. © Hadoram Shirihai.*

grey-blue head and back with paler, sometimes yellowish, patches on sides and belly (microscopic algae), scattered white spots on throat, and white underside and leading edge to long pointed flipper, with distinctly angled bend. If visible, baleen plates jet black, bristles greyer with age. **Pygmy Blue Whale** smaller, probably 15–20 m at maturity, and more compact. Quite rotund in middle third, even somewhat right whale-like, with proportionately shorter more rounded rostrum, and very short and slender tailstock. Dorsal fin on final third to quarter of back, c.3 m forward of flukes, highlighting how much shorter it is than true Blue Whales. Fluke width c.¼ of body length and flippers proportionately long. Perhaps overall less mottled and more uniform grey-blue. **Age/sex variation** (true Blue Whale) impossible to gauge, aside of estimating size, which requires care and preferably experience; sexually mature at 5–15 (mostly 8–10) years when 22–24 m, reaches max. only several years later.

Physical notes: (true Blue Whale) 20.0–33.6 m and 80–150 (exceptionally 190) tonnes; female slightly larger than male. At birth 6–7 m and 2.5–4.0 tonnes (when fully weaned may be 21 tonnes and c.16 m).

Chief identification at sea: Blows tall, dense and upright, 9–12 m high, every 10–20 seconds over 2–6 minutes. Usually settles quietly with very little of body above surface, though huge size, relatively massive shoulder, rostrum and splashguard briefly detectable. Note tiny fin and paler, greyer, more mottled body. On sunny days, body below surface appears as turquoise silhouette. Breaks surface with rostrum/splashguard and shoulders, or smooth mid-body rolls. Splashguard/shoulders sometimes still visible when fin breaks surface, though latter more often seen after final blow

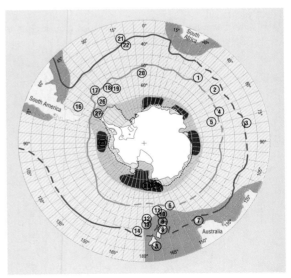

Blowing Pygmy Blue Whale Balaenoptera (musculus) brevicauda, *here whilst travelling into the wind, making tall blow appear more diffuse; note the characteristic turquoise reflection of the rear body below the syrface (a feature not unique to blue whales). Peruvian Current, Oct 2003. © Hadoram Shirihai.*

■ Approximate main Antarctic (non-breeding) occurrences during the austral summer
▨ Approximate Antarctic (non-breeding) lower density range during the austral summer
▨ Approximate non-breeding/migratory ranges
■ Approximate winter/breeding range

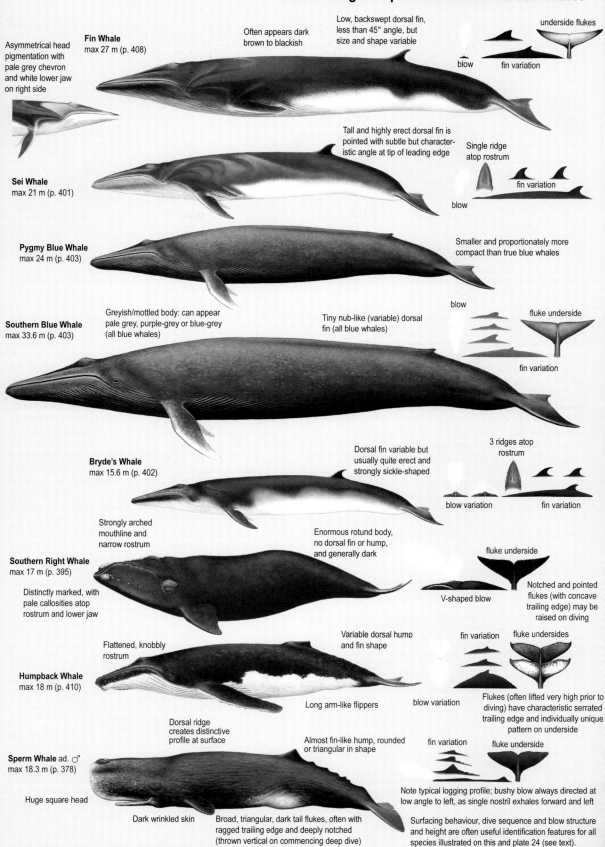

Plate 35 Large rorquals and robust-bodied whales

Fin Whale
max 27 m (p. 408)

Asymmetrical head pigmentation with pale grey chevron and white lower jaw on right side

Often appears dark brown to blackish

Low, backswept dorsal fin, less than 45° angle, but size and shape variable

underside flukes

blow   fin variation

Sei Whale
max 21 m (p. 401)

Tall and highly erect dorsal fin is pointed with subtle but characteristic angle at tip of leading edge

Single ridge atop rostrum

blow   fin variation

Pygmy Blue Whale
max 24 m (p. 403)

Smaller and proportionately more compact than true blue whales

Southern Blue Whale
max 33.6 m (p. 403)

Greyish/mottled body: can appear pale grey, purple-grey or blue-grey (all blue whales)

Tiny nub-like (variable) dorsal fin (all blue whales)

blow

fluke underside

fin variation

Bryde's Whale
max 15.6 m (p. 402)

Dorsal fin variable but usually quite erect and strongly sickle-shaped

3 ridges atop rostrum

blow variation   fin variation

Southern Right Whale
max 17 m (p. 395)

Strongly arched mouthline and narrow rostrum

Distinctly marked, with pale callosities atop rostrum and lower jaw

Enormous rotund body, no dorsal fin or hump, and generally dark

fluke underside

V-shaped blow

Notched and pointed flukes (with concave trailing edge) may be raised on diving

Humpback Whale
max 18 m (p. 410)

Flattened, knobbly rostrum

Variable dorsal hump and fin shape

fin variation   fluke undersides

Long arm-like flippers   blow variation

Flukes (often lifted very high prior to diving) have characteristic serrated trailing edge and individually unique pattern on underside

Sperm Whale ad. ♂
max 18.3 m (p. 378)

Dorsal ridge creates distinctive profile at surface

Almost fin-like hump, rounded or triangular in shape

fin variation   fluke underside

Huge square head

Note typical logging profile; bushy blow always directed at low angle to left, as single nostril exhales forward and left

Dark wrinkled skin

Broad, triangular, dark tail flukes, often with ragged trailing edge and deeply notched (thrown vertical on commencing deep dive)

Surfacing behaviour, dive sequence and blow structure and height are often useful identification features for all species illustrated on this and plate 24 (see text).

Presumed Southern Blue Whale Balaenoptera (musculus) intermedia *in smooth body roll, with miniature fin (set well back on body) emerging last with rear back and tailstock (both more often visible after final blow when preparing for a deep dive). The largest blue whales are apparently intermedia in Antarctic waters. © Paula A. Olsen.*

when preparing for deep dive; body appears to bend strongly and dorsal fin briefly emerges, with strongly arched tailstock slightly above surface. Fluking usually low. In evasive manoeuvre, accelerates with up to 50–60% of fore-body visible, pushing a mass of water in front and to sides of head.

Similar species: Blow usually denser and taller than Fin Whale, and dorsal fin lower and less falcate; also paler and more mottled (blue to pale grey and mottled, but dark and sleek in Fin, with some overlap principally due to light). Arching on rolls less obvious and frequent than Fin and, unlike latter, sometimes slightly raises flukes prior to deep dives. Can appear extremely broad and bulky compared to Fin, but take into account age/sex differences and that Pygmy Blue is overall as long as Fin. In good views Fin's head is clearly narrower, with diagnostic white patch on right-hand side. Both may show an almost identical turquoise silhouette below surface. Much smaller Sei and Bryde's have narrower heads and more prominent, less set-back dorsal fins, stronger dorsal/ventral contrast, and very different diving behaviours.

Distribution and biology

Distribution, movements and population: Isolated populations in N Pacific, N Atlantic and Southern Ocean. Latter summers to pack-ice (below 40°S, reported to 78°S), moving north in austral winter as far as Ecuador, S Brazil, South Africa and (less commonly) Australia and New Zealand. Population perhaps fewer than 9000 of which c.5000 estimated in S Indian Ocean and 710–1255 in Antarctica (1994 figures). Pygmy Blue most frequent in subantarctic Indian and SW Pacific Oceans, and Humboldt Current, but perhaps also S Atlantic.

Diet and feeding techniques: Takes only larger zooplankton in polar waters by gulp-feeding, consuming 3–8 tonnes daily, mostly near surface in evening and up to 100 m below during daytime (though surface-feeding never uncommon). Relies on blubber during austral autumn/winter.

Main social behaviour: Usually alone or in twos, and on migration groups of 2–5, with loose aggregations of up to c.50 at feeding grounds. Sometimes with Fin Whales. Breaching rare or partial in Southern Ocean (at 45°, landing on belly or sides, but such behaviour more frequent in young), and at low latitudes animals more prone to raise their tail flukes on diving.

Breathing and diving: Several shallow dives of 10–20 min at 12–20-second intervals frequent, usually followed by a 10–30-minute deep dive; may reach 150–200 m but capable of deeper dives to 500 m (50 min).

Breeding biology: Breeds every 2–3 years. Mates from late austral autumn (peaks Jul in Southern Ocean) and calves born in winter

Presumed Southern Blue Whale Balaenoptera (musculus) intermedia: *note massive head (up to a quarter of total body length and very broad), with U-shaped rostrum and prominent splashguard appearing as separate rounded hump in profile. On left, note the typical, paler, pale grey-mottled skin, which at certain angles and in some lights, can appear darker and more uniform, especially the head (right). © Paula A. Olsen.*

Mother and calf (left) and ad (right) Northern Blue Whale B. m. musculus of the NE Pacific stock, of which there an estimated c.3,000 (c.2,000 summer off California); it is the only blue whale population showing signs of a steady recovery. This form shows some structural similarities to intermedia (especially the elongated, less compact appearance). Gulf of California, Mexico, Mar 1998, 2001. © Hiroya Minakuchi/Sphere Magazine.

in warmer waters, following 10–12-month gestation; weaned at c.7 months.

Conservation Endangered (also CITES Appendix I). Already 'Commercially extinct' prior to international protection in 1966, due to its attractiveness to whalers once the explosive harpoon had been developed in late-19th century, with most being taken in first third of 20th century (nearly 30,000 in 1930–1). The mainstay of Southern Ocean whaling, most of which took place close to polar ice.

Taxonomy Four subspecies, but within our region I prefer to recognize two species: Southern Blue Whale *B. (m.) intermedia* of S Hemisphere (north to 22ºS off S America and 6ºS off W Africa), and Pygmy Blue Whale *B. (m.) brevicauda* (SE Pacific, but with similar 'pygmy'-like populations apparently scattered in subantarctic to temperate waters of S Hemisphere), including *indica* (very restricted range in N Indian Ocean). Recent work suggests that *brevicauda* and *indica* are almost identical morphologically (but apparently not genetically), and if lumped the name *indica* has priority. Furthermore, morphological and genetic differences between stocks of small animals suggest that Pygmy Blue is more variable and involves several distinctive populations, e.g. Chilean whales are intermediate in size between Pygmy and Antarctic blue whales, and maybe warrant subspecific status. Whales in the NE Pacific are more similar in size to Pygmy Blue than *intermedia*. Preliminary genetic data parallels this association with those from the SE Pacific. Based on whaling data, blue whales were/are longer in high latitudes of the N Pacific (and perhaps W Pacific), but smaller than Antarctic blues. The relationship between Southern and Pygmy Blue Whales, especially their winter and Antarctic summer ranges are almost unknown, and their taxonomic status and scientific names are likely to experience future upheaval. Northern Blue Whale *B. m. musculus* of N Hemisphere is also highly variable, at least genetically, but not recorded in our region. Hybrids: Blue × Fin is rarely recorded.

Northern Blue Whale B. m. musculus, like other blue whales, emits spectacular vertical blows which can reach up to 10 m tall (left) and, unlike Fin Whale, often raises the flukes at a shallow angle on diving (right); note also the very broad tailstock. Gulf of California, Mexico, Mar 1998, 2001. © Hiroya Minakuchi/Sphere Magazine.

Fin Whale *Balaenoptera physalus*   **Plate 35**

Identification

Confusion risks: Blue *B. musculus*, Sei *B. borealis* and Bryde's Whales *B. edeni*.

Main characters: The second largest of the rorquals and among the fastest-swimming great whales. Long streamlined body, flat head with diagnostic white lower right jaw and broad, noticeably ridged tailstock. Head shape from above is a rather acute V and the narrow longitudinal rostrum and blowhole ridges are less massive than in Blue Whale. Dorsal fin set three-quarters of way along back, small but usually clearly taller and more hooked than in Blue Whale, with long, low angle to leading edge. Body dark grey to brownish-black dorsally (often with darker line from flipper to eye and variable greyish-white chevrons from flipper to shoulder, usually more prominent on right side of body) and white ventrally, undersides of short narrow flippers and broad triangular tail flukes also white. Lower jaw dark on left side and creamy-white on the right with the white extending onto the upper jaw. Flukes relatively small with narrow tips and clear notch in base. Up to 100 darkish throat grooves extend beyond navel. Baleen alternately yellowish-white and bluish-grey. **Age/sex variation** may perhaps be judged only on size and ads more prone to possess scarring on rear body; sexually mature at 6–12 years old when 19–20 m, reaches max. size at 9–13 years old.

Physical notes: 17–27 m and 30.4–81.2 tonnes, female perhaps up to 5 m longer than male. Calf at birth 6–7 m and 1.0–1.9 tonnes (at 6–8 months may reach 11–13 m).

Chief identification at sea: Tall, narrow upright blows 4–8 m high (denser and higher than all but Blue Whale and dorsal fin appears above surface soon after), given 2–5 times at intervals of 10–20 seconds before diving. When surfacing, rises obliquely, top of head first and, following blows, arches vertically to dive, exposing rear body and dorsal fin; flukes seldom visible. May breach and

Accelerating, head-on Fin Whale Balaenoptera physalus quoyi. *Note the flattish, V-shaped rostrum, prominent splashguard (albeit less obvious than Blue Whale's* B. musculus*), and diagnostic creamy-white right side to the lower jaw.* © Paula A. Olsen.

leap (at varying angles and with large splash) but rarely given to spectacular behaviour (see below).

Similar species: In combination the following characters should

Fin Whale Balaenoptera physalus quoyi *showing all the essential features for correct identification: a large, streamlined, essentially dark grey to brownish-black rorqual, with a relatively small, backward-pointing fin (usually appears well after head submerged), flattish V-shaped rostrum, creamy-white right side to lower jaw, and tall, narrow blow.* © Paula A. Olsen.

Fin Whale Balaenoptera physalus: *in rolling to dive arches back (animal in background), rear body and dorsal fin usually appear well after head submerged, with tailstock normally disappearing after the fin. The surfacing animal in the foreground has a broad, flat rostrum and quite prominent splashguard. Mexico. © Tui de Roy/Minden Pictures, Mexico.*

eliminate Blue, Sei and Bryde's Whales (note that, in the Southern Ocean, this species ranges farther south than Sei but not as far south as Blue or Antarctic Minke *B. bonaerensis*): in particular note the asymmetrical head pigmentation, the lower mouth cavity and some baleen plates being white on the right side and uniform grey on the left; also the large size, small backward-sloping dorsal fin (in Sei it is erect and very tall, in Bryde's highly variable but always has a convex leading edge, and intermediate in size, and Blue often has a nubbin), tall narrow blow, greyish-white chevron behind head and single longitudinal ridge on head, as well as characteristic surfacing technique. In addition, Sei Whale shows as much

body as the height of the dorsal fin when diving, Fin Whale twice as much (or more) body as the height of the dorsal.

Distribution and biology

Distribution, movements and population: Deep offshore waters of the Pacific, Atlantic and Indian Oceans, reaching far north and south into polar regions, though rarely penetrating beyond ice edge. Restricted and well-demarcated migrations (of up to 3700 km) performed by small groups, moving north in austral autumn from seas between 47°S and 60°S to warmer, temperate seas of the S Pacific, off South America (north to Brazil and Peru), off W South Africa and in the S Indian Ocean around Kerguelen and Heard at 20–40°S. Different ages/sexes apparently move separately, with pregnant females initiating such movements, and larger/older individuals generally reaching further south in austral summer. Total population estimated at 119,000 in recent years, and perhaps 24,000 in Southern Ocean south of 30°S.

Diet and feeding techniques: Largely feeds on krill and other crustaceans, fish (e.g. herring and lanternfish) and squid but diet varies seasonally and according to locality. Generally uses engulfing method to capture prey and sometimes feeds at surface. Relatively often feeds on its right side, when half the tail (the left fluke) may be visible above the surface. Fasts in winter.

Main social behaviour: Groups of 3–20, occasionally aggregations of 100 or more in productive feeding areas in Southern Ocean. Only strong social bond is between mother and calf. Appears indifferent to presence of boats. Breaching is rare or partial in Antarctic waters and tail-end of body nearly always remains below surface.

Breathing and diving: Dives last 3–15 minutes, sometimes up to 30 minutes, and reach depths of 100–230 m (max. 474 m). A series of 2–5 shallow, 10–20-second dives may be followed by a much longer period below surface.

Breeding biology: Breeds every 2–3 years. Mating season largely Jun–Aug in Southern Hemisphere, and gestation occupies 11 months. Cows give birth in warmer waters (probably largely outside our region) in May–Jul, and calves grow rapidly, being weaned at 6–8 months and ready to migrate to polar waters with ads in Jul–Aug.

■ Approximate Antarctic (non-breeding) main occurrences during the austral summer
▨ Approximate Antarctic (non-breeding) lower density range during the austral summer
▨ Approximate non-breeding/migratory during the austral summer
➤ Presumed migration/origin of feeding Antarctic summer populations

Humpback Whales Megaptera novaeangliae at different stages of surfacing: the rostrum and prominent splashguard first, with blow, thereafter part of the upper body and dorsal fin. Note distinctive sloping back and stubby fin (varies in size and shape, from small triangular knob to larger 'sickle'). S Atlantic, Jan 2001. © Hadoram Shirihai.

Conservation Endangered and listed on CITES Appendix I. Fin Whale is rapidly reaching extinction with a moratorium being proposed only in the 1980s, largely due to being the largest and thus most productive and profitable of exploitable whales. Up to 30,000 were taken annually in 1935–70. In the Southern Hemisphere, Fin Whales are estimated to have declined to 20% of their original numbers.

Taxonomy The 1.0–1.5-m larger populations of Southern Hemisphere (with longer, narrower flippers) are occasionally accorded subspecific status as *B. p. quoyi*. They are apparently genetically isolated as the two forms are not known to overlap. Known to hybridize with Blue Whale.

Humpback Whale
Megaptera novaeangliae   Plate 35

Identification
Confusion risks: Superficially similar to other large rorquals.
Main characters: Stocky body with broad, rounded head and extremely long flippers up to 5 m and one-third of total length. Upperparts generally black (some grey/blue coloration may be apparent). Series of knobbly protuberances (tubercles) on head, jaws and flippers often have large barnacles growing on their summits. Flippers and underside of broad serrated tail flukes largely white, and fluke pattern is individually unique. Flippers wholly dark

Humpback Whale Megaptera novaeangliae blows are highly visible, although bushy and very broad. Antarctic Peninsula, Feb 2002. © Morten Jørgensen.

Humpback Whale Megaptera novaeangliae in spectacular tail-slapping manouevre. Kaikoura, South I, New Zealand. © Dennis Buurman.

Fluking Humpback Whales Megaptera novaeangliae: *the pattern on the underside of the flukes is individually unique. After the final blow, it performs a steep, arching roll of the body, culminating in the raised tailstock and flukes (at variable angle). The flukes, however, are rarely exposed prior to shallow dives.* © Morten Jørgenson, except bottom right © Hadoram Shirihai.

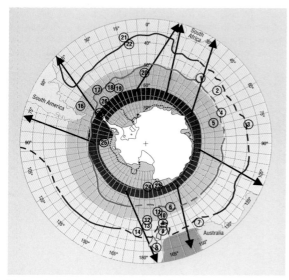

■ Approximate Antarctic (non-breeding) main occurrences during the austral summer
▨ Approximate Antarctic (non-breeding) lower density range during the austral summer
▢ Approximate non-breeding/migratory during the austral summer
▩ Approximate winter/breeding range
↗ Presumed migration/origin of feeding Antarctic summer populations

or mainly white above, but always whiter below (see taxonomy). Underparts including broad throat grooves (up to 36, reaching well beyond navel) also individually variable: some wholly black but most possess conspicuous white patch, often covering entire area of the grooves (as in Plate 35), or has only partial black area across centre. Some pink coloration is often visible within the white parts of the grooves. Very low stubby dorsal fin with

Humpback Whale Megaptera novaeangliae *flipper-waving and slapping (white undersides to long flippers clearly visible in social activities). Antarctic Peninsula, Jan 2001.* © Hadoram Shirihai.

411

Humpback Whales Megaptera novaeangliae *are often very active at the surface, breaching (as here), spyhopping, lobtailing and tail- and flipper-slapping are all frequently observed in our region, especially around the Antarctic Peninsula, Jan 2001. © Morten Jørgenson.*

pronounced hump at front. Double-blowholes and splashguard rather prominent but central rostrum ridge indistinct. Large baleen plates mainly black to brown but often admixed paler. Some individuals, especially males, scarred with thin whitish lines on black upperparts. **Age/sex variation** perhaps estimable by overall size (female possesses grapefruit-like lobe at rear of genital slit); sexually mature mainly at 5–11 years old when 11.5–12.0 m, and reaches max. size up to ten years later.

Physical notes: 11–19 m and 25.4–35.5 tonnes, male usually 1.0–1.5 m shorter than female. Calf at birth 4.0–4.6 m and c.1–2 tonnes (at 10–11 months reaches 7.5–10.0 m).

Chief identification at sea: Very active at surface where breaches, lobtails and flipper-slaps. Often spyhops and exhibits little fear of boats (sometimes even aggressive towards vessels). Very visible, bushy and distinctive blows, 2.5–3.0 m tall, being relatively broad comparative to overall height, given 4–8 times (3–6 times on breeding grounds) at 15–30-second intervals before diving. Blow on rare occasions is split and V-shaped. Body strongly arched and

Humpback Whale Megaptera novaeangliae *is large and uniquely shaped, especially the flattened, knobbly rostrum and extremely long, arm-like flippers, which are often visible underwater; note inconspicuous, single central rostrum ridge. Kaikoura, South I, New Zealand. © Dennis Buurman.*

Mother and calf Humpback Whales Megaptera novaeangliae*: note incredibly long, wing-like flippers; fore flippers, tail flukes and slender head covered by knobbly protuberances and barnacles (near tip of lower jaw). Kaikoura, South I, New Zealand. © Stephen Wong.*

Humpback Whale Megaptera novaengliae *'lunge-feeding', which is often undertaken cooperatively. Antarctic Peninusla, Jan 1999.* © Hiroya Minakuchi/Sphere Magazine.

humped for deep dives; serrated tail flukes (with distinctive undulating trailing edge and variable white pattern below) lifted very high for most dives.

Similar species: Almost unmistakable due to incredibly long flippers, knobbly head and uniquely serrated tail flukes. When commencing long dives, Sperm Whale *Physeter macrocephalus* typically also arches, humps and raise its flukes nearly vertically, while Southern Right Whale *Eubalaena australis* often throws the flukes high, but both have very different shape and pattern to flukes, mainly in the straight trailing edge and their being all dark. Humpback blows may occasionally appear V-shaped as in Southern Right Whale.

Distribution and biology

Distribution, movements and population: Widespread in all oceans, with separate stocks in N Pacific and N Atlantic Oceans and 5–6 subpopulations in Southern Ocean. Research in the 1950s revealed precise migration routes between Balleny Is feeding grounds and breeding area between New Zealand and Tonga, though not all animals may move every year. Other wintering areas of Southern Ocean populations are off Brazil; W Africa; Madagascar; W Australia; the Coral Sea; and off W South America north as far as the Galápagos. More frequently occurs within inshore waters on migration. Population 20,000–30,000 (15,000–20,000 in Northern Hemisphere) in recent years with perhaps 2500 of these in the Southern Ocean.

Diet and feeding techniques: Takes small schooling fish and krill, and makes shallow, spiral dives under shoal of food, to contain it within a 'bubble net'. Up to 45 m wide, this 'net' herds the krill or fish into a concentrated area, making it easier to engulf by swimming through it at speed. Also frequently lunge-feeds.

Main social behaviour: Groups of up to 12–15, sometimes larger aggregations in favoured feeding areas, but often in much smaller social units of mother and calf. Breaching, lobtailing and flipper-slapping all apparently important within social communication, and all are not infrequently observed in Antarctic waters. Breaches vary from full leap clear of water to leisurely surge in which less than half of body is visible. Usually lands on back but sometimes emerges dorsal-side up and performs a belly flop.

Breathing and diving: Dives last 3–15 minutes but capable of remaining underwater for up to 21 minutes, and reaching depths of up to 148 m.

Breeding biology: Among the most familiar of all whales, males

have extremely long, complex songs given on breeding grounds. Males remain longer in these areas and may attempt to mate with several females. Winters in tropical oceans where cows give birth every 2–3 years (though occasionally in successive years) in late autumn/early winter. Gestation occupies 11–12 months. Calves weaned at 6–12 months and return to natal area but subsequently may wander between breeding areas. Some females may remain on summer feeding grounds.

Conservation Vulnerable and placed on CITES Appendix I. Formerly abundant but foreign whaling ships extensively hunted Humpbacks off New Zealand, as did Australian shore-based whalers from the 1840s. Given its propensity to be slow moving, it was easy prey for whalers. Possibly as many as 200,000 were taken in the Southern Ocean but since moratorium in 1966 some stocks in this region have increased by up to 10%. Because the species is often found near shore and is very active at the surface, it is often the focus of whale-watching tourism.

Taxonomy Atlantic and Pacific Humpbacks have differently coloured flippers, with the former usually having largely white flippers on both sides and only some black markings, while those in the Pacific have a black upperside and white underside (the two may perhaps occasionally meet in Antarctic waters; M. Jørgensen pers. comm.). Southern Hemisphere populations have been named *M. n. lalandii* with those in Australian and New Zealand waters accorded the name *M. n. novaezelandiae* but neither proposal appears certainly warranted.

Pygmy Right Whale *Caperea marginata*   Plate 34

Identification

Confusion risks: Dwarf Minke *Balaenoptera [acutorostrata]* unnamed subspecies/allospecies and Antarctic Minke Whales *B. laenoptera bonaerensis*.

Main characters: The smallest baleen whale, with a poorly known (perhaps even fragmented) range, and is also the least studied. Medium-sized, rather long-bodied, arched, tapered rostrum with small ridge from near blowhole to tip of snout, distinct tail notch, small narrow flippers with slightly rounded tips and contrasting dark upper surface, and small sickle-shaped dorsal fin. Pale underside to tail flukes, bordered dark. Dark grey or blue-grey head, which is one-quarter of body length and broadest at eyes, and back (often heavily pock-marked with cookie-cutter shark bites),

Pygmy Right Whale Caperea marginata: *surfacing behaviour and blow (small and oval) generally inconspicuous, unless followed closely; note arched mouthline.* © Kenji Tuda.

Pygmy Right Whale Caperea marginata is the smallest of all baleen whales. The back and sickle-shaped dorsal fin usually surface very briefly, after the blow has dissipated; note tapered rostrum with small ridge, arched mouthline and pale chevrons behind head. © Kenji Tuda.

and pale grey/white undersides. Baleen ivory-coloured, pale lower jaw is somewhat arched with rounded lump at base of throat. Two throat grooves correspond to lower jawline. **Age/sex variation** may perhaps be judged according to size, although this is always difficult at sea. Age of sexual maturity unknown but occurs when c.5 m and dorsal and sides become darker, and lower jaw and arch of back appear more exaggerated with age. Calf proportionally slimmer with smaller head and averages paler.

Physical notes: 5.5–6.5 m and 2.8–3.5 tonnes, and female slightly larger than male. Calf at birth estimated to be 1.6–2.2 m and reaches 3.0–3.5 m at weaning (c.5–6 months).

Chief identification at sea: Does not breach or lobtail, and usually surfaces very briefly, with fin and back mostly below surface, but these briefly appear when travelling; and flukes never raised clear of water. Usually swims slowly when proportionately rather small head and elongated rear body may appear, with somewhat large-dolphin-like slow undulating movements and profile; blow a small, inconspicuous oval. Contrasting broad whitish baleen and other pale elements in mouth visible at very close range, as snout typically breaks surface when swimming leisurely.

Similar species: Ads stouter than other rorquals. Minke Whales are the principal confusion species, but Pygmy Right Whale has a strongly arched jawline and lacks white in flippers of Dwarf Minke.

Distribution and biology

Distribution, movements and population: All records are between 31°S and 55°S in waters with temperatures of 5–20°C, with strandings reported from Tierra del Fuego, South Africa, S and W Australia and both main islands of New Zealand. At-sea records from the Falklands, Crozet, S Atlantic and south of Australia. Perhaps never penetrates south of the Antarctic Convergence. Some evidence that juvs move to inshore waters in spring and summer (regular seasonal observations, perhaps in response to food availability, off S Australia, New Zealand and South Africa) but some populations, at least, may be year-round residents (e.g. around Tasmania). No estimates of population size.

Diet and feeding techniques: Copepods, euphausiids and other tiny crustaceans.

Main social behaviour: Small groups of up to ten but most sightings have been of singles or pairs, though groups of 30–80 reported. Observed in company of dolphins and pilot whales *Globicephala*, and once a Sei Whale *Balaenoptera borealis*.

Breathing and diving: Dives last between 40 seconds and four minutes, and usually only surfaces briefly.

Breeding biology: Largely unknown but season possibly extends throughout year. Gestation occupies 12 months.

Conservation Placed on CITES Appendix I but recently (1996) removed from the IUCN Red Data list. Insufficiently known but probably not rare. Few data concerning threats or population trends, though some incidental mortality has been noted off South Africa where the species is occasionally trapped in nets, and some deliberate inshore fishing for this species is known.

Taxonomy Monotypic.

▨ Presumed overall range

Subantarctic islands off South America

Three groups are included here, the Falklands, South Georgia and the isolated and rarely visited Shag Rocks, which are considered part of the UK's South Georgia and South Sandwich Islands territory. The latter are almost unvegetated, but do possess some nesting birds. On the other hand, both South Georgia and the Falklands are among the most frequently visited parts of the subantarctic region. These archipelagos possess long histories including a strong element of human interference in, and destruction of, the environment, with both whaling and sealing having been important economic activities in the region. However, the Falklands are perhaps best known for the 1982 Anglo–Argentine war and South Georgia for its strong association with the British Antarctic explorer and hero, Ernest Shackleton. Their climate and vegetation are typical of the entire subantarctic region, but their avifaunas are outstanding. Unsurprisingly, that of the Falklands possesses a strong South American component; in addition to a number of endemic forms, most of which are currently classified as subspecies of relatively widespread mainland taxa, the islands also support internationally important populations of several species now considered rare and very local on the South American mainland, and also regularly receive vagrants and overshoots from the latter region. These are perhaps just the 'icing on the cake' to the islands' important concentrations of seabirds, which attract large numbers of ecotourists on an annual basis. Overall, the Falklands possess one of the richest avifaunas within the entire region covered by this book; currently 210 species have been reliably reported from the islands. South Georgia has long been the home for much research into subantarctic avifaunas and it too is internationally important for its impressive seabird colonies. While its total avifauna is unsurprisingly less rich than that of the Falklands (due to its geographical location), it also supports a number of endemic forms that clearly derive from ancestral South American stock. Add to this both islands' importance for other forms of wildlife, principally cetaceans, and their popularity with wildlife enthusiasts is assured.

The Falkland Islands

Location and main features The Falklands, at 51°00′S–52°54′S 57°42′W–61°27′W, are 490 km east of Argentine Patagonia and comprise 778 islands covering 12,173 km². Two main islands, East and West Falkland dominate the archipelago's geography. The former is the location of the capital, Stanley, the international airport and is the better served by roads and communications. The islands are of major importance for marine mammals and birds, including many seabirds and 14 endemic taxa, two of which are currently recognized as species, and are the stronghold of Ruddy-headed Goose, Striated Caracara, Blackish Cinclodes and Black-throated Finch, all of which are highly range restricted, very rare and, in some cases, extremely difficult to find in mainland South America.

Landform, climate and habitat The archipelago is hilly and poorly drained with the exception of Lafonia, the southern part of East Falkland. The highest peaks are Mount Usborne (705 m) on East Falkland and Mount Adam (700 m) on West Falkland. Coastlines

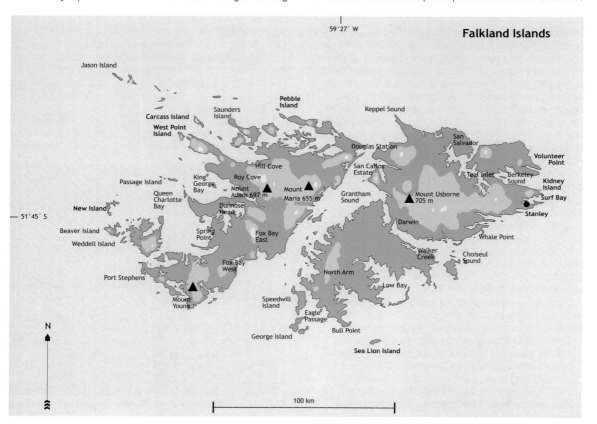

Striated Caracara Phalcobaenus australis *in the Falklands scavenges around penguin colonies and is encountered at such sites, where it can be approached very closely. The archipelago harbours the bulk of the species' world population. Falklands, Dec 1990.* © René Pop.

are deeply indented with many rocky promontories and sheltered bays. The vegetation is predominantly oceanic heath with shrubs, grasses and low-growing plants, broken by areas of shattered rock known as 'stone runs' on many hillsides. These latter comprise white quartzite boulders and were created during the last Ice Age, and arose as a result of innumerable separate freezing and thawing events that broke up the rock, then moved and sorted it, transporting the rocks downhill during seasonal thaws. Plants are able to colonize the stony soil that separate 'stone runs' (which may be up to 4 km long and several hundred metres across); the resultant patterns are best appreciated from the air, but even at ground level they are a striking feature of the landscape, particularly of East Falkland.

The flora of 364 species exhibits strong affinities with that of Patagonia and includes 13 endemic plants and 176 alien introductions. Soils are generally cold and acidic, very peaty and of relatively low fertility, and there are no native trees. Most of the vegetation can be described as either hard or soft 'camp', a corruption of the Spanish 'campo' (countryside). At higher elevations, above 500–600 m, peat gives way to stony or clay soils that support feldmark and cushion plants such as *Bolax gummifera*, *Azorella monantha* and *Valeriana sedifolia*, while in lower valleys and some coastal areas the peat soils are of higher than average fertility and support lush grasses and sedges.

Oceanic heath formations dominate much of the rest of the landscape of the two principal islands, with dense White Grass Cortaderia pilosa interspersed by rushes and mosses on poorly drained soils (soft camp) and dwarf shrubs, typically Diddle-dee or Red Crowberry *Empetrum rubrum*, Mountain Berry *Gaultheria pumila* and Christmas Bush *Baccharis magellanica*, more widespread in better drained areas of hard camp. On such well-drained

slopes or in soils overlying 'stone runs', fern beds may form, principally of Small Fern *Blechnum penna-marina* and Tall Fern *B. magellanicum*. Around streams in valley bottoms a denser vegetation of Native Rush *Juncus scheuchzerioides* and Cinnamon Grass *Hierochloë redolens* may develop, and these and several other species of rush may form the transition between heath and littoral communities.

Tussac grass *Poa flabellata* was formerly widespread on coasts, extending to 800 m inland and to 200 m above sea level. It requires highly fertile soils and a moist salt-laden environment.

Colony of Black-browed Albatross Thalassarche [melanophrys] melanophrys, *Falklands.* © Hans Reinhard.

Mixed Black-browed Albatross Thalassarche [melanophrys] melanophrys *and Rockhopper Penguin* Eudyptes [chrysocome] chrysocome *colonies are a feature in the Falklands, with the opportunity to these two species almost meet 'face to face'. © Hadoram Shirihai.*

Approximately 80% of the tussac fringe has been destroyed and serious coastal soil erosion has resulted from more than two centuries of uncontrolled grazing by cattle and sheep, and by accidental or deliberate burning, often started by 18th century sealers. Nowadays tussac largely survives on smaller offshore islands and on several small island farms, where individual owners or managers have replanted and fenced coastal paddocks since the late 19th century. Nonetheless, it persists on more than 300 islands and stacks within the Falklands, growing to 3 m in height and in places forming near-impenetrable thickets of up to 300 ha, which are important nesting areas for many bird species. In such well-developed old stands, the plant community is monospecific, the tall tussac forming a canopy through which virtually no light penetrates, but in peripheral areas other species including Wild Celery *Apium australe* and Sword Grass *Carex trifida* are often present.

Of some importance to birds, especially several passerines, are the trees and bushes established for ornamental and windbreak purposes around settlements. Gorse *Ulex europaeus*, *Cupressus macrocarpa* and Native Boxwood *Hebe elliptica* all provide cover for breeding species. Boxwood persists in the wild on coasts of West Falkland and several outlying islands, but in its naturalized form grows up to 3 m in height and is quite common around settlements.

Birds The Falklands are probably best known for their internationally important seabird colonies, particularly of Black-browed Albatross and Gentoo and Rockhopper Penguins, but a total of at least 63 species has nested in the archipelago, which is of global importance for a number of landbird forms. Approximately 500 pairs of King Penguin breed in the main colony on Volunteer Green, East Falkland, and a few at isolated sites near Gentoo colonies. Though such numbers are insignificant within a global

context, the Falklands are the most accessible area in the world to see this impressive species. Macaroni Penguin also breeds in very small numbers. The 113,000 pairs of breeding Gentoo Penguin, on the other hand, are perhaps second only to South Georgia in importance and the 272,000 pairs of Rockhopper Penguin, in 52 colonies, make the archipelago the most important place on Earth for this species. A fifth species of penguin, Magellanic, is also very common and widespread. As it burrows in coastal slopes, often under dense tussac, it is impossible to make accurate counts. However, an estimate of between 76,000 and 142,000 pairs was made from records submitted to the Breeding Birds Survey (1983–93).

Eighty per cent of global populations of Black-browed Albatross breed in the Falklands. Several colonies have increased over the past 20 years, including the largest which reached c.204,000 pairs on Steeple Jason I in 1995–6. However, the first complete census, undertaken by Falklands Conservation in Oct–Nov 2000, recorded a significant overall decline since 1995–6: the population has fallen from c.468,000 to c.382,000 pairs, with the greatest loss of c.47,000 pairs from Steeple Jason I. Other major colonies of this species involve over 103,050 pairs on Beauchêne I, c.10,000 pairs on Bird I, 52,700 pairs on Grand Jason I and 14,600 pairs on West Point I. Additional populations amounting to 54,660 pairs exist at eight other sites.

Significant numbers of Southern Giant Petrel are also present in the Falklands, with 5000–10,000 pairs estimated during the Breeding Birds Survey (1983–93); all breeders appear to be of the commoner dark morph, though the white morph is occasionally recorded in Falkland waters and a white chick was seen on Sea Lion I in 1987. Northern Giant Petrel appears to be a rare visitor, but there are unconfirmed rumours of breeding on Beauchêne I.

Typical hilly landscape and beaches on New I, which is one of the most attractive and wildlife-rich sites in the group. Falklands, Dec 1990. © René Pop.

The Breeding Birds Survey produced few breeding records of the other tubenoses in the archipelago, though several colonies were noted for the first time. The most easily accessible nesting area for Slender-billed Prions is on New I, from which most birds apparently depart north for the winter, while the only known colony of Fairy Prion, on Beauchêne I, numbered possibly 10,000 pairs. Sooty Shearwater and Common Diving-petrel may also breed in large numbers, while White-chinned Petrel, Grey-backed Storm-petrel and Wilson's Storm-petrel are perhaps locally numerous, though there are few breeding records, and Great Shearwater has only a tiny colony with Sooty Shearwater on one island. The distribution and status of most tubenoses within the archipelago has been little investigated, particularly on the many offshore islands.

Among other seabirds, both Rock and Imperial Shags are very widespread in the Falklands, occurring in all coastal waters. Data from the Breeding Birds Survey led to a population estimate of 32,000–59,000 pairs of Rock Shag, many nesting solitarily and the largest colony being only a few hundred pairs, while Imperial Shag appeared even more numerous (45,000–84,000 pairs), with several colonies totalling 1000–2000 pairs. Falkland Skua is very widespread in coastal regions, with an estimated total of 5000–9000 pairs. South Polar and Chilean Skuas are rarely seen visitors or migrants to the archipelago, although there is evidence that the former has occasionally bred. A few thousand pairs of Dolphin Gull breed in coastal regions, but it is far outnumbered by the more catholic Kelp Gull, with the only other breeding gull, Brown-hooded, much the least abundant species. South American Tern is a common colonial breeder, with 6000–12,000 pairs estimated in the Breeding Birds Survey, while three other terns occur as vagrants or non-breeding visitors.

A number of principally South American species breed in the Falklands, with waterfowl being perhaps the most obvious group. White-tufted Grebe (of the endemic, larger nominate subspecies) is widely distributed but not numerous, with an estimated 750–1400 breeding pairs, while Silvery Grebe has its strongholds in East Falkland; both species frequently occur on the same freshwater lakes. Among wildfowl, three species of geese, the extremely widespread and common Upland (endemic subspecies leucoptera, 46,000–85,000 pairs), Kelp (endemic subspecies malvinarum, 10,000–18,000 pairs), and most of the world population of Ruddy-headed Goose (14,000–27,000 pairs in 1983–93), are particularly noticeable. Ashy-headed Goose is a frequent vagrant that occasionally breeds. Other species include Black-necked Swan and Flying Steamer Duck, both widespread but not numerous; however, the endemic Falkland Steamer Duck is very widespread in coastal areas, and Speckled Teal and Crested

Duck are also very common. Chiloe Wigeon, Yellow-billed Pintail (of the race *spinicauda*) and Silver Teal are uncommon, while Cinnamon Teal is a very rare breeder.

Turkey Vulture is the commonest bird of prey, though it was formerly heavily persecuted. Red-backed Hawk, Southern (Crested) Caracara and Peregrine Falcon are all widespread in the islands, but the Falklands' most important raptor species is Striated Caracara. It is probable that most of the world population breeds here. Elsewhere, it is restricted to the extreme southernmost points of Tierra del Fuego and offshore islands. Between 1983 and 1993, the population was estimated to be 500–900 pairs. Approximately half of the population breeds in the Jason I group, with other strongholds at Beauchêne and Bird Is, both ungrazed tussac islands remote from farmed land.

Five species of South American shorebirds are also obvious in the archipelago: Magellanic and Blackish Oystercatchers, Two-banded Plover, the attractive Rufous-chested Dotterel, which is very common throughout East and West Falkland, and on several offshore islands, and Magellanic Snipe. The latter, which is sometimes treated within *G. gallinago* but is increasingly considered specifically distinct, apparently suffers predation by the Falklands' feral cat population.

Breeding passerines are comparatively few and, as expected, exhibit strong Neotropical affinities. Blackish Cinclodes (of the endemic nominate race) and Black-throated (Canary-winged) Finch (also of the nominate and endemic form) are among the principal prizes for visiting birders. The finch is extremely widespread throughout both of the main islands, with an estimated overall population of 7000–14,000 pairs (in 1983–93), while the cinclodes (known locally as the Tussacbird) is more patchily distributed, being largely restricted to rat-free coasts and offshore islands, but was the most abundant passerine in the archipelago, numbering 15,000–28,000 pairs in 1983–93. It differs in size and bill shape from the form *maculirostris*, which principally occurs on islands south of Tierra del Fuego. Other passerine breeders are more common in South America: Dark-faced Ground-tyrant

This pair of Rockhopper Penguins Eudyptes [chrysocome] chrysocome *is taking a 'rest', but it is unclear if the bottom bird is taking advantage of the shade offered by its partner, or the top bird is merely enjoying a softer 'bed'. Falklands. © Hadoram Shirihai.*

Southern Giant Petrel Macronectes giganteus *(right) and Turkey Vulture* Cathartes aura *(left) represent the most aggressive scavengers on the archipelago's coasts. Falklands, Jan 1991. © René Pop.*

(the endemic nominate race) is widespread and occurs in most habitats from sea level to the tops of mountains, Correndera Pipit (of the endemic subspecies *grayi*), Austral Thrush (the endemic nominate race is highly adaptive and occurs in most habitats) and Long-tailed Meadowlark (the endemic subspecies *falklandica* has a longer and heavier bill than mainland South American forms) is fairly widespread and the Falklands' second-most abundant passerine, while Black-chinned Siskin is mostly associated with settlements where there are trees. Grass Wren (of the endemic form falklandicus) is widespread in boggy valleys, but achieves highest densities in mature tussac grass. Some of these taxa require further study of their relationships and evolutionary history, which may result in their being upgraded to specific status. Cobb's Wren is considered Vulnerable by BirdLife International, with the population estimated at 1300–2400 pairs, in 1983–93, on rat- and cat-free islands. Carcass I and the Sea Lion group hold particularly important concentrations of the species. More recent field work (1997–98) demonstrated that Cobb's Wren was present on 29 of 57 islands surveyed, with an estimated population of c.6000 pairs. It was absent from the 23 islands where the presence of rats was confirmed. Finally, among breeding forms, House Sparrow arrived in the first quarter of the 20th century and is now numerous in Stanley and reasonably well established at several other settlements on both major islands.

Of the total Falklands list of 210 species, c.20 may be considered annual visitors or regular migrants, including several waders and waterfowl, Pale-faced Sheathbill, Blue Petrel, Grey-headed Albatross and Antarctic Prion. Given the significant recent increase in birdwatching activity in the islands, including many tour visits, it is unsurprising that more vagrants have been recorded; these range from Emperor Penguin and several of the New Zealand species of penguin, through a broad spectrum of seabirds, many shorebirds such as Tawny-throated Dotterel, Magellanic Plover and two species of seedsnipe, as well as a host of passerines, some of which are Neotropical migrants, but others, such as the two species of swift that have occurred, and Tawny-headed Swallow, might be considered less expected. Falklands Conservation publishes new and interesting bird records for the islands in its newsletter and Robin Woods is producing a detailed checklist.

Marine mammals As always on the Southern Ocean islands, pinnipeds are the most obvious marine mammals. South American Sea Lion is relatively widely distributed in the archipelago, with c.60 breeding sites having been documented, including several on mainland East Falkland and West Falkland. However, there is evidence for a recent and unexplained decline; while 30,000

animals were located in 1965, a similar survey in 1990 produced just 3385 individuals. A more comprehensive survey in 1995 found more than 5500 sea lions, suggesting either a slight recovery or that the 1990 survey had produced an unduly pessimistic result. The fur seal here is usually recognized as a subspecies of South American Fur Seal; the other taxon being *australis*, on Chilean, Argentine and S Brazilian coasts. Ten breeding sites are known in the islands, some holding 1000–3000 animals and a total population estimated at 18,000–20,000 individuals. Southern Elephant Seal is the least common of the three Falklands breeding species, having only become re-established on the islands during the last 50 years following its near extinction in the early 1800s. In recent years, numbers have noticeably increased with up to 5000 pups being born annually in the last decades and colonies of 200–300 ads exist at a number of sites on northwest, north, east and southeast coasts. For breeding, it prefers sand or shingle beaches with a gradually shelving sea-bottom approach. Leopard Seal was formerly a regular visitor to certain Falkland beaches, with an unconfirmed breeding record, but is now significantly less common, being most frequent in winter. Weddell Seal is only a rare vagrant to the islands.

Falkland waters are rich in cetaceans and other mammals. At least 16 species of whales have been recorded including Pygmy Right (rare), Blue (formerly regular but now rare), several species of the poorly known beaked whales, and Killer Whale (regular in small numbers, especially off Sea Lion). In addition, seven species of dolphin and porpoise are known from the archipelago, namely Dusky, Hourglass (uncommon), Peale's (fairly common), Bottlenose (two records of strandings), Commerson's (fairly common) and Southern Right Whale Dolphins (groups of up to 1000 recorded), and Spectacled Porpoise.

Southern Sea Otter *Lutra felina* was introduced to the Falklands in the 1930s and a number of sightings in the southwest and southeast of the archipelago suggest that a small population persists in more remote coastal regions.

Of interest is the presence of Basking *Cetorhinus maximus* and Blue Sharks *Prionace glauca* around the islands, with Thresher Shark *Alopias vulpinus* possibly occurring.

Main conservation issues Sheep farming has had a major influence on the islands' vegetation structure since the mid-19th century. Man's arrival was soon followed by the predictable host of alien mammal introductions, including goats, pigs, hares, rabbits, rats, mice and cats, some of which were already widespread by the 1830s. Patagonian Foxes *Dusicyon griseus* and Guanacos

Late season, a lone ad Rockhopper Penguin Eudyptes chrysocome *stands amid abandoned nests of King Cormorant* Phalacrocorax [atriceps] atriceps. *Falklands, Mar 2001. © Morten Jørgensen.*

Lama guanicoe followed later, by which time the island's endemic fox, known as the Warrah *Dusicyon antarctius*, had largely been exterminated. Pigs also contributed to the decline of the tussac grass communities both directly and indirectly. Whalers and others hunted the pigs with dogs, sometimes using fire to drive their quarry from cover, which inevitably destroyed yet more areas of biologically important tussac grass. Rats are found on many offshore islands, where they can survive very successfully in the peat beneath dense tussac grass and are probably present at all settlements, including Stanley. Rabbits have only survived on a few islands and in 2–3 areas on East and West Falkland.

From the mid-18th century Man began to harvest the incredibly rich wildlife of the Falklands. Whaling lasted for approximately 75 years until the 1850s, but most such ships used the archipelago only as a base. Fur and elephant seals, and sea lions offered much more lucrative hunting, both for oil and fur. The seals received the brunt of the early exploitation until, by the late 1850s with their populations depleted, commercial attention switched to sea lions, continuing periodically until 1964. At the same time as sea lions acquired economic importance, attempts to harvest penguin oil (which were perhaps initiated as early as 1820) started in earnest. This industry lasted just 16 years, from 1864 to 1880, so intense was the slaughter, which is estimated to have required the deaths of 1.5–2.0 million birds. Penguin and albatross eggs had been collected almost as long as humans had been present on the Falklands and by the mid-19th century were proving to be important sources of food, as well as income. While even very large hauls appear to have had no long-lasting detrimental affects on overall Black-browed Albatross numbers, local declines certainly did occur. Penguin and albatross eggs were still being collected in large numbers in the 1950s.

While wildlife and bird protection laws were first introduced in 1913 and fur seals were afforded complete protection in 1921, it is only within the last quarter of the 20th century that significant progress has been made in the conservation of what remains of the Falklands natural resources (though some farmers on West Point and Carcass started replanting tussac grass and protecting it within fenced coastal paddocks as long ago as 1890; this work took many years and undoubtedly improved habitats for birds on both islands). In 1964 a Nature Reserves Ordinance was introduced and, as of 1987, there were 56 reserves (both government and privately owned) protecting 21,467 ha, including 580 ha of tussac-grass habitat. Most such reserves are in West Falkland and include many of the important seabird colonies, such as Steeple Jason I. In addition there are a number of Seal Reserves, which harbour the bulk of the Falklands fur seal breeding populations and have a separate status to other reserves. The new Conservation of Wildlife and Nature Ordinance enacted in late 1999 changed the status of the above reserves; all Sanctuary Orders and Nature Reserves Orders continued as if they had been made as National Nature Reserve Orders on commencement of the 1999 Ordinance.

While the period of excessive depredation of the Falklands wildlife may be long since over, and ecotourism is playing an increasingly important role in the islands economic development, new threats are emerging. Oil exploration has taken place in offshore waters and poses a potential future threat should optimistic expectations be matched by findings. Fishing is lucrative, but the squid and finfish fleets are mostly foreign and under strict license from the Falklands government to fish only within a zone up to 150–200 miles offshore.

Human history There is inconclusive evidence to suggest that Patagonian Indians reached the Falklands prior to the earliest

In the Antarctic region the attractive Dolphin Gull Larus scoresbii *only breeds in the Falklands. S Argentina, Mar 2003. © Hadoram Shirihai.*

European discovery, in Aug 1592 by John Davis in the Desire. (A Portuguese chart of 1522 indicates that the islands may have been reached by an earlier European expedition.) The first recorded landing was in 1690 by Captain Strong of the *Welfare*. Thereafter French settlers constructed a garrison at Port Louis on East Falkland, in 1764. (The islands Spanish name of Islas Malvinas originates from that given to the archipelago by French mariners from St-Malo, Les Malouines.) Virtually concurrently, the English established a base at Port Egmont on Saunders I, although the Treaty of Tordesillas had attempted to divide rights to the New World between Spain and Portugal. Indeed, the Spanish bought out the French relatively soon after, and then evicted the British in 1767. However, when Britain threatened war, Spain restored Port Egmont, only for the British to abandon the settlement a few years later. The Spanish maintained the settlement at Port Louis until the early 1800s, whereupon the islands were only visited by occasional whalers and sealers until a military government was established by the United Provinces of the River Plate in the early 1820s. Thereafter a Buenos Aires entrepreneur, Louis Vernet, attempted to control sealing and ensure that commercial exploitation was performed sustainably. His seizure of three North American sealers caused a US naval officer to attack and destroy the Port Louis settlement in 1831. Buenos Aires continued to maintain a force in the Falklands until 1833, when it was ousted by the British. From the mid-1800s, under British control, sheep and their wool assumed major economic importance in the history of the islands, replacing cattle. The Falkland Islands Company was established by an Englishman from Montevideo, Samuel Lafone, who quickly became the largest landowner in the archipelago, while other immigrants had acquired rights to all available areas for pastoralism by the 1870s. Most of the new arrivals were English and Scottish and lived in Stanley, although rural settlements, tiny hamlets based around a sheltered harbour, which served as a model for the Argentine estancias, did develop in what is now known as the 'Camp', namely all of the Falklands outside Stanley. The population reached 2392 in 1931. Wool exports dominated the islands' economy until 1986.

In the minds of many people, the most significant event in Falklands history was the war between Britain and Argentina, caused by the latter's invasion of the islands in early Apr 1982. Argentina has never formally renounced its claim to the Falklands, which is not recognized by the British government, although a process was developed, commencing in 1971, whereby Argentina was permitted to arrange limited communications and supplies to the islands. While Falkland islanders and their supporters in Britain viewed such developments with alarm, this gradual process was considered too little and too slow by the military junta of General Galtieri, which decided to take the islands by force. The subsequent response reclaimed the Falklands for their inhabitants, albeit at considerable cost in lives and equipment. Subsequent Argentine governments have not renounced their claim to the islands, though the use of further military force has been ruled out for the present.

In the census of 2001, there were 2491 inhabitants of the Falklands, of which 80% lived in Stanley and only 20% in the Camp. Another 500 civilians are associated with the military forces at the Mount Pleasant Airfield complex. A governor appointed from London administers the islands and the British government controls all defence matters, although an elected eight-person Legislative Council (five from Stanley and three from Camp) deals with most internal matters. Fishing has recently assumed paramount importance in the Falklands economy, with licenses being issued to Asian and European countries to catch squid and finfish in the archipelago's waters. Offshore seismic surveys for oil were initiated in the 1990s and licenses for petroleum exploration are under consideration. Revenue from fishing, along with funds from the British government, has paid for many improvements to public services. Most people still work either for the government or for the Falkland Islands Company, which continues to provide shipping and other services, but has sold its pastoral rights to the government and local people.

Visiting the islands The Falklands are one of the few areas covered by this book that are comparatively easily (if expensively) visited by the independent traveller (there being a twice-weekly military flight, with limited space for civilians, from RAF Brize Norton in England to the islands, calling at Ascension I en route). Some independent travellers fly via Santiago and Punta Arenas on the weekly flight provided by LanChile. However, most naturalists still join a conventional cruise-ship tour. Falklands Conservation has recently published a comprehensive visitor's guide to 13 of the best wildlife sites in the archipelago (Summers, D., 2001, *A Visitor's Guide to the Falkland Islands*; available via www.falklandsconservation.com).

Adult Magellanic Penguin Spheniscus magellanicus with two well-grown chicks. The Falklands is a key site for the species. Jan 2001. © Hadoram Shirihai.

Two Commerson's Dolphins Cephalorhynchus commersonii; the rear, slightly greyer, animal is younger than the mature individual in front. Falklands, Feb 2001. © Morten Jørgensen.

This 112-page book will prove invaluable to anyone travelling to the group containing, as it does, useful introductory sections on photography and other aspects of travel to the islands.

Birding can start right around **Stanley** (51°42'S 57°50'W), the capital of the Falklands, with Upland Goose, Dolphin and Kelp Gulls, Rock Shag, Southern Giant Petrel and Falkland Steamer Duck all conspicuous inhabitants of the shoreline. Austral Thrush, Long-tailed Meadowlark and Black-chinned Siskin, among the few passerines, can be found around **Government House**, while Black-throated Finch is often seen on **Stanley Common** (51°43'S 57°51'W). Governor Moody named Stanley after the 14th Earl of Derby (1799–1869), who was the British Prime Minister in 1852, 1858 and 1866–68. It was Lord Stanley, as he then was, who on the advice of the Admiralty ordered the removal (in 1843–4) of the chief settlement of the Colony from Port Louis to Port Jackson, the previous name for the area. This name probably honoured Andrew Jackson, President of the USA in 1829–37. Earlier the French under de Bougainville had named it Beau Port.

Just 5 km east of Stanley, a visit to **Penguin Walk** and **Surf Bay** (51°42'S 57°46'W) should produce Gentoo and Magellanic Penguins, Two-banded Plover and White-rumped Sandpiper (the latter only in summer), as well as South American Tern, Sooty Shearwater and Black-browed Albatross offshore. Also from Stanley it is possible to visit **Volunteer Point** (51°28'S 57°49'W) and **Kidney I** (51°37'S 57°45'W). Scheduled trips are usually confined to weekends and the crossing has the capacity to produce interesting seabirds including Great Shearwater, White-chinned and Cape Petrels, Wilson's Storm-petrel, Common Diving-petrel, and even Grey-headed, Wandering or Royal Albatrosses. The two first-named species, as well as Sooty Shearwater and Grey-backed Storm-petrel, breed on Kidney. Peale's and Commerson's Dolphins are comparatively regular in the area known as the Narrows. The point itself, which can also be reached by a difficult four-hour overland drive from Stanley, has three species of penguin, including a small colony of absurdly tame King Penguin c.1 km from the sandy beach, as well as Magellanic and Blackish Oystercatchers, Rufous-chested Dotterel, Speckled Teal and Dark-faced Ground-tyrant. Other birds in the area include Ruddy-headed Goose, Magellanic Snipe, Dolphin Gull, South American Tern and Correndera Pipit. Mammals include South American Fur Seal and, less commonly, Southern Elephant Seal. Note that landings at Volunteer Point can be difficult due to the often poor weather conditions.

Kidney I, which is only a few km from Stanley, is a Falkland Islands government-owned National Nature Reserve. Authorization to visit must be obtained from the Environmental Planning Office at the Secretariat, who will supply guidelines for visitors. Kidney is an excellent example of a rat-free tussac island. It has Magellanic Penguins, a small colony of Rockhopper Penguins on the northern cliffs, Common Diving-petrels and Grey-backed Storm-petrels, many thousands of Sooty Shearwaters and hundreds of White-chinned Petrels. Other species include Imperial Shag and most of the nine breeding Falkland passerines; especially numerous are Blackish Cinclodes, Austral Thrush and both wrens, while the others breed in smaller numbers.

Pebble I (51°18'S 59°35'W), which lies immediately north of West Falkland, is also directly accessible from Stanley, this time by a light aircraft of the Falkland Islands Government Air Service (FIGAS). It is another essential destination for naturalists, boasting a strong cast of waterfowl, including both breeding grebes and Flying Steamer Duck, both caracaras including the rare Striated (though only Southern breeds), Grass Wren and Black-chinned Siskin, and has also demonstrated a strong propensity for hosting vagrants to the archipelago. Seabirds and shorebirds are also strongly represented on Pebble, with Pale-faced Sheathbills around the South American Sea Lion colonies in summer, while Rockhopper Penguin, Imperial Shag, Dolphin Gull, Falkland Skua and South American Tern are all present along shorelines. Rufous-chested Dotterel, Black-crowned Night-heron and Magellanic Snipe are also frequently seen.

Most tour groups also make time for a visit to **Sea Lion I** (52°25'S 59°04'W), which is 16 km south of East Falkland. There are no birds that cannot be seen elsewhere, though populations are noticeably high due to the absence of rats, mice or cats, and both Blackish Cinclodes and Black-throated Finch are easily found here. A few pairs of Striated Caracara breed on the island and Cobb's Wren, Rock Shag and Magellanic Penguin are other conspicuous features of the local avifauna. The island supports possibly the largest colony in the Falklands of Southern Elephant Seal, while South American Sea Lion also breeds, and there is a good chance of seeing Killer Whale and Peale's Dolphin cruising in the shallows.

Visits to **New**, **West Point** or **Carcass islands** in the extreme west of the archipelago offer the best chance to see other breeding seabirds, such as Black-browed Albatross and Slender-billed Prion, with the constant possibility of something unexpected. Landbirds on these remote islands include Correndera Pipit, Dark-faced Ground-tyrant and Red-backed Hawk, while Striated Caracaras lurk around the fringes of the Rockhopper Penguin colonies. A visit to **Carcass** (51°16'S 60°33'W), which is included in the itinerary of a number of tour groups, is the high point of any journey to the archipelago and offers a relative feast of birding, from Ruddy-headed, Upland and Kelp Geese, Gentoo (near the landing beach) and Magellanic Penguins in and around their burrows, Falkland Steamer Duck, Rock and Imperial Cormorants and South American Tern to all of the native resident passerines, including 14 pairs of Striated Caracara, the ultra-confiding Blackish Cinclodes, Grass and Cobb's Wrens, Black-chinned Siskin, Austral Thrush and super-attractive Black-throated Finch. Black-crowned Night-heron nests in the cliffs close to the boathouse at the settlement, near one of the three the landing points. In addition, South American Sea Lion, and Commerson's and Peale's Dolphins are regular offshore and frequently sighted during zodiac cruises. Carcass supports large populations of birds because it is free of mammalian predators.

West Point I (51°21'S 60°41'W), off the northwest corner of West Falkland, possesses an impressive landscape, with rugged cliffs that rise high from the sea, topped by rolling pastures. It was among the first outlying islands to be farmed, in the late 1870s,

and had previously been well known among sealers and penguin hunters. From the landing site, close to the Napier family settlement, where Peale's Dolphin and South American Sea Lion are frequently seen, it is possible to walk over the surrounding heath through pastures of vivid green balsam bog and other cushion plants. Striated Caracara is frequently observed on West Point, and the species often follows visitors. The cliff edge at Devil's Nose supports a mixed colony of 500 pairs of Rockhopper Penguin and 2100 pairs of Black-browed Albatross.

On **New I** (51°42'S 61°17'W), which was so-named by American sealers from the eastern seaboard, it is possible to hike from the landing point at the settlement alongside a hedgerow of yellow gorse and over grazed fields dotted with Upland Goose families to a cliff brimming with Rockhopper Penguins and Black-browed Albatross. A Rockhopper runway from the upper colony to the cliff is a popular visitor attraction, with a steady stream of penguins arriving from or returning to the ocean via the boulder-strewn path. New I boasts 41 breeding bird species, including many thousands of Slender-billed Prion, both caracaras, Ruddy-headed Goose, both oystercatchers, Austral Thrush and Blackish Cinclodes, as well as fur seals and South American Sea Lion. Several breeding groups of Peale's Dolphin occur in offshore waters. The island has a long history of human settlement, dating from the late 18th century, initially being used by sealers and whalers, but since the 1860s has been leased for farming. However, grazing has been greatly decreased since the early 1970s by the present owners, Tony and Kim Chater and the New Island South Conservation Trust, and the island currently comprises two reserves, North Nature Reserve and South Wildlife Reserve.

The increase in pelagic birding in Falkland waters within recent years has substantially improved our knowledge of the status of a number of seabirds; many species formerly considered to be rare or uncommon in the archipelago have been proven to be more or less regular, e.g. Shy and Light-mantled Sooty Albatrosses, Grey Petrel, Little Shearwater and Arctic Skua. During strong easterly winds even species such as Kerguelen Petrel may be pushed west as far as the Falklands. Genuine rarities recorded in this area of ocean in recent years have included three Buller's Albatross at the entrance to Falkland Sound and a Mottled Petrel southeast of the islands.

Shag Rocks

Location and main features These are the smallest of the subantarctic islands considered part of the UK's South Georgia and South Sandwich Islands territory. They lie 240 km west of South Georgia and 1500 km east of Tierra del Fuego and comprise eight very isolated rocks, some separated from each other by 20 km. Black Rock and another low rock lie 18.5 km southeast of the main group of six islets.

Landform, climate and habitat Shag Rocks rise directly from the sea, reaching a highest point of 71 m and are entirely guano-covered. There is no vegetation on the islets.

Birds Given this small archipelago's name it is entirely appropriate that 2000 pairs of South Georgian Shag nest here (1996 count), but this is the only breeding bird. Wandering Albatross, prions and most other seabirds common in this area of the S Atlantic have also been observed around the rocks, particularly because of upwellings around the ocean plateau and the frequent presence of grounded icebergs, but more data would be welcome.

Marine mammals Antarctic Fur Seals are commonly seen in the vicinity and haul out in small numbers (but don't breed), when sea state permits. A number of cetaceans have been recorded over the ocean plateau.

Main conservation issues No threats are known to these very rarely visited rocks.

Human history Given their isolation and relative lack of attractions to humans, it is unsurprising that Shag Rocks have been rarely visited. The islands' discoverer, the Spaniard Joseph de la Llana, captain of the Aurora, incorrectly mapped what he named the Aurora Islands' position in 1762, which confused an American sealer, Sheffield, who came across Shag Rocks when searching for the islands in 1819. These were, however, the same group. The first landing was made as recently as 1956 by an Argentine geologist, who was winched down from a helicopter for a few hours.

Visiting the islands Landings on these rocks are virtually impossible unless the sea is flat calm, although the first tourist visit was in 1991 and observations can be made from the surrounding sea. Close in, on a relatively calm day, they present a marvellous spectacle.

South Georgia

Location and main features Located at 53°30'S–55°00'S 35°30'W–38°40'W and 350 km south of the Antarctic Convergence, South Georgia is a 170 km x 40 km and 3755 km² island which played an important role in the development of Antarctic exploration and was a key base for S Atlantic sealing and whaling industries. It is also of enormous importance for wildlife, with an endemic passerine, South Georgia Pipit, and huge numbers of several species of breeding seabird.

Landform, climate and habitat The island is exceptionally rugged; though not of direct volcanic origin its rocks derive from a series of volcanoes active 110–140 million years ago, such as on Annenkov I and its neighbouring islets. Sediments washed down

South Georgia Pipit Anthus antarcticus *is the only indigenous passerine and is endemic to the archipelago. South Georgia, Nov 2001. © Hadoram Shirihai.*

from these became established as sandstones and shales on a basement of ocean-floor volcanic and older metamorphic rocks. A total of 57% of South Georgia is glaciated and the dramatic peaks of the Allardyce Range, the island's central spine, dominate the landscape, the highest being Mount Paget at 2934 m. Glaciers have largely been retreating since the 1880s. Temperatures range from -19°C to 24°C, although the annual range of mean monthly temperatures is only c.7°C, but weather varies over the island, with more sunshine on the north coast, which is better sheltered from prevailing winds. Winters are, unsurprisingly, colder. Indeed,

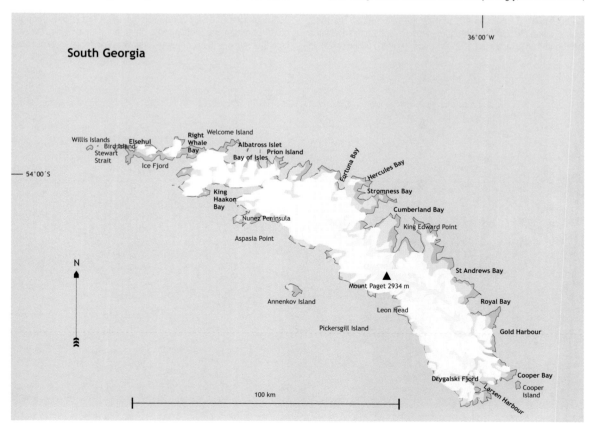

36°00'W

South Georgia

Willis Islands
Bird Island
Stewart Strait
Elsehul
Right Whale Bay
Welcome Island
Albatross Islet
Prion Island
Bay of Isles
Ice Fjord
Fortuna Bay
Hercules Bay
54°00'S
King Haakon Bay
Stromness Bay
Cumberland Bay
Nunez Peninsula
King Edward Point
Aspasia Point
St Andrews Bay
N
Mount Paget 2934 m
Royal Bay
Annenkov Island
Leon Head
Pickersgill Island
Gold Harbour
Drygalski Fjord
Cooper Bay
Cooper Island
Larsen Harbour
100 km

the island lies in the track of deep atmospheric depressions, which reach the Atlantic via the Drake Passage, and rain may fall at any season, with up to 100 mm possible in a day. In winter snow cover is complete, but frosts and snowfalls also occur in summer. However, most bays and harbours are ice-free year-round with the exception of parts of the extreme southeast of the island. Vegetation extends from sea level to approximately 250 m and is represented by 26 indigenous vascular plants and 54 aliens (of which 35 persist), with most of the latter around the former whaling stations. There are also 125 mosses, 85 liverworts, 200 lichens and 50 fungi. The flora is closely related to that found in southern South America and the Falklands. Tussac grass up to 2 m in height grows along most of the coastline, but vegetation becomes less dense inland, where herbs and mosses predominate, while grassy heaths with burnets are extensive on better drained ground, and wet meadows, bogs and pools (dominated by rushes and wet mosses) are evident in areas close to the water table. Most plants take more than one year to flower here; e.g., the introduced grass *Poa annua* is usually an annual, but is perennial on South Georgia.

There are several offshore islets, Bird I and the Willis Is off the northwest coast, Annenkov I off the southwest coast, Cooper I on the east side and Clerke Rocks 72 km southeast of South Georgia (the latter reach a max. elevation of 331 m). The whaling stations were all constructed on the northeast coast, where the many sheltered fjords provide a safe haven for ships.

Birds Among the 30 species recorded nesting on the island, there are regular breeding populations of four species of penguin on South Georgia. Thirty-four colonies of King Penguin, totalling 122,000 pairs, were recorded in 1984–5 and numbers are thought to be increasing at the rate of 5% per annum, bringing the estimated number of pairs to 400,000 by the mid-1990s. The most recent complete Gentoo Penguin census, conducted between 1985 and 1988, indicated 102,000 pairs in over 200 colonies. In

The rugged island of South Georgia is sometimes the setting for quite spectacular sunsets. NW side of South Georgia, Mar 2003. © Hadoram Shirihai.

1987–8, there was a total of 6000 pairs of Chinstrap Penguin at the principal colony in the southeast of the main island. The most numerous species is Macaroni Penguin, of which 5.4 million pairs were estimated in the late 1970s at colonies in the southeast and northwest of the main island and on the Willis Is, but numbers had apparently decreased to just 2.7 million pairs in 1985–6. Rockhopper Penguin is considered a sporadic breeder in tiny numbers, and moulting imms were present during most seasons among the Macaroni Penguins on Bird I, but there have been no records for a number of years. One pair of Adélie Penguin was present in the mid-1990s on Annenkov I.

South Georgia is also of key importance to albatrosses. Steadily decreasing numbers of Wandering Albatross nest, with less than 1000 pairs on Bird I by 2000 (25 other sites are known throughout the archipelago, holding 864 pairs in the mid-1980s, the last time that more or less complete data were available, though some

Black-browed Albatross Thalassarche melanophrys *with Roché Peak and Freshwater Bay at rear, Bird I. South Georgia, Feb 1980. © John Croxall.*

Incubating Gentoo Penguin Pygoscelis papua *above Holmestrand, South Georgia.* © Grant Dixon.

colonies were counted in the mid-1990s when the suggested overall population was 4000 pairs). Bird I also has a decreasing population of Black-browed Albatross, censused at 9539 pairs in 1995–6; the total estimated population for South Georgia in 1986–7 was 100,000 pairs, in colonies principally at the southeast and northwest extremities of the main island and on Annenkov I. The decline in numbers of these two species is almost certainly largely the result of longlining. There were 6857 pairs of Grey-headed Albatross on Bird I in 1990–1 (the total estimated population for South Georgia in 1986–7 was 80,000 pairs, in colonies principally at the northwest extremity), but numbers are apparently decreasing at a rate of 2% per annum, and 5000–7500 Light-mantled Sooty Albatross in the entire group, just 150 of these on Bird I.

There is a host (13) of breeding tubenoses (all counts relate to the period 1985–8, date of the most recent island-wide seabird census). Both giant petrels breed, with some evidence of a recent increase of the less widespread and common Northern Giant Petrel (3000 pairs) at Bird I. Cape (10,000 pairs), Snow (3000 pairs), Blue (70,000 pairs) and White-chinned Petrels (two million) are all reasonably widespread and common breeders. Among small petrels, Antarctic Prion, despite predation by rats and destruction of its breeding habitat by Antarctic Fur Seal (which may also be affecting Blue Petrel), is an extremely abundant and widespread breeder (22 million), but Fairy Prion (1000 pairs) is much less widespread. Wilson's Storm-petrel is abundant (600,000 pairs) and Black-bellied Storm-petrel a common but local breeder (10,000 pairs), while Grey-backed Storm-petrel is a very rare breeder, with no confirmed nesting records since 1972. Both South Georgian (50,000) and Common Diving-petrels (3.8 million pairs) are very abundant breeders.

Of the remainder, South Georgian Shag is another common and widespread breeder (7500 pairs), and Speckled Teal (1–10 pairs) and Brown Pintail (1000 pairs) both breed, though the former is restricted to the Cumberland Bay area. Kelp Gull (2000 pairs), Subantarctic Skua (2000 pairs, perhaps almost one-seventh of the world population) and Pale-faced Sheathbill (2000 pairs, or one-fifth of the world population, scattered over 200 sites) are prevalent on coasts, with 10,000 pairs of Antarctic Tern. The sole breeding passerine is the endemic South Georgia Pipit, which numbers 3000–4000 pairs but is restricted to rat-free areas, namely parts of the south coast and offshore islands.

As on the Falklands, the increasing numbers of birdwatchers active at sea around the islands, and between here, Shag Rocks and Antarctica, have contributed somewhat to our knowledge

of pelagic-bird distributions in this region. Great-winged, White-headed and Atlantic Petrels are among the interesting recent reports from the vicinity of South Georgia and sea area between it and the Falklands.

Prince & Croxall (1996) recently provided a complete checklist of all bird species recorded at South Georgia. Of the 79 taxa listed, almost half are vagrants or scarce visitors, including four species of penguins, several petrels, three egrets, two ducks, two raptors, two gallinules, six shorebirds, two skuas, Eared Dove and six passerines, among them House Sparrow. Regular non-breeding seabird visitors include Southern Fulmar, Antarctic Petrel, Kerguelen Petrel, Soft-plumaged Petrel and Great Shearwater. Since the publication of the Prince and Croxall list, four species have certainly occurred, Spotted Sandpiper, Rufous-chested Dotterel, Franklin's Gull (all at Bird I) and Barn Owl (an individual of which has recently wintered), and a couple more require confirmation.

Marine mammals Despite the intensive hunting, a few Antarctic Fur Seals were sighted at Bird I in 1927 and by 1956 4500 breeding females were present. Numbers have continued to increase almost exponentially since then, spreading inland from the beaches and eroding areas of tussac in the process. By the early 1980s the population was considered to number over 300,000 individuals, while a census in 1990–1 estimated the population

King Penguin Aptenodytes patagonicus *chick: this inexperienced youngster appears to be trying to 'figure out' the cause of the white substance falling from the sky! South Georgia, Nov 2001.* © Hadoram Shirihai.

Gold Harbour, with the Bertrab Glacier in the background. For wildlife, this is unquestionably one of the most spectacular sites on South Georgia, and the shore and coastal plain can be packed with breeding King Penguins Aptenodytes patagonicus *and many seals. Mar 2006. © Hadoram Shirihai.*

at 1.8 million, and it is thought there were over three million by the late 1990s. Subantarctic Fur Seal is a regular vagrant. Over 300,000 Southern Elephant Seals breed at South Georgia, and their population appears to be stable. Numbers of Leopard Seal haul out in winter. Approximately 100 Weddell Seals are resident at South Georgia, with small numbers breeding at Larsen Harbour in the southeast of the main island. Sei Whale is reasonably common offshore in late summer and autumn, while Southern Right, Minke, Humpback and Sperm Whales have all become more regular in recent years, and Blue and Fin Whales are also occasionally recorded. Other cetaceans include Southern Bottlenose Whale (regular), Arnoux's Beaked Whale (known only from strandings), Killer Whale, Long-finned Pilot Whale, Peale's, Hourglass and Commerson's Dolphins (no recent records of the first- and last-named dolphin species) and Spectacled Porpoise (few records). The best area for whales is off the northeast coast where stocks of krill are concentrated.

Main conservation issues The 19th century whalers brought the usual assortment of mammalian introductions and their stations soon became infested with mice and rats. Horses, pigs, dogs and cats all followed, but were always restricted to those areas close to habitation, and have now been extirpated. Mice have failed to spread and though rats are widespread they have not reached the main offshore islands and do not appear to prey on larger seabirds at least. A sheep farm, established in 1905, was abandoned within three months, but two herds of reindeer totalling over 2000 animals, first introduced in 1911, still graze two separate areas. Egg collecting by whalers and sealers, especially in the 1920s and 1930s, was common practice but such direct exploitation has now ceased. However, Black-browed, Grey-headed and Wandering Albatross are now threatened by the recent increase in longline fishing. Bottom trawling has been banned in South Georgian waters, but seals and seabirds are still caught in nets placed in offshore seas. The creation of the South Georgia

Maritime Zone (SGMZ), in 1993, has brought additional protection to the marine ecosystem around the islands. The SGMZ encapsulates a region of 200 nautical miles around South Georgia and the South Sandwiches, within which all fishing vessels must be licensed. Longline fishing is now very strictly regulated, with government observers present aboard all vessels and incidental seabird mortality has been reduced to c.30 individual birds per year for the entire fishery. The South Georgia Government patrols the area to prevent unlicensed fishing boats. Three protected areas were designated in 1975—Cooper, Annenkov and Bird Is. Cooper is a Specially Protected Area and the others are Sites of Special

The waters around South Georgia, especially those southwest of the island, are very rich in tubenoses, with Cape Petrel Daption capense *being one of the most frequently observed species. South Georgia, Nov 2001. © Hadoram Shirihai.*

Scientific Interest (these may only be visited by specifically autho-rised scientific groups). In 2000, the South Georgia Environmental Management Plan proposed many additional areas for protection. the commissioner for South Georgia and the South Sandwich Islands must approve all visits to the island, and all tourists attract a GBP 50 per head fee.

Human history South Georgia was probably first sighted in 1675 by London-born Antoine de la Roché, who had been blown off course by a storm while travelling between South America and England, via Cape Horn. The island next makes an appearance in history books as Isla de San Pedro, being so-named by the Spaniard Gregorio Jerez, who saw the island in 1756. The first landing was made by Cook in Jan 1775, who claimed it for the British crown and named it after George III, although he found it a curiously unattractive, inhospitable and barren place. Nonethe-less, when news of the large numbers of fur seals he had found there was made public two years later, it caused a rush of sealers, both British and US, in the years following 1786. Fur seal skins and elephant seal oil were both sought. Within five years over 100 ships were exploiting the region. One British vessel took 3000 barrels of oil and 50,000 skins in 1792–3, and several US ships exported skins as far afield as China. Such vigorous exploitation had expected consequences: while the US sealer Fanning was able to take 57,000 skins in 1800–2, by 1831 another US party that visited the island for eight months found few seals. The final fur sealing visit to South Georgia appears to have occurred in 1909, the Daisy also found seals to be scarce, just 170 were taken in five months. The elephant seal harvest appears to have remained commercially viable for significantly longer: 15,000 bar-rels were taken by the *Trinity* in 1877–8, but just 60 barrels of oil were extracted by the *Express* in 1885–6.

As sealing activities folded, whaling commenced a new period of exploitation. Beginning in 1904, when a Norwegian-operated but Argentine-owned company, established a station at the famous Grytviken, the South Georgian whaling industry swiftly rose to ex-ceptional prominence and marked the start of the island's per-manent occupation. Six onshore whaling bases were eventually established on the island, with Leith Harbour the last to close, in Dec 1965, and an anchorage for floating factory ships, at Godthul, operational in 1908–17 and 1922–9. Whalers introduced reindeer to South Georgia (a population of over 2000 animals remains to-day) in 1911. Peak seasons in the slaughter were in 1925–6, when 7825 whales yielded 404,457 barrels of oil, and 1926–7, when 5215 whales produced 417,292 barrels. The worldwide depres-sion, which commenced in 1929, caused a slowdown in whaling that ironically permitted the industry to survive for longer, as com-mercial exploitation at the same rate as in the years immediately preceding this would have been unsustainable. The Norwegians, who dominated the industry in South Georgia, withdrew from the is-land in 1961–2, their place being briefly taken by the Japanese, but they had within three years also discovered the unprofitablity of the business. Elephant seals were again exploited towards the end of this period, their oil being sometimes mixed with lower quality whale oil. Between 1905 and 1964 a further 498,870 seals were killed. Whale catches totalled 175,250 (of the five principal species, Blue, Fin, Humpback, Sei and Sperm Whales) during 1904 to 1966.

Such massive destruction was not without a human cost, as the wrecks of at least eight ships in South Georgian waters tes-tify, and the eight cemeteries on the island contain the graves of over 200 whalers and others, their most famous inhabitant being Ernest Shackleton, who died of a heart attack while at anchor in King Edward Cove during the ill-conceived Quest expedition.

The British claim to the islands was consolidated in 1908, when the government created a territory named the Falkland Islands Dependencies, comprising South Georgia, as well as the South Orkneys, South Shetlands, South Sandwiches and Graham Land on the Antarctic Peninsula. Following the German International Polar Year Expedition, which established a base at Royal Bay for

King Penguin Aptenodytes patagonicus *is a year-round breeder, making Gold Harbour always a busy place. South Georgia, Mar 2006. © Hadoram Shirihai.*

Ad and chick King Penguins Aptenodytes patagonicus *and Southern Elephant Seals* Mirounga leonina *are typical components of the coastal wildlife of South Georgia.* © Hans Reinhard.

Incubating King Penguins Aptenodytes patagonicus; *at this stage in the season the colonies are less crowded and breeders are evenly spaced, South Georgia.* © Hans Reinhard.

'Double penguin': *two ad* King Penguins Aptenodytes patagonicus *enlarging their chests and stretching their necks during a social interaction. Gold Harbour, South Georgia, Mar 2006.* © Hadoram Shirihai.

13 months in 1882–3, the next major scientific efforts at South Georgia came in 1925–39 when the Discovery Committee created a marine biological station at King Edward Point. The base assumed responsibility for meteorological observations, which had been made continuously since 1905. The many whaling and sealing ships visiting the island ironically facilitated other, less intensive scientific research, including natural history. Ongoing seabird and seal research is now well funded and operates from a permanent and well-equipped base on Bird I, with the British Antarctic Survey personnel working there overwintering at King Edward Point between 1969 and 1982. However, during the Falklands War, an Argentine force briefly took possession of South Georgia, in Apr 1982, but were swiftly evicted once a British task force arrived at the island. Since 1982 Bird I has been open year-round and nearly all seabird and marine mammal work has been based there, the only notable exceptions being studies of King Penguin and Southern Elephant Seal (at Husvik), glaciological and geological investigations throughout the island, and a few brief studies in the Bay of Isles and at Stromness.

Fishing is now the principal economic activity of the island. Large-scale commercial exploitation commenced in the late 1960s

The enormous King Penguin Aptenodytes patagonicus *colony at Salisbury Plain, in the Bay of Isles, South Georgia, Nov 2001.* © Hadoram Shirihai.

King Penguins Aptenodytes patagonicus *on glacier with Nordenskjöld peak (2356 m) in the background. St Andrews Bay, South Georgia. © Grant Dixon.*

and swiftly depleted stocks of Marbled Rockcod *Notothenia rossi*. Currently the main species of interest are Patagonian Toothfish *Dissostichus eleginoides* and Mackerel Icefish *Champsocephalus gunnari* with, until the early 1990s, Lanternfish *Electrona guntheri*. The island is also among the global centres for krill fishing, with 100,000–200,000 tonnes being taken annually, principally by Russian and Japanese trawlers. With this in mind, the British Antarctic Survey research station re-opened on 22 Mar 2001, at King Edward Point; the centre is designed to provide sound scientific advice to the government of South Georgia and the South Sandwich Islands on the sustainable management of commercial fisheries around the island.

Visiting the islands All vessels intending to visit South Georgia are required to contact the Marine Officer at King Edward Point in Cumberland East Bay, as soon as practicable upon entering the 200-nautical mile Maritime Zone around South Georgia. Other regulations governing visits include the following. Cruise ships, smaller charter vessels and cruising yachts must be accompanied by someone with subantarctic or equivalent experience of operating in remote areas. All tourist operations must be ship based, with no overnight stays ashore unless approved by the Commissioner. Deteriorating weather or sea conditions may, for example, make return to the ship hazardous and necessitate a longer stay ashore than planned. Shore parties must always be supported by their expedition vessel. No on-shore accommodation is provided for visitors and there are no hospital facilities or rescue services. Visitors, including passengers, staff and crews of all vessels visiting South Georgia must always respect the Conservation Guidelines. Entry to Cooper I, Bird I and Annenkov I is strictly prohibited, except for scientific research, for which a permit from the Commissioner is required. Visitors are prohibited from entering or approaching within 200 m of the former whaling stations at Prince Olav Harbour, Leith Harbour, Stromness and Husvik, which are in a dangerous state of disrepair and wind-blown debris including asbestos dust is a hazard. Selected areas of interest to visitors are as follows.

Elsehul (54°01'S 37°59'W) was briefly a study site for British Antarctic Survey botanists, but has now been abandoned to the exceptionally dense population of fur seals. Only zodiac cruising is possible (except late in the season), below the steep cliffs and tussac-grass slopes where Macaroni Penguin, and Black-browed, Sooty and Grey-headed Albatrosses nest. Snow Petrel also occurs, King Penguin may be founding a small breeding colony in the area and giant petrels are frequently observed offshore. The area consists of a small cove on the north side of a peninsula,

which forms the most westerly point of mainland South Georgia. The name dates to 1905–12, and was probably applied by Norwegian sealers and whalers working the area. The shores of this dramatic and picturesque bay are one of the main breeding grounds for South Georgia's fur seal population and between Nov and Mar, when they haul out to breed, both bulls (which mostly depart by mid-Jan) and cows are particularly aggressive.

Right Whale Bay (54°00'S 37°42'W) was presumably named for the large number of right whales once found here. This stunningly beautiful arena has a large King Penguin colony, and fur and elephant seals, against the backdrop of a cascading waterfall. It is possible to land on a sand beach and make the short uphill walk to the penguin nesting area.

The **Bay of Isles**, on the northwest coast holds two large breeding King Penguin colonies, the most commonly visited being at Salisbury Plain (see below) behind a flat sandy beach with many fur seals. Also in this general area are Gentoo Penguin, Wandering and Light-mantled Sooty Albatrosses, Southern and Northern Giant Petrels, Cape Petrel, Antarctic Prion, Blue and White-chinned Petrels, Wilson's Storm-petrel, Common Diving-petrel, Brown Pintail, Pale-faced Sheathbill, Subantarctic Skua, Kelp Gull, Antarctic Tern and South Georgia Pipit.

Albatross I (54°01'S 37°20'W) is located c.3 km southeast of Cape Buller within the Bay of Isles. It was charted by *Murphy*, aboard the brig *Daisy*, who afforded the islet this name for the Wandering Albatrosses he observed there. There are several landing sites, but the walk from all of these up to the nests is via a wet rocky gully, which is often heavily occupied by fur seals that should be treated with respect and given a wide berth. The seals have also been steadily colonizing the island's southern beaches in recent years. Other inhabitants include South Georgia Pipit in the tussac grass and Brown Pintail on the small tarns. The northwest point of the island is off-limits to visitors as it is being used as a control area in an experiment to determine whether tourist visits affect breeding success.

Salisbury Plain (54°03'S 37°19'W) lies within the Bay of Isles. It was here that American ornithologist Robert Cushman Murphy undertook much of his research in 1912–13. Two glaciers flank Salisbury Plain; Murphy named the Grace Glacier to the west for his wife, while that to the east is known as the Lucas Glacier. This

Dispute over food between two Southern Giant Petrels Macronectes giganteus. *Salisbury Plain, South Georgia, Nov 2001. © Hadoram Shirihai.*

The archipelago holds several million pairs of Macaroni Penguins Eudyptes chrysolophus. *South Georgia. © Hans Reinhard.*

Wandering Albatross Diomedea [exulans] exulans *Albatross I, South Georgia. © Hans Reinhard.*

exciting location is home to one of South Georgia's largest King Penguin colonies. The black-sand beach is very exposed and landing here is often difficult (and wet) due to large waves.

Also within the Bay of Isles, **Prion I** (54°01'S 37°15'W) is c.2.5 km north-northeast of Luck Point. It too was charted by Murphy, who so named it after the prions he observed around the island, which is also a nesting ground for Wandering Albatross.

Fortuna Bay (54°08'S 36°49'W) marks the point where Shackleton descended towards Stromness. It is a broad bay with mossy slopes, where many of the introduced reindeer graze. There are two landing options, one outside the bay where there is a large King Penguin rookery in front of a glacier. This landing is very weather dependent, requiring calm seas. The other landing point is inside the bay on a sandy beach, with a stunning backdrop and much wildlife, including another King Penguin colony and Light-mantled Sooty Albatross on the cliffs above the landing site.

Hercules Bay (54°07'S 36°40'W) is a small inlet, almost 1 km wide, which lies 1.5 km from Cape Saunders on the north coast. Norwegian whalers named it after the *Hercules*, a whale catcher that had visited the bay. This scenic and dramatic location is home to numerous Macaroni Penguins. Light-mantled Sooty Albatross and Southern Giant Petrel nest on the higher ramparts, where the bay's fantastic geology is exposed in striking detail. Visitors normally cruise this area by zodiac as this can produce the best views of Macaroni Penguin in South Georgia, but it is also possible to land just inside the entrance to the bay and climb through the tussac to the breeding area.

King Haakon Bay (54°07'S 37°17'W), on the south coast, is where Shackleton commenced his epic crossing of the island and holds several breeding species, including Wandering Albatross and Blue Petrel.

Around **Stromness Bay** (54°09'S 36°42'W) are several colonies of Gentoo Penguin. Stromness was established as a floating factory in Dec 1907. The building of the land-based station commenced in 1912 and by the following year it was fully operational. The station was finally closed in 1961. The British government undertook a partial clean-up operation of the abandoned stations at Husvik, Grytviken, Stromness and Leith in 1990–1. It is forbidden to approach within 200 m of any of these stations, which have fallen into disrepair and are considered dangerous. It is possible to walk from Stromness through the valley that Shackleton descended, passing elephant and fur seals, a small Gentoo colony, moulting King Penguins and terns.

Within **Cumberland Bay** (54°16'S 36°30'W), the most regularly visited area on the island, lies King Edward Cove, site of the government's Administrative Centre and Research Station, and of the Grytviken Whaling Station and South Georgia Museum. This is also an important area for birds: the surrounding mountains have breeding Wilson's and Black-bellied Storm-petrels, South Georgian Diving-petrel and Snow Petrel, although only the first of these is easy to see, and a dusk visit is essential. Most tourists may, however, with local knowledge see Light-mantled Sooty Albatross, giant petrels (at Greene Peninsula and Harpoon Bay), Kelp Gull, Subantarctic Skua, South Georgian Shag and Antarctic Tern (of the endemic South Georgia subspecies). Brown Pintail is common, but Speckled Teal is now very difficult to see, except in winter. Of course, most visitors will wish to visit Grytviken (54°16'S 36°30'W) for its historical interest. The old whaling station nestling in a corner of Cumberland East Bay (54°13'S 36°28'W) has resident fur and elephant seals in front of the final resting place of Sir Ernest Shackleton, who died aboard the *Quest* while at anchor on 5 Jan 1922.

St Andrew's Bay (54°26'S 36°11'W) is home to the largest King Penguin colony on South Georgia, over 100,000 pairs are estimated to be resident here. In 1911 Norwegian whalers imported Reindeer to the island. Several small herds are still present and can sometimes be seen feeding on tussac in this area. This is a great spot for an early-morning landing but surf can make these difficult.

Royal Bay's (54°32'S 36°00'W) south shore hosts a large

Female Southern Elephant Seal Mirounga leonina *with newborn pup, whilst Subantarctic Skuas* Catharacta [skua] antarctica *subsp.* lonnbergi *scavenge the placenta. Salisbury Plain, South Georgia, Nov 2001. © Hadoram Shirihai.*

Moulting Southern Elephant Seal Mirounga leonina, *Cumberland Bay, South Georgia. © Grant Dixon, South Georgia.*

Bull and cow Southern Elephant Seals Mirounga leonina. *South Georgia is one of the world's major breeding grounds for this species. Oct 2001. © Hadoram Shirihai.*

Pair of Southern Elephant Seal Mirounga leonina *prior to copulation, South Georgia, Jan 2001. © Maria San Román.*

King Penguin colony on a flat beach. Also here are nesting Light-mantled Sooty Albatross, giant petrels, South Georgian Shag, Brown Pintail, and elephant seals. On the south side of the bay there is a small colony of Macaroni Penguin. The area is historically important, it being the site of the first land-based scientific visit to South Georgia, the German International Polar Year Expedition of 1882–3, which established a station of prefabricated buildings, the remains of which can still be seen adjacent to Moltke Harbour.

Eleven men overwintered here, studying aspects of meteorology, geology, geophysics, glaciology, zoology and botany. Aided by good weather, they recorded the transit of Venus and observations were synchronized by the first telegraph system in the Antarctic.

Gold Harbour (54°37'S 35°56'W) on the east side of South Georgia is often referred to as the 'jewel in the island's crown'. Dramatic mountain scenery and the hanging Bertrab Glacier make it a spectacular setting. In addition to the large resident King Penguin colony, elephant and fur seals, Gentoo Penguin and giant petrels can be expected, with perhaps even a Light-mantled Sooty Albatross. Leopard Seal is occasionally seen in this area, preying on the many penguins.

Cooper Bay (54°47'S 35°49'W) is located in Cooper Sound at the southeast tip of South Georgia and consists of three shallow coves. Captain Cook named it for his First Lieutenant, Robert Palliser Cooper. In the southwest corner is a small Chinstrap Penguin colony, among the few such on South Georgia. There are Macaroni Penguin and numerous Gentoo Penguin colonies located within the bay, and South Georgia Pipit is occasionally observed here. A short distance to the south lies Cooper I, which is an SPA and landings are consequently forbidden. South Georgia Pipit also occurs here, as well as at the previous site.

Larsen Harbour (54°50'S 36°00'W), in the southeast of the island offers scenic zodiac cruising and Weddell Seal can be observed at its only South Georgian breeding site, with Crabeater Seal being very occasionally seen here. **Drygalski Fjord** (54°47'S 36°03'W) is another highly picturesque area. A number of the peaks visible in this region have never been subject to the grinding, smoothing effects of glaciers, being dramatic and sharp-peaked.

Sir Ernest Shackleton's grave at Cumberland Bay (near Grytviken), South Georgia. © Hadoram Shirihai.

Checklist of Falkland Islands birds

This checklist, prepared by Robin Woods, includes all 227 species known to have occurred on the Falklands or within the Falkland Islands Designated Area of surface waters surrounding the archipelago. Order and nomenclature follows that used elsewhere in this book (see checklist on pp. 31–34).

The following codes or symbols indicate status:
e = Endemic race
E = Endemic species
B = Breeds in the Falkland Islands
N = Non-breeding regular visitor
V = Irregular vagrant
X = Lost breeding species: not recorded recently
M = Migrates regularly to and from the islands or adjacent waters
? = Status in doubt due to lack of information
* = Introduced species

Order PODICIPEDIFORMES
    Family **Podicipedidae**
V?   Pied-billed Grebe *Podilymbus podiceps*
B   White-tufted Grebe *Rollandia rolland*
V   Great Grebe *Podiceps major*
B   Silvery Grebe *Podiceps occipitalis*
Order SPHENISCIFORMES
    Family **Spheniscidae**
B   King Penguin *Aptenodytes patagonicus*
V   Emperor Penguin *Aptenodytes forsteri*
B   Gentoo Penguin *Pygoscelis papua*
V   Adélie Penguin *Pygoscelis adeliae*
V   Chinstrap Penguin *Pygoscelis antarctica*
BM   Rockhopper Penguin *Eudyptes chrysocome*
V   Snares Penguin *Eudyptes robustus*
V   Erect-crested Penguin *Eudyptes sclateri*
BM   Macaroni Penguin *Eudyptes chrysolophus*
BM   Magellanic Penguin *Spheniscus magellanicus*
Order PROCELLARIIFORMES
    Family **Diomedeidae**
N   Wandering Albatross *Diomedea [exulans] exulans*
N   Southern Royal Albatross *Diomedea [epomophora] epomophora*
V   Northern Royal Albatross *Diomedea (epomophora) sanfordi*
BM   Black-browed Albatross *Thalassarche [melanophrys] melanophrys*
V   White-capped Albatross *Thalassarche [cauta] cauta*
V   Buller's Albatross *Thalassarche [bulleri] bulleri*
N   Grey-headed Albatross *Thalassarche chrysostoma*
V   Atlantic Yellow-nosed Albatross *Thalassarche [chlororhynchos] chlororhynchos*
V   Sooty Albatross *Phoebetria fusca*
N   Light-mantled Sooty Albatross *Phoebetria palpebrata*
    Family **Procellariidae**
BM   Southern Giant Petrel *Macronectes giganteus*
NB?   Northern Giant Petrel *Macronectes halli*
N   Southern Fulmar *Fulmarus glacialoides*
V   Antarctic Petrel *Thalassoica antarctica*
N   Cape Petrel *Daption capense*
N   Snow Petrel *Pagodroma nivea*
V   Great-winged Petrel *Pterodroma [macroptera] macroptera*
V   White-headed Petrel *Pterodroma lessonii*
V   Atlantic Petrel *Pterodroma incerta*
N   Kerguelen Petrel *Pterodroma brevirostris*
V   Herald Petrel *Pterodroma arminjoniana*
V   Soft-plumaged Petrel *Pterodroma mollis*
V   Mottled Petrel *Pterodroma inexpectata*
N   Blue Petrel *Halobaena caerulea*
N   Broad-billed Prion *Pachyptila vittata*
N   Antarctic Prion *Pachyptila desolata*
BM   Slender-billed Prion *Pachyptila belcheri*
BM?   Fairy Prion *Pachyptila turtur*
BM   White-chinned Petrel *Procellaria aequinoctialis*
V   Spectacled Petrel *Procellaria conspicillata*
V   Westland Petrel *Procellaria westlandica*
V   Grey Petrel *Procellaria cinerea*
V   Cory's Shearwater *Calonectris diomedea*
BM   Great Shearwater *Puffinus gravis*
BM   Sooty Shearwater *Puffinus griseus*

V   Manx Shearwater *Puffinus puffinus*
V   Little Shearwater *Puffinus assimilis*
    Family **Hydrobatidae**
V   European Storm-petrel *Hydrobates pelagicus*
BM   Wilson's Storm-petrel *Oceanites oceanicus*
BM   Grey-backed Storm-petrel *Garrodia nereis*
V   White-faced Storm-petrel *Pelagodroma marina*
N   Black-bellied Storm-petrel *Fregetta tropica*
V   White-bellied Storm-petrel *Fregetta grallaria*
V   Leach's Storm-petrel *Oceanodroma leucorhoa*
    Family **Pelecanoididae**
V?   South Georgian Diving-petrel *Pelecanoides georgicus*
BM?e Common Diving-petrel *Pelecanoides urinatrix*
N?   Magellanic Diving-petrel *Pelecanoides magellani*
Order PELECANIFORMES
    Family **Sulidae**
V   Peruvian Booby *Sula variegata*
    Family **Phalacrocoracidae**
V   Neotropic Cormorant *Phalacrocorax olivaceus*
B   Imperial Shag *Phalacrocorax [atriceps] atriceps*
B   Rock Shag *Phalacrocorax magellanicus*
V   Red-legged Shag *Phalacrocorax gaimardi*
Order CICONIIFORMES
    Family **Ardeidae**
V   Cocoi Heron *Ardea cocoi*
V   Great Egret *Ardea alba*
V   Snowy Egret *Ardea thula*
V   Striated Heron *Ardea striatus*
N   Cattle Egret *Bubulcus ibis*
Be   Black-crowned Night-heron *Nycticorax nycticorax*
    Family **Ciconiidae**
V   Maguari Stork *Ciconia maguari*
    Family **Threskiornithidae**
V   Black-faced Ibis *Theristicus melanopsis*
V   Roseate Spoonbill *Ajaia ajaja*
Order PHOENICOPTERIFORMES
    Family **Phoenicopteridae**
V   Chilean Flamingo *Phoenicopterus chilensis*
Order ANSERIFORMES
    Family **Anatidae**
B   Coscoroba Swan *Coscoroba coscoroba*
B   Black-necked Swan *Cygnus melancoryphus*
B*   Feral Domestic Goose *Anser anser*
Be   Upland Goose *Chloephaga picta*
Be   Kelp Goose *Chloephaga hybrida*
BM?   Ashy-headed Goose *Chloephaga poliocephala*
B   Ruddy-headed Goose *Chloephaga rubidiceps*
V   White-faced Whistling Duck *Dendrocygna viduata*
B   Flying Steamer Duck *Tachyeres patachonicus*
BE   Falkland Steamer Duck *Tachyeres brachypterus*
B   Crested Duck *Lophonetta specularioides*
B   Chiloe Wigeon *Anas sibilatrix*
B   Speckled Teal *Anas flavirostris*
V   Spectacled Duck *Anas specularis*
B   Yellow-billed Pintail *Anas georgica spinicauda*
V   White-cheeked Pintail *Anas bahamensis*
B   Silver Teal *Anas versicolor*
B   Cinnamon Teal *Anas cyanoptera*
V   Red Shoveler *Anas platalea*
V   Rosy-billed Pochard *Netta peposaca*
V   Black-headed Duck *Heteronetta atricapilla*
V   Lake Duck *Oxyura vittata*
Order CATHARTIFORMES
    Family **Cathartidae**
B   Turkey Vulture *Cathartes aura*
Order ACCIPITRIFORMES
    Family **Accipitridae**
V   Long-winged Harrier *Circus buffoni*
X?V   Cinereous Harrier *Circus cinereus*
V   Sharp-shinned Hawk *Accipiter striatus*
B   Red-backed Hawk *Buteo polyosoma*
Order FALCONIFORMES
    Family **Falconidae**
B   Southern (Crested) Caracara *Caracara plancus*
B   Striated Caracara *Phalcoboenus australis*

V	Chimango Caracara *Milvago chimango*
V/B?	American Kestrel *Falco sparverius*
V	Aplomado Falcon *Falco femoralis*
B	Peregrine Falcon *Falco peregrinus*

Order GRUIFORMES
    Family **Rallidae**

V	Austral Rail *Rallus antarcticus*
V	Speckled Rail *Coturnicops notatus*
V	Plumbeous Rail *Pardirallus sanguinolentus*
V	Purple Gallinule *Porphyrio martinica*
V	White-winged Coot *Fulica leucoptera*
V	Red-gartered Coot *Fulica armillata*
V	Red-fronted Coot *Fulica rufifrons*

Order CHARADRIIFORMES
    Family **Chionididae**

N	Pale-faced Sheathbill *Chionis alba*

    Family **Haematopodidae**

B	Magellanic Oystercatcher *Haematopus leucopodus*
B	Blackish Oystercatcher *Haematopus ater*

    Family **Recurvirostridae**

V	Black-winged Stilt *Himantopus himantopus melanurus*
V	Black-necked Stilt *Himantopus himantopus mexicanus*

    Family **Charadriidae**

V	American Golden Plover *Pluvialis dominica*
B	Two-banded Plover *Charadrius falklandicus*
BM?	Rufous-chested Dotterel *Charadrius modestus*
V	Tawny-throated Dotterel *Eudromias (Oreopholus) ruficollis*
V	Magellanic Plover *Pluvianellus socialis*
V	Southern Lapwing *Vanellus chilensis*

    Family **Scolopacidae**

BM?	Magellanic Snipe *Gallinago paraguaiae magellanica*
B?	Fuegian Snipe *Gallinago stricklandii*
V	Hudsonian Godwit *Limosa haemastica*
V	Eskimo Curlew *Numenius borealis*
N	Whimbrel *Numenius phaeopus hudsonicus*
V	Greater Yellowlegs *Tringa melanoleuca*
V	Lesser Yellowlegs *Tringa flavipes*
V	Ruddy Turnstone *Arenaria interpres*
V	Red Knot *Calidris canutus*
N	Sanderling *Calidris alba*
V	Semipalmated Sandpiper *Calidris pusilla*
N	White-rumped Sandpiper *Calidris fuscicollis*
N	Baird's Sandpiper *Calidris bairdii*
V	Pectoral Sandpiper *Calidris melanotos*
V	Stilt Sandpiper *Micropalama himantopus*
V	Upland Sandpiper *Bartramia longicauda*
V	Surfbird *Aphriza virgata*
V	Grey Phalarope *Phalaropus fulicaria*
V	Wilson's Phalarope *Phalaropus tricolor*

    Family **Thinocoridae**

X?V	White-bellied Seedsnipe *Attagis malouinus*
B?	Least Seedsnipe *Thinocorus rumicivorus*

    Family **Stercorariidae**

BM	Falkland Skua *Catharacta antarctica antarctica*
NB?	Chilean Skua *Catharacta chilensis*
N?	South Polar Skua *Catharacta maccormicki*
V	Arctic Jaeger *Stercorarius parasiticus*
V	Long-tailed Jaeger *Stercorarius longicaudus*

    Family **Laridae**

B	Dolphin Gull *Larus scoresbii*
B	Kelp Gull *Larus dominicanus*
V	Band-tailed Gull *Larus belcheri*
V	Grey Gull *Larus modestus*
V	Grey-headed Gull *Larus cirrocephalus*
B	Brown-hooded Gull *Larus maculipennis*
V	Franklin's Gull *Larus pipixcan*

    Family **Sternidae**

V	Elegant Tern *Sterna elegans*
V	Sandwich Tern *Sterna sandvicensis*
V	Common Tern *Sterna hirundo*
N	Arctic Tern *Sterna paradisea*
N?	Antarctic Tern *Sterna vittata*
BM	South American Tern *Sterna hirundinacea*
V	Trudeau's Tern *Sterna trudeaui*
V	Sooty Tern *Sterna fuscata*
V	Black Noddy *Anous minutus*

Order COLUMBIFORMES
    Family **Columbidae**

V	Chilean Pigeon *Columba araucana*
V	Eared Dove *Zenaida auriculata*
V	Ruddy Ground-dove *Columbina talpacoti*
V	Blue Ground-dove *Claravis pretiosa*

Order PSITTACIFORMES
    Family **Psittacidae**

V	Burrowing Parrot *Cyanoliseus patagonus*
V	Austral Parakeet *Enicognathus ferrugineus*

Order CUCULIFORMES
    Family **Cuculidae**

V	Dark-billed Cuckoo *Coccyzus melacoryphus*
V	Yellow-billed Cuckoo *Coccyzus americanus*

Order STRIGIFORMES
    Family **Tytonidae**

B	Barn Owl *Tyto alba*

    Family **Strigidae**

V	Magellanic Horned Owl *Bubo magellanicus*
V	Burrowing Owl *Athene cunicularia*
Be	Short-eared Owl *Asio flammeus*

Order CAPRIMULGIFORMES
    Family **Caprimulgidae**

V	Band-winged Nightjar *Caprimulgus longirostris*

Order APODIFORMES
    Family **Apodidae**

V	White-collared Swift *Streptoprocne zonaris*
V	Ashy-tailed Swift *Chaetura andrei*

    Family **Trochilidae**

V	Green-backed Firecrown *Sephanoides sephaniodes*

Order PASSERIFORMES
    Family **Furnariidae**

Be	Blackish Cinclodes *Cinclodes antarcticus*
V	Bar-winged Cinclodes *Cinclodes fuscus*
X?	Thorn-tailed Rayadito *Aphrastura spinicauda*

    Family **Rhinocryptidae**

X?	Magellanic Tapaculo *Scytalopus magellanicus*

    Family **Phytotomidae**

V	Rufous-tailed Plantcutter *Phytotoma rara*

    Family **Tyrannidae**

V	White-crested Elaenia *Elaenia albiceps*
V	Tufted Tit-tyrant *Anairetes parulus*
V	Fire-eyed Diucon *Pyrope pyrope*
V	Black-billed Shrike-tyrant *Agriornis montana*
V	White-browed Ground-tyrant *Muscisaxicola albilora*
Be	Dark-faced Ground-tyrant *Muscisaxicola macloviana*
V	Cattle Tyrant *Machetornis rixosus*
V	Austral Negrito *Lessonia rufa*
V	Great Kiskadee *Pitangus sulphuratus*
V	Eastern Kingbird *Tyrannus tyrannus*
V	Fork-tailed Flycatcher *Tyrannus savana*

    Family **Motacillidae**

BM?e	Correndera Pipit *Anthus correndera*

    Family **Ploceidae**

B*	House Sparrow *Passer domesticus*

    Family **Fringillidae**

B	Black-chinned Siskin *Carduelis barbata*

    Family **Emberizidae**

V	Mourning Sierra-finch *Phrygilus fruticeti*
V	Patagonian Sierra-finch *Phrygilus patagonicus*
Be	Black-throated (Canary-winged) Finch *Melanodera melanodera*
X?	Yellow-bridled Finch *Melanodera xanthogramma*
V	Rufous-collared Sparrow *Zonotrichia capensis*
V	Patagonian Yellow Finch *Sicalis lebruni*

    Family **Mimidae**

V	Patagonian Mockingbird *Mimus patagonicus*

    Family **Troglodytidae**

Be	Grass Wren *Cistothorus platensis*
BE	Cobb's Wren *Troglodytes cobbi*

    Family **Hirundinidae**

V	Brown-chested Martin *Progne tapera*
V	Southern Martin *Progne modesta*
V	Purple Martin *Progne subis*
V	Grey-breasted Martin *Progne chalybea*
V	White-rumped Swallow *Tachycineta leucorrhoa*
B/N	Chilean Swallow *Tachycineta leucopyga*
V	Blue-and-white Swallow *Notiochelidon cyanoleuca*
V	Sand Martin *Riparia riparia*
V	Southern Rough-winged Swallow *Stelgidopteryx ruficollis*
V	Tawny-headed Swallow *Alopochelidon fucata*
V	Cliff Swallow *Petrochelidon pyrrhonota*
V	Barn Swallow *Hirundo rustica*

    Family **Muscicapidae**

V	Wood Thrush *Hylocichla mustelina*
Be	Austral Thrush *Turdus falcklandii*

    Family **Icteridae**

Be	Long-tailed Meadowlark *Sturnella loyca falklandica*
V	Shiny Cowbird *Molothrus bonariensis*

Table 1. Breeding bird and mammal checklist for the subantarctic islands off South America.

	Falklands	Shag Rocks	South Georgia
Grebes			
White-tufted Grebe *Rollandia rolland*	X		
Silvery Grebe *Podiceps occipitalis*	X		
Penguins			
King Penguin *Aptenodytes patagonicus*	X		X
Gentoo Penguin *Pygoscelis papua*	X		X
Adélie Penguin *P. adeliae*			X
Chinstrap Penguin *P. antarctica*			X
Rockhopper Penguin *Eudyptes chrysocome*	X		X
Macaroni Penguin *E. chrysolophus*	X		X
Magellanic Penguin *Spheniscus magellanicus*	X		
Albatrosses			
Wandering Albatross *Diomedea [exulans] exulans*			X
Black-browed Albatross *Thalassarche [melanophrys] melanophrys*	X		X
Grey-headed Albatross *T. chrysostoma*			X
Light-mantled Sooty Albatross *Phoebetria palpebrata*			X
Petrels and prions			
Southern Giant Petrel *Macronectes giganteus*	X		X
Northern Giant Petrel *M. halli*			X
Cape Petrel *Daption capense*			X
Snow Petrel *Pagodroma nivea*			X
Blue Petrel *Halobaena caerulea*			X
Antarctic Prion *Pachyptila desolata*			X
Slender-billed Prion *P. belcheri*	X		
Fairy Prion *P. turtur*	X		X
White-chinned Petrel *Procellaria aequinoctialis*			X
Shearwaters			
Great Shearwater *Puffinus gravis*	X		
Sooty Shearwater *P. griseus*	X		
Storm-petrels			
Wilson's Storm-petrel *Oceanites oceanicus*	X		X
Grey-backed Storm-petrel *O. nereis*	X		X
Black-bellied Storm-petrel *Fregetta tropica*	X		X
Diving-petrels			
South Georgian Diving-petrel *Pelecanoides georgianus*			X
Common Diving-petrel *P. urinatrix*	X		X
Shags			
Imperial Shag *Phalacrocorax [atriceps] albiventer*	X		
South Georgian Shag *P. [a.] georgianus*		X	X
Rock Shag *P. magellanicus*	X		
Herons			
Black-crowned Night-heron *Nycticorax nycticorax*	X		
Swans, geese and ducks			
Black-necked Swan *Cygnus melanocoryphus*	X		
Coscoroba Swan *Coscoroba coscoroba*	X		
Upland Goose *Chloephaga picta*	X		
Kelp Goose *C. hybrida*	X		
Ashy-headed Goose *C. poliocephala*	X		
Ruddy-headed Goose *C. rubidiceps*	X		
Flying Steamer Duck *Tachyeres patachonicus*	X		
Falkland Steamer Duck *T. brachydactyla*	X		
Crested Duck *Lophonetta specularioides*	X		
Chiloe Wigeon *Anas sibilatrix*	X		
Speckled Teal *A. flavirostris*	X		X
Yellow-billed Pintail *A. georgica* (*A. g. spinicauda* in the Falklands and nominate *georgica* on South Georgia)	X		X

	Falklands	Shag Rocks	South Georgia
Silver Teal *A. versicolor*	X		
Cinnamon Teal *A. cyanoptera*	X		
Red Shoveler *A. platalea* (unconfirmed)	X		
New World Vultures			
Turkey Vulture *Cathartes aura*	X		
Hawks and Falcons			
Red-backed Hawk *Buteo polyosoma*	X		
Striated Caracara *Phalcoboenus australis*	X		
Southern (Crested) Caracara *Caracara plancus*	X		
Peregrine Falcon *Falco peregrinus*	X		
Sheathbills			
Pale-faced Sheathbill *Chionis alba*			X
Shorebirds			
Magellanic Oystercatcher *Haematopus leucopodus*	X		
Blackish Oystercatcher *H. ater*	X		
Two-banded Plover *Charadrius falklandicus*	X		
Rufous-chested Dotterel *C. modestus*	X		
Magellanic Snipe *Gallinago magellanica*	X		
Fuegian Snipe *G. stricklandii*	X?		
Skuas			
Falkland Skua *Catharacta antarctica antarctica*	X		
Subantarctic Skua *C. a. lonnbergi*			X
Gulls and terns			
Dolphin Gull *Larus scoresbii*	X		
Kelp Gull *L. dominicanus*	X		X
Brown-hooded Gull *L. maculipennis*	X		
South American Tern *Sterna hirundacea*	X		
Antarctic Tern *S. vittata*			X
Owls			
Barn Owl *Tyto alba*	X		
Short-eared Owl *Asio flammeus*	X		
Ovenbirds			
Blackish Cinclodes *Cinclodes antarcticus antarcticus*	X		
Tyrant-flycatchers			
Dark-faced ground-tyrant *Muscisaxicola macloviana macloviana*	X		
Pipits			
Correndera Pipit *Anthus correndera grayi*	X		
South Georgia Pipit *A. antarcticus*			X
Old World Sparrows			
House Sparrow *Passer domesticus*	X		
Finches			
Black-throated Finch *Melanodera melanodera melanodera*	X		
Black-chinned Siskin *Carduelis barbata*	X		
Rufous-collared Sparrow *Zonotrichia capensis*	X (unconfirmed)		
Wrens			
Grass Wren *Cistothorus platensis falklandicus*	X		
Cobb's Wren *Troglodytes cobbi*	X		
Hirundines			
Chilean Swallow *Tachycineta leucopyga*	X		
Thrushes			
Austral Thrush *Turdus falcklandii falcklandii*	X		
New World Blackbirds			
Long-tailed Meadowlark *Sturnella loyca falklandica*	X		
Seals			
South American Fur Seal *Arctocephalus australis*	X		
Antarctic Fur Seal *A. gazella*			X
South American Sea Lion *Otaria flavescens*	X		
Weddell Seal *Leptonychotes weddelli*			X
Southern Elephant Seal *Mirounga leonina*	X		X

South Shetland Islands, Antarctic Peninsula and the Weddell Sea

These areas comprise two of the most visited parts of Antarctica and one of its least known areas. While the number of tourist ships that explore the South Shetlands and Antarctic Peninsula each summer has grown almost exponentially within the last decade, few penetrate further than the extreme northwest part of the Weddell Sea, which is a barren and inhospitable region for wildlife and humans alike. The South Orkneys and South Sandwiches are UK-controlled, but comparatively little visited except by researchers; they too are extremely rich in breeding seabirds and other wildlife, and in general climate, geology and landform are rather similar to the South Shetlands. While the Peninsula constitutes the warmest and certainly most accessible part of the Antarctic continent, it nonetheless boasts a harsh climate. Virtually the only plants that can survive the rigours of the winter are a grass and a pink, and moss and lichens constitute the bulk of the vegetational communities. Despite this the South Shetlands and Peninsula offer among the visually most exciting wildlife spectacles on Earth, with huge numbers of most of the relatively small number of bird species that breed within the Antarctic Circle. The voyage from South America, departing either Ushuaia in Argentina or Punta Arenas in Chile, across the Drake Passage, also provides the opportunity to see almost innumerable whales and an exciting diversity and number of seabirds, especially tubenoses (see Gateways to the Antarctic), making a visit to this region essential (at least once in a lifetime) for the keen birder and those with a general interest in natural history alike.

South Shetland Islands and Antarctic Peninsula

Location and main features The northernmost tip of the Antarctic Peninsula is located 800 km south of South America at Cape Dubouzet (63°16'S 64°00'W) and the Peninsula lies on a north-east–southwest axis, with its southern extent being the northern part of Marguerite Bay (68°18'S 67°11'W). Offshore are a number of islands, the principal ones being the South Shetlands (63°00'S 60°00'W) and related Elephant I (61°30'S 55°00'W); the former group is separated from the Peninsula by the 160 km-wide Bransfield Strait and consists of 11 major islands and many smaller rocks, scattered across 539 km north to south. The South Shetlands often provide visitors with their first glimpse of the true Antarctic. The northern portion of the Peninsula is known as Graham Land, and the southern part as Palmer Land. The Peninsula is the most frequently visited part of Antarctica by tourists, due to its relative ease of accessibility from the southernmost port in South America, Ushuaia (Argentina), and its spectacular concentrations of wildlife, particularly penguins and seals. In addition, many seabirds and whales can be observed during the (weather dependent) 2–3-day crossing of the Drake Passage, which separates Cape Horn from the South Shetlands (see Gateways to the Antarctic).

Landform, climate and habitat The Antarctic Peninsula separates the continent's two great bays, the Weddell and Ross Seas, each of which possess large ice shelves, the Ronne Ice Shelf and the Ross Ice Shelf. During the breakup of the super-continent Gondwana, the Antarctic Peninsula and South Shetlands region

Massive geological structures and several huge volcanic craters characterize the South Shetlands. © Hans Reinhard.

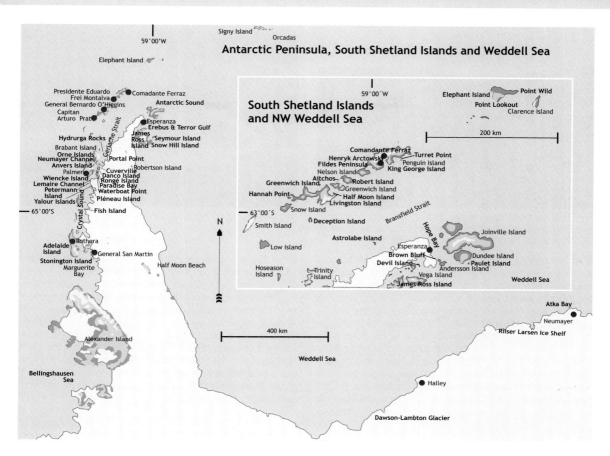

Antarctic Peninsula, South Shetland Islands and Weddell Sea

South Shetland Islands and NW Weddell Sea

remained abutted to southern South America until c.40 million years ago. Continued continental drift gradually separated these regions and formed the Drake Passage. The Peninsula, which is also known as the 'Banana Belt' because of its milder and wetter climate than the rest of the continent, in consequence supports a much wider range of wildlife than most areas of Antarctica, as well as a vista of endless icebergs, ice-clad mountains and still-active volcanoes. For many, the Peninsula epitomises Antarctica, despite its differences from much of the rest of the region. Summer temperatures rarely fall below freezing, though wet, 60-kph

Breaching Humpback Whale Megaptera novaeangliae. *Antarctic Peninsula, Feb 2002. © Morten Jørgensen.*

winds can spring up virtually unnoticed within minutes, causing rapid changes in temperature and conditions.

The South Shetlands are a mountainous group, the highest peak being at 2105 m on Smith I, mostly of volcanic origin with coastlines varying from high sheer ice cliffs to broad beach terraces. Deep fjords, ice fields and glaciers characterize their terrain, which is similar to that of the Peninsula. Some islands have small freshwater lakes and Deception I, where volcanic activity was detected as recently as 1970, has many hot springs, fumaroles and steaming beaches. The largest of the group are King George and Livingston, which are both c.75 km long and up to 25 km wide, and the total land area of the group is 4700 km². They possess a climate typical of the maritime Antarctic with mean annual temperatures reaching just -3°C, and extremes of 15°C (summer) and -30°C (winter). Rainfall is high and snow and frosts can occur year-round; the islands are surrounded by dense pack ice in winter. Mean daily sunshine is usually low, with fog commonly present and strong westerly winds a dominant feature.

The Peninsula and the South Shetlands are not well known for their flora, but there are two flowering plants in the region, a grass Deschampsia antarctica and the cushion-forming pearlwort Colobanthus quitensis. Both grow patchily in more sheltered areas. In mid- to late summer blooms of unicellular snow algae, which are either red, green or occasionally yellow are particularly noticeable in some parts of the Peninsula. The principal vegetational components of the region are lichen, of which more than 150 species are known, and mosses (50 species). There are three major lichen forms in this part of Antarctica: *Xanthoria* and *Caloplaca* spp. are the brightly coloured (orange, yellow and green) forms commonly

The South Shetlands, being located north of the Peninsula, are more extensively vegetated, such as the large green moss bed depicted here. South Shetland Is, Feb 2002. © Morten Jørgensen.

King George I, South Shetland Is. © Frank S. Todd.

found on exposed coastal rocks, while *Usnea* spp. are fruticose lichens that are rather stringy in their appearance and occur from sea level to high elevations, and foliose lichens which are leaf-like and possess distinct lobes. A number of mosses and liverworts are restricted to areas with geothermal activity on Deception I.

Birds There are large colonies of several species of penguin, but the only Emperor Penguin colony in this region, which is the smallest known of this species and numbered just 85 pairs in 1978, on the Dion Is, is off-limits to visitors. However, huge numbers of Adélie Penguins breed, 685,000 pairs were estimated in the Peninsula and Scotia Sea in the 1980s, with almost 124,000 pairs at Hope Bay in 1985. A number of Peninsula colonies have declined during the past decade or so, with some authorities suggesting that this may be due, at least in part, to global warming with a resultant loss of annual sea ice and possibly increased snow. (However, local increases have been detected for several breeding species in the Peninsula and South Shetlands since the date of the most recent cross-region count available for the area; these are not necessarily mentioned here.) Loss of sea ice does not benefit Adélie, but favours Chinstrap Penguin, of which numbers are even more enormous, with almost 160 colonies known, principally in the northern half of the Peninsula and the South Shetlands. The largest colonies are virtually all in the latter archipelago, where 938,000 pairs were estimated in the mid- to late 1980s (localized indices of abundance available from more recent years, e.g. 89,685 pairs at Harmony Point, Nelson I, in 1995–6, suggest some recent decrease in overall numbers), with 115,000 pairs in the Peninsula. Almost 70 colonies of Gentoo Penguin are known in the two areas, with 20,000 pairs in the Peninsula and 17,200 pairs on the South Shetlands: this area marks the southernmost extent of its breeding range. One certain breeding site, with just one pair in 1985, for Macaroni Penguin is known in the Peninsula, at Humble I, off Anvers I. The South Shetlands boast eight colonies of this species, with a total population of c.14,000 pairs based on counts in the 1970s and 1980s.

Tubenoses are represented by the following breeders: Southern Giant (7310 pairs in 1984, the vast majority on the South Shetlands), Cape (55,000–65,000 pairs, almost all on Elephant I) and Snow Petrels (small numbers on the offshore islands and 1000–10,000 pairs on the Peninsula), Southern Fulmar (100–1000 pairs in the Peninsula with unknown numbers in the rest of the South Shetlands, but 71,000 pairs on Elephant I), Antarctic Prion (1000–10,000 pairs) and Wilson's Storm-petrel (perhaps several million pairs, with large numbers breeding throughout the Peninsula and South Shetlands, and recent survey work in some areas finding

larger than suspected colonies), with Black-bellied Storm-petrel restricted, in this region, to the South Shetlands where reasonably common (c.21,000 pairs on Elephant I alone). Antarctic Petrel plausibly breeds on Adelaide I, but this requires confirmation; large numbers are often seen in the Bellingshausen Sea west of Adelaide. Antarctic Shag is also a common nesting bird throughout, with at least 10,000 pairs in 56 colonies in the Peninsula, 205 pairs on Elephant I and 700 pairs in 21 colonies in the South Shetlands; with the exception of the various penguins, this species is the most common, obvious bird in this part of the continent, though there is evidence for 6–9% per annum decreases from several sites during the last decade.

Among shoreline scavengers, Pale-faced Sheathbill is found at many sites, but generally in small numbers: 200 pairs nest at 17 sites in the Peninsula, with 650 pairs at 26 sites in the rest of the South Shetlands and, most significantly, c.1450 pairs on Elephant I at 152 sites. There is a significant population of South Polar Skua scattered through the Peninsula, where c.650 pairs are known (mainly on the southern half of the west side, and on the east side), with c.100–150 in the South Shetlands, being outnumbered in the latter by the 420 pairs of Subantarctic Skua. A further 150 pairs of the latter species are found in the Peninsula and 190 pairs on Elephant I. Several thousand pairs of Kelp Gull breed in the region (2100 pairs in the South Shetlands and unknown numbers in the Peninsula), which is of much greater importance for Antarctic Tern; the majority of the world's total population of c.50,000 pairs breeds here, with 35,000 pairs (including 9000 on Livingston I) on the South Shetlands alone.

Black-browed and Grey-headed Albatrosses regularly reach 64°S in this region and Northern Giant Petrel is occasionally noted off Anvers I. King and Rockhopper Penguins are considered vagrants to the Peninsula and accidental on the South Shetlands, with one record of Magellanic Penguin from King George I. There have been records of Chiloe Wigeon and Brown Pintail from both areas and a Black-necked Swan on Adelaide I, in January 1996 (with others at Palmer Station, Marguerite Bay and elsewhere in 1998–9). Leach's Storm-petrel was recently recorded at King George I. Large numbers of Arctic Tern are occasionally seen this far south, e.g. c.7600 migrated past Horseshoe I, on 7–9 Mar 1989. Landbird vagrants rarely stray so far south, but have included several dead individuals of Cattle Egret since the mid-1980s, a Least Seedsnipe on Nelson I, in Dec 1996, two ship-assisted Barn Swallows in Nov 1993 and an Austral Negrito landed on a ship during a blizzard off Adelaide I in Nov 1999. Other vagrant shorebirds have included Upland (Deception I), White-rumped (on several of the

Ice-covered peak in the Antarctic Peninsula. © Hans Reinhard.

of plastic banding from ships at sea may lead to the entrapment of seals, notably fur seals, which become entangled in these bands, resulting in severe lesions and often death. Human disturbance and associated habitat destruction, e.g. in the development of research stations, has undoubtedly led to local depletions in the numbers of some species, particularly shyer birds such as giant petrels. Even numbers of penguins, which to the casual eye may appear to be unaffected by human intrusion into their wilderness, may diminish in time around areas that are regularly used or visited by humans (though numbers of Gentoo Penguins have increased or remained stable at some such sites). No introduced predators have yet reached the Peninsula or South Shetlands, but increased human visits to seabird colonies will inevitably favour natural predators of chicks and eggs, such as sheathbills and skuas, which also locally benefit from rubbish around human bases, though all stations must abide by the Environmental Protocol and therefore no garbage should be exposed at any station. Heavy metal residues and organochlorine compounds have been increasingly reported in Antarctic birds and their eggs, especially

Gentoo Penguin Pygoscelis papua *in typical Antarctic Peninsula landscape. © Hans Reinhard.*

South Shetlands) and Pectoral Sandpipers (Rothera Point), and Wilson's (at Alexander I, the southernmost record of any shorebird) and Grey Phalaropes. Pomarine Jaeger has wandered as far south as Marguerite Bay on several occasions. One of the most remarkable occurrences in these waters must be the single Lake Duck recorded at Deception I, in 1916–7.

En route to the Peninsula from the Falklands or direct from Ushuaia, in southernmost Argentina, your cruise ship will pass through the Drake Passage. This is a superb region for seabird observations. A multitude of species is possible including Wandering (as well as smaller numbers of Gibson's and rarely Antipodean), Southern Royal (occasionally Northern Royal), Black-browed, Grey-headed and Light-mantled Sooty Albatrosses, Southern and Northern Giant Petrels, Southern Fulmar, Cape and Soft-plumaged Petrels, Antarctic, Broad-billed and Slender-billed Prions, Sooty Shearwater, Wilson's and Black-bellied Storm-petrels. Given calm conditions, which are unfortunately quite rare in these seas, large numbers of birds may be seen on the water.

Marine mammals The most obvious are, as almost throughout the region covered by this book, the seals. Five species occur: Antarctic Fur and Southern Elephant Seals are both relatively ubiquitous in this area, but Weddell Seal is also frequently seen on many beaches and there are several areas where Crabeater Seal can be encountered. Leopard Seal is one of the least frequent of the seals found in the Peninsula, but there are several known sites. Ross Seal is rare in dense pack ice in the S Peninsula region. The first four species are all reasonably common in the South Shetlands. During the Antarctic summer this region and the Drake Passage are also fantastic and challenging areas for those who thrill to cetaceans. The following are all possible: Sei, Fin, Humpback, Sperm, Southern Bottlenose and Killer Whales, and Gray's Beaked and Cuvier's Beaked Whales.

Main conservation issues While existing fisheries appear to pose few threats to seabirds, the Antarctic Krill *Euphausia superba* industry in the S Scotia Sea appears likely to offer a much longer term and more significant threat to many species, especially Chinstrap, Adélie and Macaroni Penguins and Antarctic Prions, which rely heavily on krill. It has been estimated that birds take 10–12 million tonnes annually. The increasing numbers of cruise ships using some anchorages, and fishing activities, are undoubtedly bringing greater general pollution in the form of litter and vessels cleaning their engines, which may affect breeding penguins, shags and perhaps terns in nearby areas. The discarding

Argentine base below a thick glacier, Antarctic Peninsula, Jan 1997. © Daisy Gilardini.

439

During summer, partially open sea-ice makes several key areas around the Antarctic Peninsula (including the northwest Weddell Sea) accessible for observing ice formation and many types and stages of icebergs. Left © Gordon Petersen; right © Daisy Gilardini.

among those that move further north during the non-breeding season, but recent trend data is unavailable. The development of the Antarctic Treaty in 1961 has permitted the growth of biological research in the entire region south of 60°S and the development of a protected areas system, as well as providing guidelines for the sustainable development of the continent, including restrictions on tourist numbers and waste disposal. A total of six Specially Protected Areas (SPAs) and 20 Sites of Special Scientific Interest (SSSIs, 15 terrestrial and five marine) had been designated by the end of the 20th century; these are now categorized within the Antarctic Specially Protected Areas (ASPAs) scheme, each with its own management plan. More are clearly required, as are additional controls on disturbance and predator control around several important bird colonies.

Oil pollution is, as yet, a rarely reported problem, and the establishment of the Antarctic Treaty placed interest in Antarctic oil reserves in abeyance until the mid-20th century. Nonetheless, it is possible that the long-term future may hold a disaster to rival some of these reported in the Northern Hemisphere in recent decades. In Jan 1989 an Argentina navy supply ship, the *Bahía Paraíso*, ran aground on a submerged reef near Anvers I. A total of 645,000 litres of diesel fuel was spilt, causing apparently significant losses among Adélie Penguins, and total failure of Antarctic Shag and South Polar Skua breeding colonies. While local populations of most species have now rebounded, that of Antarctic Shag appears to have been affected long term.

Human history Both British and US sealers were already operating in the waters south of Cape Horn when, in Feb 1819, William Smith discovered the South Shetlands. These islands swiftly became the focus of sealing operations in the 1820s and, in 1829, were also the first islands in the Antarctic to be visited by a scientist. The next year, Bransfield, who had been despatched by the British Admiralty to survey the South Shetlands, Palmer, a sealer from Connecticut and the Estonian Baron Bellinghausen, all set eyes on the Antarctic Peninsula. Only the latter conducted extensive explorations in the region, also discovering Peter I Øy and mapping considerable areas of coast, though he remarkably failed to find land until after crossing the Antarctic Circle. No significant progress in exploratory terms was made in this region of the continent until Biscoe's 1830–3 voyage, which found what is probably modern-day Anvers I and stretches of Graham Land (named for the then First Lord of the Admiralty), and Dumont d'Urville's expedition of 1838, which though failing in its stated aim to find the South Magnetic Pole made a number of interesting discoveries,

including Louis Philippe Land and Joinville I off the Peninsula. He was swiftly followed by an American, Charles Wilkes, who successfully followed the Antarctic coast for 2000 km, despite the loss of a ship off Chile and almost running his flagship aground on Elephant I. Quite remarkably, petty jealousies among his junior officers led not to a hero's welcome but to an eventually quashed court martial!

The mid-years of the 19th century witnessed a hiatus in the push south, but this was reinvigorated first by a Norwegian expedition, led by Larsen, which explored both coasts of the northern Peninsula and became the first Antarctic survey to deploy skis, and then by the Belgian, de Gerlache, who in Dec 1897 commenced an extensive survey of the west coast of the Peninsula, discovering and naming many of the modern tourist landing sites, including the strait that now bears his name. This expedition became the first to winter within the Antarctic Circle, though it apparently brought many of its members to near insanity and the crew was also forced to battle the ever-constant risk of scurvy; de Gerlache's ship, *Belgica*, only regained Punta Arenas, in Chile, in Mar 1899. The expedition brought back important lessons concerning survival in the Antarctic winter climate, including that of establishing food and supply depots. It was followed by a Swedish party, including Larsen and led by Nordenskjöld, which made a number of important geographical discoveries on the west side of the Peninsula in early 1902. Upon attempting to penetrate the Weddell Sea and being rebuffed by thick pack ice, six men wintered in a prefabricated hut on Snow Hill I, while their ship, *Antarctic*, went north to the Falklands and South Georgia. The adventurers made further fossil discoveries, bolstering Larsen's earlier discoveries, on Seymour I, but by Dec 1902 were becoming increasingly concerned about the fate of their ship, which had failed to return. The fate of the *Antarctic* and the subsequent tale of survival against the odds are among the earliest stories of remarkable human bravery in Antarctica. The *Antarctic* had been crushed and sunk in pack ice near Paulet I to which its crew had managed to sledge and establish a camp. A three-man party headed for Snow Hill I across the ice and miraculously met Nordenskjöld in so doing. Meanwhile search parties had been despatched from Argentina, France and Sweden. The first of these rescued the entire expedition (with the exception of one man who had died on Paulet) by Nov 1903.

Such tales of heroism and endurance did little to damper expeditionary ardour, and although interest in Antarctica was switching to the opposite side of the continent and 'the race for the pole', others continued the geographical exploration of the Peninsula. A

French physician, Charcot, who had inherited a fortune and decided to mount an expedition heard of Nordenskjöld's disappearance in the Weddell Sea area and elected to head south to assist in the rescue attempts. His plans did not change upon reaching Argentina, where he was informed that the Swedish party had been rescued, and on this and a subsequent expedition four years later he spent long periods exploring the western part of the Peninsula and its offshore islands. Remarkably both expeditions were beset by mishaps, in which his ships hit rocks and, during the earlier voyage, were forced to return to South America. Charcot undertook two voluntary winters in Antarctica, at Booth I and the other on Petermann I, and reached as far south as Marguerite Bay, named for his second wife, during the 1910 voyage. His most treasured discovery, a new landmass that he named Charcot Land, for his father, disappointingly proved to be a small island.

Following the conquest of the Pole and the end of the First World War, interest in other areas of Antarctica renewed (see The History of Antarctic Exploration). The first flights over Antarctica, by Wilkins in 1928 and Ellsworth in 1935, commenced in the South Shetlands. The modern age has seen the establishment of 16 year-round stations in this region of Antarctica, nine of these on King George I, with 11 different countries involved in the research: Argentina (three bases), Brazil (one), Chile (four), China, Poland, Russia, South Korea, Uruguay, the USA, UK and Ukraine (all single bases).

Visiting the area Most cruise ships spend 3–7 days exploring the Peninsula and its offshore islands, and during an average-length visit to the area it may be possible to briefly explore approximately ten or more of the areas mentioned here. In addition to those sites detailed below, **Antarctic Sound** (63°30'S 56°30'W), **Gerlache Strait** (64°16'S 61°34'W), **Neumayer Channel** (64°47'S 63°30'W), **Lemaire Channel** (65°06'S 64°00'W) and **Crystal Sound** (66°22'S 66°41'W) are all of magnificent scenic interest, often containing many icebergs and with good possibilities for whale sightings. The principal sites of interest to the visitor landing on the South Shetlands and Peninsula are as follows.

Turret Point (62°05'S 57°55'W), on **King George I** and nearby Penguin I, harbour Chinstrap (8120 pairs in 1980) and Adélie Penguins (c.1000 pairs in 1997), Southern Giant Petrel (including a very high percentage of white-morph birds compared to other locations in this region), Antarctic Shag, Wilson's Storm-petrel (probable breeder), Kelp Gull, skuas and Antarctic Tern, with Southern Elephant, Weddell and Antarctic Fur Seals also present. The latter increase as summer progresses. There is also significant

botanical interest, including both flowering plants, cushion mosses and lichens, on these islands, and King George is peppered with research bases, with five of these around Maxwell Bay in the south of the island alone. Two stations of interest, both in Admiralty Bay, are the visitor-welcoming **Arctowski** (Poland, 62°09'S 58°28'W) on the easily walked **Half Moon Beach** (69°29'S 60°47'W), which is close to a SSSI and has a Southern Elephant Seal moulting 'wallow' in late summer, and Brazil's **Ferraz** (62°05'S 58°23'W) located in Martel Inlet, where Antarctic Terns nest close to a reconstructed whale skeleton and there are extensive moss beds. The **Fildes Peninsula** (62°13'S 58°54'W), at the southern end of King George I, is a SSSI, with populations of nine breeding species (numbers in brackets refer to counts in 1995–6): Cape Petrel (1500 pairs), Southern Giant Petrel (115 pairs), Wilson's (2000–3000 pairs) and Black-bellied Storm-petrels (30 pairs), Pale-faced Sheathbill (four pairs), Subantarctic and South Polar Skuas (total of 150 pairs), Kelp Gull (136 pairs) and Antarctic Tern (500 pairs).

The **Aitchos** (62°24'S 59°44'W) are a small group of islands at the northern entrance to the English Strait and also support colonies of Chinstrap (3500-plus pairs) and Gentoo Penguins (1177 pairs), and Southern Giant Petrel. Visitor activity concentrates on an unnamed island northwest of Cecilia I, where a pebble-and-sand beach makes for a comfortable landing site. Nearby Whale Beach, just to the southwest, is a favourite spot and an easy hike, though due to the proximity of the island to the Drake Passage there may be a considerable amount of human garbage on the shoreline. Snow may remain on the island until Jan and mist and cloud frequently reduce the view. Three species of seal have been recorded in front of the dramatic cliffs that dominate Whalebone Beach and the island's flora is comparatively rich.

Robert I (62°28'S 59°23'W) has a rather exposed and difficult landing site at its southeast tip. The scenery is extremely wild and rugged, even by Antarctic standards, and holds 2500 pairs of Chinstrap Penguin, breeding Cape Petrels and Kelp Gulls, while Southern Elephant Seals haul-out in summer and both Antarctic Fur and Weddell Seals are possible in the area.

Half Moon I (62°36'S 59°55'W), between Livingston and Greenwich islands, is a small crescent-shaped islet that offers some excellent walking opportunities, though snow cover may occasionally make this less enjoyable than it might otherwise be. It harbours a small but increasing colony of Chinstrap Penguin (3342 pairs in 1995–6; all other counts relate to the same season), Cape Petrel (eight pairs), Wilson's (377 pairs) and Black-bellied Storm-petrels (seven pairs), Antarctic Shag (29 pairs), Pale-faced

Crabeater Seal Lobodon carcinophaga (left) and Leopard Seal Hydrurga leptonyx (right); together with Weddell Seal Leptonychotes weddellii, these species are the true seals of the region's pack ice. Antarctic Peninsula, Jan 1997. © Daisy Gilardini.

Adélie Penguins Pygoscelis adeliae, *Antarctic Peninsula, Jan 1997.*
© *Daisy Gilardini.*

Sheathbill (11 pairs), Subantarctic (three pairs) and South Polar Skuas (103 pairs), Kelp Gull (39 pairs) and Antarctic Tern (125 pairs), as well as some dramatic basaltic columns, while Antarctic Fur, Weddell and Southern Elephant Seals haul-out on the island's beaches. The Argentine summer base, Camara, is located on the far side of the landing beach. The scenic Roche Dome Glacier on Livingston I makes a perfect backdrop to a splendid wildlife site.

On **Greenwich I** (62°32'S 59°47'W) it is possible to land at Yankee Harbour, which was well known to sealers as early as 1820. There is an abandoned Argentine shelter close to the landing beach, above which more than 4000 pairs of Gentoo Penguins and skuas breed. Pale-faced Sheathbill possibly nests here. Four species of seal may be found hauled-out, especially in late summer, and should be treated with caution and respect. There are some well-developed moss communities close to the old hut.

Hannah Point (62°39'S 60°37'W), at the southwest end of **Livingston I**, where colonies of Chinstrap (up to 1200 pairs), Macaroni (small numbers) and Gentoo Penguins (more than 1000 pairs), Southern Giant and Cape Petrels, Antarctic Shag, Kelp Gull, Antarctic Tern and Pale-faced Sheathbill, along with Wilson's Storm-petrel (which presumably breeds in the scree slopes) and Southern Elephant, Weddell and Antarctic Fur Seals, vie for the naturalist's attention. Most of the 'action' takes place at the western end of the point but the whole area is a microcosm of Antarctic fauna. In addition to the natural history there are many fossils on the far side of the island from the landing area, on a long mossy beach, and an interesting geological feature of the island is a red jasper spur close to Hannah Point.

Other regularly visited sites in this region include **Deception I** (62°55'S 60°37'W), which is most noted for its geology, being the largest of three volcanic centres in the South Shetlands. Tourists often land in **Whaler's** (62°59'S 60°34'W) and **Telefon Bays** (62°56'S 60°40'W). The former has both an old whaling station and is the site of a former British Antarctic Survey station; Cape

Petrel nests nearby at the evocatively named Neptune's Bellows and Kroner Lake is a SSSI, which visitors should respect. **Pendulum Cove** (62°56'S 60°36'W), where it is almost possible to take a bath in the few cm of warm water, is another popular landing spot. Both Crabeater and Leopard Seals sporadically occur at **Baily Head** (62°58'S 60°30'W), along with a huge colony of Chinstrap Penguin (100,000 pairs in 1989, but probably fewer than 75,000 in recent years), as well as breeding Subantarctic Skuas and a large group of young male fur seals on a black volcanic beach. However, landings may not always be possible at this site due to the steep high-energy beach, heavy offshore swell or bad weather.

The more northerly **Elephant I** can be problematic to visit due to rough seas and consequently difficult landings, but is a notable destination for both naturalists and students of Antarctic history. **Point Lookout** (61°17'S 55°13'W) is a steep 240 m-high cliff at the south end of the island and is a noted haul-out point for Southern Elephant and Antarctic Fur Seals, with Weddell Seal sometimes also in attendance. All should be treated with caution and should not be approached too closely. The landing beach is narrow and the exposed area of water is subject to high swell and wind, making zodiac rides potentially difficult and wet. This is a wild-looking area with numerous rock towers and spires, and three glaciers spill down from Mount White, a highly crevassed tower of snow that rises almost 1000 m above the beach. Birds include

Antarctic Minke Whale Balaenoptera bonaerensis *spyhopping (above) and Humpback Whale* Megaptera novaeangliae *surfacing (below) are the two frequent baleen whales seen off the Antarctic Peninsula during the austral summer.* © *Morten Jørgensen.*

Ad white-morph Southern Giant Petrel Macronectes giganteus *with chick at nest. South Shetlands, Jan 2001. © Morten Jørgensen.*

10,700 pairs of Chinstrap Penguin, with much smaller numbers of Gentoo and Macaroni Penguins. Cape Petrel is common offshore, while Wilson's Storm-petrel and Pale-faced Sheathbill are both confirmed breeders. **Point Wild** (61°06'S 54°52'W) on the east coast of the same island is a noted site for history buffs, it being the starting point for Shackleton's epic rescue mission following the loss of the *Endurance*. The site is named in honour of Frank Wild who led the party that remained on the island for four months until Shackleton was able to bring a rescue boat. Some of the same bird and mammal species present at Point Lookout also occur here, including 4000 pairs of Chinstrap Penguins.

The northeast part of the Peninsula holds a number of remarkable wildlife areas. **Hope Bay** (63°23'S 57°00'W), which opens onto Antarctic Sound where whales are often found, is the site of the modern-day Argentine Esperanza Station, and is also the site of the Swedish Antarctic Expedition (1901–4) hut and a Uruguayan base. There is a large colony of almost 130,000 Adélie Penguins nesting inland of the Argentine station (most of it off-limits to visitors), a large Kelp Gull colony, and Pale-faced Sheathbill probably also breeds.

Astrolabe I 63°17'S 58°40'W), in the Bransfield Strait, is a nearly 5 km-long island ideal for those who like to be able to walk about more than is possible on many Antarctic beaches, as there are relatively few fur seals at this location. Birds include breeding Chinstrap Penguin (3400 pairs in steep locations), Southern Fulmar (which nests from c.10 m above sea level) and Subantarctic Skua on the main island, Antarctic Shag on offshore islets and probably Wilson's Storm-petrel. Weddell Seal is regular here.

Further south, in the northwest portion of the Peninsula there is a heavily indented, fjord-like coastline with numerous offshore rocks and islets, among them **Hydrurga Rocks** (64°08'S 61°37'W), which has Chinstrap Penguin, Antarctic Shag, Subantarctic Skua and Kelp Gull among its avifauna. However, many of the nesting areas are comparatively inaccessible due to deep-lying snow and difficult terrain, and overall visitor space is comparatively restricted.

Portal Point (64°30'S 61°46'W), on the west shore of Graham Land, overlooking the Gerlache Strait, is not particularly well known for its wildlife, but Gentoo Penguin, Southern Giant Petrel, Antarctic Shag, Subantarctic Skua and Kelp Gull, along with Weddell and Crabeater Seals on shores or offshore ice floes, all occur. The strait itself often has whales, including Humpbacks and Antarctic Minkes, within its waters. Nearby Charlotte Bay may be

filled with icebergs and large glacial tongues extend to sea level.

Continuing south into the Errera Channel, there is the small, rocky island of **Cuverville** (64°41'S 62°38'W), where the largest Gentoo Penguin colony in the region (4818 pairs in 1994), Southern Giant (and probably Cape and Snow Petrels) and Wilson's Storm-petrels, Antarctic Shag, Pale-faced Sheathbill, South Polar and Subantarctic Skuas, Kelp Gull and Antarctic Tern all breed. The area is also known for its dramatic scenery, including nearby glaciers and icebergs, along with its beautiful mosses. The area was discovered by Gerlache's expedition of the late 1890s. The scenic channel is a good area for whales and onshore, at higher elevations and on steep slopes, is a reasonable selection of Antarctic flora.

In the same area, **Danco I** (64°44'S 62°37'W), **Georges Point**, on **Rongé I** (64°40'S 62°40'W) and the **Orne islets** (64°40'S 62°40'W) are all regularly visited. Though none hold the comparative wealth of wildlife evident on Cuverville, Danco, which is close to Cuverville, has a Gentoo colony (1637 pairs in 1994) and is the site of an old British Antarctic Survey hut, which is off-limits to visitors. Chinstrap Penguin nests on the Ornes, Gentoo and Chinstrap Penguins and Pale-faced Sheathbills breed at Georges Point, while Weddell and Crabeater Seals may haul-out at the latter site. The landing beach easily accesses the penguin colonies and there may be a substantial blooming of snow algae, though extensive snow cover is often prevalent early in the season and makes walking difficult. Norwegian whalers apparently regularly fished the Ornes. The large island of **Anvers** (64°49'S 63°49'W) boasts the US Palmer research base at its southern end, which is a regular port of call for cruise ships, often in conjunction with a visit to the **Togerson I** Adélie colony.

Nearby **Wiencke I** offers a couple of landing possibilities, at **Dorian Bay** and **Port Lockroy** (64°49'S 63°30'W). The French Antarctic Expedition of 1904 discovered Port Lockroy; both areas have Gentoo colonies and the latter also Antarctic Shag, skuas and Kelp Gull. The Port Lockroy harbour is the site of Goudier I, where the first British station was constructed in 1944. The original huts are intact and have been renovated by the UK Antarctic Heritage Trust. The island is a regular destination for tour ships, e.g. in the 2000/1 summer, Nov–Mar, 81 cruise ships and 29 private yachts called at Port Lockroy, with 6417 visitors landing on the island. The shores of the bay are strewn with old whale bones. A colony of c.1600 pairs of Gentoo Penguin above the landing point at Port Lockroy is situated close to the old huts. Similar numbers of this penguin breed at Dorian Bay, where the landing site is reasonably easily accessed. There are many large glaciers in the area, including a particularly large flat area that has served as a landing site for British Antarctic Survey Twin Otter aircraft. There is also a former British Antarctic Survey hut and emergency depot here; if the ship was unable to penetrate the pack ice and reach Adelaide I base or Rothera Station, personnel would be landed here, possibly staying several days until an aircraft could fly from the stations to collect them.

On the east side of **Paradise Bay** (64°54'S 62°52'E), which separates Wiencke from the Peninsula and often holds Killer Whales, is the Chilean González Videla Station at **Waterboat Point** (64°49'S 62°51'W). The Belgian Antarctic Expedition of 1897–9 first surveyed this coast, along with much of the rest of this part of the Peninsula. The landing site and station are actually sited on a small group of islands just offshore. The entire region is scenically splendid and, if that were not sufficient, there are still large numbers of Gentoo Penguin breeding, while Chinstrap Penguin also breeds, though in greatly reduced numbers since the 1920s (fewer than ten pairs), along with Pale-faced Sheathbill. Skuas, Antarctic Shag and Kelp Gull are all regularly noted, but do

Panic-stricken Adélie Penguins Pygoscelis adeliae *escaping from a Leopard Seal* Hydrurga leptonyx. *Paulet I, Antarctic Peninsula, Dec 2001.* © *Hadoram Shirihai.*

not apparently nest at the locality. Seals occasionally haul-out on the rocks close to the station.

Nearby **Almirante Brown Station** (64°53'S 62°52'W) is an Argentine base that was almost completely destroyed by fire a number of years ago. The area is a popular location for zodiac cruises given the impressive backdrop. Three species of seal, including Leopard Seal, may be encountered on the numerous ice flows in this area, although there is no suitable haul-out beach in this part of the bay, which is well protected and deep. Indeed, there are often icebergs in the bay, as well as nesting Cape Petrel in the cliffs close to the base. Other breeding birds include Antarctic Shag, whose colonies just upslope of the station are easily viewed from zodiacs, Gentoo Penguin, Pale-faced Sheathbill, skuas, Kelp Gull and Antarctic Tern. As summer progresses a reasonable flora of moss and lichens becomes evident.

The southwest of the Peninsula has rather fewer crucial wildlife sites, but the small and heavily indented Petermann I (65°10'S 64°10'W), in addition to having important historical sites, has breeding populations of Adélie (c.1000 pairs) and Gentoo Penguins (more than 1200 pairs at this, the species' southernmost location), Antarctic Shag and South Polar Skua. As snow cover recedes later in the summer a flora of lichens and cushion mosses becomes evident, but note that snow may be extensive and last well into the season at this locality. Most visits commence at Port Circumcision hut, which is a good area for birdwatching, though the building itself is off-limits to visitors. The nearby **Yalour Is** (65°14'S 64°09'W) also have breeding Adélies (8000 pairs in 1982), though not on all islands, but are better known for the possibilities for zodiac cruising, during which there are chances to observe whales and seals. The islands are small and low-lying and are the one of the southernmost sites for grass in Antarctica. The **Pléneau I** (65°06'S 64°04'W) Gentoo colony occasionally attracts imm Emperor Penguins. Kelp Gull and South Polar Skua also breed here. Typical Antarctica flora may be observed in late season. The Fish Is (66°02'S 65°25'W), just north of the Antarctic Circle and situated in the Pendleton Strait to the west of Graham Land, are one of the southernmost regularly visited sites in the Peninsula, possessing remarkable glaciated scenery and being an admirable place for zodiac cruising, usually among the islets known as the Minnows just

to the east of Flounder I. Both Adélie Penguin (4000 pairs in 1984) and Antarctic Shag breed there. Tour ships occasionally reach as far south as Marguerite Bay (67°45'S–68°45'S) and visit stations as far south as Stonington I (68°11'S 67°00'W), both of which are now World Heritage Sites; the major avian prize in this region is the occasional sighting of an Emperor Penguin from the species' most isolated and smallest colony.

Weddell Sea

Location and main features Situated to the east of the Antarctic Peninsula, between it and Coats Land, the Weddell Sea lies principally to the south of 66°S and within the Antarctic Circle. It is dominated by heavy pack ice, making it among the least-visited areas covered by this guide, although it harbours a number of important Emperor Penguin colonies. Two large ice shelves, the Ronne Ice Shelf (named by the leader of an American naval expedition of 1947–8 for his wife) and Filchner Ice Shelf (which was originally named, in Jan 1912, for the German emperor Kaiser Wilhelm who decided that the honour should belong to the discoverer), mark the sea's southern boundary. On the west edge of the sea, the Riiser-Larsen Ice Shelf (named for the Norwegian pilot of the Christensen expeditions of 1933–4, which overflew the area) constitutes another formidable barrier.

Landform, climate and habitat The climate and coastal topography of the region is similar to that of the southwestern Peninsula (see above). However, ashore the flora and fauna are incredibly sparse, with few species, the richest areas being on James Ross I and neighbouring islands off the NE Trinity Peninsula. The sea is dominated by heavy pack ice most of the year, and consequently is seldom visited and has received comparatively little scientific attention.

Birds While a long-since extinct 1.5–2.0 m-tall penguin may no longer exist, the area still harbours perhaps the most impressive of extant species of penguin, the Emperor, which has many colonies in the region, of which three are at Norselbukta, the Brunt Ice Shelf and Halley Bay. In summer, Antarctic Petrel and Southern Fulmar can be extremely numerous at the northern limit of the pack ice, but their numbers appear to negatively correlate, while Antarctic Tern is widespread and relatively numerous in east and

Cape Petrels Daption capense capense *in front of a tabular iceberg in a stormy ocean, which is nonetheless extremely rich in breeding seabirds and other wildlife. South Orkneys, Nov 2001. © Hadoram Shirihai.*

central parts of the sea. Seabird observations from the region are comparatively few, with most from the north and east, but among other expected species are Adélie Penguin, Cape and Snow Petrels, Antarctic Prion, Wilson's Storm-petrel and South Polar Skua, with more surprising observations including Wandering Albatross, Blue and Atlantic Petrels and Southern Giant Petrel. Adélie Penguin, Snow and Cape Petrels, and probably Antarctic Petrel and Wilson's Storm-petrel breed on the islands off the Trinity Peninsula, as does Antarctic Shag, both breeding skuas, Kelp Gull and Antarctic Tern.

Marine mammals Fossil whales have been found on Seymour I, and a veloceraptor-type of dinosaur on James Ross and Vega Is. In addition, palaeontologists working on Seymour I have discovered fossilized starfish, crabs, molluscs and, more impressively, a small primitive marsupial and a 40–45 million-year-old sea turtle, which was the size and shape of a Volkswagen Beetle car! Present-day inhabitants of the Weddell Sea are rather less outlandish, but include Crabeater, Weddell, Leopard and Ross Seals. In the northern part of the Weddell Sea, the most frequently observed cetaceans in summer are Humpback, Southern Right, Killer and Antarctic Minke Whales.

Main conservation issues Given the general inhospitability of the region, it is not surprising that it has been little subject to disturbance from humans. As yet there are few, if any conservation issues specific to this area, and others that are significant in other parts of Antarctica, for instance tourist disturbance and pressures at seabird colonies, are virtually unknown here.

Human history The sea takes its name from the British sealer James Weddell, captain of the *Jane*, who was first to enter the area in Feb 1823. He named it 'King George IV Sea' for his monarch, but a German Antarctic historian, Karl Fricker, proposed its current patronymic in 1900. The next important visitant was James Clark Ross, in 1843, who discovered Snow Hill and Seymour Is, although it was left to subsequent, Norwegian, explorers, in 1892–3 and 1902, to discover their insular nature. Seymour is

of extreme importance to palaeontologists and geologists, as its western slopes are almost wholly paved in fossils (see above for some of the important discoveries). Argentina has maintained a station, equipped with one of only five rock airstrips in Antarctica, on the island since 1969–70. Other bases in the region include the German-operated Neumayer station, which was established in 1982 and is situated on the Ronne Ice Shelf. The Ronne shelf was discovered by the American commander of the Ronne Antarctic Research Expedition, Finn Ronne, in 1947–8, while the Filchner Ice Shelf, from which it is separated by Berkner I, was located by a German explorer, William Filchner, in Jan 1912. Berkner marks the starting point for most transantarctic skiing expeditions. Two other bases operate in the region. The Argentine General Belgrano II is a year-round station constructed in 1979 at the site of a previous US meteorological base, Ellsworth, established in 1954–5, which was virtually destroyed by snow build-up. Halley is a British operation, initiated in 1956, on the Brunt Ice Shelf, which is floating and therefore makes regular renewal of the station a necessity, as the ice in this region moves c.2 m per day. Halley is famous for being the place where ozone depletion was first recognised, in 1985, and also near the point from which Sir Vivian Fuchs' 1956–7 Trans-Antarctic Expedition departed.

The Weddell Sea is perhaps best known for having claimed Shackleton's *Endurance*, which became trapped in heavy pack ice in Jan 1915 and eventually sank in Nov that year, before his expedition to cross the Antarctic continent could even commence. The rescue operation, which involved the first crossing of South Georgia and a 1300-km open-sea small-boat journey is the stuff of legend, and is grippingly recounted in Shackleton's book South and Lansing's *Endurance*. At least four other ships have suffered similar fates in the Weddell Sea, including Nordenskjöld's *Antarctic* in 1902 (see the relevant section in the South Shetlands and Antarctic Peninsula).

Visiting the area Several of the sites mentioned here are often included within Peninsula itineraries. A huge colony of 95,000–

The west and south Weddell Sea holds several small to medium-sized Emperor Penguin Aptenodytes forsteri *colonies. Dawson-Lambton Glacier, Nov 1998. © David Tipling/Windrush Photos.*

105,000 pairs (1999) of Adélie Penguin occurs on the rugged, often ice-encrusted 3.5 km-long **Paulet I** (63°35'S 55°47'W) beach, while the hillsides above hold breeding Wilson's Storm-petrel and Snow Petrel. Antarctic Shag, Pale-faced Sheathbill and Subantarctic Skua also breed; Kelp Gull is a regular, apparently non-breeding visitor, and Weddell and Leopard Seals are both frequently observed here. The landing site is a pebble beach on the north-central side of the island, close to the remains of the historic Nordenskjöld Expedition hut. Just upslope of the old base is a lake thronged with yet more penguins, and close by are colonies of shags and sheathbills. Visitors should beware of rockslides and keep away from the screes, which shelter breeding petrels.

The 745 m-high **Brown Bluff** (63°32'S 56°55'W) on the Tabarin Peninsula, so named for its rust-coloured basalt stones and scenic cliffs, which harbour several mosses and lichens, also holds many Adélies (20,000 chicks were counted in Jan 1995), along with c.600 Gentoo Penguin nests, Cape and Snow Petrels, skuas and Kelp Gull. Rockslides are frequent in this area and visitors should take care; landings can also be difficult, as there may be thick brash ice around the beach.

Further south, the narrow 1.5 km-wide **Devil I** (63°48'S 57°17'W), off the north coast of the larger Vega I, has another huge colony of Adélie Penguins (10,320 chicks in 1996) and yet more Subantarctic Skua, along with Kelp Gull and Wilson's Storm-petrel (breeding by the latter two species has not been confirmed), and sometimes Leopard Seal on the offshore ice-flows. This small island possesses two towering mountains, several lichens and offers a dramatic vista across the surrounding region, including the waterfalls on Vega I; it was also the site of the miraculous reunifi-

Ice shelf between the Weddell and King Haakon VII Seas. © Daisy Gilardini.

Female and pup Weddell Seal Leptonychotes weddellii. *Dawson-Lambton Glacier, Nov 1998. © David Tipling/Windrush Photos.*

The impressive summer waterfalls on the north coast of Vega I offer visible proof of receding glaciers and ice cap. Northwest Weddell Sea, Feb 2002. © Morten Jørgensen.

Emperor Penguin Aptenodytes forsteri *brooding chick on feet. Dawson-Lambton Glacier, Nov 1998. © David Tipling/Windrush Photos.*

Ad Emperor Penguin Aptenodytes forsteri *with well-fed chick. Dawson-Lambton Glacier, Nov 1998. © David Tipling/Windrush Photos.*

cation of the two halves of the Nordenskjöld Expedition in 1903.

Across **Erebus & Terror Gulf**, which marks the centre of the nearly 300,000-pair-strong Adélie Penguin population in this region, is **Seymour I** (64°18'S 56°45'W). This lies adjacent to **James Ross I** (64°10'S 57°45'W), the site of an Argentine facility, Marambio Station, where Nordenskjöld made many of his fossil penguin discoveries. Adélie Penguin breeds in the southeast of the island and Antarctic Tern probably to the north of the station. Emperor Penguin has been sighted on several occasions between Nov and Jan on ice floes near James Ross I, suggesting that an undiscovered colony may exist in this area.

Nearby **Snow Hill I** (64°28'S 57°12'W) appears to have no breeding wildlife, but South Polar Skua, Kelp Gull and Antarctic Tern have all been observed, and fossils of marine invertebrates are easily found. There is a refuge hut, dating once again from the Nordenskjöld Expedition, which is maintained by Argentina and contains a number of exhibits from the Swedish visit (though most items were illegally removed to Buenos Aires sometime ago). Hiking must be undertaken with care in order not to damage the fossil areas. Most of the islands in this region have a hidden danger to walkers, quick mud. This is a very fine, soft viscous mud, which appears perfectly innocent, but is very liable to engulf boots and legs up to the knee or deeper. Extricating oneself can be very difficult and likely to result in loss of footwear, as well as delaying the field party.

Today, among the main reasons to visit the Weddell Sea is the

hope of seeing Emperor Penguin. Best known from the Ross Sea area, several colonies were discovered in 1986 in the E Weddell Sea, and new breeding areas continue to be found. One, of c.5600 pairs, is at the **Riiser-Larsen Ice Shelf** (72°09'S 15°07'W), while another (8000 pairs in 1986 but many fewer in 2001) is close by at **Atka Bay** (70°30'S 09°00'W, the landing point for the German-operated Neumayer Station), but is impossible to visit unless in an icebreaker, and by Christmas the colonies are abandoned. The **Dawson-Lambton Glacier** (76°30'S 29°00'W) has 4000–6000 pairs of Emperors and may sometimes be visited by Twin Otter plane from Patriot Hills, the Adventure Network International base camp, generally in Nov or early Dec. Among non-breeding seabirds, Grey-headed Albatross is reasonably regular in the northern part of the sea, and several other species of smaller albatross have also been observed in this area.

South Orkney Islands

Location and main features Comprising five major islands, Coronation, Signy, Powell, Fredriksen and Laurie, and several minor islets and rocks, situated at 61°00'N 45°00'W, as well as the Inaccessible Is, 29 km to the west, the South Orkneys cover 622 km² and lie 700 km east and slightly north of the tip of the Antarctic Peninsula. They are situated 800 km south of the Antarctic Convergence. The archipelago is important for breeding seabirds, with enormous numbers of breeding penguins and petrels.

Emperor Penguin Aptenodytes forsteri *chicks. Dawson-Lambton Glacier, Nov 1998. © David Tipling/Windrush Photos.*

Emperor Penguins Aptenodytes forsteri. *During blizzards the crèches concentrate into tight assemblies for warmth. Dawson-Lambton Glacier, Nov 1998. © David Tipling/Windrush Photos.*

Landform, climate and habitat The islands are 85% ice-covered, with a highest point, Mount Nivea, of 1265 m on Coronation, which is also the largest island, being 48 km by 12 km. Coronation, Laurie (24 km long and rising to 940 m) and Powell (11 x 3 km and up to 620 m high) have extensive permanent ice caps, but Signy, a smaller island of 20 km² rising to 279 m, now has only the remnant of such a covering. This occupies the centre of the island, with a large glacier reaching the sea on the south coast and a smaller field on its east side; the ice fields have been receding since the 1950s. The island's coastal areas are undulating, being formed by ancient glaciers and now carpeted with a luxuriant covering of lichens and mosses, with sparser fell-field vegetation at higher altitudes. The huge numbers of non-breeding male fur seals, which visit the island in summer from South Georgia, have destroyed much of the coastal vegetation. Post-glacial weathering has given rise to a variety of soils, which are snow-free in summer but remain saturated with melt water. Pack ice surrounds all of the islands in May–Dec but most small islets in the group are ice free with steep cliffs. Signy has a mean annual temperature of -3.8°C (range 19.8°C to -39.3°C), with winds up to 59 kph, extreme winds on 60 days per year, snow on 120 days and rain on 95 days. Prevailing winds are westerly as at all islands in this region.

Birds Decreasing numbers of Adélie and Chinstrap Penguins breed in the South Orkneys. At least 20 breeding areas for the former are known, ten of which are on Laurie, totalling 200,000–300,000 pairs in 1983. Chinstrap Penguin numbered c.600,000 pairs in the entire group in the 1980s. Two other species of penguin also breed in the group: five islands host colonies totalling 10,940 pairs of Gentoo Penguin, and 50+ pairs of Macaroni Penguin breed on three islets in the archipelago. Many petrels breed in the group, with up to 8755 pairs of Southern Giant Petrel (the apparently stable or slightly increasing population consists of both colour phases), as well as huge concentrations of Southern Fulmar (100,000 to one million pairs), Cape (10,000–100,000 pairs) and Snow Petrels (1000 pairs, of which approximately 20% are on Signy), Antarctic Prion (hundreds of thousands of pairs), and Wilson's (c.97,000 pairs on Signy alone and breeds on many other islands in the group) and Black-bellied Storm-petrels (100–200 pairs on Signy and also breeds on Larson and Laurie, with almost certainly a few pairs at most ice-free rocky headlands and screes). Antarctic Shag also nests, with ten colonies located in the 1980s holding 2000 pairs, but is perhaps declining as early visitors reported more than this total on Laurie I alone (more regular counts on Signy indicate the population there to be stable). Both

Iceberg in the lee of Laurie I. The South Orkneys is one of the best areas to encounters massive icebergs. © Keith Robinson.

South Polar and Subantarctic Skuas have been found nesting, with just ten pairs of the former on Signy being outnumbered by 300 pairs of *lonnbergi*, of which 143 pairs breed on Signy. Approximately half of the estimated world population of 10,000 pairs of Pale-faced Sheathbill is known from the archipelago, c.5500 pairs at just six sites in the early 1980s, but only small numbers of Kelp Gull nest, c.500 pairs during the same period. Antarctic Tern, with 150–200 pairs prior to 1988, appears to be declining; c.1000 individuals were recorded breeding on the islands in the 1930s (though the accuracy of this estimate is open to question).

King Penguin is an occasional, perhaps annual visitor in Nov–Feb, Emperor Penguin appears to be an occasional visitor from its Weddell Sea colonies, and Magellanic and Rockhopper Penguins have also been recorded, but the former apparently only once (in 1986). There have been several records of Wandering Albatross since the mid-1970s, and there are also records of Black-browed, Grey-headed and Light-mantled Sooty Albatrosses from the archipelago. Northern Giant Petrel has been recorded in small numbers, but with greater regularity in recent years, perhaps as a result of the increasing numbers nesting on South Georgia, and Antarctic Petrel is an at least annual visitor to the group. Few other vagrants and visitors have appeared on the islands, in part due to the low observer coverage, but among these have been Cattle Egret, Chiloe Wigeon, Brown Pintail, Upland (unconfirmed), Least and Baird's Sandpipers, and Wilson's and Grey Phalaropes, and Arctic Jaeger. Kerguelen, Soft-plumaged and White-chinned

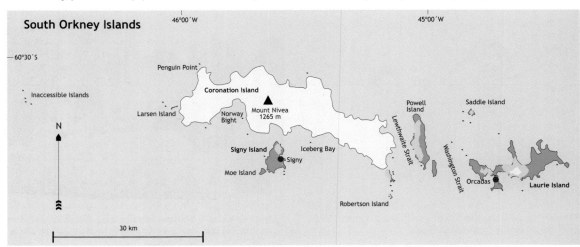

South Orkney Islands

46°00′W

45°00′W

60°30′S

Penguin Point

Inaccessible Islands

Coronation Island

Larsen Island

Norway Bight

▲ Mount Nivea 1265 m

N

Signy Island

Iceberg Bay

Signy

Moe Island

Robertson Island

Lewthwaite Strait

Powell Island

Saddle Island

Washington Strait

Orcadas

Laurie Island

30 km

Petrels, and Common Diving-petrel are all apparently regular but scarce visitors to nearby waters.

Marine mammals Weddell Seal is a common breeder in the archipelago (several hundred animals). A tiny number of Southern Elephant Seal pups are born on some beaches, though there are large numbers of non-breeders (several hundred on Signy alone). There are also a few very small breeding colonies of Antarctic Fur Seal, but the summer influx of non-breeding young males from South Georgia is a recent phenomenon. Before the mid-1970s only a few dozens of these seals were seen each year, then a population explosion of summer immigrants resulted in numbers increasing annually. Since c.1990 until the present over 30,000 invaded the lowland ice-free terrain of the islands, two-thirds of which come ashore on Signy. Regularly recorded cetaceans in summer are Humpback, Antarctic Minke and Killer Whales.

Main conservation issues These are very similar to those outlined above for the Peninsula. Four Specially Protected Areas—Moe, Lynch, North Coronation and Southern Powell and adjacent islands—have been designated within the archipelago.

Human history The islands were discovered in Dec 1821 by separate groups of US and British sealers. On 6 Dec, the American Nathaniel Palmer, sailing in the James Monroe, and the British sealer George Powell, in the Dove, came upon the islands. Powell named the group for himself and took possession for the British crown the following day when making landfall on Coronation I. Just a few days later, on 12 Dec, the British sealer, Michael McLeod in the *Beaufoy*, also reached the South Orkneys, which received their present name in Feb 1822 when yet another British sealer, James Weddell, visited the group and recognised that their southerly latitude mirrored the position of the Scottish islands in the Northern Hemisphere. Sealers were the only visitors in the 19th century. The first scientific visit to the group occurred in 1903, when the Scottish National Antarctic Expedition under Bruce wintered on Laurie I, establishing a meteorological station subsequently operated by Argentina and which is the longest continually run research station in Antarctica. Britain claimed the South Orkneys as part of the Falkland Islands Dependencies in 1908, but Argentina challenged this in 1925. Whalers arrived in Jan 1912, with the Norwegians taking the lead. Floating factory ships were principally used to process the catch, which numbered approximately 3500 animals during the 1920s, but a land base was also established on Signy I, which was named by Petter Sørlle, captain of the first ship to take a whale within the group, for his wife. A new meteorological station was founded in 1946–7 by Britain, on Signy, with its remit subsequently being expanded to include ecological work. The station was permanently staffed until 1995, whereupon the operation became a summer-only programme.

Visiting the islands The first tourists to visit the South Orkneys arrived in 1933, when an Argentine relief ship for the meteorological station on Laurie I brought a number of visitors. Among the important tourist landing sites are **Shingle Cove**, part of Iceberg Bay on **Coronation I** (60°38'S 45°35'W), where elephant and fur seals haul-out on the shingle beach. Above here, there is a fine display of mosses and grasses on the large boulders. In addition to a comparatively small colony of Adélie Penguin (c.4000 pairs), the island is a breeding site for Cape and Snow Petrels, Subantarctic Skua and Antarctic Tern, and there is British refuge hut, built in 1963, which remains in very good condition. In addition, **Laurie I** (60°44'S 44°37'W) houses the Argentine weather station, **Orcadas** (60°44'S 44°42'W), which is the oldest continuously operated such station in Antarctica. Visits are possible with prior arrangement. The British Antarctic Survey operates a major biological research station on **Signy I** (60°45'S 45°36'W), where scientists conduct

Waves lash at grounded icebergs in the lee of Laurie I, South Orkneys. © Cherry Alexander.

long-term studies of terrestrial and freshwater biology, as well as researching the seabird populations and Antarctic marine life. One of the principal studies at Signy is the long-term Penguin Monitoring Programme, and the island is also an important monitoring site for the Antarctic Treaty Convention. **Point Martin** is one of the most frequently visited sites. Formerly, there were facilities for diving beneath the ice in winter, supported by sledge and skidoo transport, but these were disbanded in 1996/7.

South Sandwich Islands

Location and main features The South Sandwiches lie 530 km east-southeast of South Georgia and 800 km east-northeast of

Chinstrap Penguin Pygoscelis antarctica colony on Saunders I, South Sandwiches, Nov 2001. © Maria San Román.

Chinstrap Penguin Pygoscelis antarctica *colony on the slopes of Saunders I, South Sandwiches, Nov 2001. © Daisy Gilardini.*

the South Orkneys, 1000 km south of the Antarctic Convergence, and are included within the maritime Antarctic biogeographical zone. The 11 islands of the South Sandwich group are scattered

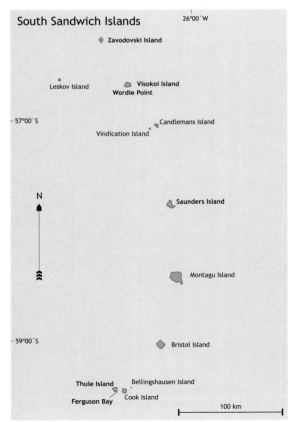

South Sandwich Islands

26°00´W

Zavodovski Island

Leskov Island
Visokoi Island
Wordie Point

−57°00´S
Candlemans Island
Vindication Island

N

Saunders Island

Montagu Island

−59°00´S
Bristol Island

Thule Island   Bellingshausen Island
Ferguson Bay   Cook Island

100 km

in a 375 km north to south arc, centred on 58°00'N 27°00'W, and cover 310 km². They are, from north to south: Zavodovski, Leskov (the smallest, 2.4 km in circumference), Visokoi, Candlemas, Vindication, Saunders, Montagu (the largest, 12 km in diameter), Bristol, Bellinghausen, Cook and Thule. The first three are collectively known as the Traversay Is, Vindication and Candlemas are known as the Candlemas Is, and the southernmost three are known as Southern Thule. Their ornithological importance is principally in the huge numbers of Chinstrap Penguin that breed virtually throughout the group.

Landform, climate and habitat The South Sandwiches are a product of geologically recent volcanic events, and all but Vindication, Montagu and Cook have witnessed 20th-century activity, with some of the more dramatic eruptions occurring in 1908, 1956 and 1962. Many of the physical features of both Zavodovski and Candlemas have been named in recognition of the sights (and smells) associated with such activity. Most islands are single or complex volcanic cones, which have been heavily glaciated and possess sheer, vertical rock or ice cliffs at sea level. Five islands, Visokoi, Montagu, Bristol, Cook and Thule, are almost entirely ice-covered, Candlemas and Saunders, are more than half ice-covered, but the remainder are virtually ice-free. The summer climate is similar to that of the South Orkneys, with strong winds, low cloud and swirling fog and rain on many days; calm and sunshine are rare. Air temperatures hover around freezing, but frequently rise a few degrees above. Pack ice from the south reaches the archipelago, especially around the more southerly islands, in winter (May–Nov). Vegetation, as at the South Orkneys, is sparse, with a green alga *Prasiola* being widespread but few moss or lichen communities, although *Deschampsia antarctica* grows on Candlemas. The archipelago's highest point, Mount Belinda at 1375 m, is on Montagu. A deepwater trench, which reaches 8265 m, is situated east of the islands and marks the margin of a major tectonic plate.

Birds Adélie Penguin breeds on six islands with a maximum population of up to 70,000 pairs estimated in a census of seabirds conducted in 1996–7. They are vastly outnumbered by the population of Chinstrap Penguin, which was estimated at 1.5 million during the same survey, with colonies on all islands except Leskov. Gentoo Penguin breeds on four islands and numbered 1500 pairs, and Macaroni Penguin nests on all but Leskov and Cook, the vast majority (52,000 pairs) being on Zavadovski. King Penguin occasionally visits the islands and was recently proven to breed, and there is at least one record of Emperor Penguin. Other seabirds recorded during the most recent census were Southern Giant Petrel, the majority nesting on Candlemas (1500 pairs) with 25 pairs on Zavodovski, Southern Fulmar (an estimated 90,000 pairs mainly on Visokoi, Montagu, Bristol and Cook), Cape (12,000 pairs) and Snow Petrels (3200 pairs). Small numbers of Antarctic Prion are thought to nest on Leskov, with Wilson's Storm-petrel (probably 10,000 pairs and breeding on most islands), South Georgian Shag (365 pairs in three colonies, on Montagu, Bristol and Zavodovski), Subantarctic Skua (300–400 pairs, nesting on most islands), Kelp Gull (c.85 pairs on several islands) and Antarctic Tern (c.12 pairs). Black-bellied Storm-petrel was recorded nesting in small numbers on Candelmas and single sheathbills were seen on Zavodovski and Freezland. Great Shearwater occasionally penetrates as far south as the northernmost islands in the chain and one visitor reported Kerguelen Petrel as being abundant in Dec.

Table 1. Breeding bird and mammal checklist for the South Shetland Islands, Antarctic Peninsula, the Weddell Sea, South Orkney Islands and South Sandwich Islands.

	South Shetlands & Antarctic Peninsula	Weddell Sea	South Orkney Islands	South Sandwich Islands
Penguins				
Emperor Penguin *Aptenodytes forsteri*	X	X		
Gentoo Penguin *Pygoscelis papua*	X		X	X
Adélie Penguin *P. adeliae*	X	X	X	X
Chinstrap Penguin *P. antarctica*	X		X	X
Macaroni Penguin *Eudyptes chrysolophus*	X		X	X
Petrels and prions				
Southern Giant Petrel *Macronectes giganteus*	X		X	X
Southern Fulmar *Fulmarus glacialoides*	X		X	X
Antarctic Petrel *Thalassoica antarctica*	X?	X		
Cape Petrel *Daption capense*	X		X	X
Snow Petrel *Pagodroma nivea*	X	X	X	X
Antarctic Prion *Pachyptila desolata*	X		X	X
Storm-petrels				
Wilson's Storm-petrel *Oceanites oceanicus*	X	X	X	X
Black-bellied Storm-petrel *Fregetta tropica*	X		X	X
Shags				
Antarctic Shag *Phalacrocorax [atriceps] bransfieldensis*	X		X	
South Georgian Shag *P. [a.] georgianus*		X		X
Sheathbills				
Pale-faced Sheathbill *Chionis alba*	X		X	
Skuas				
Subantarctic Skua *Catharacta antarctica lonnbergi*	X		X	X
South Polar Skua *C. maccormicki*	X	X	X	
Gulls and terns				
Kelp Gull *Larus dominicanus*	X	X	X	X
Antarctic Tern *Sterna vittata*	X	X	X	X
Seals				
Antarctic Fur Seal *Arctocephalus gazella*	X		X	X
Leopard Seal *Hydrurga leptonyx*	X	X		
Weddell Seal *Leptonychotes weddellii*	X	X	X	
Crabeater Seal *Lobodon carcinophaga*	X	X	X	
Southern Elephant Seal *Mirounga leonina*	X		X	X
Ross Seal *Ommatophoca rossii*		X		

Marine mammals Five species of seal, Antarctic Fur, Southern Elephant, Weddell, Crabeater and Leopard Seals, are known from the environs of the group, but only the two first-named have been confirmed to breed.

Main conservation issues Like other areas of Antarctica, fishing around the islands has been monitored and controlled by the Convention on the Conservation of Antarctic Marine Living Resources (CCAMLR) since 1984. This regulates catch sizes, bans the exploitation of some species and establishes mesh sizes for nets. But the creation of the South Georgia and South Sandwich Islands Maritime Zone (SGMZ) in 1993 has brought additional protection to the marine ecosystem around the islands. The SGMZ encapsulates a region of 200 nautical miles around South Georgia and the South Sandwiches. Vessels can only fish inside the zone with the authority of a licence issued by the government (see below).

Human history As with so many islands in the region covered by this book, the early history of the South Sandwiches is associated with Captain Cook, who discovered the eight southernmost islands in Jan 1775 and afforded them the name 'Sandwich Land' after the fourth Earl of Sandwich, who was the First Lord of the Admiralty at the time. Sealers typically made the first landings, in this instance in 1818, and the following year the Russian explorer Bellinghausen discovered the present-day Traversay Is, landing on Zavadovski, which he named for the captain of his flagship, the *Vostok*. Only sealers and whalers visited the group for much of the 19th and early part of the 20th century. Like other groups within this sector of the S Atlantic, territorial rights are claimed by Britain, who consider the islands part of the South Georgia and South Sandwich Islands territory, and Argentina, who regard them as part of its Islas del Atlántico Sur. This dispute erupted as the Falklands War. In 1954–5 an Argentine refuge hut was erected on Hewison Point, Thule, and a larger naval station (Corbeta Uruguay) was illegally built in 1976; it remained operational until Jun 1982, when it was removed by British forces. In Jan 1983, the Argentine flag was discovered flying again at the base, which was then destroyed by British troops. The uninhabited archipelago is part of the British Overseas Territory of South Georgia and the South Sandwich Islands (SGSSI). Until 1985 these groups were administered as Dependencies of the Falkland Islands. On 3 October 1985, SGSSI became a British Overseas Territory in its own right and is now managed by the SGSSI government. Legal, financial and administrative arrangements for the government of SGSSI are the responsibility of the Commissioner (Governor of the Falkland Islands), while international relations and defence are the responsibility of the Commissioner and the British Foreign and Commonwealth Office.

Visiting the islands Permission to land at these islands is required from the Commissioner of South Georgia and the South Sandwich Islands. Poor weather and rough seas often prevent landings, and there have been very few tourist visits. The first cruise ship visit to the group was in 1982 and most, if not all, subsequent landings have been made at **Zavodovski** (56°18'S 27°36'W). Other sites include **Wordie Point** (56°44'S 27°15'W), on Visokoi, **Saunders I** (57°47'S 26°37'W), which was first visited in the 1999–2000 season, and **Ferguson Bay** (59°29'S 27°29'W), at the southeast corner of Thule I, where Adélie, Gentoo and Chinstrap Penguins all breed on the lava beach, which has a scant flora of algae and lichens.

South Atlantic Islands

For ornithologists Tristan da Cunha exerts an easily explained and very strong attraction; together with Gough the islands harbour some of the most fascinating and enigmatic insular landbird endemics on Earth, along with a vast array of breeding seabirds, including several globally threatened species. While the Tristan group and Gough are unequivocally subantarctic in their affinities (some of the breeding landbirds obviously derive from ancestral South American stock, while others may be African in origin and still other taxa are unclear in their biogeographic histories), the highly isolated Norwegian territory of Bouvetøya is unequivocally Antarctic, being largely ice-capped and possessing a vegetation solely of lichens and mosses. They are grouped within the same chapter due to their similar longitudinal position within the South Atlantic, despite their quite different ecological characters. As yet, Bouvetøya's avifauna is still relatively poorly known, a consequence of the lack of visits. While our collective knowledge of Tristan natural history is relatively substantial, with much research having been conducted in recent years, principally by South African workers, the islands are still comparatively infrequently visited by tourists, largely due to their relative remoteness.

Tristan da Cunha and Gough

Location and main features At 37°06'S–37°25'S 12°13'W–12°42'W, on the border between the subantarctic and subtropical climatic zones, the Tristan da Cunha group lies virtually midway between South Africa and Argentina. The main island of Tristan is unquestionably the most remote inhabited island on Earth. Of

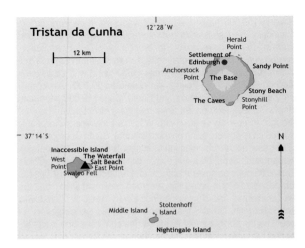

the group, which along with Tristan (96 km²) consists of Inaccessible (16 km²), 40 km to the southwest, nearby Nightingale (4 km²) and its tiny satellites, Middle (or Alex) and Stoltenhoff, and remote Gough (40°21'S 09°53'W; 65 km²), 450 km southeast of Tristan da Cunha, only Tristan is inhabited. Approximately 300 people live in the settlement of Edinburgh. Despite the usual tale of destruction wrought by commercial sealers and Man's inopportune alien introductions, the islands are of considerable biological importance, harbouring six endemic landbirds of which Gough Moorhen, Inaccessible Island Rail and Inaccessible, Nightingale, Grosbeak and Gough Buntings are globally threatened, as well as important populations of a number of globally threatened seabirds, including Tristan Albatross and Atlantic Petrel (both virtually restricted to Gough) and Spectacled Petrel (known to breed only on Inaccessible), as well as being the only breeding location for Atlantic Yellow-nosed Albatross.

Landform, climate and habitat Tristan, the main island of the group, reaches 2060 m, but most land below 300 m, including the settlement plain, has been developed for pastureland, with many imported alien grasses present. Seaward cliffs rise to 600 m, with just four low-lying coastal areas (Edinburgh Settlement, Sandy Point, where there is an orchard and conifer plantation, Stony Beach and Cave Point), all of which appear to be very young in origin; that at the Settlement may be just 6000 years old. Above 750 m (on steep slopes natural vegetation occurs to c.100 m in places and to almost sea level in others) stunted *Phylica arborea* trees (endemic) and the endemic cycad-like bog fern *Blechnum palmiforme* persist, giving way around 900 m to a wet heath of grasses, including the aliens *Rumex acetosella* and *Holcus lanatus*, sedges, *Blechnum penna-marina*, *Empetrum rubrum* and *Rhacomitrium langinosum*. However, on the volcano's largely unvegetated central cone (from which lava last flowed in 1961) some small patches of *Empetrum* and bryophytes persist as high as 2000 m. Forty species of flowering plants are considered native to the island and there are more than 100 species of alien vascular plants.

A number of younger volcanic cones are scattered around the Base, all of which are probably younger than 25,000 years old. Permanent running water is found only on the Settlement plain, though there are some small waterbodies, including three crater lakes, on the Base plateau and one in the central cone. The cli-

Atlantic Yellow-nosed Albatrosses Thalassarche [chlororhynchos] chlororhynchos *and flying Sooty Albatross* Phoebetria fusca *on Inaccessible I, Dec 1999. © Peter Ryan.*

mate is typical of the subantarctic islands, with high rainfall (1676 mm in 250 days at Edinburgh), heavy cloud cover, especially around the peak, and strong winds, which gust and veer violently, regularly reaching gale force. The mean annual temperature is 14.5°C. Snow may lie on the highest ground throughout the winter, but is much less common at lower levels down to 600 m, and frost is virtually unknown at sea level.

The lower slopes of Inaccessible are dominated by up to 3 m-tall tussac grass *Spartina arundinacea* (endemic), giving way above 200 m on the island's steep-sided cliffs to a fernbush of *Phylica arborea*, *Blechnum penna-marina* and *Histiopteris incisa*, with wet heath carpeting areas above this. The island's highest point, Swales Fell, is c.600 m and there is a plateau at 300–500 m where *Spartina* tussac is comparatively scarce and the tree fern *Blechnum palmiforme* and *Phylica* trees dominate the vegetation. *Peperomia tristanensis* is a curiosity of the island, being found at only one location on Inaccessible and in the Juan Fernández group off Chile. New Zealand Flax *Phormium tenax* has been introduced and is spreading on cliffs above the Waterfall. More than 25 other introduced plants occur on the island but few are widespread (e.g. *Holcus lanatus* and *Rumex obtusifolius*). Three principal drainage systems dominate the plateau, with numerous additional dry ravines and gullies. Wetter areas have *Empetrum* and mossy *Scirpus* at higher levels and *Azolla filiculoides* at sea level. In total 40 species of flowering plants and 30 ferns (including one endemic species) are native to the island. Inaccessible is a volcanic remnant that arose three million years ago and its shoreline is dominated by sheer cliffs that rise to 300 m in places, with narrow boulder beaches virtually throughout, except at Salt Beach and Waterfall Beach. A landslide at West Point forms the only area of relatively level land at sea level on the island, and a 400-year-old bog is the only patch of fresh water, with the excep-

tion of pools in many Spectacled Petrel colonies. The climate is similar to Tristan and other subantarctic islands, with only minor seasonal variations in temperature, frequent cloud cover and high rainfall, which increase dramatically with altitude on this island.

Nightingale lies 38 km southwest of Tristan and 22 km southeast of Inaccessible, and reaches 366 m at High Ridge. The vegetation is dominated by 2–3 m-tall tussac grass, with a few scattered *Phylica arborea*. The island is a volcanic skeleton with little trace of its original form, though a broad, shallow, submerged platform off the north coast may mark some of its original extent. There is evidence of volcanic activity as recently as 250,000 years ago. New Zealand Flax was formerly present, but due to its negative affect on the growth of tussac grass was finally removed in the 1970s, and the native vegetation has otherwise been little altered by Man (though there is some flax around one of the ponds); 19 species of flowering plants and six alien vascular plant species have been recorded. A small grove of *Phylica* is present. Boggy valleys with standing water occur in parts and five such areas in the centre of the island are known locally as The Ponds. There is no running water on the island. The climate has not been fully studied but is considered to be warmer and drier than Tristan, with less cloud cover.

The 0.5 km² Middle (or Alex) I lies just 100 m away and rises to 46 m. It has the oldest rocks in the group, dating back 18 million years. There are some boggy areas but most of the island is covered by tussac grass and is the site of a large penguin colony. Stoltenhoff lies 1.5 km north of Nightingale and covers just 0.2 km². It reaches 99 m at its south end, where there are two large offshore stacks. Most of the rest of the island is covered in low tussac, which increases in height at the eastern end, where there are many rocky outcrops. A single *Phylica* tree has been noted.

Gough is an unglaciated, 13 km-long steep-sided island, particularly on its west side where the cliffs reach 460 m, and has a

Edinburgh Settlement Plain, Tristan da Cunha, Nov 1999. © Peter Ryan.

Cone I, off Gough, Oct 1990. © Peter Ryan.

Albatross Plain, Gough, Sep 1999. © Peter Ryan.

Nightingale I, Dec 1989. © Peter Ryan.

number of offshore pillars and rocks, most within 100 m of the main island and none at a distance greater than 1 km. The largest stacks support vascular plants and breeding seabirds. The northern and eastern sides of the island form a deeply dissected landscape of narrow ridges and steep-sided valleys known as Glens. This portion of the island has been estimated to be five million years old, much of the rest of the island is considerably younger and apparently the result of secondary volcanic activity. The island's climate is the wettest and coldest of the entire group. Mean temperature close to sea level is 11.3°C with little seasonal variation (extremes are -3°C and 25°C) and the mean relative humidity is 80%. In association with cyclonic depressions, frontal precipitation falls throughout the year. Mean annual precipitation near sea level is 3397 mm with relatively little inter-annual variation and rain on 296 days. In winter (Jun–Aug) snow falls on high ground above 300 m but does not accumulate. As on most subantarctic islands strong winds are a near-permanent feature. The highest point is Edinburgh Peak at 910 m, closely followed by Gonçalo Alvarez (recently renamed in honour of the island's discoverer) at 894 m, with only the southern part of the island being below 200 m. Boulder beaches are found below cliffs.

Gough is carpeted by lush vegetation comprising 63 vascular plants, of which several probable aliens have been recorded (but only six survive), and there are several subantarctic and Fuegian species not found in the Tristan group, e.g. the tussac grass *Poa flabellata*. It also supports an intriguing population of *Sophora microphylla* trees, restricted to a single glen on the east coast, a species which otherwise occurs only in coastal S Chile. Twelve species are considered endemic and an additional 49 are restricted to Gough and the Tristan group. The marine area can be divided into two distinct algal zones. From sea level to 5 m depth, the algae

consist mainly of bull kelp *Durvillea antarctica*, and beyond 20 m the dominants are *Laminaria pallida* and giant kelp *Macrocystis pyrifera*. Of 40 species of algae, two are endemic to the island. Mosses and tussac grass, which reach 300 m on the western cliffs but only 100 m in the east, are replaced by some of the 25 species of ferns that occur on the island and predominate below c.500 m, especially *Histiopteris incisa*, while the tree *Phylica arborea* persists in sheltered gullies. Above the upper limits of the fernbush communities, wet heath becomes the dominant vegetation type up to 800 m. This is a diverse assemblage, characterized by ferns, sedges, grasses, angiosperms and mosses. *Blechnum palmiforme*, *Empetrum rumbrum* and grasses and sedges are the most important constituents of wet heath. Above 600 m peat bogs are widespread. These reach depths of up to 5 m in some valleys and are dominated by *Sphagnum* mosses. *Tetroncium magellanicium* and *Scirpus* spp. are the only abundant vascular plants to occur in bogs, though the margins are more diverse. Above 600 m feldmark and montane rock communities are also found. These consist of cushion-forming or crevice plants, found on exposed areas such as ridges.

Birds Penguins are, in contrast to many subantarctic islands, a less significant component of the avifauna of these islands. Nevertheless, the sole representative of this family, Northern Rockhopper Penguin, breeds in large and increasing numbers, with 150,000–160,000 pairs in the Tristan da Cunha archipelago (principally late-1980s counts, which found major concentrations on the main island, Nightingale, Middle and Inaccessible) and 144,000 pairs on Gough (in 1984). On the other hand, the islands are of immense importance for their albatross populations. Tristan Albatross, which now breeds nowhere else but Gough (mean annual breeding population c.1000 pairs) and Inaccessible I (2–3 pairs in 1990, formerly several hundred pairs in the early 1870s, when it also bred in some numbers on the main island of Tristan) appears stable and has been so for c.50 years. However, the status of another endemic breeder, Atlantic Yellow-nosed Albatross, is unclear. Its populations very crudely totalled 27,200–46,300 pairs in 1972–4, with the majority of these (20,000–30,000 pairs, despite formerly being much exploited for food) on the main island, where concentrated on southeast slopes of the Base, at 200–800 m, and on Gough, where most breed on steep slopes at 60–300 m. Smaller numbers also occur on Inaccessible (1100 pairs), Nightingale, Middle and Stoltenhoff (2000–5000 pairs). Sooty Albatross also breeds in highly significant numbers, with colonies on Tristan, Inaccessible, Nightingale, Stoltenhoff and Gough perhaps totalling 10,000 pairs in recent years. Most colonies are on high sea-cliffs and on inland slopes and crags, occurring between 15 m

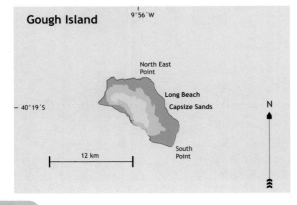

Gough Island

9°56′W

North East Point

Long Beach

Capsize Sands

N

40°19′S

South Point

12 km

and 1200 m on Tristan and at 50–500 m on Gough.

Among petrels, Great-winged nests on Gough, Tristan, possibly on Inaccessible and in small numbers on Gough. Following near-extermination on the main island it increased sufficiently to be considered common again in the 1950s (1000–3000 pairs in 1972–4). Kerguelen Petrel breeds uncommonly on Inaccessible (50–500 pairs in 1988–9) and abundantly on Gough (where Richardson estimated a near-incredible 1–10 million pairs in 1972–4). The endemic Atlantic Petrel is common on Gough (tens to hundreds of thousands of pairs), but occurs sparingly on Tristan (100–200 pairs in 1972–4) and possibly Inaccessible. Soft-plumaged Petrel is common throughout the group (it numbered 1–10 million pairs on Gough, 100–500 pairs on Tristan and 1000–5000 pairs on Nightingale in the 1970s, and was recently confirmed to breed on Inaccessible, where >10,000 pairs were estimated in 1988–9). Grey Petrel nests on Tristan (50–100 pairs in 1972–4), Gough (perhaps hundreds of thousands of pairs in the 1970s) and almost certainly on Inaccessible, and the globally threatened Spectacled Petrel breeds on Inaccessible, where c.10,000 pairs nest on the banks of river valleys in the western plateau. Both Spectacled and White-chinned Petrels are relatively numerous at sea around Inaccessible, with some of the former remaining in the vicinity year-round. Both Great-winged and Atlantic Petrels are unusual in being mid-altitude winter breeders, while Grey Petrel also breeds at this season, but on higher slopes. Many expeditions, which visit the islands in summer, tend to 'miss' these species.

Great, Sooty and Little Shearwaters all nest: the former being perhaps the commonest seabird in the group with c.2 million pairs thought to breed on Nightingale, >2 million pairs on Inaccessible and 600,000 to three million pairs on Gough. It probably bred in much smaller numbers on the main island of Tristan in the 1940s. Most of the world's population of this species thus uses the islands for breeding (with elsewhere only small numbers at the Falklands). Sooty Shearwater has recently been confirmed to nest in very small numbers at Big Green Hill, on the main island of Tristan (and may breed on Inaccessible). Little Shearwater was confirmed to breed on Inaccessible in the late 1980s, where it is abundant (>5000 pairs estimated in 1988–9) and skuas predate large numbers; it also breeds on Nightingale (a few hundred pairs), perhaps on Middle and Stoltenhoff, and on Gough (perhaps hundreds of thousands in the early 1970s).

Of the smaller tubenoses, Broad-billed Prion nests at Tristan (1000–10,000 pairs), Inaccessible (>50,000 pairs in 1988–9), Nightingale, probably Middle and Stoltenhoff (perhaps similar numbers), and Gough (where possibly millions of pairs and considered the most common tubenose in the 1970s). White-faced and White-bellied Storm-petrels also nest, with White-bellied an abundant late-summer breeder throughout the group. Its status has previously been confused with that of Black-bellied Storm-petrel, as birds breeding in the Tristan group possess measurements in line with those previously presented for the latter species and some display more pronounced and elevated nostrils. However, none that has been examined during recent seabird research in the islands has possessed a black median line on the belly. Nonetheless, some researchers insist that both species occur in the group, perhaps occasionally hybridizing and plausibly segregated altitudinally. White-faced Storm-petrel is another seabird that due to recent more intensive research has been confirmed to breed within the Tristan group. In Oct 1989 several burrows were discovered at Blenden Hall, on Inaccessible, some in close proximity to those of the previous species; more than 5000 pairs were estimated to be nesting on the island at this time. It was also judged to occur in its thousands at Nightingale and Gough in the

Atlantic Yellow-nosed Albatross Thalassarche [chlororhynchos] chlororhynchos *colony with chicks. Nightingale I, Feb 2000. © Peter Ryan.*

early 1970s. Grey-backed Storm-petrel is assumed to breed on Gough; it is common offshore there in Oct and its occurrence is sufficiently regular to consider it a probable breeder. It was thought to be nesting on the main island of Tristan in the 1950s. Common Diving-petrel breeds on Nightingale (tens of thousands of pairs in the 1970s), Inaccessible Is (>1000 pairs in 1988–9) and Gough (where it occurs in large numbers).

Southern Giant Petrel formerly bred on the main island of Tristan, but both species of *Macronectes* now appear to be non-breeding visitors to the archipelago, with at-sea data suggesting that Southern predominates. The latter species does still breed on Gough (60 pairs in the 1970s). There are a small number of recent shore-based and at-sea sightings of Cory's Shearwater in the Tristan group, and one from Gough. Other seabird visitors to the archipelago include Black-browed and Light-mantled Sooty Albatrosses, Southern Fulmar, Cape and White-headed Petrels, Antarctic Prion, Leach's and Wilson's Storm-petrels, Arctic and Long-tailed Jaegers, Kelp Gull and Arctic Tern.

The breeding skuas on these islands are *Catharacta antarctica hamiltoni*, with the majority of the 2500 pairs on Gough, just 200 pairs on Tristan da Cunha, where numbers have significantly decreased due to persecution, and 80 pairs on Inaccessible. At least 86 pairs of Antarctic Tern nested on Inaccessible in 1982–3 along with 50 pairs of Common Noddy. Other populations of the latter were noted on Tristan (30–50 pairs), Nightingale (200–500 pairs) and possibly 100 pairs on Stoltenhoff in the 1970s, as well as on Gough. As for Antarctic Tern, in the 1970s there were 50–70 pairs on Tristan, 100–300 pairs on Nightingale, 100–400 pairs on Inaccessible, c.100 pairs on Stoltenhoff and 500–1000 pairs on Gough.

The breeding landbirds are small in number but of great interest to visiting birders because of their extraordinary level of endemicity.

Atlantic Yellow-nosed Albatrosses Thalassarche [chlororhynchos] chlororhynchos, *with Tristan I in the background. Inaccessible I, Dec 1999. © Peter Ryan.*

The flightless Gough Moorhen, which in plumage is very similar to the more familiar, smaller and faster moving Common Moorhen *Gallinula chloropus*, numbers 4500–6500 individuals and is increasing. The flightless Tristan Moorhen (indistinguishable from the Gough Moorhen) lived on the main island and reportedly became extinct at the end of the 19th century. Indeed, some Gough Moorhens were introduced to Tristan in 1956. But, it has never been proven that the moorhens found on Tristan in the 1970s were descendants of these introductions or genuine survivors of the original stock. The islanders today deny its former existence, but eyewitness accounts and the history of the first specimens leave no doubt concerning its former occurrence there. It requires adequate cover, being found in fernbush and tussac on Gough up to c.300 m; and is restricted to fernbush on Tristan, where it has

spread widely across the Base and almost to sea level at Sandy Point.

Restricted to the island of the same name, Inaccessible Island Rail is also flightless and surely one of the most tantalizing names for a bird ever coined: limited to a near-inaccessible island and being a rail, it throws down a considerable gauntlet to birders. Ecologically it is more like a mouse than a bird, inhabiting tunnels under the grass. Even the feathers are almost hair-like. The population is estimated at 8400 pairs.

Tristan Thrush, which appears to be most closely related to some of the South American thrushes (perhaps being an offshoot of *Turdus* and also bearing a similarity to the West Indian genus *Cichlherminia*, though the Tristan form's resemblance to the Groundscraper Thrush *Psophocichla litsipsirupa* of E and S Africa

The volcanic Tristan da Cunha (2060 m), Mar 2006. © Hadoram Shirihai.

is also notable), numbered 6000 birds in the 1980s. Some weak geographical variation is recognized: the three races occur on the main island of Tristan (where it is decreasing), on Inaccessible and on Nightingale, Middle and Stoltenhoff islands. Four buntings, Gough, Inaccessible, Nightingale and Grosbeak Buntings, also derive from South American stock. All are considered globally threatened. The former is restricted to Gough and numbered at most 1500 pairs in 1991, while Inaccessible Bunting is much commoner, being found on Inaccessible, and formerly on the main island of Tristan, and currently numbers 10,000 pairs. It became extinct on Tristan in the 19th century; the cause of its demise there is unclear, because it occurred prior to the arrival of rats and before its favoured tussac grass was destroyed by cattle and sheep. The recently split Nightingale Bunting numbers c.4000 pairs and occurs on Nightingale, Middle and Stoltenhoff. Grosbeak Bunting is the rarest of the four, being restricted to Inaccessible and Nightingale and with a pure-bred population of just 500 individuals (it hybridizes widely with Inaccessible Bunting on Inaccessible).

Among records of vagrants on the islands the following are perhaps most noteworthy: King (at least two records) and Macaroni Penguins, Grey-headed Albatross (which appears to be occasional at both Tristan da Cunha and Gough), and there is a record of an unidentified frigatebird from Mar 1951. A ringed Wandering Albatross from South Georgia has been recovered on Gough and another was seen at sea off Inaccessible, while 'Shy' Albatross has been seen off Tristan. Recent additions to the list of seabirds recorded in Tristan waters have been Slender-billed Prion and Leach's Storm-petrel. Among landbirds, the main island of Tristan has hosted Striated Heron, Great, Snowy and Cattle Egrets, Paint-billed Crake, Purple Gallinule (comparatively regular in Mar–Jul), many shorebirds including Rufous-chested Dotterel, Ruddy Turnstone, Solitary, Sharp-tailed, Pectoral, Upland and Spotted Sandpipers, Franklin's Gull, Common Nighthawk and Barn Swallow. Non-marine vagrants recorded at Inaccessible are Purple Gallinule, White-rumped Sandpiper and Barn Swallow. Yellow-billed Teal and Cocoi Heron have been recorded on Gough.

Marine mammals Subantarctic Fur Seal breeds on Inaccessible, Nightingale and Tristan, where numbers are increasing following the cessation of sealing activities which decimated the original populations on Tristan da Cunha and Gough. Southern Elephant Seal was formerly common but almost extirpated by hunting. Individuals haul-out occasionally on the northern islands, and there is a recent pup record at Tristan (Boat Harbour Bay). Both species occur on Gough (where in recent years there were 200,000 and 100 individuals respectively) and fur seals have been increasing throughout the islands since at least the 1950s. On Gough, elephant seals are restricted to a sheltered beach on the island's east coast; numbers decreased slowly but steadily until the 1990s, then stabilized at their current low levels. Leopard Seal has been occasionally reported from Tristan da Cunha. An increase in numbers of Southern Right Whale was noted off Tristan and Nightingale in the mid-20th century, when at least 100 were present in 1951 between Jul and Dec, but numbers decreased during the 1960s, perhaps due to pirate Russian whaling during the period when Tristan was evacuated. This species also occurs off Gough along with Dusky Dolphin. Other cetaceans known from the group include Humpback, Long-finned Pilot, Killer, False Killer and Sperm Whales (the latter stranded). Beaked whales are seen quite regularly at Tristan, and stranded animals include several specimens of the little-known Shepherd's Beaked Whale.

Main conservation issues Both Tristan da Cunha and Gough are of international biological importance, not only for their breeding seabirds but also for a number of landbird endemics, some of which are globally threatened. Gough was declared a strict Wildlife Reserve in 1976, following the first thorough scientific investigation of the island in 1955–6, and subsequently, in 1995, a World Heritage Site, following adoption of a comprehensive management plan. Its landbirds have been protected under a Tristan ordinance dating from 1950. World Heritage Site status has since been accorded to several other subantarctic islands, principally in the New Zealand region. Conservation efforts in the Tristan group have steadily mounted, by 1997 44% of the land area, including all of Inaccessible, was officially protected.

Exploitation of the large albatross colonies on Tristan has been long term; sustained slaughter of Tristan Albatross on the main island from the early-19th century led to its extirpation there by

Northern Rockhopper Penguins Eudyptes [chrysocome] moseleyi *possess highly luxuriant crests; this form is restricted to Tristan, Gough and, in the Indian Ocean, Amsterdam and Saint Paul. Nightingale Mar 2003. © Hadoram Shirihai.*

Sooty Albatross Phoebetria fusca *is one of the most exciting tubenoses found in the South Atlantic. Off Inaccessible, Mar 2006. © Hadoram Shirihai.*

1907, though there have been recent sightings since. Yellow-nosed and Sooty Albatrosses and their eggs did not escape the islanders' attentions, and by the early-20th century concerns were being voiced for these populations. Numbers of mollymawks taken annually on Tristan in the mid-1920s were between 3700 and 5000, and by this period attention was largely switching to the other islands and their still dense colonies! By 1942 it was necessary to place a total ban on such harvesting on Tristan and introduce a quota system for Nightingale. Such measures failed to work; the ban was lifted in 1949–50 and while the killing of ads was officially discouraged, chicks and eggs continued to be seen as 'fair game'. Despite various wildlife ordinances, quotas on Nightingale continued to go unobserved and Sooty Albatrosses on Tristan lost approximately half of their chicks each year to the harvest in the early 1950s, with smaller numbers still being taken as late as 1968. Further piecemeal ordinances followed, providing protection for some species on some islands, but it was only in 1986 that complete protection was accorded to all three species of albatross throughout the group. In contrast, on Gough, only sealers and other mariners occasionally took albatrosses and their eggs, and crayfish fishermen also took some, but their effects do not appear to have been significant. However, exploitation of the eggs and chicks of the Great Shearwater continues, with two trips annually to Nightingale (an egging trip and a 'fattening trip'—the greatest delicacy on Tristan is potato cakes fried in petrel fat).

House Mouse *Mus musculus*, which appears to have arrived in the Tristan group in the early-19th century, is the only alien mammal on Gough; the animals are unusually large (up to 50 g), widespread and take *Phylica* seeds and invertebrates (especially at the summit), as well as small-petrel eggs and chicks. Inaccessible

formerly supported populations of pigs and sheep, and Nightingale a herd of the latter, but these and other occasional alien introductions, mainly as a result of efforts to establish farming settlements, have all failed or been removed. Indeed, pigs were described as widespread on Inaccessible in the 1950s, but subsequent visitors have not noticed them, and they appear to have died out naturally. Such introductions have been more difficult to control on the main island. Goats and pigs were introduced as early as the late-18th century while rats reached Tristan in 1882, following the wreck of a cattle ship, and by 1962 were estimated to number 400,000 and to be the cause of mortality of many small birds. Feral cats and dogs were both eradicated by the early 1960s, but there are domesticated dogs in Edinburgh.

Human history The Tristan da Cunha group was discovered in 1506, by a Portuguese admiral, one Tristão da Cunha (although Gough had been probably sighted a year previously by another Portuguese captain, Gonçalo Alvarez), while a Dutchman, Bierenbroodspot, made the first recorded landing in Feb 1643. One source claims that another Dutch mariner, van Amsterdam, apparently visited both Gough and Tristan in 1655–6 (but significant doubt is attached to this claim). More certain is that the London-born merchant Antoine de la Roché probably made the first landing on Gough in May 1675; however, this island takes its name from another British captain, Charles Gough, who rediscovered it on 3 Mar 1732. No formal claim was made on Tristan until 1775, when Bolts took possession for the Emperor of Austria, Joseph II. Sealing then briefly flourished: the first ship, the US *Industry*, arrived in 1790–1 and took 5600 fur seals, but by 1801–02 the numbers available were pitifully low. At Gough sealers and penguin hunters exacted a toll on the island's wildlife throughout the 19th century, with the first visits being in 1806; they had exhausted the island's fur seal potential by 1891 and then turned to boiling penguins for their oil. Unsuccessful South African diamond prospectors replaced them in 1919.

Despite the Austrian claim, three men from the sealing ship *Baltic* were the first to establish a settlement on Tristan, in 1810, with a certain Jonathan Lambert styling himself emperor. However, following a drowning incident in 1812 only Thomas Curri (or Curry) remained alive, though two British sailors joined him in Mar 1813. During the British–American war of 1812–5 the islands were occasionally the scene for US naval raids on British vessels. Fearing the French might occupy Tristan da Cunha to organize the escape of Napoleon Bonaparte, imprisoned on St Helena, the British formally annexed Tristan (and Ascension) and established

Gough Moorhen Gallinula [nesiotis] comeri: *the origin of those moorhens on Tristan is subject to discussion, though the modern-day population apparently solely comprises Gough Moorhens. Gough. © Peter Ryan.*

Inaccessible Island Rail Atlantisia rogersi: *one of the 'dream' endemics of the region. Only very recently has Inaccessible become open to, very limited, landings by visitors. Mar 2003. © Hadoram Shirihai.*

a short-lived garrison to prevent such a possibility. The settlement of Edinburgh came into being in the years shortly after this. The island's single men negotiated that a ship's captain obtain wives for them from St Helena, 2435 km to the northeast, and it was only with their arrival that a settled population was established. Prior to this (1827), there was only one couple on the island (William Glass, the founder of Edinburgh and a former member of the British garrison, and his wife). All the first wives (including Glass') were of mixed race. Following this, shipwrecked seamen augmented the population, especially if free daughters of a suitable age were available. Indeed, there were a total of at least 19 such groundings between 1817 and 1898. (The Tristinians, willingness to come to the aid of such beleaguered mariners led the British government to send occasional provisions and supplies in gratitude, and to supply a lifeboat in 1884, despite reduced sea traffic calling at the island due to the decline in S Atlantic whaling and the opening of the Suez Canal in 1869.)

These developments led a British naval expedition to remove

45 inhabitants in 1857, in an effort to prevent overpopulation. This evacuation was instigated by a reverend unable to believe that Tristan was inhabitable, due to some severe winters, which brought serious food shortages. Such measures could, of course, backfire on an island with a small population: in 1885 15 men drowned in the lifeboat, leaving just three men alive on the island. Following this, another parson made a second attempt to remove everyone from the island, but he too failed in this endeavour. Whaling took place in the waters off Gough between 1830 and 1870, but the island remained uninhabited.

Annual voyages to bring mail and provisions to Tristan were initiated by the British Colonial Office in 1927, and in Mar 1938 the Tristan group and Gough were claimed as a British Possession and defined as Dependencies of St Helena. Meteorological and radio stations were established during the Second World War, partially to prevent use of the islands by Nazi warships, which did attempt to use Gough once. With the end of the war the British detachment was withdrawn from Tristan and the South African

Male Gough Bunting Rowettia goughensis*: Gough and Tristan harbour some of the most interesting landbirds of the region, especially the buntings (see pp. 305–308). Gough, Nov 2004. © Peter Ryan.*

Weather Bureau assumed responsibility for the base. The latter also took responsibility for meteorological work on Gough in May 1956, following a British scientific survey expedition initiated the previous year; the 1956 base being relocated in 1962–3 and then enlarged in the mid-1980s. In 1961 a volcanic eruption forced the temporary evacuation of all humans from Tristan, initially to Nightingale, then Cape Town and eventually England, before returning to the island in 1963.

A largely elected Island Council, overseen by an Administrator appointed by the Governor of St Helena, currently governs Tristan da Cunha. Edinburgh is nowadays a small town with most expected amenities: a library, social centre, pub, churches, a school, supermarket, museum and even a golf course. The island's government employs most people, processing rock lobsters for export or engaged in handicraft production, also for overseas. In contrast to most parts of the world, crime is unknown and the egalitarian code created by the original settlers is still broadly adhered to.

Visiting the islands Even in 2001 access to these remote and fascinating islands can be problematic. Most opportunities arise on voyages by Antarctic tourist ships at the end of the southern summer season, but such visits are extremely brief, normally just hours. Approximately six expedition cruises per year call at the group. The only regular ships calling at Tristan, from Cape Town, are the fishing vessels *Kelso* and *Edinburgh*, each c.3 times a year and with a stay around the islands of 1–3 months. Berths on these vessels are extremely difficult to secure and islanders have preference. Two other vessels call just once a year, also out of Cape Town. They are the South African polar supply ship *SA Agulhas*, in Sep–Oct, on its Gough relief voyage (which takes 2.5–3.0 weeks, but coincides with the start of the main fishing season and a period of often rough seas, making it difficult to reach other islands), and the *RMS St Helena*, in Jan–Feb, which has also called at Gough. The *RMS St Helena* is the easiest way of getting to Tristan, but the call is only c.3 days, and passengers overnight aboard. Tristan has no hotels or other commercial accommodation, but it is possible to stay in islanders' homes (cost is usually c.UK£20, including meals). All visitors must first call at **Edinburgh**

(37°03'S 12°18'W), the settlement on the main island, and clear customs and immigration, where a UK£10 entrance fee is payable to land on Tristan itself. Contact the island on Channel 16 or Channel 10 (VHF marine bands) to arrange clearance (the police will usually come out in their vessel). Further details are available from Inspector Conrad Glass at hmg@cunha.demon.co.uk (mail should be marked for attention of Conrad).

Landing is relatively easy in the harbour at the settlement, but is weather dependent (the entrance to the harbour is shallow and can be used only in relatively calm weather). Access is best on calm days or when the wind and weather is from the south (the harbour faces north). There is little reason to want to land elsewhere on the main island, but there are reasonable landing sites (depending on sea state) at **Sandy Point** (37°05'S 12°12'W), **Stony Beach** (37°08'S 12°15'W) and the **Caves** (37°08'S 21°18'W). However, you must be accompanied by a Tristan islander to venture ashore anywhere in the group. (It should be noted that all expeditions involving landings in the archipelago have been accompanied by at least one Tristan islander.) Steep cliffs reach the sea around most of the island, making zodiac trips (if possible) of relatively little value. There are a few fur seal or Northern Rockhopper Penguin colonies, but these are not spectacular. To see Tristan Thrush (which is scarce) you ideally need to reach the Base (use an island guide and be aware that it is a stiff 1.5-hour climb), though there are a few pairs in the bottom of gulches behind the potato patches (again ask for guidance). The introduced Gough Moorhen is common on the Base (where easy to locate by their loud clucking calls).

Access to **Gough** is prohibited unless prior written approval has been obtained from the Administrator of Tristan da Cunha, and landings are difficult even on the coast adjacent to the meteorological station. It has been suggested that signs be erected on the island, indicating the conservation objectives, and that detailed, informative literature be produced for any permitted visitors to the island, but there are no tourist facilities. Tour vessels do visit and if weather permits put zodiacs out to cruise close inshore, typically along the eastern side (which is sheltered from the prevailing westerlies), where there is spectacular scenery (waterfalls, offshore stacks and cliffs), and large numbers of fur seals and Northern Rockhopper Penguin. The small numbers of elephant seals on **Capsize Sands** (40°19'S 9°54'W) and/or **Long Beach** (40°18'S 9°55'W) should be left undisturbed: numbers have decreased steadily and now appear to have stabilized at a very low level (10–15 pups per year). It is also possible to observe moorhens and buntings foraging along the shore, but some luck will be required.

Inaccessible is off-limits to tourists, but this may change (a draft management plan considers limited tourist landings possible if well controlled and accompanied by Tristan guides, as at Nightingale). Fairly easy landings, given prevailing westerly conditions, are possible on the eastern shore at **The Waterfall** (37°17'S 12°39'W) and **Salt Beach** (37°17'S 12°39'W; both of which are sheltered bays with pebble/small-boulder beaches). Access from these sites is limited to the immediate coastal strip at the foot of the precipitous cliffs, but it is possible to see Tristan Thrush, Tristan Bunting and Inaccessible Island Rail quite easily (the latter is impossible to see unless you are able to land on the island). There are also many Northern Rockhopper Penguins and fur seals, as well as skuas, noddies and Antarctic Terns. There is excellent scenery (cliffs, trachyte plugs and stacks) along the southwest coast, but this is best observed from ship unless conditions are exceptionally calm.

Weather permitting, a landing can be made on **Nightingale** for a day excursion, but you are obliged to hire an island guide for every eight passengers and there may be a landing fee. Contact James Glass, Chief Islander and Head of Natural Resources Department (e-mail as Conrad Glass) to arrange such visits. Landings are possible at two sites, the main area being at the northeast end of the island adjacent to the huts (37°25'S 12°28'W) and the 'west landing' (37°25'S 12°28'W) in the channel opposite Middle (Alex). Both sites are rock ledges (which can can be very slippery) with adjacent deep water. From either there is a path through the tussac to the trail to The Ponds (with many Atlantic Yellow-nosed Albatross and all of the landbirds).

Being nature reserves, both Gough and Inaccessible have strict management plans in place. While Nightingale does not have the same reserve status, ad hoc landings on this island are strictly forbidden, especially as the huts on Nightingale used by Tristan islanders have not yet been repaired following the hurricane that hit the group on 21 May 2001.

Bouvetøya

Location and main features Located at 54°25'S 03°21'E, 1600 km from the nearest land of the Antarctic continent, 2600 km southwest of South Africa and 4800 km east of Cape Horn, Bouvetøya is the most isolated island in the world. It covers 49 km² and is among the most rarely visited places on Earth. Its avifauna, dominated by two species of penguin, is in consequence not well known, although four recent summer expeditions have greatly expanded our knowledge. Bouvetøya possesses a tiny outlier, Larsøya, to the southwest, but another, Thompson, to the northeast, which was mentioned in some 19th century reports concerning the area, is speculated to have been destroyed as a result of volcanic activity in 1895–6 (or was perhaps simply an iceberg). Further disturbances (or perhaps a landslide) sometime in 1955–8 produced a low-lying lava shelf, Nyrøysa (new rock) and flat beach (Westwindstranda), on the island's west coast, which forms a seabird and important seal breeding area, and measures 1.6 km from north to south and 400 m east to west. This area is unstable and the seaward margin is rapidly being eroded by a combination of wave action and collapse.

Landform, climate and habitat Bouvetøya is volcanic in origin and forms the tip of a comparatively young volcano that rises from the Southern Ocean at the southern end of the Mid-Atlantic Ridge. While geothermal activity persists, the volcano has not erupted recently. Glaciers cover 93% of the island and there are steep cliffs reaching 490 m on its north and west sides. Numer-

Bouvetøya is a Periantarctic island; note the year-round icebergs surrounding it. © R. Wanless.

ous offshore rocks exist. Bouvetøya reaches 780 m (Olavtoppen) and this and another high summit surround the ice-filled crater of the volcano, which is known as the Wilhelm II plateau. Bouvetøya has a maritime Antarctic climate, with a mean temperature of -1°C (mean monthly temperatures at sea level range between -2.7°C to 1.6°C). Typically it is cloaked in clouds or thick fog. In 1978 a temperature of 25°C was recorded 30 cm below the surface of the ground. The vegetation, which is largely restricted to coastal cliffs, capes and boulder beaches, consists mainly of mosses and lichens, with some fungi, algae and liverworts. There are no records of any introduced flora or fauna.

The Nyrøysa platform is the best-studied part of the island (due to its relative accessibility). The higher area (25 m above sea level) consists of a broken terrain of large boulders, mixed with large to small rocks. In parts there is a peaty 'soil', which together with the rocky terrain appears to rest on subterranean ice. In summer, as this ice melts, sink holes form. A significant portion of the higher ground (the southern part) is covered in moss and bears the name Grøndal ('Green Valley'). The best-vegetated parts of the island are Rustadkollen and Moserygyen. At the southern end of Nyrøysa a glacier flows into the sea, beyond which the smaller of the two beaches begins. The significantly larger northern beach extends from the north side of the higher ground towards Kapp Circoncision. The cliffs that back the platform are largely composed of avalanche debris and scree, and can be climbed to 200 m, above which the terrain becomes progressively steeper, with permanent ice and glaciers forming a spectacular lip that rims the entire inland portion of the platform. Such a formation lends support to the theory that the platform is of avalanche origin, though it may be of combined avalanche and volcanic origin.

Birds Very small numbers (max. 60 pairs in 1978/9, but none in 1989/90) of Adélie Penguin occasionally bred at Nyrøysa, but the majority of the island's penguins (up to 100,000 pairs in 1978/9; recent estimates suggest considerably lower numbers) breed at Kapp Circoncision. The majority are Macaroni Penguins, but up to 8200 pairs of Chinstrap Penguin were also present in the late-1970s, though numbers in the following decade were around 7000 pairs. The local penguin population decline at Nyrøysa (from a peak of 20,000 pairs in 1981 to just 3925 pairs in 2001) may be directly attributed to an increase in the Antarctic Fur Seal population, with the behaviourally more sensitive Chinstrap Penguin most adversely affected, and is perhaps the reason for the lack of recent breeding records of Adélie Penguin. Moulting King Penguins have been recorded in Dec–Jan and are apparently frequent visi-

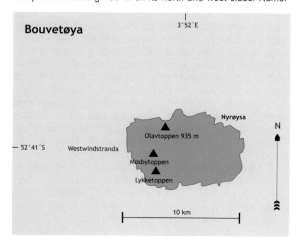

Bouvetøya

3°52'E

Nyrøysa

Olavtoppen 935 m

Westwindstranda

Mosbytoppen

Lykketoppen

N

52°41'S

10 km

Young Southern Elephant Seal Mirounga leonina, *cooling on a sunny day at Bouvetøya.* © R. Wanless.

tors, but do not breed here, with Gentoo Penguin being much less frequently noted. There are apparently no nesting albatrosses, but yellow-nosed albatrosses, presumably of the Atlantic form, are very occasional in offshore waters (no recent observations), while Wandering, Black-browed, Grey-headed and Light-mantled Sooty Albatrosses are frequent summer visitors to nearby waters.

Other breeding species at Bouvetøya include Southern Giant Petrel (one pair in 1981 and considered common in Dec 1980, but apparently extirpated due to the increasing Antarctic Fur Seal population at Nyrøysa), Cape and Snow Petrels (perhaps as many as 10,000 pairs of the former, but no recent confirmed evidence for the latter), Antarctic Prion, Southern Fulmar (at least 100,000 pairs over the entire island in 1998/9), Wilson's and Black-bellied Storm-petrels (at least 1000 pairs of the latter at Nyrøysa in 1998/9), small numbers of Subantarctic Skua (30–45 breeding groups at Nyrøysa in 1996–2001), Kelp Gull (not confirmed as a breeder) and Antarctic Tern (no recent confirmation of nesting). Antarctic, Kerguelen and Blue Petrels are considered regular offshore visitors, while White-headed and Soft-plumaged Petrels have been recorded within 20 km of the island, and Slender-billed Prion is strongly suspected to breed at Nyrøysa. Records of the following species also exist for Bouvetøya: Sooty Albatross, Northern Giant Petrel, Fairy Prion, White-chinned Petrel, Great Shearwater, Common Diving-petrel, South Polar Skua and Arctic Jaeger.

Marine mammals The island has breeding populations of two species of seal: Antarctic Fur and Southern Elephant Seals. While the elephant seal breeding population remains small (88 pups at Nyrøysa in 1998), the Antarctic Fur Seal population is growing exponentially, with at least 13,000 pups being born there in recent years (compared to the 950 pups counted in summer 1978/9), and a total of 74,966 animals at Nyrøysa in 2001. Weddell, Crabeater and Leopard Seals and Subantarctic Fur Seal have been sighted

and are probably occasional visitors, as is Killer Whale during summer. Humpback Whale is common around the island during the latter season.

Main conservation issues Fur sealing was prohibited on Bouvetøya in 1929. In 1935 all seals in the area were declared protected species, and in 1971 the island and adjacent territorial waters were designated a nature reserve, affording complete protection to the rich and distinctive plant and animal life. It was recently included within a BirdLife International Important Bird Areas (IBA) inventory. Given the infrequency of visits to this remote outpost few direct threats to the island's wildlife are current, though the increasing fur seal population is impacting penguin numbers and continuing erosion of the Nyrøysa platform could have negative consequences for several breeding birds. The platform is suffering marine erosion and subterranean ice melt, which cumulatively total a mean rate of 3 m per annum (thus its raised portion is unlikely to survive very long). The area experiences frequent landslides/avalanches with large boulders sometimes falling onto the narrow beach, leading to the loss of cliff-edge nesting sites (and often eggs/chicks) of Macaroni and Chinstrap Penguins, Cape Petrel and Southern Fulmar, and the death of seals. The area has been declared a Commission for the Conservation of Antarctic Marine Living Resources (CCAMLR) Ecosystem Monitoring Programme site and a draft management plan for the area exists. CCAMLR approved plans for a longline toothfish *Dissostichus* fishery in the sea area of Bouvetøya in 1997, but no catches had been reported by Jun 1998.

Human history Bouvetøya is named after the Frenchman, Bouvet de Lozier, who was the first to sight the island, on 1 Jan 1739, and spent 12 days unsuccessfully attempting to determine whether it was connected to a mainland or was merely an island. The British captains Lindsay and Hopper, of Enderby Brothers whalers, established its insular nature in 1808 but its

Table 1. Breeding bird and mammal checklist for the subantarctic islands in the South Atlantic Ocean.

	Tristan	Inaccessible	Nightingale	Gough	Bouvetøya
Penguins					
Adélie Penguin *Pygoscelis adeliae*					X
Chinstrap Penguin *P. antarctica*					X
Northern Rockhopper Penguin					
Eudyptes [chrysocome] moseleyi	X	X	X	X	
Macaroni Penguin *E. chrysolophus*					X
Albatrosses					
Tristan Albatross *Diomedea [exulans] dabbenena*	extinct	X		X	
Atlantic Yellow-nosed Albatross					
Thalassarche [chlororhynchos] chlororhynchos	X	X	X	X	
Sooty Albatross *Phoebetria fusca*	X	X	X	X	
Petrels and prions					
Southern Giant Petrel *Macronectes giganteus*	extinct			X	X
Southern Fulmar *Fulmarus glacialoides*					X
Cape Petrel *Daption capense*					X
Snow Petrel *Pagodroma nivea*					X
Great-winged Petrel					
Pterodroma [macroptera] macroptera	X	X?		X	
Atlantic Petrel *P. incerta*	X	X?		X	
Kerguelen Petrel *P. brevirostris*	X?	X		X	
Soft-plumaged Petrel *P. mollis*	X	X	X	X	
Broad-billed Prion *Pachyptila vittata*	X	X	X	X	
Antarctic Prion *P. desolata*					X
Spectacled Petrel *Procellaria conspicillata*		X			
Grey Petrel *P. cinerea*	X	X?		X	
Shearwaters					
Great Shearwater *Puffinus gravis*	?extinct	X	X	X	
Sooty Shearwater *P. griseus*	X				
Little Shearwater *P. assimilis*	?extinct	X	X	X	
Storm-petrels					
Wilson's Storm-petrel *Oceanites oceanicus*					X
Grey-backed Storm-petrel *O. nereis*		X?		X	
White-faced Storm-petrel *Pelagodroma marina*		X	X	X	
Black-bellied Storm-petrel *Fregetta tropica*					X?
White-bellied Storm-petrel *F. grallaria*		X	X	X	
Diving-petrels					
Common Diving-petrel *Pelecanoides urinatrix*		X	X	X	
Rails					
Inaccessible Island Rail *Atlantisia rogersi*		X			
Gough Moorhen *Gallinula [nesiotis] comeri*	X (introduced)			X	
Skuas					
Tristan Skua *Catharacta antarctica hamiltoni*	X	X	X	X	
Subantarctic Skua *C. a. lonnbergi hamiltoni*					X
Gulls and terns					
Kelp Gull *Larus dominicanus*					X?
Antarctic Tern *Sterna vittata*	X	X	X	X	X
Common Noddy *Anous stolidus*		X	X	X	
Finches					
Gough Bunting *Rowettia goughensis*				X	
Inaccessible/Tristan Bunting *Nesospiza acunhae*	extinct	X			
Nightingale Bunting *Nesospiza questi*			X		
Grosbeak Bunting *N. wilkinsi*			X		
Thrushes					
Tristan Thrush *Nesocichla eremita*	X	X	X		
Seals					
Antarctic Fur Seal *Arctocephalus gazella*					X
Subantarctic Fur Seal *A. tropicalis*	X	X	X	X	
Southern Elephant Seal *Mirounga leonina*	only 1 recent record	extinct as a breeder		X	X

precise position remained undetermined until as late as 1898, when the German Deep Sea Exploration Expedition correctly established it. Bouvet's failure to correctly register the island's coordinates had led Cook to search unsuccessfully for the island in both 1772 and 1775. The few other recorded visits in the 19th century were virtually all made by sealers and whalers (though a claim by the American Morrell to have landed on the island in 1822 is generally regarded as dubious). Men from the British ships *Sprightly* and *Lively* made the first documented landing in 1825 and claimed the island, which the sealers named Liverpool, for the British crown. A Norwegian scientific expedition visited in 1927 and this country's government formally annexed the island on 27 Feb 1930; the British government renounced its claim later the same year. In 1979 a small Norwegian research and weather station was established on Bouvetøya, with three huts being erected by a research expedition. A new building was built in 1997. Scientists visiting the island used a large container equipped as a research station (with four bunk beds and small office and kitchen areas) in 1996/7, 1998/9, 2000/1 and 2001/2. In Sep 1979 a thermonuclear device appears to have been detonated in the waters west of the island, though no country has ever admitted responsibility.

Visiting the island Special permission is required, even by scientists, to land on Bouvetøya. The presence of glaciers on the south and east coasts, and steep-sided cliffs in the north and west, leave few places where landings can be attempted even in favourable weather, while offshore rocks pose additional hazards to the navigator. All research on Bouvetøya has been conducted at Nyrøysa (54°25'S 03°30'E), a 650 m-long platform, which formed between 1955 and 1958 (see above), and is the most accessible part of the island, as well as supporting breeding populations of seabirds and seals. Only the north and south beaches of **Nyrøysa** should be considered as landing sites, albeit dangerous ones. Given that most of the island's Antarctic Fur Seals use the north beach, which is very rocky and broken, landings at the south beach are more advisable, though here there is an extremely strong backwash and strong, predominantly north-flowing current. Hidden rocks are a further hazard. Only minimal scientific work is permitted due to the potentially hazardous impact on the wildlife. The managing authority for Bouvetøya is the Norwegian Polar Institute.

463

Subantarctic islands in the Indian Ocean

The southern Indian Ocean islands represent some of the richest areas for seabirds in the world, in particular supporting a host of tubenoses. All are part of the Territoire des Terres Australes et Antarctiques Françaises, except the Prince Edward Is, which are owned by South Africa and the Heard and MacDonald Is, which are under Australian jurisdiction. With the exception of Amsterdam and St Paul, all are located in close proximity to the Antarctic Convergence and share a similar climate of cold, wet and windy conditions, marked by little or no seasonal variation. Several of these islands are famed for the number of shipwrecks, a factor that, along with the usual tales of sealing and failed farming projects, contributed to human devastation of their natural resources. Amsterdam was perhaps most severely affected, with the vast majority of the island's once luxuriant forest cover being destroyed by a series of fires that were deliberately or inadvertently started by human visitors. Despite such ravages and the effects of the many introduced predators to have reached these islands, most retain important colonies of seabirds, though landbirds, in comparison to other subantarctic islands at similar latitudes are almost entirely absent. Indeed, the islands are commemorated in the names of several species that are endemic breeders to this region, e.g. Amsterdam Albatross and Kerguelen Tern. However, most are comparatively rarely visited by casual tourists, as opposed to scientific researchers, and because of strict enforcement of protective measures for Amsterdam's remaining seabirds, those visitors that do reach the island are still not assured of seeing its fabled albatross.

Prince Edward and Marion Islands

Location and main features Collectively known as the Prince Edward Is, these volcanic islets covering 335 km² and part of South Africa's Western Cape province, are located at 46°54'S 37°45'E or 2180 km southeast of Cape Town, with the larger Marion being 19 km southwest of Prince Edward. They lie 925 km west of the Crozets and 220 km north of the Antarctic Convergence. Given the comparatively limited number of accidental and deliberate introductions of non-native species, it is unsurprising that the islands are of major importance to wildlife, supporting important populations of several species of penguin and tubenoses, as well as fur and elephant seals.

Landform, climate and habitat These c.500,000 year-old islands are subject to a prevailing climate of cloudy conditions (mean sunshine is 3.6 hours per day), strong westerly winds (reaching gale force on a mean 107 days per annum), low temperatures (mean monthly temperatures are near 0°C year-round) and heavy snow and rain (>2500 mm per annum, with Aug–Oct being the driest months). There is little seasonal variation, e.g. even in winter temperatures rarely fall below -4°C. Marion at 290 km² is the larger of the two and presents a landscape of low, rolling hills, including the archipelago's highest point, the frequently ice-capped State President Swart Peak (1230 m), and lakes. The central highland (mean elevation 1000 m) and island slope are separated from the volcanic coastal plain by a 400 m-high escarpment. Much of the landscape is covered by old grey lava, with some more recent black lava in places; the most recent eruption was in 1980. Three glacial episodes have been detected on Marion, with ice cover finally disappearing c.12,000 years ago; in contrast there is no evidence for glacial activity on Prince Edward. There is a single perennial stream on Marion. Prince Edward is smaller (45 km²), lower (the highest point is 672 m), but much more vertical in aspect, having 490 m-high sea-cliffs on its south-west coast. The islands vegetation is comparatively depauperate, with just 38 vascular species recorded, of which 14 are alien and none are endemic. Totals of 72 species of moss, 35 liverworts and 100 species of lichen are known from the group. Forty-one different plant communities have been identified. Coastal cliffs and slopes exposed to sea spray on both islands support tussac grass, *Crassula moschata* and *Cotula plumosa*, while the relatively level and poorly drained coastal plains are dominated by the grass *Agrostis magellanica* and herb *Acaena magellanica*, but near seal or penguin colonies communities of *Callitriche antarctica* and *Poa cooki* are more common. Mires and bogs are characterised by *Juncus scheuchzerioides* and *Blepharidophyllum densifolium*. Drained slopes of the interior hold the fern *Blechnum penna-marina* and above 300 m there is a feldmark of *Andreaea*, *Racomitrium crispulum*, mosses, lichens and cushions of *Azorella selago*.

Birds Four species of penguin breed on the islands. In the mid-1970s c.220,000 pairs of King Penguin bred on Marion and Prince Edward in seven colonies. Totals of 1543 pairs of Gentoo Penguin (1984 count), 415,500 pairs of Macaroni Penguin in 33 colonies on Marion in 1984 (17,000 pairs were counted on Prince Edward in the mid-1970s) and 161,500 pairs of Rockhopper Penguin on Marion in 1987 (35,000 pairs were present on Prince Edward in the mid-1970s) make the islands of key importance for this family. Large albatrosses are represented by an overall apparently stable population of Wandering Albatross, 1794 pairs on Marion (in 1995), most on flat, mossy areas below 100 m, with a major colony being sited at Goney Plain on the north coast, and 913 pairs on Prince Edward (in 1985), where it is most numerous in the east of the island, especially in the appropriately-named Albatross Valley. In addition, 7000 pairs of Indian Yellow-nosed Albatross bred on Prince Edward in 1979, with a probably stable population of Grey-headed Albatross, numbering 6217 pairs, on

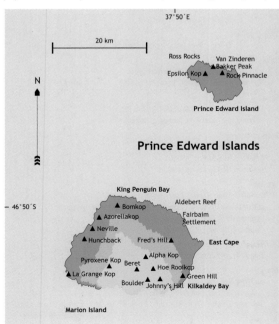

First red hill. Marion, Apr 2000. © Peter Ryan.

the south coast of Marion (in 1995) and 1500 on Prince Edward (in 1979), where it breeds in mixed colonies with the former species on cliffs of the north coast (this population is subject to considerable inter-annual variation). Both sooty albatrosses breed on the islands: Sooty Albatross numbered 2055 pairs on Marion in 1987 with 700 on Prince Edward (in 1972), and there were 201 pairs of Light-mantled Sooty Albatross on Marion (in 1987) and 40 pairs on Prince Edward in the 1980s. On Marion both sooty albatrosses are widespread on grey lava cliffs on northern and eastern coasts, but on Prince Edward Sooty is restricted to three areas on the northern coastal cliffs, while Light-mantled is more widespread, also using inland slopes.

Like most other islands in the S Indian Ocean, spectacular numbers of tubenoses breed (all population estimates from 1984, unless otherwise stated): Southern (1473 pairs in 2000/1 on Marion) and Northern Giant Petrels (540 pairs), Great-winged (>10,000 pairs, principally on Marion, in 1979–80), White-headed (unconfirmed but possible breeder on both islands), Kerguelen (>10,000 pairs, principally on Marion), Soft-plumaged (perhaps 1000 pairs) and Blue Petrels (up to 100,000 pairs, with most on Prince Edward), Salvin's (up to 100,000 pairs) and Fairy Prions (up to 100 pairs), White-chinned (perhaps 10,000 pairs) and Grey Petrels (up to 1000 pairs), Grey-backed (100 pairs) and Black-bellied Storm-petrels (1000 pairs), and small numbers of South Georgian and Common Diving-petrels.

Crozet Shag has a highly restricted world range, but breeds on both islands, with a population of 670 pairs, of which most are apparently on Marion. Subantarctic Skua numbers 960 pairs on the islands, sharing the shores with 1400 pairs of Black-faced Sheathbill (most on Marion), 230 pairs of Kelp Gull (of which 200 are on Marion) and 50 pairs of Antarctic and c.30 pairs of Kerguelen Terns.

Among vagrants, the Prince Edwards have hosted singles of Australasian Gannet, Intermediate Egret, White Stork, Eaton's Pintail, Corncrake, Ringed and Three-banded Plovers, Wood and Common Sandpipers, Little Stint, Grey Phalarope, Arctic Jaeger, Franklin's and Sabine's Gulls, Arctic Tern, European, Cape and Laughing Turtle-doves (origin of these records unknown), with increasing records of Chinstrap Penguin and Cattle Egret (at least 20 individuals in total). Other wanderers to the islands are as follows: Blacksmith Lapwing, Whimbrel, Common Greenshank, Terek Sandpiper, Ruddy Turnstone, Pectoral Sandpiper, Lesser Black-backed and Hartlaub's Gulls *L. hartlaubi* (latter unconfirmed), European Cuckoo (the specimen was originally identified and published as an African Cuckoo *Cuculus gularis*), Common Swift, Sand and Northern House Martins, Barn Swallow, Yellow Wagtail, Mountain Chat, Common Whitethroat, Willow Warbler,

Red-backed Shrike and House Sparrow. In addition there are records of a pipit *Anthus* and *Muscicapa* flycatcher not identified to species. Non-breeding seabirds include Royal Albatross (sensu lato), Black-browed Albatross (two records, the second was a bird that formed a mixed pair with a Grey-headed Albatross; the resultant egg failed), Antarctic Petrel, which is occasional off Marion in Aug–Oct, Cape Petrel, which is regularly seen feeding off Kildalkey Bay (Marion), Snow Petrel (one record) and Cory's and Little Shearwaters.

Marine mammals Subantarctic and Antarctic Fur Seals breed and to a certain extent, interbreed on both islands. Subantarctic Fur Seal, with in excess of 50,000 individuals at Marion, far outnumbers its rapidly increasing (17% per annum) counterpart, which is mostly colonizing the island's southern and southeastern beaches. Subantarctic Fur Seals are most numerous on western shores, while Southern Elephant Seals occur mostly on leeward eastern beaches. The Marion elephant seal population has declined by 83% since 1951 and by 37.2% in recent years, from 2120 individuals in 1986 to 1330 in 1994, with a 5.8% annual rate of change. Some 430 elephant seal pups have been born annually since 1994, and its population has since stabilized. Killer Whales abound in inshore waters and have been seen with very small calves. They take advantage of the large numbers of seals during spring and early summer, and exhibit an annual visitation cycle, some individuals returning to the islands. Vagrant Leopard Seals come ashore occasionally, and single Weddell and South African Fur Seals have been recorded. Southern Right and Humpback Whales have also been sighted very close to Marion.

Main conservation issues As on other subantarctic islands, recent conservation efforts have been directed toward putting right the damage caused by 19th- and 20th-century introductions of alien species. House Mouse *Mus musculus* which arrived on Marion (Prince Edward is fortunately free of this species) with early sealing visitors has harmed plant and insect life, preying on an endemic flightless moth *Pringleophaga marioni*, which may have led to decreases in the endemic subspecies marionensis of Black-faced Sheathbill, as they compete for invertebrate resources in winter. Records show that the islands are slowly becoming warmer and drier, which could lead to increased mice populations, as well as making the islands more susceptible to alien plant introductions, of which 12 species have already become established. The three most significant are *Agrostis stolonifera*, *Poa annua* and *Sagina procumbens*, which are all widespread. In addition, 12 alien insect species have become naturalized. The most significant of these is the Diamond-back Moth *Plutella xylostella*, which causes widespread damage to Kerguelen Cabbage *Pringlea antiscorbutica*.

The descendents of five cats, brought to control rodents on Marion in 1949, caused near-catastrophic damage to breeding seabird populations. By 1977 the cats numbered 2100, but have since been exterminated by introduction of a feline virus, as well as trapping, poisoning and shooting, being finally eradicated in 1991. Several burrow-nesting seabirds have shown improved breeding success as a result. Longline fishing was sanctioned off Prince Edward in 1996 and the following season over 900 seabirds of at least nine species (only 393 individuals were examined by scientists) were killed, including five albatross species and both giant petrels. However, illegal or 'pirate' longlining was rampant prior to the sanctioned fishery. It is estimated that illegal operators set more than four times the number of hooks set by the legal fishery in the first year. Seabird bycatch from the legal fishery is thus probably small compared to that of the 'pirate fishery'. Longline fishing in more distant waters (i.e. at the Subtropical Convergence and in continental waters of South Africa and Australia) also threatens

Prince Edward I. © Peter Ryan.

albatrosses and petrels, which cover vast distances during their breeding and especially their non-breeding seasons.

The Southern Elephant Seal population has experienced a population decline that has tentatively been linked to food shortages, while inshore-feeding populations of Gentoo and Rockhopper Penguins and Crozet Shag also appear to be suffering population decreases, perhaps linked to local changes in feeding conditions, due to climatic change.

Access to Prince Edward is severely restricted even to *bona fide* scientific researchers. Human visits are permitted only once every 3–5 years, when a maximum of four people is granted leave to stay four days. In contrast, a meteorological station has operated continuously on Marion since 1947 and has a constant population of just under than 20 people, swelling to 50 in autumn (April). Biological studies now constitute part of the station's work. The Seabirds and Seals Protection Act was enforced on the islands from 1973, while plans for an airstrip on Marion, investigated in 1987, were shelved due to environmental reasons. Both islands were declared Special Nature Reserves by the South African government in 1995 and a management plan and committee for their continued development and protection are in place.

Human history First sighted by a Dutchman, Lam in the *Maerseveen*, on 4 Mar 1663, the islands were not rediscovered until January 1772, when the Frenchman, Marion du Fresne, in the *Mascarin*, initially failed to realise that they were islands and mistook nesting albatrosses for sheep! The archipelago's next visitor, Captain Cook, who after failing to find the islands in 1775, finally located them in December 1776, gave them their name, the Prince Edward Is. Subsequently, sealers applied the name Marion to the larger. The date of the first landing on the islands is unclear, but may have been in 1799. What is clear is that sealers exploited them during the 19th and early-20th centuries, the slaughter reaching a peak in 1840, with seal numbers largely exhausted by 1870 and a brief revival around 1909 lasting barely two years. Many sailors were shipwrecked on the islands during the

19th century with some being forced to spend years on Marion. Scientists on board the *Challenger* took the first photographs of Wandering Albatross in 1873, also on Marion. By 1908 the British government considered it able to assume territorial rights, granting William Newton an unrealized licence to exploit the islands' guano. Subsequently, in 1926–30, the Kerguelen Sealing & Whaling Co., based in Cape Town, acquired exclusive rights to fish for seals and whales, take guano and extract minerals on these islands, and Heard and McDonald. In 1947, South Africa secretly mounted Operation Snoektown, which claimed the archipelago for the country, a regime that persists to the present.

Visiting the islands In response to growing pressure from tourism companies for new Antarctic destinations, the South African Department of Environmental Affairs and Tourism recently conducted an Environmental Impact Assessment of Tourism to Marion. The department's final recommendation was that small, special interest tours (<100 visitors) should be permitted to visit Marion, subject to a list of conditions. Despite this development no tour parties have visited Marion to date. Potential visitors to the latter are advised to study the *Prince Edwards Islands Management Plan* (1996) and *An Introductory Guide to the Marion and Prince Edward Island Special Nature Reserves* (1998), both of which are published by the South African Department of Environmental Affairs and Tourism.

Prince Edward is one of the least disturbed subantarctic islands and is thus strictly off-limits to visitors. Under no circumstances should anyone attempt to land or even cruise inshore by zodiac.

Marion is a large, relatively unspectacular island in terms of landforms and scenery. Boot Rock off the north coast is the only stack of note. Huge penguin colonies exist, and there are large numbers of fur seals (*tropicalis* and some *gazella*) and elephant seals. The best zodiac sites are probably the big penguin colonies, at **Kildalkey** in the southeast, which is the largest, but where the sea state is often rather rough. Difficult sea conditions are also often the case at the large colonies on the north coast (**King Penguin Bay**). The easiest area to work is around the base, between Ship's Cove and Archway (near **East Cape**), which tends to be calm in prevailing westerly conditions. In this area it is possible to see all four penguins, as well as Black-faced Sheathbill, the shag and Kerguelen Tern.

Crozet Islands

Location and main features Crozet consists of five main islands situated at 45°57'S–46°30'S 50°20'E–52°20'E, namely the largest Île de la Possession (145 km²), Île de l'Est, Île aux Cochons, and the smaller Île des Pingouins (3 km²) and Îlots des Apôtres (2 km²). The group is situated 400 km north of the Antarctic Convergence. The archipelago is frequently subdivided into the western group, consisting of the three last-named islands and the reefs Brisants de l'Héroïne, while the eastern group, 100 km distant, comprises the two larger, first-named islands. In total, Crozet covers 325 km² and lie 6500 km west of Fremantle, Western Australia, where a message attached to a young Wandering Albatross by a group of castaways on the islands in 1887 was eventually recovered. Discovered by a French expedition in the late-18th century and now part of the Territoire des Terres Australes et Antarctiques Françaises, the islands are of extreme importance for breeding seabirds, some being completely undisturbed.

Landform, climate and habitat Climate is typical of the S Indian Ocean territories being cold (3°C in winter, 8°C in summer), wet (>2400 mm of rain per year), windy and heavily overcast, though winters are rarely severe. The highest point in the group is

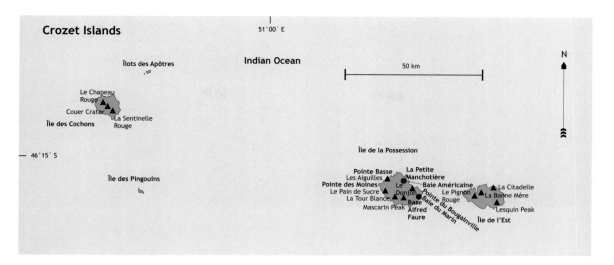

the 1050-m Mont Marion-Dufresne, on Île de l'Est. While coastal vegetation is dominated by tussac grass, inland smaller tussacs are replaced by a short-grass heath of *Deschampsia antarctica*, with burnet *Acaena magellanica* and *Blechnum penna-marina* ferns. The islands are unglaciated, lack ice caps and the highest areas are dominated by feldmark with cushions of *Azorella selago*. While Possession is dominated by huge sea-cliffs, inland there are green hills and valleys, and Île de l'Est is much rockier with jagged ridges and peaks interspersed by broad valleys and rivers. The Île aux Cochons is a former volcanic cone.

Birds Large numbers of penguins use the islands for breeding, including half of the world's two million plus pairs of King Penguin. A total of one million pairs was present in the group in the 1990s, by which time numbers were considered to have stabilized following a period of increasing numbers. The 2.4–3.87 million pairs of Macaroni Penguin that use the islands make the archipelago the second-most important breeding area for this species in the world, after South Georgia. There are large colonies on all five main islands. Rockhopper Penguin also nests throughout the group, though the total population of at least 264,000 pairs constitutes a comparatively small percentage of the overall world population of 3.67 million pairs. A total of 9000–17,000 pairs of Gentoo Penguin

King Penguin Aptenodytes patagonicus *colony, Île de la Possession, Crozets. © Michel Gauthier-Clerc.*

Île de l'Est, Crozets. © Gordon Petersen.

Typical landscape in the Crozets, with hills covered by various tussac grasses. Possession I, Mar 2004. © Hadoram Shirihai.

breeds on three of the five islands, including both of those in the eastern group, but with the largest numbers (5000–6000 pairs) on Île aux Cochons (1990s counts).

Albatrosses are another important and obvious component of the breeding avifauna. The Wandering population halved in the two decades prior to 1985, with 1963 pairs in the 1981–2 season, but numbers have been slowly recovering since 1986 at the rate of 4% per year, with the most recent estimate for the group being 2085 pairs. Black-browed Albatross breeds on three islands (Île de l'Est, Île des Pingouins and Îlots des Apôtres), with c.980 pairs in the early 1980s. Numbers of both Grey-headed and Indian Yellow-nosed Albatrosses are considerably higher, with 5940 of the former on four islands, of which just ten pairs were on Possession and most on Île de l'Est (in 1981–2), and 5800 of the latter on Île des Pingouins, in the 1990s, and 1230 on Îlots des Apôtres, in 1981–2 (with a total population estimate for the group of 7030 pairs). Previously observed infrequently at sea around the archipelago, four pairs of Salvin's Albatross (one of which had been ringed as a visitor on Bird I, South Georgia, in Feb 1981) were discovered breeding on Île des Pingouins in late 1986, the first recorded nesting away from the Australasian region. Both sooty albatrosses breed on all five principal islands: Sooty Albatross totalled 2668 pairs in 1980–1, with the best recent estimate being 2620–2740 pairs; and Light-mantled Sooty Albatross numbered 2305 pairs in the same season and the only figures available since, from Possession and Pingouins, suggestive of a slight decrease on the former (1.7% per annum until 1995) and a tenfold increase, from 30 pairs to 300 pairs in 1996 on the latter.

Tubenoses are represented by staggering numbers of the following species (all population estimates from 1981–2 unless otherwise stated): Southern (1017 pairs) and Northern Giant Petrels (1613–1663 pairs in the late 1990s, though numbers decreased by 33% between 1981 and 1994), Cape (200–300 pairs), Great-winged (tens of thousands of pairs, principally on Île de l'Est), White-headed (100–200 pairs), Kerguelen (tens of thousands of pairs, with nesting recorded on most islands), Soft-plumaged (colonies on four of the five main islands may total 30,000–50,000 pairs) and Blue Petrels (40,000–180,000 pairs in the 1990s), Salvin's (perhaps as many as 5.3 million pairs in the 1990s), Antarctic (100–200 pairs), Slender-billed (10–20 pairs) and Fairy Prions (70,000–290,000 pairs), White-chinned (breeds on four of the five major islands with a total population perhaps approaching 100,000 pairs) and Grey Petrels (2000–5000 pairs), Wilson's (20,000–90,000 pairs in the 1990s), Grey-backed (200–900 pairs in the 1990s) and Black-bellied Storm-petrels (2000–9000 pairs in the same decade), and

several million pairs each of South Georgian and Common Diving-petrels, which are both extremely abundant throughout the group. Little Shearwater may breed; it is regularly seen around Île de la Possession and Île de l'Est in summer and winter.

Crozet Shag, which takes its name from these islands, is not a strict endemic (it also occurs on Prince Edward and Marion), but numbers here are greater, with 815 pairs in the early 1980s being scattered throughout the archipelago. Recent winter studies at Possession demonstrate the highly sedentary nature of this bird. Another globally threatened species, Eaton's Pintail is restricted to Kerguelen and Crozet, where it occurs on all five principal islands and may number 600–700 pairs.

An estimated 2000–3000 pairs of Black-faced Sheathbill occur, with over one-third of these on Possession, where the species appears to be increasing, presumably in response to the population expansion in King Penguin noted on the same island. Subantarctic Skua breeds on all five main islands with a total of c.900 pairs, Kelp Gull may number as many as 800 pairs, four colonies of Antarctic Tern are known, totalling 103 pairs, and there are at least 150 pairs of Kerguelen Tern in three colonies.

Vagrants are comparatively few, but include Chinstrap Penguin, Australasian Gannet, Cattle Egret, Whimbrel, Greenshank, Green (unconfirmed), Curlew, Terek and Common Sandpipers, Ruddy Turnstone, Yellow-legged and Sabine's Gulls, Arctic Tern, Brown Noddy, Common Cuckoo, Sand Martin and Barn Swallow. Antarctic Petrel appears to be regular in small numbers at sea off the Crozets in Aug–Sep. White-necked Petrel has been reported

Black-faced Sheathbill Chionis minor crozettensis, Crozets. © Michel Gauthier-Clerc.

King Penguin Aptenodytes patagonicus *and Northern Giant Petrel* Macronectes halli, *the former protecting its egg from the top scavenger in the subantarctic islands. Possession I, Crozets, Mar 2004.* © Hadoram Shirihai.

Juvenile Gentoo Penguins Pygoscelis papua, *Île de la Possession, Crozets, Nov 1999.* © Hadoram Shirihai.

once at sea, off Île des Pingouins (the only Indian Ocean record). Southern Fulmar sometimes appears in considerable numbers in winter (e.g. perhaps several thousand were present in Aug 1996), while Cape Petrel is common at this season and Great Shearwater regularly reaches this far east in small numbers. In the late 1990s the distribution of seabirds off Possession in winter received some attention, providing valuable new information from this season. A remarkable record of a Laysan Albatross, between Crozet and Réunion in Dec 1984, illustrates the potential for future discoveries in this area and elsewhere within the S Indian Ocean. [For updated population trends and other recent data concerning the avifauna of the French-administered subantarctic islands, i.e. Crozet, Amsterdam, St Paul and Kerguelen, see Duriez *et al.* 2005.]

Marine mammals Three species of seal breed: Southern Elephant, Antarctic and Subantarctic Fur Seals. Leopard Seal is regular in small numbers, particularly in Sep–Nov. The following cetaceans have been recorded within French subantarctic waters and clearly all are possible in this group: Blue, Fin, Sei, Antarctic Minke, Humpback, Southern Right, Pygmy Right, Sperm, Southern Bottlenose, Arnoux's Beaked, Killer and Long-finned Pilot Whales, along with Commerson's, Dusky and Hourglass Dolphins.

Main conservation issues Whaling and sealing, both of which peaked in the first half of the 19th century, took a heavy toll, though seal numbers at least have now largely recovered. Penguins and albatrosses were also harvested on the Crozets, though rarely systematically. Longer lasting have been the affects of introduced alien predators. As early as 1805, Henry Fanning and other sealers brought pigs, cats, rabbits, rats and house mice to the islands. Though goats, which were introduced on Possession, and pigs, on Cochons, both died out due to their destroying the vegetation on which they were supposed to subsist, the other introductions have left more permanent legacies in the greatly reduced numbers of breeding seabirds. The islands were declared a national park in 1938 and intensive research into the archipelago's avian riches commenced, in earnest, in the mid-20th century. They were recently incorporated within the French Southern Territories Important Bird Area, as defined by BirdLife International, and all except Île de la Possession are Specially Protected Areas under Territoire des Terres Australes et Antarctiques Françaises (TAAF) regulations.

Human history The islands were discovered in Jan 1772 by Marion Dufresne, in the *Mascarin*, who named the group for his second-in-command and landed on Possession, which he claimed for France. Sealers took just over 30 years to reach the group, but by 1804–5 were shipping the fur seal skins direct to Canton, in S China, for processing and sale. Typically, within the space of

just a single generation the slaughter was near complete; a US sealer visiting the archipelago in 1835 found only two fur seals. Sealing was hazardous and the first of many recorded shipwrecks occurred in 1821, with at least two groups of mariners spending 17–21 months on the islands. As late as 1875, the surviving passengers from the *Strathmore*, which ran aground within the Îlots des Apôtres while en route for New Zealand, were forced to spend seven months on Île Grande, where they chiefly subsisted on a diet of young albatrosses before their rescue by a US whaling vessel. Indeed, whaling swiftly became the chief economic interest of the islands. By 1841 12 whalers were at work around the archipelago and just a couple of years later the number of US whalers alone had grown to 20. Such intensive exploitation again proved unsurprisingly short-lived and the islands remained little visited for much of the rest of the century, with most early

Macaroni Penguins Eudyptes chrysolophus, *Crozets, Nov 1999.* © Hadoram Shirihai.

Chick Wandering Albatross Diomedea [exulans] exulans, *Île de la Possession, Crozets, Nov 1999. © Hadoram Shirihai.*

information concerning the group's flora and fauna the result of information gathered by shipwrecked sailors. Only with the 20th century did real scientific interest in these and other islands in the S Indian Ocean gather pace. Possession was visited for such purposes in 1929, 1939 and 1957, when a photo-reconnaissance was performed. In 1959, more detailed work on the island's Wandering Albatrosses was undertaken and a permanent French base housing up to 35 people was constructed at Port Alfred in 1963–4, with continuous seabird research, which continues to the present, being initiated in 1966. Ornithological research on other islands in the group has been more erratic. The French government formally confirmed their claim to the Crozets by incorporating the group, along with the other islands in this region into the Territoire des Terres Australes et Antarctiques Françaises in 1955.

Visiting the islands The islands are highly protected and landings are not permitted without written authorisation from Monsieur l'Administrateur Supérieur, Terres Australes et Antarctiques Françaises, rue Gabriel Dejean, 97 410 Saint-Pierre, La Réunion, or alternatively Monsieur le Chef de District, Base Alfred Faure, Crozet, Territoire des Terres Australes et Antarctiques Françaises, and the services of a guide (such as those aboard the *Marion Dufresne*). The best way to access the islands is on the *Marion Dufresne* (there are no flights), one of the largest oceanographic boats in the world (120 m), which can accommodate 110 passengers. There are usually four voyages per year, in Nov, Dec, Mar and Jul, but these may be subject to change. Tourists are limited to 15 people each trip to avoid excessive disturbance to the avifauna and to the scientific bases, and visits must be supervised by a researcher from the station.

The landing site is at **Baie du Marin** (46°25'S 51°53'E), on Île de la Possession, a bay 500 m from the base, **Port-Alfred** (46°26'S 51°52'E). Thousands of King Penguin throng the landing site along with a few Gentoo Penguins and Southern Elephant Seals. Also in this area it is possible to see Crozet Shag, Black-faced Sheathbill, Subantarctic Skua, Kelp Gull and Eaton's Pintail. The path to the base winds through nests of Wandering Albatross. While Killer Whales are regularly seen in the Baie du Marin, the best place to watch them is **Baie Américaine** (46°23'S 51°49'E) where several groups cruise the coast in search of young Southern Elephant Seals and King Penguins, which breed in this area. The bay is close to **La petite manchotière** (46°23'S 51°49'E) where there is another colony of King Penguin, and Gentoo Penguin and Wandering Albatross also breed along this coast. Landing is possible by zodiac or by walking from the base. Cliff-nesting Sooty Albatrosses can be seen at **Pointe du Bougainville** (46°26'S 51°51'E), a 30-minute walk from the base. One of the key sites for breeding birds is **Pointe Basse** (46°21'S 51°42'E), in the north of the island, where long-term studies of Wandering and Sooty Albatrosses are being conducted. This is a protected area and permission is only given to scientific visits. At the west tip of the island, **Pointe des Moines** (46°23'S 51°39'E) is a cape of sharp dark rocks emerging from the ocean and also the main area for breeding fur seals; thus it too is protected.

The largest King Penguin colony in the world is on **Île des Cochons** (46°06'S 50°14'E) but this island, as well as **Île de l'Est** (46°25'S 52°13'E), **Îlots des Apôtres** (45°58'S 50°27'E) and **Île des Pingouins** (50°26'S 45°58'E), is fully protected and no landing is permitted, but most of the tubenoses mentioned in the birds section are readily observed, often in huge numbers, while cruising around the archipelago.

Amsterdam and Saint Paul Islands

Location and main features Lying 700 km north of the Subtropical Convergence and almost at the centre of the Indian Ocean, these islets are important seabird havens and zoogeographically most closely related to Tristan da Cunha in the Atlantic Ocean. Amsterdam (37°50'S 77°31'E) covers 55 km², while St Paul (38°43'S 77°30'E), 89 km to the south, occupies just 8 km². Both are administered by France, as part of the country's Terres Australes et Antarctiques Françaises, and difficult of access, being 3200 km from Australia, 3000 km from Madagascar and 3300 km from Antarctica. Even having reached Amsterdam it still requires a mini-expedition to reach the protected nesting grounds of the extremely rare Amsterdam Albatross, for which the island is best known among birders. Consequently ornithological research in the group commenced in earnest as recently as 1973 (previous visits with a natural history emphasis were limited to the 'Passage of Venus' expedition in 1874 and the work of Paulian in the 1950s). Human impacts on these islands, which at 3000 km from the nearest continental land are among the most isolated on Earth, have been perhaps surprisingly severe; only ten of the total of 22 species known to have bred on Amsterdam persist there in the present day.

Landform, climate and habitat Both islands have not been subject to glacier action and are volcanic. The risk of volcanic activity is still present. Climate is typically dominated by wind and rain (239 days per annum and a mean total of 1120 mm, with a short dry season in Feb–Mar), with high humidity (82% in November) and significant cloud cover also noticeable features. Snow is rare and is usually confined to Amsterdam's summit. Being located in the subtropical zone, 500 km north of the Subtropical Convergence, mean seawater temperatures are 12–17°C, and on-land temperatures also vary little; the mean annual record is 13.7°C.

Tiny St Paul is a volcanic cone of which the eastern third has disappeared, either as a result of wave action or an eruption. Steep cliffs, up to 200 m high, characterize this side of the island, but the western and southern slopes are less steep, ending in 30-m sea cliffs, with an entrance to the central lagoon in the east corner of the crater. The island's highest point is the 268-m Crête de la Novara. Most slopes are covered by near-impenetrable sedge *Scirpus nodosus*.

Amsterdam is considerably lusher, and is one of the few subantarctic islands to support trees, principally *Phylica nitida*, but deliberate forest fires have destroyed much of these and modern-day, semi-wild descendents of introduced cattle have damaged much of the rest, outside of fenced-off areas. The accounts of shipwrecked sailors and early scientific expeditions have permitted a reasonable reconstruction of the island's native flora, the vast majority of which has now been lost. Amsterdam is oval in shape, with a central plateau (the former volcano's floor) of 264 ha and c.550–600 m high, and high points at 881 m (Mont de la Dives) and 742 m (La Grande Marmite), which were formerly part of the rim of the volcano's crater. This area of the island has many peat bogs dominated by a moss and sphagnum flora, as well as *Lycopodium saururus*, *Uncinia compacta*, *Poa fueguiana* and *Scirpus aucklandicus*. Lava flows radiate from the central plateau, generally reaching the sea as 20–80 m-high cliffs above narrow shingle beaches, except in the west, where the cliffs reach up to 700 m.

Birds One species of penguin, Northern Rockhopper Penguin breeds on the islands, with the population on Amsterdam varying between 17,400 and 39,871 pairs in 1988–93 and 9000 on St Paul in the 1990s, but numbers have apparently halved since the late 1960s. This form differs from *E. chrysocome* in phenology, voice and head-feather patterns, and clearly deserves further attention, being considered an allospecies here. Amsterdam Albatross is slowly increasing, and numbered 15 breeding pairs (perhaps equating to c.120 individuals, an increase of 25 since the 1980s) in 2000. Smaller albatrosses are represented by a declining (at the rate of 7% per year) population of c.18,990 pairs of Indian Yellow-nosed Albatross on Amsterdam in the late 1990s, where they nest on tussac-grass slopes at 50–400 m on the west coast, with a tiny group of 3–4 pairs on St Paul (in 2001), and 240 pairs of Sooty Albatross on Amsterdam (1995 count) and 21 pairs on St Paul. The majority of these two species breed on Entrecasteaux cliffs, from where there is a record of an Atlantic Yellow-nosed Albatross at the colony.

Few species of petrel survive (perhaps as many as six have been lost, including possibly Spectacled Petrel), all in presumably greatly reduced numbers since the arrival of humans. Just 10–50 pairs of Soft-plumaged Petrel and 5–10 pairs of Grey Petrel possibly persist on cliffs and steep slopes away from cattle-grazed areas, but have not been confirmed to breed. The endemic Saint Paul Prion (which is sometimes considered a race of Salvin's Pri-

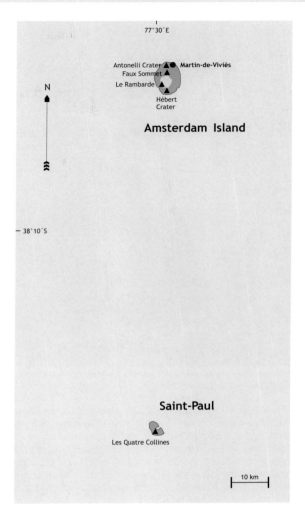

on) is known to breed only on Roche Quille, a small rock adjacent to St Paul (an estimated 150–200 pairs), which also harbours colonies of Fairy Prion (10–20 pairs), Great-winged Petrel (50 pairs), Little Shearwater (10–20 pairs) and White-bellied Storm-petrel (20–70 pairs). Wilson's Storm-petrel has been heard ashore on St Paul. Flesh-footed Shearwater has also been reported breeding in small numbers (532 pairs in 2001), but Common Diving-petrel has been extirpated from St Paul, though calling birds have been found on Amsterdam. There have been several recent (all since 1987) breeding attempts by Cape and Australasian Gannets (1–8 pairs) on St Paul, but only that in 2000 was successful. Eaton's Pintail was introduced in 1959, 1970, 1980 and 1981 but has failed to become established. Other survivors are Antarctic Tern, of which 200 pairs remain, and Subantarctic Skua with just 15–23 pairs in the late 1980s, though late-19th century reports indicate that it was formerly abundant. Sooty Tern breeds on Roche Quille, and there are at least three sightings from Amsterdam. Five introductions, the first in 1977 and the most recent in 1985, have led to the arrival of Amsterdam's only breeding passerine, Common Waxbill, which now numbers c.50 pairs around the base.

Among seabirds recorded offshore, Wandering, Black-browed and Shy Albatrosses are regularly observed year-round, Northern and Southern Giant Petrels are frequent visitors (most common in Jul–Dec), Cape Petrel is regular in Jul–Oct, Great-winged

Aerial view of Amsterdam. © TAFF collection.

Northern Rockhopper Penguins Eudyptes [chrysocome] moseleyi. St Paul, Nov 1999. © Hadoram Shirihai.

(Feb–Apr and Jul–Sep), White-headed (Feb, Apr, Sep and Nov) and White-chinned Petrels (Sep–Apr) have all been recorded with some degree of frequency, and Cory's Shearwater is also known from these waters. Southern Fulmar and Arctic Tern have each been recorded once and Common Diving-petrel twice, but Sooty Shearwater and Wilson's and White-faced Storm-petrels are regular offshore and Black-bellied Storm-petrel has been noted on a few occasions. Vagrant shorebirds include Large Sand Plover, Bar-tailed Godwit, Whimbrel, Common Greenshank, Common Sandpiper, Grey-tailed Tattler, Ruddy Turnstone, Curlew Sandpiper (regular), Red Knot and Sanderling, and other remarkable records from the islands include Cattle Egret, Black-crowned Night-heron, Hobby, Peregrine Falcon and Lesser and Red-chested Cuckoos. A number of other observations, including that of an apparent *Campethera woodpecker*, in May 1984, cannot be attributed to species.

Marine mammals Subantarctic Fur Seal was once numerous at Amsterdam, so common that landings could be problematic. Between 1789 and 1835 over 150,000 were slaughtered and by 1893 the species had apparently been extirpated. But in 1905 a colony was discovered on the northwest coast and, by 1983, 81% of the available coast was again being utilized by the species, with numbers stabilizing between 1982 and 1993 at 35,000 animals. Southern Elephant Seal is a summer visitor to the islands and Leopard Seal a winter visitor. Cetaceans recorded from French subantarctic waters and possible in these waters include: Blue, Fin, Sei, Antarctic Minke, Humpback, Southern Right, Pygmy Right, Sperm, Southern Bottlenose, Arnoux's Beaked, Killer and Long-finned Pilot Whales, Commerson's, Dusky and Hourglass Dolphins.

Main conservation issues The islands were recently incorporated within the French Southern Territories Important Bird Area, as defined by BirdLife International, and the most important breeding areas for birds, Plateau des Tourbières and Entrecasteaux

cliffs, are Specially Protected Areas under Terres Australes et Antarctiques Françaises (TAAF) regulations. The once-considerable tree cover on Amsterdam has been substantially affected by human actions. A large forest fire was noted as early as 1792, and two Tasmanian sealers started another fire in 1825–6 which raged for several months. Shipwrecked sailors, from the US-based *Lady Munro*, caused yet more devastation in 1833. Forest cover once occupied 27% of the island's land area, but had declined to just 5% by 1875 and only fragments of the once-extensive forests have persisted until the modern age, and these have been subject to further degradation as a result of browsing by introduced cattle (brought to the island in the late-19th century) and their descendents. Cats, one of six mammalian introductions as a result of Man's arrival on the island, still take significant numbers of birds in some areas, but current predation levels on the remaining seabirds are considered likely to be small. Most small, burrow-nesting procellariids have already been extirpated from Amsterdam. While major commercial fishing is not conducted around Amsterdam, given that some species range long distances on fishing trips, their bycatch is currently one of the most important conservation problems facing the island's seabirds.

Amsterdam Albatross was formerly much more widespread on the island, but habitat degradation due to fires and the introduction of cattle in 1871 has restricted the availability of suitable breeding areas. Goats and pigs, which first arrived on both islands in 1799 have also altered the habitat, and the latter is presumably responsible for local seabird extinctions, destroying burrows and eating birds and their eggs.

Given the effect of human introductions on the native avifauna and that most seabirds are now restricted to the peat soils of the central plateau, a management plan has been developed for the future conservation of Amsterdam. A fence dividing the island was erected in 1987 and over 1000 cattle were removed from the southern half the following year. In 1992 a second fence was constructed in order to prevent the remaining 400 cattle reaching the central plateau. A reforestation programme has also been initiated in the southern half of the island. Monitoring and research studies of the remaining flora, invertebrates and seabirds, with particular attention being paid to the endemic albatross, also form part of the management plan. Rats and rabbits were recently (1997–9) eradicated on St Paul, permitting the return of ground-nesting seabirds (notably prions), and on Amsterdam rats and mice are now the principal prey of feral cats in most areas (the cats having so thoroughly depleted the local seabirds).

Excavations for subfossil bones on Amsterdam have been richly rewarded. Unfortunately this research has also revealed just how much of the island's avifauna has been lost: 12 species appear

Roche Quille: this tiny rock stack off Saint Paul is the main breeding site of the endemic Saint Paul Prion Pachyptila [vittata/salvini] macgillivrayi. Nov 1999. © Hadoram Shirihai.

dated 1559, also appears to mark the position of St Paul, although the first clearly recorded sighting of the latter belongs to a Dutchman, Haevik Klaaszoon, on 19 Apr 1618. It was also left to another Dutchman, van Diemen, to name Amsterdam, on 17 Jun 1633. The Dutch were also first to land on Amsterdam, in 1696, when it was reportedly impossible to land without first killing the fur seals that carpeted the beach. Sealers initiated the systematic slaughter of the vast majority of the island's seals in the 1800s, with two US ships taking 150,000 skins on Amsterdam alone (to be sold in S China) before the market collapsed in 1809. There was also more-limited whaling activity at the islands until at least the 1830s.

At least nine shipwrecks occurred on the islands during the 19th century, during which time a Polish settler took up residence on St Paul, between 1819 and 1830. Fishermen from Réunion and Mauritius, and sealers from elsewhere also occasionally based themselves on St Paul, with 50 present in 1843 (by which time up to 300 goats were at large there), and 500 British troops were temporarily forced to camp on the island in 1871 when their transport ship developed a leak. At the same time, a Frenchman, his family and several employees attempted to start a cattle ranch on Amsterdam, though the attempt was abandoned within a few months, leaving the animals behind. In 1928–31, a French-based company commenced commercial exploitation of the abundant rock lobsters around St Paul; the industry at its peak employed up to 150 people seasonally, but appears to have been badly managed and eventually collapsed, leaving the staff marooned and starving. While the fishery continues to operate it is now wholly ship-based. Rock lobsters have also been exploited off Amsterdam since 1948. France established a permanent scientific station on the north side of Amsterdam in 1949, and annexed the islands as part of the Terres Australes et Antarctiques Françaises (TAAF) in 1955 (St Paul was first claimed by the French, replacing the Dutch in this region of the Indian Ocean, in 1893). Amsterdam is currently served by boat four times a year, with a permanent French staff of 15–20 at the research station, of which none remain longer than 18 months. The first natural history observations

Cape d'Entrecasteaux, Amsterdam I, Jan 1998. © Alfred van Cleef.

to have been extirpated from the island, including an endemic flightless duck (*Anas marecula*), a storm-petrel, a *Pterodroma* and *Procellaria* petrel. Similar research is planned on St Paul, where the early sealers are known to have hunted a small brown duck.

Human history The Portuguese were apparently first to discover both islands. Elcano (or del Cano), second-in-command to Magellan and commander of his Spanish fleet following the latter's death, first saw Amsterdam on 18 Mar 1522. A Portuguese chart,

Amsterdam Albatrosses Diomedea [exulans] amsterdamensis *displaying on their breeding island; access to this part of the island is strictly controlled. Amsterdam, Mar 2004. © Hadoram Shirihai.*

were made on St Paul and Amsterdam in 1874, but little intensive work was conducted until recent decades.

Visiting the islands As with most other islands in the region, the archipelago is fully protected and managed by the French authorities, and landing is only permitted at the base jetty at **Martin-de-Viviès** (37°50'S 77°34'E) and by complying with TAAF procedures. Visiting the fenced area of the plateau on **Amsterdam I** (see map), where Amsterdam Albatross nests is not permitted, unless you are part of a research team undertaking a regular monitoring visit. Most visitors to the island arrive on the *Marion Dufresne*; both the onshore team and the personnel onboard are very helpful, and can often assist you cruise around the island to the vast colonies of Indian Yellow-nosed Albatross on the cliffs at the southwest tip. Nearby at sea, especially to the west, there are often huge feeding concentrations of this species and petrels. Occasionally, at certain seasons, Amsterdam Albatross may be attracted to these congregations. To maximize your chance of seeing this bird you will need to visit from just before the onset of breeding (in late Feb), until when the parents are still regularly feeding the young. If you are fortunate, you may spot an individual approaching the island or flying over it, even over the base area. Around the base there is huge fur seal colony, which affords great opportunities to study this sociable animal at very close quarters. The *Marion Dufresne* has a helicopter and you may be able to charter it in order to explore the island from the air, but again it is not permitted to fly over the Amsterdam Albatross colony or Entrecasteaux cliffs.

St Paul is a beautiful and dramatically shaped island, to which access is also highly controlled, in order to minimize disturbance to the vast colonies of Northern Rockhopper Penguin, albatrosses and other seabirds. However, there are opportunities to photograph Indian Yellow-nosed Albatross and the penguin at very close quarters. Visiting vessels usually anchor outside the cone, but a small boat and zodiac can cruise into it on the east side of the island, where there is small jetty for easy landing (close to the small research quarters). From here, a c.20-minute climb will bring you to the heart of the colonies. Visits are only permitted if accompanied by conservation officers, and you must follow their instructions in order to avoid disturbance. The helicopter on the *Marion Dufresne* may sometimes be used for a very dramatic aerial exploration of the island.

Kerguelen Islands

Location and main features This archipelago lies at 48°35'S–49°44'S 68°43'E–70°35'E and consists of a main island, Grande Terre, and approximately 300 islets and rocks. It is the most extensive archipelago in the Southern Ocean with the exception of the Falklands. The group lies 2000 km north of Antarctica, 1800 km west of Australia, 3300 km southeast of Madagascar and Heard I is 500 km to the southeast. A long submarine shelf, submerged at a depth of 200 m, off the north coast of the main island indicates that the archipelago once constituted a much larger landmass. The group currently covers 7215 km², extending 195 km north to south and 145 km west to east. The islands are of extreme importance for breeding seabirds despite the depredations of the usual assortment of previous miscalculated and mismanaged introductions.

Landform, climate and habitat These volcanic islands, which have been subject to a series of extreme glacial events, enjoy typical subantarctic climatic conditions of rain (less than 800 mm per year in the east of the main island, but more than 3200 mm on the west coast), heavy cloud, cold (mean annual temperature is 4.5°C) and wind (100 km/h winds occur in all months). Prevailing westerlies regularly reach gale-force strength. Grande Terre is, at

The volcanic Kerguelen group is characterized by mountains, plains, deep valleys and lakes, all the products of intensive glacial activity, and mostly covered by low vegetation. Mar 2004. © Hadoram Shirihai.

its widest points, approximately 100 km north to south and 120 km west to east, but due to its heavily indented coastline, especially in the northeast and southeast, nowhere is more than 21 km from the sea. Deep valleys and lakes, the products of intensive glacier action, punctuate the island's high mountains and plateaux, while the Calotte Glaciaire Cook covers 10% of the west of the island, and is a remnant of the ice sheet that presumably once covered all of Grande Terre. Three such ice caps exist in the archipelago, all in the western part. The highest point on the main island is Grand Ross, at 1850 m, and the only flat low-lying area is the Courbet Peninsula in the east, which is marshy and has many ponds. Wind erosion has reduced most areas to a desert-like terrain, though valleys are dotted with pools and braided rivers. Shorelines largely comprise steep cliffs, dissected by innumerable fjords and inlets. Well-vegetated areas occur only below 300 m, where the principal native vascular plants, among the 29 species known to occur, are *Acaena magellanica*, *Azorella selago*, *Blechnum pennamarina*, *Cotula plumosa*, *Poa cooki* (tussac grass) and *Pringlea antiscorbutica* (Kerguelen Cabbage). One species is endemic to the archipelago, *Lyallia kerguelensis*. Mosses predominate in damper areas. Cover is very sparse or non-existent at higher altitudes.

Birds Penguins and albatrosses are important constituents of the breeding avifauna. King Penguin numbers are increasing, with 173,000 pairs in nine colonies counted in 1985–7 (given that the species breeds only twice every three years, up to 280,000 pairs may use the islands). The largest colonies, with nearly 100,000

Steep rocky islands and rough seas are features of the Kerguelen archipelago. Nov 1999. © Hadoram Shirihai.

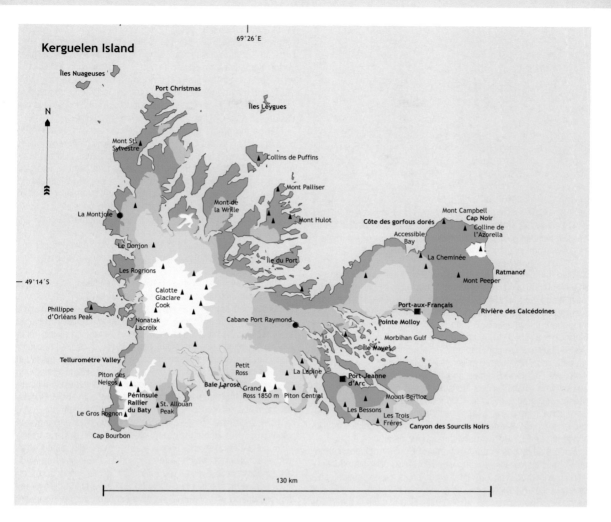

Kerguelen Island

Îles Nuageuses
Port Christmas
Îles Leygues
Mont St Sylvestre
Collins de Puffins
Mont Palliser
Mont de la Wrille
Côte des gorfous dorés
Mont Campbell
Cap Noir
Mont Hulot
Accessible Bay
Colline de l'Azorella
La Montjoie
La Cheminée
Le Donjon
Île du Port
Ratmanof
Les Rogrions
Mont Peeper
Calotte Glaciare Cook
Phillippe d'Orléans Peak
Port-aux-Français
Rivière des Calcédoines
Nonatak Lacroix
Cabane Port Raymond
Pointe Molloy
Morbihan Gulf
Île Mayes
Telluromètre Valley
Piton des Neiges
Petit Ross
La Lapine
Port-Jeanne d'Arc
Baie Larose
Grand Ross 1850 m
Piton Central
Péninsule Rallier du Baty
St. Allouan Peak
Mount Berlioz
Le Gros Rognon
Les Bessons
Les Trois Frères
Canyon des Sourcils Noirs
Cap Bourbon

69°26′E
N
49°14′S
130 km

and 30,000 pairs, are at Cape Ratmanof and Feu de Joie Beach. The population on Kerguelen has recently been demonstrated to be genetically highly distinct from that on Crozet and the birds at Kerguelen are also smaller in several measurements. The 10,000–15,000 pairs of Gentoo Penguin that breed in the archipelago are widely scattered, though it is particularly abundant on the Courbet Peninsula (8800 pairs recently). Numbers appear to have decreased markedly in recent years. More than 1.81 million pairs of Macaroni Penguin are present in 41 colonies, and numbers are increasing, while 15,000–200,000 pairs of Rockhopper Penguin were also counted in the late 1990s, when numbers had obviously increased since a 1985 count. Most of the latter nest in small colonies, with nearly 30% of these on the Courbet Peninsula.

Among albatrosses, there were 1455 pairs of Wandering Albatross in 1992 (numbers appear to be increasing in recent years), with most breeding on the Courbet and Rallier du Baty Peninsulas (combined total of 1050 pairs at these sites in recent years). Decreasing numbers of Black-browed Albatross (placed at 3115 pairs in 1995) also breed, with the majority on Croy I in the 1980s. Fifty pairs of Indian Yellow-nosed Albatross were discovered within the large albatross colony on Croy I, in 1984–5. Totals of 7860 pairs of Grey-headed Albatross (almost all on Croy in close association with Black-browed Albatrosses) and 4000 widely scattered pairs of Light-mantled Sooty Albatross were counted during the same

period, with some inland at altitudes up to 400 m and up to 20 km from the open sea, while c.6 pairs of Sooty Albatross bred annually in the 1990s on the Jeanne D'Arc Peninsula, at Canyon des Sourcils Noirs (150 m altitude). This tiny outpost is the most southerly and easterly known locality for the species.

There are populations of both giant petrels within the archipelago: Northern is by far the more numerous with a population of 1450–1800 pairs in the 1980s, most in the east of the main island, and just 3–5 pairs of Southern breeding among its congener at Feu de Joie Beach and in the Telluromètre Valley. Kerguelen is a significant breeding ground for tubenoses: Cape Petrel (1000–2000 pairs) nests on rocky cliffs throughout the archipelago, while among *Pterodroma* petrels Great-winged (perhaps 100,000–200,000 pairs), White-headed (10,000–30,000 pairs and especially abundant on islands in the Morbihan Gulf), Kerguelen (breeds throughout with 50,000–100,000 pairs) and Soft-plumaged Petrels (colonies containing several hundreds of pairs were discovered on Foch and Howe Is in the 1980s) are all known to breed. Huge numbers (100,000–200,000 pairs) of Blue Petrel nest, although the species is now most abundant on the Morbihan Gulf islands. Three species of prion, Antarctic, Slender-billed and Fairy breed, with numbers of the two first-named almost certainly exceeding several million pairs. Fairy Prion is far rarer, with 1000–2000 pairs on Croy and 50+ pairs on Howe. Both White-

A female Wandering Albatross Diomedea [exulans] exulans returns from a long foraging trip. Kerguelen, Apr 1996. © Frédéric Jiguet.

chinned and Grey Petrels are abundant, with perhaps as many as 30,000–60,000 pairs of the former, principally in the east of the main island, and 10,000–20,000 of the latter species. Large numbers (400,000–800,000 pairs) of Wilson's Storm-petrel also breed throughout the archipelago, with much smaller concentrations of Black-bellied (5000–10,000 pairs) and Grey-backed Storm-petrels (1000–2000 pairs) reported to nest. Total numbers of Common Diving-petrel may reach three million pairs, with the densely vegetated Morbihan Gulf islands again constituting an extremely important and cat-free refuge for this species. At sea in this area it is possible to see groups of up to 1000 individuals on the water. South Georgian Diving-petrel is apparently even more numerous, with 2–5 million pairs. It tends to breed at more inland localities than its congener, and on rocky ground throughout the archipelago.

Recent advances in the taxonomy of Southern Ocean cormorants have favoured affording specific status to isolated populations and that breeding on Kerguelen is no exception. Like several other *Phalacrocorax* taxa within our region, numbers of Kerguelen Shag are small; just 10,000–12,000 pairs in the 1990s scattered through most areas in the archipelago. Eaton's Pintail, which is currently considered globally threatened, was still reasonably common in suitable habitat throughout the archipelago in the 1980s (when still hunted; it is now protected), though most abundant (up to 5000 pairs) in the eastern part of the Courbet Peninsula. Mallard was introduced in 1959, but had disappeared five years later and similar, subsequent introductions also appear to have failed. Other seabird breeders are: Black-faced Sheathbill (scattered along most shorelines, with a significant proportion of the world's population, 3000–5000 pairs breeding throughout the group, often at low densities and in close proximity to breeding penguins or shags), Subantarctic Skua (2000–4000 pairs), which is particularly common given the large numbers of breeding petrels in the Morbihan Gulf, Kelp Gull (common throughout with perhaps 3000–5000 pairs), and Kerguelen (2500 pairs in small colonies throughout the group) and Antarctic Terns (1000–2000 pairs).

Vagrants have included Emperor (singles in 1898 and 1973), Adélie, Chinstrap and Erect-crested Penguins and an unverified report of Yellow-eyed Penguin, Campbell Albatross, an unidentified pratincole *Glareola* sp., three Large Sand Plovers together, several Common Greenshanks and Ruddy Turnstones, Common and Curlew Sandpipers (the latter apparently a regular visitor), Sanderling, South Polar and Chilean Skuas (the latter unconfirmed) and a dead Broad-billed Roller. An ad Salvin's Albatross has frequented a Black-browed Albatross colony for several

years, even building a nest in 1996. In common with other islands in this region there are comparatively few data concerning seabirds off Kerguelen, but Southern Fulmar appears to be regular visitor, sometimes in large numbers (1035 moulting individuals were observed in a fjord in the north of the archipelago in Nov 1987) and may be regular at most other islands in the region too, though there are fewer data to support this. Antarctic Petrel is occasional in Aug–Oct and Snow Petrel rare in summer.

Marine mammals Since the cessation in sealing, numbers of both Antarctic Fur and Southern Elephant Seals have rebounded, and these species are currently increasing, although their numbers are still well below those of the early-19th century. Leopard Seal is regularly present in winter on Kerguelen, and Weddell and Crabeater Seals are rare visitors. Among cetaceans recorded in French subantarctic waters the following are possible offshore: Blue, Fin, Sei, Antarctic Minke, Humpback, Southern Right, Pygmy Right, Sperm, Southern Bottlenose (known from this group as a beached animal stranded in 1996), Arnoux's Beaked, Killer and Long-finned Pilot Whales, along with Commerson's, Dusky and Hourglass Dolphins.

Main conservation issues Both fur and elephant seal colonies suffered enormously at the hands of sealers in the 19th century. Penguins and albatrosses were also harvested, with both eggs and ads being taken during the same period. Efforts to reverse the effects of the predictable catalogue of introduced aliens (12 in total) have commenced in recent years. Mice, which are principally restricted to areas close to human settlements, and cats arrived in the 19th century and the latter have taken a toll on burrow nesters, their eggs and chicks. Cats have also had an effect since their arrival in 1956; they are now widespread south of a line bordering the southern edge of the Cook glacier. Rabbits, deliberately introduced in 1874, have been the scourge of the native flora and are very widespread throughout the group, although tussac grass is largely immune to their attentions. Pigs, cattle, dogs, ponies, mules, mink and even reindeer, which were released in 1955, have all made an appearance on Grande Terre. Mouflon, a wild sheep from Corsica, persist on one island (Île Haute) and several hundred sheep are present on Île Longue. Cat and rat control programmes were commenced in 1972, especially on small isolated islands but have not been wholly successful, while myxamotosis was deliberately introduced twice in the mid-1950s to curb the numbers of rabbits. Following a rapid decline, numbers quickly bounced back, but it

King Penguins Aptenodytes patagonicus returning to the sea. Ratmanof, Kerguelen, Nov 1999. © Hadoram Shirihai.

was successfully extirpated from three islets in the Golfe du Morbihan between 1992 and 1994 (Îles Verte, Guillou and Cochons), and rat and mice eradication programmes on some islets are set to commence in 2002. As through most of the region, longline fishing (for *Dissostichus eleginoides*) commenced recently, with the usual risks to seabird populations; thus far, diving species and several albatross species have been caught. The islands were recently incorporated within the French Southern Territories Important Bird Area, as defined by BirdLife International, and some islands and sites are Specially Protected Areas under Terres Australes et Antarctiques Françaises (TAAF) regulations.

Human history Kerguelen's discovery, in Feb 1772, by the French captain Kerguélen-Trémarec is infamous in the annals of Antarctic exploration for the considerable misrepresentation with which the finding was announced. Kerguélen-Trémarec considered that he had discovered the long-speculated Antarctic continent, and on his arrival at the court of Louis XV embellished his account of the discovery by several magnitudes, declaring that the lands held the promise of rich farming and mining, including precious stones, as well as 'men of a different species'. Given such exciting news it is scarcely surprising that Kerguélen was despatched on a second voyage the following year with a larger fleet and 700 men to colonize 'La France Australe'. Unfortunately for Kerguélen, the second landing proved how fanciful his initial report had been. Upon his return to France he was sentenced to prison for 20 years (a sentence subsequently commuted to six years). Captain Cook was next to visit, in Dec 1776, and thereafter the first sealers, from the US, arrived in 1791. By 1817, sealers had completed the destruction of the profitable fur seal colonies, forcing subsequent commercial adventurers to turn their attention to elephant seals, which they exploited for their blubber. One US ship took 3700 barrels of oil in 1838–40 and, indeed, US-based ships from the port of New London, Connecticut held a near-monopoly on this trade until 1875. Expeditions from the US, Britain and Germany all visited the archipelago in Dec 1874 to observe the transit of Venus across the face of the sun, and a British company attempted, briefly, to establish a coal-mining operation on Grande Terre in 1877. Quite a number of scientific expeditions visited the islands during the second half of the 19th century, but surprisingly little was known of their avifauna until recent decades. The French government formally annexed Kerguelen in 1893, whereupon it issued a 50-year sealing and whaling lease to a French company, who established a station on Grande Terre between 1908 and 1925. Further such bases were operated in 1951–6 and 1956–60. During the Second

World War, the Allies, concerned at the possibility of Axis forces using the archipelago as a warship or submarine base, mined several of the deeper fjords, making these dangerous anchorages even today. Both in the late 1920s and early 1930s, and again following the war, the French geologist Aubert de la Rüe spent long periods working on the geography and vegetation of the group. Formerly administered as a dependency of Madagascar, the islands were included within the Terres Australes et Antarctiques Françaises (TAAF) in 1955. A permanently occupied station was established on the east coast of Grand Terre in 1949, and the French National Center for Space Studies founded a satellite-tracking station in 1994. Currently up to 120 personnel summer on the islands, with up to 70 wintering there.

Visiting the islands All visits require permission from the administrative department of the Terres Australes et Antarctiques Françaises (either from Monsieur l'Administrateur Supérieur, Terres Australes et Antarctiques Françaises, rue Gabriel Dejean, 97 410 Saint-Pierre, La Réunion, or alternatively Monsieur le Chef de District, Port-aux-Français, Kerguelen, Terres Australes et Antarctiques Françaises) and the services of a guide. For details concerning travel to the islands see the relevant section under the Crozets.

The landing site is situated at **Port-aux-Français** (49°21'S 70°13'E), Baie du Morbihan and several shelters (capable of accommodating up to 12 people) have been constructed there for tourists. Several seabird colonies are very closely protected and even people working on the islands must be accompanied by an ornithologist when visiting these, in order not to disturb them.

Among the best places on Kerguelen is **Ratmanof** (49°14'S 70°33'E), which is situated on a long beach of the Courbet Peninsula and is the site of a huge King Penguin colony close to a river. It also harbours many small colonies of Gentoo Penguin, Black-faced Sheathbill, Subantarctic Skua, Kelp Gull and giant petrels in considerable numbers, as well as breeding Wandering Albatross on a well-vegetated flat plateau (mostly *Acaena adscendens*). Look also for Eaton's Pintail on the ponds here. There are many cats and rabbits in this area and consequently few nesting petrels, except some White-chinned and White-headed. It is also a very good area for Southern Elephant Seal (especially between late Sep and mid-Dec) and Leopard Seal in winter. Landing is only possible by helicopter but the anchorage is far from the coast.

Between Ratmanof and a small headland to the south, known as **Rivière des Calcédoines** (49°20'S 70°30'E), there can be many moulting penguins and migrant shorebirds: Common Greenshank, Curlew Sandpiper and Sanderling are annual. On the north

Kerguelen Petrel Pterodroma (Aphrodroma *or* Lugensa) brevirostris *at a nesting area. Kerguelen, Feb 1996. © Frédéric Jiguet.*

Incubating White-chinned Petrel Procellaria aequinoctialis, *Kerguelen, Oct 1996. © Frédéric Jiguet.*

Eaton's Pintail Anas eatoni. *Kerguelen, Jan 1996.* © Frédéric Jiguet.

coast of Péninsule Courbet is **Cap Noir** (49°04'S 70°27'E), which has one of the largest fur seal colonies, as well as breeding Light-mantled Sooty Albatross. Further northwest on Courbet is the **Côte des gorfous dorés** (49°04'S 70°16'E), where there are thousands of Macaroni Penguins and always a few black-chested 'Royal Penguin'.

Situated on the Morbihan Gulf, west of Port-aux-Français, **Pointe Molloy** (49°22'S 70°05'E) is a small protected bay with a tiny peninsula. Gentoo Penguin nests there, and there is a splendid view of the gulf and its islands. On the opposite side of the bay, Rockhopper Penguin nests among the boulders at the edge of the cliffs. Landing is possible by zodiac in calm seas and the best time to visit is 15 Nov–15 Feb.

Port Jeanne d'Arc (49°33'S 69°49'E) is located at the very tip of the Morbihan Gulf and is well sheltered. The remains of an old whaling station can be seen and Antarctic and Kerguelen Terns nest here. This is good area for Eaton's Pintail, and Gentoo Penguin has occasionally been recorded on the beach. Easy zodiac landings are possible. One of the most highly protected sites is **Île Mayes** (49°28'S 69°55'E) in th Morbihan Gulf. It is among the best-preserved islands, with original vegetation and only introduced mice ashore. Hundreds of thousands of petrels breed here, including almost every species breeding on Kerguelen. Like Bird I in South Georgia, Mayes is a specially protected area where long-term ornithological studies have been conducted since 1985.

Another protected site is the **Canyon des Sourcils Noirs** (49°50'S 70°14'E), on the Jeanne-d'Arc Peninsula, which has a large colony of Black-browed Albatross mixed with Rockhopper Penguin, along with many Light-mantled Sooty Albatross on the cliffs and a few pairs of Sooty Albatross. A Salvin's Albatross has been returning to this area for several years. There are also tiny numbers of visiting Grey-headed Albatross and a colony of Kerguelen Shag on the cliffs. Landing is impossible (there being no beach, huge rocks and a heavy swell) and in any case forbidden, but it is possible to take a zodiac cruise along the edge of the cliffs.

The **Baie Larose** (49°33'S 69°20'E) is a beautiful bay with splendid scenery. King Penguin nests here, and there are Southern Elephant and a few Antarctic Fur Seals on the sandy beach. It is well known among tourists for the Doigt de St Anne, an eroded rock with a shark-tooth shape close to the beach. Landing is possible by zodiac, depending on the swell, and it is best visited in Oct–Dec.

In the southwest of the main island is the **Péninsule Rallier du Baty** (49°09'S 69°00'E), which is fully protected and has a huge colony of Macaroni Penguins (situated at Cap Bourbon) and stunning scenery of volcanic peaks and mountains. The Tell**uromètre**

Valley (49°32'S 68°52'E) on the same peninsula is one of the best landing spots within the archipelago, with a breath-taking view of the nearby volcanic peaks, and dense subantarctic vegetation. There is a colony of King Penguin and many Wandering Albatross nests. Leopard Seal is often seen in the vicinity of the penguin colony. The area is free of cats and rabbits, and in consequence there are many burrow-nesting prions and diving petrels at this site. Landing is prohibited but cruising offshore can be rewarding.

Port Christmas (48°41'S 69°04'E, which is known as Baie de l'Oiseau on some maps) is at the northern tip of the island and offers a protected anchorage in westerly winds. Its name results from the season of its discovery by Cook. There is a small King Penguin colony and Gentoo Penguin nests on the vegetated slopes. Light-mantled Sooty and Black-browed Albatrosses nest on the steepest slopes, but this is very dangerous terrain. Landing is possible by zodiac in favourable conditions.

Other excellent and fully protected sites are the **Îles Nuageuses** (48°38'S 68°43'E) and **Îles Leygues** (48°41'S 69°29'E), in the north of the archipelago, with their large colonies of Black-browed and Grey-headed Albatrosses, and fur seals.

Heard and McDonald Islands

Location and main features These volcanic islands, now an external Australian territory, comprise Heard, the tiny Shag which has been visited only once, 11 km to the north, and the three islands of McDonald (Flat and McDonald, and Meyer Rock), 43 km to the west at 53°02'S 73°36'E. Heard, the most significant of the group, lies at 53°05'S 73°30'E. The islands are physically remote, 4120 km southwest of Australia and 4740 km southeast of South Africa. In summer the Antarctic Convergence is c.180 km to the north of the islands. Like other Indian Ocean subantarctic islands, this group is of major importance to breeding seabirds, with the globally threatened Heard Shag being endemic to the archipelago.

Landform, climate and habitat The largest island of the group, 45 km long and 25 km wide and covering 375 km², Heard is a broadly circular active volcano, known as Big Ben, which erupted four times in the 20th century, most recently in 1992–3; and volcanic activity was evident in 1997 on McDonald. Steam constantly rises from the volcano and low cloud almost constantly shrouds its upper slopes, which reach 2745 m at Mawson Peak. Approximately 70% of the island is glaciated, but some glaciers are now in recession. Disturbing the island's otherwise neat globular shape

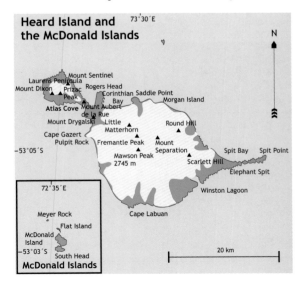

is the 10 km-long Laurens Peninsula in the northwest and 7 km-long Elephant Spit in the southeast. The island's climate is typical of the subantarctic islands, with a mean annual temperature of 1.2°C, annual rainfall of 1380 mm and mean annual wind speed of c.12 km/s. Eleven species of vascular plants are known from Heard, with tussac grass, *Poa cooki*, Kerguelen Cabbage *Pringlea antiscorbutica* and *Azorella selago* locally common, and cushions of *Colobanthus* abundant. The entirely ice-free McDonald group probably forms part of a volcanic cone that has been breached and partially destroyed by the sea. The islands are still poorly known, being rarely visited; five species of vascular plants occur, tussac grass, Kerguelen Cabbage and *Azorella selago* being the most common and forming luxuriant ground vegetation in some areas. The group totals 4.8 km², with the highest point being 212 m.

Birds The islands relatively untouched state means that substantial seabird colonies survive in the group. Full data from the most recent survey of Heard during summer 2000/1 (with further work planned for 2003/4) is not yet available, though some of the general results have been reported in the online *Australian Antarctic Magazine*. The most obvious constituents of the avifauna are the penguins and albatrosses, with more than 25,000 pairs of King (following the species' successful recolonization of Heard in 1948 the population has increased rapidly, doubling every 5–6 years and the 2000/1 survey indicates that this continues), c.16,000 pairs of Gentoo, one million pairs of Macaroni, principally at Long Beach (which holds perhaps the world's largest colony of this species) and on the scree slopes of the Laurens Peninsula, and c.10,000 pairs of Rockhopper Penguins on Heard in 1987–8. Additional concentrations of one million Macaroni existed on the McDonald Is in 1980. Most intriguing is the occasional appearance of white-faced birds, apparently Royal Penguins, within Macaroni Penguin colonies. This phenomenon has also been reported on several of the Kerguelen group and, perhaps erroneously, from Marion and the Falklands.

Among albatrosses, Heard harboured 600–700 pairs of Black-browed Albatross in four colonies, all in the northeast of the island (1987–8 count), with the southern cliffs of McDonald and nearby Meyer Rock supporting 82–89 pairs in 1981. Heard also held 200–500 pairs of Light-mantled Sooty Albatross in 1947–55 (based on late-1980s field work the lower figure now appears more likely), where it is known from at least seven localities, including the Laurens Peninsula, with possibly further colonies on the McDonald Is. A male Wandering Albatross was found brooding a chick at Cape Gazert, on Heard, in 1980 and two old nest mounds were discovered at the same time, but subsequent visits have failed to discover any additional breeding evidence.

Southern Giant Petrel breeds though numbers are declining, with 1700 pairs on Heard, in 1987–8 (there were 3500 pairs in 1951), and 1400–1600 pairs on McDonald in 1980. There is a record of Northern Giant Petrel, Southern Fulmar is considered accidental and Kerguelen Petrel has been recorded once or twice during the breeding season. Antarctic Petrel occurs in small numbers in Jul–Nov. Between 1000 and 10,000 pairs of Cape Petrel nest on Heard, but numbers appear to have declined since the mid-20th century. Antarctic Prion and Wilson's Storm-petrel are both reasonably abundant, with the former perhaps numbering over 10,000 pairs and considered to be probably the commonest of the burrow-nesting petrels in the 1950s, but accurate population estimates are unavailable for either species. Heard is the only island away from the New Zealand region with a breeding population of Fulmar Prion, which totalled thousands of pairs in the 1950s. Large numbers of South Georgian (at least 10,000 pairs on Heard, McDonald and Flat Is) and Common Diving-petrels (in excess of

King Penguin Aptenodytes patagonicus *colony. Heard I. © Eric Woehler.*

1000 pairs on Heard and McDonald) breed. True numbers may be commensurate with other colonies in the S Indian Ocean.

One of the principal reasons for visiting the islands is the endemic Heard Shag, which numbers just 2500–3500 individuals in four areas on Heard, with the largest colony (1000) on Pillar Rock, on the periphery of a Macaroni Penguin colony, only being located in Nov 2000. The other colonies are at Red Island in the northwest (c.30 pairs), Saddle Point, on the central-north coast (c.80 pairs) and Stephenson Lagoon on the northeast coast (c.100 pairs). One hundred pairs of Subantarctic Skua occur on Heard, with smaller numbers on McDonald and Shag, and possibly as many 1000 pairs of Black-faced Sheathbill occur on the same island, but there are few precise data available on the latter species. It is also been recorded on most of the other islands in the group. Kelp Gull numbers at least 100 pairs on Heard, but as with many of the seabirds breeding in these islands few concrete and precise data are available. Fewer than 100 pairs of Antarctic Tern also breed on Heard and at least some of this population has recently been demonstrated to winter in South Africa. The lack of ornithological coverage has led to few records of vagrants, but these have included two Emperor Penguins, regular records of Adélie and Chinstrap Penguins in the late 1940s and early 1950s, Common Greenshank and South Polar Skua, while Arctic Tern is considered a regular passage migrant.

Marine mammals Antarctic Fur Seal is plentiful on McDonald's beaches, with much smaller numbers of Southern Elephant Seal, numbers of which have declined by up to 60% since the 1950s. Both species also breed on Heard, where female Leopard Seals also pup. The resident winter population of up to 750 animals

Heard I. © Eric Woehler.

at this island is the densest concentration reported north of the pack ice. Commerson's Dolphin, which is otherwise restricted to extreme S South America, the Falklands and Kerguelen, has recently been discovered off Heard.

Main conservation issues This is the only major subantarctic island group free of introduced species (with the exception of the grass, *Poa annua*, which has recently reached Heard), and negligible modification by humans. Due to these qualities, other ecological and biological values, and their outstanding geophysical attributes, the islands were inscribed on the World Heritage list in 1997 (as the Heard Island Wilderness Reserve). Maintaining their integrity and unmodified status is the main conservation issue.

As yet the islands have escaped the problems caused by the arrival of introduced predators (though seals, skuas and sheathbills take some seabirds) and strict visitor guidelines and controls have been implemented to try and ensure that this remains the case. McDonald is completely closed to tourism and has been managed by The Territory of Heard Island and McDonald Islands Environmental Protection and Management Ordinance 1987. The islands, including waters to 12 nautical miles offshore are subject to a management plan, which has legal force under the ordinance. Copies of this can be obtained from the Australian Antarctic Division, which is responsible for administering the territory, while the Australian Fisheries Management Authority is charged with fisheries administration in this region. Some direct but low-level exploitation of penguin and shag eggs was made by members of the Australian National Antarctic Research Expedition (ANARE) base in the mid-20th century (see below) and commercial fishing activities offshore commenced in 1997, but have thus far been intermittent (though worth c.30 million Australian dollars per annum); an Economic Exclusion Zone (EEZ) was declared in 1979. Fuel drums, discarded when the ANARE base was closed in 1955, and some fishing and plastic debris have been cleared as part of major clean-up efforts in the mid- to late 1980s and again in 2000. The Nullabor Plain adjacent to the ANARE station, is the major breeding area for South Georgian Diving-petrel and is particularly sensitive to disturbance.

Plans to establish a Commonwealth Reserve of 7.6 million ha in the region were announced in Jan 2001; the proposed reserve includes the World Heritage-listed islands and associated territo-

rial sea, in addition to several distinctive marine areas, extending in parts to the 200 nautical mile EEZ boundary, and is intended to protect outstanding and representative habitats, geographical features, and terrestrial and marine species and their foraging grounds. Once proclaimed, a new management plan will be prepared for both the marine area and land reserve.

Global warming is having a considerable affect on Heard, with a marked retreat of more than 1600 m upslope having been noted in some glaciers. Mean ocean temperatures have increased by 1°C since 1947.

Human history Some dispute surrounds the archipelago's first observation. Cook possibly registered land around the correct position in 1773, and Heard was possibly sighted by another Briton, Kemp in 1833, and a North American, Long in 1848. It was left to John Heard, of the US, to unequivocally discover the island that bears his name in Nov 1853. Two months later, another Briton, McDonald, also found Heard and the adjacent McDonalds. Further visits followed in Dec 1854 (three) and 1857, all made by crews who thought they had discovered the islands. A North American, Rogers also made the first recorded landing on Heard, in Jan 1855, and his harvest of fur seal skins and elephant seal oil naturally encouraged others to follow suit. Because Heard offered no safe anchorages (at least seven ships were wrecked there between 1856 and 1880), elephant seal blubber was often transported to Kerguelen for extraction of the oil. Up to 15 ships worked the rich seal fishing grounds off Elephant Spit in 1858. The islands were formally annexed by the British government in 1908, who established Admiralty Hut on Heard in 1929, and their sovereignty was formally passed to Australia in Dec 1947. ANARE established a base on Heard in 1947–55, whereupon personnel and equipment was transferred to Mawson Station on the Antarctic continent. Since then, an Australian and a US expedition have visited Heard and two recorded landings (the only ones) have been made on McDonald by Australian researchers, in 1970 and 1980.

Visiting the islands Permits to visit Heard are granted by the Australian Antarctic Division, and limited to a maximum of 400 visitors per annum (with many fewer actually visiting due to the remoteness of the territory and hazardous landing conditions). At the **Atlas Cove Main Use Area**, maximum numbers ashore are restricted to 60 people in groups of 15. At all other sites numbers ashore must not exceed 15. McDonald, as mentioned above, is completely closed to tourism.

Rockhopper Penguin Eudyptes chrysocome filholi *colony, Heard I. © Eric Woehler.*

Table 1. Breeding bird and mammal checklist for the subantarctic islands of the Indian Ocean.

	Prince Edward and Marion	Crozet Islands	Amsterdam and Saint Paul	Kerguelen Islands	Heard and the McDonald Islands
Penguins					
King Penguin *Aptenodytes patagonicus*	X	X		X	X
Gentoo Penguin *Pygoscelis papua*	X	X		X	X
Rockhopper Penguin *Eudyptes chrysocome*	X	X		X	X
Northern Rockhopper Penguin *E. [c.] moseleyi*			X		
Macaroni Penguin *E. chrysolophus*	X	X		X	X
Albatrosses					
Wandering Albatross *Diomedea [exulans] exulans*	X	X		X	X
Amsterdam Albatross *D. [e.] amsterdamensis*			X		
Black-browed Albatross *Thalassarche [melanophrys] melanophrys*	X		X	X	
Salvin's Albatross *T. [cauta] salvini*		X			
Grey-headed Albatross *T. chrysostoma*	X			X	
Indian Yellow-nosed Albatross *T. [chlororhynchos] carteri*	X	X	X	X	
Sooty Albatross *Phoebetria fusca*	X	X	X	X	
Light-mantled Sooty Albatross *P. palpebrata*	X	X		X	X
Petrels and prions					
Southern Giant Petrel *Macronectes giganteus*	X	X		X	X
Northern Giant Petrel *M. halli*	X	X		X	
Cape Petrel *Daption capense*		X		X	X
Great-winged Petrel *Pterodroma [macroptera] macroptera*	X	X	X	X	
White-headed Petrel *P. lessonii*	X?	X		X	
Kerguelen Petrel *P. brevirostris*	X	X		X	
Soft-plumaged Petrel *P. mollis*	X	X	X	X	
Blue Petrel *Halobaena caerulea*	X	X		X	
Salvin's Prion *Pachyptila salvini salvini*	X	X			
Saint Paul Prion *P. [vittata/salvini] macgillivrayi*			X		
Antarctic Prion *P. desolata*		X		X	X
Slender-billed Prion *P. belcheri*		X		X	
Fairy Prion *P. turtur*	X	X	X	X	
Fulmar Prion *P. crassirostris*					X
White-chinned Petrel *Procellaria aequinoctialis*	X	X		X	
Grey Petrel *P. cinerea*	X	X	X	X	
Shearwaters					
Flesh-footed Shearwater *Puffinus carneipes*			X		
Little Shearwater *P. assimilis*			X		
Storm-petrels					
Wilson's Storm-petrel *Oceanites oceanicus*				X	X
Grey-backed Storm-petrel *O. nereis*	X	X		X	
Black-bellied Storm-petrel *Fregetta tropica*	X	X		X	
White-bellied Storm-petrel *F. grallaria*			X		
Diving-petrels					
South Georgian Diving-petrel *Pelecanoides georgianus*	X	X		X	X
Common Diving-petrel *P. urinatrix*	X	X		X	X
Gannets					
Cape Gannet *Sula capensis*			occasional		
Australasian Gannet *S. serrator*			occasional		
Shags					
Heard Shag *Phalacrocorax [atriceps] nivalis*					X
Crozet Shag *P. [a.] melanogenis*	X	X			
Kerguelen Shag *P. [a.] verrucosus*				X	
Ducks					
Eaton's Pintail *Anas eatoni*		X		X	
Sheathbills					
Black-faced Sheathbill *Chionis minor*	X	X		X	X
Skuas					
Subantarctic Skua *Catharacta antarctica lonnbergi*	X	X	X	X	X
Gulls and terns					
Kelp Gull *L. dominicanus*	X	X		X	X
Antarctic Tern *Sterna vittata*	X	X	X	X	X
Kerguelen Tern *S. virgata*	X	X		X	
Sooty Tern *S. fuscata*			X		
Waxbills					
Common Waxbill *Estrilda astrild*			X		
Seals					
Antarctic Fur Seal *Arctocephalus gazella*	X	X		X	X
Subantarctic Fur Seal *A. tropicalis*	X	X	X		X
Southern Elephant Seal *Mirounga leonina*	X	X		X	X

Subantarctic islands south of New Zealand

These islands, which are taken here to include the Chathams and the Australian territory of Macquarie, collectively offer a stupendous wildlife spectacle. Those with a fascination for seabirds, especially penguins and albatrosses, scarce insular endemics or simply remote, wild places will probably feel an irresistible tug in their direction. With the exception of Macquarie, they are owned by New Zealand and all have suffered long periods of human disturbance and interference in their fragile ecosystems, which have led to the loss of a number of avian forms and severely reduced the populations of many seabirds, as well as those of seals, which are still recovering their former abundances. Like other subantarctic islands, they have wet, windy and largely uniform climates, that show little, if any, seasonal differentiation. Ornithologically, however, each is unique. The Chathams especially, with their rich diversity of endemic taxa, including several seriously threatened seabirds and shorebirds, as well as landbirds (the most famous of which is, of course, Black Robin), are of particular importance and of international interest. While the Chathams may be singled out for specific recognition, all of the islands covered within this chapter are of outstanding importance for wildlife (especially given recent developments in albatross taxonomy), and visitors to the region will wish to select an itinerary that encompasses as many of these as possible, in order to gain as complete an understanding and appreciation of their faunas and history.

Chatham Islands

Location and main features This group, famous among birders throughout the world, totals 96,500 ha and consists of two larger islands, the main island of 90,000 ha known simply as Chatham, and the next largest, Pitt at 6300 ha, 17 km to the southeast, in addition to the smaller islets of South East (also known as Rangatira; 218 ha), Mangere (113 ha), Little Mangere, the Sisters, Forty Fours and Pyramid, which is home to virtually the entire world's breeding Chatham Albatrosses (in recent years one pair has bred on the Snares). Centred on 44°S 176°W and located 870 km east of New Zealand, the archipelago is not officially included within New Zealand's subantarctic territories, but is frequently incorporated within cruises to the region (and hence its appearance here). The two larger islands are permanently inhabited (total population c.700). Despite being situated on the same eastward

and southward extension of the New Zealand continental shelf as the subantarctic islands, Chatham's terrestrial fauna and flora exhibit a clear affinity with those of mainland New Zealand. The more temperate climate results from their proximity to the Subtropical Convergence. Associated steep gradients in temperature and salinity have produced a particularly rich marine biome, with aquatic fauna and flora from both zones. Despite the familiar tale of ecological damage wrought by humans, the group still boasts a number of exciting endemics, large numbers of seabirds, including several globally threatened species, and for those fascinated by island avifaunas they are an important place of pilgrimage.

Landform, climate and habitat The islands' basement metamorphic rocks were uplifted during a substantial movement c.140 million years ago (when they were still connected to New Zealand). Subsequently, during the Cretaceous period (135–65 million years ago), as the Earth's crusts separated and sea gaps appeared, the former New Zealand landmass experienced massive erosion and Chatham was isolated as a result. For the period of the Tertiary (65–2 million years ago) the islands were probably amalgamated, but periodic marine sandstone, limestone and green sand deposition, and two volcanic activities, early and late in this era, were responsible for creating the islands of today. Few areas of the world can boast such a prolonged history of volcanic activity within such a small area.

Climate is temperate, though dominated by strong winds that blow for much of the year. Nonetheless, temperatures are usually in the low 20°Cs in midsummer, dipping to 5–8°C in winter.

It may come as a surprise to those who have never visited the group that almost 25% of the land area of the islands consists of lagoons and lakes, with the largest waterbody being Te Whanga lagoon on the east side of the main island. The islands possess a highly distinctive native flora, which appears to be entirely a result of long-distance dispersal. Of the c.320 species, at least 40 (12%) vascular plants constitute endemic forms (of which 19 are trees, with two ferns, three grasses, two sedges or rushes and 14 herbs), but most derive from C New Zealand, with c.4% having clear N New Zealand or subantarctic affinities. Botanists consider 27 plants found on the islands as being under some degree of threat. Quite a number of non-native species (chiefly from other temperate regions of the world) have become established,

Pyramid Rock (left) with its huge cave is the sole breeding locality of the Chatham Albatross Thalassarche [cauta] eremita; *on the right is a close up of the cave and the tightly clustered nests, from where the albatrosses glide in and out at speed and from sea level look like swifts flying around a nesting cliff. Chatham, Dec 1997 and Jan 2007. © Hadoram Shirihai*

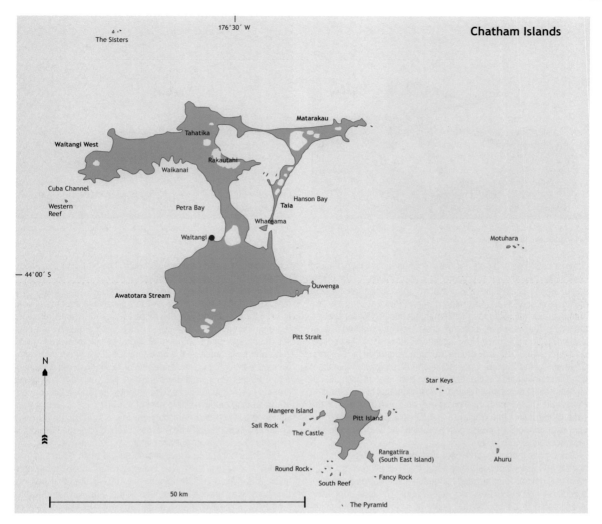

Chatham Islands

principally as accidental imports, though others are presumably escapes from gardens, with Chilean Guava *Ugni molinae* (which was apparently introduced deliberately by 19th-century whalers) of most concern as it has the capacity to become a serious pest.

Originally the most widespread vegetation, *Dracophyllum* forest, dominated by the endemic *D. arboreum* tree, formerly covered much of the hill country and rolling uplands, where higher rainfall and cloud favoured peat formation. Now it is reduced to comparatively small fragments. Other canopy species are also few, to the benefit of the harsh tree fern *Dicksonia squarrosa*, which has become an important feature of the understorey. *Sporadanthus–Olearia* shrub–rush peat communities are dominated by *S. traversii*, as well as the purple-flowered Chatham Island Aster *Olearia semidentata* and *Dracophyllum paludosum*. Intensive firing and stocking have considerably reduced the amount of *Sporadanthus* during the last ten years, but high-quality stands persist in the lowlands and Southern Tablelands. In hill country, wherever the incline is sufficient to reduce peat formation, mixed broadleaf forest is present. Formerly these diverse and productive forests were dominated by *Coprosma chathamica*, *Melicytus chathamicus*, *Pseudopanax chathamicus*, *Corokia macrocarpa*, *Myrsine chathamica*, tree ferns of the genera *Cyathea* and *Dicksonia*, and the endemic *Brachyglottis huntii*. Nikau Palms were

locally common in moist fertile areas. On coastal slopes *Melicytus chathamicus* and *Olearia traversii* increased, with occasional Nikau. These forests supported significant bird populations, but were largely cleared following the arrival of European settlers. Kopi (the local name for *Corynocarpus laevigatus*) forests were prevalent in well-drained fertile lowlands and some sand dunes, while very fertile sites held *Plagianthus chathamicus*, with *Sophora microphylla* on calcareous sediments. These areas have been almost entirely converted to agriculture, and only fragments remain. *Olearia chathamica* scrub formerly occurred on exposed rocky coasts, particularly on cliffs, serving as a hedge to mixed broadleaf scrub or forest, but proved vulnerable to the attentions of livestock and is now much reduced on Chatham.

Birds Around 100 bird taxa have been reported from Chatham, of which c.60 breed and the rest occur only at sea, or as vagrants or non-breeding migrants. New additions to the avifauna are made with comparative frequency, among the most recent being a Wrybill in Jun 1999. Of the 20 that have colonized in European times, at least six were directly introduced by Man, including California Quail and Weka, and the others originated from stock brought to the New Zealand mainland from Europe, North America or Australia. Of indigenous bird taxa ever recorded on Chatham approximately 40% are endemic. However, since European settlement

Ad Chatham Albatross Thalassarche [cauta] eremita, *Pyramid Rock, Chatham, Dec 1997.* © *Hadoram Shirihai.*

Ad Chatham Albatross Thalassarche [cauta] eremita *off Pyramid Rock, Chatham, Dec 1997.* © *Hadoram Shirihai.*

commenced, nine bird taxa, including four endemics (two of them *Gallirallus* rails and most enigmatically the Chatham Island sea eagle, as well as a bellbird and a fernbird), have been lost from the main island and seven (six endemics) from Pitt. Between the first human arrival and European settlement an additional four species have been lost, including a swan, a crow, the New Zealand (Black-backed) Little Bittern and New Zealand Scaup (which still persists on the mainland). Several others are greatly reduced in numbers. Chatham Island Pigeon, Chatham Island Red-crowned Parakeet and Chatham Island Tui are now rare on both islands, with the latter now extinct on the main island. Two indigenous birds, Chatham Petrel and Shore Plover, now occur only on South East and (in the case of the latter) the Western Reef. Chatham Island Snipe occurs naturally on South East, Star Keys and has been successfully reintroduced to Mangere.

Among the endemic and near-endemic extant breeders are Northern Royal Albatross which, with the exception of up to 20 pairs that nest at Taiaroa Head, Dunedin, and a few on Enderby I, breeds only on the Sisters and Forty Fours. The total population is estimated to be 6500–7000 pairs, of which most nest annually due to high nest-failure rates on the storm-damaged breeding grounds. Pacific Albatross breeds only on the Sisters and Forty Fours, with a tiny population (up to 20 pairs) on Three Kings I, north of New Zealand. The total population is c.18,000 pairs. Chatham Albatross nests only on Pyramid Rock, 8 km south of Pitt, where space is so restricted that some ads scarcely have suf-

The Castle and Mangere Islands, Chatham. © *Andris Apse.*

ficient room to stand beside their nests. The breeding population currently numbers up to 5333 pairs.

Chatham Petrel breeds only on South East, where it is very rare but regularly seen; there are only occasional records at sea. In 1995 the population was estimated at 600–1000 birds. Magenta Petrel is increasing slowly due to determined efforts by the conservation department, with a new colony being discovered in Nov 2000 and some additional burrows in Feb 2001, when total numbers were thought to be in the region of 120 individuals. Chatham Island Fulmar Prion was discovered in 1937, when it was found breeding on Pyramid Rock. Subsequently, in 1954, it was discovered breeding on the easternmost of the Sister Islets (where possibly now extinct) and remains were found in 1983 on the Forty Fours and Murumurus, where it most probably breeds but work is required to establish its current status.

Pitt Shag occurs on rocky shores on the main islands. Some are nearly always present near Waitangi wharf and the total population was placed at 729 pairs in the 1997–8 breeding season. Chatham Shag breeds on the main island, Star Keys and Rabbit I (off Pitt). Unlike Pitt Shag, it prefers to nest in dense colonies on level platforms, with the largest, on Star Keys, holding 339 nests in 1997–8, in which season the total population was 842 pairs.

Other seabirds that also breed include Little Penguin (endemic subspecies), Northern Giant Petrel, Broad-billed (among the world's largest population) and Fairy Prions, Sooty Shearwater, Grey-backed and White-faced Storm-petrels, Common Diving-petrel, Subantarctic Skua (c.259 birds, comprising 72 breeding pairs, 14 breeding trios and two larger breeding groups), Kelp and Red-billed Gulls, and White-fronted Tern. Much scarcer are Cape Petrel (only on the Forty Fours), Black-winged Petrel (only on Mangere), Little Shearwater and Great Cormorant.

Chatham Island Oystercatcher occurs on coasts in very low numbers (probably fewer than 200 in 2000/01, but numbers are responding well to predator control) and Shore Plover, which originally occurred in small numbers throughout New Zealand and the Chatham group but is another wader in decline; it is currently confined to South East, where there are c.130, with c.20 individuals being found recently on the Western Reef. Attempts to reintroduce it to Mangere in the 1970s failed, but a new attempt using juv birds commenced in 2001. Among other shorebirds, Chatham Island Snipe was once common throughout the group, but with the arrival of cats and rats vanished from all islands except South East (where c.1300 ads were found in a May 2001 census). Since the 1890s it was thought confined to this islet, but was discovered on

Ad and chick Chatham Albatross Thalassarche [cauta] eremita. *Pyramid Rock, Chatham, Dec 1997. © Hadoram Shirihai.*

Star Keys in the 1970s (fewer than 20 pairs during same recent survey, based on quantity of suitable habitat) and in 1970 reintroduced to Mangere (200–250 pairs), from where, in 1972, it colonized nearby Little Mangere (less than 30 pairs). Double-banded Plover also breeds. Pacific Golden Plover, Bar-tailed Godwit, Red Knot (groups of 500–1500 individuals have been recorded) and Ruddy Turnstone are generally scarce, but comparatively regular non-breeding visitors, while South Island Pied Oystercatcher, Grey Plover, Red-necked Stint, Sharp-tailed Sandpiper, Whimbrel, Lesser Yellowlegs, Oriental Plover, Hudsonian Godwit, and Grey-tailed and Wandering Tattlers are all vagrants.

Landbird populations are among the most interesting and diverse of the entire region covered by this book, and include three endemic species and five subspecies, some of which, at least, may be worthy of taxonomic reassessment. Forbes' Parakeet, only recently recognized as a species-level taxon (the most recent research suggests that it is sufficiently distinct to be considered well apart from the Yellow-crowned Parakeet group), currently numbers 500–700 individuals on Mangere and Little Mangere. Once one of the rarest birds in the world, Black Robin has staged a remarkable and well-publicized comeback from the very brink of extinction and currently (1999) numbers 259 individuals on Mangere and South East. Chatham Island Warbler is still common in wooded parts in the south of the main island, Pitt, Mangere, South East and Star Keys. Chatham's isolation has not spared it from the attentions of Shining Bronze-cuckoo, which uses it as a host. Chatham Island Red-crowned Parakeet persists in small numbers in the remnant bush patches on the main island, but like several other landbirds would greatly benefit from increased predator control. A significant population survives on South East. Though reasonably large tracts of bush remain on Pitt, the taxon is scarce there due to cat predation. Chatham Island Pigeon, a distinct taxon that has long been speculated as worthy of species status (and treated as such here), is now very rare and found only in the extreme south of the main island, and (very rarely) on Pitt (five birds) and South East (two birds), in remnant bush, though such areas are rapidly degenerating. Chatham Island Tomtit, another distinct taxon not yet recognized at species level (though treated as an allospecies here), is still abundant on South East, but was recently (c.1976) extirpated from the main island (a translocation attempt to re-establish it proved unsuccessful) and survives in only tiny numbers in wooded areas of Mangere and Pitt. Two other subspecies, Chatham Island Fantail and Chatham Island Tui, are doing better. The former is quite common throughout, except on Mangere, which was only recently colonized. The tui is probably now extinct on the main island but is more plentiful on Pitt and South East, and was recently found breeding on Mangere.

Natural colonists include White-faced Heron, Pied Stilt, Masked Lapwing and Welcome Swallow (which have become established only during the last two decades), as well as Mallard, Dunnock, Silvereye, Common Blackbird, Song Thrush, Yellowhammer, Common Chaffinch, European Greenfinch, European Goldfinch and Common Redpoll. Direct introductions include Black Swan (1890), Skylark in 1893, Weka in 1905, and subsequently House Sparrow and Common Starling. Swamp Harrier and New Zealand Pipit are reasonably common native breeders, while among less common

Chatham Albatross Thalassarche [cauta] eremita, *Pyramid Rock, Chatham, Dec 1997. © Hadoram Shirihai.*

Pacific Albatross Thalassarche [bulleri] *sp. Chatham, Dec 1997. © Hadoram Shirihai.*

Chatham Island Snipe Coenocorypha pusilla *is endemic to Chatham, with only tiny extant populations on a few offshore islets. Mangere, Chatham, Oct 2001. © Hadoram Shirihai.*

Black Robin Petroica traverse *almost became extinct but due to conservation efforts is now recovering. Mangere, Chatham, Oct 2001. © Hadoram Shirihai.*

or scarce nesting species (some only very irregularly) are Indian Yellow-nosed and White-capped Albatrosses, Spotless Crake, Purple Swamphen and Shining Bronze-cuckoo (irregular migrant). The list of non-breeding visitors is extensive, including Southern Royal Albatross, various populations of Wandering Albatross, Black-browed and Salvin's Albatrosses (which has recently been discovered ashore on Pyramid, where it may be breeding), White-chinned, Westland, Soft-plumaged, White-headed and Mottled Petrels, Flesh-footed, Buller's and Fluttering Shearwaters, Antarctic Prion, Wilson's, Black-bellied and Leach's Storm-petrels, Australasian Gannet and Arctic Jaeger. The vagrant list is also long, but some of the more regular and extraordinary include Erect-crested and Yellow-eyed Penguins (one of the latter has regularly occurred on South East for over a decade), Grey Petrel, Lesser Frigatebird, Eastern Reef Egret (formerly established but not seen for 25 years), Paradise and Australian Shelducks, Antarctic Tern, Long-tailed Cuckoo and Sacred Kingfisher. Rockhopper Penguin is a vagrant, with a record of one at a nest on South East in Nov 1970.

Marine mammals New Zealand Fur Seal breeds on some outlying islands and is still recovering from previous decades of exploitation; c.2100 animals were estimated to be present in 1981, including 700 on The Sisters and c.270 on the Forty Fours. New Zealand (Hooker's) Sea Lion was obviously fairly common in the past (judging by the number of bones discovered in Moriori middens), but is

Magenta Petrel Pterodroma magentae *was long thought to be extinct but following its recent rediscovery and due to conservation efforts is now recovering its numbers. The extant population breeds in a highly protected patch of forest on the main Chatham island.* © Peter Reese.

very rare now. Southern Elephant Seal is a regular non-breeding visitor and Leopard Seal an infrequent visitor. Sperm Whale is regularly sighted in tiny numbers (just 3–4 animals) each summer, but Long-finned Pilot Whale is the commonest whale in these waters, with large numbers sometimes being stranded. A number of other cetaceans have also been recorded in the waters around Chatham and many strand (for details see the species accounts). (The insect fauna of Chatham is also rich, between 750 and 800 species have been recorded of which approximately one-fifth is endemic.)

Main conservation issues The histories of South East and Mangere graphically illustrate the damage that humans and introduced animals are capable of inflicting upon island avifaunas. Both islands have been greatly modified by fire, wind and livestock over a similar period, and their avifauna exploited by commercial collectors. Land mammals in the Chatham group include Australian Brush-tail Possum *Trichosurus vulpecula* on the main island, along with feral cats, *Rattus norvegicus*, *R. exulans* and *R. rattus*, and European Hedgehog *Erinaceus europaeus*. Feral cats and House Mice *Mus musculus* occur on both the main island and Pitt. Polynesian Rat *Rattus exulans*, which presumably first arrived in the canoes of Polynesian settlers, was rediscovered in 1992 and is commonly caught in traps set in the Southern Tablelands during pest-control operations. Cattle, sheep, goats, pigs and horses occur in both a domestic and feral state on the main island and all, except goats, also persist on Pitt. Given the distribution of such introductions, it is unsurprising that South East, which has never had cats and rats, has apparently retained a greater proportion of its indigenous species, despite moderately extensive habitat destruction. The history of bird extinctions on this island is virtually unknown, but there were probably several. In contrast, Mangere, which was formerly inhabited by cats and possibly rats, lost 22 forms, of which 15 were endemic. The more complete destruction of the latter's scrub and forest cover presumably accounts for the extirpation of Chatham Island Pigeon, Chatham Island Bellbird and Chatham Island Tui, but fails to explain the disappearance of shore- and ground-dwelling forms, and its breeding petrels.

South East served as an onshore whaling base for a short period in the mid-19th century, and by 1880–1900 sheep were present. Subsequently it was overrun by goats until, in 1915, it was again leased for grazing and the goats eradicated. Lowland areas were burnt and sown, while over the following 40 years a flock of 700–1200 sheep and a few cattle were maintained. Eventually the island was acquired by the Crown and declared a reserve for the

Chatham Island Pigeon Hemiphaga chathamensis, *Chatham, Oct 2001.* © *Hadoram Shirihai.*

Weka Gallirallus australis, *Chatham, Oct 2001.* © *Hadoram Shirihai.*

preservation of flora and fauna in 1954 (now Nature Reserve), though the grazing lease was permitted to naturally expire in 1957. Cattle were removed in 1956 and virtually all of the sheep by Mar 1959; the remainder being destroyed by a Wildlife Service team in 1961, making the island free of all introduced mammals.

Mangere was long grazed by sheep, goats and rabbits, though fire and wind were probably the major causes of the removal of most bush in the early-20th century. Cats had been introduced just prior to this, to deal with the accidentally introduced rabbits and (and possibly rats), which they did effectively. However, prior to the eradication of these pests, cats had also contrived to destroy the greater part of the terrestrial avifauna, as well as populations of White-faced Storm-petrel (which has since recolonized Mangere) and Common Diving-petrel. Eleven forms (eight of which were Chatham endemics) were exterminated, including the last-known populations of Chatham Island Rail, Chatham Island Bellbird and Chatham Island Fernbird. Too late to avert the irreversible, the government bought Mangere in 1966 and the following year it was declared a reserve for the preservation of flora and fauna. By 1968 the Wildlife Service had destroyed all of the sheep and in consequence entirely rid the island of introduced mammals. Only small areas of natural vegetation exist on rock ledges and remnant coastal forest among boulders at the foot of the north bluffs, but in the late 1970s a re-vegetation programme commenced and a large area is now covered by young *Olearia* forest that will eventually support several of the endemics.

A total of 20 reserves, covering 4700 ha (or 5% of the islands' total land area), has already been established, usually as gifts by concerned landowners. Acquisition is generally considered a last option because the islanders largely resent the idea of the government 'grabbing' land. Conservation efforts are therefore focused on maximizing the potential of those areas already designated as reserves, as well as any land that is offered in the future. Work is required to fence those reserves on the main island and Pitt, to prevent stock from grazing the understorey, as well as to commence re-vegetation projects, control weeds and predators, and manage populations by nest manipulation and translocations of birds to new habitats. Where this has been done, the positive impact on native bird populations has been impressive. Fortunately, in Oct 2000, the New Zealand government announced a NZ$100,000 increase in monies for protection and restoration of Chatham's biodiversity, with some of this funding being made available for additional trapping of introduced predators and intensive nest

monitoring, which has already produced the exciting discovery of several new nest burrows of Magenta Petrel. Other threatened species currently subject to active management include Chatham Petrel, Chatham Island Oystercatcher, Shore Plover, Forbes' Parakeet, Black Robin and Chatham Island Pigeon.

Human history The *Discovery* and *Chatham* left Dusky Sound, in S New Zealand, on 21 Nov 1791. Lieutenant Broughton, in the latter, first co-discovered the Snares and subsequently Chatham, where he was met by the Morioris (who numbered c.2000 people at this time). These were East Polynesians who had settled there either directly and via New Zealand, probably in the 13th or 14th centuries. Upon the European arrival they were isolated from other populations and had developed a unique culture. The next visitors were sealers, but whether Chatham ever yielded comparable quantities of skins to the subantarctic islands is unknown, although the earliest sealing records from Chatham did closely follow huge hauls at the Antipodes and Aucklands.

It was only following heavy fishing of the C Pacific in the 1820s that whalers turned their attention to Chatham. Such activity in the group dates from 1830–1, when at least two ships searched for Southern Right Whales in these waters. From Feb 1835 numbers of visiting whalers gradually increased and the 1839–40 season was a bonanza for the 50-plus ships that patrolled offshore waters for Sperm Whales, which were processed at sea, and inshore for right whales. An abrupt decline in this formerly lucrative business occurred in the following decade, but a greatly reduced industry persisted, with the last whaling ship visiting these waters in Apr

Chatham Island Oystercatcher Haematopus chathamensis. *Chatham, Oct 2001.* © *Hadoram Shirihai.*

The race of Tui Prosthemadera novaeseelandiae chathamensis *is endemic to the Chathams. Pitt I, Jan 2007, © Hadoram Shirihai.*

Male Shore Plover Thinornis novaeseelandiae, *Chatham, Oct 2001. © Hadoram Shirihai.*

1888. Records exist of at least 250 whaling visits to Chatham and the total catch of Sperm Whales was probably c.1000. Numbers of Southern Right Whales taken in these and other New Zealand waters are unclear, but the Chatham fishery was apparently exhausted within just six seasons, in 1835–41.

Maori arrived in 1835, taking hostages to force whalers to take them to the islands. Two tribes were involved, and 900 men, women and children landed at Whangaroa and formally claimed the Chathams. Approximately 300 Moriori were slaughtered in the struggle, prior to their subjugation. The Moriori declined rapidly as a result of further killings, enslavement and demoralization (with the last dying in 1933), though some of their mixed-race descendents are alive in the present day.

European and Maori settlers farmed large areas, but during periods of low demand for wool or meat permitted livestock to wander, with the result that wild sheep, cattle and pigs now occur almost throughout. Fishing has always been important; between 1910 and the mid-1950s blue cod was the major catch. In the late 1960s crayfish assumed key importance and, most recently, paua and scallops. Farming and fishing continue to constitute the islands' economic backbone, which are no longer reliant on central government for subsidised transport and other services, but operate their own airline and shipping services, and enjoy some self-determination.

Visiting the islands The New Zealand subantarctic islands are administered by the Department of Conservation (DOC). Tour operators, individual tourists and researchers must apply for permits to enter the nature reserves, pay a tourism impact fee, and most vessels are required to carry a government representative aboard. The department has a minimum impact code in order to restrict disturbance to wildlife. There are quarantine procedures to limit alien introductions, no specimen collecting or souvenirs are permitted, and wildlife must not be approached closer than 5 m. The Chathams arguably are among the ultimate Southern Hemisphere birding experiences, especially if you possess a passion for island endemics. A visit in Oct–Apr, when many pelagics occur offshore, is unquestionably best. Most tourists visit in Dec–Feb, which are the warmer summer months, but the weather is still very unpredictable and can change rapidly, so alpine survival clothes are required. Offshore islands possess the richest avifaunas, but access to some, including South East, Mangere and Little Mangere, is prohibited for this very reason. The Sisters, Forty Fours, Star Keys and Pyramid are privately owned, but permission to visit them is occasionally granted. It is thus necessary to bird most of Chatham by boat, especially as many endemics, e.g. Shore Plover, are observable from zodiacs. Local fishing boats can be arranged as transport, but these are almost invariably expensive. Heritage Expeditions includes the Chathams in its itineraries as

Ad (right) and juv Chatham Island Warbler Gerygone albofrontata. *Although closely related to Grey Warbler* G. igata *of mainland New Zealand, this is a very distinctive species, best observed in the forest on Main Island. Oct 2001 (left) and Jan 2007. © Hadoram Shirihai.*

Nesting Buller's Albatross Thalassarche [bulleri] bulleri *on the Snares.* © Andris Apse.

well as the 2–4-day voyage between New Zealand and Chatham, which offers an exciting opportunity to practice tubenose identification, especially midway between the islands and the mainland where one can expect more western and northern species such as Westland, Great-winged and Cook's Petrels.

Opportunities for birding the main Chatham island or Pitt are limited due to wholesale habitat modification, and large areas are privately owned and require permission to enter. In the north of the main island the endemic shags and oystercatchers can be seen at **Matarakau** (43°44'S 176°21'W, private land). Do not approach the shag colony as it is declining, possibly as a result of human disturbance. Oystercatchers can also be seen at **Wharekauri** (private land). At **Waitangi West** (43°46'S 176°49'W, free public access) it is possible to observe Double-banded Plover, oystercatchers and other waterbirds. Waders occur on the main lagoon in season, but **Taia** (43°53'S 176°24'W, which is private land) is better than the west side for observing these. In the south, where the **South Coast** Road meets the **Awatotara Stream** (44°03'S 176°41'W), there is a forested valley (private land) where Chatham Island Pigeon, Chatham Island Warbler, Chatham Island Fantail and Chatham Island Red-crowned Parakeet can often be seen from the road.

There are three nature reserves: Tuku (in the south of the main island), South East and Mangere. Permits to visit these are only issued for approved management and research purposes. A Visitor Information booklet has recently (Feb 2001) been published by Chatham Islands Council (P.O. Box 24, Tuku Road, Waitangi, Chatham Islands, New Zealand). The booklet provides information on services, useful telephone numbers, reserves, tours, general information and a map of Chatham.

Snares Islands

Location and main features The Snares (48°01'S 166°36'E) are 209 km southwest of Bluff (the southernmost town in mainland New Zealand) and 105 km south-southwest of Stewart I, and consist of two small rocky islands, North East (2.8 km^2) and Broughton (48 ha), as well as several rocks, including the five islets known as the Western Chain: Tahi, Rua, Toru, Wha and Rima.

Landform, climate and habitat The islands are low lying, North East reaches 130 m and Broughton 90 m, though the well-vegetated coastal cliffs reach 50 m in places. Four major

catchments drain the east side of North East, where they form bays enclosed by more gentle slopes than found elsewhere on the larger islands. The only rock is a moderately coarse, even-grained muscovite granite, which dates from the Cretaceous (100 million years ago) and is similar to that found on southern Stewart I. Indeed, the islands are located within an extensive belt of such rocks stretching from South I to Marie Byrd Land in E Antarctica. In colour, they are almost white, but with weathering acquire a pink or reddish tint. The island's surface is entirely covered by peat to a mean depth of c.2 m. Indigenous plants are few, with just 22 species of flowering plants and ferns being known from the group, including three woody species, and these demonstrate a close affinity with the S New Zealand flora. But the milder climate (mean annual temperatures reach as high as 11°C), soil and birds (the excreta of nesting Snares Penguins can destroy the vegetation surrounding their breeding areas) have created obvious communities. *Olearia lyalli* forest, with a canopy of 6–8 m,

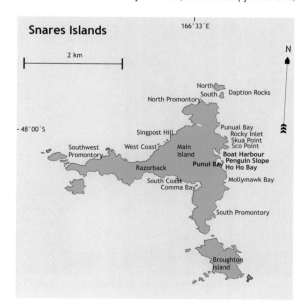

Snares Islands

166°33'E

2 km

N

North Promontory
North
South   Daption Rocks

48°00'S

Singpost Hill
Southwest Promontory
West Coast
Main Island
Razorback
South Coast
Comma Bay

Punual Bay
Rocky Inlet
Skua Point
Sco Point
Boat Harbour
Penguin Slope
Ho Ho Bay
Mollymawk Bay

Punui Bay

South Promontory

Broughton Island

covers the interiors of the two main islands, extending in places to the cliffs, where *Hebe elliptica* also grows, and occupies gullies and the majority of sheltered slopes. North East is the only island among the subantarctic groups to possess a predominant forest vegetation cover. In the east *Brachyglottis stewartiae* becomes a more common feature of the forest canopy. Undergrowth is virtually non-existent, largely because of the nest-burrowing activities of the Sooty Shearwaters that use the islands, but what there is consists of *Polystichum*, *Asplenium* or *Blechnum* ferns, and *Callitriche antarctica* and *Crassula moschata* herbs. Tussac meadows comprise two distinct formations, *Poa astonii* and *P. tennantiana*, which dominate the landscape of the west of the main island and also appear on the largest islet, Alert Stack, while the Western Chain, though almost entirely devoid of vegetation, has remnants of *P. astonii* on two of these. *Stilbocarpa robusta* grows as isolated specimens in hollows and sheltered areas or in broad patches mixed with *Asplenium* and *Blechnum* ferns. The many vivid green cushions of *Colobanthus muscoides* dominate rocky coastal communities, with the succulent *Crassula moschata* in crevices and forming bright green mats on adjacent wet peat, along with much *Callitriche antarctica* and *Scirpus nodosus*. The single endemic plant, *Anisotome acutifolia* is rather uncommon, but the threatened Cook's Scurvy Grass *Lepidium oleraceum*, which is now rare in mainland New Zealand, is still common here. Two introduced plants, *Poa annua* and *Stellaria media*, are very locally established on North East.

Birds Being free of introduced predators the Snares support huge numbers of breeding birds, including most famously the endemic Snares Penguin (c.23,300 breeding pairs in 1985, of which c.20,000 occur on North East) and large colonies of Buller's Albatross (8877 breeding pairs in 1997) on North East and Broughton

Breeding Salvin's Albatrosses Thalassarche [cauta] salvini, *Snares, Dec 1984. © Colin Miskelly.*

and their outlying rocks and stacks, with tiny numbers located on Toru in 1984. The colony of Salvin's Albatross on Toru and Rima, in the Western Chain (585 chicks in Feb 1984), is one of two in the New Zealand region (Bounty has the world's largest population). Black-browed Albatross has been present in several breeding seasons since the 1980s, with one pair breeding in 1984 and 1986 on Toru, and Chatham Albatross has attempted breeding at least once (in Oct 1995) on the same islet. Cape Petrel, distinctive in this region due to the restricted white in the upperwing, breeds at many localities on North East, on offshore stacks and in the Western Chain (total numbers estimated at 7385 pairs in 1984). An estimated 2.75 million pairs of Sooty Shearwater bred in 1969–71, though a c.37% decline in the number of burrows was registered in 1996–2000, while Mottled Petrel and Common Diving-petrel nest in reasonable numbers (with perhaps tens of thousands of the former and c.250,000 pairs of the latter), and Broad-billed Prion in small numbers (2000–5000 pairs on North East). Both Fairy (c.4000 pairs on the Snares, principally on North East) and Fulmar Prions (in the Western Chain, where perhaps as many as 400–600 pairs nest) also breed in the group. Pacific Black Duck nests in small numbers on North East. New Zealand Snipe of the endemic form *huegeli* is known from North East, Broughton and Alert Stack, but the small population, c.1100 individuals, is source for considerable conservation concern. Subantarctic Skua (84 pairs in the mid-1980s) is scattered throughout the Snares, and Kelp Gull (which colonized the islands sometime between 1987 and 1992 and now breeds in very small numbers), Red-billed Gull

Snares Penguins Eudyptes robustus *at the 'Penguin Slope', North East I, Snares, Nov 1987. © Colin Miskelly.*

Snares Penguins Eudyptes robustus *and New Zealand Fur Seal* Arctocephalus forsteri, *Snares, Dec 1999. © Hadoram Shirihai.*

The Snares hold one of the world's largest concentrations of nesting Sooty Shearwater Puffinus griseus. Left © Colin Miskelly; right © Andris Apse.

(160 pairs in 1984) and Antarctic Tern (70 pairs in 1984–5) occur in small, scattered colonies, in the Snares.

Landbirds are led by an endemic and very distinctive, all-black, race of New Zealand Tomtit (*dannefaerdi*), which was conservatively estimated to number 500 pairs in the 1980s. An endemic race of Fernbird (*caudata*) is also common, with c.1500 pairs. Silvereye breeds commonly throughout (100–200 pairs), as does New Zealand Fantail (now c.300 pairs, though not recording breeding prior to 1982). Several European species introduced to New Zealand breed on the islands: Mallard (which hybridizes with Pacific Black Duck), Song Thrush, Common Blackbird, Common Redpoll and Common Starling. Common Chaffinch and House Sparrow have bred on a couple of occasions, while Skylark, Dunnock, European Greenfinch, European Goldfinch and Yellowhammer are only occasional visitors.

Non-breeding visitors include small numbers of Fiordland and Erect-crested Penguins that moult here, both Northern and Southern Royal Albatrosses, which occur in surrounding waters, and Northern Giant Petrel, which is frequently seen ashore, though breeding is unconfirmed. Migrant shorebirds involve small numbers of overshoots, such as Pied Oystercatcher, Masked Lapwing, Latham's Snipe, Bar-tailed Godwit, Ruddy Turnstone, Sharp-tailed Sandpiper and Common Greenshank.

The total number of bird species recorded at the Snares is 99 and in the last two decades, regular and more extended visits by ornithologists have brought more sightings of migrants and stragglers: Hoary-headed Grebe (the first New Zealand record), King,

Gentoo, Yellow-eyed, two forms of Rockhopper, Little, Royal and Macaroni Penguins, Grey and Blue Petrels, Salvin's Prion, Little Shearwater, White-faced and Black-bellied Storm-petrels, Australasian Gannet, Great, Little and Pied Cormorants, Auckland Shag (present from Jul 1994 to at least 2001), White-faced Heron, Great and Cattle Egrets, Canada Goose, Australian Shelduck, Maned Duck, Grey Teal, Swamp Harrier, Black-billed Gull, Black-fronted, White-fronted and Arctic Terns, Oriental, Long-tailed and Shining Bronze-cuckoos, Southern Boobook, White-throated Needletail, Red-crowned Parakeet, Welcome Swallow, Tree Martin and Grey Warbler. Other seabirds frequently seen offshore include Light-mantled Sooty Albatross, Southern Fulmar, White-chinned and White-headed Petrels and Grey-backed Storm-petrel.

Marine mammals New Zealand Fur Seal was almost eradicated during the sealing period, but continues to breed and significantly increased in the 1950s and 1960s, though numbers have probably stabilized since. New Zealand (Hooker's) Sea Lion is a regular visitor, with a few breeding most years. Leopard and Southern Elephant Seals are also regular visitors.

Main conservation issues Currently free of introduced animals, the arrival of rats on the islands would represent an ecological disaster; thus, only limited numbers of researchers are permitted to visit, a measure which also limits damage to the heavily burrowed soils. Fishing boats that traditionally moored offshore have been prevented from doing so, except three licensed boats, whose permits will expire when their current owners retire.

Ad Snares Island Snipe Coenocorypha [aucklandica] huegeli with chick. Snares, Jan 1987. © Colin Miskelly.

Snares Island Fernbird Bowdleria [punctata] caudate. Snares. © Peter Reese.

491

Human history The islands were discovered independently, on 23 Nov 1791, by Vancouver and Broughton, who were travelling in convoy from Dusky Sound, New Zealand, but had become separated in a storm. Vancouver was in command of a two-ship expedition whose goal was to explore NW North America. He named this group the Snares, a title that has lasted. The activities of sealers who obviously worked the group during the same period are little known, and no shipwrecks were recorded. Four escaped convicts from Norfolk I were marooned on the Snares in 1810–17 from the ship *Adventure*. Left with just a few potatoes, one became deranged, leading the others, who were eventually rescued by an American ship, the *Enterprise*, to push him off a cliff. In 1842 the islands became a New Zealand dependency and from 1867 to 1927 government steamers regularly checked for castaways and replenished a supply depot established there. Serious biological studies were initiated in 1947, when a team led by Falla and Murphy visited the islands for two weeks, incorporating a very brief visit to Rua. The Snares became a nature reserve in 1961, a status that was upgraded to National Nature Reserve in 1986, and World Heritage Site in 1998. Recent decades have seen the University of Canterbury construct a field station, based around the old castaways' depot on North East, which since the early 1970s has been occupied on a near-annual basis. A complete biological exploration of the Western Chain was a part of this work. Mention here should be made of research on Snares Penguin, Buller's Albatross and various petrels by John Warham and his students, and in recent years Paul Sagar and his co-workers have conducted work on the impact of fisheries bycatch on Buller's Albatross, while they, Colin Miskelly and others have made ecological and population studies on many other species using the islands.

Visiting the islands The Snares are administered by the Regional Conservator, Southland Conservancy, Department of Conservation, P.O. Box 743, Invercargill, New Zealand. A World Heritage Site of exceptional importance due to the lack of introduced animals, only two species of introduced plant occur. Essentially, the islands are pristine, with endemic forms of fernbird, tomtit, snipe and penguin, and provide safe nesting for huge numbers of seabirds. All landings require a permit, which are not issued for tourist visits; primarily to minimize damage to the islands' extensively burrowed surfaces. However, zodiac cruising along the east side of the main island, especially around **Boat Harbour** (48°01'S 166°37'E), **HoHo Bay** (48°01'S 166°37'E) and off **Penguin Slope** (48°00'S 166°36'E) permits good to excellent views of all the island endemics, with the exception of the snipe. Snares Penguin can be seen in large numbers at their landing places in Boat Harbour and above the cave in HoHo Bay. However, the most spectacular views are obtained off Penguin Slope, where hundreds ascend and descend the steep 150 m-high cliff. From mid-Dec, Buller's Albatross may be seen nesting on the cliffs around the island and close views can be had from zodiacs cruising close to the cliffs in HoHo Bay and **Punui Bay** (48°01'S 166°37'E, the latter en route to Penguin Slope). Tomtits and fernbirds forage on coastal vegetation and rocks, and are probably most easily seen at Boat Harbour and HoHo Bay. Antarctic Tern, Subantarctic Skua, Cape Petrel, Sooty Shearwater, and Fairy and Broad-billed Prions feed close inshore. Prevailing weather is from the west and so, unless strong northwest winds are blowing, access by zodiac is usually possible along the east coast of the main island. As is typical for New Zealand, the weather is variable, with the possibility of all four seasons in a day.

Auckland Islands

Location and main features This, the largest of the subantarctic island groups off New Zealand, located c.450 km south of Bluff at 50°30'S, comprises two main islands, Auckland (c.51,000 ha, highest point 644 m) and Adams (c.10,100 ha, 705 m), and several small islets, such as Disappointment (500 ha, 316 m) and Enderby (700 ha, 43 m).

Landform, climate and habitat The islands are dominated by two partially dissected basaltic volcanoes dating from the Miocene (12–23 million years ago), on a north–south axis, which reach 705 and 644 m. These rest on older lava rocks (principally 15–25 million years old) within a depression that has been locally exposed by erosion. Many reminders of the group's volcanic origin and history are evident, particularly the many lava and basalt flows on the islands shores. There are some fossiliferous sediments and unfossiliferous granites (dating from 95–100 million years ago) at Tagua Bay and Camp Cove, and the entire group appears grounded on a basement of biotite granite (95 million years old).

Given the lack of permanent ice and the considerable rainfall, vegetation is the richest of New Zealand's subantarctic islands (196 indigenous and 37 introduced vascular plants have been recorded), with coastal rocks, Rata forest, *Olearia* forest (apparently recently introduced, but locally dominant around Erebus Cove and on Ewing, though not dense and appears to be spreading only very slowly), scrub formations, *Poa* sp. grasslands, close-cropped sward and areas of grazing-induced *Bulbinella rossii* being segregated altitudinally. Rata forest fringes sheltered areas of coast, but in exposed areas there is a tussac land of *Poa litorosa* and/or *P. foliosa* with associated herbs and herb turf in the salt-spray zone. In addition to Southern Rata *Metrosideros umbellata*, woody plants are *Dracophyllum longifolium*, *Coprosma foetidissima*, *Myrsine divaricata* and *Pseudopanax simplex*, and on north-facing slopes continuous scrub occurs either above the Rata forest,

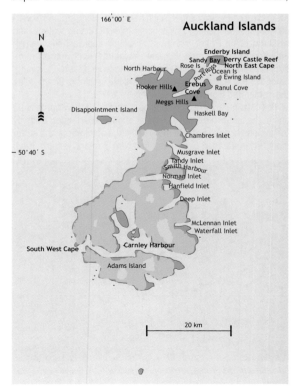

View of Fly Harbour, with nesting Light-mantled Sooty Albatross Phoebetria palpebrata, Auckland. © Andris Apse.

or from sea level on steeper, more exposed slopes to c.130 m. The understorey in such areas is generally limited to mosses and liverworts. Immediately above the taller forest is a dense subalpine shrubland of *Cassinia vauvilliersii*, *Coprosma ciliata* and *C. cuneata*, with associated ferns, mosses and herbs. This mosaic gives way to tussac grassland and scrub, with occasional 'windlanes', which also penetrate some southern valleys. The transition to predominantly tussac grassland *Chionochloa antarctica* takes place at c.200 m, sometimes lower. Undisturbed closed grassland is up to 1 m tall and species poor, except in swampy places or where albatrosses have nested, when the grassland becomes sufficiently open to support a greater diversity of herbs, including *Damnamenia vernicosa*, *Hebe benthamii* and *Gentiana concinna*. Fell field commences at c.460 m and occurs atop lateral ridges and along the main ridge, where the megaherb *Pleurophyllum hookeri* is predominant, but scattered rocky outcrops support a more diverse flora.

On Enderby, and near Erebus and Terror Coves, vegetation has been considerably modified by pigs, cattle and rabbits, locally by goats and by humans on all islands except Adams, and given the lack of introduced mammals on the latter the three *Pleurophyllum* megaherbs occur in much greater profusion: *P. criniferum* in boggy situations between sea level (e.g. at Magnetic Survey Bay and Fairchild's Garden) and 400 m; *P. hookeri* at 200–640 m, principally on exposed ridges and occasionally in swampy situations; while *P. speciosum* is largely confined to a mistbelt at 460–640 m and favours rock-slides on south-facing slopes. In addition, above 200 m, wet tussac grass dominated by *Chionochloa antarctica* is common.

Birds Two species of penguin certainly breed, including Yellow-eyed Penguin (at least 520–570 pairs), which occurs in loose concentrations throughout the group, but the population centre appears to be Enderby. Rockhopper Penguin has declined but traditional colonies still exist on east and west coasts. Occasional Erect-crested Penguins have been recorded within Rockhopper colonies but there are no records since 1972. King Penguin is occasionally seen ashore.

For birders one of the principal attractions is the fantastic range of albatrosses and tubenoses. These islands are the major

View of South Cape, with chick Gibson's Albatross Diomedea [exulans] gibsoni, *Auckland*. © Andris Apse.

View from South West Cape, with White-capped Albatross Thalassarche [cauta] steadi, *Auckland. © Andris Apse.*

breeding ground of White-capped Albatross (70,000–80,000 pairs based on aerial counts in 1994, virtually all on Disappointment). The endemic form, Gibson's Albatross (mean 5800 pairs per annum, with counts in the 1990s ranging from 4826 to 7417 pairs, the vast majority on Adams) also breeds. Very small numbers of Southern Royal Albatross nest (72 pairs on Enderby, Adams and Auckland in the early 1990s); almost the entire world population breeds on nearby Campbell. Black-browed and Buller's Albatross are frequently observed at sea. Light-mantled Sooty Albatross numbered c.5000 pairs in the early 1970s, with most in the south of the main island, but no recent population estimates are available. Northern Giant Petrel breeds commonly and occurs in moderate concentrations in nearby seas. Other tubenoses are: Cape (c.200 pairs, mainly on Beacon Rocks) and White-headed Petrels, Antarctic (of the form banksi) and Fulmar Prions (all breeding largely throughout and apparently numerous), White-chinned Petrel (with the exception of Antarctic Prion, petrels are confined to smaller cat-free islands and have a patchy distribution even on these), Sooty Shearwater (perhaps one million pairs, largely on the offshore islands of Disappointment and Adams), Grey-backed, White-faced and Black-bellied Storm-petrels (perhaps widespread, though few colonies are known), the subantarctic form of Common Diving-petrel (numerous, especially around coasts) and possibly South Georgian Diving-petrel (which formerly bred on Enderby and Dundas, but not since the 1940s).

If this was not enough to tempt birders, the Auckland group harbours one of the rarest endemics in the world, Auckland Shag, which breeds throughout, as well as Auckland Teal, which is holding its own on predator-free islets, breeding on all outlying islands but not the main island, which has pigs and cats. Pacific Black Duck and New Zealand Falcon nest in small numbers (ten pairs of the latter in 1990), with most in the south of the main island. Recently rediscovered, following its mid-1800s extinction from the main island, Auckland Island Rail is now known to breed on Adams, where located in 1989 (several hundred individuals) and Disappointment (population of c.500 found in 1993), but its status is poorly known. New Zealand Snipe has also recovered and currently numbers c.25,000 individuals (two-thirds of the total population of this species, which has always been highly vulnerable to introduced predators). It breeds regularly on most offshore islands with the majority on Ewing, Disappointment, Adams and Enderby.

Several other breeders are easily found, e.g. the local race

of Double-banded Plover (*exilis*), while Subantarctic Skua (100 pairs) occurs throughout the group. Moderate numbers of Kelp and Red-billed Gulls breed throughout, and White-fronted and Antarctic Terns form small colonies. Red-crowned Parakeet predominates on larger offshore islands, but Yellow-crowned Parakeet is commoner on Auckland. The local form of New Zealand Pipit *aucklandicus* is common, mainly on coasts, and Silvereye and Auckland Island Tomtit numerous throughout. New Zealand Bellbird is probably the most abundant bush bird, but Tui also occurs throughout. Recent arrivals are Mallard, Skylark, Dunnock, Song Thrush, Common Blackbird, Common Chaffinch, European Goldfinch, Common Redpoll, House Sparrow and Common Starling, and vagrants include Shining Bronze-cuckoo, Long-tailed Cuckoo and Welcome Swallow.

Migrant and vagrant shorebirds include Pacific Golden Plover, Ruddy Turnstone, Bar-tailed and Black-tailed Godwits, Red Knot, Red-necked Stint, and Sharp-tailed and Curlew Sandpipers. White-faced Heron and Swamp Harrier are stragglers and Arctic Tern occasional.

Marine mammals New Zealand Fur Seal breeds and is still slowly recovering from 19th-century exploitation. Auckland is the major breeding ground of New Zealand (Hooker's) Sea Lion, with c.14,000 animals producing 1800 pups annually in three colonies, on Enderby, Dundas and Figure of Eight. As on other subantarctic islands within the New Zealand region, Leopard Seal is a regular winter visitor and Hourglass Dolphin has been recorded.

Main conservation issues Studies of New Zealand (Hooker's) Sea Lion and Gibson's Albatross are ongoing, as they fall victim to boats trawling for squid and longlining for tuna and other fisheries. Provision exists to halt squid fishing should too many sea lions be caught, but much work is still required to prevent albatross losses. One of the greatest threats is the accidental introduction of rats, and for this reason all landings are restricted. The successful eradication of rabbits (which formerly thrived on Enderby and Rose), cattle (removed in 1993), mice and goats in recent years has highlighted what can be achieved. Removing the pigs and cats from the main island is currently being investigated, but will be a major undertaking. Adams and Disappointment have fortunately not been subject to the depredations of such aliens.

Human history Auckland has suffered prolonged human interference in its ecosystem and, like other groups within New Zealand's subantarctic islands, may have been known to early Maori. Credit for their discovery, however, goes to Abraham Bristow of the whaler *Ocean*, who sighted the islands on 18 Aug 1806 and returned the following year in the *Sarah*, anchoring in the sound now

Southern Royal Albatrosses Diomedea [epomophora] epomophora, *Auckland, Jan 2000. © Hadoram Shirihai.*

known as Port Ross, where he liberated pigs for the potential use of castaways. He named the islands 'Lord Auckland's Groupe'. At this time fur seals and sea lions abounded but were swiftly slaughtered for their skins and oil, with parties from New South Wales and America making numerous visits, especially in 1822–3, until by 1830 seals were almost extinct.

The explorers Wilkes, Dumont D'Urville and James Ross all visited in 1840, the latter's party making an early collection of the flora. They released pigs and rabbits, and discovered that pigs, cats and mice were already well established on the main island. Thereafter a group of 40 Chatham Maoris, with 26 Moriori slaves, arrived at Port Ross in the brig *Hannah*, in summer 1842–3, with the intention of settling. Subsequently, they divided into two parties (totalling 23 Maori and all 26 Moriori), on Enderby and the other in the northeast of the main island, where the settlement of Hardwicke briefly came into being in 1849 when the Southern Whale Fishery Company leased the islands from the Crown. The chief commissioner of the company, Charles Enderby (who had been fired-up by the favourable reports of Ross and others) and his British colonists soon encountered the native population, who kept dogs and pigs of which many ran free. While the short-lived whale fishery settlement was sited on the main island, most stock was kept on Enderby, including 80 cattle, c.700 sheep and three horses. The British abandoned the settlement in Aug 1852 (whale stocks were already exhausted and the climate had proved unconducive to farming), taking the horses and some other livestock, but leaving many pigs, sheep and cattle on Enderby. Apart from the cattle, these soon disappeared, probably being eaten by the Maoris, who departed in Mar 1856. By 1863, Enderby's rights had been formally cancelled and the islands became part of New Zealand by imperial statute. Subsequently, in 1904, 2000 sheep were released in the Carnley Harbour area of the main Auckland island, only to quickly perish in the harsh wet climate; an earlier attempt at farming on Enderby, in 1894, had also came to naught.

Between 1833 and 1907 no fewer than ten, possibly more, ships were wrecked within the group, with the loss of over 100 lives. Most were bound from Australia to England, via Cape Horn, and had come south to take advantage of the westerly winds at these latitudes. In the frequent stormy conditions they were unable to sight the sun to determine their position, a situation compounded by the islands being incorrectly marked on charts. Among the more infamous wrecks was the *General Grant* (1866), which was reputedly carrying a large quantity of gold that has never been recovered. The survivors of the *Grafton* (1864) eked out a meagre

Ad Auckland Shag Phalacrocorax [campbelli] colensoi, *Auckland, Dec 1999. © Hadoram Shirihai.*

existence for 18 months before sailing a dinghy to New Zealand. The latter country constructed a number of castaway depots on the Aucklands (and other subantarctic islands) that were regularly checked by government steamers until 1929, but the opening of the Panama Canal meant that ships no longer used the Cape Horn route and effectively brought this era to a close. These voyages to the castaways' depots were also popular tours for governors and their guests, and were occasionally joined by visiting naturalists.

The group was declared a reserve for the protection of native flora and fauna in 1934 (Adams had already been gazetted as a reserve in 1910). In 1939 the crew of a German freighter cut firewood in Carnley Harbour to enable her to reach a neutral country (being in Dunedin when war was declared). Fears that enemy shipping might use the islands as a staging post to attack New Zealand led, in 1941, to coastal watch parties being estab-

Female Auckland Teal Anas [aucklandica] aucklandica, *Auckland, Jan 2000. © Hadoram Shirihai.*

Ad Auckland Double-banded Plover Charadrius bicinctus exilis, *Auckland, Jan 2000. © Hadoram Shirihai.*

Silvereye Zosterops lateralis *is one of mainland New Zealand's typical forest species that also occurs on some of the subantarctic islands to the south.* © Klaus Bjerre.

Auckland Island Snipe Coenocorypha aucklandica aucklandica, *Auckland.* © Peter Reese.

lished on Auckland, as well as on Campbell (known collectively as 'The Cape Expedition'). Bases in Port Ross and Carnley Harbour were manned until the end of the war, gathering valuable scientific information. Thereafter expeditions organised by the Dominion Museum, DSIR, Wildlife Service, Department of Lands and Survey and Department of Conservation have visited the islands regularly, especially between 1954 and 1966, the early 1970s and 1990s, though there have been very few landings on Disappointment (the albatross colonies being counted and photographed from the air). The archipelago acquired National Nature Reserve status in 1986 and in common with other New Zealand subantarctic islands was designated a World Heritage Site in 1998.

Visiting the islands The New Zealand subantarctic islands are administered by the Department of Conservation (DOC). Tour operators, individual tourists and researchers must apply for permits to enter the nature reserves, pay a tourism impact fee, and most vessels are required to carry a government representative aboard. The department has a minimum impact code to restrict disturbance to wildlife. There are quarantine procedures to limit alien introductions, no specimen collecting or souvenirs are permitted, and wildlife must not be approached closer than 5 m. Most tourists visit in Dec–Feb, which are the warmer summer months, but the weather is still very unpredictable and can change rapidly, so alpine survival clothes are required.

The principal landing sites are at **Erebus Cove** (50°33'S 166°13'E), at the northeast end of the main Auckland I, **Carnley Harbour** (50°50'S 166°05'E), which separates the latter from Adams I, and **Sandy Bay** (50°30'S 166°17'E) on Enderby I. The former is important historically, being the site of the English settlement of **Hardwicke**, which was briefly established in the mid-19th century, and has Rata and *Olearia* forests. Carnley Harbour may be full of Sooty Shearwaters and Yellow-eyed Penguin is fairly common here. The forests in this region of the main Auckland I hold most of the breeding landbirds. Nearby, the **South West Cape** (50°50'S 165°53'E) has most of the breeding albatrosses, including a colony of White-capped and scattered Gibson's, as well as Subantarctic Skuas. For the naturalist, **Enderby** (50°30'S 166°18'E) is significantly more interesting. It is possible to land by zodiac on rocky platforms or through the surf at Sandy Bay. This is probably the best opportunity to see a good variety of plants and wildlife, and it receives the best weather of any of the islands. Under supervision from researchers stationed on the island, it

is possible to view New Zealand (Hooker's) Sea Lion, while a round-island walk permits views of Southern Royal Albatross, Yellow-eyed Penguin, New Zealand Snipe, Auckland Teal and Light-mantled Sooty Albatross. From Sandy Bay it is possible to walk to **Derry Castle Reef** (50°29'S 166°18'E) and the **North East Cape** (50°30'S 166°19'E), where many of the shags nest. Despite the depredations of the many introduced mammals in the past, Enderby still has some important stands of Southern Rata forest.

Campbell Island

Location and main features Situated at 52°33'S 169°09'E, Campbell is the southernmost of New Zealand's subantarctic islands, being c.700 km south of Bluff. The second largest of New Zealand's subantarctic island groups, there is a main island and several small islets, covering 11,400 ha and reaching a peak altitude of 569 m.

Landform, climate and habitat Campbell is the dissected remnant of a 6–11 million year-old volcanic dome (its flows cover nearly two-thirds of the island and in some places form dramatic cliffs and stacks) situated on basement sandstone, mudstone and limestone sediments dating from the Cretaceous–Cenozoic and Paleozoic schist. The latter are among the oldest known from the Campbell Plateau and are similar to those in Marie Byrd Land, Antarctica and in Westland, New Zealand. Most of the western

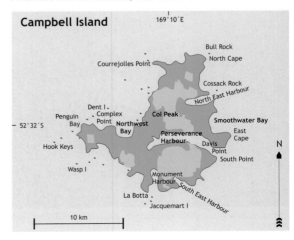

New Zealand (Hooker's) Sea Lions Phocarctos hookeri *breed mainly on Auckland and Campbell, where they prefer sandy beaches. The single bull (dark animal in centre) controls a harem of up to 25 females. Auckland Is, Dec 1999. © Hadoram Shirihai.*

half of the volcano has disappeared through marine erosion, while in the east the 'drowning' of radial valleys has created a series of fjord-like inlets separated by gently sloping ridges. Coasts are mainly cliffs, with many outlying stacks, rocks and islets. Ice action dating from the Pleistocene (two million years ago) is evident, but the origins of glacial landforms are debated.

Vegetation reflects the island's generally harsh climate (mean annual temperature is 6°C, with extremes of 21°C and -7°C being recorded, accompanied by high winds of 63 km/h on 280 days per annum, a low annual sunshine total and a mean 1360 mm of rain per year), being predominantly tussac grassland, shrub land and herbfield. Overall floral diversity (213 species of vascular plants, of which only 128 are native) and tree height are lower than at Auckland due to the high winds and cool temperatures, though *Dracophyllum* spp., *Coprosma* spp. and *Myrsine divaricata* approach 5 m tall in parts. An introduced spruce *Sicea sitchensis* (planted in 1907 by Lord Plunkett), the most isolated tree in the world, has reached c.6 m tall and there are six endemic plant taxa, includ-

ing a tussac grass *Poa aucklandica campbellensis*. Coastal turf is scattered through the salt-spray zone. Elsewhere vegetation is best divided into three latitudinal zones: upper alpine, lower alpine and subalpine. Tall rush/herbfield predominates in the high-alpine mosaic. The rush *Marsippospermum gracile* and *Bulbinella rossii* are most obvious but many grasses, forbs, lichens, bryophytes, as well as other rushes form a dense cushion. Prior to the introduction of grazing, *Pleurophyllum hookeri*, *Anisotome antipoda* (above 300 m, with *A. latifolia* abundant at sea level and up to this altitude) and dwarf *Stilbocarpa polaris* would have been common in such areas. *Pleurophyllum speciosum* occurs below 300 m altitude and *P. criniferum* in the low-altitude bogs. The lower alpine zone is still characterized, in places, by stands of tall *Chionochloa antarctica* tussac grassland with deep peat bogs, but sheep grazing has reduced most areas within this zone to grass meadows of *Poa litorosa*. Dwarf forest of *Dracophyllum scoparium* and *D. longifolium* dominates the subalpine zone up to c.180 m, at least in sheltered areas. *Dracophyllum* has greatly increased its

Southern Royal Albatross Diomedea [epomophora] epomophora *on Gomez I, Campbell. © Andris Apse.*

Campbell Shag Phalacrocorax [campbelli] campbelli. © *Peter Reese.*

range since the 1940s, invading tussac meadows made vulnerable through burning and grazing of *Chionochloa* tussac.

Birds Numbers of Rockhopper Penguin have declined by 94% since the late 1950s, when the population was estimated at 1.6 million breeders (determined using photographs and nest densities) and was perhaps the most important in the world. The crash is attributed to lack of food caused by a southward shift of the nutrient-rich convergence zone. The island remains important for Yellow-eyed Penguin (fluctuating in numbers from 610 to 890 pairs in 1988 to 250–540 pairs in 1992, and now increasing again).

Campbell is of key importance for breeding tubenoses, among them several globally threatened albatross forms. It holds almost the entire population of Southern Royal Albatross (c.7800 pairs in 1996) and is the sole nesting area for Campbell Albatross (19,000–26,000 pairs in the 1990s), which nest in association with 6000–9000 pairs of Grey-headed Albatross, the majority on the north coast, between Northeast Harbour and Courrejolles Point, but in the latter area the two species are difficult to distinguish in aerial counts). Between three and 24 pairs of Black-browed Albatross nest (1975–95 data), occasionally interbreeding with Campbell Albatross, but with relatively little success (though a mixed pair nested successfully each year in 1991–1996). A relict, but apparently highly stable population (six pairs in 1995) of Antipodean Albatross also uses the island. Completing the albatrosses are c.1600 pairs (in 1995) of Light-mantled Sooty Albatross, which is widespread on coasts and offshore islets.

Perhaps increasing numbers of Northern Giant Petrel breed, largely in the south, with 234 pairs estimated in 1996–7. A winter breeder (chiefly in the Mt Eboule area and perhaps on some offshore small islands), Grey Petrel is apparently represented by fewer than 100 pairs. Sooty Shearwater is greatly reduced on the main island through rat predation, while Cape Petrel breeds at two sites and the now globally threatened White-chinned Petrel is common on offshore islands. Grey-backed Storm-petrel and Common Diving-petrel breed, but mainly on offshore islands, where they are not subject to rat predation, and Black-bellied Storm-petrel may do so, though there are no confirmed records ashore. Prions are present on some offshore stacks (birds were seen in burrows in the 1980s), but have not been identified to species (they are either Antarctic or Fairy). White-headed Petrel has been recorded occasionally in these seas, which is one of the richest tubenose areas in the region, with other foragers including Gibson's Albatross. Many of New Zealand's albatrosses, petrels and shearwaters occur between Campbell and the Aucklands, sometimes in large numbers, making this area hugely interesting to seabird fanatics.

The New Zealand region is particularly rich in cormorant taxa and this archipelago possesses the endemic Campbell Shag (c.8000 birds). Another endemic, Campbell Teal was rediscovered in 1976 on Dent (estimated population 30–50 individuals). In Nov 1997 a previously undescribed subspecies of New Zealand Snipe was discovered on Jacquemart, which is rat-free. Regular breeders also include Pacific Black Duck, Subantarctic Skua (c.100 pairs in 1984–6), Kelp and Red-billed Gulls, Antarctic Tern and Silvereye. Little Pied Cormorant bred until the 1980s. New Zealand Pipit (perhaps an endemic subspecies) survives on Dent, Monowai and Jacquemart, but rats have probably exterminated it on the main island. Introduced breeders have included Mallard, Skylark (since the late 1960s), Song Thrush, Common Blackbird, Dunnock, European Goldfinch, Common Redpoll, Common Starling, House Sparrow (breeding confirmed mid-1960), Common Chaffinch and Yellowhammer, but several of these have disappeared with the removal of sheep from the island.

With even greater ornithological attention in recent years, additional species have been recorded for the archipelago list, including King, Gentoo and Macaroni Penguins, which are all annual in appearance, and there were two Chinstrap in Jan 1996, while Royal, Erect-crested, Snares and Fiordland Penguins have all been recorded. Other stragglers are Great Cormorant, Great Egret, White-faced Heron, Australian Shelduck, Swamp Harrier, New Zealand Falcon, Purple Swamphen, South Island Pied Oystercatcher, Double-banded Plover, Masked Lapwing, Common Greenshank, South Polar Skua, White-fronted and Arctic Terns, White-throated Needletail, Fork-tailed Swift and Welcome Swallow. Migrant shorebirds are less common than on some of the other islands in this region, but include Bar-tailed and Hudsonian Godwits (the latter record is unconfirmed), Red Knot and Ruddy Turnstone.

Marine mammals New Zealand Fur Seal is slowly recovering from the over-exploitative years. Southern Elephant Seal has declined dramatically since the early 1970s and by 97% since 1947, with fewer than five pups now born annually. The decline may be related to the shifting of the convergence zone. Significant numbers of New Zealand (Hooker's) Sea Lions also breed, with c.120 pups being produced per annum and 200–350 animals present in 1988. Leopard Seal is comparatively regular in winter. The majority of the New Zealand population of Southern Right Whale is found in these waters and Hourglass Dolphin also occurs.

Main conservation issues Having been subject to introductions of pigs, goats, domestic fowl, sheep, cattle and cats at various stages in its history, it is perhaps surprising that so much of

Southern Elephant Seal Mirounga leonina, *Campbell, Jan 1998. © Hadoram Shirihai.*

Campbell's native flora and fauna survives. The first three, which all arrived in the 1860s, failed to survive long, and sheep and cattle were removed following a fencing programme commenced in 1970 and completed in 1992, while cats, which reached the main island sometime after 1916, appear to have died out naturally. Rats, which have had a disastrous effect on birdlife, were all that remained; they were already numerous by 1868 and may have reached the islands within just a few years of their discovery. Recent successes in removing rats from other islands led the Department of Conservation to seriously consider the possibility of their eradication from Campbell. Funding of $2.5 million was approved and the project was completed in Jun–Jul 2001. With their removal, several exciting possibilities exist, including the reintroduction of the teal, snipe, pipit and some smaller petrels, prions and shearwaters.

Human history Frederick Hasselborough, a sealer from Sydney in command of the *Perseverance*, discovered the main island in Jan 1810 (naming it for the ship's owner). By this time sealing was already declining in some areas of the subantarctic, though cheap licences for such exploitation continued to be issued until the mid-1920s, and the practice persisted on Campbell until 1842. Amazingly both Hasselborough and his ship met their end at Campbell: the captain drowned in Perseverance Harbour later the same year and his former ship was wrecked in North West Bay in 1829 (which is considered the most likely means for Norway Rat *Rattus norvegicus* to have colonized the group). During the 19th century several expeditions paused at Campbell, beginning with that of James Clark Ross in 1840–2. His scientists, Hooker and Lyall, and surgeon Robert McCormick compiled the first fauna and flora inventories of Campbell. Other visiting naturalists followed later in the century aboard New Zealand government steamers (in the period 1883 to 1927), but the first detailed studies of the island's albatrosses were not conducted until the 1940s: between 1943 and 1970 over 20,000 Southern Royal Albatross were ringed.

As on other islands in the region, prior to 1895 sheep, goats and pigs were occasionally liberated to provide sustenance to the shipwrecked, but none of these introductions survived long. In contrast, rats had reportedly reached plague proportions on the main island by 1874. Accidental or deliberate fires were started occasionally, but it was not until 1895, when a farm was established, that large-scale modification of the vegetation commenced. The main island appeared to hold much better prospects for agriculturalists than neighbouring groups, and 300–400 sheep were re-introduced in 1895, when the island was leased to J. Gordon for 21 years. Two small whaling stations were established in 1909

and 1911 at Northwest Bay and North East Harbour; these took up to 60 Southern Right Whales. The former lasted until 1916 and the latter closed in 1914 with the advent of the First World War. Unreliable transport and worldwide recession also forced the farmers to finally withdraw in 1931, leaving c.4000 sheep and 20–30 cattle unattended.

In 1954 the islands were declared a reserve for the preservation of flora and fauna (though calls for their protection had been advanced as early as 1907). In order to eradicate the sheep, a dividing fence was constructed in 1970 and the animals removed from half of the island to permit long-term comparisons of plant and animal populations. These monitoring studies established the success of the project, so that sheep were further restricted in 1984 by erection of another fence, and were wholly removed in 1992. Cattle were also eradicated in 1984. In addition, a general management plan has operated since 1983, a boardwalk to one of the albatross colonies has been constructed and in 1998 Campbell was declared a World Heritage Site.

Visiting the islands The New Zealand subantarctic islands are administered by the Department of Conservation (DOC). Tour operators, individual tourists and researchers must apply for permits to enter the nature reserves, pay a tourism impact fee, and most vessels are required to carry a government representative aboard. The department operates a minimum impact code to limit disturbance to wildlife. Quarantine procedures are designed to prevent alien introductions, and no specimen collecting or souvenirs are permitted. Wildlife must not be approached closer than 5 m. Most tourists visit in Dec–Feb, which are the warmer summer months but the climate can still change rapidly, so alpine clothes are necessary. Of New Zealand's true subantarctic islands, it is only possible to make landings on Auckland and Campbell, where it is possible to visit the former (closed 1995) at the west end of **Perseverance Harbour** (52°33'S 169°11'E) via the old wharf. By climbing **Col Peak** (52°32'S 169°08'E) to the north of the station, via an easy boardwalk, it is possible within an hour to reach the rapidly recovering megaherb fields (flowering peaks in Jan), site of the world's largest Southern Royal Albatross colony. It is usually possible to see Southern Elephant Seal and New Zealand (Hooker's) Sea Lion on the coast in this region as well, and the loneliest tree in the world is found near the harbour. A more vigorous walk (5–6

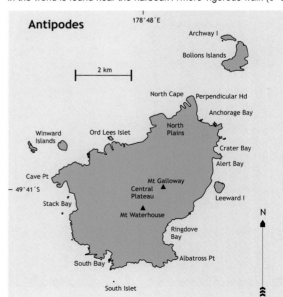

Ad (possibly male) Antipodean Albatross Diomedea [exulans] antipodensis. *Off the Antipodes, Jan 2000. © Hadoram Shirihai.*

hours) takes the visitor to **Northwest Bay** (52°33'S 169°05'E), where it is possible to see Yellow-eyed Penguin. Nearby, **Smoothwater Bay** (52°32'S 169°14'E) has Rockhopper Penguin.

Antipodes Islands

Location and main features At 49°41'S 178°45'E, this is the most remote of New Zealand's subantarctic island groups, being c.870 km southeast of Bluff. The Antipodes cover c.2100 ha, comprising the main island and several small rocky islets, of which the largest, Bollons, covers 50 ha and reaches 200 m.

Landform, climate and habitat Entirely volcanic in origin, only a few fragments of underlying basement granite have been found in the Antipodes. The main island was formed during two volcanic periods and is overlain by ash and basaltic lava flows, which slope to its centre, forming spectacular and inaccessible cliffs peaking at 366 m and encircling the island. These are especially dramatic on the east and west coasts. The central volcanic cone is Quaternary and there are smaller volcanic vents at Crater Bay, Leeward I,

the Windward Is, as well as Bollons. There is a prominent raised beach around most coasts of the main island.

The group has significantly lower rainfall than for instance the Aucklands and this may contribute to its small flora, c.166 species, of which four are endemic and 68 indigenous vascular plants. Three introduced higher plant species are all very localized, being restricted to areas of greatest human disturbance. Vegetation is almost entirely tussac grassland dominated by *Poa litorosa*, but is often very lush and due to the recent lack of grazing frequently in good condition. Littoral tussacs are particularly large and dense, reaching 2 m, but on exposed sectors of coast or in areas that have been heavily burrowed by seabirds, are interspersed by ferns and several megaherbs. Localized bogs are largely free of tussac grass but have much *Anisotome antipoda*, *Stilbocarpa polaris* and patches of *Coprosma purpusilla* and *Hymenophyllum multifidum*. At higher elevations the fern *Polystichum vestitum*, in its semi-tree form, is an important constituent of grasslands but there is also much *Anisotome antipoda* (which also occurs on coasts), *Acaena minor* and the fern *Histiopteris incisa*. Sheltered areas may have dense stands of *Stilbocarpa polaris* and patches of *Coprosma antipoda*; it and three congeners are the only species of woody plants to occur in the group, and in places they form near-impenetrable clumps. Where giant petrels have manured the ground and areas of seepage occur the endemic herb *Senecio antipoda* is abundant.

Birds The islands host approximately two-thirds of the world population of Erect-crested Penguin, which often breeds in mixed colonies with Rockhopper Penguin (4000 pairs); the former had declined to 49,000–57,000 pairs in 1995. The Antipodes are the world's principal breeding area for the sexually dimorphic Antipodean Albatross (5148 pairs in 1996). There is a small colony of Black-browed Albatross (115 pairs in 1995) on Bollons, in which some observers have also reported tiny numbers of White-capped Albatross (six pairs in 1993 and 18 pairs in 1995). Light-mantled Sooty Albatross breeds largely on the main island's coastal cliffs (c.1000 pairs in 1969, 200–300 pairs in 1995, but just 169 pairs in 1997).

Other breeding seabirds include 230 breeding pairs of Northern Giant Petrel (in 2000), which often attack the penguins, and

Colony of Erect-crested Penguin Eudyptes sclateri. *Antipodes. © Andris Apse.*

Incubating Erect-crested Penguin Eudyptes sclateri. *Antipodes.* © *Andris Apse*

Antipodes Island Snipe Coenocorypha aucklandica meinertzhagenae. *Antipodes.* © *Andris Apse.*

scavenge eggs and chicks of other seabirds. Breeding throughout the group, numbers of Grey Petrel are the largest in New Zealand waters; approximately 56,000 pairs were estimated in Jun 2001. Cape, White-chinned, Soft-plumaged and White-headed Petrels, and Little Shearwater are (with the exception of the latter, which is restricted to offshore islands) widespread and, based on numbers at sea, quite numerous. Common Diving-petrel and Black-bellied Storm-petrel breed in numbers (the latter is possibly the commonest breeding species), with relatively small populations of Sooty Shearwater, Grey-backed Storm-petrel and Fairy Prion (chiefly in coastal caves and rock-falls) mostly on offshore islands.

Among landbirds, the islands are the breeding ground for one of the world's rarest parakeets; the population of Antipodes Parakeet is currently stable at 2000–3000 birds. The Antipodes also support endemic races of Red-crowned Parakeet (*hochstetteri* currently numbers 4000–5000 individuals) and New Zealand Snipe (*meinertzhagenae*, numbering c.8000 individuals) that breed commonly throughout virtually the entire group. Scattered breeders are Subantarctic Skua (50 pairs), Kelp and Red-billed Gulls and Antarctic Tern, while New Zealand Pipit is abundant. A few other colonists have arrived, namely Mallard, Dunnock, Common Chaffinch, European Goldfinch, Common Redpoll, Silvereye, Common Blackbird, Song Thrush, and Common Starling. Ruddy Turnstone and Bar-tailed Godwit have been recorded as accidentals.

Marine mammals Small numbers of New Zealand Fur Seal breed but they do not appear to be increasing as swiftly as elsewhere. Even smaller numbers of Southern Elephant Seal breed; as the island is so rarely visited, no recent census information is available but the population appears stable at about 100 pups per annum, in marked contrast to those elsewhere in this region, on Macquarie and Campbell. The only extant introduced mammal is House Mouse *Mus musculus*, on the main island, which has had major impacts on the larger invertebrates.

Main conservation issues Due to the comparative infrequency of visits, the threat of introductions reaching shore is not as great as at some islands in this region. Greater care, however, is required to avoid the introduction of plants; stricter quarantine provisions for visitors being the most obvious limiting procedure. Work is underway to clarify whether breeding albatrosses are affected by mortality caused by fisheries bycatch, and similar research has recently begun for Grey Petrel, as large numbers drown on longlines.

Human history Originally named the Penantipodes by their discoverer, Waterhouse in the *Reliance*, who sighted the islands on 26 Mar 1800, the first sealers were ashore in 1804. They spent

more than a year there, collecting almost 60,000 fur seal pelts. Given such rapacious slaughter, it is unsurprising that by the 1830s seals were virtually extinct, bringing the exploitation to an end. The islands were declared a dependency of New Zealand in 1842 and from 1882 government steamers regularly visited the group to check for potential castaways. A hut, constructed at Anchorage Bay in 1886 to aid such hapless souls, is still standing. It was not until the early 1880s that interest in the islands renewed, as large numbers of penguin skins were taken to meet a fashionable demand for ladies' muffs. On 4 Sep 1893 *Spirit of the Dawn* carrying a cargo of rice was wrecked off the Antipodes; five crew including the captain drowned and the shipwrecked men failed to locate the government depot 4–5 hours walk from their camp, which held clothing and provisions that would have made their enforced stay of 87 days less unpleasant. Early bird-collecting expeditions visited the archipelago in 1901 and, subsequently, the indefatigable Rollo Beck, in 1926. More detailed avifaunal research commenced in the 1950s, though Bollons went unvisited until a six-week expedition in 1978–9. In 1961 the islands were declared a nature reserve, with National Nature Reserve status (1986) and World Heritage Site categorization (1998) thereafter.

Visiting the islands The New Zealand subantarctic islands are administered by the Department of Conservation (DOC). The department has a minimum impact code to restrict disturbance to wildlife. Quarantine procedures limit alien introductions, and no specimen collecting or souvenirs are permitted. Wildlife must not be approached closer than 5 m. Landings are not permitted on the main island but it is possible to make zodiac cruises within the group, allowing visitors to gain an appreciation of the seabirds present around the islands. Given calm weather it may be possible to see Antipodes Island Parakeet feeding on the grass between the rocks as you cruise the shoreline. However, for observing many of the breeding tubenoses it is best to seawatch from your vessel, especially close to dusk when petrel activity peaks.

Most visitors visit the archipelago in Dec–Feb, which are the warmer summer months, but the weather is still very unpredictable and can change rapidly, at times being very cold and windy. Heritage Expeditions include the Antipodes within at least one of its itineraries each year, but other operators rarely visit the area.

Bounty Islands

Location and main features The smallest of New Zealand's subantarctic island groups, the Bounties are situated at 47°45'S 179°03'E and c.600 km southeast of Bluff. They occupy c.135 ha

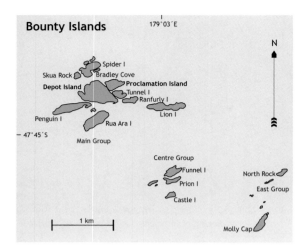

Bounty Islands

Salvin's Albatrosses Thalassarche [cauta] salvini; *the Bounties are the world's principal breeding ground for this species. Off the Bounties, Jan 2000. © Hadoram Shirihai.*

and comprise three distinct subgroups totalling 20 islets of various sizes, as well as a number of exposed rocks: Main Group with the largest island, Depot, Central Group and East Group. Despite their lack of vegetation, the islands are of critical importance for four seabirds: Erect-crested Penguin, Salvin's Albatross, Fulmar Prion and Bounty Shag.

Landform, climate and habitat Like the Snares, these islands are non-volcanic and consist entirely of basement biotite granite, with occasional finer grained variations, which date from the early Jurassic (being 180–190 million years old) and have no obvious correlations with rocks in nearby groups, instead appearing to be distantly related to those of Thurston I in West Antarctica. The islands are wholly devoid of higher vegetation; only algae and

lichens persist. The highest point is just 73 m.

Birds One of the world's only two colonies of Erect-crested Penguin (c.28,000 pairs in 1997) is found here in association with the world's principal colony of Salvin's Albatross (c.30,750 pairs in 1997). One of the rarest cormorants, Bounty Shag (c.500 pairs) is easily observed but entirely restricted to this barren group. Cape Petrel and Fulmar Prion (for which these islands are the most important breeding area in the world) are also common nesters, while Subantarctic Skua (erratic), Kelp and Red-billed Gulls (latter perhaps doubtful), and Antarctic Tern also breed. Vagrants have included Rockhopper Penguin (1997), Black-winged Stilt (two undated specimens), Masked Lapwing, Common Starling and Common Chaffinch. The seas north and south of here are apparently

Erect-crested Penguins Eudyptes sclateri; *the Bounties and the Antipodes are the sole breeding ground for this species. Bounties. © Hadoram Shirihai.*

Fulmar Prion Pachyptila crassirostris *is one of the few small tubenoses that is active during daylight at the nesting grounds. Bounties.* © Frank S. Todd.

important feeding areas for petrels. White-chinned, Soft-plumaged and White-headed Petrels, Grey-backed and Black-bellied Storm-petrels, Common Diving-petrel and Little Shearwater are often seen, and Kerguelen and Juan Fernández Petrels have also been recorded. Northern Giant Petrel appears to be reasonably numerous offshore. In addition, on 1 Jan 2000, Tony Palliser, Rodney Russ and myself recorded 11 Chatham Petrels with several Great-winged, Black-winged and Cook's Petrels, along with large numbers of White-faced Storm-petrel, feeding with Broad-billed and Fulmar Prions, and smaller numbers of Grey-backed Storm-petrel. During the day virtually all of New Zealand's albatrosses were observed following the ship, including Antipodes, Gibson's, and Northern and Southern Royal Albatrosses.

Marine mammals The only breeding mammal is New Zealand Fur Seal, which was hunted almost to extinction but has now largely recovered. The population is currently placed at 24,000 animals following a recent aerial census.

Main conservation issues Fortunately, the threat of introduced animals surviving in the islands' harsh environment is low. One of the most critical issues is the interaction between fur seals, penguins and albatrosses, especially as numbers of the former continue to increase.

Human history Discovered on 9 Sep 1788 by Captain William Bligh, who named the islands after his famous ship (though he did not approach the islands, observing them only at some distance), the next visitors did not arrive until 1807 when a Sydney vessel, the *Santa Anna* (with a Maori chief aboard whose ambition was to visit the British king, George III), arrived in the archipelago. The chieftain, Ruatara, and others disembarked to kill seals, while the ship searched elsewhere; three men died of starvation, thirst and exposure on the waterless island during the interim. The rest amassed a total of 8000 seal pelts and within the first two years of sealing c.50,000 seals had been killed. Such slaughter, as usual, proved unsustainable and by 1831, at the height of the breeding season, Biscoe could find only five fur seals. Declared a New Zealand dependency in 1842, Captain George Palmer of the Rosario formally took possession of the islands for Britain in 1870 and from then until 1927 the islands were regularly visited by government steamers that checked for castaways and replenished store depots established on the Bounties and other subantarctic islands off New Zealand. Given the archipelago's complete lack of vegetation, the government plan to create a sheep run on the islands, in 1894, is both amusing and bizarre. Ornithological and biological

surveys were undertaken in 1950, 1978 and 1997, and in 1961 the islands were declared a nature reserve, with World Heritage Site status being acquired in 1998.

Visiting the islands The New Zealand subantarctic islands are administered by the Department of Conservation (DOC). The department has a minimum impact code to restrict disturbance to wildlife (see previous accounts). Landings were formerly permitted on **Depot** and **Proclamation islands** within the Main Group, but in recent years all visits to the archipelago have been restricted to offshore zodiac cruises, which offer a better means to view the wildlife while avoiding undue disturbance.

Macquarie Island

Location and main features Lying approximately at the junction between the S Indian and Pacific Oceans, this Australian-controlled territory of c.12,785 ha, is situated at 54°30'S 158°57'E and 1,466 km southeast of Hobart. The island boasts a superb flora and wildlife, including 20 species of breeding seabirds. Ecologically and climatologically Macquarie fits well within the north–south gradient of New Zealand-owned island groups covered above. However, its closeness to the Antarctic Convergence exerts a strong influence on the composition of the flora and fauna (see below). The main island is elongated and measures 33 km by 5 km. In addition to a number of offshore stacks and reefs, a small group of islands, the Judge and Clerk Islets, lies 11 km north of Macquarie and the Bishop and Clerk Islets 37 km to the south. Earthquakes are common in the area, with a mean one per annum measuring above 6.2 on the Richter scale.

Landform, climate and habitat Macquarie is a geologically unusual and recent event; the present island emerged above sea level <700,000 years ago and is a rare example of uplifted oceanic crust, which formed c.20 million years ago, at depths of 2000–4000 m. As such, it is perhaps the best-preserved fragment of deep oceanic crust known above sea level; the island represents a tiny visible section of the long north–south marine ridge that extends between New Zealand and the Balleny Is. The same oceanic crust that forms Macquarie also covers most of the Earth's surface, but the rocks are deep below the surface of the sea. Only here is the oceanic crust visible above sea level. Mount Hamilton

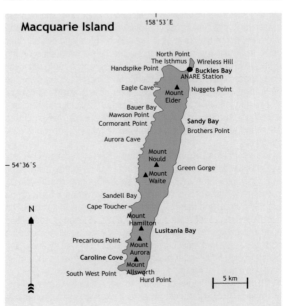

King Penguins Aptenodytes patagonicus *and Southern Elephant Seals* Mirounga leonina *near Green Gorge, Macquarie. © Andris Apse.*

is the island's highest point at 433 m, but there are several other peaks in excess of 400 m and most of the island consists of a plateau between 200 and 300 m.

The climate of Macquarie is very similar to that of other subantarctic islands north of the Antarctic Convergence, with little seasonal variation, except in day length. Cool, moist, cloudy and windy conditions predominate for much of the year. Long periods of sunshine are rare, but snow rarely accumulates for more than a few days. Precipitation is a near-daily feature, but daytime temperatures rarely fall below freezing even in higher areas.

Forty-six species of vascular plants are known from the island, of which three are endemic and five are introductions, two of which have since been removed. In addition, more than 80 mosses, 50 hepatic and 100 lichens have been noted on Macquarie. There are several large lakes with a combined area of 200 ha, the most important being Major Lake at 46 ha. The main vegetation types are tall, tussac grassland which occurs to c.330 m, herbfields, which grow in sheltered areas as high as 380 m (including short tussac grassland), mire, incorporating fen and bog on valley floors, and feldmark, which occurs in all areas above 180 m and occasionally down to 90 m. Tussac grassland is the tallest vegetation on the island (which has no trees or tall shrubs), and is dominated by *Poa foliosa* and *Stilbocarpa polaris*. Such communities occur on better-drained sections of the coastal terraces, most steep coastal slopes and in sheltered well-drained areas. Coastal communities, especially on rocky areas, are heavily influenced by exposure to wave and salt-spray action, but comprise many of the same constituents.

Heavy grazing by rabbits impacted extensive areas of tall tussac grassland but this has regained much of its former distribution with the implementation of a rabbit control programme. Feldmark is the most widespread vegetation type, covering c.50% of the island's plateau and most exposed montane areas. In some places it forms extensive terraces, formed by a combination of frost action and wind exposure. Mires occupy most raised beach terraces on northwest and southeast coasts, as well as many valley floors and plateau bogs. With water at or near the surface, vegetation often floats on a layer of unstable peat over 6 m deep in places.

Birds Given its close proximity to the Antarctic Convergence, the island's cold surrounding waters support an avifauna reminiscent of those occurring on islands at a similar latitude elsewhere in the Southern Ocean (e.g. Kerguelen). Thus, Macquarie possesses a remarkable density and diversity of seabirds. In all, at least 72 species have been noted, of which 29 have bred, including four penguins. Most important are the world's only breeding Royal Penguins, currently estimated at 810,000–960,000 pairs in 57 colonies, which are mainly coastal, with some occurring inland up to 200 m. King Penguin numbers appear to have significantly recovered since harvesting for oil ceased, and is the second-most abundant penguin (at least 100,000 breeding pairs). When ads return to the colonies and join the previous season's young, up to 0.5 million individuals may be present, and numbers were increasing in the 1990s. Rockhopper Penguin mainly breeds on the west coast (estimates of the breeding population vary from 100,000 to 500,000 pairs), while Gentoo Penguin forms small colonies of up to 300 pairs (total population 3000–5000 pairs).

Tubenoses include Wandering Albatross (15 pairs in 1999) of the very white-looking form, Snowy Albatross. Light-mantled Sooty Albatross is the most common albatross on the island (1150 pairs in 1994), while Black-browed Albatross breeds in the southwest of the island (45 pairs in 1999), and on Bishop and Clerk (141 pairs in 1993), often among the colony (78 pairs in 1999) of Grey-headed Albatross.

In this region Macquarie is the only island to host significant numbers of both Southern (2293 pairs in 1999) and Northern Giant Petrels (1485 pairs in 1999), of which a small percentage of the former are pure white. Both species may be in decline, the former more markedly so. Cape Petrel was discovered breeding here in 2001. White-headed Petrel (8000 burrows) is probably the commonest breeding gadfly petrel and is often observed at sea, but the status of Soft-plumaged Petrel is unconfirmed. Blue Petrel (500–600 pairs) has colonies at Langdon Point, Green Gorge and Caroline Cove, but Grey Petrel (two pairs in 1999 and six fledged young in 2000) did not breed on the island for many years due to the presence of introduced predators. Fairy (40 pairs) and Slender-billed Prions also nest. Birds that appeared to be Fulmar Prions were caught on the island in winter 2000 and may also breed. Antarctic Prion (49,000 pairs) is the most numerous and widespread of the burrow nesters (despite the considerable attentions of feral cats), being most abundant in the centre of the island. Moderate colonies of Sooty Shearwater (totalling nearly 1800 pairs) exist at North Head, Handspike Point, Langdon Point and Caroline Cove.

Macquarie's plateau. © Grant Dixon.

Royal Penguins Eudyptes schlegeli. *© Frank S. Todd.*

Grey-backed Storm-petrel (100 pairs) and Common Diving-petrel (20 pairs) complete the list of breeding tubenoses.

The endemic Macquarie Shag breeds in 23 colonies and is a relatively obvious feature of the breeding avifauna, though its numbers total only c.660 pairs. A few Pacific Black Duck breed among tussac on coastal terraces, as does Mallard (which arrived unaided by humans from New Zealand) on inland lakes. They occasionally interbreed. Other breeding species include Subantarctic Skua (550 pairs), which is common for nine months of the year, but most disperse in early winter. Kelp Gull is resident but uncommon (just 50–100 breeding pairs), while 20–50 pairs of Antarctic Tern are also present year-round. Common Redpoll and Common Starling, the only passerines to nest on Macquarie, became established in the early 1900s and are now widespread and common.

Few other tubenoses have been reported from surrounding waters, e.g. Antarctic and Snow Petrels (winter 2000), and Shy Albatross, while South Polar Skua is apparently also only a vagrant (though perhaps overlooked during migration). Among vagrants, Snares and Erect-crested Penguins, Great Cormorant, White-faced Heron and Swamp Harrier have all been recorded on several occasions, there is a single, doubtful record of New Zealand Falcon, a certain record of Baillon's Crake, at least eight each of Eurasian Coot and Black-winged Stilt, as well as Grey Plover, a group of four Spur-winged Lapwing in winter 2000 (apparently the first record in the *HANZAB* region), and Latham's Snipe, Bar-tailed Godwit, Common Greenshank, Ruddy Turnstone, Red Knot, White-fronted and Arctic Terns, Pallid Cuckoo, Shining Bronze-cuckoo, White-throated Needletail, Fork-tailed Swift, Welcome Swallow (winter 2000), Song Thrush, Silvereye and European Goldfinch have all been documented, some more than once.

Marine mammals Small numbers of fur seals were present on the island when the Australian National Antarctic Research Expedition (ANARE) base was established in 1948, though none was breeding. In 1954, 130 years after the cessation of sealing, the first fur seal pup was born. Annual pup production increased slowly up until the 1980s when the population began to increase exponentially. Macquarie is unique among fur seal breeding islands in that three species are present, Antarctic, Subantarctic and New Zealand Fur Seals. The tiny breeding population consists mainly of Antarctic and Subantarctic Fur Seals, though male New Zealand Fur Seals have breeding territories and females occasionally breed. The recent rapid increase in pup production at Macquarie is primarily driven by expanding Antarctic Fur Seal numbers (c.13% per year), which account for c.65% of the entire population. In recent seasons the Subantarctic Fur Seal population has begun to show a significant annual increase (9% per year) and

now accounts for c.20% of the entire fur seal population. All three fur seals hybridize at Macquarie, with animals of mixed parentage accounting for c.15% of the population. One of several long-term research programmes is a study, which commenced in 1986 and is based at La Trobe University, to monitor the recovery and biology of the fur seal population. Each summer, 2–3 researchers spend around five months on the island, assessing among other things annual changes in pup production of each species, and the extent and trends in hybridization. In 1985 an estimated 86,500 Southern Elephant Seal pups were born on the island, making Macquarie among the species' major breeding sites. As at other sites the species was exploited for oil, harvesting occurred between 1810 and 1919. Pre-sealing numbers were estimated to be in excess of 100,000. By 1950 the population had recovered and exceeded that number, with 180,000+ seals on the island. However, between 1949 and 1985 the population declined by 50%, and this decline continues. Both Weddell and Crabeater Seals have appeared as vagrants, and Leopard Seal is regular between Jun and Jan; New Zealand (Hooker's) Sea Lion is a frequent visitor in winter. Six species of whale have been recorded from the island's waters, with Killer Whale the most frequent and Southern Right and Sperm Whales also seen.

Main conservation issues Eleven alien mammals have been accidentally or intentionally introduced onto the island, but only four are extant: rabbits, cats, rats and mice (horses, donkeys, goats, sheep, pigs and domestic ducks and fowl have all been successfully removed). Sealers introduced Wekas as a food source, but these flightless rails predate the eggs and young of ground-nesting birds, and have now been removed. Rabbits,

King Penguin Aptenodytes patagonicus *colony at Lusitania Bay, Macquarie, Dec 1999. © Hadoram Shirihai.*

Incubating Southern Giant Petrel Macronectes giganteus. Macquarie. © *Alan Wiltshire.*

Bull Southern Sea Elephant Mirounga leonina. Macquarie, Feb 1997. © *Daisy Gilardini.*

which were first liberated in 1875–8, have been dramatically reduced: 150,000 were thought to be present in 1978, though only 10,000 are estimated to still survive. A campaign, initiated in 1974, had reduced cat numbers to a low level by 1995, and had been almost wholly successful by 2001 (just one animal was seen and killed in 2000). In the early 1970s the island's 250–500 cats were estimated to be killing c.60,000 petrels per year, despite their principal prey being rabbits. Rats and mice, which arrived in the 1890s are also still present, the former taking some petrels. Nonetheless, smaller tubenoses, such as petrels, have already started to recolonize and increase as a result of work by the Tasmanian Nature Conservation Branch and Parks & Wildlife Service. The long-term goal is to remove all introduced animals from Macquarie. The current control programme is the Integrated Vertebrate Pest Management—the aim of which is to eliminate all introduced vertebrate pests.

Another issue is the impact of researchers on the small populations of fur seals and albatrosses, or those of declining species (e.g. Southern Elephant Seal). The nature of research should be consistent with the conservation status of the species. The impact of the station on, for instance, Southern Elephant Seal, requires investigation, as it was constructed on a prime breeding site for the latter species, excluding the seals. General human disturbance (e.g. by visitors) should also be addressed.

Human history Discovered, on 11 Jul 1810, by the Sydney-based sealer Hasselborough in the *Perseverance*, who six months previously had found Campbell; it was named Macquarie after the governor of New South Wales. Hasselborough landed eight sealers with nine months provisions. The island proved excellent for sealing and by Dec the same year three additional sealing gangs had landed. It has been estimated that Macquarie had between 200,000 and 400,000 fur seals at this time; what is clear is that in the first 18 months at least 120,000 were killed. By 1815 Macquarie had been 'written off' the sealers map: perhaps as many as 193,000 fur seal skins were taken and one species may have been locally exterminated. During the same period, in 1820, a Russian expedition led by Bellinghausen made a small collection of flora and fauna.

Elephant seals, whose blubber contained oil used as a fuel for lighting, lubricant for iron machinery and in tanning and rope manufacture, were next to suffer at the hands of Man. By 1826 such production appears to have been the only commercial operation, but by 1829 all accessible beaches had been worked. An 1867

visiting crew killed seals and introduced the Weka. Rabbits were also released as food for humans in the 1870s. Sealing resumed in 1874 and by 1889 humans were resident on the island. The first systematic scientific studies began when Scott, from the University of Otago, spent several days on the island in 1883. He was followed by Augustus Hamilton, who made a short visit in 1894. Meanwhile a sealer, Joseph Hatch, who had worked Macquarie since 1890, acquired exclusive sealing rights to the island in 1902. Between 1890 and 1919 his company made 75 voyages to Macquarie and he also attempted to exploit King Penguins for their oil. This venture failed commercially but was successful in reducing the birds' numbers to low levels. Hatch therefore turned to the Royal Penguins, exploiting huge numbers between at least 1905 and 1919. Finally, in 1920, the Tasmanian government declined to renew his licence.

As the period of commercial exploitation drew to a close, additional scientific work was undertaken on Macquarie. British Antarctic explorers such as Scott, under whom Wilson collected some specimens in 1901, and Shackleton in 1909 paused on the island, while in 1911–4, the great Australian researcher Douglas Mawson established a scientific station, the first such base in the region, on Macquarie. In 1948, the Australian government founded the first permanent scientific station there, following the island's declaration as a wildlife sanctuary under Tasmanian law in 1933. The ANARE station continues to operate to the present day. The island became a Conservation Area in 1971, a status that was upgraded to state reserve the following year and, in 1978, renamed Macquarie Island Nature Reserve, which includes all of the offshore islets and stacks. A management plan for the island was formulated in 1991 and in 1997 it became a World Heritage Site.

Visiting the island Careful guidelines have been developed by the Nature Conservation Branch and Parks & Wildlife Service of Tasmania for visiting the reserve, to minimize disturbance to wildlife and reduce the risk of further exotics arriving on the island. Permits must be applied for in advance of any visit; your tour operator should handle this. **Caroline Cove**, which harbours the few remaining Wandering Albatrosses, is closed to general visitors. However, there is much to be seen around the research station in the extreme south of the island, including all four breeding penguins, giant petrels and Southern Elephant Seal. The most interesting and regularly visited sites, by zodiac, include **Lusitania Bay** (with its King Penguins), **Sandy Bay** (King and Royal Penguins, Macquarie Shag, Subantarctic Skua and Southern Elephant Seal) and **Buckles Bay** (Gentoo Penguin).

Table 1. Breeding bird and mammal checklist for subantarctic islands south of New Zealand.

	Snares	Auckland	Macquarie	Campbell	Antipodes	Bounty	Chatham
Penguins							
King Penguin *Aptenodytes patagonicus*			X				
Gentoo Penguin *Pygoscelis papua*			X				
Rockhopper Penguin *Eudyptes chrysocome*		X	X	X	X		
Snares Penguin *E. robustus*	X						
Erect-crested Penguin *E. sclateri*					X	X	
Royal Penguin *E. schlegeli*			X				
Yellow-eyed Penguin *Megadyptes antipodes*		X		X			
Little Penguin *Eudyptula minor*							X
Albatrosses							
Wandering Albatross *Diomedea [exulans] exulans*			X				
Antipodean Albatross *D. [e.] antipodensis*				X	X		
Gibson's Albatross *D. [e.] gibsoni*		X					
Southern Royal Albatross *D. [epomophora] epomophora*		X		X			
Northern Royal Albatross *D. [e.] sanfordi*		X					X
Black-browed Albatross *Thalassarche [melanophrys] melanophrys*	X		X	X	X		
Campbell Albatross *T. [m.] impavida*				X			
Grey-headed Albatross *T. chrysostoma*			X	X			
White-capped Albatross *T. [c.] steadi*		X			X		
Salvin's Albatross *T. [c.] salvini*	X					X	
Chatham Albatross *T. [c.] eremita*							X
Buller's Albatross *T. [bulleri] bulleri*	X						
Pacific Albatross *T. [b.] sp.*							X
Light-mantled Sooty Albatross *Phoebetria palpebrata*		X	X	X	X		
Petrels and prions							
Southern Giant Petrel *Macronectes halli*			X				
Northern Giant Petrel *M. giganteus*		X	X	X	X		X
Cape Petrel *Daption capense australe*	X	X	X	X	X	X	X
White-headed Petrel *Pterodroma lessonii*		X	X		X		
Magenta Petrel *P. magentae*							X
Soft-plumaged Petrel *P. mollis*			X		X		
Mottled Petrel *P. inexpectata*	X						
Black-winged Petrel *P. nigripennis*							X
Chatham Petrel *P. axillaris*							X
Blue Petrel *Halobaena caerulea*			X				
Broad-billed Prion *Pachyptila vittata*	X						X
Antarctic Prion *P. desolata banksi*		X	X	X?			
Slender-billed Prion *P. belcheri*			X?				
Fairy Prion *P. turtur*	X		X	X?	X		X
Fulmar Prion *P. crassirostris*	X	X				X	X
White-chinned Petrel *Procellaria aequinoctialis*		X	X	X	X		
Grey Petrel *P. cinerea*			X	X	X		
Shearwaters							
Sooty Shearwater *Puffinus griseus*	X	X	X	X	X		X
Little Shearwater *P. assimilis elegans*					X		X
Storm-petrels							
Grey-backed Storm-petrel *Oceanites nereis*		X	X	X	X		X
White-faced Storm-petrel *Pelagodroma marina*		X					X
Black-bellied Storm-petrel *Fregetta tropica*		X		X?	X		
Diving-petrels							
South Georgian Diving-petrel *Pelecanoides georgicus*	X?						
Common Diving-petrel *P. urinatrix*	X	X	X	X	X		X
Shags							
Great Cormorant *Phalacrocorax carbo*							X
Pitt Shag *P. featherstoni*							X
Macquarie Shag *P. [atriceps] purpurascens*			X				
Chatham Shag *P. [carunculatus] onslowi*							X
Auckland Shag *P. [campbelli] colensoi*		X					
Campbell Shag *P. [c.] campbelli*				X			
Bounty Shag *P. [c.] ranfurlyi*						X	
Herons							
White-faced Heron *Egretta novaehollandiae*							X
Swans and Ducks							
Black Swan *Cygnus atratus*							X
Auckland Teal *Anas [aucklandica] aucklandica*		X					
Campbell Teal *A.[a.] nesiotis*				X			
Mallard *A. platyrhynchos*	X	X	X	X	X		X
Pacific Black Duck *A. superciliosa*	X	X	X	X			X
Harriers and falcons							
Swamp Harrier *Circus approximans*							X
New Zealand Falcon *Falco novaeseelandiae*		X					
Gamebirds							
California Quail *Lophortyx californica*							extinct

	Snares	Auckland	Macquarie	Campbell	Antipodes	Bounty	Chatham
Rails							
Weka *Gallirallus australis*			extinct				X
Spotless Crake *Porzana tabuensis*							X
Auckland Island Rail *Dryolimnas [pectoralis] muelleri*		X					
Purple Swamphen *Porphyrio porphyrio*							X
Shorebirds							
Chatham Island Oystercatcher *Haematopus chathamensis*							X
Double-banded Plover *Charadrius bicinctus bicinctus*							X
Auckland Island Banded Plover *C. bicinctus exilis*		X					
Shore Plover *Thinornis novaeseelandiae*							X
Masked Lapwing *Vanellus miles novaehollandiae*							X
Chatham Island Snipe *Coenocorypha pusilla*							X
New Zealand Snipe *C. aucklandica*	X	X		X	X		
Skuas							
Subantarctic Skua *Catharacta antarctica lonnbergi*	X	X	X	X	X	X	X
Gulls and terns							
Kelp Gull *Larus dominicanus*	X	X	X	X	X	X	X
Red-billed Gull *L. scopulinus*	X	X		X	X	X?	X
White-fronted Tern *Sterna striata*		X					X
Antarctic Tern *S. vittata*	X	X	X	X	X	X	
Pigeons							
Chatham Island Pigeon *Hemiphaga chathamensis*							X
Parakeets							
Antipodes Parakeet *Cyanoramphus unicolor*					X		
Red-crowned Parakeet *C. [novaezelandiae] novaezelandiae*		X					
Chatham Island Red-crowned Parakeet *C. [n.] chathamensis*							X
Antipodes Red-crowned Parakeet *C. [n.] hochstetteri*					X		
Yellow-crowned Parakeet *C. auriceps*		X					
Forbes' Parakeet *C. [novaezelandiae/auriceps] forbesi*							X
Cuckoos							
Shining Bronze-cuckoo *Chalcites lucidus*							X
Honeyeaters							
New Zealand Bellbird *Anthornis melanura*		X					
Tui *Prosthemadera novaeseelandiae novaeseelandiae*	X						
Chatham Island Tui *P. n. chathamensis*							X
Australasian warblers							
Chatham Island Warbler *Gerygone albofrontata*							X
Flycatchers							
Chatham Island Tomtit *Petroica [macrocephala] chathamensis*						X	
Auckland Islands Tomtit *P. [m.] marrineri*		X					
Snares Tomtit *P. [m.] dannefaerdi*	X						
Black Robin *P. traversi*							X
New Zealand Fantail *Rhipidura fuliginosa fuliginosa*	X						
Chatham Island Fantail *R. f. penitus*							X
Larks							
Skylark *Alauda arvensis*		X		extinct			X
Pipits							
New Zealand Pipit *Anthus novaeseelandiae*		X		X	X		X
Accentors							
Dunnock *Prunella modularis*		X		X	X		X
Old World Sparrows							
House Sparrow *Passer domesticus*	X?	X		extinct			X
Old World Finches							
Common Chaffinch *Fringilla coelebs*	X	X		extinct	X		X
European Greenfinch *Carduelis chloris*							X
European Goldfinch *C. carduelis*		X		extinct	X		X
Common Redpoll *C. flammea*	X	X	X	X	X		X
Yellowhammer *Emberiza citrinella*				extinct			X
Hirundines							
Welcome Swallow *Hirundo neoxena*							X
Warblers							
Snares Island Fernbird *Bowdleria [punctata] caudata*	X						
White-eyes							
Silvereye *Zosterops lateralis*	X	X		X	X		X
Thrushes							
Common Blackbird *Turdus merula*	X	X		X	X		X
Song Thrush *T. philomelos*	X	X		extinct	X		X
Starlings							
Common Starling *Sturnus vulgaris*	X	X	X	X	X		X
Seals							
New Zealand Fur Seal *Arctocephalus forsteri*	X	X	X	X	X	X	X
Antarctic Fur Seal *A. gazella*			X				
Subantarctic Fur Seal *A. tropicalis*			X				
New Zealand (Hooker's) Sea Lion *Phocarctos hookeri*	X	X		X			
Southern Elephant Seal *Mirounga leonina*		X	X		X		

The Ross Sea

Being the arena of some of the most famous heroics of the Golden Age of Antarctic exploration, the Ross Sea sector of the continent exerts an almost irresistible fascination on those with any interest in Antarctic history. Sites in and around the Ross Sea Ice Shelf marked the starting point for many of the most famous journeys to the inhospitable Antarctic interior; several of the early explorers' huts are still standing and permit tourists a remarkable insight into the lives of Scott, Shackleton and others. As these early expeditions discovered, the Ross Sea is also remarkable for its huge concentrations of wildlife. What it lacks in species, it gains in huge overall numbers of individuals, especially penguins, most notably Emperor Penguin, and some petrels. While vegetation is limited, due to the extreme cold, especially in winter, to a few patches of moss and lichens, this region of Antarctica is one of the most scenically dramatic regions on the planet, and this combined with its strong historical associations and rich natural history make it an increasingly visited part of the continent. Conveniently, at least some companies offer itineraries that permit visitors to combine the Ross Sea with a tour of the subantarctic islands south of New Zealand.

Location and main features The Ross Sea is a large bay of 770,000 km², contained by Victoria Land in the west, which stretches 800 km from 71°S to the Ross Ice Shelf at 77°S; the latter feature continues a further 700 km south towards the South Pole. The shelf occupies an area the size of France, being 830 km wide at its open sea edge where it links S Victoria Land to the Edward VII Peninsula in Marie Byrd Land. Waters are generally rather shallow, 300–900 m, but in the north of the sea reach up to 4000 m.

Landform, climate and habitat This region, part of East Antarctica, experiences a climate very similar to that elsewhere in this half of the continent. Its landform, geology, climate and habitat are described in the chapter dealing with East Antarctica as well as the general introductory chapters to this book. The Ross Sea is one of two large embayments, the other being the Weddell Sea, of the Antarctic continent, but despite a moderating sea influence this area is subject to a harsh climate and even algae, mosses and lichens survive in just a few tiny patches in a handful of areas.

Birds The region is of supreme importance for Antarctic birds, with ten or 11 breeding species, of which only six nest south of the Balleny Is and Scott I. Of Emperor Penguin, approximately 40% or c.70,000 pairs of the global population breed in this region, with the largest colonies at Cape Washington (24,000 pairs in 1990) and on Coulman I, in Victoria Land (28,000 pairs in the same year) being the most important in the world. Adélie Penguin nests at 38 breeding sites totalling c.1 million pairs or 40% of the overall population, but numbers in this region alone, including non-breeders may be up to seven times greater than this figure: the largest colonies are at Cape Adare (c.250,000 pairs) and Cape Crozier (c.130,000 pairs), but some number just a few thousand pairs. Post-1980s data suggest that the overall population in this region is stable.

Information on numbers and distribution of petrels breeding in the Ross Sea is very limited, largely because, unlike penguins and skuas, very little sustained effort has been applied to survey their breeding sites, primarily because of their inaccessibility and remoteness from scientific bases. Nevertheless, it is possible that as many as five million Antarctic Petrels occur in this region, being strongly associated with the pack-ice zone, though no confirmed breeding sites are known, with the exception of Mount Paterson on the Rockefeller Plateau. Snow Petrel numbers are also sub-

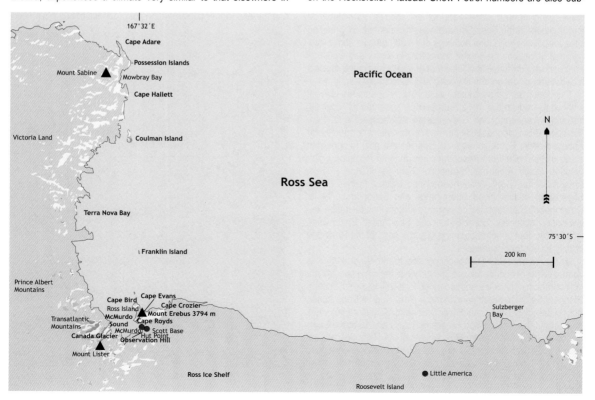

Killer Whales Orcinus orca *spyhopping in McMurdo Sound, Ross Sea, Jan 1992. © Kim Westerskov.*

ject to speculation but as many as c.2 million pairs may inhabit the Ross Sea; this species is also strongly associated with pack ice. More is known concerning the breeding sites of this species, with colonies having been found in the Morozumi Range, on Duke of York I, Cape Adare, Cape Hallet, Edisto Inlet, Felsite I, Crater Cirque, Washington Ridge and Mount Paterson. Wilson's Storm-petrel, of which the total population is estimated at 128,000 pairs, is associated with open water and open leads in pack ice. It breeds at Cape Adare, the Possession Is, Cape Hallet and Moubray Bay, with records from Edisto Inlet, Felsite I, Crater Cirque and Franklin I. The only other breeding species is the near-appropriately named South Polar Skua; with almost 6000 pairs in the region, this is the most important area of the world for the species. Its distribution and numbers in the Ross Sea are well documented: 55 breeding sites are known, with total numbers of 15,000 despite some local declines. It vacates the region completely in winter and evidence from banded individuals indicates that at least some of the region's breeders reach Japan, the N Pacific and Alaskan coasts.

The Antarctic Convergence, at c.60°S, appears to prevent southward movement of a number of subantarctic species, including Wandering and Grey-headed Albatrosses, and Slender-billed Prion, and restricts northward movement of open-water Antarctic birds. Some subantarctic species are able to penetrate south of the polar front in summer and autumn including Light-mantled Sooty Albatross, Southern Giant and Cape Petrels, Antarctic Prion, Grey, White-headed and Mottled Petrels, Sooty Shearwater, Black-bellied Storm-petrel and Subantarctic Skua. Other infrequently reported or vagrant seabirds include Indian Yellow-nosed Albatross, Black Petrel and Short-tailed Shearwater, while Arctic Tern is not uncommon in some parts of the Ross Sea during the southern summer.

Marine mammals Four species of seal breed: Weddell Seal is characteristic of fast-ice around coasts, while the other species are only common in pack ice and are much less well known. Southern Elephant Seal has been found in the N Ross Sea, at Cape Adare, but no breeding sites are known. Crabeater Seal is commonest, breeding in the N Ross Sea, whereas Ross's and Leopard Seals are particularly little known. Most whales of the Ross Sea are baleen whales, with Antarctic Minke and Blue Whales penetrating to the continental ice edge in pursuit of food during summer. Southern Right and Humpback Whales are uncommon in the Ross Sea, as are Fin and Sei Whales. The only toothed whales are Killer Whale,

which roams in family pods, and Long-finned Pilot Whale, with a doubtful report of False Killer Whale. Generally only male Sperm Whales occur in the Southern Ocean and very rarely reach the Ross Sea. Several species of beaked whales have been reported in the Ross Sea, among them Arnoux's, Strap-toothed, Southern Bottlenose and Gray's Beaked Whales. Among dolphins, the following have been recorded: Southern Right Whale Dolphin, Hourglass Dolphin, Commerson's Dolphin and Spectacled Porpoise.

Main conservation issues Pollution, such as oiling, and poisoning, from organochlorine compounds and heavy metals, are relatively recent phenomena within the Ross Sea (and throughout the Southern Ocean), but have been noted in breeding penguins and petrels. Higher concentrations of organochlorines have been

Emperor Penguin Aptenodytes forsteri *colony at Cape Crozier, Ross I, Sep 1991. © Kim Westerskov.*

noted in those species such as Wilson's Storm-petrel that move well beyond the Antarctic Convergence in the non-breeding season. Habitat disturbance and destruction through human visits to colonies, both on foot and by helicopter, have caused birds to desert colonies or to lay them open to nest predators such as skuas. Construction of a research station at Cape Hallet forced 8000–10,000 pairs, of a 40,000-pair colony of Adélie Penguins, to move elsewhere. Fouling at sea should discharges occur is another potentially serious problem, as is the seabird bycatch in fisheries, particularly longline fishing for toothfish.

On the positive side, a number of Specially Protected Areas (SPA) and Sites of Special Scientific Interest (SSSI) have been established in the region, including Capes Royds, Crozier and Hallet, and Beaufort I, while outlines for future survey and research projects were formulated 20 years ago.

The Antarctic Treaty, which came into force on 23 Jun 1961, formalized and guaranteed free access and research rights to all countries, both claimant and non-claimant, to work cooperatively for common, peaceful causes in the continent. A major feature of the treaty is the consultative system which it established. Many recommendations have been adopted, most dealing with conservation and environmental protection. Of even greater significance was the adoption (1991) and enforcement (1998) of the Protocol on Environmental Protection to the Antarctic Treaty, which establishes mandatory standards through technical annexes on conservation of fauna and flora, waste disposal, prevention of marine pollution and area protection. Fuller details of these can be found in the introductory chapter, Conservation in the Region, but the most comprehensive relate to the preservation and protection of all living resources. Thus far, the Treaty has commenced to tackle the challenges of mineral exploration and exploitation, the conservation of marine living resources, and tourism. And, as always, recommendations will require renegotiation in the light of new data concerning novel pressures, such as over-fishing in the

'Quintessential Antarctica': Adélie Penguin Pygoscelis adeliae *colony bustling with activity, with icebergs, sea ice and ice cliffs in the background, Cape Bird, Ross I, Ross Sea. © Kim Westerskov.*

Beacon Valley within the Dry Valleys region of the Ross Sea, Jan 1992. © Kim Westerskov.

continent's seas. The importance and role of conservation within the Treaty is one of the major issues facing the Antarctic and, given the developing ozone-hole problem, the world.

Human history It was left to James Clark Ross to fully explore the sea, subsequently named in his honour, in 1841, during which he also discovered Ross I and the 3794 m-high Mount Erebus. (Previously, in 1831, a Liverpool merchant, Samuel Harvey, had penetrated to 72°S in this region.) Half a century passed before others were moved to make a mark in this sea of near-impenetrable pack ice, until, on 24 Jan 1895, crew from the whaler *Antarctica* landed at Cape Adare. One of these, Carsten Borchgrevink, a Norwegian living in Australia sought to return. He gained the financial backing of Sir George Newnes and purchased a whaler which was renamed *Southern Cross*, with the object of returning to the Ross Sea in order to find the South Magnetic Pole. *Southern Cross* dropped anchor off Cape Adare on 17 Feb 1899 and two prefabricated huts were constructed to house the expedition's scientific programme, which made observations in meteorology, magnetism and marine biology throughout the following winter. In Jan 1900 the expedition was able to continue into the Ross Sea, making landings on Possession I, Coulman I and near Mount Melbourne, and sledging over the Ross Ice Shelf to c.78°50'S.

Borchgrevink's expedition had been a considerable success, despite the loss of one member of the party and considerable personal differences between the leader and some of his men, and paved the way for Scott's National Antarctic Expedition and thereafter 'the race to the pole'. Indeed, because of expectations surrounding Scott's first expedition, which departed south shortly after Borchgrevink's return, the latter was somewhat overshadowed and his achievements went rather unrecognized for several years. Despite finance difficulties, the *Discovery* was built and stocked with equipment and a team of 48 men selected, of which 32 were from the navy. Following a winter at McMurdo Sound, the spring and summer sledging season included the 93-day farthest south, achieved by Scott, Wilson and Shackleton, who reached 82°17'S, and the first ascent of the Polar Plateau, by Armitage. Though it proved impossible to free the Discovery, which had been deliberately allowed to become frozen within the pack ice, the arrival of the *Morning* with further supplies permitted another winter on the continent during which observations on meteorology, botany and geology continued. In Oct 1903, a second party, this time led by Scott, again scaled the Polar Plateau. With the arrival, in Jan 1904, of two relief ships, it finally proved possible to free the *Discovery*, which permitted the expedition's departure.

Scott was assured of a hero's welcome on his return to Britain,

Mountains, Ross Sea region. © Daisy Gilardini.

party found Scott's last camp, in Nov 1912. Now only the last great journey remained, the crossing of the Antarctic continent.

Thus in 1914 Shackleton, whose reputation as simply 'the Boss' was by now well established, launched the Imperial Trans-Antarctic Expedition consisting of two parties: that led by him was to enter the Weddell Sea and sledge the 2600 km to McMurdo Sound, while the other was to go direct to the latter and lay depots as far inland as the foot of the Beardmore Glacier. But the expedition was soon in difficulties: in Nov 1915, the *Endurance* was crushed by pack ice and sank in the Weddell Sea. Miraculously the entire party survived and was rescued following a winter on the ice, the small-boat voyage to, and then the crossing on foot of, South Georgia. It demonstrated, once again, Shackleton's heroism and compassion for his men. Meanwhile, in McMurdo Sound matters also did not go to plan. The support ship *Aurora* was driven seawards during a winter blizzard and was forced to drift in the pack ice for nine months. Nonetheless, the following summer depot laying, commenced the previous autumn, was completed but at the cost of three lives. *Aurora* eventually reached New Zealand, where it was repaired, and returned to rescue the survivors in Jan 1917.

The next major initiatives in Antarctic exploration to touch upon the Ross Sea came in 1947 and 1948, when the USA launched operations High Jump and Windmill, which conducted extensive aerial photographic surveys of the entire continent's coastline. Three nations now have permanent bases in the Ross Sea region. In 1955, the US operation Deep Freeze established McMurdo Station, at Hut Point, in preparation for the International Geophysical Year (IGY) of 1957–8. It has operated year-round since then. Concurrently, New Zealand opened Scott Base just 2 km from McMurdo Base to support the Commonwealth Trans-Antarctic Expedition, in which Sir Vivien Fuchs finally crossed the continent from the Weddell Sea to Ross I. New Zealand continues to maintain a science and research programme there. Subsequent research projects have included Terra Nova Bay Station, which was established by Italy in summer 1986–7, and which operates from mid-Oct until late Feb annually. In addition, Greenpeace established the short-term World Park Base on Ross I in 1987 and maintained it year-round until 1992 to monitor human impacts on the Antarctic environment.

Visiting the region Each year several cruise companies visit the Ross Sea, and there are many possible landings at coastal sites and islands between Cape Adare and Ross I, but icebreakers and ships equipped with helicopters offer greater opportunities to explore more inaccessible areas, such as the Dry Valleys. Most voyages last 3–4 weeks and operate in Dec–Feb but in recent years special Emperor Penguin cruises have been operated earlier in the season in order to visit their massive colonies in Nov. The following are the key sites for wildlife in the Ross Sea.

but it was Shackleton, whose gargantuan but somewhat understated role in the history of Antarctic exploration is overshadowed by Scott's better known but not necessarily more successful exploits, who now seized the initiative and announced the British Antarctic Expedition (1907–09). With limited funds, the ship *Nimrod*, a motor car, ponies and dogs were procured; Shackleton also enlisted a competent scientific team. Upon arrival, in Jan 1908, a base was established at Cape Royds and Mount Erebus scaled. That winter the scientific programme continued and the following spring the main sledging parties departed. Shackleton and his party crossed the Ross Ice Shelf via the Beardmore Glacier and south to 88°23'S, less than 200 km from the pole. But, suffering from insufficient food, dysentery and exhaustion, Shackleton made the difficult decision to return to Cape Royds. It cost him the chance of reaching the pole and immortality, but perhaps proved him to be the true hero, as his decision saved the lives of his men. The other party, a three-man team including Mawson reached the South Magnetic Pole, on 15 Jan 1909. The expedition earned Shackleton a knighthood.

With the way still clear, Scott's British Antarctic Expedition (1910–13), in addition to an ambitious scientific programme, had the clearly stated aim of reaching the South Pole. With the Terra Nova, a formidable team of scientists, three motor tractors, dogs, ponies and buildings at his disposal, Scott left England in Jun 1910, receiving news, en route in Melbourne of Amundsen's plans to reach the South Pole. The race had been joined! The expedition's 25-man shore party disembarked at Cape Evans and immediately commenced its meteorological, glaciological, zoological and geological work. A second, much smaller base was also erected at Cape Adare. Meanwhile Amundsen had established his base operation at the Bay of Whales on the Ross Ice Shelf. Scott's five-man party and support teams started for the pole on 1 Nov breaking Shackleton's furthest south on 9 Jan 1912. Little did they know it, but even by this date Amundsen had already departed from the South Pole to his base camp, having achieved the seemingly impossible on 14 Dec 1911. It was not until over a month later, on 17 Jan, that Scott, Wilson, Bowers, Oates and Evans could plant a British flag next to the Norwegian standard. The achievement must have seemed hollow; to have come second was almost to not have run and the immense demoralization is almost evident on the men's faces as they posed for their Polar photograph. The return journey is arguably the most famous in the history of Antarctic exploration; it brought the deaths of the entire party and provides the great discussion point of Antarctic history. Was Scott reckless, ill-prepared, both of or none of these? What is clear is that a search

Breaking Ross Ice Shelf. © Hans Reinhard.

McMurdo Station, Ross Sea. © Hans Reinhard.

Inside Shackleton's hut at Cape Royds, Ross I, still looking as if 'The Boss' might walk in any minute. © Kim Westerskov.

Cape Adare (71°17'S 170°14'E) is the site of the first recorded landing on the Antarctic continent and that of the first expedition to winter there (in 1898); it is thus of major historical importance. The cape marks the extreme point of a north-facing peninsula of Victoria Land and was named, by James Clark Ross, for his friend Viscount Adare. Borchgrevink's rather ill-starred Southern Cross expedition, which wintered there, constructed a 6.5 x 5.5-m hut at the cape that has been preserved by the New Zealand Antarctic Heritage Trust. A large gravel spit, Ridley Beach (named for Borchgrevink's mother), holds the largest Adélie Penguin colony in Antarctica, with c.250,000 breeding pairs and is also the burial site of the first human to die on the Antarctic continent, Nicolai Hansen, biologist with the Southern Cross expedition. In addition, there is a large South Polar Skua colony and Southern Giant Petrels are often seen on the beach.

Part of **Cape Hallett** (72°18'S 179°19'E) has been designated as a SPA due to its unusually rich flora. The avifauna is also interesting with a large Adélie Penguin colony at Seabee Hook, the landing point, on the northwest corner of the cape. The site was among James Clark Ross' numerous discoveries and was named for his purser, Thomas Hallet. The highest point in the region is 1770 m above sea level and the area is generally similar in appearance and structure to Cape Adare. From 1957 to 1973 a scientific station, a joint New Zealand and USA venture, operated in the area, but the disused buildings have since been removed. Zodiac cruises are possible but helicopter landings are forbidden.

Possession Is (71°56'S 171°12'E) comprise two main islets and at least seven rocky pillars (up to 90 m tall), 8 km from the coast of Victoria Land. Possession itself, named by James Clark Ross to commemorate the planting of the British flag, was discovered on 12 Jan 1841. Foyn, named by a Norwegian expedition after its most generous financier, is the more southerly of the two islands. A total population of c.300,000 pairs of Adélie Penguin breeds here, with Southern Giant Petrel a frequent, apparently non-breeding visitor. Wilson's Storm-petrel has bred on Possession.

Coulman I (73°28'S 169°45'E), part of an extinct volcano, was another of Sir James Clark Ross' discoveries and was named for his father-in-law. Borchgrevink made the first landing in Feb 1900, and Scott also called at the island in Jan 1902. Thirty km long, 13 km wide and rising to 2000 m, with few landing places, the island possesses four Adélie Penguin colonies totalling c.24,000 pairs. In addition a huge Emperor Penguin colony uses the fast ice close to the island to breed in winter, and some are usually still present in the vicinity in summer.

Terra Nova Bay (74°50'S 164°30'E) is sited between Cape Washington and the Drygalski ice tongue. An Italian base constructed at the southern end of the Gerlache Inlet in 1986/7 is capable of housing up to 70 people and on the north side of the bay Mount Melbourne (named by James Clark Ross in honour of a British Prime Minister), at 2730 m, is among the few volcanoes on the Antarctic continent. Usually ice-free, the bay was discovered by Scott's British National Antarctic Expedition and named after its relief ship. The huge Emperor Penguin colony at Cape Washington produced c.24,000 chicks in 1990, making it the largest in existence. Elsewhere within the bay there is an Adélie colony in the Northern Foothills, with c.13,000 pairs, and another at Inexpressible I containing 29,000 pairs. A cave on the latter was used as a base by Scott's Northern Party in Feb–Sep 1912 when ice conditions prevented their ship from returning, and is a rather dreary spot; naturalists, however, will enjoy the Weddell Seals that are regularly sighted here.

Franklin (76°05'S 168°19'E) is a low, 12-km long volcanic island 105 km northeast of Cape Bird. It was named by its discoverer Ross after Sir John Franklin, governor of Tasmania and a noted Arctic explorer who perished in the search for the Northwest Passage. There is a low gravel spit on the island's western side supporting up to c.70,000 breeding pairs of Adélie Penguin. South Polar Skua nests on the summit and to the north there is a large ice-cape, near where Snow Petrel possibly breeds. A small Emperor Penguin colony (2500 chicks in 1990) is located in the south of the island.

Cape Bird (77°10'S 166°43'E) marks the northernmost extremity of Ross I. Named in honour of Edward Bird of the Erebus, it is another famous site in the annals of Antarctic history, and New Zealand maintains a field station that among other research has conducted long-term work on the Adélie Penguin (c.41,000 pairs in 1990) and South Polar Skua colonies there. The area known as New College Valley is both a SPA and SSSI.

Cape Crozier (77°28'S 169°28'E), at the extreme east end of Ross I and abutting the Ross Ice Shelf, is accessible by air from either McMurdo Station or Scott Base (see below) and is a SSSI measuring c.19 km². There are gravel slopes on the northeast side of the cape but much of the remainder is covered by ice. Long-term studies of Emperor (up to several thousand pairs) and Adélie Penguin (over 175,000 pairs in two main colonies) are being conducted at the site. The Emperor colony was that visited by Wilson, Bowers and Cherry-Garrard during the Terra Nova expedition, and which Cherry-Garrard described, without any exaggeration, as 'the worst journey in the world'. McMurdo Sound

Emperor Penguins Aptenodytes forsteri, *Ross Sea. © Hans Reinhard.*

Adélie Penguins Pygoscelis adeliae, *Ross Sea. © Hans Reinhard.*

(77°30'S 165°00'E), which is 148 km long and 74 km broad at its widest point, lies at the junction of the Ross Sea and its ice shelf, between Ross I and Victoria Land, and is perhaps best known for Hut Point, on a rocky promontory near Cape Armitage. Scott established his base for the 1901–04 Discovery Expedition here and the shelter was subsequently used in 1908, 1911 and 1915. The hut which is just 9.3 m square still stands and was subject to restoration work in 1964, but is overshadowed by the modern US base constructed in the mid-1950s and, just 5 km distant by gravel road, at Pram Point, New Zealand's Scott Base, which was built in 1955–8 and through subsequent enlargement in 1976 is now capable of housing up to 86 personnel in summer. Scott Base and Ross I are part of the New Zealand Ross Dependency, the only piece of the Antarctic continent to be under this country's stewardship, having been originally claimed by the UK in 1923 but subsequently placed in the custody of the New Zealand government. Both bases were initially constructed as part of the IGY and some of the original buildings remain, but the American base has grown near-exponentially in recent decades, being served by transport aircraft from Christchurch (New Zealand) and even boasting a supermarket, church, cinema and two airfields! Up to several thousand personnel may be based there in summer, with several hundred remaining in winter. Above the station is the 230-m high Observation Hill (77°51'S 166°40'E), which is regularly visited by tourists, the commemorative cross at its summit was constructed in honour of Scott and the other members of the ill-fated polar party. The sound marks the southern limit of summer fast ice and is a reliable area to observe the first Emperor Penguins in mid- to late Feb, while Southern Giant Petrel can be common. Killer and Minke Whales are regularly reported.

Cape Royds (77°33'S 166°09'E) at the western extremity of Ross I is another must-visit site for those with even a passing interest in Antarctic history. This low prominence was named for the lieutenant of the Discovery. Shackleton established his 1907–09 base here and the 7 x 6 m hut, which housed 14 men, is maintained by the New Zealand Antarctic Heritage Trust. The area thus became a base for the successful conquest of nearby Mount Erebus (77°25'S 167°25'E), the ascent of the Beardmore Glacier and pinpointing of the South Magnetic Pole. It was visited by Scott's British Antarctic Expedition a few years later and then again in 1947, by which date the base was in severe disrepair; restoration work commenced in 1960 and the result is perhaps one of the most interesting monuments to the golden age of Antarctic exploration. The walls are autographed by several of the heroes of the period, including both Mawson and Shackleton and, in general, the hut possesses much more personality and human interest than those occupied by Scott's

expeditions. A small Adélie colony (4000 pairs) constitutes the species' southernmost breeding site and is protected as a SSSI, although the early explorers viewed it as a source of food!

Cape Evans (77°38'S 166°24'E) is synonymous with Scott's second expedition (and was named after his second-in-command), which established its base here at the southernmost point it was possible to reach. Following the departure of Scott's British Antarctic Expedition, the base was occupied by the stranded men from Shackleton's Aurora, who decamped here for 20 months before their rescue in Jan 1917. The hut was visited again in the 1940s. Restoration work commenced in 1960 and the Antarctic Heritage Trust maintains the 15.25 x 7.6 m hut, which is an essential port of call for anyone visiting the region. Indeed, it is possible to enter the hut, which has been preserved as closely as possible to appear as it would have been, thus providing a unique insight into the trials and cramped conditions associated with early Antarctic exploration (up to ten men shared this small space, though it should be remembered that, at the time, this was the most lavishly constructed Antarctic base to have been constructed). Naturalists will also enjoy the opportunity to study the South Polar Skuas nesting in the area.

The **Ross Ice Shelf** (78°00'S 169°E–170°W) and **Dry Valleys** are among other notable sites in this region. The massive floating Ross Ice Shelf was originally named the Victoria Barrier, after Queen Victoria, by its discoverer James Clark Ross. Its present-day name has only been acquired with the passage of time. It has inspired both fear and wonder among its beholders and perhaps the most telling words written about the shelf are those of Roald Amundsen, in Jan 1911, 'It is altogether a thing which can hardly be described...'. The first of the Dry Valleys to be discovered was Taylor Valley, by Scott in Dec 1903, who described it as 'a valley of the dead'. Lying in S Victoria Land, there are three main valleys, Victoria, Wright and Taylor, and their collective name is certainly no misnomer, rainfall has been unknown in this area for at least two (possibly four) million years! The valleys cover 3000 km² and have no snow or ice, although an unusual assemblage of lakes and ponds in the region possess some life, mainly algae, and some of the plants here are perhaps 200,000 years old. The terrain in this region has been compared to Mars, with highly sculpted rocks, as well as many mummified seals (and even penguins) their carcasses freeze-dried by the exceptional aridity and thereafter eroded by the wind. One site is a SSSI, the **Canada Glacier** (77°37'S 163°05'E), within the Taylor Valley, which has a comparatively rich flora. Most of the area is protected under the Antarctic Treaty and even scientists are not permitted to visit, but tourists are able to fly into Taylor Valley by helicopter.

Adélie Penguin Pygoscelis adeliae *colony. Cape Bird, Ross I, Ross Sea.*
© *Kim Westerskov.*

South Polar Skua Catharacta [skua] maccormicki *chick in a rare, heavy midsummer snowfall. Observation Hill, Ross I, Ross Sea, Jan 1992.* © *Kim Westerskov.*

Scott Island

Location and main features This small volcanic island, located at 67°24'S 179°55'W, lies north of the Ross Sea, c.560 km northeast of Cape Adare and 2420 km southeast of New Zealand. Well south of the Antarctic convergence, it more or less marks the northern limit of pack ice in summer.

Landform, climate and habitat Scott measures c.400 x 200 m, aligned on a north to south axis, with a maximum elevation of 50 m (in the north) and consists of a crater and volcanic plug. Vertical wave-cut cliffs that virtually encircle the island are c.30–40 m high in the northwest, but slope to c.10 m in the south. There is a large arch in the northwest headland of the main island. Small, steep boulder beaches are present on the north and west sides. Entirely snow- and ice-covered in winter, in summer much of the higher part is ice-free. A rocky, 62.5 m-high sheer-sided stack, Haggits Pillar, lies c.730 m west of the main island.

Birds Scott I and Haggits Pillar possess a tiny breeding avifauna consisting of Southern Fulmar, Cape and Snow Petrels, Antarctic Prion (at least 200 pairs) and Wilson's Storm-petrel. Antarctic Petrel may also breed. There are a number of reports of Blue Petrel in the immediate vicinity of Scott, which may indicate possible breeding there. The only ornithological observations are the casual notes of Colbeck, in 1902, who noted large numbers of many of the above-mentioned species around the northern cone, those of Harper, in Feb 1962, who discovered Antarctic Prions breeding in rock fissures near the summit of both the main island and in Haggits Pillar, with Snow Petrels also nesting on the latter. In Jan 1982, Cape Petrel was added to the list of breeders and, in 1996, Southern Fulmar on Haggits Pillar.

Marine mammals Southern Elephant Seal has recently been found at Scott, but is not known to breed there.

Main conservation issues None are known.

Human history Discovered, in Dec 1902, by Colbeck in the *Morning*, when coming to the relief of Scott's Discovery Expedition, his is one of only five recorded landings on the island, of which two have been made by helicopter. Scott, which is named after the explorer, is characterized by steep cliffs and icy slopes which, with the surrounding rough seas, usually combine to prevent landings, but Colbeck was able to land on the southeast shore.

Visiting the islands No landings have been made on the island by ornithologists and the only ornithological observations are those mentioned above.

Balleny Islands

Location and main features Consisting of three main islands (Sturge, Buckle and Young) and numerous smaller islands (including Row, Borradaile and Sabrina), 300 km northwest of Cape Adare, in Victoria Land, the Balleny Is straddle the Antarctic Circle. These form a c.160 km-long chain, aligned on a northwest to southeast axis, between 66°15'S and 162°15'–164°45'E.

Landform, climate and habitat The islands total less than 400 km² and all are high, steep and of volcanic origin, rising sharply from the ocean floor; depths of 2000 m occur within five nautical miles of the group. Volcanic activity was reported in the early-19th century but there has been none since, although there was recently a major earthquake in the area. The most northerly of the group is Young, a 30.5 km-long and 6.5 km-wide island, its coastline consisting of alternating cliffs and glaciers. Just to the southeast is Row, a small island (1.6 km in diameter) encrusted in glacial ice, with a small beach. Next is Borradaile (3.2 x 1.6 km) which is capped by a glacier and has beaches on the northwest

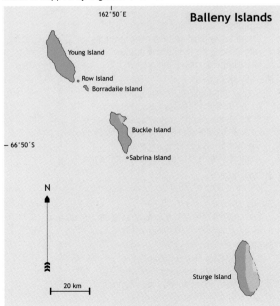

Balleny Islands

162°50'E

Young Island

Row Island
Borradaile Island

Buckle Island

– 66°50'S

Sabrina Island

N

20 km

Sturge Island

Antarctic Minke Whales Balaenoptera bonaerensis *spyhopping in McMurdo Sound, Ross Sea, Jan 1992. © Kim Westerskov.*

and southwest coasts that may offer landing places. One of the three large islands of the group, Buckle is c.21 km long and 5 km wide. It too is covered by glacial ice and possesses a coastline of alternating cliffs and glaciers. Sabrina is tiny, less than 2 km wide, with a small permanent ice-cap covering c.25% of its area. Associated are two rocky islets, Monolith to the south and Chinstrap to the northeast; the former is dominated by a spectacular 78 m-high volcanic plug and is connected by a boulder spit to Sabrina. Sturge is the largest (c.32 x 6.5 km), highest (Brown Peak reaches 1705 m) and most southerly of the group. It is almost completely ice-covered, with the exception of several cliffs on the west and south coasts. Pack ice from the Ross Sea regularly drifts towards the islands and surrounds the group in winter. The islands are cloud-covered for much of the year and vegetation is generally very sparse. Though terrestrial algae are common, lichens are generally rare and mosses absent from the group.

Birds Seabirds are scattered throughout the group, with five species known to breed (all counts are from 1984). Three colonies of Adélie Penguin totalling 1357 pairs occur on Buckle, with 3500 pairs on Sabrina, c.2000 pairs on Chinstrap and perhaps ten pairs on a rocky promontory at Cape Symth, on Sturge. Chinstrap Penguin nest, appropriately enough only on Chinstrap, where there is a tiny colony of c.10 pairs. Small numbers of Southern Fulmar nest on Young and there is a colony of c.6000 on the northeast coast of Row, with unknown numbers present on Borradaile and 10,000–20,000 pairs on the northwest coast of Sturge. Cape and Snow Petrels both nest on Young, Borradaile, the Beale Pinnacle just to the southeast of the latter island, and Buckle, with the former also breeding on Sabrina, Chinstrap and perhaps Sturge, where a large colony of up to 10,000 Snow Petrels is present on the central-west coast. Those breeding at the Balleny Is are apparently all Greater Snow Petrels, but as detailed in the species accounts there is still much to learn concerning this form and its relationship to the Lesser Snow Petrel.

Species observed near the Balleny Is include Emperor Penguin, Southern Giant Petrel, Antarctic Petrel, Antarctic Prion, Sooty Shearwater, Arctic Tern and Subantarctic Skua. Some may even breed.

Marine mammals Weddell, Crabeater and Southern Elephant Seals have been observed on the beaches of Borradaile, while Weddell Seal has been recorded on Row's only beach.

Main conservation issues Largely undisturbed by direct human influence, the Balleny archipelago's biological diversity exceeds that of any other site in this region and has led to Sabrina being designated as a Specially Protected Area (SPA). The New Zealand government is currently proposing that the entire group and a substantial marine area around the archipelago be designated as a SPA. This would afford the group much greater protection.

Human history Discovered in Feb 1839 by the British captain John Balleny, 19 recorded landings have been made on the islands and some have witnessed volcanic eruptions. Most have been associated with scientific expeditions.

Visiting the islands Three of the most recent landings were made by those on tourist ships. Special permission is required to land on Sabrina but going ashore on any of the group is comparatively difficult due to the paucity of suitable beaches.

Table 1. Breeding bird and mammal checklist for the Ross Sea.

	Ross Sea	Balleny	Scott
Penguins			
Emperor Penguin *Aptenodytes forsteri*	X		
Adélie Penguin *Pygoscelis adeliae*	X	X	
Chinstrap Penguin *P. antarctica*		X	
Petrels and prions			
Southern Fulmar *Fulmarus glacialoides*	X	X	X
Antarctic Petrel *Thalassoica antarctica*	X	X?	X?
Cape Petrel *Daption capense*		X	
Lesser Snow Petrel *Pagodroma [nivea] minor*	X		X
Greater Snow Petrel *P. [n.] major*		X	
Antarctic Prion *Pachyptila desolata banksi*		X?	X
Storm-petrels			
Wilson's Storm-petrel *Oceanites oceanicus*	X	X?	X
Skuas			
Subantarctic Skua *Catharacta antarctica lonnbergi*		X?	
South Polar Skua *C. maccormicki*	X		
Seals			
Leopard Seal *Hydrurga leptonyx*	X		
Weddell Seal *Leptonychotes weddellii*	X	X	
Crabeater Seal *Lobodon carcinophaga*	X		
Ross Seal *Ommatophoca rossii*	X		

East Antarctica

Tourists, principally because of the relative lack of historical landmarks or specific wildlife stopping-off points, very rarely visit this harsh, inhospitable area, which includes the South Pole. Most of the region is also somewhat remote in comparison to the more frequently visited Ross Sea and Peninsula regions. East Antarctica, which is divided into Norwegian, Australian and French-claimed territory, is the oldest landmass on the planet and most is a permanently ice-covered, vast wasteland plateau, with many underground freshwater lakes, but few patches of vegetation (even moss or lichens). It is the site of the lowest-ever recorded temperature on Earth, at almost -90°C. As mentioned above, opportunities for wildlife viewing are very limited and are restricted to the same species as found in the Ross Sea region. However, there are number of spectacular penguin and other bird colonies in the region, including the largest known colony of Antarctic Petrel.

Location and main features The area known as East (or Greater) Antarctica occupies by the far greater part of the polar landmass, and takes its better known name as a result of the majority lying within the Eastern Hemisphere. It includes the South Pole, as well as large regions claimed by Norway (Dronning Maud Land), Australia (Australian Antarctic Territory) and France (Terre Adélie). A number of other countries also maintain scientific stations within this part of the continent, which principally consists of a high plateau covered by a vast, deep ice field, separated from West (or Lesser) Antarctica by the Transantarctic Mountains. Birdlife in this region arguably is most appealingly manifest, at least to casual visitors, in the form of several large penguin colonies.

Landform, climate and habitat East Antarctica is apparently the oldest landmass on the planet, with some of its rocks estimated at over 3.8 million years old. The vast majority of the region, over 99%, is permanently ice covered. In places the ice is 4.8 km deep and the region contains the world's largest glacier, Lambert, at 400 km long and 65 km wide. While a number of mountain ranges are in close proximity to the sea, much of the interior, including the South Pole, is a vast wasteland plateau. East Antarctica is the site of the lowest-ever-recorded temperature on Earth, -89.6°C, at Vostock Station, in Jul 1983. Vostock has a vast, 280 km long, 60 km wide and perhaps 500 m deep, under-ice lake, one of 79 such freshwater lakes that have formed in some basins, caused by ice

melt as a result of rising geothermal heat from the Earth's core. Some of these lakes may be hundreds of thousands of years old. Physically, Dronning Maud Land is typical of this region of Antarctica, being characterized by ice that floats out into the sea, forming an almost unbroken wall 30 m high. Disembarkation from a ship is only possible in a few places. One hundred to 200 km inland, mountain ranges rise through the 2000 m-plus-thick ice cap.

Birds The principal and most obvious feature is the two breeding penguins: Emperor (27 colonies, the largest, of 17,000 pairs at Haswell I, in Wilkes Land, in 1970 may since have declined) and Adélie (55 colonies, with many exceeding 10,000 pairs and most in Princess Elizabeth Land, where the four colonies totalled c.325,000 pairs in the early 1980s).

Norwegian-claimed territory has, until recently, received very little ornithological attention, with mid-1990s research focusing on Antarctic Petrel. Despite the great distance from the open sea, there are numerous nesting cliffs inhabited by seabirds. What is thought to be the largest colony of birds on the entire Antarctic continent is the perhaps almost one-million-strong colony of Antarctic Petrels situated at Svarthamaren in the Mühlig-Hoffmanfjella, 200 km from the coast (though counts in the mid-1980s put the total at 207,000 pairs). Other large colonies of Antarctic Petrel are also known in Dronning Maud Land, with e.g. 2000 pairs at Jutulsessen in 1984–5. Snow Petrel is probably the most abundant species in the interior of western Dronning Maud Land, with several colonies being known and the species has been recorded up to 400 km from the sea. Unfortunately no breeding-colony counts are available. Wilson's Storm-petrel may breed in the west of the Norwegian territory, as may South Polar Skua, which might be expected to nest in close proximity to some of the Snow Petrel colonies. This species has also been recorded far inland in this region.

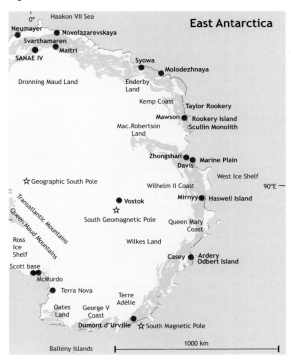

Emperor Penguin Aptenodytes forsteri *chicks in blizzard, East Antarctica.*
© Gordon Petersen.

Ice-wall formation in East Antarctica. © Gordon Petersen.

Adélie Penguins Pygoscelis adeliae, Shirley I, East Antarctica. © Grant Dixon.

The ornithology of the Australian-claimed territory (AAT) is perhaps best known. Comparatively detailed data are available for the period 1958–87 and most counts given below refer to this era. Fourteen colonies of Emperor Penguin are known, totalling 59,335 pairs or c.30% of the overall breeding population; the largest containing 15,000 pairs in 1960 is on Penguin I. In comparison, just 3120 pairs breed in the French-claimed territory. Short-term increases have been documented at two colonies, but other data do not permit any interpretation of overall trends. A similar proportion of the global population of Adélie Penguin breeds in the Australian region, 684,600 pairs inhabiting 27 colonies, the largest with 196,592 pairs being in the Vestfold Hills, and early 1990s counts suggest the overall population is increasing. All four colonies of Southern Giant Petrel known from the Antarctic continent are within East Antarctica, three of them in the Australian-controlled region, with two pairs at the Rookery Is, in 1993, 21 pairs at Hawker I, in 1988, and 174 pairs at the Frazier Is, in 1989–90. Numbers of Antarctic Petrel breeding in the AAT are of crucial importance: 11 nesting sites are now known, containing a minimum of 164,520 pairs (large colonies at Mount Biscoe and Cape Hunter have yet to be counted) or 43% of the estimated world population. Its overall trends are unknown with local increases and decreases reported. Scullin Monolith, which harbours 157,000 breeding pairs (1987 data) is the most important site for this species. Twenty-nine thousand pairs of Southern Fulmar are known to breed in the AAT, with increases reported from at least three colonies, the most significant being on the Rauer Is, which numbered 14,170 pairs in 1985. Thirteen breeding areas, with a minimum population of 4000 pairs of Cape Petrel have been documented. Four colonies remain uncounted, one of which, at Cape Pigeon Rocks, may be significant. Similarly, only four of the 20 known nesting sites for Snow Petrel in the AAT have been accurately or recently surveyed. These produced a total of 8599 pairs, with the majority (an estimated 5000) in the Vestfold Hills. A few pairs of Antarctic Prions were discovered at Cape Denison in Dec 1913, the only known nesting area for this species in the entire continent, but when the area was next visited, in Jan 1982, the species could not be located. The 20 breeding localities for Wilson's Storm-petrel have also received little adequate coverage, with population estimates available from only six of these areas; the largest, estimated at 40,000 pairs is in the Vestfold Hills, while the others number just 1624 pairs. South Polar Skua appears relatively stable in the AAT, with a minimum 357 pairs (considered a significant underestimate) being strongly associated with penguin and petrel colonies.

King Penguin has been recorded on at least four occasions in recent years in Terre Adélie and there is a record, involving two individuals (one of which was collected) of Royal Penguin. There were at least 40 non-breeding records of Chinstrap Penguin on the Pointe Géologie archipelago between 1976 and 1986, with breeding records from Terre Adélie in 1988, 1991 and 1992. A colony of Southern Giant Petrel exists in Terre Adélie, where up to 14 pairs breed on the Pointe Géologie archipelago. They shared the islands in 1999 with 54 pairs of Southern Fulmar, 897 breeding pairs of Snow and 453 pairs of Cape Petrels (with another 1000 pairs of the two latter species elsewhere in this region), and similar numbers of Wilson's Storm-petrel, which totals 1600–2355 pairs in this region but reaches its highest density within Terre Adélie at the site, as well as 46 pairs of South Polar Skua in 1999 (numbers of the latter total just 60–80 pairs in the entire region). In recent years a single Subantarctic Skua has successfully interbred with a South Polar Skua, the resulting hybrid also breeding with a *maccormicki*. Elsewhere, in Terre Adélie, c.50 pairs of Southern Fulmar breed near the base on Île des Petrels.

The following seabirds, which do not breed in the region, have been reported from Antarctic waters in the vicinity of Terre Adélie: Black-browed and Light-mantled Sooty Albatrosses, White-headed, Mottled and Blue Petrels (the latter rare) and Slender-billed and Antarctic Prions, Sooty Shearwater and Black-bellied Storm-petrel.

Nesting Antarctic Petrel Thalassoica antarctic. East Antarctica. © Gordon Petersen.

Glacier in East Antarctica. © Brett Jarrett.

Marine mammals Considerable populations of seals breed in this region. A population of 15 million Crabeater Seals has been estimated for the entire Antarctic coastline. Leopard and Weddell Seals also occur in large numbers throughout East Antarctica.

Main conservation issues Human disturbance in Terre Adélie has led to declines in the numbers of Adélie Penguins and Southern Giant Petrels nesting in the region, and may have adversely affected numbers of Wilson's Storm and Snow Petrels breeding in some parts of the AAT, e.g. due to quarrying operations at Casey Station. Regular tourist visits are currently not envisaged to the AAT, though Australia recently indicated that a blue-ice runway at Casey should be operational in 2003/4. Husky dogs have been recorded taking both species of penguin, as well as Snow Petrels, but other predators, seals and skuas, are natural. Commercial fisheries, taking fin fish and Antarctic krill, are currently small scale and likely to be of comparatively little threat, despite their taking species on which several bird species are strongly dependent. Direct human exploitation of penguin eggs has been reported in the past, but strict regulations preventing such activities are now in place. The Prince Charles Mountains and Prydz Bay area have been identified as the most promising areas for future mineral exploration, with both iron ore and coal being considered as potentially viably exploitable mineral resources within the AAT, though development of mining interests is currently banned for 50 years under the terms of the Madrid Protocol.

Perhaps the greatest threats to Antarctic birds, especially in this region with its many bases, are pollution and poisoning: pesticides and mercury residues in birds and their eggs are low in most breeding species, but significantly high in Southern Giant Petrel, Wilson's Storm-petrel and South Polar Skua, and may

have negatively impacted upon the former. Rubbish dumps and associated burns provide a threat to scavenging skuas, but major clean-up operations have been implemented at many stations, significantly reducing the risks of such avian hazards.

Thus far, three Specially Protected Areas and four Sites of Special Scientific Interest have been declared within the AAT under the Agreed Measures for the Conservation of Fauna and Flora (1964), which were a part of the conservation outline as defined by the 1960 Antarctic Treaty Act (and updated within the Madrid Protocol). Though significant numbers of Southern Fulmar are protected by these areas, only three Emperor Penguin colonies receive any protection and the bulk of the populations of most breeding species, while nominally protected by the 1964 act which prohibits the killing or harming of any bird and attempts to minimize harmful by-products of human activities, remain effectively at risk.

Human history Some of the greatest legends of human Antarctic history belong, of course, to the conquest of the South Pole. These are described separately under the Ross Sea section, from where these journeys largely originated. Much of East Antarctica is claimed by three nations: Norway (which lays claim to the area from 20°W to 45°E), Australia (that from 45°E to 136°E and from 142°E to 160°E) and France (136°E to 142°E, i.e. the land sandwiched entirely between the two parts of the AAT). AAT covers six million km^2 or 42% of the continent. Norway annexed Dronning Maud Land on 14 Jan 1939. To the west the territory borders the British Antarctic Territory while limits to the south and within offshore waters are undefined. The territory was named after Queen Maud (1869–1938), and was annexed in order to protect the country's whaling industry from being shut out or disadvantaged by the actions of other states (a German claim to the same area was considered likely).

Humans are a recent arrival in much of East Antarctica. In 1911–12 the Australasian Antarctic Expedition, led by Douglas Mawson, made a number of significant scientific discoveries, including the first Antarctic meteorite, and a number of new territories, including King George V Land, though the expedition is perhaps best-remembered for an ill-fated sledging expedition that cost two lives and very nearly Mawson's. Undeterred, Mawson returned to East Antarctica in 1929, discovering Mac.Robertson Land (so-named for an expedition sponsor, MacPherson Robertson, whose full name was deemed too long for maps) during this visit. Norwegian whaling ships formerly fished the waters offshore from the country's modern claim, naming much of the coast for members of the Norwegian royal family. Sovereignty for that

Broken sea ice, East Antarctica. © Grant Dixon.

and ultimately came to naught; a wave inundated equipment support building in Jan 1994 and the French government thereafter abandoned plans to use the airstrip. The base currently comprises 49 buildings on a 1.5-km site and is capable of accommodating up to 120 personnel in summer.

Japan has operated a base at **Syowa** (69°00'S 39°35'E), on East Ongul I, near continuously since 1959 and its 47 buildings now house up to 60 personnel in summer. The first live television broadcast from Antarctica was made here in 1979, while during the first seasons following the base's construction two dogs remarkably managed to survive for a year without human assistance. A South African National Antarctic Expedition (SANAE) base was first established in 1959. The current incarnation, **SANAE IV** (71°40'S 02°49'W; built in 1997–8), is one of the most modern stations on the continent and is situated on Ahlmann Ridge, c.170 km from the north coast of Dronning Maud Land, and at an altitude of 650 m; it is capable of housing up to 80 personnel in summer. **Casey Station** (66°17'S 110°31'E; Australia), established in 1969, in Wilkes Land and just outside the Antarctic Circle, replaced the original **Wilkes Station**, constructed in 1957 by the USA but in considerable disrepair by 1964. Casey was modernized and rebuilt during the 1980s and is now capable of accommodating up to 70 personnel in summer. **Novolazarevskaya Station** (70°46'S 11°51'E; Russia, 1961) further to the east and 75 km from the coast is named after the second-in-command of the Bellinghausen expedition, and accommodates up to 70 people in summer, while another Russian base, **Molodezhnaya Station** (67°40'S 45°51'E; 1962), has been established in Enderby Land. **Neumayer Station** (70°38'S 8°15'W; Germany, 1981) situated on the Ekström Ice Shelf, in Dronning Maud Land, is largely hidden below ground and is perhaps chiefly famous for being staffed by the first all-female group to winter in Antarctica. In the same area is **Maitri Station** (70°45'S 11°44'E; India, 1989), which stands on ice-free rock in the Schirmacher Hills. The base houses up to 65 personnel and among its research projects is a study of the geology of Gondwana. China established a 60-man base, **Zhongshan** (69°22'S 76°22'E), in the Larsemann Hills in Feb 1989, where there are also summer, 1980s-built, Australian and Russian bases.

Visiting the area As mentioned above, East Antarctica holds large numbers of the Antarctic true seals, large colonies of the two Antarctic penguins, Emperor and Adélie, and several concentrations of Snow and, especially, Antarctic Petrels, all within an extremely inhospitable icy wilderness of spectacular glaciers, ice shelves and icy seas. Among Specially Protected Areas are the Emperor Penguin colony (2900 pairs in 1988) at **Taylor**

Weddell Seal Leptonychotes weddellii, *East Antarctica, 1997. © Daisy Gilardini.*

territory currently claimed by Australia was transferred from the British crown in 1933.

Within the last 50 years a number of scientific stations have been established in East Antarctica. The oldest continuously occupied Antarctic base is **Mawson Station** (67°36'S 62°52'E; Australia, 1954), within Horseshoe Harbour in Mac.Robertson Land, which has been substantially modernized in recent years, as has the same country's **Davis Station** (68°34'S 77°58'E; 1957), named after the ship's captain of both Mawson and Shackleton, and situated in the Vestfold Hills. These hills were the site of the landing by the first woman to set foot in Antarctica, the Norwegian Karoline Mikkelsen, who came ashore on this, the largest ice-free area on the Antarctic coast, in Feb 1935. The base is the largest Australian station in Antarctica. The first Russian base to be established was **Mirnyy Station** (66°33'S 93°00'E), in 1956, on the Wilhelm II Coast, with their next, **Vostok Station** (78°28'S 106°48'E), being erected at the South Geomagnetic Pole (1399 km from the sea) the following year. Both are still operational but their activities have been reduced due to the current state of the Russian economy, although Mirnyy is capable of housing up to 169 personnel. Haswell I adjacent to the latter harbours an Emperor Penguin colony (17,000 pairs in 1970 but reported to have decreased since). France also created a base in 1956, **Dumont D'Urville Station** (66°39'S 140°00'E), in Terre Adélie, which replaced an earlier (1952) construction at Point Martin and is perhaps best known for a ten-year programme to construct a large airstrip to serve the base. The project, eventually completed in 1993, caused international objections on environmental grounds

Snow Petrels Pagodroma [nivea]*, East Antarctica. © Brett Jarrett.*

South Polar Skua Catharacta [skua] maccormicki, *East Antarctica.* © Brett Jarrett.

Rookery in Mac.Robertson Land (67°26'S 60°50'E), **Rookery Is**, **Holme Bay** (67°37'S 62°33'E, which hold six breeding bird species including Southern Giant Petrel) and **Ardery** and **Odbert Is** (66°22'S 110°28'E), which have breeding Antarctic Petrel and Southern Fulmar. The remarkable **Scullin Monolith**, also in Mac. Robertson Land, lies 160 km east of Mawson Station and is a 430 m-high lonely block of dark gneiss. It has a dense population of birds, including Adélie Penguin and many petrels. Sites of Special Scientific Interest include **Haswell I** (66°31'S 93°00'E), which holds all of the region's breeding birds, **Svarthamaren** (71°44'S 05°12'E), in Dronning Maud Land, which has breeding Antarctic and Snow Petrels and South Polar Skua, and **Marine Plain** (68°38'S 78°08'E), in the Vestfold Hills, where a new genus of fossil dolphin was discovered in the 1990s. The first tourist ships to visit this region called at a number of stations within the Australian-claimed territory in 1992/3, but aside of station-supply icebreakers and scientific vessels very few people visit these remote areas, although every few years Quark Expedition makes a circumnavigation of Antarctica that involves several landings in this region.

Table 1. Breeding bird and mammal checklist for East Antarctica.

	Dronning Maud Land	Australain-Antarctic Territory	Terre Adélie
Penguins			
Emperor Penguin *Aptenodytes forsteri*	X	X	X
Adélie Penguin *Pygoscelis adeliae*	X	X	X
Petrels and prions			
Southern Giant Petrel			
Macronectes giganteus		X	X
Southern Fulmar *Fulmarus glacialoides*	X	X	X
Antarctic Petrel *Thalassoica antarctica*		X	
Cape Petrel *Daption capense*		X	X
Snow Petrel *Pagodroma nivea*	X	X	X
Antarctic Prion *Pachyptila desolata*		Historical record	
Storm-petrels			
Wilson's Storm-petrel			
Oceanites oceanicus		X	X
Skuas			
South Polar Skua			
Catharacta maccormicki		X	X
Seals			
Leopard Seal *Hydrurga leptonyx*	X	X	X
Weddell Seal *Leptonychotes weddellii*	X	X	X
Crabeater Seal *Lobodon carcinophaga*	X	X	X
Ross Seal *Ommatophoca rossii*	X	X	X

Peter I Øy

Location and main features This is the only oceanic island in the extreme S Pacific zone of the Southern Ocean. It lies west of the Antarctic Peninsula and south of the Antarctic Circle, at 68°50'S 90°35'W, in the Bellingshausen Sea. Peter I Øy is surrounded by dense pack ice almost year-round; the nearest land, in West Antarctica, is 450 km away.

Landform, climate and habitat Almost 95% glaciated, ice fields extend to the sea at most points around the island, although there are three small, exposed rocky beaches where it is possible to make landings. The climate is harsh with strong winds, freezing temperatures and snow; in consequence the vegetation consists almost exclusively of mosses and lichens that have adapted to the extreme climatic conditions. Except in late summer, the island is surrounded by dense pack ice year-round. Peter I is 18 km long and 8 km wide, covers 156 km² and rises to 1755 m at Lars Christensen peak, which is an extinct volcano with an ice-filled crater 100 m wide. Some of the island's rocks date from 13 million years ago and Peter I marks the highest point of single huge but extinct volcano. Two ice-free, flat-topped columnar rocks, the Tvistein Pillars, lie just east of the steepest coast of the island. A high central piedmont plateau dominates the west, while gradual shelves of glacial ice characterize much of the north and south coasts.

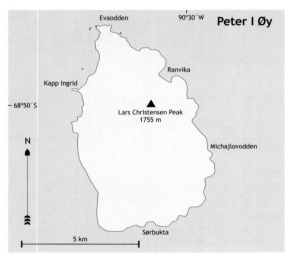

Birds There are a few data available for this rarely visited island: a tiny population of Adélie Penguin has been noted on several occasions (20 pairs in 1948 and 50 pairs in 1990), while Chinstrap Penguin has also been reported breeding (four pairs in 1948, but none found in 1990). South Polar Skua also nests, as well as large numbers of cliff-breeding Southern Fulmars. Possible nesters are Snow Petrel and Wilson's Storm-petrel. There are several records of Arctic Tern from the Bellingshausen Sea during the southern summer.

Marine mammals Large numbers of seals are found both on land and in the surrounding waters, particularly Crabeater and Leopard Seals. In 1999 a two-year-old Southern Elephant Seal, which had been tagged on Macquarie I, was discovered on a tiny beach on the island.

Main conservation issues No threats to the island's fauna and flora are known.

Human history Discovered by the Russian, Bellinghausen, on 21 Jan 1821 and named for Czar Peter I, founder of the country's navy, there were no landings on the island until 2 Feb 1929, when Ola Olstad, in the second *Norvegia* expedition, claimed it for Norway. The island was formally declared a Norwegian dependency in 1931. At the time of its initial discovery it was the first land to be found south of the Antarctic Circle. In Feb 1948, H. Holgersen visited the island, from whose observations much of our early knowledge of the island's avifauna comes.

Visiting the islands Several tourist ships have brought visitors since 1980 but there have been no regular landings.

Table 1. Breeding bird and mammal checklist for Peter I Øy.

	Peter I Øy
Penguins	
Adélie Penguin *Pygoscelis adeliae*	X
Chinstrap Penguin *P. antarctica*	X
Petrels and prions	
Southern Fulmar *Fulmarus glacialoides*	X
Snow Petrel *Pagodroma nivea*	X?
Storm-petrels	
Wilson's Storm-petrel *Oceanites oceanicus*	X?
Skuas	
South Polar Skua *Catharacta maccormicki*	X

Other Regions and Islands

In defining the northern limits of our region (see Synopsis of the Region, pp. 13 and 15) several island groups that harbour a number of 'classic' Southern Ocean seabirds were, of necessity, excluded from the regional accounts. These islands are in three main areas, off S Chile and S Argentina, Tasmania, and within the New Zealand region. The first two are treated selectively and in brief here, but only those islands that hold pure Southern Ocean species, e.g. Rockhopper Penguin and Black-browed Albatross (off S South America), and Shy Albatross (Tasmania), are covered. Furthermore, because of their position, some of the South American islands can be considered to be within subantarctic waters, while

Tasmania lies only just north of the Subtropical Convergence, although both areas are close to continental landmasses, explaining their otherwise comparatively rich landbird avifaunas. Here, however, the focus is mainly on describing these islands' importance to Southern Ocean seabirds. On the other hand, virtually the entire New Zealand region is located north of the Subtropical Convergence and therefore not included here, because its avifauna is well beyond the scope of this book (and well covered elsewhere). However, within the species accounts all oceanic birds breeding in New Zealand and its offshore islands are covered, principally because they also occur in subantarctic waters to the south, e.g.

Cook's and Black Petrels. The first part of this chapter (Islands off southern Chile and southern Argentina) was jointly prepared by Guy Kirwan, Roger Kirkwood, Ricardo Matus, Julieta Rajlevsky, Graham Robertson and José Valencia, while that covering Tasmania was devised by Alan Wiltshire and Sheryl Hamilton.

Islands off southern Chile and southern Argentina

Isla Diego de Almagro (Chile)

Location and main features Situated within a sensitive military area, at 51°26'S 75°15'W, Isla Diego de Almagro is one of the outermost islands within the Chilean fjordland, lying north of the Pacific entrance to the Strait of Magellan.

Landform, climate and habitat The island comprises metamorphosed sedimentary rocks, is rugged and, at 40 km long, relatively large. The highest peak is over 1200 m and there is permanent snow cover above c.800 m. There is a range of vegetation types including *Nothofagus* forest, dense scrub, *Azorella* and tussac grass. Rainfall is high with several metres per annum and it is rare to have days without rain.

Birds Poorly known due to it being a sensitive area, but at least 45 species have been recorded including most of the typical Patagonian forest and coastal species, as well as Striated Caracara. Black-browed Albatross was found breeding in large numbers in the mid-1980s, with 10–15,000 pairs estimated in 1983 and 1985 at six localities on the west coast of the island, on steep rocky cliffs at 15–170 m. Perhaps as many as 30,000 pairs were present at these sites in 2001.

Marine mammals The only data is from 2001 when South American Sea Lion was seen regularly, along with Southern Elephant Seal, Peale's and Commerson's Dolphins, and Killer Whale.

Main conservation issues No specific issues are currently recognized, but all islands in the southern Chilean sector require accurate and up-to-date seabird population census work. There is much fisheries debris on some beaches.

Human history The 2001 visit found no evidence of any previous human habitation or visitation. Fishing vessels occasionally anchor in some sheltered coves. **Visiting the islands** It is not possible to visit the island without special permission from the Chilean authorities.

Islas Ildefonso (Chile)

Location and main features These Chilean-owned islands located at 55°44'S 69°26'W have been visited by a number of famous ornithologists. They lie 96 km west of Isla Hermite, part of Tierra del Fuego and consist of nine stacks, within two groups, strung out over 6 km on a northwest–southeast axis. More than 50% of the land area comprises the large single southern stack that is 970 m long and 80–200 m wide.

Landform, climate and habitat These are steep, largely rocky islands covered in tussac grass, which reach a maximum altitude of 120 m, although only the southernmost stack has been subject to a detailed and prolonged visit. Deep soil and luxuriant tussac growth occur over one-fifth of this island. Rock (sandstone) is the dominant substrate. Wind speeds of 60–70 knots per hour are regular.

Birds Rockhopper Penguin breeds on the grass-covered plateau of one island, in a mixed colony with Magellanic Penguin. Estimated at c.8000 pairs (in 1983), 17,000 pairs (in 1985) and 15,000–30,000 pairs (in 2001), there is a significant breeding population of Black-browed Albatross in the archipelago, with colonies on all three of the larger islands. In addition, there were eight pairs

of Grey-headed Albatross at the northwest end of the second-largest island in 2001 and at least one of this species was present within a colony of the previous species in Dec 1914. Imperial Shag is a common breeder on the southernmost stack in the group.

Marine mammals South American Sea Lion has been recorded in waters around the islands but probably does not breed.

Main conservation issues No specific issues are currently recognized, but all islands in the southern Chilean sector require accurate and up-to-date seabird population census work. The islands are self-protecting, by virtue of their steepness and the roughness of the surrounding ocean. The main threat comes from mortality to albatrosses in local and distant-water longline fisheries. In 2001, birds with fishing-line traces in their wings, gapes and nests were observed.

Human history It is possible that Islas Ildefonso were encountered by Francis Drake, in the *Golden Hind*, as he sailed northwest from Cape Horn in Sep 1578, but we cannot be certain of this. Ornithologist visitors in the 20th century included Rollo Beck (Dec 1914), Castellanos (1935), Meade-Cabot (1971–2), Peter Harrison (1985), Chebez and Bertonatti (1994), and Roger Kirkwood, Kieren Lawton and Graham Robertson et al. in 2001.

Visiting the islands The southern stack of Ildefonso appears to have no exotic animals or plants, and it is important that this state is preserved. It is advisable that future visitants are screened by the Chilean authorities and that proper controls are set in place to ensure that no exotics are introduced. In spring the stack is so densely packed with birds that it is impossible to move about without causing disturbance. Landing is exceptionally difficult (and inadvisable—you have to swim to get ashore) and only by special permit.

Islas Diego Ramírez (Chile)

Location and main features The Islas Diego Ramírez comprise two small groups of islets and rocks in the Drake Passage, at 56°31'S 68°44'W or 112 km southwest of Cape Horn. They lie over the southern edge of the continental shelf, extend over 10 km on a northwest–southeast axis, and are perhaps rather better known and more frequently visited than the other islands considered within this chapter.

Landform, climate and habitat The southerly group comprises Isla Bartolomé (which covers 93 ha and reaches a maximum height of 190 m) and Isla Gonzálo (38 ha and 139 m), which are separated by a narrow channel, and at least 11 other named, small islets and several rocks. The two main islands are hilly, with coastal cliffs on their west sides and steep rocky slopes in the east. Eight species of vascular plants are known, with 1–2 m-high coastal tussac grass *Poa flabellata* decreasing in height and being replaced, further inland, by the cushion plants *Plantago barbata* and *Colobanthus quitensis*. Approximately 4 km to the north lies the smaller and less vegetated of the two groups that comprise Islas Diego Ramírez, this consisting of Isla Norte and four other smaller, named islets and several rocks.

Birds Macaroni (25,000 known from the Cape Horn area), Rockhopper (150,000 individuals in the Cape Horn area) and Magellanic Penguins (common) nest in the archipelago. Black-browed (19,195 pairs in 1980) and Grey-headed Albatrosses (8396 pairs in the same year) breed on three islands within the southern part of the archipelago. Four major colonies of the former are known (two of these on Isla Bartolomé), with Grey-headed Albatross being more widely scattered through the tussac grass. Among tubenoses, Southern Giant Petrel (182 individuals), Sooty Shearwater (considered abundant), Common and Magellanic Diving-petrels (unknown abundances, but both probably common) and possibly as many as two million individuals of Blue Petrel breed. Other resident or breeding birds include Rock and Imperial Shags (the latter scarce and perhaps only a visitor), Kelp Goose, Striated Caracara, Chilean Skua, Dolphin and Kelp Gulls (both common), Blackish Cinclodes (reasonably common) and Thorn-tailed Rayadito. Seasonal visitors or vagrants to the archipelago include King (more frequent in recent years) and Chinstrap Penguins, Wandering (two in Dec 2001), Chatham (one in Nov 2001) and Light-mantled Sooty Albatrosses (summer), Northern Giant Petrel (summer), Cape Petrel, Black-crowned Night-heron, Chiloe Wigeon (common in summer), Yellow-billed Pintail, Southern (Crested) Caracara, American Kestrel, Pale-faced Sheathbill (regular in winter), Rufous-chested Dotterel (summer), Upland Sandpiper, Arctic and Bridled Terns *Sterna anaethetus* (one collected in Jan 1969), Bar-winged Cinclodes (summer), White-crested Elaenia (common in summer), Fire-eyed Diucon, and Chilean (summer) and Barn Swallows.

Marine mammals The following species have been recorded in recent years: Southern Right Whale, Killer Whale, Hourglass Dolphin, South American Sea Lion, Leopard Seal, Southern Elephant Seal and South American Fur Seal.

Main conservation issues No specific issues are currently recognized, but all islands in the southern Chilean sector require accurate and up-to-date seabird population census work.

Human history The two largest islands of the group are named after their co-discoverers. In Feb 1619 the Portuguese brothers Bartolomé and Gonzálo de Nodal, in the *Nuestra Señora de Achoa* and *Nuestra Señora de Buen Succeso*, completed the first successful circumnavigation of Tierra del Fuego, discovering this group in the process, which they named for the expedition's cosmographer. Sealers reached the islands in the 1820s and the first scientific visits were in 1826 and 1830, when the *Adventure* and *Beagle* called at the group. A treaty of 1881 confirmed their ownership as Chilean, but it was not until 1951 that a small meteorological station was established on Isla Gonzálo, which has been occupied ever since and is resupplied by naval vessels several times per annum. Additional scientific visits were made, for one day in 1958, by the Frenchman Edgar Aubert de la Rüe, and for three months in 1980–1 by Roberto Schattler, while José Valencia and others have made ornithological observations in the group over the course of the most recent four spring and summer seasons.

Visiting the islands Difficult, though some yachts may be able to land visitors on Gonzálo, weather permitting. The tourist ship Bremen visits Gonzálo annually given favourable weather conditions, landing tourists to see the nesting birds and the lighthouse.

Isla de los Estados (Argentina)

Location and main features Isla de los Estados is the name given to a group of islands and islets located at 54°52'S 64°39'W, 30 km east of Tierra del Fuego across the Le Maire Channel. The Isla de los Estados itself, with a total surface area of 63,000 ha, is the largest and best known of these islands, extending over 75 km on an east–west axis.

Landform, climate and habitat Several of the islands known as Isla de los Estados (Observatorio, Elizalde, Alferez Goffré and Zeballos) are grouped under the name of Islas de Año Nuevo, with Observatorio (54°38'S 64°08'W) the largest, having a total surface area of 400 ha. Isla de los Estados is part of a mountain range at the southeast end of the Fuegian Mountains. Deep valleys and steep slopes characterize the central-east, while broader valleys and gentler slopes can be found in the west of the island. The coast is mainly rocky with steep cliffs to the ocean. Climate is typically oceanic and very humid, with over 200 mm of

rain per annum. Winds are persistent, mainly from the northwest and southwest. Vegetation comprises forests and steppes, with swamps of Cyperaceae (e.g. *Marsippospermum grandiflorum*) and Juncaceae (mainly *Sphagnum*) and tussac communities (*Poa flabellata*). Forests are characteristic of the Magellanic District of the Patagonia Fitogeographic Province, being dominated by *Nothofagus betuloides* and *Drymis winterii*. Several other species, such as *Lebethantus myrsinites*, *Chiliotrichum diffusum*, *Berberis ilicifolia* and *B. buxifolia* also occur in these forests. *Senecio websterri* is endemic to these islands.

Birds Rockhopper (over 176,000 pairs in Bahía Franklin in 1999, with a smaller colony in San Juan) and Magellanic Penguins (common, over 120,000 pairs on Islas Observatorio and Alferez Goffré in 1997) nest on the islands. Black-browed Albatross nests on Observatorio and Alferez Goffré (probably common), as well as on the main island. Southern Giant Petrel (200–1000 pairs in 1997) breeds in two colonies, in Bahía Franklin and on Observatorio. Magellanic Diving-petrel breeds on San Juan, Puerto Hoppner and Puerto Año Nuevo (but numbers are unknown). Rock Shag (common) nests along all coasts in small colonies, and a large number of Imperial Shag (2500 pairs in 1997 on Observatorio) can be found on the Islas de Año Nuevo. Other resident or breeding species include Neotropic Cormorant *Phalacrocorax brasilensis*, Black-crowned Night-heron (common), Kelp and Ashy-headed Geese, Flightless Steamer-duck, Crested Duck, Turkey Vulture, Andean Condor *Vultur gryphus*, Striated and Southern (Crested) Caracaras, Blackish and Magellanic Oystercatchers, South Polar Skua, Dolphin and Kelp Gulls (the latter very common), Dark-bellied *Cinclodes patagonicus*, Grey-flanked *C. oustaleti* and Bar-winged Cinclodes, Dark-faced Ground-tyrant, Austral Thrush, Patagonian Sierra-finch *Phrygilus patagonicus*, Rufous-collared Sparrow and Black-chinned Siskin. Seasonal visitors or vagrants include King and Gentoo Penguins (summer), Cape Petrel (winter), Southern Fulmar (winter), Sooty Shearwater, Wilson's Storm-petrel (summer), Sharp-shinned and Red-backed Hawks (summer), Peregrine Falcon (spring and summer), Plumbeous Rail (summer) and South American Tern (summer).

Marine mammals South American Fur Seal breeds in four colonies, at Islas Dampier, Punta Achaval, Punta Jira and Punta Leguizamo (with a total of over 2500 individuals in 1997), and can also be seen at Caleta Ojeda and Cabo Furneaux. Numbers were severely reduced by hunting in the 18th and 19th centuries, and some colonies are known to have disappeared completely, although numbers have noticeably recovered in recent years. The latter is not true of South American Sea Lion, which has apparently not recovered from such intense hunting, and is only a scarce breeder, on Observatorio, Goffre and Cabo San Antonio (total of c.200 individuals in 1997). Southern Sea *Lutra felina* and Large River Otters *L. provocax* are often observed around the main island (e.g. at Puerto Parry, Puerto Roca and Puerto San Juan among others), although their abundances are unknown. Southern Elephant Seal perhaps breeds in the Islas de Año Nuevo, where it is frequently observed.

Main conservation issues The IUCN has declared it a priority to obtain status information for both Southern Sea and Large Rivers Otters in Isla de los Estados. Rockhopper Penguin has one of its largest colonies on the island. During the course of the 19th century, both accidental and deliberate introductions occurred, among them, mice, wild goats, rabbits and deer are still easily seen in Isla de los Estados. Accurate and up-to-date population census work, as well as management plans for both natural and introduced species are required.

Human history Isla de los Estados was 'discovered' in 1616 by Schouten and Le Maire, although human presence dates from pre-Hispanic times. In 1868, the Argentine government awarded Isla de los Estados to a naval commander, Luis Piedrabuena, who unsustainably exploited the many penguin and sea lion colonies. A colony of more than 10,000 pairs of King Penguin at Puerto Roca is known to have disappeared as a result. In the late-19th century, a permanent population inhabited the island, first in San Juan and subsequently in Puerto Cook, where a navy post was established, along with a maximum-security prison. Between 1906 and 1977, when the prison was moved to Ushuaia, only occasional sailors lived on the islands. In 1977, a new navy post was founded at Puerto Parry, where four officers have been based since. In 1991, Isla de los Estados was declared a reserve by the Constitution of Tierra del Fuego Province but no regulations for its use and management have been established.

Visiting the islands Access to Isla de los Estados is currently very limited, and there is almost no demand for transportation to the islands by visitors. A good boat and an experienced sailor capable of dealing with the dangerous conditions of the Le Maire Channel and the strong winds in this area are required. There are no facilities for visitors, and tourists would need to sleep aboard ship.

Bahía Franklin (54°53'S 64°39'W), on the western side of Isla de los Estados itself, is a Site of Special Scientific Interest, with colonies of Southern Giant Petrel (100–500 pairs), and Magellanic (100–500 pairs) and Rockhopper Penguins (over 176,000 pairs). Its exposure to high winds makes it a rarely visited and dangerous place to anchor and land.

Puerto San Juan (54°44'S 63°51'W), a protected bay at the northeast end of the island, is a safe place to anchor and an interesting area to visit. Two beaches at the end of the fjord permit landings. Southern Sea Otter can often be observed near the coastal cliffs, which are dominated by forest. A replica of the 19th-century lighthouse, which reportedly inspired Jules Verne's novel *The Lighthouse at the End of the World* stands on its original site, offering shelter and a great view to visitors. An old cemetery is situated in the woods behind the beach.

Isla Observatorio (54°44'S 63°51'W), the largest of the Islas de Año Nuevo, has a protected anchoring area on its east side. Its flat surface is covered by low vegetation dominated by *Chiliotrichum diffusum*, *Poa flabellata*, *Pernettya mucronata* and *Empetrum rubrum*, among others. Major colonies of Magellanic Penguins (over 105,000 pairs) and Southern Giant Petrels (over 181 pairs) nest on the island. Rock (32 pairs) and Imperial Shags (over 2500 pairs) also breed on Observatorio. South American Fur Seal (over 80 individuals) breeds on the northeast side of the island. Several old buildings still stand in the centre of the island, among them the lighthouse which offers a panoramic view of the northern side of Isla de los Estados.

Tasmania Group

Location and main features Tasmania is an island state of Australia, separated from the mainland by the 240-km wide Bass Strait. The main island of Tasmania (40°38'S–43°39'S, 144°36'E–148°23'E) covers an area of 63,447 km². The group also includes two large islands, King (1094 km²) off the northwest coast of Tasmania, and Flinders (1354 km²) to the northeast. There are a further 334 smaller islands surrounding Tasmania. The main island (population 470,000), King (population c.2000) and Flinders (population c.1000) are all permanently inhabited, as are many of the smaller islands. Many important seabird colonies are known both from the main island and the offshore islands. Over 30% of the state is reserved within national parks and there are more than 2000 km of walking tracks.

Landform, climate and habitat Tasmania has a temperate, maritime climate. The coastline is c.5400 km long, with many protected bays and waterways. It is a mountainous island with numerous lakes, highland tarns, streams and rivers. The west coast and highlands are cool, wet and cloudy and the east coast and lowlands milder, drier and sunnier. Much of the lowlands is dominated by farming landscapes, but natural habitats range from coastal heaths, including vast button-grass plains in the south-west, wetlands, estuaries, dry and wet *Eucalyptus* forests and ancient rainforests of myrtle *Nothofagus cunninghamii*, sassafras *Atherosperma moschatum* and huon pine *Dacrydium franklinii*.

Birds The Tasmanian avifauna consists of over 220 species of resident or regular visitors, including 13 endemic species. Another 18 forms are considered endemic at the subspecific level. Short-tailed Shearwater is the most abundant and widespread species in Tasmania, with an estimated population of 14.7 million breeding pairs. There are a number of colonies of Short-tailed Shearwater and Little Penguin on the main island. The breeding endemic Shy Albatross nests on three islands off the Tasmanian coast—The Mewstone (7000 pairs), Albatross Island (5000 pairs) and Pedra Branca (250 pairs). Other breeding seabirds include Fairy Prion, Common Diving-petrel, Soft-plumaged Petrel, Sooty Shearwater, White-faced Storm-petrel, Australasian Gannet, Australian Pelican *Pelecanus conspicillatus*, Black-faced Shag *Phalacrocorax fuscescens*, Caspian *Sterna caspia*, Crested *S. bergii*, Fairy *S. nereis*, Little *S. albifrons* and White-fronted Terns, and Pacific *Larus pacificus*, Kelp and Silver Gulls *L. novaehollandiae*.

Marine mammals Both Australian *Arctocephalus* [*pusillus*] *doriferus* and New Zealand Fur Seals breed on islands around Tasmania. Southern Elephant Seal (large breeding colonies in the Bass Strait were exterminated in the 19th century but occasional pups are still born in the state), Leopard Seal and Crabeater Seal are occasional visitors to coasts. Southern Right and Humpback Whales pass the Tasmanian coastline during their migrations in spring and autumn.

Main conservation issues In the past, habitat modification has probably had the biggest impact on native fauna, and continues to threaten many Tasmanian species. Due to a history of human habitation, the main island, along with many of its offshore islands, are severely modified. Predation by introduced species, recreational and commercial gill-netting, coastal development, unregulated ecotourism and human disturbance threaten many seabird populations. Introduced vertebrates include cats, rabbits, rats and, most recently, Red Fox *Vulpes vulpes*. Agriculture is extensive with large parts of the landscape converted to pasture or crops. The greatest threat to Shy Albatross is through accidental deaths from longline fishing. Short-tailed Shearwater is subject to commercial and recreational exploitation of chicks for food. Human history Tasmanian Aborigines have inhabited the islands for thousands of years and the islands provided abundant natural food resources such as shellfish, seals and seabirds. The European discoverer of Tasmania was the Dutchman Abel Jansz Tasman, in 1642. Tasmania was originally named Van Dieman's Land and was settled by Europeans in 1883. Many of the early settlers were convicts transported from Britain.

Visiting the islands There are a number of opportunities on the main islands, both self-guided and through commercial tours, to observe Short-tailed Shearwater and Little Penguin at their breeding colonies. Many of the offshore islands are either privately owned or are reserved land, and require permission for access. Several commercial operators provide day trips to observe seals, whales and seabirds. The three Shy Albatross colonies are all on reserve land administered by the state government conservation agency.

Gateways to the Antarctic: pelagic and other birds and marine mammals in southern South America, South Africa, Australia and New Zealand

Most visitors to the Southern Ocean usually visit the region via one of several main portals, Ushuaia in S Argentina (or from Punta Arenas in S Chile or Stanley in the Falklands), Cape Town in South Africa, and various points in Australia (e.g. Hobart, Tasmania) and New Zealand (e.g. Christchurch and Invercargill/Bluff). In preparing this work, it therefore appeared meritorious to present some brief information concerning bird- and mammal-watching opportunities in each of these areas. That presented here is a summation of the experience of several people and their many colleagues, principally Peter Ryan (South Africa), Tony Palliser (Australia), Dennis Buurman and Sav Saville (New Zealand) and Guy Kirwan (S South America).

The main aim in presenting this information is to give readers a flavour of the possibilities for yet more pelagic birding activities in each of the regions at either end of their trip, if their appetites have not been satiated by a visit to the Southern Ocean. Although it might be deemed to be somewhat outside the scope of the present work, I consider that the following brief summaries of the possibilities available to those with additional time at their disposal enhance the overall usefulness of the book to the visitor.

Ushuaia, the Beagle Channel and south of Tierra del Fuego

This section mainly introduces the possibilities for finding some of those species which otherwise, within our region, occur only in the Falklands. Nonetheless, Tierra del Fuego also harbours several subantarctic breeders, e.g. Rockhopper Penguin and Black-browed Albatross, and several of the Southern Ocean tubenoses are regular non-breeding visitors, making the area a famed birding destination in its own right. Despite rich seabird and marine mammal communities, no regular or long-term pelagic birding or whale-watching has been conducted in this region (aside of the many Antarctic cruises that emanate from Ushuaia and Punta Arenas). Further information on selected islands off S Argentina and S Chile is presented within Other Regions and Islands (pp. 522–525).

Ushuaia area

Many voyages to the Antarctic Peninsula, South Shetlands and South Georgia commence in Ushuaia, which is the southernmost town in South America. It is a pleasant, busy little town, very much geared to tourism, with a range of shops, restaurants, hotels and services that belie its size. Anyone undertaking an Antarctic trip from here is advised to spend a few days at the end of their voyage to explore the island of Tierra del Fuego, on which Ushuaia is situated, and for keen birders planning a S Argentina itinerary, it is an essential port of call.

Just around Ushuaia harbour it should be possible to find a range of interesting species, including Great Grebe, Upland Goose, Flying and Flightless Steamer Ducks *Tachyeres pteneres*, Crested Duck, Chiloe Wigeon, Rock and Imperial Shags, Magellanic and Blackish Oystercatchers, Southern Lapwing, White-rumped Sandpiper, Kelp and Dolphin Gulls, and South American Tern. Overhead there should be Chilean Skua, Southern Giant Petrel, which patrol the boats, and Chimango Caracara, while

passerines are represented by Correndera Pipit, Austral Negrito, Chilean Swallow, Black-chinned Siskin, Rufous-collared Sparrow and Long-tailed Meadowlark.

At the harbour you can also arrange a small-boat trip into the Beagle Channel. Several local operators offer such trips, and most, if not all, have offices close to the waterfront. These are principally geared to naturalists, but some also include a visit to the historical Estancia Harberton. If you wish to look specifically for birds and mammals let the staff know as they will usually be happy to design a trip around your needs or, if you are alone, at least recommend you take a pre-arranged tour that most suits your requirements. For those en route to or from Antarctica the range of species to be seen in the Channel is far from exceptional, but may be still worthwhile, as such a trip is usually a guaranteed means of observing Magellanic Diving-petrel. Regular seabirds include Magellanic Penguin, Southern Giant Petrel and many Black-browed Albatross, South American Tern and Chilean Skua; less frequent are White-chinned Petrel and Pale-faced Sheathbill. During the austral winter the diversity and possibilities increase considerably. Some of those species recorded in the Channel are as follows: Wandering (accidental), Grey-headed and Light-mantled Sooty Albatrosses (both occasional), Southern Fulmar, Cape Petrel (both regular non-breeding visitors) and Blue Petrel (uncommon). Some of the rocky islets have colonies of shags and gulls, as well as South American Sea Lion. A lone King Penguin was present in this region the 1990s, and there is an outside chance of finding Blackish Cinclodes on the islands; check the shorelines and tidewrack carefully.

Just west of Ushuaia is Tierra del Fuego National Park (small entrance fee). A number of roads transect the area and virtually all are worthy of exploration. This is an extensively forested area, with many lakes and rivers, and it is often difficult to get far from the road, which can be frustrating as the park is also popular with more conventional tourists. The picnic sites and stopping places around Lago Roca, which lies adjacent to the main road through the park, should be worked for the majestic Magellanic Woodpecker *Campephilus magellanicus*, which is not uncommon, the abundant Thorn-tailed Rayadito, White-throated Treerunner *Pygarrhichas albogularis* and Magellanic Tapaculo, with other regular species including Black-faced Ibis *Theristicus melanopis*, Chiloe Wigeon, Yellow-billed Pintail, Speckled Teal, Andean Condor *Vultur gryphus*, Black-chested Buzzard-eagle *Geranoaetus melanoleucos*, Chilean Hawk *Accipiter chilensis*, Austral Parakeet, Bar-winged, Grey-flanked *Cinclodes oustaleti* and Dark-bellied Cinclodes *C. patagonicus*, Fire-eyed Diucon, Dark-faced Ground-tyrant, White-crested Elaenia, Tufted Tit-tyrant, Correndera Pipit, Austral Thrush, Patagonian Sierra-finch *Phrygilus patagonicus*, Black-chinned Siskin and House Wren *Troglodytes aedon*. Check the lakes for the rather uncommon Spectacled Duck. A nocturnal visit may produce Rufous-legged Owl *Strix rufipes*. En route to the park, it is worth stopping in the vicinity of the Ushuaia municipal dump as this is as reliable a place as any for White-throated Caracara *Phalcoboenus albogularis*.

Immediately above Ushuaia is the imposing Martial Glacier. This is a famous site among birders, it being one of the most

Table 1. Tubenoses observed between 1995 and 2002 in the Beagle Channel, off Cape Horn and within the Drake Passage, or between the Falklands and Tierra del Fuego (from summaries supplied by other observers and HS' observations mainly in summer): A = abundant, C = common, F = frequent in small numbers, S = scarce and R = rare. Vagrants are not included (* indicates more frequent occurrences outside of summer or an apparently rare species that is possibly overlooked).

	Beagle Channel	Cape Horn & the Drake Passage	Between Tierra del Fuego & the Falklands
Wandering Albatross Diomedea [exulans] exulans	R/S	F	C
Tristan Albatross D. [e.] dabbenena		R*	R*
Southern Royal Albatross D. [epomophora] epomophora		R	R
Northern Royal Albatross D. [e.] sanfordi	R	S	S
Black-browed Albatross Thalassarche [melanophrys] melanophrys	C	A	A
Campbell Albatross T. [m.] impavida		R*	
Shy (Tasmanian) T. [cauta] cauta or White-capped Albatrosses T. [c.] steadi		R*	
Grey-headed Albatross T. chrysostoma	R/S	F	F
Atlantic Yellow-nosed Albatross T. [chlororhynchos] chlororhynchos		R*	R/S*
Indian Yellow-nosed Albatross T. [c.] carteri		R*	R*
Sooty Albatross Phoebetria fusca			R*
Light-mantled Sooty Albatross P. palpebrata		F	R/S
Southern Giant Petrel Macronectes giganteus	C	C	C
Northern Giant Petrel M. halli	R/S	F	F
Southern Fulmar Fulmarus glacialoides	R*	C*	S*
Antarctic Petrel Thalassoica antarctica		R/S*	
Cape Petrel Daption capense	F	A	A
Lesser Snow Petrel Pagodroma [nivea] nivea		R*	
Great-winged Petrel Pterodroma [macroptera] macroptera		R/S*	R/S*
White-headed Petrel P. lessonii			R*
Atlantic Petrel P. incerta		R*	R*
Kerguelen Petrel P. brevirostris		R*	R*
Soft-plumaged Petrel P. mollis		S/F*	S/F
Blue Petrel Halobaena caerulea		S/F	S/F
Antarctic Prion Pachyptila desolata		C/A	R/S*
Slender-billed Prion P. belcheri		C/A	F/C
White-chinned Petrel Procellaria aequinoctialis	F	F	A
Westland Petrel P. westlandica		R	
Grey Petrel P. cinerea		R/S*	F/C*
Great Shearwater Puffinus gravis		F	C
Sooty Shearwater P. griseus	F	A	A
Manx Shearwater P. puffinus			R*
Little Shearwater P. assimilis		R*	R*
Wilson's Storm-petrel Oceanites oceanicus	F	A	C/A
Grey-backed Storm-petrel O. nereis		S/F	S/F
Black-bellied Storm-petrel Fregetta tropica		S/F	R/S
Common Diving-petrel Pelecanoides urinatrix		S/F	S/F
Magellanic Diving-petrel P. magellani	F	R/S	R/S

But, unfortunately, the species is no easier to find here, and it will require some determination on the behalf of would-be observers, as the birds can be anywhere on the slopes of a long, rock-strewn valley northwest of the road, and there is no ski-lift providing easier access to the higher parts. Yellow-bridled Finch and Ochre-naped Ground-tyrant are again numerous in this area, and several of the woodland species mentioned for Tierra del Fuego National Park can be found close to the car-parking area.

Just south of Paso Garibaldi is the road to Puerto Almanza. Beyond the latter settlement, the road follows the northern shore of the Beagle Channel past Estancia Harberton and beyond as far as Estancia Moat. This area is well worth exploring: the scenery alongside the Beagle Channel is highly attractive and there are plenty of birds, including Ashy-headed, Upland and Kelp Geese, many other waterfowl, Great Grebe, Black-faced Ibis, White-chinned Petrel, both oystercatchers, Chilean Swallow, Grass Wren, Austral Negrito and Correndera Pipit. There are several small, marshy wetlands alongside this route, especially near Estancia Moat, and these should be checked for Magellanic Snipe and the localized Fuegian Snipe. These species are rather poorly covered in the available literature and can represent something of an identification challenge. Beyond Estancia Moat lies the Mitre (Hell) Peninsula, the stronghold of Striated Caracara in Tierra del Fuego. However, even here it is not common and, as befits the area's name, the nature of the rugged terrain and lack of roads, it requires a venture of almost expedition-style proportions to have a chance of seeing the species. Most visitors will probably be content to visit the Falklands, where it is much more easily encountered, or simply concentrate on the more easily visited sites in Tierra del Fuego, which still offer a chance of the species, albeit a very slim possibility.

Pelagic birds and cetaceans off Tierra del Fuego

As mentioned above, the seas of this region have not been subject to regular pelagic or land-based seabird observations. Coverage of the area has mainly occurred en route to the Antarctic Peninsula, and a list of those tubenoses observed between 1995 and 2002 in the Beagle Channel, around Cape Horn, in the Drake Passage and between Tierra del Fuego and Falklands is presented (Table 1). Readers should also refer to *Birds of the Beagle Channel and Cape Horn* (Couve & Vidal 2000) which was used in the preparation of the table. Little has been published on the marine mammals using these waters, but over the years many of the wide-ranging baleen whales, Sperm Whale and some of the beaked whales, as well as oceanic dolphins, have been recorded in this region. As always, much depends on wind/sea conditions and season as to which of these the observer might see. One voyage that serves to illustrate the extraordinary abundance of cetaceans in the area took place in Jan 2001 between Cape Horn, across the Drake Passage, to the Peninsula, South

easily accessible sites to try and find the cryptically plumaged and highly unobtrusive White-bellied Seedsnipe, which in the breeding season is restricted to high-altitude stony slopes and bleak moorland; some fortune will be required and many come away empty handed. Fortunately, a ski-lift permits relatively easy access to the upper, largely snow-covered slopes beloved of the seedsnipe, but even from here it is a considerable hike to the most favoured areas. There are few other birds to be found above the tree-line, but Andean Condor, Ochre-naped Ground-tyrant and the stunning Yellow-bridled Finch are all readily seen. Should you be one of the many not to find a seedsnipe you can, at least on a sunny day, console yourself with some marvellous views over the Beagle Channel. Another site for the seedsnipe is Paso Garibaldi, approximately 50 km east of Ushuaia, on the road towards Río Grande.

Georgia and the Falklands. Over 450 whales and c.140 dolphins were represented by the following species: Antarctic Minke, Sei, Fin, Humpback, Southern Right, Sperm, Killer, Long-finned Pilot, Southern Bottlenose, Cuvier's and Gray's Beaked Whales, and Hourglass and Peale's Dolphins (Morten Jorgensen and HS pers. obs.). More regular observations should provide better data concerning the occurrence of birds and marine mammals around Tierra del Fuego, Cape Horn and within the Drake Passage, and between the former and the Falklands.

Seabird and whale viewing off South Africa

Although Cape Agulhas, the southern tip of Africa, is lower than 35°S, South Africa offers some excellent land- and boat-based pelagic bird and cetacean viewing. Many Southern Ocean species visit the productive waters off the coast of this part of Africa. Most are non-breeding visitors and are abundant in the austral winter, but many occur year-round, and some, such as White-chinned Petrel, even commute from their breeding sites in the subantarctic to forage off South Africa while nesting. The productive Benguela Upwelling Zone also supports several endemic seabirds (African Penguin *Spheniscus demersus*, Cape *Phalacrocorax capensis*, Bank *P. neglectus* and Crowned Cormorants *P. coronatus*, Cape Gannet, Hartlaub's Gull *Larus hartlaubi* and Damara Tern *Sterna balaenarum*) and marine mammals (Haviside's Dolphin *Cephalorhynchus heavisidii* and South African Fur Seal), providing added incentive to visit the region.

Land-based observations

Several pelagic species are fairly easily observed from land. Chief among these are the many Southern Right Whales that visit coastal waters to calf and mate each winter. They often occur within 100 m of the shore, and are perhaps best observed from land, though boat-based whale-watching trips operate from several centres on west and south coasts. Most animals arrive in Jun and depart in early Nov, but some occur throughout the year. Sep–Oct is the best time for viewing, as this is when they are most active, often breaching and generally performing in their quest for mates. They are common from the Olifants River, on the west coast, to East London, on the east coast, and are most abundant in sheltered bays, especially off the south coast. Hermanus is perhaps the best-known site, but for sheer numbers the De Hoop Nature Reserve, east of Cape Agulhas, takes some beating.

The endemic Haviside's Dolphin occurs off the west coast north of Cape Town, typically in small pods just beyond the surf zone. It is best observed in the sheltered bays from Cape Columbine north to St Helena Bay, and boat-based trips for this species operate from Lambert's Bay. Other cetaceans commonly seen from land include Humpback and Bryde's Whales, Common, Dusky (south and west coasts), Bottlenose and Indo-Pacific Humpbacked Dolphins *Sousa chinensis* (south and east coasts). South African Fur Seal is common off west and south coasts, and can be seen from the shore or hauled out on offshore rocks or in the harbour at Cape Town's waterfront. A short boat ride from Hout Bay takes you to a breeding island, which can be viewed at close range from the boat.

Many seabirds can also be seen from land. Indeed, for coastal birds such as cormorants, gulls and terns, this is the best way to see these species. The endemic coastal seabirds are restricted to the cold, nutrient-rich upwelling waters off west and south coasts. Bank and Crowned Cormorants are most restricted, only just reaching Cape Agulhas, whereas African Penguin, Cape Cormorant, Cape Gannet and Damara Tern breed east to Algoa Bay (Port Elizabeth). Hartlaub's Gull is common on the west coast, becoming increasingly rare east of Cape Agulhas.

All four marine cormorants (including White-breasted *Phalacrocorax carbo lucidus*) are easily observed at Kommetjie on the west coast of the Cape Peninsula. This is also a good site to observe gulls and terns, including Antarctic Tern during the austral winter (May–Oct). But the endemic Damara Tern is extremely local in South Africa, breeding in small numbers in the Northern Cape (Port Nolloth being the most accessible site), Western Cape (between Struisbaai and De Mond, east of Cape Agulhas) and Eastern Cape (near the Sundays River, Algoa Bay). It is much more abundant in Namibia, being easily observed from Walvis Bay northwards.

African Penguin is arguably best seen at Boulders Beach, Simon's Town, on the Cape Peninsula. It only started breeding at this mainland site in 1982, but due largely to immigration the colony now supports c.1000 pairs. The birds are extremely tolerant of humans and permit much closer approach than those at other colonies. Other accessible penguin breeding sites include Robben I (regular tours depart from Cape Town's waterfront), Betty's Bay and Bird I, in Lambert's Bay (only a few pairs). Cape Gannet is easy to see from shore around much of the coast, but only breeds at six islands off South Africa and Namibia. Two of these are accessible to the public. Bird I, in Lambert's Bay is linked to the mainland by a harbour wall, and has an excellent viewing platform right next to the gannet colony. Malgas I, at the entrance to Saldanha Bay, is part of the West Coast National Park—contact the park office for access details.

Seawatching for pelagic seabirds also can be rewarding, especially from promontories during strong onshore winds. The most productive areas are those where the continental shelf is relatively narrow, which excludes the west coast north of Cape Columbine and much of the south coast between False Bay and Port Elizabeth. The best-known sites are on the Cape Peninsula, where Cape Point (southeast–southwest winds), the Cape of Good Hope (south–west winds) and Kommetjie (southwest–northwest) are perhaps most rewarding. Birding is best early in the morning, when birds generally occur closer to shore.

White-chinned Petrel and Sooty Shearwater are common year-round, as is 'Shy' Albatross. Giant petrels often patrol close inshore, but are usually too distant to identify to species with certainty, even with a telescope. Summer often sees large numbers of Cory's Shearwater, as well as northern skuas and Sabine's Gull. The persistent observer may find Manx and Flesh-footed Shearwaters, and perhaps the occasional Great-winged and Soft-plumaged Petrels. Winter is usually more productive, with large

Seabirds around a trawler during a Cape pelagic trip, off South Africa. © Peter Ryan.

numbers of albatrosses ('Shy', Black-browed and a few Yellow-nosed) pushed inshore by storms. Other species seen regularly include prions (presumably mostly Antarctic), Wilson's Storm-petrel, Cape Petrel and Subantarctic Skua. During or immediately after especially severe weather you may see seabirds that typically occur much farther offshore, such as Soft-plumaged and Great-winged Petrels, Little Shearwater, or real vagrants to South African waters, such as Southern Fulmar.

Boat-based observations

Going to sea is undoubtedly the best way to get to grips with Southern Ocean birds and the Cape in particular offers some of the best boat-based seabirding in the world. It's not for the faint-hearted or weak of stomach—the seas are often rough, and the small boats used on most trips often take a fair amount of spray. However, these discomforts are forgotten once you locate a fishing boat with its attendant flock of thousands of albatrosses and petrels. Drifting slowly among hundreds of squabbling albatrosses must rate among the spectacles of the birding world.

Given the rough seas and paucity of offshore islands, there are few options for getting to sea other than on specialist birding trips. The ferry to Robben I (which departs several times daily from Cape Town's waterfront) takes c.25 minutes to cross Table Bay and often produces Sabine's Gull and northern jaegers (mostly Arctic) in summer. You may also see White-chinned Petrel and Sooty Shearwater, as well as the occasional 'Shy' Albatross, especially in winter. Some coastal whale-watching trips also advertise seabirds, but keen birders are unlikely to see anything very interesting. These trips stay close inshore, chiefly in the sheltered bays favoured by Southern Right Whale, and

Table 1. The seasonal occurrence of pelagic seabirds seen from one-day boat trips from Cape Town. Scores denote frequency of observation: 5 = seen on >80% of trips, 4 = 50–80%, 3 = 25–50%, 2 = 5–25% and 1 = <5%. These are based on means achieved over several years; some less common species differ in occurrence between years, being seen regularly in some and not at all in others.

Species	J	F	M	A	M	J	J	A	S	O	N	D
'Wandering' Albatross Diomedea [exulans]	1	1	1	1	2	3	3	3	3	2	1	1
Northern Royal Albatross D. [epomophora] sanfordi	1	1	1	1	3	3	3	3	3	2	1	1
Black-browed Albatross Thalassarche [melanophrys] melanophrys	5	5	5	5	5	5	5	5	5	5	5	5
'Shy' Albatross T. [cauta]	5	5	5	5	5	5	5	5	5	5	5	5
Grey-headed Albatross T. chrysostoma					1	2	2	1	1			
Atlantic Yellow-nosed Albatross T. [chlororhynchos] chlororhynchos	5	5	5	5	4	3	3	3	5	5	5	5
Indian Yellow-nosed Albatross T. [c.] carteri	5	5	5	5	4	3	4	3	4	5	5	5
Southern Giant Petrel Macronectes giganteus	3	3	3	3	4	5	5	5	5	4	4	3
Northern Giant Petrel M. halli	3	3	3	3	4	5	5	5	5	4	4	3
Southern Fulmar Fulmarus glacialoides					1	2	2	1	1			
Cape Petrel Daption capense					3	5	5	5	5	4	2	1
Great-winged Petrel Pterodroma macroptera [macroptera]	5	5	5	4	3	3	2	2	3	4	4	5
Soft-plumaged Petrel P. mollis	1	1	1	1	2	2	2	3	3	2	1	1
Antarctic Prion Pachyptila desolata			3	5	5	5	2					
White-chinned Petrel Procellaria aequinoctialis	5	5	5	5	5	5	5	5	5	5	5	5
Spectacled Petrel P. [a.] conspicillata	2	2	2	1	1	1	1	1	1	1	1	2
Cory's Shearwater Calonectris diomedea	5	5	5	5	4	1	1				4	5
Flesh-footed Shearwater Puffinus carneipes	2	2	2	1	1	1				1	2	2
Great Shearwater P. gravis	5	5	5	5	4	2	1	2	5	5	5	5
Sooty Shearwater P. griseus	5	5	5	5	5	5	5	5	5	5	5	5
Manx Shearwater P. puffinus	3	3	3	2	1	1	1	1	1	2	3	3
Little Shearwater P. assimilis	1	1	1	1							1	1
European Storm-petrel Hydrobates pelagicus	5	5	5	5	3				2	3	5	5
Wilson's Storm-petrel Oceanites oceanicus	5	5	5	5	5	5	5	5	5	5	5	5
Black-bellied Storm-petrel Fregetta tropica					2				3	2		
Leach's Storm-petrel Oceanodroma leucorhoa	1	1	1	2	1					1	2	1
Cape Gannet Sula capensis	5	5	5	5	5	5	5	5	5	5	5	5
Subantarctic Skua Catharacta [skua] lonnbergi	5	5	5	5	5	5	5	5	5	5	5	5
Pomarine Jaeger Stercorarius pomarinus	3	2	2	2	1					1	2	3
Arctic Jaeger S. parasiticus	5	5	5	4	2				1	4	5	5
Long-tailed Jaeger S. longicaudus	2	2	3	3	2					2	2	2
Sabine's Gull Larus sabini	5	5	5	4				1	1	3	5	5
Arctic Tern Sterna paradisaea	4	4	5	5	3	1	1	1	5	4	4	4

the chances of seeing even the more common pelagic species is remote. To see interesting seabirds, you really need to reach the edge of the continental shelf or beyond.

Most dedicated boat-based birding takes place out of Simon's Town, with boats heading to the fishing grounds at the edge of the continental shelf c.25–30 nautical miles southwest of Cape Point. Scheduled trips depart every couple of weeks and are planned for Saturdays, with Sunday being held in reserve should weather conditions be unsuitable on the first day. Those signing-up for a trip are expected to be available on both days (there is no refund if the trip is moved to Sunday). The boat sails at 07h00 and returns around 15h00 (max. 12 passengers). Groups may wish to charter their own trip, with vessels available from both Simon's Town and Hout Bay. Visit www.capetownpelagics.com for a full listing of scheduled tours, as well as booking details and other relevant information.

Table 1 summarizes the seasonal occurrence of the more regularly observed species seen on these day trips. It excludes inshore species such as penguins and cormorants. Winter (May–Sep) is the best time to see vast numbers of birds and offers the best chance of southern vagrants such as Grey-headed Albatross and Southern Fulmar. However, spring (Sep–Nov) and autumn (Apr–May) can be more productive in terms of numbers of species, when several birds occur on passage (e.g. Black-bellied Storm-petrel and Arctic Tern). Summer has the smallest numbers of birds, but also generally produces higher total species counts than winter trips, due to the influx of northern migrants, as well as warmer water species such as Flesh-footed Shearwater Puffinus carneipes.

In addition to those species listed in Table 1, there is always the chance of finding something really unusual, which of course adds to the excitement of pelagic birding. Recent years have seen the first South African records of Buller's, Salvin's and Chatham Albatrosses, as well as Balearic Shearwater Puffinus mauretanicus. Other rarely recorded species seen include Southern Royal Albatross, Grey Petrel and South Polar Skua. Some known to occur in South African waters at least occasionally have yet to be seen during these day trips (e.g. Light-mantled Sooty Albatross and Antarctic, Blue and Kerguelen Petrels).

The chances of sighting cetaceans on these dedicated birding trips depend largely on sea conditions—they are much easier to spot when the sea is relatively calm. In addition to Southern Right Whale, Bryde's Whale is often seen inside False Bay or relatively close to Cape Point, where it feeds on pelagic schooling fish such as anchovies and sardines. Inshore waters are also good for Humpback Whales, and Common and Dusky Dolphins. Farther offshore, you may encounter Sperm Whale (often at the shelf-break in c.1000 m of water), Long-finned Pilot Whale, and

Providence Petrel Pterodroma solandri, *off Australia.* © *Tony Palliser.*

the occasional pod of Risso's Dolphin or Killer Whale. South African Fur Seal is common at fishing boats, where they join the seabirds in scavenging fish, and there is always a chance of seeing a vagrant Subantarctic Fur Seal.

Some birds that are seldom seen on the one-day trips occur more commonly in oceanic waters farther offshore (e.g. 'Wandering' Albatross, Soft-plumaged Petrel, Little Shearwater and Leach's Storm-petrel), and the chances of seeing regional rarities also increase as you head farther from land (e.g. Sooty Albatross, White-headed Petrel and White-bellied Storm-petrel). 2001 witnessed the first of what is hoped to be regular trips using the South African Antarctic supply ship *SA Agulhas* to reach oceanic waters. This midwinter trip reported Sooty Albatross as well as several Southern and Northern Royal Albatrosses, and large numbers of Little Shearwater. Future trips are planned for passage seasons, when there is a chance of finding some of the region's rarer storm-petrels.

Finally, some birding trips are run from Durban and, more recently, from Saldanha Bay, Mossel Bay, Port Elizabeth and East London. These typically experience better sea conditions than off Cape Town, but see many fewer birds. Most Durban pelagics operate in winter, when Southern Ocean species penetrate these tropical waters. Indian Yellow-nosed Albatross, White-chinned Petrel and Subantarctic Skua are regular, and Black-browed and 'Shy' Albatrosses, and Cape Petrel occur sporadically. The east coast is much better for Flesh-footed Shearwater and there is always the chance of turning-up a tropical seabird, such as Wedge-tailed Shearwater *Puffinus pacificus*, boobies, tropicbirds and frigatebirds. Durban pelagics have also yielded several firsts for the southern African region, including Streaked Shearwater *Calonectris leucomelas* and Matsudaira's Storm-petrel *Oceanodroma matsudairae*. Bottlenose Dolphins are common and there is a fair chance of seeing Humpback Whale, as it migrates along the KwaZulu-Natal coast.

Scheduled Durban pelagics are listed on www.capetownpelagics.com. However, to stand a reasonable chance of seeing warm-water pelagics, the best option is to take a cruise in the Mozambique Channel. In addition to boobies, tropicbirds and frigatebirds, some lucky birders have seen Jouanin's *Bulweria fallax* and Barau's Petrels *Pterodroma baraui*.

Observing Southern Ocean seabirds and cetaceans off Australia

It is possible to observe many Southern Ocean seabirds and mammals from the Australian continent and there is little doubt that the most effective method of doing this is aboard a pelagic catering for birders.

Pelagic trips have been operating regularly from Wollongong and Sydney along the New South Wales east coast for many years, and over this time an impressive list of both tropical and subantarctic species has been compiled (Table 1 illustrates the approximate occurrence and abundance of each species by month). The list of *Pterodroma* species in particular is unique and the combination of many tropical species with those from the cooler Southern Ocean establishes the east coast of Australia as one of the world's premier locations for the seabird enthusiast. Other ports around Australia also offer pelagic trips for birders. Key ports at the time of writing include: Eden (New South Wales), Port Fairy (Victoria), Eaglehawk Neck (Tasmania), Southport (Queensland) and Perth (Western Australia). Interested parties are advised to contact local ornithological societies or search related websites for the most up-to-date information. As off South Africa, most Southern Ocean species such as albatrosses are winter visitors (Apr–Oct) to the New South Wales coast, though some can be seen all year, particularly off Tasmania or Victoria.

Offshore territories such as Macquarie and Heard are very remote and generally not accessible to the general public, except as part of an expensive cruise (mostly from New Zealand). Lord Howe and Norfolk Is, on the other hand, are only a short flight from the mainland and well worth the effort for those interested in seabirds, breathtaking scenery and a great holiday. Weekend packages to both islands are readily available from travel agents at reasonable prices. Lord Howe I is the primary breeding location of Providence Petrel *Pterodroma solandri* and many thousands can be seen circling the slopes of Mount Gower at the right season. Black-winged Petrels patrol the headlands along with boobies and Red-tailed *Phaethon rubricauda* and White-tailed Tropicbirds *P. lepturus*, and the forested portions support large colonies of Flesh-footed and Wedge-tailed Shearwaters *Puffinus pacificus*.

Land-based observations

Until recently land-based observations have been somewhat infrequent. Though, as in other parts of the world, if one puts in the time on a suitable headland the rewards can be substantial. Seawatches from headlands in Sydney during onshore winds, particularly in winter and spring (Jun–Oct), can produce most of the species likely to be encountered on boat trips. Numerous headlands along the New South Wales and Victoria coast are productive, of which Green Cape, close to the New South Wales/Victoria border is perhaps the best. But the remoteness of this location and paucity of observers means the area does not receive the recognition that it deserves. There are several undocumented observations involving many thousands of albatrosses and shearwaters. Seawatches from northern locations are generally not quite as productive, though areas north of Brisbane on the east coast or Broome on the west are sheltered by reefs and offer more tropical species such as terns and boobies. North Stradbroke I off the coast of SE Queensland has been well watched and consequently has produced many difficult species such as Streaked Shearwater *Calonectris leucomelas*, White-necked Petrel, Kermadec Petrel *P. neglecta* and more, but again the number of species encountered is relative to the amount of time spent seawatching. Busselton in Western Australia is another area producing some impressive sightings. Most parts of S Tasmania are too remote or too sheltered for land-based seawatching. Therefore, organised pelagic trips are the most productive means of getting to grips with seabirds, albeit they are somewhat infrequent. One of the most spectacular sights in Australia is to watch the annual migration of Short-tailed Shearwaters as they head to their breeding grounds in Tasmania. Vast numbers can be seen in Sep–Oct wheeling south. Up to 11 million pairs are estimated to breed on the islands around Tasmania.

Table 1. Approximate seasonal occurrence of pelagic seabirds seen from one-day boat trips from Wollongong and Sydney off the New South Wales coast. Scores denote frequency of observation but not abundance: 5 = seen on >80% of trips, 4 = 50–80%, 3 = 25–50%, 2 = 5–25% and 1 = <5%. Inshore species such as penguins, cormorants, pelican and some terns have been omitted.

	J	F	M	A	M	J	J	A	S	O	N	D
Wandering Albatross Diomedea [exulans] exulans	2	2	2	3	4	5	5	5	5	5	5	3
Royal Albatross D. [epomophora]						2	1	1			1	
Black-browed Albatross Thalassarche [melanophrys] melanophrys		2	2	4	5	5	5	5	5	5	5	3
Shy Albatross T. [cauta]	2			3	3	4	5	5	4	4	3	1
Buller's Albatross T. [bulleri] bulleri					2	2	1		1	2	1	2
Grey-headed Albatross T. chrysostoma					2	2	1	2	2			
Indian Yellow-nosed Albatross T. [chlororhynchos] carteri		1		3	5	5	5	5	4	3	1	
Sooty Albatross Phoebetria fusca					1	1						
Light-mantled Sooty Albatross P. palpebrata						1	1	1	1	1		
Southern Giant Petrel Macronectes giganteus						3	3	5	4	3	2	1
Northern Giant Petrel M. halli						2	2	3	3	2	2	
Southern Fulmar Fulmarus glacialoides							1	1	2	1		
Cape Petrel Daption capense					2	4	5	5	5	3		
Great-winged/Grey-faced Petrels Pterodroma [macroptera] macroptera/gouldi	5	5	5	5	4	4	4	5	5	5	5	5
White-headed Petrel P. lessonii		1	2	2	3	3	3	4	4	2		
Providence Petrel P. solandri	2	1	4	5	5	5	5	5	5	5	5	3
Tahiti Petrel P. rostrata	2	2	1							1	1	1
Kermadec Petrel P. neglecta		1	2	3			1	1		2		1
Herald Petrel P. heraldica			2					1	1			
Kerguelen Petrel P. brevirostris						1	1	1				
Soft-plumaged Petrel P. mollis						1	1		2			
Mottled Petrel P. inexpectata	1								2	1	1	
Juan Fernández Petrel P. externa							1					
White-necked Petrel P. cervicalis	3	3							1			1
Black-winged Petrel P. nigripennis	2	1		2						1	1	1
Cook's Petrel P. cooki	1	1		2						1	2	1
Gould's Petrel P. leucoptera	4	4	3	2								3
Blue Petrel Halobaena caerulea						1	1					
Salvin's Prion Pachyptila salvini						1	1					
Antarctic Prion P. desolata						2	3	3	2	2		
Slender-billed Prion P. belcheri						2	2	3	2	1		
Fairy Prion P. turtur			3		3	5	5	5	4	2		
White-chinned Petrel Procellaria aequinoctialis										2	1	2
Westland Petrel P. westlandica										1	1	1
Black Petrel P. parkinsoni		2								2	4	1
Streaked Shearwater Calonectris leucomelas	2	2	3	1							1	
Wedge-tailed Shearwater Puffinus pacificus	5	5	5	5				4	5	5	5	5
Buller's Shearwater P. bulleri	4	3	2						1	2	2	3
Flesh-footed Shearwater P. carneipes	5	5	5	5				3	5	5	5	
Pink-footed Shearwater P. creatopus				1								
Sooty Shearwater P. griseus	4	4	4	3	3	3	2	1	3	4	5	5
Short-tailed Shearwater P. tenuirostris	5	5	5	5	4	3	2	1	5	5	5	5
Manx Shearwater P. puffinus									1			
Fluttering Shearwater P. gavia	5	5	5	4	5	5	5	5	5	5	5	4
Hutton's Shearwater P. huttoni	3	4	3	3	3	3	3	4	5	5	5	3
Audubon's Shearwater P. lherminieri	1	1										
Little Shearwater P. assimilis						1	1	1	1	1	1	1
Wilson's Storm-petrel Oceanites oceanicus	3	2	4	4	3	3	3	2	1	5	5	4
Grey-backed Storm-petrel O. nereis								2	1			
White-faced Storm-petrel Pelagodroma marina	3	2	1	2	1	1	3	4	4	3	4	4
Black-bellied Storm-petrel Fregetta tropica		1				2	1	1	3	2	2	1
White-bellied Storm-petrel F. grallaria					1							
Tristram's Storm-petrel Oceanodroma tristrami									1			
Common Diving-petrel Pelecanoides urinatrix	1				1		1	1	1			
Australasian Gannet Sula serrator	5	5	5	5	5	5	5	5	5	4	4	3
Brown Booby S. leucogaster			1								1	1
Red-tailed Tropicbird Phaethon rubricauda			1	1	1	1						
White-tailed Tropicbird P. lepturus	1	2	2	1								
Great Skua Catharacta skua			2	3	4	4	5	4	3	4	1	
South Polar Skua C. [s.] maccormicki			1	1	1			1				
Pomarine Jaeger Stercorarius pomarinus	5	5	5	4	2				2	4	5	5
Arctic Jaeger S. parasiticus	5	5	5	4	1			1	3	4	5	5
Long-tailed Jaeger S. longicaudus	5	4	4	4						2	3	4
Pacific Gull Larus pacificus					1	1		1				
Kelp Gull L. dominicanus	5	5	5	5	5	5	5	5	5	5	5	5
Silver Gull L. novaehollandiae	5	5	5	5	5	5	5	5	5	5	5	5
Sabine's Gull L. sabini					1		1					
Crested Tern Sterna bergii	5	5	5	5	5	5	5	5	5	5	5	5
White-fronted Tern S. striata				2	1			4	4	4	3	2
Common Tern S. hirundo	3	2	2	2	1				3	3	3	4
Arctic Tern S. paradisaea				2		1	1	1	2	1		
Bridled Tern S. anaethetus										1		
Sooty Tern S. fuscata	2	2	1	1					2	2	3	3
Common Noddy Anous stolidus			1							1		
Black Noddy A. minutus										1		1
Grey Ternlet Procelsterna cerulea	2	3	2									
White Tern Gygis alba		2	2	1								

Whales and dolphins

Cetaceans are regularly observed off Australian coasts and whale-watching is fast becoming a primary tourist attraction, particularly during migration (May–Jun and Sep–Oct). Of the larger species, most sightings involve Humpback and Sperm Whales, though any number of other species may be encountered. From late Jul–early Nov, Hervey Bay (300 km north of Brisbane) in SE Queensland is privileged to have the magnificent Humpback Whale visit its clear waters, and day trips are available throughout the season. Up to several hundred animals use the area during the course of a year. Bottlenose and, occasionally, Risso's Dolphins also frequent this site. Several other sites in Queensland also host the species in Jun–Nov. Sites to find Humpbacks on migration in New South Wales include Wollongong (also a famous pelagic birding destination, see below) in Jun–Nov, with chances also for Sperm, Pilot, Minke and beaked whales, and Eden, within Twofold Bay (476 km south of Sydney), where Humpbacks are present in Oct–Dec, Southern Right Whale in May–Oct and there is the chance to see Killer, Blue and Minke Whales. A variety of commoner dolphin species can also be seen in most of these areas. Logan's Beach, at Warrnambool (260 km southwest of Melbourne), in Victoria, attracts large numbers of visitors due to the presence of a Southern Right Whale nursery there (Blue Whale is a rare visitor), and there are also several other opportunities for quality land-based views of these whales in South Australia (especially off Twin Rocks and the coast between Bunda Cliffs and Nullabor National Park, where the Head of Bight is considered to be among the best shore-based whale observation points) and Western Australia (off Albany in May–Oct). A total of 25 species of cetacean have been recorded off S Australia and this area is one of the few places in the world where Pygmy Right Whale appears to be reasonably regular. Streaky Bay, just over 700 km west of Adelaide has Common and Bottlenose Dolphins and an Australian Sea Lion Neophoca cinerea colony. Monkey Mia, 750 km north of Perth, at the southern end of Shark Bay, in Western Australia, attracts huge numbers of visitors each year, who come to see Bottlenose Dolphins at close quarters (by just wading into the water; Apr–Oct is the best period), as well as Humpback (Jun–Nov) and Southern Right Whales (May–Oct), with other species of whales possible. Both land-based observations and short boat trips are possible. Southern Right and Humpback Whales can even be seen off Rottnest I, just south of Perth, and Dwarf Minke may also be regular in this region in May–Jul, with Blue Whale an irregular visitor.

Boat-based observations

Specific birding trips to the continental shelf anywhere off Australia can be rewarding irrespective of season. The species list tends to vary considerably according to conditions and locality. Trips from Sydney and Wollongong (79 km to the south) on the New South Wales coast are the most convenient and reliable. Luxury liners operate to Pacific islands such as Vanuatu, Fiji, New Caledonia and may permit observation of a wide range of tropical species, including Tahiti *Pterodroma rostrata* and Herald Petrels *P. heraldica*, Pink-footed *Puffinus creatopus* and Audubon's Shearwaters *P. lherminieri* and Tristram's Storm-petrel *Oceanodroma tristrami*, but unfortunately there are no regular ferry trips to suit the needs of the birder. The ferries that operate between Melbourne and Tasmania travel only at night so are of little value.

Table 1 summarizes the seasonal occurrence of species seen on these day trips. Winter (May–Sep) and spring (Sep–Oct) are the best times to see many of the Southern Ocean species, though a wide selection can be encountered at any season.

Seabird and marine mammal viewing around New Zealand

New Zealand is often described as the seabird capital of the world. The three main islands (North, South and Stewart) stretch c.2000 km between 34°S and 46°S, and offshore waters hold c.75% of the world's albatrosses and petrels, and half of the shearwaters. Ferries offer excellent opportunities for birding, but commercial pelagic trips offer unrivalled opportunities to observe seabirds—important for separating some confusing species e.g. Westland, Black and White-chinned Petrels, Sooty and Short-tailed Shearwaters and the different Wandering Albatrosses. Seawatching from shore can be highly productive, with uncountable numbers of various shearwaters, as well as smaller—but still impressive—totals of albatrosses and petrels. The spectacular rediscovery of the 'extinct' New Zealand Storm-petrel *Pealeornis maoriana* in 2003 has provided another incentive to visit New Zealand (see www. wrybill-tours.com).

Marine mammals

The well-known tourist operation at Kaikoura in the east of South I offers the best chance of Sperm Whale, but other whales are quite frequently seen from land and the Cook Strait ferry—notably Killer, Humpback and Long-finned Pilot Whales—whilst, as numbers increase, whales are now being occasionally seen in places like Wellington Harbour, from where there have been several sightings of Southern Right Whale recently. In northern parts of North I, especially Hauraki Gulf, Bryde's Whale is reasonably common. New Zealand Fur Seal was rare until the mid-1970s, but there are now many colonies, mostly on South I (Kaikoura, Ohau Point just north of there, and Cape Foulwind at Westport are perhaps most accessible), and New Zealand Sea Lion can be found on Stewart I and in the southeast of South I (The Catlins coast is favourite). Southern Elephant and Leopard Seals are much rarer, but occur occasionally. Dolphins are numerous; Bottlenose off all coasts, Common and Dusky as far south as Kaikoura and the endemic Hector's Dolphin *Cephalorhynchus hectori* particularly at the very top end of South I (Cloudy Bay), around the Banks Peninsula (Christchurch) and Kaikoura, with all three home to commercial dolphin-watching tours.

Hauraki Gulf and northern New Zealand

A pelagic trip to the outer Hauraki Gulf offers a fine introduction to New Zealand's seabirds. The gulf stretches from Auckland to the Poor Knights Is, Great Barrier I, and the continental shelf edge. The list of species is impressive and complements that further south (e.g. Kaikoura, Stewart I). Seabirds common in the gulf include: Buller's (present year-round), Flesh-footed (some year-round), Fluttering (year-round), Sooty (Aug–Apr), Short-tailed (Aug–May) and Little Shearwaters (Feb–Dec), Black, Cook's, Pycroft's and Black-winged Petrels (all Sep–Apr); Grey-faced Petrel (present year-round), Common Diving-petrel (fairly common all year), Fairy Prion (Sep–May), White-faced Storm-petrel (Sep–Apr), Little Penguin (year-round), Australasian Gannet (all year), Grey Ternlet (Dec–Apr) and White-faced Tern (year-round). The breeding ground(s) for the New Zealand Storm-petrel is unknown, but is believed to be in the Hauraki Gulf (Oct–May). Mammals include: Bryde's Whale, Killer, Common and Bottlenose Dolphins, and occasionally New Zealand Fur Seal. Pterodroma Pelagics (www. nzseabirds.com) operate seabird tours from Leigh or Sandspit.

Kaikoura

As some Australian birders have put it, 'three hours on a boat off Kaikoura can summarize a year off Sydney for the major Southern Ocean species'. Kaikoura is on the southeast coast of South I and virtually all of the tubenoses, including all of the albatrosses of this region, occur just offshore in large numbers. It is special principally because a vast underwater canyon lies very close to shore, where warm and cold currents meet. Prior to 1988, Kaikoura relied upon fishing and agriculture for employment, but the community has been transformed into a thriving tourist centre and is internationally recognized for marine ecotourism (see www. oceanwings.co.nz). Whilst numbers and variety of seabirds are spectacular at all times of year (see Figs. 1–5), in winter, when albatross numbers peak, Fairy Prion, Southern Fulmar and Great-winged and Grey Petrels also appear. Other species found year-round include both giant Petrels (Northern is abundant) and Cape Petrel. Only the smaller storm-petrels are less common. In spring, large flocks of Hutton's Shearwater return to Kaikoura, prior to breeding in burrows in the mountains immediately inland (the only nesting site in the world), and the endemic Westland Petrel, with White-chinned Petrel and Sooty Shearwater followed slightly later by Flesh-footed Shearwater.

The following are among the seabirds that may be seen off Kaikoura: Yellow-eyed Penguin (very rare Jul–Oct), Little Penguin (year-round), Northern Royal Albatross (year-round but less regular Oct–Nov), Southern Royal Albatross (also year-round, mostly May–Jul), Gibson's Albatross (common year-round), Antipodean Albatross (common year-round), Wandering Albatross (year-round), White-capped Albatross (common year-round but less numerous May–Jun), Salvin's Albatross (common year-round except May–Jun), Black-browed Albatross (common year-round), Campbell Albatross (quite scarce, Feb–Mar best), Buller's/Pacific Albatross (Feb–Jul), Chatham Albatross (very rare), Indian Yellow-nosed Albatross (vagrant), Northern Giant Petrel (common year-round), Southern Giant Petrel (mainly Jul–Dec, scarce rest of year), Westland (up to c.50 most days Sep–Jun but rare Jul–Aug), White-chinned (up to c.15 most days Oct–Apr but rare May–Sep), Grey (rare, chiefly Jul–Aug), Cape (common year-round), Great-winged (most days Aug–Dec but rare other months), Soft-plumaged (rare), Black-winged (rare, early summer) and Cook's Petrels (rare, summer), Common Diving-petrel (mainly Apr–Sep, rare in summer), White-faced Storm-petrel (rare, mostly Oct), Grey-backed Storm-petrel (rare), Short-tailed (scarce Oct–Mar, rare other months), Pink-footed *Puffinus creatopus* (vagrant), Flesh-footed (small numbers, mainly spring/summer), Fluttering (mainly spring and summer), Hutton's (common year-round, especially Sep–Mar) and Buller's Shearwaters (common Nov–May but rare other months), Southern Fulmar (seen most days May–Nov

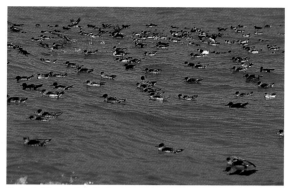

Hutton's Shearwaters Puffinus huttoni, *off Kaikoura, South I, New Zealand, Feb 2001. © Hadoram Shirihai.*

but rare other months), Fairy Prion (common May–Mar, sporadic Dec–Feb), Subantarctic Skua (scarce Aug–Mar), Red-billed Gull (common year-round), Black-billed Gull (year-round), White-fronted (common year-round) and Black-fronted Terns (common Feb–Sep, scarce other months). Other species recorded off Kaikoura are Adélie and Fiordland Penguins, and Kermadec Petrel *Pterodroma neglecta*, indicating the potential for vagrants. Opportunities for observing marine mammals are also diverse and the following species have been recorded: Sperm Whale (year-round up to c.20 young males, less easily found Sep–Nov), Humpback Whale (regular late May–Jul and occasional Nov–Dec), Antarctic Minke Whale (singles May–Jun, rare other months), Southern Right Whale Dolphin (rare), Fin Whale (scarce), Blue Whale (just two sightings 1998–2001), Dusky (readily found year-round, sometimes in pods exceeding 1000), Hector's (regular inshore just north and south of the peninsula), Common (up to c.20 Jan–Jun but rare other months, generally with previous species) and Bottlenose Dolphins (scarce, mainly Nov–Feb), Killer Whale (up to c.30 Sep–May, rare other months), Long-finned Pilot Whale (up to c.200 Sep–May, scarcer in other months), Southern Right Whale (scarce, mainly Sep–Oct) and New Zealand Fur Seal (common on the Kaikoura coast).

All trips are weather-dependent, so bear this in mind. It is also important to book well in advance for these tours and you should aim to spend a few days in Kaikoura in order to avoid disappointment. The following companies offer tours by either sea or air: Albatross Encounters (seabird watching), Dolphin Encounters (swimming with and observing dolphins), Whale Watch Kaikoura, Kaikoura Helicopters and Wings Over Whales (all whale watching), and several other operations run trips to swim with fur seals. Information can be obtained from Kaikoura Information Centre.

Stewart Island

New Zealand's third-largest island is renowned for its fine forests and scenery. Less well known, it is also one of New Zealand's finest destinations for seabirds, with half-day, full-day and overnight boat trips offered. Southern seabirds include the following species: Buller's Albatross (common Dec–Jun), Southern and Northern Royal Albatrosses (year-round), Gibson's and White-capped Albatrosses (year-round), Salvin's Albatross (year-round except Apr/May), Mottled (Oct–Apr), Cook's (Oct–Apr), White-headed (scarce Mar–May) and Cape Petrels (year-round), Broad-billed (Oct–May) and Fairy Prions (all year), Hutton's Shearwater (Feb–Apr), Common and South Georgian Diving-petrels, White-faced (common in some areas Oct–Mar), Grey-backed (scarce, Feb–Mar) and Black-bellied Storm-petrels (scarce Nov/Apr),

Fiordland (Jul–Feb), Yellow-eyed (year-round), Little (all year) and Snares Penguins (vagrant), Pied, Stewart Island and Spotted Shags (year-round), and Antarctic, White-fronted (year-round) and Black-fronted Terns (Feb–Aug). Boat trips are offered by Aurora Charters and Bravo Adventures who are used to working with seabird enthusiasts. Also check out Pterodroma Pelagics for ambitious seabird birdwatching trips.

Other boat opportunities

Several companies currently run seabird- or sea mammal-watching trips throughout New Zealand, and the selection is growing steadily (www.wrybill-tours.com, etc.). Some of the more noteworthy operations (and target species) are listed below but visitors should seek up-to-date information. Boats quite suitable for birding can be hired in almost any harbour. In all cases they will stay relatively close to land, usually within c.10 nautical miles, thus true pelagic birding in New Zealand is an unknown quantity as yet. The following are just a few of the key areas for sea/pelagic birding with selected species. **Off North Cape**: many subtropical species, including Black-winged Petrel, and northern vagrants in late summer, e.g. White-necked, Gould's, Kermadec and Providence Petrels *P. solandri*, White Tern, Red-tailed Tropicbird; Cook's and Pycroft's Petrels *P. pycrofti* are common, while many of the other New Zealand seabirds (e.g. most albatrosses, petrels, prions and shearwaters) are abundant at certain times of the year. Pterodroma Pelagics started running trips in 2004 and operate 2–3-night trips from Houhora each year. **Off Doubtless Bay**: as North Cape. **Off Ahipara Bay**: as North Cape and Doubtless Bay but fewer petrels. **Paihia, Bay of Islands**: notable numbers of Fluttering, Buller's and Flesh-footed Shearwaters; many other New Zealand seabirds, e.g. most albatrosses, petrels, prions and shearwaters, are abundant at certain seasons, whilst several of the region's commoner cetaceans, e.g. Bottlenose and Common Dolphins, and Killer Whale also occur. **Tutukaka (Poor Knights Islands)**: these islands are nature reserves and the breeding grounds of Buller's Shearwaters. Visitors in summer can see vast rafts of these shearwaters, often feeding in association with schools of fish. Other seabirds include: Little Penguin, Fairy Prion, Flesh-footed Shearwater, Fluttering Shearwater, Cook's, Pycroft's and Black Petrels, and White-faced Storm-petrel. Inquire at Dive Tutukaka for boat trips. **Whitianga, Coromandel Peninsula**: Pycroft's Petrel, while many of New Zealand's tubenoses are abundant at different periods. **Off Hicks and Araroa Bay**: as previous three localities but also notable for its good land-based seawatching. **Tolaga Bay**: Great-winged, Black and Cook's Petrels, White-faced Storm-petrel, Fluttering and Flesh-footed Shearwaters, and Fairy Prion. During summer potential for subtropical vagrants (e.g. White-necked Petrel in Feb). **Cook Straight**: see above for ferry across Cook Straight. **Picton, Marlborough Sounds**: King Shag; Fluttering Shearwater, Fairy Prion and Common Diving-petrel are rather common; also Hector's and Dusky Dolphins. **Kaikoura**: see above. **Akaroa, Christchurch**: White-flippered Penguin *Eudyptula* [*minor*] *albosignata*; also Hector's Dolphin. **Dunedin**: Northern Royal Albatross and Stewart Shag. **Off Bluff**: many southern tubenoses, whilst Sooty Shearwater and Buller's Albatross are among the most obvious species; also various cetaceans.

Land-based seawatching

Non-pelagic seabirds (gulls, terns and cormorants) and penguins are most easily seen from land. All three New Zealand gull species (Kelp, Red-billed and the endemic Black-billed) are numerous and can be seen from all coasts, along with White-fronted Tern. The endemic Black-fronted Tern breeds only on South I where it is quite common, and a few winter on North I. Caspian Tern *Sterna caspia* is widespread, Little Tern *S. albifrons* is mostly confined to the far north and is a summer visitor. Fairy Tern *S. nereis* breeds at only two localities on North I with a tiny population of just c.25 individuals. Around the south of Stewart I are Antarctic Terns, but they are highly sedentary and reaching their breeding areas is time-consuming (or very expensive). All of the cormorants are easy to find on coasts, except King Shag *Phalacrocorax [carunculatus] carunculatus*, which breeds on just a couple of rocky islands in Marlborough Sounds and can only be seen with certainty from a boat (the commercial operation out of Picton offers King Shag, and, in season, Hector's, Bottlenose and Dusky Dolphins), and Stewart Shag *Phalacrocorax [carunculatus] chalconotus*, which, though common, is restricted to southern South I and Stewart I. Three species of penguin breed: Little is commonest and the most widespread and can be seen at many localities, with a guaranteed site at Oamaru in the east of South I (the Cook Straight Ferry—see below—is also a good bet). Yellow-eyed Penguin also occurs at Oamaru and around Dunedin and Catlins, as well as on Stewart. Fiordland Penguin breeds in the southwest of South I and on Stewart, and can be found easily in the Haast, Milford and Doubtful Sounds, among other places, between August and November. Taiaroa Head on Otago Peninsula, near Dunedin, has the world's only mainland albatross colony, where excellent views of Northern Royal Albatross can be had, as well as nearby Yellow-eyed Penguin, and Stewart Shag at the northern edge of its range. Seawatching can be excellent with other albatrosses, both giant petrels and particularly Sooty Shearwater likely. Many headlands can be rewarding for those seeking pelagic species, especially in onshore winds, with species seen being determined mostly by latitude—subtropical breeders such as Buller's, Flesh-footed and Fluttering Shearwaters in the north, and subantarctic breeders (most of the albatrosses, giant petrels, Hutton's and Sooty Shearwaters) further south. However, as always with seabirds, almost anything can and does turn up. There are several mainland sites for Australasian Gannet, with the most accessible being at Muriwai just north of Auckland and at Cape Kidnappers near Napier in the east of North I. The latter has also held a single Cape Gannet in the summers of 1997–2006.

Inter-island ferries

Three regular passenger ferries run at times that make day-return trips feasible if time is limited. That from Auckland to Great Barrier I (c.2 hours) traverses the Hauraki Gulf and provides chances of Black and Cook's Petrel, Flesh-footed, Buller's and Fluttering Shearwaters, and White-faced Storm-petrel. These waters are far more productive in the austral summer. The Cook Strait ferry takes three hours and runs between North and South Is (the fast ferry should be avoided if possible, as viewing conditions are less good and less time is spent in open sea). The expected species change with season. Wandering, Royal, Black-capped, White-capped and Salvin's Albatrosses are common, as are White-fronted Tern, Fluttering Shearwater, Fairy Prion, Common Diving-petrel, Westland Petrel, Spotted Shag, Pied Cormorant and Little Penguin. There are more albatrosses (sometimes hundreds) in autumn and winter, when Cape Petrel can also be numerous, but summer has Arctic Jaeger, Buller's, Flesh-footed and Sooty Shearwaters. Again, there is always the possibility of a surprise for the lucky observer; Grey-headed Albatross, Subantarctic Skua, Soft-plumaged and Grey Petrel, and Southern Fulmar are occasionally seen. The ferry to Stewart from Bluff is relatively small and crosses a particularly rough stretch of water. The journey takes c.1 hour and, if the

weather permits you to stand outside, the birds can be quite spectacular. Summer crossings are recommended (for birds and better weather) when Buller's and Shy Albatrosses are common, Cape Petrel, Common Diving-petrel and Sooty Shearwaters are abundant, and there is a chance of Little Shearwater and Mottled and Cook's Petrels. Spotted and Stewart Shags will both be seen, and all three penguins are possible, along with Subantarctic Skua, which breeds on Stewart.

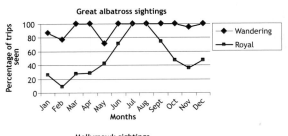

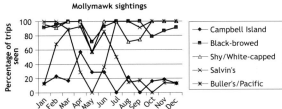

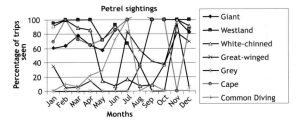

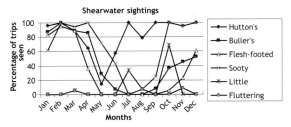

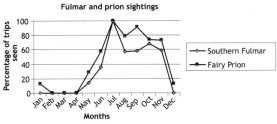

Figures 1–5. Summaries of three years of pelagic seabird observations off Kaikoura, New Zealand, with reference to the most frequently observed tubenoses (mention of Wandering and Royal Albatrosses refers to the entire Wandering complex and both forms of Royal; Giant Petrel includes both Southern and Northern).

Bibliography

Ainley, D.G., O'Conner, E.F. and Boekleheide, R.J. 1984. *The Marine Ecology of Birds in the Ross Sea, Antarctica*. Washington DC: American Ornithologists' Union.

Alberts, F.G. 1981. *Geographical Names of the Antarctic*. Washington DC: US Government Printing Office.

American Ornithologists' Union 1998. *Check-list of North American Birds*. Seventh edition. Lawrence, KS: American Ornithologists' Union.

American Ornithologists' Union 2000. Forty-second supplement to the American Ornithologist's Union Check-list of North American Birds. *Auk* 117: 847–858.

Amundsen, R. 1912. *The South Pole*. London, UK: John Murray.

Anon. 1984. *A la découverte des Terres Australes et Antarctiques Françaises*. Marseille: Mus. Hist. Nat. Marseille.

Anon. 2001. Seabird agreement signed. *World Birdwatch* 23 (3): 7.

Auburn, F.M. 1982. *Antarctic Law and Politics*. London, UK: Hurst.

Ausilio, E. and Zotier, R. 1989. Vagrant birds at Iles Kerguelen, southern Indian Ocean. *Cormorant* 17: 9–18.

Bachmann, S. 1999. Pingüino de Barbijo (*Pygoscelis antarctica*) y Pingüino Rey (*Aptenodytes patagonicus*) en la provincia de Buenos Aires, Argentina. *Nuestras Aves* 40: 8.

Bailey, A.M. and Sorenson, J.H. 1962. *Subantarctic Campbell Island*. Denver, CO: Denver Museum.

Baker, A.N. 1990. *Whales and Dolphins of New Zealand and Australia—An Identification Guide*. Melbourne: Victoria University Press.

Baker, P.E. 1967. Historical and geological notes on Bouvetøya. *Brit. Antarctic Survey Bull.* 13: 71–84.

Baker, P.E. and Tomblin, J.F. 1964. A recent volcanic eruption on Bouvetøya, South Atlantic Ocean. *Nature* 203: 1055–1056.

Barbraud, C. and Baker, S.C. 1998. Fulmarine petrels and South Polar Skua *Catharacta maccormicki* populations on Ardery Island, Windmill Islands, Antarctica. *Emu* 98: 234–236.

Barbraud, C., Mariani, A. and Jouventin, P. 2000. Variations in call properties of the snow petrel, *Pagodroma nivea*, in relation to sex and body size. *Australian J. Zool.* 48: 421–430.

Barbraud, C., Weimerskirch, H., Guinet, C. and Jouventin, P. 2000. Effect of sea-ice extent on adult survival of an Antarctic top predator: the snow petrel *Pagodroma nivea*. *Oecologia* 125: 483–488.

Barnes, J.N. 1982. *Let's Save Antarctica!* Victoria: Greenhouse Publications.

Beck, J.R. 1968. Unusual birds at Signy Island, South Orkney Islands, 1966–67. *Brit. Antarctic Survey Bull.* 18: 81–82.

Beck, P. 1986. *The International Politics of Antarctica*. London, UK: Croom Helm.

Beintema, A.J. 1972. The history of the Island Hen (*Gallinula nesiotis*), the extinct flightless gallinule of Tristan da Cunha. *Bull. Brit. Orn. Club* 92: 106–113.

Bell, B.J. and Robertson, C.J.R. 1994. Seabirds of the Chatham Islands. In: Nettleship, D.N., Burger, J. and Gochfeld, M. (eds.) *Seabirds on Islands: Threats, Case Studies and Action Plans*. Cambridge, UK: BirdLife International.

Bell, D. and Bell, M. 2000. Discovery of a second natural wild population of the New Zealand Shore Plover (*Thinornis novaeseelandiae*). *Notornis* 47: 166–167.

Bell, M. and Bell, D. 2000. First Wrybill (*Anarhynchus frontalis*) record from the Chatham Islands. *Notornis* 47: 6.

Bell, M. and Bell, D. 2000. Census of the three shag species in the Chatham Islands. *Notornis* 47: 148–153.

Belton, W. 1985. Birds of Rio Grande do Sul, Brazil, 2. *Bull. Amer. Mus. Nat. Hist.* 180 (1): 1–241.

Berta, A. and Sumich, J.L. 1999. *Marine Mammals: Evolutionary Biology*. London, UK: Academic Press.

Black, A.D., Gillon, K.W. and White, R.W. (2000) Uncommon seabirds in Falkland Island waters, 1998–1999. *Sea Swallow* 49: 36–42.

Blake, E.R. 1977. *Manual of Neotropical Birds*, 1. Chicago: University of Chicago Press.

Bonner, N. 1990. *The Natural History of Seals*. New York: Facts on File.

Bonner, W.N. and Walton, D.W.H. (eds.) 1985. *Key Environments: Antarctica*. New York: Pergamon Press.

Boon, W.M., Kearvell, J.C., Daugherty, C.H. and Chambers, G.K. 2000. Molecular systematics of New Zealand *Cyanoramphus* parakeets: conservation of Orange-fronted and Forbes' Parakeets. *Bird Conserv. Intern.* 10: 211–239.

Borchgrevink, C.E. 1901. *First on the Antarctic Continent: being an account of the British Antarctic Expedition, 1898–1900*. London, UK: George Newnes.

Borrow, N. and Demey, R. 2002. *Birds of Western Africa*. London, UK: A. & C. Black.

Bourne, W.R.P. 1999. Birds attracted by lights and killed by skuas on Gough Island, South Atlantic Ocean, and their zonal affinities. *Sea Swallow* 48: 53–58.

Bourne, W.R.P. 2000. The South Indo-Atlantic Fregetta storm-petrels. *Sea Swallow* 49: 54–56.

Bourne, W.R.P. 2001. The status of the genus *Lugensa* Matthews and the birds collected by Carmichael on Tristan da Cunha in 1816–1817. *Bull. Brit. Orn. Club* 121: 215–216.

Bourne, W.R.P. in press. The classification of albatrosses. *Australasian Seabird Group Newsletter*.

Bourne, W.R.P. and Curtis, W.F. 1985. South Atlantic seabirds. *Sea Swallow* 34: 18–28.

Bourne, W.R.P. and David, A.C.F. 1995. The early history and ornithology of St Paul and Amsterdam Islands, southern Indian Ocean. *Gerfaut* 85: 19–36.

Bourne, W.R.P. and Warham, J. 1999. Letters: Albatross taxonomy. *Birding World* 12: 123–124.

Bretagnolle, V. and Genevois, F. 1997. Geographic variation in the call of the Blue Petrel: effects of sex and geographical scale. *Condor* 99: 985–989.

Bretagnolle, V. and Thomas, T. 1990. Seabird distribution between Tasmania and Adélie Land (Antarctica), and comparison with nearby Antarctic sectors. *Emu* 90: 97–107.

Bretagnolle, V., Zotier, R. and Jouventin, P. 1990. Comparative population biology of four prions (genus *Pachyptila*) from the Indian Ocean and consequences for their taxonomic status. *Auk* 107: 305–316.

Bried, J. and Jouventin, P. 1997. Morphological and vocal variation among subspecies of the Black-faced Sheathbill. *Condor* 99: 818–825.

Bried, J. and Mougeot, F. 1994. Premier cas de mélanisme chez un Procellariiforme: le Pétrel tempête à croupion gris *Garrodia nereis*. *Alauda* 311–312.

Brinkley, E.S., Howell, S.N.G., Force, M.P., Spear, L.B. and Ainley, D.C. 2000. Status of the Westland Petrel (*Procellaria westlandica*) off South America. *Notornis* 47: 179–183.

Brothers, N., Pemberton, D., Prior, H. and Halley, V. 2001. *Tasmania's Offshore Islands:*

Seabirds and Other Natural Features. Tasmania: Tasmanian Museum and Art Gallery.

Brown, L.H., Urban, E.K. and Newman, K. (eds.) 1982. *The Birds of Africa*, 1. London, UK: Academic Press.

Burger, A.E., Williams, A.J. and Sinclair, J.C. 1980. Vagrants and the paucity of land bird species at the Prince Edwards Islands. *J. Biogeogr.* 7: 305–310.

Buurman, D. and Shirihai, H. in press. Kaikoura, New Zealand: the world's no.1 site for seabird and marine mammals. *Birding World*.

Cameron, I. 1974. *Antarctica: The Last Continent*. London, UK: Cassell.

Campbell, D. 1992. *The Crystal Desert: Summers in Antarctica*. Boston, MA: Houghton Mifflin.

Capdeville, D., Huin, N. and Jacquet, L. 1995. First record of a Chinstrap Penguin *Pygoscelis antarctica* breeding in Adelie Land, Antarctica. *Marine Orn.* 22: 245–246.

Carwardine, M. and Camm, M. 1995. *Whales, Dolphins and Porpoises*. London, UK: Dorling Kindersley.

Carwardine, M., Hoyt, E., Fordyce, R.E. and Gill, P. 1998. *Collins Whales and Dolphins: The Ultimate Guide to Marine Mammals*. London, UK: HarperCollins.

Casaux, R. and Baroni, A. 2000. Sexual size dimorphism in the Antarctic Shag. *Waterbirds* 23: 489–493.

Catard, A. 2001. French Southern Territories. In: Fishpool, L.D.C. and Evans, M.I. *Important Bird Areas in Africa and Associated Islands: Priority Sites for Conservation*. Cambridge, UK: BirdLife International & Newbury: Pisces Publications.

Chatham Islands Conservation Board 1996. *The Chatham Islands: Heritage and Conservation*. Christchurch: Canterbury University Press.

Chaturvedi, S. 1995. *The Polar Regions: A Political Geography*. London UK: John Wiley.

Cherel, Y., Weimerskirch, H. and Duhamel, G. 1996. Interactions between longline vessels and seabirds in Kerguelen waters and a method to reduce seabird mortality. *Biol. Conserv.* 75: 63–70.

Cherry-Garrard, A. 1922. *The Worst Journey in the World*. London, UK: Constable & Co.

Cheshire, N.G. 1990. Notes on species. *Sea Swallow* 39: 20–36.

Chilton, C. (ed.) 1909. *The Subantarctic Islands of New Zealand*, 1 & 2. Wellington: Philosophical Institute of Canterbury.

Chu, P.C. 1998. A phylogeny of the gulls (Aves: Larinae) inferred from osteological and integumentary characteristics. *Cladistics* 14: 1–43.

Clement, P., Harris, A. and Davis, J. 1993. *Finches and Sparrows. An Identification Guide*. London, UK: A. & C. Black.

Clement, P. and Hathway, R. 2000. *Thrushes*. London, UK: A. & C. Black.

Clements, J.F. 2000. *Birds of the World: A Checklist*. Robertsbridge: Pica Press.

Cobley, N. 1989. First recorded sighting of the Imperial Cormorant *Phalacrocorax atriceps* at Zavadovski Island, South Sandwich Islands. *Cormorant* 17: 78.

Convey, P., Morton, A. and Poncet, J. 1999. Survey of marine birds and mammals of the South Sandwich Islands. *Polar Record* 35 (193): 107–124.

Cooper, J. 2000. Keeping albatrosses off the hook. *Brit. Birds* 93: 260–262.

Cooper, J., Brooke, M. de L., Burger, A.E., Crawford, R.J.M., Hunter, S. & Williams, A.J. (2001) Aspects of the breeding biology of the Northern Giant Petrel (*Macronectes halli*) and the Southern Giant Petrel (*M. giganteus*) at sub-Antarctic Marion Island. *Intern. J. Orn.* 4: 53–68.

Couve, E. and Vidal, C. 2000. *Birds of the Beagle Channel and Cape Horn*. Punta Arenas: Fantastico Sur.

Cramp, S. and Simmons, K.E.L. (eds.) 1983. *The Birds of the Western Palearctic*, 3. Oxford: Oxford University Press.

Cresswell, G. and Walker, D. 2001. *Whales and Dolphins of the European Atlantic*. Old Basing: WildGuides.

Crockett, D.E. 1994. Rediscovery of Chatham Island Taiko *Pterodroma magentae*. *Notornis* (Suppl.) 41: 49–60.

Croxall, J.P. and Gales, R. 1997. An assessment of the conservation status of albatrosses. In: Robertson, G. and Gales, R. (eds.) *Albatross Biology and Conservation*. Chipping Norton: Beatty & Sons.

Croxall, J.P., Prince, P.A., Hunter, I., McInnes, S.J. and Copestake, P.G. 1984. The seabirds of the Antarctic Peninsula, islands of the Scotia Sea, and Antarctic Continent between 80°W and 20°W: their status and conservation. In: Croxall, J.P., Evans, P.G.H. and Schreiber, R.W. (eds.) *Status and Conservation of the World's Seabirds*. Cambridge, UK: International Council for Bird Preservation.

Croxall, J.P., Prince, P.A., Rothery, P. and Wood, A.G. 1997. Population changes in albatrosses at South Georgia. In: Robertson, G. and Gales, R. (eds.) *Albatross Biology and Conservation*. Chipping Norton: Beatty & Sons.

Cumpston, T.S. 1968. *Macquarie Island*. Canberra: Department of External Affairs.

Curtis, W.F. 1988. First occurrence of Buller's Albatross in the Atlantic Ocean. *Sea Swallow* 37: 62–63.

Curtis, W.F. 1995. Mottled Petrel Pterodroma inexpectata near the Falkland Islands. *Sea Swallow* 44: 63–64.

Daugherty, C.H., Williams, M. and Hay, J.M. 1999. Genetic differentiation, taxonomy and conservation of Australasian teals Anas spp. *Bird Conserv. Intern.* 9: 29–42.

Davis, A. 1994. Status, distribution and population trends of the New Zealand Shore Plover *Thinornis novaeseelandiae*. *Notornis* (Suppl.) 41: 179–194.

Davis, A. 1994. Breeding biology of the New Zealand Shore Plover *Thinornis novaeseelandiae*. *Notornis* (Suppl.) 41: 195–208.

Department of Conservation 1999. *New Zealand Subantarctic Islands*. Auckland: Reed.

Department of Environment and Land Management 1997. *Macquarie Island Nature Reserve*. Hobart: Department of Environment and Land Management.

Devillers, P. 1977. The skuas of the North American Pacific coast. *Auk* 94: 417–429.

Devillers, P. 1978. Distribution and relationships of South American skuas. *Gerfaut* 68: 374–417.

Dove, C.J. and Banks, R.C. 1999. A taxonomic study of Crested Caracaras (Falconidae). *Wilson Bull.* 111: 330–339.

Duriez, O., Jornvall, H. & Shirihai, H. (2005) Birds and wildlife of the French subantarctic islands: Crozet, Kerguelen and Amsterdam & St Paul. *Dutch Birding* 27: 87–115.

Dyer, B. in prep. A possible sighting of Lesser Beaked Whale in southern Indian Ocean waters.

Ebels, E.B. 2001. Amsterdam and its albatrosses. *Dutch Birding* 23: 7–12.

Eber, G. 1961. Vergleichende Untersuchungen am flugfähigen Teichhun Gallinula chl. chloropus und an der flugunfähigen Inselralle Gallinula nesiotis. *Bonn. zool. Beitr.* 12: 247–315.

Eden, A.W. 1955. Islands of Despair. *Being an Account of a Survey Expedition to the Sub-Antarctic Islands of New Zealand*. London, UK: Andrew Melrose.

Edwards, G. 1967. Bird observations in the Weddell Sea. *Sea Swallow* 19: 30–34.

Elliott, H.F.I. 1957. A contribution to the ornithology of the Tristan da Cunha group. *Ibis* 99: 545–586.

Elliott, H.F.I. 1958. The fauna of Tristan da Cunha. *Oryx* 2: 41–53.

Enticott, J.W. 1991. Distribution of the Atlantic Petrel *Pterodroma incerta* at sea. *Marine Orn.* 19: 49–60.

Enticott, J.W. and O'Connell, M. 1985. The distribution of the spectacled form of the White-chinned Petrel (*Procellaria aequinoctialis conspicillata*) in the South Atlantic Ocean. *Brit. Antarctic Survey Bull.* 66: 83–86.

Enticott, J. and Tipling, D. 1997. *Photographic Handbook of the Seabirds of the World*. London, UK: New Holland.

Ertel, R. and Rose, B. 1997. Erstnachweis eines Bulleralbatrosses *Diomedea bulleri* für Afrika. *Limicola* 11: 306–309.

Euson, K. 1974. *The Wreck of the General Grant*. Wellington: A.H. & A.W. Reed.

Evans, P. 1987. *The Natural History of Whales and Dolphins*. London, UK: Christopher Helm.

Evans, P. 1990. *Whales*. London, UK: Whitten Books.

Evans, P. 1994. *Dolphins*. London, UK: Whitten Books.

Evans, P.G.H. and Raga, J.A. (eds.) 2001. *Marine Mammals: Biology and Conservation*. Netherlands: Kluwer.

Falla, R.A., Sibson, R.B. and Turbott, E.G. 1983. *The New Guide to the Birds of New Zealand and Outlying Islands*. Auckland & London, UK: Collins.

Favero, M. 1994. Biologia reproductiva del Gaviotín Antártico, *Sterna vittata*, en Península Potter, Isla 25 de Mayo (King George), Islas Shetland del Sur, Antártida. *Riv. ital. Orn.* 64: 62–70.

Favero, M. 2001. Características morfológicas y dimorfismo sexual en la Paloma Antárctica (*Chionis alba*). *Orn. Neotrop.* 12: 173–179.

Favero, M. and Silva, M.P. 1999. First record of the Least Seedsnipe *Thinocorus rumicivorus* in the Antarctic. *Orn. Neotrop.* 10: 107–109.

Ferguson-Lees, J. and Christie, D. A. 2001. *Raptors of the World*. London, UK: A. & C. Black.

Flood, B. 2003. The New Zealand storm petrel is not extinct. *Birding World* 16: 479–483.

Fjeldså, J. and Krabbe, N. 1990. *Birds of the High Andes*. Copenhagen: Zool. Mus., University of Copenhagen & Svendborg: Apollo Books.

Fothergill, A. 1993. *Life in the Freezer: A Natural History of the Antarctic*. London, UK: BBC Books.

Franeker, J.A. van, Gavrilo, M., Mehlum, F., Veit, R.R. and Woehler, E.J. 1999. Distribution and abundance of the Antarctic Petrel. *Waterbirds* 22: 14–28.

Fraser, C. 1986. *Beyond the Roaring Forties*. Auckland: Woolmore Printing.

Fraser, M.W. and Briggs, D.J. 1992. New information on the *Nesospiza* buntings at Inaccessible Island, Tristan da Cunha, and notes on their conservation. *Bull. Brit. Orn. Club* 112: 191–205.

Fraser, M.W., Ryan, P.G., Dean, W.R.J., Briggs, D.J. and Moloney, C.L. 1994. Biology of the Tristan Thrush *Nesocichla eremita*. *Ostrich* 65: 14–25.

Fraser, M.W., Ryan, P.G. and Watkins, B.P. 1988. The seabirds of Inaccessible Island, South Atlantic Ocean. *Cormorant* 16: 7–33.

Freeman, A.N.D. 1994. Landbirds recorded at the Chatham Islands, 1940 to December 1993. *Notornis* (Suppl.) 41: 127–142.

Fuchs, V. 1991. *A Time to Speak: An Autobiography*. London, UK: Nelson.

Furness, R.W. 1987. *The Skuas*. Calton: T. & A.D. Poyser.

Gales, R. 1997. Albatross populations: status and threats. In: Robertson, G. and Gales, R. (eds.) *Albatross Biology and Conservation*. Chipping Norton: Beatty & Sons.

Gantlett, S. and Harrap, S. 1992. Identification forum: South Polar Skua. *Birding World* 5: 256–270.

Garcia Esponda, C.M., Coria, N.R. and Montalti, D. 2000. Breeding birds at Half Moon Island, South Shetland Islands, Antarctica, 1995/96. *Marine Orn.* 28: 59–62.

Gaskin, C.P. & Baird, K.A. 2005. Observations of black and white storm petrels in the Hauraki Gulf, November 2003 to June 2005; were they of New Zealand storm petrels? *Notornis* 52: 181–194.

Gauthier-Clerc, M. and Lambert, N. in press. Bird observations at Possession Island (Crozet Archipelago) during winters 1996 and 1997. *Marine Orn.*

Genevois, F. and Bretagnolle, V. 1995. Sexual dimorphism of voice and morphology in the Thin-billed Prion (*Pachyptila belcheri*). *Notornis* 42: 1–10.

Genevois, J.E. and Buffard, E. 1994. Sites de nidification et caractéristiques des terriers chez deux espèces sympatriques aux îles Kerguelen: le Petrel blue Halobaena caerulea et le Prion de Belcher Pachyptila belcheri. *Alauda* 62: 123–134.

Gill, P. and Burke, C. 1999. *Whale Watching in Australian and New Zealand Waters*. Sydney: New Holland.

Given, D.R. and Williams, P.A. 1985. *Conservation of Chatham Island Flora and Vegetation Botany*. Christchurch: D.S.I.R. Publishing.

Government of South Georgia and the South Sandwich Islands 1997. *South Georgia*. Stanley: Government of South Georgia and the South Sandwich Islands.

Green, R.H. 1995. *The Fauna of Tasmania: Birds*. Tasmania: Potoroo Publishing.

Gregory, P. 1990. Birding the Falklands. *Birding World* 2: 428–432.

Guinard, E., Weimerskirch, H. and Jouventin, P. 1998. Population changes and demography of the Northern Rockhopper Penguin on Amsterdam and Saint Paul islands. *Colonial Waterbirds* 21: 222–228.

Haase, B. 1994. A Chatham Island Mollymawk off the Peruvian coast. *Notornis* 41: 51–60.

Hagen, Y. 1952. *Birds of Tristan da Cunha*. Oslo: Norske Videnskaps-Akademi.

Hahn, S., Peter, H.-U., Quillfeldt, P. and Reinhardt, K. 1998. The birds of the Potter Peninsula, King George Island, South Shetland Islands, Antarctica, 1965–1998. *Marine Orn.* 26: 1–6.

Hahn, S. and Quillfeldt, P. 1998. First record of Leach's Storm Petrel *Oceanodroma leucorhoa* for King George Island, South Shetlands, Antarctica. *Marine Orn.* 26: 80.

Hall, C.M. and Johnston, M.E. (eds.) 1995. *Polar Tourism: Tourism in the Arctic and Antarctic Regions*. London, UK: John Wiley.

Hänel, C. and Chown, S. 1998. *An Introductory Guide to the Marion and Prince Edward Island Special Nature Reserves*. Pretoria: Department of Environmental Affairs and Tourism.

Harper, P.C. and Kinsky, F.C. 1978. *Southern Albatrosses and Petrels—An Identification Guide*. Melbourne: Victoria University Press.

Harper, P.C., Knox, G.A., Spurr, E.B., Taylor, R.H., Wilson, G.J. and Young, E.C. 1984. The status and conservation of birds in the Ross Sea sector of Antarctica. In: Croxall, J.P., Evans, P.G.H. and Schreiber, R.W. (eds.) *The Status and Conservation of the World's Seabirds*. Cambridge, UK: International Council for Bird Preservation.

Harris, G. 1998. *A Guide to the Birds and Mammals of Coastal Patagonia*. Princeton, NJ: Princeton University Press.

Harris, M.P. 1982. Seabird counts made during a crossing of the southern Indian and Atlantic Oceans. *Brit. Antarctic Survey Bull.* 55: 105–109.

Harrison, P. 1983. Seabirds of the World. Beckenham: Croom Helm.

Harrowfield, D. 1995. *Icy Heritage. Christchurch*: Antarctic Heritage Trust.

Hatherton, T. (ed.) 1990. *Antarctica, the Ross Sea region*. Wellington: D.S.I.R. Publishing.

Hay R.F., Mutch, A.R. and Walters, W.A. 1970. *Geology of Chatham Islands*. New Zealand Geological Survey Bull. MW Series 83.

Hayman, P., Marchant, J. and Prater, T. 1986. *Shorebirds. An Identification Guide to the Waders of the World*. Beckenham: Croom Helm.

Headland, B.K. 1989. *Chronological List of Antarctic Expeditions and Related Historical Events. Studies in Polar Research*. Cambridge, UK: Cambridge University Press.

Headland, R.K. 2001. *Protected Areas in the Antarctic Treaty Region*. Cambridge, UK: Scott Polar Research Institute.

Heather, B. and Robertson, H. 1997. *The Field Guide to the Birds of New Zealand*. New York: Oxford University Press.

Hemmings, A.D. 1994. Cooperative breeding in the skuas (Stercorariidae); history, distribution and incidence. *J. Royal Soc. New Zealand* 24: 245–260.

Heydenrych, R. and Jackson, S. 2000. *Environmental Impact Assessment of Tourism on Marion Island*. Pretoria: Department of Environmental Affairs and Tourism.

Higgins, P.J. (ed.) 1999. *Handbook of Australian, New Zealand and Antarctic Birds*, 4. Melbourne: Oxford University Press.

Higgins, P.J. and Davies, S.J.J.F. (eds.) 1996. *Handbook of Australian, New Zealand and Antarctic Birds*, 3. Melbourne: Oxford University Press.

Higham, T. (ed.) 1991. *Subantarctic Islands—A Guide Book*. Invercargill: Craig Printing.

Hilary, E. 1961. *No Latitude for Error*. London, UK: Hodder & Stoughton.

Hockey, P. 2001. *The African Penguin: a Natural History*. Cape Town: Struik.

Hofmeyr, G., Krafft, B.A., Kirkman, S., Kovacs, K.M., Bester, M. and Gjertz, I. 2001. Increase in the Antarctic fur seal population at Bouvetøya. In: *Proc. Zool. Soc. Southern Africa Conference* 2001: 16.

Holgersen, H. 1957. *Ornithology of the 'Brategg' Expedition*. Bergen: John Griegs.

Howell, S.N.G. 1996. *A Checklist of the Birds of Chile*. Colorado Springs, CO: American Birding Association.

del Hoyo, J., Elliott, A. and Sargatal, J. (eds.) 1992. *Handbook of the Birds of the World*, 1. Barcelona: Lynx Edicions.

del Hoyo, J., Elliott, A. and Sargatal, J. (eds.) 1994. *Handbook of the Birds of the World*, 2. Barcelona: Lynx Edicions.

del Hoyo, J., Elliott, A. and Sargatal, J. (eds.) 1996. *Handbook of the Birds of the World*, 3. Barcelona: Lynx Edicions.

del Hoyo, J., Elliott, A. and Sargatal, J. (eds.) 1997. *Handbook of the Birds of the World*, 4. Barcelona: Lynx Edicions.

del Hoyo, J., Elliott, A. and Sargatal, J. (eds.) 1999. *Handbook of the Birds of the World*, 5. Barcelona: Lynx Edicions.

Hoyt, E. 1998. *Whale and Dolphin Watching*. Hamburg: Vier Pfoten.

Humphrey, P.S., Bridge, D., Reynolds, P.W. and Peterson, R.T. 1970. *Birds of Isla Grande (Tierra del Fuego)*. Washington DC: Smithsonian Institution.

Huntford, R. 1979. *Scott and Amundsen*. London, UK: Hodder & Stoughton.

Huntford, R. 1985. *Shackleton*. London, UK: Hodder & Stoughton.

Huxley, E. 1977. *Scott of the Antarctic*. London, UK: Cox & Huxley.

Huyser, O. 2001. Bouvetøya. In: Fishpool, L.D.C. and Evans, M.I. *Important Bird Areas in Africa and Associated Islands: Priority Sites for Conservation*. Cambridge, UK: BirdLife International & Newbury: Pisces Publications.

Huyser, O., Dyer, B.M., Isaksen, K., Ryan, P.G. and Cooper, J. 1997. Breeding biology of and diet of Pintado Petrels *Daption capense* at Bouvetøya during the summer of 1996/1997. CCAMLR Working Group Paper.

Imber, M.J. 1994. Seabirds recorded at the Chatham Islands, 1960 to May 1993. *Notornis (Suppl.)* 41: 97–108.

Imber, M.J., Taylor, G.A., Grant, A.D. and Munn, A. 1994. Chatham Island Taiko *Pterodroma magentae* management and research, 1987–1993: predator control, productivity, and breeding biology. *Notornis (Suppl.)* 41: 61–68.

Inskipp, T., Lindsey, N. and Duckworth, W. 1996. *An Annotated Checklist of the Birds of the Oriental Region*. Sandy: Oriental Bird Club.

IUCN 1985. *Conservation of Islands in the Southern Ocean: A Review of the Protected Areas of Insulantarctica*. Gland & Cambridge, UK: International Union for Conservation of Nature and Natural Resources.

Jacka, E.F. and Jacka, E.A. 1988. *Mawson's Antarctic Diaries*. Adelaide: University of Adelaide.

Jahncke, J., Goya, E. and Guillen, A. 2001. Seabird by-catch in small-scale longline fisheries in northern Peru. *Waterbirds* 24: 137–141.

Jaramillo, A. and Burke, P. 1999. *New World Blackbirds: The Icterids*. London, UK: A. & C. Black.

Jehl, J.R., Todd, F.S., Rumboll, M.A.E. and Schwartz, D. 1979. Pelagic birds in the South Atlantic Ocean and at South Georgia in the austral autumn. *Gerfaut* 69: 13–27.

Jefferson, T.A., Leatherwood, S. and Webber, M.A. 1993. *Marine Mammals of the World: FAO Species Identification Guide*. Gland: UNEP & FAO.

Jiguet, F. 1997. Identification of South Polar Skua: the Brown Skua pitfall. *Birding World* 10: 306–310.

Jiguet, F. 2000. Identification and ageing of Black-browed Albatross at sea. *Brit. Birds* 93: 263–276.

Jiguet, F. 2000. The two giant petrels. *Birding World* 13: 108–115.

Jiguet, F., Chastel, O. and Barbraud, C. 1999. A hybrid South Polar Skua x Brown Skua. *Birding World* 12: 118–122.

Jones, D.R.C. 1973. *Scott Island and its discovery*. Antarctic 6: 437–440.

Jonsson, L. 1992. *Birds of Europe*. London, UK: Christopher Helm.

Jouventin, P. 1982. *Visual and vocal signals in penguins, their evolution and adaptive characters*. Hamburg: Paul Parey.

Jouventin, P. 1988. Shy Albatross *Diomedea cauta salvini* breeding on Penguin Island, Crozet archipelago, Indian Ocean. *Ibis* 132: 126.

Jouventin, P. 1994. Past, present and future of Amsterdam Island (Indian Ocean) and its avifauna. In: Nettleship, D.N., Burger, J. and Gochfeld, M. (eds.) *Seabirds on Islands: Threats, Case Studies and Action Plans*. Cambridge, UK: BirdLife International.

Jouventin, P. and Bried, J. 2001. The effect of mate choice on speciation in snow petrels. *Animal Behav.* 62: 123–132.

Jouventin, P., Stahl, J.C., Weimerskirch, H. and Mougin, J.L. 1984. The seabirds of the French subantarctic islands and Adélie Land: their status and conservation. In: Croxall, J.P., Evans, P.G.H. and Schreiber, R.W. (eds.) *Status and Conservation of the World's Seabirds*. Cambridge, UK: International Council for Bird Preservation.

Juniper, T. and Parr, M. 1998. *Parrots. A Guide to the Parrots of the World*. Robertsbridge: Pica Press.

Kasamatsu, F. and Joyce, G.G. 1995. Current status of odontocetes in the Antarctic. *Antarctic Sci.* 7: 365–379.

Kasamatsu, F., Joyce, G.G., Ensor, P. and Mermoz, J. 1996. Current occurrence of baleen whales in Antarctic waters. *Report Intern. Whaling Comm.* 46: 293–304.

Keith, D.G., Hofmeyr, G.J.G., Harck, B.I.B. and Mehlum, F. 2001. Dynamics of penguin–fur seal interactions at Bouvetøya. In: *Proc. Zool. Soc. Southern Africa Conference* 2001: 64.

Kerr, I.S. 1976. *Campbell Island: A History*. Wellington: A.H. & A.W. Reed.

Kerr, I.S. and Judd, N. 1978. *Marlborough Whalers at Campbell Island, 1909–1916*. Wellington: Department of Lands and Survey.

King, C.M. (ed.) 1990. *The Handbook of New Zealand Mammals*. Oxford: Oxford University Press.

King, J.R. 1983. *Seals of the World*. London, UK: Brit. Mus. (Natural History).

Knox, G.A. 1994. *The Biology of the Southern Ocean*. Cambridge, UK: Cambridge University Press.

König, C., Weick, F. and Becking, J.-H. 1999. *Owls. A Guide to the Owls of the World.* Robertsbridge: Pica Press.

Laws, R. 1989. *Antarctica: The Last Frontier*. London, UK: Boxtree.

Laws, R.M. (ed.) 1993. *Antarctic Seals Research Methods and Techniques*. Cambridge UK: Cambridge University Press.

Leatherwood, S. and Reeves, R.R. 1983. *The Sierra Club Handbook of Whales and Dolphins*. San Francisco: Sierra Club.

Lequette, B., Bertreaux, D. and Judas, J. 1995. Presence and first breeding attempts of southern gannets *Morus capensis* and *M. serrator* at Saint Paul Island, southern Indian Ocean. *Emu* 95: 134–137.

Lewis, D. 1979. *Voyage to the Ice*. London, UK: William Collins Sons & Co.

Lewis Smith, R.I., Walton, D.W.H. and Dingwall, P.R. 1994. *Developing the Antarctic Protected Area System*. Gland: IUCN.

Lucas, M. 1996. *Antarctica*. London, UK: New Holland.

Lumpe, P. and Weidinger, K. 2000. Distribution, numbers and breeding of birds at the northern ice-free areas of Nelson Island, South Shetland Islands, Antarctica, 1990–1992. *Marine Orn.* 28: 41–46.

MacMillan, L.B. 1977. *This Accursed Land*. Adelaide: University of Adelaide.

Madge, S. and Burn, H. 1988. *Wildfowl*. London, UK: A. & C. Black.

Marchant, S. and Higgins, P.J. (eds.) 1990. *Handbook of Australian, New Zealand and Antarctic Birds*, 1. Melbourne: Oxford University Press.

Marchant, S. and Higgins, P.J. (eds.) 1993. *Handbook of Australian, New Zealand and Antarctic Birds*, 2. Oxford: Oxford University Press.

Mawson, D. 1977. *The Home of the Blizzard*. London, UK: Heinemann.

May, J. (ed.) 1988. *The Greenpeace Book of Antarctica*. London, UK: Dorling Kindersley.

Mazar Barnett, J. and Pearman, M. 2001. *Annotated Checklist of the Birds of Argentina*. Barcelona: Lynx Edicions.

McGonigal, D. and Woodworth, L. 2001. *The Complete Story: Antarctica*. Noble Park: The Five Mile Press.

Mear, R. and Swan, R. 1987. *In the Footsteps of Scott*. London, UK: Jonathan Cape.

Mearns, B. and Mearns, R. 1998. *The Bird Collectors*. London, UK: Academic Press.

Micol, T. and Jouventin, P. 2001. Long-term population trends in seven Antarctic seabirds at Pointe Géologie (Terre Adélie). Human impact compared with environmental change. *Polar Biol.* 24: 175–185.

Milius, N. 2000. The birds of Rothera, Adelaide Island, Antarctic Peninsula. *Marine Orn.* 28: 63–67.

Millener, P.R. and Powlesland, R.G. 2001. The Chatham Islands Pigeon (Parea) deserves full species status; *Hemiphaga chathamensis* (Rothschild 1891); Aves: Columbidae. *J. Roy. Soc. New Zealand* 31: 365–383.

Minasian, S.M., Balcomb, K.C. and Foster, L. 1984. *The World's Whales. The Complete Illustrated Guide*. Washington DC: Smithsonian Institution.

Miskelly, C.M. 2000. Historical records of snipe from Campbell Island, New Zealand. *Notornis* 47: 131–140.

Miskelly, C.M., Sagar, P.M., Tennyson, A.J.D. and Schofield, R.P. 2001. Birds of the Snares Islands, New Zealand. *Notornis* 48: 1–40.

Moir, G.D. 1993. *The History of the Falklands*. Privately published.

Moore, P.J. and Battam, H. 2000. Procellariiforms killed by fishers in Chile to obtain bands. *Notornis* 47: 168–169.

Moss, S. 1988. *Natural History of the Antarctic Peninsula*. New York: Columbia University Press.

Murphy, R.C. (1936) *Oceanic Birds of South America*. New York: American Museum of Natural History.

Murphy, R.C. and Harper, F. 1921. A review of the diving petrels. *Bull. Amer. Mus. Nat Hist.* 44:495–554.

Naveen, R. 1997. *The Oceanites Site Guide to the Antarctic Peninsula*. Chevy Chase: Maryland.

Naveen, R. 1997. *Compendium of Antarctic Peninsula Visitor Sites: A Report to the Governments of the United States and the United Kingdom. Washington: US Department of State & London*, UK: Foreign and Commonwealth Office.

Naveen, R., Forrest, S.C., Dagit, R., Blight, L.K., Trivelpiece, W.Z. and Trivelpiece, S.G. 2000. Censuses of penguin, blue-eyed shag, and southern giant petrel populations in the Antarctic Peninsula region, 1994–2000. *Polar Record* 36: 323–334.

Naveen, R., Forrest, S.C., Dagit, R., Blight, L.K., Trivelpiece, W.Z. and Trivelpiece, S.G. 2001. Zodiac landings by tourist ships in the Antarctic Peninsula region, 1989–99. *Polar Record* 37: 121–132.

Naveen, R., Monteath, C., de Roy, T. and Jones, M. 1990. *Wild Ice: Antarctic Journeys*. Washington DC: Smithsonian Press.

Neves, T.S. and Olmos, F. 2001. Tristan Albatross (*Diomedea dabbenena*) in Brazil. *Nattereria* 2: 19–20.

Nixon, A.J. 1994. Feeding ecology of hybridizing parakeets on Mangere Island, Chatham Islands. *Notornis (*Suppl.) 41: 5–18.

Novatti, R. 1960. *Observaciones sobre aves oceanicas en el mar de Weddell durante el verano 1959–60*. Buenos Aires: Instituto Antártico Argentino.

Novatti, R. 1962. *Distribución pelágica de aves en el mar de Weddell*. Buenos Aires: Instituto Antártico Argentino.

Nunn, G.B. and Stanley, S.E. 1998. Body size effects and rates of cytochrome *b* gene evolution in tube-nosed seabirds. *Molecular Biol. and Evol.* 15: 1360–1371.

Olmos, F. 1997. Seabirds attending bottom long-line fishing off southeastern Brazil. *Ibis* 139: 685–691.

Olsen, K.M. and Larsson, H. 1997. *Skuas and Jaegers*. Robertsbridge: Pica Press.

Olson, S.L. 1973. Evolution of the rails of the South Atlantic Islands. *Smithsonian Contrib. Zool.* 152: 1–53.

Olson, S.L. 2000. A new genus for the Kerguelen Petrel. *Bull. Brit. Orn. Club* 120: 59–62.

Olson, S.L. and Jouventin, P. 1996. A new species of small flightless duck from Amsterdam Island, southern Indian Ocean (Anatidae, *Anas*). *Condor* 98: 1–9.

Onley, D. and Bartle, S. 1999. *Identification of Seabirds of the Southern Ocean*. Wellington: Te Papa Press.

Orgeira, J.L. 2001. Nuevos registros del Petrel Atlántico (*Pterodroma incerta*) en Océano Atlántico Sur y Antártida. *Orn. Neotrop.* 12: 165–171.

Ornithological Society of New Zealand 1990. *Checklist of the Birds of New Zealand*. Auckland: Random Century.

Parkinson, B. 2000. *Field Guide to New Zealand Seabirds*. Auckland: New Holland.

Parmalee, D.F. 1980. *Bird Island in Antarctic Waters*. Minneapolis, MN: University of Minneapolis Press.

Parmalee, D.F. 1992. *Antarctic Birds: Ecological and Behavioural Approaches*. Minneapolis, MN: University of Minneapolis Press.

Parmalee, D.F. and Rimmer, C.C. 1985. Ornithological observations at Brabant Island, Antarctica. *Brit. Antarctic Survey Bull.* 67: 7–12.

Paulian, P. 1953. *Pinnipèdes, Cétacés, Oiseaux des Iles Kerguelen et Amsterdam*. Mém. Institut Sci. Madagascar 8.

Payne, M.R. & Prince, P.A. 1979. Identification and breeding biology of the diving petrels *Pelecanoides georgicus* and *P. urinatrix exsul* at South Georgia. *NZ Zool.* 6: 299–318.

Perrin, W.F., Würsig, B and Thewissen, J.G.M. (eds.) 2002. *Encyclopedia of Marine Mammals*. San Diego: Academic Press.

Phillips, A.V. and Stirling, I. 2001. Vocal repertoire of South American Fur Seal Arctocephalus australis: structure, function, and context. *Can. J. Zool.* 79: 420–437.

Ponting, H.G. 1921. *The Great White South*. London, UK: Duckworth.

Pop, R. and Ebels, E.B. 2001. Falkland Islands. *Dutch Birding* 23: 12–24.

Prince Edward Islands Management Plan Working Group (compilers) 1996. Prince *Edwards Islands Management Plan*. Pretoria: Department of Environmental Affairs and Tourism.

Prince, P.A. and Croxall, J.P. 1996. The birds of South Georgia. *Bull. Brit. Orn. Club* 116: 81–104.

Prince, P.A. and Rodwell, S.P. 1994. Ageing immature Black-browed and Grey-headed Albatrosses using moult, bill and plumage characteristics. *Emu* 94: 246–254.

Rand, A.L. 1955. The origin of the land birds of Tristan da Cunha. *Fieldiana Zool.* 37: 139–166.

Reader's Digest 1985. *Antarctica—The Extraordinary History of Man's Conquest of the Frozen Continent*. Sydney: Reader's Digest.

Redwood, R. 1950. *Forgotten Islands of the South Pacific*. Wellington: A.H. & A.W. Reed.

Reeves, R.R., Stewart, B.S., Clapham, P.J. and Powell, J.A. 2002. *National Audubon Guide to Marine Mammals of the World*. New York: A. A. Knopf.

Reeves, R.R., Stewart, B.S. and Leatherwood, S. 1992. *The Sierra Club Handbook of Seals and Sirenians*. San Francisco: Sierra Club.

Rice, D.W. 1998. *Marine Mammals of the World: Systematics and Distribution*. Lawrence, KS: Allen Press.

Richardson, M.E. 1984. Aspects of the ornithology of the Tristan da Cunha group and Gough Island, 1972–1974. *Cormorant* 12: 123–201.

Ridgely, R.S. and Greenfield, P.J. 2001. *The Birds of Ecuador*. London, UK: A. & C. Black.

Ridgely, R.S. and Tudor, G. 1989. *The Birds of South America*, 1. Oxford: Oxford University Press.

Ridgely, R.S. and Tudor, G. 1994. *The Birds of South America*, 2. Oxford: Oxford University Press.

Ridgway, H. and Harrison, R.J. 1981–98. *Handbook of Marine Mammals*, 1–6. London, UK: Academic Press.

Riedman, M. 1990. *The Pinnipeds. Seals, Sea Lions and Walruses*. Berkeley: California University Press.

Roberts, B. 1967. *Edward Wilson's Birds of the Antarctic*. London, UK: Blandford Press.

Robertson, C.J.R. and Bell, B.D. 1984. Seabird status and conservation in the New Zealand region. In: Croxall, J.P., Evans, P.G.H. and Schreiber, R.W. (eds.) *Status and Conservation of the World's Seabirds*. Cambridge, UK: International Council for Bird Preservation.

Robertson, C.J.R., Bell, D. and Nicholls, D.G. 2000. The Chatham Albatross (*Thalassarche eremita*): at home and abroad. *Notornis* 47: 174.

Robertson, C.J.R. and Nicholls, D.G. 2000. Round the world with the Northern Royal Albatross. *Notornis* 47: 176.

Robertson, C.J.R. and Nunn, G.B. 1998. Towards a new taxonomy for albatrosses. In: Robertson, G. and Gales, R. (eds.) *Albatross Biology and Conservation*. Chipping Norton: Beatty & Sons.

Robertson, C.J.R. & van Tets, G. (1982) The status of birds at the Bounty Islands. *Notornis* 29: 311–336.

Robertson, G. 1998. The culture and practice of longline tuna fishing: implications for seabird by-catch mitigation. *Bird Conserv. Intern.* 8: 211–221.

Rootes, D.M. 1988. The status of birds at Signy Island, South Orkney Islands. *Brit. Antarctic Survey Bull.* 80: 87–119.

Rounsevell, D.E. and Brothers, N.P. 1984. The status and conservation of seabirds at Macquarie Island. In: Croxall, J.P., Evans, P.G.H. and Schreiber, R.W. (eds.) *Status and Conservation of the World's Seabirds*. Cambridge, UK: International Council for Bird Preservation.

Roux, J.-P. 1988. Second record of a Laysan Albatross *Diomedea immutabilis* in the Indian Ocean. *Cormorant* 16: 56.

Roux, J.-P. and Martinez, J. 1987. Rare, vagrant and introduced birds on Amsterdam and Saint Paul Islands, southern Indian Ocean. *Cormorant* 14: 3–19.

Rowlands, B.W. 2001. St Helena and the dependencies of Ascension Island and Tristan da Cunha, including Gough Island. In: Fishpool, L.D.C. and Evans, M.I. *Important Bird Areas in Africa and Associated Islands: Priority Sites for Conservation*. Cambridge, UK: BirdLife International & Newbury: Pisces Publications.

Rubin, J. 2000. *Antarctica*. Melbourne: Lonely Planet.
Russ, R. and Shirihai, H. 2000. The birds, marine mammals, habitat and history of the subantarctic islands off New Zealand. *Alula* 6: 82–147.
Ryan, P.G. 1989. Common Nighthawk *Chordeiles minor* and new records of seabirds from Tristan da Cunha and Gough Islands. *Bull. Brit. Orn. Club* 109: 147–149.
Ryan, P.G. 1998. The taxonomic and conservation status of the Spectacled Petrel *Procellaria conspicillata*. *Bird Conserv. Intern.* 8: 223–235.
Ryan, P.G. 1999. Sexual dimorphism, moult and body condition of seabirds killed by longline vessels around the Prince Edward Islands, 1996–97. *Ostrich* 70: 187–192.
Ryan, P.G. 2000. Gull relationships all at sea. *Africa—Birds & Birding* 5 (4): 20–21.
Ryan, P.G. 2000. Separating albatrosses: Tristan or Wandering? *Africa—Birds & Birding* 5 (4): 35–39.
Ryan, P.G. 2002. Chatham Albatross *Thalassarche eremita*: new to Africa. *Bull. ABC* 9: 43–44.
Ryan, P.G. (ed.) 2007. *Field guide to the animals and plants of Tristan da Cunha and Gough Island*. Newbury: Pisces Publications.
Ryan, P.G. in press. Taxonomic and conservation implications of ecological speciation in *Nesospiza* buntings at Tristan da Cunha. *Bird Conserv. Intern.*
Ryan, P.G., Bloomer, P., Moloney, C.L., Grant, T. & Delport, W. 2007. Ecological speciation in South Atlantic island finches. *Science* 315: 1420–1423.
Ryan, P.G., Cooper, J. and Glass, J.P. 2001. Population status, breeding biology and conservation of the Tristan Albatross *Diomedea [exulans] dabbenena*. *Bird Conserv. Intern.* 11: 35–48.
Ryan, P.G., Dean, W.R.J., Moloney, C.L., Watkins, B.P. and Milton, S.J. 1990. New information on seabirds at Inaccessible Island and other islands in the Tristan da Cunha group. *Marine Orn.* 18: 43–54.
Ryan, P.G. and Glass, J.P. 2001. *Inaccessible Island Nature Reserve Management Plan*. Edinburgh: Government of Tristan da Cunha.
Ryan, P.G., Moloney, C.L. and Hudon, J. (1994) Color variation and hybridization among *Nesospiza* buntings on Inaccessible Island, Tristan da Cunha. *Auk* 111: 314–327.
Ryan, P.G. and Watkins, B.P. 1988. Birds of the inland mountains of western Dronning Maud Land, Antarctica. *Cormorant* 16: 34–40.
Sagar, P.M. and Warham, J. 1997. Breeding biology of Southern Buller's Albatrosses at The Snares, New Zealand. In: Robertson, G. and Gales, R. (eds.) *Albatross Biology and Conservation*. Chipping Norton: Beatty & Sons.
Sampaio, C.L.S. and Castro, J.O. 1998. Registros de *Phoebetria palpebrata* (Foster, 1785) no litoral da Bahia, Nordeste do Brasil (Procellariiformes: Diomedidae). *Ararajuba* 6: 136–137.
Sangster, G. 1998. Trends in systematics. Purple Swamp-hen is a complex of species. *Dutch Birding* 20: 13–22.
Sangster, G. 1999. Trends in systematics. Relationships among gulls: new approaches. *Dutch Birding* 21: 207–218.
Savigny, C. in press. Observaciones sobre aves marinas en aguas argentinas, sudeste Bonaerense y Patagonia. *Cotinga* 18.
Saville, S., Stephenson, B. & Southey, I. 2003. A possible sighting of an 'extinct' bird – the New Zealand storm petrel. *Birding World* 16: 173–175.
Savours, A. (ed.) 1974. *Scott's Last Voyage through the Antarctic Camera of Herbert Ponting*. London, UK: Sidgwick & Jackson.
Schlatter, R.P. 1984. The status and conservation of seabirds in Chile. In: Croxall, J.P., Evans, P.G.H. and Schreiber, R.W. (eds.) *Status and Conservation of the World's Seabirds*. Cambridge, UK: International Council for Bird Preservation.
Scott, R.F. 1905. *The Voyage of the 'Discovery'*. London, UK: Smith Elder.
Scott, R.F. 1964. *Scott's Last Expedition*. London, UK: The Folio Society.
Selkirk, P.M., Seppelt, R.D. and Selkirk, D.R. 1990. *Subantarctic Macquarie Island Environment and Biology*. Cambridge, UK: Cambridge University Press.
Serventy, D.L., Serventy, V. and Warham, J. 1971. *The Handbook of Australian Seabirds*. Wellington: A.H. & A.W. Reed.
Shackleton, R. 1985. *The Heart of the Antarctic*. London, UK: Heinemann.
Sibley, C.G. 1996. *Birds of the World 2.0*. Cincinnati: Thayer Birding Software.
Sibley, C.G. and Monroe, B.L. 1990. *Distribution and Taxonomy of the Birds of the World*. New Haven & London, UK: Yale University Press.
Silva, M.P., Favero, M., Casaux, R. and Baroni, A. 1998. The status of breeding birds at Harmony Point, Nelson Island, Antarctica in summer 1995/96. *Marine Orn.* 26: 75–78.
Sitwell, N. and Ritchie, T. 1997. *Antarctica Primer*. Connecticut: Quark Expeditions.
Soave, G.E., Coria, N.R., Montalti, D. and Curtosi, A. 2000. Breeding flying birds in the region of the Fildes Peninsula, King George Island, South Shetland Islands, Antarctica, 1995/96. *Marine Orn.* 28: 37–40.
Soper, T. and Scott, D. 1994. *Antarctica. A Guide to the Wildlife*. Chalfont St Peter: Bradt Travel Guides.
Sorensen, J.H. 1951. *Wildlife in the Subantarctic*. London: Whitcombe & Tombs Ltd.
Stattersfield, A.J. and Capper, D.R. (eds.) 2000. *Threatened Birds of the World*. Cambridge, UK: BirdLife International & Barcelona: Lynx Edicions.
Stattersfield, A.J., Crosby, M.J., Long, A.J. and Wege, D.C. 1998. *Endemic Bird Areas of the World: Priorities for Biodiversity Conservation*. Cambridge, UK: BirdLife International.
Stewardson, C.L. 1997. *Mammals of the Ice*. Braddon: Sedona Publishing.
Stonehouse, B. 1972. *Animals of the Antarctic: the Ecology of the Far South*. London, UK: Peter Lowe
Stonehouse, B. (ed.) 1975. *The Biology of the Penguins*. London, UK: Macmillan.
Stonehouse, B. 1990. *North Pole, South Pole: A Guide to the Ecology and Resources of the Arctic and Antarctic*. London, UK: Prion Press.
Stonehouse, B. 2000. *The Last Continent: Discovering Antarctica*. Burgh Castle: SCP Books.
Strange, I.J. 1992. *A Field Guide to the Wildlife of the Falkland Islands and South Georgia*. London, UK: HarperCollins.
Summers, D. and Falklands Conservation 2001. *A Visitor's Guide to the Falkland Islands*. Stanley & London, UK: Falklands Conservation.
Suter, K. 1991. *Antarctica: Private Property or Public Heritage*? London, UK: Zed Books.
Swales, M.K. 1965. The sea-birds of Gough Island. *Ibis* 107: 17–42, 215–229.
Taylor, B. and van Perlo, B. 1998. *Rails. A Guide to the Rails, Crakes, Gallinules and Coots of the World*. Robertsbridge: Pica Press.
Taylor, R.H., Wilson P.R. and Thomas B.W. 1990. *Status and Trends of the Adelie Penguin populations in the Ross Sea region*. Polar Record 26.
Thomas, R. 2000. Longlining: a major threat to the world's seabirds. *World Birdwatch* 22 (2): 10–13.
Tickell, W.L.N. 1999. The tail patterns of Northern Royal Albatross. *Australasian Seabird Group Newsletter* 33: 14–15.
Tickell, W.L.N. 2000. *Albatrosses*. Robertsbridge: Pica Press.
Tickell, W.L.N. submitted. The Latin name of the Eastern Yellow-nosed Albatross. *Marine Orn.*
Todd, B. 1999. *Whales & Dolphins. Kaikoura New Zealand*. Privately published.
Trewick, S.A. 1997. Flightlessness and phylogeny amongst endemic rails (Aves: Rallidae) of the New Zealand region. *Phil. Trans. Roy. Soc. London* B 352: 429–446.
Triggs, G.D. 1987. *The Antarctic Treaty Regime*. Cambridge, UK: Cambridge University Press.
Turner, A. and Rose, C. 1989. *A Handbook to the Swallows and Martins of the World*. London, UK: A. & C. Black.
Valencia, J. 1995. Conservation status of the Archipelago Diego Ramírez. In: Dingwall, P. (ed.) *Progress in Conservation of the Subantarctic Islands*. SCAR-IUCN Publication Conservation of the Southern Polar Region 2.
Vaurie, C. 1980. Taxonomy and geographical distribution of the Furnariidae (Aves, Passeriformes). *Bull. Amer. Mus. Nat. Hist.* 166 (1): 1–357.
Veit, R.R., Whitehouse, M.J. and Prince, P.A. 1996. Sighting of a Leach's Storm Petrel *Oceanodroma leucorhoa* near the Antarctic Polar Front. *Marine Orn.* 24: 41–42.
Verheyden, C. 1994. First record of the Tawny-headed Swallow (*Alopochelidon fucata*) at the Falkland Islands. *Alauda* 62: 148–150.
Voisin, J.-F. 1968. Les petrels géants (*Macronectes halli* et *Macronectes giganteus*) de l'île de la Possession. *L'Oiseau et R.F.O.* 38: 95–122.
Voisin, J.-F. 1990. Movements of giant petrels *Macronectes* spp. banded as chicks at Iles Crozet and Kerguelen. *Marine Orn.* 18: 27–36.
Wace, N.M. and Holdgate, M.W. 1976. *Man and Nature in the Tristan da Cunha Islands*. Morges: IUCN.
Waller, G. (ed.) 1996. *Sealife. A Complete Guide to the Marine Environment*. Robertsbridge: Pica Press.
Walton, D. (ed.) 1987. *Antarctic Science*. Cambridge, UK: Cambridge University Press.
Ward, V.L. 1998. Antarctic Petrel *Thalassoica antarctica* records from the Prince Edward Islands and South Africa. *Marine Orn.* 26: 86–87.
Warham, J. 1991. *The Petrels: Their Ecology and Breeding Systems*. London, UK: Academic Press.
Warham, J. 1996. *The Behaviour, Population Biology and Physiology of the Petrels*. London, UK: Academic Press.
Waterhouse, E.J. (ed.) 2001. *Ross Sea region 2001: a state of the environment report for the Ross Sea region of Antarctica*. Christchurch: New Zealand Antarctic Institute.
Watkins, B.P. and Cooper, J. 1983. Scientific research at Gough Island, 1869–1982: a bibliography. *S. Afr. J. Antarctic Res.* 13: 54–58.
Watkins, B.P. and Furness, R.W. 1985. Population status, breeding and conservation of the Gough Moorhen. *Ostrich* 57: 32–36.
Watkins, B.P., Cooper, J. and Newton, I.P. 1984. Research into the natural sciences at the Tristan da Cunha islands, 1719–1983: a bibliography. *S. Afr. J. Antarctic Res* 14: 40–47.
Watson, G.E. 1975. *Birds of the Antarctic and Subantarctic*. Washington DC: American Geophysical Union.
Watson, L. 1981. *Sea Guide to Whales of the World*. New York: E.P. Dutton.
Watts, D. 1999. *Field Guide to Tasmanian Birds*. Sydney: New Holland Publishers.
Wee Ming Boon, Kearvell, J.C., Daugherty, C.H. and Chambers, G.K. 2001. Molecular systematics and conservation of kakariki (*Cyanoramphus* spp.). *Sci. for Conserv.* 176.
Weimerskirch, H. and Jouventin, P. 1997. Changes in population sizes and demographic parameters of six albatross species breeding on the French sub-Antarctic islands. In: Robertson, G. and Gales, R. (eds.) *Albatross Biology and Conservation*. Chipping Norton: Beatty & Sons.
Weimerskirch, H., Zotier, R. and Jouventin, P. 1988. The avifauna of the Kerguelen Islands. *Emu* 89: 15–29.
Wetmore, A. 1926. Observations on the birds of Argentina, Paraguay, Uruguay, and Chile. *US Natl. Mus. Bull.* 133: 1–448.
Wheeler, S. 1997. *Antarctica, The Falklands and South Georgia*. London, UK: Cadogan Travel Guides.
Wijpkema, J. and Wijpkema, T. 1999. Fuegan [sic] Snipe. *Dutch Birding* 21: 205–206.
Wildlife Management Section Biodiversity Group 1999. *Recovery Plan for Albatrosses and Giant Petrels*. Canberra: Department of the Environment & Heritage.
Williams, A.J. 1984. The status and conservation of seabirds on some islands in the African sector of the Southern Ocean. In: Croxall, J.P., Evans, P.G.H. and Schreiber, R.W. (eds.) *Status and Conservation of the World's Seabirds*. Cambridge, UK: International Council for Bird Preservation.
Williams, T.D. 1995. *The Penguins*. Oxford: Oxford University Press.
Wilson, E. 1987. *Birds of the Antarctic*. Dorset: New Orchard.
Wiltshire, A. and Hamilton, S. submitted. Population estimate of Northern Giant Petrels on Antipodes Island, New Zealand. *Emu*.
Wiltshire, A.J. and Scofield, R.P. 2000. Population estimate of breeding Northern Giant Petrels *Macronectes halli* on Campbell Island, New Zealand. *Emu* 100: 186–191.
Woehler, E.J. 1990. First records of Kerguelen Petrel *Pterodroma brevirostris* at Heard Island. *Marine Orn.* 18: 70–71.
Woehler, E.J. 1991. Status and conservation of the seabirds of Heard Island and the McDonald Islands. In: Croxall, J.P. (ed.) *Seabird Status and Conservation: a Supplement*. Cambridge, UK: International Council for Bird Preservation.
Woehler, E.J. 1993. *The Distribution and Abundance of Antarctic and Subantarctic Penguins*. Cambridge, UK: Scientific Committee on Antarctic Research.
Woehler, E.J. 1993. Antarctic seabirds: their status and conservation in the AAT. *Wingspan* Suppl. 12.
Woehler, E.J. and Cooper, J. 1999. A continental undertaking: an IBA inventory for the Antarctic Continent. *BirdLife S. Afr. News* 26: 8 & 10.
Woehler, E.J. and Croxall, J.P. 1997. The status and trends of Antarctic and sub-Antarctic seabirds. *Marine Orn.* 25: 43–66.
Woehler, E.J. and Johnstone, G.W. 1991. Status and conservation of the seabirds of the Australian Antarctic Territory. In: Croxall, J.P. (ed.) *Seabird Status and Conservation: a Supplement*. Cambridge, UK: International Council for Bird Preservation.
Woods, R.W. 1988. *Guide to Birds of the Falkland Islands*. Oswestry: Anthony Nelson.
Woods, R.W. 1993. Cobb's Wren *Troglodytes (aedon) cobbi* of the Falkland Islands. *Bull. Brit. Orn. Club* 113: 195–207.
Woods, R.W. 2001. A survey of the number, size and distribution of islands in the Falklands archipelago. *The Falkland Islands J.* 7: 1–25.
Woods, R.W. and Woods, A. 2006. *Birds and Mammals of the Falkland Islands*. Hampshire: WildGuides.
Woods, R.W. and Woods, A. 1997. *Atlas of Breeding Birds of the Falkland Islands*. Oswestry: Anthony Nelson.
Yaldwyn, J.C. (ed.) 1975. *Preliminary Results of the Auckland Islands Expedition 1972–73*. Auckland: Department of Lands and Survey.

Organizations and Contacts in the Region

1. Conservation and research bodies

Antarctica Project: This organization promotes conservation of Antarctica's resources by lobbying governments and attending Antarctic Treaty System meetings. It also publishes resources concerning the continent for schools, and provides a secretariat for the Antarctic and Southern Ocean Coalition (ASOC), an umbrella organization of over 250 bodies from 49 countries. www.asoc.org.

British Antarctic Survey: Part of the Natural Environment Research Council (NERC), the BAS has undertaken most of Britain's research in the Southern Ocean. It employs over 400 staff, with three stations in Antarctica and two on South Georgia. It has the ice-strengthened ships *RRS James Clark Ross* (for oceanographic research) and *RRS Ernest Shackleton* (primarily to re-supply stations), whilst *HMS Endurance* provides logistic support). The Antarctic Funding Initiative provides access to Antarctica for BAS and NERC staff, and universities. www.antarctica.ac.uk.

Department of Conservation: New Zealand government dept that manages the country's subantarctic islands, national parks and nature reserves. Administers permit applications for reserves, undertakes conservation of subantarctic islands and wildlife habitats, and manages visitors. Address: P.O. Box 10420, Wellington, New Zealand.

Greenpeace NZ Inc: Campaigns for the protection of the environment, especially marine mammals in the Southern Ocean and protection of Antarctica from mining and other resource exploitation. Greenpeace International www.greenpeace.org/oceans / Greenpeace Australia www.greenpeace.org.au.

Heritage Antarctica: Coordinates the preservation of historic sites in the Ross Sea. A sister organization, the United Kingdom Antarctic Heritage Trust, is developing such a programme elsewhere. www.heritage-antarctica.org.

National Institute of Water and Atmospheric Research Ltd: New Zealand government enterprise that undertakes applied research on oceanic topics including environmental change in the Southern Ocean. Address: P.O. Box 14-901, Kilbirnie, Wellington, New Zealand.

Royal Forest and Bird Protection Society of New Zealand Inc: Conservation body that campaigns to protect New Zealand's flora and fauna, and lobbies government and industry to protect seabirds and marine mammals. Address: 172 Taranaki Street, Wellington, New Zealand.

World Conservation Union (IUCN): International headquarters and various specialist programmes based in Gland, Switzerland, with various global commissions and specialist committees, several of which have an interest in Antarctica and the subantarctic, particularly the Antarctic Advisory Committee and the World Commission on Protected Areas (wcpa.iucn.org). National committees (e.g. in New Zealand and Australia) take a particular interest in the subantarctic islands. Membership comprises both governments and NGOs, and is represented at Antarctic Treaty Consultative Meetings, and has Observer status at meetings of the CCAMLR. Actively participates with scientific, environmental, management and legal bodies associated with the Antarctic Treaty System—and domestically with appropriate government entities. www.iucn.org

Worldwide Fund for Nature (New Zealand): Non-profit conservation organization that funds research on New Zealand's native flora and fauna, and runs international public awareness campaigns. Address: PO Box 6237, Wellington, New Zealand.

2. Other relevant organizations

Antarctican Society: www.antarctican.com/
Antarctic Co-operative Research Centre: www.antcrc.utas.edu.au
Antarctic Society of Australia: www.es.mq.edu.au/physgeog/antsoc.htm
AARC Arctic and Antarctic Research Center, UCSD: www.arcane.ucsd.edu
Australian Antarctic Division: www.aad.gov.au
Australian National Antarctic Research Expeditions: www.anareclub.org.au
BirdLife International Seabird Conservation Programme: www.savethealbatross.org.za
Byrd Polar Research Center: www.bprc.mps.ohiostate.edu
Falklands Conservation: Internet: www.falklandconservation.com
International Southern Ocean Longline Fisheries Information Clearing House: www.isofish.org.au
New Zealand Antarctic Institute: www.antarcticanz.govt.nz
Scientific Committee on Antarctic Research: www.scar.org
Scott Polar Research Institute: www.spri.cam.ac.uk
Tasmanian Polar Network: www.tpn.aq
UK Overseas Territories Conservation Forum: www.ukotfc.org
World Wide Fund for Nature International Endangered Seas Campaign: www.panda.org

3. Antarctic Treaty

This came into force on 23 Jun 1961 and has been ratified by 45 countries. Its articles provide for the peaceful and sustainable use of Antarctica, and are designed to continue the international cooperation initiated during the 1957–8 International Geophysical Year. One of the most important aspects is that the territorial claims of those countries that maintain official designs upon parts of the continent have agreed to 'freeze' these claims indefinitely. Military operations are prohibited under the Treaty, which also provides a baseline for the free exchange of scientific information and resources in the region. For more information see the Conservation in the Region chapter.

4. IAATO and tour companies visiting Antarctica

Most accredited tour companies are members of the International Association of Antarctica Tour Operators (IAATO). Founded in 1991, IAATO now consists of 46 member and associate companies in 11 countries. Further details of most members, their tours and history can be found at www.iaato.org. IAATO is fosters appropriate, safe and environmentally sound travel to the Antarctic. The organization aims to represent Antarctic tour operators and others conducting travel to the Antarctic to the Antarctic Treaty Parties, the international conservation community and the public at large. IAATO also coordinates itineraries so that no more than 100 people are ashore at anytime in any place; seeks to enhance public awareness and concern for the conservation of the Antarctic environment; to support science in Antarctica through cooperation with national Antarctic programmes; and to ensure that the best-qualified staff and field personnel are employed by IAATO members. Finally, it endeavours to develop international acceptance of evaluation, certification and accreditation programmes for Antarctic personnel.

Biographies

About the author

Hadoram Shirihai (45) is well known for his work on the identification and migration of Western Palearctic birds. A founder of the International Birding & Research Center Eilat, where much of the groundbreaking research into raptor migration between Africa and the Palearctic has been conducted, his main works are *The Birds of Israel* (1996, Academic Press), *The Macmillan Birder's Guide to European and Middle Eastern Birds* (1996, Macmillan), and *Sylvia Warblers* (2001, Helm), all of which, plus the first edition of *A Complete Guide to Antarctic Wildlife*, have featured in the Best Bird Book of the Year awards of *British Birds* and *Birdwatch* magazines. Over the years he has served as an editorial consultant to most leading birding magazines in Europe including *Dutch Birding*. His long-held interest in seabirds and marine mammals has led to an in-progress monograph of the *Tubenoses: A Guide to the Albatrosses, Petrels and Shearwaters of the World* (Helm), and the highly acclaimed *Whales, Dolphins and Seals: A Field Guide to the Marine Mammals of the World* (2006, A & C Black). A companion volume, *Seabirds of the World* (Helm), is in preparation. Hadoram has visited nearly all of the subantarctic islands and many parts of Antarctica to study wildlife, but in recent years he has also explored many of the world's seas observing and photographing nearly all of the seabirds and marine mammals. He is also involved in several other major projects, particularly *The Photographic Handbook to the Birds of the Western Palearctic* with Lars Svensson and *Geographical Variation in Palearctic Birds* with Kees Roselaar (both Helm). Recently, Hadoram has commenced work on *The Photographic Handbook to the Birds of the World* (Helm), with Hans Jornvall; in consequence, he is now traveling year-round throughout the globe, to experience and photograph birds in the world's wildest places.

The author during a recent visit to South Georgia

About the artists

Brett Jarrett (42) spent his formative years in Portland, SE Australia, and is a naturalist of unique standing amongst wildlife painters and illustrators. Twenty-nine years of first-hand knowledge of his most beloved subjects—marine birds and mammals—and 11 years as a wildlife artist provided the basis for the present work. Balancing his time between painting and research, he has extensively travelled the Australian coast, the Australasian part of the Southern Ocean, Antarctica and throughout the eastern tropical Pacific. Brett's masterful illustrations of marine mammals have also appeared in Hadoram's *Whales, Dolphins and Seals: A Field Guide to the Marine Mammals of the World* (2006, A & C Black).

John Cox (40) is a world-class bird artist whose work has appeared in several books, including the well-regarded *Pheasants, Partridges and Grouse* and *Pigeons and Doves* (both Helm). However, researching and illustrating seabirds have been always his passions, and his plates adorned Michael Brooke's *Albatrosses and Petrels across the World* (Oxford University Press, 2004). Recently he has commenced work for Hadoram's forthcoming monograph to the *Tubenoses: A Guide to the Albatrosses, Petrels and Shearwaters of the World* (Helm).

About the editor

Guy Kirwan (39) is an ornithological editor and author, who manages or has managed the production of *Sandgrouse, Bulletin of the African Bird Club, Cotinga* and *Bulletin of the British Ornithologists' Club*, one of the longest-running and most respected ornithological periodicals. He is also the author of numerous contributions on the status and distribution of the birds of Turkey, and the senior author of a forthcoming major review of this country's birdlife. With Hadoram, he has also co-authored several other publications on Middle Eastern birds, and he has collaborated on a number of major publishing projects, notably two volumes of the acclaimed *Handbook of the Birds of the World* series, the electronic version of Sibley & Monroe's *Distribution and Taxonomy of the Birds of the World* and the award-winning *Sylvia Warblers*. He currently spends long periods of each year in Latin America, researching and tour-leading, often working with Hadoram in connection with *The Photographic Handbook to the Birds of the World*.

BirdLife
INTERNATIONAL

From every copy sold of this and future editions of this book, the author's royalties will be donated for the conservation of the albatrosses of the Southern Ocean. The author invites readers to support the Save the Albatross Campaign and BirdLife International (www.savethealbatross.net), in order to tackle the disastrous and rapid declines of albatrosses throughout the world.

Index